HOLT

SCIENCE SPECTRUM®

Physical Science

Integrating

- Chemistry
- Physics
- Earth Science
- Space Science
- Mathematics

Ken Dobson, Ph.D.
Former Head of Science
Woodberry Down School
London, United Kingdom

John Holman, Ph.D.
Professor of Chemical Education
Director of the Science Curriculum Centre
University of York
York, United Kingdom

Michael Roberts, Ph.D.
Science Writer
Bristol, United Kingdom

HOLT, RINEHART AND WINSTON
A Harcourt Education Company
Orlando • **Austin** • New York • San Diego • Toronto • London

About the Authors

Ken Dobson, Ph.D.

Dr. Dobson studied physics and education at Manchester and began teaching in 1956. At Wilson's grammar school in Camberwell he developed an early form of "self-study" for physics students. He has also served as head of science for Woodberry Down School in Hackney and Chief Awarder for Nuffield A-level Physics. He later was instrumental in developing the basic principles of "Suffolk Science," which became a national program for teaching science in over 600 schools in England. Dr. Dobson also served as a member of the Working Group that established the first National Curriculum in science. He has served as Honorary Editor of *Physics Education* from 1996 to 2000.

John Holman, Ph.D.

Dr. Holman studied natural sciences at the University of Cambridge and then taught chemistry at a number of independent and state schools. He has worked as a writer and science education specialist for Science and Technology in Society (SATIS), Salters Advanced Chemistry, Science Across the World, and other projects. He was head of Watford Grammar School for Boys, where he also taught chemistry. Currently, he is professor of chemical education and director of the Science Curriculum Centre at the University of York.

Michael Roberts, Ph.D.

Dr. Roberts was educated at Epsom College and Queens' College in England. He performed postgraduate research on the neurophysiology of annelids. He was a lecturer at the University of California at Santa Barbara and then head of biology at Marlborough College. During this time, he was also an external examiner in biology at the University of Botswana and Swaziland and the National University of Lesotho. Dr. Roberts was a research associate at Chelsea College (now King's College) and head of biology at Cheltenham College. He is now retired and focuses a great deal of time on writing textbooks.

This adaptation of **Nelson Balanced Science** and **Nelson Science** is published by arrangement with Thomas Nelson & Sons Ltd., Walton-on-Thames, UK.

Printed in the United States of America

ISBN 0-03-039093-1

2 3 4 5 6 7 048 08 07 06 05

Acknowledgements

Contributing Authors

Robert Davisson
Science Writer
Albuquerque, New Mexico

Mary Kay Hemenway, Ph.D.
Research Associate and Senior Lecturer
Department of Astronomy
The University of Texas at Austin
Austin, Texas

William G. Lamb, Ph.D.
Winningstad Chair in the Physical Sciences
Oregon Episcopal School
Portland, Oregon

Contributing Writers

David Bethel
Science Writer
Austin, Texas

Meredith Phillips
Science Writer
Brooklyn, New York

Rosemary Previte
Science Writer
Lexington, Massachusetts

Tracy Schagen
Science Writer
Austin, Texas

Inclusion Specialists

Joan A. Solorio
Special Education Director
Austin Independent School District
Austin, Texas

John A. Solorio
Multiple Technologies Lab Facilitator
Austin Independent School District
Austin, Texas

Feature Development

John M. Stokes
Science Writer
Socorro, New Mexico

Andrew Strickler
Science Writer
Oakland, California

Teacher Edition Development

Maria Hong
Science Writer
Austin, Texas

Bob Roth
Science Writer
Pittsburgh, Pennsylvania

Academic Reviewers

Mead Allison, Ph.D.
Associate Professor
Department of Geology and Earth Sciences
Tulane University
New Orleans, Louisiana

Eric Anslyn, Ph.D.
Professor of Chemistry
Department of Chemistry and Biochemistry
The University of Texas
Austin, Texas

Paul Asimow, Ph.D.
Assistant Professor of Geology and Geochemistry
Division of Geological and Planetary Sciences
California Institute of Technology
Pasadena, California

John A. Brockhaus, Ph.D.
Director of Mapping, Charting, and Geodesy Program
Department of Geography and Environmental Engineering
United States Military Academy
West Point, New York

Thomas Connolley, Ph.D.
Visiting Assistant Professor
Department of Mechanical Engineering
The University of Texas
San Antonio, Texas

Scott W. Cowley, Ph.D.
Associate Professor
Department of Chemistry and Geochemistry
Colorado School of Mines
Golden, Colorado

Nels F. Forsman, Ph.D.
Associate Professor of Geochemistry
Department of Physics and Astrophysics
University of North Dakota
Grand Forks, North Dakota

Gina Frey, Ph.D.
Professor of Chemistry
Department of Chemistry
Washington University
St. Louis, Missouri

Frank Guziec
Dishman Professor of Science
Department of Chemistry
Southwestern University
Georgetown, Texas

Vicki Hansen, Ph.D.
Professor of Geological Sciences
Department of Geology
Southern Methodist University
Dallas, Texas

Richard Hey, Ph.D.
Professor of Geophysics
School of Ocean and Earth Sciences Technology
University of Hawaii
Honolulu, Hawaii

Guy Indebetouw, Ph.D.
Professor of Physics
Department of Physics
Virginia Polytechnic Institute and State University
Blacksburg, Virginia

Wendy L. Keeney-Kennicutt, Ph.D.
Associate Professor of Chemistry
Chemistry Department
Texas A&M University
College Station, Texas

Samuel P. Kounaves
Associate Professor of Chemistry
Department of Chemistry
Tufts University
Medford, Massachusetts

David Lamp, Ph.D.
Associate Professor of Physics
Physics Department
Texas Tech University
Lubbock, Texas

Phillip LaRoe
Instructor
Department of Physics and Chemistry
Central Community College
Grand Isle, Nebraska

Joel Leventhal, Ph.D.
Emeritus Scientist
U.S. Geological Survey and Diversified Geochemistry
Lakewood, California

Joseph McClure, Ph.D.
Professor of Physics, Emeritus
Department of Physics
Georgetown University
Washington, D.C.

Gary Mueller, Ph.D.
Associate Professor of Nuclear Engineering
Department of Engineering
University of Missouri
Rolla, Missouri

Emily Neimeyer, Ph.D.
Assistant Professor of Chemistry
Department of Chemistry
Southwestern University
Georgetown, Texas

Hilary Olsen, Ph.D.
Research Scientist
Institute of Geophysics
The University of Texas
Austin, Texas

Brian Pagenkopf, Ph.D.
Professor of Chemistry
Department of Chemistry and Biochemistry
The University of Texas
Austin, Texas

Per F. Peterson, Ph.D.
Professor and Chair
Department of Nuclear Engineering
University of California
Berkeley, California

Barron Rector, Ph.D.
Assistant Professor and Extension Range Specialist
Texas Agricultural Extension Service
Texas A&M University
College Station, Texas

Dork Sahagian
Research Professor, Stratigraphy and Basin Analysis, Geodynamics
Global Analysis, Interpretation, and Modeling Program
University of New Hampshire
Durham, New Hampshire

Charles Scaife, Ph.D.
Chemistry Professor
Department of Chemistry
Union College
Schenectady, New York

Fred Seaman, Ph.D.
Research Scientist and Chemist
Department of Pharmacological Chemistry
The University of Texas
Austin, Texas

Miles Silman, Ph.D.
Associate Professor of Biology
Department of Biology
Wake Forest University
Winston-Salem, North Carolina

Spencer Steinberg, Ph.D.
Associate Professor, Environmental Organic Chemistry
Chemistry Department
University of Nevada
Las Vegas, Nevada

Richard Storey, Ph.D.
Dean of the Faculty and Professor of Biology
Colorado College
Colorado Springs, Colorado

Jack B. Swift, Ph.D.
Associate Professor of Physics
Department of Physics
The University of Texas
Austin, Texas

Acknowledgments continued on page 902.

Contents in Brief

Table of CONTENTS

CHAPTER 3

States of Matter 68

CHAPTER 4

Atoms and the Periodic Table 102

3
Li
Lithium
6.941

11
Na
Sodium
22.989.770

19
K
Potassium
39.0983

37
Rb
Rubidium
85.4678

55
Cs
Cesium
132.905 43

CHAPTER 5

The Structure of Matter 142

CHAPTER 6

Chemical Reactions 182

CHAPTER 7

Solutions 222

CHAPTER 8

Acids, Bases, and Salts 254

INTEGRATING TECHNOLOGY and Society

CHAPTER 9

Nuclear Changes 282

INTEGRATING TECHNOLOGY and Society

CHAPTER 10

Motion 316

CHAPTER 11

Forces 344

CHAPTER 12

Work and Energy 376

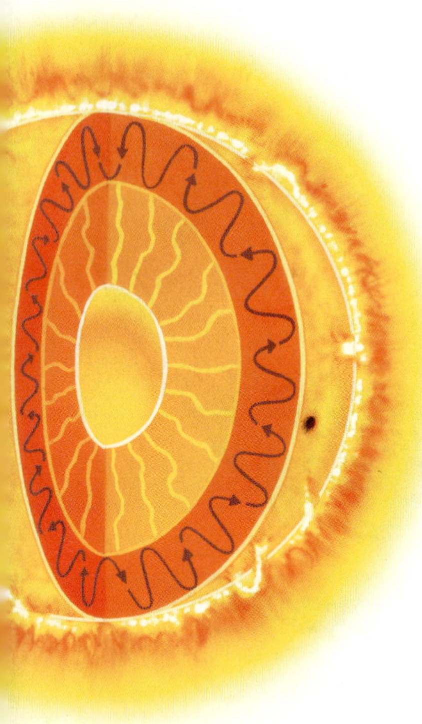

Reference Section

Laboratory Experiments

Quick Lab

Quick Activity

How to Use Your Textbook

Your Roadmap for Success with *Holt Science Spectrum*

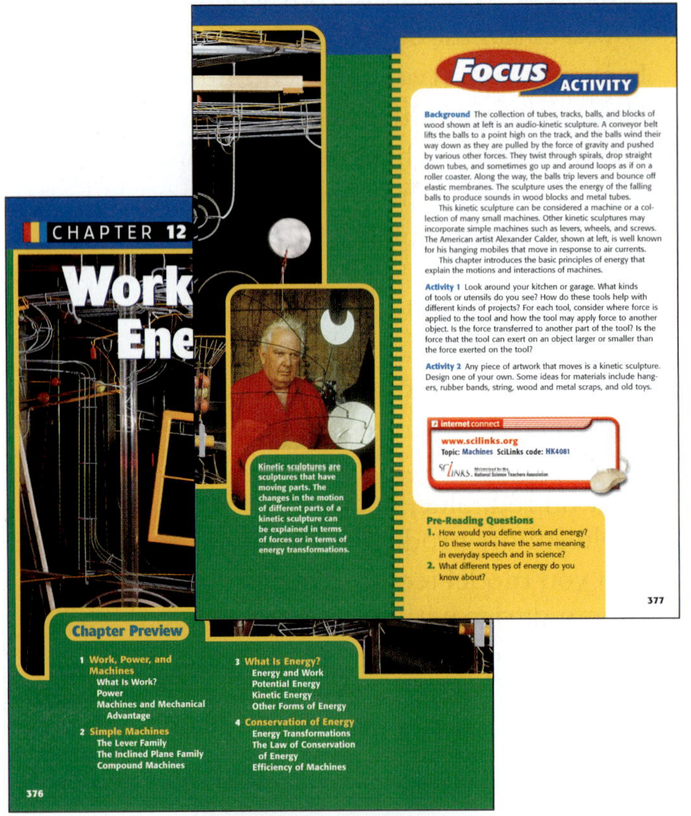

CHAPTER 12

Work … Ene…

Focus ACTIVITY

Background The collection of tubes, tracks, balls, and blocks of wood shown at left is an audio-kinetic sculpture. A conveyor belt lifts the balls to a point high on the track, and the balls wind their way down as they are pulled by the force of gravity and pushed by various other forces. They twist through spirals, drop straight down tubes, and sometimes go up and around loops as if on a roller coaster. Along the way, the balls trip levers and bounce off elastic membranes. The sculpture uses the energy of the falling balls to produce sounds in wood blocks and metal tubes.

This kinetic sculpture can be considered a machine or a collection of many small machines. Other kinetic sculptures may incorporate simple machines such as levers, wheels, and screws. The American artist Alexander Calder, shown at left, is well known for his hanging mobiles that move in response to air currents.

This chapter introduces the basic principles of energy that explain the motions and interactions of machines.

Activity 1 Look around your kitchen or garage. What kinds of tools or utensils do you see? How do these tools help with different kinds of projects? For each tool, consider where force is applied to the tool and how the tool may apply force to another object. Is the force transferred to another part of the tool? Is the force that the tool can exert on an object larger or smaller than the force exerted on the tool?

Activity 2 Any piece of artwork that moves is a kinetic sculpture. Design one of your own. Some ideas for materials include hangers, rubber bands, string, wood and metal scraps, and old toys.

internet connect
www.scilinks.org
Topic: Machines SciLinks code: HK4081

Kinetic sculptures are sculptures that have moving parts. The changes in the motion of different parts of a kinetic sculpture can be explained in terms of forces or in terms of energy transformations.

Pre-Reading Questions
1. How would you define work and energy? Do these words have the same meaning in everyday speech and in science?
2. What different types of energy do you know about?

377

Chapter Preview

1 Work, Power, and Machines
What Is Work?
Power
Machines and Mechanical Advantage

2 Simple Machines
The Lever Family
The Inclined Plane Family
Compound Machines

3 What Is Energy?
Energy and Work
Potential Energy
Kinetic Energy
Other Forms of Energy

4 Conservation of Energy
Energy Transformations
The Law of Conservation of Energy
Efficiency of Machines

376

Get Organized

Answer the **Pre-Reading Questions** at the beginning of each chapter to help prepare you to read the material in the chapter. Read the **Background** in the **Focus Activity** at the beginning of each chapter to understand what is shown in the photograph and how it relates to what you will learn in the chapter.

STUDY TIP Use the **Chapter Preview** outline at the beginning of the chapter to organize your notes on the chapter content in a way that you understand.

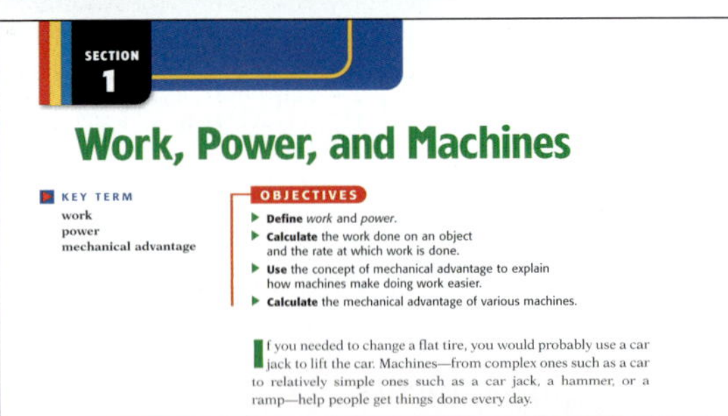

SECTION 1

Work, Power, and Machines

KEY TERM
work
power
mechanical advantage

OBJECTIVES
- **Define** *work* and *power*.
- **Calculate** the work done on an object and the rate at which work is done.
- **Use** the concept of mechanical advantage to explain how machines make doing work easier.
- **Calculate** the mechanical advantage of various machines.

If you needed to change a flat tire, you would probably use a car jack to lift the car. Machines—from complex ones such as a car to relatively simple ones such as a car jack, a hammer, or a ramp—help people get things done every day.

Read for Meaning

Read the **Objectives** at the beginning of each section because they will tell you what you'll need to learn. **Key Terms** are also listed for each section. Each key term is highlighted in the text and defined in the margin. After reading each section, read the **Summary** at the end of the section for a quick review of the section's main concepts.

STUDY TIP If you don't understand a definition, reread the page on which the term is introduced. The surrounding text should help make the definition easier to understand.

Be Resourceful, Use the Web

Internet Connect boxes in your textbook take you to resources that you can use for science projects, reports, and research papers. Go to **scilinks.org** and type in the **SciLinks code** to get information on a topic.

Visit go.hrw.com

Find worksheets and reference materials that go with your textbook at **go.hrw.com.** Enter the keyword **HK6 Home** to access the home page for your textbook.

Work the Problems

Build your reasoning and problem-solving skills by following the worked-out example problems in **Math Skills.** Then you can practice those skills in the associated **Practice** problems.

Prepare for Tests

Section Reviews and **Chapter Reviews** test your knowledge of the main points of the chapter. Thinking Critically items challenge you to think about the material in different ways and in greater depth. The **Standardized Test Prep** that is located after each Chapter Review helps you sharpen your test-taking abilities.

STUDY TIP Reread the Objectives and the section summaries when studying for a test to be sure you know the material.

Use the Appendix

Your **Appendix** contains a variety of resources designed to enhance your learning experience. These resources include **Study Skills,** which can help sharpen your reading, math, graphing, and lab skills. **Useful Data** is a collection of information that can come in handy during your study of physical science. **Problem Bank** provides additional practice problems on key skills. **Selected Answers** is the place to check your final answers for some problems, allowing you to quickly catch and to correct mistakes you might be making.

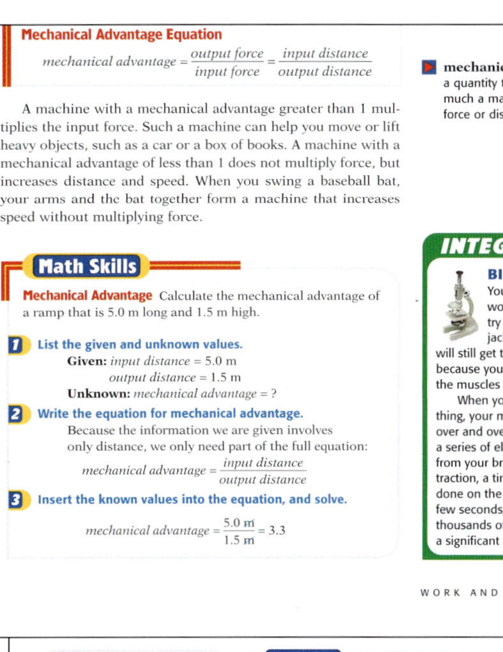

Mechanical Advantage Equation

$$\text{mechanical advantage} = \frac{\text{output force}}{\text{input force}} = \frac{\text{input distance}}{\text{output distance}}$$

A machine with a mechanical advantage greater than 1 multiplies the input force. Such a machine can help you move or lift heavy objects, such as a car or a box of books. A machine with a mechanical advantage of less than 1 does not multiply force, but increases distance and speed. When you swing a baseball bat, your arms and the bat together form a machine that increases speed without multiplying force.

mechanical advantage a quantity that measures how much a machine multiplies force or distance

Math Skills

Mechanical Advantage Calculate the mechanical advantage of a ramp that is 5.0 m long and 1.5 m high.

1 List the given and unknown values.
Given: *input distance* = 5.0 m
output distance = 1.5 m
Unknown: *mechanical advantage* = ?

2 Write the equation for mechanical advantage.
Because the information we are given involves only distance, we only need part of the full equation:

$$\text{mechanical advantage} = \frac{\text{input distance}}{\text{output distance}}$$

3 Insert the known values into the equation, and solve.

$$\text{mechanical advantage} = \frac{5.0\ \text{m}}{1.5\ \text{m}} = 3.3$$

INTEGRATING BIOLOGY

You may not do any work on a car if you try to lift it without a jack, but your body will still get tired from the effort because you are doing work on the muscles inside your body.

When you try to lift something, your muscles contract over and over in response to a series of electrical impulses from your brain. With each contraction, a tiny bit of work is done on the muscles. In just a few seconds, this can add up to thousands of contractions and a significant amount of work.

WORK AND ENERGY 383

Practice HINT

- The mechanical advantage equation can be rearranged to isolate any of the variables on the left.
- For practice problem 4, you will need to rearrange the equation to isolate output force on the left.
- For practice problem 5, you will need to rearrange to isolate output distance. When rearranging, use only the part of the full equation that you need.

Practice

Mechanical Advantage

1. Calculate the mechanical advantage of a ramp that is 6.0 m long and 1.5 m high.
2. Determine the mechanical advantage of an automobile jack that lifts a 9900 N car with an input force of 150 N.
3. A sailor uses a rope and pulley to raise a sail weighing 140 N. The sailor pulls down with a force of 140 N on the rope. What is the mechanical advantage of the pulley?
4. Alex pulls on the handle of a claw hammer with a force of 15 N. If the hammer has a mechanical advantage of 5.2, how much force is exerted on a nail in the claw?
5. While rowing in a race, John pulls the handle of an oar 0.80 m on each stroke. If the oar has a mechanical advantage of 1.5, how far does the blade of the oar move through the water on each stroke?

SECTION 1 REVIEW

SUMMARY

- Work is done when a force causes an object to move. This meaning is different from the everyday meaning of *work*.
- Work is equal to force times distance. The most commonly used SI unit for work is joules.
- Power is the rate at which work is done. The SI unit for power is watts.
- Machines help people by redistributing the work put into them. They can change either the size or the direction of the input force.

1. Define work and power. How are work and power related to each other?
2. Determine if work is being done in these situations:
   a. lifting a spoonful of soup to your mouth
   b. holding a stack of books motionless over your head
   c. letting a pencil fall to the ground
3. **Describe** how a ramp can make lifting a box easier without changing the amount of work being done.
4. **Critical Thinking** A short ramp and a long ramp both reach a height of 1 m. Which has a greater mechanical advantage?

Math Skills

5. How much work in joules is done by a person who uses a force of 25 N to move a desk 3.0 m?
6. A bus driver applies a force of 55.0 N to the steering wheel, which in turn applies 132 N of force on the steering column. What is the mechanical advantage of the steering wheel?

Visit Holt Online Learning

If your teacher gives you a special password to log onto the **Holt Online Learning** site, you'll find your complete textbook on the Web. In addition, you'll find some great learning tools and practice quizzes. You'll be able to see how well you know the material from your textbook.

Safety in the Laboratory

Andy Christiansen/HRW

Systematic, careful lab work is an essential part of any science program. The equipment and apparatus you will use involve various safety hazards, just as they do for working scientists. Your instructor will guide you in properly using the equipment and carrying out the experiments, but you must also take responsibility for your safety.

Anything can be dangerous if it is misused. Always follow the instructions and pay close attention to the safety notes.

These safety rules always apply in the lab

1. **Wear safety goggles, gloves, and a lab apron.**
   Wear these safety devices whenever you are in the lab. Keep the lab apron strings tied. If your safety goggles are uncomfortable or cloud up, ask for help.
2. **Do not wear contact lenses in the lab.**
   Contact lenses should not be worn during any investigations using chemicals (even if you are wearing goggles). In the event of an accident, chemicals can get behind contact lenses and cause serious eye damage. If your doctor requires that you wear contact lenses, you should wear eye-cup safety goggles in the lab.
3. **NEVER work alone in the lab.**
   Work in the lab only when supervised. Do not leave equipment unattended while it is in operation.
4. **Wear the right clothing for lab work.**
   Necklaces, neckties, dangling jewelry, long hair, and loose clothing can get caught in moving parts or catch on fire. Remove your wristwatch, and wear shoes that will protect your feet from chemical spills and falling objects.
5. **Only books and notebooks needed for the experiment should be in the lab.**
   Keep other items in your desk or locker.
6. **Read the entire experiment before entering the lab.**
   Memorize the safety precautions. Be familiar with the instructions for the experiment. Only authorized materials and equipment should be used. If you are not sure of something, ask your instructor about it.
7. **Always heed safety symbols and cautions listed in the experiments, listed on handouts, posted in the room, and given verbally by your instructor.**
   They are provided for a reason: YOUR SAFETY.
8. **Read chemical labels.**
   Follow the instructions and safety precautions stated on the labels.
9. **Be alert, and walk with care in the lab.**
10. **Know proper fire drill procedures and the location of fire exits and emergency equipment.**
    Make sure you know the procedures to follow in case of a fire or emergency.
11. **Know the location of and how to operate safety showers and eyewash stations.**
12. **If your clothing catches on fire, do not run; WALK to the safety shower, stand under it, and turn it on.**
    Alert your instructor while you do this.

13. **If you get a chemical in your eyes, walk immediately to the eyewash station, turn it on, and lower your head so that your eyes are in the running water.**
Hold your eyelids open with your thumbs and fingers, and roll your eyes. You have to flush your eyes continuously for at least 15 minutes. Alert your instructor while you do this.

14. **If you spill a chemical on your skin, wash it off with lukewarm water, and alert your instructor.**
If you spill a solid chemical on your clothing, brush it off carefully without scattering it. If you get liquid on your clothing, wash it off right away using the sink faucet. If the spill is on your pants or somewhere else that will not fit under the sink faucet, use the safety shower. Remove the affected clothing while under the shower.

15. **Report all accidents and spills, no matter how minor, to the instructor IMMEDIATELY.**
In addition, tell your instructor if you get a headache, feel sick to your stomach, or feel dizzy.

16. **The best way to prevent an accident is to stop it before it happens.**
If you have a close call, tell your instructor so that you can find a way to prevent it from happening again.

17. **DO NOT perform unauthorized experiments or use equipment and apparatus in a manner for which they were not intended.**
Use only materials and equipment listed in the instructions. Procedures should only be performed as described.

18. **Food, beverages, chewing gum, and tobacco products are NEVER permitted in the lab.**

19. **For all chemicals, take only what you need.**
However, if you happen to take too much and have some left over, DO NOT put it back into the container. Ask your instructor what to do with any leftover chemicals.

20. **NEVER taste chemicals. Do not touch chemicals or allow them to contact areas of bare skin.**

21. **Use a sparker to light a Bunsen burner.**
Do not use matches. Be sure that all gas valves are turned off when you leave the lab.

22. **Use extreme caution when working with hot plates or other heating devices.**
Keep your head, hands, hair, and clothing away from the flame or heating area, and turn the devices off when they are not in use. Remember that metal surfaces connected to the heated area will become hot by conduction. Remember that many metal, ceramic, and glass items do not always look hot when they are hot. Allow all items to cool before storing.

23. **Do not use electrical equipment with frayed or twisted wires.**

24. **Be sure your hands are dry before using electrical equipment.**
The area under and around electrical equipment should be dry; cords should not lie in puddles of spilled liquid.

25. **Do not let electrical cords dangle from work stations.**
Before plugging an electrical cord into a socket, be sure the equipment is turned OFF. When you are finished with the device, turn it off and unplug the device.

26. **Horseplay and fooling around in the lab are very dangerous.**

27. **Keep work areas and apparatus clean and neat.**
Always clean up any clutter made during the course of lab work, put away apparatus in an orderly manner, and report any damaged or missing items to your instructor.

28. **Always thoroughly wash your hands with soap and water at the conclusion of each lab.**

Safety in the Laboratory

Safety Symbols

The following symbols will appear in the laboratory experiments to emphasize important additional areas of caution.

EYE PROTECTION

- Wear safety goggles, and know where the eyewash station is located and how to use it. Contents under pressure may become projectiles and cause serious injury.
- Never look directly at the sun through any optical device or use direct sunlight to illuminate a microscope.
- If any substance gets into your eyes, notify your instructor immediately and flush your eyes with running water for at least 15 minutes.

CLOTHING PROTECTION

- Secure loose clothing, and remove dangling jewelry. Do not wear open-toed shoes or sandals in the lab.
- Wear an apron or lab coat to protect your clothing when you are working with chemicals.
- If a spill gets on your clothing, rinse it off immediately with water for at least 5 minutes while notifying your instructor.

CAUSTIC SUBSTANCES

- If a chemical gets on your skin, on your clothing, or in your eyes, rinse it immediately and alert your instructor.
- If a chemical is spilled on the floor or lab bench, alert your instructor, but do not clean it up yourself unless your instructor directs you to do so.

CHEMICAL SAFETY

- Always use caution when working with chemicals.
- Always wear appropriate protective equipment. Always wear eye goggles, gloves, and a lab apron or lab coat when you are working with any chemical or chemical solution.

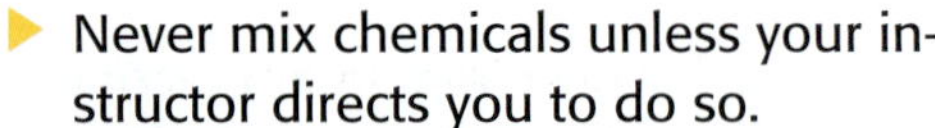

- Never mix chemicals unless your instructor directs you to do so.
- Never taste, touch, or smell chemicals unless your instructor directs you to do so.
- Add an acid or base to water; never add water to an acid or base.
- Never return an unused chemical to its original container.
- Never transfer substances by sucking on a pipet or straw; use a suction bulb.
- Follow instructions for proper disposal.

ELECTRICAL SAFETY

- Never close a circuit until it has been approved by your instructor. Never rewire or adjust any element of a closed circuit.
- If the pointer of any kind of meter moves off the scale, open the circuit immediately by opening the switch.
- Do not place electrical cords in walking areas or let cords hang over a table edge in a way that could cause equipment to fall if the cord is accidentally pulled.
- Do not use equipment that has frayed electrical cords or loose plugs.
- Be sure that equipment is in the "off" position before you plug it in.
- Never use an electrical appliance around water or with wet hands or clothing.
- Be sure to turn off and unplug electrical equipment when you are finished using it.

HEATING SAFETY

- Avoid wearing hair spray or hair gel on lab days.
- Whenever possible, use an electric hot plate instead of an open flame as a heat source.
- When heating materials in a test tube, always angle the test tube away from yourself and others.
- Glass containers used for heating should be made of heat-resistant glass.

- Never leave a hot plate unattended while it is turned on.
- Wire coils may heat up rapidly during experiments. If heating occurs, open the switch immediately, and handle the equipment with heat-resistant gloves.
- Allow all equipment to cool before storing it.

SHARP OBJECTS

- Use knives and other sharp instruments with extreme care.
- Never cut objects while holding them in your hands. Place objects on a suitable work surface for cutting.
- Never use a double-edged razor in the lab.

HAND SAFETY

- To avoid burns, wear heat-resistant gloves whenever instructed to do so.
- Always wear protective gloves when working with an open flame, chemicals, and solutions.
- If you do not know whether an object is hot, do not touch it.
- Use tongs when heating test tubes. Never hold a test tube in your hand to heat the test tube.

EXPLOSION SAFETY

- Use flammable liquids only in small amounts.
- When working with flammable liquids, be sure that no one else in the lab is using or plans to use a lit Bunsen burner. Make sure that no other heat sources are present.

FIRE SAFETY

- Know the location of laboratory fire extinguishers and fire-safety blankets.
- Know your school's fire-evacuation routes.

GAS SAFETY

- Do not inhale any gas or vapor unless directed to do so by your instructor. Do not breathe pure gases.
- Handle materials prone to emit vapors or gases in a well-ventilated area. This work should be done in an approved chemical fume hood.

GLASSWARE SAFETY

- Check the condition of glassware before and after using it. Inform your instructor of any broken, chipped, or cracked glassware, because it should not be used.
- Do not pick up broken glass with your bare hands. Place broken glass in a specially designated disposal container.
- If a thermometer breaks, notify your instructor immediately.
- If a light bulb breaks, notify your instructor immediately. Do not remove broken bulbs from sockets.

WASTE DISPOSAL

- Clean and decontaminate all work surfaces and personal protective equipment as directed by your instructor.
- Dispose of all broken glass, contaminated sharp objects, and other contaminated materials in special containers as directed by your instructor.

HYGIENIC CARE

- Keep your hands away from your face and mouth.
- Always wash your hands thoroughly when you are done with an experiment.

CHAPTER 1

Introduction to Science

Chapter Preview

Laser-induced fusion is being studied as a way to produce energy for our growing needs. Lasers and fusion reactions were developed using the same approach to the scientific method used in 1896 by Dr. George Washington Carver at the Tuskeegee Institute.

Focus ACTIVITY

Background Imagine that it is 1895 and you are a scientist working in your laboratory. Outside, people move about on foot, on bicycles, or in horse-drawn carriages. A few brave and rich people have purchased the new invention called an automobile. They ride along the street, but their auto sputters, pops, puffs smoke, and frightens both horses and people.

Your laboratory is filled with coils of wire, oddly shaped glass tubes, magnets of all sorts, and many heavy glass jars containing liquid and metal plates (batteries). A few dim electric bulbs are strung along the ceiling. Additional light comes from daylight through windows or from the old gas lamps along the wall.

It's an exciting time in science because new discoveries about matter and energy are being made almost every day. A few European scientists are even beginning to pay attention to those upstart scientists from America. However, some people believe that humans have learned nearly everything that is worth knowing about the physical world.

Activity 1 Interview someone old enough to have witnessed many technological changes. Ask the person what scientific discoveries have made the biggest differences in his or her life. Which changes do you think have been the most important?

Activity 2 Using a meterstick, measure the length and width of your desk surface. To what fraction of a unit can you reliably measure? Multiply your two measurements to calculate the surface area of your desk. Compare your results with those of other students. What might be the reasons for differences in calculations?

internet connect

www.scilinks.org
Topic: New Discoveries in Science
SciLinks code: HK4093

SCILINKS. Maintained by the National Science Teachers Association

Pre-Reading Questions

1. How do scientific discoveries contribute to the development of new technology?
2. What are some problems that have been solved by science and technology in the last 10 years? What new problems have these technological changes caused?

SECTION 1

The Nature of Science

KEY TERMS

science
technology
scientific law
scientific theory

OBJECTIVES

- **Describe** the main branches of natural science and relate them to each other.
- **Describe** the relationship between science and technology.
- **Distinguish** between scientific laws and scientific theories.
- **Explain** the roles of models and mathematics in scientific theories and laws.

Generally, scientists describe the universe using basic rules, which can be discovered by careful, methodical study. A scientist may perform experiments to find a new aspect of the natural world, to explain a known phenomenon, to check the results of other experiments, or to test the predictions of current theories.

How Does Science Take Place?

Imagine that it is 1895 and you are experimenting with cathode rays. These mysterious rays were discovered almost 40 years before, but in 1895 no one knows what they are. To produce the rays, you create a vacuum by pumping the air out of a sealed glass tube that has two metal rods at a distance from each other, as shown in ***Figure 1A.*** When the rods are connected to an electrical source, electric charges flow through the empty space between the rods, and the rays are produced.

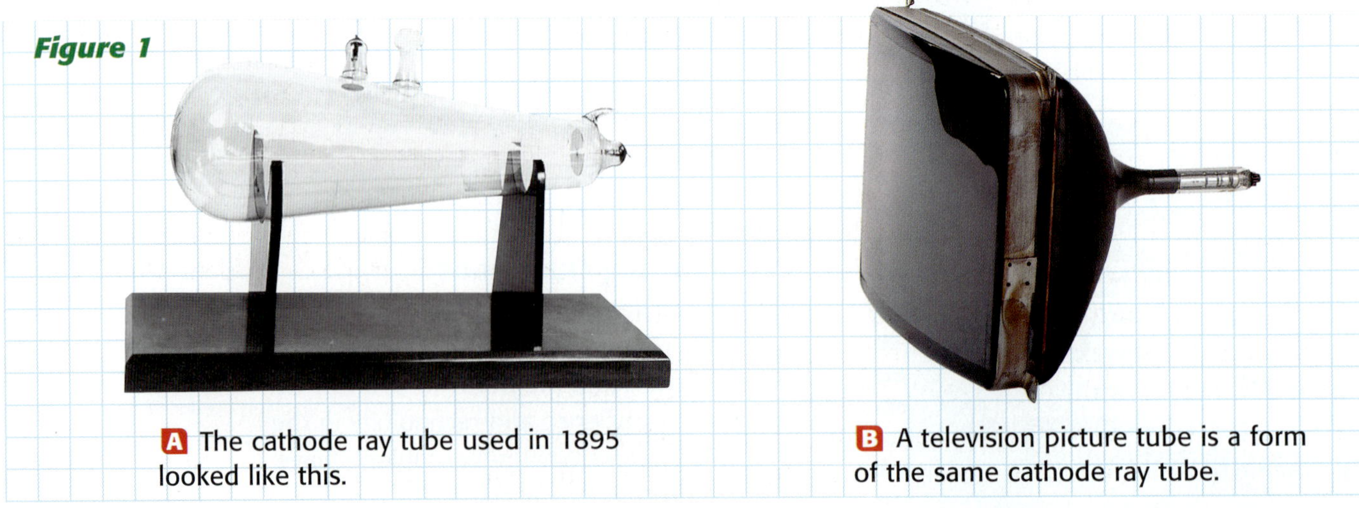

Figure 1

A The cathode ray tube used in 1895 looked like this.

B A television picture tube is a form of the same cathode ray tube.

Scientists investigate

You have learned from the work of other scientists and have conducted experiments of your own. From these, you know that when certain minerals are placed inside the tube, the cathode rays make them fluoresce (glow). Pieces of cardboard coated with powder made from these minerals are used to detect the rays. With a very high voltage, even the glass tube itself glows.

Other scientists have found that cathode rays can pass through thin metal foils, but they travel in our atmosphere for only 2 or 3 cm. You wonder if the rays could pass through the glass tube. Others have tried this experiment and have found that cathode rays don't go through glass. But you think that the glow from the glass tube might have outshined any weak glow from the mineral-coated cardboard. So, you decide to cover the glass tube with heavy black paper.

VOCABULARY Skills Tip

Cathode rays *got their name because they come from the cathode, the rod connected to the negative terminal of the electricity source. The positive terminal is called the* anode.

Scientists plan experiments

Before experimenting, you write your plan in your laboratory notebook and sketch the equipment you are using. You make a table in which you can write down the electric power used, the distance from the tube to the fluorescent detector, the air temperature, and anything you observe. You state the idea you are going to test: At a high voltage, cathode rays will be strong enough to be detected outside the tube by causing the mineral-coated cardboard to glow.

Scientists observe

Everything is ready. You want to be sure that the black-paper cover doesn't have any gaps, so you darken the room and turn on the tube. The black cover blocks the light from the tube. Just before you switch off the tube, you glimpse a light nearby. When you turn on the tube again, the light reappears.

Then you realize that this light is coming from the mineral-coated cardboard you planned to use to detect cathode rays. The detector is already glowing, and it is on a table almost 1 m away from the tube. You know that 1 m is too far for cathode rays to travel in air. You suspect that the tube must be giving off some new rays that no one has seen before. What do you do now?

This is the question Wilhelm Roentgen had to ponder in Würzburg, Germany, on November 8, 1895, when all this happened to him. Should he call the experiment a failure because it didn't give the results he expected? Should he ask reporters to cover this news story? Maybe he should send letters about his discovery to famous scientists and invite them to come and see it.

INTEGRATING

BIOLOGY

In 1928, the Scottish scientist Alexander Fleming was investigating disease-causing bacteria when he saw that one of his cultures contained an area where no bacteria were growing. Instead, an unknown organism was growing in that area. Rather than discarding the culture as a failure, Fleming investigated the unfamiliar organism and found that it was a type of mold. This mold produced a substance that prevented the growth of many disease bacteria. What he found by questioning the results of a "failed" experiment became the first modern antibiotic, penicillin. Major discoveries are often made by accident when trying to find something else.

Scientists always test results

Because Roentgen was a scientist, he first repeated his experiment to be sure of his observations. His results caused him to begin thinking of new questions and to design more experiments to find the answers.

He found that the rays passed through almost everything, although dense materials absorbed them somewhat. When he held his hand in the path of the rays, the bones were visible as shadows on the fluorescent detector, as shown in ***Figure 2.*** When Roentgen published his findings in December, he still did not know what the rays were. He called them *X rays* because *x* represents an unknown in a mathematical equation.

Within three months of Roentgen's discovery, a doctor in Massachusetts used X rays to help set properly the broken bones in a boy's arm. After a year, more than a thousand scientific articles about X rays had been published. In 1901, Roentgen received the first Nobel Prize in physics for his discovery.

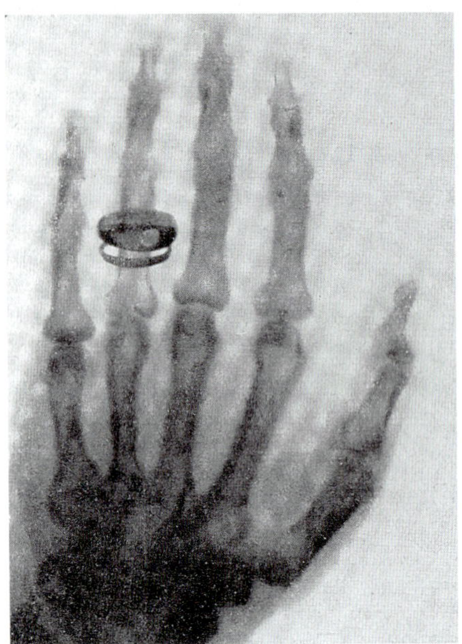

Figure 2

Roentgen included this X ray of his wife's hand in one of the first papers he wrote on X rays.

Science has many branches

Roentgen's work with X rays illustrates how scientists work, but what is **science** about? Science is observing, studying, and experimenting to find the nature of things. You can think of science as having two main branches: social science, which deals with individual and group human behavior, and natural science. Natural science tries to understand how "nature," which really means "the whole universe," behaves. Natural science is usually divided into life science, physical science, and Earth science, as shown in ***Figure 3.***

science the knowledge obtained by observing natural events and conditions in order to discover facts and formulate laws or principles that can be verified or tested

Life science is *biology.* Biology has many branches, such as *botany,* the science of plants; *zoology,* the science of animals; and *ecology,* the science of balance in nature. Medicine and agriculture are branches of biology too.

Figure 3

This chart shows one way to look at science. Modern science has many branches and specialties.

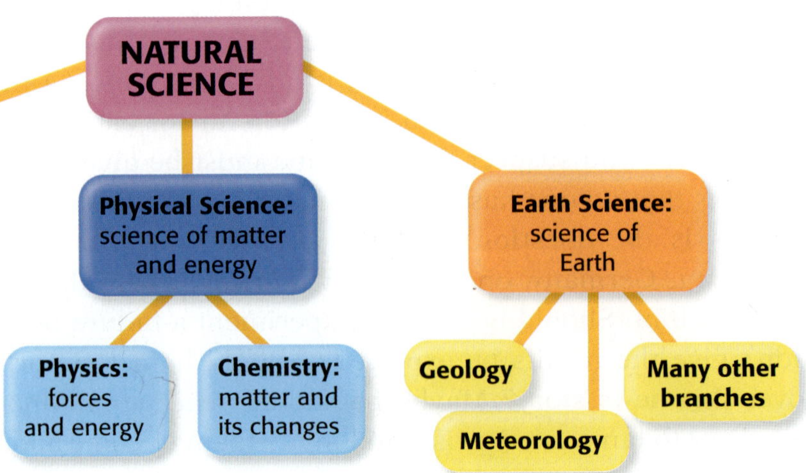

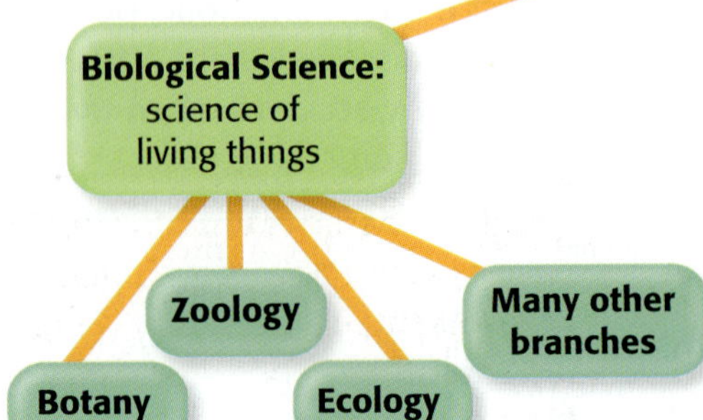

Physical science has two main branches—*chemistry* and *physics*. Chemistry is the science of matter and its changes, and physics is the science of forces and energy. Both depend greatly on mathematics.

Some of the branches of Earth science are *geology,* the science of the physical nature and history of the Earth, and *meteorology,* the science of the atmosphere and weather.

This classification of science appears very tidy, like stacks of boxes in a shoe store, but there's a problem with it. As science has progressed, the branches of science have grown out of their little boxes. For example, chemists have begun to explain the workings of chemicals that make up living things, such as DNA, shown in **Figure 4.** This science is *biochemistry,* the study of the matter of living things. It is both a life science and a physical science. In the same way, the study of the forces that affect the Earth is *geophysics,* which is both an Earth science and a physical science.

Figure 4
Our DNA (deoxyribonucleic acid) makes each of us unique.

Science and technology work together

Scientists who do experiments to learn more about the world are practicing *pure science*. Engineers look for ways to use this knowledge for practical applications. This application of science is called **technology.** Certain technologies can be important to some people, but may have little impact on others. For example, very few students used personal computers when they were first created in the 1970's. Now, computers are found in many classroms in the United States, but are not as available to students in all other countries.

technology the application of science for practical purposes

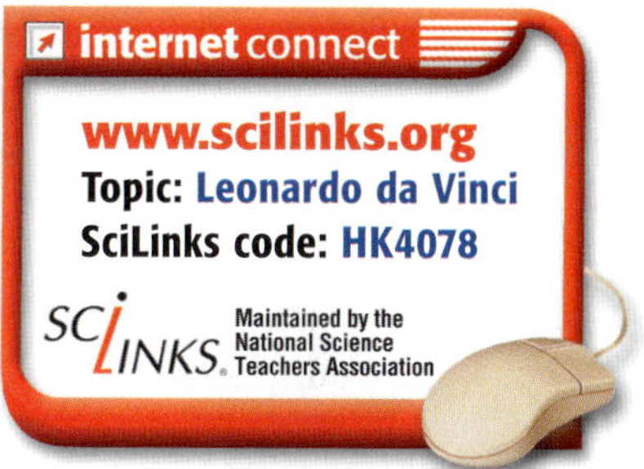

Technology and science depend on one another, as illustrated by some of Leonardo da Vinci's drawings in **Figure 5.** For instance, scientists did not know that tiny organisms such as bacteria even existed until the technology to make precision magnifying lenses developed in the late 1600s.

Figure 5
Some of Leonardo da Vinci's ideas could not be built until twentieth-century technology developed. Some examples are: **A** a design for a parachute and **B** a design for a glider.

Scientific Laws and Theories

▶ **scientific law** a summary of many experimental results and observations; a law tells how things work

▶ **scientific theory** an explanation for some phenomenon that is based on observation, experimentation, and reasoning

People sometimes say things like, "My theory is that we'll see Jaime on the school bus," when they really mean, "I'm guessing that we'll find Jaime on the school bus." People use the word *theory* in everyday speech to refer to a guess about something. In science, a theory is much more than a guess.

Laws and theories are supported by experimental results

When you place a hot cooking pot in a cooler place, does the pot become hotter as it stands? No, it will always get cooler. This illustrates a **scientific law** that states that warm objects always become cooler when they are placed in cooler surroundings. A scientific law describes a process in nature that can be tested by repeated experiments. A law allows predictions to be made about how a system will behave under a wide range of conditions.

However, a law does not *explain* how a process takes place. In the example of the hot cooking pot, nothing in the law tells why hot objects become cooler in cooler surroundings. Such an explanation of how a natural process works must be provided by a **scientific theory.**

Scientific theories are always being questioned and examined. To be valid, a theory must continue to pass several tests.

- A theory must explain observations clearly and consistently. The theory that heat is the energy of particles in motion explains how the far end of a metal tube gets hot when you hold the tip over a flame, as shown in ***Figure 6A.***
- Experiments that illustrate the theory must be repeatable. The far end of the tube always gets hot when the tip is held over a flame, whether it is done for the first time or the thirty-first time.
- You must be able to predict from the theory. You might predict that anything that makes particles move faster will make the object hotter. Sawing a piece of wood will make the metal particles in the saw move faster. If, as shown in ***Figure 6B,*** you saw rapidly, the saw will get hot to the touch.

A

B

Figure 6

The kinetic theory of heat explains many things that you can observe, such as why both the far end of the tube A and the saw blade B get hot.

Mathematics can describe physical events

How would you state the law of gravitation? You could say that something you hold will fall to Earth when you let go. This *qualitative* statement describes with words something you have seen many times. But many scientific laws and theories can be stated as mathematical equations, which are *quantitative* statements.

Rectangle Area Equation

$$A = l \times w$$

The rectangle area equation works for all rectangles, whether they are short, tall, wide, or thin.

Universal Gravitation Equation

$$F = G\frac{m_1 m_2}{d^2}$$

In the same way, the universal gravitation equation describes how big the force will be between two galaxies or between Earth and an apple dropped from your hand, as shown in ***Figure 7.*** Quantitative expressions of the laws of science make communicating about science easier. Scientists around the world speak and read many different languages, but mathematics, the language of science, is the same everywhere.

Theories and laws are always being tested

Sometimes theories have to be changed or replaced completely when new discoveries are made. Over 200 years ago, scientists used the *caloric theory* to explain how objects become hotter and cooler. Heat was thought to be an invisible fluid, called caloric, that could flow from a warm object to a cool one. People thought that fires were fountains of caloric, which flowed into surrounding objects, making them warmer. The caloric theory could explain everything that people knew about heat.

During the 1800s, after doing many experiments, some scientists suggested a new theory based on the idea that heat was a result of the motion of particles. Like many new ideas, this new theory was strongly criticized and not accepted at first by the scientific community. But the caloric theory couldn't explain why rubbing two rough surfaces together made them warmer. Because this theory, the *kinetic theory,* explained the old observations as well as the new ones, it was kept and the caloric theory was discarded.

Models can represent physical events

When you see the word *model,* you may think of a small copy of an airplane or a person who shows off clothing. Scientists use models too. A scientific model is a representation of an object or event that can be studied to understand the real object or event. Sometimes, like a model airplane, models represent things that are too big, too small, or too complex to study easily.

Figure 7

Gravitational attraction is described as a force that varies depending on the mass of the objects and the distance that separates them.

A model of water is shown in ***Figure 8A.*** Chemists use models to study how water forms an ice crystal, such as a snowflake. Models can be drawings on paper. The spring shown in ***Figure 8B*** serves as a model of a sound wave moving through matter. Also, a model can be a mental "picture" or a set of rules that describes what something does. After you have studied atoms in Chapter 3, you will be able to picture atoms in your mind and use models to predict what will happen in chemical reactions.

Scientists and engineers also use computer models. These can be drawings such as the one shown in ***Figure 9A;*** more often, they are mathematical models of complex systems. Computer models can save time and money because long calculations are done by a machine to predict what will happen.

Figure 8

A Models can be used to describe a water molecule (top right) and to study how water molecules are arranged in a snowflake.

B Experiments show that this model depicts how a sound wave moves through matter.

Figure 9

Crash tests give information that is used to make cars safer. Now, models **A** can replace some real-world crash tests **B**.

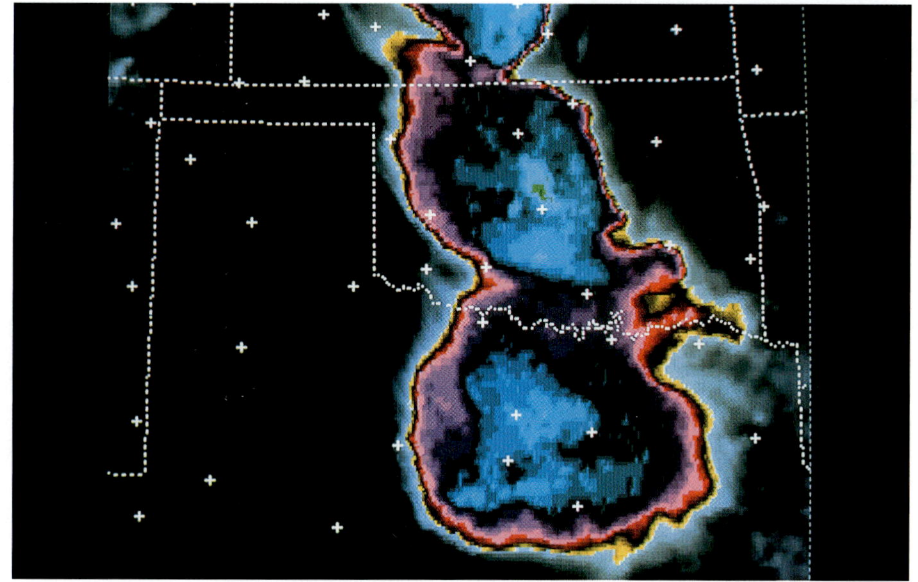

Figure 10
Models help forecast the weather and, in cases of dangerous storms, can help save lives.

Computer models have a variety of applications. For example, they can be used instead of expensive crash tests to study the effects of motion and forces in car crashes, as shown in ***Figure 9.*** Engineers use the predictions from the models to improve the design of cars. *Meteorologists* have computer models such as the one shown in ***Figure 10,*** which uses information about wind speed and direction, air temperature, moisture levels, and ground shape to help forecast the weather.

SECTION 1 REVIEW

SUMMARY

- A scientist makes objective observations.
- A scientist confirms results by repeating experiments and learns more by designing and conducting new experiments.
- Scientific laws and theories are supported by repeated experiments but may be changed when results are not consistent with predictions.
- Models are used to represent real situations and to make predictions.

1. **Compare and Contrast** the two main branches of physical science.
2. **Explain** how science and technology depend on each other.
3. **Explain** how a scientific theory differs from a guess or an opinion.
4. **Define** *scientific law* and give an example.
5. **Compare and Contrast** a scientific law and a scientific theory.
6. **Compare** quantitative and qualitative descriptions.
7. **Describe** how a scientific model is used, and give an example of a scientific model.
8. **Creative Thinking** How do you think Roentgen's training as a scientist affected the way he responded to his discovery?
9. **Creative Thinking** Pick a common happening, develop an explanation for it, and describe an experiment you could perform to test your explanation.

SECTION 2

The Way Science Works

KEY TERMS

critical thinking
scientific method
variable
length
mass
volume
weight

OBJECTIVES

- **Understand** how to use critical thinking skills to solve problems.
- **Describe** the steps of the scientific method.
- **Know** some of the tools scientists use to investigate nature.
- **Explain** the objective of a consistent system of units, and identify the SI units for length, mass, and time.
- **Identify** what each common SI prefix represents, and convert measurements.

critical thinking the ability and willingness to assess claims critically and to make judgments on the basis of objective and supported reasons

Throwing a spear accurately to kill animals for food or to ward off intruders was probably a survival skill people used for thousands of years. In our society, throwing a javelin is an athletic skill, and riding a bicycle or driving a car is considered almost a survival skill. The skills that we place importance on change over time, as society and technology change.

Science Skills

Although pouring liquid into a test tube without spilling is a skill that is useful in science, other skills are more important. Identifying problems, planning experiments, recording observations, and correctly reporting data are some of these more important skills. The most important skill is learning to think critically.

Critical thinking

If you were doing your homework and the lights went out, what would you do? Would you call the electric company immediately? A person who thinks like a scientist might first ask questions and make observations. Are lights on anywhere in the house? If so, what would you conclude? Suppose everything electrical in the house is off. Can you see lights in the neighbors' windows? If their lights are on, what does that mean? What if everyone's lights are off?

If you approach the problem this way, you are thinking logically. This kind of thinking is very much like **critical thinking.** You do this kind of thinking when you consider if the giant economy-sized jar of peanut butter is really less expensive than the regular size, as shown in ***Figure 11,*** or consider if a specific brand of soap makes you more attractive.

Figure 11
Making thoughtful decisions is important in scientific processes as well as in everyday life.

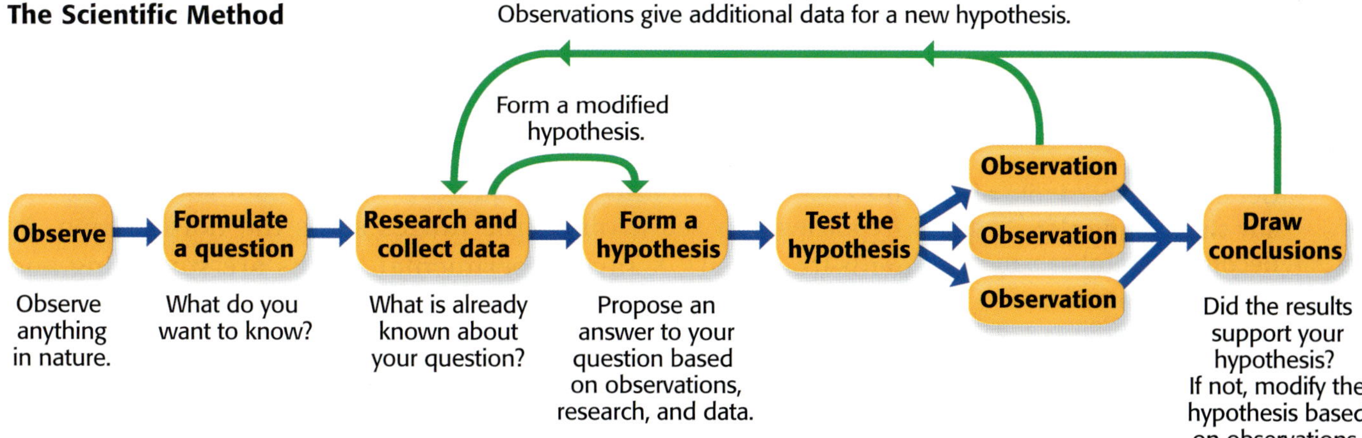

Figure 12
The scientific method is a general description of scientific thinking rather than an exact path for scientists to follow.

When the lights go out, if you get more facts before you call the power company, you're thinking critically. You're not making a reasonable conclusion if you immediately assume there is a citywide power failure. You can make observations and use logic.

Using the scientific method

In the **scientific method,** critical thinking is used to solve scientific problems. The scientific method is a general way to help organize your thinking about questions that you might think of as scientific. Using the scientific method helps you find and evaluate possible answers. The scientific method is often followed as a series of steps like those in ***Figure 12.***

scientific method a series of steps followed to solve problems including collecting data, formulating a hypothesis, testing the hypothesis, and stating conclusions

Most scientific questions begin with observations—simple things you notice. For example, you might notice that when you open a door, you hear a squeak. You ask the question: Why does this door make noise? You may gather data by checking other doors and find that the other doors don't make noise. So you form a *hypothesis,* a possible answer that you can test in some way. For instance, you may think that if the door makes a noise, the source of the noise is the doorknob.

Testing hypotheses

Scientists test a hypothesis by doing a *controlled experiment*. In a controlled experiment, all **variables** that can affect the outcome of the experiment are kept constant, or controlled, except for one. Only the results of changing one given variable are observed.

variable a factor that changes in an experiment in order to test a hypothesis

When you change more than one thing at a time, it's harder to make reasonable conclusions. If you remove the knob, sand the frame, and put oil on the hinges, you may stop the squeak, but you won't know what was causing the squeak. Even if you test one thing at a time, you may not find the answer on the first try. If you take the knob off the door and the door still makes noise, was your experiment a failure?

Quick ACTIVITY

Making Observations

1. Get an ordinary candle of any shape and color.
2. Record all the observations you can make about the candle.
3. Light the candle, and watch it burn for 1 minute.
4. Record as many observations about the burning candle as you can.
5. Share your results with your class, and find out how many different things were observed.

Conducting experiments

In truth, no experiment is a failure because all observations of events in the natural world can be used to revise a hypothesis and to plan tests of a different variable. For example, once you know that the doorknob did not cause the squeak, you can revise your hypothesis to see if oiling the hinges stops the noise. Often, as with Roentgen's X rays, experimental results are surprising and lead scientists in new directions.

Scientists always keep the question to be tested in mind. To avoid coming to false conclusions, scientists must carefully search for bias in the design or analysis of their experiments. Scientists who work together tend to see things from a similar point of view, and should seek opinions from those outside of their own working group. Research that has been examined and critiqued by other scientists is said to have been *peer reviewed*.

In addition to personal bias, scientists should keep in mind and disclose conflicts of interest. Government agencies, private foundations, and industrial interests frequently fund scientific research. Scientists must guard against reaching false conclusions that are desired by their sources of funding.

Some questions, such as how Earth's continents have moved over millions of years, cannot be answered with experimental data. Instead of doing experiments, geologists make observations all over Earth. They also use models, such as the one shown in ***Figure 13,*** based on the laws of physics.

Using scientific tools

Of course, logical thinking isn't the only skill used in science. Sometimes special tools, provided through developments in technology, are used to make observations. Scientists must know how to use these tools, what the limits of the tools are, and how to interpret data from them.

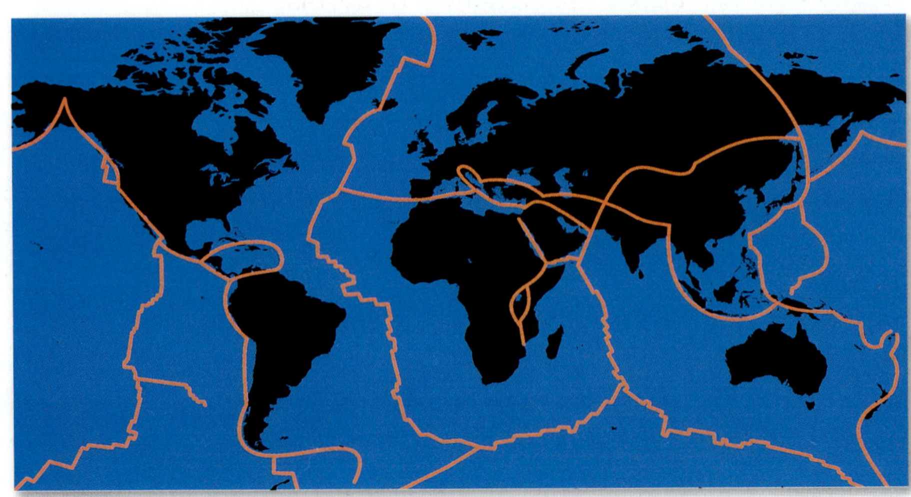

Figure 13

Computer models of Earth's crust help geologists understand how the continental plates (outlined in red) moved in the past and how they may move in the future.

Figure 14

A The Gemini North observatory in Hawaii is a new tool for scientists. Its 8.1 m mirror is used to view distant galaxies.

B The Whirlpool galaxy (M51) and its companion NGC5195 are linked by a trail of gas and dust, which NGC5195 has pulled from M51 by gravitational attraction.

Astronomers, for example, use *telescopes* with lenses and mirrors such as the one shown in **Figure 14A** to magnify objects that appear small because they are far away, such as the distant galaxies shown in **Figure 14B.** Other kinds of telescopes do not form images from visible light. *Radio telescopes* detect the radio signals emitted by distant objects. Some of the oldest, most distant objects in the universe have been found with radio telescopes. Radio waves from those objects were emitted almost 15 billion years ago.

Several different types of *spectroscopes* break light into a rainbowlike *spectrum.* A chemist can learn a great deal about a substance from the light it absorbs or emits. Physicists use *particle accelerators* to make fragments of atoms move extremely fast and then let them smash into atoms or parts of other atoms. Data from these collisions give us information about the structure of atoms.

Units of Measurement

As you learned in Section 1, mathematics is the language of science, and mathematical models rely on accurate observations. But if your scientific measurements are in inches and gallons, some scientists may not understand because they do not use these units. For this reason scientists use the International System of Units, abbreviated SI, which stands for the French phrase *le Système Internationale d'Unités.*

Connection to LANGUAGE ARTS

The word *scope* comes from the Greek word *skopein,* meaning "to see." Science and technology use many different scopes to see things that can't be seen with unaided eyes. For example, the telescope gets its name from the Greek prefix *tele-* meaning "distant" or "far." So a telescope is a tool for seeing far.

Making the Connection

Use a dictionary to find out what is seen by a microscope, a retinoscope, a kaleidoscope, and a hygroscope.

SI units are used for consistency

When all scientists use the same system of measurement, sharing data and results is easier. SI is based on the metric system and uses the seven SI base units that you see listed in ***Table 1.***

Perhaps you noticed that the base units do not include area, volume, pressure, weight, force, speed, and other familiar quantities. Combinations of the base units, called *derived units,* are used for these measurements.

Suppose you want to order carpet for a floor that measures 8.0 m long and 6.0 m wide. You know that the area of a rectangle is its length times its width.

$$A = l \times w$$

The area of the floor can be calculated as shown below.

$$A = 8.0 \text{ m} \times 6.0 \text{ m} = 48 \text{ m}^2$$

(or 48 square meters)

The SI unit of area, m^2, is a derived unit.

Did You Know?

SI started with the metric system in France in 1795. The meter was originally defined as 1/10 000 000 of the distance between the North Pole and the Equator.

Table 1 **SI Base Units**

Quantity	Unit	Abbreviation
Length	meter	m
Mass	kilogram	kg
Time	second	s
Temperature	kelvin	K
Electric current	ampere	A
Amount of substance	mole	mol
Luminous intensity	candela	cd

Table 2 **Prefixes Used for Large Measurements**

Prefix	Symbol	Meaning	Multiple of base unit
kilo-	k	thousand	1000
mega-	M	million	1 000 000
giga-	G	billion	1 000 000 000

Table 3 **Prefixes Used for Small Measurements**

Prefix	Symbol	Meaning	Multiple of base unit
deci-	d	tenth	0.1
centi-	c	hundredth	0.01
milli-	m	thousandth	0.001
micro-	μ	millionth	0.000 001
nano-	n	billionth	0.000 000 001

SI prefixes are for very large and very small measurements

Look at a meterstick. How would you express the length of a bird's egg in meters? How about the distance you traveled on a trip? The bird's egg might be 1/100 m, or 0.01 m, wide. Your trip could have been 800 000 m in distance. To avoid writing a lot of decimal places and zeros, SI uses prefixes to express very small or very large numbers. These prefixes, shown in ***Table 2*** and ***Table 3,*** are all *multiples* of 10.

Using the prefixes, you can now say that the bird's egg is 1 cm (1 *centi*meter is 0.01 m) wide and your trip was 800 km (800 *kilo*meters are 800 000 m) long. Note that the base unit of mass is the *kilo*gram, which is already a multiple of the gram.

It is easy to convert SI units to smaller or larger units. Remember that to make a measurement, it takes more of a small unit or less of a large unit. A person's height could be 1.85 m, a fairly small number. In centimeters, the same height would be 185 cm, a larger number.

So, if you are converting to a smaller unit, multiply the measurement to get a bigger number. To write 1.85 m as *centi*meters, you multiply by 100, as shown below.

$$1.85\ \cancel{m} \times \frac{100\ cm}{1\ \cancel{m}} = 185\ cm$$

If you are converting to a larger unit, divide the measurement to get a smaller number. To change 185 cm to meters, divide by 100, as shown in the following.

$$185\ \cancel{cm} \times \frac{1\ m}{100\ \cancel{cm}} = 1.85\ m$$

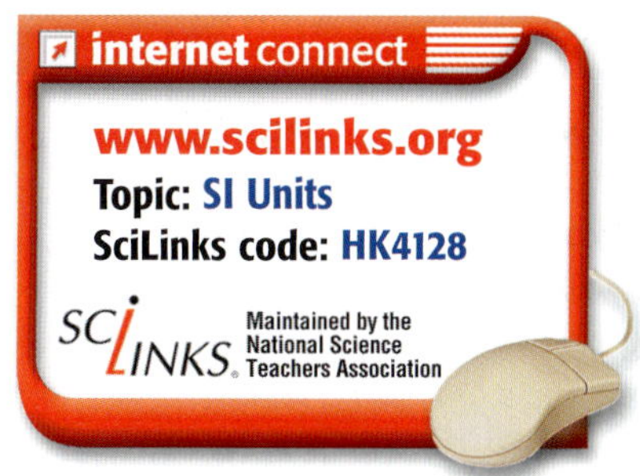

Math Skills

Conversions A roll of copper wire contains 15 m of wire. What is the length of the wire in centimeters?

1 List the given and unknown values.

Given: *length in meters*, $l = 15$ m

Unknown: *length in centimeters* = ? cm

2 Determine the relationship between units.

Looking at **Table 1-3,** you can find that 1 cm = 0.01 m. This also means that 1 m = 100 cm.

You will multiply because you are converting from a larger unit (meters) to a smaller unit (centimeters).

3 Write the equation for the conversion.

$$length\ in\ cm = m \times \frac{100\ cm}{1\ m}$$

4 Insert the known values into the equation, and solve.

$$length\ in\ cm = 15\ \cancel{m} \times \frac{100\ cm}{1\ \cancel{m}}$$

$$length\ in\ cm = 1500\ cm$$

If you have done the conversions properly, all the units above and below the fraction will cancel except the units you need.

Practice

Conversions

1. Write 550 *milli*meters as meters.
2. Write 3.5 seconds as *milli*seconds.
3. Convert 1.6 *kilo*grams to grams.
4. Convert 2500 *milli*grams to *kilo*grams.
5. Convert 4 *centi*meters to *micro*meters.
6. Change 2800 *milli*moles to moles.
7. Change 6.1 amperes to *milli*amperes.
8. Write 3 *micro*grams as *nano*grams.

Did You Know?

A unit used for measuring the mass of precious metals and gems is the carat. The word *carat* comes from the word *carob.* Originally, the carat was the mass of one seed from the carob plant. It is now defined as 200 mg.

Figure 15 Quantitative Measurements

	Time	Length
SI unit	second, s	meter, m
Other units	milliseconds, ms minutes, min hours, h	millimeter, mm centimeter, cm kilometer, km
Examples		91m 2 cm 1 mm
Tools		

Making measurements

Many observations rely on quantitative measurements. The most basic scientific measurements generally answer questions such as how much time did it take and how big is it?

Often, you will measure time, **length,** **mass,** and **volume.** The SI units for these quantities, examples of each quantity, and the tools you may use to measure them are shown in ***Figure 15.***

Although you may hear someone say that he or she is "weighing" an object with a balance, **weight** is not the same as mass. Mass is the quantity of matter and weight is the force with which Earth's gravity pulls on that quantity of matter.

In your lab activities, you will use a graduated cylinder to measure the volume of liquids. The volume of a solid that has a specific geometric shape can be calculated from the measured lengths of its surfaces. Small volumes are usually expressed in cubic centimeters, cm^3. One cubic centimeter is equal to 1 mL.

length a measure of the straight-line distance between two points

mass a measure of the amount of matter in an object

volume a measure of the size of a body or region in three-dimensional space

weight a measure of the gravitational force exerted on an object

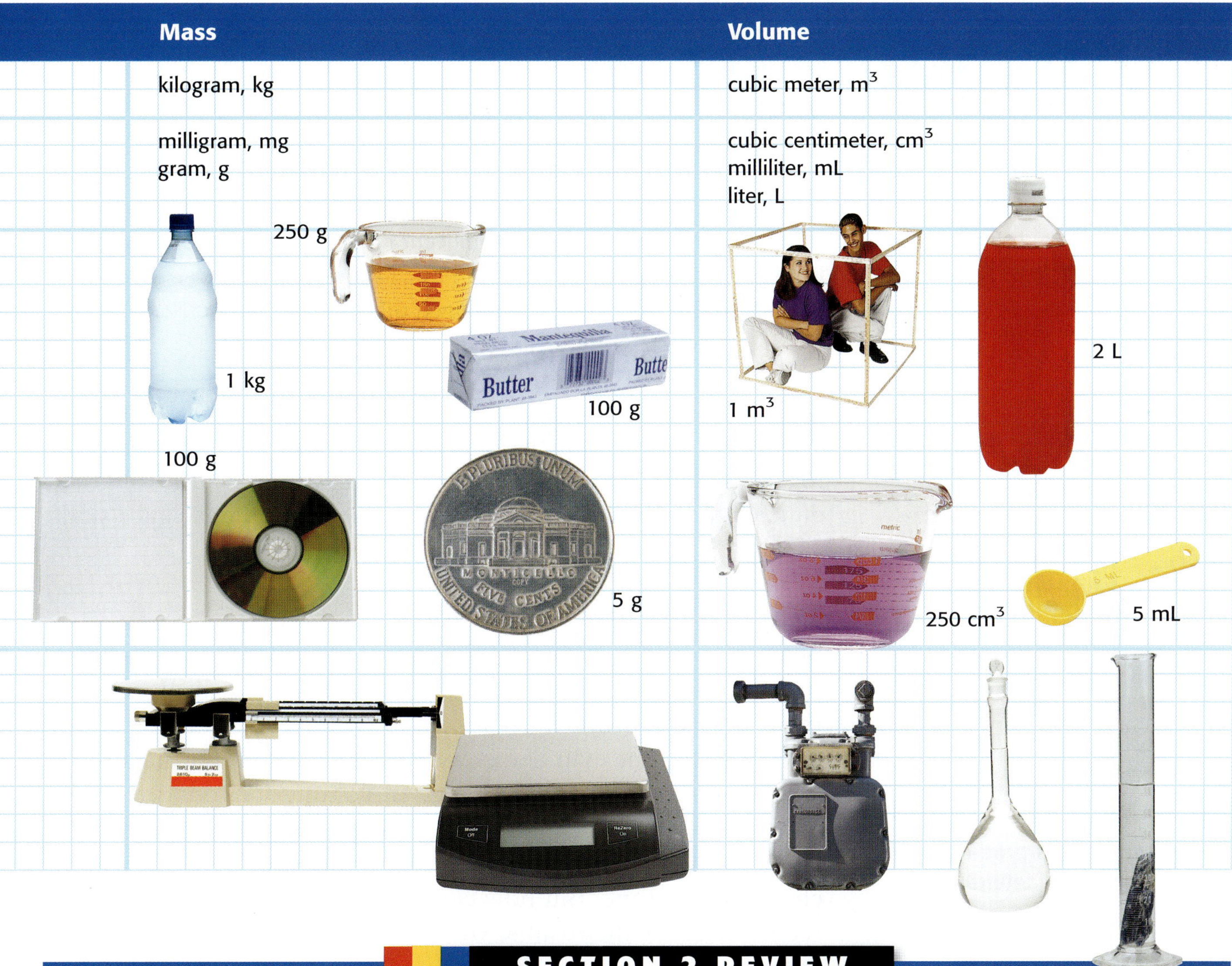

SECTION 2 REVIEW

SUMMARY

- In the scientific method, a person asks a question, collects data about the question, forms a hypothesis, tests the hypothesis, draws conclusions, and if necessary, modifies the hypothesis based on results.
- In an ideal experiment, only one factor, the variable, is tested.
- SI has seven base units.

1. **List** three examples each of things that are commonly measured by mass, by volume, and by length.
2. **Explain** why the scientific method is said to involve critical thinking.
3. **Describe** a hypothesis and how it is used. Give an example of a hypothesis.
4. **Explain** why no experiment should be called a failure.
5. **Relate** the discussion of scientists' tools to how science and technology depend on each other.
6. **Explain** the difference between SI base units and derived units. Give an example of each.
7. **Critical Thinking** Why do you think it is wise to limit an experiment to test only one factor at a time?

SECTION 3

Organizing Data

KEY TERMS

scientific notation
precision
significant figures
accuracy

OBJECTIVES

- **Interpret** line graphs, bar graphs, and pie charts.
- **Use** scientific notation and significant figures in problem solving.
- **Identify** the significant figures in calculations.
- **Understand** the difference between precision and accuracy.

One thing that helped Roentgen discover X rays was that he could read about the experiments other scientists had performed with the cathode ray tube. He was able to learn from their data. Organizing and presenting data are important science skills.

Presenting Scientific Data

Suppose you are trying to determine the speed of a chemical reaction that produces a gas. You can let the gas displace water in a graduated cylinder, as shown in ***Figure 16.*** You read the volume of gas in the cylinder every 10 seconds from the start of the reaction until there is no change in volume for four successive readings. ***Table 4*** shows the data you collect in the experiment.

Because you did the experiment, you saw how the volume changed over time. But how can someone who reads your report see it? To show the results, you can make a graph.

Figure 16

The volume of gas produced by a reaction can be determined by measuring the volume of water the gas displaces in a graduated cylinder.

Table 4 **Experimental Data**

Time (s)	Volume of gas (mL)	Time (s)	Volume of gas (mL)
0	0	90	116
10	3	100	140
20	6	110	147
30	12	120	152
40	25	130	154
50	43	140	156
60	58	150	156
70	72	160	156
80	100	170	156

Line graphs are best for continuous changes

Many types of graphs can be drawn, but which one should you use? A *line graph* is best for displaying data that change. Our example experiment has two variables, time and volume. Time is the *independent variable* because you chose the time intervals to take the measurements. The volume of gas is the *dependent variable* because its value depends on what happens in the experiment.

Line graphs are usually made with the x-axis showing the independent variable and the y-axis showing the dependent variable. **Figure 17** is a graph of the data that is in **Table 4.**

A person who never saw your experiment can look at this graph and know what took place. The graph shows that gas was produced slowly for the first 20 s and that the rate increased until it became constant from about 40 s to 100 s. The reaction slowed down and stopped after about 140 s.

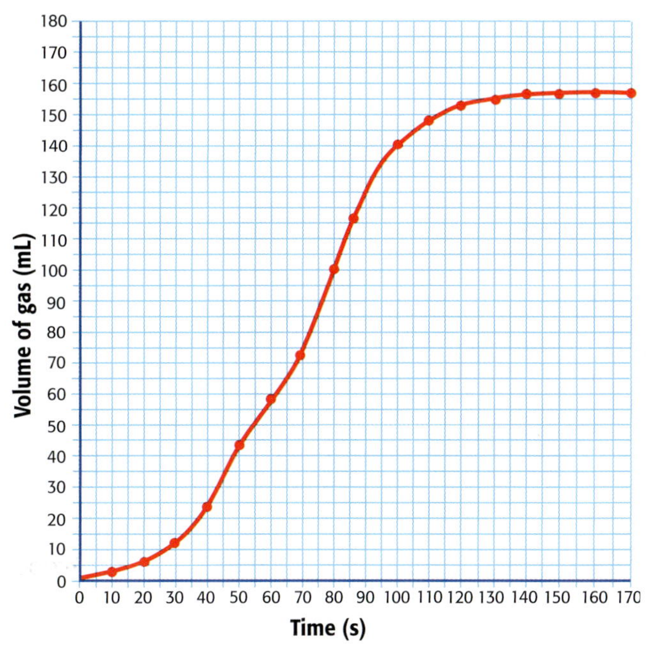

Figure 17

Data that change over a range are best represented by a line graph. Notice that many in-between volumes can be estimated.

Bar graphs compare items

A *bar graph* is useful when you want to compare similar data for several individual items or events. If you measured the melting temperatures of some metals, your data could be presented in a way similar to that in **Table 5. Figure 18** shows the same values as a bar graph. A bar graph often makes clearer how large or small the differences in individual values are.

Table 5 Melting Points of Some Metals

Element	Melting temp. (K)
Aluminum	933
Gold	1337
Iron	1808
Lead	601
Silver	1235

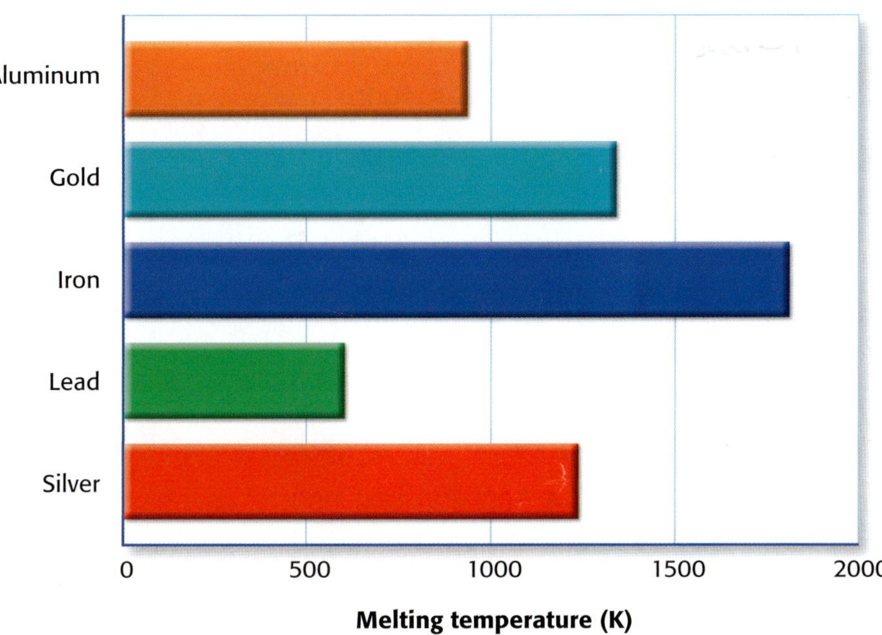

Figure 18

A bar graph is best for data that have specific values for different events or things.

Composition of Calcite

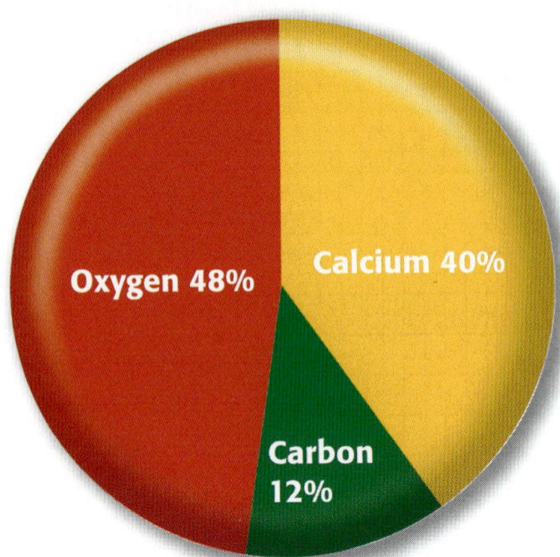

Figure 19

A pie chart is best for data that represent parts of a whole, such as the percentage of each element in the mineral calcite.

Pie charts show the parts of a whole

A *pie chart* is ideal for displaying data that are parts of a whole. Suppose you have analyzed a compound to find the percentage of each element it contains. Your analysis shows that the compound consists of 40 percent calcium, 12 percent carbon, and 48 percent oxygen. You can draw a pie chart that shows these percentages as a portion of the whole pie, the compound, as shown in ***Figure 19.*** To construct a pie chart, refer to the Graphing Skills Refresher in Appendix A and the skills page at the end of this chapter.

Writing Numbers in Scientific Notation

Scientists sometimes need to express measurements using numbers that are very large or very small. For example, the speed of light through space is about 300 000 000 m/s. Suppose you want to calculate the time required for light to travel from Neptune to Earth when Earth and Neptune are 4 500 000 000 000 m apart. To find out how long it takes, you would divide the distance between Earth and Neptune by the distance light travels in 1 s.

$$t = \frac{\text{distance from Earth to Neptune (m)}}{\text{distance light travels in 1 s (m/s)}}$$

$$t = \frac{4\,500\,000\,000\,000 \text{ m}}{300\,000\,000 \text{ m/s}}$$

This is a lot of zeros to keep track of when performing a calculation.

To reduce the number of zeros, you can express values as a simple number multiplied by a power of 10. This is called **scientific notation.** Some powers of 10 and their decimal equivalents are shown below.

scientific notation a method of expressing a quantity as a number multiplied by 10 to the appropriate power

$$10^4 = 10\,000$$
$$10^3 = 1000$$
$$10^2 = 100$$
$$10^1 = 10$$
$$10^0 = 1$$
$$10^{-1} = 0.1$$
$$10^{-2} = 0.01$$
$$10^{-3} = 0.001$$

In scientific notation, 4 500 000 000 000 m can be written as 4.5×10^{12} m. The speed of light in space is 3.0×10^8 m/s. Refer to the Math Skills Refresher in Appendix A for more information on scientific notation.

Using scientific notation

When you use scientific notation in calculations, you follow the math rules for powers of 10. When you multiply two values in scientific notation, you add the powers of 10. When you divide, you subtract the powers of 10.

So the problem about Earth and Neptune can be solved more easily as shown below.

$$t = \frac{4.5 \times 10^{12} \text{ m}}{3.0 \times 10^{8} \text{ m/s}}$$

$$t = \left(\frac{4.5}{3.0} \times \frac{10^{12}}{10^{8}}\right) \frac{\text{m}}{\text{m/s}}$$

$$t = (1.5 \times 10^{(12-8)})\text{s}$$

$$t = 1.5 \times 10^{4} \text{ s}$$

Math Skills

Writing Scientific Notation The adult human heart pumps about 18 000 L of blood each day. Write this value in scientific notation.

1 List the given and unknown values.

Given: *volume,* $V = 18\ 000$ L

Unknown: *volume,* $V = ? \times 10^{?}$ L

2 Write the form for scientific notation.

$V = ? \times 10^{?}$ L

3 Insert the known values into the form, and solve.

First find the largest power of 10 that will divide into the known value and leave one digit before the decimal point. You get 1.8 if you divide 10 000 into 18 000 L. So, 18 000 L can be written as $(1.8 \times 10\ 000)$ L.

Then write 10 000 as a power of 10. Because $10\ 000 = 10^4$, you can write 18 000 L as 1.8×10^4 L.

$V = 1.8 \times 10^4$ L

Practice

Writing Scientific Notation

1. Write the following measurements in scientific notation:

a. 800 000 000 m

b. 0.0015 kg

c. 60 200 L

d. 0.000 95 m

e. 8 002 000 km

f. 0.000 000 000 06 kg

2. Write the following measurements in long form:

a. 4.5×10^3 g

b. 6.05×10^{-3} m

c. 3.115×10^6 km

d. 1.99×10^{-8} cm

- A shortcut for scientific notation involves moving the decimal point and counting the number of places it is moved. To change 18 000 to 1.8, the decimal point is moved four places to the left. The number of places the decimal is moved is the correct power of 10.

$18\ 000 \text{ L} = 1.8 \times 10^4 \text{ L}$

- When a quantity smaller than 1 is converted to scientific notation, the decimal moves to the right and the power of 10 is *negative.* For example, suppose an *E. coli* bacterium is measured to be 0.000 0021 m long. To express this measurement in scientific notation, move the decimal point to the right.

$0.000\ 0021 \text{ m} = 2.1 \times 10^{-6} \text{ m}$

Math Skills

Using Scientific Notation Your state plans to buy a rectangular tract of land measuring 5.36×10^3 m by 1.38×10^4 m to establish a nature preserve. What is the area of this tract in square meters?

1 List the given and unknown values.

Given: *length,* $l = 1.38 \times 10^4$ m

width, $w = 5.36 \times 10^3$ m

Unknown: *area,* $A = ?$ m^2

2 Write the equation for area.

$A = l \times w$

3 Insert the known values into the equation, and solve.

$A = (1.38 \times 10^4 \text{ m})(5.36 \times 10^3 \text{ m})$

Regroup the values and units as follows.

$A = (1.38 \times 5.36)(10^4 \times 10^3)(\text{m} \times \text{m})$

When multiplying, add the powers of 10.

$A = (1.38 \times 5.36)(10^{4+3})(\text{m} \times \text{m})$

$A = 7.3968 \times 10^7 \text{ m}^2$

$A = 7.40 \times 10^7 \text{ m}^2$

Practice HINT

Because not all devices can display superscript numbers, scientific calculators and some math software for computers display numbers in scientific notation using E values. That is, 3.12×10^4 may be shown as 3.12 E4. Very small numbers are shown with negative values. For example, 2.637×10^{-5} may be shown as 2.637 E–5. The letter E signifies exponential notation. The E value is the exponent (power) of 10. The rules for using powers of 10 are the same whether the exponent is displayed as a superscript or as an E value.

Practice

Using Scientific Notation

1. Perform the following calculations.
   - **a.** $(5.5 \times 10^4 \text{ cm}) \times (1.4 \times 10^4 \text{ cm})$
   - **b.** $(2.77 \times 10^{-5} \text{ m}) \times (3.29 \times 10^{-4} \text{ m})$
   - **c.** $(4.34 \text{ g/mL}) \times (8.22 \times 10^6 \text{ mL})$
   - **d.** $(3.8 \times 10^{-2} \text{ cm}) \times (4.4 \times 10^{-2} \text{ cm}) \times (7.5 \times 10^{-2} \text{ cm})$
2. Perform the following calculations.
   - **a.** $\dfrac{3.0 \times 10^4 \text{ L}}{62 \text{ s}}$
   - **b.** $\dfrac{6.05 \times 10^7 \text{ g}}{8.8 \times 10^6 \text{ cm}^3}$
   - **c.** $\dfrac{5.2 \times 10^8 \text{ cm}^3}{9.5 \times 10^2 \text{ cm}}$
   - **d.** $\dfrac{3.8 \times 10^{-5} \text{ kg}}{4.6 \times 10^{-5} \text{ kg/cm}^3}$

Using Significant Figures

Suppose you measure a length of wire with two tape measures. One tape is marked every 0.001 m, and the other is marked every 0.1 m. The tape marked every 0.001 m gives you more **precision,** because with it you can report a length of 1.638 m. The other tape is only precise to 1.6 m.

To show the precision of a measured quantity, scientists use **significant figures.** The length of 1.638 m has four significant figures because the digits 1638 are known for sure. The measurement of 1.6 m has two significant figures.

precision the exactness of a measurement

significant figure a prescribed decimal place that determines the amount of rounding off to be done based on the precision of the measurement

A Good accuracy (near post) and good precision (close together)

B Good accuracy (near post) and poor precision (spread apart)

C Poor accuracy (far from post) and good precision (close together)

D Poor accuracy (far from post) and poor precision (spread apart)

Figure 20

A ring toss is a game of skill, but it is also a good way to visualize accuracy and precision in measurements.

If the tip of your tape measure has broken off, you can read 1.638 m precisely, but that number is not **accurate.** A measured quantity is only as accurate as the tool used to make the measurement. One way to think about the accuracy and precision of measurements is shown in ***Figure 20.***

accuracy a description of how close a measurement is to the true value of the quantity measured

Math Skills

Significant Figures Calculate the volume of a room that is 3.125 m high, 4.25 m wide, and 5.75 m long. Write the answer with the correct number of significant figures.

1 List the given and unknown values.

Given: *length,* $l = 5.75$ m

width, $w = 4.25$ m

height, $h = 3.125$ m

Unknown: *Volume,* $V = ?\ \text{m}^3$

2 Write the equation for volume.

Volume, $V = l \times w \times h$

3 Insert the known values into the equation, and solve.

$V = 5.75\ \text{m} \times 4.25\ \text{m} \times 3.125\ \text{m}$

$V = 76.367\ 1875\ \text{m}^3$

The answer should have three significant figures because the value with the smallest number of significant figures has three significant figures.

$V = 76.4\ \text{m}^3$

Practice

Significant Figures

Perform the following calculations, and write the answer with the correct number of significant figures.

1. 12.65 m × 42.1 m
2. 3.02 cm × 6.3 cm × 8.225 cm
3. 3.7 g ÷ 1.083 cm^3
4. 3.244 m ÷ 1.4 s

Practice HINT

When rounding to get the correct number of significant figures, do you round up or down if the last digit is a 5? Your teacher may have other ways to round, but one very common way is to round to get an even number. For example, 3.25 is rounded to 3.2, and 3.35 is rounded to 3.4. Using this simple rule, half the time you will round up and half the time you will round down. See the Math Skills Refresher in Appendix A for more about significant figures and rounding.

When you use measurements in calculations, the answer is only as precise as the least precise measurement used in the calculation—the measurement with the fewest significant figures. Suppose, for example, that the floor of a rectangular room is measured to the nearest 0.01 m (1 cm). The measured dimensions are reported to be 5.871 m by 8.14 m.

If you use a calculator to multiply 5.871 by 8.14, the display may show 47.789 94 as an answer. But you don't really know the area of the room to the nearest 0.000 01 m^2, as the calculator showed. To have the correct number of significant figures, you must round off your results. In this case the correct rounded result is A = 47.8 m^2, because the least precise value in the calculation had three significant figures.

When adding or subtracting, use this rule: the answer cannot be more precise than the values in the calculation. A calculator will add 6.3421 s and 12.1 s to give 18.4421 as a result. But the least precise value was known to 0.1 s, so round to 18.4 s.

SECTION 3 REVIEW

SUMMARY

- Representing scientific data with graphs helps you and others understand experimental results.
- Scientific notation is useful for writing very large and very small measurements because it uses powers of 10 instead of strings of zeros.
- Accuracy is the extent to which a value approaches the true value.
- Precision is the degree of exactness of a measurement.
- Expressing data with significant figures tells others how precisely a measurement was made.

1. **Describe** the kind of data that is best displayed as a line graph.
2. **Describe** the kind of data that is best displayed as a pie chart. Give an example of data from everyday experiences that could be placed on a pie chart.
3. **Explain** in your own words the difference between accuracy and precision.
4. **Critical Thinking** An old riddle asks, "Which weighs more, a pound of feathers or a pound of lead?" Answer the question, and explain why you think people sometimes answer incorrectly.

Math Skills

5. **Convert** the following measurements to scientific notation:
   a. 15 400 mm^3
   b. 0.000 33 kg
   c. 2050 mL
   d. 0.000 015 mol
6. **Calculate** the following:
   a. 3.16×10^3 m $\times$ 2.91×10^4 m
   b. 1.85×10^{-3} cm $\times$ 5.22×10^{-2} cm
   c. 9.04×10^5 g $\div$ 1.35×10^5 cm^3
7. **Calculate** the following, and round the answer to the correct number of significant figures.
   a. 54.2 cm^2 $\times$ 22 cm
   b. 23 500 m $\div$ 89 s

Constructing a Pie Chart

Unlike line or bar graphs, pie charts require special calculations to accurately display data. The steps below show how to construct a pie chart from this data.

Wisconsin Hardwood Trees

Type of tree	Number found
Oak	600
Maple	750
Beech	300
Birch	1200
Hickory	150
Total	3000

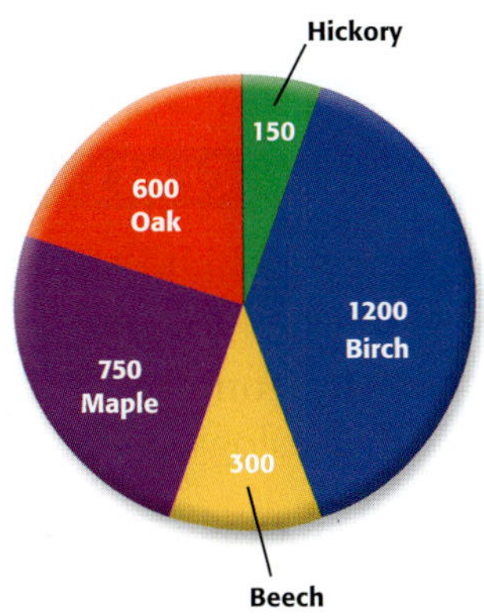

1 First, find the percentage of each type of tree. To do this, divide the number of each type of tree by the total number of trees and multiply by 100.

$$\frac{600 \text{ oak}}{3000 \text{ trees}} \times 100 = 20\% \text{ oak} \qquad \frac{750 \text{ maple}}{3000 \text{ trees}} \times 100 = 25\% \text{ maple}$$

Continuing these calculations for the rest of the trees, you find that 10% of the trees are beech, 40% are birch, and 5% are hickory. Check to make sure the sum is 100.

2 Now determine the size of the pie shapes that will make up the chart. Use the conversion factor 360°/100% to convert from percentage to degrees of a circle.

$$20\% \text{ oak} \times \frac{360°}{100\%} = 72° \text{ oak} \qquad 25\% \text{ maple} \times \frac{360°}{100\%} = 90° \text{ maple}$$

$$10\% \text{ beech} \times \frac{360°}{100\%} = 36° \text{ beech} \qquad 40\% \text{ birch} \times \frac{360°}{100\%} = 144° \text{ birch}$$

$$5\% \text{ hickory} \times \frac{360°}{100\%} = 18° \text{ hickory}$$

Check to make sure that the sum of all angles is 360°.

3 Use a compass to draw a circle and mark the circle's center. Then use a protractor to draw an angle of 144°. Mark this angle. From this mark, measure an angle of 90°. Continue marking angles from largest to smallest until all the angles have been marked. Finally, label each part of the chart, and choose an appropriate title for the graph.

Practice

1. A recipe for a loaf of bread calls for 474 g water, 9.6 g yeast, 28.3 g butter, 10 g salt, 10 g honey, and 907 g flour. Make a pie chart showing what percentage of the bread each of these ingredients is.

Chapter Highlights

Before you begin, review the summaries of key ideas of each section, found at the end of each section. The vocabulary terms are listed on the first page of each section.

UNDERSTANDING CONCEPTS

1. Which of the following is not included in physical science?
a. physics **c.** astronomy
b. chemistry **d.** zoology

2. What science deals most with energy and forces?
a. biology **c.** botany
b. physics **d.** agriculture

3. Using superconductors to build computers is an example of
a. technology. **c.** pure science.
b. applied biology. **d.** an experiment.

4. A balance is a scientific tool used to measure
a. temperature. **c.** volume.
b. time. **d.** mass.

5. Which of the following units is an SI base unit?
a. liter **c.** kilogram
b. cubic meter **d.** centimeter

6. The composition of the mixture of gases that makes up our air is best represented on what kind of graph?
a. pie chart **c.** line graph
b. bar graph **d.** variable graph

7. In a controlled experiment,
a. the outcome is controlled.
b. one variable is fixed while all others are changed.
c. one variable is changed while all others remain fixed.
d. results are obtained by computer models.

USING VOCABULARY

8. *Physical science* was once defined as the science of the nonliving world. Write a paragraph suggesting why that definition is no longer sufficient. **WRITING SKILL**

9. Explain why the observation that the sun sets in the west could be called a scientific law.

10. Explain why the rotation of Earth could be considered a *scientific theory*. Use it to account for the answer in item 9, as well as to explain the motion of stars in the night sky.

11. The volume of a bottle has been measured to be 465 mL. Use the terms *significant figures* and *precision* to explain what you know and do not know about the measured volume. How does the *accuracy* of the measurement affect the value?

12. Explain why *mass* and *weight* are not the same. How would the units in which they are measured differ?

BUILDING MATH SKILLS

13. Graphing The graph at right shows the changes in temperature during a chemical reaction. Study the graph and answer the following questions:

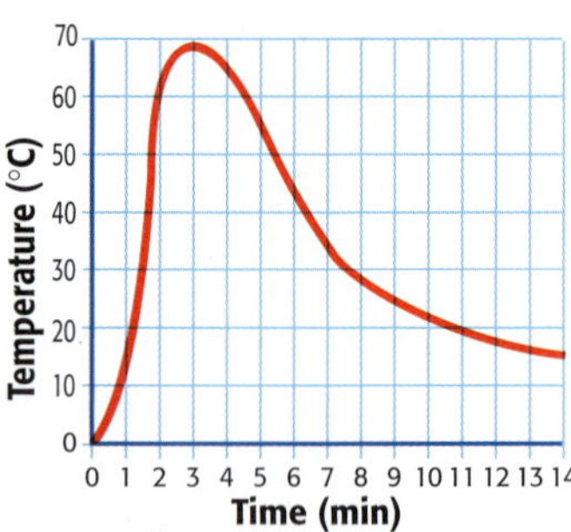

a. What was the highest temperature reached during the reaction?
b. How many minutes passed before the highest temperature was reached?
c. During what period of time was the temperature increasing?
d. Did heating or cooling occur faster?

14. Graphing Silver solder is a mixture of 40 percent silver, 40 percent tin, 14 percent copper, and 6 percent zinc. Draw a graph that shows the composition of silver solder.

15. Scientific Notation Write the following measurements in scientific notation:

a. 22 000 mg　　**c.** 65 900 000 m
b. 0.005 km　　**d.** 0.000 0037 kg

16. Scientific Notation Do the following calculations, and write the answers in scientific notation:

a. 37 000 000 A $\times$ 7 100 000 s
b. 0.000 312 $m^3 \div$ 486 s

17. Significant Figures Round the following measurements to the number of significant figures shown in parentheses:

a. 7.376 m (2)　　**c.** 0.087 904 85 g (1)
b. 48 794 km (3)　　**d.** 362.003 06 s (5)

18. Significant Figures Do the following calculations, and write the answers with the correct number of significant figures:

a. 15.75 m $\times$ 8.45 m
b. 5650 L $\div$ 27 min

19. SI Prefixes Express each of the following quantities using an appropriate SI prefix before the proper units.

a. 0.004 g　　**b.** 75 000 m

THINKING CRITICALLY

20. Applying Knowledge Today, scientists must do a search through scientific journals before performing an experiment or making metho-dical observations. Where would this step take place in the diagram of the scientific method?

21. Creative Thinking At an air show, you are watching a group of skydivers when a friend says, "We learned in science class that things fall to Earth because of the law of gravitation." Tell what is wrong with your friend's statement, and explain your reasoning.

22. Applying Knowledge You have decided to test the effects of five different garden fertilizers by applying some of each to five separate rows of radishes. What is the independent variable? What factors should you control? How will you measure the results?

23. Interpreting and Communicating A person points to an empty, thick-walled glass bottle and says that the volume is 1200 cm^3. Explain why the person's statement is not as clear as it should be.

DEVELOPING LIFE/WORK SKILLS

24. Interpreting Graphics A consumer magazine has tested several portable stereos and has rated them according to price and sound quality. The data are summarized in the bar graph shown below. Study the graph and answer the following questions:

a. Which brand has the best sound?
b. Which brand has the highest price?
c. Which brand do you think has the best sound for the price?
d. Do you think that sound quality corresponds to price?
e. If you can spend as much as $150, which brand would you buy? Explain your answer.

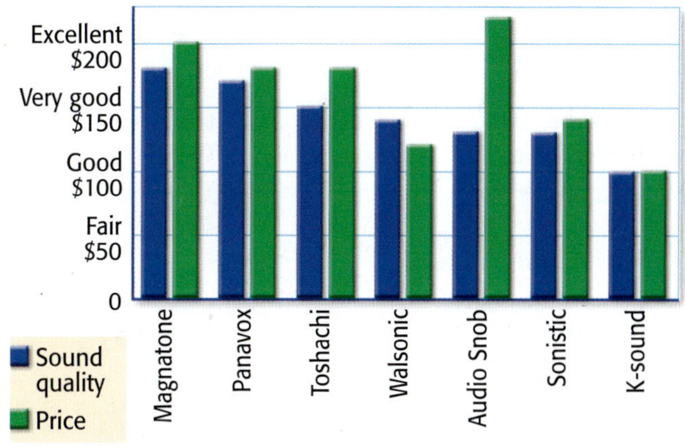

25. **Making Decisions** You have hired a painter to paint your room with a color that must be specially mixed. This color will be difficult to match if more has to be made. The painter tells you that the total length of your walls is 26 m and all walls are 2.5 m tall. You determine the area ($A = l \times w$) to be painted is 65 m^2. The painter says that 1 gal of paint will cover about 30 m^2 and that you should order 2 gal of paint. List at least three questions you should ask the painter before you buy the paint.

26. **Applying Technology** Scientists discovered how to produce laser light in 1960. The substances in lasers emit an intense beam of light when electrical energy is applied. Find out what the word *laser* stands for, and list four examples of technologies that use lasers.

INTEGRATING CONCEPTS

27. **Integrating Biology** One of the most important discoveries involving X rays came in the early 1950s, when the work of Rosalind Franklin, a British scientist, provided evidence for the structure of a critical substance. Do library research to learn how Franklin used X rays and what her discovery was.

28. **Concept Mapping** Copy the unfinished concept map given below onto a sheet of paper. Complete the map by writing the correct word or phrase in the lettered box.

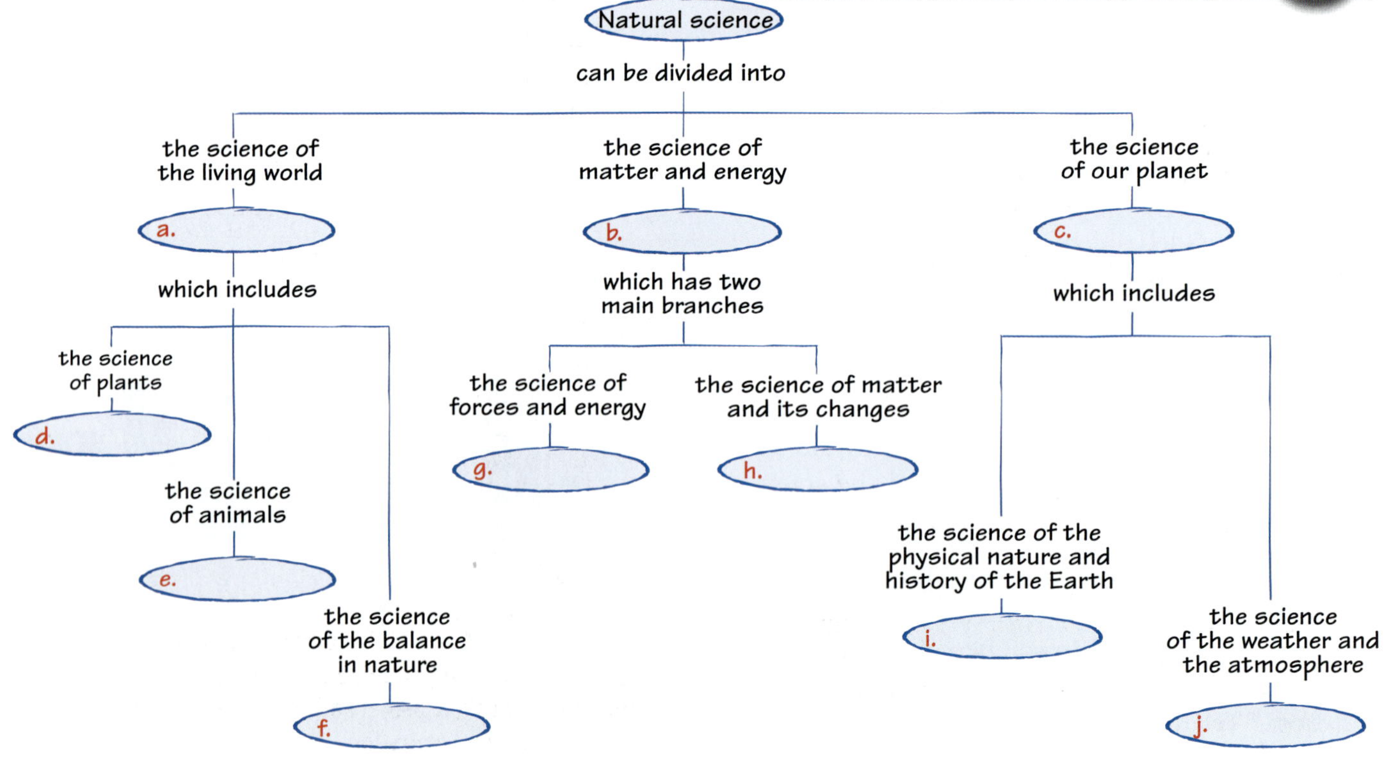

Standardized Test Prep

Understanding Concepts

Directions (1–3): **For *each* question, write on a separate sheet of paper the letter of the correct answer.**

1 During a storm, rainwater depth is measured every 15 minutes. Which of these terms describes the depth of the water?
- **A.** controlled variable
- **B.** dependent variable
- **C.** independent variable
- **D.** significant variable

2 Why were scientists unable to form a theory that diseases are caused by bacteria before the late fifteenth century?
- **F.** No one tried to understand the cause of disease until then.
- **G.** Earlier scientists were not intelligent enough to understand the existence of bacteria.
- **H.** The existence of microbes could not be discovered until the technology to make high-quality lenses had been developed.
- **I.** Doctors believed they understood the disease process, so they would not accept new ideas about the causes.

3 What is a scientific theory?
- **A.** A theory is a guess as to what will happen.
- **B.** A theory is a summary of a scientific fact based on observations.
- **C.** A theory is an explanation of how a process works based on observations.
- **D.** A theory describes a process in nature that can be repeated by testing.

Directions (4): **Write a short response to the question.**

4 When designing a new airplane, experienced pilots use computer simulations to determine how changes from previous designs affect the plane's handling in flight. What is the advantage of computer simulation over actually building the plane and having pilots test it in actual flight situations?

Reading Skills

Directions (5): **Read the passage below. Then answer the question.**

Two thousand years ago Earth was believed to be unmoving and at the center of the universe. The moon, sun, each of the known planets, and all of the stars were believed to be located on the surfaces of rotating crystal spheres. Motion of the celestial objects could be predicted based on the complex movement of the spheres that had been determined using observations recorded over many years.

5 Demonstrate why this description of the universe was a useful model to ancient astronomers but not to present-day astronomers.

Interpreting Graphics

Directions (6): **Base your answer to question 6 on the graph below.**

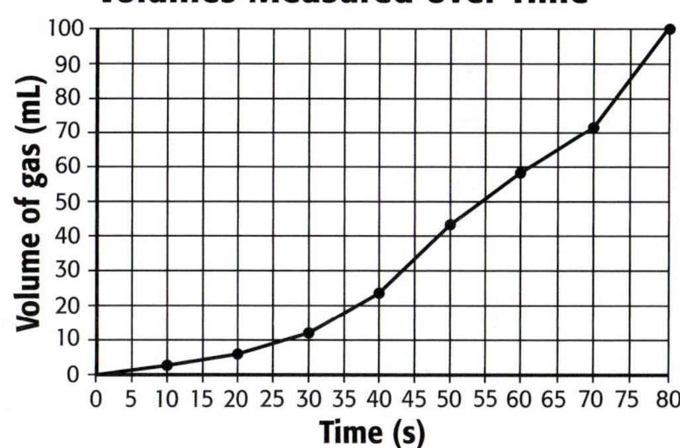

6 What is the volume of the gas 40 seconds into the experiment?
- **F.** 15 mL
- **G.** 24 mL
- **H.** 27 mL
- **I.** 50 mL

Test TIP

When answering short-response or extended-response questions, be sure to write in complete sentences. When you have finished writing your answer, be sure to proofread for errors in spelling, grammar, and punctuation.

Skills Practice Lab

Making Measurements

Introduction

How can you use laboratory tools to measure familiar objects?

Objectives

- ***Measure*** mass, length, volume, and temperature.
- ***Organize*** data into tables and graphs.

Materials

balance, platform or triple-beam
basketball, volleyball, or soccer ball
graduated cylinder, 25 mL
meterstick or metric ruler marked with centimeters and millimeters
small beaker
small block or box
small rock or irregularly-shaped object
sodium chloride (table salt)
sodium hydrogen carbonate (baking soda)
string
test tubes
wall thermometer

Procedure

Preparing for Your Experiment

1. In this laboratory exercise, you will use a meterstick to measure length, a graduated cylinder to measure volume, a balance to measure mass, and a thermometer to measure temperature. You will determine volume by liquid displacement.

Measuring Temperature

2. At a convenient time during the lab, go to the wall thermometer and read the temperature. Be sure no one else is recording the temperature at the same time. On the chalkboard, record your reading and the time at which you read the temperature. At the end of your lab measurements, you will make a graph of the temperature readings made by the class.

Measuring Length

3. Measure the length, width, and height of a block or box in centimeters. Record the measurements in a table like ***Table 6,*** shown below. Using the equation below, calculate the volume of the block in cubic centimeters (cm^3), and write the volume in the table.

   Volume = length (cm) × width (cm) × height (cm)

   $$V = l \times w \times h$$

   $$V = ?\ cm^3$$

4. Repeat the measurements twice more, recording the data in your table. Find the average of your measurements and the average of the volume you calculated.

Table 6 **Dimensions of a Rectangular Block**

	Length (cm)	Width (cm)	Height (cm)	Volume (cm^3)
Trial 1				
Trial 2				
Trial 3				
Average				

5. To measure the circumference of a ball, wrap a piece of string around the ball and mark the end point. Measure the length of the string using the meterstick or metric ruler. Record your measurements in a table like ***Table 7,*** shown below. Using a different piece of string each time, make two more measurements of the circumference of the ball, and record your data in the table.
6. Find the average of the three values and calculate the difference, if any, of each of your measurements from the average.

Table 7 **Circumference of a Ball**

	Circumference (cm)	Difference from average (cm)
Trial 1		
Trial 2		
Trial 3		
Average		

Measuring Mass

7. Place a small beaker on the balance, and measure the mass. Record the value in a table like ***Table 8,*** shown below. Measure to the nearest 0.01 g if you are using a triple-beam balance and to the nearest 0.1 g if you are using a platform balance.
8. Move the rider to a setting that will give a value 5 g more than the mass of the beaker. Add sodium chloride (table salt) to the beaker a little at a time until the balance just begins to swing. You now have about 5 g of salt in the beaker. Complete the measurement (to the nearest 0.01 or 0.1 g), and record the total mass of the beaker and the sodium chloride in your table. Subtract the mass of the beaker from the total mass to find the mass of the sodium chloride.
9. Repeat steps 7 and 8 two times, and record your data in your table. Find the averages of your measurements, as indicated in ***Table 8.***

Table 8 **Mass of Sodium Chloride**

	Mass of beaker and sodium chloride (g)	Mass of beaker (g)	Mass of sodium chloride (g)
Trial 1			
Trial 2			
Trial 3			
Average			

10. Make a table like ***Table 8,*** substituting sodium hydrogen carbonate for sodium chloride. Repeat steps 7, 8, and 9 using sodium hydrogen carbonate (baking soda), and record your data.

Measuring Volume

11. Fill one of the test tubes with tap water. Pour the water into a 25 mL graduated cylinder.
12. The top of the column of water in the graduated cylinder will have a downward curve. This curve is called a *meniscus* and is shown in the figure at right. Take your reading at the bottom of the meniscus. Record the volume of the test tube in a table like ***Table 9.*** Measure the volume of the other test tubes, and record their volumes. Find the average volume of the three test tubes.

Table 9 **Liquid Volume**

	Volume (mL)
Test tube 1	
Test tube 2	
Test tube 3	
Average	

Measuring Volume by Liquid Displacement

13. Pour about 10 mL of tap water into the 25 mL graduated cylinder. Record the volume as precisely as you can in a table like ***Table 10,*** shown below.

Table 10 **Volume of an Irregular Solid**

	Total volume (mL)	Volume of water only (mL)	Volume of object (mL)
Trial 1			
Trial 2			
Trial 3			
Average			

14. Gently drop a small object, such as a stone, into the graduated cylinder; be careful not to splash any water out of the cylinder. You may find it easier to tilt the cylinder slightly and let the object slide down the side. Measure the volume of the water and the object. Record the volume in your table. Determine the volume of the object by subtracting the volume of the water from the total volume.

Analysis

1. On a clean sheet of paper make a line graph of the temperatures that were measured with the wall thermometer over time. Did the temperature change during the class period? If it did, find the average temperature, and determine the largest rise and the largest drop.

Conclusions

2. On a clean sheet of paper make a bar graph using the data from the three calculations of the mass of sodium chloride. Indicate the average value of the three determinations by drawing a line that represents the average value across the individual bars. Do the same for the sodium hydrogen carbonate masses. Using the information in your graphs, determine whether you measured the sodium chloride or the sodium hydrogen carbonate more precisely.
3. Suppose one of your test tubes has a capacity of 23 mL. You need to use about 5 mL of a liquid. Describe how you could estimate 5 mL.
4. Why is it better to align the meterstick with the edge of the object at the 1 cm mark rather than at the end of the stick?

5. Why do you think it is better to measure the circumference of the ball using string than to use a flexible metal measuring tape?

CHAPTER 2

Matter

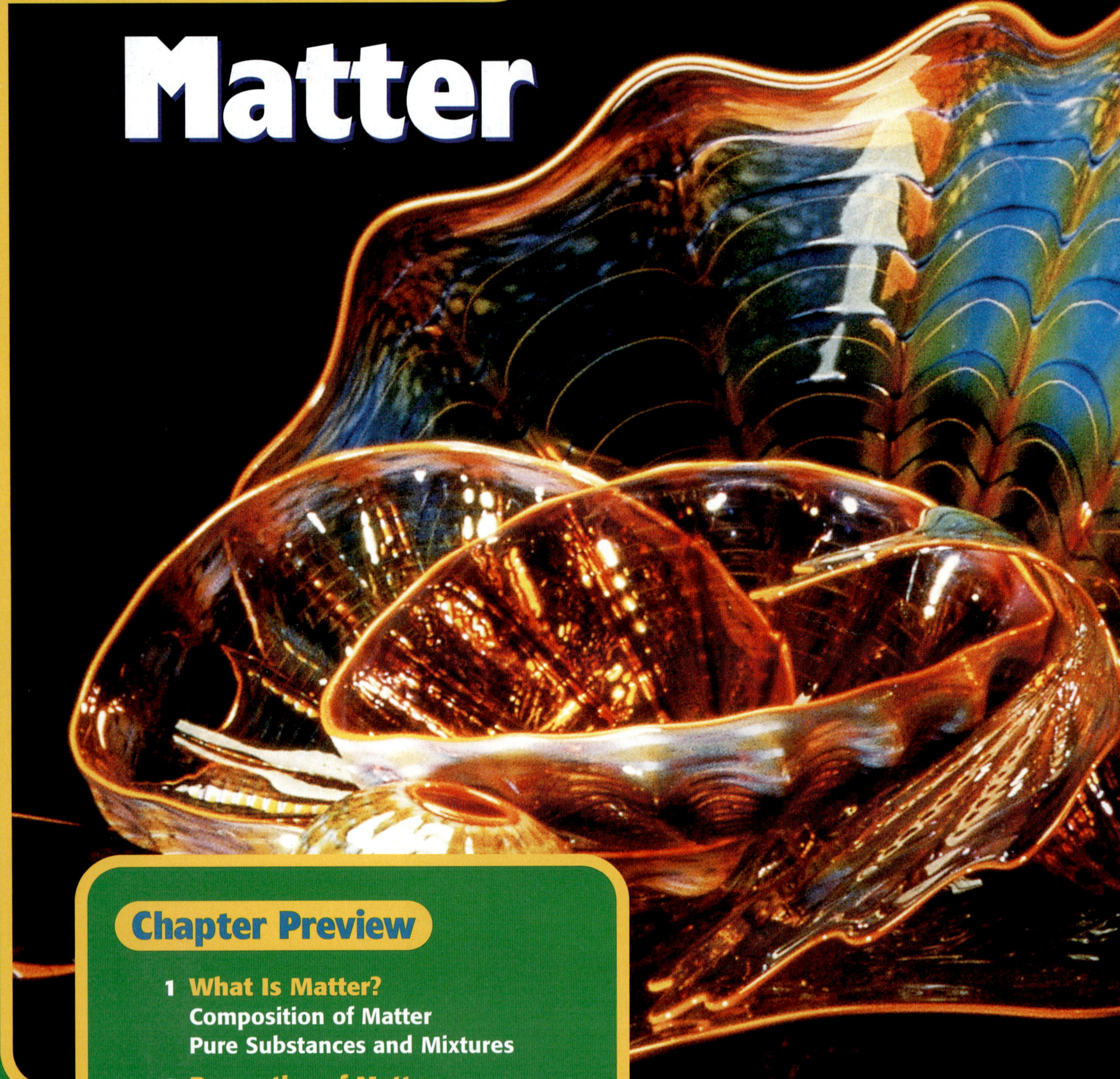

Chapter Preview

Focus ACTIVITY

Background People have been making glass for thousands of years. Glass making begins when sand is mixed with finely ground limestone and a powder called *soda ash.* When the mixture is heated to about 1500°C, the sand mixture becomes transparent and flows like honey.

A glass blower dips a hollow iron blowpipe into the red-hot mixture and picks up a gob of molten glass. By turning the sticky glob and blowing into the tube, the glass blower creates a hollow bulb that can be pulled, twisted, and blown into different shapes. When the finished shape is broken from the tube, a beautiful glass sculpture has been created. Through heating and cooling, glass changes from a solid to a liquid and back to a solid.

Activity 1 Your teacher will provide several samples of glass. Look at the different types of glass on display. Write down (a) the different characteristics of the glass (such as shape, color, texture, and density) and (b) possible uses for each type of glass.

Activity 2 Look at different types of plastic and plastic containers. List the differences you can observe between the examples of glass and plastic. Even though we have plastics and other materials to use in containers and other products, why do you think glass is still used?

Dale Chihuly is the glass artist who created the sculptures in both of these photographs.

internet connect

www.scilinks.org
Topic: Glass **SciLinks code:** HK4064

SCILINKS® Maintained by the National Science Teachers Association

Pre-Reading Questions

1. Look around the room, and find several examples of matter. Can you find examples that are not matter?
2. Can matter ever change forms? Can one substance change into another? Explain how you think this change happens, and give examples.

SECTION 1

What Is Matter?

KEY TERMS

- chemistry
- matter
- element
- atom
- compound
- molecule
- chemical formula
- pure substance
- mixture

OBJECTIVES

- **Explain** the relationship between matter, atoms, and elements.
- **Distinguish** between elements and compounds.
- **Describe** molecules, and explain how they are formed.
- **Interpret** and write some common chemical formulas.
- **Categorize** materials as pure substances or mixtures.

Making glass, as shown in ***Figure 1,*** is the process of changing the raw materials sand, limestone, and soda ash into a different substance. Such processes are what **chemistry** is all about: what things are made of, what their properties are, and how they interact and change. Chemistry is an important part of your daily life. Everything you use, from soaps to foods to carbonated drinks to books, you choose because of chemistry—what the object is made of, what its properties are, or how it changes.

Glass is used as a building material because its properties of being transparent, solid, and waterproof meet the needs we have for windows. The properties of sand, on the other hand, do not meet these needs. Chemistry helps you recognize how the differences in materials' properties relate to what the materials are composed of.

chemistry the scientific study of the composition, structure, and properties of matter and the changes that matter undergoes

matter anything that has mass and takes up space

Composition of Matter

You are made of **matter.** This book is also matter. All the materials you can hold or touch are matter. Matter is anything that has mass and occupies space. The air you are breathing is matter even though you cannot see it. Light and sound are not matter. Unlike air, they have no mass or volume.

Figure 1

Glass blowers have been practicing their craft for more than 2000 years. Raw materials are changed into a new substance during the glass making process.

Atoms are matter

Figure 2

This diamond is made of carbon atoms.

Wood is matter. Because it is rigid and lightweight, wood is a good choice for furniture and buildings. When wood gets hot enough, it chars—its surface turns black. The wood surface breaks down to form carbon, another kind of material that has different properties. The carbon in the charred remains will not decompose by further chemical reactions because carbon is an **element** and each element is made of only one kind of **atom.**

Diamonds, such as the one shown in ***Figure 2,*** are made of atoms of the element carbon. The shiny foil wrapped around a baked potato is made of atoms of the element aluminum. The elements that are most abundant on Earth and in the human body are shown in ***Figure 3.*** Each element is designated by a one- or two-letter symbol that is used worldwide. Symbols for elements are always a single capital letter or a capital letter followed by a lowercase letter. There are no exceptions! For example, the symbol for carbon is C, iron is Fe, copper is Cu, and aluminum is Al. Each of the more than 110 elements that we know of is unique and has different properties from the rest.

element a substance that cannot be seperated or broken down into simpler substances by chemical means

atom the smallest unit of an element that maintains the properties of that element

compound a substance made of atoms of two or more different elements that are chemically combined

Elements combine chemically to form a compound

Many familiar substances, such as aluminum and iron, are elements. Nylon is a familiar substance, but it is not an element. Nylon is a **compound.** The basic unit that makes up nylon contains carbon, hydrogen, nitrogen, and oxygen atoms, but each strand contains many of these units linked together.

Figure 3

Earth and the human body differ in the kind and proportion of elements they are composed of.

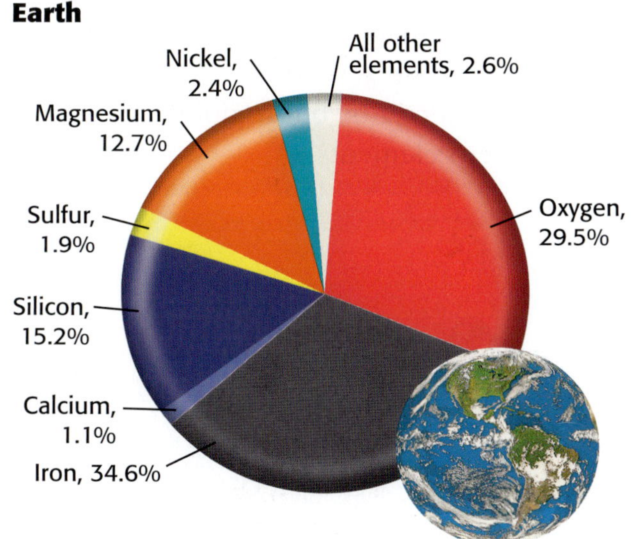

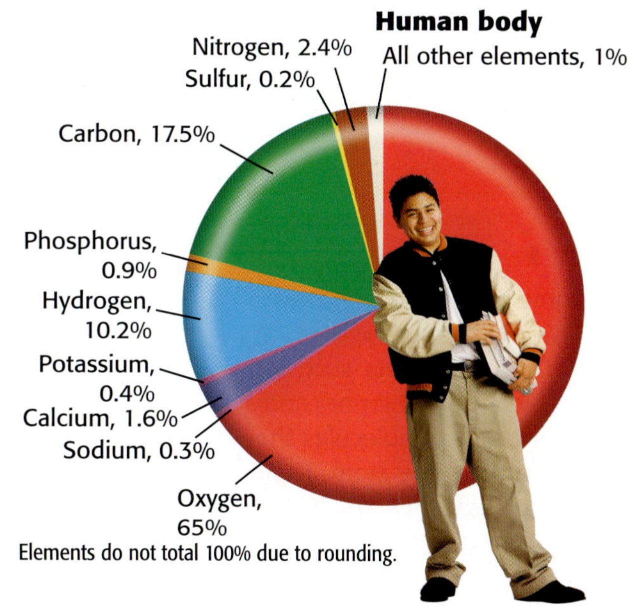

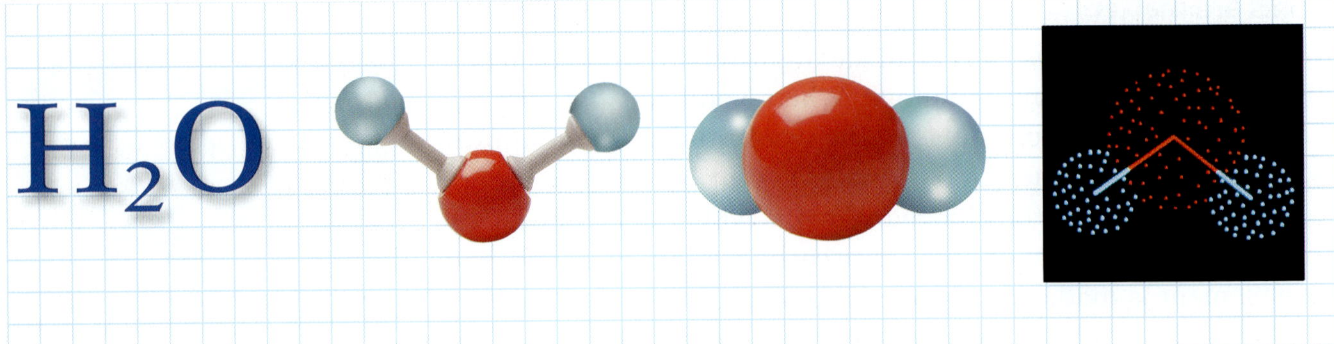

Figure 4

A water molecule can be represented by a formula, physical models, or computer images.

Compounds have unique properties

Every compound is different from the elements it contains. For example, the elements hydrogen, oxygen, and nitrogen occur in nature as colorless gases. Yet when they combine with carbon to form nylon, the strands of nylon are a flexible solid.

When elements combine to make a specific compound, the elements always combine in the same proportions. For example, iron(III) oxide, which we see often as rust, always has two atoms of iron for every three atoms of oxygen.

A molecule acts as a unit

molecule the smallest unit of a substance that keeps all of the physical and chemical properties of that substance

Atoms can join together to make millions of **molecules** like letters of the alphabet combine to form different words. A molecular substance you are familiar with is water. A water molecule is made of two hydrogen atoms and one oxygen atom, as shown in ***Figure 4.***

When oxygen and hydrogen atoms form a molecule of water, the atoms combine and act as a unit. That is what a molecule is—the smallest unit of a substance that behaves like the substance. Most molecules are made of atoms of different elements, such as water. But a molecule may also be made of atoms of the same element, such as those shown in ***Figure 5.*** A compound is made of atoms of two or more different elements, but a molecule may be of the same elements or different elements.

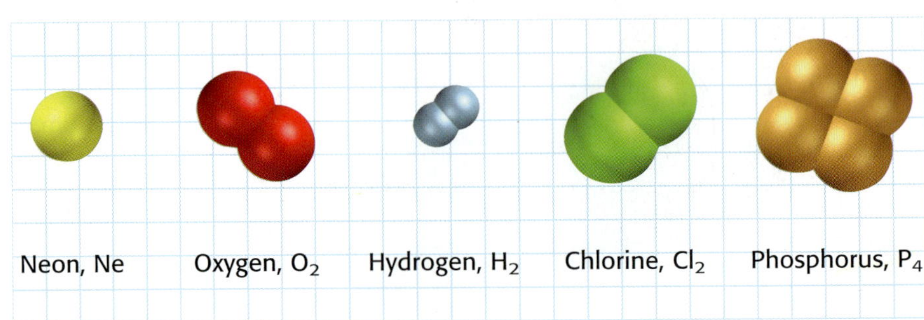

Figure 5

The atoms of elements such as neon, Ne, are found singly in nature. Other elements, such as oxygen, hydrogen, chlorine, and phosphorus, form molecules that have more than one atom. Their unit molecules are O_2, H_2, Cl_2, and P_4.

Chemical formulas represent compounds and molecules

Indigo is the dye first used to turn jeans blue. The **chemical formula** for a molecule of indigo, $C_{16}H_{10}N_2O_2$, is shown in ***Figure 6.*** A chemical formula shows how many atoms of each element are in a unit of a substance. In a chemical formula, the number of atoms of each element is written after the element's symbol as a *subscript*. If only one atom of an element is present, no subscript number is used.

Numbers placed in front of the chemical formula show the number of molecules. So, three molecules of table sugar are written as $3C_{12}H_{22}O_{11}$. Each molecule of sugar contains 12 carbon atoms, 22 hydrogen atoms, and 11 oxygen atoms.

Figure 6

The chemical formula for a molecule of indigo shows that it is made of four elements and 30 atoms.

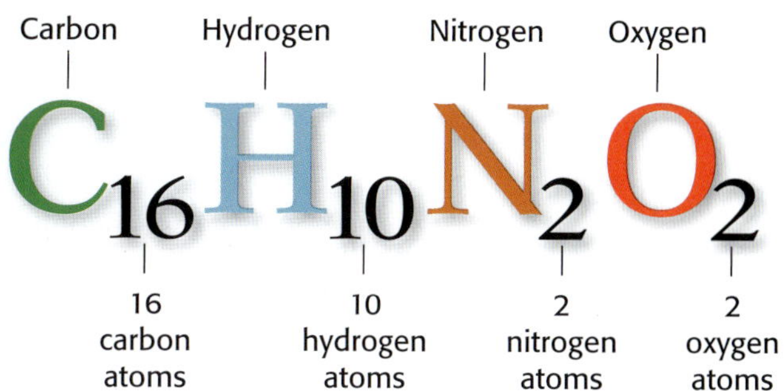

Pure Substances and Mixtures

The word *pure* often means "not mixed with anything." For example, "pure grape juice" contains the juice of grapes and nothing else. In chemistry, the word *pure* has another meaning. A **pure substance** is matter that has a fixed composition and definite properties.

So, grape juice actually is not a pure substance. It is a **mixture** of many pure substances, such as water, sugars, and vitamins. The composition of grape juice is not fixed; it can have different amounts of water or sugar. Elements and compounds are pure substances, but mixtures are not. Many of the foods we eat are mixtures. The air we breathe is a mixture of gases.

Figure 7 shows a mixture and a pure substance. A mixture, such as grape juice, can be separated into its components. The components of water, a pure substance, are chemically combined and cannot be separated in the same way that the components of grape juice can be separated.

chemical formula a combination of chemical symbols and numbers to represent a substance

pure substance a sample of matter, either a single element or a single compound, that has definite chemical and physical properties

mixture a combination of two or more substances that are not chemically combined

Figure 7

Grape juice is a mixture, and water is a pure substance. The components of grape juice, such as sugar and water, are not chemically combined. Water is a pure substance made up of the elements hydrogen and oxygen, which are chemically combined.

Figure 8

A Flour is suspended in water.

B Powdered sugar is dissolved in water.

Mixtures are formed by mixing pure substances

While a compound is different from the elements that it is composed of, a mixture may have properties that are similar to the pure substances that form it. Although you cannot see the different pure substances in grape juice, the mixture has chemical and physical properties in common with its components. Grape juice is a liquid like the water that it contains, and it is sweet like the sugar that it also contains.

Mixtures are classified by how thoroughly the substances mix

Some mixtures are made by putting solids and liquids together. In **Figure 8,** two white, powdery solids—flour and powdered sugar—are each mixed with water. Although these solids look similar, the mixtures they form with water are different.

The flour and water form a cloudy white mixture. The flour does not dissolve in water. A mixture like this is called a *heterogeneous mixture.* The substances aren't mixed uniformly and are not evenly distributed.

The sugar-water mixture looks very different from the flour-water mixture. You cannot see the sugar, and the mixture is clear. Powdered sugar dissolves in water. If you leave the mixture for a long time, the sugar will not settle out. Sugar and water form a *homogeneous mixture* because the components are evenly distributed, and the mixture is the same throughout.

Gasoline is a liquid mixture—a homogeneous mixture of at least 100 liquids. Thus, gasoline is composed of *miscible* liquids.

If you shake a mixture of oil and water, the oil and water will not mix well together, and the water will settle out. Oil and water are *immiscible.* You can see two layers in the mixture.

INTEGRATING

BIOLOGY

The pure substance indigo is a natural dye made from plants of the genus *Indigofera,* which is in the pea family. Before synthetic dyes were developed, indigo plants were widely grown in the East Indies, in India, and in the Americas. Most indigo species are shrubs 1 to 2 m tall. The leaves and branches are fermented to yield a paste, which is formed into blocks and then ground. The blue color develops when the material is exposed to air.

Dry Cleaning: How Are Stains Dissolved?

Why do some clothes need to be dry cleaned, while others do not? Washing with water and detergents cleans most clothes. But if your clothes have a stubborn stain—such as ink or rust—if you have spilled something greasy on them, or if the label on the clothing recommends dry cleaning, then dry cleaning may be necessary. Dry cleaning is recommended for clothing made of fabrics that do not respond well to water. These fabrics, such as silk and wool, are usually cleaned without water because water causes them to shrink, to take on stubborn wrinkles, or to lose their shape.

Stain Removal

By knowing the composition of a stain, dry cleaners can decide how to treat the stain. Removing a stain that does not dissolve in water, such as oil or grease, requires two steps. First, the stain is treated with a substance that loosens the stain. Then, the stain is removed when the garment is washed in a mechanical dry-cleaning machine.

If a stain is water soluble, it will dissolve in water. A water-soluble stain is first treated with a stain remover that is specific to that stain. The stain is then flushed away with a steam gun. After the garment is dry, it is cleaned in a dry-cleaning machine to remove any stains that do not dissolve in water.

Once a fabric has been treated for tough stains, the garment is "washed" in a dry-cleaning machine.

Dry Cleaning Isn't Really Dry

In spite of its name, dry cleaning does involve liquids. But instead of water, another liquid is used to dissolve stains. It is always difficult to remove fats, greases, and oils from fabrics with water-based washing.

A good dry-cleaning substance must dissolve oil and grease, which can be trapped in the cloth fibers. The most commonly used dry-cleaning solvent is tetrachloroethylene, C_2Cl_4. Tetrachloroethylene dissolves oil, grease, and alcohols. Also, tetrachloroethylene is not flammable, and it evaporates easily, so it can be recycled by the process of distillation.

In distillation, the components of a liquid mixture are separated based on their rates of evaporation. Upon heating, the component that evaporates fastest is the first to vaporize and separate from the mixture. When the vapors are cooled, they condense to form a purified sample of that component.

Tetrachloroethylene is suspected of causing some kinds of cancer. To meet the standards of the U.S. Occupational Safety and Health Administration (OSHA) and other federal guidelines, dry-cleaning machines must be airtight so that no C_2Cl_4 escapes.

Your Choice

1. **Critical Thinking** Why is it difficult to remove greasy stains from fabrics with water-based cleaners?
2. **Critical Thinking** C_2Cl_4 evaporates faster than the fats and oils it dissolves. How can C_2Cl_4 be recycled by distillation?

internet connect

www.scilinks.org
Topic: Dry Cleaning
SciLinks code: HK4033

Figure 9

The meringue in this pie is a mixture of air and liquid egg white that has been beaten and then heated to form a solid foam.

Gases can mix with liquids

Air is a mixture of gases consisting mostly of nitrogen and oxygen. You inhale oxygen every time you breathe because the gases mixed in air form a homogeneous mixture. Carbonated drinks are also homogeneous mixtures. They contain sugar, flavorings, and carbon dioxide gas, CO_2, dissolved in water.

Even a liquid that is not carbonated can contain dissolved gases. For example, if you let a glass of cold water stand overnight, you may see bubbles on the sides of the glass the next morning. The bubbles form when some of the air that was dissolved in the cold water comes out of solution as the water warms up.

Carbonated drinks often have a foam on top. A foam is a kind of gas-liquid mixture. The gas is not dissolved in the liquid but has formed tiny bubbles in it. The bubbles join together to form bigger bubbles that escape from the foam, which causes the foam to collapse.

Other foams are stable and last for a long time. For example, if you whip egg whites with enough air, you get a foam. If you bake that foam in an oven, the liquid egg white dries and hardens, and you have a solid foam—meringue, shown in ***Figure 9.***

SECTION 1 REVIEW

SUMMARY

- Matter has mass and occupies space.
- An element is a substance that cannot be broken down into simpler substances.
- An atom is the smallest unit of an element that has the properties of the element.
- Atoms can combine to form molecules or compounds.
- Chemical formulas represent the atoms in compounds and molecules.
- A mixture is a combination of two or more pure substances. Mixtures can be categorized as heterogeneous or homogeneous.

1. **State** the relationship between atoms and elements. Are both atoms and elements matter?
2. **List** the two types of pure substances.
3. **Describe** matter, and explain why light is not matter. Is light made of atoms and elements?
4. **Define** *molecule*, and give examples of a molecule formed by one element and a molecule formed by two elements.
5. **Classify** each of the following as an element or a compound.
   a. sulfur, S_8
   b. methane, CH_4
   c. carbon monoxide, CO
   d. cobalt, Co
6. **State** the chemical formula of water.
7. **Compare and Contrast** mixtures and pure substances. Give an example of each.
8. **Critical Thinking** David says, "'Pure honey' means it has nothing else added." Susan says, "The honey is not really pure. It is a mixture of many substances." Who is right? Explain your answer.

SECTION 2

Properties of Matter

OBJECTIVES

- **Distinguish** between the physical and chemical properties of matter, and give examples of each.
- **Perform** calculations involving density.
- **Explain** how materials are suited for different uses based on their physical and chemical properties, and give examples.
- **Describe** characteristic properties, and give examples.

KEY TERMS

melting point
boiling point
density
reactivity
flammability

The frame and engine of a car are made of steel. Steel is a mixture of iron, other metallic elements, and carbon. It is a strong solid that provides structure. The tires are made of a flexible solid that cushions your ride. You may not think of the cars you see in ***Figure 10*** as examples of chemistry. However, the properties and changes that make steel, gasoline, and other substances useful in cars are explained by chemistry.

Physical Properties

Some properties of matter, such as color and shape, are called *physical properties*. Physical properties are often very easy to observe. You rely on physical properties to identify things. You recognize your friends by their physical properties, such as height and hair color. When playing sports, you choose a ball that has the shape and mass suitable for your game. Mass, volume, and density are physical properties of matter. Matter can also be described in terms of the absence of a physical property. A physical property of air is that it is colorless.

Figure 10

The physical and chemical properties of substances determine how they are used in these cars.

Figure 11

These models show water in three states. The molecules are close together in the solid and liquid states but far apart in the gas state. The molecules in the solid state are relatively fixed in position, but those in the liquid and gas states can flow around each other.

Physical properties describe matter

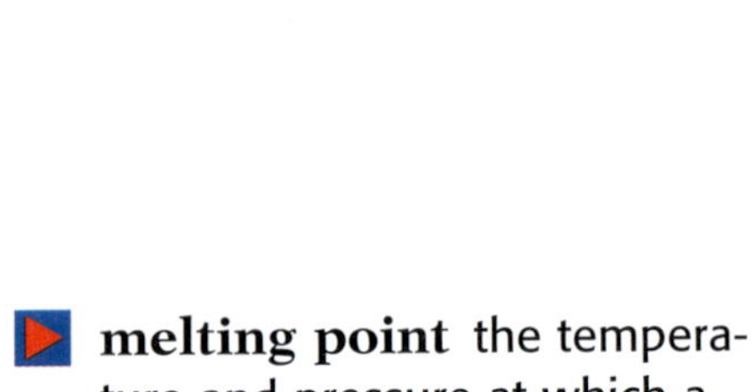

melting point the temperature and pressure at which a solid becomes a liquid

boiling point the temperature at which a liquid becomes a gas

Many physical properties can be observed or measured to help identify a substance. You can use your senses to observe some of the basic physical properties of a substance: shape, color, odor, and texture. Other physical properties, such as **melting point, boiling point,** strength, hardness, and the ability to conduct electricity, magnetism, or heat, can be measured.

Because many physical properties remain constant for pure substances, you can use your observations or measurements of these properties to identify substances. At room temperature and atmospheric pressure, all samples of pure water are colorless and liquid; pure water is never a powdery green solid.

A characteristic of any pure substance is that its boiling point and its melting point are constant if the pressure remains the same. At sea level, water boils at 100°C and freezes at 0°C. It doesn't matter if you have a lot of water or a little water; these physical properties of the water are the same regardless of the mass or volume involved. This statement is true for all pure substances.

An easily observed physical property is *state*—the physical form in which a substance exists. Solids, liquids, and gases are three common states of matter. ***Figure 11*** shows the solid, liquid, and gas states of water at the molecular level.

Density is a physical property

Density is a measurement of how much matter is contained in a certain volume of a substance. A substance that has a low **density** is "light" in comparison with something else of the same volume. The balloons in ***Figure 12*** float because they are less dense than the air around them. A substance that has a high density is "heavy" in comparison with another object of the same volume. A stone sinks to the bottom of a pond because the stone is more dense than the water around it.

You can compare the density of two objects of the same volume by holding one in each hand. The lighter one is less dense; the heavier one is more dense. If you held a brick in one hand and an equal-sized piece of sponge in the other hand, you would know instantly that the brick is more dense than the sponge. Remember that weight and density are different. Two pounds of feathers are heavier than one pound of steel. But the feathers are less dense than the steel, so two pounds of feathers have a greater volume than one pound of steel.

Density determines whether an object will float or sink. An object will float when placed in water if it is less dense than water. If an object is more dense than water, the object will sink.

Table 1 lists the densities of some common substances. The density of an object is calculated by dividing the object's mass by its volume.

Figure 12

Helium-filled balloons float upward because helium is less dense than air is. Similarly, hot-air balloons rise because hot air is less dense than cool air is.

$$D = m/V$$

$$density = mass/volume$$

density the ratio of the mass of a substance to the volume of a substance

Table 1 **Densities of Some Substances**

Substance	Chemical formula	Density in g/cm^3
Air, dry	mixture	0.00129
Brick, common	mixture	1.9
Gasoline	mixture	0.7
Helium	He	0.00018
Ice	H_2O	0.92
Iron	Fe	7.86
Lead	Pb	11.3
Nitrogen	N_2	0.00125
Steel	mixture	7.8
Water	H_2O	1.00

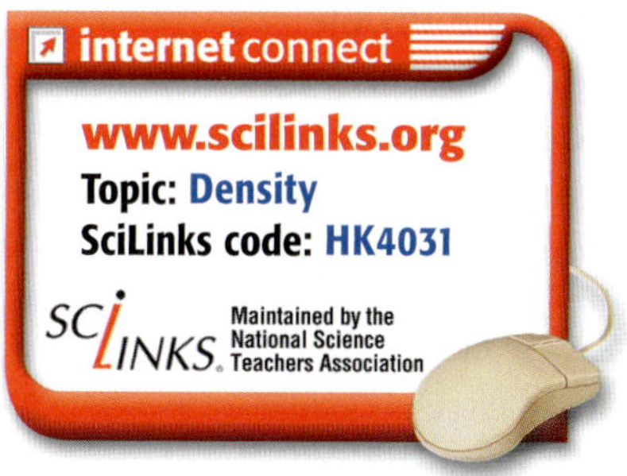

Figure 13

A golf ball is denser than a table-tennis ball because the golf ball contains more matter in about the same volume.

Density is often measured in units of g/cm³

A golf ball and a table tennis ball are shown in ***Figure 13.*** Which ball is more dense? The two balls have a similar volume, but the mass of a golf ball is 45.9 g and the mass of a table tennis ball is 2.5 g. The golf ball has more mass per unit of volume than a table tennis ball has, and therefore the golf ball is more dense.

The density of a liquid or a solid is usually reported in units of grams per cubic centimeter (g/cm^3). For example, 10.0 cm^3 of water has a mass of 10.0 g. Its density is 10.0 g for every 10.0 cm^3, or 1.00 g/cm^3. A cubic centimeter contains the same volume as a milliliter. You may see the density of water expressed as 1 g/mL.

Math Skills

Density If 10.0 cm^3 of ice has a mass of 9.17 g, what is the density of ice?

1 List the given and the unknown values.

Given: *mass,* $m = 9.17$ g

volume, $V = 10.0\ cm^3$

Unknown: *density,* $D = ?\ g/cm^3$

2 Write the equation for density.

$D = \frac{m}{V}$ **or** *density = mass/volume*

3 Insert the known values into the equation, and solve.

$D = 9.17\ g/10.0\ cm^3$

$D = 0.917\ g/cm^3$

Practice HINT

- When a problem requires you to calculate density, you can use the density equation. $D = \frac{m}{V}$
- You can solve for mass by multiplying both sides of the density equation by volume. $DV = \frac{mV}{V}$ $\quad m = DV$
- You will need to use this form of the equation in Practice Problem 3.
- You can solve for volume by dividing both sides of the equation shown above by density. $\frac{m}{D} = \frac{DV}{D}$ $\quad V = \frac{m}{D}$

Practice

Density

1. A piece of tin has a mass of 16.52 g and a volume of 2.26 cm^3. What is the density of tin?
2. A man has a 50.0 cm^3 bottle completely filled with 163 g of a slimy green liquid. What is the density of the liquid?
3. A piece of metal has a density of 11.3 g/cm^3 and a volume of 6.7 cm^3. What is the mass of this piece of metal?

Physical properties help determine uses

Every day, you use physical properties to identify substances. Physical properties help you determine whether your socks are clean (odor), whether you can fit all your books into your backpack (volume), or whether your shirt matches your pants (color).

In industry, physical properties are used to select substances that may be useful. Copper is used in electrical power lines, telephone lines, and electric motors because it conducts electricity well. Antifreeze, which contains ethylene glycol (a poisonous liquid), remains a liquid at temperatures that would freeze or boil water in a car radiator. As shown in ***Figure 14,*** aluminum is used in foil because it is lightweight yet durable, water resistant, and flexible.

Can you think of other physical properties that help us determine how we can use a substance? Some substances have the ability to conduct heat, while others do not. Plastic-foam cups do not conduct heat well, so they are often used for holding hot drinks. What would happen if you poured hot tea into a metal cup?

Figure 14

Aluminum is light, strong, and durable, which makes it ideal for use in foil.

Quick Lab

How are the mass and volume of a substance related?

Materials

- *100 mL graduated cylinder*
- *250 mL beaker with 200 mL water*
- *balance*
- *graph paper*

1. Make a data table that has 3 columns and 12 rows. In the first row, label the columns "Volume of H_2O (mL)," "Mass of cylinder (g) and H_2O (g)," and "Mass of H_2O (g)." In the remaining spaces of the first column, write 0, 10, 20, 30, 40, 50, 60, 70, 80, 90, and 100.
2. Measure the mass of the empty graduated cylinder, and record it on a piece of paper.
3. For each amount of water listed in column one, pour the water from the beaker into the graduated cylinder. Then, use the balance to find the mass of the graduated cylinder with the water. Record each value in column two of your data table.
4. On graph paper, make a graph and label the horizontal *x*-axis "Volume of water (mL)." Mark the *x*-axis in 10 equal increments for 10, 20, 30, 40, 50, 60, 70, 80, 90 and 100 mL. Label the vertical *y*-axis "Mass of water (g)." Mark the *y*-axis in 10 equal increments for 10, 20, 30, 40, 50, 60, 70, 80, 90, and 100 g.
5. Plot a graph of your data either on graph paper, on a graphing calculator, or by using a graphing/spreadsheet computer program.

Analysis

1. What is the mass of the graduated cylinder?
2. Use your graph to estimate the mass of 55 mL of water and 85 mL of water.
3. Use your graph to predict the volume of 25 g of water and 75 g of water.
4. How could you use your data table or graph to calculate the density of water? Which method do you think gives better results? Why?

Chemical Properties

Some elements, such as sodium, react very easily with other elements and usually are found as compounds in nature. Other elements, like gold, are much less reactive and often are found uncombined in nature. Magnesium is so reactive that it is used to make emergency flares. Light bulbs are filled with argon gas because argon is not reactive, so the tungsten filament lasts longer. All of these are examples of *chemical properties*. Chemical properties are generally not as easy to observe as physical properties.

reactivity the ability of a substance to combine chemically with another substance

flammability the ability of a substance to react in the presence of oxygen and burn when exposed to a flame

Chemical properties describe how a substance reacts

Although iron has many useful physical and chemical properties, one property that can cause problems for people is its reactivity with oxygen. When iron is exposed to oxygen, it rusts. You can see rust on the old car shown in ***Figure 15.*** The steel parts of a car rust when iron atoms in the steel react with oxygen in air to form iron(III) oxide. The painted and chromium parts of the car do not rust because they do not react with oxygen.

Chemical properties are related to the specific elements that make up substances. The elements in steel, paint, and chrome have different chemical properties. A chemical property describes how a substance changes into a new substance, either by combining with other elements or by breaking apart into new substances. Chemical properties include the **reactivity** of elements or compounds with oxygen, acid, water, or other substances.

Another chemical property is **flammability**—the ability to burn. For example, wood can be burned to create new substances (ash and smoke) with properties that are different from the original wood. A substance that does not burn, such as gold, has the chemical property of nonflammability. Remember that even when wood is not actually burning, it is still flammable because flammability is one of wood's chemical properties. A substance always has its chemical properties, even when you cannot observe them.

Figure 15

A This hole started as a small chip in the paint, which exposed the iron in the car to oxygen. The iron rusted and crumbled away.

B Paint does not react with oxygen, so it provides a barrier between oxygen and the iron in the car's steel.

C This bumper is rust free because it is coated with chromium, which is nonreactive with oxygen.

Comparing Physical and Chemical Properties

It is important to remember the differences between physical and chemical properties. You can observe physical properties without changing the identity of the substance. But you can observe chemical properties only in situations in which the identity of the substance changes.

Table 2 summarizes the physical and chemical properties of some common substances. As you can see, many substances have very similar physical properties but completely different chemical properties. For example, baking soda and powdered sugar are both white powders, but baking soda reacts with vinegar, whereas sugar does not.

Did You Know?

Galvanized steel is steel that is coated with zinc to prevent rusting. It is used in buckets and nails. Steel coated with tin is used in food cans and containers. Today, most canned carbonated beverages are packaged in aluminum cans instead of steel cans.

Table 2 **Comparing Physical and Chemical Properties**

Substance	Physical property	Chemical property
Helium	less dense than air	nonflammable
Wood	grainy texture	flammable
Baking soda	white powder	reacts with vinegar to produce bubbles
Powdered sugar	white powder	does not react with vinegar
Rubbing alcohol	clear liquid	flammable
Red food coloring	red color	reacts with bleach and loses color
Iron	malleable	reacts with oxygen

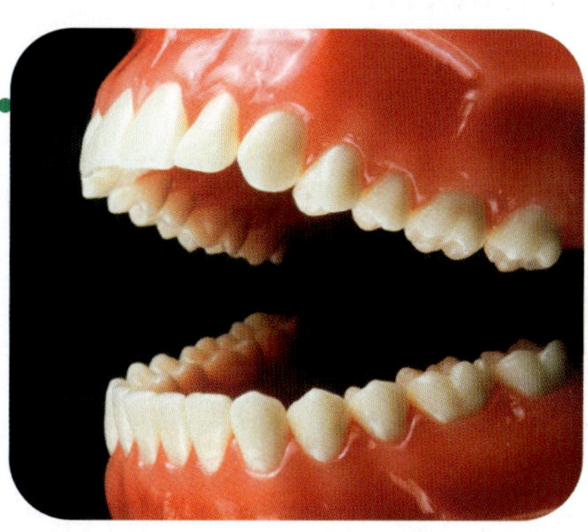

Choosing Materials Materials are chosen because their properties are suitable for use. For example, white acrylic plastic can be used to make false teeth. Sometimes, porcelain is used. Metals are less commonly used, although gold teeth are still made sometimes. False teeth have a demanding job to do. They are constantly bathed in saliva, which is corrosive. They must withstand the forces from chewing hard objects, such as popcorn or hard candy. The material chosen has to be nontoxic, hard, waterproof, unreactive, toothlike in appearance, and affordable. Acrylic plastic satisfies these requirements.

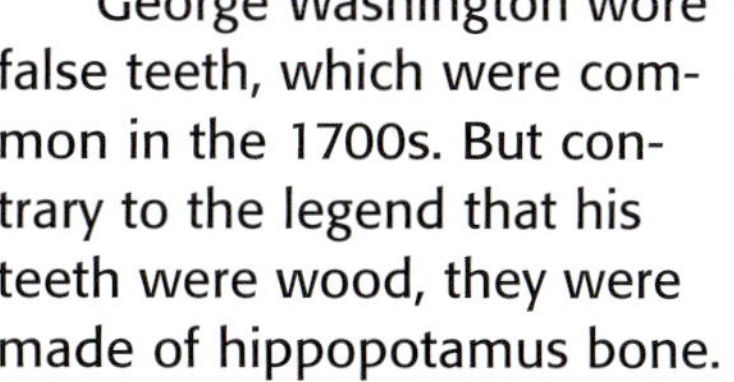

George Washington wore false teeth, which were common in the 1700s. But contrary to the legend that his teeth were wood, they were made of hippopotamus bone.

Applying Information

1. Compare the advantages and disadvantages of gold false teeth and Washington's bone teeth.
2. Identify some advantages of acrylic plastic teeth.

Figure 16
Helium is used in blimps because it is less dense than air and is nonflammable.

Characteristic properties help to identify and classify substances

You can describe matter by both physical and chemical properties. The properties that are most useful in identifying a substance, such as density, solubility (whether or not it dissolves), and reactivity with acids, are its *characteristic properties.* Characteristic properties include both types—physical and chemical properties. The characteristic properties of a substance are always the same whether the sample you are observing is large or small.

The blimp in ***Figure 16*** is filled with helium. The characteristic properties of helium, such as its density and nonflammability, make helium very useful for blimp flight.

SECTION 2 REVIEW

SUMMARY

- Physical properties can be observed or measured without changing the composition of matter.
- Physical properties help determine how substances are used.
- The density of a substance is equal to its mass divided by its volume.
- Chemical properties describe how a substance reacts; they can be observed when one substance reacts with another.
- Scientists use characteristic properties to identify and classify substances.

1. **Classify** the following as either chemical or physical properties.
   a. is shiny and silvery
   b. melts easily
   c. has a density of 2.3 g/cm^3
   d. tarnishes in moist air
2. **Identify** which of the following properties *are not* chemical properties.
   a. reacts with water
   b. boils at 100°C
   c. is red
   d. does not react with hydrogen
3. **Describe** several uses for plastic, and explain why plastic is a good choice for these purposes.
4. **Describe** characteristic properties, and explain why they are important. List some characteristic properties.

Math Skills

5. **Calculate** the density of a rock that has a mass of 454 g and a volume of 100 cm^3.
6. **Calculate** the density of a substance in a sealed 2500 cm^3 flask that is full to capacity with 0.36 g of a substance.
7. **Critical Thinking** Suppose you need to build a raft. Write a paragraph describing the physical and chemical properties of the raft that would be important to ensure your safety.

SECTION 3

Changes of Matter

OBJECTIVES

- **Explain** physical change, and give examples of physical changes.
- **Explain** chemical change, and give examples of chemical changes.
- **Compare and contrast** physical and chemical changes.
- **Describe** how to detect whether a chemical change has occurred.

KEY TERMS

physical change
chemical change

Some materials benefit us because they stay in the same state and do not change under normal conditions. Surgical steel pins are used to reinforce broken bones because surgical steel remains the same even after years in the human body. Concrete and glass are used as building materials because they change very little under most weather conditions. Other materials are valued for their ability to change states easily. Water is turned into steam to heat homes and factories. Liquid gasoline is changed into a gas so it can burn in car engines. The physical and chemical properties of a substance determine how the substances behave under different conditions.

physical change a change of matter from one form to another without a change in chemical properties

Physical Changes

A **physical change** affects one or more physical properties of a substance without changing its identity. For example, if you break a piece of chalk in two, you change its physical properties of size and shape. But no matter how many times you break it, chalk would still be chalk and the chemical properties of the chalk would remain unchanged. Each piece of chalk would still produce bubbles if you placed it in vinegar.

Figure 17 shows a physical change taking place. The girl in the picture is getting her hair cut, but the chemical nature of her hair is not changing. The haircut will affect only the physical properties of her hair. Other examples of physical changes are dissolving sugar, melting ice, sanding a piece of wood, crushing an aluminum can, and mixing oil and vinegar.

Figure 17
Is this haircut a physical or a chemical change?

Figure 18

When sugar dissolves in water, water particles attract and pull apart sugar particles, so the sugar particles spread out in the water.

Physical changes do not change a substance's identity

Both quartz crystals and sand are made of SiO_2, but they look different. When quartz is crushed into sand, a physical change takes place. During physical changes, energy is absorbed or released. After a physical change, a substance may look different, but the arrangement of atoms that make up the substance are not changed.

Pounding a gold nugget into a ring results in physical changes. But physical changes do not change all the properties of a substance. For example, the color of the gold, its melting point, and its density do not change. Melting, freezing, and evaporating—all changes of state—are physical changes, too, because the identity of the substance does not change.

Dissolving is a physical change

When you stir sugar into water, the sugar dissolves and seems to disappear. But the sugar is still there; you can taste the sweetness when you drink the water. ***Figure 18*** shows sugar and water molecules dissolving. When sugar dissolves, it seems to disappear because the sugar particles become spread out between the particles of the water. The molecules of the sugar have not changed because dissolving is a physical change. Dissolving a solid in a liquid, a gas in a liquid, or a liquid in a liquid are all physical changes.

Quick Lab

How can you separate a mixture?

Materials
- ✔ *distilled water*
- ✔ *clear plastic cups*
- ✔ *filter funnel*
- ✔ *plastic spoon*
- ✔ *filter paper*
- ✔ *5 g sample of mixture*
- ✔ *magnet*
- ✔ *paper towels*

1. Design an experiment in which the given materials are used to separate the components of the sample mixture. (**Hint:** Consider physical properties such as solubility, density, and magnetism.)
2. Once you have separated the components of the sample mixture, describe them by their physical properties.

Analysis

1. What properties did you observe in each of the components of the mixture?
2. How did these properties help you to separate the components of the sample?
3. Did any of the components share similar properties?
4. Based on your observations, what do you think the mixture was composed of?

Figure 19

These pictures show ways that physical changes can be used to separate mixtures.

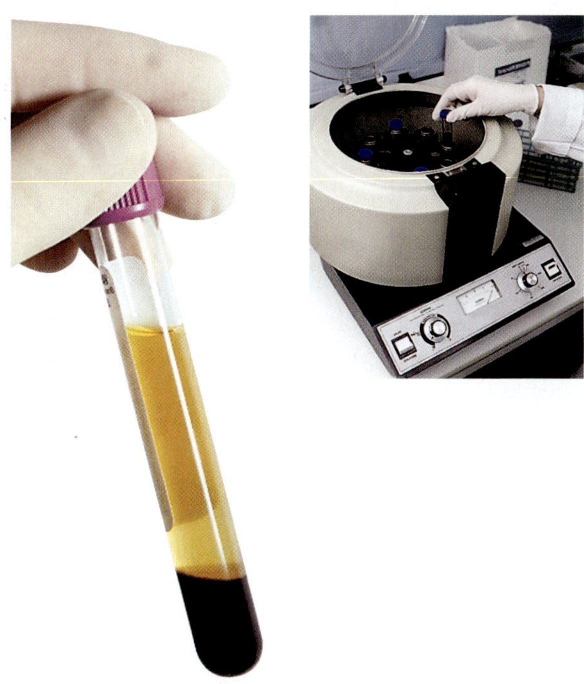

A A centrifuge is a tool used to separate mixtures. It spins a sample of a mixture rapidly until the components of the mixture separate. You can see different layers in this sample of blood because it has been separated into its components.

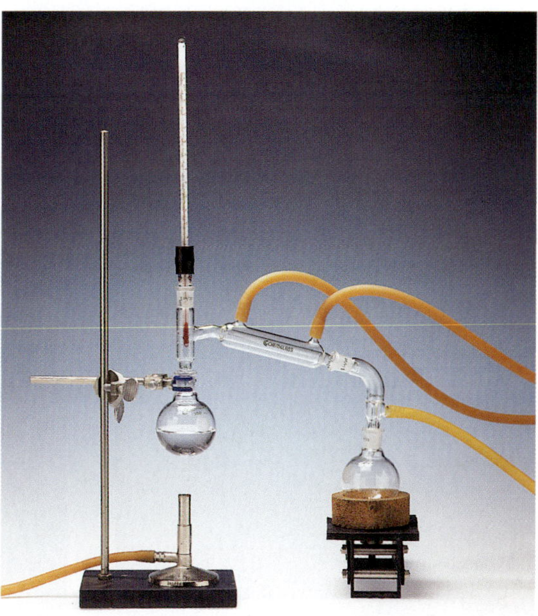

B The distillation device shown here can separate components of mixtures that have different boiling points. When heated, the component that boils and evaporates first, separates from the mixture and collects in the receiving flask.

Mixtures can be physically separated

Because mixtures are not chemically combined, each component of a mixture has the same chemical makeup it had before the mixture was formed. Each substance in a mixture keeps its identity. In some mixtures, such as a slice of pizza, you can easily see the individual components. In other mixtures, such as salt water, you cannot see all the components.

You can remove the mushrooms on a pizza, which results in a physical change. The identities of the substances in the pizza would not change. Unlike mixtures, compounds can be broken down only through chemical changes.

Not all mixtures are as easy to separate as a pizza. You cannot pick salt out of a saltwater mixture, but you can separate the salt from the water by heating the mixture. When the water evaporates, the salt remains behind. Several common techniques for separating mixtures are shown in ***Figure 19.***

C Magnets can be used to separate mixtures that have components containing iron. In this mixture of nails, the magnet attracts and separates the nails containing iron from the nails that do not contain iron.

Figure 20
Examples of Chemical Changes

A Soured milk smells bad because bacteria have formed new substances in the milk.

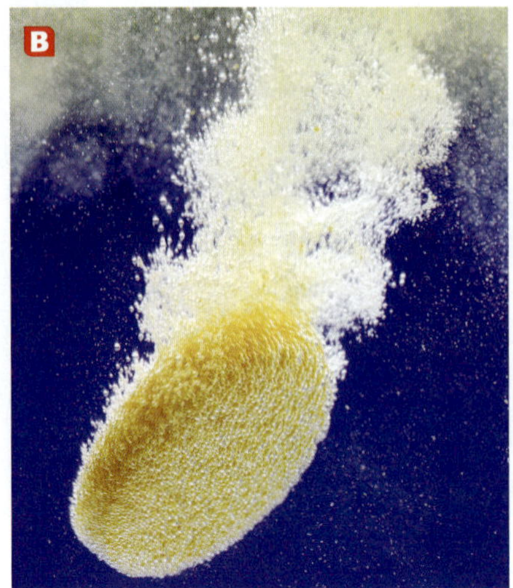

B Effervescent tablets bubble when the citric acid and baking soda in them react with water to produce CO_2.

C The Statue of Liberty is made of shiny, orange-brown copper. But the metal's interaction with carbon dioxide and water has formed new substances, including green copper compounds.

Chemical Changes

Some materials are useful because of their ability to change and combine to form new substances. For example, the compounds in gasoline burn in the presence of oxygen to form carbon dioxide and water, which releases energy. This is a **chemical change.** A chemical change occurs when one or more substances are changed into entirely new substances that have different properties.

chemical change a change that occurs when a substance changes composition by forming one or more new substances

Chemical changes happen everywhere

You see chemical changes happening more often than you may think. When a battery "dies," the chemicals inside the battery have changed, so the battery can no longer supply energy. The oxygen you inhale is used in a series of chemical reactions in your body. After it has undergone a chemical change by reacting with carbon, the oxygen is then exhaled as part of the compound carbon dioxide. Chemical changes occur when fruits and vegetables ripen and when the food you eat is digested. ***Figure 20*** shows some examples of other chemical changes that may be familiar to you.

Chemical changes form new substances that have different properties

A fun (and tasty) way to observe a chemical change is to bake a cake. When you bake a cake, you combine eggs, flour, sugar, butter, milk, baking powder, and other ingredients. Each ingredient has its own set of properties. For example, when baking powder combines with a liquid such as milk or water, it releases carbon dioxide, which causes the cake to rise. When you mix all of the ingredients and add heat by baking the cake batter, you get something completely different. The heat of the oven and the interaction of the ingredients cause chemical changes, which results in a cake with properties that are completely different from the properties of the original ingredients.

Figure 21

Table sugar is a compound made of carbon, hydrogen, and oxygen. When table sugar is heated, it caramelizes. When heated to a high temperature, it breaks down completely into carbon and water.

Chemical changes can be detected

When a chemical change takes place, there are often clues that suggest that a chemical change has happened. A change in odor or color is a good clue that a substance is changing chemically. When food burns, you can often smell the gases given off by the chemical changes. When paint fades, you can observe the effects of chemical changes in the paint. Chemical changes often cause color changes, fizzing or foaming, or the production of sound, heat, light, or odor.

Figure 21 shows table sugar being heated in a test tube. When sugar is heated to a high temperature, it breaks down into carbon and water. How do you know a chemical change is taking place in ***Figure 21***? The sugar has changed color, bubbles are forming, and a caramel smell is filling the air.

Chemicals changes cannot be reversed by physical changes

Because new substances are formed in a chemical change, you cannot reverse chemical changes by using physical changes. You cannot "unbake" a cake by separating out each ingredient. Most of the chemical changes you observe in your daily life, such as a cake baking, milk turning sour, or iron rusting, are impossible to reverse. Imagine trying to unbake a cake! While some physical changes can be easily undone, chemical changes are often more difficult to undo.

However, some chemical changes can be reversed under the right conditions by other chemical changes. For example, the water formed in a space shuttle's rockets can be split back into the starting materials—hydrogen and oxygen—by using an electric current to initiate a reaction that separates the hydrogen and oxygen atoms in the water molecules.

Quick ACTIVITY

Compound Confusion

1. Measure 4 g each of compounds A and B; place each in a clear plastic cup.
2. Observe the color and texture of each compound. Record your observations.
3. Add 5 mL of vinegar to each cup. Record your observations.
4. Baking soda reacts with vinegar, but powdered sugar does not. Which of these two substances is compound A, and which is B?

Compounds can be broken down through chemical changes

Some compounds can be broken down into elements through chemical changes. When the compound mercury(II) oxide is heated, it breaks down into the elements mercury and oxygen. If an electric current is passed through melted table salt, the elements sodium and chlorine are produced.

Other compounds undergo chemical changes to form simpler compounds. Carbonic acid is a compound that gives carbonated soda a tart taste and adds "fizz." In an unopened bottle of soda, you don't see bubbles because carbon dioxide is present in the form of carbonic acid. When you open a bottle of soda, the carbonic acid breaks down into carbon dioxide and water. The carbon dioxide escapes as bubbles. Through additional chemical changes, the carbon dioxide and water can be further broken down into the elements carbon, oxygen, and hydrogen.

SECTION 3 REVIEW

SUMMARY

- Physical changes are changes in the physical properties of a substance that do not change the identity of the substance.
- Changes of state are physical changes.
- Dissolving is a physical change.
- Physical changes are often easily reversed.
- Chemical changes form new substances that have new properties. Chemical changes can be reversed only through chemical reactions.
- Chemical changes often cause changes in color or produce sound, light, odor, or heat.

1. **Classify** the following as a chemical or a physical change.
   a. adding sugar to lemonade
   b. plants using CO_2 and H_2O to form O_2 and sugar
   c. boiling water
   d. frying an egg
   e. rust forming on metal
   f. fruit rotting
   g. removing salt from water by evaporation
2. **Explain** why changes of state are physical changes.
3. **Describe** how you would separate the components of a mixture, and state whether your methods would be physical or chemical changes.
4. **Define** physical change and chemical change, and give examples of each.
5. **Explain** why physical changes can easily be reversed but chemical changes cannot.
6. **Identify** two ways to break down a compound into simpler substances.
7. **List** three clues that indicate a chemical change.
8. **Critical Thinking** Describe the difference between physical and chemical changes in terms of what happens to the particles.

Study Skills

Two-Column Notes

Two-column notes help you learn or review details of specific concepts.

1 Identify the main ideas using the section objectives.

The objectives from Section 1 will be used as a source for main ideas on matter.

2 Divide a blank sheet of paper into two columns, write the main ideas and detail numbers in the left-hand column, and write the detail notes in the right-hand column.

Main idea	Detail notes
Elements (2 characteristic properties)	contain one type of atom simplest form of substance
Compounds (2 characteristic properties)	made of two or more elements chemical properties differ from its elements
Pure substances (3 characteristic properties)	fixed composition definite properties examples: elements and compounds
Molecules (4 characteristic properties)	act as a unit smallest unit of a substance that has the same properties of the substance some molecules made of different elements are also compounds some molecules are made of atoms of the same element
Mixtures (3 characteristic properties)	combination of pure substances heterogeneous mixture: non-uniform homogeneous mixture: uniform

Practice

Use concepts from Section 3 to create a table of two-column notes. In the detail notes, include examples of physical and chemical changes, and explain how these changes can be distinguished.

CHAPTER 2 REVIEW

Chapter Highlights

Before you begin, review the summaries of the key ideas of each section, found at the end of each section. The vocabulary terms are listed on the first page of each section.

UNDERSTANDING CONCEPTS

1. Matter is
- **a.** any visible solid that has mass.
- **b.** any liquid that takes up space and has mass.
- **c.** anything that takes up space and has mass.
- **d.** any liquid or solid that takes up space.

2. What is the chemical formula for iron(III) oxide?
- **a.** Fe^{2+}
- **b.** NaCl
- **c.** I_2
- **d.** Fe_2O_3

3. Which of the following is a mixture?
- **a.** air
- **b.** salt
- **c.** water
- **d.** sulfur

4. Compounds and elements are
- **a.** always solids.
- **b.** mixtures.
- **c.** pure substances.
- **d.** dense.

5. Which of the following is a physical change?
- **a.** melting ice cubes
- **b.** burning paper
- **c.** rusting iron
- **d.** burning gasoline

6. Which of the following is a pure substance?
- **a.** grape juice
- **b.** salt water
- **c.** table salt
- **d.** gasoline

7. If you add oil to water and shake the two liquids together, you will form a
- **a.** pure substance.
- **b.** miscible liquid.
- **c.** heterogeneous mixture.
- **d.** homogeneous mixture.

USING VOCABULARY

8. List four properties that can be used to classify elements.

9. Compare the following sets of terms:
- **a.** an *atom* and a *molecule*
- **b.** a *molecule* and a *compound*
- **c.** a *compound* and a *mixture*

10. When wood is burned, heat, ash, and smoke are produced. Describe this reaction, and explain what type of change is occurring. Use the terms *flammability, chemical property,* and *physical change* or *chemical change.*

11. When sugar is added to water, the sugar dissolves and the resulting liquid is clear. Have the combined sugar and water formed a *pure substance* or a *mixture*? Explain your answer.

12. When water and rubbing alcohol are mixed together, they completely dissolve. Are the two liquids *miscible* or *immiscible*? Explain the difference.

13. The figure below shows magnesium burning in the presence of oxygen. Give some evidence from the figure that a *chemical change* is occurring.

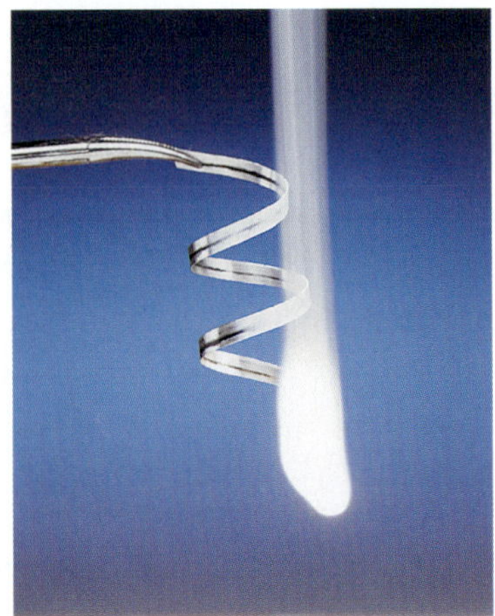

14. Make a table that has two columns. Label one column "Physical properties" and the other "Chemical properties." Put each of the following terms in the proper column: *color, density, reactivity, magnetism, melting point, corrosion, flammability, dissolving, conducting electricity,* and *boiling point.*

BUILDING GRAPHING SKILLS

15. **Graphing** Make a graph that shows the relationship between the mass and volume of aluminum samples of different sizes. Use the y-axis to plot mass and the x-axis to plot volume. What does the shape of the graph tell you about the density of aluminum?

Block number	Mass (g)	Volume (cm^3)
1	1.20	0.443
2	3.59	1.33
3	5.72	2.12
4	12.4	4.60
5	15.3	5.66
6	19.4	7.17
7	22.7	8.41
8	24.1	8.94
9	34.0	12.6
10	36.4	13.5

BUILDING MATH SKILLS

16. **Calculating Density** A piece of titanium metal has a mass of 67.5 g and a volume of 15 cm^3. What is the density of titanium?

17. **Calculating Density** A sample of a substance with a mass of 85 g occupies a volume of 110 cm^3. What is the density of the substance? Will the substance float in water? Explain your answer.

18. **Calculating Volume** The density of a piece of brass is 8.4 g/cm^3. If the mass of the brass is 510 g, find the volume of the brass.

19. **Calculating Mass** What mass (in grams) of water will fill a tank that is 100.0 cm long, 50.0 cm wide, and 30.0 cm high?

20. **Calculating Volume and Mass** A graduated cylinder is filled with water to a level of 40.0 mL. When a piece of copper is lowered into the cylinder, the water level rises to 63.4 mL. Find the volume of the copper sample. If the density of the copper is 8.9 g/cm^3, what is the copper's mass?

THINKING CRITICALLY

21. **Applying Knowledge** A jar contains 30 mL of glycerin (mass = 37.8 g) and 60 mL of corn syrup (mass = 82.8 g). Which liquid is on the top layer? Explain your answer.

22. **Applying Knowledge** Describe a procedure to separate a mixture of salt, finely ground pepper, and pebbles.

23. **Applying Knowledge** A light-green powder is heated in a test tube. A gas is given off while the solid becomes black. In which category of matter does the green powder belong? Explain your reasoning.

24. **Creative Thinking** Suppose you are planning a journey to the center of Earth in a self-propelled tunneling machine. List properties of the special materials that would be needed to build the machine, and explain why each property would be important.

DEVELOPING LIFE/WORK SKILLS

25. Making Decisions The frame of a tennis racket needs to be strong and stiff yet light. Tennis racket frames were once made of wood. But to be strong and stiff, the frame had to be thick and heavy. Now rackets can be made from different materials. Make a table of the advantages and disadvantages of each of the materials described in the graph below.

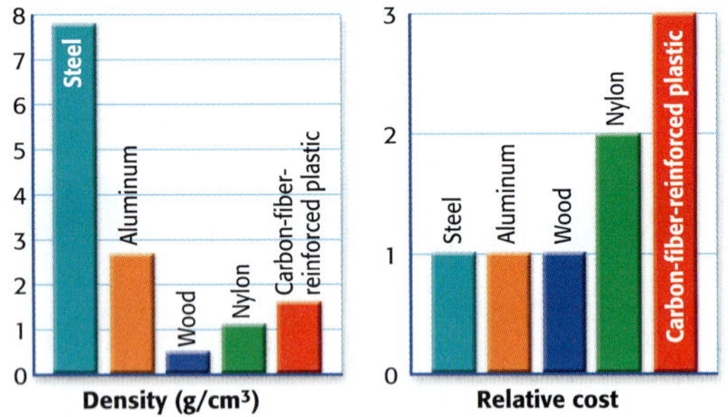

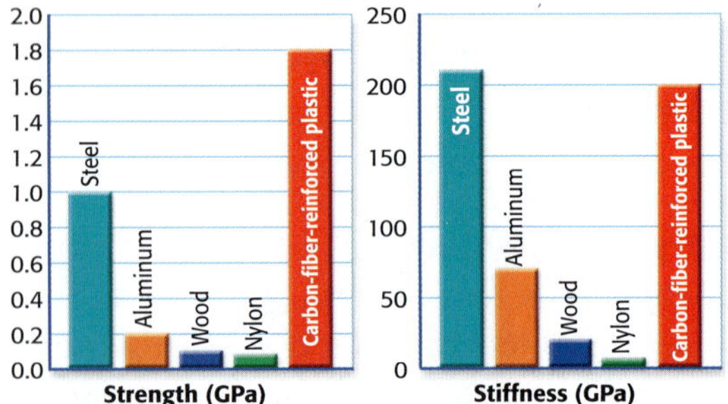

26. Applying Technology COMPUTER SKILL Use a computer drawing program to illustrate a chemical change in which one atom and one molecule interact to form two molecules.

27. Working Cooperatively Suppose you are given a piece of a material that is painted black so you cannot tell its normal appearance. Work in a small group to plan tests you would do on the material to decide whether it is metal, glass, plastic, or wood.

INTEGRATING CONCEPTS

28. Connection to Biology Explain why the process of digestion involves mainly chemical changes. Research what the starting materials of digestion are and the final end products, and find out if physical changes are also involved. Why is digestion necessary?

29. Connection to Language Arts An element is sometimes named for one of its properties, an interesting fact about the element, or for the person who first discovered the element. Research the origin of the name of each of the following elements: promethium, oxygen, iridium, fermium, curium, tantalum, silver, polonium, ytterbium, and hafnium.

30. Concept Mapping Copy the unfinished concept map below onto a sheet of paper. Complete the map by writing the correct word or phrase in the lettered boxes.

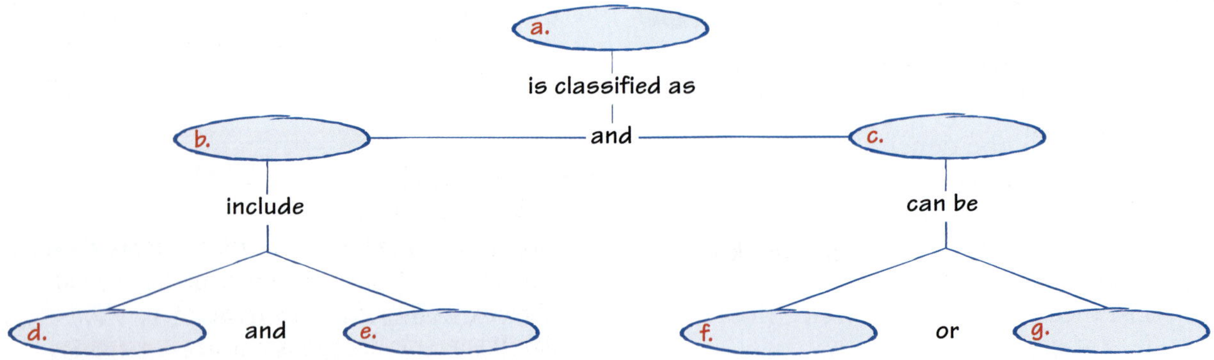

Standardized Test Prep

Understanding Concepts

***Directions (1–3):* For *each* question, write on a separate sheet of paper the letter of the correct answer.**

1. Which of the following substances is a compound?
   A. air
   B. carbon dioxide
   C. nitrogen
   D. oxygen

2. If vinegar is poured into two test tubes containing white powders that look identical, which of the following statements is a reasonable conclusion as to why bubbles form in one tube but not the other?
   F. The test tubes contain two different mixtures.
   G. The contents of the test tubes are two different pure substances.
   H. The materials in the two test tubes cannot be the same substance.
   I. One test tube contains an element, and the other contains a compound.

3. Which of these is a physical change?
   A. the combustion of gasoline in an engine
   B. the expansion of air in a balloon when it is heated
   C. the conversion of milk to yogurt by microorganisms
   D. the change in color of a bronze statue from copper-colored to green

***Directions (4–5):* For *each* question, write a short response.**

4. Iron, gold, copper, and silver are all elements that are metals. Based on these elements, what are some of the physical properties that could be used to classify a substance as a metal?

5. How could an engineer use the physical properties of water and dissolved salts to develop a system for producing drinking water from seawater?

Reading Skills

***Directions (6):* Read the passage below. Then answer the question.**

Most of the elements were originally discovered on Earth, but helium was first found in the sun. Every element emits light at specific wavelengths when it is heated. The first evidence that helium existed was a line in the spectrum of the sun that did not match any produced by known elements. The astronomer who discovered helium was examining a spectrum of sunlight taken during an eclipse, when only the outer part of the sun is visible. Helium was not isolated from Earth's atmosphere until more than 20 years after its discovery.

6. How could scientists know that helium was a different element from any previously discovered, without having isolated any helium on Earth?

Interpreting Graphics

***Directions (7):* Base your answer to question 7 on the illustration below.**

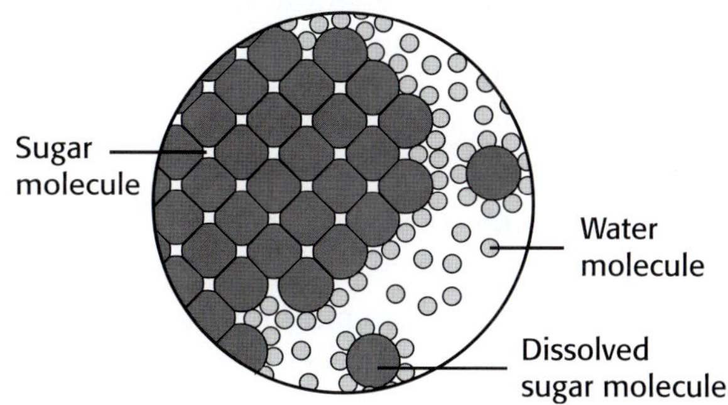

7. Examine the illustration of sugar molecules in water. Why is it that sugar does not dissolve immediately when it is placed in water?

Test TIP

Take time to read each question completely on a standardized test, including all of the answer choices. Consider each answer choice before determining which one is correct.

Skills Practice Lab

Testing the Conservation of Mass

Introduction

How can you show that mass is conserved in a chemical reaction between two household substances—vinegar and baking soda?

Objectives

- USING SCIENTIFIC METHODS ***Measure*** the masses of reactants and products in a chemical reaction.
- ***Design*** an experiment to test the law of conservation of mass.

Materials

balance (with standard masses, if necessary)
baking soda (sodium bicarbonate)
beaker, 400 mL (optional)
clear plastic cups (capable of holding at least 150 mL each) (2)
graduated cylinder, 100 mL
plastic sandwich bag with zipper-type closure
twist tie
vinegar (acetic acid solution)
weighing papers (2)

▶ Procedure

Observing the Reaction Between Vinegar and Baking Soda

1. On a blank sheet of paper, prepare a table like the one shown below.

	Initial mass (g)	Final mass (g)	Change in mass (g)
Trial 1			
Trial 2			

SAFETY CAUTION Put on a lab apron, safety goggles, and gloves. If you get a chemical on your skin or clothing, wash it off at the sink while calling to your teacher. If you get a chemical in your eyes, immediately flush it out at the eyewash station while calling to your teacher. When mixing chemicals, use a rimmed tray with a paper lining to catch and absorb spills.

2. Place a piece of weighing paper on the balance. Place about 4 to 5 g of baking soda on the paper. Carefully transfer the baking soda to a plastic cup.
3. Using the graduated cylinder, measure about 50 mL of vinegar. Pour the vinegar into the second plastic cup.
4. Place both cups on the balance, and determine the combined mass of the cups, baking soda, and vinegar to the nearest 0.01 g. Record the combined mass in the first row of your table under "Initial mass."
5. Take the cups off the balance. Carefully and slowly pour the vinegar into the cup that contains the baking soda. To avoid splattering, add only a small amount of vinegar at a time. Gently swirl the cup to make sure the reactants are well mixed.

6. When the reaction has finished, place both cups back on the balance. Determine the combined mass to the nearest 0.01 g. Record the combined mass in the first row of your table under "Final mass."
7. Subtract the final mass from the initial mass, and record the result in the first row of your table under "Change in mass."

Designing Your Experiment

8. Examine the plastic bag and the twist ties. With your lab partners, develop a procedure that will test the law of conservation of mass more accurately than Trial 1 did. Which products' masses were not measured? How can you be sure you measure the masses of all of the reaction products?
9. In your lab report, list each step you will perform in your experiment.
10. Before you carry out your experiment, your teacher must approve your plan.

Performing Your Experiment

11. After your teacher approves your plan, perform your experiment using approximately the same quantities of baking soda and vinegar you used in Trial 1.
12. Record the initial mass, final mass, and change in mass in your table.

▶ Analysis

1. Compare the changes in mass you calculated for the first and second trials. What value would you expect to obtain for a change in mass if both trials validated the law of conservation of mass?
2. Was the law of conservation of mass violated in the first trial? Explain your reasoning.
3. If the results of the second trial were different from those of the first trial, explain why.

▶ Conclusions

4. Suppose someone performs an experiment like the one you designed and finds that the final mass is much less than the initial mass. Would that prove that the law of conservation of mass is wrong? Explain your reasoning.

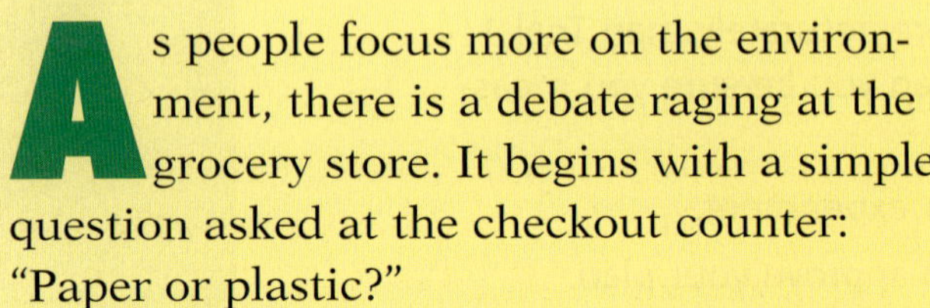

viewpoints

Paper or Plastic at the Grocery Store?

As people focus more on the environment, there is a debate raging at the grocery store. It begins with a simple question asked at the checkout counter: "Paper or plastic?"

Some say that paper is a bad choice because making paper bags requires cutting down trees. Yet these bags are naturally biodegradable, and they recycle easily.

Others say that plastic is not a good choice because plastic bags are made from nonrenewable petroleum products. But recent advances have made plastic bags that can break down when exposed to sunlight. Many stores collect used plastic bags and recycle them to make new ones.

How should people decide which bags to use? What do you think?

PAPER!

> FROM: Jaclyn M., Chicago, IL

I think people should choose paper bags because they can be recycled and reused. There should be a mandatory law that makes sure each community has a weekly recycling service for paper bags.

> FROM: Eric S., Rochester, MN

When it comes down to it, both types of bags can be recycled. However, as we know, not everybody recycles bags. Therefore, paper is a better choice because it is a renewable resource.

PLASTIC!

> FROM: Ashley A., Dyer, IN

Plastic is not necessarily better, but it is a lot more convenient. You can reuse plastic bags as garbage bags or bags to carry anything you need to take with you. Plastic is also easier to carry when you leave the store. Plastic bags don't get wet in the rain and break, causing you to drop your groceries on the ground.

> FROM: Christy M., Houston, TX

I believe we should use more plastic bags in grocery stores. By using paper, we are chopping down not only trees but also the homes of animals and plants.

> FROM: Andrew S., Bowling Green, KY

People should be able to use the bags they want. People that use paper bags should try to recycle them. People that use plastic bags should reuse them. We should be able to choose, as long as we recycle the bags in some way.

> FROM: Alicia K., Coral Springs, FL

Canvas bags would be a better choice than the paper or plastic bags used in stores. Canvas bags are made mostly of cotton, a very renewable resource, whereas paper bags are made from trees, and plastic bags are made from nonrenewable petroleum products.

BOTH or NEITHER!

Your Turn

1. **Critiquing Viewpoints** Select one of the statements on this page that you *agree* with. Identify and explain at least one weak point in the statement. What would you say to respond to someone who brought up this weak point as a reason you were wrong?
2. **Critiquing Viewpoints** Select one of the statements on this page that you *disagree* with. Identify and explain at least one strong point in the statement. What would you say to respond to someone who brought up this point as a reason they were right?
3. **Creative Thinking** Make a list of at least 12 additional ways for people to reuse their plastic or paper bags.
4. **Life/Work Skills** Imagine that you are trying to decrease the number of bags being sent to the local landfill. Develop a presentation or a brochure that you could use to convince others to reuse or recycle their bags.

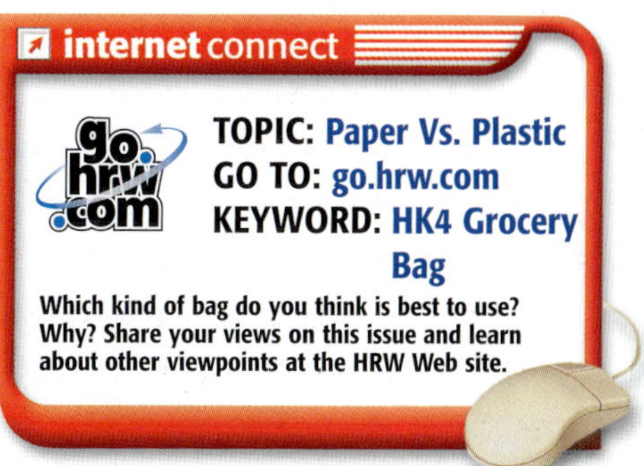

CHAPTER 3

States of Matter

Chapter Preview

Carbon dioxide changes directly from a solid to a gas under standard conditions.

Focus ACTIVITY

Background Do you notice something unique about the castle shown to the left? This castle is made of blocks of ice! Water exists in many forms, such as steam rising from a tea kettle, dew collecting on grass, crystals of frost forming on the windows in winter, and blocks of ice in an ice castle. But no matter what form you see, water always contains the same elements—hydrogen and oxygen.

In this chapter, you'll learn more about the many different properties of matter, such as the various forms water takes. Although you may not always be aware of them, changes of matter take place all around you. The atoms and molecules that make up all matter are in constant motion, whether the matter is a solid, a liquid, or a gas. This is true even in solid ice. Ice consists of water molecules held firmly in a rigid structure. Although they do not move about freely, ice molecules are able to vibrate back and forth.

Activity 1 Use the materials your teacher provides to make models of water molecules in ice.

Activity 2 Use the same materials to make models of liquid water molecules breaking away from ice crystals during melting.

Pre-Reading Questions

1. What three states of matter are you familiar with? Give examples of each.
2. Can you think of an example of matter changing from one state to another? What would cause a substance to change from one state to another?

SECTION 1

Matter and Energy

KEY TERMS

plasma
energy
thermal energy
evaporation
sublimation
condensation

OBJECTIVES

- **Summarize** the main points of the kinetic theory of matter.
- **Describe** how temperature relates to kinetic energy.
- **Describe** four common states of matter.
- **List** the different changes of state, and describe how particles behave in each state.
- **State** the laws of conservation of mass and conservation of energy, and explain how they apply to changes of state.

If you visit a restaurant kitchen, such as the one in ***Figure 1,*** you can smell the food cooking even if you are a long way from the stove. One way to explain this phenomenon is to make some assumptions. First, assume that the particles (atoms and molecules) within the food substances are always in motion and are constantly colliding. Second, assume that the particles move faster as the temperature rises. A theory based on these assumptions, called the kinetic theory of matter, can be used to explain things such as why you can smell food cooking from far away.

When foods are cooking, energy is transferred from the stove to the foods. As the temperature increases, some particles in the foods move very fast and actually spread through the air in the kitchen. In fact, the state, or physical form, of a substance is determined, partly by how its particles move.

Figure 1

The ingredients in foods are chemicals. A skilled chef understands how the chemicals in foods interact and how changes of state affect cooking.

Kinetic Theory

Here are the main points of the kinetic theory of matter:

- All matter is made of atoms and molecules that act like tiny particles.
- These tiny particles are always in motion. The higher the temperature of the substance, the faster the particles move.
- At the same temperature, more-massive (heavier) particles move slower than less massive (lighter) particles.

The kinetic theory helps you visualize the differences among the three common states of matter: solids, liquids, and gases.

Figure 2

Common States of Matter

A Here, the element sodium is shown as the solid metal.

B This is sodium melted as a liquid.

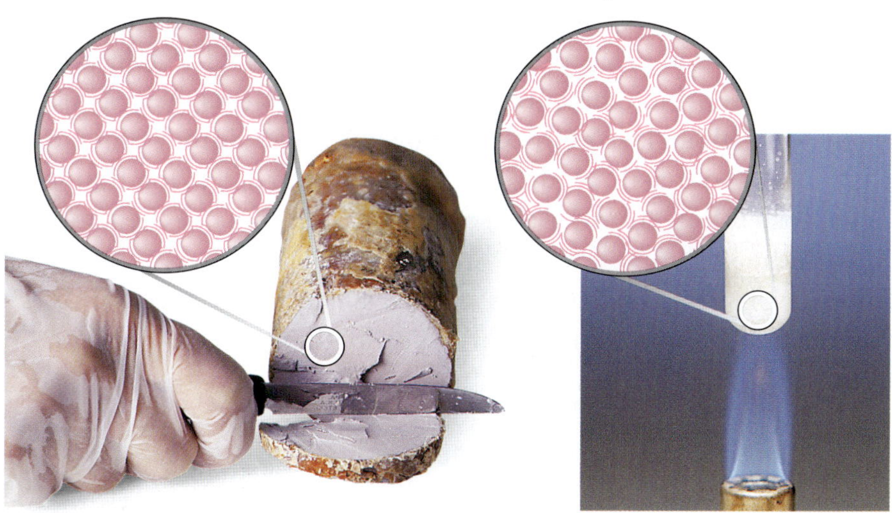

C Sodium exists as a gas in a sodium-vapor lamp.

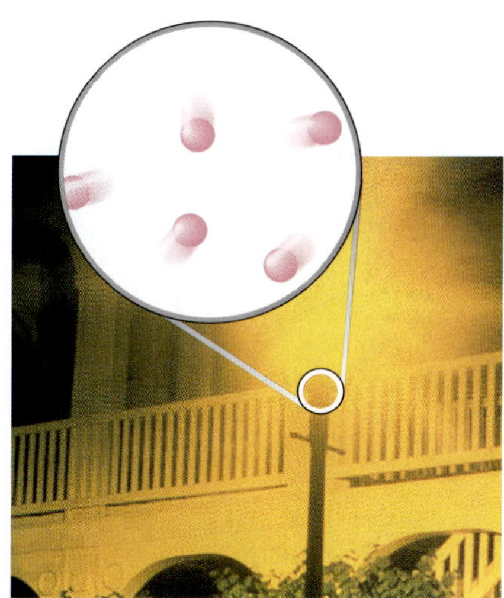

The states of matter are physically different

The models for solids, liquids, and gases shown in ***Figure 2*** differ in the distances between the atoms or molecules and in how closely these particles are packed together. Particles in a solid, such as iron, are in fixed positions. In a liquid, such as cooking oil, the particles are closely packed, but they can slide past each other. Gas particles are in a constant state of motion and rarely stick together. Most matter found naturally on Earth is either a solid, a liquid, or a gas, although matter also exists in other states.

Figure 3

Particles in a crystalline solid have an orderly arrangement.

Solids have a definite shape and volume

Take an ice cube out of the freezer. The ice cube has the same volume and shape that it had in the ice tray. Unlike gases and liquids, a solid does not need a container in order to have a shape. The structure of a solid is rigid, and the particles have almost no freedom to change position. The particles in solids are held closely together by strong attractions, yet they vibrate.

Solids are often divided into two categories—crystalline and amorphous. *Crystalline solids* have an orderly arrangement of atoms or molecules. Examples of crystalline solids include iron, diamond, and ice. *Amorphous solids* are composed of atoms or molecules that are in no particular order. Each particle is in a particular place, but the particles are in no organized pattern. Examples of amorphous solids include rubber and wax. ***Figure 3*** and ***Figure 4*** illustrate the differences in these two types of solids.

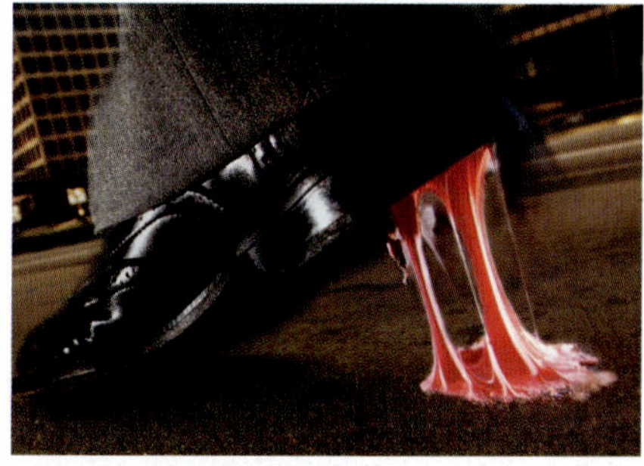

Figure 4

The particles in an amorphous solid do not have an orderly arrangement.

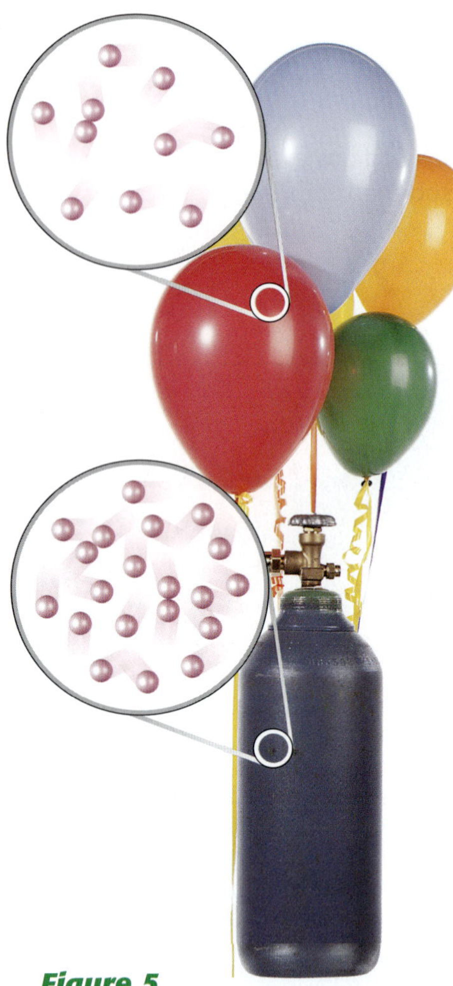

Figure 5

The particles of helium gas, He, in the cylinder are much closer together than the particles of the gas in the balloons.

Liquids change shape, not volume

Liquids have a definite volume, but they change shape. The particles of a liquid can slide past one another. And the particles in a liquid move more rapidly than those in a solid—fast enough to overcome the forces of attraction between them. This allows liquids to flow freely. As a result, the liquids are able to take the shape of the container they are put into. You see this every time you pour yourself a glass of juice. But even though liquids change shape, they do not easily change volume. The particles of a liquid are held close to one another and are in contact most of the time. Therefore, the volume of a liquid remains constant.

Another property of liquids is *surface tension,* the force acting on the particles at the surface of a liquid that causes a liquid, such as water, to form spherical drops.

Gases are free to spread in all directions

If you leave a jar of perfume open, particles of the liquid perfume will escape as gas, and you will smell it from across the room. Gas expands to fill the available space. And under standard conditions, particles of a gas move rapidly. For example, helium particles can travel 1200 m/s.

One cylinder of helium, as shown in ***Figure 5,*** can fill about 700 balloons. How is this possible? The volume of the cylinder is equal to the volume of only five inflated balloons. Gases change both their shape and volume. The particles of a gas move fast enough to break away from each other. In a gas, the amount of empty space between the particles changes. The helium atoms in the cylinder in ***Figure 5,*** for example, have been forced close together. But, as the helium fills the balloon, the atoms spread out, and the amount of empty space in the gas increases.

plasma a state of matter that starts as a gas and then becomes ionized

Plasma is the most common state of matter

Scientists estimate that 99% of the known matter in the universe, including the sun and other stars, is made of matter called **plasma.** Plasma is a state of matter that does not have a definite shape and in which the particles have broken apart.

Plasmas are similar to gases but have some properties that are different from the properties of gases. Plasmas conduct electric current, while gases do not. Electric and magnetic fields affect plasmas but do not affect gases. Natural plasmas are found in lightning, fire, and the aurora borealis, shown in ***Figure 6.*** The glow of a fluorescent light is caused by an artificial plasma, which is formed by passing electric currents through gases.

Figure 6

Auroras form when high-energy plasma collides with gas particles in the upper atmosphere.

Figure 7

The particles in the steam have the most kinetic energy, but the ocean has the most total thermal energy because it contains the most particles.

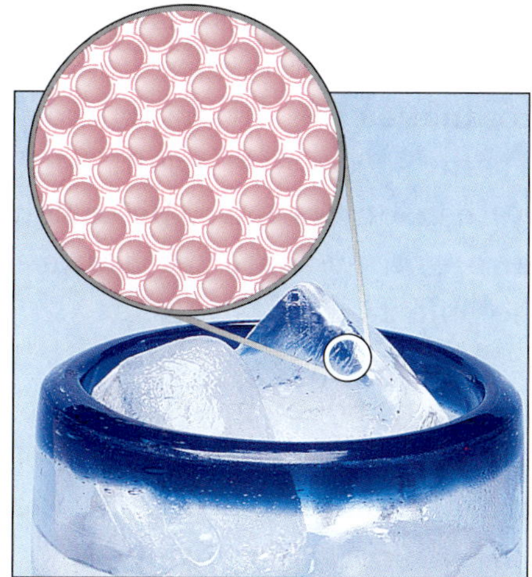

A The particles in an ice cube vibrate in fixed positions; therefore, they do not have a lot of kinetic energy.

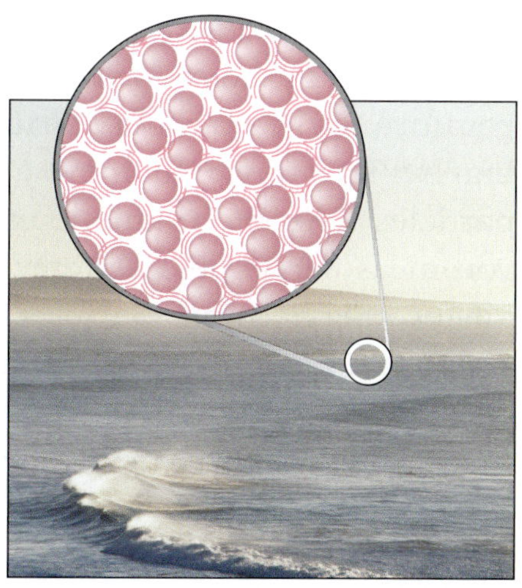

B The particles in ocean water move around; therefore, they have more kinetic energy than the particles in an ice cube.

C The particles in steam move around rapidly; therefore, they have more kinetic energy than the particles in ocean water.

Energy's Role

What sources of energy would you use if the electricity were off? You might use candles for light and batteries to power a clock. Electricity, candles, and batteries are sources of energy. The food you eat is also a source of energy. Chemical reactions that release heat are another source of energy. You can think of **energy** as the ability to change or move matter. Later, you will learn how energy can be described as the ability to do work.

energy the capacity to do work

thermal energy the kinetic energy of a substance's atoms

Thermal energy is the total kinetic energy of a substance

According to the kinetic theory, all matter is made of particles—atoms and molecules—that are constantly in motion. Because the particles are in motion, they have *kinetic energy,* or energy of motion. **Thermal energy** is the total kinetic energy of the particles that make up an object. The more kinetic energy the particles in the object have, the more thermal energy the object has. At higher temperatures, particles of matter move faster. The faster the particles move, the more kinetic energy they have, and the greater the object's thermal energy is. Thermal energy also depends on the number of particles in a substance. Look at **Figure 7.** Which substance do you think has the most thermal energy? The answer might surprise you.

Temperature is a measure of average kinetic energy

Do you think of temperature as a measure of how hot or cold something is? Scientifically, temperature is a measure of the average kinetic energy of the particles in an object. The more kinetic energy the particles of an object have, the higher the temperature of the object is. Particles of matter are constantly moving, but they do not all move at the same speed. As a result, some particles have more kinetic energy than others have. So, when you measure an object's temperature, you measure the average kinetic energy of the particles in the object.

The temperature of a substance is not determined by how much of the substance you have. For example, a teapot contains more tea than a mug does, but the temperature, or average kinetic energy of the particles in the tea, is the same in both containers. However, the total kinetic energy of the particles in each container is different.

Quick ACTIVITY

Hot or Cold?

You will need three buckets: one with warm water, one with cold water, and one with hot water. **SAFETY:** Test a drop of the hot water to make sure it is not too hot.

Put both your hands into a bucket of warm water, and note how it feels. Now put one hand into a bucket of cold water and the other into a bucket of hot water. After a minute, take your hands out of the hot and cold water, and put them back in the warm water. Can you rely on your hands to determine temperature? Explain your observations.

Energy and Changes of State

A change of state—the conversion of a substance from one physical form to another—is a physical change. The identity of a substance does not change during a change of state, but the energy of a substance does change. In ***Figure 8,*** the ice, liquid water, and steam are all the same substance—water, H_2O—but they all have different amounts of energy.

If energy is added to a substance, its particles move faster, and if energy is removed, its particles move slower. The temperature of a substance is a measure of its energy. Therefore, steam, for example, has a higher temperature than liquid water does, and the particles in steam have more energy than the particles in liquid water do. A transfer of energy known as *heat* causes the temperature of a substance to change, which can lead to a change of state.

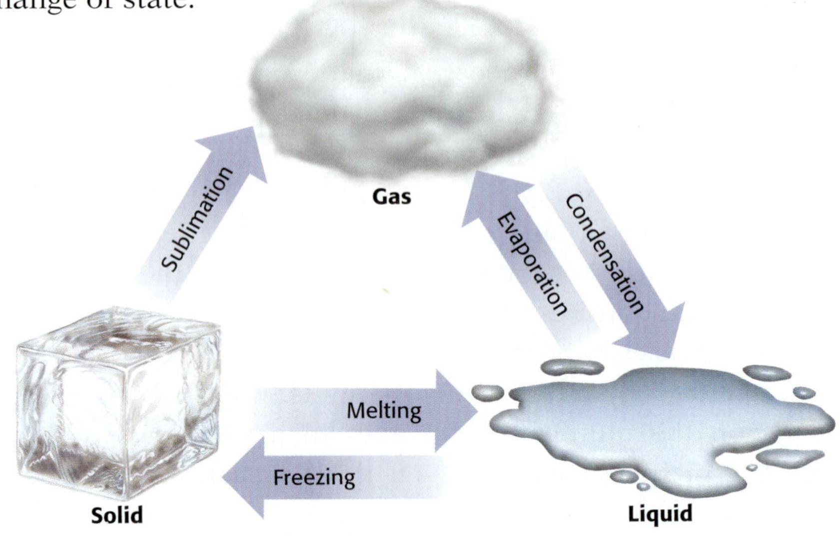

Figure 8

This figure shows water undergoing five changes of state: freezing, melting, sublimation, evaporation, and condensation.

Some changes of state require energy

Changes, such as melting, that require energy are called *endothermic changes*. A solid changes to a liquid by melting. Heating a solid transfers energy to the atoms, which vibrate faster as they gain energy. Eventually, they break from their fixed positions, and the solid melts. The *melting point* is the temperature at which a substance changes from a solid to a liquid. The melting point of water is 0°C. Table salt has a melting point of 801°C.

Evaporation is the change of a substance from a liquid to a gas. Boiling is evaporation that occurs throughout a liquid at a specific temperature and pressure. The temperature at which a liquid boils is the liquid's *boiling point*. Like the melting point, the boiling point is a characteristic property of a substance. The boiling point of water at sea level is 100°C, and the boiling point of mercury is 357°C.

Figure 9

Your body's heat provides the energy for sweat to evaporate.

You can feel the effects of an energy change when you sweat. Energy from your body is transferred to sweat molecules as heat. When this transfer occurs, your body cools off. The molecules of sweat on your skin gain energy and move faster, as shown in ***Figure 9.*** Eventually, the fastest-moving molecules break away, and the sweat evaporates. Energy is needed to separate the particles of a liquid to form a gas.

Solids can also change to gases. ***Figure 10*** shows solid carbon dioxide undergoing **sublimation,** that is, the process by which a solid turns directly into a gas. Sometimes ice sublimes to form a gas. When left in the freezer for a while, ice cubes get smaller as the ice changes from a solid to a gas.

evaporation the change of a substance from a liquid to a gas

sublimation the process in which a solid changes directly into a gas (the term is sometimes also used for the reverse process)

Figure 10

Dry ice (solid carbon dioxide) sublimes to form gaseous carbon dioxide.

Figure 11

Gaseous water in the air will become liquid when it contacts a cool surface.

Energy is released in some changes of state

When water vapor becomes a liquid, or when liquid water freezes to form ice, energy is released from the water to its surroundings. For example, the dew drops in ***Figure 11*** form as a result of **condensation,** which is the change of state from a gas to a liquid. During this energy transfer, the water molecules slow down. For a gas to become a liquid, large numbers of atoms clump together. Energy is released from the gas and the particles slow down.

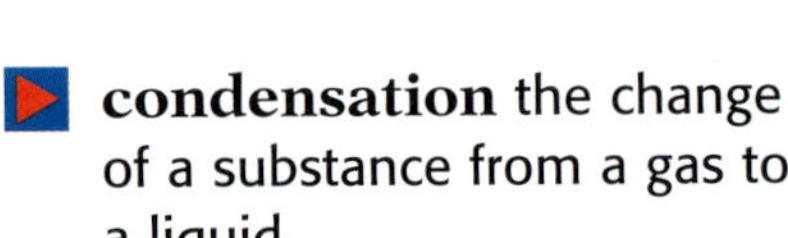

condensation the change of a substance from a gas to a liquid

Condensation sometimes takes place when a gas comes in contact with a cool surface. Have you ever noticed drops of water forming on the outside of a glass containing a cool drink? The *condensation point* of a substance is the temperature at which the gas becomes a liquid.

Energy is also released during freezing, which is the change of state from a liquid to a solid. The temperature at which a liquid changes into a solid is its *freezing point.* Freezing is the reverse of melting, so freezing and melting occur at the same temperature, as shown in ***Figure 12.*** For a liquid to freeze, the motion of its particles must slow down, and the attractions between the particles must overcome their motion. Like condensation, freezing is an *exothermic change* because energy is released from the substance as it changes state.

Figure 12

Liquid water freezes at the same temperature that ice melts: 0°C.

Temperature change versus change of state

When a substance loses or gains energy, either its temperature changes or its state changes. But the temperature of a substance does not change during a change of state, as shown in ***Figure 13.*** For example, if you add heat to ice at 0°C, the temperature will not rise until all the ice has melted.

Figure 13

Changes of State for Water

Energy must be added to separate the particles as ice melts; the same amount of energy is released when water freeezes.

Energy is absorbed when water vaporizes; the same amount of energy is released when the water vapor condenses.

Gaseous steam

Energy released to condense

Energy absorbed to vaporize

Liquid water

Energy released to solidify

Energy absorbed to melt

Solid ice

Relative energy: 0, 10, 20, 30, 40, 50, 60, 70, 80, 90, 100

Temperature (°C): −20, 0, 20, 40, 60, 80, 100, 120

Conservation of Mass and Energy

Look at the changes of state shown in ***Figure 13.*** Changing the energy of a substance can change the state of the substance, but it does not change the composition of a substance. Ice, water, and steam are all made of H_2O. When an ice cube melts, the mass of the liquid water is the same as the mass of the ice cube. When water boils, the number of molecules stays the same even as the liquid water loses volume. The mass of the steam is the same as the mass of the water that evaporated.

Mass cannot be created or destroyed

In chemical changes, as well as in physical changes, the total mass of matter stays the same before and after the change. Matter changes, but the total mass stays the same. The law of conservation of mass states that mass cannot be created or destroyed. For instance, when you burn a match, it seems to lose mass. The ash has less mass than the match. But there is also mass in the oxygen that reacts with the match, in the tiny smoke particles, and in the gases formed in the reaction. The total mass of the reactants (the match and oxygen) is the same as the total mass of the products (the ash, smoke, and gases).

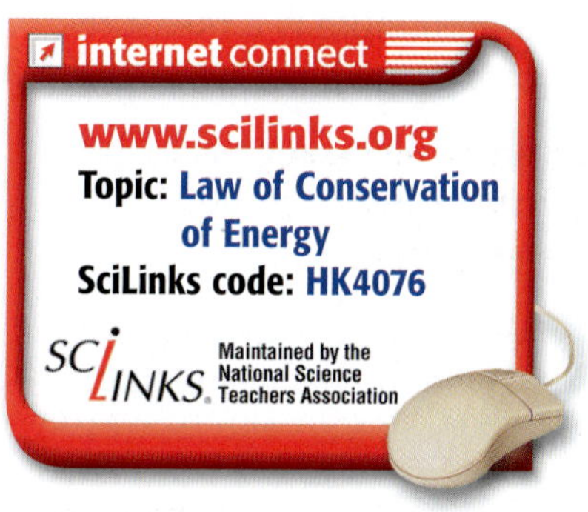

INTEGRATING

SPACE SCIENCE

Studies of the chemical changes that stars and nebulae undergo are constantly adding to our knowledge. Present estimates are that hydrogen makes up more than 90% of the atoms in the universe and constitutes about 75% of the mass of the universe. Helium atoms make up most of the remainder of the mass. The total of all the other elements contributes very little to the total mass of the universe.

Energy cannot be created or destroyed

Energy may be converted to another form during a physical or chemical change, but the total amount of energy present before and after the change is the same. The law of conservation of energy states that energy cannot be created or destroyed.

Starting a car may seem to violate the law of conservation of energy. For the small amount of energy needed to turn the key in the ignition, a lot of energy results. But the car needs gasoline to run. Gasoline releases energy when it is burned. Because of the properties of chemicals that make up gasoline, it has stored energy. When the stored energy is considered, the energy before you start the car is equal to the energy that is produced.

When you drive a car, gasoline is burned to produce the energy needed to power the car. However, some of the energy from the gasoline is transferred to the surroundings as heat. That is why a car's engine gets hot. The total amount of energy released by the gasoline is equal to the energy used to move the car, plus the energy transferred to the surroundings as heat.

SECTION 1 REVIEW

SUMMARY

- The kinetic theory states that all matter is made of tiny, moving particles.
- Solids have a definite volume and shape. Liquids have a definite volume but a variable shape. Gases have a variable shape and volume.
- Thermal energy is the total kinetic energy of the particles of a substance.
- Temperature is a measure of average kinetic energy.
- A change of state is a physical change that requires or releases energy.
- Mass and energy are conserved in changes of state.

1. **List** three main points of the kinetic theory of matter.
2. **Describe** the relationship between temperature and kinetic energy.
3. **State** two examples for each of the four common states of matter.
4. **Describe** the following changes of state, and explain how particles behave in each state.
   a. freezing **c.** sublimation
   b. boiling **d.** melting
5. **State** whether energy is released or energy is required for the following changes of state to take place.
   a. melting **c.** sublimation
   b. evaporation **d.** condensation
6. **Compare** the shape and volume of solids, liquids, and gases.
7. **Describe** the role of energy when ice melts and when water vapor condenses to form liquid water. Portray each state of matter and the change of state using a computer drawing program. COMPUTER SKILL
8. **State** the law of conservation of mass and the law of conservation of energy, and explain how they apply to changes of state.
9. **Critical Thinking** Use the kinetic theory to explain how a dog could find you by your scent.

Refrigeration

Today the refrigerator is the most common kitchen appliance around. You can find one in more than 99% of American homes, but it wasn't always like this. Refrigerators didn't become widely available until 1916. Before that, people stored foods in "ice boxes" that held slabs of ice. This ice was often cut from frozen mountain lakes and carried long distances to be sold in cities. Ice was a luxury, but it played the same important role that refrigeration does today. Cold prevents the growth of bacteria that spoils food. If eaten, some bacteria can also cause sickness and even death.

erators help keep food fresh

Ice Cold Science

Modern refrigeration systems use refrigerants to keep cool. A *refrigerant* is a substance that evaporates (and transfers energy) at a very low temperature. If a refrigerant can evaporate at a low temperature, it takes an input of less energy for the refrigerant to change from a liquid to a gas. On the back of a refrigerator, coiled tubes contain a refrigerant that alternately evaporates from a liquid into a gas and is then condensed back into a liquid. Through each cycle of evaporation, the refrigerant draws heat out of the air in the refrigerator, causing the air temperature in the refrigerator to go down.

Refrigerants

The first refrigerators used toxic gases such as ammonia as refrigerants, and leaking refrigerators were responsible for several deaths in the 1920s. In 1928, a "miracle" refrigerant made from organic compounds called chlorofluorocarbons (CFCs) was introduced. Freon® not only was an efficient refrigerant but also was odorless and nonflammable.

Unfortunately, the "miracle" refrigerant was too good to be true. In the 1980s, scientists were alarmed to learn that the ozone layer, a protective layer of gases in Earth's atmosphere, was disappearing. Evidence linked CFCs to the ozone loss. Freon manufacture was banned in the United States, forcing companies to develop new, safer refrigerants.

Refrigerator Magnet

Scientists have recently discovered a way to use a magnet and the "magnetocaloric" element gadolinium to cool air. Magnetocaloric materials change temperature when in contact with a magnetic field. Because the device uses water instead of refrigerant, scientists are hopeful that the magnet refrigerator will one day be a safe, efficient form of refrigeration.

Your Choice

1. **Applying Knowledge** Why was the manufacture of Freon banned in the United States?
2. **Critical Thinking** Why is it important that a refrigerant evaporates at a low temperature?

SECTION 2

Fluids

KEY TERMS

fluid
buoyant force
pressure
Archimedes' principle
pascal
Pascal's principle
viscosity

OBJECTIVES

- **Describe** the buoyant force and explain how it keeps objects afloat.
- **Define** Archimedes' principle.
- **Explain** the role of density in an object's ability to float.
- **State** and apply Pascal's principle.
- **State** and apply Bernoulli's principle.

What do liquids and gases have in common? Liquids and gases are states of matter that do not have a fixed shape. They have the ability to flow, and they are both referred to as **fluids.** Fluids are able to flow because their particles can move past each other easily. Fluids, especially air and water, play an important part in our lives. The properties of fluids allow huge ships to float, divers to explore the ocean depths, and jumbo jets to soar across the skies.

Buoyant Force

Why doesn't a rubber duck sink to the bottom of a bath tub? Even if you push a rubber duck to the bottom, it will pop back to the surface when you release it. A force pushes the rubber duck to the top of the water. The force that pushes the duck up is the **buoyant force**—the upward force that fluids exert on matter. When you float on an air mattress in a swimming pool, the buoyant force keeps you and the air mattress afloat. A rubber duck and a large steel ship, such as the one shown in ***Figure 14,*** both float because they are less dense than the water that surrounds them and because the buoyant force pushes against them to keep them afloat.

fluid a nonsolid state of matter in which the atoms or molecules are free to move past each other, as in a gas or liquid

buoyant force the upward force exerted on an object immersed in or floating on a fluid

Figure 14
Despite its large size and mass, this ship is able to float because its density is less than that of the water and because the buoyant force keeps it afloat.

Buoyancy explains why objects float

The buoyant force, which keeps the ice in ***Figure 15*** floating, is a result of pressure. All fluids exert **pressure,** which is the amount of force exerted on a given area. The pressure of all fluids, including water, increases as the depth increases. The water exerts fluid pressure on all sides of each piece of ice. The pressure exerted horizontally on one side of the ice is equal to the pressure exerted horizontally on the opposite side. These equal pressures cancel one another. The only fluid pressures affecting the pieces of ice are above and below. Because pressure increases with depth, the pressure below the ice is greater than the pressure on top of the ice. Therefore, the water exerts a net upward force—the buoyant force—on the ice above it. Because the buoyant force is greater than the weight of the ice, the ice floats.

Figure 15

Ice floats in water because it is less dense than water and because of the upward buoyant force on the ice.

Determining buoyant force

Archimedes, a Greek mathematician in the third century BCE, discovered a method for determining buoyant force. **Archimedes' principle** states that the buoyant force on an object in a fluid is an upward force equal to the weight of the fluid that the object displaces. For example, imagine that you put a brick in a container of water, as shown in ***Figure 16.*** A spout on the side of the container at the water's surface allows water to flow out of the container. As the object sinks, the water rises and flows through the spout into another container. The total volume of water that collects in the smaller container is the displaced volume of water from the larger container. The weight of the displaced fluid is equal to the buoyant force acting on the brick. An object floats only when it displaces a volume of fluid that has a weight equal to the object's weight—that is, an object floats if the buoyant force on the object is equal to the object's weight.

pressure the amount of force exerted per unit area of a surface

Archimedes' principle the principle that states that the buoyant force on an object in a fluid is an upward force equal to the weight of the volume of fluid that the object displaces

Figure 16

A An object is lowered into a container of water.

B The object displaces water, which flows into a smaller container.

C When the object is completely submerged, the volume of the displaced water equals the volume of the object.

Figure 17

Helium in a balloon floats in air for the same reason a duck floats in water—the helium and the duck are less dense than the surrounding fluid.

An object will float or sink based on its density

By knowing the density of a substance, you can determine if the substance will float or sink. For example, the density of a brick is 1.9 g/cm^3, and the density of water is 1.00 g/cm^3. The brick will sink because it is denser than the water.

One substance that is less dense than air is helium, a gas. Helium is about seven times less dense than air. A given volume of helium displaces a volume of air that is much heavier, so helium floats. That is why helium is used in airships and parade balloons, such as the one shown in ***Figure 17.***

Steel is almost eight times denser than water. And yet huge steel ships cruise the oceans with ease, and they even carry very heavy loads. But hold on! Substances that are denser than water will sink in water. So, how does a steel ship float?

The shape of the ship allows it to float. Imagine a ship that was just a big block of steel, as shown in ***Figure 18.*** If you put that steel block into water, it would sink because it is denser than water. Ships are built with a hollow shape, as shown below. The amount of steel is the same, but the hollow shape decreases the boat's density. Water is denser than the hollow boat, so the boat floats.

INTEGRATING

BIOLOGY

Some fish can adjust their density so that they can stay at a certain water depth. Most fish have an organ called a *swim bladder,* which is filled with gases. The inflated swim bladder increases the fish's volume, decreases its overall density, and keeps it from sinking. The fish's nervous system controls the amount of gas in the bladder according to the fish's depth in the water. Some fish, such as sharks, do not have a swim bladder, so they must swim constantly to keep from sinking.

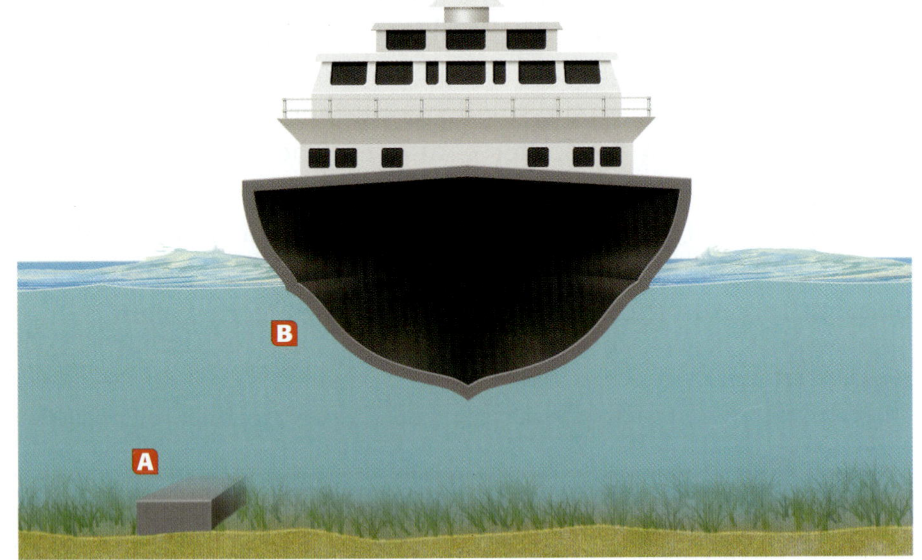

Figure 18

A A block of steel is denser than water, so it sinks.

B Shaping the block into a hollow form increases the volume occupied by the same mass, which results in a reduced overall density. The ship floats because it is less dense than water.

Fluids and Pressure

You probably have heard the terms *air pressure, water pressure,* and *blood pressure.* Air, water, and blood are all fluids, and all fluids exert pressure. So, what is pressure? For instance, when you pump up a bicycle tire, you push air into the tire. Inside the tire, tiny air particles are constantly pushing against each other and against the walls of the tire, as shown in ***Figure 19.*** The more air you pump into the tire, the more the air particles push against the inside of the tire, and the greater the pressure against the tire is. Pressure can be calculated by dividing force by the area over which the force is exerted:

$$pressure = \frac{force}{area}$$

The SI unit for pressure is the **pascal.** One pascal (Pa) is the force of one newton exerted over an area of one square meter (1 N/m^2). You will learn more about newtons, but remember that a newton is a measurement of force. Weight is a force, and an object's weight can be given in newtons.

When you blow a soap bubble, you blow in only one direction. So, why does the bubble get rounder as you blow, instead of longer? The shape of the bubble is due partly to an important property of fluids: fluids exert pressure evenly in all directions. The air you blow into the bubble exerts pressure evenly in all directions, so the bubble expands in all directions and creates a round sphere.

Figure 19
The force of air particles inside the tire creates pressure, which keeps the tire inflated.

pascal the SI unit of pressure; equal to the force of 1 N exerted over an area of 1 m^2 (abbreviation, Pa)

Density on the Move A submarine is a type of ship that can travel both on the surface of the water and underwater. Submarines have special ballast tanks that control their buoyancy. When the submarine dives, the tanks can be opened to allow sea water to flow in. This water adds mass and increases the submarine's density, so the submarine can descend into the ocean. The crew can control the amount of water taken in to control the submarine's depth. To bring the submarine through the water and to the surface, compressed air is blown into the ballast tanks to force the water out. The first submarine, *The Turtle,* was used in 1776 against British warships during the American War of Independence. It was a one-person, hand-powered, wooden vessel. Most modern submarines are built of metals and use nuclear power, which enables them to remain submerged almost indefinitely.

Applying Information

1. Identify the advantages of using metals instead of wood in the construction of today's submarines.

Pascal's Principle

Have you ever squeezed one end of a tube of paint? Paint usually comes out the opposite end. When you squeeze the sides of the tube, the pressure you apply is transmitted throughout the paint. So, the increased pressure near the open end of the tube forces the paint out. This phenomenon is explained by Pascal's principle, which was named for the 17th-century scientist who discovered it. **Pascal's principle** states that a change in pressure at any point in an enclosed fluid will be transmitted equally to all parts of the fluid. Mathematically, Pascal's principle is stated as $p_1 = p_2$ or $pressure_1 = pressure_2$.

Pascal's principle the principle that states that a fluid in equilibrium contained in a vessel exerts a pressure of equal intensity in all directions

Math Skills

Pascal's principle

A hydraulic lift, shown in ***Figure 20,*** makes use of Pascal's principle, to lift a 19,000 N car. If the area of the small piston (A_1) equals 10.5 cm^2 and the area of the large piston (A_2) equals 400 cm^2, what force needs to be exerted on the small piston to lift the car?

1 List the given and unknown values.

Given: $F_2 = 19{,}000\text{ N}$

$A_1 = 10.5\text{ cm}^2$

$A_2 = 400\text{ cm}^2$

Unknown: F_1

2 Write the equation for Pascal's principle.

According to Pascal's principle, $p_1 = p_2$

$$\frac{F_1}{A_1} = \frac{F_2}{A_2} \quad F_1 = \frac{(F_2)(A_1)}{A_2}$$

3 Insert the known values into the equation, and solve.

$$F_1 = \frac{(19{,}000\text{ N})(10.5\text{ cm}^2)}{400\text{ cm}^2}$$

$$F_1 = 500\text{ N}$$

Pressure, Force, and Area

The pressure equation

$$pressure = \frac{force}{area}$$

can be used to find pressure or can be rearranged to find force or area.

$$force = (pressure)(area)$$

$$area = \frac{force}{pressure}$$

Practice

Pascal's principle

1. In a car's liquid-filled hydraulic brake system, the master cylinder has an area of 0.5 cm^2, and the wheel cylinders each have an area of 3.0 cm^2. If a force of 150 N is applied to the master cylinder by the brake pedal, what force does each wheel cylinder exert on its brake pad?

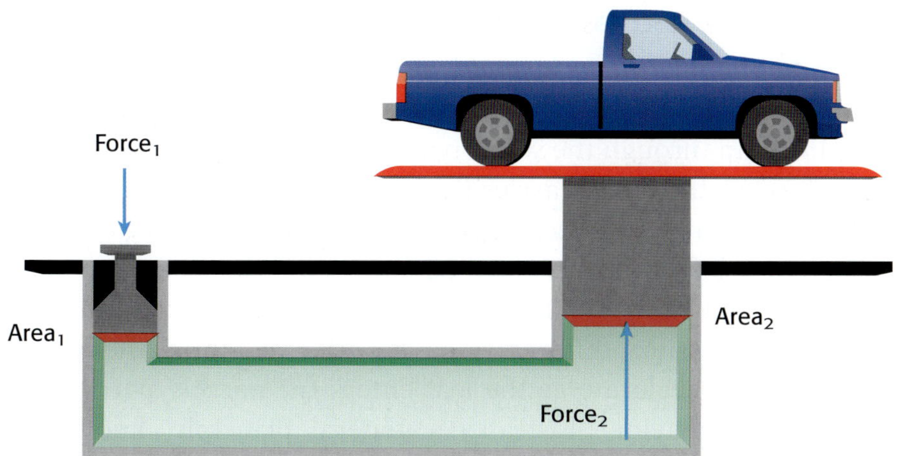

Figure 20
Because the pressure is the same on both sides of the enclosed fluid in a hydraulic lift, a small force on the smaller area (left) produces a much larger force on the larger area (right).

Hydraulic devices are based on Pascal's principle

Devices that use liquids to transmit pressure from one point to another are called *hydraulic devices*. Hydraulic devices use liquids because liquids cannot be compressed, or squeezed, into a much smaller space. This property allows liquids to transmit pressure more efficiently than gases, which can be compressed.

Hydraulic devices can multiply forces. For example, in ***Figure 20,*** a small downward force (F_1) is applied to a small area. This force exerts pressure on the liquid in the device, such as oil. According to Pascal's principle, this pressure is transmitted equally to a larger area, where it creates a force (F_2) larger than the initial force. Thus, the initial force can be multiplied many times.

Fluids in Motion

Examples of moving fluids include liquids flowing through pipes and air moving as wind. Have you ever used a garden hose? What happens when you place your thumb over the end of the hose? Your thumb blocks some of the area through which the water flows out of the hose, so the water exits at a faster speed. Fluids move faster through smaller areas than through larger areas, if the overall flow rate remains constant. Fluid speed is faster in a narrow pipe and slower in a wider pipe.

Figure 21
The honey shown above has a higher viscosity than water.

Viscosity is resistance to flow

Liquids vary in the rate at which they flow. For example, honey flows more slowly than lemonade. **Viscosity** is a liquid's resistance to flow. In general, the stronger the attraction between a liquid's particles the more viscous the liquid is. Honey flows more slowly than lemonade because it has a higher viscosity than lemonade. ***Figure 21*** shows a liquid that has a high viscosity.

viscosity the resistance of a gas or liquid to flow

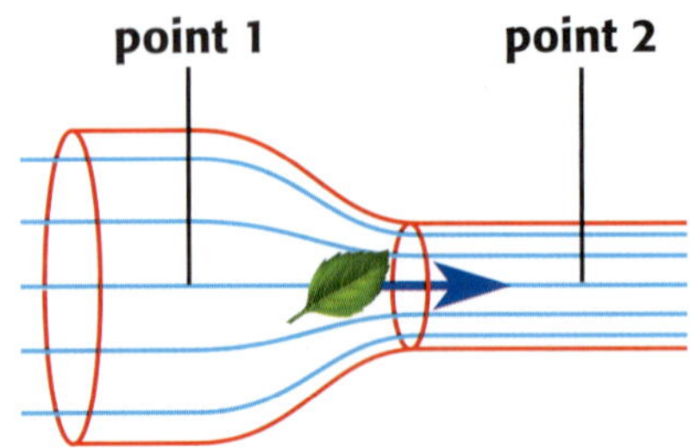

Figure 22

As a leaf passes through the drainage pipe, it speeds up. The water pressure on the right is less than the pressure on the left.

Fluid pressure decreases as speed increases

Figure 22 shows a water-logged leaf being carried along by water in a pipe. The water will move faster through the narrow part of the pipe than through the wider part, which is a property of fluids. Therefore, as the water carries the leaf into the narrow part of the pipe, the leaf moves faster. If you measure the pressure at point 1 and point 2, labeled in ***Figure 22,*** you would find that the water pressure in front of the leaf is less than the pressure behind the leaf. The pressure difference causes the leaf and the water around it to accelerate as the leaf enters the narrow part of the tube. This behavior illustrates a general principle, known as *Bernoulli's principle,* which states that as *the speed of a moving fluid increases, the pressure of the moving fluid decreases.* This property of moving fluids was first described in the 18th century by Daniel Bernoulli, a Swiss mathematician.

SECTION 2 REVIEW

SUMMARY

- Gases and liquids are fluids.
- Buoyancy is the tendency of a less dense substance to float in a denser liquid; buoyant force is the upward force exerted by fluids.
- Archimedes' principle states that the buoyant force on an object equals the weight of the fluid displaced by the object.
- Pressure is a force exerted on a given area; fluids exert pressure equally in all directions.
- Pascal's principle states that a change in pressure at any point in an enclosed fluid will be transmitted equally to all parts of the fluid.
- Bernoulli's principle states that fluid pressure decreases as the speed of a moving fluid increases.

1. **Explain** how differences in fluid pressure create buoyant force on an object.
2. **State** Archimedes' principle and give an example of how you could determine a buoyant force.
3. **State** Pascal's principle, and give an example of its use.
4. **Compare** the viscosity of milk and molasses.
5. **Define** the term *fluids.* What does Bernoulli's principle state about fluids?
6. **Critical Thinking** Two ships in a flowing river are sailing side-by-side with only a narrow space between them.
   a. What happens to the fluid speed between the two boats?
   b. What happens to the pressure between the boats?
   c. How could this change lead to a collision of the boats?

Math Skills

7. A water bed that has an area of 3.75 m^2 weighs 1025 N. Find the pressure that the water bed exerts on the floor.
8. An object weighs 20 N. It displaces a volume of water that weighs 15 N. (a) What is the buoyant force on the object? (b) Will the object float or sink? Explain.
9. Iron has a density of 7.9 g/cm^3. Mercury has a density of 13.6 g/cm^3. Will iron float or sink in mercury? Explain.

SECTION 3

Behavior of Gases

OBJECTIVES

- **Explain** how gases differ from solids and liquids.
- **State and explain** the following gas laws: Boyle's law, Charles's law, and Gay-Lussac's law.
- **Describe** the relationship between gas pressure, temperature, and volume.

KEY TERMS

Boyle's law
Charles's law
Gay-Lussac's law

Because many gases are colorless and odorless, it is easy to forget that they exist. But, every day you are surrounded by gases. Earth's atmosphere is a gaseous mixture of elements and compounds. Some examples of gases in Earth's atmosphere are nitrogen, oxygen, argon, helium, and carbon dioxide, as well as methane, neon and krypton. In the study of chemistry, as in everyday life, gases are very important. In this section, you will learn how pressure, volume, and temperature affect the behavior of gases.

Properties of Gases

As you have already learned, the properties of gases are unique. Some important properties of gases are listed below.

- Gases have no definite shape or volume, and they expand to completely fill their container, as shown in ***Figure 23.***
- Gas particles move rapidly in all directions.
- Gases are fluids.
- Gas molecules are in constant motion, and they frequently collide with one another and with the walls of their container.
- Gases have a very low density because their particles are so far apart. Because of this property, gases are used to inflate tires and balloons.
- Gases are compressible.
- Gases spread out easily and mix with one another. Unlike solids and liquids, gases are mostly empty space.

Figure 23

As you can see in this photo of chlorine gas, gases take the shape of their container.

Gases exert pressure on their containers

A balloon filled with helium gas is under pressure. The gas in the balloon is pushing against the walls of the balloon. The kinetic theory helps to explain pressure. Helium atoms in the balloon are moving rapidly and they are constantly hitting each other and the walls of the balloon, as shown in ***Figure 24.*** Each gas particle's effect on the balloon wall is small, but the battering by millions of particles adds up to a steady force. The pressure inside the balloon is the measure of this force per unit area. If too many gas particles are in the balloon, the battering overcomes the force of the balloon holding the gas in, and the balloon pops.

If you let go of a balloon that you have held pinched at the neck, most of the gas inside rushes out and causes the balloon to shoot through the air. A gas under pressure will escape its container if possible. If there is a lot of pressure in the container, the gas can escape with a lot of force. For this reason, gases in pressurized containers, such as propane tanks for gas grills, can be dangerous and must be handled carefully.

Did You Know?

The ability of gas particles to move and the relative sizes of gas particles have practical applications. Garrett Morgan was an African American born in Kentucky in 1875. Although he had only six years of formal education, he was an inventor of many useful products. For example, he invented a gas mask that allowed air, but not harmful gases, to pass through it. The mask received little recognition until Morgan used it to rescue 30 workers who were trapped underground in a tunnel that contained poisonous gases.

Gas Laws

You can easily measure the volume of a solid or liquid, but how do you measure the volume of a gas? The volume of a gas is the same as the volume of its container but there are other factors, such as pressure, to consider.

The gas laws describe how the behavior of gases is affected by pressure and temperature. Because gases behave differently than solids and liquids, the gas laws will help you understand and predict the behavior of gases in specific situations.

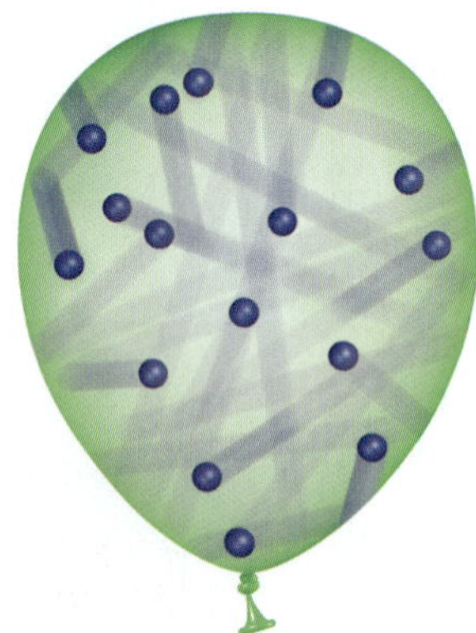

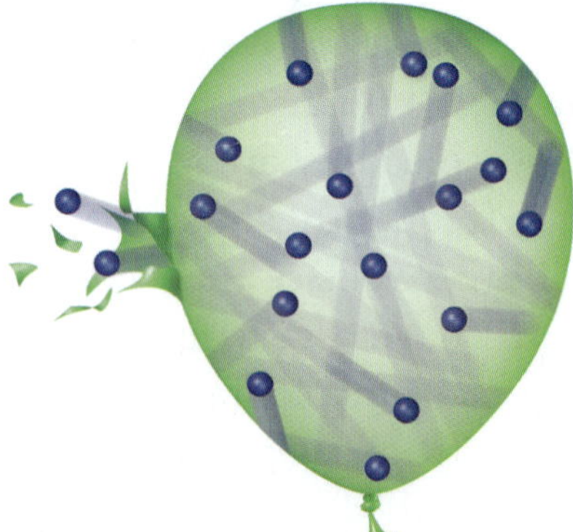

Figure 24

A Gas particles exert pressure by hitting the walls of the balloon.

B The balloon pops because the internal pressure is more than the balloon can hold.

Figure 25

Boyle's law Each illustration shows the same piston and the same amount of gas at the same temperature.

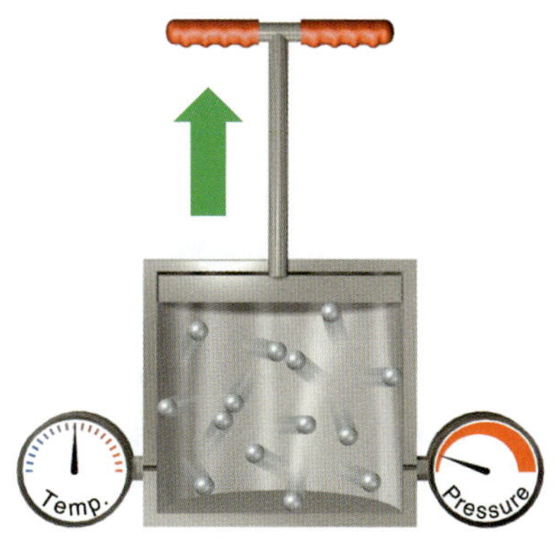

A Lifting the plunger decreases the pressure of the gas; the gas particles spread farther apart.

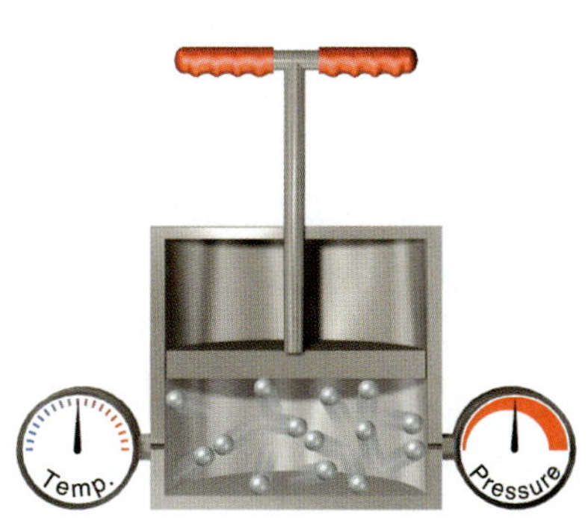

B Releasing the plunger allows the gas to change to an intermediate volume and pressure.

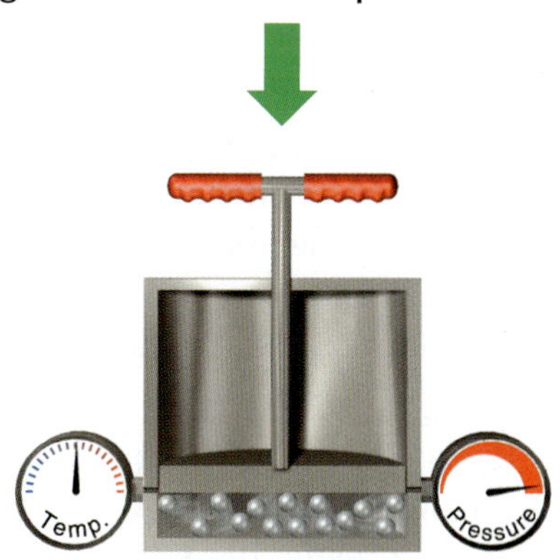

C Pushing the plunger increases the pressure, and decreases the volume of the gas.

Boyle's law relates the pressure of a gas to its volume

A diver at a depth of 10 m blows a bubble of air. As the bubble rises, its volume increases. When the bubble reaches the water's surface, the volume of the bubble will have doubled because of the decrease in pressure. The relationship between the volume and pressure of a gas is known as **Boyle's law.** Boyle's law states that for a fixed amount of gas at a constant temperature, the volume of a gas increases as its pressure decreases. Likewise, the volume of a gas decreases as its pressure increases. Boyle's law is illustrated in ***Figure 25.*** Boyle's law can be expressed as: $(pressure_1)(volume_1) = (pressure_2)(volume_2)$ or $P_1V_1 = P_2V_2$.

Boyle's law the law that states that for a fixed amount of gas at a constant temperature, the volume of the gas increases as the pressure of the gas decreases and the volume of the gas decreases as the pressure of the gas increases

Quick Lab

Does temperature affect the volume of a balloon?

Materials

- *aluminum pans (2)*
- *ice*
- *balloon*
- *hot plate*
- *beaker 250 ml*
- *ruler*
- *gloves*
- *water*

1. Fill an aluminum pan with 5 cm of water. Put the pan on the hot plate.
2. Fill another pan with 5 cm of ice water.
3. Blow up a balloon inside a beaker. The balloon should fill the beaker but should not extend outside it. Tie the balloon at its opening.
4. Place the beaker and balloon in the ice water. Record your observations.
5. Remove the balloon and beaker from the ice water. Observe the balloon for several minutes, and record any changes.
6. Next, put the beaker and balloon in the hot water. Record your observations.

Analysis

1. How did changing the temperature affect the volume of the balloon?
2. Is the density of a gas affected by temperature?

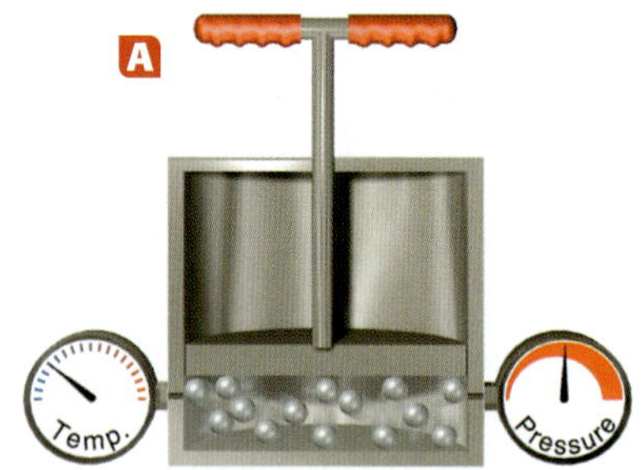

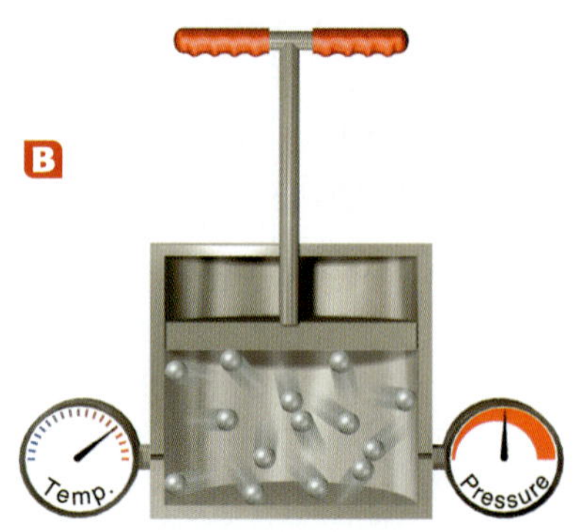

Figure 26

Each illustration shows the same piston and the same amount of gas at the same pressure.

A Decreasing the temperature causes the gas particles to move more slowly; they hit the sides of the piston less often and with less force. As a result, the volume of the gas decreases.

B Raising the temperature of the gas causes the particles to move faster. As a result, the volume of the gas increases.

Charles's law relates the temperature of a gas to its volume

An inflated balloon will also pop when it gets too hot which demonstrates another gas law—Charles's law. **Charles's law** states that for a fixed amount of gas at a constant pressure, the volume of the gas increases as its temperature increases. Likewise, the volume of the gas decreases as its temperature decreases. Charles's law is illustrated by the model in ***Figure 26.*** You can see Charles's law in action by putting an inflated balloon in the freezer and waiting about 10 minutes to see what happens!

As shown in ***Figure 27,*** if the gas in an inflated balloon is cooled (at constant pressure), the gas will decrease in volume and cause the balloon to deflate.

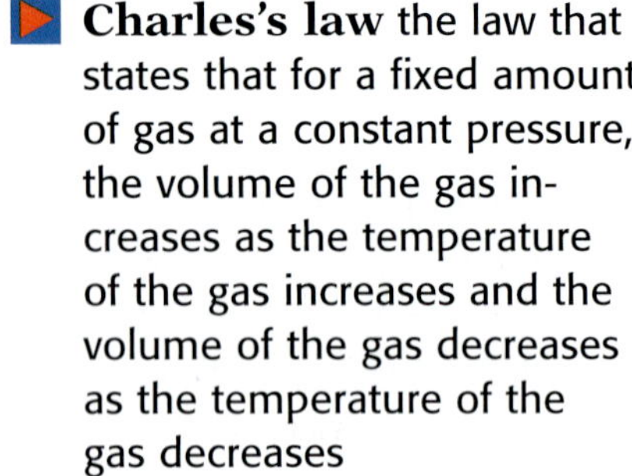

Charles's law the law that states that for a fixed amount of gas at a constant pressure, the volume of the gas increases as the temperature of the gas increases and the volume of the gas decreases as the temperature of the gas decreases

Figure 27

A Air-filled balloons are exposed to liquid nitrogen.

B The balloons shrink in volume.

C The balloons are removed from the liquid nitrogen and are warmed. The balloons expand to their original volume.

Math Skills

Boyle's Law

The gas in a balloon has a volume of 7.5 L at 100 kPa. The balloon is released into the atmosphere, and the gas expands to a volume of 11 L. Assuming a constant temperature, what is the pressure on the balloon at the new volume?

1 **List the given and unknown values.**

Given: $V_1 = 7.5$ L

$P_1 = 100$ kPa

$V_2 = 11$ L

Unknown: P_2

2 **Write the equation for Boyle's law, and rearrange the equation to solve for P_2.**

$$P_1V_1 = P_2V_2$$

$$P_2 = \frac{P_1V_1}{V_2}$$

3 **Insert the known values into the equation, and solve.**

$$P_2 = \frac{(100 \text{ kPa})(7.5 \text{ L})}{11 \text{ L}}$$

$$P_2 = 68 \text{ kPa}$$

Boyle's Law

The equation for Boyle's law can be rearranged to solve for volume in the following way. Use the equation $P_1V_1 = P_2V_2$ Divide both sides by P_2

$$\frac{P_1V_1}{P_2} = \frac{\cancel{P_2}V_2}{\cancel{P_2}}$$

$$\frac{P_1V_1}{P_2} = V_2$$

You will need to use this form of the equation in Practice Problems 2, 3, and 4.

Practice

Boyle's Law

1. A flask contains 155 cm^3 of hydrogen collected at a pressure of 22.5 kPa. Under what pressure would the gas have a volume of 90.0 cm^3 at the same temperature? (Recall that 1 cm^3 = 1 mL.)
2. If the pressure exerted on a 300.0 mL sample of hydrogen gas at constant temperature is increased from 0.500 atm to 0.750 atm, what will be the final volume of the sample?
3. A helium balloon has a volume of 5.0 L at a pressure of 101.3 kPa. The balloon is released and reaches an altitude of 6.5 km at a pressure of 50.7 kPa. If the gas temperature remains the same, what is the new volume of the balloon? Assume that the pressures are the same inside and outside of the balloon.
4. A sample of oxygen gas has a volume of 150 mL at a pressure of 0.947 atm. What will the volume of the gas be at a pressure of 1.000 atm if the temperature remains constant?

Gay-Lussac's law relates gas pressure to temperature

You have just learned about the relationship between the volume and temperature of a gas at constant pressure. What would you predict about the relationship between the pressure and temperature of a gas at constant volume? Remember that pressure is the result of collisions of gas molecules against the walls of their containers. As temperature increases, the kinetic energy of the gas particles increases. The energy and frequency of the collision of gas particles against their containers increases. For a fixed quantity of gas at constant volume, the pressure increases as the temperature increases.

Joseph Gay-Lussac is given credit for recognizing this property in 1802. **Gay-Lussac's law** states that the pressure of a gas increases as the temperature increases if the volume of the gas does not change. So if pressurized containers that hold gases, such as spray cans, are heated, they may explode. You should always be careful to keep containers of pressurized gas away from heat.

Gay-Lussac's law the law that states that the pressure of a gas at a constant volume is directly proportional to the absolute temperature

SECTION 3 REVIEW

SUMMARY

- Gases are fluids, their particles are in constant motion, they have low density, they are compressible, and they expand to fill their container.
- Gas pressure increases as the number of collisions of gas particles increases.
- Boyle's law states that the volume of a gas increases as the pressure decreases if the temperature does not change.
- Charles's law states that the volume of a gas increases as the temperature increases if the pressure does not change.
- Gay-Lussac's law states that the pressure of a gas increases as the temperature increases if the volume does not change.

1. **List** four properties of gases.
2. **Explain** why the volume of a gas can change.
3. **Describe** how gases are different from solids and liquids and give examples.
4. **Identify** what causes the pressure exerted by gas molecules on their container.
5. **Restate** Boyle's law, Charles's law, and Gay-Lussac's law.
6. **Identify** a real-life example for each of the three gas laws.
7. **Critical Thinking** When scientists record the volume of a gas, why do they also record the temperature and the pressure?
8. **Critical Thinking** Predict what would happen to the volume of a balloon left on a sunny windowsill. Which gas law predicts this result?

Math Skills

9. A partially inflated weather balloon has a volume of 1.56×10^3 L and a pressure of 98.9 kPa. What is the volume of the balloon when it is released to a height where the pressure is 44.1 kPa?

Graphing Skills

Percentages of Tin and Lead at Given Melting Points

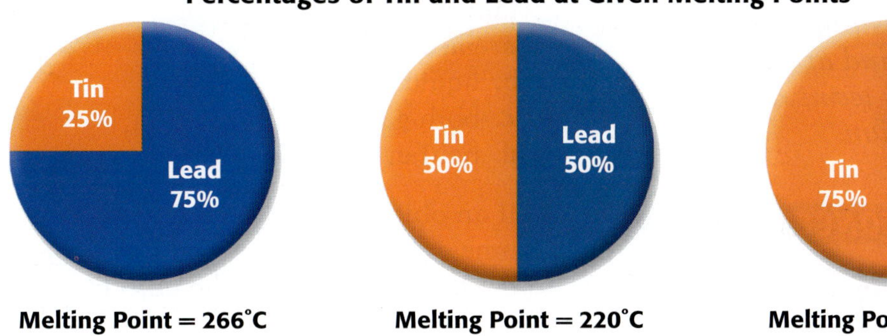

Melting Point = 266°C **Melting Point = 220°C** **Melting Point = 192°C**

Melting Point of Pure Lead = 326°C Melting Point of Pure Tin = 232°C

In most cases, when two pure substances with melting points that are not extremely different are mixed, the melting point of the mixture is lower than the melting points of either pure substances. Examine the graphs and answer the following questions.

1. What type of graphs are these?
2. Identify the quantities given in each graph. What important quantities relate the two graphs to each other?
3. By examining the graphs, what can you tell about the melting point of lead-tin alloys?
4. From the information given, estimate the percentages of tin and lead that would have the lowest melting temperature.
5. Suppose you wish to make a tin-lead solder that melts below 200°C. How might you find the limiting range of percentages for tin and lead for such a solder?
6. Construct a graph best suited for the information listed in the table below. Near what percentage mixture of metals is the melting point lowest?

Percentage of aluminum in Al-Cu alloy	Melting point (°C)
0	1084
20	930
40	610
60	540
80	600
100	650

CHAPTER 3 REVIEW

Chapter Highlights

Before you begin, review the summaries of the key ideas of each section, found at the end of each section. The vocabulary terms are listed on the first page of each section.

UNDERSTANDING CONCEPTS

1. Which of the following assumptions is *not* part of the kinetic theory?
- **a.** All matter is made up of tiny, invisible particles.
- **b.** The particles are always moving.
- **c.** Particles move faster at higher temperatures.
- **d.** Particles are smaller at lower pressure.

2. Three common states of matter are
- **a.** solid, water, and gas.
- **b.** ice, water, and gas.
- **c.** solid, liquid, and gas.
- **d.** solid, liquid, and air.

3. During which change of state do atoms or molecules become more ordered?
- **a.** boiling
- **b.** condensation
- **c.** melting
- **d.** sublimation

4. Which of the following describes what happens as the temperature of a gas in a balloon increases?
- **a.** The speed of the particles decreases.
- **b.** The volume of the gas increases and the speed of the particles increases.
- **c.** The volume decreases.
- **d.** The pressure decreases.

5. Fluid pressure is always directed
- **a.** up.
- **b.** down.
- **c.** sideways.
- **d.** in all directions.

6. Materials that can flow to fit their containers include
- **a.** gases.
- **b.** liquids.
- **c.** both gases and liquids.
- **d.** neither gases nor liquids.

7. If an object weighing 50 N displaces a volume of water with a weight of 10 N, what is the buoyant force on the object?
- **a.** 60 N
- **b.** 50 N
- **c.** 40 N
- **d.** 10 N

USING VOCABULARY

8. Compare *endothermic* and *exothermic* changes.

9. For each pair of terms, explain the difference in meaning.
- **a.** *solid/liquid*
- **b.** *Boyle's law/Charles's law*
- **c.** *Gay-Lussac's law/Pascal's principle*

10. Describe four states of matter using the terms *solid, liquid, gas,* and *plasma*. Describe the behavior of particles in each state.

11. State the *law of conservation of energy* and the *law of conservation of mass* and explain what happens to energy and mass in a change of state.

12. Describe the *buoyant force* and explain how it relates to *Archimedes principle.*

13. Explain how fluid pressure is affected by the speed of the fluids by restating *Bernoulli's principle.*

14. Describe how *pressure* is exerted by fluids.

15. Why are liquids used in *hydraulic* brakes instead of gases?

BUILDING GRAPHING SKILLS

16. **Graphing** The graph below shows the effects of heating on ethylene glycol, the liquid commonly used as antifreeze. Until the temperature is 197°C, is the temperature increasing or decreasing? What physical change is taking place when the ethylene glycol is at 197°C? Describe what is happening to the ethylene glycol molecules at 197°C. How can you tell?

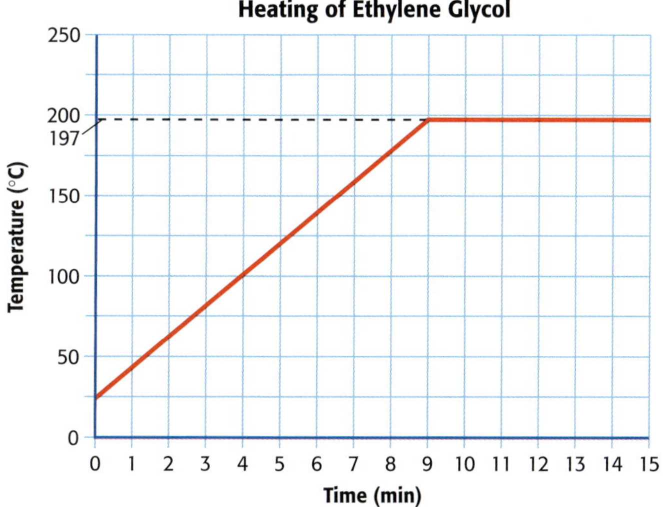

17. **Interpreting Data** Kate placed 100 mL of water in five different pans. She then placed the pans on a windowsill for a week, and measured how much water evaporated. Draw a graph of her data, shown below, with surface area on the *x*-axis. Is the graph linear or nonlinear? What does this tell you?

Pan number	1	2	3	4	5
Surface area (cm^2)	44	82	20	30	65
Volume evaporated (mL)	42	79	19	29	62

BUILDING MATH SKILLS

18. **Pressure** Calculate the area of a 1500 N object that exerts a pressure of 500 Pa. Then calculate the pressure exerted by the same object over twice that area. Be sure to express your answer in the correct SI unit.

19. **Pressure** A box, half full of books, rests on the ground. The area where the box comes in contact with the floor is 1 m^2. The box weighs 110 N. How much pressure is the box exerting on the floor? Express your answer in pascals.

20. **Pascal's principle** One of the largest helicopters in the world weighs 1.0×10^6 N. If you were to place this helicopter on a large piston of a hydraulic lift, what force would need to be applied to the small piston, with an area of 0.7 m^2, in order to lift the helicopter? The area of the large piston is 140 m^2.

21. **Boyle's law** A sample of neon gas occupies a volume of 2.8 L at 1.8 atm. What will its volume be at 1.2 atm?

22. **Boyle's law** 2.2 L of hydrogen at 6.5 atm pressure is used to fill a balloon at a final pressure of 1.15 atm. What is its final volume?

23. **Boyle's law** A sample of oxygen gas has a volume of 150 mL when its pressure is 0.947 atm. If the pressure is increased to 0.987 atm and the temperature remains constant, what will the new gas volume be?

THINKING CRITICALLY

24. **Applying Knowledge** After taking a shower, you notice that small droplets of water cover the mirror. Explain how this happens, describing where the water comes from and the changes it goes through.

25. Understanding Systems An iceberg is floating, partially submerged, in the ocean. At what part of the iceberg is the water pressure the greatest?

26. Understanding Systems Use Boyle's Law to explain why "bubble wrap" pops when you squeeze it.

27. Applying Knowledge Compared with an empty ship, will a ship loaded with plastic-foam balls float higher or lower in the water? Explain.

28. Critical Thinking Inside all vacuum cleaners is a high-speed fan. Explain how this fan causes dirt to be picked up by the vacuum cleaner.

DEVELOPING LIFE/WORK SKILLS

29. Allocating Resources Use the Internet or library references to find out how using a pressure cooker can preserve the nutritional value of food. Prepare an illustrated report that explains the science behind pressure-cooking.

30. Locating Information Use the Internet or library references to find out why changes must be made in some recipes for cooking and baking at high elevations. Make a poster presentation that compares recipes for sea level and high altitude preparations.

INTEGRATING CONCEPTS

31. Connection to Biology Your body uses the food you eat to do work. However, some of the food energy is lost as heat. How does your body give off this heat?

32. Connection to Environmental Science Research the process of glass and metal recycling. Visit a metal salvage yard or recycling center. Find out what types of metal and glass are recycled and how the recycled material is bought and sold. Work with a group to set up a glass and metal collection site at your school.

33. Concept Mapping Copy the unfinished concept map below onto a sheet of paper. Complete the map by writing the correct word or phrase in the lettered boxes.

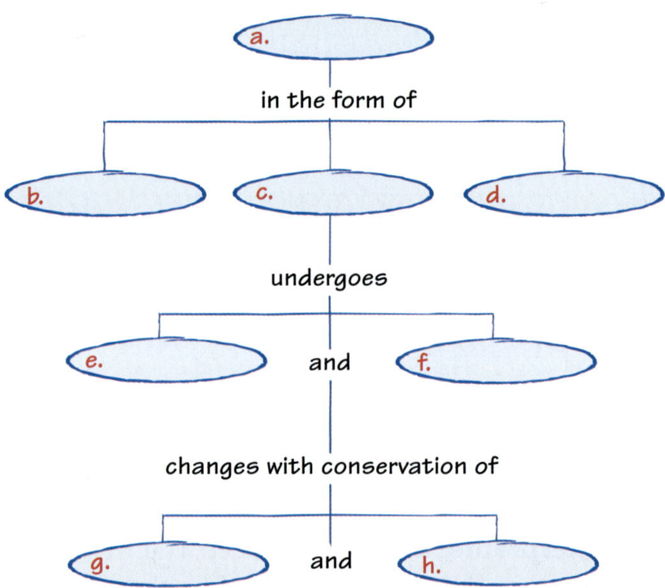

Standardized Test Prep

Understanding Concepts

Directions (1–3): **For *each* question, write on a separate sheet of paper the letter of the correct answer.**

1 Which of these following changes of state is exothermic?

A. evaporation
B. freezing
C. melting
D. sublimation

2 Which of these statements describes the particles of a liquid?

F. Particles are far apart and move freely.
G. Particles are close together and vibrate in place.
H. Particles are far apart and unable to change location.
I. Particles are close together and move past each other easily.

3 As the plunger is depressed, the volume of a syringe filled with helium gas is reduced from 25 mL to 10 mL. If the initial pressure is 150 kPa, what is the final pressure, in kPa, assuming constant temperature?

Reading Skills

Directions (4): **Read the passage below. Then answer the question.**

If the temperature in a citrus orchard drops below −2°C for several hours, the fruit will freeze and be destroyed. Citrus growers spray tiny droplets of water to protect the crop if a freeze is predicted. Protection comes from the heat released as the heated water cools. However, much of the heat that protects trees from freezing is released as the water freezes.

4 Based on the energy changes that occur when materials change state, determine how water freezing on the fruit can protect it from becoming too cold.

When analyzing a graph, pay attention to its title, which should tell you what is plotted on the graph.

Interpreting Graphics

Directions (5–8): **Base your answers to questions 5 through 8 on the graph below.**

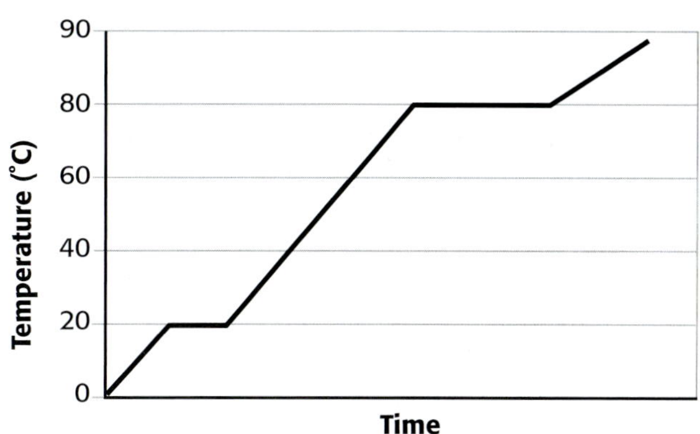

5 What is the boiling point of the substance shown on the graph?

A. 20°C
B. between 20°C and 80°C
C. 80°C
D. above 80°C

6 In what state is the substance at a temperature of 30°C?

F. gas and liquid mix
G. liquid
H. solid
I. solid and liquid mix

7 How will the substance change if energy is added to the liquid substance at 20°C?

A. The liquid will freeze.
B. The liquid will vaporize.
C. The liquid will become warmer.
D. The liquid will not undergo any change.

8 What occurs to the substance as energy is added to the liquid at 80°C?

F. The liquid will freeze.
G. The liquid will vaporize.
H. The liquid will become warmer.
I. The liquid will not undergo any change.

Skills Practice Lab

Boiling and Freezing

Introduction

When you add or remove energy from a substance, does the substance's temperature always change? Investigate this question with a common substance—water.

Objectives

- USING SCIENTIFIC METHODS ***Test your hypothesis*** by measuring the temperature of water as it boils and freezes.
- ***Graph*** data, and interpret the slopes of the graphs.

Materials

beaker, 250 or 400 mL
coffee can, large
crushed ice
gloves, heat-resistant
graduated cylinder, 100 mL
graph paper
hot plate
rock salt
stopwatch
thermometer
water
wire-loop stirring device

Procedure

Preparing for Your Experiment

1. Make a prediction: what happens to the temperature of boiling water as the boiling process continues?
2. Make a prediction: what happens to the temperature of freezing water as the freezing process continues?
3. Prepare two data tables like the one shown at right.

Boiling Water

4. Fill the beaker about one-third to one-half full with water.

5. Put on heat-resistant gloves. Turn on the hot plate, and put the beaker on the plate. Put the thermometer in the beaker.
   SAFETY CAUTION Be careful not to touch the hot plate. Also be careful not to break the thermometer.
6. In your first data table, record the temperature of the water every 30 seconds. Continue doing this until about one-fourth of the water boils away. Note the first temperature reading at which the water is steadily boiling.
7. Turn off the hot plate. Let the beaker cool for a few minutes, then use heat-resistant gloves to pick up the beaker. Pour the warm water out, and rinse the warm beaker with cool water.
   SAFETY CAUTION Even after cooling, the beaker may still be too hot to handle without gloves.

Freezing Water

8. Put approximately 20 mL of water in the graduated cylinder.
9. Put the graduated cylinder in the coffee can, and fill in around the graduated cylinder with crushed ice. Pour rock salt on the ice around the graduated cylinder. Slide the tip of the thermometer through the loop on the wire-loop stirring device and put the thermometer and the wire-loop stirring device in the graduated cylinder.

Temperature of Water

Time (s)	30	60	90	120	150	180	etc.
Temperature (°C)							

10. As the ice melts and mixes with the rock salt, the level of ice will decrease. Add ice and rock salt to the can as needed.
11. In your second data table, record the temperature of the water in the graduated cylinder every 30 s. Stir the water occasionally by moving the wire-loop stirring device up and down along the thermometer.
    SAFETY CAUTION Do not stir in a circular motion with the thermometer.
12. Once the water begins to freeze, stop stirring. Do not try to pull the thermometer out of the solid ice in the graduated cylinder.
13. Note the temperature when you first notice ice crystals forming in the water. Continue taking readings until the water in the graduated cylinder is frozen.
14. After you record your final reading, pour warm water into the can. Then wait until the ice in the graduated cylinder has melted. Pour the water out of the cylinder, and rinse the cylinder with water. Pour out the contents of the can, and rinse the can with water. Put away all equipment as directed by your instructor.

Analysis

1. **Constructing Graphs** Make a graph of temperature (*y*-axis) versus time (*x*-axis) for the boiling-water data from the first table. Draw an arrow to the temperature reading at which the water started to boil.
2. **Constructing Graphs** Make a graph of temperature (*y*-axis) versus time (*x*-axis) for the freezing-water data from the second table. Draw an arrow to the temperature reading at which the water started to freeze.
3. What does the slope of the line on each graph represent?
4. In your first graph, how does the slope when the water is boiling compare to the slope before the water starts to boil?
5. In your second graph, how does the slope when the water is freezing compare to the slope before the water starts to freeze?

Conclusions

6. Explain what happens to the energy that is added to the water while the water is boiling.
7. When water freezes, energy is removed from the water. What role do you think this energy played in the water before the energy was removed? Where does the energy go?

Science in ACTION

Plasma

We are surrounded by matter in one of three states: solid, such as wood and plastic; liquid, such as milk and seawater; and gas, such as oxygen and helium. But almost everything in the universe (99.9% of all matter) including the sun and all other stars, is a *plasma*. Plasma is a strange state of matter that has some unexpected effects on your daily life.

An artificial plasma was created in the plasma globe shown here by applying an electrical charge to a gas.

The lightning over Sydney, Australia, is an example of a natural plasma.

What Is Plasma?

Matter in the plasma state is a collection of free-moving electrons and ions (atoms that have lost electrons). Like gases, plasmas do not have a definite shape or volume. But unlike gases, plasmas conduct electricity and are affected by magnets. Plasmas require an energy source to exist. This energy may be a heat source, such as the heat of the sun; an electrical current; or a strong light, such as a laser. Some plasmas, including lightning and fire, do occur naturally on Earth. Artificial plasmas, including fluorescent and neon lights, are created by running an electrical current through a gas to change the gas into a plasma that emits light. When the current is removed the plasma becomes a gas again.

Space Weather

The sun is a giant ball of super heated plasma. On its surface, violent eruptions send waves of plasma streaming out into space at high speeds. As you read this book, Earth is bathed in waves of plasma known as solar wind. The most spectacular evidence of plasma in space is an aurora. When the highly charged plasma from the sun comes in contact with Earth's ionosphere (the uppermost region of Earth's atmosphere), the plasma produces an electrical discharge. This discharge, known as an aurora, lights up the sky.

After periods of disturbance on the surface of the sun, strong solar winds can disrupt radio and telephone communications, damage orbiting satellites, and cause electrical blackouts. Scientists are working to understand the forces behind solar wind and hope to better forecast damaging solar wind headed toward Earth.

Aurora borealis, also known as the Northern Lights, results from solar wind interacting with the Earth's atmosphere.

Science and You

1. **Understanding Concepts** Describe one way that a plasma is similar to a gas. Describe one way plasma is different from gas.
2. **Understanding Concepts** Name one common technology that uses plasma.
3. **Critical Thinking** Do you think that auroras occur at the same time as eruptions on the surface of the sun? Explain.
4. **Critical Thinking** Why do you think scientists want to predict solar winds in Earth's atmosphere?
5. **Acquiring and Evaluating** Some scientists believe that plasma may be a key to source of energy in the future. Research the Tokamak Fusion Reactor, and answer the following questions: What do scientists hope to achieve with this research? How are magnets involved in containing the plasma? What challenges do scientists face when studying plasma?

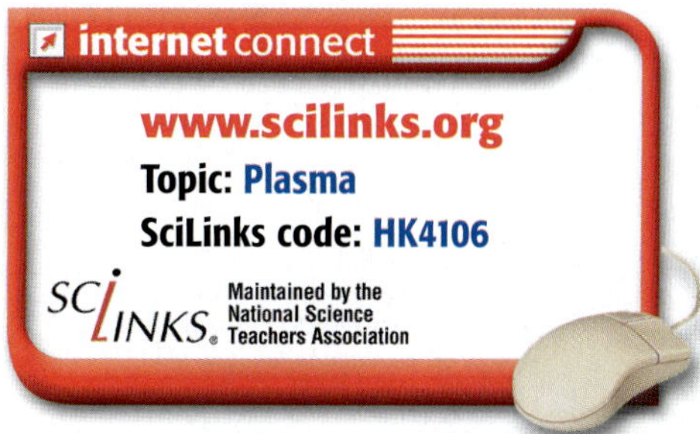

CHAPTER 4

Atoms and the Periodic Table

Chapter Preview

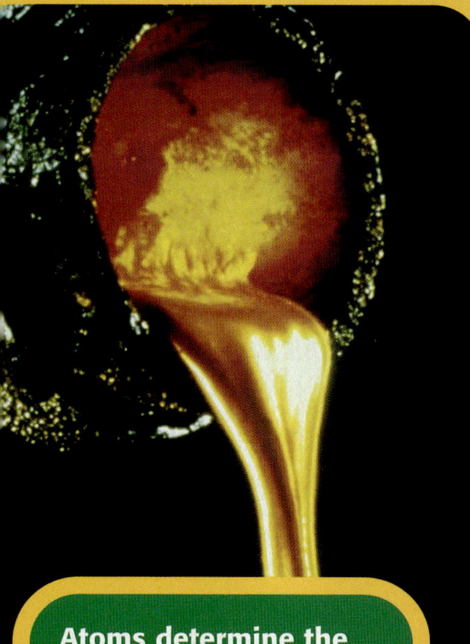

Atoms determine the properties of objects. For example, metal atoms give gold its shine and the ability to be worked into different shapes.

Focus ACTIVITY

Background Have you ever wondered why most metals shine? Metals shine because they are made of elements that reflect light. Another property of metals is that they do not shatter. Metals bend as they are pressed into thin, flat sheets during the coin-making process. All metals share some similarities, but each metal has its own unique chemical and physical properties.

The unique building shown on the opposite page is the Guggenheim Museum in Bilboa, Spain. This art museum is covered in panels made of titanium. Titanium is a strong, durable metallic element that can be used for a variety of purposes.

Metals, like everything around us, are made of trillions of tiny units that are too small to see. These units are called atoms. Atoms determine the properties of all substances. For example, gold atoms make gold softer and shinier than silver, which is made of silver atoms. Pennies get their color from the copper atoms they are coated with. In this chapter, you will learn what determines an atom's properties, why atoms are considered the smallest units of elements, and how elements are classified.

Activity 1 What metals do you see during a typical day? Describe their uses and their properties.

Activity 2 Describe several different ways to classify the metals shown on the opposite page.

Pre-Reading Questions

1. How are the atoms of all elements alike?
2. How does the periodic table help us learn about atoms and elements?
3. Which elements does your body contain?

SECTION 1

Atomic Structure

KEY TERMS

nucleus
proton
neutron
electron
orbital
valence electron

OBJECTIVES

- **Explain** Dalton's atomic theory, and describe why it was more successful than Democritus's theory.
- **State** the charge, mass, and location of each part of an atom according to the modern model of the atom.
- **Compare** and contrast Bohr's model with the modern model of the atom.

Atoms are everywhere. They make up the air you are breathing, the chair you are sitting in, and the clothes you are wearing. This book, including this page you are reading, is also made of atoms.

Disc One, Module 2:
Models of the Atom
Use the Interactive Tutor to learn more about this topic.

What Are Atoms?

Atoms are tiny units that determine the properties of all matter. The aluminum cans shown in ***Figure 1*** are lightweight and easy to crush because of the properties of the atoms that make up the aluminum.

Our understanding of atoms required many centuries

In the fourth century BCE, the Greek philosopher Democritus suggested that the universe was made of invisible units called atoms. The word *atom* is derived from the Greek word meaning "unable to be divided." He believed movements of atoms caused the changes in matter that he observed.

Although Democritus's theory of atoms explained some observations, Democritus was unable to provide the evidence needed to convince people that atoms really existed. Throughout the centuries that followed, some people supported Democritus's theory. But other theories were also proposed. As the science of chemistry was developing in the 1700s, more emphasis was put on making careful and repeated measurements in scientific experiments. As a result, more-reliable data were collected and used to favor one theory over another.

Aluminum Atoms

Figure 1
The atoms in aluminum, seen here as an image from a scanning tunneling electron microscope, give these aluminum cans their properties.

John Dalton developed an atomic theory

In 1808, an English schoolteacher named John Dalton proposed his own atomic theory. Dalton's theory was developed with a scientific basis, and some parts of his theory still hold true today. Like Democritus, Dalton proposed that atoms could not be divided. Today, we know that atoms are actually made up of even smaller particles! According to Dalton, all atoms of a given element were exactly alike. Dalton also stated that atoms of different elements could join to form compounds. Today, Dalton's theory is considered the foundation for modern atomic theory.

internet connect
www.scilinks.org
Topic: Atomic Theory
SciLinks code: HK4011
SCILINKS. Maintained by the National Science Teachers Association

Atoms are the building blocks of molecules

An atom is the smallest part of an element that still has the element's properties. Imagine dividing a coin made of pure copper until the pieces were too small for you to see. If you were able to continue dividing these pieces, you would be left with the simplest units of the coin—copper atoms. All the copper atoms would be alike. Each copper atom would have the same chemical properties as the coin you started with.

You have learned that atoms can join. ***Figure 2*** shows atoms joined together to form molecules of water. The water we see is actually made of a very large number of water molecules. Whether it gushes downstream in a riverbed or is bottled for us to drink, water is always the same: each molecule is made of two hydrogen atoms and one oxygen atom.

Figure 2

A The water that we see, no matter what its source, is made of many molecules.

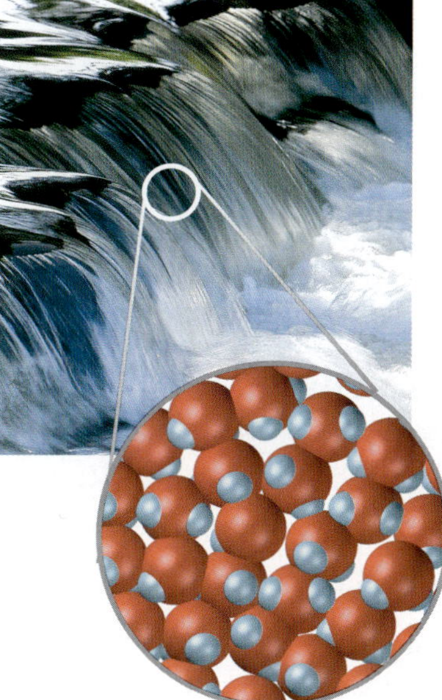

B Each molecule of water is made of two hydrogen atoms and one oxygen atom.

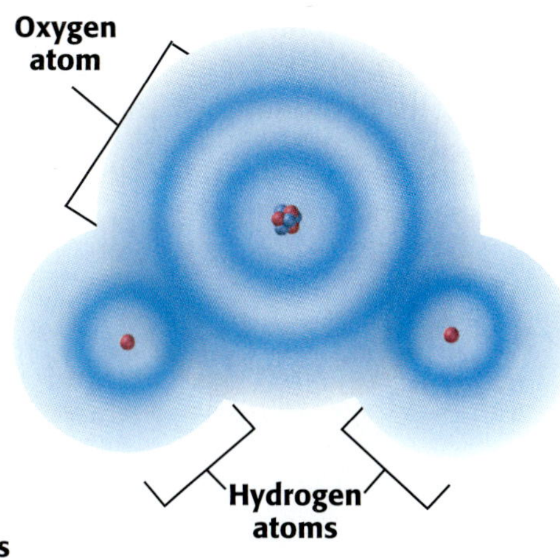

Figure 3

If the nucleus of an atom were the size of a marble, the whole atom would be the size of a football stadium

nucleus an atom's central region which is made up of protons and neutrons

proton a subatomic particle that has a positive charge and that is found in the nucleus of an atom

neutron a subatomic particle that has no charge and that is found in the nucleus of an atom

electron a subatomic particle that has a negative charge

Figure 4

A helium atom is made of two protons, two neutrons, and two electrons ($2e^-$).

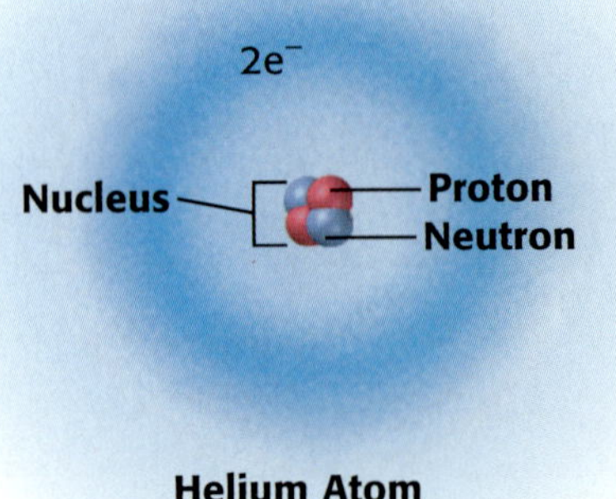

What's in an Atom?

Less than 100 years after Dalton published his atomic theory, scientists determined that atoms consisted of still smaller particles and could be broken down even further. While we now know that atoms are made up of many different subatomic particles, we need to study only three of these particles to understand the chemistry of most substances.

Atoms are made of protons, neutrons, and electrons

At the center of each atom is a small, dense **nucleus** with a positive electric charge. The nucleus is made of **protons** and **neutrons.** These two subatomic particles are almost identical in size and mass, but protons have a positive electric charge while neutrons have no electric charge at all. Moving around outside the nucleus is a cloud of very tiny negatively charged subatomic particles with very little mass. These particles are called **electrons.** To get an idea of how far from the nucleus an electron can be, see ***Figure 3.*** If the nucleus of an atom were the size of a marble, the whole atom would be the size of a football stadium! A helium atom, shown in ***Figure 4,*** has one more proton and one more electron than a hydrogen atom has. The number of protons and electrons an atom has is unique for each element.

Unreacted atoms have no overall charge

You might be surprised to learn that atoms are not charged even though they are made of charged protons and electrons. Atoms do not have a charge because they have an equal number of protons and electrons whose charges exactly cancel. A helium atom has two protons and two electrons. The atom is neutral because the positive charge of the two protons exactly cancels the negative charge of the two electrons.

Charge of two protons:	+2
Charge of two neutrons:	0
Charge of two electrons:	–2
Total charge of a helium atom:	0

Subatomic Particles

Particle	Charge	Mass (kg)	Location in the atom
Proton	+1	1.67×10^{-27}	In the nucleus
Neutron	0	1.67×10^{-27}	In the nucleus
Electron	–1	9.11×10^{-31}	Moving around outside the nucleus

Models of the Atom

Democritus in the fourth century BCE and later Dalton, in the nineteenth century, thought that the atom could not be split. That theory had to be modified when it was discovered that atoms are made of protons, neutrons, and electrons. Like most scientific models and theories, the model of the atom has been revised many times to explain such new discoveries.

VOCABULARY Skills Tip

Remember that **protons** *have a* ***positive*** *charge and* **neutrons** *are* ***neutral.***

Bohr's model compares electrons to planets

In 1913, the Danish scientist Niels Bohr suggested that electrons in an atom move in set paths around the nucleus much like the planets orbit the sun in our solar system. In Bohr's model, each electron has a certain energy that is determined by its path around the nucleus. This path defines the electron's energy level. Electrons can only be in certain energy levels. They must gain energy to move to a higher energy level or lose energy to move to a lower energy level.

One way to imagine Bohr's model is to compare an atom to the stairless building shown in ***Figure 5.*** Imagine that the nucleus is in a very deep basement and that the electronic energy levels begin on the first floor. Electrons can be on any floor of the building but not between floors. Electrons gain energy by riding up in the elevator and lose energy by riding down in the elevator. Bohr's description of energy levels is still considered accurate today.

Electrons act more like waves

By 1925, Bohr's model of the atom no longer explained electron behavior. So a new model was proposed that no longer assumed that electrons orbited the nucleus along definite paths like planets orbiting the sun. In this modern model of the atom, it is believed that electrons behave more like waves on a vibrating string than like particles.

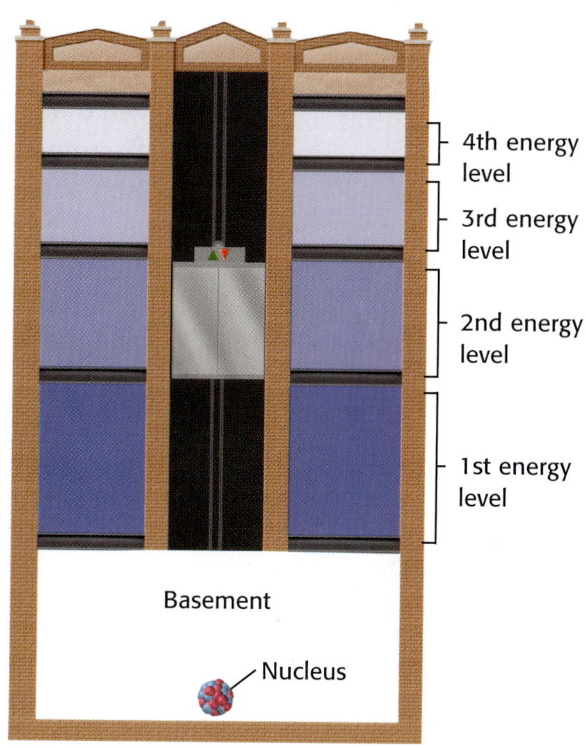

Figure 5

The energy levels of an atom are like the floors of the building shown here. The energy difference between energy levels decreases as the energy level increases.

Figure 6

The exact location of any of the blades of this fan is difficult to determine. The exact location of an electron is impossible to determine.

An electron's exact location cannot be determined

Imagine the moving blades of a fan, like the one shown in ***Figure 6.*** If you were asked where any one of the blades was located at a certain instant, you would not be able to give an exact answer. It is very difficult to know the exact location of any of the blades because they are moving so quickly. All you know for sure is that each blade could be anywhere within the blurred area you see as the blades turn.

It is impossible to determine both the exact location of an electron in an atom and the electron's speed and direction. The best scientists can do is calculate the chance of finding an electron in a certain place within an atom. One way to visually show the likelihood of finding an electron in a given location is by shading. The darker the shading, the better the chance of finding an electron at that location. The whole shaded region is called an electron cloud.

Electrons exist in energy levels

Within the atom, electrons with different amounts of energy exist in different energy levels. There are many possible energy levels that an electron can occupy. The number of filled energy levels an atom has depends on the number of electrons. The first energy level holds two electrons, and the second energy level holds eight. So, a lithium atom, with three electrons, has two electrons in its first energy level and one in the second. ***Figure 7*** shows how the first four energy levels are filled.

Figure 7

Electrons can be found in different energy levels. Each energy level holds a certain number of electrons.

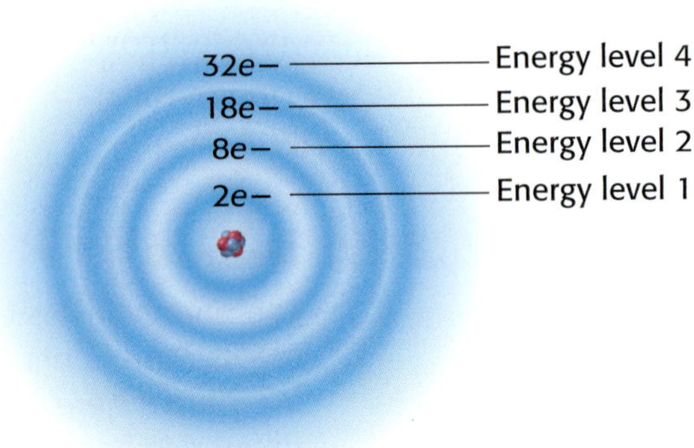

Quick ACTIVITY

Constructing a Model

A scientific model is a simplified representation based on limited knowledge that describes how an object looks or functions. In this activity, you will construct your own model.

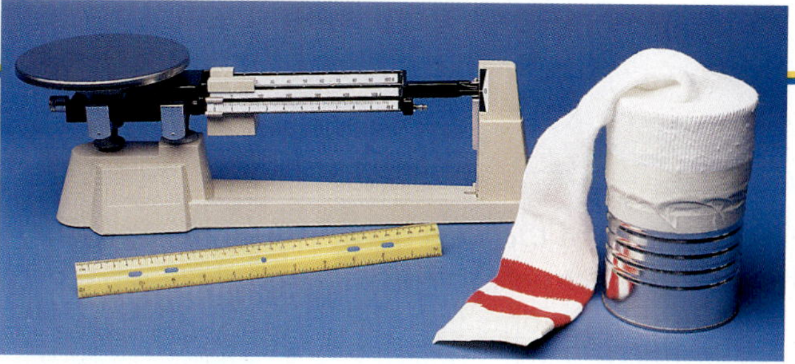

1. Obtain from your teacher a can that is covered by a sock and sealed with tape. An unknown object is inside the can.
2. Without unsealing the container, try to determine the characteristics of the object inside by examining it through the sock. What is the object's mass? What is its size, shape, and texture? Record all of your observations in a data table.
3. Remove the taped sock so that you can touch the object without looking at it. Record these observations as well.
4. Use the data you have collected to draw a model of the unknown object.
5. Finally remove the object to see what it is. Compare and contrast the model you made with the object it is meant to represent.

Electrons are found in orbitals within energy levels

The regions in an atom where electrons are likely to be found are called **orbitals.** Within each energy level, electrons occupy orbitals that have the lowest energy. The four different kinds of orbitals are the *s, p, d,* and *f* orbitals. The simplest kind of orbital is an *s* orbital. An *s* orbital can have only one possible orientation in space because it has a shape like a sphere, as shown in ***Figure 8.*** An *s* orbital has the lowest energy and can hold two electrons.

A *p* orbital, on the other hand, is dumbbell shaped and can be oriented three different ways in space, as shown in ***Figure 9.*** The axes on the graphs are drawn to help you picture how these orbitals look in three dimensions. Imagine the *y*-axis being flat on the page. Imagine the dotted lines on the *x*- and *z*-axes going into the page, and the darker lines coming out of the page. A *p* orbital has more energy than an *s* orbital has. Because each *p* orbital can hold two electrons, the three *p* orbitals can hold a total of six electrons.

The *d* and *f* orbitals are much more complex. There are five possible *d* orbitals and seven possible *f* orbitals. An *f* orbital has the greatest energy. Although all these orbitals are very different in shape, each can hold a maximum of two electrons.

orbital a region in an atom where there is a high probability of finding electrons

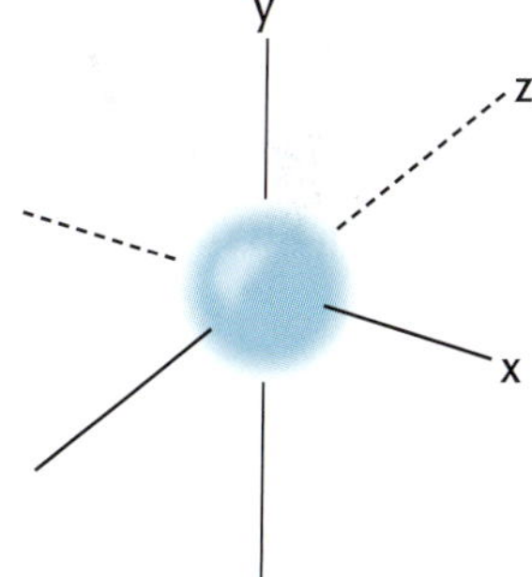

Figure 8

An *s* orbital is shaped like a sphere, so it has only one possible orientation in space. An *s* orbital can hold a maximum of two electrons.

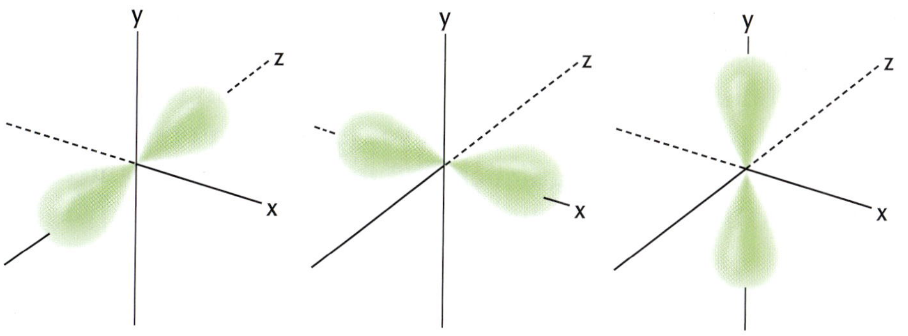

Figure 9

Each of these *p* orbitals can hold a maximum of two electrons, so all three together can hold a total of six electrons.

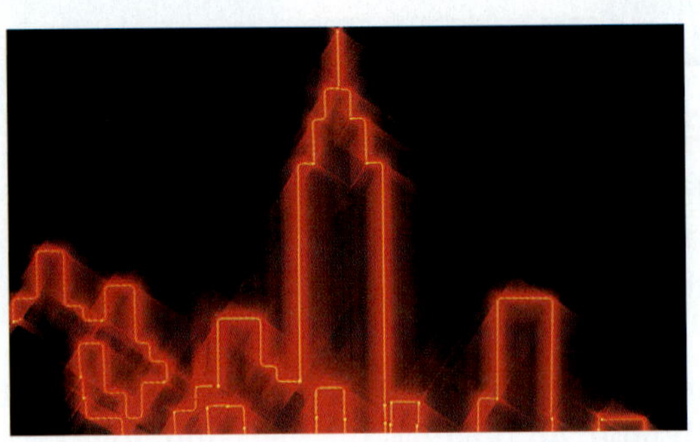

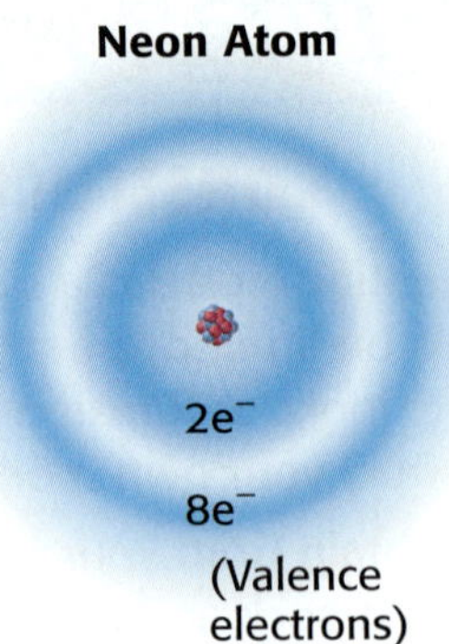

Figure 10

The neon atoms of this sign have eight valence electrons. The sign lights up because atoms first gain energy and then release this energy in the form of light.

Every atom has between one and eight valence electrons

valence electron an electron that is found in the outermost shell of an atom and that determines the atom's chemical properties

An electron in the outermost energy level of an atom is called a **valence electron.** Valence electrons determine an atom's chemical properties and its ability to form bonds. The single electron of a hydrogen atom is a valence electron because it is the only electron the atom has. The glowing red sign shown in ***Figure 10*** is made of neon atoms. In a neon atom, which has 10 electrons, 2 electrons fill the lowest energy level. Its valence electrons, then, are the 8 electrons that are farther away from the nucleus in the atom's second (and outermost) energy level.

SECTION 1 REVIEW

SUMMARY

- Elements are made of very small units called atoms.
- The nucleus of an atom is made of positively charged protons and uncharged neutrons.
- Negatively charged electrons surround the nucleus.
- Atoms have an equal number of protons and electrons.
- In Bohr's model of the atom, electrons orbit the nucleus in set paths.
- In the modern atomic model, electrons are found in orbitals within each energy level.
- Electrons in the outermost energy level are called valence electrons.

1. **Summarize** the main ideas of Dalton's atomic theory.
2. **Explain** why Dalton's theory was more successful than Democritus's theory.
3. **List** the charge, mass, and location of each of the three subatomic particles found within atoms.
4. **Explain** why oxygen atoms are neutral.
5. **Compare** an atom's structure to a ladder. What parts of the ladder correspond to the energy levels of the atom? Identify one way a real ladder is not a good model for the atom.
6. **Explain** how the path of an electron differs in Bohr's model and in the modern model of the atom.
7. **Critical Thinking** In the early 1900s, two associates of New Zealander Ernest Rutherford bombarded thin sheets of gold with positively charged subatomic particles. They found that most particles passed right through the sheets but some bounced back as if they had hit something solid. Based on their results, what do you think an atom is made of? What part of the atom caused the particles to bounce back? (**Hint:** Positive charges repel other positive charges.)

SECTION 2

A Guided Tour of the Periodic Table

OBJECTIVES

- **Relate** the organization of the periodic table to the arrangement of electrons within an atom.
- **Explain** why some atoms gain or lose electrons to form ions.
- **Determine** how many protons, neutrons, and electrons an atom has, given its symbol, atomic number, and mass number.
- **Describe** how the abundance of isotopes affects an element's average atomic mass.

KEY TERMS

periodic law
period
group
ion
atomic number
mass number
isotope
atomic mass unit (amu)
average atomic mass

When you are in a store, are your favorite items placed randomly on the shelves? Usually similar items are grouped together, as shown in ***Figure 11,*** so that you can find what you need quickly. The periodic table organizes the elements in a similar way.

Organization of the Periodic Table

The periodic table groups similar elements together. This organization makes it easier to predict the properties of an element based on where it is in the periodic table. In the periodic table shown in ***Figure 12,*** elements are represented by their symbols and are arranged in a certain order. The order is based on the number of protons an atom of that element has in its nucleus.

A hydrogen atom has one proton, so hydrogen is the first element listed in the periodic table. A helium atom has two protons and is the second element listed. Elements are listed in this order in the periodic table because the **periodic law** states that when elements are arranged this way, similarities in their properties will occur in a regular pattern.

periodic law the law that states that the repeating chemical and physical properties of elements change periodically with the atomic numbers of the elements

Figure 11
In many stores, similar items are grouped so that they are easier to find.

Figure 12

The Periodic Table of the Elements

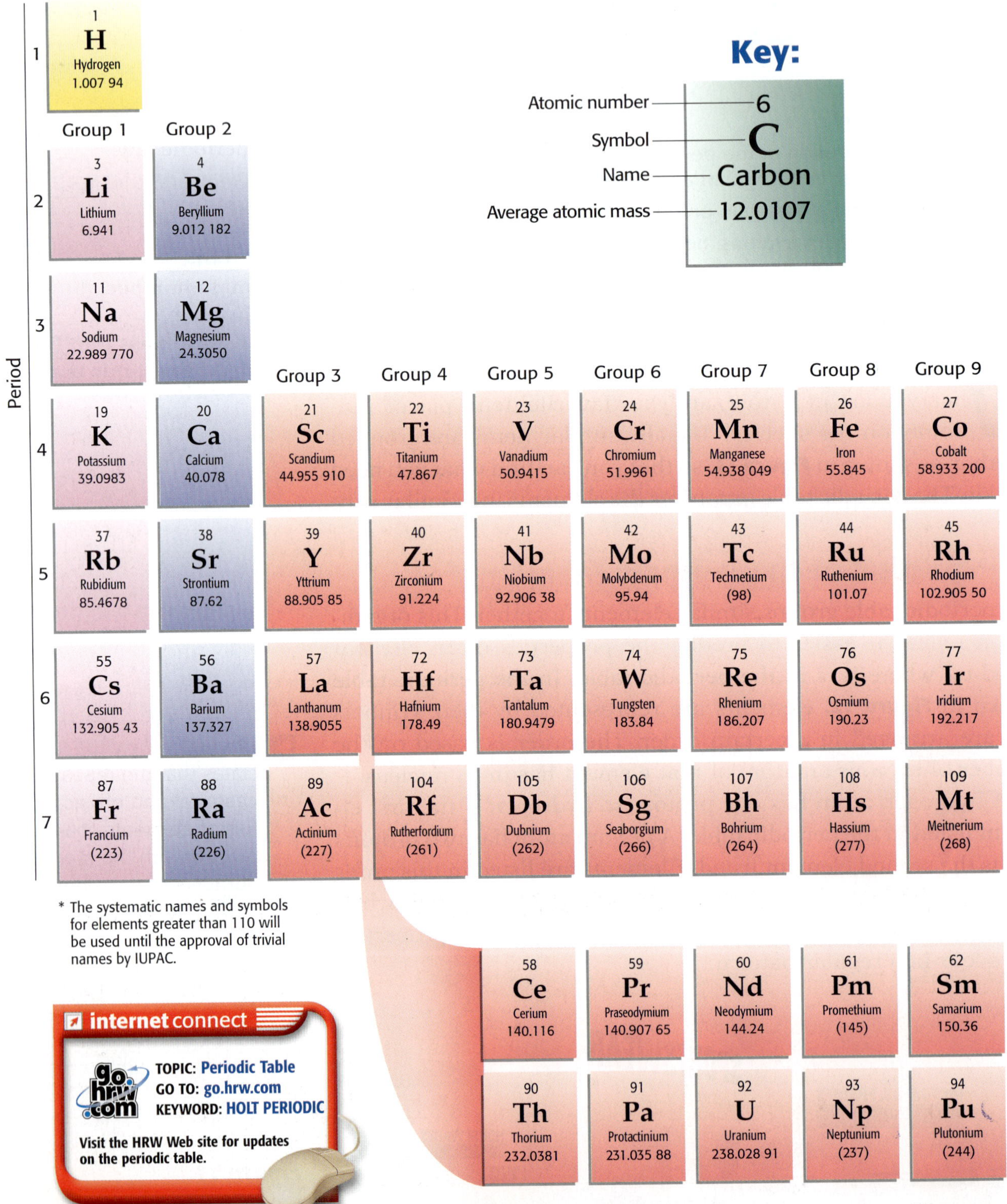

Hydrogen
Semiconductors
(also known as *metalloids*)

Metals
Alkali metals
Alkaline-earth metals
Transition metals
Other metals

Nonmetals
Halogens
Noble gases
Other nonmetals

Group 10	Group 11	Group 12	Group 13	Group 14	Group 15	Group 16	Group 17	Group 18
								2 **He** Helium 4.002 602
			5 **B** Boron 10.811	6 **C** Carbon 12.0107	7 **N** Nitrogen 14.0067	8 **O** Oxygen 15.9994	9 **F** Fluorine 18.998 4032	10 **Ne** Neon 20.1797
			13 **Al** Aluminum 26.981 538	14 **Si** Silicon 28.0855	15 **P** Phosphorus 30.973 761	16 **S** Sulfur 32.065	17 **Cl** Chlorine 35.453	18 **Ar** Argon 39.948
28 **Ni** Nickel 58.6934	29 **Cu** Copper 63.546	30 **Zn** Zinc 65.409	31 **Ga** Gallium 69.723	32 **Ge** Germanium 72.64	33 **As** Arsenic 74.921 60	34 **Se** Selenium 78.96	35 **Br** Bromine 79.904	36 **Kr** Krypton 83.798
46 **Pd** Palladium 106.42	47 **Ag** Silver 107.8682	48 **Cd** Cadmium 112.411	49 **In** Indium 114.818	50 **Sn** Tin 118.710	51 **Sb** Antimony 121.760	52 **Te** Tellurium 127.60	53 **I** Iodine 126.904 47	54 **Xe** Xenon 131.293
78 **Pt** Platinum 195.078	79 **Au** Gold 196.966 55	80 **Hg** Mercury 200.59	81 **Tl** Thallium 204.3833	82 **Pb** Lead 207.2	83 **Bi** Bismuth 208.980 38	84 **Po** Polonium (209)	85 **At** Astatine (210)	86 **Rn** Radon (222)
110 **Ds** Darmstadtium (281)	111 **Uuu*** Unununium (272)	112 **Uub*** Ununbium (285)	113 **Uut*** Ununtrium (284)	114 **Uuq*** Ununquadium (289)	115 **Uup*** Ununpentium (288)			

A team at Lawrence Berkeley National Laboratories reported the discovery of elements 116 and 118 in June 1999. The same team retracted the discovery in July 2001. The discovery of elements 113, 114, and 115 has been reported but not confirmed.

63 **Eu** Europium 151.964	64 **Gd** Gadolinium 157.25	65 **Tb** Terbium 158.925 34	66 **Dy** Dysprosium 162.500	67 **Ho** Holmium 164.930 32	68 **Er** Erbium 167.259	69 **Tm** Thulium 168.934 21	70 **Yb** Ytterbium 173.04	71 **Lu** Lutetium 174.967
95 **Am** Americium (243)	96 **Cm** Curium (247)	97 **Bk** Berkelium (247)	98 **Cf** Californium (251)	99 **Es** Einsteinium (252)	100 **Fm** Fermium (257)	101 **Md** Mendelevium (258)	102 **No** Nobelium (259)	103 **Lr** Lawrencium (262)

The atomic masses listed in this table reflect the precision of current measurements. (Values listed in parentheses are the mass numbers of those radioactive elements' most stable or most common isotopes.)

The periodic table helps determine electron arrangement

period a horizontal row of elements in the periodic table

group (family) a vertical column of elements in the periodic table

Horizontal rows in the periodic table are called **periods.** Just as the number of protons an atom has increases by one as you move from left to right across a period, so does its number of electrons. You can determine how an atom's electrons are arranged if you know where the corresponding element is located in the periodic table.

Hydrogen and helium are both located in Period 1 of the periodic table. ***Figure 13*** shows that a hydrogen atom has one electron in an *s* orbital, while a helium atom has one more electron, for a total of two. Lithium is located in Period 2. The electron arrangement for lithium is just like that for a helium atom, except that lithium has a third electron in an *s* orbital in the second energy level, as follows:

Energy level	Orbital	Number of electrons
1	*s*	2
2	*s*	1

As you continue to move to the right in Period 2, you can see that a carbon atom has electrons in s orbitals and *p* orbitals. The locations of the six electrons in a carbon atom are as follows:

Energy level	Orbital	Number of electrons
1	*s*	2
2	*s*	2
2	*p*	2

A nitrogen atom has three electrons in *p* orbitals, an oxygen atom has four, and a fluorine atom has five. ***Figure 13*** shows that a neon atom has six electrons in *p* orbitals. Each orbital can hold two electrons, so all three *p* orbitals are filled.

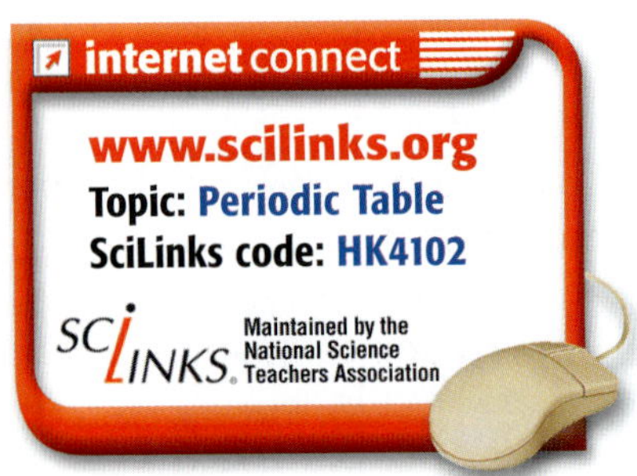

Elements in the same group have similar properties

Valence electrons determine the chemical properties of atoms. Atoms of elements in the same **group,** or column, have the same number of valence electrons, so these elements have similar properties. Remember that these elements are not exactly alike, though, because atoms of these elements have different numbers of protons in their nuclei and different numbers of electrons in their filled inner energy levels.

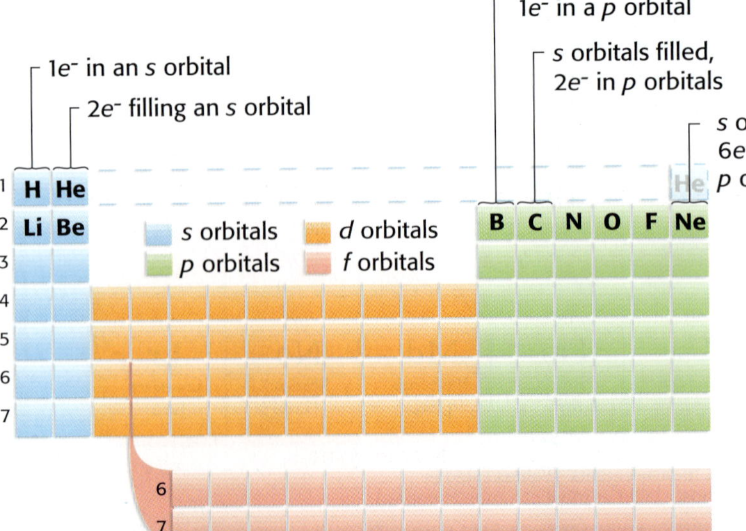

Figure 13

The electronic arrangement of atoms becomes increasingly more complex as you move further right across a period and further down a group of the periodic table.

Some Atoms Form Ions

Atoms of Group 1 elements are reactive because their outermost energy levels contain only one electron. Atoms that do not have filled outer *s* and *p* orbitals may undergo a process called ionization. That is, they may gain or lose valence electrons so that they have a full outermost *s* and/or *p* orbital. If an atom gains or loses electrons, it no longer has the same number of electrons as it does protons. Because the charges do not cancel completely as they did before, the **ion** that forms has a net electric charge, as shown for the lithium ion in ***Figure 14.*** Sodium chloride, or table salt, shown in ***Figure 15*** is made of sodium and chloride ions.

-1e⁻
Electron lost
Lithium atom
Lithium ion
+

Figure 14

The valence electron of a reactive lithium atom may be removed to form a lithium ion, Li^+, with a 1+ charge.

A lithium atom loses one electron to form a 1+ charged ion

Lithium is located in Group 1 of the periodic table. It is so reactive that it even reacts with the water vapor in the air. An electron is easily removed from a lithium atom, as shown in ***Figure 14.*** The atomic structure of lithium explains its reactivity. A lithium atom has three electrons. Two of these electrons occupy the first energy level in the *s* orbital, but only one electron occupies the second energy level. This single valence electron makes lithium very reactive. Removing this electron forms a positive ion, or *cation.*

A lithium ion, written as Li^+, is much less reactive than a lithium atom because it has a full outer *s* orbital. Atoms of other Group 1 elements also have one valence electron. They are also reactive and behave similarly to lithium.

ion an atom or group of atoms that has lost or gained one or more electrons and has a negative or positive charge

Figure 15

Table salt is made of sodium and chloride ions.

A fluorine atom gains one electron to form a 1– charged ion

Like lithium, fluorine is also very reactive. However, instead of losing an electron to become less reactive, an atom of the element fluorine gains one electron to form an ion with a 1– charge. Fluorine is located in Group 17 of the periodic table, and each atom has nine electrons. Two of these electrons occupy the first energy level, and seven valence electrons occupy the second energy level. A fluorine atom needs only one more electron to have a full outermost energy level. An atom of fluorine easily gains this electron to form a negative ion, or *anion,* as shown in ***Figure 16.***

Ions of fluorine are called fluoride ions and are written as F^-. Because atoms of other Group 17 elements also have seven valence electrons, they are also reactive and behave similarly to fluorine.

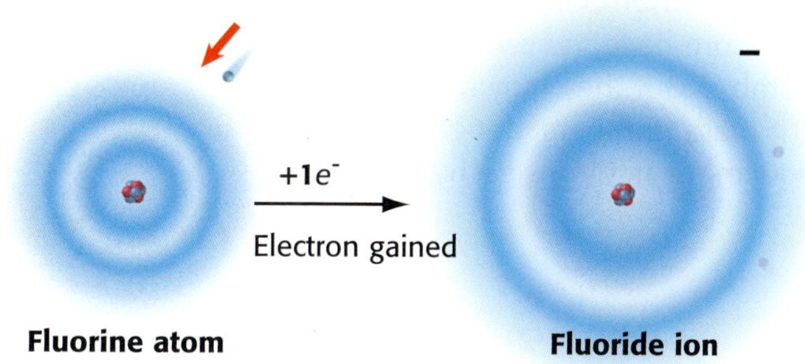

Figure 16

A fluorine atom easily gains one valence electron to form a fluoride ion, F^-, with a 1– charge.

How Do the Structures of Atoms Differ?

Disc One, Module 3:
Periodic Properties
Use the Interactive Tutor to learn more about these topics.

As you have seen with lithium and fluorine, atoms of different elements have their own unique structures. Because these atoms have different structures, they have different properties. An atom of hydrogen found in a molecule of swimming-pool water has properties very different from an atom of uranium in nuclear fuel.

Atomic number equals the number of protons

The **atomic number,** Z, tells you how many protons are in an atom. Remember that atoms are always neutral because they have an equal number of protons and electrons. Therefore, the atomic number also equals the number of electrons the atom has. Each element has a different atomic number. For example, the simplest atom, hydrogen, has just one proton and one electron, so for hydrogen, $Z = 1$. The largest naturally occurring atom, uranium, has 92 protons and 92 electrons, so $Z = 92$ for uranium. The atomic number for a given element never changes.

atomic number the number of protons in the nucleus of an atom

mass number the sum of the numbers of protons and neutrons in the nucleus of an atom

Mass number equals the total number of subatomic particles in the nucleus

The **mass number,** A, of an atom equals the number of protons plus the number of neutrons. A fluorine atom has 9 protons and 10 neutrons, so $A = 19$ for fluorine. Oxygen has 8 protons and 8 neutrons, so $A = 16$ for oxygen. This mass number includes only the number of protons and neutrons (and not electrons) because protons and neutrons provide most of the atom's mass. Although atoms of an element always have the same atomic number, they can have different mass numbers. ***Figure 17*** shows which subatomic particles in the nucleus of an atom contribute to the atomic number and which contribute to the mass number.

Mass number, A = number of protons + number of neutrons

Atomic number, Z = number of protons

Nucleus

Figure 17
Atoms of the same element have the same number of protons and therefore have the same atomic number. But they may have different mass numbers, depending on how many neutrons each atom has.

Figure 18

Protium has only a proton in its nucleus. Deuterium has both a proton and a neutron in its nucleus, while tritium has a proton and two neutrons.

Isotopes of Hydrogen

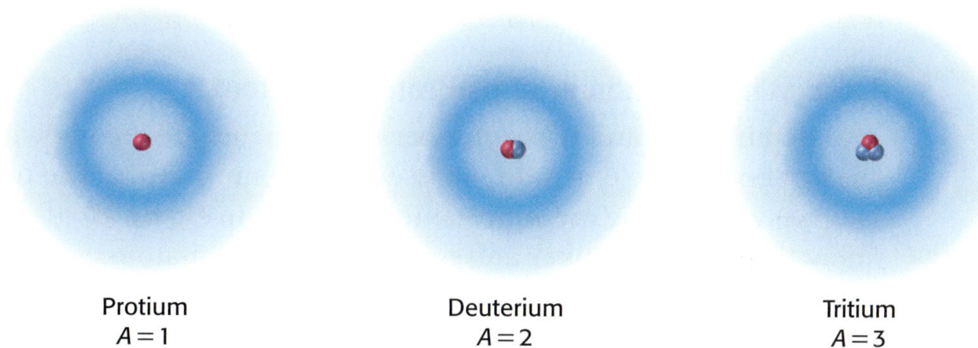

Isotopes of an element have different numbers of neutrons

Neutrons can be added to an atom without affecting the number of protons and electrons the atom is made of. Many elements have only one stable form, while other elements have different "versions" of their atoms. Each version has the same number of protons and electrons as all other versions but a different number of neutrons. These different versions, or **isotopes,** vary in mass but are all atoms of the same element because they each have the same number of protons.

isotope an atom that has the same number of protons as other atoms of the same element do but that has a different number of neutrons

The three isotopes of hydrogen, shown in ***Figure 18,*** have the same chemical properties because each is made of one proton and one electron. The most common hydrogen isotope, protium, has only a proton in its nucleus. A second isotope of hydrogen has a proton and a neutron. The mass number, *A,* of this second isotope is two, and the isotope is twice as massive. In fact, this isotope is sometimes called "heavy hydrogen." It is also known as deuterium, or hydrogen-2. A third isotope has a proton and two neutrons in its nucleus. This third isotope, tritium, has a mass number of three.

Some isotopes are more common than others

Hydrogen is present on both the sun and on Earth. In both places, protium (the hydrogen isotope without neutrons in its nucleus) is found most often. Only a very small fraction of the less common isotope of hydrogen, deuterium, is found on the sun and on Earth, as shown in ***Figure 19.*** Tritium is an unstable isotope that decays over time, so it is found least often.

Figure 19

A Hydrogen makes up less than 1% of Earth's crust. Only 1 out of every 6000 of these hydrogen atoms is a deuterium isotope.

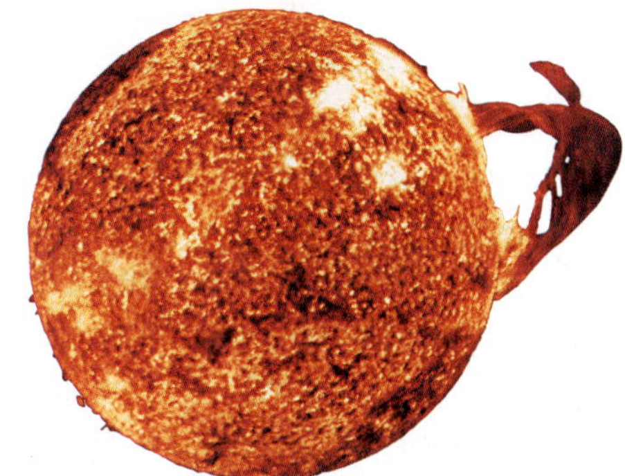

B Seventy-five percent of the mass of the sun is hydrogen, with protium isotopes outnumbering deuterium isotopes 50 000 to 1.

Figure 20
One isotope of chlorine has 18 neutrons, while the other isotope has 20 neutrons.

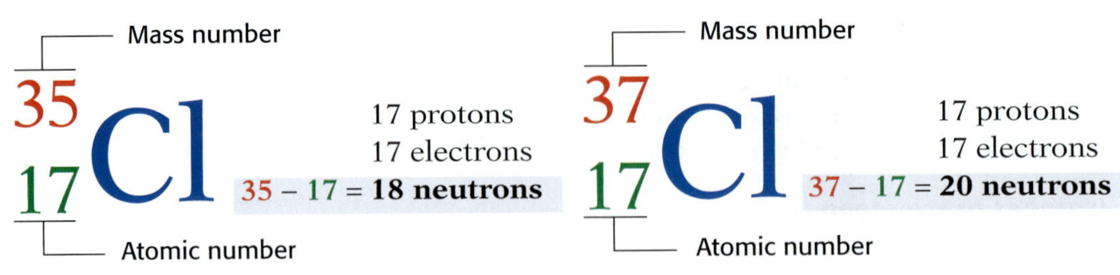

Calculating the number of neutrons in an atom

Atomic numbers and mass numbers may be included along with the symbol of an element to represent different isotopes. The two isotopes of chlorine are represented this way in ***Figure 20.*** If you know the atomic number and mass number of an atom, you can calculate the number of neutrons it has.

Uranium has several isotopes. The isotope that is used in nuclear reactors is uranium-235, or $^{235}_{92}U$. Like all uranium atoms, it has an atomic number of 92, so it must have 92 protons and 92 electrons. It has a mass number of 235, which means its number of protons and neutrons together is 235. The number of neutrons must be 143.

Mass number (A):	235
Atomic number (Z):	− 92
Number of neutrons:	143

atomic mass unit (amu) a unit of mass that describes the mass of an atom or molecule; it is exactly one-twelfth of the mass of a carbon atom with mass number 12

average atomic mass the weighted average of the masses of all naturally occurring isotopes of an element

The mass of an atom

The mass of a single atom is very small. A single fluorine atom has a mass less than one trillionth of a billionth of a gram. Because it is very hard to work with such tiny masses, atomic masses are usually expressed in atomic mass units. An **atomic mass unit (amu)** is equal to one-twelfth of the mass of a carbon-12 atom. This isotope of carbon has six protons and six neutrons, so individual protons and neutrons must each have a mass of about 1.0 amu because electrons contribute very little mass.

Often, the atomic mass listed for an element in the periodic table is an average atomic mass for the element as it is found in nature. The **average atomic mass** for an element is a weighted average, so the more commonly found isotopes have a greater effect on the average than rare isotopes.

Figure 21 shows how the natural abundance of chlorine's two isotopes affects chlorine's average atomic mass. The average atomic mass of chlorine is 35.45 amu. This mass is much closer to 35 amu than to 37 amu. That's because the atoms of chlorine with masses of nearly 35 amu are found more often and therefore contribute more to chlorine's average atomic mass than chlorine atoms with masses of nearly 37 amu.

Quick ACTIVITY

Isotopes

Calculate the number of neutrons there are in the following isotopes. (Use the periodic table to find the atomic numbers.)

1. carbon-14
2. nitrogen-15
3. sulfur-35
4. calcium-45
5. iodine-131

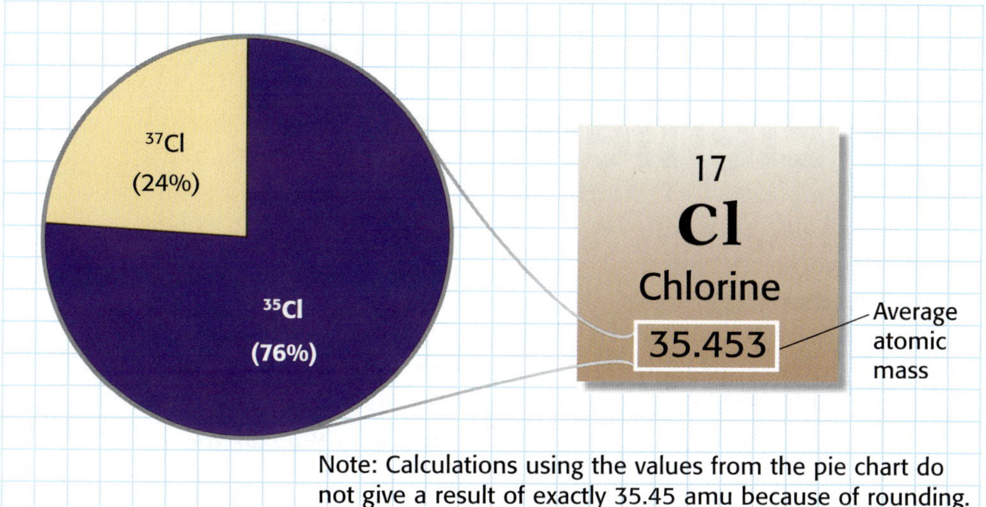

Figure 21

The average atomic mass of chlorine is closer to 35 amu than it is to 37 amu because ^{35}Cl isotopes are found more often than ^{37}Cl isotopes.

SECTION 2 REVIEW

SUMMARY

- Elements are arranged in order of increasing atomic number so that elements with similar properties are in the same column, or group.
- Elements in the same group have the same number of valence electrons.
- Reactive atoms may gain or lose valence electrons to form ions.
- An atom's atomic number is its number of protons.
- An atom's mass number is its total number of protons and neutrons in the nucleus.
- Isotopes of an element have different numbers of neutrons, and therefore have different masses.
- An element's average atomic mass is a weighted average of the masses of its naturally occurring isotopes.

1. **Explain** how you can determine the number of protons, electrons, and neutrons an atom has from an atom's mass number and its atomic number.
2. **Calculate** how many neutrons a phosphorus-32 atom has.
3. **Name** the elements represented by the following symbols:
   a. Li **d.** Br **g.** Na
   b. Mg **e.** He **h.** Fe
   c. Cu **f.** S **i.** K
4. **Compare** the number of valence electrons an oxygen, O, atom has with the number of valence electrons a selenium, Se, atom has. Are oxygen and selenium in the same period or group?
5. **Explain** why some atoms gain or lose electrons to form ions.
6. **Predict** which isotope of nitrogen is more commonly found, nitrogen-14 or nitrogen-15. (**Hint:** What is the average atomic mass listed for nitrogen in the periodic table?)
7. **Describe** why the elements in the periodic table are arranged in order of increasing atomic number.
8. **Critical Thinking** Before 1937, all naturally occurring elements had been discovered, but no one had found any trace of element 43. Chemists were still able to predict the chemical properties of this element (now called technetium), which is widely used today for diagnosing medical problems. How were these predictions possible? Which elements would you expect to be similar to technetium?

Families of Elements

KEY TERMS

- metal
- nonmetal
- semiconductor
- alkali metal
- alkaline-earth metal
- transition metal
- halogen
- noble gas

OBJECTIVES

- **Locate** alkali metals, alkaline-earth metals, and transition metals in the periodic table.
- **Locate** semiconductors, halogens, and noble gases in the periodic table.
- **Relate** an element's chemical properties to the electron arrangement of its atoms.

You may have wondered why groups in the periodic table are sometimes called families. Consider your own family. Though each member is unique, you all share certain similarities. All members of the family shown in ***Figure 22A,*** for example, have a similar appearance. Members of a family in the periodic table have many chemical and physical properties in common because they have the same number of valence electrons.

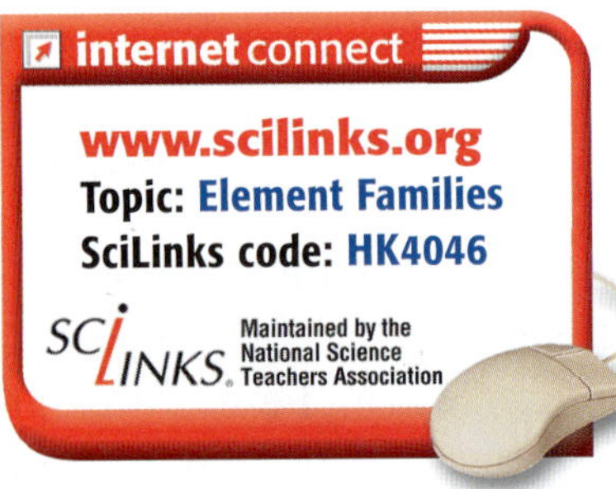

How Are Elements Classified?

Think of each element as a member of a family that is also related to other elements nearby. Elements are classified as metals or nonmetals, as shown in ***Figure 22B.*** This classification groups elements that have similar physical and chemical properties.

Figure 22

A Just like the members of this family,
B elements in the periodic table share certain similarities.

A

B

Metals
Nonmetals

	1	2	3	4	5	6	7	8	9	10	11	12	13	14	15	16	17	18
1	1 H																	2 He
2	3 Li	4 Be											5 B	6 C	7 N	8 O	9 F	10 Ne
3	11 Na	12 Mg											13 Al	14 Si	15 P	16 S	17 Cl	18 Ar
4	19 K	20 Ca	21 Sc	22 Ti	23 V	24 Cr	25 Mn	26 Fe	27 Co	28 Ni	29 Cu	30 Zn	31 Ga	32 Ge	33 As	34 Se	35 Br	36 Kr
5	37 Rb	38 Sr	39 Y	40 Zr	41 Nb	42 Mo	43 Tc	44 Ru	45 Rh	46 Pd	47 Ag	48 Cd	49 In	50 Sn	51 Sb	52 Te	53 I	54 Xe
6	55 Cs	56 Ba	57 La	72 Hf	73 Ta	74 W	75 Re	76 Os	77 Ir	78 Pt	79 Au	80 Hg	81 Tl	82 Pb	83 Bi	84 Po	85 At	86 Rn
7	87 Fr	88 Ra	89 Ac	104 Rf	105 Db	106 Sg	107 Bh	108 Hs	109 Mt	110 Ds	111 Uuu*	112 Uub*	113 Uut*	114 Uuq*	115 Uup*			

58 Ce	59 Pr	60 Nd	61 Pm	62 Sm	63 Eu	64 Gd	65 Tb	66 Dy	67 Ho	68 Er	69 Tm	70 Yb	71 Lu
90 Th	91 Pa	92 U	93 Np	94 Pu	95 Am	96 Cm	97 Bk	98 Cf	99 Es	100 Fm	101 Md	102 No	103 Lr

Note: Sometimes the boxed elements toward the right side of the periodic table are classified as a separate group and called semiconductors or metalloids.

Elements are classified into three groups

As you can see in ***Figure 22B,*** most elements are **metals.** Most metals are shiny solids that can be stretched and shaped. They are also good conductors of heat and electricity. All **nonmetals,** except for hydrogen, are found on the right side of the periodic table. Nonmetals may be solids, liquids, or gases. Solid nonmetals are typically dull and brittle and are poor conductors of heat and electricity. But some elements that are classified as nonmetals can conduct under certain conditions. These elements are sometimes considered to be their own group and are called **semiconductors** or metalloids.

metal an element that is shiny and conducts heat and electricity well

nonmetal an element that conducts heat and electricity poorly

semiconductor an element or compound that conducts electric current better than an insulator but not as well as a conductor does

alkali metal one of the elements of Group 1 of the periodic table

Metals

Many elements are classified as metals. To further classify metals, similar metals are grouped together. There are four different kinds of metals. Two groups of metals are located on the left side of the periodic table. Other metals, like aluminum, tin, and lead, are located toward the right side of the periodic table. Most metals, though, are located in the middle of the periodic table.

The alkali metals are very reactive

Sodium is found in Group 1 of the periodic table, as shown in ***Figure 23A.*** Like other **alkali metals** it is soft and shiny and reacts violently with water. Sodium must be stored in oil, as in ***Figure 23B,*** to prevent it from reacting with moisture in the air.

An atom of an alkali metal is very reactive because it has one valence electron that can easily be removed to form a positive ion. You have already seen in Section 2 how lithium, another alkali metal, forms positive ions with a 1+ charge. Similarly, the valence electron of a sodium atom can be removed to form the positive sodium ion Na^+.

Because alkali metals such as sodium are so reactive, they are not found in nature as elements. Instead, they combine with other elements to form compounds. For example, the salt you use to season your food is actually the compound sodium chloride, NaCl.

Figure 23

A The alkali metals are located on the left edge of the periodic table.

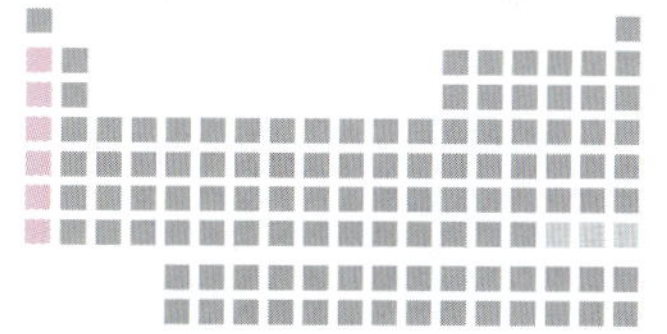

Alkali Metals

B The alkali metal sodium must be stored in oil. Otherwise, it will react violently with moisture and oxygen in the air.

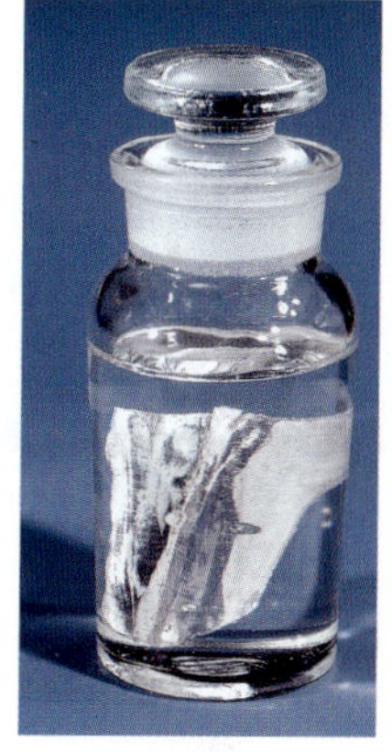

Group 1

3
Li
Lithium
6.941

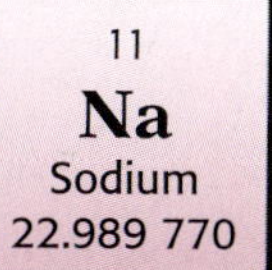

11
Na
Sodium
22.989 770

19
K
Potassium
39.0983

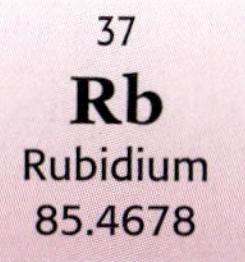

37
Rb
Rubidium
85.4678

55
Cs
Cesium
132.905 43

87
Fr
Francium
(223)

Quick ACTIVITY

Elements in Your Food

1. For 1 day, make a list of the ingredients in all the foods and drinks you consume.
2. Identify which ingredients on your list are compounds.
3. For each compound on your list, try to figure out what elements it is made of.

Alkaline-earth metals form compounds that are found in limestone and in the human body

Calcium is in Group 2 of the periodic table, as shown in ***Figure 24A,*** and is an **alkaline-earth metal.** Atoms of alkaline-earth metals, such as calcium, have two valence electrons. Alkaline-earth metals are less reactive than alkali metals, but they may still react to form positive ions with a 2+ charge. When the valence electrons of a calcium atom are removed, a calcium ion, Ca^{2+}, forms. Alkaline-earth metals like calcium also combine with other elements to form compounds.

alkaline-earth metal one of the elements of Group 2 of the periodic table

Calcium compounds make up the hard shells of many sea animals. When the animals die, their shells settle to form large deposits that eventually become limestone or marble, both of which are very strong materials used in construction. Coral is one example of a limestone structure. The "skeletons" of millions of tiny animals combine to form sturdy coral reefs that many fish rely on for protection, as shown in ***Figure 24B.*** Your bones and teeth also get their strength from calcium compounds.

Magnesium is another alkaline-earth metal that has properties similar to calcium. Magnesium is the lightest of all structural metals and is used to build some airplanes. Magnesium, as Mg^{2+}, activates many of the enzymes that speed up processes in the human body. Magnesium also combines with other elements to form many useful compounds. Two magnesium compounds are commonly used medicines—milk of magnesia and Epsom salts.

Group 2

4 **Be** Beryllium 9.012 182
12 **Mg** Magnesium 24.3050
20 **Ca** Calcium 40.078
38 **Sr** Strontium 87.62
56 **Ba** Barium 137.327
88 **Ra** Radium (226)

Figure 24

A The alkaline-earth metals make up the second column of elements from the left edge of the periodic table.

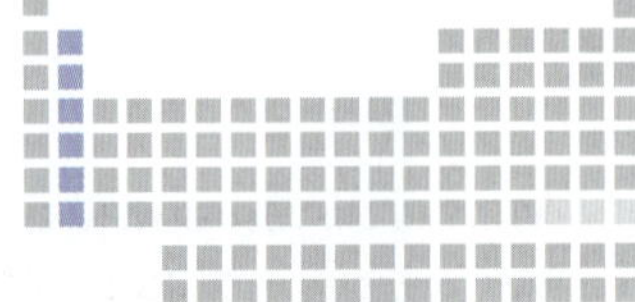

Alkaline-earth Metals

B Fish can escape their predators by hiding among the hard projections of limestone coral reefs that are made of calcium compounds.

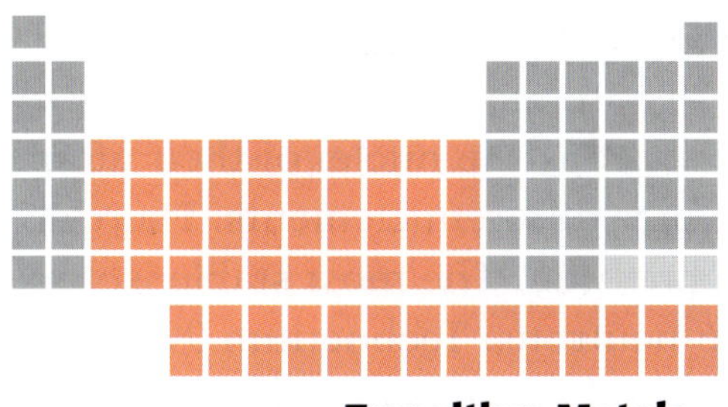

Figure 25

A The transition metals are located in the middle of the periodic table.

B The transition metals platinum, gold, and silver are often shaped to make jewelry.

Gold, silver and platinum are transition metals

Gold is a valuable **transition metal.** ***Figure 25A*** shows that the transition metals are located in Groups 3–12 of the periodic table. Unlike most other transition metals, gold is not found combined with other elements as an ore but as the free metal.

transition metal one of the elements of Groups 3–12 of the periodic table

Transition metals, like gold, are much less reactive than sodium or calcium, but they can lose electrons to form positive ions too. There are two possible cations that a gold atom can form. If an atom of gold loses only one electron, it forms Au^{+}. If the atom loses three electrons, it forms Au^{3+}. Some transition metals can form as many as four differently charged cations because of their complex arrangement of electrons.

All metals, including transition metals, conduct heat and electricity. Most metals can also be stretched and shaped into flat sheets, or pulled into wire. Because gold, silver, and platinum are the shiniest metals, they are often molded into different kinds of jewelry, as shown in ***Figure 25B.***

VOCABULARY Skills Tip

The properties of transition metals *gradually transition, or shift, from being more similar to Group 2 elements to being more similar to Group 13 elements as you move from left to right across a period.*

There are many other useful transition metals. Copper is often used for electrical wiring or plumbing. Light bulb filaments are made of tungsten. Iron, cobalt, copper, and manganese play vital roles in your body chemistry. Mercury, shown in ***Figure 26,*** is the only metal that is a liquid at room temperature. It is often used in thermometers because it flows quickly and easily without sticking to glass.

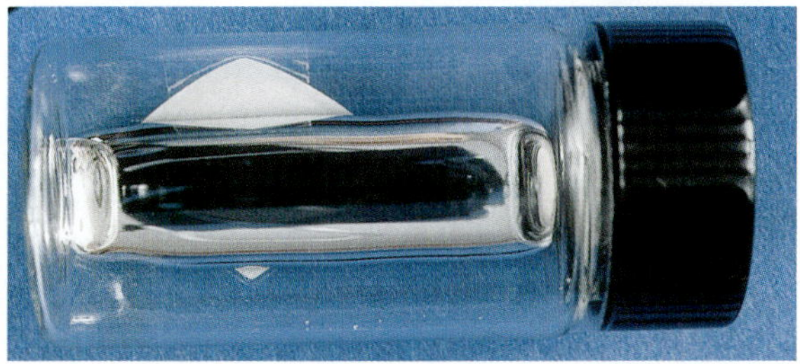

Figure 26

Mercury is an unusual metal because it is a liquid at room temperature. Continued exposure to this volatile metal can harm you because if you breathe in the vapor, it accumulates in your body.

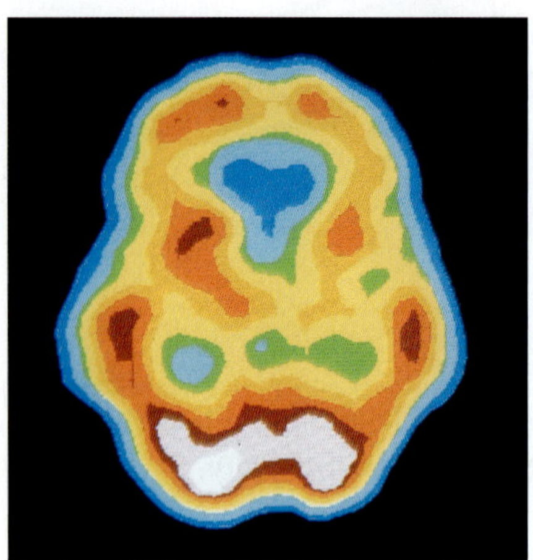

Figure 27

With the help of the radioactive isotope technetium-99, doctors are able to confirm that this patient has a healthy brain.

Technetium and promethium are synthetic elements

Technetium and promethium are both man-made elements. They are also both *radioactive,* which means the nuclei of their atoms are continually decaying to produce different elements. There are several different isotopes of technetium. The most stable isotope is technetium-99, which has 56 neutrons. Technetium-99 can be used to diagnose cancer as well as other medical problems in soft tissues of the body, as shown in ***Figure 27.***

When looking at the periodic table, you might have wondered why part of the last two periods of the transition metals are placed toward the bottom. This keeps the periodic table narrow so that similar elements elsewhere in the table still line up. Promethium is one element located in this bottom-most section. Its most useful isotope is promethium-147, which has 86 neutrons. Promethium-147 is an ingredient in some "glow-in-the-dark" paints.

All elements with atomic numbers greater than 92 are also man-made and are similar to technetium and promethium. For example, americium, another element in the bottom-most section of the periodic table, is also radioactive. Tiny amounts of americium-241 are found in most household smoke detectors. Although even small amounts of radioactive material can affect you, americum-241 is safe when contained inside your smoke detector.

Quick Lab

Why do some metals cost more than others?

1. The table at right gives the abundance of some metals in Earth's crust. List the metals in order from most to least abundant.
2. List the metals in order of price, from the cheapest to the most expensive
3. Create a spreadsheet that can be used to calculate how many grams of each metal you could buy with $100.

Metal	Abundance in Earth's crust (%)	Price ($/kg)
Aluminum (Al)	8.2	1.55
Chromium (Cr)	0.01	0.06
Copper (Cu)	0.0060	2.44
Gold (Au)	0.000 0004	11 666.53
Iron (Fe)	5.6	0.03
Silver (Ag)	0.000 007	154.97
Tin (Sn)	0.0002	6.22
Zinc (Zn)	0.007	1.29

Analysis

1. If the price of a metal depends on its abundance, you would expect the order to be the same on both lists. How well do the two lists match? Mention any exceptions.
2. The order of reactivity of these metals, from most reactive to least reactive, is aluminum, zinc, chromium, iron, tin, copper, silver, and gold. Use this information to explain any exceptions you noticed in item 3.

Nonmetals

Except for hydrogen, nonmetals are found on the right side of the periodic table. They include some elements in Groups 13–16 and all the elements in Groups 17 and 18.

Carbon is found in three different forms and can also form many compounds

Carbon and other nonmetals are found on the right side of the periodic table, as shown in ***Figure 28A.*** Although carbon in its pure state is usually found as graphite (pencil "lead") or diamond, the existence of fullerenes, a third form, was confirmed in 1990. The most famous fullerene consists of a cluster of 60 carbon atoms, as shown in ***Figure 28B.***

Carbon can also combine with other elements to form millions of carbon-containing compounds. Carbon compounds are found in both living and nonliving things. Glucose, $C_6H_{12}O_6$, is a sugar in your blood. A type of chlorophyll, $C_{55}H_{72}O_5N_4Mg$, is found in all green plants. Many gasolines contain isooctane, C_8H_{18}, while rubber tires are made of large molecules with many repeating C_5H_8 units.

Connection to ARCHITECTURE

The discoverers of the first and most famous fullerene named the molecule *buckminsterfullerene.* Its structure resembles a geodesic dome, a kind of structure designed by American engineer and inventor R. Buckminster Fuller. A geodesic dome encloses the most space using the fewest materials. Any strains caused by the ground shifting or strong winds have little affect on a geodesic dome. That's because the strains are spread evenly throughout the entire structure. These sturdy structures have been used successfully as radar towers in Antarctica in winds as strong as 90 m/s (200 mi/h) for over 25 years. Geodesic domes provide the framework for some sports arenas, theaters, greenhouses, and even some homes.

Making the Connection

1. How does the shape of a geodesic dome differ from a more typical building?
2. Explain why energy savings are greater in this kind of structure than in a boxlike building that encloses the same amount of space.

Nonmetals and their compounds are plentiful on Earth

Oxygen, nitrogen, and sulfur are other common nonmetals. Each may form compounds or gain electrons to form the negative ions oxide, O^{2-}, sulfide, S^{2-}, and nitride, N^{3-}. The most plentiful gases in the air are the nonmetals nitrogen and oxygen. Although sulfur itself is an odorless yellow solid, many sulfur compounds, like those in rotten eggs and skunk spray, are known for their terrible smell.

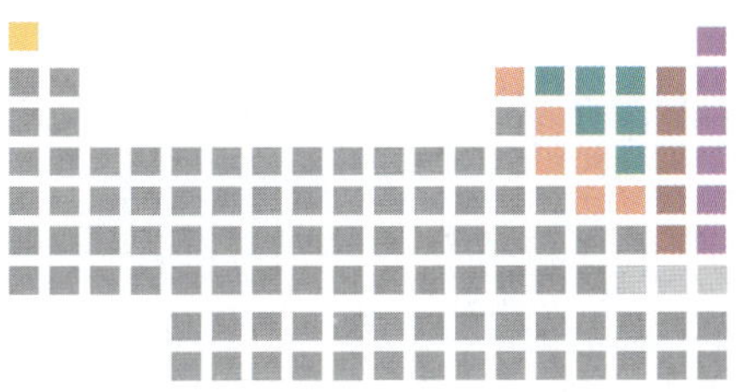

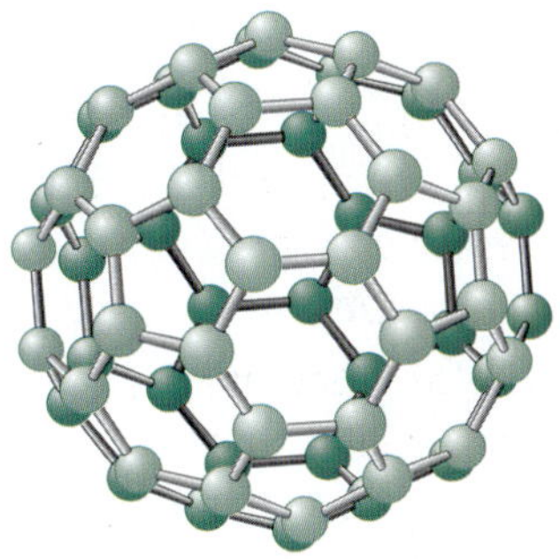

Figure 28

A Most nonmetals are located on the right side of the periodic table.

B The way carbon atoms are connected in the most recently discovered form of carbon resembles the familiar pattern of a soccer ball.

halogen one of the elements of Group 17 of the periodic table

INTEGRATING

EARTH SCIENCE

Eighty-one elements have been detected in sea water. Magnesium and bromine are two such elements. To recover an element from a sample of sea water, you must evaporate some of the water from the sample. Sodium chloride then crystallizes and the liquid that remains becomes more concentrated in bromide, magnesium, and other ions than the original sea water was, making their recovery easier.

Chlorine is a halogen that protects you from harmful bacteria

Chlorine and other **halogens** are located in Group 17 of the periodic table, as shown in ***Figure 29A.*** You have probably noticed the strong smell of chlorine in swimming pools. Chlorine is widely used to kill bacteria in pools, like the one shown in ***Figure 29B,*** as well as in drinking-water supplies.

Like fluorine atoms, which you learned about in Section 2, chlorine atoms are very reactive. As a result, chlorine forms compounds. For example, the chlorine in most swimming pools is added in the form of the compound calcium hypochlorite, $Ca(OCl)_2$. Elemental chlorine is a poisonous yellowish green gas made of pairs of joined chlorine atoms. Chlorine gas has the chemical formula Cl_2. A chlorine atom may also gain an electron to form a negative chloride ion, Cl^-. The attractions between Na^+ ions and Cl^- ions form table salt, NaCl.

Fluorine, bromine, and iodine are other Group 17 elements. Fluorine is a poisonous yellowish gas, bromine is a dark red liquid, and iodine is a dark purple solid. Atoms of each of these elements can also form compounds by gaining an electron to become negative ions. A compound containing the negative ion fluoride, F^-, is used in some toothpastes and added to some water supplies to help prevent tooth decay. Adding a compound containing iodine as the negative ion iodide, I^-, to table salt makes "iodized" salt. You need this ion in your diet for your thyroid gland to function properly.

Group 17

9 **F** Fluorine 18.998 4032
17 **Cl** Chlorine 35.453
35 **Br** Bromine 79.904
53 **I** Iodine 126.904 47
85 **At** Astatine (210)

Figure 29

A The halogens are in the second column from the right of the periodic table.

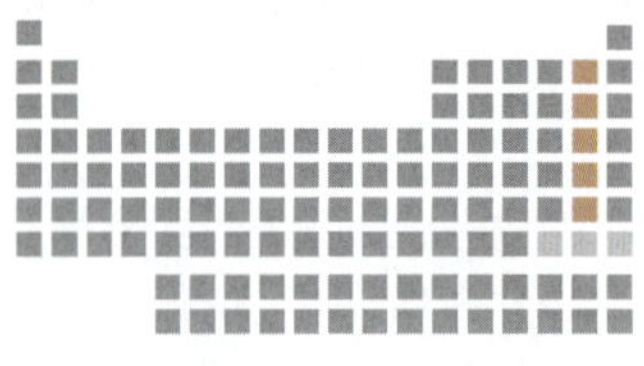

Halogens

B Chlorine keeps pool water bacteria-free for swimmers to enjoy.

The noble gases are inert

Neon is one of the **noble gases** that make up Group 18 of the periodic table, as shown in ***Figure 30A.*** It is responsible for the bright reddish orange light of "neon" signs. ***Figure 30B*** shows how mixing neon with another substance, such as mercury, can change the color of a sign.

The noble gases are different from most elements that are gases because they exist as single atoms instead of as molecules. Like other members of Group 18, neon is inert, or unreactive, because its *s* and *p* orbitals are full of electrons. For this reason, neon and other noble gases do not gain or lose electrons to form ions. They also don't join with other atoms to form compounds under normal conditions.

Helium and argon are other common noble gases. Helium is less dense than air and is used to give lift to blimps and balloons. Argon is used to fill light bulbs because its lack of reactivity prevents filaments from burning.

Figure 30

A The noble gases are located on the right edge of the periodic table.

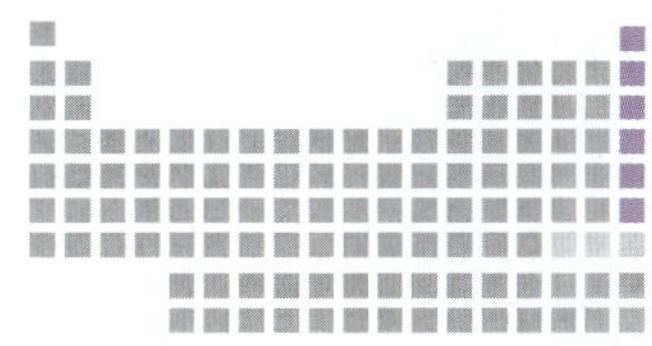

Noble Gases

B A neon sign is usually reddish orange, but adding a few drops of mercury makes the light a bright blue.

Group 18

2
He
Helium
4.002 602

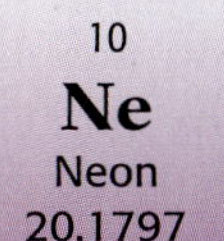

18
Ar
Argon
39.948

36
Kr
Krypton
83.798

54
Xe
Xenon
131.293

86
Rn
Radon
(222)

Semiconductors are intermediate conductors of heat and electricity

Figure 31 shows that the elements sometimes referred to as semiconductors or metalloids are clustered toward the right side of the periodic table. Only six elements—boron, silicon, germanium, arsenic, antimony, and tellurium—are semiconductors. Although these elements are classified as nonmetals, each one also has some properties of metals. And as their name implies, semiconductors are able to conduct heat and electricity under certain conditions.

Boron is an extremely hard element. It is often added to steel to increase steel's hardness and strength at high temperatures. Compounds of boron are often used to make heat-resistant glass. Arsenic is a shiny solid that tarnishes when exposed to air. Antimony is a bluish white, brittle solid that also shines like a metal. Some compounds of antimony are used as fire retardants. Tellurium is a silvery white solid whose ability to conduct increases slightly with exposure to light.

noble gas an unreactive element of Group 18 of the periodic table

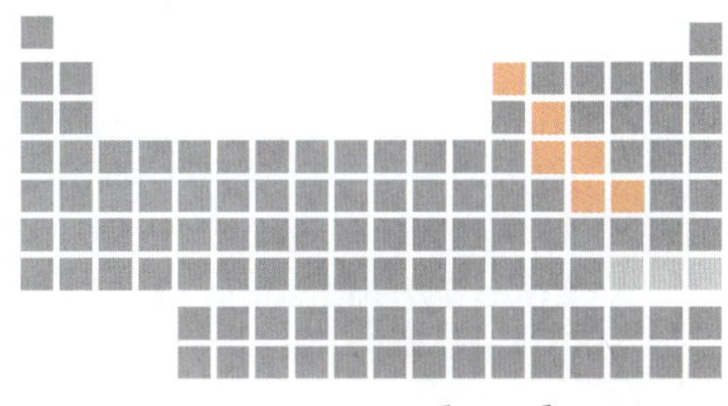

Semiconductors

Figure 31

Semiconductors are located toward the right side of the periodic table.

Figure 32

Silicon chips are the basic building blocks of computers.

Silicon is the most familiar semiconductor

Silicon atoms, usually in the form of compounds, account for 28% of the mass of Earth's crust. Sand is made of the most common silicon compound, called silicon dioxide, SiO_2. Small chips made of silicon, like those shown in ***Figure 32,*** are used in the internal parts of computers.

Silicon is also an important component of other semiconductor devices such as transistors, LED display screens, and solar cells. Impurities such as boron, aluminum, phosphorus, and arsenic are added to the silicon to increase its ability to conduct electricity. These impurities are usually added only to the surface of the chip. This process can be used to make chips of different conductive abilities. This wide range of possible semiconductor devices has led to great advances in electronic technology.

SECTION 3 REVIEW

SUMMARY

- Metals are shiny solids that conduct heat and electricity.
- Alkali metals, located in Group 1 of the periodic table, are very reactive.
- Alkaline-earth metals, located in Group 2, are less reactive than alkali metals.
- Transition metals, located in Groups 3–12, are not very reactive.
- Nonmetals usually do not conduct heat or electricity well.
- Nonmetals include the inert noble gases in Group 18, the reactive halogens in Group 17, and some elements in Groups 13–16.
- Semiconductors are nonmetals that are intermediate conductors of heat and electricity.

1. **Classify** the following elements as alkali, alkaline-earth, or transition metals based on their positions in the periodic table:
   a. iron, Fe
   b. potassium, K
   c. strontium, Sr
   d. platinum, Pt
2. **Predict** whether cesium forms Cs^+ or Cs^{2+} ions.
3. **Describe** why chemists might sometimes store reactive chemicals in argon, Ar. To which family does argon belong?
4. **Determine** whether the following elements are more likely to be a metal or nonmetal:
   a. a shiny substance used to make flexible bed springs
   b. a yellow powder from underground mines
   c. a gas that does not react
   d. a conducting material used within flexible wires
5. **Describe** why atoms of bromine, Br, are so reactive. To which family does bromine belong?
6. **Predict** the charge of a beryllium ion.
7. **Identify** which element is more reactive: lithium, Li, or beryllium, Be.
8. **Creative Thinking** Imagine you are a scientist who has just discovered a new element. You have confirmed that the element is a metal but are unsure whether it is an alkali metal, an alkaline-earth metal, or a transition metal. Write a paragraph describing the additional tests you can do to further classify this metal.

WRITING SKILL

SECTION 4

Using Moles to Count Atoms

OBJECTIVES

- **Explain** the relationship between a mole of a substance and Avogadro's constant.
- **Find** the molar mass of an element by using the periodic table.
- **Solve** problems converting the amount of an element in moles to its mass in grams, and vice versa.

KEY TERMS

mole
Avogadro's constant
molar mass
conversion factor

Counting objects is one of the very first things children learn to do. Counting is easy when the objects being counted are not too small and there are not too many of them. But can you imagine counting the grains of sand along a stretch of beach or the stars in the night-time sky?

Counting Things

When people count out large numbers of small things, they often simplify the job by using counting units. For example, when you order popcorn at a movie theater, the salesperson does not count out the individual popcorn kernels to give you. Instead, you specify the size of container you want, and that determines how much popcorn you get. So the "counting unit" for popcorn is the size of the container: small, medium, or large.

There are many different counting units

The counting units for popcorn are only an approximation and are not exact. Everyone who orders a large popcorn will not get exactly the same number of popcorn kernels. Many other items, however, require more-exact counting units, as shown in ***Figure 33.*** For example, you cannot buy just one egg at the grocery store. Eggs are packaged by the dozen. Copy shops buy paper in reams, or 500-sheet bundles.

An object's mass may sometimes be used to "count" it. For example, if a candy shopkeeper knows that 10 gumballs have a mass of 21.4 g, then the shopkeeper can assume that there are 50 gumballs on the scale when the mass is 107 g (21.4 g × 5).

Figure 33

Eggs are counted by the dozen, and paper is counted by the ream.

Did You Know?

Did you know that Avogadro never knew his own constant? Count Amedeo Avogadro (1776–1856) was a lawyer who became interested in mathematics and physics. Avogadro's constant was actually determined by Joseph Loschmidt, a German physicist in 1865, nine years after Avogadro's death.

The mole is useful for counting small particles

Because chemists often deal with large numbers of small particles, they use a large counting unit—the **mole,** abbreviated *mol.* A mole is a collection of a very large number of particles.

About 602 213 670 000 000 000 000 000!

This number is usually written as 6.022×10^{23}/mol and is referred to as **Avogadro's constant.** The constant is named in honor of the Italian scientist Amedeo Avogadro. Avogadro's constant is defined as the number of particles, 6.022×10^{23}, in exactly 1 mol of a pure substance.

One mole of gumballs is 6.022×10^{23} gumballs. One mole of popcorn is 6.022×10^{23} kernels of popcorn. This amount of popcorn would cover the United States and form a pile about 500 km (310 mi) high! It is unlikely that you will ever come in contact with this much gum or popcorn, so it does not make sense to use moles to count either of these items. The mole is useful, however, for counting atoms.

You might wonder why 6.022×10^{23} represents the number of particles in 1 mol. The mole has been defined as the number of atoms in 12.00 grams of carbon-12. Experiments have shown that 6.022×10^{23} is the number of carbon-12 atoms in 12.00 g of carbon-12. One mole of carbon consists of 6.022×10^{23} carbon atoms, with an average atomic mass of 12.01 amu.

Moles and grams are related

The mass in grams of 1 mol of a substance is called its **molar mass.** For example, 1 mol of carbon-12 atoms has a molar mass of 12.00 g. But a mole of an element will usually include atoms of several isotopes. So the molar mass of an element in grams is the same as its average atomic mass in amu, which is listed in the periodic table. The average atomic mass for carbon is 12.01 amu. One mole of carbon, then, has a mass of 12.01 g. ***Figure 34*** demonstrates this idea for magnesium.

mole the SI base unit used to measure the amount of a substance whose number of particles is the same as the number of atoms of carbon in 12 g of carbon-12

Avogadro's constant equals 6.022×10^{23}/mol; the number of particles in 1 mol

molar mass the mass in grams of 1 mol of a substance

12
Mg
Magnesium
24.3050

Figure 34
One mole of magnesium (6.022×10^{23} Mg atoms) has a mass of 24.30 g. Note that the balance is only accurate to one-tenth of a gram, so it reads 24.3 g.

Calculating with Moles

Because the amount of a substance and its mass are related, it is often useful to convert moles to grams, and vice versa. You can use **conversion factors** to relate units.

conversion factor a ratio that is derived from the equality of two different units and that can be used to convert from one unit to another

Using conversion factors

How did the shopkeeper mentioned on the previous page know the mass of 50 gumballs? He multiplied by a conversion factor to determine the number of gumballs on the scale from their combined mass. Multiplying by a conversion factor is like multiplying by 1 because both parts of the conversion factor are always equal.

The shopkeeper knows that exactly 10 gumballs have a combined mass of 21.4 g. This relationship can be written as two equivalent conversion factors, both of which are shown below.

$$\frac{10 \text{ gumballs}}{21.4 \text{ g}} \qquad \frac{21.4 \text{ g}}{10 \text{ gumballs}}$$

The shopkeeper can use one of these conversion factors to determine the mass of 50 gumballs because mass increases in a predictable way as more gumballs are added to the scale, as you can see from ***Figure 35.***

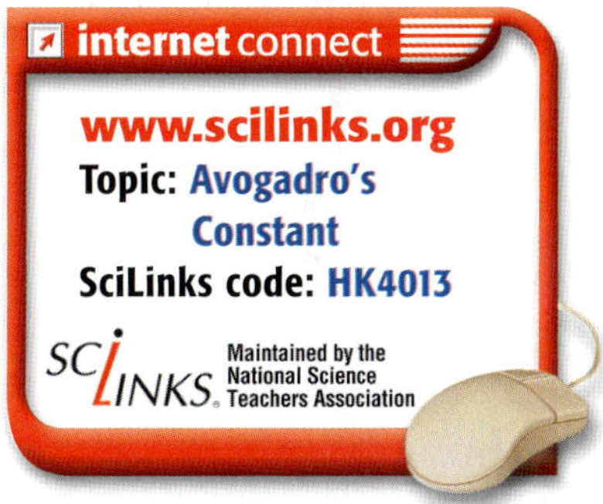

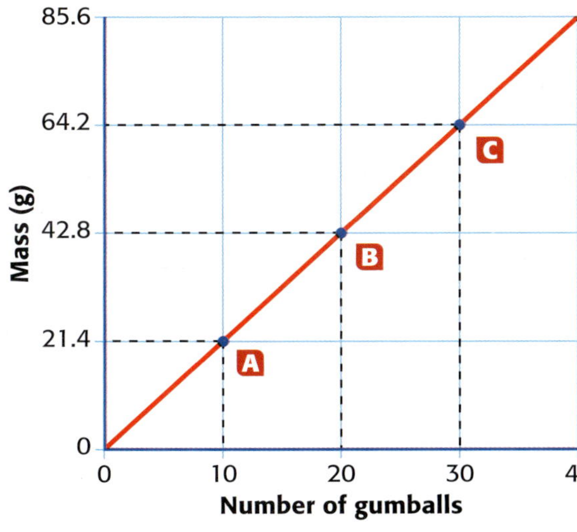

Figure 35
There is a direct relationship between the number of gumballs and their mass. Ten gumballs have a mass of 21.4 g, 20 gumballs have a mass of 42.8 g, and 30 gumballs have a mass of 64.2 g.

A

B

C

Math Skills

Conversion Factors What is the mass of exactly 50 gumballs?

1 List the given and unknown values.

Given: mass of 10 gumballs = 21.4 g
Unknown: mass of 50 gumballs = ? g

2 Write down the conversion factor that converts number of gumballs to mass.

The conversion factor you choose should have the unit you are solving for (g) in the numerator and the unit you want to cancel (number of gumballs) in the denominator.

$$\frac{21.4 \text{ g}}{10 \text{ gumballs}}$$

3 Multiply the number of gumballs by this conversion factor, and solve.

$$50 \cancel{\text{gumballs}} \times \frac{21.4 \text{ g}}{10 \cancel{\text{gumballs}}} = 107 \text{ g}$$

Practice

Conversion Factors

1. What is the mass of exactly 150 gumballs?
2. If you want 50 eggs, how many dozens must you buy? How many extra eggs do you have to take?
3. If a football player is tackled 1.7 ft short of the end zone, how many more yards does the team need to get a touchdown?

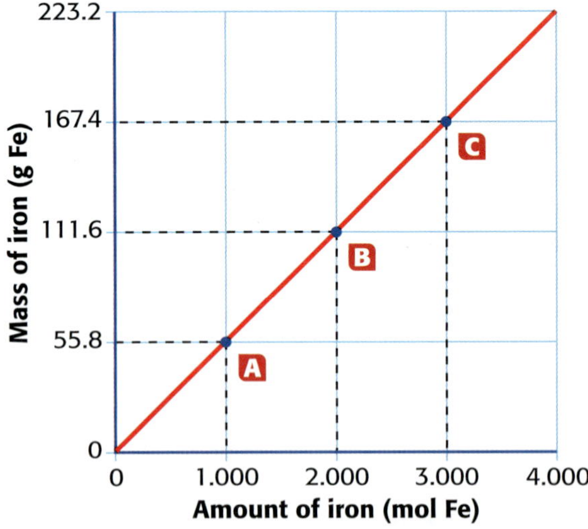

Relating amount to mass

Just as in the gumball example, there is also a relationship between the amount of an element in moles and its mass in grams. This relationship is graphed for iron nails in ***Figure 36.*** Because the amount of iron and the mass of iron are directly related, the graph is a straight line.

An element's molar mass can be used as if it were a conversion factor. Depending on which conversion factor you use, you can solve for either the amount of the element or its mass.

A

B

C

Figure 36
There is a direct relationship between the amount of an element and its mass.

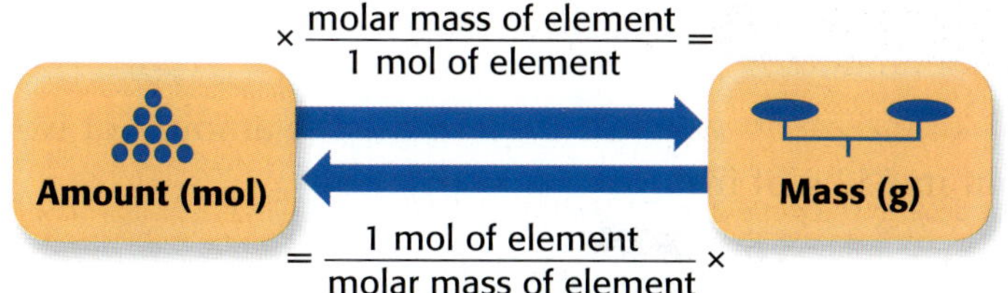

Figure 37
The molar mass of an element allows you to convert between the amount of the element and its mass.

Converting moles to grams

Converting between the amount of an element in moles and its mass in grams is outlined in ***Figure 37.*** For example, you can determine the mass of 5.50 mol of iron by using ***Figure 37*** as a guide. First you must find iron in the periodic table. Its average atomic mass is 55.85 amu. This means iron's molar mass is 55.85 g/mol Fe. Now you can set up the problem using the molar mass as if it were a conversion factor, as shown in the sample problem below.

Math Skills

Converting Amount to Mass Determine the mass in grams of 5.50 mol of iron.

1 List the given and unknown values.

Given: amount of iron = 5.50 mol Fe

molar mass of iron = 55.85 g/mol Fe

Unknown: mass of iron = ? g Fe

2 Write down the conversion factor that converts moles to grams.

The conversion factor you choose should have what you are trying to find (grams of Fe) in the numerator and what you want to cancel (moles of Fe) in the denominator.

$$\frac{55.85 \text{ g Fe}}{1 \text{ mol Fe}}$$

3 Multiply the amount of iron by this conversion factor, and solve.

$$5.50 \cancel{\text{mol Fe}} \times \frac{55.85 \text{ g Fe}}{1 \cancel{\text{mol Fe}}} = 307 \text{ g Fe}$$

Notice how iron's molar mass, 55.85 g/mol Fe, includes units (g/mol) and a chemical symbol (Fe). The units specify that this mass applies to 1 mol of substance. The symbol for iron, Fe, clearly indicates the substance. Remember to always include units in your answers and make clear the substance to which these units apply. Otherwise, your answer has no meaning.

Practice

Converting Amount to Mass

What is the mass in grams of each of the following?

1. 2.50 mol of sulfur, S
2. 1.80 mol of calcium, Ca
3. 0.50 mol of carbon, C
4. 3.20 mol of copper, Cu

Math Skills

Converting Mass to Amount Determine the amount of iron present in 352 g of iron.

1 List the given and unknown values.

Given: mass of iron = 352 g Fe

molar mass of iron = 55.85 g/mol Fe

Unknown: amount of iron = ? mol Fe

2 Write down the conversion factor that converts grams to moles.

The conversion factor you choose should have what you are trying to find (moles of Fe) in the numerator and what you want to cancel (grams of Fe) in the denominator.

$$\frac{1 \text{ mol Fe}}{55.85 \text{ g Fe}}$$

3 Multiply the mass of iron by this conversion factor, and solve.

$$352 \text{ g Fe} \times \frac{1 \text{ mol Fe}}{55.85 \text{ g Fe}} = 6.30 \text{ mol Fe}$$

Once you have learned how to convert mass to amount, you should use this sample problem to check your answers to the practice on the previous page.

SECTION 4 REVIEW

SUMMARY

- One mole of a substance has as many particles as there are atoms in exactly 12.00 g of carbon-12.
- Avogadro's constant, 6.022×10^{23}/mol, is equal to the number of particles in 1 mol.
- Molar mass is the mass in grams of 1 mol of a substance.
- An element's molar mass in grams is equal to its average atomic mass in amu.
- An element's molar mass can be used to convert from amount to mass, and vice versa.

1. **Define** Avogadro's constant. Describe how Avogadro's constant relates to a mole of a substance.
2. **Determine** the molar mass of the following elements:
   a. manganese, Mn
   b. cadmium, Cd
   c. arsenic, As
   d. strontium, Sr
3. **List** the two equivalent conversion factors for the molar mass of silver, Ag.
4. **Explain** why a graph showing the relationship between the amount of a particular element and the element's mass is a straight line.
5. **Critical Thinking** Which has more atoms: 3.0 g of iron, Fe, or 2.0 g of sulfur, S?

Math Skills

6. What is the mass in grams of 0.48 mol of platinum, Pt?
7. How many moles are present in 620 g of mercury, Hg?
8. How many moles are present in 11 g of silicon, Si?
9. How many moles are present in 205 g of helium, He?

Math Skills

Conversion Factors

A chemical reaction requires 5.00 mol of sulfur as a reactant. What is the mass of this sulfur in grams?

1 List all given and unknown values.

Given: amount of sulfur, 5.00 mol S
molar mass of sulfur, 32.07 g/mol S

Unknown: mass of sulfur (g)

2 Write the conversion factor for moles to grams.

The conversion factor you choose should have the unit you are solving for (g S) in the numerator and the unit you want to cancel (mol S) in the denominator.

$$\frac{32.07 \text{ g S}}{1 \text{ mol S}}$$

3 Multiply the number of moles by this conversion factor, and solve.

$$5.00 \text{ mol} \times \frac{32.07 \text{ g S}}{1 \text{ mol S}} = 160.4 \text{ g S}$$

Therefore, 160.4 grams of sulfur are needed for the reaction.

Practice

Molar Masses	
Copper	63.55 g/mol
Oxygen	16.00 g/mol
Sulfur	32.07 g/mol
Lead	207.2 g/mol

Using the example above, calculate the following:

1. If 4.00 mol of copper are needed as a reactant, what is the copper's mass in grams?
2. A combustion reaction requires 352 g of oxygen. What is the amount of oxygen atoms in moles?
3. If 622 g of lead are required for a reaction, what is the amount of the lead in moles?

Chapter Highlights

Before you begin, review the summaries of the key ideas of each section, found at the end of each section. The key vocabulary terms are listed on the first page of each section.

UNDERSTANDING CONCEPTS

1. Which of Dalton's statements about the atom was later proven false?
- **a.** Atoms cannot be subdivided.
- **b.** Atoms are tiny.
- **c.** Atoms of different elements are not identical.
- **d.** Atoms join to form molecules.

2. Which statement is not true of Bohr's model of the atom?
- **a.** The nucleus can be compared to the sun.
- **b.** Electrons orbit the nucleus.
- **c.** An electron's path is not known exactly.
- **d.** Electrons exist in energy levels.

3. According to the modern model of the atom,
- **a.** moving electrons form an electron cloud.
- **b.** electrons and protons circle neutrons.
- **c.** neutrons have a positive charge.
- **d.** the number of protons an atom has varies.

4. If an atom has a mass of 11 amu and contains five electrons, its atomic number must be
- **a.** 55.
- **b.** 16.
- **c.** 6.
- **d.** 5.

5. Which statement about atoms of elements in the same group of the periodic table is true?
- **a.** They have the same number of protons.
- **b.** They have the same mass number.
- **c.** They have similar chemical properties.
- **d.** They have the same number of total electrons.

6. The majority of elements in the periodic table are
- **a.** nonmetals.
- **b.** conductors
- **c.** synthetic.
- **d.** noble gases.

7. An atom of which of the following elements is unlikely to form a positively charged ion?
- **a.** potassium, K
- **b.** selenium, Se
- **c.** barium, Ba
- **d.** silver, Ag

8. Which of the following statements about krypton is not true?
- **a.** Its molar mass is 83.80 g/mol Kr.
- **b.** Its atomic number is 36.
- **c.** One mole of krypton atoms has a mass of 41.90 g.
- **d.** It is a noble gas.

USING VOCABULARY

9. How many *protons* and *neutrons* does a silicon, Si, atom have, and where are each of these subatomic particles located? How many *electrons* does a silicon atom have?

10. Identify the particles that make up an atom. How do these particles relate to the identity of an atom?

11. Explain why different atoms of the same element always have the same *atomic number* but can have different *mass numbers*. What are these different atoms called?

12. Distinguish between the following:
- **a.** an *atom* and a *molecule*
- **b.** an *atom* and an *ion*
- **c.** a *cation* and an *anion*

13. List several familiar *transition metals* and their uses.

14. How is the *periodic law* demonstrated with the *halogens?*

15. Explain why *semiconductors,* or metalloids, deserve their name.

16. Distinguish between *alkali metals* and *alkaline-earth metals,* and give several examples of how they are used.

17. State *Avogadro's constant* and explain its relationship to the *mole.*

18. What does an element's *molar mass* tell you about the element?

BUILDING MATH SKILLS

19. **Graphing** Use a graphing calculator, a computer spreadsheet, or a graphing program to plot the atomic number on the *x*-axis and the average atomic mass in amu on the *y*-axis for the transition metals in Period 4 of the periodic table (from scandium to zinc). Do you notice a break in the trend near cobalt? Explain why elements with larger atomic numbers do not necessarily have larger atomic masses.

COMPUTER SKILL

20. **Converting Mass to Amount** For an experiment you have been asked to do, you need 1.5 g of iron. How many moles of iron do you need?

21. **Converting Amount to Mass** Robyn recycled 15.1 mol of aluminum last month. What mass of aluminum in grams did she recycle?

THINKING CRITICALLY

22. **Critical Thinking** Why is it difficult to measure the size of an atom?

23. **Creative Thinking** Some forces push two atoms apart while other forces pull them together. Describe how the subatomic particles in each atom interact to produce these forces.

24. **Applying Knowledge** Explain why magnesium forms ions with the formula Mg^{2+}, not Mg^{+} or Mg^{-}.

25. **Evaluating Data** The figure below shows relative ionic radii for positive and negative ions of elements in Period 2 of the periodic table. Explain the trend in ion size as you move from left to right across the periodic table. Why do the negative ions have larger radii than the positive ions?

0.60	0.31	1.71	1.40	1.36
Li^{+}	Be^{2+}	N^{3-}	O^{2-}	F^{-}

26. **Problem Solving** What would happen to poisonous chlorine gas if the following alterations were made to the chlorine?
    - **a.** A proton is added to each atom.
    - **b.** An electron is added to each atom.
    - **c.** A neutron is added to each atom.

DEVELOPING LIFE/WORK SKILLS

27. **Locating Information** Some "neon" signs contain substances other than neon to produce different colors. Design your own lighted sign, and find out which substances you could use to produce the colors you want your sign to be.

28. **Communicating Effectively** The study of the nucleus produced a new field of medicine called nuclear medicine. Pretend you are writing an article for a hospital newsletter. Describe how radioactive substances called tracers are sometimes used to detect and treat diseases.

29. Applying Knowledge You read a science fiction story about an alien race of silicon-based life-forms. Use information from the periodic table to hypothesize why the author chose silicon over other elements. (**Hint:** Life on Earth is carbon based.)

INTEGRATING CONCEPTS

30. Connection to Health You can keep your bones healthy by eating 1200–1500 mg of calcium a day. Use the table below to make a list of the foods you might eat in a day to satisfy your body's need for calcium. How does your typical diet compare with this?

Item, serving size	Calcium (mg)
Plain lowfat yogurt, 1 cup	415
Ricotta cheese, 1/2 cup	337
Skim milk, 1 cup	302
Cheddar cheese, 1 ounce	213
Cooked spinach, 1/2 cup	106
Vanilla ice cream, 1/2 cup	88

internet connect
www.scilinks.org
Topic: Origin of Elements SciLinks code: HK4097
SCILINKS. Maintained by the National Science Teachers Association

31. Concept Mapping Copy the unfinished concept map below onto a sheet of paper. Complete the map by writing the correct word or phrase in the lettered boxes.

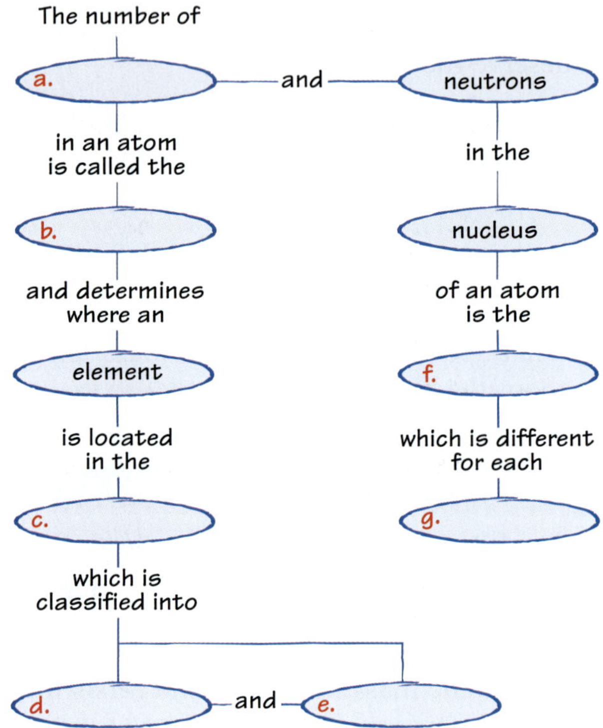

32. Connection to Physics Research the origins of the elements. The big bang theory suggests that the universe began with an enormous explosion. What was formed as a result of the big bang? Describe the matter that was present after the explosion. How much time passed before the elements as we know them were formed?

33. Connection to Earth Science The isotope carbon-14 is used in radiocarbon- dating of animal and plant fossils. Scientists use other isotopes to tell the ages of rocks and meteorites. Do some research and find out which isotopes are used to date rocks and meteorites.

Standardized Test Prep

Understanding Concepts

Directions (1–3): **For *each* question, write on a separate sheet of paper the letter of the correct answer.**

1 Why do atoms gain or lose electrons?

A. to balance the charges between the nucleus and the electron cloud
B. to obtain a more stable electron configuration through a full outermost orbital
C. to place electrons in higher energy levels than are occupied in the atom
D. to reduce the amount of energy required to bring atoms closer together

2 Why are the Group 18 elements nonreactive?

F. They have no valence electrons.
G. They combine to form stable molecules.
H. Their outermost energy levels are completely filled.
I. They are too rare to react with significant amounts of other elements.

3 Antimony is a shiny, brittle solid that conducts electricity under some conditions but does not conduct under other conditions. How is antimony classfied on the modern periodic table?

A. metal
B. nonmetal
C. semiconductor
D. transition element

Directions (4): **Write a short response to the question.**

4 Beryllium is located on the same row of the periodic table as fluorine, while iodine is located in the same column. Identify which element, beryllium or iodine, will form an ion by gaining one electron, as fluorine does, and explain your answer.

Test TIP

For multiple-choice questions, try to eliminate any answer choices that are obviously incorrect, and then consider the remaining answer choices.

Reading Skills

Directions (5): **Read the passage below. Then answer the question.**

Particle accelerators are devices that speed up charged particles to speeds close to the speed of light in order to smash them together and observe the results. In many cases, these collisions form a new atomic nucleus. This nucleus attracts electrons and becomes a neutral atom. Atoms formed this way can either be an isotope of a known element or a previously unknown element.

5 Determine how scientists can judge whether the newly formed material is a new element or a new isotope of an existing element.

Interpreting Graphics

Directions (6): **Base your answer to question 6 on the illustration below, which shows the ionization of a fluorine atom.**

Formation of a Fluoride Ion

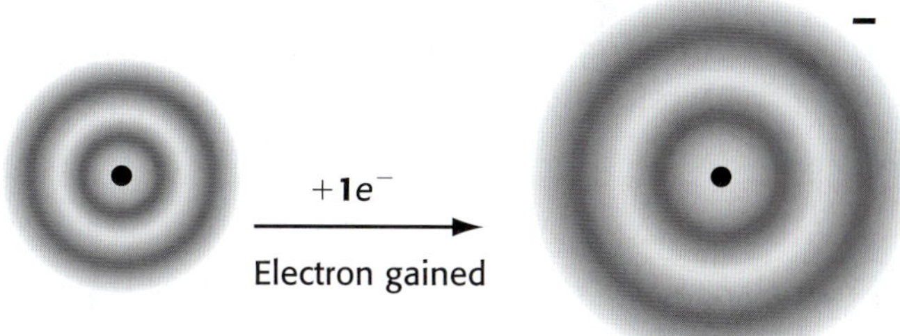

6 Why is the fluoride ion larger than the fluorine atom?

F. The electrons experience a greater electrical repulsion.
G. The interaction between the electrons and the protons is stronger.
H. The ion has more protons than electrons so it is not as stable as the atom.
I. The addition of another electron makes the ion substantially more massive than the atom.

Skills Practice Lab

Introduction

How can you distinguish metal elements by analyzing their physical properties?

Objectives

- USING SCIENTIFIC METHODS ***Hypothesize*** which physical properties can help you ***distinguish*** between different metals.
- ***Identify*** unknown metals by ***comparing*** the data you collect with reference information.

Materials

balance
beakers (several)
graduated cylinder
hot plate
ice
magnet
metal samples, unidentified (several)
metric ruler
stopwatch
water
wax

Comparing the Physical Properties of Elements

Procedure

Identifying Metal Elements

1. In this lab, you will identify samples of unknown metals by comparing the data you collect with reference information listed in the table at right. Use at least two of the physical properties listed in the table to identify each metal.

Deciding Which Physical Properties You Will Analyze

2. Density is the mass per unit volume of a substance. If the metal is box-shaped, you can measure its length, width, and height, and then use these measurements to calculate the metal's volume. If the shape of the metal is irregular, you can add the metal to a known volume of water and determine what volume of water is displaced.
3. Relative hardness indicates how easy it is to scratch a metal. A metal with a higher value can scratch a metal with a lower value, but not vice versa.
4. Relative heat conductivity indicates how quickly a metal heats or cools. A metal with a value of 100 will heat or cool twice as quickly as a metal with a value of 50.
5. If a magnet placed near a metal attracts the metal, then the metal has been magnetized by the magnet.

Designing Your Experiment

6. With your lab partner(s), decide how you will use the materials provided to identify each metal you are given. There is more than one way to measure some of the physical properties that are listed, so you might not use all of the materials that are provided.
7. In your lab report, list each step you will perform in your experiment.
8. Have your teacher approve your plan before you carry out your experiment.

Physical Properties of Some Metals

Metal	Density (g/mL)	Relative hardness	Relative heat conductivity	Magnetized by magnet?
Aluminum (Al)	2.7	28	100	no
Iron (Fe)	7.9	50	34	yes
Nickel (Ni)	8.9	67	38	yes
Tin (Sn)	7.3	19	28	no
Tungsten (W)	19.3	100	73	no
Zinc (Zn)	7.1	28	49	no

Performing Your Experiment

9. After your teacher approves your plan, carry out your experiment. Keep in mind that the more careful your measurements are, the easier it will be for you to identify the unknown metals.
10. Record all the data you collect and any observations you make in your lab report.

Analysis

1. Make a table listing the physical properties you compared and the data you collected for each of the unknown metals.
2. Which metals were you given? Explain the reasoning you used to identify each metal.
3. Which physical properties were the easiest for you to measure and compare? Which were the hardest? Explain why.
4. What would happen if you tried to scratch aluminum foil with zinc?
5. Explain why it would be difficult to distinguish between iron and nickel unless you calculate each metal's density.
6. Suppose you find a metal fastener and determine that its density is 7 g/mL. What are two ways you could determine whether the unknown metal is tin or zinc?

Conclusions

7. Suppose someone gives you an alloy that is made of both zinc and nickel. In general, how do you think the physical properties of the alloy would compare with those of each individual metal?

CHAPTER 5

The Structure of Matter

Chapter Preview

Focus ACTIVITY

Background Suddenly, a glass object slips from your hand and crashes to the ground. You watch it break into many tiny pieces as you hear it hit the floor. Glass is a brittle substance. When enough force is applied, it breaks into many sharp, jagged pieces. Glass behaves the way it does because of its composition.

A glass container and a stained glass window have some similar properties because both are made mainly from silicon dioxide. But other compounds are responsible for the window's beautiful colors. Adding a compound of nickel and oxygen to the glass produces a purple tint. Adding a compound of cobalt and oxygen makes the glass deep blue, while adding a compound of copper and oxygen makes the glass dark red.

Activity 1 There are many different kinds of glass, each with its own use. List several kinds of glass that you encounter daily. Describe the ways that each kind of glass differs from other kinds of glass.

Activity 2 Research other compounds that are sometimes added to glass. Describe how each of these compounds changes the properties of glass. Write a report on your findings.

Glass is a brittle substance that is made from silicon dioxide, a compound with a very rigid structure. The addition of small amounts of other compounds changes the color of the glass, "staining" it.

Pre-Reading Questions

1. How does atomic structure affect the properties of a substance?
2. Can bonds between atoms be broken?

SECTION 1

Compounds and Molecules

KEY TERMS

chemical bond
chemical structure
bond length
bond angle

OBJECTIVES

- **Distinguish** between compounds and mixtures.
- **Relate** the chemical formula of a compound to the relative numbers of atoms or ions present in the compound.
- **Use** models to visualize a compound's chemical structure.
- **Describe** how the chemical structure of a compound affects its properties.

If you step on a sharp rock with your bare foot, you feel pain. That's because rocks are hard substances; they don't bend. Many rocks are made of quartz. Table salt and sugar look similar; both are grainy, white solids. But they taste very different. In addition, salt is hard and brittle and breaks into uniform cubelike granules, while sugar does not. Quartz, salt, and sugar are all compounds. Their similarities and differences result from the way their atoms or ions are joined.

What Are Compounds?

Table salt is a compound made of two elements, sodium and chlorine. When elements combine to form a compound, the compound has properties very different from those of the elements that make it. ***Figure 1*** shows how the metal sodium combines with chlorine gas to form sodium chloride, NaCl, or table salt.

Figure 1

A The silvery metal sodium combines with **B** poisonous, yellowish green chlorine gas in a violent reaction **C** to form **D** white granules of table salt that you can eat.

+

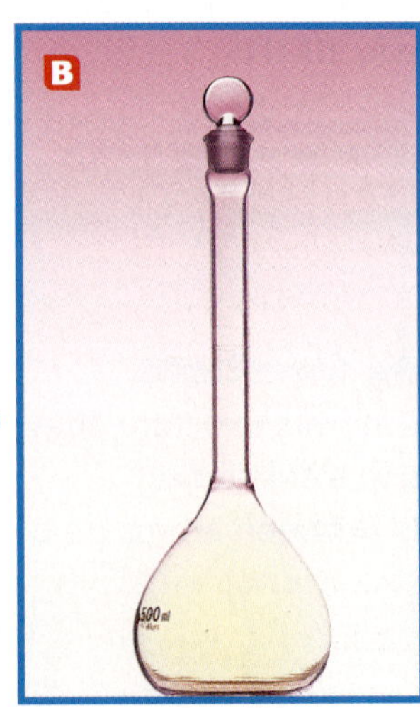

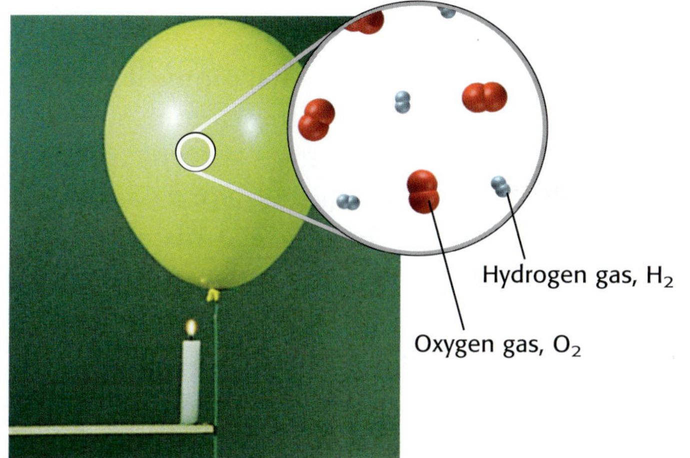

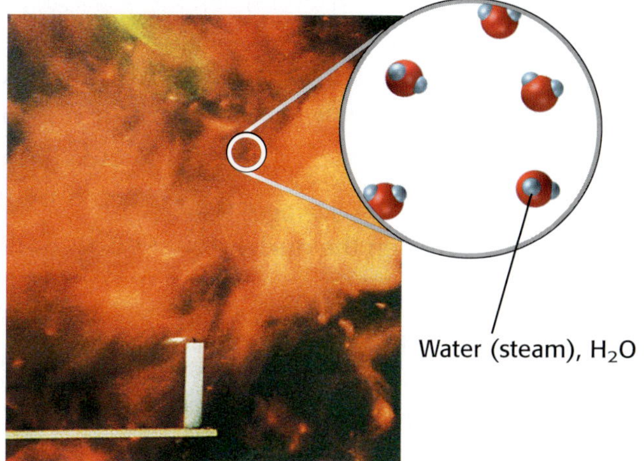

Figure 2

A Placing a lit candle under a balloon containing hydrogen gas and oxygen gas causes the balloon to melt, releasing the mixed gases.

B The mixed gases are ignited by the candle flame, and water is produced.

Chemical bonds distinguish compounds from mixtures

The attractive forces that hold different atoms or ions together in compounds are called **chemical bonds.** Recall how compounds and mixtures are different. Mixtures are made of different substances that are just placed together. Each substance in the mixture keeps its own properties.

chemical bond the attractive force that holds atoms or ions together

For example, mixing blue paint and yellow paint makes green paint. Different shades of green can be made by mixing the paints in different proportions, but both original paints remain chemically unchanged.

Figure 2 shows that when a mixture of hydrogen gas and oxygen gas is heated, a violent reaction takes place and a compound forms. Chemical bonds are broken, and atoms are rearranged. New bonds form water, a compound with properties very different from those of the original gases.

A compound always has the same chemical formula

The chemical formula for water is H_2O, and that of table sugar is $C_{12}H_{22}O_{11}$. The salt you season your food with has the chemical formula NaCl. A chemical formula shows the types and numbers of atoms or ions making up the simplest unit of the compound.

There is another important way that compounds and mixtures are different. Compounds are always made of the same elements in the same proportion. A molecule of water, for example, is always made of two hydrogen atoms and one oxygen atom. This is true for all water. That means water frozen in a comet in outer space and water at 37°C (98.6°F) inside the cells of your body both have the same chemical formula—H_2O.

chemical structure the arrangement of atoms in a substance

bond length the average distance between the nuclei of two bonded atoms

bond angle the angle formed by two bonds to the same atom

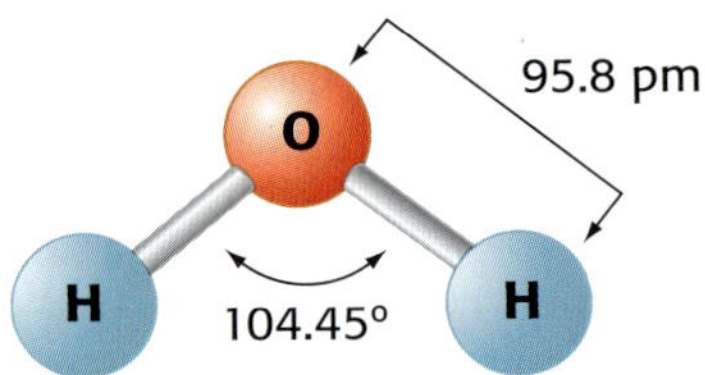

Figure 3

The ball-and-stick model in this figure is a giant representation of one molecule of water. A picometer (pm) is equal to 1×10^{-12} m.

Chemical structure shows the bonding within a compound

Although water's chemical formula tells us what atoms it is made of, it doesn't reveal anything about the way these atoms are connected. You can see how a compound's atoms or ions are connected by its **chemical structure.** The structure of a compound can be compared to that of a rope. The kinds of fibers used to make a rope and the way the fibers are intertwined determine how strong the rope is. Similarly, the atoms in a compound and the way the atoms are arranged determine many of the compound's properties.

Two terms are used to specify the positions of atoms relative to one another in a compound. A **bond length** gives the distance between the nuclei of two bonded atoms. And when a compound has three or more atoms, **bond angles** tell how these atoms are oriented in space. ***Figure 3*** shows the chemical structure of a water molecule. You can see that the way hydrogen and oxygen atoms bond to form water looks more like a boomerang than a straight line.

Models of Compounds

Figure 3 is a ball-and-stick model of a water molecule. Ball-and-stick models, as well as other kinds of models, help you "see" a compound's structure by showing you how the atoms or ions are arranged in the compound.

Some models give you an idea of bond lengths and angles

In the ball-and-stick model of water shown in ***Figure 3,*** the atoms are represented by balls. The bonds that hold the atoms together are represented by sticks. Although bonds between atoms aren't really as rigid as sticks, this model makes it easy to see the bonds and the angles they form in a compound.

Structural formulas can also show the structures of compounds. Notice how water's structural formula, which is shown below, is a lot like its ball-and-stick model. The difference is that only chemical symbols are used to represent the atoms.

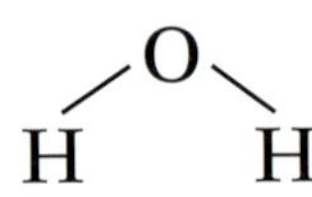

Connection to FINE ARTS

Clay has a layered structure of silicon, oxygen, aluminum, and hydrogen atoms. Artists can mold wet clay into any shape because water molecules let the layers slide over one another. When clay dries, water evaporates and the layers can no longer slide. To keep the dry, crumbly clay from breaking apart, artists change the structure of the clay by heating it. The atoms in one layer bond to atoms in the layers above and below. When this happens, the clay hardens, and the artist's work is permanently set.

Making the Connection

1. Think of other substances that can be shaped when they are wet and that "set" when they are dried or heated.
2. Write a paragraph about one of these substances and why it has these properties. WRITING SKILL

Space-filling models show the space occupied by atoms

Figure 4 shows another way chemists picture a water molecule. It is called a space-filling model because it shows the space that is occupied by the oxygen and hydrogen atoms. The problem with this model is that it is harder to "see" bond lengths and angles.

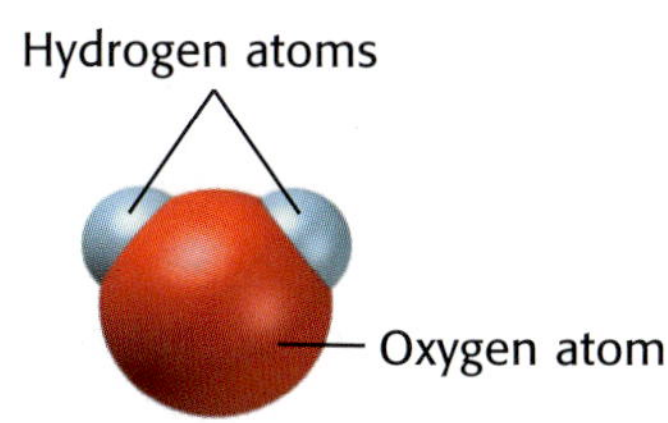

Figure 4

This space-filling model of water shows that the two hydrogen atoms take up much less space than the oxygen atom.

How Does Structure Affect Properties?

Some compounds, such as the quartz found in many rocks, exist as a large network of bonded atoms. Other compounds, such as table salt, are also large networks, but of bonded positive and negative ions. Still other compounds, such as water and sugar, are made of many separate molecules. Different structures give these compounds different properties.

Compounds with network structures are strong solids

Quartz is sometimes found in the form of beautiful crystals, as shown in ***Figure 5.*** Quartz has the chemical formula SiO_2, and so does the less pure form of quartz, sand. ***Figure 5*** shows that every silicon atom in quartz is bonded to four oxygen atoms. The bonds that hold these atoms together are very strong. All of the Si—O—Si and O—Si—O bond angles are the same. That is, each one is 109.5°. This arrangement continues throughout the substance, holding the silicon and oxygen atoms together in a very strong, rigid structure.

This is why rocks containing quartz are hard and inflexible solids. Silicon and oxygen atoms in sand have a similar arrangement. It takes a lot of energy to break the strong bonds between silicon and oxygen atoms in quartz and sand. That's why the melting point and boiling point of quartz and sand is so high, as shown in ***Table 1.***

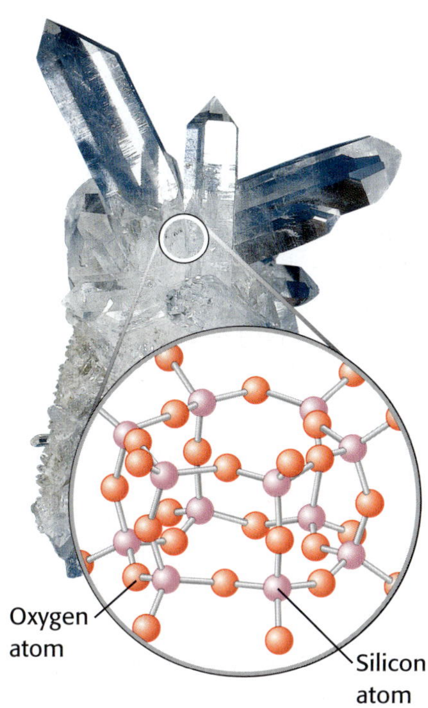

Figure 5

Quartz and sand are made of silicon and oxygen atoms bonded in a strong, rigid structure.

Table 1 **Some Compounds with Network Structures**

Compound	State (25°C)	Melting point (°C)	Boiling point (°C)
Silicon dioxide, SiO_2 (quartz)	solid	1700	2230
Magnesium fluoride, MgF_2	solid	1261	2239
Sodium chloride, NaCl (table salt)	solid	801	1413

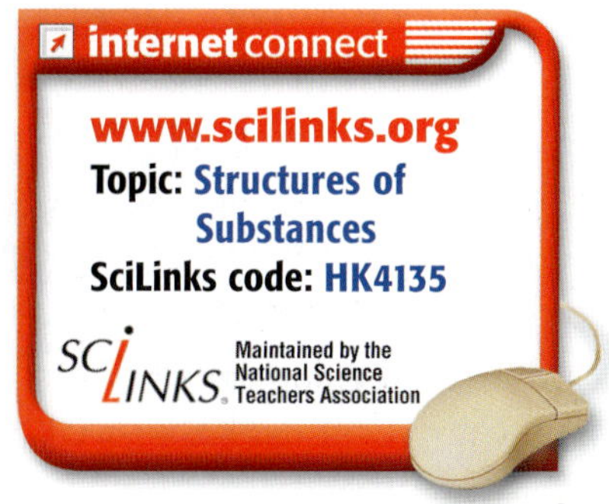

Figure 6

Each grain of table salt, or sodium chloride, is composed of a tightly packed network of Na^+ ions and Cl^- ions.

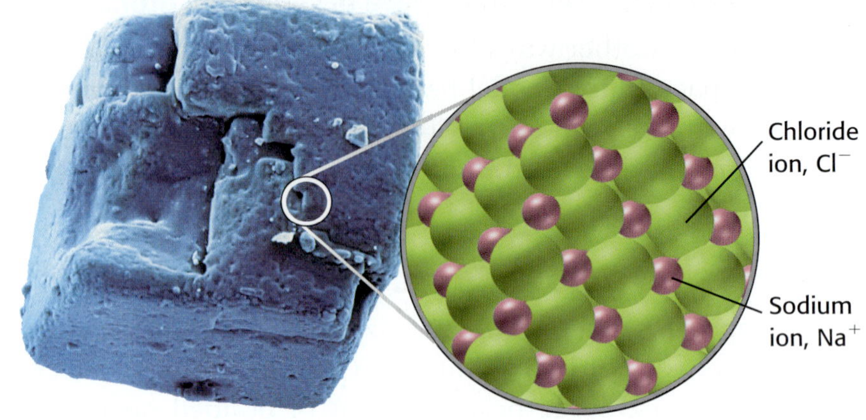

Some compounds are made of networks of bonded ions

Like some quartz, table salt—sodium chloride—is found in the form of regularly shaped crystals. Crystals of sodium chloride are cube shaped. Like quartz and sand, sodium chloride is made of a repeating network connected by strong bonds. The network is made of tightly packed, positively charged sodium ions and negatively charged chloride ions, as shown in ***Figure 6.*** The strong attractions between the oppositely charged ions cause table salt and other similar compounds to have high melting points and boiling points, as shown in ***Table 1.***

Some compounds are made of molecules

Salt and sugar are both white solids you can eat, but their structures are very different. Unlike salt, sugar is made of molecules. A molecule of sugar, shown in ***Figure 7,*** is made of carbon, hydrogen, and oxygen atoms joined by bonds. Molecules of sugar do attract each other to form crystals. But these attractions are much weaker than those that hold bonded carbon, hydrogen, and oxygen atoms together to make a sugar molecule.

Figure 7

Sugar, $C_{12}H_{22}O_{11}$, is made of molecules.

We breathe nitrogen, N_2, oxygen, O_2, and carbon dioxide, CO_2, every day. All three substances are colorless, odorless gases made of molecules. Within each molecule, the atoms are so strongly attracted to one another that they are bonded. But the molecules of each gas have very little attraction for one another. Because the molecules of these gases are not very attracted to one another, they spread out as much as they can. That is why gases can take up a lot of space.

Table 2 **Comparing Compounds Made of Molecules**

Compound	State (25°C)	Melting point (°C)	Boiling point (°C)
Sugar, $C_{12}H_{22}O_{11}$	Solid	185–186	——
Water, H_2O	Liquid	0	100
Dihydrogen sulfide, H_2S	Gas	–86	–61

The strength of attractions between molecules varies

Compare sugar, water, and dihydrogen sulfide in ***Table 2.*** Although all three compounds are made of molecules, their properties are very different. Sugar is a solid, water is a liquid, and dihydrogen sulfide is a gas. That means that sugar molecules have the strongest attractions for each other, followed by water molecules. Dihydrogen sulfide molecules have the weakest attractions for each other. The fact that sugar and water have such different properties probably doesn't surprise you. Their chemical structures are not at all alike. But what about water and dihydrogen sulfide, which do have similar chemical structures?

Which melts more easily, sugar or salt?

Materials
- ✓ *table salt*
- ✓ *Bunsen burner*
- ✓ *stopwatch*
- ✓ *table sugar*
- ✓ *2 test tubes*
- ✓ *tongs*

SAFETY CAUTION Wear safety goggles and gloves. Tie back long hair, confine loose clothing, and use tongs to handle hot glassware. When heating a substance in a test tube, always point the open end of the test tube away from yourself and others.

1. Use your knowledge of structures to make a hypothesis about whether sugar or salt will melt more easily.
2. To test your hypothesis, place about 1 cm^3 of sugar in a test tube.
3. Using tongs, position the test tube with sugar over the flame, as shown in the figure at right. Move the test tube back and forth slowly over the flame. Use a stopwatch to measure the time it takes for the sugar to melt.
4. Repeat steps 2 and 3 with salt. If your sample does not melt within 1 minute, remove it from the flame.

Analysis

1. Which compound is easier to melt? Was your hypothesis right?
2. How can you relate your results to the structure of each compound?

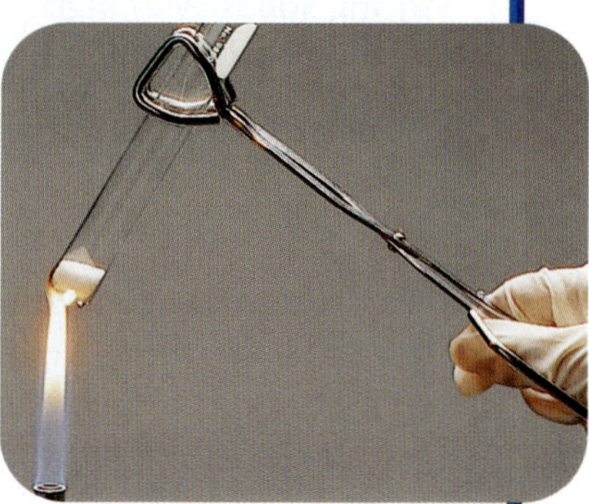

Attractions between water molecules are called hydrogen bonds

The higher melting and boiling points of water suggest that water molecules attract each other more than dihydrogen sulfide molecules do. ***Figure 8*** shows how an oxygen atom of one water molecule is attracted to a hydrogen atom of a neighboring water molecule. This attraction is called a *hydrogen bond*. Water molecules attract each other, but these attractions are not as strong as the bonds holding oxygen and hydrogen atoms together within a molecule.

Figure 8

Dotted lines indicate the *inter*molecular attractions that occur *between* water molecules, which is often referred to as "hydrogen bonding." Water is a liquid at room temperature because of these attractions.

SECTION 1 REVIEW

SUMMARY

- Atoms or ions in compounds are joined by chemical bonds.
- A compound's chemical formula shows which atoms or ions it is made of.
- A model represents a compound's structure visually.
- Substances with network structures are usually strong solids with high melting and boiling points.
- Substances made of molecules have lower melting and boiling points.
- Whether a molecular substance is a solid, a liquid, or a gas at room temperature depends on the attractions between its molecules.

1. **Classify** the following substances as mixtures or compounds:
   a. air
   b. CO
   c. SnF_2
   d. pure water
2. **Explain** why silver iodide, AgI, a compound used in photography, has a much higher melting point than vanillin, $C_8H_8O_3$, a sweet-smelling compound used in flavorings.
3. **Draw** a ball-and-stick model of a boron trifluoride, BF_3, molecule. In this molecule, a boron atom is attached to three fluorine atoms. Each F—B—F bond angle is 120°, and all B—F bonds are the same length.
4. **Predict** which molecules have a greater attraction for each other, C_3H_8O molecules in liquid rubbing alcohol or CH_4 molecules in methane gas.
5. **Explain** why glass, which is made mainly of SiO_2, is often used to make cookware. (**Hint:** What properties does SiO_2 have because of its structure?)
6. **Critical Thinking** A picometer (pm) is equal to 1×10^{-12} m. O—H bond lengths in water are 95.8 pm, while S—H bond lengths in dihydrogen sulfide are 135 pm. Why are S—H bond lengths longer than O—H bond lengths? (**Hint:** Which is larger, a sulfur atom or an oxygen atom?)

SECTION 2

Ionic and Covalent Bonding

OBJECTIVES

- **Explain** why atoms sometimes join to form bonds.
- **Explain** why some atoms transfer their valence electrons to form ionic bonds, while other atoms share valence electrons to form covalent bonds.
- **Differentiate** between ionic, covalent, and metallic bonds.
- **Compare** the properties of substances with different types of bonds.

KEY TERMS

ionic bond
metallic bond
covalent bond
polyatomic ion

When two atoms join, a bond forms. You have already seen how bonded atoms form many kinds of substances. Atoms bond in different ways to form these many substances. The type of bonds that the atoms of a substance form affect the substance's properties.

What Holds Bonded Atoms Together?

Three different kinds of bonds describe the way atoms bond in most substances. In many of the models you have seen so far, the bonds that hold atoms together are represented by sticks. But what bonds atoms in a real molecule?

Bonded atoms usually have a stable electron configuration

Atoms bond when their valence electrons interact. You have learned that atoms with full outermost *s* and *p* orbitals are more stable than atoms with only partly filled outer *s* and *p* orbitals. Generally, atoms join to form bonds so that each atom has a stable electron configuration. When this happens, each atom has an electronic structure similar to that of a noble gas.

When two hydrogen atoms bond, as shown in ***Figure 9,*** the positive nucleus of one hydrogen atom attracts the negative electron of the other hydrogen atom, and vice versa. This attraction pulls the two atoms closer together. Soon the electron clouds of the hydrogen atoms cross each other. The shared electron cloud of the molecule that forms has two electrons (one from each atom). A hydrogen molecule, which consists of two hydrogen atoms bonded together, has an electronic structure similar to the noble gas helium. The molecule will not fall apart unless enough energy is added to break the bond.

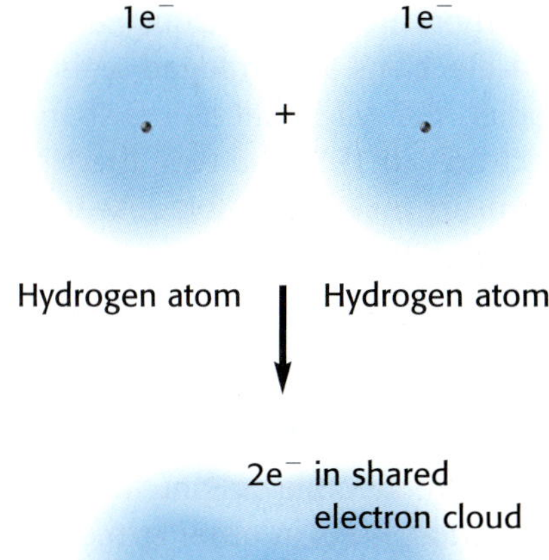

Figure 9
When two hydrogen atoms are very close together, their electron clouds overlap, and a bond forms. The two electrons of the hydrogen molecule that forms are in the shared electron cloud.

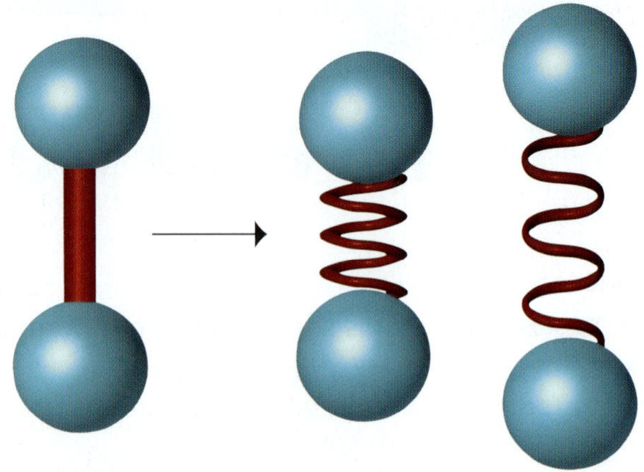

Figure 10

Chemists often use a solid bar to show a bond between two atoms, but real bonds are flexible, like stiff springs.

Bonds can bend and stretch without breaking

Although some bonds are stronger and more rigid than others, all bonds behave more like flexible springs than like sticks, as ***Figure 10*** shows. The atoms move back and forth a little and their nuclei do not always stay the same distance apart. In fact, most reported bond lengths are averages of these distances. Although bonds are not rigid, they still hold atoms together tightly.

ionic bond a bond formed by the attraction between oppositely charged ions

Ionic Bonds

Ionic bonds are formed between oppositely charged ions. Atoms of metal elements, such as sodium and calcium, form the positively charged ions. Atoms of nonmetal elements, such as chlorine and oxygen, form the negatively charged ions.

Ionic bonds are formed by the transfer of electrons

Some atoms do not share electrons to fill their outermost energy levels completely. Instead, they transfer electrons. One of the atoms gains the electrons that the other atom loses. Both ions that form usually have stable electron configurations. The result is a positive ion and a negative ion, such as the Na^+ ion and the Cl^- ion in sodium chloride.

These oppositely charged ions attract each other and form an ionic bond. Each positive sodium ion attracts several negative chloride ions. These negative chloride ions attract more positive sodium ions, and so on. Soon a network of these bonded ions forms a crystal of table salt.

Connection to SOCIAL STUDIES

American scientist Linus Pauling studied how electrons are arranged within atoms. He also studied the ways that atoms share and exchange electrons. In 1954, he won the Nobel Prize in chemistry for his valuable research.

Later, Pauling fought to ban nuclear weapons testing. Pauling was able to convince more than 11 000 scientists from 49 countries to sign a petition to stop nuclear weapons testing. Pauling won the Nobel Peace Prize in 1962 for his efforts. A year later, a treaty outlawing nuclear weapons testing in the atmosphere, in outer space, and underwater went into effect.

Making the Connection

1. *Electronegativity* is an idea first thought of by Pauling. It tells how easily an atom accepts electrons. Which is more electronegative, a fluorine atom or a calcium atom? Why?
2. Nuclear weapons testing can harm living things because of the resulting radiation. Write a paragraph explaining how high levels of radiation can affect your body. **WRITING SKILL**

Ionic compounds are in the form of networks, not molecules

Because sodium chloride is a network of ions, it does not make sense to talk about "a molecule of NaCl." In fact, every sodium ion is next to six chloride ions, as shown in **Figure 6.** Instead, chemists talk about the smallest ratio of ions in ionic compounds. Sodium chloride's chemical formula, NaCl, tells us that there is one Na^+ ion for every Cl^- ion, or a 1:1 ratio of ions. This means the compound has a total charge of zero. One Na^+ ion and one Cl^- ion make up a *formula unit* of NaCl.

Not every ionic compound has the same ratio of ions as sodium chloride. An example is calcium fluoride, which is shown in **Figure 11.** The ratio of Ca^{2+} ions to F^- ions in calcium fluoride must be 1:2 to make a neutral compound. That is why the chemical formula for calcium fluoride is CaF_2.

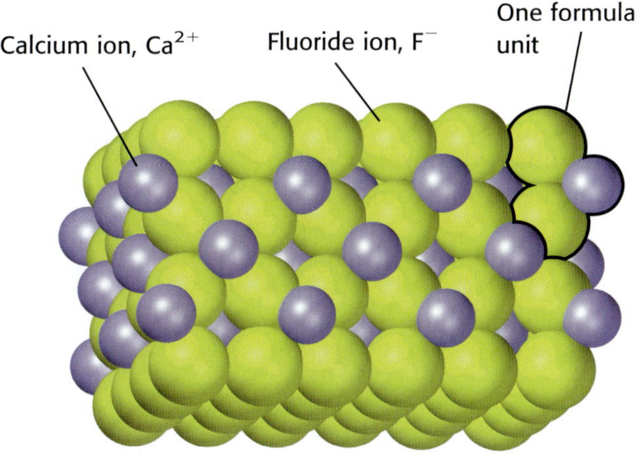

Figure 11

There are twice as many fluoride ions as calcium ions in a crystal of calcium fluoride, CaF_2. So one Ca^{2+} ion and two F^- ions make up one formula unit of the compound.

When melted or dissolved in water, ionic compounds conduct electricity

Electric current is moving charges. Solid ionic compounds do not conduct electricity because the charged ions are locked into place, causing the melting points of ionic compounds to be very high—often well above 300°C. But if you dissolve an ionic compound in water or melt it, it can conduct electricity. That's because the ions are then free to move, as shown in **Figure 12.**

Figure 12

Like other ionic compounds, sodium chloride conducts electricity when it is dissolved in water.

Figure 13

Copper is a flexible metal that melts at 1083°C and boils at 2567°C. Copper conducts electricity because electrons can move freely between atoms.

Metallic Bonds

Metals, like copper, shown in ***Figure 13,*** can conduct electricity when they are solid. Metals are also flexible, so they can bend and stretch without breaking. Copper, for example, can be hammered flat into sheets or stretched into very thin wire. What kind of bonds give copper these properties?

Electrons move freely between metal atoms

metallic bond a bond formed by the attraction between positively charged metal ions and the electrons around them

The atoms in metals like copper form **metallic bonds.** The attraction between one atom's nucleus and a neighboring atom's electrons packs the atoms closely together. This close packing causes the outermost energy levels of the atoms to overlap, as shown in ***Figure 13.*** Therefore, electrons are free to move from atom to atom. This model explains why metals conduct electricity so well. Metals are flexible because the atoms can slide past each other without their bonds breaking.

Quick ACTIVITY

Building a Close-Packed Structure

Copper and other metals have close-packed structures. This means their atoms are packed very tightly together. In this activity, you will build a close-packed structure using table-tennis balls.

1. Place three books flat on a table so that their edges form a triangle.
2. Fill the triangular space between the books with the spherical "atoms." Adjust the books so that the atoms make a one-layer, close-packed pattern, as shown at right.
3. Build additional layers on top of the first layer. How many other atoms does each atom touch? Where have you seen other arrangements that are similar to this one?

Covalent Bonds

Compounds that are made of molecules, like water and sugar, have **covalent bonds.** Compounds existing as networks of bonded atoms, such as silicon dioxide, are also held together by covalent bonds. Covalent bonds are often formed between nonmetal atoms.

covalent bond a bond formed when atoms share one or more pairs of electrons

Covalent compounds can be solids, liquids, or gases. Except for silicon dioxide and other compounds with network structures, most covalent compounds have low melting points—usually below 300°C. In compounds that are made of molecules, the molecules are free to move when the compound is dissolved or melted. But most of these molecules remain intact and do not conduct electricity because they are not charged.

Atoms joined by covalent bonds share electrons

Some atoms, like the hydrogen atoms in ***Figure 9,*** bond to form molecules. ***Figure 14A*** shows how two chlorine atoms bond to form a chlorine molecule, Cl_2. Before bonding, each atom has seven electrons in its outermost energy level. The atoms don't transfer electrons to one another because each needs to gain an electron. If each atom shares one electron with the other atom, then both atoms together have a full outermost energy level. That is, both atoms together have eight valence electrons. The way electrons are shared depends on which atoms are sharing the electrons. Two chlorine atoms are exactly alike. When they bond, electrons are equally attracted to the positive nucleus of each atom. Bonds like this one, in which electrons are shared equally, are called *nonpolar covalent bonds.*

VOCABULARY Skills Tip

Covalent bonds *form when atoms share pairs of* valence *electrons.*

The structural formula in ***Figure 14B*** shows how the chlorine atoms are connected in the molecule that forms. A single line drawn between two atoms indicates that the atoms share two electrons and are joined by one covalent bond.

Figure 14

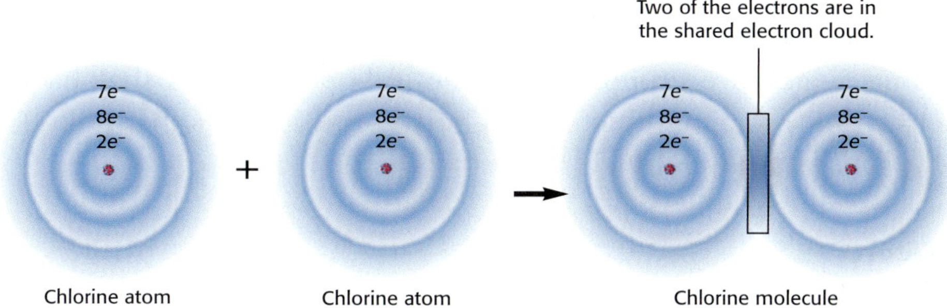

A Two chlorine atoms share electrons equally to form a *nonpolar covalent bond.*

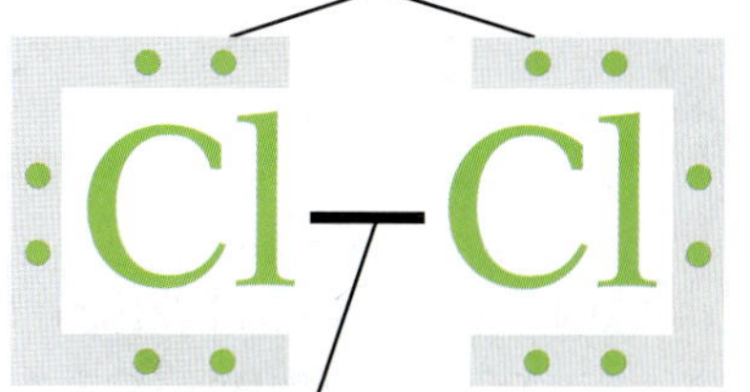

B A single line drawn between two chlorine atoms shows that the atoms share two electrons. Dots represent electrons that are not involved in bonding.

Figure 15

The elements oxygen and nitrogen have covalent bonds. Electrons not involved in bonding are represented by dots.

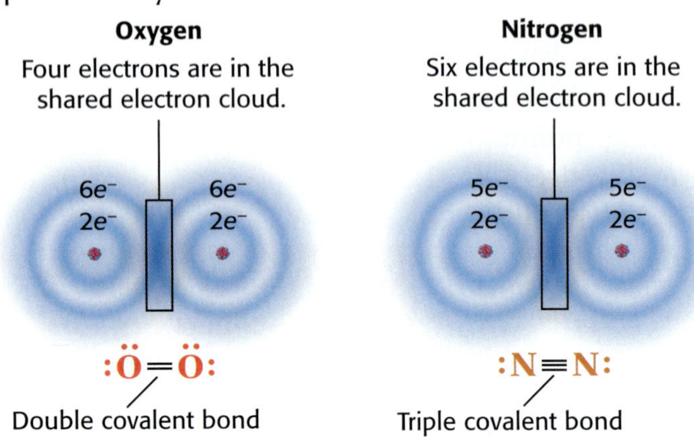
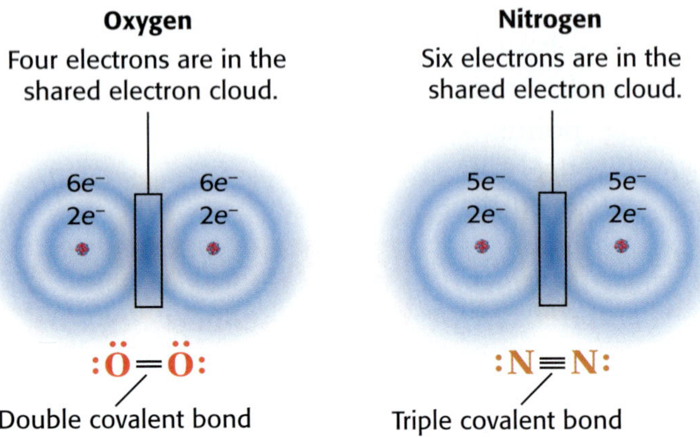

Atoms may share more than one pair of electrons

Figure 15 shows covalent bonding in oxygen gas, O_2 and nitrogen gas, N_2. Notice that the bond joining two oxygen atoms is represented by two lines. This means that two pairs of electrons (a total of four electrons) are shared to form a double covalent bond.

The bond joining two nitrogen atoms is represented by three lines. Two nitrogen atoms form a triple covalent bond by sharing three pairs of electrons (a total of six electrons).

The bond between two nitrogen atoms is stronger than the bond between two oxygen atoms. That's because more energy is needed to break a triple bond than to break a double bond. Triple and double bonds are also shorter than single bonds.

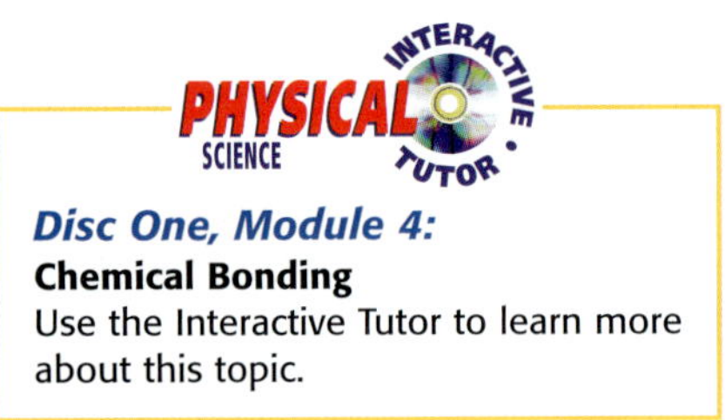

Disc One, Module 4:
Chemical Bonding
Use the Interactive Tutor to learn more about this topic.

Atoms do not always share electrons equally

When two different atoms share electrons, the electrons are not shared equally. The shared electrons are attracted to the nucleus of one atom more than the other. An unequal sharing of electrons forms a *polar covalent bond*.

Usually, electrons are more attracted to atoms of elements that are located farther to the right and closer to the top of the periodic table. The shading in ***Figure 16*** shows that the shared electrons in the ammonia gas, NH_3, in the headspace of this container, are closer to the nitrogen atom than they are to the hydrogen atoms.

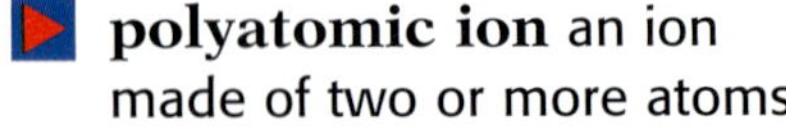

polyatomic ion an ion made of two or more atoms

Polyatomic Ions

Until now, we have talked about compounds that have either ionic or covalent bonds. But some compounds have both ionic and covalent bonds. Such compounds are made of **polyatomic ions,** which are groups of covalently bonded atoms that have either lost or gained electrons. A polyatomic ion acts the same as the ions you have already encountered.

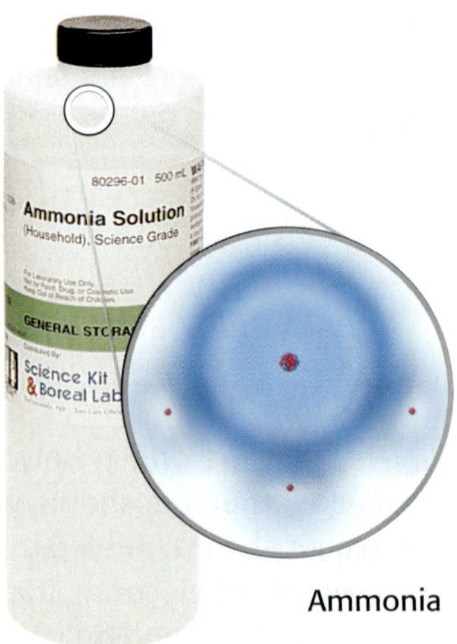

Figure 16

The darker shading around the nitrogen atom as compared to the hydrogen atoms shows that electrons are more attracted to nitrogen atoms than to hydrogen atoms. So the bonds in ammonia are *polar covalent bonds.*

There are many common polyatomic ions

Many compounds you use either contain or are made from polyatomic ions. For example, your toothpaste may contain baking soda. Another name for baking soda is sodium hydrogen carbonate, $NaHCO_3$. Hydrogen carbonate, HCO_3^-, is a polyatomic ion. Sodium carbonate, Na_2CO_3, is often used to make soaps and other cleaners and contains the carbonate ion, CO_3^{2-}. Sodium hydroxide, NaOH, has hydroxide ions, OH^-, and is also used to make soaps. A few of these polyatomic ions are shown in ***Figure 17.***

Oppositely charged polyatomic ions, like other ions, can bond to form compounds. Ammonium nitrate, NH_4NO_3, and ammonium sulfate, $(NH_4)_2SO_4$, both contain positively charged ammonium ions, NH_4^+. Nitrate, NO_3^-, and sulfate, SO_4^{2-}, are both negatively charged polyatomic ions.

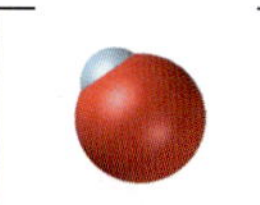

Hydroxide ion, OH^-

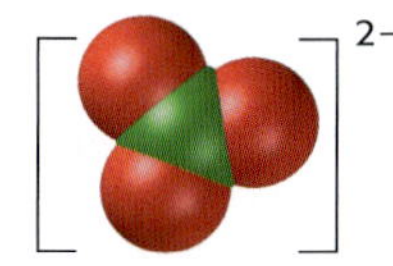

Carbonate ion, CO_3^{2-}

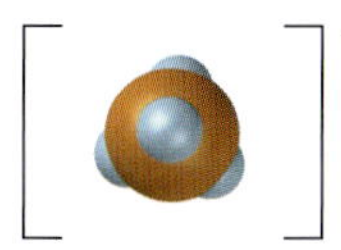

Ammonium ion, NH_4^+

Figure 17

The hydroxide ion (OH^-), carbonate ion (CO_3^{2-}), and ammonium ion (NH_4^+) are all polyatomic ions.

Parentheses group the atoms of a polyatomic ion

You might be wondering why the chemical formula for ammonium sulfate is written as $(NH_4)_2SO_4$ instead of as $N_2H_8SO_4$. The parentheses around the ammonium ion are there to remind you that it acts like a single ion. Parentheses group the atoms of the ammonium ion together to show that the subscript 2 applies to the whole ion. There are two ammonium ions for every sulfate ion. Parentheses are not needed in compounds like ammonium nitrate, NH_4NO_3, because there is a 1:1 ratio of ions.

Always keep in mind that a polyatomic ion's charge applies not only to the last atom in the formula but to the entire ion. The carbonate ion, CO_3^{2-}, has a 2− charge. This means that CO_3, not just the oxygen atom, has the negative charge.

Some polyatomic anion names relate to their oxygen content

You may have noticed that many polyatomic anions are made of oxygen. Most of their names end with *-ite* or *-ate*. These endings do not tell you exactly how many oxygen atoms are in the ion, but they do follow a pattern. Think about sulfate (SO_4^{2-}) and sulfite (SO_3^{2-}), nitrate (NO_3^-) and nitrite (NO_2^-), and chlorate (ClO_3^-) and chlorite (ClO_2^-). The charge of each ion pair is the same. But notice how the ions have different numbers of oxygen atoms. Their names also have different endings.

An *-ate* ending is used to name the ion with one more oxygen atom. The name of the ion with one less oxygen ends in *-ite*. ***Table 3,*** on the next page, lists several common polyatomic anions. As you look at this table, you'll notice that not all of the anions listed have names that end in *-ite* or *-ate*. That's because some polyatomic anions, like hydroxide (OH^-) and cyanide (CN^-), are not named according to any general rules.

INTEGRATING

SPACE SCIENCE

Most of the ions and molecules in space are not the same as those that are found on Earth or in Earth's atmosphere. C_3H, C_6H_2, and HCO^+ have all been found in space. So far, no one has been able to figure out how these unusual molecules and ions form in space.

Table 3 Some Common Polyatomic Anions

Ion name	Ion formula	Ion name	Ion formula
Acetate ion	$CH_3CO_2^-$	Hydroxide ion	OH^-
Carbonate ion	CO_3^{2-}	Hypochlorite ion	ClO^-
Chlorate ion	ClO_3^-	Nitrate ion	NO_3^-
Chlorite ion	ClO_2^-	Nitrite ion	NO_2^-
Cyanide ion	CN^-	Phosphate ion	PO_4^{3-}
Hydrogen carbonate ion	HCO_3^-	Phosphite ion	PO_3^{3-}
Hydrogen sulfate ion	HSO_4^-	Sulfate ion	SO_4^{2-}
Hydrogen sulfite ion	HSO_3^-	Sulfite ion	SO_3^{2-}

SECTION 2 REVIEW

SUMMARY

- Atoms bond when their valence electrons interact.
- Cations and anions attract each other to form ionic bonds.
- When ionic compounds are melted or dissolved in water, moving ions can conduct electricity.
- Atoms in metals are joined by metallic bonds.
- Metals conduct electricity because electrons can move from atom to atom.
- Covalent bonds form when atoms share electron pairs. Electrons may be shared equally or unequally.
- Polyatomic ions are covalently bonded atoms that have either lost or gained electrons. Their behavior resembles that of simple ions.

1. **Determine** if the following compounds are likely to have ionic or covalent bonds.
   a. magnesium oxide, MgO
   b. strontium chloride, $SrCl_2$
   c. ozone, O_3
   d. methanol, CH_3OH
2. **Identify** which two of the following substances will conduct electricity, and explain why.
   a. aluminum foil
   b. sugar, $C_{12}H_{22}O_{11}$, dissolved in water
   c. potassium hydroxide, KOH, dissolved in water
3. **Draw** the structural formula for acetylene. Atoms bond in the order HCCH. Carbon and hydrogen atoms share two electrons, and each carbon atom must have a total of four bonds. How many electrons do the carbon atoms share?
4. **Predict** whether a silver coin can conduct electricity. What kind of bonds does silver have?
5. **Describe** how it is possible for calcium hydroxide, $Ca(OH)_2$, to have both ionic and covalent bonds.
6. **Explain** why electrons are shared equally in oxygen, O_2, but not in carbon monoxide, CO.
7. **Analyze** whether dinitrogen tetroxide, N_2O_4, has covalent or ionic bonds. Describe how you reached this conclusion.
8. **Critical Thinking** *Bond energy* measures the energy per mole of a substance needed to break a bond. Which element has the greater bond energy, oxygen or nitrogen? (**Hint:** Which element has more bonds?)

SECTION 3

Compound Names and Formulas

OBJECTIVES

- **Name** simple ionic and covalent compounds.
- **Predict** the charge of a transition metal cation in an ionic compound.
- **Write** chemical formulas for simple ionic compounds.
- **Distinguish** a covalent compound's empirical formula from its molecular formula.

KEY TERMS

empirical formula
molecular formula

Just like elements, compounds have names that distinguish them from other compounds. Although the compounds BaF_2 and BF_3 may appear to have similar chemical formulas, they have very different names. BaF_2 is *barium fluoride,* and BF_3 is *boron trifluoride.* When talking about these compounds, you have little chance for confusing their names. You can see that the names of these compounds reflect the elements from which the compounds are formed.

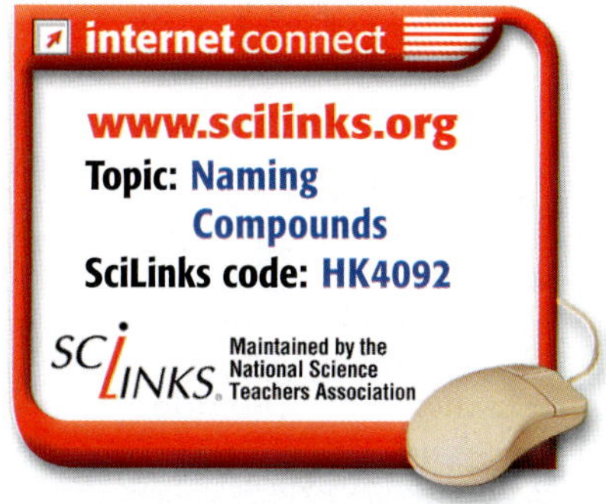

Naming Ionic Compounds

Ionic compounds are formed by the strong attractions between cations and anions. Both ions are important to the compound's structure, so it makes sense that both ions are included in the name.

Names of cations include the elements of which they are composed

In many cases, the name of the cation is just like the name of the element from which it is made. You have already seen this for many cations. For example, when an atom of the element *sodium* loses an electron, a *sodium ion,* Na^+, forms. Similarly, when a *calcium* atom loses two electrons, a *calcium ion,* Ca^{2+}, forms. And when an *aluminum* atom loses three electrons, an *aluminum ion,* Al^{3+}, forms. These and other common cations are listed in **Table 4.** Notice how ions of Group 1 elements have a 1+ charge and ions of Group 2 elements have a 2+ charge.

Table 4 Some Common Cations

Ion name and symbol	Ion charge
Cesium ion, Cs^+	1+
Lithium ion, Li^+	
Potassium ion, K^+	
Rubidium ion, Rb^+	
Sodium ion, Na^+	
Barium ion, Ba^{2+}	2+
Beryllium ion, Be^{2+}	
Calcium ion, Ca^{2+}	
Magnesium ion, Mg^{2+}	
Strontium ion, Sr^{2+}	
Aluminum ion, Al^{3+}	3+

Table 5 Some Common Anions

Element name and symbol	Ion name and symbol	Ion charge
Fluor~~ine~~, F	Fluoride ion, F^-	1−
Chlor~~ine~~, Cl	Chloride ion, Cl^-	
Brom~~ine~~, Br	Bromide ion, Br^-	
Iod~~ine~~, I	Iodide ion, I^-	
Ox~~ygen~~, O	Oxide ion, O^{2-}	2−
Sulf~~ur~~, S	Sulfide ion, S^{2-}	
Nitr~~ogen~~, N	Nitride ion, N^{3-}	3−

Names of anions are altered names of elements

An anion that is made of one element has a name similar to the element. The difference is the name's ending. **Table 5** lists some common anions and shows how they are named. Just like most cations, anions of elements in the same group of the periodic table have the same charge.

NaF is made of sodium ions, Na^+, and fluoride ions, F^-. Therefore, its name is *sodium fluoride.* **Figure 18** shows how calcium chloride gets its name.

Some cation names must show their charge

Think about the compounds FeO and Fe_2O_3. According to the rules you have learned so far, both of these compounds would be named *iron oxide,* even though they are not the same compound. Fe_2O_3, a component of rust, is a reddish brown solid that melts at 1565°C. FeO, on the other hand, is a black powder that melts at 1420°C. These different properties tell us that they are different compounds and should have different names.

Iron is a transition metal. Transition metals may form several cations—each with a different charge. A few of these cations are listed in **Table 6.** The charge of the iron cation in Fe_2O_3 is different from the charge of the iron cation in FeO. In cases like this, the cation name must be followed by a Roman numeral in parentheses. The Roman numeral shows the cation's charge. Fe_2O_3 is made of Fe^{3+} ions, so it is named *iron(III) oxide.* FeO is made of Fe^{2+} ions, so it is named *iron(II) oxide.*

$CaCl_2$

Ca^{2+} Cl^-

Calcium — Chloride

Figure 18

Ionic compounds are named for their positive and negative ions.

Table 6 Some Transition Metal Cations

Ion name	Ion symbol	Ion name	Ion symbol
Copper(I) ion	Cu^+	Chromium(II) ion	Cr^{2+}
Copper(II) ion	Cu^{2+}	Chromium(III) ion	Cr^{3+}
Iron(II) ion	Fe^{2+}	Cadmium(II) ion	Cd^{2+}
Iron(III) ion	Fe^{3+}	Titanium(II) ion	Ti^{2+}
Nickel(II) ion	Ni^{2+}	Titanium(III) ion	Ti^{3+}
Nickel(III) ion	Ni^{3+}	Titanium(IV) ion	Ti^{4+}

Determining the charge of a transition metal cation

How can you tell that the iron ion in Fe_2O_3 has a charge of 3+? Like all compounds, ionic compounds have a total charge of zero. This means that the total positive charges must equal the total negative charges. An oxide ion, O^{2-}, has a charge of 2−. Three of them have a total charge of 6−. That means the total positive charge in the formula must be 6+. For two iron ions to have a total charge of 6+, each ion must have a charge of 3+.

Writing Formulas for Ionic Compounds

You have seen how to determine the charge of each ion in a compound if you are given the compound's formula. Following a similar process, you can determine the chemical formula for a compound if you are given its name.

Math Skills

Writing Ionic Formulas What is the chemical formula for aluminum fluoride?

1 List the symbols for each ion.

Symbol for an aluminum ion from ***Table 4:*** Al^{3+}
Symbol for a fluoride ion from ***Table 5:*** F^-

2 Write the symbols for the ions with the cation first.

$Al^{3+}F^-$

3 Find the least common multiple of the ions' charges.

The least common multiple of 3 and 1 is 3. To make a neutral compound, you need a total of three positive charges and three negative charges.

To get three positive charges: you need only one Al^{3+} ion because $1 \times 3+ = 3+$.
To get three negative charges: you need three F^- ions because $3 \times 1- = 3-$.

4 Write the chemical formula, indicating with subscripts how many of each ion are needed to make a neutral compound.

$\mathbf{AlF_3}$

Once you have determined a chemical formula, always check the formula to see if it makes a neutral compound. For this example, the aluminum ion has a charge of 3+. The fluoride ion has a charge of only 1−, but there are three of them for a total of 3−.

(3+) + (3−) = 0, so the charges balance, and the formula is neutral.

Practice

Writing Ionic Formulas

Write formulas for the following ionic compounds.

1. lithium oxide
2. beryllium chloride
3. titanium(III) nitride
4. cobalt(III) hydroxide

Table 7 Prefixes Used to Name Covalent Compounds

Number of atoms	Prefix
1	*mono-*
2	*di-*
3	*tri-*
4	*tetra-*
5	*penta-*
6	*hexa-*
7	*hepta-*
8	*octa-*
9	*nona-*
10	*deca-*

N_2O_4

Dinitrogen tetroxide

Figure 19

One molecule of *di*nitrogen *tetr*oxide has *two* nitrogen atoms and *four* oxygen atoms.

empirical formula the composition of a compound in terms of the relative numbers and kinds of atoms in the simplest ratio

Naming Covalent Compounds

Covalent compounds, like SiO_2 (silicon dioxide) and CO_2 (carbon dioxide), are named using different rules than those used to name ionic compounds.

Numerical prefixes are used to name covalent compounds of two elements

For two-element covalent compounds, numerical prefixes tell how many atoms of each element are in the molecule. **Table 7** lists some of these prefixes. If there is only one atom of the first element, it does not get a prefix. Whichever element is farther to the right in the periodic table is named second and ends in *-ide.*

There are one boron atom and three fluorine atoms in *boron trifluoride,* BF_3. *Dinitrogen tetroxide,* N_2O_4, is made of two nitrogen atoms and four oxygen atoms, as shown in **Figure 19.** Notice how the *a* in *tetra* is dropped to make the name easier to say.

Chemical Formulas for Covalent Compounds

Emeralds, shown in **Figure 20,** are made of a mineral called beryl. The chemical formula for beryl is $Be_3Al_2Si_6O_{18}$. But how did people determine this formula? It took some experiments. Chemical formulas like this one were determined by first measuring the mass of each element in the compound.

A compound's simplest formula is its empirical formula

Once the mass of each element in a sample of the compound is known, scientists can calculate the compound's **empirical formula,** or simplest formula. An empirical formula tells us the smallest whole-number ratio of atoms that are in a compound. Formulas for most ionic compounds are empirical formulas.

Covalent compounds have empirical formulas, too. The empirical formula for water is H_2O. It tells you that the ratio of hydrogen atoms to oxygen atoms is 2:1. Scientists have to analyze unknown compounds to determine their empirical formulas.

Figure 20

Emerald gemstones are cut from the mineral beryl. Very tiny amounts of chromium(III) oxide impurity in the gemstones gives them their beautiful green color.

Determining empirical formulas

If a 142 g sample of an unknown compound contains only the elements phosphorus and oxygen and is found to contain 62 g of P and 80 g of O, its empirical formula is easy to calculate. This process is shown in ***Figure 21.***

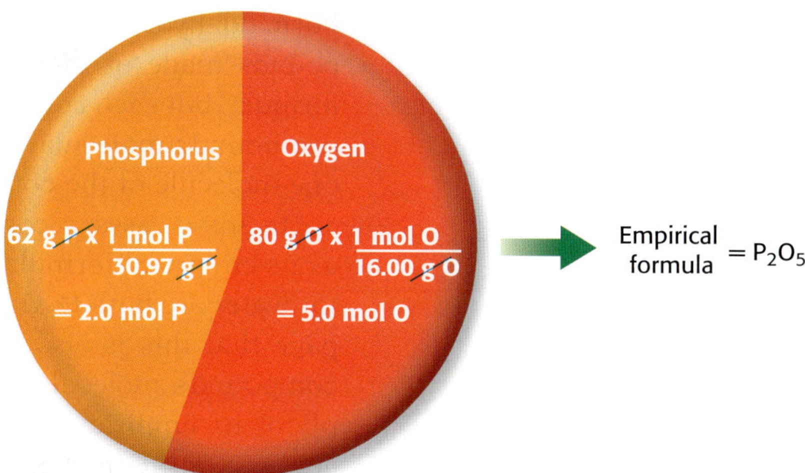

Figure 21

Once you determine the mass of each element in a compound, you can calculate the amount of each element in moles. The empirical formula for the compound is the ratio of these amounts.

Different compounds can have the same empirical formula

It's possible for several compounds to have the same empirical formula because empirical formulas only represent a ratio of atoms. Formaldehyde, acetic acid, and glucose all have the empirical formula CH_2O, as shown in ***Table 8.*** These three compounds are not at all alike, though. Formaldehyde is sometimes used to keep dead organisms from decaying so that they can be studied. Acetic acid gives vinegar its sour taste and strong smell. And glucose is a sugar that plays a very important role in your body chemistry. Some other formula must be used to distinguish these three very different compounds.

Table 8 **Empirical and Molecular Formulas for Some Compounds**

Compound	Empirical formula	Molar mass	Molecular formula	Structure
Formaldehyde	CH_2O	30.03 g/mol	CH_2O	
Acetic acid	CH_2O	60.06 g/mol	$2 \times CH_2O = C_2H_4O_2$	
Glucose	CH_2O	180.18 g/mol	$6 \times CH_2O = C_6H_{12}O_6$	

Molecular formulas are determined from empirical formulas

Formaldehyde, acetic acid, and glucose are all covalent compounds made of molecules. They all have the same empirical formula, but each compound has its own **molecular formula.** A compound's molecular formula tells you how many atoms are in one molecule of the compound.

molecular formula
a chemical formula that shows the number and kinds of atoms in a molecule, but not the arrangement of atoms

In some cases, a compound's molecular formula is the same as its empirical formula. The empirical and molecular formulas for water are both H_2O. You can see from ***Table 8*** on the previous page that this is also true for formaldehyde. In other cases, a compound's molecular formula is a small whole-number multiple of its empirical formula. The molecular formula for acetic acid is two times its empirical formula, and that of glucose is six times its empirical formula.

SECTION 3 REVIEW

SUMMARY

- To name an ionic compound, first name the cation and then the anion.
- If an element can form cations with different charges, the cation name must include the ion's charge. The charge is written as a Roman numeral in parentheses.
- Prefixes are used to name covalent compounds made of two different elements.
- An empirical formula tells the relative numbers of atoms of each element in a compound.
- A molecular formula tells the actual numbers of atoms in one molecule of a compound.
- Covalent compounds have both empirical and molecular formulas.

1. **Name** the following ionic compounds, specifying the charge of any transition metal cations.
   a. FeI_2 **c.** $CrCl_2$
   b. MnF_3 **d.** CuS
2. **Name** the following covalent compounds:
   a. As_2O_5 **c.** P_4S_3 **e.** SeO_2
   b. SiI_4 **d.** P_4O_{10} **f.** PCl_3
3. **Explain** why Roman numerals must be included in the names of MnO_2 and Mn_2O_7. Name both of these compounds.
4. **Identify** how many fluorine atoms are in one molecule of sulfur hexafluoride.

Math Skills

5. **Critical Thinking** An unknown compound contains 49.47% C, 5.20% H, 28.85% N, and a certain percentage of oxygen. What percentage of the compound must be oxygen? (**Hint:** The sum of the percentages should equal 100%.)
6. What is the charge of the cadmium cation in cadmium cyanide, $Cd(CN)_2$, a compound used in electroplating? Explain your reasoning.
7. Determine the chemical formulas for the following ionic compounds:
   a. magnesium sulfate **c.** chromium(II) fluoride
   b. rubidium bromide **d.** nickel(I) carbonate

SECTION 4

Organic and Biochemical Compounds

INTEGRATING TECHNOLOGY and Society

OBJECTIVES

- **Describe** how carbon atoms bond covalently to form organic compounds.
- **Identify** the names and structures of groups of simple organic compounds and polymers.
- **Identify** what makes up the polymers that are essential to life.

KEY TERMS

organic compound
polymer
carbohydrate
protein
amino acid

The word *organic* has many different meanings. Most people associate the word *organic* with living organisms. Perhaps you have heard of or eaten organically grown fruits or vegetables. What this means is that they were grown using fertilizers and pesticides that come from plant and animal matter. In chemistry, the word *organic* is used to describe certain compounds.

Organic Compounds

An **organic compound** is a covalently bonded compound made of molecules. Organic compounds contain carbon and, almost always, hydrogen. Other atoms, such as oxygen, nitrogen, sulfur, and phosphorus, are also found in some organic compounds.

organic compound a covalently bonded compound that contains carbon, excluding carbonates and oxides

Many ingredients of familiar substances are organic compounds. The effective ingredient in aspirin is a form of the organic compound acetylsalicylic acid, $C_9H_8O_4$. Sugarless chewing gum also has organic compounds as ingredients. Two ingredients are the sweeteners sorbitol, $C_6H_{14}O_6$, and aspartame, $C_{14}H_{18}N_2O_5$, both of which are shown in ***Figure 22.***

Figure 22
The organic compounds sorbitol and aspartame sweeten some sugarless chewing gums.

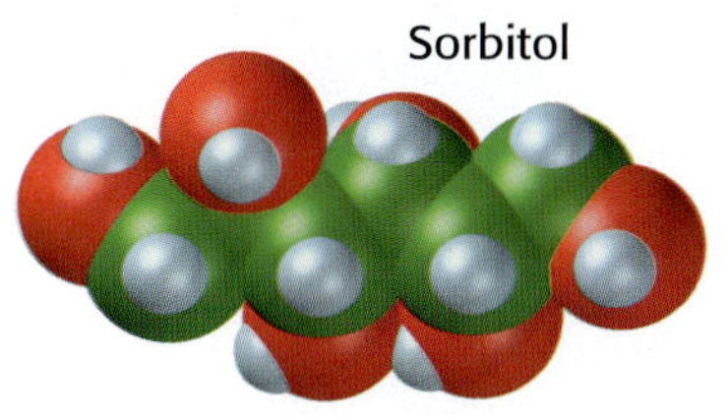

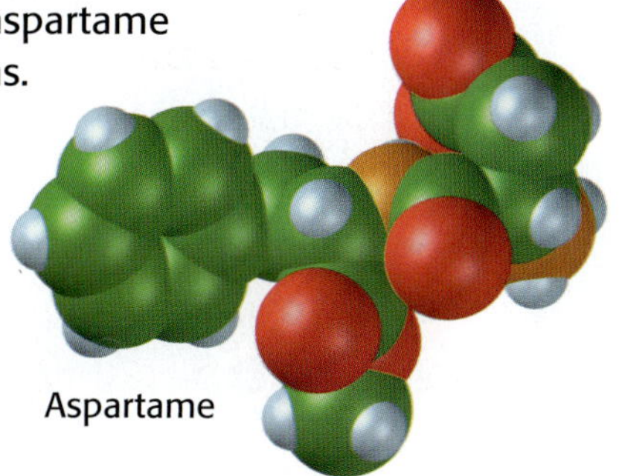

Carbon atoms form four covalent bonds in organic compounds

When a compound is made of only carbon and hydrogen atoms, it is called a *hydrocarbon*. Methane, CH_4, is the simplest hydrocarbon. Its structure is shown in **Figure 23.** Methane gas is formed when living matter, such as plants, decay, so it is often found in swamps and marshes. The natural gas used in Bunsen burners is also mostly methane. Carbon atoms have four valence electrons to use for bonding. In methane, each of these electrons forms a different C—H single bond.

A carbon atom may also share two of its electrons with two from another atom to form a double bond. Or a carbon atom may share three electrons to form a triple bond. However, a carbon atom can never form more than a total of four bonds.

Figure 23
Methane is an alkane that has four C—H bonds.

Alkanes have single covalent bonds

Alkanes are hydrocarbons that have only single covalent bonds. **Figure 23** shows that methane, the simplest alkane, has only C—H bonds. But alkanes can also have C—C bonds. You can see from **Figure 24** that ethane, C_2H_6, has a C—C bond in addition to six C—H bonds. Notice how each carbon atom in both of these compounds bonds to four other atoms.

Many gas grills are fueled by another alkane, propane, C_3H_8. Propane is made of three bonded carbon atoms. Each carbon atom on the end of the molecule forms three bonds with three hydrogen atoms, as shown in **Figure 25.** Each of these end carbon atoms forms its fourth bond with the central carbon atom. The central carbon atom shares its two remaining electrons with two hydrogen atoms. You can see only one hydrogen atom bonded to the central carbon atom in **Figure 25** because the second hydrogen atom is on the other side.

Figure 24
Ethane, another alkane, has one C—C bond and six C—H bonds.

Figure 25
This camper is preparing his dinner on a gas grill fueled by propane. Propane is an alkane that has two C—C bonds and eight C—H bonds.

Arrangements of carbon atoms in alkanes

The carbon atoms in methane, ethane, and propane all line up in a row because that is their only possible arrangement. When there are more than three bonded carbon atoms, the carbon atoms do not always line up in a row. When they do line up, the alkane is called a *normal alkane,* or *n*-alkane for short. **Table 9** shows chemical formulas for the *n*-alkanes that have up to 10 carbon atoms. *Condensed structural formulas* are also included in the table to show how the atoms bond.

The carbon atoms in any alkane with more than three carbon atoms can have more than one possible arrangement. Carbon atom chains may be branched or unbranched, and they can even form rings. **Figure 26** shows some of the possible ways six carbon atoms can be arranged when they form hydrocarbons with only single covalent bonds.

Table 9 First 10 *n*-Alkanes

n-Alkane	Molecular formula	Condensed structural formula
Methane	CH_4	CH_4
Ethane	C_2H_6	CH_3CH_3
Propane	C_3H_8	$CH_3CH_2CH_3$
Butane	C_4H_{10}	$CH_3(CH_2)_2CH_3$
Pentane	C_5H_{12}	$CH_3(CH_2)_3CH_3$
Hexane	C_6H_{14}	$CH_3(CH_2)_4CH_3$
Heptane	C_7H_{16}	$CH_3(CH_2)_5CH_3$
Octane	C_8H_{18}	$CH_3(CH_2)_6CH_3$
Nonane	C_9H_{20}	$CH_3(CH_2)_7CH_3$
Decane	$C_{10}H_{22}$	$CH_3(CH_2)_8CH_3$

Alkane chemical formulas usually follow a pattern

Except for cyclic alkanes like cyclohexane, the chemical formulas for alkanes follow a special pattern. The number of hydrogen atoms is always two more than twice the number of carbon atoms. This pattern is shown by the chemical formula C_nH_{2n+2}.

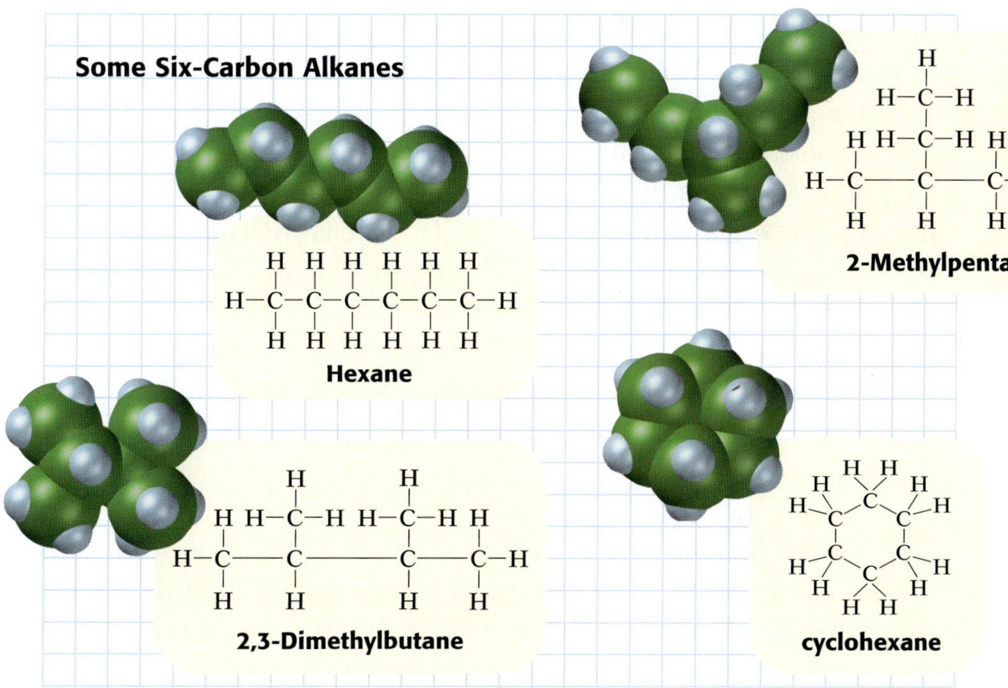

Figure 26

Hexane, 2-methylpentane, 2,3-dimethylbutane, and cyclohexane are some of the forms six carbon atoms with single covalent bonds may take.

Figure 27
The peaches in this plastic container, which is made by joining propene molecules, release ethene gas as they ripen.

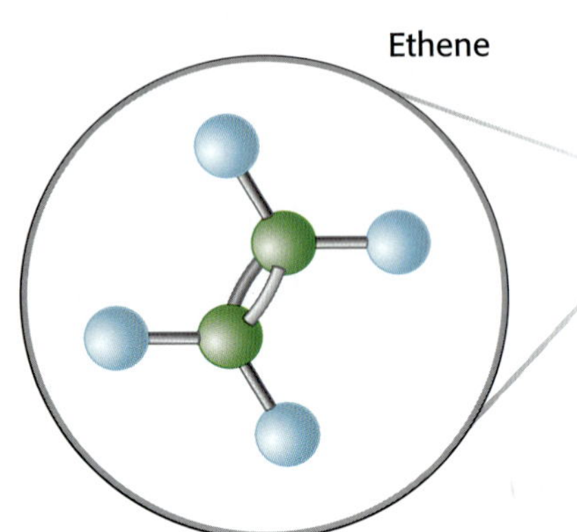

Alkenes have double carbon-carbon bonds

Alkenes are also hydrocarbons. Alkenes are different from alkanes because they have at least one double covalent bond between carbon atoms. This is shown by C=C. Alkenes are named like alkanes but with the *-ane* ending replaced by *-ene*.

The simplest alkene is ethene (or ethylene), C_2H_4. Ethene is formed when fruit ripens. Propene (or propylene), C_3H_6, is used to make rubbing alcohol and some plastics. The structures of both compounds are shown in **Figure 27.**

Alcohols have −OH groups

Alcohols are organic compounds that are made of oxygen as well as carbon and hydrogen. Alcohols have *hydroxyl,* or −OH, groups. The alcohol methanol, CH_3OH, is sometimes added to another alcohol ethanol, CH_3CH_2OH, to make denatured alcohol. Denatured alcohol is found in many familiar products, as shown in **Figure 28.** Isopropanol, which is found in rubbing alcohol, has the chemical formula C_3H_8O, or $(CH_3)_2CHOH$. You may have noticed how the names of these three alcohols all end in *-ol.* This is true for most alcohols.

Figure 28
Many products contain a mixture of the alcohols methanol and ethanol. This mixture is called "denatured alcohol."

Alcohol molecules behave similarly to water molecules

A methanol molecule is like a water molecule except that one of the hydrogen atoms is replaced by a methyl, or $-CH_3$, group. Just like water molecules, neighboring alcohol molecules are attracted to one another. That's why many alcohols are liquids at room temperature. Alcohols have much higher boiling points than alkanes of similar size.

Polymers

What do the DNA inside the cells of your body, rubber, wood, and plastic milk jugs have in common? They are all made of large molecules called **polymers.**

Many polymers have repeating subunits

Some small organic molecules bond to form long chains called polymers. Polyethene, which is also known as polyethylene or polythene, is the polymer plastic milk jugs are made of. The name *polyethene* tells its structure. *Poly* means "many." *Ethene* is an alkene whose chemical formula is C_2H_4. Therefore, polyethene is "many ethenes," as shown in ***Figure 29.*** The original molecule, in this case C_2H_4, is called a *monomer.*

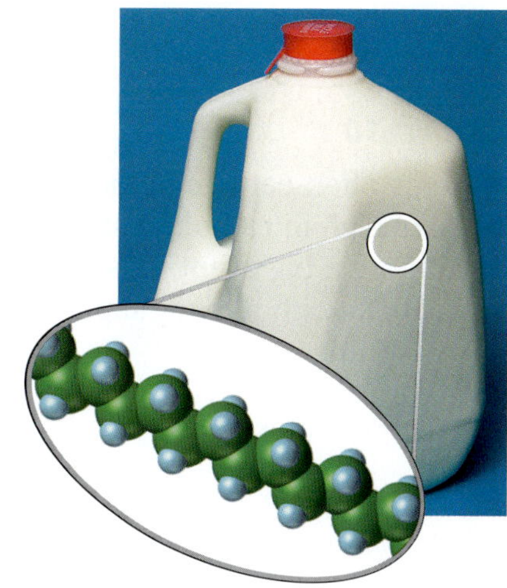

Figure 29 Polyethene

Polyethene is a polymer made of many repeating ethene units. As the polymer forms, ethene's double bonds are replaced by single bonds.

Some polymers are natural; others are man-made

Rubber, wood, cotton, wool, starch, protein, and DNA are all natural polymers. Man-made polymers are usually either plastics or fibers. Most plastics are flexible and easily molded, whereas fibers form long, thin strands.

Some polymers can be used as both plastics and fibers. For example, polypropene (polypropylene) is molded to make plastic containers, like the one shown in ***Figure 27,*** as well as some parts for cars and appliances. It is also used to make ropes, carpet, and artificial turf for athletic fields.

polymer a large molecule that is formed by more than five monomers, or small units

The elasticity of a polymer is determined by its structure

As with all substances, the properties of a polymer are determined by its structure. Polymer molecules are like long, thin chains. A small piece of plastic or a single fiber is made of billions of these chains. Polymer molecules can be likened to spaghetti. Like a bowl of spaghetti, the chains are tangled but can slide over each other. Milk jugs are made of polyethene, a plastic made of such noodlelike chains. You can crush or dent a milk jug because the plastic is flexible. Once the jug has been crushed, though, it does not return to its original shape. That's because polyethene is not elastic.

When the chains are connected to each other, or cross-linked, the polymer's properties change. Some become more elastic and can be likened to a volleyball net. Like a volleyball net, an elastic polymer can stretch. When the polymer is released, it returns to its original shape. Rubber bands are elastic polymers. As long as a rubber band is not stretched too far, it can shrink back to its original form.

Quick ACTIVITY

Polymer Memory

Polymers that return to their original shape after stretching can be thought of as having a "memory." In this activity, you will compare the memory of a rubber band with that of the plastic rings that hold a six-pack of cans together.

1. Which polymer stretches better without breaking?
2. Which one has better memory?
3. Warm the stretched six-pack holder over a hot plate, being careful not to melt it. Does it retain its memory?

Figure 30

Athletes often eat lots of foods that are high in carbohydrates the day before a big event. This provides them with a ready supply of stored energy.

Biochemical Compounds

Biochemical compounds are naturally occurring organic compounds that are very important to living things. Carbohydrates give you energy. Proteins form important parts of your body, like muscles, tendons, fingernails, and hair. The DNA inside your cells gives your body information about what proteins you need. Each of these biochemical compounds is a polymer.

- **carbohydrate** any organic compound that is made of carbon, hydrogen, and oxygen and that provides nutrients to the cells of living things
- **protein** an organic compound that is made of one or more chains of amino acids and that is a principal component of all cells
- **amino acid** any one of 20 different organic molecules that contain a carboxyl and an amino group and that combine to form proteins

Many carbohydrates are made of glucose

The sugar glucose is a **carbohydrate.** Glucose provides energy to living things. Starch, also a carbohydrate, is made of many bonded glucose molecules. Plants store their energy as chains of starch.

Processes in the human body involve specific biochemical reactions governed by biochemical principles. For example, when you eat starchy foods, such as potatoes and pasta noodles, enzymes in your body break down the starch. This makes glucose available as a nutrient for your cells. Glucose that is not needed right away is stored as *glycogen.* When you become active, glycogen breaks apart and glucose molecules give you energy. Athletes often eat starchy foods so they will have more energy when they exert themselves later on, as shown in ***Figure 30.***

Proteins are polymers of amino acids

Starch is made of only glucose. **Proteins,** on the other hand, are made of many different molecules that are called **amino acids.** Amino acids are made of carbon, hydrogen, oxygen, and nitrogen. Some amino acids also contain sulfur. There are 20 amino acids found in naturally occurring proteins. The way these amino acids combine determines which protein is made.

Proteins are long chains made of amino acids. A small protein, insulin, is shown in ***Figure 31.*** Many proteins are made of thousands of bonded amino acid molecules. This means that millions of different proteins can be made with very different properties. When you eat foods that contain proteins, such as cheese, your digestive system breaks down the proteins into individual amino acids. Later, your cells bond the amino acids in a different order to form whatever protein your body needs.

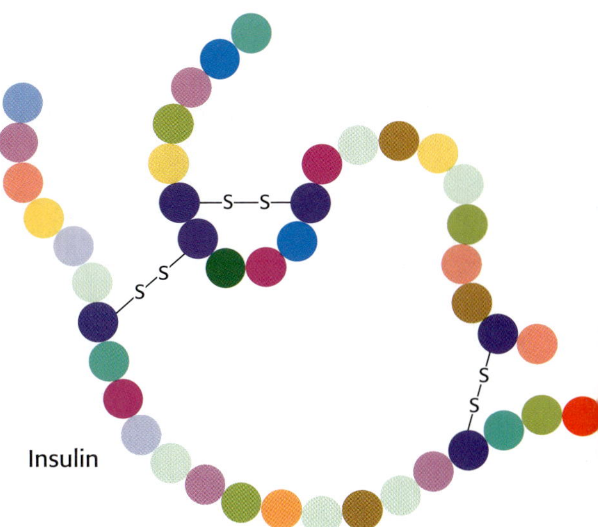

Figure 31

Insulin controls the use and storage of glucose in your body. Each color in the chain represents a different amino acid.

DNA is a polymer with a complex structure

Your DNA determines your entire genetic makeup. It is made of organic molecules containing carbon, hydrogen, oxygen, nitrogen, and phosphorus.

Figuring out the complex structure of DNA was one of the greatest scientific challenges of the twentieth century. Instead of forming one chain, like many proteins and polymers, DNA is in the form of paired chains, or strands. It has the shape of a twisted ladder known as a *double helix*.

What properties does a polymer have?

Materials
- *water*
- *white glue*
- *borax*
- *250 mL beakers (2)*
- *plastic spoons*
- *plastic sandwich bags*

SAFETY CAUTION Wear safety goggles, gloves, and a laboratory apron. Be sure to work in an open space and wear clothes that can be cleaned easily.

1. In one beaker, mix 4 g borax with 100 mL water, and stir well.
2. In the second beaker, mix equal parts of glue and water. This solution will determine the amount of new material made. The volume of diluted glue should be between 100 and 200 mL.
3. Pour the borax solution into the beaker containing the glue, and stir well using a plastic spoon.
4. When it becomes too thick to stir, remove the material from the cup and knead it with your fingers. You can store this new material in a plastic sandwich bag.

Analysis

1. What happens to the new material when it is stretched, or rolled into a ball and bounced?
2. Compare the properties of the glue with those of the new material.
3. The properties of the new material resulted from the bonds between the borax and the glue particles. If too little borax were used, in what way would the properties of the new material differ?
4. Does the new material have the properties of a polymer? Explain how you reached this conclusion.

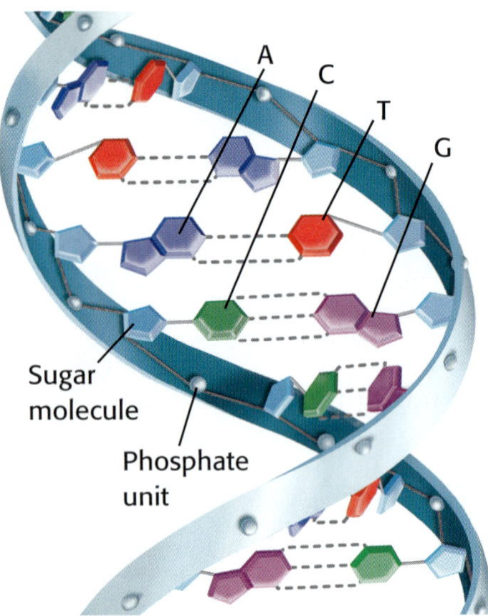

Figure 32

In DNA, cytosine, C, always pairs with guanine, G. Adenine, A, always pairs with thymine, T.

Your body has many copies of your DNA

Most cells in your body have a copy of your genetic material in the form of chromosomes made of DNA. For new cells to have the right amount of DNA, the DNA must be copied. Copying cannot happen unless the two DNA strands are first separated.

Proteins called helicases unwind DNA by separating the paired strands. Proteins called DNA polymerases then pair up new monomers with those already on the strand. At the end of this process, there are two strands of DNA.

DNA's structure resembles a twisted ladder

DNA's structure can be likened to a ladder. Alternating sugar molecules and phosphate units correspond to the ladder's sides, as shown in ***Figure 32.*** Attached to each sugar molecule is one of four possible DNA monomers—adenine, thymine, cytosine, or guanine. These DNA monomers pair up with DNA monomers attached to the opposite strand in a predictable way, as shown in ***Figure 32.*** Together, the DNA monomer pairs make up the rungs of the ladder.

SECTION 4 REVIEW

SUMMARY

- Alkanes have C–C and C–H bonds.
- Alkenes have C=C and C–H bonds.
- Alcohols have one or more –OH groups.
- Polymers form when small organic molecules bond to form long chains.
- Biochemical compounds important to living things are often polymers.
- Sugars and starches are carbohydrates that provide energy.
- Amino acids bond to form polymers called proteins.
- DNA is a polymer shaped like a twisted ladder.

1. **Identify** the following compounds as alkanes, alkenes, or alcohols based on their names:
   a. 2-methylpentane
   b. 3-methyloctane
   c. 1-nonene
   d. 2-butanol
   e. 3-heptene
   f. cyclohexanol
2. **Explain** why the compound CBr_5 does not exist. Give an acceptable chemical formula for a compound made of only carbon and bromine.
3. **Determine** how many hydrogen atoms a compound has if it is a hydrocarbon and its carbon atom skeleton is C=C–C=C.
4. **Compare** the structures and properties of carbohydrates with those of proteins.
5. **Identify** which compound is an alkane: CH_2O, C_6H_{14}, or C_3H_4. Explain your reasoning.
6. **Critical Thinking** *Alkynes,* like alkanes and alkenes, are hydrocarbons. Alkynes have carbon-carbon triple covalent bonds, or C≡C bonds. Draw the structure of the alkyne that has the chemical formula C_3H_4. Can you guess the name of this compound?

Study Skills

KWL Notes

KWL stands for "what I **K**now—what I **W**ant to know—what I **L**earned". The KWL strategy helps you relate your new ideas and concepts with those you have already learned.

1. **Read the section objectives.**

   We'll use the first objective, "Distinguish between compounds and mixtures," from Section 1.

2. **Divide a blank sheet of paper into three columns, and label the columns "What I know," "What I want to know," and "What I learned."**

3. **In the first column, write what information you know about the objective.**

4. **In the second column, write the information that you want to know about the objective.**

5. **After you have read the section, write in the third column what you have learned.**

What I know	What I want to know	What I have learned
water is a compound mixtures can be separated grape juice is a mixture	how to distinguish between compounds and mixture	Compounds are held together by chemical bonds, but mixtures are not. Compounds are always made of the same proportion of elements, but mixtures are not. Substances in mixtures keep their own identities.

Practice

Use the remaining objectives from Section 1 to create a table of KWL notes. Compare the ideas you wrote down in the first column with the items in the third column. If some of your initial ideas are incorrect, cross them out.

CHAPTER 5 REVIEW

Chapter Highlights

Before you begin, review the summaries of the key ideas of each section, found at the end of each section. The key vocabulary terms are listed on the first page of each section.

UNDERSTANDING CONCEPTS

1. Which of the following is not true of compounds made of molecules?
   a. They may exist as liquids.
   b. They may exist as solids.
   c. They may exist as gases.
   d. They always have very high melting points.

2. Compounds are different from mixtures because
   a. compounds are held together by chemical bonds.
   b. each substance in a compound maintains its own properties.
   c. each original substance in a compound remains chemically unchanged.
   d. mixtures are held together by chemical bonds.

3. Crystals of salt, called sodium chloride, are
   a. made of molecules.
   b. made of a network of ions.
   c. chemically similar to sugar crystals.
   d. weak solids.

4. Ionic solids
   a. are formed by networks of ions that have the same charge.
   b. melt at very low temperatures.
   c. have very regular structures.
   d. are sometimes found as gases at room temperature.

5. A chemical bond can be defined as
   a. a force that joins atoms together.
   b. a force blending nuclei together.
   c. a force caused by electric repulsion.
   d. All of the above

6. Which substance has ionic bonds?
   a. CO
   b. CO_2
   c. KCl
   d. O_2

7. The chemical formula for calcium chloride is
   a. CaCl.
   b. $CaCl_2$.
   c. Ca_2Cl.
   d. Ca_2Cl_2.

8. All organic compounds
   a. come only from living organisms.
   b. contain only carbon and hydrogen.
   c. are biochemical compounds.
   d. have atoms connected by covalent bonds.

USING VOCABULARY

9. Compare the chemical structure of oxygen difluoride with that of carbon dioxide. Which compound has the larger bond angle?

Carbon dioxide

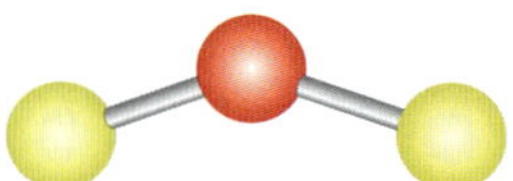
Oxygen difluoride

10. Name the following *covalent* compounds:
   a. SF_4
   b. N_2O
   c. PCl_3
   d. P_2O_5

11. Explain why *proteins* and *carbohydrates* are *polymers*. What is each polymer made of?

12. Compare *ionic bonds* and *covalent bonds*, and list two differences between them.

13. What does an *organic compound* contain? List several organic compounds that can be found in your body or in your daily life.

14. What is a *hydroxyl* group? What organic compound contains a hydroxyl group?

15. What is a *hydrocarbon* made of? Name the most simple hydrocarbon.

BUILDING MATH SKILLS

16. Graphing Which of the graphs below shows how bond length and bond energy are related? Describe the flawed relationships shown by each of the other graphs.

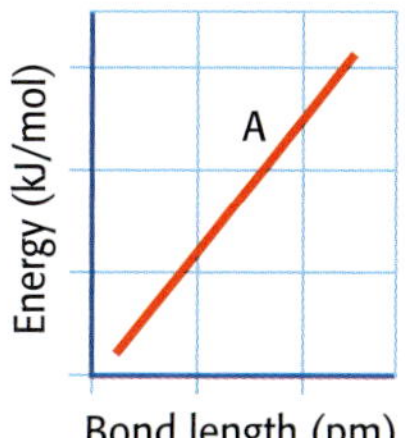

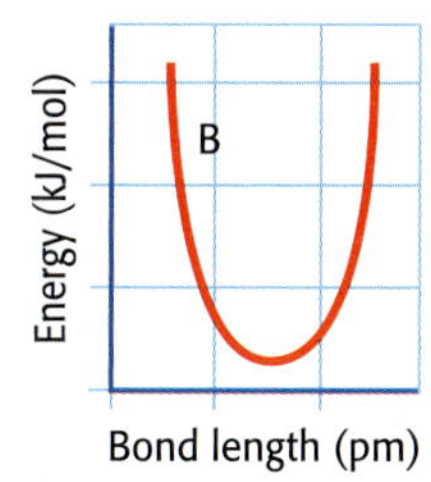

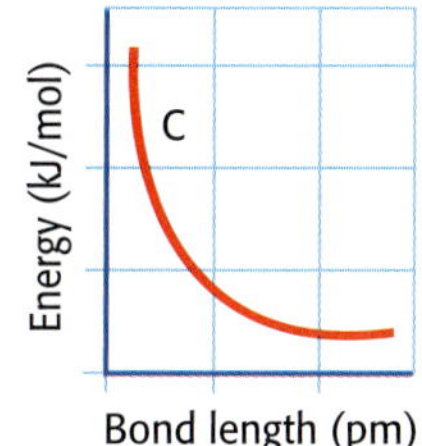

17. Graphing The melting points of elements in the same group of the periodic table follow a pattern. A similar pattern is also seen among the melting points of ionic compounds when the cations are made from elements that are in the same group. To see this, plot the melting point of each of the ionic compounds in the table below on the *y*-axis and the average atomic mass of the element that the cation is made from on the *x*-axis.

- **a.** What trend do you notice in the melting points as you move down Group 2?
- **b.** $BeCl_2$ has a melting point of 405°C. Is this likely to be an ionic compound like the others? Explain. (**Hint:** Locate beryllium in the periodic table.)
- **c.** Predict the melting point of the ionic compound $RaCl_2$. (**Hint:** Check the periodic table, and compare radium's location with the location of magnesium, calcium, strontium, and barium.)

Compound	Melting point (°C)
$MgCl_2$	714
$CaCl_2$	782
$SrCl_2$	875
$BaCl_2$	963

18. Writing Ionic Formulas Determine the chemical formula for each of the following ionic compounds:

- **a.** strontium nitrate, an ingredient in some fireworks, signal flares, and matches
- **b.** sodium cyanide, a compound used in electroplating and treating metals
- **c.** chromium(III) hydroxide, a compound used to tan and dye substances

THINKING CRITICALLY

19. Evaluating Data A substance is a solid at room temperature. It is unable to conduct electricity as a solid but can conduct electricity as a liquid. This compound melts at 755°C. Would you expect this compound to have ionic, metallic, or covalent bonds?

20. Creative Thinking Dodecane is a combustible organic compound used in jet fuel research. It is an *n*-alkane made of 12 carbon atoms. How many hydrogen atoms does dodecane have? Draw the structural formula for dodecane.

21. Applying Knowledge The length of a bond depends upon its type. Predict the relative lengths of the carbon-carbon bonds in the following molecules, and explain your reasoning.

```
   H  H          H       H
   |  |           \     /
H—C—C—H            C=C          H—C≡C—H
   |  |           /     \
   H  H          H       H
```

Ethane | **Ethene** | **Ethyne**

22. Critical Thinking A classmate insists that sodium gains a positive charge when it becomes an ion because it gains a proton. Explain this student's error.

23. **Critical Thinking** Describe what attractive force(s) must be overcome to melt ice.

DEVELOPING LIFE/WORK SKILLS

24. **Working Cooperatively** For one day, write down all of the ionic compounds listed on the labels of the foods you eat. Also write down the approximate mass you eat of each compound. As a class, make a master list in the form of a computer spreadsheet that includes all of the ionic compounds eaten by the whole class. Identify which compounds were eaten by the most people. Together, create a poster describing the dietary guidelines for the ionic compound that was eaten most often. **COMPUTER SKILL**

25. **Making Decisions** People on low-sodium diets must limit their intake of table salt. Luckily, there are salt substitutes that do not contain sodium. Research different kinds of salt substitutes, and describe how each one affects your body. Determine which salt substitute you would use if you were on a low-sodium diet.

26. **Locating Information** Numerical recycling codes identify the composition of a plastic so that it can be sorted and recycled. For each of the recycling codes, 1–6, identify the plastic, its physical properties, and at least one product made of this plastic.

27. **Interpreting and Communicating** Covalently bonded solids, such as silicon, an element used in computer components, are harder than some pure metals. Research theories that explain the hardness of covalently bonded solids and their usefulness in the computer industry. Present your findings to the class.

INTEGRATING CONCEPTS

28. **Connection to Health** The figure below shows how atoms are bonded in a molecule of vitamin C. Which elements is vitamin C made of? What is its molecular formula? Write a paragraph explaining some of the health benefits of taking vitamin C supplements. **WRITING SKILL**

29. **Concept Mapping** Copy the unfinished concept map below onto a sheet of paper. Complete the map by writing the correct word or phrase in the lettered boxes.

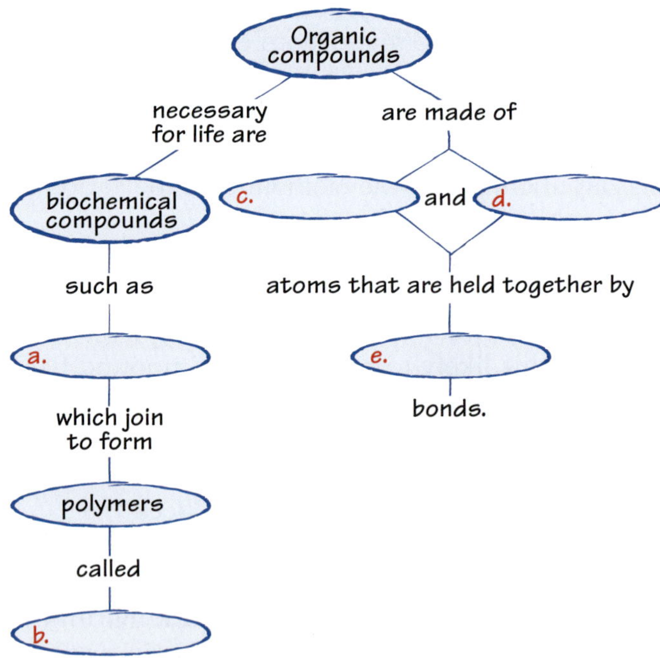

Standardized Test Prep

Understanding Concepts

Directions (1–3): **For *each* question, write on a separate sheet of paper the letter of the correct answer.**

1 What causes atoms to form chemical bonds with other atoms?
- **A.** They want to have filled outer orbitals.
- **B.** When two atoms get close together, they merge into one.
- **C.** The interaction of valence electrons forms a more stable configuration.
- **D.** The attraction of the nuclei for one another causes atoms to share electrons.

2 Which of the following pairs of atoms is most likely to form a covalently bonded compound?
- **F.** bromine and lithium
- **G.** helium and fluorine
- **H.** nitrogen and iodine
- **I.** nitrogen and copper

3 Which of the following statements about covalent compounds is true?
- **A.** Covalent compounds generally exist as molecules.
- **B.** Covalent compounds are good electrical conductors in solution.
- **C.** The valence electrons are always shared equally by the two atoms in a covalent bond.
- **D.** Covalent bonds generally involve two atoms that are very different, such as a metal and a nonmetal.

Directions (4): **Write a short response to the question.**

4 The three different types of chemical bonds–covalent, ionic, and metallic–differ in what happens to valence electrons within the chemical bond. Compare the three types of bonds based on valence electrons.

Test TIP

When possible, use the text in multiple choice questions to help you "jump start" your thinking.

Reading Skills

Directions (5): **Read the passage below. Then answer the question.**

Spider silk, a long polymer made of a chain of amino acids, is one of the strongest known fibers. It is strong enough to support the spider and has enough elasticity to absorb the energy of the collision of a flying insect. The strength comes from the covalent bonds between units of the chain and the elasticity is the result of interactions between different parts of the molecule. Coils or folds in the polymer expand on impact. Spiders can make at least seven different kinds of silk for different purposes by varying the amino acids. Scientists studying the silk structure have identified some of the structures that account for its properties but still have more to learn from spiders.

5 How is the specific order of amino acids in the polymer related to the characteristics of different kinds of silk?

Interpreting Graphics

Directions (6): **Base your answer to question 6 on the illustration below, which models how water molecules are arranged in the liquid state.**

Interaction of Water Molecules in the Liquid State

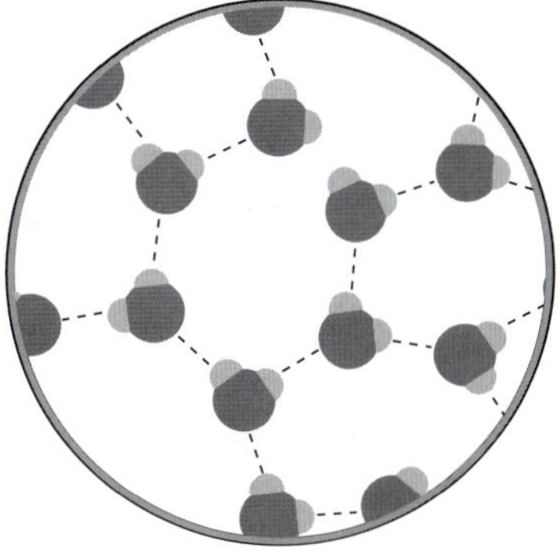

6 Compare the forces of attraction between the atoms of a water molecule to those between two water molecules.

Skills Practice Lab

Introduction

Many polymers are able to "bounce back" after they are stretched, bent, or compressed. In this lab, you will compare the bounce heights of two balls made from different polymers.

Objectives

- ***Synthesize*** two different polymers, ***shape*** each into a ball, and ***measure*** how high each ball bounces.
- USING SCIENTIFIC METHODS ***Conclude*** which polymer would make a better toy ball.

Materials

acetic acid solution (vinegar), 5%
container, 2 L
ethanol solution, 50%
graduated cylinder, 10 mL
graduated cylinders, 25 mL (2)
liquid latex
meterstick
paper cups, medium-sized (2)
paper towels
sodium silicate solution
water, deionized
wooden craft sticks (2)

Comparing Polymers

Procedure

1. Prepare a data table in your lab report similar to the one shown at right.

Making Latex Rubber

SAFETY CAUTION If you get a chemical on your skin or clothing, wash it off with lukewarm water while calling to your teacher. If you get a chemical in your eyes, flush it out immediately at the eyewash station and alert your teacher.

2. Pour 1 L of deionized water into a 2 L container.
3. Use a 25 mL graduated cylinder to pour 10 mL of liquid latex into one of the paper cups.
4. Clean the graduated cylinder thoroughly with soap and water, then rinse it with deionized water and use it to add 10 mL of deionized water to the liquid latex.
5. Use the same graduated cylinder to add 10 mL of acetic acid solution to the liquid latex-water mixture.
6. Stir the mixture with a wooden craft stick. As you stir, a "lump" of the polymer will form around the stick.
7. Transfer the stick and the attached polymer to the 2 L container. While keeping the polymer underwater, gently pull it off the stick with your gloved hands.
8. Squeeze the polymer underwater to remove any unreacted chemicals, shape it into a ball, and remove the ball from the water.
9. Make the ball smooth by rolling it between your gloved hands. Set the ball on a paper towel to dry while you continue with the next part of the lab.

Bounce Heights of Polymers

Polymer	Trial 1	Trial 2	Bounce height (cm) Trial 3	Trial 4	Trial 5	Average
Latex rubber						
Ethanol-silicate						

10. Wash your gloved hands with soap and water, then remove the gloves and dispose of them. Wash your hands again with soap and water.

Making an Ethanol-silicate Polymer

SAFETY CAUTION Put on a fresh pair of gloves. Ethanol is flammable, so make sure there are no flames or other heat sources anywhere in the laboratory.

11. Use a clean 25 mL graduated cylinder to pour 12 mL of sodium silicate solution into the clean paper cup.
12. Use a 10 mL graduated cylinder to add 3 mL of the ethanol solution to the sodium silicate solution.
13. Stir the mixture with the clean wooden craft stick until a solid polymer forms.
14. Remove the polymer with your gloved hands, and gently press it between your palms until you form a ball that does not crumble. This activity may take some time. Occasionally dripping some tap water on the polymer might be helpful.
15. When the ball no longer crumbles, dry it very gently with a paper towel.
16. Repeat step 10, and put on a fresh pair of gloves.
17. Examine both polymers closely. Record in your lab report how the two polymers are alike and how they are different.
18. Use a meterstick to measure the highest bounce height of each ball when each is dropped from a height of 1 m. Drop each ball five times, and record the highest bounce height each time in your data table.

▶ Analysis

1. Calculate the average bounce height for each ball by adding the five bounce heights and dividing by 5. Record the averages in your data table.
2. Based on only their bounce heights, which polymer would make a better toy ball?

▶ Conclusions

3. Suppose that making a latex rubber ball costs 22 cents and that making an ethanol-silicate ball costs 25 cents. Does this fact affect your conclusion about which polymer would make a better toy ball? Besides cost, what are other important factors that should be considered?

CareerLink

Analytical Chemist

Have you ever looked at something and wondered what chemicals it contained? That's what analytical chemists do for a living. They use a range of tests to determine the chemical makeup of a sample. To find out more about analytical chemistry as a career, read the interview with analytical chemist Roberta Jordan, who works at the Idaho National Engineering and Environmental Laboratory, in Idaho Falls, Idaho.

In addition to working as an analytical chemist, Roberta Jordan mentors students regularly in the local schools.

"Chemistry is in everything we do. Just to take a breath and eat a meal involves chemistry."

What is your work as an analytical chemist like?

We deal with radioactive waste generated by old nuclear power plants and old submarines, and we try to find a safe way to store the waste. I'm more like a consultant. A group of engineers that are working on a process will come to me. I tell them what things they need to analyze for and why they need to do that. On the flip side, I'll tell them what techniques they need to use.

What do you like best about your work?

It forces me to stay current with any new techniques, new areas that are going on in analytical chemistry. And I like the team approach because it allows me to work on different projects.

What do you find most interesting about your work?

Probably the most interesting thing is to observe how different industries and different labs conduct business. It gives you a broad feel for how chemistry is done.

What qualities does a good chemist need?

I think you do need to be good at science and math and to like those subjects. You need to be fairly detail-oriented. You have to be precise. You need to be analytical in general, and you need to be meticulous.

What part of your education do you think was most valuable?

I think it was worthwhile spending a lot of energy on my lab work. With any science, the most important part is the laboratory experience, when you are applying those theories that you learn. I'm really a proponent of being involved in science-fair activities.

What advice do you have for students who are interested in analytical chemistry?

It's worthwhile to go to the career center or library and do a little research. Take the time to find out what kinds of things you could do with your degree. You need to talk to people who have a degree in that field.

Do you think chemistry has a bright future?

I think that there are a lot of things out there that need to be discovered. My advice is to go for it and don't think that everything we need to know has been discovered. Twenty to thirty years down the road, we will have to think of a new energy source, for example.

internet connect

www.scilinks.org
Topic: Analytical Chemistry
SciLinks code: HK4006

SCILINKS. Maintained by the National Science Teachers Association

"One of the things necessary to be a good chemist is you have to be creative. You have to be able to think above and beyond the normal way of doing things to come up with new ideas, new experiments."

—Roberta Jordan

CHAPTER 6

Chemical Reactions

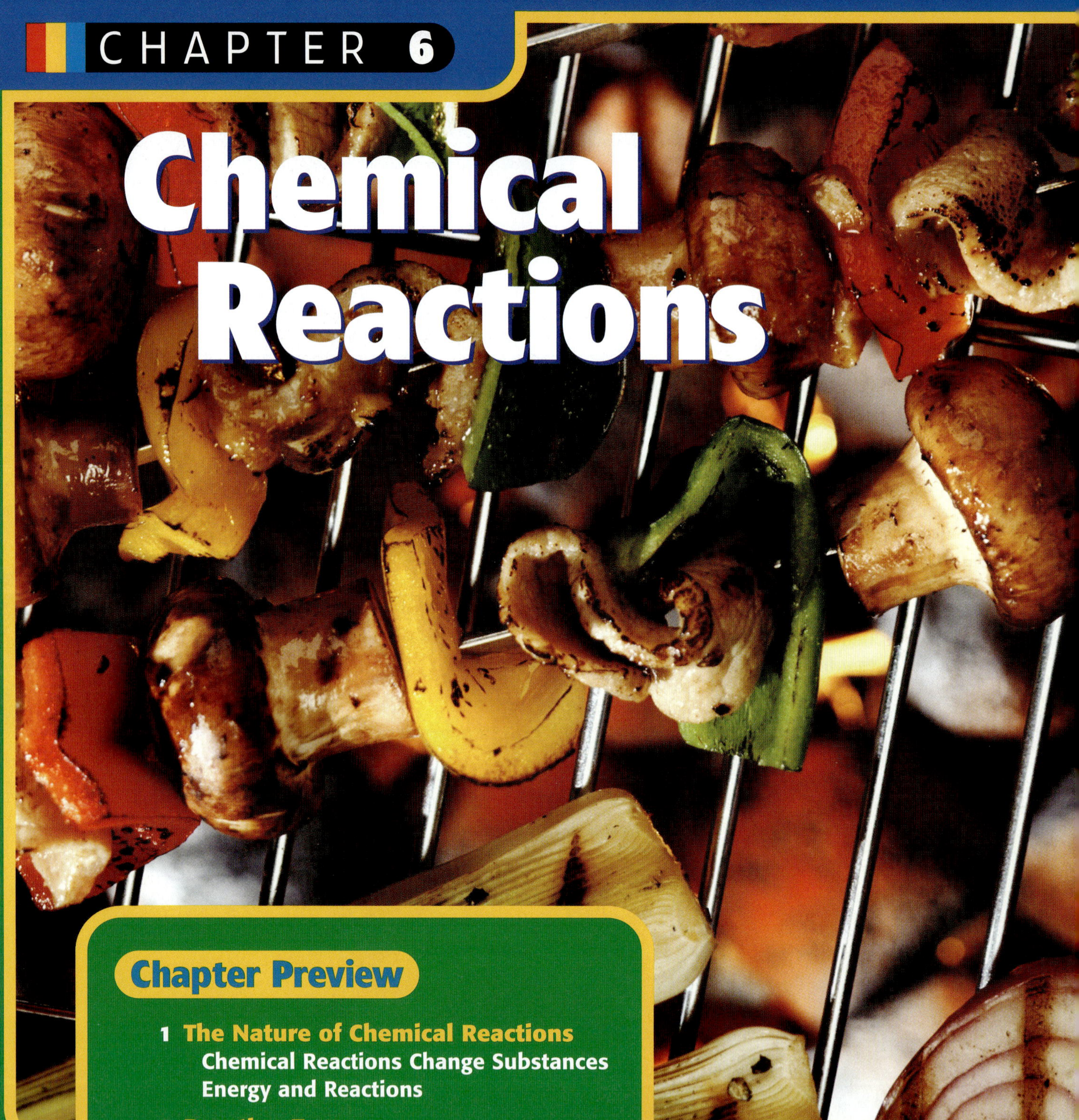

Chapter Preview

1 **The Nature of Chemical Reactions**
Chemical Reactions Change Substances
Energy and Reactions

2 **Reaction Types**
Classifying Reactions
Electrons and Chemical Reactions

3 **Balancing Chemical Equations**
Describing Reactions
Determining Mole Ratios

4 **Rates of Change**
Factors Affecting Reaction Rates
Equilibrium Systems

The energy in charcoal is stored in chemical bonds. When charcoal is burned, the stored energy is released as heat and light.

Focus ACTIVITY

Background Many people look forward to summer as prime "grilling time." Although there are many ways to prepare food on a grill, the basic principle is the same: raw food is cooked to make it tastier, easier to digest, and safer to eat.

One method of grilling uses charcoal as a fuel. Charcoal is produced by heating wood or other plant matter to high temperatures in the absence of air. When charcoal is burned on a grill, the matter in the charcoal and oxygen in the air combine in a chemical reaction to produce light and heat energy that cooks the food.

Some food can be "cooked" using chemical reactions that are not caused by heat. For example, ceviche, which is usually served cold, contains fish that is "cooked" with lime juice. But in all cases, when food is cooked, chemical reactions make the energy in food easier to release when you eat it.

Activity 1 Obtain three freshly cut slices of apple. Cover one completely with water, and wrap another slice with clear plastic wrap. Allow the third slice to remain exposed to the air. Do the slices look the same after one hour? After six hours? Why or why not?

Activity 2 Sodium bicarbonate, also known as baking soda, is used to make pancakes, cookies, and other baked goods light and fluffy. Pour a small amount of vinegar into a cup and add a pinch of baking soda to the cup. What changes do you observe? How might the same reaction cause pancakes to rise?

Pre-Reading Questions

1. When food is cooked, what are some signs to look for to indicate that the food is ready to eat?
2. Wood is sometimes used as a fuel to provide heat and light. What other things in addition to wood are required to start a fire?

SECTION 1

The Nature of Chemical Reactions

KEY TERMS

reactant
product
chemical energy
exothermic reaction
endothermic reaction

OBJECTIVES

- **Recognize** some signs that a chemical reaction may be taking place.
- **Explain** chemical changes in terms of the structure and motion of atoms and molecules.
- **Describe** the differences between endothermic and exothermic reactions.
- **Identify** situations involving chemical energy.

If someone talks about chemical reactions, you might think about scientists doing experiments in laboratories. But words like *grow, ripen, decay,* and *burn* describe chemical reactions you see every day. Even your own health is due to chemical reactions taking place inside your body. The food you eat reacts with the oxygen you inhale in processes such as respiration and cell growth. The carbon dioxide formed in these reactions is carried to your lungs, and you exhale it into the environment.

Chemical Reactions Change Substances

When sugar, water, and yeast are mixed into flour to make bread dough, a chemical reaction takes place. The yeast acts on the sugar to form new substances, including carbon dioxide and lactic acid. You know that a chemical reaction has happened because lactic acid and carbon dioxide are different from sugar.

Chemical reactions occur when substances undergo chemical changes to form new substances. Often you can tell that a chemical reaction is happening because you will be able to see changes, such as those in ***Figure 1.***

Figure 1

Signs of a Chemical Reaction

A When the calcium carbonate in a piece of chalk reacts with an acid, bubbles of carbon dioxide gas are given off.

B When solutions of sodium sulfide and cadmium nitrate are mixed, a solid—yellow cadmium sulfide—settles out of the solution.

C When ammonium dichromate decomposes, energy is released as light and heat.

Production of gas and change of color are signs of chemical reactions

In bread making, the carbon dioxide gas that is produced expands the dough, causing the bread to rise. This release of gas is a sign that a chemical reaction may be happening.

As the dough bakes, old bonds break and new bonds form. Chemical reactions involving starch and protein make food turn brown when heated. A chemical change happens almost every time there is a change in color.

Chemical reactions rearrange atoms

When gasoline is burned in the engine of a car or boat, a lot of different reactions happen with the compounds that are in the mixture we call gasoline. In a typical reaction, isooctane, C_8H_{18}, and oxygen, O_2, are the **reactants.** They react and form two **products,** carbon dioxide, CO_2, and water, H_2O.

The products and reactants contain the same types of atoms: carbon, hydrogen, and oxygen. New product atoms are not created, and old reactant atoms are not destroyed. Atoms are rearranged as bonds are broken and formed. In all chemical reactions, mass is always conserved.

reactant a substance or molecule that participates in a chemical reaction

product a substance that forms in a chemical reaction

Energy and Reactions

Filling a car's tank with gasoline would be very dangerous if isooctane and oxygen could not be in the same place without reacting. Like most chemical reactions, the isooctane-oxygen reaction needs energy to get started. A small spark provides enough energy to start this reaction. That is why smoking or having any open flame near a gas pump is not allowed.

Energy must be added to break bonds

In each isooctane molecule, like the one shown in ***Figure 2,*** all the bonds to carbon atoms are covalent. In an oxygen molecule, a covalent bond holds the two oxygen atoms together. For the atoms in isooctane and oxygen to react, all of these bonds have to be broken. This takes energy.

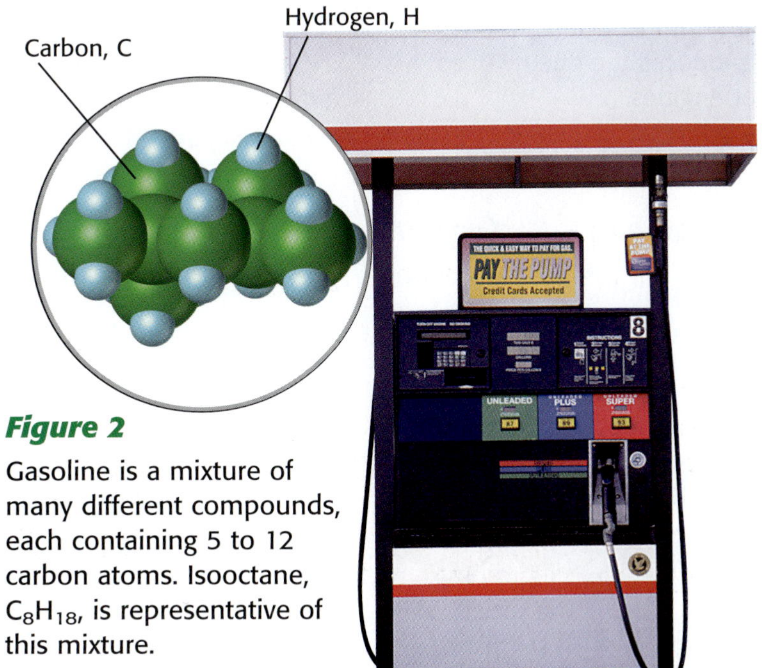

Figure 2
Gasoline is a mixture of many different compounds, each containing 5 to 12 carbon atoms. Isooctane, C_8H_{18}, is representative of this mixture.

Figure 3

A Light passing through a camera lens causes silver bromide crystals on the film to form darker elemental silver on the negative.

B Light passing through the negative onto black and white photographic paper causes another reaction that forms the photograph.

A Negative

B Photo (positive image)

Many forms of energy can be used to break bonds. Sometimes the energy is transferred as heat, like the spark that starts the isooctane-oxygen reaction. Energy also can be transferred as electricity, sound, or light, as shown in ***Figure 3.*** When molecules collide and enough energy is transferred to separate the atoms, bonds can break.

Forming bonds releases energy

Once enough energy is added to start the isooctane-oxygen reaction, new bonds form to make the products, as shown in ***Figure 4.*** Each carbon dioxide molecule has two oxygen atoms connected to the carbon atom with a double bond. A water molecule is made when two hydrogen atoms each form a single bond with the oxygen atom.

When new bonds form, energy is released. When gasoline burns, energy in the form of heat and light is released as the products of the isooctane-oxygen reaction and other gasoline reactions form. Other chemical reactions can produce electrical energy.

Figure 4

The formation of carbon dioxide and water from isooctane and oxygen produces the energy used to power engines.

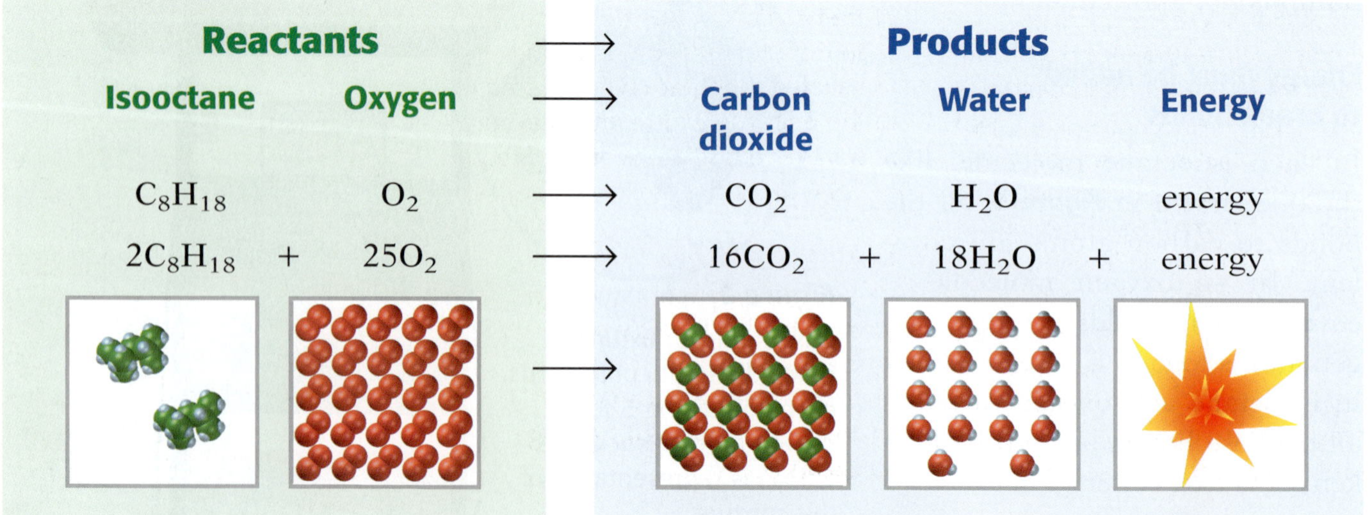

Energy is conserved in chemical reactions

Energy may not appear to be conserved in the isooctane reaction. After all, a tiny spark can set off an explosion. The energy for that explosion comes from the bonds between atoms in the reactants. Often this stored energy is called **chemical energy.** The total energy of isooctane, oxygen, and their surroundings includes this chemical energy. The total energy before the reaction is equal to the total energy of the products and their surroundings.

internet connect

www.scilinks.org
Topic: Corrosion
SciLinks code: HK4029
SCILINKS. Maintained by the National Science Teachers Association

Reactions that release energy are exothermic

In the isooctane-oxygen reaction, more energy is released as the products form than is absorbed to break the bonds in the reactants. Like all other combustion reactions, this is an **exothermic reaction.** After an exothermic reaction, the temperature of the surroundings rises because energy is released. The released energy comes from the chemical energy of the reactants.

Reactions that absorb energy are endothermic

If you put hydrated barium hydroxide and ammonium nitrate together in a flask, the reaction between them takes so much energy from the surroundings that water in the air will condense and then freeze on the surface of the flask. This is an **endothermic reaction**—more energy is needed to break the bonds in the reactants than is given off by forming bonds in the products.

chemical energy the energy released when a chemical compound reacts to produce new compounds

exothermic reaction a chemical reaction in which heat is released to the surroundings

endothermic reaction a chemical reaction that requires heat

REAL WORLD APPLICATIONS

Self-Heating Meals

Corrosion, the process by which a metal reacts with the oxygen in air or water, is not often desirable. However, corrosion is encouraged in self-heating meals so that the energy from the exothermic reaction can be used. Self-heating meals, as the name implies, have their own heat source.

Each meal contains a package of precooked food, a bag that holds a porous pad containing a magnesium-iron alloy, and some salt water. When the salt water is poured into the bag, the salt water soaks through the holes in the pad of metal alloy and begins to corrode the metals vigorously. Then the sealed food package is placed in the bag. The exothermic reaction raises the temperature of the food by 38°C in 14 minutes.

Applying Information

1. List some people for whom self-heating meals would be useful.
2. What other uses can you think of for this self-heating technology?

Figure 5

Energy must be added to start both exothermic and endothermic reactions.

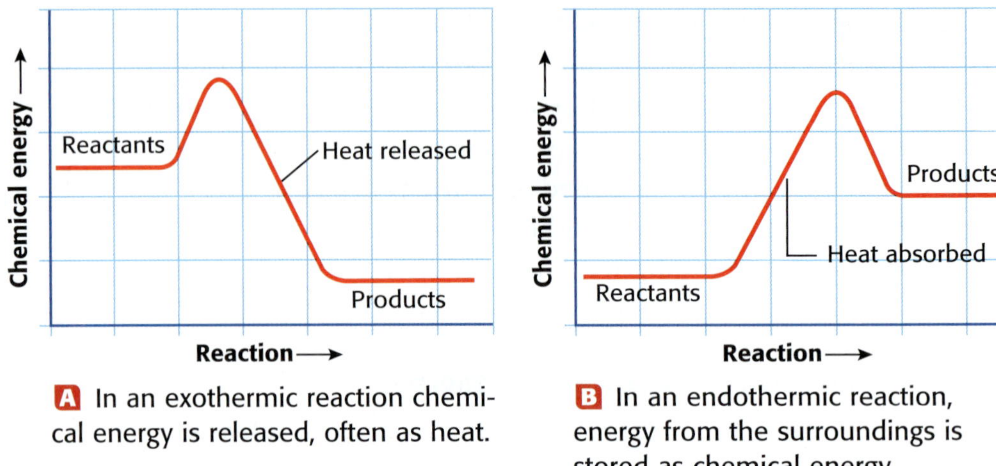

A In an exothermic reaction chemical energy is released, often as heat.

B In an endothermic reaction, energy from the surroundings is stored as chemical energy.

When an endothermic reaction occurs, you may be able to notice a drop in temperature. Some endothermic reactions cannot get enough energy as heat from the surroundings to happen; so energy must be added as heat to cause the reaction to take place. The changes in chemical energy for an exothermic reaction and for an endothermic reaction are shown in ***Figure 5.***

Photosynthesis, like many reactions in living things, is endothermic. In photosynthesis, plants use energy from light to convert carbon dioxide and water to glucose and oxygen, as shown in ***Figure 6.***

Figure 6

All of the food you eat comes directly or indirectly from the products of photosynthesis.

Plants Use the Energy from Light

Carbon dioxide, CO_2

Oxygen, O_2

Water, H_2O

Glucose, $C_6H_{12}O_6$

Sometimes, reactions are described as exergonic or endergonic. These terms refer to the ease with which the reactions occur. In most cases in this book, exergonic reactions are exothermic and endergonic reactions are endothermic. Bioluminescence, shown in ***Figure 7,*** and respiration are exergonic reactions, and photosynthesis is an endergonic reaction.

Figure 7

A Some living things, such as this firefly, produce light through a chemical process called bioluminescence.

B The comb jelly *(Mnemiopsis leidyi)*, shown above, is about 10 cm wide and is native to the Atlantic coast. Comb jellies are not true jellyfish.

INTEGRATING

BIOLOGY

People are charmed by fireflies because these common insects give off light. Scientists have found that fireflies are not alone in this. Some kinds of bacteria, worms, squids, and jellyfish also give off light. This process, called bioluminescence, involves an exothermic reaction made possible by the enzyme luciferase. Scientists can use bacteria that contain luciferase to track the spread of infection in the human body.

SECTION 1 REVIEW

SUMMARY

- During a chemical reaction, atoms are rearranged.
- Signs of a chemical reaction include any of the following: a substance that has different properties than the reactants have; a color change; the formation of a gas or a solid precipitate; or the transfer of energy.
- Mass and energy are conserved in chemical reactions.
- Energy can be released or absorbed in a chemical reaction.
- Energy must be added to the reactants for bonds between atoms to be broken.

1. **Identify** which of the following is a chemical reaction:
   a. melting ice
   b. burning a candle
   c. rubbing a marker on paper
   d. rusting iron
2. **List** three signs that could make you think a chemical reaction might be taking place.
3. **List** four forms of energy that might be absorbed or released during a chemical reaction.
4. **Classify** the following reactions as exothermic or endothermic:
   a. paper burning with a bright flame
   b. plastics becoming brittle after being left in the sun
   c. a firecracker exploding
5. **Predict** which atoms will be found in the products of the following reactions:
   a. mercury(II) oxide, HgO, is heated and decomposes
   b. limestone, $CaCO_3$, reacts with hydrochloric acid, HCl
   c. table sugar, $C_{12}H_{22}O_{11}$, burns in air to form caramel
6. **Critical Thinking** Calcium oxide, CaO, is used in cement mixes. When water is added, heat is released as CaO forms calcium hydroxide, $Ca(OH)_2$. What signs are there that this is a chemical reaction? Which has more chemical energy, the reactants or the products? Explain your answer.

SECTION 2

Reaction Types

KEY TERMS

synthesis reaction
decomposition reaction
electrolysis
combustion reaction
single-displacement reaction
double-displacement reaction
oxidation-reduction reaction
radical

OBJECTIVES

- **Distinguish** among five general types of chemical reactions.
- **Predict** the products of some reactions based on the reaction type.
- **Describe** reactions that transfer or share electrons between molecules, atoms, or ions.

In the last section, you saw how CO_2 is made from sugar by yeast, how isooctane from gasoline burns, and how photosynthesis happens. These are just a few examples of the many millions of possible reactions.

synthesis reaction a reaction in which two or more substances combine to form a new compound

Classifying Reactions

Even though there are millions of unique substances and many millions of possible reactions, there are only a few general types of reactions. Just as you can follow patterns to name compounds, you also can use patterns to identify the general types of chemical reactions and to predict the products of the chemical reactions.

Synthesis reactions combine substances

Polyethene, a plastic often used to make trash bags and soda bottles, is produced by a **synthesis reaction** called polymerization. In polymerization reactions, many small molecules join together in chains to make larger structures called polymers. Polyethene, shown in ***Figure 8,*** is a polymer formed of repeating ethene molecules.

Hydrogen gas reacts with oxygen gas to form water. In a synthesis reaction, at least two reactants join to form a product. Synthesis reactions have the following general form.

$$A + B \longrightarrow AB$$

The following is a synthesis reaction in which the metal sodium reacts with chlorine gas to form sodium chloride, or table salt.

$$2Na + Cl_2 \longrightarrow 2NaCl$$

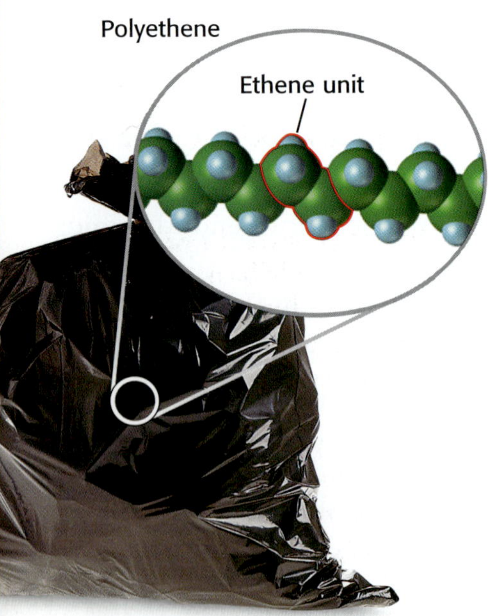

Figure 8
A molecule of polyethene is made up of as many as 3500 units of ethene.

Synthesis reactions always join substances, so the product is a more complex compound than the reactants.

Photosynthesis is another kind of synthesis reaction—the synthesis reaction that goes on in plants. The photosynthesis reaction is shown in ***Figure 9.***

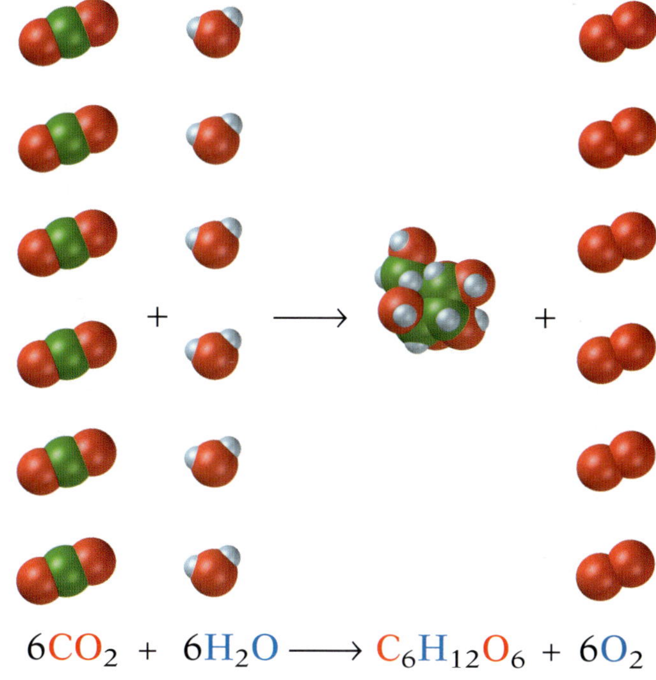

$$6CO_2 + 6H_2O \longrightarrow C_6H_{12}O_6 + 6O_2$$

Figure 9

Photosynthesis is the synthesis of glucose and oxygen gas from carbon dioxide and water.

Decomposition reactions break substances apart

Digestion is a series of reactions that break down complex foods into simple fuels your body can use. Similarly, in what is known as "cracking" crude oil, large molecules made of carbon and hydrogen are broken down to make gasoline and other fuels. Digestion and "cracking" oil are **decomposition reactions,** reactions in which substances are broken apart. The general form for decomposition reactions is as follows.

$$AB \longrightarrow A + B$$

The following shows the decomposition of water.

$$2H_2O \longrightarrow 2H_2 + O_2$$

The **electrolysis** of water is a simple decomposition reaction—water breaks down into hydrogen gas and oxygen gas when an electric current flows through the water.

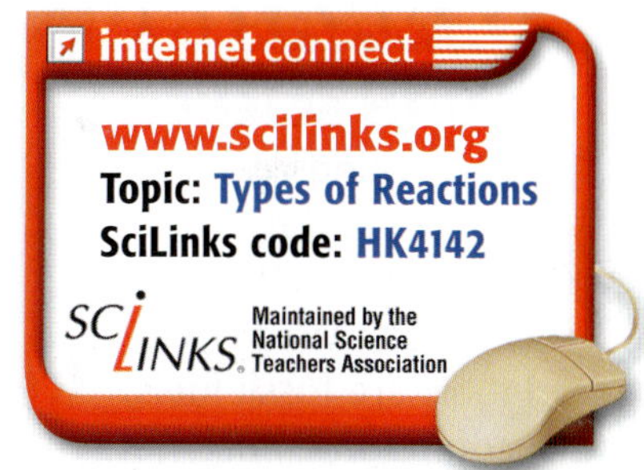

Combustion reactions use oxygen as a reactant

Isooctane forms carbon dioxide and water during combustion. Oxygen is a reactant in every **combustion reaction,** so at least one product of such reactions always contains oxygen. Water is a common product of combustion reactions.

If the air supply is limited when a carbon-containing fuel burns, there may not be enough oxygen gas for all the carbon to form carbon dioxide. In that case, some carbon monoxide may form. Carbon monoxide, CO, is a poisonous gas that lowers the ability of the blood to carry oxygen. Carbon monoxide has no color or odor, so you can't tell when it is present. When there is not a good air supply during a combustion reaction, not all fuels are converted completely to carbon dioxide. In some combustion reactions, you can tell if the air supply is limited because the excess carbon is given off as small particles that make a dark, sooty smoke.

decomposition reaction a reaction in which a single compound breaks down to form two or more simpler substances

electrolysis the process in which an electric current is used to produce a chemical reaction, such as the decomposition of water

combustion reaction the oxidation reaction of an organic compound, in which heat is released

In combustion the products depend on the amount of oxygen

To see how important a good air supply is, look at a series of combustion reactions for methane, CH_4. Because methane has only one carbon atom, it is the simplest carbon-containing fuel. Methane is the primary component in natural gas, the fuel often used in stoves, water heaters, and furnaces.

Methane reacts with oxygen gas to make carbon dioxide and water. In the balanced form of the chemical equation, four molecules of oxygen gas are needed for the combustion of two molecules of methane, as shown below.

$$2CH_4 + 4O_2 \longrightarrow 2CO_2 + 4H_2O$$

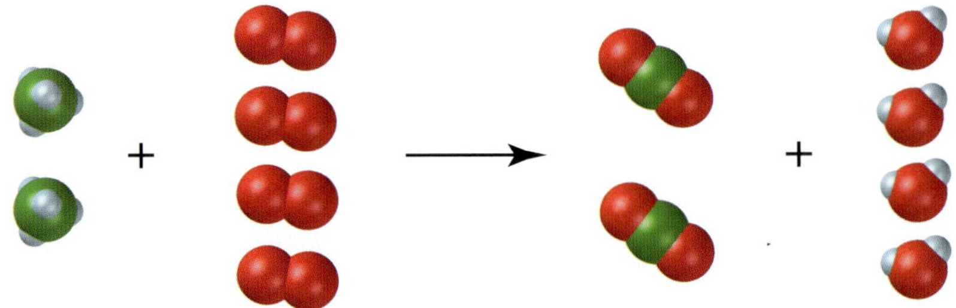

Did You Know?

In the United States, natural gas supplies one-fifth of the energy used. The pipelines that carry this natural gas, if laid end-to-end, would stretch to the moon and back twice.

Now look at what happens when less oxygen gas is available. If there are only three molecules of oxygen gas for every two molecules of methane, water and carbon monoxide may form, as shown in the following reaction.

$$2CH_4 + 3O_2 \longrightarrow 2CO + 4H_2O$$

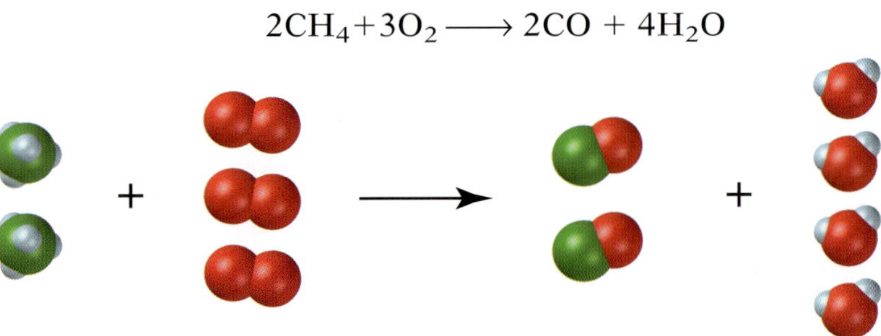

When the air supply is very limited and only two molecules of oxygen gas are available to react with two molecules of methane, water and tiny bits of carbon, or soot, are formed as follows.

$$2CH_4 + 2O_2 \longrightarrow 2C + 4H_2O$$

INTEGRATING

EARTH SCIENCE

Compounds containing carbon and hydrogen are often called hydrocarbons. Most hydrocarbon fuels are fossil fuels, that is, compounds that were formed millions of years before dinosaurs existed. When prehistoric organisms died, they decomposed, and many were slowly buried under layers of mud, rock, and sand. During the millions of years that passed, the once-living material formed different fuels, such as oil, natural gas, or coal, depending on the kind of material present, the length of time the material was buried, and the conditions of temperature and pressure that existed when the material was decomposing.

Fire Extinguishers: Are They All The Same?

A fire is a combustion reaction in progress that is speeded up by high temperatures. Three things are needed for a combustion reaction to occur: a fuel, some oxygen, and an ignition source. If any of these three is absent, combustion cannot occur. So the goal of firefighting is to remove one or more of these parts. Fire extinguishers are effective in firefighting because they separate the fuel from the oxygen supply, which is most commonly air.

Fire extinguishers display codes indicating which types of fires they can put out.

Classes of Fires

A fire is classified by the type of fuel that combusts to produce it. Class A fires involve solid fuels, such as wood and paper. The fuel in a Class B fire is a flammable liquid, like grease, gasoline, or oil. Class C fires involve "live" electric circuits. And Class D fires are fueled by the combustion of flammable metals.

Types of Fire Extinguishers

Different types of fuels require different firefighting methods. Water extinguishers are used on Class A fires, which involve fuels such as most flammable building materials. The steam that is produced helps to displace the air around the fire, preventing the oxygen supply from reaching the fuel.

A Class B fire, in which the fuel is a liquid, is best put out by cold carbon dioxide gas, CO_2. Because carbon dioxide is more dense than air, it forms a layer underneath the air, cutting off the oxygen supply for the combustion reaction.

Class C fires, which involve a "live" electric circuit, can also be extinguished by CO_2. Liquid water cannot be used, or there will be a danger of electric shock. Some Class C fire extinguishers contain a dry chemical that smothers the fire. The dry chemical smothers the fire by reacting with the intermediates that drive the chain reaction that produces the fire. This stops the chain reaction and extinguishes the fire.

Finally, Class D fires, which involve burning metals, cannot be extinguished with CO_2 or water because these compounds may react with some hot metals. For these fires, nonreactive dry powders are used to cover the metal and keep it separate from oxygen. In many cases, the powders used in Class D extinguishers are specific to the type of metal that is burning.

Most fire extinguishers can be used with more than one type of fire. Check the fire extinguishers in your home and school to find out the kinds of fires they are designed to put out.

Your Choice

1. **Making Decisions** Aside from displacing the air supply, how does water or cold CO_2 gas reduce a fire's severity?
2. **Critical Thinking** How is the chain reaction in a Class C fire interrupted by the contents of a dry chemical extinguisher?

In single-displacement reactions, elements trade places

Copper(II) chloride dissolves in water to make a bright blue solution. If you add a piece of aluminum foil to the solution, the color fades, and clumps of reddish brown material form. The reddish brown clumps are copper metal. Aluminum replaces copper in the copper(II) chloride, forming aluminum chloride. Aluminum chloride does not make a colored solution, so the blue color fades as the amount of blue copper(II) chloride decreases, as shown in ***Figure 10.***

At first, the copper atoms are in the form of copper(II) ions, as part of copper(II) chloride, and the aluminum atoms are in the form of aluminum metal. After the reaction, the aluminum atoms become ions, and the copper atoms become neutral in the copper metal. Because the atoms of one element appear to move into a compound, and atoms of the other element appear to move out, this is called a **single-displacement reaction.** Single-displacement reactions have the following general form.

single-displacement reaction a reaction in which one element or radical takes the place of another element or radical in a compound

$$AX + B \longrightarrow BX + A$$

The single-displacement reaction between copper(II) chloride and aluminum is shown as follows.

$$3CuCl_2 + 2Al \longrightarrow 2AlCl_3 + 3Cu$$

Generally, in a single-displacement reaction, a more reactive element will take the place of a less reactive one.

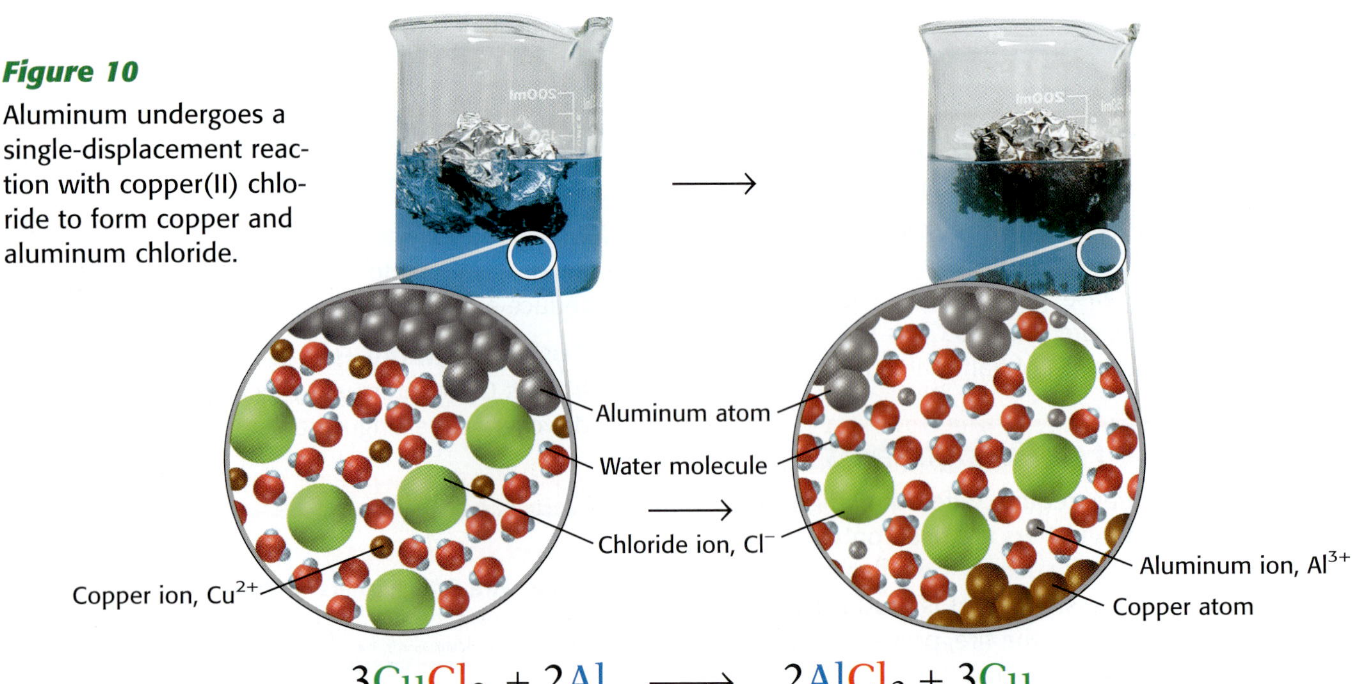

Figure 10
Aluminum undergoes a single-displacement reaction with copper(II) chloride to form copper and aluminum chloride.

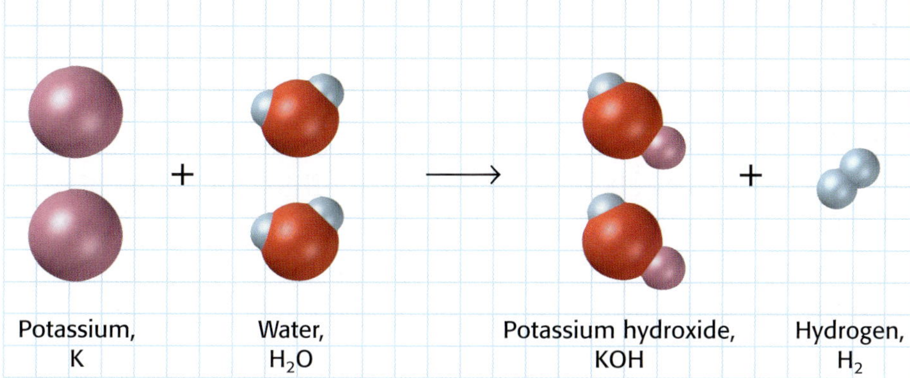

Figure 11

Potassium reacts with water in a single-displacement reaction.

Alkali metals react with water to form ions

Potassium metal is so reactive that it undergoes a single-displacement reaction with water. A potassium ion appears to take the place of one of the hydrogen atoms in the water molecule. Potassium ions, K^+, and hydroxide ions, OH^-, are formed. The hydrogen atoms displaced from the water join to form hydrogen gas, H_2.

The potassium and water reaction, shown in ***Figure 11,*** is so exothermic that the H_2 may explode and burn instantly. All alkali metals and some other metals undergo single-displacement reactions with water to form hydrogen gas, metal ions, and hydroxide ions.

All of these reactions happen rapidly and give off heat but some alkali metals are more reactive than others. Lithium reacts steadily with water to form lithium ions, hydroxide ions, and hydrogen gas. Sodium and water react vigorously to make sodium ions, hydroxide ions, and hydrogen gas. Rubidium and cesium are so reactive that the hydrogen gas will explode as soon as they are put into water.

In double-displacement reactions, ions appear to be exchanged between compounds

The yellow lines painted on roads are colored with lead chromate, $PbCrO_4$. This compound can be formed by mixing solutions of lead nitrate, $Pb(NO_3)_2$, and potassium chromate, K_2CrO_4. In solution, these compounds form the ions Pb^{2+}, NO_3^-, K^+, and CrO_4^{2-}. When the solutions are mixed, the yellow lead chromate compound that forms doesn't dissolve in water, so it settles to the bottom. A **double-displacement reaction,** such as this one, occurs when two compounds appear to exchange ions. The general form of a double-displacement reaction is as follows.

$$AX + BY \longrightarrow AY + BX$$

The double-displacement reaction that forms lead chromate is as follows.

$$Pb(NO_3)_2 + K_2CrO_4 \longrightarrow PbCrO_4 + 2KNO_3$$

double-displacement reaction a reaction in which a gas, a solid precipitate, or a molecular compound forms from the apparent exchange of atoms or ions between two compounds

Electrons and Chemical Reactions

The general classes of reactions described earlier in this section were used by early chemists, who knew nothing about the parts of the atom. With the discovery of the electron and its role in chemical bonding, another way to classify reactions was developed. We can understand many reactions as transfers of electrons.

oxidation-reduction reaction any chemical change in which one species is oxidized (loses electrons) and another species is reduced (gains electrons); also called *redox reaction*

radical an organic group that has one or more electrons available for bonding

Electrons are transferred in redox reactions

The following **oxidation-reduction reaction** is an example of electron transfer. When the metal iron reacts with oxygen to form rust, Fe_2O_3, each iron atom loses three electrons to form Fe^{3+} ions, and each oxygen atom gains two electrons to form the O^{2-} ions.

Substances that accept electrons are said to be *reduced;* substances that give up electrons are said to be *oxidized.* One way to remember this is that the gain of electrons will reduce the positive charge on an ion or will make an uncharged atom a negative ion. Reduction and oxidation are linked. In all redox reactions, one or more reactants is reduced and one or more is oxidized.

Some redox reactions do not involve ions. In these reactions, oxidation is a gain of oxygen or a loss of hydrogen, and reduction is the loss of oxygen or the gain of hydrogen. Respiration and combustion are redox reactions because oxygen gas reacts with carbon compounds to form carbon dioxide. Carbon atoms in CO_2 are oxidized, and oxygen atoms in O_2 are reduced.

Radicals have electrons available for bonding

Many synthetic fibers, as well as plastic bags and wraps, are made by polymerization reactions, as you have already learned. Polymerization reactions can occur when **radicals** are formed.

When a covalent bond is broken such that at least one unpaired electron is left on each fragment of the molecule, these fragments are called radicals. Because an uncharged hydrogen atom has one electron available for bonding, it is a radical. Radicals react quickly to form covalent bonds with other substances, making new compounds. Often, when you see chemical radicals mentioned in the newspaper or hear about them on the radio or television, they are called free radicals.

Connection to FINE ARTS

Metal sculptures often corrode because of redox reactions. The Statue of Liberty, which is covered with 200 000 pounds of copper, was as bright as a new penny when it was erected. However, after more than 100 years, the statue had turned green. The copper reacted with the damp air of New York harbor. More importantly, oxidation reactions between the damp, salty air and the internal iron supports made the structure dangerously weak. The statue was closed for several years in the 1980s while the supports were cleaned and repaired.

Making the Connection

1. Metal artwork in fountains often rusts very quickly. Suggest a reason for this.
2. Why do you think the most detailed parts of a sculpture are the first to appear worn away?

Radicals are part of many everyday reactions besides the making of polymers, such as those shown in ***Figure 12.*** Radicals can also be formed when coal and oil are processed or burned. The explosive combustion of rocket fuel is another reaction involving the formation of radicals.

Figure 12

Radical reactions are used to make polystyrene. Polystyrene foam is often used to insulate or to protect things that can break.

SECTION 2 REVIEW

SUMMARY

- Synthesis reactions make larger molecules.
- Decomposition breaks compounds apart.
- In combustion, substances react with oxygen.
- Elements appear to trade places in single-displacement reactions.
- In double-displacement reactions, ions appear to move between compounds, resulting in a solid that settles out of solution, a gas that bubbles out of solution, and/or a molecular substance.
- In redox reactions, electrons transfer from one substance to another.

1. **Classify** each of the following reactions by type:
   a. $S_8 + 8O_2 \longrightarrow 8SO_2 + \text{heat}$
   b. $6CO_2 + 6H_2O \longrightarrow C_6H_{12}O_6 + 6O_2$
   c. $2NaHCO_3 \longrightarrow Na_2CO_3 + H_2O + CO_2$
   d. $Zn + 2HCl \longrightarrow ZnCl_2 + H_2$
2. **Identify** which element is oxidized and which element is reduced in the following reaction.
   $$Zn + CuSO_4 \longrightarrow ZnSO_4 + Cu$$
3. **Define** *radical.*
4. **Compare and Contrast** single-displacement and double-displacement reactions based on the number of reactants. Use the terms *compound, atom* or *element,* and *ion.*
5. **Explain** why charcoal grills or charcoal fires should never be used for heating inside a house. (**Hint:** Doors and windows are closed when it is cold, so there is little fresh air.)
6. **Contrast** synthesis and decomposition reactions.
7. **List** three possible results of a double-displacement reaction.
8. **Creative Thinking** Would you expect larger or smaller molecules to be components of a more viscous liquid? Which is likely to be more viscous, crude oil or oil after cracking?

SECTION 3

Balancing Chemical Equations

KEY TERMS

chemical equation
mole ratio

OBJECTIVES

- **Demonstrate** how to balance chemical equations.
- **Interpret** chemical equations to determine the relative number of moles of reactants needed and moles of products formed.
- **Explain** how the law of definite proportions allows for predictions about reaction amounts.
- **Identify** mole ratios in a balanced chemical equation.
- **Calculate** the relative masses of reactants and products from a chemical equation.

You may have seen a combustion reaction in the lab or at home if you have a gas stove. When natural gas burns, methane, the main component, reacts with oxygen gas to form carbon dioxide and water. Energy is also released as heat and light, as shown in ***Figure 13A.***

chemical equation a representation of a chemical reaction that uses symbols to show the relationship between the reactants and the products

Describing Reactions

You can describe this reaction in many ways. You could take a photograph or make a videotape. One way to record the products and reactants of this reaction is to write a word equation.

$$\text{methane} + \text{oxygen} \longrightarrow \text{carbon dioxide} + \text{water}$$

Chemical equations summarize reactions

In Section 1, you learned that all chemical reactions are rearrangements of atoms. This is shown clearly in ***Figure 13B.*** A better way to write the methane combustion reaction is as a **chemical equation,** using the formulas for each substance.

Figure 13

A A methane flame is used to polish the edges of these glass plates.

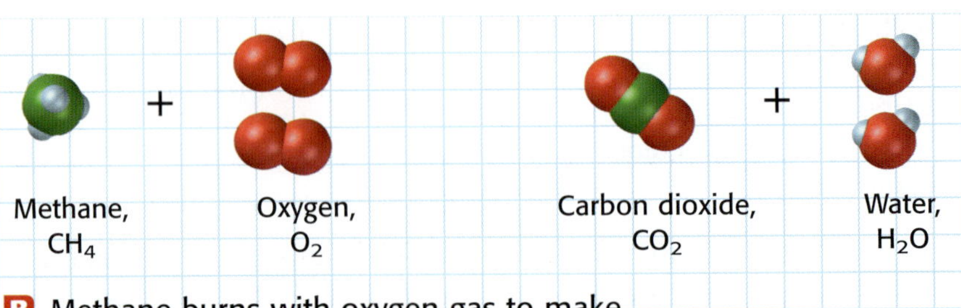

B Methane burns with oxygen gas to make carbon dioxide and water.

Unbalanced Chemical Equation

$CH_4 + O_2$	$\longrightarrow$	$CO_2 + H_2O$
reactants	"give" or "yield"	products

In a chemical equation, such as the one above, the reactants, which are on the left-hand side of the arrow, form the products, which are on the right-hand side. When chemical equations are written, $\longrightarrow$ means "gives" or "yields." People all over the world write chemical equations the same way, as shown in ***Figure 14.***

Figure 14

This student is giving a talk on reactions that use copper. You can read the chemical equations even if you can't read Japanese.

Balanced chemical equations account for the conservation of mass

The chemical equation shown above can be made more useful. As written, it does not tell you anything about the amount of the products that will be formed from burning a given amount of methane. When the number of atoms of each element on the right-hand side of the equation matches the number of atoms of each element on the left, then the chemical equation is said to be *balanced.* A balanced chemical equation is the standard way of writing equations for chemical reactions because it follows the law of conservation of mass.

How to balance chemical equations

In the previous equation, the number of atoms on each side of the arrow did not match for all of the elements in the equation. Carbon is balanced because one carbon atom is on each side of the equation. However, four hydrogen atoms are on the left, and only two are on the right. Also, two oxygen atoms are on the left, and three are on the right. This can't be correct because atoms can't be created or destroyed in a chemical reaction.

Remember that you cannot balance an equation by changing the chemical formulas. You have to leave the subscripts in the formulas alone. Changing the formulas would mean that different substances were in the reaction. An equation can be balanced only by putting numbers, called coefficients, in front of the chemical formulas.

Because there is a total of four hydrogen atoms in the reactants, a total of four hydrogen atoms must be in the products. Instead of a single water molecule, this reaction makes two water molecules to account for all four hydrogen atoms. To show that two water molecules are formed, a coefficient of 2 is placed in front of the formula for water.

$$CH_4 + O_2 \longrightarrow CO_2 + 2H_2O$$

Connection to SOCIAL STUDIES

No one can be sure when fireworks were first used. When the Mongols attacked China in 1232, the defenders used "arrows of flying fire," which some historians think were rockets fired by gunpowder. The Arabs probably used rockets when they invaded the Spanish peninsula in 1249. For hundreds of years, the main use of rockets was to add terror and confusion to battles. In the late 1700s, rockets were used with some success against the British in India. Because of this, Sir William Congreve began to design rockets for England. Congreve's rockets were designed to explode in the air or be fired along the ground.

Making the Connection

British forces used Congreve's rockets during the War of 1812. Research the battle of Fort McHenry. Find out what happened, who won the battle, and what lyrics the rockets inspired.

Next look at the oxygen. There is a total of four oxygen atoms in the products. Two are in the CO_2, and each water molecule contains one oxygen atom. To get four oxygen atoms on the left side of the equation, two oxygen molecules must react. That would account for all four oxygen atoms.

Balanced Chemical Equation

$$CH_4 + 2O_2 \longrightarrow CO_2 + 2H_2O$$

Now the numbers of atoms for each element are the same on each side, and the equation is balanced, as shown below.

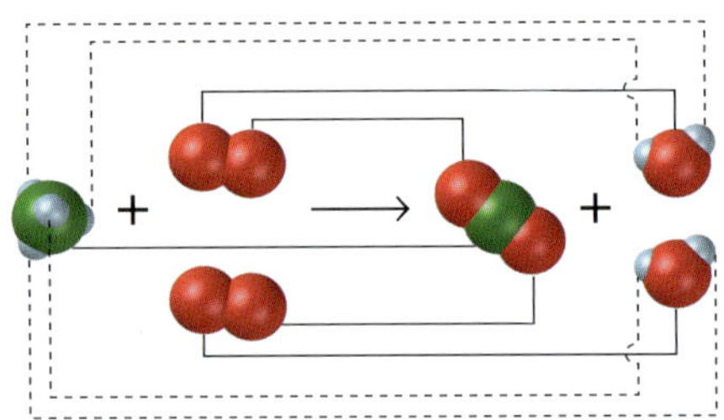

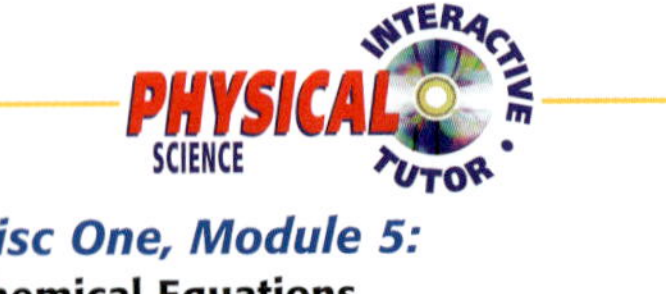

Disc One, Module 5:

Chemical Equations

Use the Interactive Tutor to learn more about this topic.

Information from a balanced equation

You can learn a lot from a balanced equation. In our example, you can tell that each molecule of methane requires two oxygen molecules to react. Each methane molecule that burns forms one molecule of carbon dioxide and two molecules of water. Balanced chemical equations are the standard way chemists write about reactions to describe both the substances in the reaction and the amounts involved.

If you know the formulas of the reactants and products in a reaction, like the one shown in ***Figure 15,*** you can always write a balanced equation, as shown on the following pages.

Figure 15

Magnesium in these fireworks gives off energy as heat and light when it burns to form magnesium oxide.

Math Skills

Balancing Chemical Equations Write the equation that describes the burning of magnesium in air to form magnesium oxide.

1 Identify the reactants and products.

Magnesium and oxygen gas are the reactants that form the product, magnesium oxide.

2 Write a word equation for the reaction.

$$\text{magnesium} + \text{oxygen} \longrightarrow \text{magnesium oxide}$$

3 Write the equation using formulas for the elements and compounds in the word equation.

Remember that some gaseous elements, like oxygen, are molecules, not atoms. Oxygen in air is O_2, not O.

$$Mg + O_2 \longrightarrow MgO$$

4 Balance the equation one element at a time.

The same number of each kind of atom must appear on both sides. So far, there is one atom of magnesium on each side of the equation.

Atom	Reactants	Products	Balanced?
Mg	1	1	✔
O	2	1	✘

But there are two oxygen atoms on the left and only one on the right. To balance the number of oxygen atoms, you need to double the amount of magnesium oxide:

$$Mg + O_2 \longrightarrow 2MgO$$

Atom	Reactants	Products	Balanced?
Mg	1	2	✘
O	2	2	✔

This equation gives you two magnesium atoms on the right and only one on the left. So you need to double the amount of magnesium on the left, as follows.

$$2Mg + O_2 \longrightarrow 2MgO$$

Atom	Reactants	Products	Balanced?
Mg	2	2	✔
O	2	2	✔

Now the equation is balanced. It has an equal number of each type of atom on both sides.

▶ Sometimes changing the coefficients to balance one element may cause another element in the equation to become unbalanced. So always check your work.

Practice

Balancing Chemical Equations

1. Copper(II) sulfate, $CuSO_4$, and aluminum react to form aluminum sulfate, $Al_2(SO_4)_3$, and copper. Write the balanced equation for this single-displacement reaction.
2. In a double-displacement reaction, sodium sulfide, Na_2S, reacts with silver nitrate, $AgNO_3$, to form sodium nitrate, $NaNO_3$, and silver sulfide, Ag_2S. Balance this equation.
3. Hydrogen peroxide, H_2O_2, is sometimes used as a bleach or as a disinfectant. Hydrogen peroxide decomposes to give water and molecular oxygen. Write a balanced equation for the decomposition reaction.

Determining Mole Ratios

Look at the reaction of magnesium with oxygen to form magnesium oxide.

$$\text{magnesium} + \text{oxygen} \longrightarrow \text{magnesium oxide}$$

$$2Mg + O_2 \longrightarrow 2MgO$$

The single molecule of oxygen in the equation might be shown as $1O_2$. However, a coefficient of 1 is never written.

Balanced equations show the conservation of mass

Other ways of looking at the amounts in the reaction are shown in ***Figure 16.*** Notice that there are equal numbers of magnesium and oxygen atoms in the product and in the reactants. The total mass of the reactants is always the same as the total mass of the products.

Figure 16 **Information from the Balanced Equation: $2Mg + O_2 \longrightarrow 2MgO$**

Equation:	2Mg	+	O_2	$\longrightarrow$	2MgO
Amount (mol)	2		1	$\longrightarrow$	2
Molecules	$(6.022 \times 10^{23}) \times 2$		$(6.022 \times 10^{23}) \times 1$	$\longrightarrow$	$(6.022 \times 10^{23}) \times 2$
Mass (g)	24.3 g/mol × 2 mol		32.0 g/mol × 1 mol	$\longrightarrow$	40.3 g/mol × 2 mol
Total mass (g)	48.6		32.0	$\longrightarrow$	80.6
Model				$\longrightarrow$	

The law of definite proportions

What if you want 4 mol of magnesium to react completely? If you have twice as much magnesium as the balanced equation calls for, you will need twice as much oxygen. Twice as much magnesium oxide will be formed. No matter what amounts of magnesium and oxygen are combined or how the magnesium oxide is made, the balanced equation does not change. This follows the law of definite proportions, which states:

A compound always contains the same elements in the same proportions, regardless of how the compound is made or how much of the compound is formed.

Mole ratios can be derived from balanced equations

Whether the magnesium-oxygen reaction starts with 2 mol or 4 mol of magnesium, the proportions remain the same. One way to understand this is to look at the **mole ratios** from the balanced equation. For 2 mol of magnesium and 1 mol of oxygen, the ratio is 2:1. If 4 mol of magnesium is present, 2 mol of oxygen is needed to react. The ratio is 4:2, which reduces to 2:1.

mole ratio the relative number of moles of the substances required to produce a given amount of product in a chemical reaction

The mole ratio for any reaction comes from the balanced chemical equation. For example, in the following equation for the electrolysis of water, the mole ratio for H_2O:H_2:O_2, using the coefficients, is 2:2:1.

$$2H_2O \longrightarrow 2H_2 + O_2$$

As you can see in ***Figure 17,*** the hydrogen gas produced occupies twice the volume of the oxygen gas. That is because there are twice as many molecules of hydrogen gas produced in electrolysis as there are molecules of oxygen gas.

Figure 17

Electrical energy causes the decomposition of water into oxygen (in the test tube on the left) and hydrogen (on the right).

Mole ratios allow you to calculate the mass of the reactants

If you know the mole ratios of the substances involved in a reaction, you can determine the relative masses of the substances required to react completely.

The most convenient way to determine the relative masses is by multiplying the molecular mass of each substance by the mole ratio from the balanced equation. For example, for the reaction shown in ***Figure 16,*** the atomic mass of magnesium, 24.3 g/mol, is multiplied by 2 to get a total mass of 48.6 g. The mass of molecular oxygen, 32.0 g/mol, is multiplied by 1. This means that in order for magnesium to react completely with oxygen, there must be 32 g of oxygen available for every 48.6 g of magnesium.

Can you determine the products of a reaction?

Materials
- 7 test tubes
- test-tube rack
- labels or wax pencil
- 10 mL graduated cylinder
- bottles of the following solutions: sodium chloride, NaCl; potassium bromide, KBr; potassium iodide, KI; and silver nitrate, $AgNO_3$

SAFETY CAUTION Wear safety goggles and an apron. Silver nitrate will stain your skin and clothes.

1. Label three test tubes, one each for NaCl, KBr, and KI.
2. Using the graduated cylinder, measure 5 mL of each solution into the properly labeled test tube. Rinse the graduated cylinder between each use.
3. Add 1 mL of $AgNO_3$ solution to each of the test tubes. Record your observations.

Analysis

1. What did you observe as a sign that a double-displacement reaction was occurring?
2. Identify the reactants and products for each reaction.
3. Write the balanced equation for each reaction.
4. Which ion(s) produced a solid with silver nitrate?
5. Does this test let you identify all the ions? Why or why not?

SECTION 3 REVIEW

SUMMARY

- A chemical equation shows the reactants that combine and the products that result from the reaction.
- Balanced chemical equations show the proportions of reactants and products needed for the mass to be conserved.
- A compound always contains the same elements in the same proportions, regardless of how the compound is made or how much of the compound is formed.
- A mole ratio relates the amounts of any two or more substances involved in a chemical reaction.

1. **Identify** which of the following is a complete and balanced chemical equation:
   a. $H_2O \longrightarrow H_2 + O_2$
   b. $NaCl + H_2O$
   c. $Fe + S \longrightarrow FeS$
   d. $CaCO_3$
2. **Balance** the following equations:
   a. $KOH + HCl \longrightarrow KCl + H_2O$
   b. $Pb(NO_3)_2 + KI \longrightarrow KNO_3 + PbI_2$
   c. $NaHCO_3 \longrightarrow H_2O + CO_2 + Na_2CO_3$
   d. $NaCl + H_2SO_4 \longrightarrow Na_2SO_4 + HCl$
3. **Explain** why the numbers in front of chemical formulas, not the subscripts, must be changed to balance an equation.
4. **Describe** the information needed to calculate the mass of a reactant or product for the following balanced equation:

$$FeS + 2HCl \longrightarrow H_2S + FeCl_2$$

5. **Critical Thinking** Ammonia is manufactured by the Haber process in the reaction shown below:

$$N_2 + 3H_2 \rightleftarrows 2NH_3 + \text{heat}$$

This involves the reaction of nitrogen with hydrogen. What mass of nitrogen is needed to make 34 g of ammonia?

SECTION 4

Rates of Change

OBJECTIVES

- **Describe** the factors affecting reaction rates.
- **Explain** the effect a catalyst has on a chemical reaction.
- **Explain** chemical equilibrium in terms of equal forward and reverse reaction rates.
- **Apply** Le Châtelier's principle to predict the effect of changes in concentration, temperature, and pressure in an equilibrium process.

KEY TERMS

catalyst
enzyme
substrate
chemical equilibrium

Chemical reactions can occur at different speeds or rates. Some reactions, such as the explosion of nitroglycerin, shown in ***Figure 18,*** are very fast. Other reactions, such as the burning of carbon in charcoal, are much slower. But what if you wanted to slow down the nitroglycerin reaction to make it safer? What if you wanted to speed up the reaction by which yeast make carbon dioxide, so bread would rise in less time? If you think carefully, you may already know some things about how to change reaction rates.

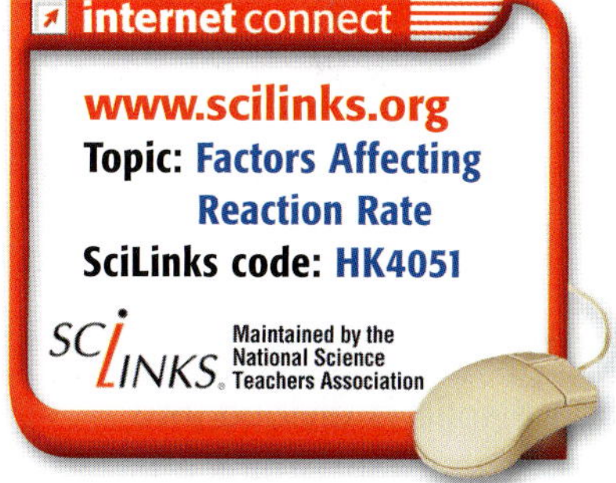

Factors Affecting Reaction Rates

Think about the following observations:

- A potato slice takes 5 minutes to fry in oil at 200°C but takes 10 minutes to cook in boiling water at 100°C. Therefore, potatoes cook faster at higher temperatures.
- Potato slices take 10 minutes to cook in boiling water, but whole potatoes take about 30 minutes to cook. Therefore, potatoes cook faster if you cut them up into smaller pieces.

These observations relate to the speed of chemical reactions. For any reaction to occur, the particles of the reactants must collide with one another. In each situation where the potatoes cooked faster, the contact between particles was greater, so the cooking reaction went faster.

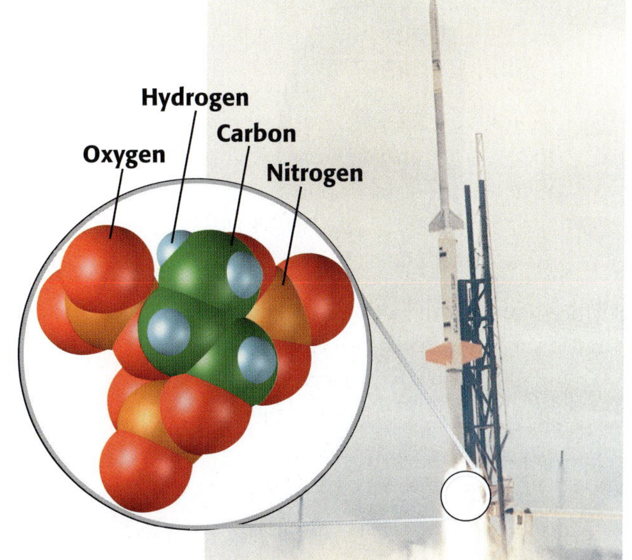

Figure 18

Nitroglycerin can be used as a rocket fuel as well as a medicine for people with heart ailments.

Figure 19

A Mold will grow on bread stored at room temperature. **B** Bread stored in the freezer for the same length of time will be free of mold when you take it out.

Most reactions go faster at higher temperatures

Heating food speeds up the chemical reactions that happen in cooking. Cooling food slows down the chemical reactions that result in spoiling, as shown in ***Figure 19.***

The kinetic theory states that particles move faster at higher temperatures. The faster moving particles collide more often, and there are more chances for the particles to react. Therefore, the reaction will be faster.

A large surface area speeds up reactions

When a whole potato is placed in boiling water, only the outside is in direct contact with the boiling water. The energy transferred from the water takes longer to reach the center of the potato than it would if the potato were sliced. As ***Figure 20*** shows, cutting potatoes into pieces allows parts that were inside the potato to be exposed. In other words, the *surface area* of the potato is increased. The surface area of a solid is the amount of the surface that is exposed. Generally solids that have a large surface area react more rapidly because more particles can come in contact with the other reactants.

Figure 20

When a solid is divided into pieces, the total surface area becomes larger.

Concentrated solutions react faster

Think about a washing machine full of clothes with grass stains on them. If you put a drop of bleach in the water, little will happen to the dirty clothes. If you pour a bottle of bleach into the washing machine, the stained clothes will be clean. The more concentrated solution has more bleach particles. This means a higher chance for particle collisions with the stains.

Reactions are faster at higher pressure

The concentration of a gas can be thought of as the number of particles in a given volume. A gas at high pressure is more concentrated than the same amount of a gas at a low pressure because the gas at high pressure has been squeezed into a smaller volume. Gases react faster at higher pressures; the particles have less space, so they have more collisions.

Massive, bulky molecules react slower

The size and shape of the reactant molecules affect the rate of reaction. You know from the kinetic theory of matter that massive molecules move more slowly than less massive molecules at the same temperature. This means that for equal numbers of massive and "light" molecules of about the same size, the molecules with more mass collide less often with other molecules.

Some molecules, such as large biological compounds, must fit together in a particular way to react. They can collide with other reactants many times, but if the collision occurs on the wrong end of the molecule, they will not react. Generally these compounds react very slowly because many unsuccessful collisions may occur before a successful collision begins the reaction.

internet connect

www.scilinks.org
Topic: Catalysts
SciLinks code: HK4018
SCILINKS. Maintained by the National Science Teachers Association

Catalysts change the rates of chemical reactions

Why add a substance to a reaction if the substance may not react? This is done all the time in industry when **catalysts** are added to make reactions go faster. Catalysts are not reactants or products. They speed up or slow reactions. Catalysts that slow reactions are called *inhibitors*. Catalysts are used to help make ammonia, to process crude oil, and to accelerate making plastics. Catalysts can be expensive and still be profitable because they can be cleaned or renewed and reused. Sometimes the name of the catalyst is written over the reaction arrow of a chemical equation when a catalyst is present.

Catalysts work in different ways. Most solid catalysts, such as those in car exhaust systems, speed up reactions by providing a surface where the reactants can collect and react. Then the reactants can form new bonds to make the products. Most solid catalysts are more effective if they have a large surface area.

catalyst a substance that changes the rate of a chemical reaction without being consumed or changed significantly

enzyme a type of protein that speeds up metabolic reactions in plants and animals without being permanently changed or destroyed

Enzymes are biological catalysts

Enzymes are proteins that are catalysts for chemical reactions in living things. Enzymes are very specific. Each enzyme controls one reaction or set of similar reactions. Some common enzymes and the reactions they control are listed in ***Table 1***. Most enzymes are fragile. If they are kept too cold or too warm, they tend to decompose. Most enzymes stop working above 45°C.

Table 1 **Common Enzymes and Their Uses**

Enzyme	Substrate	What the enzyme does
Amylase	starch	breaks down long starch molecules into sugars
Cellulase	cellulose	breaks down long cellulose molecules into sugars
DNA polymerase	nucleic acid	builds up DNA chains in cell nuclei
Lipase	fat	breaks down fat into smaller molecules
Protease	protein	breaks down proteins into amino acids

Catalase, an enzyme produced by humans and most other living organisms, breaks down hydrogen peroxide. Hydrogen peroxide is the **substrate** for catalase.

substrate a part, substance, or element that lies beneath and supports another part, substance, or element; the reactant in reactions catalyzed by enzymes

$$2H_2O_2 \xrightarrow{\text{catalase}} 2H_2O + O_2$$

For an enzyme to catalyze a reaction, the substrate and the enzyme must fit exactly—like a key in a lock. This fit is shown in ***Figure 21.*** Enzymes are very efficient. In 1 minute, one molecule of catalase can catalyze the decomposition of 6 million molecules of hydrogen peroxide.

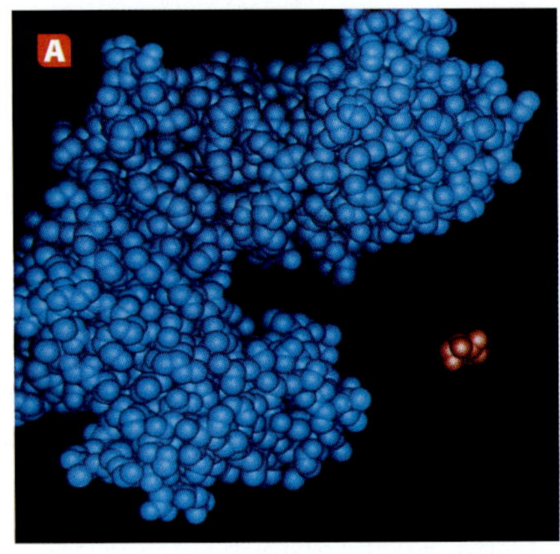

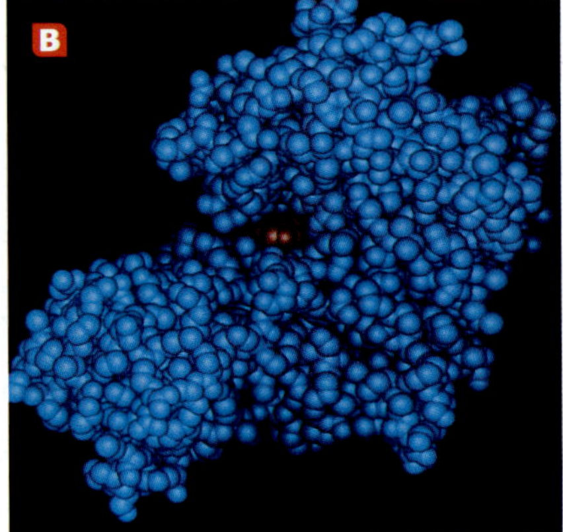

Figure 21

The enzyme hexokinase catalyzes the addition of phosphate to glucose. This model shows the enzyme, in blue, before **A** and after **B** it fits with a glucose molecule, shown in red.

Quick Lab

What affects the rates of chemical reactions?

Materials

- *Bunsen burner*
- *paper clip*
- *6 test tubes*
- *paper ash*
- *sandpaper*
- *tongs*
- *matches*
- *2 sugar cubes*
- *steel wool ball, 2 cm diameter*
- *graduated cylinder*
- *vinegar*
- *magnesium ribbon, copper foil strip, zinc strip; each 3 cm long, uniform width*

SAFETY CAUTION Wear safety goggles and an apron.

1. Label three test tubes 1, 2, and 3. Place 10 mL of vinegar in each test tube. Sandpaper the metals until they are shiny. Then add the magnesium to test tube 1, the zinc to test tube 2, and the copper to test tube 3. Record your observations.
2. Using tongs, hold a paper clip in the hottest part of the burner flame for 30 s. Repeat with a ball of steel wool. Record your observations.
3. Label three more test tubes A, B, and C. To test tube A, add 10 mL of vinegar; to test tube B, add 5 mL of vinegar and 5 mL of water; and to test tube C, add 2.5 mL of vinegar and 7.5 mL of water. Add a piece of magnesium ribbon to each test tube. Record your observations.
4. Using tongs, hold a sugar cube and try to ignite it with a match. Rub paper ash on another cube and try again. Record your observations.

Analysis

1. Describe and interpret your results.
2. For each step, list the factor(s) that influenced the rate of reaction.

Equilibrium Systems

When nitroglycerin explodes, not much nitroglycerin is left. When an iron nail rusts, given enough time, all the iron is converted to iron(III) oxide and only the rust remains. Even though an explosion occurs rapidly and rusting occurs slowly, both reactions go to completion. Most of the reactants are converted to products, and the amount that is not converted is not noticeable and usually is not important.

Some changes are reversible

You may get the idea that all chemical reactions go to completion if you watch a piece of wood burn or see an explosion. However, reactions don't always go to completion; some are reversible.

For example, carbonated drinks, such as the soda shown in ***Figure 22,*** contain carbon dioxide. These drinks are manufactured by dissolving carbon dioxide in water under pressure. To keep the carbon dioxide dissolved, you need to maintain the pressure by keeping the top on the bottle. Opening the soda allows the pressure to decrease. When this happens, some of the carbon dioxide comes out of solution, and you see a stream of carbon dioxide bubbles. This carbon dioxide change is reversible.

$$CO_2 \text{ (gas above liquid)} \underset{\text{decrease pressure}}{\overset{\text{increase pressure}}{\rightleftarrows}} CO_2 \text{ (gas dissolved in liquid)}$$

The physical change can go in either direction. The $\rightleftarrows$ sign indicates a reversible change. Compare it with the arrow you normally see in chemical reactions, $\longrightarrow$, which indicates a change that goes in one direction—toward completion.

> **Quick ACTIVITY**
>
> **Catalysts in Action**
>
> 1. Pour 2% hydrogen peroxide into a test tube to a depth of 2 cm.
> 2. Pour 2 cm of water into another test tube.
> 3. Drop a small piece of raw liver into each test tube.
> 4. Liver contains the enzyme catalase. Watch carefully, and describe what happens. Explain your observations.
> 5. Repeat steps 1–4 using a piece of liver that has been boiled for 3 minutes. Explain your result.
> 6. Repeat steps 1–4 again using iron filings instead of liver. What happens?

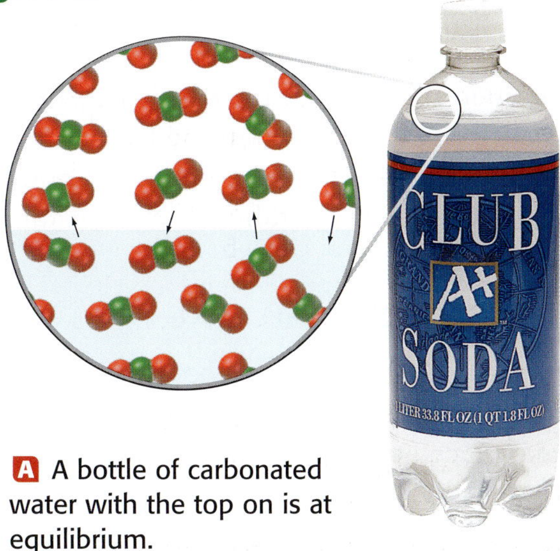

A A bottle of carbonated water with the top on is at equilibrium.

B When the top is removed, the carbonated water is no longer at equilibrium.

chemical equilibrium a state of balance in which the rate of a forward reaction equals the rate of the reverse reaction and the concentrations of products and reactants remain unchanged

VOCABULARY Skills Tip

Equilibrium comes from the Latin aequilibris *meaning equally balanced. In Latin,* aequil *means equal, and* libra *means a balance scale. You may have seen the constellation called Libra. The stars in the constellation roughly represent a balance.*

Equilibrium results when rates balance

When a carbonated drink is in a closed bottle, you can't see any changes. The system is in **chemical equilibrium**—a balanced state. This balanced state is dynamic. No changes are apparent, but changes are occurring. If you could see individual molecules in the bottle, you would see continual change. Molecules of CO_2 are coming out of solution constantly. However, CO_2 molecules from the air above the liquid are dissolving at the same time and the same rate.

The result is that the amount of dissolved and undissolved CO_2 doesn't change, even though individual CO_2 molecules are moving in and out of the solution. This is similar to the number of players on the field for a football team. Although different players can be on the field at any time, eleven players are always on the field for each team.

Systems in equilibrium respond to minimize change

When the top is removed from a carbonated drink, the drink is no longer at equilibrium, and CO_2 leaves as bubbles. For equilibrium to be reached, none of the reactants or products can escape.

The conversion of limestone, $CaCO_3$, to lime, CaO, is a chemical reaction that can lead to equilibrium. Limestone and seashells, which are also made of $CaCO_3$, were used to make lime more than 2000 years ago. By heating limestone in an open pot, lime was produced to make cement. The ancient buildings in Greece and Rome, such as the one shown in ***Figure 23,*** were probably built with cement made by this reaction.

$$CaCO_3 + heat \longrightarrow CaO + CO_2$$

Because the CO_2 gas can escape from an open pot, the reaction proceeds until all of the limestone is converted to lime.

However, if some dry limestone is sealed in a closed container and heated, the result is different. As soon as some CO_2 builds up in the container, the reverse reaction starts. Once the concentrations of the $CaCO_3$, CaO, and CO_2 stabilize, equilibrium is established.

$$CaCO_3 \rightleftharpoons CaO + CO_2$$

If there aren't any changes in the pressure or the temperature, the forward and reverse reactions continue to take place at the same rate. The concentration of CO_2 and the amounts of $CaCO_3$ and CaO in the container do not change.

Figure 23

Cement for ancient buildings, like this one in Limeni, Greece, probably contained lime made from seashells.

Table 2 **The Effects of Change on Equilibrium**

Condition	Effect
Temperature	Increasing temperature favors the reaction that absorbs energy.
Pressure	Increasing pressure favors the reaction that produces fewer molecules of gas.
Concentration	Increasing the concentration of one substance favors the reaction that produces less of that substance.

Le Châtelier's principle predicts changes in equilibrium

Le Châtelier's principle is a general rule that describes the behavior of equilibrium systems.

If a change is made to a system in chemical equilibrium, the equilibrium shifts to oppose the change until a new equilibrium is reached.

The effects of different changes on an equilibrium system are shown in ***Table 2.***

Ammonia is a chemical building block used to make fertilizers, dyes, plastics, cosmetics, cleaning products, and fire retardants, such as those you see being applied in ***Figure 24.*** The Haber process, which is used to make ammonia industrially, is exothermic; it releases energy.

$$\text{nitrogen} + \text{hydrogen} \rightleftarrows \text{ammonia} + \text{heat}$$

$$N_2\ (\text{gas}) + 3H_2\ (\text{gas}) \rightleftarrows 2NH_3\ (\text{gas}) + \text{heat}$$

At an ammonia-manufacturing plant production chemists must choose the conditions that favor the highest yield of NH_3. In other words, the equilibrium should favor the production of NH_3.

INTEGRATING

ENVIRONMENTAL SCIENCE

All living things need nitrogen, which cycles through the environment. Nitrogen gas, N_2, is changed to ammonia by bacteria in soils. Different bacteria in the soil change the ammonia to nitrites and nitrates. Nitrogen in the form of nitrates is needed by plants to grow. Animals eat the plants and deposit nitrogen compounds back in the soil. When plants or animals die, nitrogen compounds are also returned to the soil. Additional bacteria change the nitrogen compounds back to nitrogen gas, and the cycle can start again.

Figure 24

Ammonium sulfate and ammonium phosphate are being dropped from the airplane as fire retardants. The red dye used for identification fades away after a few days.

Figure 25

Ammonia, which is manufactured in plants such as this, is used to make ammonium perchlorate—one of the space shuttle's fuels.

Le Châtelier's principle can be used to control reactions

If you raise the temperature, Le Châtelier's principle indicates that the equilibrium will shift to the left, the direction that absorbs energy and makes less ammonia. If you raise the pressure, the equilibrium will move to reduce the pressure according to Le Châtelier's principle. One way to reduce the pressure is to have fewer gas molecules. This means the equilibrium moves to the right—more ammonia—because there are fewer gas molecules on the right side. So to get the most ammonia from this reaction, you need to use a high pressure and a low temperature. The Haber process is a good example of balancing equilibrium conditions to make the most product. A manufacturing plant that uses the Haber process to produce ammonia is shown in ***Figure 25.***

SECTION 4 REVIEW

SUMMARY

- Increasing the temperature, surface area, concentration, or pressure of reactants may speed up chemical reactions.
- Catalysts alter the rate of chemical reactions. Most catalysts speed up chemical reactions. Others, called inhibitors, slow reactions down.
- In a chemical reaction, chemical equilibrium is achieved when reactants change to products and products change to reactants at the same time and the same rate.
- At chemical equilibrium, no changes are apparent even though individual particles are reacting.
- Le Châtelier's principle states that for any change made to a system in equilibrium, the equilibrium will shift to minimize the effects of the change.

1. **List** five factors that may affect the rate of a chemical reaction.
2. **Describe** what can happen to the reaction rate of a system that is heated and then cooled.
3. **Compare and Contrast** a catalyst and an inhibitor.
4. **Analyze** the error in reasoning in the following situation: A person claims that because the overall amounts of reactants and products don't change, a reaction must have stopped.
5. **Decide** which way an increase in pressure will shift the following equilibrium system involving ethane, C_2H_6, oxygen, O_2, water, H_2O, and carbon dioxide, CO_2.
   $$2C_2H_6\text{ (gas)} + 7O_2\text{ (gas)} \rightleftharpoons 6H_2O\text{ (liquid)} + 4CO_2\text{ (gas)}$$
6. **Identify and Explain** an example of Le Châtelier's principle.
7. **Identify** the effect of the following changes on the system in which the reversible reaction shown below is taking place:
   $$4HCl\text{ (gas)} + O_2\text{ (gas)} \rightleftharpoons 2Cl_2\text{ (gas)} + 2H_2O\text{ (gas)} + \text{heat}$$
   a. the pressure of the system is increased
   b. the pressure of the system is decreased
   c. the concentration of O_2 is decreased
   d. the temperature of the system is increased
8. **Critical Thinking** Consider the decomposition of solid calcium carbonate to solid calcium oxide and carbon dioxide gas.
   $$\text{heat} + CaCO_3 \rightleftharpoons CaO + CO_2\text{ (gas)}$$
   What conditions of temperature and pressure would you choose to get the most decomposition of $CaCO_3$? Explain.

Math Skills

Using Mole Ratios to Calculate Mass

Determine the mass of hydrogen gas, H_2, and oxygen gas, O_2, produced by 4 mol of water, H_2O, in the following chemical reaction:

$$2H_2O \longrightarrow 2H_2 + O_2$$

1 Write down the mole ratio for the balanced equation and multiply the ratio to obtain the number of moles of H_2O.

There are 4 mol of H_2O, so multiply each number in the ratio by 2.

Equation	$2H_2O$	$\longrightarrow$	$2H_2$	+	O_2
Mole ratio	2	:	2	:	1
Amount (mol)	4		4		2

2 Determine the mass per mol of each substance.

Look up the atomic mass of each element first. Since there are 2 hydrogen atoms and 1 oxygen atom in each molecule of H_2O, the mass per mol of H_2O is 2×1 g/mol + 16 g/mol = 18 g/mol. Similarly, the mass of H_2 is 2 g/mol, and the mass of O_2 is 32 g/mol.

3 Multiply the number of moles by the mass per mol of each substance.

The total mass of the reactants should match the total mass of the products.

Equation	$2H_2O$	$\longrightarrow$	$2H_2$	+	O_2
Mole ratio	2	:	2	:	1
Amount (mol)	4		4		2
Mass per mol	18 g/mol		2 g/mol		32 g/mol
Mass	18 g/mol $\times$ 4 mol	=	2 g/mol $\times$ 4 mol	+	32 g/mol $\times$ 2 mol
Total mass	72 g	=	8 g	+	64 g

4 mol of H_2O (72 g) will produce 8 g of H_2 and 64 g of O_2.

Practice

1. Determine the mass of H_2SO_4 produced when 1 mol of H_2O reacts with 1 mol of SO_3 in the following reaction:

$$H_2O + SO_3 \longrightarrow H_2SO_4$$

2. Determine the mass of $ZnSO_4$ produced in the following reaction if 2 mol of Zn reacts with 2 mol of $CuSO_4$.

$$Zn + CuSO_4 \longrightarrow ZnSO_4 + Cu$$

CHAPTER 6 REVIEW

Chapter Highlights

Before you begin, review the summaries of the key ideas of each section, found at the end of each section. The key vocabulary terms are listed on the first page of each section.

UNDERSTANDING CONCEPTS

1. When a chemical reaction occurs, atoms are never
- **a.** ionized.
- **b.** rearranged.
- **c.** destroyed.
- **d.** vaporized.

2. In an exothermic reaction,
- **a.** energy is conserved.
- **b.** the formation of bonds in the product releases more energy than is required to break the bonds in the reactants.
- **c.** energy is released as bonds form.
- **d.** All of the above

3. Radicals
- **a.** form ionic bonds with other ions.
- **b.** result from broken covalent bonds.
- **c.** usually break apart to form smaller components.
- **d.** bind molecules together.

4. Hydrogen peroxide, H_2O_2, decomposes to produce water and oxygen gas. The balanced equation for this reaction is
- **a.** $H_2O_2 \longrightarrow H_2O + O_2$.
- **b.** $2H_2O_2 \longrightarrow 2H_2O + O_2$.
- **c.** $2H_2O_2 \longrightarrow H_2O + 2O_2$.
- **d.** $2H_2O_2 \longrightarrow 2H_2O + 2O_2$.

5. Most reactions speed up when
- **a.** the temperature is lowered.
- **b.** equilibrium is achieved.
- **c.** the concentration of the products is increased.
- **d.** the reactants are in small pieces.

6. A system in chemical equilibrium
- **a.** has particles that don't move.
- **b.** responds to minimize change.
- **c.** is undergoing visible change.
- **d.** is stable only when all of the reactants have been used.

USING VOCABULARY

7. Explain what it means when a system in equilibrium shifts to favor the products.

8. When wood is burned, energy is released in the forms of heat and light. Describe the reaction, and explain why this change does not violate the law of conservation of energy. Use the terms *combustion, exothermic,* and *chemical energy.* **WRITING SKILL**

9. Translate the following chemical equation into a sentence.

$$CH_4 + 2O_2 \longrightarrow CO_2 + 2H_2O$$

10. How does a *combustion* reaction differ from other chemical reactions?

11. Use the *kinetic theory* to explain how an increase in the surface area of a reactant and higher temperatures can increase the rate of a chemical reaction.

12. For each of the following changes to the equilibrium system below, predict which reaction will be favored—forward (to the right), reverse (to the left), or neither.

$$H_2\ (\text{gas}) + Cl_2\ (\text{gas}) \rightleftharpoons 2HCl\ (\text{gas}) + \text{heat}$$

- **a.** addition of Cl_2
- **b.** removal of HCl
- **c.** increased pressure
- **d.** decreased temperature
- **e.** removal of H_2

BUILDING GRAPHING SKILLS

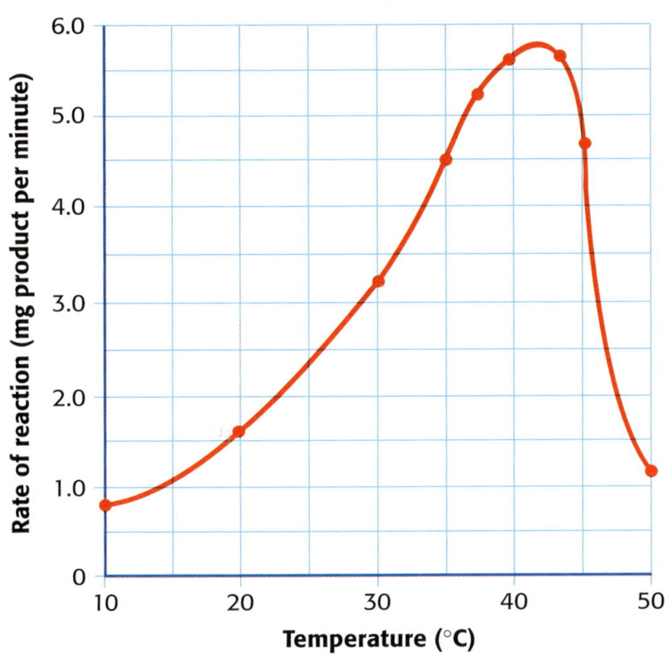

13. **Graphing** A technician carried out an experiment to study the effect of increasing temperature on a certain reaction. Her results are shown in the graph above.
    a. Between which temperatures does the rate of the reaction rise?
    b. Between which temperatures does the rate of the reaction slow down?
    c. At what temperature is the rate of the reaction fastest?

BUILDING MATH SKILLS

14. **Chemical Equations** In 1774, Joseph Priestly discovered oxygen when he heated solid mercury(II) oxide, HgO, and produced the element mercury and oxygen gas. Write and balance this equation.

15. **Chemical Equations** Write the balanced chemical equation for methane, CH_4, reacting with oxygen gas to produce water and carbon dioxide.

16. **Chemical Equations** Sucrose, $C_{12}H_{22}O_{11}$, is a sugar used to sweeten many foods. Inside the body, it is broken down to produce H_2O and CO_2.

$$C_{12}H_{22}O_{11} + 12O_2 \longrightarrow 12CO_2 + 11H_2O$$

List all of the mole ratios that can be determined from this equation.

17. **Chemical Equations** Sulfur burns in air to form sulfur dioxide.

$$S + O_2 \longrightarrow SO_2$$

    a. What mass of SO_2 is formed from 64 g of sulfur?
    b. What mass of sulfur is necessary to form 256 g of SO_2?

18. **Chemical Formulas** What is the mass of 25 moles of water, H_2O?

THINKING CRITICALLY

19. **Designing Systems** Paper consists mainly of cellulose, a complex compound made up of simple sugars. Suggest a method for turning old newspapers into sugars using an enzyme. What problems would there be? What precautions would need to be taken?

20. **Applying Knowledge** Molecular models of some chemical reactions are pictured below. Correct the drawings by adding coefficients or drawing molecules with a computer drawing program to reflect balanced equations.

COMPUTER SKILL

a.

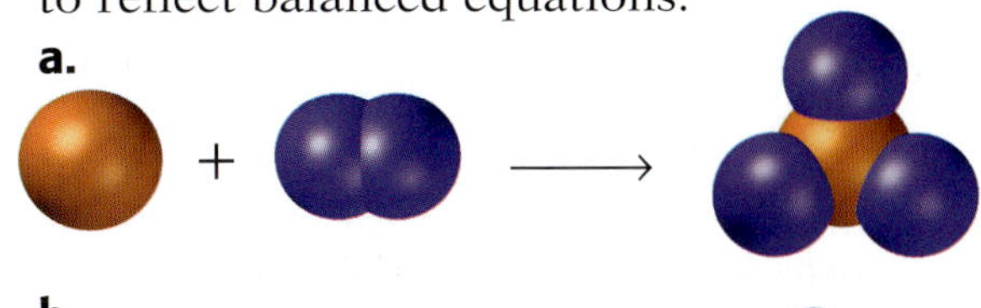

b.

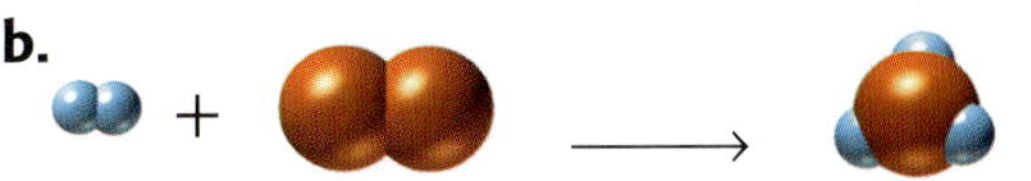

c.

21. **Creative Thinking** Explain why hydrogen gas is given off when a reactive metal undergoes a single-displacement reaction with water.

22. **Applying Knowledge** Classify each of the following reactions as synthesis, decomposition, single-displacement, double-displacement, or combustion:
    a. $N_2 + 3H_2 \longrightarrow 2NH_3$
    b. $2Li + 2H_2O \longrightarrow 2LiOH + H_2$
    c. $2NaNO_3 \longrightarrow 2NaNO_2 + O_2$
    d. $2C_6H_{14} + 19O_2 \longrightarrow 12CO_2 + 14H_2O$
    e. $NH_4Cl \longrightarrow NH_3 + HCl$
    f. $BaO + H_2O \longrightarrow Ba(OH)_2$
    g. $AgNO_3 + NaCl \longrightarrow AgCl + NaNO_3$

DEVELOPING LIFE/WORK SKILLS

23. **Making Decisions** Cigarette smoke contains carbon monoxide. Why do you think carbon monoxide is in the smoke? Why is smoking bad for your health?

24. **Interpreting and Communicating** Choose several items labeled "biodegradable," and research the decomposition reactions involved. Write balanced chemical equations for the decomposition reactions. Be sure to note any conditions that must occur for the substance to biodegrade. Present your information to the class to inform the students about what products are best for the environment.

INTEGRATING CONCEPTS

25. **Integrating Biology** Research the enzymes listed in the table called "Common Enzymes and Their Uses" in Section 4. Write a paragraph on each one, describing in what way it acts as a catalyst.

26. **Integrating Physics** Explain how a balanced chemical equation illustrates that mass is never lost or gained in a chemical reaction.

27. **Concept Mapping** Copy the unfinished concept map given below onto a sheet of paper. Complete the map by writing the correct word or phrase in the lettered box.

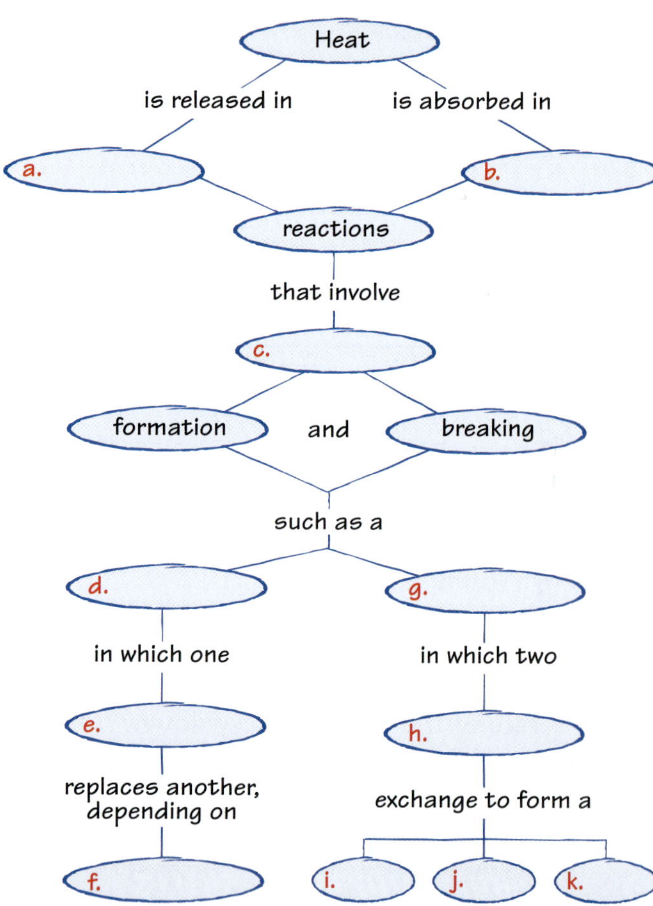

Standardized Test Prep

Understanding Concepts

***Directions (1–3):* For *each* question, write on a separate sheet of paper the letter of the correct answer.**

1 $Mg(s) + Cl_2(g) \longrightarrow MgCl_2(s)$ is an example of what type of chemical reaction?
- **A.** synthesis reaction
- **B.** decomposition reaction
- **C.** single-displacement reaction
- **D.** double-displacement reaction

2 Which of the following changes will not increase the rate of a chemical reaction?
- **F.** using an enzyme in a reaction
- **G.** adding an inhibitor to the reaction mixture
- **H.** increasing the concentration of the reactants
- **I.** grinding a solid reactant to make a fine powder

3 Which of the following is an endothermic chemical reaction?
- **A.** fireworks exploding in the sky
- **B.** photosynthesis in plant cells
- **C.** respiration in animal cells
- **D.** wood burning in a fireplace

***Directions (4–5):* For *each* question, write a short response.**

4 Most chemical reactions proceed faster if the reactants are heated. How does the added heat affect reactant atoms or molecules?

5 The reaction of glucose and oxygen to form carbon dioxide and water produces the same amount of energy inside living cells as it does by combustion. Analyze how this reaction can occur at body temperature in the cells, but not in the open air.

Test TIP

When using a diagram to answer a question, look in the image for evidence that supports your potential answer.

Reading Skills

***Directions (6):* Read the passage below. Then answer the question.**

Some metals react with water to form new compounds by displacing hydrogen from water molecules. Alkali metals are sufficiently reactive that this chemical reaction happens at room temperature. If a piece of cesium is placed in water, an explosion occurs as the hydrogen gas reacts with oxygen in the air.

6 Hydrogen and oxygen gases do not react spontaneously when they are mixed, unless energy is added to start the reaction. What is the source of energy that causes hydrogen to react explosively when cesium is added to water?

Interpreting Graphics

***Directions (7):* The graphs below plot energy changes during two different types of chemical reactions. Base your answer to question 7 on the graphs.**

Energy Changes During Chemical Reactions

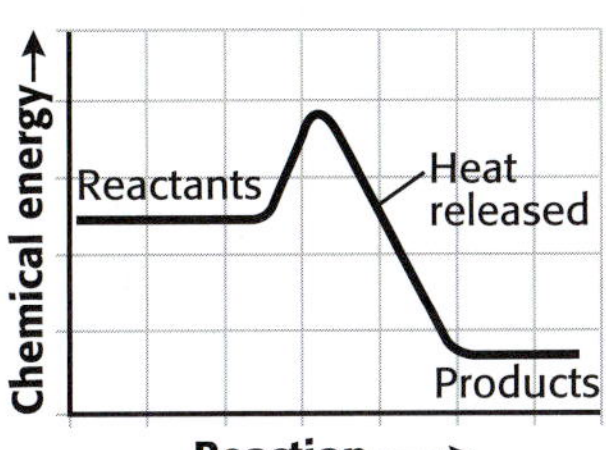

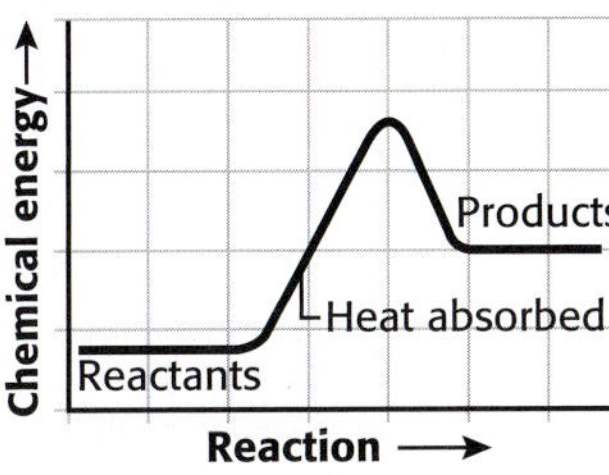

7 In each of these reactions, the chemical energy increases and then decreases, during the course of the reaction. What does the height of this "hill" on each graph represent?
- **F.** energy that must be added to start the reaction
- **G.** energy released as reactant molecules approach one another
- **H.** the potential energy of the chemical bonds in the molecules of the reactants
- **I.** the change in total chemical energy between the reactants and the products

Skills Practice Lab

Introduction

How can you show that the rate of a chemical reaction depends on the temperature of the reactants?

Objectives

- ***Measure*** the volume of gas evolved to determine the average rate of the reaction between zinc and hydrochloric acid.
- USING SCIENTIFIC METHODS ***Determine*** how the rate of this reaction depends on the temperature of the reactants.

Materials

beaker to hold a 10 mL graduated cylinder
graduated cylinder, 10 mL
graduated cylinder, 25 mL
heavy scissors
hydrochloric acid, 1.0 M
ice
metric ruler
rubber tubing
sidearm flasks with rubber stoppers (2)
stopwatch
strips of thick zinc foil, 10 mm wide
thermometer
water bath to hold a sidearm flask

Measuring the Rate of a Chemical Reaction

Procedure

Observing the Reaction Between Zinc and Hydrochloric Acid

1. On a blank sheet of paper, prepare a table like the one shown at right.
   SAFETY CAUTION Hydrochloric acid can cause severe burns. Wear a lab apron, gloves, and safety goggles. If you get acid on your skin or clothing, wash it off at the sink while calling to your teacher. If you get acid in your eyes, immediately flush it out at the eyewash station while calling to your teacher. Continue rinsing for at least 15 minutes or until help arrives.

2. Fill a 10 mL graduated cylinder with water. Turn the cylinder upside down in a beaker of water, taking care to keep the cylinder full. Place one end of the rubber tubing under the spout of the graduated cylinder. Attach the other end of the tubing to the arm of the flask. Place the flask in a water bath at room temperature. Record the initial gas volume of the cylinder and the temperature of the water bath in your data table.
3. Cut a piece of zinc about 50–75 mm long. Measure the length, and record this in your data table. Place the zinc in the sidearm flask.
4. Measure 25 mL of hydrochloric acid in a graduated cylinder.
5. Carefully pour the acid from the graduated cylinder into the flask. Start the stopwatch as you begin to pour. Stopper the flask as soon as the acid is transferred.
6. Record any signs of a chemical reaction you observe.
7. After 15 minutes, determine the amount of gas given off by the reaction. Record the volume of gas in your data table.

	Length of zinc strip (mm)	Initial gas volume (mL)	Final gas volume (mL)	Temperature (°C)	Reaction time (s)
Reaction 1					
Reaction 2					

Designing Your Experiment

8. With your lab partners decide how you will answer the question posed at the beginning of the lab. By completing steps 1–7, you have half the data you need to answer the question. How can you collect the rest of the data?
9. In your lab report, list each step you will perform in your experiment. Because temperature is the variable you want to test, the other variables in your experiment should be the same as they were in steps 1–7.
10. Before you carry out your experiment, your teacher must approve your plan.

Performing Your Experiment

11. After your teacher approves your plan, carry out your experiment. Record your results in your data table.
12. How do the two reactions differ?

Analysis

1. Express the rate of each reaction as mL of gas evolved in 1 minute.
2. Which reaction was more rapid?
3. Divide the faster rate by the slower rate, and express the reaction rates as a ratio.
4. According to your results, how does decreasing the temperature affect the rate of a chemical reaction?

Conclusions

5. How could you test the effect of temperature on this reaction without using an ice bath?
6. How can you express the rate of each of the two reactions you conducted as a function of the surface area of the zinc?
7. How would you design an experiment to test the effect of surface area on this reaction?

viewpoints

How Should Life-Saving Inventions Be Introduced?

Researchers are developing better fireproof materials to use inside passenger airplanes. But the new materials are much more expensive than the ones currently used.

Should the Federal Aviation Administration (FAA) require that the new materials be used on all new and old planes, or should it be up to the plane manufacturers and airlines to decide whether to use the new materials?

A similar debate occurs whenever life-saving inventions are introduced, from automobile airbags to better child-safety seats. If the inventions should be used, who should bear the cost? Should it be the federal government, an insurance company, a manufacturer, or the customers?

If the device shouldn't be required at all times, how do you decide when it should be used? When are the risks so small that it doesn't make sense to spend money on another safety device?

What do you think?

> FROM: Stacey F., Rochester, MN.

It should be up to the plane manufactuers because not all companies would be able to afford the cost. The FAA should look into the budgets of all plane companies and companies that can afford it should be required to use the new material.

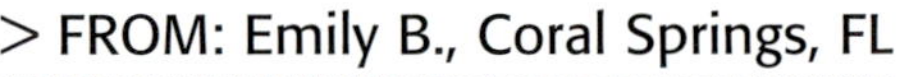

> FROM: Emily B., Coral Springs, FL

I think it should be up to the plane manufacturers and airlines. The new materials shouldn't be required on planes that are already built or on planes that are being built, because of expenses. However, it would be to an airline's advantage to have the best safety material possible for their customers' sake.

> FROM: Virginia M., Houston, TX

The airlines are responsible for the lives of their passengers, so they should decide. But the FAA should pass a law stating that if the airlines refuse new safety measures, the airlines will accept total responsibility for any accidents that occur.

Leave the Decisions to the Companies Involved

Require Safety Immediately

> FROM: April R., Coral Springs, FL

If it can save just one life, it's worth spending money and time on. Eventually the technology will be required on all planes anyway. If an airline chose not to use these materials and there were an accident, there would be liability cases because lives might have been saved. Most people will have no problem spending more for a plane ticket if their safety is ensured.

> FROM: Carlene de C., Chicago, IL

The FAA should require that all planes—those currently in use and those being built—have fireproof materials. Otherwise, passengers could sue the airline company if they were hurt in a fire and it could have been prevented.

> FROM: Shannon B., Bowling Green, KY.

They should put the new fireproof materials on all planes, even the ones that have already been built. The public's health is at risk if a plane malfunctions, and the airlines should want to keep everybody safe. Otherwise they will lose customers.

Your Turn

1. **Critiquing Viewpoints** Select one of the statements on this page that you agree with. Explain at least one weak point in the statement. How would you respond to someone who used this point as a reason you were wrong?
2. **Critiquing Viewpoints** Select one of the statements on this page that you disagree with. Explain one strong point in the statement. How would you respond to someone who used this point as a reason they were right?
3. **Evaluating Science** Identify and describe another example of research into new materials or technologies that resulted in a life-saving invention. Evaluate the impact this research or invention had on society.
4. **Life/Work Skills** Imagine that you are preparing to testify in a congressional hearing about this matter. Choose the four most important points you'd make, and draft a statement that explains all of them persuasively.

CHAPTER 7

Solutions

Chapter Preview

Background Paramedics rush to the scene of an accident. Someone has been injured, and the person's blood pressure has become dangerously low. Paramedics pump a *saline solution*, a mixture of water and sodium chloride that is similar to blood, into the person's veins. This mixture maintains the blood pressure that is needed to keep the person alive on the way to the hospital.

Shots called *vaccines* are mixtures that help protect you from many diseases. Vaccines have a tiny amount of the disease-causing organism you are trying to protect yourself from. The shot you get is harmless because the organism contained in it is dead, or inactivated. But the shot keeps you from getting the disease because your body can now recognize this harmful bacterium or virus again and fight it.

Activity 1 Look up the word *saline* in the dictionary. Which group of elements in the periodic table form ionic compounds that can be described by the word *saline*? Explain how the word *saline* applies to sodium chloride.

Activity 2 Fill a clear plastic cup with water. After the water settles, add table salt one teaspoon at a time to the water. Stir after you add each spoonful until all of the salt dissolves. How much salt are you able to dissolve before it stops dissolving and settles to the bottom of the cup? Perform this activity again, but this time use sugar instead of salt. Does the same amount of sugar dissolve? If not, what might explain the difference?

Many solutions can be life-saving. Some solutions replace vital fluids in your body if you are injured, while others protect you from deadly diseases.

Pre-Reading Questions

1. The label on some drinks reads "Shake well before serving." Why do you need to shake these drinks? Why don't you need to shake all drinks?
2. Frozen orange juice must be mixed with water before you can drink it. Why is frozen orange juice referred to as *orange juice concentrate*?

SECTION 1

Solutions and Other Mixtures

KEY TERMS

suspension
colloid
emulsion
solution
solute
solvent
alloy

OBJECTIVES

- **Distinguish** between heterogeneous mixtures and homogeneous mixtures.
- **Compare** the properties of suspensions, colloids, and solutions.
- **Give** examples of solutions that contain solids or gases.

Any sample of matter is either a pure substance or a mixture of pure substances. You can easily tell that fruit salad is a mixture because it is a blend of different kinds of fruit. But some mixtures look like they are pure substances. For example, a mixture of salt and water looks the same as pure water. Air is a mixture of several gases, but you cannot see different gases in the air.

Figure 1

Fruit salad is a heterogeneous mixture. Each spoonful has a different composition of fruit because the fruits are not distributed evenly throughout the salad.

Heterogeneous Mixtures

The amount of each substance in different samples of a *heterogeneous mixture* varies, just as the amount of each kind of fruit varies in each spoonful of fruit salad, as shown in ***Figure 1.*** If you compared two shovels full of dirt from a garden, they would not be exactly the same. Each shovelful would have a different mixture of rock, sand, clay, and decayed matter.

Another naturally occurring heterogeneous mixture is granite, a type of igneous rock shown in ***Figure 2.*** Granite is a mixture of crystals of the minerals quartz, mica, and feldspar. Because a mixture has no fixed composition, samples of granite from different locations can vary greatly in appearance because the samples have different proportions of minerals.

Figure 2

These paperweights are made from granite, which is a mixture of quartz, black mica, and feldspar.

Figure 3 **Orange Juice: A Heterogeneous Mixture**

A The pulp in the orange juice is spread throughout the mixture right after the orange juice is shaken.

B Over time, the pulp does not stay mixed with the water molecules. The pulp settles to the bottom, and two layers form.

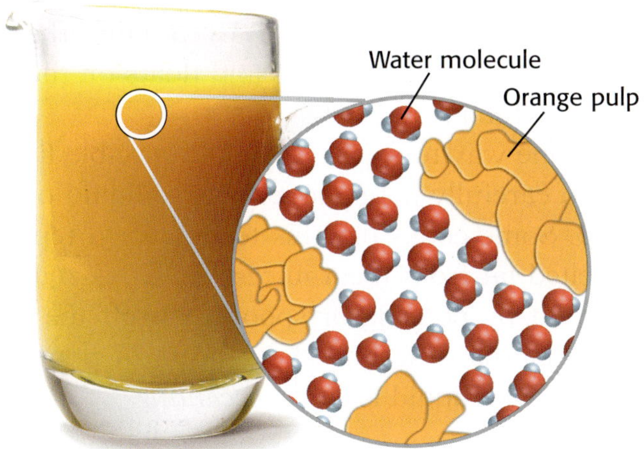

Particles in a suspension are large and eventually settle out

Have you ever forgotten to shake the orange juice carton before pouring yourself a glass of juice? The juice probably tasted thin and watery. Natural orange juice is a **suspension** of orange pulp in a clear liquid that is mostly water, as shown in ***Figure 3A.*** A property of a suspension is that the particles settle out when the mixture is allowed to stand. So if the orange juice carton is not shaken, the top layer of the juice in the carton is mostly water because all the pulp has settled to the bottom.

Orange juice is clearly a heterogeneous mixture because after it settles, the liquid near the top of the container is not the same as the liquid near the bottom. Shaking the container mixes the pulp and water, but the pulp pieces are big enough that they will eventually settle out again, as shown in ***Figure 3B.***

suspension a mixture in which particles of a material are more or less evenly dispersed throughout a liquid or gas

Particles in a suspension may be filtered out

Particles in suspensions are usually the size of or larger than the tip of an extremely sharp pencil, which has a diameter of about 1000 nm, or about the size of a bacterial cell. Particles of this size are large enough that they can be filtered out of the mixture. For example, a filter made of porous paper can be used to catch the suspended pulp in orange juice. That is, the pulp stays in the filter, while water molecules pass through the filter easily. You can classify a mixture as a suspension if the particles settle out or can be filtered out.

Figure 4

Some salad dressings are made with oil and vinegar, which form a suspension when shaken. Oil and vinegar mixtures separate after standing for a few minutes.

Some mixtures of two liquids will separate

Oil, vinegar, and flavorings can be shaken together to make salad dressing. But when the dressing stands for a few minutes, two layers form, as shown in ***Figure 4.*** The two liquids separate because they are *immiscible,* which means they do not mix. Eventually, the oil, which is less dense, rises and floats on the vinegar, which is denser.

One way to separate two immiscible liquids is to carefully pour the less dense liquid off the top. Some cooks use this technique to separate melted fat from meat juices. The cook removes the fat by pouring or spooning it off the meat juices, which are denser than the fat. The process of pouring a lighter liquid off of a heavier liquid is called *decanting.*

Particles in a colloid are too small to settle out

Latex paint is an example of another kind of heterogeneous mixture called a **colloid.** Latex paint is a thick combination of solid particles of pigment dispersed in water and other substances that make the pigment stick to a surface. The difference between colloids and suspensions is that the particles in colloids are smaller than those in suspensions—ranging from only 1 to 100 nm in diameter. Because the particles in colloids are so small, they pass through ordinary filters and stay dispersed throughout the mixture. However, the particles are large enough to scatter light that passes through the colloid, even though the colloid may look like clear water, as shown in ***Figure 5.*** This scattering of light is called the *Tyndall effect.*

colloid a mixture consisting of tiny particles that are intermediate in size between those in solutions and those in suspensions and that are suspended in a liquid, solid, or gas

Figure 5

The liquid in the jar on the right is a colloid. Colloids exhibit the Tyndall effect, in which light is scattered by the invisible particles.

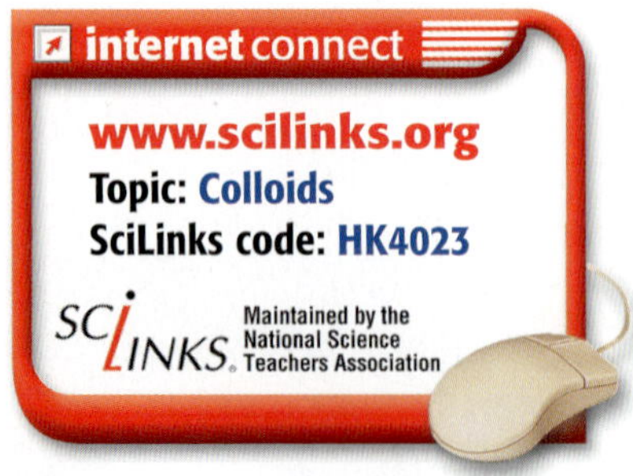

Making Butter

Cream is a lipid-in-water emulsion. Churning or shaking cream causes lipid droplets to stick to one another, which forms butter. You can make your own butter in the following way.

1. Pour 250 mL (about 1/2 pint) of heavy cream into an empty 500 mL container.
2. Add a clean marble, and seal the container tightly so that it does not leak.
3. Take turns shaking the container. When the cream becomes very thick, you will no longer hear the marble moving.
4. Open the container to look at the substance that formed. Record your observations.
5. If the butter is made of joined lipid droplets, what must make up most of the liquid that is left behind?

Other familiar materials are also colloids

The particles in most colloids are composed of many atoms, ions, or molecules, but individual protein molecules are also large enough to form colloids. Examples of protein colloids include gelatin desserts, egg whites, and blood plasma. These colloids consist of protein molecules dispersed in a liquid.

Other examples of colloids include whipped cream, which is made by dispersing a gas in a liquid, and marshmallows, which are made by dispersing a gas in a solid. Fog consists of small droplets of water dispersed in air, and smoke contains small solid particles dispersed in air.

emulsion any mixture of two or more immiscible liquids in which one liquid is dispersed in the other

Some immiscible liquids can form colloids

Mayonnaise is a colloid consisting of very small droplets of oil suspended in vinegar. Vinegar-and-oil salad dressings separate into two layers, but the vinegar and oil in mayonnaise do not separate. Mayonnaise has another ingredient that keeps the oil and vinegar together—egg yolk. Egg yolk coats the oil droplets, which keeps them from joining to form a separate layer. Mayonnaise is an **emulsion,** a colloid in which liquids that normally do not mix are spread throughout each other. Another example of an emulsion is found in your body. Bile salts cause fats to form an emulsion in the small intestine. Then digestive enzymes are able to break down the smaller fat particles.

Like other colloids, an emulsion has particles so small that it may appear to be uniform. But a closer look shows that it is not. For example, cream does not form separate layers, so it looks like a pure substance. Cream is really a mixture of oily fats, proteins, and carbohydrates dispersed in water. The lipid droplets are coated with a protein. The protein is an *emulsifier* that keeps the lipid droplets dispersed in the water so that they can spread throughout the entire mixture, as shown in ***Figure 6.***

Figure 6
Cream may look like a pure substance, but when cream is magnified, you can see that it is an emulsion of droplets of fats, or lipids, dispersed in water.

Connection to ENGINEERING

Ink is a complicated mixture of substances. Some inks, such as those used in printing books and magazines, contain *pigments* that give the ink most of its color. Pigments are added to a liquid as finely ground, solid particles to form a suspension. The ink is then applied to the paper on a printing press and allowed to dry.

The ink used in some ballpoint pens is different from ink used in printing. The ink in pens contains a dissolved iron salt, such as ferrous sulfate, and an organic substance called *tannic acid.* Tannic acid and the iron salt mix to form a dark blue solution that gives the ink its blue-black color.

Making the Connection

1. In a library or on the Internet, research two different types of inks used in printing. How do the properties of the inks differ? What properties make them good choices for printing different materials?

Homogeneous Mixtures

Homogeneous mixtures not only look uniform but *are* uniform. Salt water is an example of a homogeneous mixture. If you add pure salt to a glass of water and stir, the mixture soon looks like pure water. The mixture looks uniform even when you examine it under a microscope. That's because the individual components of the mixture are too small to be seen. The mixture is made of sodium ions and chloride ions surrounded by water molecules, as shown in **Figure 7.** Because the number of ions will be the same throughout the salt water, the mixture is homogeneous.

When salt and water are mixed, no chemical reaction occurs. For this reason, the two substances can be easily separated by evaporating the water. As the water evaporates, the sodium and chloride ions of the salt begin to rejoin to form salt crystals like those that originally dissolved. When all the water evaporates, only salt is left.

Figure 7

A Plain water is homogeneous because it is a single substance. **B** Salt water is also homogeneous because it is a uniform mixture of water molecules, sodium ions, and chloride ions.

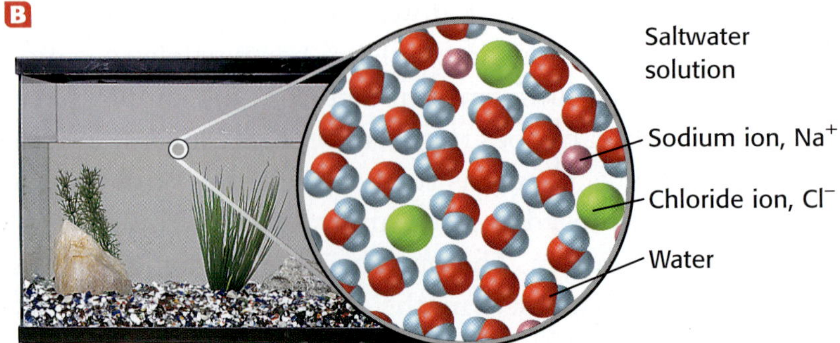

Homogeneous mixtures are solutions

When you add aquarium salt to water and stir, the solid seems to disappear. What really happens is that salt has *dissolved* in water to form a **solution.** In this particular solution, aquarium salt is the **solute,** the substance that dissolves. Water is the **solvent,** the substance in which the solute dissolves. When a solute has dissolved in a solvent, the dissolved particles are so small that you can't see them, even with a powerful microscope. They are invisible because they are the smallest particles of the substance—atoms, ions, or molecules. Mixtures are homogeneous when the smallest particles of one substance are uniformly spread among similar particles of another substance. This description of a homogeneous mixture is also a description of a solution, so all homogeneous mixtures are also solutions.

solution a homogeneous mixture of two or more substances uniformly dispersed throughout a single phase

solute in a solution, the substance that dissolves in the solvent

solvent in a solution, the substance in which the solute dissolves

Miscible liquids mix to form solutions

Two or more liquids that form a single layer when mixed are said to be miscible. Some solutions of two liquids are useful. For example, water mixed with isopropanol makes a solution called *rubbing alcohol,* and some skin lotions contain a solution of glycerol and water.

Chemists often have to separate miscible liquids when purifying substances in the laboratory. Because miscible liquids do not separate into layers, they are not as easy to separate as immiscible liquids are. One way to separate miscible liquids is by a process called *distillation,* which involves an apparatus such as the one shown in **Figure 8.** Distillation works only when the two miscible liquids have different boiling points. For example, a mixture of methanol and water can be separated by distillation because methanol boils at 64.5°C and water boils at 100.0°C. When this mixture is heated in a distillation apparatus, the methanol boils away first, leaving most of the water behind.

Disc One, Module 8:
Solutions
Use the Interactive Tutor to learn more about this topic.

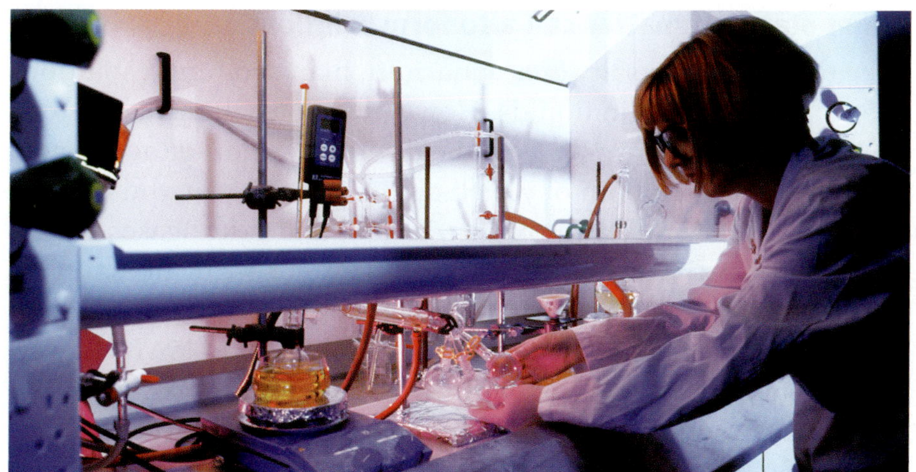

Figure 8
A solution of miscible liquids that have different boiling points may be separated by distillation in an apparatus such as this one.

Chromatography Chromatography is often used to separate mixtures that can't be separated by simpler methods. The figure at right shows how paper chromatography can be used to separate colored dyes in three different samples of black ink.

First, ink marks are made on absorbent paper. Then the paper is put in a jar holding a small volume of solvent. The solvent travels upward through the paper, carrying the ink with it. The finished *chromatogram* reveals which dyes make up each of the inks.

Each dye has a different chemical structure. Dyes that have structures more like that of the paper than that of the solvent stick to the paper and travel slower. Dyes that have structures more like that of the solvent move upward with the solvent and therefore travel farther.

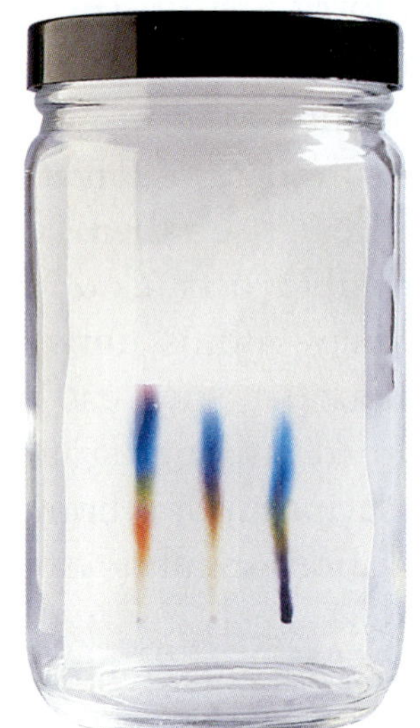

Applying Information

1. Does the blue dye in each sample have a structure more like that of the paper or the solvent? Explain your answer.
2. How would the result differ if the inks were made from a single dye instead of a mixture of several dyes?

Liquid solutions sometimes contain no water

Many examples of solutions of liquids in other liquids do not contain water. For example, some kinds of fingernail-polish removers and paint strippers are mixtures of liquid substances that contain no water. Fuels such as gasoline, diesel fuel, and kerosene are homogeneous mixtures of several different liquid substances. These fuels are made from a liquid solution called petroleum, which is also called *crude oil.* Petroleum is a solution of many different carbon compounds. Fuels and other useful materials are made from petroleum by distillation. For example, gasoline is a solution containing several liquid substances distilled from petroleum.

Other states of matter can also form solutions

Like the water in a saltwater aquarium, many common solutions are solids dissolved in liquids. However, solutes and solvents can be in any state. For instance, vinegar is a solution of acetic acid dissolved in water, both of which are liquids. The air you breathe is a solution of nitrogen, oxygen, argon, and other gases. Gases can also dissolve in liquids. For example, a soft drink contains carbon dioxide gas dissolved in liquid water. Mothballs, which are made of a solid substance called *naphthalene,* slowly give off vapor that forms a solution with air. The liquid element mercury dissolves in solid silver to form a solution called an *amalgam,* which can be used to fill cavities in teeth.

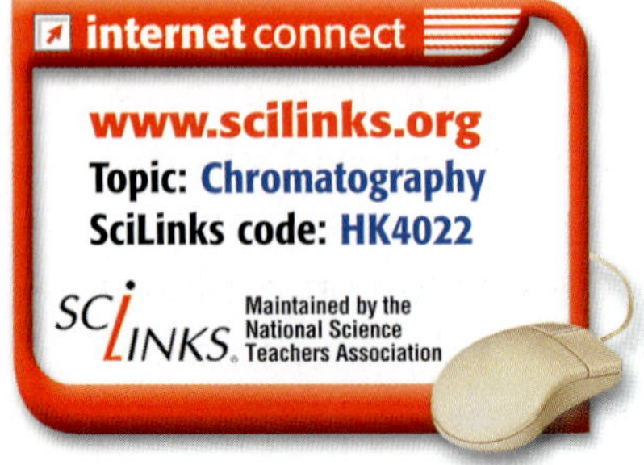

Solids can dissolve in other solids

The musical instrument shown in ***Figure 9*** is made of brass, a solution of zinc metal dissolved in copper metal. Brass is an example of an **alloy,** a homogeneous mixture that is usually composed of two or more metals. Of course, the metals must be melted to liquids and then mixed, but when the mixture cools, the result is a solid solution of one metal in another metal.

Alloys are important because they have properties that the individual metals do not have. For example, pure copper is too soft and bends too easily to be used to make a sturdy musical instrument. When zinc is dissolved in copper, the resulting brass is harder and tougher than copper, but the brass is still easy to form into complicated shapes. Bronze, an alloy of tin in copper, is harder than tin or copper alone. Bronze resists corrosion, so bronze has been used since ancient times to make sculptures and other objects meant to last a long time. Not all alloys contain only metals. Some types of steel are alloys containing the nonmetal element carbon.

alloy a solid or liquid mixture of two or more metals

Figure 9
This cornet is made of the alloy brass, which is a solid solution.

SECTION 1 REVIEW

SUMMARY

- A heterogeneous mixture is a nonuniform blend of two or more substances.
- The particles in a suspension settle out of the mixture or may be filtered out.
- The dispersed particles in a colloid are too small to settle out or to be filtered out.
- A homogeneous mixture, or solution, is a uniform blend of substances.
- In a solution, the solute is dissolved in the solvent.
- Solutions may be formed from solids, liquids, or gases.

1. **Classify** the following mixtures as heterogeneous or homogeneous:
   a. orange juice without pulp
   b. sweat
   c. cinnamon sugar
   d. concrete
2. **Explain** the difference between a suspension and a colloid.
3. **List** three examples of solutions that are not liquids.
4. **Identify** the solvent and solute in a solution made by dissolving a small quantity of baking soda in water.
5. **Arrange** the following mixtures in order of increasing particle size: muddy water, sugar water, and egg white.
6. **Explain** why distillation would not be an effective way to separate a mixture of the miscible liquids formic acid, which boils at 100.7°C, and water, which boils at 100.0°C.
7. **Critical Thinking** A small child watches you as you stir a spoonful of sugar into a glass of clear lime-flavored drink. The child says she believes that the sugar went away because it seemed to disappear. How would you explain to the child what happened to the sugar, and how could you show her that you can get the sugar back?

SECTION 2

How Substances Dissolve

KEY TERMS

polar compound
hydrogen bonding
nonpolar compound

OBJECTIVES

- **Explain** how the polarity of water enables it to dissolve many different substances.
- **Relate** the ability of a solvent to dissolve a solute to the relative strengths of forces between molecules.
- **Describe** three ways to increase the rate at which a solute dissolves in a solvent.
- **Explain** how a solute affects the freezing point and boiling point of a solution.

Suppose you and a friend are drinking iced tea. You add one spoonful of loose sugar to your glass of tea, stir, and all of the sugar dissolves quickly. Your friend adds a sugar cube to her tea and finds that she must stir longer than you did to dissolve all of the sugar cube. Why does the sugar cube take longer to dissolve? Why does sugar dissolve in water at all?

polar compound a molecule that has an uneven distribution of electrons

Water: A Common Solvent

Two-thirds of Earth's surface is water. The liquids you drink are mostly water, and three-fourths of your body weight is water. Many different substances can dissolve in water. For this reason, water is sometimes called the *universal solvent.*

Water can dissolve ionic compounds because of its structure

To understand what makes water such a good solvent, consider the structure of water. A water molecule is made up of two hydrogen atoms bonded to one oxygen atom by covalent bonds. But electrons are not evenly distributed throughout a water molecule because oxygen atoms strongly attract electrons. The oxygen atom pulls electrons away from the hydrogen atoms, giving them a partial positive charge. The electrons are then bunched around the oxygen atom, giving it a partial negative charge. This uneven distribution of electrons, combined with a water molecule's bent shape, causes it to be a **polar compound**, as shown in ***Figure 10.*** A polar molecule has distinct positively and negatively charged sides, which are indicated by $\delta+$ and $\delta-$ in ***Figure 10.*** Water molecules attract both the positive and negative ions of an ionic compound.

Figure 10

Water is a polar molecule because the oxygen atom strongly attracts electrons, which leaves the hydrogen atoms with a positive charge.

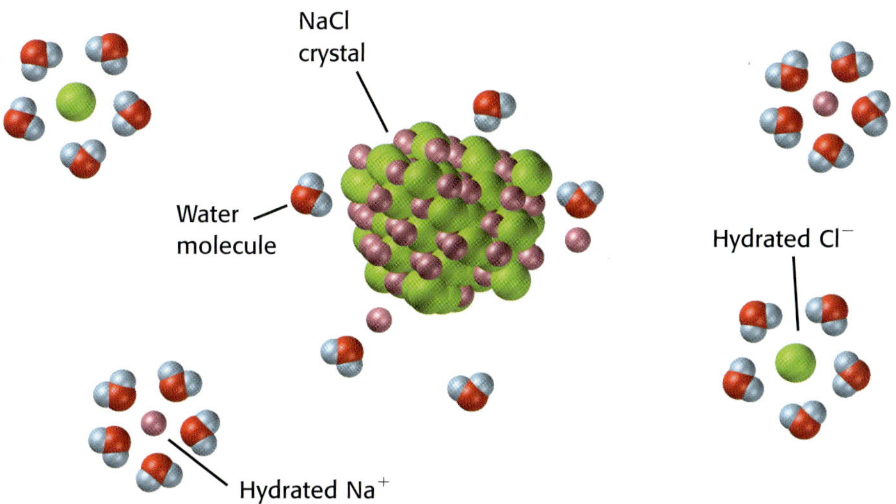

Figure 11

Polar water molecules attract the positive sodium ions and negative chloride ions, pulling the ions away from the crystal of NaCl. Notice that the negative oxygen atoms of the water molecules are attracted to the positive sodium ion and that the positive hydrogen atoms are attracted to the negative chloride ions.

Polar water molecules pull ionic crystals apart

Figure 11 shows how a sodium chloride, NaCl, crystal dissolves in water. First, the partially negative oxygen atoms of water molecules attract the positively charged sodium ions at the surface of the sodium chloride crystal. The partially positive hydrogen atoms of water molecules also attract the negatively charged chloride ions. As more water molecules attract the ions, the force of attraction between the ions and the water molecules increases. Finally, this force becomes stronger than the force of attraction between the sodium and chloride atoms in the crystal. Then, the ions are pulled away from the crystal and surrounded by water molecules. Eventually, all of the ions in the crystal are pulled into solution, and the substance is completely dissolved.

Dissolving depends on forces between particles

Water dissolves baking soda and many other ionic compounds in exactly the same way that water dissolves sodium chloride. The attraction of water molecules pulls the crystals apart into individual ions. Many other ionic compounds, though, do not dissolve in water. Silver chloride, unlike sodium chloride, is an ionic compound that does not dissolve in water.

Why does one ionic compound dissolve in water, but another ionic compound does not? The answer is related to forces of attraction. To dissolve an ionic substance, water molecules must exert a force on the ions that is more attractive than the force between the ions in the crystal. This principle applies not only to water molecules and ionic compounds but also to any solvent and any substance. To dissolve a substance, solvent molecules must exert more force on the particles of the substance than the particles exert on one another.

INTEGRATING

BIOLOGY

When a solute dissolves in water, the random movement of particles called *diffusion* ensures that the solute spreads out evenly through the solution. Cells rely on diffusion to transport molecules. When the concentration of a solute is greater inside a cell than it is outside, the solute moves out of the cell through the cell membrane.

Not all substances can diffuse across a cell membrane. Sodium ions and potassium ions, for example, are transported into and out of cells through structures called *sodium-potassium pumps.* These ions give many cells an electrical charge that makes it possible for the cells to send electrical signals to different parts of the body.

Figure 12

As water slowly dissolves the sugar cube, streams of denser sugar solution move downward. Table sugar, or sucrose, is a molecular compound.

Water dissolves many molecular compounds

Water has a low molecular mass, but it is a fairly dense liquid that has a high boiling point. Water has these properties because **hydrogen bonding** occurs between water molecules. Recall that electrons are pulled away from the hydrogen atoms of water by the oxygen atom. As a result, the hydrogen atom of one water molecule attracts electrons from the oxygen atom of another water molecule to form a partial covalent bond. This hydrogen bond pulls water molecules close together.

hydrogen bonding the intermolecular force occurring when a hydrogen atom that is bonded to a highly electronegative atom of one molecule is attracted to two unshared electrons of another molecule

Besides ionic compounds, water also dissolves many molecular compounds, such as ethanol, ascorbic acid (vitamin C), and table sugar, as shown in ***Figure 12.*** These molecular compounds are polar because they have hydrogen atoms bonded to oxygen, which attract electrons strongly. Ethanol, for example, has a polar $-OH$ group in its structure, CH_3CH_2OH. As a result, the negative oxygen atom of a water molecule attracts the positive hydrogen atom of an ethanol molecule. The positive hydrogen atom of a water molecule also attracts the negative oxygen atom of an ethanol molecule. This attraction is one force that pulls an ethanol molecule into water solution.

Hydrogen bonding plays a large part in the dissolving of other molecular compounds such as sucrose, $C_{12}H_{22}O_{11}$ as shown in ***Figure 13.*** Water molecules form hydrogen bonds with the $-OH$ groups in the sucrose molecule and easily pull the sucrose molecules away from the sugar crystal and into solution.

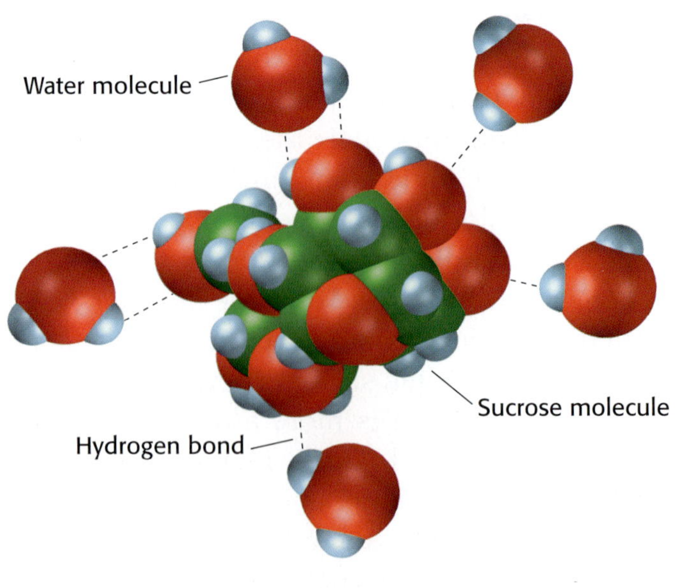

Figure 13

Water molecules form hydrogen bonds with the $-OH$ groups of a sucrose molecule. These forces pull the sucrose molecule away from the sugar crystal and into solution.

What dissolves a nonpolar substance?

Some elements, such as oxygen, nitrogen, and chlorine exist as diatomic molecules. These molecules are completely nonpolar because neither atom in the molecule attracts electrons more strongly. Iodine, I_2, is a nonpolar molecule. In this activity, you will determine whether water or ethanol dissolves iodine better.

1. Dip a cotton swab in tincture of iodine, and make two small spots on the palm of your hand. Let the spots dry. The spots that remain are iodine.
2. Dip a second cotton swab in water, and wash one of the iodine spots with it. What happens to the iodine spot?
3. Dip a third cotton swab in ethanol, and wash the other iodine spot with it. What happens to the iodine spot?
4. Did water or ethanol dissolve the iodine spot better? Is water more polar or less polar than ethanol? Write a paragraph explaining your reasoning. **WRITING SKILL**

Like dissolves like

A rule of thumb in chemistry is that like dissolves like. This rule means that a solvent will dissolve substances that are like the solvent in molecular structure. For example, water is a polar molecule because it has positive and negative ends. So, water dissolves ions and polar molecules, which also have charges.

Nonpolar compounds usually will not dissolve in water. Nonpolar molecules do not have charges on opposite sides, like water molecules have. For example, olive oil is not soluble in water because it is a mixture of nonpolar compounds. Water does not attract nonpolar molecules enough to overcome the attractive forces between the nonpolar molecules. So, nonpolar solvents must be used to dissolve nonpolar materials, as shown in ***Figure 14.*** Nonpolar solvents that are distilled from petroleum are often used to dissolve nonpolar materials.

nonpolar compound a compound whose electrons are equally distributed among its atoms

Figure 14

Nonpolar substances, such as oil-based paint, must be dissolved by a like solvent. This means that a nonpolar solvent must be used.

The Dissolving Process

According to the kinetic theory of matter, water molecules in a glass of tea are always moving. When sugar is poured into the tea, water molecules collide and transfer energy to the sugar molecules at the surface of the sugar crystal. This energy, as well as the attractive forces between water and sugar molecules, causes molecules at the surface of the crystal to dissolve.

Every time a layer of sugar molecules leaves the crystal, another layer of sugar molecules is uncovered. Sugar molecules break away from the crystal layer by layer in this way until the crystal completely dissolves.

Solutes with a larger surface area dissolve faster

When a solid is crushed into small pieces, it dissolves faster than the same substance in large pieces. Breaking the solid into smaller pieces exposes more surface area, uncovering more of the solute. More molecules exposed to a solvent leads to more solute-solvent collisions. Therefore, the solid dissolves faster.

Figure 15 shows how breaking a solid into many smaller pieces increases the total exposed surface area. The large crystal is a cube that is 1 cm on each edge, so each face of the crystal has an area of 1 cm^2. A cube has six surfaces, so the total surface area is 6 cm^2. Suppose the large cube is cut into 1000 cubes that are 0.1 cm on each edge. The face of each small cube has an area of $0.1 \text{ cm} \times 0.1 \text{ cm} = 0.01 \text{ cm}^2$, so each cube has a surface area of 0.06 cm^2. The total surface area of the small cubes is $1000 \times 0.06 \text{ cm}^2 = 60 \text{ cm}^2$, which is ten times the surface area of the large cube.

Figure 15

 This salt crystal has a small surface area compared to its total volume.

B When the salt crystal is crushed into small pieces, more of the salt can be exposed to a solute, which allows the salt to dissolve faster.

A

B

Figure 16

How Stirring Affects the Dissolving Process

A If the solution is not stirred, crystals of table sugar, or sucrose, become surrounded by dissolved sugar molecules, which prevent water molecules from reaching the undissolved sugar.

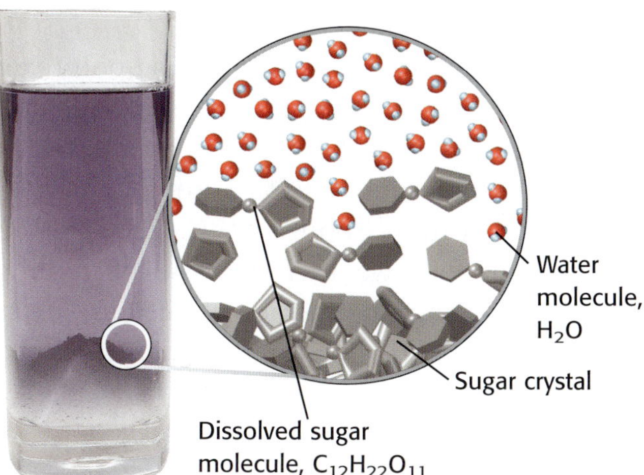

B Stirring moves the dissolved sugar molecules away from the undissolved sugar, and more water molecules can reach the undissolved sugar.

Stirring or shaking a solution helps the solute dissolve faster

If you pour sugar in a glass of water and let it sit without stirring, the sugar will take a long time to dissolve completely. The sugar takes a long time to dissolve because it is at the bottom of the glass surrounded by dissolved sugar molecules, as shown in ***Figure 16A.*** Dissolved sugar molecules will slowly *diffuse,* or spread out, throughout the entire solution. But until that happens, the dissolved sugar molecules cluster near the surface of the crystal. These dissolved molecules keep water molecules from reaching the sugar that has not yet dissolved.

Stirring or shaking the solution moves the dissolved sugar away from the sugar crystals. So, more water molecules can interact with the solid, as shown in ***Figure 16B,*** and the sugar crystals dissolve faster.

Solutes dissolve faster when the solvent is hot

Solutes dissolve faster in a hot solvent than in a cold solvent. The kinetic theory states that when matter is heated, its particles move faster. As a result of heating, particles of solvent collide with undissolved solute more often. These collisions also transfer more energy than collisions that occur when the solvent is cold. The greater frequency and energy of the collisions help "knock" undissolved solute particles away from each other and spread them throughout the solution.

Figure 17

The coolant mixture of ethylene glycol and water keeps the radiator fluid from freezing in winter and boiling in summer.

Solutes affect the physical properties of a solution

The boiling point of pure water is 100°C. But, if you dissolve 12 g of sodium chloride in 100 mL of water, you will find that the boiling point of the solution is increased to about 102°C. Also, the freezing point of the solution will be lowered to about −7°C. Many solutes increase the boiling point of a solution above that of the pure solvent. Likewise, the same solutes lower the freezing point of the solution below that of the pure solvent.

The effect of a solute on freezing point and boiling point can be useful, as shown in ***Figure 17.*** For example, a car's cooling system often contains a mixture that is 50% water and 50% ethylene glycol, a type of alcohol. This solution acts as antifreeze in cold weather because its freezing point is about −30°C. The solution also helps prevent boiling in hot weather because its boiling point is about 109°C. Adding sodium chloride to ice can lower the freezing point of the mixture to about −15°C, which is cold enough to freeze ice cream.

SECTION 2 REVIEW

SUMMARY

- Water dissolves ionic compounds and polar molecular compounds because water molecules are polar.
- To dissolve a solute, a solvent must attract solute particles more strongly than solute particles attract each other.
- Nonpolar compounds do not dissolve in water but may be dissolved by nonpolar solvents.
- Solids with a greater surface area dissolve faster.
- Stirring or heating a solvent dissolves solutes faster.
- Solutes can lower the freezing point of a solution and raise its boiling point.

1. **Explain** how water can dissolve some ionic compounds, such as ammonium chloride, NH_4Cl, as well as some molecular compounds, such as methanol.
2. **Describe** the relationship of attractive forces between molecules and the ability of a solvent to dissolve a substance.
3. **Explain** why large crystals of coarse sea salt take longer to dissolve in water than crystals of fine table salt.
4. **Use** the like dissolves like rule to predict whether glycerol, which is a polar molecular compound, is soluble in water.
5. **Describe** three methods you could use to make a spoonful of salt dissolve faster in water.
6. **Critical Thinking** You have made some strawberry-flavored drink from water, sugar, and drink mix. You decide to freeze the mixture into ice cubes, so you pour the liquid into an ice-cube tray and place it in the freezer along with another tray of plain water. Two hours later, you find the water has frozen, but the fruit drink has not. How can you explain this result?

SECTION 3

Solubility and Concentration

OBJECTIVES

- **Explain** the meaning of solubility and compare the solubilities of various substances.
- **Describe** dilute, concentrated, saturated, unsaturated, and supersaturated solutions.
- **Relate** changes in temperature and pressure to changes in solubility of solid and gaseous solutes.
- **Express** the concentration of a solution as molarity, and calculate the molarity of a solution given the amount of solute and the volume of the solution.

KEY TERMS

solubility
concentration
unsaturated solution
saturated solution
supersaturated solution
molarity

How much would you have to shake, stir, or heat the olive oil and water mixture shown in ***Figure 18*** to dissolve the oil in the water? The answer is that the oil would never dissolve in the water no matter what you did. Some substances are *insoluble* in water, meaning they do not dissolve. Other substances such as sugar and baking soda are said to be *soluble* in water because they dissolve easily in water. However, there is often a limit to how much of a substance will dissolve.

solubility the maximum amount of a solute that will dissolve in a given quantity of solvent at a given temperature and pressure

Figure 18
Olive oil and water form two layers when they are mixed because olive oil is *insoluble* in water.

Solubility in Water

Have you ever tried to dissolve several spoonfuls of salt in a glass of water? If you have tried, you may have observed that some of the salt did not dissolve, no matter how much you stirred. Unlike olive oil, salt is soluble in water, but the amount of salt that will dissolve is limited. The maximum amount of salt that can be dissolved in 100 g of water at room temperature is 36 g, or about two tablespoonfuls. The maximum mass of a solute that will dissolve in 100 g of water at 20°C and standard atmospheric pressure is known as the **solubility** of the substance in water.

Some substances such as acetic acid, methanol, ethanol, glycerol, and ethylene glycol are completely soluble in water. This means that any amount of the substance will mix with water to form a solution. Some ionic compounds, such as silver chloride, AgCl, are almost completely insoluble in water. Only 0.000 19 g of AgCl will dissolve in 100 g of water.

Table 1 Solubilities of Some Ionic Compounds in Water

Substance	Formula	Solubility in g/100 g H_2O at 20°C
Silver nitrate	$AgNO_3$	216
Silver chloride	$AgCl$	0.000 19
Sodium fluoride	NaF	4.06
Sodium chloride	$NaCl$	35.9
Sodium iodide	NaI	178
Calcium chloride	$CaCl_2$	75
Calcium sulfate	$CaSO_4$	0.32
Calcium fluoride	CaF_2	0.0015
Sodium sulfide	Na_2S	26.3
Iron(II) sulfide	FeS	0.0006

Different substances have different solubilities

Even closely related compounds can have very different solubilities. Compare the solubilities of some of the ionic compounds in **Table 1.** All compounds listed that contain sodium also contain one other element, but sodium iodide is much more soluble than either sodium chloride or sodium fluoride.

The solubility of any substance in water depends on the strength of the forces acting between water molecules and solute particles compared to the forces acting between the solute particles. Sodium iodide is more soluble than many other compounds that also contain sodium because the forces between water molecules and particles of sodium iodide are much greater than the forces between sodium iodide particles.

How much of a substance can dissolve in a solvent?

Because substances vary greatly in solubility, you need a way to specify how much solute is dissolved in a given solution. One way is to refer to a solution as *weak* if only a small amount of solute is dissolved or *strong* if a large amount of solute is dissolved. However, *weak* and *strong* mean different things to different people. For example, most people would describe the sulfuric acid solution found in automobile batteries as strong. The solution can injure the skin and react with the fiber in textiles to create holes in clothing. A chemist, though, might describe battery acid as a weak solution of sulfuric acid because the chemist knows that much stronger solutions of sulfuric acid can be prepared.

The terms *weak* and *strong* do not specify the **concentration** of a solution. Concentration is the quantity of solute dissolved in a given volume of solution. Scientists refer to a solution that contains a large amount of solute as *concentrated*. A solution that contains only a small amount of solute is *dilute*.

concentration the amount of a particular substance in a given quantity of a mixture, solution, or ore

unsaturated solution a solution that contains less solute than a saturated solution does and that is able to dissolve additional solute

Unsaturated solutions can dissolve more solute

The terms *concentrated* and *dilute* give no information about the actual quantity of solute dissolved in a solution. An **unsaturated solution** contains less than the maximum amount of solute that will dissolve in the solvent under the same conditions. The solution of sodium acetate in **Figure 19A** is unsaturated. A solution is unsaturated as long as it is able to dissolve more solute.

Figure 19

How Concentration Affects the Dissolving Process

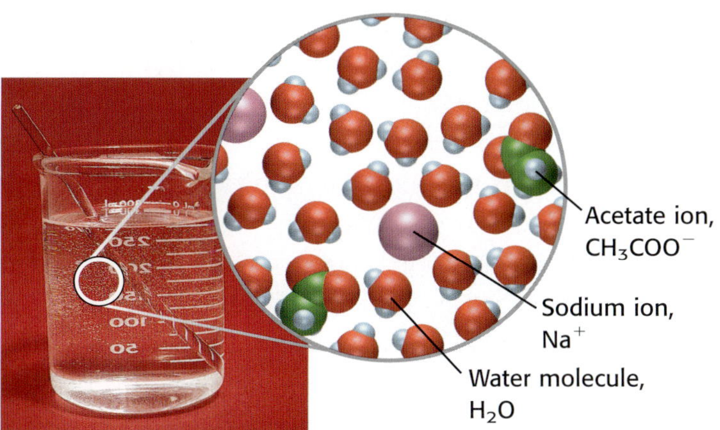

A Additional sodium acetate can dissolve when added to this unsaturated solution.

B No more sodium acetate will dissolve in this saturated solution. Any additional sodium acetate that is dissolved causes an equal amount to settle out of the solution.

At some point, most solutions become saturated with solutes

If you keep adding sodium acetate to the solution in ***Figure 19A,*** the added sodium acetate dissolves until the solution becomes saturated, as shown in ***Figure 19B.*** A **saturated solution** can dissolve no more solute. The dissolved solute is in equilibrium with undissolved solute. To be in equilibrium means that the dissolved solute re-forms crystals at the same rate that the undissolved solute dissolves. So if you add more solute, it just settles to the bottom of the container. No matter how much you stir, no more sodium acetate will dissolve in a saturated solution.

saturated solution a solution that cannot dissolve any more solute under the given conditions

supersaturated solution a solution that holds more dissolved solute than is required to reach equilibrium at a given temperature

Heating a saturated solution usually dissolves more solute

The solubility of most solutes increases as the temperature of the solution increases. If you heat a saturated solution of sodium acetate, more sodium acetate can dissolve until the solution becomes saturated at the higher temperature.

But something interesting happens when the temperature of the solution decreases again. The extra sodium acetate does not re-form crystals, but remains in solution. At the cooler temperature, this unstable **supersaturated solution** holds more solute than it normally can. Adding a small crystal of sodium acetate to the solution provides the surface that the excess solute needs to crystallize, as shown in ***Figure 20.*** The solute crystallizes out of the solution until the solution is saturated at the cooler temperature.

Figure 20

Adding a single crystal of sodium acetate to a supersaturated solution causes the excess sodium acetate to quickly crystallize out of the solution.

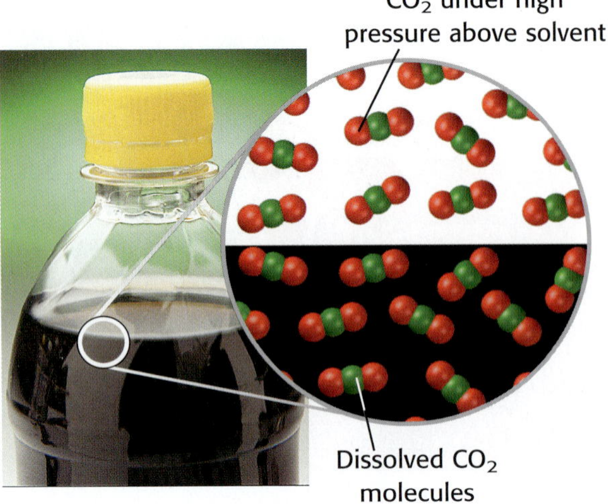

A Carbon dioxide gas is dissolved in this unopened bottle of soda.

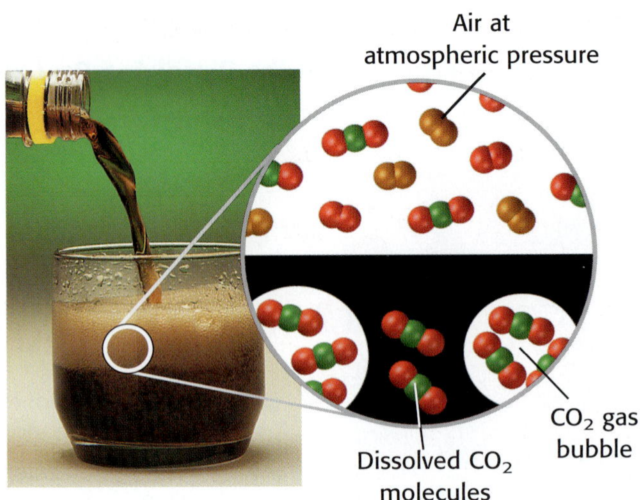

B When the bottle is opened, the pressure inside the bottle decreases. Carbon dioxide gas then forms bubbles as it comes out of solution.

Figure 21

The solubility of a gas in water depends on the pressure of the gas.

Temperature and pressure affect the solubility of gases

Gases can also dissolve. For instance, some household cleaners contain ammonia gas dissolved in water. Soda is a solution of carbon dioxide gas, sweetener, and flavorings in water. Unlike solid solutes, gaseous solutes are less soluble in warmer water. For example, soda goes flat quickly at room temperature but stays fizzy for a longer period of time when it is cold.

The solubility of gases also depends on pressure, as shown in ***Figure 21.*** Carbon dioxide is dissolved in the soda under high pressure, and the bottle is sealed. When the bottle is opened, the gas pressure decreases to atmospheric pressure and the soda fizzes as the carbon dioxide comes out of solution.

Divers must understand the solubility of gases. Increased pressure underwater causes nitrogen gas to dissolve in the blood. If the diver returns to the surface too quickly, nitrogen comes out of solution and forms bubbles in blood vessels. This condition, called the *bends,* is extremely painful and dangerous.

Concentration of Solutions

Describing a solution as concentrated, dilute, saturated, or unsaturated still does not reveal the quantity of dissolved solute. For example, only 0.173 g of calcium hydroxide will dissolve in 100 g of water. This solution is saturated but is still dilute because so little solute is present. Scientists express the quantity of solute in a solution in several ways, but one of the most useful forms of expressing this measurement is molarity.

Molarity is a precise way of measuring concentration

You have already seen that the solubility of a substance can be expressed as grams of solute per 100 grams of solvent. Concentration can also be expressed as **molarity.**

$$Molarity = \frac{moles\ of\ solute}{liters\ of\ solution}, \quad \text{or } M = \frac{mol}{L}$$

Note that molarity is expressed as moles per liter of solution, not per liter of solvent.

A 1.0 M, which is read as "one molar," solution of NaCl contains 1.0 mol of dissolved NaCl in every 1.0 L of solution. To find the molar concentration of a solute, divide the number of moles of solute by the volume of the solution in liters.

molarity an expression of the concentration of a solution in moles of dissolved solute per liter of solution

Math Skills

Molarity Calculate the molarity of sodium carbonate, Na_2CO_3, in a solution of 38.6 g of solute in 0.500 L of solution.

1 List the given and unknown values.

Given: mass of sodium carbonate = 38.6 g
volume of solution = 0.500 L

Unknown: molarity, amount of Na_2CO_3 in 1 L of solution

2 Write the equation for moles Na_2CO_3 and molarity.

$$moles\ Na_2CO_3 = \frac{mass\ Na_2CO_3}{molar\ mass\ Na_2CO_3}$$

$$molarity = \frac{moles\ Na_2CO_3}{}$$

3 Find the number of moles of Na_2CO_3 and calculate molarity.

$$molar\ mass\ Na_2CO_3 = 106\ g$$

$$moles\ Na_2CO_3 = \frac{38.6\ g}{106\ g} = 0.364\ mol\ Na_2CO_3$$

$$molarity\ of\ solution = \frac{0.364\ mol\ Na_2CO_3}{0.500\ L\ solution} = 0.728\ M$$

Practice HINT

- When calculating molarity, remember that molarity is moles per liter of solution, not moles per liter of solvent.
- If volume is given in milliliters, you must multiply by 1 L/1000 mL to change milliliters to liters. You will need to do this in Practice problems 1c and 1d.

Practice

Molarity

1. Determine the molarity of each of the following solutions:

a. 2 mol of calcium chloride, $CaCl_2$, dissolved in 1 L of solution

b. 0.75 mol of copper(II) sulfate, $CuSO_4$, dissolved in 1.5 L of solution

c. 2.25 mol of sulfuric acid, H_2SO_4, dissolved in 725 mL of solution

d. 525 g of lead(II) nitrate, $Pb(NO_3)_2$, dissolved in 1250 mL of solution

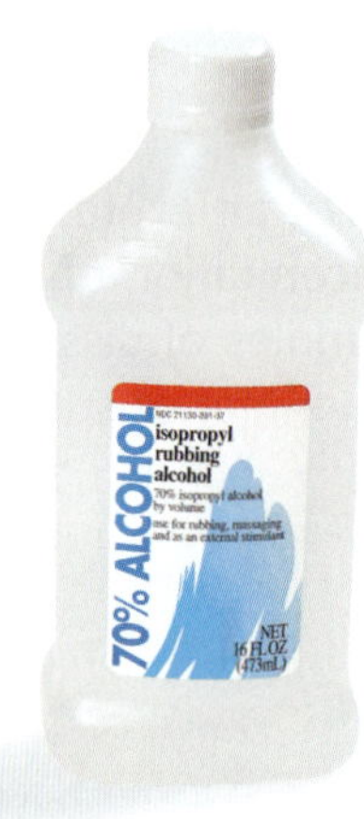

Figure 22

There are 70 grams of alcohol in every 100 g of this solution.

Other measures of solution concentration can be used

Concentration is sometimes expressed as mass percent, which is grams of solute per 100 g of solution. To make a 5.0% solution of sodium chloride, you would dissolve 5 g of sodium chloride in 95 g of water. The concentration of ordinary rubbing alcohol solution is usually 70%, as shown in ***Figure 22.***

The concentrations of solutions that contain extremely small amounts of solutes are sometimes given in parts per million, ppm, or parts per billion, ppb. Sea water contains slightly more than 1 ppm of fluoride ions, which means that every 1 000 000 g of seawater (about 1000 L) contains 1 g of dissolved fluoride ions. One million grams of water is about the mass of water in a child's plastic wading pool. Sea water also contains about 4 ppb of arsenic, or 4 g arsenic in every 1 000 000 000 g of sea water. The U.S. Environmental Protection Agency has set a maximum safe level of lead in drinking water at 15 ppb.

SECTION 3 REVIEW

SUMMARY

- The solubility of a substance is the maximum amount that can dissolve in a solvent at a certain temperature and pressure.
- The concentration of a solution is the quantity of solute dissolved per unit volume of solution.
- An unsaturated solution can dissolve more solute.
- A saturated solution cannot dissolve more solute.
- A solute's solubility is exceeded in a supersaturated solution.
- The solubility of a gas in water depends on both pressure and temperature.
- Molarity is a useful way of expressing the concentration of a solution. Molarity is moles of solute per liter of solution.

1. **Explain** how a solution can be both saturated and dilute at the same time. Use an example from ***Table 1.***
2. **Describe** how a saturated solution can become supersaturated.
3. **Propose** a way to determine whether a saltwater solution is unsaturated, saturated, or supersaturated.
4. **Compare** the solubility of olive oil and acetic acid in water. What is the solubility of olive oil? of acetic acid?
5. **Determine** whether your sweat would evaporate more quickly if the humidity were 92% or 37%. (**Hint:** When the humidity is 100%, the air is saturated with dissolved water vapor.)
6. **Express** the molarity of a solution that contains 0.5 mol of calcium acetate per 1.0 L of solution.
7. **Critical Thinking** When you fill a glass with cold water from a faucet and then let the glass sit undisturbed for two hours, you will see small bubbles sticking to the glass. What are the bubbles? Why did they form?

Math Skills

8. **Math Skills** Calculate the molarity of a solution that contains 35.0 g of barium chloride, $BaCl_2$, dissolved in 450.0 mL of solution.

Graphing Skills

Maximum Percentage of Ammonium Nitrate Dissolved in Water

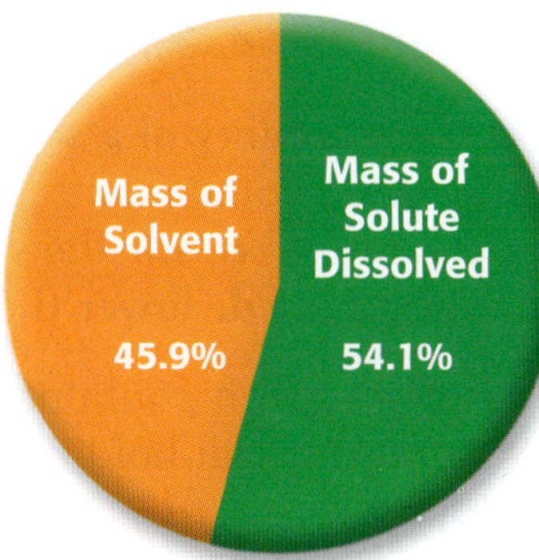

Solution Temperature = 0°C

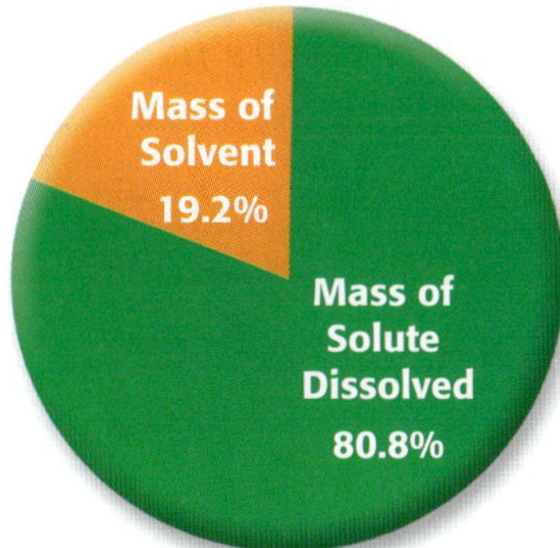

Solution Temperature = 60°C

Examine the graphs, and answer the following questions. (See Appendix A for help interpreting a graph.)

1. What type of graphs are these?
2. Identify the quantities that are given in each graph. What important quantities relate the two graphs to each other?
3. By examining the graphs, what can you tell about the solubility of ammonium nitrate?
4. Suppose 500.0 g of water is used to dissolve the ammonium nitrate. What is the maximum mass of ammonium nitrate that can be dissolved at 0°C? What is the maximum mass of ammonium nitrate that can be dissolved at 60°C?
5. From the two graphs, what might the percentage of solute dissolved be if the temperature of the solution is 30°C?
6. The information in the table below shows the solubility of calcium acetate dihydrate in water at various temperatures. Construct a graph best suited for the information listed. How does solubility vary with temperature?

Temperature (°C)	Maximum mass of solute dissolved in 100 g of water (g)
0	37.4
20	34.7
60	32.7
100	29.7

CHAPTER 7 REVIEW

Chapter Highlights

Before you begin, review the summaries of key ideas of each section, found at the end of each section. The vocabulary terms are listed on the first page of each section.

UNDERSTANDING CONCEPTS

1. Which of the following is a homogeneous mixture?
   a. tossed salad **c.** salt water
   b. soil **d.** vegetable soup

2. If the label on a bottle of medicine reads "shake well before using," the medicine is probably a
   a. solution. **c.** colloid.
   b. suspension. **d.** gel.

3. Suppose you add a teaspoon of table salt to a cool saltwater solution and stir until all of the salt dissolves. The solution you started with was
   a. unsaturated. **c.** saturated.
   b. supersaturated. **d.** concentrated.

4. Which of the following materials is an example of a solid dissolved in another solid?
   a. smoke **c.** mayonnaise
   b. bronze **d.** ice

5. The dispersed particles of a suspension are ______ than the particles of a colloid.
   a. larger **c.** lighter
   b. smaller **d.** less dense

6. Water attracts the ions of ionic compounds because water molecules are
   a. polar. **c.** magnetic.
   b. ions. **d.** nonpolar.

7. To dissolve a substance, a solvent must attract particles of the substance more strongly than the ______ attract each other.
   a. solvent particles **c.** ions
   b. water molecules **d.** solute particles

8. To cause a solute to dissolve faster, you could
   a. add more solute. **c.** stir the solution.
   b. cool the solution. **d.** saturate the solution.

9. To increase the solubility of a solid substance in a solvent, you could
   a. add more solute. **c.** stir the solution.
   b. heat the solution. **d.** lower the pressure.

10. A solution is ______ if it contains as much dissolved solute as it will hold under a given set of conditions.
    a. saturated **c.** supersaturated
    b. dilute **d.** concentrated

11. Gases are more soluble in liquids when the pressure is ______ and the temperature is ______.
    a. high, high **c.** low, high
    b. high, low **d.** low, low

12. The boiling point of a solution of sugar in water is ______ the boiling point of water.
    a. higher than **c.** the same as
    b. lower than **d.** not related to

USING VOCABULARY

13. A small amount of *solute* is added to two different solutions. Based on the figures below, which solution was *unsaturated*? Which solution was *saturated*? Explain your answer.

a.
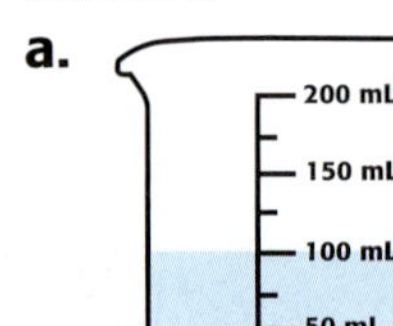

b.
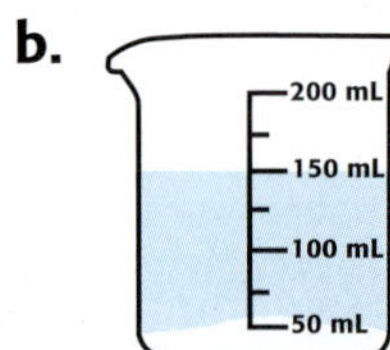

14. Explain why an *alloy* is a type of solution. Why are alloys used more often than pure metals?

15. Ethanol is completely *miscible* in water. Is it possible to prepare a *saturated solution* of ethanol in water? Explain your answer.

16. Classify the following as either a *suspension,* a *colloid,* an *emulsion,* or a *solution*: muddy water, salt water, mayonnaise, vinegar, fog, dry air, and cream.

BUILDING MATH SKILLS

17. **Molarity** How many moles of lithium chloride are dissolved in 3.00 L of a 0.200 M solution of lithium chloride?

18. **Molarity** What is the molarity of 250 mL of a solution that contains 12.5 g of dissolved zinc bromide, $ZnBr_2$?

19. **Solubility** The solubility of sodium fluoride, NaF, is 4.06 g NaF/100 g H_2O at 20°C. What mass of NaF would you have to dissolve in 1000 g H_2O to make a saturated solution?

BUILDING GRAPHING SKILLS

20. **Graphing** Make a solubility graph for $AgNO_3$ from the data in the table below. Plot temperature on the *x*-axis, and plot solubility on the *y*-axis. Answer the following questions.
    - **a.** How does the solubility of $AgNO_3$ vary with the temperature of water?
    - **b.** Estimate the solubility of $AgNO_3$ at 35°C, at 55°C, and at 75°C.
    - **c.** At what temperature would the solubility of $AgNO_3$ be 512 g per 100 g of H_2O?
    - **d.** If 100 g $AgNO_3$ were added to 100 g H_2O at 10°C, would the solution be saturated or unsaturated?

Temperature (°C)	Solubility of $AgNO_3$ in g $AgNO_3$/100 g H_2O
0	122
20	216
40	311
60	440
80	585

21. **Interpreting Graphs** The graph below shows the solubilities of two different substances, cadmium selenate, $CdSeO_4$, and cobalt(II) chloride, $CoCl_2$, over a range of temperatures. Use the graph to answer the following questions.

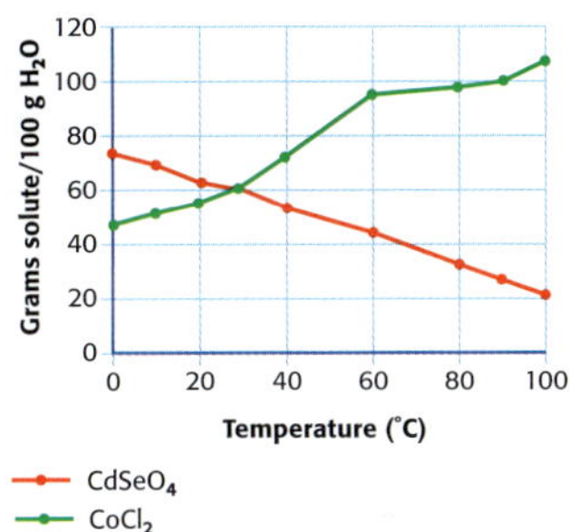

- **a.** At what temperature do both substances have the same solubility?
- **b.** At what temperature is the solubility of $CdSeO_4$ equal to 40 g $CdSeO_4$/100 g H_2O?
- **c.** Describe how the solubility of each substance changes with increasing temperature. Which substance has an unusual solubility trend? How is the trend unusual?
- **d.** Propose a way to make a supersaturated solution of $CdSeO_4$ at 50°C from a saturated solution.
- **e.** Suppose that you add 80 g $CoCl_2$ to 100 g of water at 20°C and stir until no more $CoCl_2$ dissolves. What mass of $CoCl_2$ remains undissolved at 20°C?

THINKING CRITICALLY

22. **Creative Thinking** Sea water is a solution that contains dissolved sodium chloride, dissolved magnesium chloride, and many other dissolved ions. Suppose you have a sample of seawater that contains mud and sand. What is the simplest way to get clear sea water from this mixture? Could you use distillation to separate the sea water from the mud? Explain your answer.

23. Applying Knowledge You have been investigating the nature of suspensions, colloids, and solutions and have made the observations on four unknown mixtures in the table below. From your data, decide whether each mixture is a solution, a suspension, or a colloid.

Sample	Clarity	Settles out	Scatters light
1	clear	no	yes
2	clear	no	no
3	cloudy	yes	yes
4	cloudy	no	yes

24. Designing Systems Use what you have learned about the polarity of water molecules and how ionic substances dissolve to make a three-step diagram or computer presentation showing how water molecules attract, surround, and dissolve an ionic substance.

COMPUTER SKILL

25. Problem Solving Sometimes, powerful searchlights are pointed toward the sky to draw the public's attention to grand openings of stores and restaurants. Even when the air appears clear, you can see the searchlight beam shining into the sky. Explain why these beams are visible in air.

WRITING SKILL

BUILDING LIFE/WORK SKILLS

26. Communicating Effectively When there is an oil spill, emergency-response teams use the properties of oil and water along with solubility principles to clean spills and prevent them from spreading. Describe the research behind these techniques, and evaluate the impact this research has had on the environment.

27. Interpreting Data Use a reference book to look up the solubilities of the fluoride compounds and chloride compounds made from alkali metals and alkaline-earth metals. What conclusions can you draw about the solubilities of the compounds of these metals?

INTEGRATING CONCEPTS

28. Connection to Biology Hydrogen bonding is extremely important to the function of substances within organisms. Use biology books to find three examples in which hydrogen bonds play a crucial role in the life processes of a cell.

29. Concept Mapping Copy the unfinished concept map below onto a sheet of paper. Complete the map by writing the correct word or phrase in the lettered boxes.

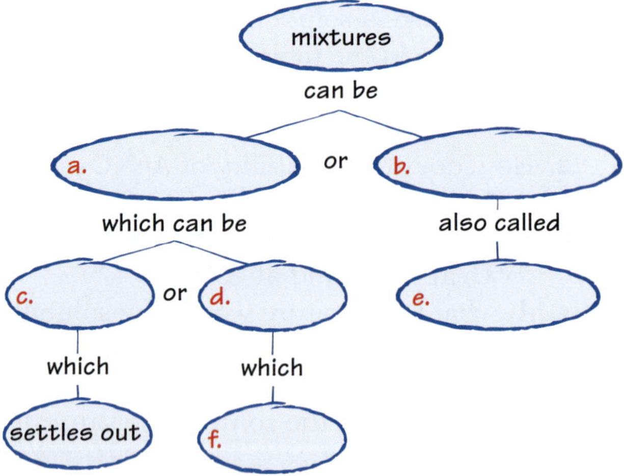

Standardized Test Prep

Understanding Concepts

***Directions (1–3):* For *each* question, write on a separate sheet of paper the letter of the correct answer.**

1 What characteristic of a molecular compound is most likely to cause the compound to be very soluble in water?
A. hydrogen content
B. low boiling point
C. high polarity
D. small size

2 What factor differentiates a colloid from a suspension?
F. Suspensions contain larger particles in solution.
G. Colloids have smaller particles that do not settle out.
H. A colloid is a type of solution, while a suspension is a type of mixture.
I. The solvent in a suspension is polar, while the solvent in a colloid is nonpolar.

3 Adding a crystal to a supersaturated solution causes crystallization of the solute because
A. as the added crystal dissolves, it causes the solution to cool
B. the added crystal provides a surface on which the solute can form crystals
C. as the added crystal dissolves, the level of supersaturation becomes too high
D. the added crystal decreases the solubility of the solute molecules, causing them to crystallize

***Directions (4):* Write a short response to the question.**

4 When paint thinner is added to latex paint, the mixture quickly separates into two distinct layers, but water mixes into the paint easily. Based on this observation, what can you infer about the type of solvents used in latex paint and in paint thinner?

Test TIP

To develop a short-response or extended-response answer, jot down your key ideas on a piece of scratch paper first.

Reading Skills

***Directions (5):* Read the passage below. Then answer the question.**

If you rinse greasy hands in water, the grease does not wash off because the molecules of the compounds in grease are nonpolar, while the molecules of water are polar. If you use soap, though, the grease washes away. The molecules of soap are long chains of atoms with a polar end and a nonpolar end. The nonpolar ends surround grease molecules, dissolving them. Then the polar ends of the soap molecules interact with water to make the whole group soluble in water.

5 When the polar end of soap reacts with calcium ions, it forms a salt that is not very soluble in water. How does this explain the observation that soap does not work well in hard water, which contains dissolved calcium ions?

Interpreting Graphics

***Directions (6):* Base your answer to question 6 on the illustration below.**

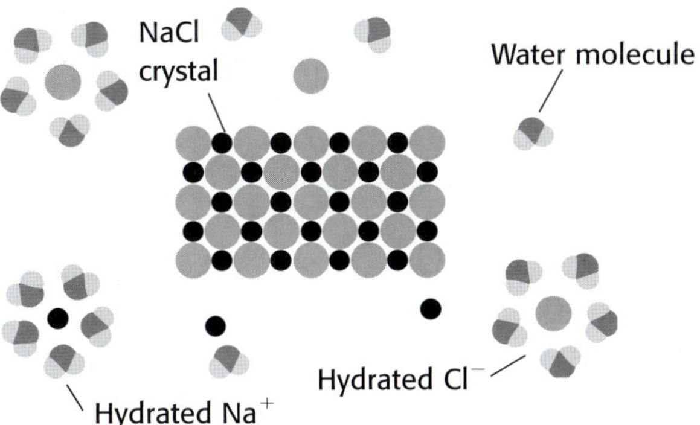

6 What happens to sodium chloride when it dissolves in water?
F. It forms a suspension of small particles.
G. The crystal breaks apart into pairs of positive and negative ions.
H. Ions separate from one another and interact with water molecules.
I. The hydrogen ends of water molecules surround the cations and the oxygen ends surround the anions.

Skills Practice Lab

Introduction

In general, a solid solute dissolves faster in a liquid solvent if the liquid is warm. In this lab, you will determine whether this is true of carbon dioxide, a gaseous solute, dissolved in a soft drink.

Objectives

- ***Compare*** the volume of carbon dioxide released from a warm soft drink with that released from a cold soft drink.
- USING SCIENTIFIC METHODS ***Draw conclusions*** to relate carbon dioxide's solubility in each soft drink to the temperature of each soft drink.

Materials

beaker, 1 L
carbonated soft drinks in plastic bottles, 2
crushed ice
flexible metric tape measure
paper towels
plastic bags, 2 small
stopwatch
thermometer
twist ties, 4

Investigating How Temperature Affects Gas Solubility

Procedure

Preparing for Your Experiment

1. Prepare a data table in your lab report similar to the one shown at right.

Testing the Solubility of Carbon Dioxide in a Warm Soft Drink

SAFETY CAUTION Wear safety goggles, gloves, and a laboratory apron.

2. Obtain a bottle of carbonated soft drink that has been stored at room temperature, and carry it to your lab table. Try not to disturb the liquid.
3. Use a thermometer to measure the temperature in the laboratory. Record this temperature in your data table.
4. Remove the bottle's cap, and quickly place the open end of a deflated plastic bag over the bottle's opening. Seal the bag tightly around the bottle's neck with a twist tie. Begin timing with a stopwatch.
5. When the bag is almost fully inflated, stop the stopwatch. Very carefully remove the plastic bag from the bottle, making sure to keep the bag sealed so the carbon dioxide inside does not escape. Seal the bag tightly with another twist tie.
6. Gently mold the bag into the shape of a sphere. Measure the bag's circumference in centimeters by wrapping the tape measure around the largest part of the bag. Record the circumference in your data table.

Soft Drink Data

	Temperature (°C)	Circumference of bag (cm)	Radius of of bag (cm)	Volume of of bag (cm^3)
Soft drink at room temp				
Chilled soft drink				

Testing the Solubility of Carbon Dioxide in a Cold Soft Drink

7. Obtain a second bottle of carbonated soft drink that has been chilled. Place the bottle in a 1 L beaker, and pack crushed ice around the bottle. Use paper towels to dry any water on the outside of the beaker, and then carefully move the beaker to your lab table.
8. Repeat step 4. Let the second plastic bag inflate for the same length of time that the first bag was allowed to inflate. Very carefully remove the bag from the bottle as you did before. Seal the plastic bag tightly with a twist tie.
9. Wait for the bag to warm to room temperature. While you are waiting, use the thermometer to measure the temperature of the cold soft drink. Record the temperature in your data table.
10. When the bag has warmed to room temperature, repeat step 6.

Analysis

1. Calculate the radius in centimeters of each inflated plastic bag by using the following equation. Record the results in your data table.

$$\text{radius (in cm)} = \frac{\text{circumference (in cm)}}{2\pi}$$

2. Calculate the volume in cubic centimeters of each inflated bag by using the following equation. Record the results in your data table.

$$\text{volume (in cm}^3\text{)} = \frac{4}{3}\pi \times [\text{radius (in cm)}]^3$$

3. Compare the volume of carbon dioxide released from the two soft drinks. Use your data to explain how the solubility of carbon dioxide in a soft drink is affected by temperature.

Conclusions

4. Suppose someone says that your conclusion is not valid because a soft drink contains many other solutes besides carbon dioxide. How could you verify that your conclusion is correct?

Science in ACTION

In Search of a Blood Substitute

When patients lose a lot of blood, doctors give them a blood transfusion, or an infusion of replacement blood. This replacement blood comes from either the patient or a blood donor. Blood donation has declined in recent years, leaving many areas with severe blood shortages. For several years, sick or injured dogs have received transfusions of a new blood substitute. Some day, blood substitutes could save human lives by alleviating blood shortages and by helping people who have rare blood types and other conditions that make traditional blood transfusions difficult.

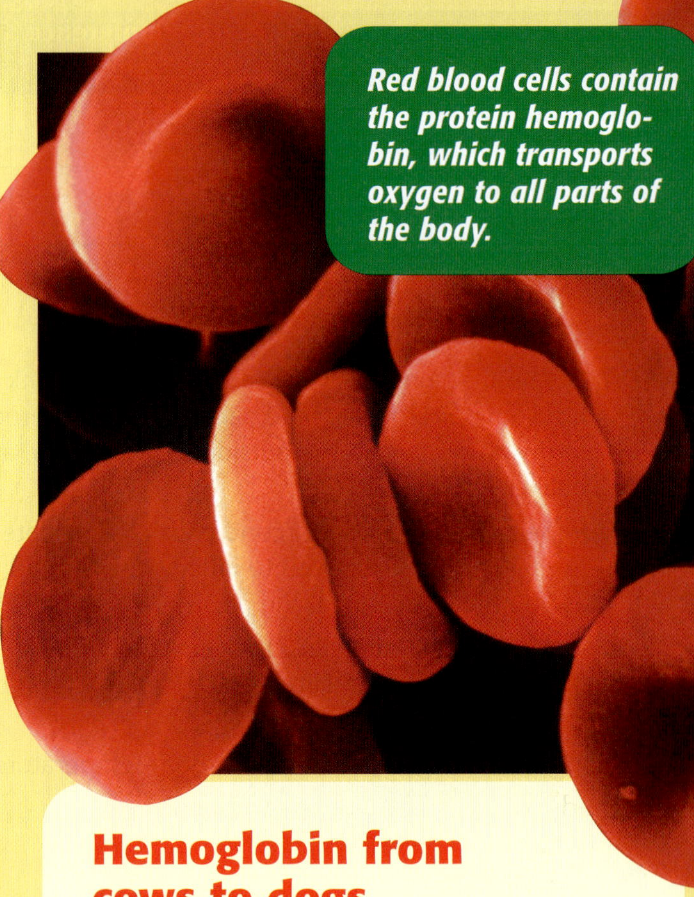

Red blood cells contain the protein hemoglobin, which transports oxygen to all parts of the body.

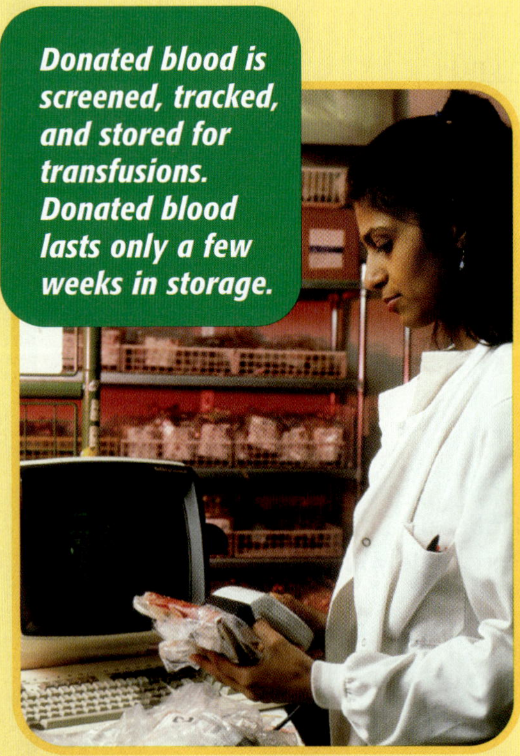

Donated blood is screened, tracked, and stored for transfusions. Donated blood lasts only a few weeks in storage.

Hemoglobin from cows to dogs

When an animal or human is injured, the number of red blood cells in the blood drops. This drop may cause the body's tissues to be starved for oxygen. The artificial blood now available for injured dogs reduces the risk of anemia by replacing the natural hemoglobin, the protein that allows blood to carry oxygen through the body. The artificial blood given to dogs is made from hemoglobin recycled from slaughtered cows. Because this hemoglobin lacks the complex, natural covering normally present in red blood cells, the hemoglobin is often absorbed by the dog's body in less than a day. These products are saving dogs' lives by giving dogs time to replace the blood they have lost and to recover from their injuries.

Artificial blood for humans

Researchers are now racing to develop a blood substitute for humans. One promising new family of substances known as *perfluorocarbons* is made from fluorine and carbon. Perfluorocarbons are oily substances that are coated with a bonding chemical that allows them to mix with a water-based saline solution. Perfluorocarbons have a major advantage over real blood because they don't have to match the patient's blood type. Perfluorocarbons also carry twice as much oxygen as human hemoglobin does. And unlike donated human blood, which must be thrown out after six weeks, artificial blood can be stored for up to two years. However, artificial blood does have one major limitation—it lacks white blood cells and platelets, a critical part of the body's defense and healing systems. For this reason, artificial blood will probably never be a permanent replacement for real blood. If approved for humans, blood substitutes will most likely be used for short-term needs (such as during surgery) until matching human blood can be found.

This mouse is "breathing" comfortably, thanks to the oxygen-carrying perfluorocarbons in this solution.

Science and You

1. **Applying Knowledge** Describe one medical condition that can be cured or helped with artificial blood.
2. **Understanding Concepts** If perfluorocarbons are more efficient at carrying oxygen through the body than natural blood is, why don't doctors expect to use perfluorocarbons as a permanent blood replacement?
3. **Critical Thinking** Do you think that the ability of artificial blood to be stored for long periods of time will help reduce blood shortages? Why or why not?
4. **Creative Thinking** Why do you think doctors don't use cow hemoglobin for human use?
5. **Acquiring and Evaluating** Research the medical condition called *sickle cell anemia,* and write a short paper that answers the following questions: What is sickle cell anemia? How are sickle cells different from healthy cells? How is the condition normally treated? How might artificial blood be used to treat people who have sickle cell anemia?

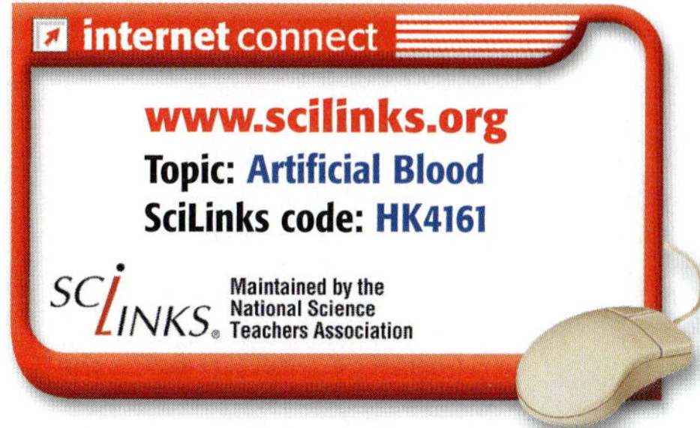

CHAPTER 8

Acids, Bases, and Salts

Chapter Preview

Focus ACTIVITY

Background Some kinds of ants can defend themselves with a quick squirt of highly irritating formic acid solution. These ants are often called *stinging ants,* but in fact the ants bite and then squirt the acid into the wound. Formic acid was identified in 1670 by a chemist who heated ants in a flask and collected the vapors given off. The name *formic acid* is from the Latin *formica*, meaning ant. Many other acids are also found in living things.

Acids also react with a type of chemical called *bases.* In many ways, acids and bases are chemical opposites. For example, the base calcium hydroxide can be used to treat lakes that are too acidic. The reaction that neutralizes the lake is similar to the reaction that happens when you take an antacid for an upset stomach.

Activity 1 Cut a lemon in half. Squeeze the lemon over a clean dish to get about a teaspoon of juice. Dip a clean finger into the juice, and taste it. Describe the taste. Do you think that lemon juice is acidic or basic? Give reasons for your decision.

Activity 2 After you have tasted the lemon juice in Activity 1, add a teaspoon of water to it, and stir with your finger. With a clean, dry spoon, add 1/2 teaspoon of baking soda to the diluted lemon juice. What happens to the juice and baking soda? Baking soda is a basic substance. What evidence do you see that a chemical reaction takes place?

Some species of ants produce formic acid and inject it into their victims when they bite. The helicopter is adding a base to an acidic lake to neutralize it.

Pre-Reading Questions

1. The orange is known as a citrus fruit because it contains *citric acid*. What other foods may contain citric acid?
2. Bee venom is also acidic. How might a solution of baking soda in water reduce the pain of a bee sting?

SECTION 1

Acids, Bases, and pH

KEY TERMS

acid
indicator
electrolyte
base
pH

OBJECTIVES

- **Describe** the ionization of strong acids in water and the dissociation of strong bases in water.
- **Distinguish** between solutions of weak acids or bases and solutions of strong acids or bases.
- **Relate** pH to the concentration of hydronium ions and hydroxide ions in a solution.

Does the thought of eating a lemon make your mouth pucker and your saliva flow? You know to expect that sour, piercing taste that can sometimes make you shudder. Eating a lime or a dill pickle may cause you to have a similar response.

What Are Acids?

Each of the foods shown in ***Figure 1*** tastes sour because it contains an **acid.** Several fruits, including lemons and limes, contain citric acid. Dill pickles are soaked in vinegar, which contains acetic acid. Other acidic foods include apples, which contain malic acid, and grapes, which contain tartaric acid.

acid any compound that increases the number of hydronium ions when dissolved in water

When acids dissolve in water, they *ionize*, which means that they form ions. Hydrogen ions, H^+, attach to water molecules to form hydronium ions, H_3O^+. These hydronium ions are responsible for the sour taste you experience. **Indicators** respond to the concentration of hydronium ions in water by changing color. Blue litmus paper contains an indicator that can help you determine if a substance is an acid. Acids turn blue litmus paper red, as shown in ***Figure 1.***

indicator a compound that can reversibly change color depending on the pH of the solution or other chemical change

Figure 1

Lemons, limes, and dill pickles taste sour because they contain acids. Acids, such as the citric acid in lemon juice, turn blue litmus paper red.

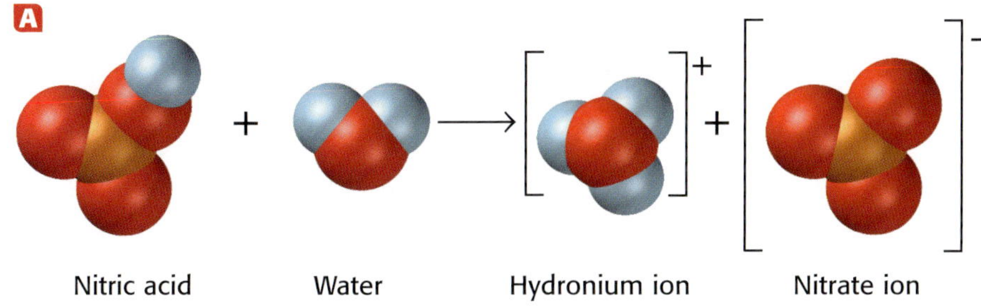

Strong acids ionize completely

All acids ionize when dissolved in water. The ionization process shown in ***Figure 2A*** occurs when nitric acid is added to water. The single arrow pointing to the right shows that nitric acid ionizes completely in water. When the acid ionizes, it forms hydronium ions and nitrate ions. These charged ions are able to move around in the solution and conduct electricity, as you see in ***Figure 2B.*** A substance that conducts electricity when dissolved in water is an **electrolyte.**

Solutions of some acids, such as nitric acid, conduct electricity well. Nitric acid, HNO_3, is a *strong acid* because it ionizes completely in water. Other strong acids behave similarly to nitric acid when dissolved in water. A solution of sulfuric acid in water, for example, conducts electric current in car batteries. Strong acids are strong electrolytes because solutions of these acids have as many hydronium ions as the acid can possibly form.

Figure 2

B Nitric acid, HNO_3, is a strong electrolyte and a strong acid because it ionizes completely in water to form hydronium, ions H_3O^+, and nitrate ions, NO_3^-.

electrolyte a substance that dissolves in water to give a solution that conducts an electric current

Weak acids do not ionize completely

Solutions of *weak acids,* such as acetic acid, CH_3COOH, do not conduct electricity as well as nitric acid. When acetic acid is added to water, the equilibrium shown in ***Figure 3A*** is reached.

When acetic acid is dissolved in water, some molecules of acetic acid combine with water molecules to form ions. Many of the ions then recombine to form molecules of acetic acid. Because there are fewer charged ions in a solution of acetic acid, it does not conduct electricity very well, as shown in ***Figure 3B.*** Acetic acid and other weak acids are weak electrolytes.

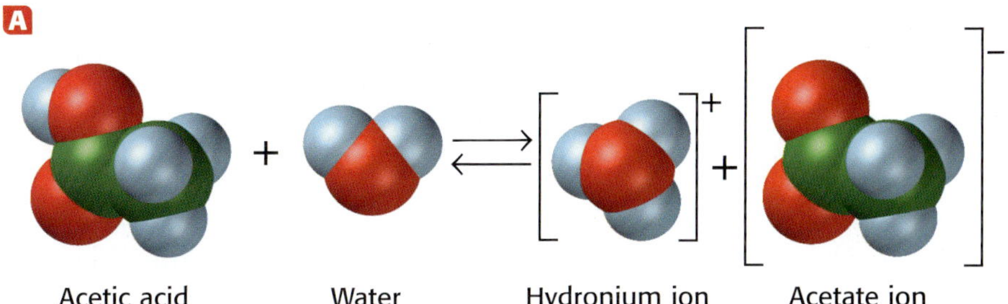

Figure 3

B Acetic acid, CH_3COOH, is a weak acid and a weak electrolyte because it ionizes only partially in water to form hydronium ions, H_3O^+, and acetate ions, CH_3COO^-.

Table 1 Some Common Acids

Acid	Formula	Strength	Uses for the acid
Hydrochloric acid	HCl	strong	cleaning masonry; treating metal before plating or painting; adjusting the pH of swimming pools
Sulfuric acid	H_2SO_4	strong	manufacturing fertilizer and chemicals; most used industrial chemical; the electrolyte in car batteries
Nitric acid	HNO_3	strong	manufacturing fertilizers and explosives
Acetic acid	CH_3COOH	weak	manufacturing chemicals, plastics, and pharmaceuticals; the acid in vinegar
Formic acid	$HCOOH$	weak	dyeing textiles; the acid in stinging ants
Citric acid	$H_3C_6H_5O_7$	weak	manufacturing flavorings and soft drinks; the acid in citrus fruits (oranges, lemons, limes)

Figure 4
These household items are bases because they produce OH^- ions in water solution.

base any compound that increases the number of hydroxide ions when dissolved in water

Any acid can be dangerous in a concentrated form

Some examples of common strong and weak acids and their uses are listed in **Table 1.** Acids are used in many manufacturing processes and are necessary to many organisms even though strong acids can damage living tissue. For example, your stomach normally contains a dilute solution of hydrochloric acid that helps you digest food, but concentrated hydrochloric acid can burn your skin.

Even weak acids are not always safe to handle. Most vinegar is a 5% solution of acetic acid in water, but concentrated acetic acid can damage the skin, and the vapors are harmful to the eyes, mouth, and lungs. To be safe, always wear safety goggles, gloves, and a laboratory apron when working with acids.

What Are Bases?

Like acids, all **bases** share common properties. Bases have a bitter, soapy taste, and solutions of bases feel slippery. **Figure 4** shows some common household substances that contain bases. Like solutions of acids, solutions of bases contain ions and can conduct electricity. Some bases contain hydroxide ions, OH^-, but others do not. Bases that do not contain hydroxide ions will react with water molecules to form hydroxide ions. Bases cause indicators to change color, such as turning red litmus paper blue.

Table 2 Some Common Bases

Base	Formula	Strength	Uses for the base
Potassium hydroxide (potash)	KOH	strong	manufacturing soap; absorbing carbon dioxide from flue gases; dyeing products
Sodium hydroxide (lye)	$NaOH$	strong	manufacturing soap; refining petroleum; cleaning drains; manufacturing synthetic fibers
Calcium hydroxide	$Ca(OH)_2$	strong	treating acidic soil; treating lakes polluted by acid precipitation; making mortar, plaster, and cement
Ammonia	NH_3	weak	fertilizing soil; manufacturing other fertilizers; manufacturing nitric acid; making cleaning solutions
Methylamine	CH_3NH_2	weak	manufacturing dyes and medicines; tanning leather
Aniline	$C_6H_5NH_2$	weak	manufacturing dyes and varnishes; used as a solvent

Many common bases contain hydroxide ions

Strong bases are ionic compounds that contain a metal ion and a hydroxide ion. These strong bases are also known as *metal hydroxides.* When a metal hydroxide is dissolved in water, the metal ions and the hydroxide ions *dissociate,* or separate.

For example, sodium hydroxide, NaOH, is a metal hydroxide that is found in some drain cleaners. Solutions of sodium hydroxide conduct electricity well, so sodium hydroxide is a strong electrolyte. The dissociation of sodium hydroxide in water is shown below.

$$NaOH \rightarrow Na^+ + OH^-$$

Some metal hydroxides, such as calcium hydroxide and magnesium hydroxide, are not very soluble in water, but the ions in the part of the metal hydroxide that does dissolve separate completely. Calcium hydroxide is used to treat soil that is too acidic. Other useful bases are listed in **Table 2.**

Like acids, bases can be very dangerous in concentrated form, and in the case of bases such as sodium hydroxide and potassium hydroxide, bases can be dangerous even in fairly dilute form. Because bases attack living tissue very rapidly, bases are in some ways more dangerous than acids. To protect yourself when working with bases in the laboratory, always wear safety goggles, gloves, and a laboratory apron. If possible, work with very dilute bases instead of concentrated ones.

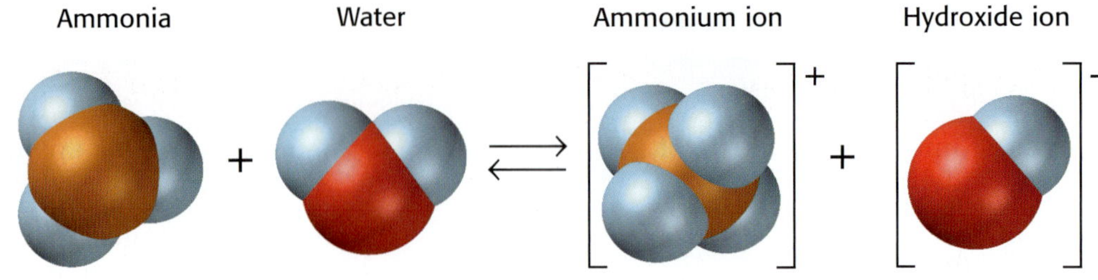

Figure 5

Ammonia produces hydroxide ions in water through ionization. An ammonia molecule accepts H^+ ions from water to form ammonium ions, NH_4^+, and hydroxide ions, OH^-.

Other bases ionize in water to form hydroxide ions

Ammonia, like other bases, forms hydroxide ions when it dissolves in water. But ammonia does not contain hydroxide ions. Instead, it forms hydroxide ions with water through an ionization process, shown in ***Figure 5.*** In this process, water acts as an acid and donates a hydrogen ion to ammonia to form an ammonium ion, NH_4^+, and leaves a hydroxide ion, OH^-, behind.

A solution of ammonia in water is a poor conductor of electricity. This shows that only some of the ammonia molecules actually become ammonium ions when the ammonia dissolves. So, an ammonia solution consists mostly of water and dissolved ammonia, along with a few ammonium ions and hydroxide ions. Ammonia is a much weaker base than potassium hydroxide, which is a metal hydroxide that dissociates completely.

Which household substances are acidic, which are basic, and which are neither?

Materials

- baking powder
- baking soda
- several 50 mL beakers
- pipet bulbs
- milk
- mineral water
- bleach
- blue litmus paper
- white vinegar
- dishwashing liquid
- soft drinks
- mayonnaise
- red litmus paper
- disposable pipets or eyedroppers
- laundry detergent
- tap water

SAFETY CAUTION Wear safety goggles, gloves, and a laboratory apron. Never pipet anything by mouth.

1. Prepare a sample of each substance you will test. If the substance is a liquid, pour about 5 mL of it into a small beaker. If the substance is a solid, place a small amount of it in a beaker, and add about 5 mL of water. Label each beaker clearly with the name of the substance that is in the beaker.
2. Use a pipet to transfer a drop of liquid from one of the samples to red litmus paper. Then transfer another drop of liquid from the same sample to blue litmus paper. Record your observations.
3. Repeat step 2 for each sample. Be sure to use a clean pipet to transfer each sample.

Analysis

1. Which substances are acidic? Which are basic? How did you determine this?
2. Which substances are not acids or bases? How did you determine this?

What Is pH?

You can tell if a solution is acidic or basic by using an indicator, such as litmus paper. But to determine exactly how acidic or basic a solution is, you must measure the concentration of hydronium (H_3O^+) ions. The **pH** of a solution indicates its concentration of H_3O^+ ions. The pH of a solution is often critical. For example, enzymes in your body work only in a narrow pH range.

VOCABULARY Skills Tip

The term pH *originates from the French words* pouvoir Hydrogène, *which means "the power of hydrogen."*

pH values correspond to the concentration of hydronium ions

pH is a measure of the H_3O^+ concentration in a solution, but pH also indicates hydroxide ion (OH^-) concentration. So a pH value can tell you how acidic or basic a solution is. A pH value can even tell you if a solution is neutral, or neither an acid nor a base.

pH a value used to express the acidity or alkalinity of a solution

Typically, the pH of solutions ranges from 0 to 14, as shown in ***Figure 6.*** In neutral solutions, or in substances such as pure water, the concentration of hydronium ions equals the concentration of hydroxide ions, and the pH is 7. Solutions that have a pH of less than 7 are acidic. In acidic solutions, such as apple juice, the concentration of hydronium ions is greater than the concentration of hydroxide ions. Solutions that have a pH of greater than 7 are basic. In basic solutions, the concentration of hydroxide ions is greater than the concentration of hydronium ions.

Figure 6

The pH of a solution is easily measured by moistening a piece of pH paper with the solution and then comparing the color of the pH paper with the color scale on the dispenser of the pH paper.

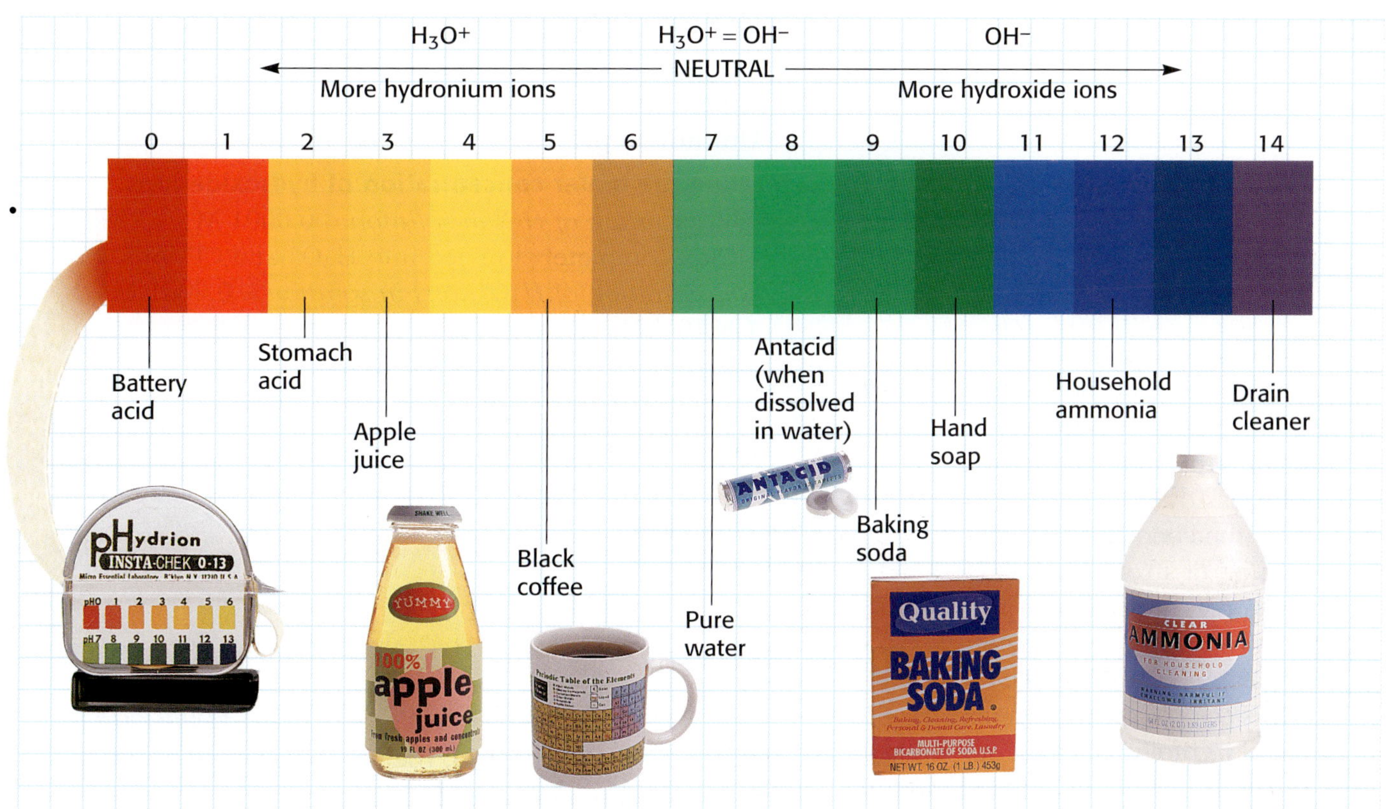

internet connect

www.scilinks.org
Topic: pH
SciLinks code: HK4103

SciLINKS. Maintained by the National Science Teachers Association

Did You Know?

Did you know that the concentration of hydronium ions and the concentration of hydroxide ions are related? In any solution made with water, the more hydronium ions there are (the more acidic the solution is), the fewer hydroxide ions there are (the less basic the solution is).

- If a solution contains a base, you should expect the pH to be greater than 7. If the solution contains an acid, the pH will be less than 7.
- To find the concentration of a solution of strong acid from its pH, multiply the pH value by –1. Then use the result as a power of 10. The result is the concentration of the acid in moles per liter (mol/L).

The concentration of a strong acid allows you to calculate pH

When you describe the concentration of a substance in a solution, you probably write the concentration as a *molarity* (M), or the number of moles of the substance per liter of solution. For example, the hydronium ion (H_3O^+) concentration of pure water at 25°C is 0.000 000 1 mol/L, or 10^{-7} M.

When the H_3O^+ concentration of a solution can be written as a power of 10, the pH is the negative of the power of 10 used to describe the concentration of hydronium ions. For example, the pH of pure water is 7, so the concentration of hydronium ions in water is 10^{-7} M. The pH of apple juice is about 3, so the concentration of H_3O^+ in apple juice is 10^{-3} M.

If you know the concentration of a solution of a strong acid, you can calculate the pH of the solution. When a strong monoprotic acid ionizes in a solution, one hydronium ion is formed for each particle of acid that dissolves. So the concentration of hydronium ions in a solution of strong acid is the same as the concentration of the acid itself, and this information allows you to find the pH of the solution.

Math Skills

Determining pH Determine the pH of a 0.0001 M solution of the strong acid HCl dissolved in water.

1 List the given and unknown values.

Given: *concentration of HCl in solution* = 0.0001 M

Unknown: pH

2 Determine the molar concentration of hydroxide ions.

concentration of HCl in solution = 0.0001 M

HCl is completely ionized into H_3O^+ and Cl^- ions.

concentration of H_3O^+ ions in solution = 0.0001 M = 1×10^{-4} M

3 Convert the H_3O^+ concentration to pH.

concentration of H_3O^+ ions = 1×10^{-4} M

pH = –(–4) = 4

Practice

Determining pH

1. Calculate the pH of a 1×10^{-4} M solution of HBr, a strong acid.
2. Determine the pH of a 0.01 M solution of HNO_3, a strong acid.
3. Nitric acid, HNO_3, is a strong acid. The pH of a solution of HNO_3 is 3. What is the concentration of the solution?

Small differences in pH mean larger differences in acidity

Because pH is the negative of the power of 10 of hydronium ion concentration, small differences in pH mean larger differences in the hydronium ion concentration. For example, the pH of apple juice differs from the pH of coffee by two pH units, so apple juice is 10^2, or 100 times, more acidic than coffee. Likewise, coffee is about 10^3, or 1000 times, more acidic than antacid tablets, which form a base with a pH of about 8 when dissolved in water.

pH can be measured in more than one way

pH paper contains several indicators that change color at different pH values. pH may also be measured with a pH meter, as shown in ***Figure 7***. Because ions in a solution have an electric charge, a pH meter can measure pH by determining the electric current created by the movement of the ions in the solution. If you use a pH meter properly, you can determine the pH of a solution more precisely than is possible if you use pH paper.

Figure 7

A pH meter measures an electric current that results from differences in H_3O^+ concentrations.

SECTION 1 REVIEW

SUMMARY

- Acids are substances that taste sour, turn blue litmus paper red, and form hydronium ions when they dissolve in water.
- Strong acids are strong electrolytes because they ionize completely in water.
- Weak acids are weak electrolytes because they ionize only slightly in water.
- Bases have a slippery feel, have a bitter taste, turn red litmus paper blue, and produce hydroxide ions when they dissolve in water.
- The pH of a solution of a strong acid can be found if you know the concentration of the solution.

1. **Explain** how a strong acid and a weak acid behave differently when each is dissolved in water.
2. **Compare** the ionization of a weak acid in water to the ionization of a weak base in water.
3. **Write** the chemical equation for the self-ionization of water.
4. **Classify** the following solutions as acidic, basic, or neutral.
   a. a soap solution, pH = 9
   b. a sour liquid, pH = 5
   c. a solution that has four times as many hydronium ions as hydroxide ions
   d. pure water
5. **Arrange** the following substances in order of increasing acidity: vinegar (pH = 2.8), gastric juices from inside your stomach (pH = 2.0), and a soft drink (pH = 3.4).
6. **Critical Thinking** A solution of an acid in water has a pH of 4, which is slightly acidic. Is this a solution of a weak acid? Explain your answer.

Math Skills

7. What is the pH of a 0.01 M solution of the strong acid $HClO_4$, perchloric acid?

SECTION 2

Reactions of Acids with Bases

KEY TERMS

neutralization reaction

salt

OBJECTIVES

- **Write** ionic equations for neutralization reactions.
- **Identify** the products of a neutralization reaction.
- **Describe** the composition of a salt.

Have you ever used an antacid to relieve the symptoms of an upset stomach or so-called heartburn? Heartburn has nothing to do with your heart. Heartburn occurs when the stomach's natural solution of hydrochloric acid (HCl) irritates the lining of the esophagus. The antacid contains a base that reacts with the acid to reduce the acidity of the solution and soothe your stomach.

neutralization reaction the reaction of the ions that characterize acids (hydronium ions) and the ions that characterize bases (hydroxide ions) to form water molecules and a salt

Acid-Base Reactions

A reaction between an acid and a base is a **neutralization reaction.** An example of neutralization is the reaction of HCl and magnesium hydroxide, which is an antacid and a base.

Neutralization is an ionic reaction

A solution of a strong acid, such as hydrochloric acid, ionizes completely, as shown below.

$$HCl + H_2O \rightarrow H_3O^+ + Cl^-$$

In a similar way, a solution of a strong base, such as sodium hydroxide, dissociates completely, as shown below.

$$NaOH \rightarrow Na^+ + OH^-$$

If the two solutions of equal concentrations and equal volumes are combined, the following neutralization reaction takes place:

$$H_3O^+ + Cl^- + Na^+ + OH^- \rightarrow Na^+ + Cl^- + 2H_2O$$

The Na^+ and Cl^- ions are called *spectator ions* because they are like spectators watching on the sidelines. These ions do not change during the reaction between H_3O^+ and OH^-. As you can see in ***Figure 8,*** energy is also released in the reaction of Na and Cl_2.

Figure 8

When Na reacts with Cl_2, sodium chloride is produced and energy is released.

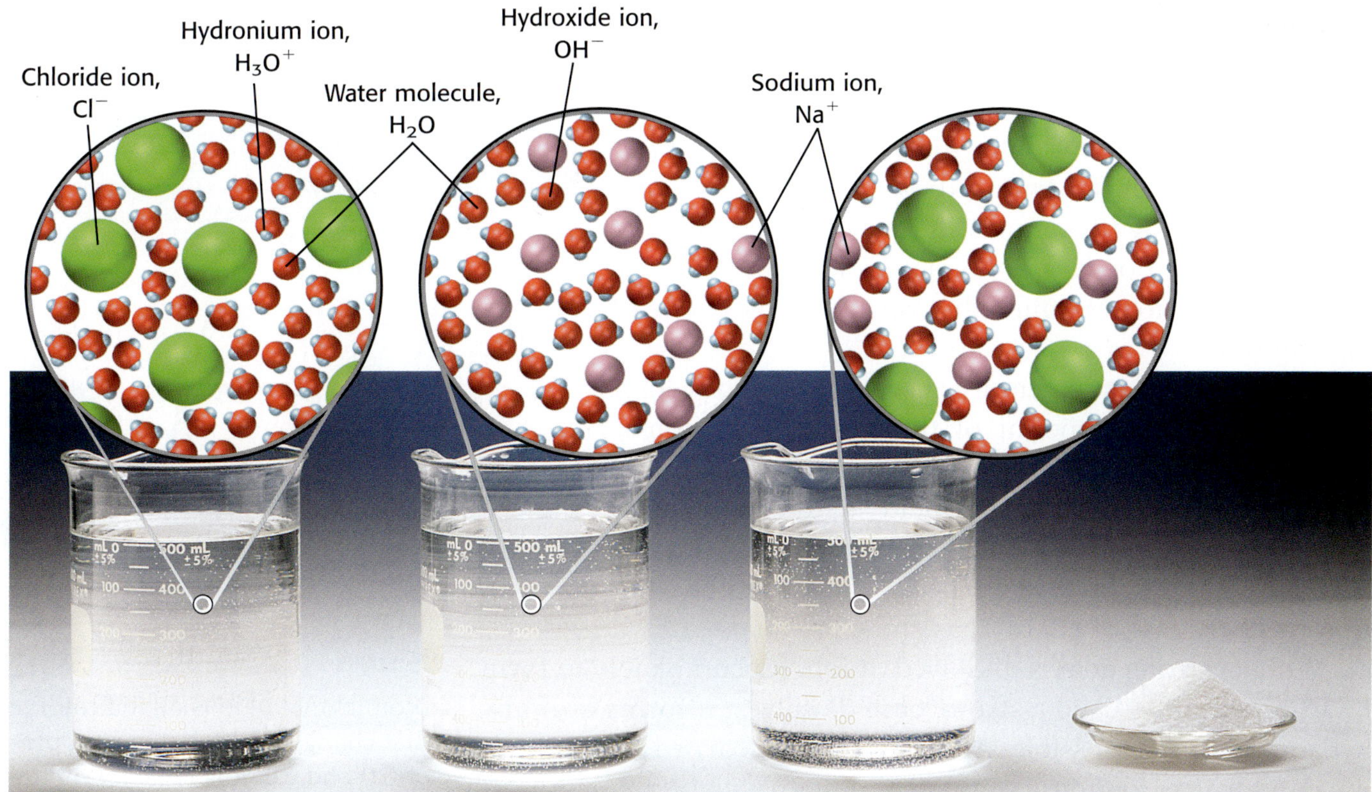

Figure 9

When a solution of HCl reacts with a solution of NaOH, the reaction produces water and leaves sodium and chloride ions in solution. When the water is evaporated, the sodium and chloride ions crystallize to form pure sodium chloride.

Strong acids and bases react to form water and a salt

If you include only the substances that react during neutralization, the equation can be written as follows:

$$H_3O^+ + OH^- \rightarrow 2H_2O$$

When an acid reacts with a base, hydronium ions react with hydroxide ions to form water. The other ions—positive ions from the base and negative ions from the acid—form an ionic compound called a **salt,** such as sodium chloride. Salts are ionic compounds that are often soluble in water, as you can see in ***Figure 9.***

salt an ionic compound that forms when a metal atom or a positive radical replaces the hydrogen of an acid

Not all neutralization reactions produce neutral solutions

Reactions between acids and bases do not always produce neutral solutions. The final pH of the solution depends on the amounts of acid and base that are combined. The pH also depends on whether the acid and base are strong or weak.

If a strong acid, such as nitric acid, reacts with an equal amount of a weak base, such as sodium hydrogen carbonate from an antacid tablet, the resulting solution will still be acidic. A similar situation occurs when a strong base reacts with a weak acid. When a strong acid reacts with an equal amount of a weak base, the resulting solution will be acidic.

Titrations are neutralization reactions

When an acid solution is added to a basic solution, a neutralization reaction occurs. If you know the concentration of the acid solution or the basic solution, a *titration* can help you determine the concentration of the other solution. A titration is the process of gradually adding one solution to another solution in the presence of an indicator to determine the concentration of one of the solutions.

In a titration, an indicator is used that changes color when the original amount of the base in solution is equal to the amount of the acid added to the solution. For example, when a strong acid is titrated with a strong base, an indicator called *bromthymol blue* is used because bromthymol blue changes color when the solution reaches a pH of about 7, as shown in **Figure 10.**

Figure 10

Bromthymol blue is an indicator that changes color between a pH of 6.0 and 7.6. It is ideal for a titration involving a strong acid and a strong base.

When a strong acid is dissolved, it ionizes completely to form hydronium ions. When a strong base dissolves, it forms as many hydroxide ions as possible. And as you have learned, hydronium ions and hydroxide ions combine in a neutralization reaction. If the number of hydronium ions is equal to the number of hydroxide ions in a solution, the product of the reaction will be neutral. The *equivalence point* in a titration of a strong acid with a strong base is reached when the original amount of the acid equals the original amount of the base and occurs at pH 7. **Figure 11** shows the change in pH during the titration of nitric acid with sodium hydroxide.

The equivalence point is not always neutral

Titrations can also be carried out with a strong acid and a weak base, or with a weak acid and a strong base. In these cases, however, the equivalence point will not be at pH 7. For example, when 1 mol of acetic acid, a weak acid, reacts in water with 1 mol of sodium hydroxide, a strong base, 1 mol of sodium acetate should form. However, some of the acetate ions react with water molecules. As a result, OH^- ions ions are formed.

When there are OH^- ions left over, a neutralization reaction does not produce a neutral solution. Neutralization occurs when water is formed from H_3O^+ ions and OH^- ions, but if there are any hydroxide ions left over, the solution will still be basic. A similar situation occurs when a strong acid is titrated with a weak base, but in this case the product is acidic and has a pH of less than 7.

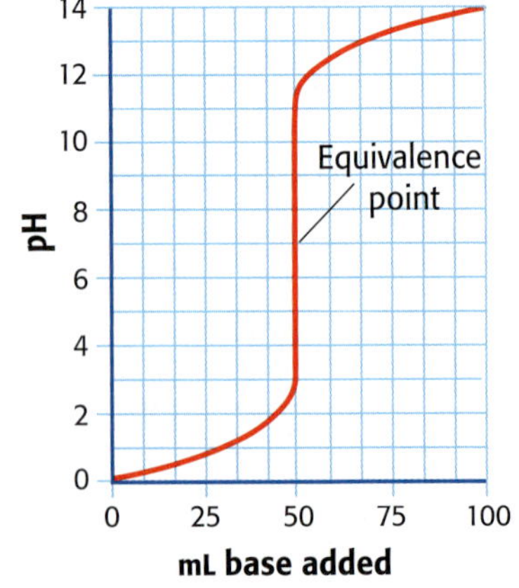

Figure 11

When a strong acid, such as nitric acid, is titrated with a strong base, the pH of the solution changes rapidly when the equivalence point is reached.

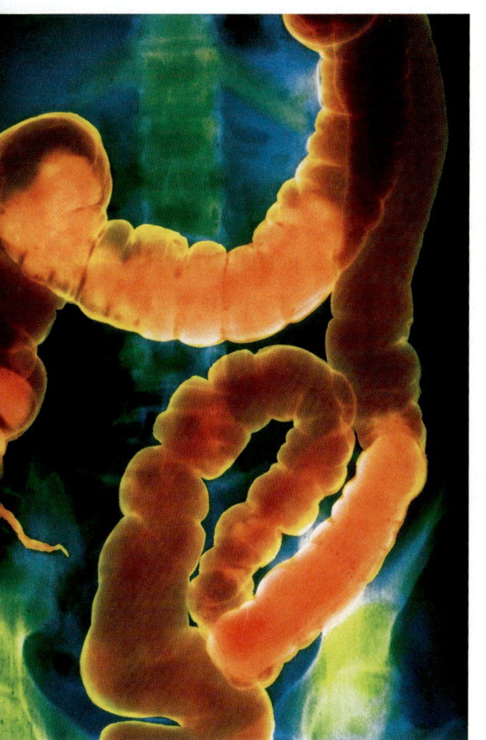

Figure 12

The salt barium sulfate, $BaSO_4$, is a highly insoluble salt that blocks X rays. After barium sulfate is placed into the large intestine, the form of the intestine shows up lighter on an X-ray photo.

Salts

When you hear the word *salt,* you probably think of white crystals that you sprinkle on food. But to a chemist, a salt can be almost any combination of cations and anions, except for hydroxides and oxides, which are bases.

Sodium chloride has many different uses

Common table salt contains sodium chloride, NaCl, which is an ionic compound that can be formed from the reaction of hydrochloric acid with sodium hydroxide. NaCl is the source of most of the sodium in your diet. It is widely used to season and preserve food. Most NaCl in the United States comes from underground deposits that were left when ancient seas dried up.

NaCl is also used in ceramic glazes, soap manufacturing, home water softeners, highway de-icing, and fire extinguishers. Many other salts also contain sodium, as you can see in ***Table 3*** below.

Salts are all around us

Salts can be formed by acid-base neutralization, but more often, they are formed from other salts. Another familiar example of a salt is baking soda, sodium hydrogen carbonate. Photographic film contains the salts silver bromide and silver iodide, which are sensitive to light. Ordinary soaps and detergents are also examples of salts. ***Figure 12*** shows a salt that is used in medical diagnosis.

Table 3 **Some Common Salts**

Salt	Formula	Uses
Aluminum sulfate	$Al_2(SO_4)_3$	purifying water; used in antiperspirants
Ammonium sulfate	$(NH_4)_2SO_4$	flameproofing fabric; used as fertilizer
Calcium chloride	$CaCl_2$	de-icing streets and highways; used in some kinds of concrete
Potassium chloride	KCl	treating potassium deficiency; used as table-salt substitute
Sodium carbonate	Na_2CO_3	manufacturing glass; added to wash to soften water
Sodium hydrogen carbonate	$NaHCO_3$	treating upset stomach; ingredient in baking powder; used in fire extinguishers
Sodium stearate	$NaOOCC_{17}H_{34}$	typical example of a soap
Sodium lauryl sulfonate	$NaSO_3C_{12}H_{25}$	typical example of a detergent

Figure 13

These butterflies can obtain the salt they need from the dried sweat on an old sneaker.

Salts are useful substances

You have probably seen a lot of chalk since you entered school, but did you know that chalk is a salt? Chalk is one form of the salt calcium carbonate, $CaCO_3$, which also makes up limestone and marble. It is likely that the walls in your house are made of slabs of gypsum, which is one form of the salt calcium sulfate, $CaSO_4$.

You often hear that a healthful diet should include minerals such as potassium, sodium, calcium, magnesium, iron, phosphorus, and iodine. However, ingesting these nutrients in the form of free elements is not very common. Instead, you get ions of these elements in their ionic form from salts. You need calcium ions, Ca^{2+}, for strong bones and teeth and for proper function of nerves and muscles. The correct proportion of potassium ions, K^+, and sodium ions, Na^+, is crucial for transmission of nerve impulses, even in insects, such as those shown in ***Figure 13.*** Phosphorus, in the form of phosphate ions, PO_4^{3-}, is needed for many processes in living cells, from transporting energy to the reproduction of the genetic code.

SECTION 2 REVIEW

SUMMARY

- Acids and bases react with each other in a process called *neutralization.*
- Neutralization is a reaction between an acid and a base to form water and a salt.
- Neutralization reactions between weak acids and strong bases result in basic solutions.
- Neutralization reactions between strong acids and weak bases result in acidic solutions.
- Salts are ionic substances composed of cations and anions other than oxide or hydroxide.

1. **Write** the chemical equation for the neutralization of nitric acid, HNO_3, with magnesium hydroxide, $Mg(OH)_2$, first with spectator ions and then without spectator ions.
2. **Determine** which acid and which base you would combine to form the salt aluminum sulfate, $Al_2(SO_4)_3$.
3. **Identify** the spectator ions in the neutralization of lithium hydroxide, LiOH, with hydrobromic acid, HBr.
4. **Predict** whether the reaction of each of the following acids and bases will yield an acidic, a basic, or a neutral solution. Explain your answer for each.
   a. sulfuric acid, H_2SO_4, and ammonia, NH_3
   b. formic acid, HCOOH, and potassium hydroxide, KOH
   c. nitric acid, HNO_3, and calcium hydroxide, $Ca(OH)_2$
5. **Critical Thinking** A classmate observes a neutralization reaction between an acid and a base. After the reaction is complete, your classmate is surprised to find that the pH of the resulting solution is 4, not 7, the pH of a neutral solution. What can you tell your classmate to help them understand what happened?

SECTION 3

INTEGRATING TECHNOLOGY and Society

Acids, Bases, and Salts in the Home

OBJECTIVES

- **Describe** the chemical structures of soaps and detergents and explain how they work.
- **Describe** the chemical composition of bleach and its uses.
- **Describe** how an antacid reduces stomach acid.
- **Identify** acidic and basic household products and their uses.

KEY TERMS

soap
detergent
disinfectant
bleach
antacid

As you have seen, you won't find acids, bases, and salts only in a laboratory. Many items in your own home, such as soaps, detergents, shampoos, antacids, vitamins, sodas, and juices in your kitchen are examples of household products that contain acids, bases, and salts.

soap a substance that is used as a cleaner and that dissolves in water

Cleaning Products

If you work on an oily bicycle chain or if you've been eating potato chips, water alone will not remove the greasy film from your hands. Water will not work because it doesn't mix with grease or oil. Something else must be added to water to improve its ability to clean.

Soaps allow oil and water to mix

Soap improves water's ability to clean because it can dissolve in both oil and in water. This property allows oil and water to form an emulsion that can be washed away by rinsing. For example, when you are washing your face with soap, as the girl in ***Figure 14*** is, the oil on your face is emulsified by the soapy water. The water you rinse with carries away both the soap and unwanted oil to leave your face clean.

Soaps are salts of sodium or potassium and fatty acids, which have long hydrocarbon chains. Soaps are made through a reaction of animal fats or vegetable oils with a solution of sodium hydroxide or potassium hydroxide. The products of the reaction are soap and an alcohol called *glycerol*.

Figure 14
When you wash with soap, you create an emulsion of oil droplets spread throughout water.

Connection to SOCIAL STUDIES

People have used soap for thousands of years. Ancient Egyptians took baths regularly with soap made from animal fats or vegetable oils and basic solutions of alkali-metal compounds. According to Roman legend, people discovered that the water in the Tiber River near Mount Sapo was good for washing. Mount Sapo was used for elaborate animal-sacrifice rituals, and the combination of animal fat and the basic ash that washed down the mountain made the river soapy.

Making the Connection

1. The process of making soap is sometimes referred to as *saponification.* How does this word relate to the Roman soap legend?
2. Homemade soap can be made from hog fat and ashes. Which material provides the base needed to make the soap?

How soap removes grease

Soap is an ionic compound. Its negative ion is a long hydrocarbon chain of the soap anion with a carboxylate group ($-COO^-$) at one end. For every negatively charged end, there is a positive sodium or potassium ion.

Soap is able to remove grease and oil because the cations and the negatively charged ends of the chains ($-COO^-$) dissolve in water, while the hydrocarbon chains dissolve in oil. Soap acts as an emulsifier by surrounding droplets of oil, as shown in ***Figure 15.*** This action causes the droplets of oil to stay suspended in water. When you are washing your hands with soap, you probably rub them together. Rubbing your hands together actually helps clean them. When you do this, you lift most of the emulsion of grease and water into the lather where it can be rinsed into the sink.

detergent a water-soluble cleaner that can emulsify dirt and oil

Figure 15

The charged ends of soap or detergent dissolve in water, and the hydrocarbon chains dissolve in oil, keeping the oil droplet in suspension.

Detergents have replaced soap in many uses

As useful as soap is for cleaning, it does not work well in hard water, that is, water containing the dissolved ions Mg^{2+}, Ca^{2+}, and Fe^{3+}. These cations combine with the fatty acid anions of soap to form an insoluble salt called *soap scum.* This soap scum settles out on clothing, dishes, your skin, and your hair. The scum also makes a ring around the bathtub or washbasin. To prevent this problem, **detergents** are used instead of soap to wash clothes and dishes. Most shampoos, liquid hand soaps, and body washes are actually detergents, not soap.

Detergents are sodium, potassium, and sometimes ammonium salts. Like anions in soaps, the anion in detergents are composed of a long hydrocarbon chain that has a negatively charged end. But the charged end of a detergent is a sulfonate group ($-SO_3^-$), not a carboxylate group. These sulfonate ions do not form scum with the ions in hard water. Detergents are also different from soaps because their hydrocarbon chains are made from petroleum products instead of from animal fats or plant oils.

Because soaps and detergents act in the same way, ***Figure 15*** represents detergents as well as soaps. The long hydrocarbon chains are soluble in oil or grease. The sulfonate ends are highly soluble in water. Water molecules attract the charged sulfonate group and keep the oil droplet suspended among the water molecules.

Many household cleaners contain ammonia

Ammonia solutions, such as the ones shown in ***Figure 16,*** are also effective cleaners. Household ammonia is a solution of ammonia gas in water. Recall that ammonia is a weak base because it ionizes only slightly in water to form ammonium ions and hydroxide ions. The hydroxide ions make the ammonia solution basic, as shown in the reaction below.

$$NH_3 + H_2O \leftrightarrows NH_4^+ + OH^-$$

Although the concentration of hydroxide ions is very low in an ammonia solution, enough of the ions are available to help emulsify thin layers of oily dirt, such as fingerprints and oily smears. In addition, many ammonia cleaners contain alcohols, detergents, and other cleaning agents.

Figure 16

Basic solutions of ammonia, such as these, can clean away light grease smears, such as fingerprints.

Bleach can eliminate stains

A **disinfectant** is a substance that kills bacteria and viruses. Household **bleach,** a very strong disinfectant, is a basic solution of sodium hypochlorite, NaOCl. You are probably familiar with the ability of bleach to remove colors and stains.

Bleach does not actually remove the substance causing the stain. Instead, it changes the substance to a colorless form. This bleaching action is carried out by the oxygen atom in the hypochlorite ion, ClO^-.

If an acid is added to a bleach solution, the acid reacts with the hydroxide ions, and the reaction reverses, giving off deadly chlorine gas. For this reason, you should never mix bleach with an acid, such as vinegar. Also, ammonia and bleach should not be mixed because noxious chloramine gas, NH_2Cl, is formed.

disinfectant a chemical substance that kills harmful bacteria or viruses

bleach a chemical compound used to whiten or make lighter, such as hydrogen peroxide or sodium hypochlorite

Detergents

Detergents help break up oil into droplets that can be washed away by water. Detergents also break up the surface tension of water so that it can wet materials more easily. In this activity, you will demonstrate this effect using a piece of wax paper, a drop of water, a toothpick, and liquid detergent.

1. Lay some wax paper on a flat surface, and put a drop of water on it. Does the water wet the surface of the wax paper? How can you tell?
2. Gently touch the drop of water with the tip of the toothpick. What happens to the drop of water?
3. Now dip the tip of the toothpick in liquid detergent.
4. Gently touch the drop of water with the tip of the toothpick after it has been dipped in detergent. What happens to the drop of water? How could this action help water clean away dirt?

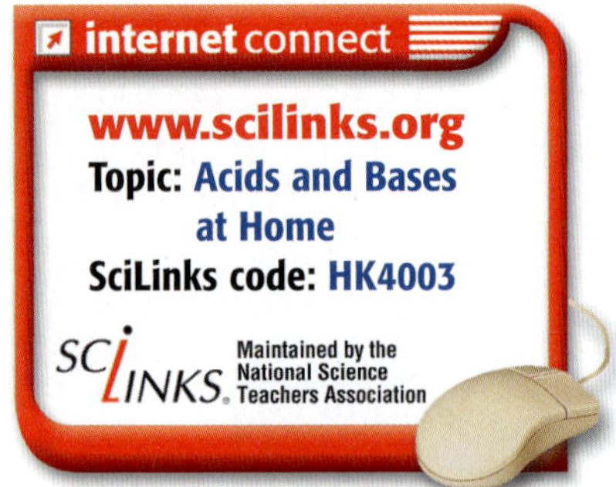

Acids, Bases, and Salts in the Household

You probably have taken many of the acidic and basic materials in your home for granted. For example, many of the clothes in your closet get their color from acidic dyes. These dyes are sodium salts of organic compounds that contain the sulfonic acid group ($-SO_3H$) or the carboxylic acid group ($-COOH$). If you have ever had an upset stomach because of excess stomach acid, you may have taken an antacid tablet to feel better. The antacid made you feel better because it neutralized the excess stomach acid. Many other useful products in your home are also acids or bases.

Many healthcare products are acids or bases

antacid a weak base that neutralizes stomach acid

In the morning before school, you may drink a glass of orange juice that contains vitamin C. Ascorbic acid is the chemical name for vitamin C, which your body needs to grow and repair bone and cartilage. Both sodium hydrogen carbonate and magnesium hydroxide (milk of magnesia) can be used as **antacids.** Antacids are basic substances that you swallow to neutralize stomach acid when you have an upset stomach. ***Figure 17*** shows how adding an antacid tablet to an acidic solution changes the pH of the solution. A similar reaction (without the color change) takes place in your stomach when you take an antacid.

What does an antacid do?

Materials

- *plastic stirrer*
- *wax paper*
- *several varieties of antacid tablets*
- *red litmus paper*
- *150 to 200 mL beakers (2)*
- *pipet bulbs*
- *vinegar*
- *spoon*
- *blue litmus paper*
- *disposable pipets*

1. Pour 100 mL of water in a beaker. Add vinegar one drop at a time while stirring. Test the solution with litmus paper after each drop is added. Record the number of drops it takes for the solution to turn blue litmus paper bright red.

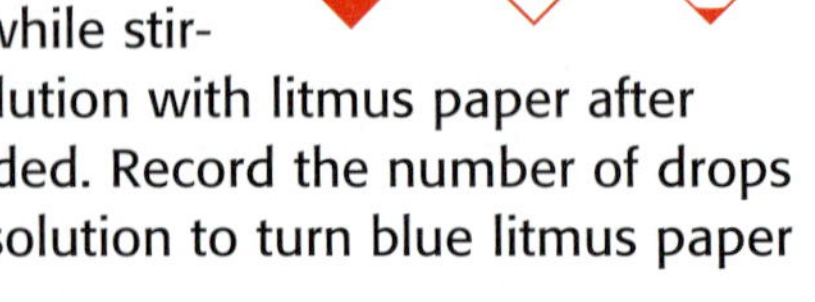

2. Use the back of a spoon to crush an antacid tablet to a fine powder on a piece of wax paper. Pour 100 mL of water in the second beaker, add the powdered tablet, and stir until a suspension forms.
3. Use litmus paper to find out whether the mixture is acidic, basic, or neutral. Record your results.
4. Now add vinegar to the antacid mixture. Record the number of drops it takes to react with the antacid and turn the blue litmus paper bright red. Compare this solution with the solution that has only vinegar and water. Compare the brand of antacid you tested with the brands of other groups.

Analysis

1. How does an antacid work to relieve the pain caused by excess stomach acid?
2. Of the brands that were tested, which brand worked the best? Explain your reasoning.

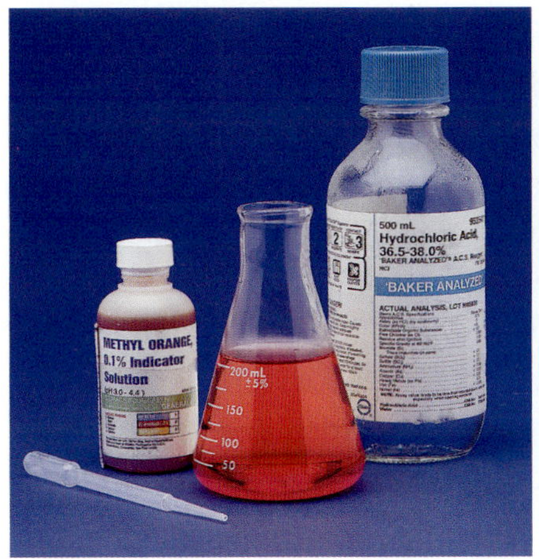

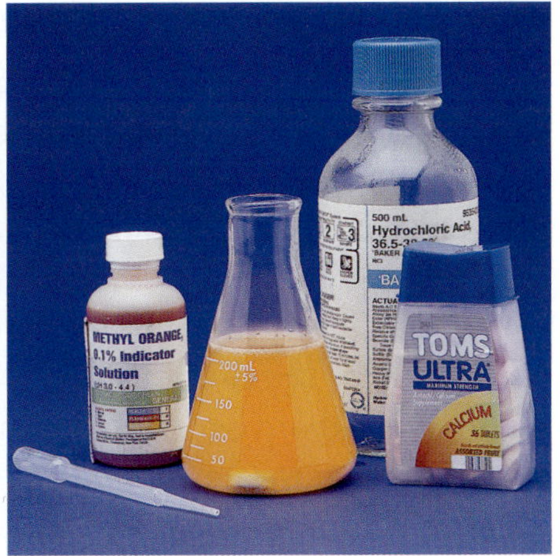

Figure 17

Stomach acid has about the same concentration of HCl as the solution in the flask in the left photo. When an antacid tablet reacts with the acid, the pH increases to a less acidic level, as shown in the photo on the right.

Did You Know ?

The fibrous protein keratin builds up in the outermost cells of your epidermis, the outer layer of your skin. Keratin in these cells makes the skin tough and almost completely waterproof. Keratin forms callouses in places on the skin where it is rubbed.

The horns, hoofs, claws, feathers, and scales of animals grow from the same type of tissue that makes up your epidermis and also consist mainly of keratin.

Shampoos are adjusted for an ideal pH

Shampoos can be made from soap. But if they are, they can leave sticky soap scum on your hair if you happen to live in an area that has hard water. Most shampoos today are made from detergents and are able to remove dirt as well as most of the oil from your hair without leaving soap scum, even when they are used with hard water. Shampoo is not meant to remove all of the oil from your hair. Some oil is needed to give your hair shine and to keep it from becoming dry and brittle.

The appearance of your hair is greatly affected by the pH of the shampoo you use. Hair—which consists of strands of a protein called *keratin*—looks best when it is kept at either a slightly acidic pH or very close to neutral. If a shampoo is too basic, it can cause strands of hair to swell, which gives them a dull, lifeless appearance. Shampoos are usually pH balanced, which means that they are made to be in a specific pH range. The pH of most shampoos is between 5 and 8. Shampoos that have higher pH values are more effective in cleaning oil from your hair. Shampoos that have lower pH values protect dry hair.

Acids keep fruit fresh longer

Some cut fruits slowly turn brown when they are exposed to air, such as the right side of the cut apple shown in ***Figure 18.*** This happens because certain molecules in the apple are oxidized to form darker substances. Both sides of the apple in ***Figure 18*** were cut at the same time, so why does the left side of the apple look like it was just cut? The left side was moistened with lemon juice shortly after it was cut. The citric acid in lemon juice helps *antioxidants* in the apple that react with oxygen before the oxygen can react with other substances in the apple. Vitamin C is another example of a natural antioxidant.

Figure 18

The left side of this cut apple was coated with lemon juice. Citric acid in the lemon juice kept the surface of the apple looking fresh.

Figure 19

Adding vinegar to milk causes the milk to curdle, because casein, the main protein in milk, becomes denatured by the acid.

Acids, bases, and salts in the kitchen

Acids have other uses in the kitchen. Acidic marinades made of vinegar or wine can be used to tenderize meats because they can *denature* proteins in the meat. That is, the acids cause the protein molecules to unravel and lose their characteristic shapes. As a result, the meat becomes more tender.

Figure 19 shows that milk curdles if you add vinegar to it. This reaction may seem undesirable, but a similar reaction occurs in the formation of yogurt. Bacteria convert lactose, a sugar in milk, into lactic acid. The lactic acid denatures the protein casein in milk and changes the milk into a thick gel known as yogurt.

There are many bases and salts in the kitchen. You can unclog a drain by using the strong base sodium hydroxide, also called *lye*. Baking soda, or sodium hydrogen carbonate, is a salt that forms carbon dioxide gas at high temperatures, which makes cookies rise when they are baked. Baking powder consists of baking soda and an acidic substance that react to release CO_2, which makes light, fluffy batter for cakes.

SECTION 3 REVIEW

SUMMARY

- Soaps and detergents can dissolve in oil and water. They are usually sodium or potassium salts of carboxylic or sulfonic acids, which have long hydrocarbon chains.
- Detergents do not form an insoluble scum in hard water as soap does.
- Bleach is an alkaline solution of sodium hypochlorite, NaOCl. Bleach is a disinfectant and oxidizes stains to a colorless form.
- Antacids are basic substances that react with hydrochloric acid in the stomach.
- Acids, bases, and salts have many practical uses in the kitchen, both in cleaning and cooking.

1. **Describe** how soap can dissolve in both oil and water. How does soap work with water to remove oily dirt?
2. **Explain** why soap scum might form in hard water that contains Mg^{2+} ions when soap is used instead of detergent to wash dishes.
3. **Explain** why the agitation of a washing machine helps a detergent clean your clothes. (**Hint:** Compare this motion to rubbing your hands together when you wash them.)
4. **Explain** why it is not necessary for bleach to actually remove the substance that causes a stain.
5. **Explain** how milk of magnesia, an antacid, can reduce acidity in stomach acid.
6. **List** three acidic household substances and three basic household substances. How are the substances most often used?
7. **Critical Thinking** Crayon companies recommend treating wax stains on clothes by spraying the stains with an oily lubricant, applying dishwashing liquid, and then washing the clothes. Explain in a paragraph why this treatment would remove the stain.

Graphing Skills

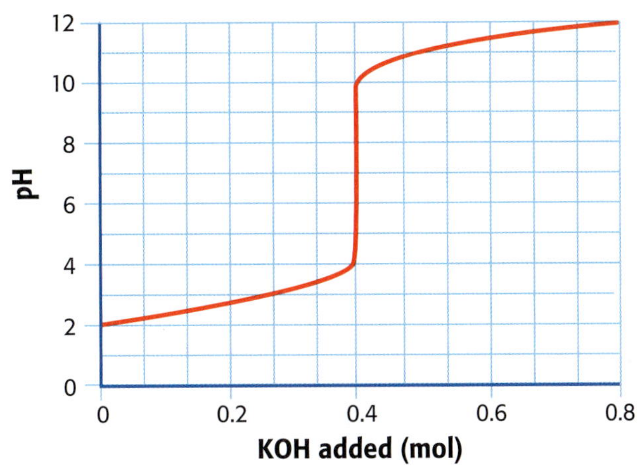

Examine the above graph, and answer the following questions. (See Appendix A for help interpreting a graph.)

1. Does the solution's acidity increase or decrease as potassium hydroxide is added? Explain your answer.

2. Identify the independent and dependent variables. What is the relationship between the two variables?

3. At what point on the graph are there equal moles of acid and base? Explain your answer.

4. Use your answer to the previous question to calculate the number of moles of acid present before the potassium hydroxide is added to the solution.

5. What is the pH of the potassium hydroxide solution added to the acid? How did you reach this conclusion?

6. A person who has a stomach disorder is advised to avoid acidic foods. Construct the type of graph best suited for the data given in the table below. Which substance is most acidic? Which substance has a pH closest to the pH of pure water?

Substance	Average pH
Bananas	4.6
Dill pickles	3.4
Eggs	7.8
Salmon	6.2
Soda crackers	7.5

CHAPTER 8 REVIEW

Chapter Highlights

Before you begin, review the summaries of key ideas of each section, found at the end of each section. The vocabulary terms are listed on the first page of each section.

UNDERSTANDING CONCEPTS

1. Which ions does an acid form in solution?
a. oxygen **c.** hydroxide
b. hydronium **d.** sulfur

2. Which ions does a base form in solution?
a. oxygen **c.** hydroxide
b. hydronium **d.** sulfur

3. When a solution of nitric acid is added to a solution of calcium hydroxide, the salt formed has the formula
a. $Ca(NO_3)_2$. **c.** H_2O.
b. $Ca(OH)_2$. **d.** CaH.

4. An antacid relieves an overly acidic stomach because antacids are
a. acidic. **c.** basic.
b. neutral. **d.** dilute.

5. Detergents have replaced soap in many uses because detergents
a. are made from animal fat.
b. do not form insoluble substances.
c. are milder than soap.
d. contain ammonia.

6. Which of the following ionic equations best represents a neutralization reaction?
a. $Na + H_2O \rightarrow Na^+ + OH^- + H_2$
b. $HNO_3 + H_2O \rightarrow H_3O^+ + NO_3^-$
c. $2OH^- + NH_4Cl \rightarrow Cl^- + H_2O + NH_3$
d. $OH^- + H_3O^+ \rightarrow 2H_2O$

7. An increase in the hydronium ion concentration of a solution ________ the pH.
a. raises **c.** does not affect
b. lowers **d.** doubles

8. Bleach removes stains by
a. changing the color of the stain.
b. covering the stain.
c. removing the stain-causing substances.
d. disinfecting the stain.

9. Which of the following is *not* an acidic material found in the kitchen?
a. baking soda **c.** vinegar
b. lemon juice **d.** vitamin C

USING VOCABULARY

10. Explain how the *ionization* of a strong acid differs from the ionization of a weak acid in a solution. Give an example of a strong acid and a weak acid. Show which ions form when each is dissolved in water.

11. Explain how you can use the *indicator* litmus, in the form of litmus paper, to determine whether a solution is *acidic, basic,* or *neutral.*

12. Explain how the molecular structure of *soaps* and *detergents* can cause water to wash away oil and grease.

13. What is the active substance in *bleach*? How is bleach made?

14. Why are most shampoos made from *detergents* rather than *soaps*?

15. Microbiologists often wipe down work areas with a *bleach* solution before working with bacterial cultures. What is the purpose of using bleach in this way?

16. Explain why a solution of a *strong acid* is a good conductor of electricity.

17. What is a *neutralization reaction*? How might the product of a neutralization reaction have a pH of less than 7?

18. How would you find the concentration of a strong acid in a *titration*? Use the terms *indicator* and *equivalence point* in your answer.

BUILDING MATH SKILLS

19. Determining pH What is the pH of a 0.001 M solution of hydrobromic acid, HBr, a strong acid?

20. Determining pH What is the pH of a solution that contains 0.10 mol of HCl in a volume of 100.0 L?

21. Using pH What is the molar concentration of hydronium ions in a solution with a pH of 6?

22. Determining pH The concentration of hydronium ions in a certain acid solution is 100 times the concentration of hydronium ions in a second acid solution. If the second solution has a pH of 5, what is the pH of the first solution?

BUILDING GRAPHING SKILLS

23. Interpreting Graphs The point at which equal amounts of an acid and a base have reacted in a neutralization reaction is called the equivalence point. Study the graph of pH versus volume of base added below, and note the pH at the equivalence point. Classify both the acid and the base in this neutralization reaction as either weak or strong. Explain your answer.

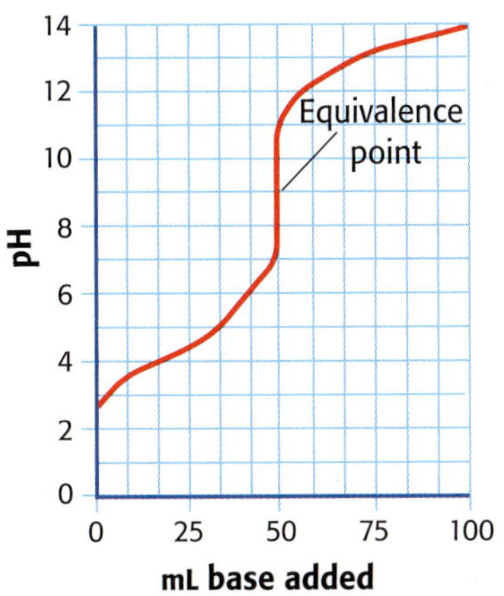

THINKING CRITICALLY

24. Applying Knowledge Baking soda, sodium hydrogen carbonate ($NaHCO_3$), is useful in the kitchen for baking and to absorb odors in the refrigerator. Baking soda can also be tossed onto a grease fire to extinguish it. How can baking soda extinguish fires?

25. Creative Thinking If you wish to change the pH of a solution very slightly, should you add a strong acid or a weak acid? Explain your answer.

26. Problem Solving Insect bites hurt because the insect injects a toxin into the victim. When certain kinds of ants bite, they inject a small amount of highly irritating formic acid. Suggest a treatment that might stop an ant bite from itching or hurting.

27. Designing Systems Suppose you measure the pH of a clear solution in a beaker and find that it has a pH of 3. You are asked to determine whether the solution is a very dilute solution of a strong acid or a stronger solution of a weak acid. Propose a method to answer the question.

28. Creative Thinking You need several grams of the substance ammonium bromide, NH_4Br, for an experiment, but you do not have any. You do, however, have a solution of hydrobromic acid, HBr, and a solution of ammonia. Suggest a way to use an acid-base reaction to make a small quantity of NH_4Br.

29. Applying Knowledge Pure water is a poor conductor of electricity. But it is still dangerous to have any sort of plugged-in appliances near the bathtub or shower. Why does this danger exist? Explain your reasoning by discussing the composition of tap water.

BUILDING LIFE/WORK SKILLS

30. Locating Information Research the invention of the pH meter by Dr. Arnold O. Beckman. Why was the pH meter invented? How does it work? Prepare a poster to present your results.

31. Applying Knowledge Design an experiment to measure the pH of four types of shampoo: baby shampoo, shampoo for extra body, shampoo for oily hair, and shampoo that contains conditioner. Also compare two brands of pH-balanced shampoo. Write a paragraph summarizing your results.

INTEGRATING CONCEPTS

32. Connection to Biology The pH of human blood is about pH 7.4 and must be kept within a few tenths of a pH unit of the normal pH. Reactions within the human body ensure that a proper pH is maintained. The equilibrium shown below between carbonic acid, H_2CO_3, and the hydrogen carbonate ion, HCO_3^-, is important to maintain the blood's pH.

$$H_2CO_3 + H_2O \rightleftharpoons HCO_3^- + H_3O^+$$

Find out what happens to keep the pH from decreasing as extra hydronium ions enter the blood. Also find out how the pH is kept from increasing as extra OH^- ions enter the blood.

33. Connection to History In the 18th century, the French chemist Antoine Lavoisier experimented with substances containing oxygen, such as CO_2 and SO_2, that formed acidic solutions when dissolved in water. His observations led him to infer that for a solution to be acidic, it must contain oxygen. Provide evidence to disprove Lavoisier's conclusion.

34. Locating Information A reaction between baking soda and a baking batter that is made of acidic ingredients produces CO_2 gas. The reaction makes the batter fluffier. Some recipes call for baking powder instead of baking soda. Find out what regular baking powder and double-acting baking powder are made of. How do they each differ from baking soda?

35. Concept Mapping Copy the unfinished concept maps below onto a sheet of paper. Complete the maps by writing the correct word or phrase in the lettered boxes.

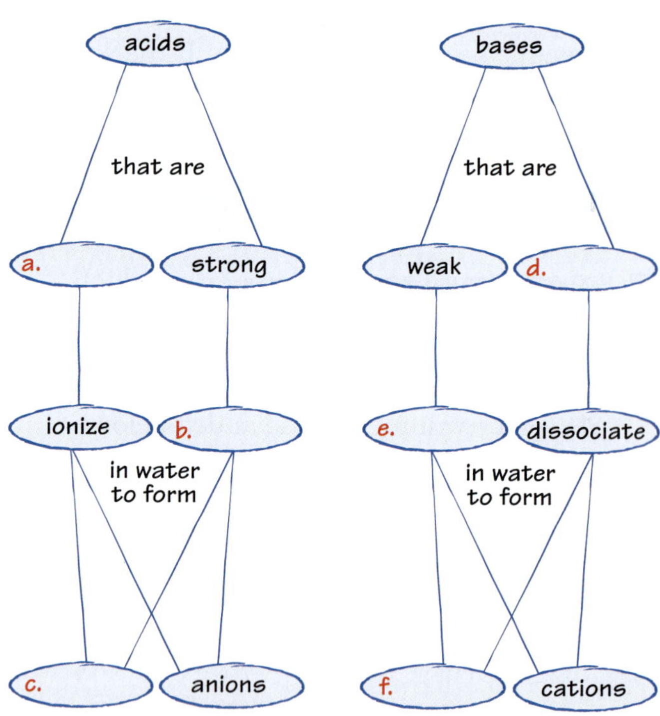

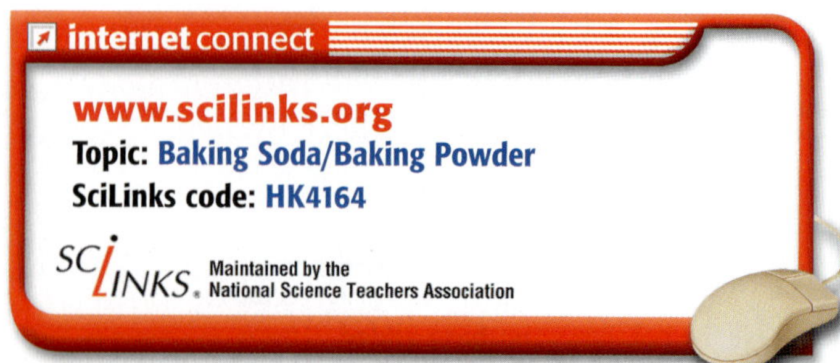

Standardized Test Prep

Understanding Concepts

Directions (1–3): **For *each* question, write on a separate sheet of paper the letter of the correct answer.**

1 What is the pH of a solution with a hydroxide ion concentration of 1×10^{-13} M?

A. –13
B. 1
C. 7
D. 13

2 Which of the following is true of weak acids?

F. They are less soluble in water than strong acids.
G. They do not ionize as completely in water as strong acids.
H. They have a pH value that is lower than that of strong acids.
I. They do not react with bases to form a salt as do strong acids.

3 Which of the following pH ranges would include the equivalence point of the titration of a strong acid with a weak base?

A. pH 2 to pH 6
B. pH 6 to pH 8
C. exactly pH 7
D. exactly pH 8

Directions (4–5): **For *each* question, write a short response.**

4 What property of detergents makes them more useful than soap for washing clothes and dishes in many parts of the country?

5 How can you determine by tasting which foods have a high concentration of one or more acidic compounds?

Test TIP

Sometimes only a portion of a graph or table is needed to answer a question. Focus only on the necessary information to avoid confusion.

Reading Skills

Directions (6): **Read the passage below. Then answer the question.**

Nitrogen and sulfur compounds formed by the combustion of fossil fuels react with oxygen and water in the air to form acids. These acids dissolve in water, forming acid precipitation, which can react with objects on which it falls. Limestone statues and decorations on buildings in areas with acidic rainfall have been severely damaged by the acid. On the other hand, granite statues and carvings tend to suffer much less damage under the same conditions.

6 Assess why one type of stone, limestone, is affected by acid precipitation much more than another type of stone, granite.

Interpreting Graphics

Directions (7): **Base your answer to question 7 on the graph below, which shows how pH changes during a titration.**

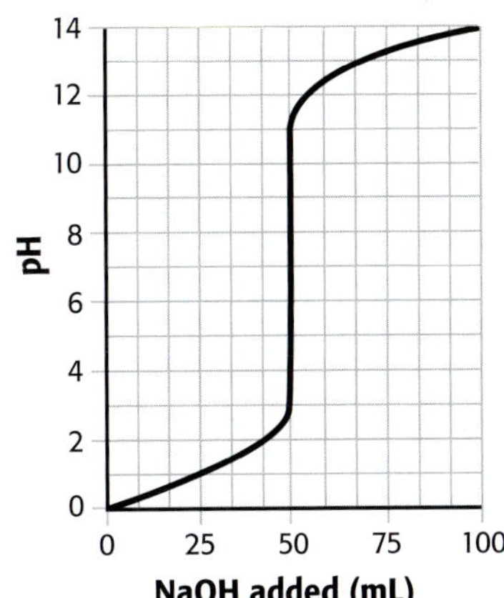

7 What is occurring between the addition of 10 mL and 20 mL of NaOH?

F. Hydrogen ion concentration is increasing.
G. Hydroxide ion concentration is increasing.
H. Hydronium ion concentration is increasing.
I. Hydrogen ion and hydroxide ion concentrations are increasing.

Skills Practice Lab

Measuring Quantities in an Acid-Base Reaction

Introduction

Acids and bases neutralize each other to form a salt and water. Phenolphthalein is a good indicator to use in the neutralization of a strong acid by a strong base. It is a good indicator because phenolphthalein changes color at a pH very near the neutral point of a reaction of a strong base and a strong acid.

Objectives

- ***Determine*** the volume of a base solution needed to neutralize a given volume of acid solution.
- USING SCIENTIFIC METHODS ***Analyze the results*** to compare the volume of base solution needed to neutralize a given volume of HCl solution with the volume needed to neutralize the same volume of H_2SO_4 solution.

Materials

0.1 M H_2SO_4 solution
0.1 M HCl solution
0.1 M NaOH solution
marker
phenolphthalein indicator solution
plastic pipets, disposable
test-tube rack
test tubes

Preparing for Your Experiment

1. On a sheet of paper, prepare a data table similar to the one shown at right.

Procedure

Neutralizing HCl with NaOH

SAFETY CAUTION Wear an apron or lab coat to protect your clothing when working with chemicals. If a spill gets on your clothing, rinse it off immediately with water for at least 5 minutes, while. Wear safety goggles and gloves when handling chemicals. If any substance gets in your eyes, immediately flush your eyes with running water for at least 15 minutes and notify your instructor. Always use caution when working with chemicals. Add an acid or a base to water; never do the opposite.

2. Use the marker to write "HCl" on the bulb of one pipet. This pipet should be used only for hydrochloric acid solution. Mark a second pipet NaOH. This pipet should be used only for sodium hydroxide solution.
3. Add 40 drops of 0.1 M HCl solution to a clean test tube at a steady rate. Do not let the tip of the pipet touch the sides of the test tube. Hold the long tube of the pipet with the other hand, if necessary.
4. Add two drops of phenolphthalein indicator to the test tube. Gently shake the test tube from side to side to mix the liquid in the tube. Be careful not to spill or splash the liquid.
5. Note the concentrations of the HCl and NaOH solutions. Predict how many drops of NaOH solution will be required to neutralize the 40 drops of HCl. Record your prediction in the data table.
6. Add 25 drops of 0.1 M NaOH solution to the test tube. You will probably see a pink color develop temporarily. This is the color of phenolphthalein in a basic solution. Remember this color. Gently swirl the test tube to mix the liquid. The pink color should disappear.

Neutralization Reaction Data			
	Number of drops	Drops NaOH needed (predicted)	Drops NaOH needed (measured)
HCl			
H_2SO_4			

7. Add more NaOH solution to the test tube two drops at a time, and mix the liquids after each addition. As the pink color starts to disappear more slowly when you mix the liquids, start adding the NaOH solution one drop at a time, and mix the solution with each addition. When the mixture remains slightly pink after the addition of a drop and does not change within 10 seconds, you have reached the end of the neutralization reaction. Record in the data table the total number of drops of NaOH solution you added.

Neutralizing H_2SO_4 with NaOH

8. Use the marker to label a third pipet "H_2SO_4." Use this pipet only for sulfuric acid solution.
9. Repeat steps 3–6, but start with 40 drops of 0.1 M H_2SO_4 solution instead of 40 drops of HCl solution. Make and record your prediction as in step 4.

Analysis

1. In the neutralization of HCl with NaOH, how close was your predicted number of drops to the actual number of drops of NaOH solution needed? If there is a large difference, explain the reasoning that led to your prediction.
2. Write a complete nonionic chemical equation for the reaction of HCl and NaOH. Then, write the ionic equation for the reaction without spectator ions.
3. In the neutralization of H_2SO_4 with NaOH, how close was your predicted number of drops to the actual number of drops of NaOH solution needed? If there is a large difference, explain the reasoning that led to your prediction.
4. Write a complete nonionic chemical equation for the reaction of H_2SO_4 and NaOH. Then, write the ionic equation for the reaction without spectator ions.

Conclusions

5. Suppose someone tries to explain your results by saying that H_2SO_4 is twice as strong an acid as HCl. How could you explain that this person's reasoning is incorrect?

CHAPTER 9

Nuclear Changes

Chapter Preview

1 **What Is Radioactivity?**
Nuclear Radiation
Nuclear Decay
Radioactive Decay Rates

2 **Nuclear Fission and Fusion**
Nuclear Forces
Nuclear Fission
Nuclear Fusion

3 **Nuclear Radiation Today**
Where Is Radiation?
Beneficial Uses of Nuclear Radiation
Possible Risks of Nuclear Radiation
Nuclear Power

Focus ACTIVITY

Background The painting "Woman Reading Music" was considered one of a series of great finds discovered by Dutch painter and art dealer Han van Meegeren in the 1930s. The previously unknown paintings were believed to be by the great seventeenth century Dutch artist Jan Vermeer. But after World War II, another painting said to be by Vermeer was found in a Nazi art collection, and its sale was traced to van Meegeren. Arrested for collaborating with the Nazis, van Meegeren confessed that both paintings were forgeries. He claimed that he had used one of the fake Vermeers to lure Nazi Germany into returning many genuine paintings to the Dutch.

Was van Meegeren lying, or had he really swindled the Nazis? Although X-ray photographs of the painting suggested that it was a forgery, conclusive evidence did not come about until 20 years later. A fraction of the lead in some pigments used in the painting proved to be radioactive. By measuring the number of radioactive lead nuclei that decayed each minute, experts were able to determine the age of the painting. The fairly rapid decay rate indicated that the paint was less than 40 years old.

Activity 1 Radiation exposes photographic film. To test this, obtain a sheet of unexposed photographic film and a new household smoke detector, which contains a radioactive sample. Remove the detector's casing. In a dark room, place the film next to the smoke detector in a cardboard box. Close the box. After a day, open the box in a dark room. Place the film in a thick envelope. Have the film processed. How does the image differ from the rest of the film? How can you tell that the image is related to the radioactive source?

Radioactive substances in the paints and canvases used in painting decay over time. These radioactive substances emit nuclear radiation. The nuclear radiation emitted can be used to determine how old the painting is and whether the painting is a forgery or not.

Pre-Reading Questions

1. What are some applications of nuclear radiation?
2. How does nuclear power compare to other sources of power?

SECTION 1

What Is Radioactivity?

KEY TERMS

radioactivity
nuclear radiation
alpha particle
beta particle
gamma ray
half-life

OBJECTIVES

- **Identify** four types of nuclear radiation and their properties.
- **Balance** equations for nuclear decay.
- **Calculate** the half-life of a radioactive isotope.

Our lives are affected by radioactivity in many ways. Technology using radioactivity has helped to detect disease and dysfunction, kill cancer cells, generate electricity, and design smoke detectors. On the other hand, there are also risks associated with too much nuclear radiation, so it is important to know where it may exist and how to counteract it. What exactly is radioactivity?

Nuclear Radiation

radioactivity the process by which an unstable nucleus emits one or more particles or energy in the form of electromagnetic radiation

nuclear radiation the particles that are released from the nucleus during radioactive decay

Many elements change through **radioactivity.** Radioactive materials have unstable nuclei, which go through changes by emitting particles or releasing energy to become stable, as shown in ***Figure 1.*** This nuclear process is called *nuclear decay.* After the changes in the nucleus, the element can transform into a different isotope of the same element or into an entirely different element. Recall that isotopes of an element are atoms that have the same number of protons but different numbers of neutrons in their nuclei. Different elements are distinguished by having different numbers of protons in their nuclei.

The released energy and matter are called **nuclear radiation.** Just as radioactivity changes the materials that undergo nuclear decay, nuclear radiation has effects on other materials. These effects depend on the type of radiation and on the properties of the materials that nuclear radiation encounters. (Note that the term *radiation* can refer to light or to energy transfer. *To avoid confusion, the term* nuclear radiation *will be used to describe radiation associated with nuclear changes.*)

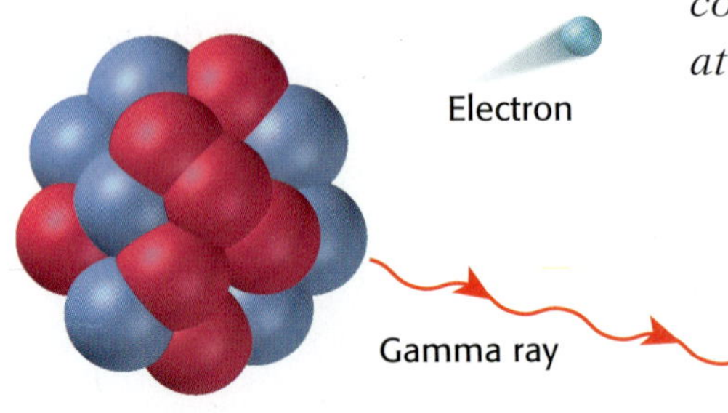

Figure 1

During radioactivity an unstable nucleus emits one or more particles or high-energy electromagnetic radiation.

Table 1 Types of Nuclear Radiation

Radiation type	Symbol	Mass (kg)	Charge
Alpha particle	${}^{4}_{2}He$	6.646×10^{-27}	+2
Beta particle	${}^{0}_{-1}e$	9.109×10^{-31}	–1
Gamma ray	γ	none	0
Neutron	${}^{1}_{0}n$	1.675×10^{-27}	0

There are different types of nuclear radiation

Essentially, there are four types of nuclear radiation: alpha particles, beta particles, gamma rays, and neutron emission. Some of their properties are listed in **Table 1.** When a radioactive nucleus decays, the nuclear radiation leaves the nucleus. This nuclear radiation interacts with nearby matter. This interaction depends in part on the properties of nuclear radiation, such as charge, mass, and energy, which are discussed below.

Alpha particles consist of protons and neutrons

Uranium is a radioactive element that naturally occurs in three isotope forms. One of its isotopes, uranium-238, undergoes nuclear decay by emitting positively charged particles. Ernest Rutherford, noted for discovering the nucleus, named them *alpha* (α) *rays*. Later, he discovered that alpha rays were actually particles, each made of two protons and two neutrons—the same as helium nuclei. **Alpha particles** are positively charged and more massive than any other type of nuclear radiation.

Alpha particles do not travel far through materials. In fact, they barely pass through a sheet of paper. One factor that limits an alpha particle's ability to pass through matter is the fact that it is massive. Because alpha particles are charged, they remove electrons from—or ionize—matter as they pass through it. This ionization causes the alpha particle to lose energy and slow down further.

alpha particle a positively charged atom that is released in the disintegration of radioactive elements and that consists of two protons and two neutrons

beta particle a charged electron emitted during certain types of radioactive decay, such as beta decay

Beta particles are electrons produced from neutron decay

Some nuclei emit another type of nuclear radiation that travels farther through matter than alpha particles do. This nuclear radiation is named the **beta particle,** after the second Greek letter, *beta* (β). Beta particles are often fast-moving electrons.

Negative particles coming from a positively charged nucleus puzzled scientists for years. However, in the 1930s, another discovery helped to clear up the mystery: neutrons, which are not charged, decay to form a proton and an electron. The electron, having very little mass, is then ejected at a high speed from the nucleus as a beta particle.

Beta particles easily go through a piece of paper, but most are stopped by 3 mm of aluminum or 10 mm of wood. This greater penetration occurs because beta particles aren't as massive as alpha particles and therefore move faster. But like alpha particles, beta particles can easily ionize other atoms. As they ionize atoms, beta particles lose energy. This property prevents them from penetrating matter very deeply.

Figure 2

In 1898, Marie Curie discovered the element radium, which was later found to emit gamma rays.

Gamma rays are very high energy

In 1898, Marie Curie, shown in ***Figure 2,*** and her husband, Pierre, isolated the radioactive element radium. In 1900, studies of radium by Paul Villard revealed that the element emitted a previously undetected form of nuclear radiation. This radiation was much more penetrating than even beta particles. Following the pattern established by Rutherford, this new kind of nuclear radiation was named the **gamma ray,** after the third Greek alphabet letter, *gamma* (γ).

gamma ray the high-energy photon emitted by a nucleus during fission and radioactive decay

Unlike alpha or beta particles, gamma rays are not made of matter and do not have an electrical charge. Instead, gamma rays consist of a form of electromagnetic energy called photons, like visible light or X rays. Gamma rays, however, have more energy than light or X rays.

Although gamma rays have no electrical charge, they can easily ionize matter. High-energy gamma rays can cause damage in matter. They can penetrate up to 60 cm of aluminum or 7 cm of lead. They are not easily stopped by clothing or most building materials and therefore pose a greater danger to health than either alpha or beta particles.

Neutron radioactivity may occur in an unstable nucleus

Like alpha and beta radiation, *neutron emission* consists of matter that is emitted from an unstable nucleus. In fact, scientists first discovered the neutron by detecting its emission from a nucleus.

Because neutrons have no charge, they do not ionize matter as alpha and beta particles do. Because neutrons do not use their energy ionizing matter, they are able to travel farther through matter than either alpha or beta particles. A block of lead about 15 cm thick is required to stop most fast neutrons emitted during radioactive decay.

Nuclear Decay

Anytime an unstable nucleus emits alpha or beta particles, the number of protons or neutrons changes. An example would be radium-226 (an isotope of radium with the mass number 226), which changes to radon-222 by emitting an alpha particle.

A nucleus gives up two protons and two neutrons during alpha decay

Nuclear decay equations are similar to those for chemical reactions. The nucleus before decay is like a reactant and is placed on the left side of the equation. Products are placed on the right side. The process of the alpha decay of radium-226 is written as follows.

$$^{226}_{88}\text{Ra} \longrightarrow {}^{222}_{86}\text{Rn} + {}^{4}_{2}\text{He} \qquad \begin{matrix} 226 = 222 + 4 \\ 88 = 86 + 2 \end{matrix}$$

The mass number of the atom before decay is 226 and equals the sum of the mass numbers of the products, 222 and 4. The atomic numbers follow the same principle. The 88 protons in radium before the nuclear decay equals the 86 protons in the radon-222 nucleus and 2 protons in the alpha particle.

A nucleus gains a proton and loses a neutron during beta decay

With beta decay, the form of the equation is the same except the symbol for a beta particle is used. This symbol, with the appropriate mass and atomic numbers, is $^{0}_{-1}e$.

Of course, an electron is not an atom and should not have an atomic number, which is the number of positive charges in a nucleus. But for the sake of convenience, since an electron has a single negative charge, an electron is given an atomic number of –1 when you write a nuclear decay equation. Similarly, the beta particle's mass is so much less than that of a proton or neutron that it can be regarded as having a mass number of 0.

A beta decay process occurs when carbon-14 decays to nitrogen-14 by emitting a beta particle.

$$^{14}_{6}\text{C} \longrightarrow {}^{14}_{7}\text{N} + {}^{0}_{-1}e \qquad \begin{matrix} 14 = 14 + 0 \\ 6 = 7 + (-1) \end{matrix}$$

In all cases of beta decay, the mass number before and after the decay does not change. Note that the atomic number of the product nucleus increases by 1. This occurs because a neutron decays into a proton, causing the positive charge of the nucleus to increase by 1.

Did You Know?

Ernest Rutherford showed that alpha particles are helium nuclei by trapping alpha particles from radon-222 decay in a glass tube. He then applied a high electric voltage across the gas, causing it to glow. The glow was identical to the glow produced by helium atoms, indicating that the two substances were the same.

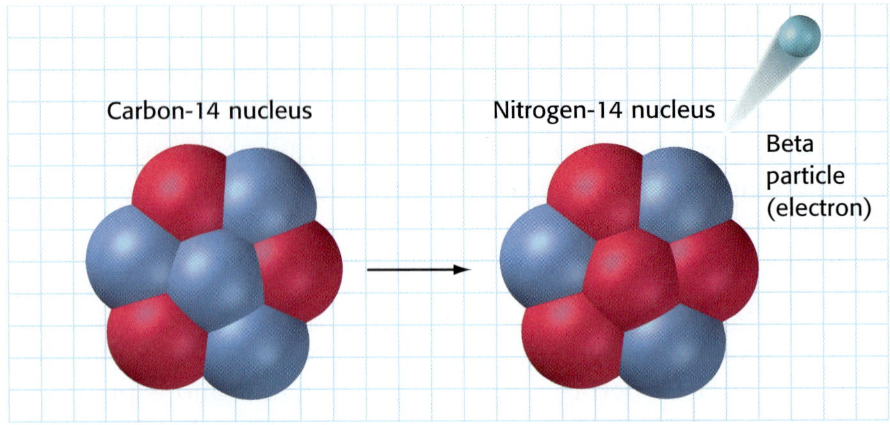

Figure 3

A nucleus that undergoes beta decay has nearly the same atomic mass afterward, except that it has one more proton and one less neutron.

Figure 3 shows how the positive charge of the nucleus increases by 1 when a neutron decays into a proton. When the nucleus undergoes nuclear decay by gamma rays, there is no change in the atomic number of the element. This is because the number of protons does not change. The atomic number is the number of protons in the nucleus of the atom. The only change is in the energy content of the nucleus.

Math Skills

Nuclear Decay Actinium-217 decays by releasing an alpha particle. Write the equation for this decay process, and determine what element is formed.

1 Write down the equation with the original element on the left side and the products on the right side.

Use the letter *X* to denote the unknown product. Note that the mass and atomic numbers of the unknown isotope are represented by the letters *A* and *Z*.

$$^{217}_{89}\mathrm{Ac} \longrightarrow {}^{A}_{Z}\mathrm{X} + {}^{4}_{2}\mathrm{He}$$

2 Write math equations for the atomic and mass numbers.

$217 = A + 4 \qquad 89 = Z + 2$

3 Rearrange the equations.

$A = 217 - 4 \qquad Z = 89 - 2$

4 Solve for the unknown values, and rewrite the equation with all nuclei represented.

$A = 213 \qquad Z = 87$

The unknown decay product has an atomic number of 87, which is francium, according to the periodic table. The element is therefore $^{213}_{87}\mathrm{Fr}$.

$$^{217}_{89}\mathrm{Ac} \longrightarrow {}^{213}_{87}\mathrm{Fr} + {}^{4}_{2}\mathrm{He}$$

Practice

Nuclear Decay

Complete the following radioactive-decay equations by identifying the isotope *X*. Indicate whether alpha or beta decay takes place.

1. ${}^{12}_{5}\mathrm{B} \longrightarrow {}^{12}_{6}\mathrm{C} + {}^{A}_{Z}\mathrm{X}$

2. ${}^{225}_{89}\mathrm{Ac} \longrightarrow {}^{221}_{87}\mathrm{Fr} + {}^{A}_{Z}\mathrm{X}$

3. ${}^{63}_{28}\mathrm{Ni} \longrightarrow {}^{A}_{Z}\mathrm{X} + {}^{0}_{-1}e$

4. ${}^{212}_{83}\mathrm{Bi} \longrightarrow {}^{A}_{Z}\mathrm{X} + {}^{4}_{2}\mathrm{He}$

Radioactive Decay Rates

If you were asked to pick up a rock and determine its age, you would probably not be able to do so. After all, old rocks do not look much different from new rocks. How, then, would you go about finding the rock's age? Likewise, how would a scientist find out the age of cloth found at the site of an ancient village?

One way to do it involves radioactive decay. Although it is impossible to predict the moment when any particular nucleus will decay, it is possible to predict the time it takes for half the nuclei in a given radioactive sample to decay. The time in which half a radioactive substance decays is called the substance's **half-life.**

half-life the time required for half of a sample of a radioactive substance to disintegrate by radioactive decay or by natural processes

After the first half-life of a radioactive sample has passed, half the sample remains unchanged, as indicated in ***Figure 4*** for carbon-14. After the next half-life, half the remaining half decays, leaving only a quarter of the sample undecayed. Of that quarter, half will decay in the next half-life. Only one-eighth will remain undecayed then.

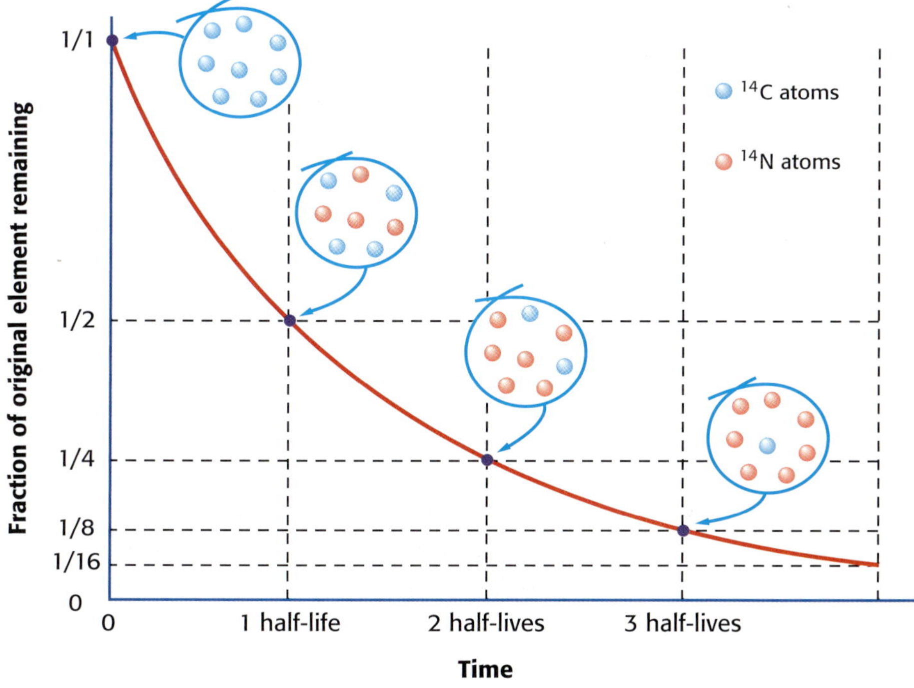

Figure 4

With each successive half-life, half the remaining sample decays to form another element.

Table 2 Half-lives of Selected Isotopes

Isotope	Half-life	Nuclear radiation emitted
Thorium-219	1.05×10^{-6} s	${}^{4}_{2}He$
Hafnium-156	2.5×10^{-2} s	${}^{4}_{2}He$
Radon-222	3.82 days	${}^{4}_{2}He$, γ
Iodine-131	8.1 days	${}^{0}_{-1}e$, γ
Radium-226	1599 years	${}^{4}_{2}He$, γ
Carbon-14	5715 years	${}^{0}_{-1}e$
Plutonium-239	2.412×10^{4} years	${}^{4}_{2}He$, γ
Uranium-235	7.04×10^{8} years	${}^{4}_{2}He$, γ
Potassium-40	1.28×10^{9} years	${}^{0}_{-1}e$, γ
Uranium-238	4.47×10^{9} years	${}^{4}_{2}He$, γ

Half-life is a measure of how quickly a substance decays

Different radioactive isotopes have different half-lives, as indicated in **Table 2.** Half-lives can last from nanoseconds to billions of years, depending on the stability of the nucleus.

Using half-lives, scientists can predict how old an object is. Using the half-lives of long-lasting isotopes, such as potassium-40, geologists calculate the age of rocks. Potassium-40 decays to argon-40, so the ratio of potassium-40 to argon-40 is smaller for older rocks than it is for younger rocks.

Modeling Decay and Half-life

For this exercise, you will need a jar with a lid, 128 pennies, pencil and paper, and a flat work surface.

1. Place the pennies in the jar, and place the lid on the jar. Shake the jar, and then pour the pennies onto the work surface.
2. Separate pennies that are heads up from those that are tails up. Count and record the number of heads-up pennies, and set these pennies aside. Place the tails-up pennies back in the jar.
3. Repeat the process until all pennies have been set aside.
4. For each trial, divide the number of heads-up pennies set aside by the total number of pennies used in the trial. Are these ratios nearly equal to each other? What fraction are they closest to?

Carbon-14 is used to date materials

Archaeologists use the half-life of radioactive carbon-14 to date more recent materials, such as the remains of an animal or fibers from ancient clothing. All of these materials came from organisms that were once alive. When plants absorb carbon dioxide during photosynthesis, a tiny fraction of the CO_2 molecules contains carbon-14 rather than the more common carbon-12. While the plant is alive, the ratio of the carbon isotopes remains constant. This is also true for animals that eat plants.

When a plant or animal dies, it no longer takes in carbon-14. The amount of carbon-14 decreases through beta decay, while the amount of carbon-12 remains constant. Thus, the ratio of carbon-14 to carbon-12 decreases with time. By measuring this ratio and comparing it with the ratio in a living plant or animal, scientists can estimate the age of the once-living organism.

Math Skills

Half-life Radium-226 has a half-life of 1599 years. How long would it take seven-eighths of a radium-226 sample to decay?

1 List the given and unknown values.

Given: half-life = 1599 years

fraction of sample decayed = $\frac{7}{8}$

Unknown: fraction of sample remaining = ?

total time of decay = ?

2 Calculate the fraction of radioactive sample remaining.

To find the fraction of sample remaining, subtract the fraction that has decayed from 1.

fraction of sample remaining = 1 – fraction decayed

fraction of sample remaining = $1 - \frac{7}{8} = \frac{1}{8}$

3 Calculate the number of half-lives.

Amount of sample remaining after one half-life = $\frac{1}{2}$

Amount of sample remaining after two half-lives

$= \frac{1}{2} \times \frac{1}{2} = \frac{1}{4}$

Amount of sample remaining after three half-lives

$= \frac{1}{2} \times \frac{1}{2} \times \frac{1}{2} = \frac{1}{8}$

Three half-lives are needed for one-eighth of the sample to remain undecayed.

4 Calculate the total time required for the radioactive decay.

Each half-life lasts 1599 years.

total time of decay = 3 half-lives $\times \frac{1599 \text{ y}}{\text{half-life}}$ = 4797 years

INTEGRATING

EARTH SCIENCE

Earth's interior is extremely hot. One reason is because uranium and the radioactive elements produced by its decay are present in amounts of about 3 parts per million beneath the surface of Earth, and their nuclear decay produces energy that escapes into their surroundings.

The long half-lives of uranium-238 and -235 allow their radioactive decay to heat Earth for billions of years. The very large distance this heat energy must travel to reach Earth's surface keeps the interior of Earth much hotter than its surface.

Practice

Half-life

1. The half-life of iodine-131 is 8.1 days. How long will it take for three-fourths of a sample of iodine-131 to decay?
2. Radon-222 is a radioactive gas with a half-life of 3.82 days. How long would it take for fifteen-sixteenths of a sample of radon-222 to decay?
3. Uranium-238 decays very slowly, with a half-life of 4.47 billion years. What percentage of a sample of uranium-238 would remain after 13.4 billion years?
4. A sample of strontium-90 is found to have decayed to one-eighth of its original amount after 87.3 years. What is the half-life of strontium-90?
5. A sample of francium-212 will decay to one-sixteenth its original amount after 80 minutes. What is the half-life of francium-212?

SECTION 1 REVIEW

SUMMARY

- Nuclear radiation includes alpha particles, beta particles, gamma rays, and neutron emissions.
- Alpha particles are helium-4 nuclei.
- Beta particles are electrons emitted by neutrons decaying in the nucleus.
- Gamma radiation is an electromagnetic wave like visible light but with much greater energy.
- In nuclear decay, the sums of the mass numbers and the atomic numbers of the decay products equal the mass number and atomic number of the decaying nucleus.
- The time required for half a sample of radioactive material to decay is called its half-life.

1. **Identify** which of the four common types of nuclear radiation correspond to the following descriptions.
   a. an electron
   b. uncharged particle
   c. can be stopped by a piece of paper
   d. high-energy light
2. **Describe** what happens when beta decay occurs.
3. **Explain** why charged particles do not penetrate matter deeply.

Math Skills

4. **Determine** the product denoted by *X* in the following alpha decay.
$$^{212}_{86}\text{Rn} \longrightarrow {}^{A}_{Z}\text{X} + {}^{4}_{2}\text{He}$$
5. **Determine** the isotope produced in the beta decay of iodine-131, an isotope used to check thyroid-gland function.
$$^{131}_{53}\text{I} \longrightarrow {}^{A}_{Z}\text{X} + {}^{0}_{-1}e$$
6. **Calculate** the time required for three-fourths of a sample of cesium-138 to decay given that its half-life is 32.2 minutes.
7. **Calculate** the half-life of cesium-135 if seven-eighths of a sample decays in 6×10^6 years.
8. **Critical Thinking** An archaeologist discovers charred wood whose carbon-14 to carbon-12 ratio is one-sixteenth the ratio measured in a newly fallen tree. How old does the wood seem to be, given this evidence?

SECTION 2

Nuclear Fission and Fusion

OBJECTIVES

- **Describe** how the strong nuclear force affects the composition of a nucleus.
- **Distinguish** between fission and fusion, and provide examples of each.
- **Recognize** the equivalence of mass and energy, and why small losses in mass release large amounts of energy.
- **Explain** what a chain reaction is, how one is initiated, and how it can be controlled.

KEY TERMS

fission
nuclear chain reaction
critical mass
fusion

In 1939, German scientists Otto Hahn and Fritz Strassman conducted experiments in the hope of forming heavy nuclei. Using the apparatus shown in ***Figure 5,*** they bombarded uranium samples with neutrons, expecting a few nuclei to capture one or more neutrons. The new elements they made had chemical properties they could not explain.

It wasn't until their colleague Lise Meitner and her nephew Otto Frisch read the results of Hahn and Strassman's work that an explanation was offered. Meitner and Frisch believed that instead of making heavier elements, the uranium nuclei had split into smaller elements.

Nuclear Forces

Protons and neutrons are tightly packed in the tiny nucleus of an atom. As we saw in the previous section, certain nuclei are unstable and undergo decay by emitting nuclear radiation. Also, an element can have both stable and unstable isotopes. For instance, carbon-12 is a stable isotope, while carbon-14 is unstable and radioactive. The stability of a nucleus depends on the nuclear forces that hold the nucleus together. These forces act between the protons and the neutrons.

Figure 5

Using this equipment, Otto Hahn and Fritz Strassman first discovered nuclear fission.

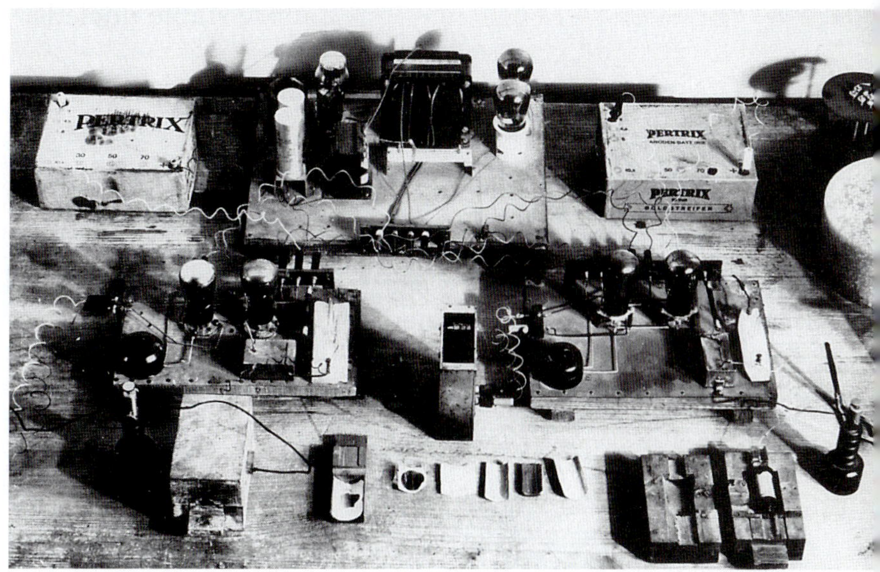

Nuclei are held together by a special force

Like charges repel, so how can so many positively charged protons fit into an atomic nucleus without flying apart?

The answer lies in the existence of the *strong nuclear force.* This force causes protons and neutrons in the nucleus to attract each other. The attraction is much stronger than the electric repulsion between protons. However, this attraction due to the strong nuclear force occurs over a very short distance, less than 3×10^{-15} m, or about the width of three protons.

Neutrons contribute to nuclear stability

Due to the strong nuclear force, neutrons and protons in a nucleus attract other protons and neutrons. Because neutrons have no charge, they do not repel each other or the protons. On the other hand, the protons in a nucleus both repel and attract each other, as shown in **Figure 6.** In stable nuclei, the attractive forces are stronger than the repulsive forces.

Too many neutrons or protons can cause a nucleus to become unstable and decay

While more neutrons can help hold a nucleus together, there is a limit to how many neutrons a nucleus can have. Nuclei with too many or too few neutrons are unstable and undergo decay.

Nuclei with more than 83 protons are always unstable, no matter how many neutrons they have. These nuclei will always decay, releasing large amounts of energy and nuclear radiation. Some of this released energy is transferred to the various particles ejected from the nucleus, the least massive of which move very fast as a result. The rest of the energy is emitted in the form of gamma rays. The radioactive decay that takes place results in a more stable nucleus.

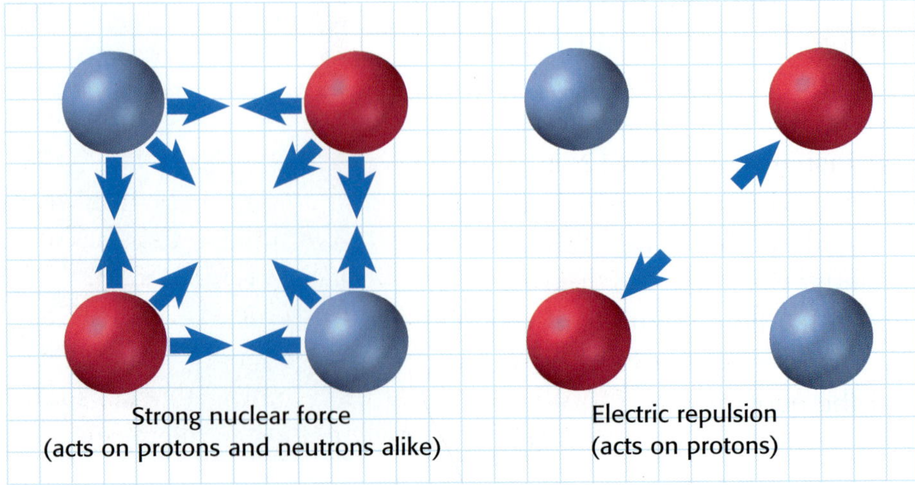

Figure 6
The nucleus is held together by the attractions among protons and neutrons. These forces are greater than the electric repulsion among the protons alone.

Nuclear Fission

The process of splitting heavier nuclei into lighter nuclei, which Hahn and Strassman observed, is called **fission.** In their experiment, uranium-235 was bombarded by neutrons. The products of this fission reaction included two lighter nuclei barium-137 and krypton-84, together with neutrons and energy.

fission the process by which a nucleus splits into two or more fragments and releases neutrons and energy

$$^{235}_{92}\text{U} + ^{1}_{0}\text{n} \longrightarrow ^{137}_{56}\text{Ba} + ^{84}_{36}\text{Kr} + 15^{1}_{0}\text{n} + \text{energy}$$

Notice that the products include 15 neutrons. Uranium-235 can also undergo fission by producing different pairs of lighter nuclei with a different number of neutrons. For example, a different fission of uranium-235 produces strontium-90, xenon-143, and three neutrons. So, in either fission process when the nucleus splits, both neutrons and energy are released.

Energy is released during nuclear fission

During fission, as shown in ***Figure 7,*** the nucleus breaks into smaller nuclei. The reaction also releases large amounts of energy. Each dividing nucleus releases about 3.2×10^{-11} J of energy. By comparison, the chemical reaction of one molecule of the explosive trinitrotoluene (TNT) releases only 4.8×10^{-18} J.

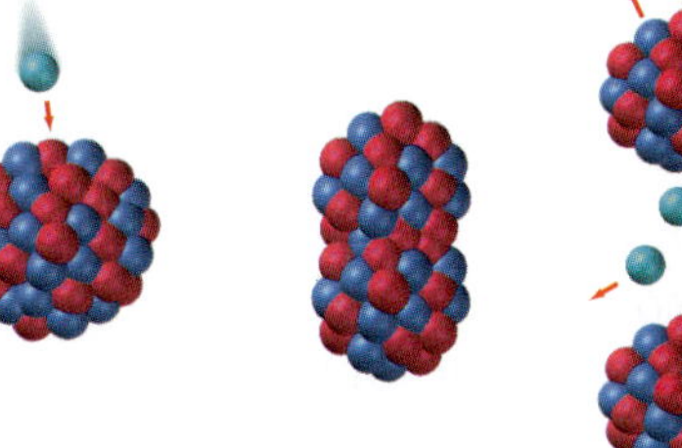

Figure 7
When the uranium-235 nucleus is bombarded by a neutron the nucleus breaks apart. It forms smaller nuclei, such as xenon-143 and strontium-90, and releases energy through fast neutrons.

In their experiment, Hahn and Strassman determined the masses of all the nuclei and particles before and after the reaction. They found that the overall mass had decreased after the reaction. The missing mass had changed into energy.

The equivalence of mass and energy observed in nature is explained by the special theory of relativity, which Albert Einstein presented in 1905. This equivalence means that matter can be converted into energy and energy into matter. This equivalence is expressed by the following equation.

Mass-Energy Equation

$$Energy = mass \times (speed\ of\ light)^2$$
$$E = mc^2$$

Because c, which is constant, has such a large value, 3.0×10^8 m/s, the energy associated with even a small mass is immense. The mass-equivalent energy of 1 kg of matter is 9×10^{16} J. This is more than the chemical energy of 22 million tons of TNT.

Obviously, it would be devastating if objects around us changed into their equivalent energies. Under ordinary conditions of pressure and temperature, matter is very stable. Objects, such as chairs and tables, never spontaneously change into energy.

Did You Know?

Enrico Fermi and his associates achieved the first controlled nuclear reaction in December 1942. The reactor was built on a racquetball court under the unused football stadium at the University of Chicago. The reactor consisted of blocks of uranium for fuel and graphite to slow the neutrons so that they could be captured by the uranium nuclei and cause fission.

When the total mass of any nucleus is measured, it is less than the individual masses of the neutrons and protons that make up the nucleus. This missing mass is referred to as the *mass defect*. But what happens to the missing mass? Einstein's equation provides an explanation—it changes into energy. However, the mass defect of a nucleus is very small.

Another way to think about mass defect is to imagine constructing a nucleus by bringing individual protons and neutrons together. During this process a small amount of mass changes into energy, as described by $E = mc^2$.

Neutrons released by fission can start a chain reaction

Have you ever played marbles with lots of marbles in the ring? When one marble is shot into the ring, the resulting collisions cause some of the marbles to scatter. Some nuclear reactions are like this, where one reaction triggers another.

nuclear chain reaction a continuous series of nuclear fission reactions

A nucleus that splits when it is struck by a neutron forms smaller product nuclei. These smaller nuclei need fewer neutrons to be held together. Therefore, excess neutrons are emitted. One of these neutrons can collide with another large nucleus, triggering another nuclear reaction. This reaction releases more neutrons, and so it is possible to start a chain reaction.

When Hahn and Strassman continued experimenting, they discovered that each dividing uranium nucleus, on average, produced between two and three additional neutrons. Therefore, two or three new fission reactions could be started from the neutrons ejected from one reaction.

If each of these three new reactions produce three additonal neutrons, a total of nine neutrons become available to trigger nine additional fission reactions. From these nine reactions, a total of 27 neutrons are produced, setting off 27 new reactions, and so on. You can probably see from **Figure 8** how the reaction of uranium-235 nuclei would very quickly result in an uncontrolled **nuclear chain reaction.** Therefore, the ability to create a chain reaction partly depends on the number of neutrons released.

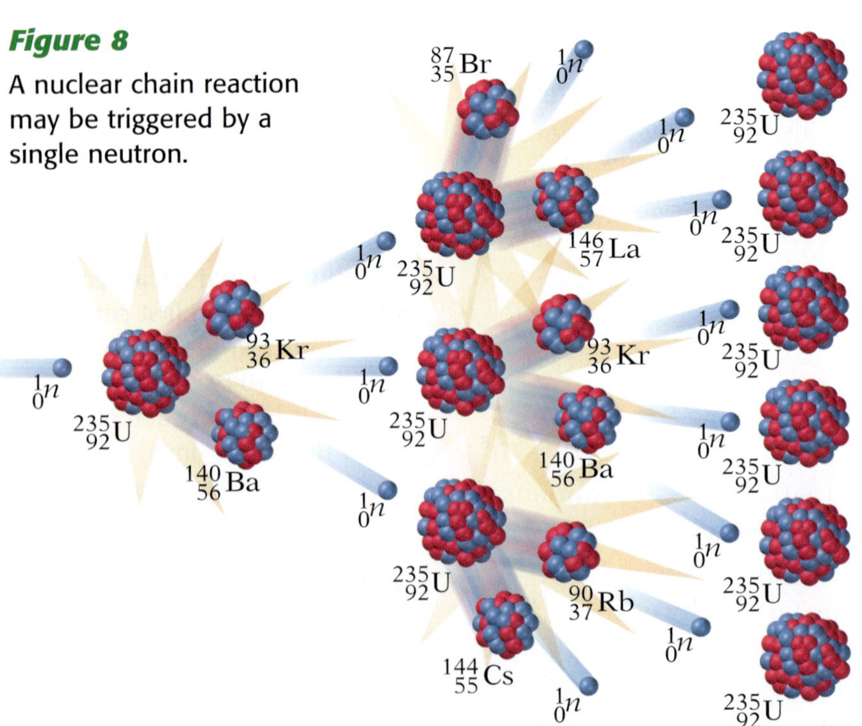

Figure 8
A nuclear chain reaction may be triggered by a single neutron.

Modeling Chain Reactions

1. To model a fission chain reaction, you will need a small wooden building block and a set of dominoes.
2. Place the building block on a table or counter. Stand one domino upright in front of the block and parallel to one of its sides, as shown at right.
3. Stand two more dominoes vertically, parallel, and symmetrical to the first domino. Continue this process until you have used all the dominoes and a triangular shape is created, as shown at right.
4. Gently push the first domino away from the block so that it falls and hits the second group. Note how more dominoes fall with each step.

Chain reactions can be controlled

Energy produced in a controlled chain reaction can be used to generate electricity. Particles released by the splitting of the atom strike other uranium atoms, splitting them. The particles that are given off split still other atoms. A chain reaction is begun, which gives off heat energy that is used to boil water. The boiling water heats another set of pipes filled with water to make steam. The steam then rotates a turbine to generate electricity. So, energy released by the chain reaction changes the atomic energy into heat energy.

The chain-reaction principle is also used in the nuclear bomb. Two or more masses of uranium-235 are contained in the bomb. These masses are surrounded by a powerful chemical explosive. When the explosive is detonated, all of the uranium is pushed together to create a **critical mass.** The critical mass refers to the minimum amount of a substance that can undergo a fission reaction and can also sustain a chain reaction. If the amount of fissionable substance is less than the critical mass, a chain reaction will not continue. Fortunately, the concentration of uranium-235 in nature is too low to start a chain reaction naturally . Almost all of the escaping neutrons are absorbed by the more common and more stable isotope uranium-238.

critical mass the minimum mass of a fissionable isotope that provides the number of neutrons needed to sustain a chain reaction

In nuclear power plants, control rods are used to regulate splitting, slowing the chain reaction. In nuclear bombs, reactions are not controlled, and almost pure pieces of the element uranium-235 or plutonium of a precise mass and shape must be brought together and held together with great force. These conditions are not present in a nuclear reactor.

fusion the process in which light nuclei combine at extremely high temperatures, forming heavier nuclei and releasing energy

Nuclear Fusion

Just as energy is obtained when heavy nuclei break apart, energy can also be obtained when very light nuclei are combined to form heavier nuclei. This type of nuclear process is called **fusion.**

In stars, including the sun, energy is primarily produced when hydrogen nuclei combine, or fuse together, and release tremendous amounts of energy. However, a large amount of energy is needed to start a fusion reaction. This is because all nuclei are positively charged, and they repel each other with an electrical force. Energy is required to bring the hydrogen nuclei close together until the electrical forces are overcome by the attractive nuclear forces between two protons. In stars, the extreme temperatures provide the energy needed to bring hydrogen nuclei together.

Four hydrogen atoms fuse together in the sun to produce a helium atom and enormous energy in the form of gamma rays. This occurs in a multistep process that involves two isotopes of hydrogen: ordinary hydrogen ($^1_1$H), and deuterium ($^2_1$H).

$$^1_1\mathrm{H} + {}^1_1\mathrm{H} \longrightarrow {}^2_1\mathrm{H} + \text{two particles}$$

$$^2_1\mathrm{H} + {}^1_1\mathrm{H} \longrightarrow {}^3_2\mathrm{He} + {}^0_0\gamma$$

$$^3_2\mathrm{He} + {}^3_2\mathrm{He} \longrightarrow {}^4_2\mathrm{He} + {}^1_1\mathrm{H} + {}^1_1\mathrm{H}$$

SECTION 2 REVIEW

SUMMARY

- Neutrons and protons in the nucleus are held together by the strong nuclear force.
- Nuclear fission takes place when a large nucleus divides into smaller nuclei.
- Nuclear fusion occurs when light nuclei combine.
- Mass is converted into energy during fusion reactions of light elements and fission reactions of heavy elements.

1. **Explain** why most isotopes of elements with a high atomic number are radioactive.
2. **Indicate** whether the following are fission or fusion reactions.
   - **a.** $^1_1\mathrm{H} + {}^2_1\mathrm{H} \longrightarrow {}^3_2\mathrm{He} + \gamma$
   - **b.** $^1_0n + {}^{235}_{92}\mathrm{U} \longrightarrow {}^{146}_{57}\mathrm{La} + {}^{87}_{35}\mathrm{Br} + 3^1_0n$
   - **c.** $^{21}_{10}\mathrm{Ne} + {}^4_2\mathrm{He} \longrightarrow {}^{24}_{12}\mathrm{Mg} + {}^1_0n$
   - **d.** $^{208}_{82}\mathrm{Pb} + {}^{58}_{26}\mathrm{Fe} \longrightarrow {}^{265}_{108}\mathrm{Hs} + {}^1_0n$
3. **Predict** whether the total mass of a nucleus of an atom of $^{56}_{26}$Fe is greater than, less than, or equal to the combined mass of the 26 protons and 30 neutrons that make up the nucleus. If the masses are not equal, explain why.
4. **Critical Thinking** Suppose a nucleus captures two neutrons and decays to produce one neutron; is this process likely to produce a chain reaction? Explain your reasoning.

SECTION 3

Nuclear Radiation Today

OBJECTIVES

- **Describe** sources of nuclear radiation, including where it exists as background radiation.
- **List** and explain three beneficial uses and three possible risks of nuclear radiation.
- **Compare** and contrast the advantages and disadvantages of nuclear energy as a power source.

KEY TERMS

background radiation
rem
radioactive tracer

It may surprise you to learn that you are exposed to some form of nuclear radiation every day. Some forms of nuclear radiation are beneficial. Others present some risks. This section will discuss both the benefits and the possible risks of nuclear radiation.

Where Is Radiation?

Nuclear radiation is all around you. This form of nuclear radiation is called **background radiation.** Most of it comes from natural sources, such as the sun, heat, soil, rocks, and plants, as shown in ***Figure 9.*** The living tissues of most organisms are adapted to survive these low levels of natural nuclear radiation.

background radiation the nuclear radiation that arises naturally from cosmic rays and from radioactive isotopes in the soil and air

Figure 9

Sources of background radiation are all around us.

Table 3

Radiation Exposure Per Location

Location	Radiation Exposure (millirems/year)
Tampa, FL	63.7
Richmond, VA	64.1
Las Vegas, NV	69.5
Los Angeles, CA	73.6
Portland, OR	86.7
Rochester, NY	88.1
Wheeling, WV	111.9
Denver, CO	164.6

Source: United States Department of Energy, Nevada Operations Office

Radiation is measured in units of rems

Levels of radiation absorbed by the human body are measured in **rems** or millirems (1 rem = 1000 millirems).

In the United States, many people work in occupations involving nuclear radiation. Nuclear engineering, health physics, radiology, radiochemistry, X-ray technology, and other nuclear medical technology all involve nuclear radiation. A safe limit for these workers has been set at 5000 millirems annually, in addition to natural background exposures.

Exposure varies from one location to another

People in the United States receive varying amounts of natural radiation. Those in higher altitudes receive more exposure to nuclear radiation from space than those in lower altitudes do. People in areas with many rocks have higher nuclear radiation exposure than people in areas without many rocks do. Because of large differences both in altitude and background radiation sources, exposure varies greatly from one location to another, as illustrated in ***Table 3.***

Some activities add to the amount of nuclear radiation exposure

Another factor that affects levels of exposure is participation in certain activities. ***Table 4*** shows actual exposure to nuclear radiation for just a few activities. There are more activities that add to the amount of nuclear radiation exposure than those in this table, but these listed are at least a few of the activities that will add nuclear radiation to the air, affecting all those in the area around these activities.

rem the quantity of ionizing radiation that does as much damage to human tissue as 1 roentgen of high-voltage X rays does

Table 4 **Radiation Exposure Per Activity**

Activity	Radiation (millirems/year)
Smoking 1 1/2 packs of cigarettes per day	8,000
Flying for 720 hours (airline crew)	267
Inhaling radon from the environment	360
Giving or receiving medical X rays	100

Source: United States Department of Energy, Nevada Operations Office

Beneficial Uses of Nuclear Radiation

Radioactive substances have a wide range of applications. In these applications, nuclear radiation is used in a controlled way to take advantage of its effects on other materials.

Smoke detectors help to save lives

Small radioactive sources are present in smoke alarms, as shown in ***Figure 10.*** They release alpha particles, which are charged and produce an electric current. Smoke particles in the air reduce the flow of the current. The drop in current sets off the alarm before levels of smoke increase.

Figure 10

In a smoke alarm, a small alpha-emitting isotope detects smoke particles in the air.

Nuclear radiation is used to detect diseases

The digital computer, ultrasound scanning, CT scanning, PET, and magnetic resonance imaging (MRI) have combined to create a large variety of diagnostic imaging techniques. Using these procedures, doctors can view images of parts of the organs and can detect dysfunction or disease.

The MRI, an imaging process, as in ***Figure 11,*** uses radio frequency pulses to provide images of even small bodily structures. Several types of nuclear radiation procedures, including CT scanning and PET, have been very helpful to medical science. An X ray once was the primary imaging technique used in medicine. An image was created by focusing X rays for 11 minutes through a part of the body and onto a single piece of film. Today, X-ray imaging is done in milliseconds.

Radioactive tracers are widely used in medicine. Tracers are short-lived isotopes that tend to concentrate in affected cells and are used to locate tumors.

radioactive tracer a radioactive material that is added to a substance so that its distribution can be detected later

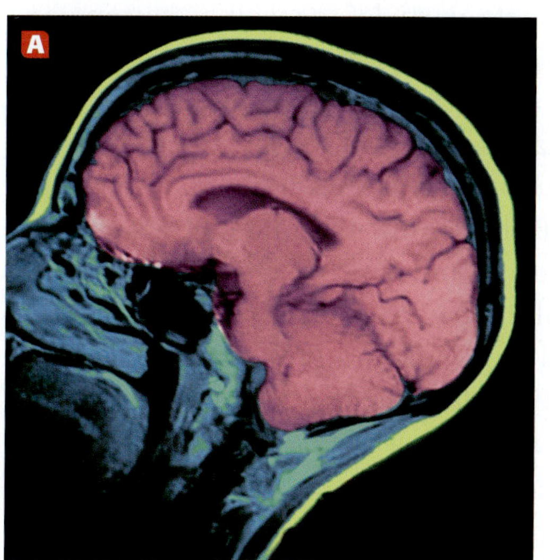

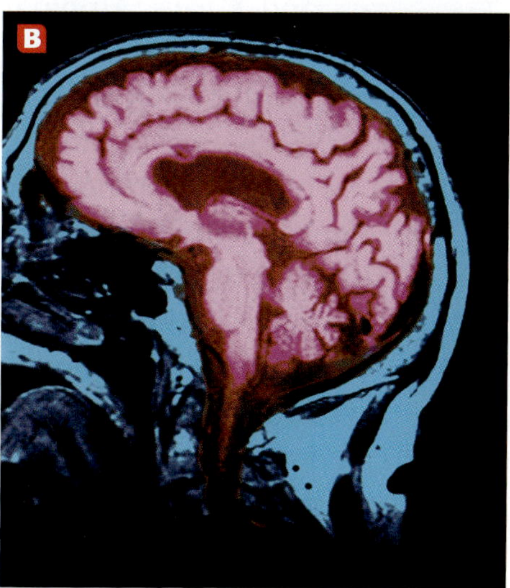

Figure 11

A This is an image of a healthy brain obtained with magnetic resonance imaging (MRI).

B Magnetic resonance imaging reveals that this brain has Alzheimer's disease.

Figure 12

Research farms use radioactive tracers to reveal water movement and other biochemical processes.

Nuclear radiation therapy is used to treat cancer

Radiotherapy is treatment that uses controlled doses of nuclear radiation for treating diseases such as cancer. For example, certain brain tumors can be targeted with small beams of gamma rays.

Radiotherapy is also used for treating thyroid cancer, using an iodine isotope. Treatment of leukemia also uses radiotherapy. The defective bone marrow is first killed with a massive dose of nuclear radiation and then replaced with healthy bone marrow from a donor.

Agriculture uses radioactive tracers and radioisotopes

On research farms, as in ***Figure 12,*** radioactive tracers in flowing water can show how fast water moves through the soil or through stems and leaves of crops. They help us to understand biochemical processes in plants. Radioisotopes are chemically identical with other isotopes of the same element. Because of that similarity, they are substituted in chemical reactions. Radioactive forms of the element can then be easily located with sensors.

Possible Risks of Nuclear Radiation

While nuclear radiation has many benefits, there are also risks. It is important to know what they are so that you can make informed decisions and exercise caution.

Nuclear radiation can ionize atoms

Nuclear radiation interacts with living tissue. This radiation includes charged particles (alpha and beta) as well as gamma rays and X rays. Alpha and beta particles, as well as gamma and X rays, can change the number of electrons in atoms in living materials. This is known as *ionization*. Molecules containing ionized atoms may form substances that are harmful to life.

The ability to penetrate matter differs among different types of nuclear radiation. A layer of clothing or an inch of air can stop alpha particles, which are heavy and slow moving. Beta particles are lighter and faster than alpha particles. Beta particles can penetrate a fraction of an inch in solids and liquids and can travel several feet in air. The ability of gamma rays to penetrate a material depends upon their energy. Several feet of material may protect you from high-energy gamma rays.

The risk depends upon amounts of radiation

The effects of low levels of nuclear radiation on living cells are so small that they may not be detected. However, studies have shown a relationship between exposure to high levels of nuclear radiation and cancer. Cancers associated with high-dose exposure include leukemia as well as breast, lung, and stomach cancers.

Radiation sickness results from high levels of nuclear radiation

Radiation sickness is an illness resulting from excessive exposure to nuclear radiation. This sickness may occur from a single massive exposure, such as a nuclear explosion, or repeated exposures to very high nuclear radiation levels.

Individuals working with nuclear radiation must protect themselves with shields and special clothing. A person working in radioactive areas should wear a *dosimeter,* a device for measuring the amount of nuclear radiation exposure.

Medical Radiation Exposure Graves' disease causes the thyroid gland to produce excess hormones. This excess induces increase in metabolism, weight loss (despite a healthy appetite), and irregular heartbeat.

Graves' disease and similar illnesses can be treated in several ways. Parts of the thyroid gland can be surgically removed, or patients can be treated with radioactive iodine-131. The thyroid cells need iodine to make hormones. When they take in the radioactive iodine-131, the overactive cells are destroyed, and hormone levels drop.

Examine the table below, which shows radiation exposures for different situations and the resulting increased risks in leukemia rates.

Applying Information

1. Given that the typical exposure for radioisotope therapy is about 10 rems, mostly delivered at once, do you think leukemia rates are likely to go up for this group? If so, estimate the expected risk.
2. The link of low-level nuclear radiations to cancers such as leukemia is still in question. Describe what other information would help you evaluate the risks. WRITING SKILL

Person tested	Radiation exposure	Measured increased leukemia risk
Hiroshima atomic bomb survivor	27 rem at once	6%
U.S. WW II radiology technician	50 rem over 2 years	0%
Austrian citizen after the nuclear accident at Chernobyl	0.025 rem	0%

Did You Know?

Radon-222 problems in homes or offices can be eliminated by sealing cracks in foundations or by installing vents that draw air out of the building.

High concentrations of radon gas can be hazardous

Colorless and inert, *radon gas* is produced by the radioactive decay of uranium-238 present in soil and rock. Radon gas emits alpha and beta particles and gamma rays. Tests have shown a correlation between lung cancer and high levels of exposure to radon gas, especially for smokers. Some areas have higher radon levels than others do. Tests for radon gas in buildings are widely available.

Nuclear Power

Today, nuclear reactors, as shown in ***Figure 13,*** are used in dozens of countries to generate electricity. Energy produced from fission is used to light the homes of millions of families. There are numerous advantages to this source of energy. There are also disadvantages.

Nuclear fission has both advantages and disadvantages

One advantage of nuclear fission is that it does not produce gaseous pollutants, and there is much more energy in the known uranium reserves than in the known reserves of coal and oil.

In nuclear fission reactors, energy is produced by triggering a controlled fission reaction in uranium-235. However, the products of fission reactions are often radioactive isotopes. Therefore, serious safety concerns must be addressed. Radioactive products of fission must be handled carefully so they do not escape in the environment and release nuclear radiation.

Another safety issue involves the safe operation of the nuclear reactors in which the controlled fission reaction is carried out. A nuclear reactor must be equipped with many safety features. The reactor requires considerable shielding and must meet very strict safety requirements. Thus, nuclear power plants are expensive to build.

Figure 13

Nuclear reactors like this are used over much of the world to generate electricity.

Nuclear waste must be safely stored

Besides the expenses that occur during the life of a nuclear power plant, there is the expense of storing radioactive materials, such as the fuel rods used in the reactors. After their use they must be placed in safe facilities that are well shielded, as shown in ***Figure 14.*** These precautions are necessary to keep nuclear radiation from leaking out and harming living things. The facilities must also keep nuclear radiation from contacting ground water.

Ideal places for such facilities are sparsely populated areas with little water on the surface or underground. These areas must be free from earthquakes.

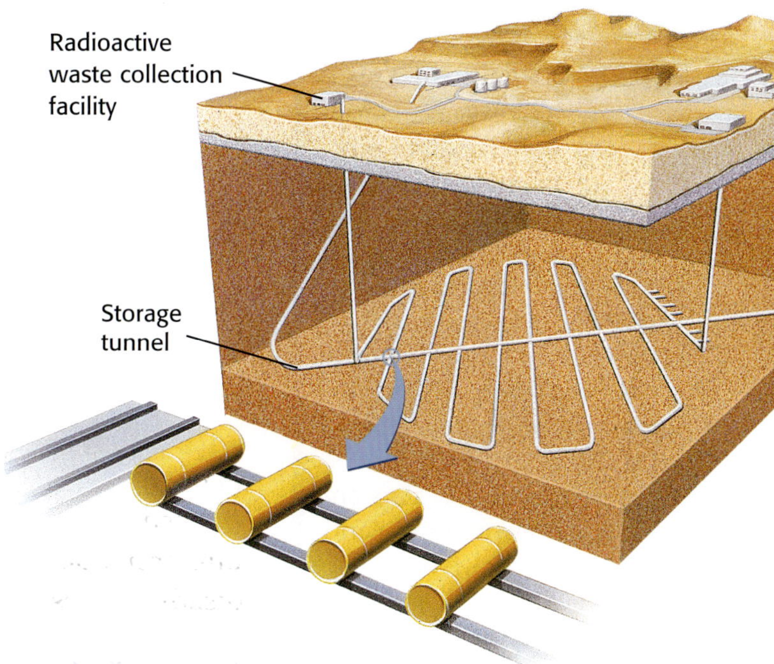

Figure 14

Storage facilities for nuclear waste must be designed to contain radioactive materials safely for thousands of years.

Nuclear fusion reactors are being tested

Another option that holds some promise as an energy source is nuclear fusion. Fusion means joining (fusing) smaller nuclei to make a larger nucleus. The sun uses the nuclear fusion of hydrogen atoms; this fusion results in larger helium atoms. This process of fusion gives off heat, light, and other radiation, otherwise known as solar energy. Solar energy can be captured by solar panels or other means to provide energy for homes and other types of buildings.

Recall from the last section that the process of fusion takes place when light nuclei, such as hydrogen, are forced together to produce heavier nuclei, such as helium, producing large amounts of energy. Some scientists estimate that 1 pound of hydrogen in a fusion reactor could release as much energy as 16 million pounds of burning coal. Nuclear fusion releases very little waste or pollution.

Because fusion requires that the electrical repulsion between protons be overcome, these reactions are difficult to produce in the laboratory. However, successful experiments have been conducted in the United States when researchers took a major step toward exploiting a safe, clean source of power that uses fuels extracted from ordinary water. Other experiments for power generated in a nuclear fusion reactor have also been carried out near Oxford, England.

INTEGRATING

SPACE SCIENCE

Unmanned space probes have greatly increased our knowledge of the solar system. Nuclear-powered probes can venture far from the sun without losing power, as solar-powered probes do. *Cassini,* which was sent to explore Saturn, is powered by the heat generated by the radioactive decay of plutonium.

INTEGRATING

SPACE SCIENCE

All heavy elements, from cobalt to uranium, are made when massive stars explode. The pressure produced in the explosion causes nearby nuclei to fuse together, in some cases more than once.

The explosion carries the newly created elements into space. These elements later become parts of new stars and planets. The elements of Earth are believed to have formed in the outer layers of an exploding star.

Nuclear fusion also has advantages and disadvantages

The most attractive feature of fusion is that the fuel for it is abundant. Hydrogen is the most common element in the universe and is plentiful in many compounds on Earth, such as water. Earth's oceans could provide enough hydrogen to meet current world energy demands for millions of years.

Unfortunately, practical fusion-based power is far from being a reality. Fusion reactions have some drawbacks. They can produce fast neutrons, a highly energetic and potentially dangerous form of nuclear radiation. Shielding material in the reactor would have to be replaced periodically, increasing the expense of operating a fusion power plant. Lithium can be used to slow down these neutrons, but it is chemically reactive and rare, making its use impractical.

Nuclear fusion is still in its infancy. Successful experiments are just beginning. Who can say what the future may hold? Perhaps scientists yet to come will find the answers to the nagging questions that plague the government today concerning the perfect fuel for United States citizens.

SECTION 3 REVIEW

SUMMARY

- Background radiation comes from natural sources and is everywhere. Living tissue adapts to background radiation in most cases.
- Beneficial uses of nuclear radiation include smoke detectors, X rays, CT, PET, radiotherapy, radioactive tracers, and radioisotopes.
- Risks of high levels of nuclear radiation include cancers and radiation sickness. High levels of radon gas can be harmful. Tests for radon gas are widely available.
- Nuclear fission is an alternative to fossil fuels as a source of energy.

1. **List** three sources of background radiation.
2. **Identify** three activities that add to background radiation under normal circumstances.
3. **Describe** how smoke detectors use alpha particles and what sets off the alarm.
4. **Name** three nuclear radiation diagnostic imaging techniques that help detect diseases.
5. **Explain** how radioactive tracers help locate tumors.
6. **Describe** how gamma rays are used in cancer therapy.
7. **Compare** and contrast the benefits and risks of radiation therapy in general.
8. **Explain** why it is important to use low levels of nuclear radiation for detection and treatment of disease.
9. **Summarize** why the testing of buildings for radon gas levels may be important, especially for smokers.
10. **Critical Thinking** Suppose uranium-238 could undergo fission as easily as uranium-235. Predict how that would change the advantages and drawbacks of fission reactors.

Math Skills

Calculating Times of Decay

A sample of francium-223 has a half-life of 22 minutes.

a. What fraction of francium-223 remains if 93.75 percent of it has undergone radioactive decay?

b. How many half-lives does it take for the sample to decay?

c. How long does it take for the sample to decay?

1 **List all given and unknown values.**

Given: fraction of sample decayed, 93.75 percent
half-life, 22 min

Unknown: fraction of sample remaining
number of half-lives (*n*)
time of decay

2 **Write down the equation relating the fraction of the sample remaining to the percentage of sample decayed, and the equation relating the time of decay to the number of half-lives.**

$$\text{fraction of sample remaining} = 1 - \text{fraction of sample decayed}$$
$$= 1 - \frac{\text{percentage of sample decayed}}{100}$$
$$= \left(\frac{1}{2}\right)^n$$

$$\text{time of decay} = n \times \text{half-life}$$

3 **Calculate the unknown quantities.**

a. $\text{fraction of sample remaining} = 1 - \frac{93.75}{100} = 1 - 0.9375 = 0.0625$

To express this as a fraction, divide the answer into 1 to find the denominator of the fraction. 1/0.0625 = 16, so the fraction of sample remaining is 1/16.

b. $\left(\frac{1}{2}\right)^n = \frac{1}{16} = \left(\frac{1}{2}\right) \times \left(\frac{1}{2}\right) \times \left(\frac{1}{2}\right) \times \left(\frac{1}{2}\right) = \left(\frac{1}{2}\right)^4$

$\text{number of half-lives} = n = 4$

c. $\text{time of decay} = 4 \times 22 \text{ min} = 88 \text{ min}$

Practice

Following the example above, calculate the following:

1. What fraction of iodine-132 remains if 87.5% has undergone radioactive decay?
2. How many half-lives does it take for the sample to decay?
3. Iodine-132 has a half-life of 2.3 hours. How long does it take for the sample to decay?

CHAPTER 9 REVIEW

Chapter Highlights

Before you begin, review the summaries of the key ideas of each section, found at the end of each section. The key vocabulary terms are listed on the first page of each section.

UNDERSTANDING CONCEPTS

1. When a heavy nucleus decays, it may emit
- **a.** alpha particles.
- **b.** beta particles.
- **c.** gamma rays.
- **d.** All of the above

2. A neutron decays to form a proton and a(n)
- **a.** alpha particle.
- **b.** beta particle.
- **c.** gamma ray.
- **d.** emitted neutron.

3. After three half-lives, __________ of a radioactive sample remains.
- **a.** all
- **b.** one-half
- **c.** one-third
- **d.** one-eighth

4. Carbon dating can be used to measure the age of each of the following except
- **a.** a 7000-year-old human body.
- **b.** a 1200-year-old wooden statue.
- **c.** a 2600-year-old iron sword.
- **d.** a 3500-year-old piece of fabric.

5. The strong nuclear force
- **a.** attracts protons to electrons.
- **b.** holds molecules together.
- **c.** holds the atomic nucleus together.
- **d.** attracts electrons to neutrons.

6. The process in which a heavy nucleus splits into two lighter nuclei is called
- **a.** fission.
- **b.** fusion.
- **c.** alpha decay.
- **d.** a chain reaction.

7. The amount of energy produced during nuclear fission is related to
- **a.** the temperature in the atmosphere during nuclear fission.
- **b.** the masses of the missing nuclei and particles released.
- **c.** the volume of the nuclear reactor.
- **d.** the square of the speed of sound.

8. Which condition is not necessary for a chain reaction to occur?
- **a.** The radioactive sample must have a short half-life.
- **b.** The neutrons from one split nucleus must cause other nuclei to divide.
- **c.** The radioactive sample must be at critical mass.
- **d.** Not too many neutrons must be allowed to leave the radioactive sample.

9. Which of the following is *not* a use for radioactive isotopes?
- **a.** as tracers for diagnosing disease
- **b.** as an additive to paints to increase their durability
- **c.** as a way of treating forms of cancer
- **d.** as a way to study biochemical processes in plants

USING VOCABULARY

10. How can *nuclear radioactivity* affect the atomic number and mass number of a nucleus that changes after undergoing decay?

11. Describe the main differences between the four main types of nuclear *radiation: alpha particles, beta particles, gamma rays,* and *neutron emission.*

12. What are two factors that cause alpha particles to lose energy and travel less distance than neutrons travel?

13. Where do beta particles come from?

14. Why do gamma rays have no mass at all?

15. Would a substance with a one-second *half-life* be effective as a *radioactive tracer?*

16. For the nuclear *fission* process, how is *critical mass* important in a *chain reaction?*

17. How does nuclear *fusion* account for the energy produced in stars?

18. What is *background radiation,* and what are its sources?

19. The amount of nuclear radiation exposure that is received into a human body is measured in *rems*. How does the amount of exposure in rems per year in Denver, Colorado, compare with the amount that has been set as a safe limit for workers in occupations with relatively high radiation exposure?

20. How can a *radioactive tracer* be used to locate tumors?

BUILDING MATH SKILLS

21. **Nuclear Decay** Bismuth-212 undergoes a combination of alpha and beta decays to form lead-208. Depending on which decay process occurs first, different isotopes are temporarily formed during the process. Identify these isotopes by completing the equations given below:

a. $^{212}_{83}\text{Bi} \longrightarrow {}^{\square}_{\square}\text{X} + {}^{4}_{2}\text{He}$

$^{\square}_{\square}\text{X} \longrightarrow {}^{208}_{82}\text{Pb} + {}^{0}_{-1}e$

b. $^{212}_{83}\text{Bi} \longrightarrow {}^{\square}_{\square}\text{X} + {}^{0}_{-1}e$

$^{\square}_{\square}\text{X} \longrightarrow {}^{208}_{82}\text{Pb} + {}^{4}_{2}\text{He}$

22. **Half-life** The ratio of carbon-14 to carbon-12 in a prehistoric wooden artifact is measured to be one-eighth of the ratio measured in a fresh sample of wood from the same region. The half-life of carbon-14 is 5715 years. Determine its age.

23. **Half-life** Health officials are concerned about radon levels in homes. The half-life of radon-222 is 3.82 days. If a sample of gas contains 4.38 μg of radon-222, how much will remain in the sample after 15.2 days?

BUILDING GRAPHING SKILLS

24. **Graphing** The first 20 elements have stable nuclei composed of equal numbers of protons and neutrons. Draw a graph entitled "Number of protons versus number of neutrons for small stable nuclei." Let the *x*-axis (horizontal axis) represent number of protons. Let the *y*-axis (vertical axis) represent number of neutrons.

25. **Graphing** Using a graphing calculator or computer graphing program, create a graph for the decay of iodine-131, which has a half-life of 8.1 days. Use the graph to answer the following questions:

COMPUTER SKILL

a. Approximately what percentage of the iodine-131 has decayed after 4 days?
b. Approximately what percentage of the iodine-131 has decayed after 12.1 days?
c. What fraction of iodine-131 has decayed after 2.5 half-lives have elapsed?
d. What percentage of the original iodine-131 remains after 3.5 half-lives?

THINKING CRITICALLY

26. **Applying Knowledge** Describe the similarities and differences between atomic electrons and beta particles.

27. **Critical Thinking** Why do people working around radioactive waste in a radioactive storage facility wear badges containing strips of photographic film?

28. **Critical Thinking** Why would carbon-14 not be a good choice to use in household smoke detectors?

29. **Critical Thinking** Would an emitter of alpha particles be useful in measuring the thickness of a brick? Explain your answer.

DEVELOPING LIFE/WORK SKILLS

30. Allocating Resources An archeologist has collected seven samples from a site: two scraps of fabric, two strips of leather, and three bone fragments. The age of each item must be determined, but the budget for carbon-14 dating is only $4500. Carbon-14 mass spectrometry is an accurate way to find a sample's age, but it costs $820 per sample. Carbon-14 dating by liquid scintillation costs only $400 a sample, but is less reliable. How would you apply either or both of these techniques to the samples to obtain the most reliable information and still stay within your budget?

31. Making Decisions Suppose you are an energy consultant who has been asked to evaluate a proposal to build a power plant in a remote area of the desert. Investigate the requirements for and possible hazards of nuclear-fission power plants, coal-burning power plants, and solar-energy farms. Study research about their environmental impacts. Using this information and what you have learned from this chapter, write a paragraph supporting your decision about which of these power plants would be best for its surroundings.

WRITING SKILL

32. Working Cooperatively Read the following, and research with a group of classmates possible solutions that make use of radioactivity. Report your findings.

A person believed to be suffering from cancer has been admitted to a hospital. What are some possible methods of diagnosing the patient's condition? Assuming that cancer is found, how might the disease be treated? Suppose you suspect that another patient is suffering from radiation poisoning. How would you be able to tell?

INTEGRATING CONCEPTS

33. Concept Mapping Copy the unfinished concept map below onto a sheet of paper. Complete the map by writing the correct word or phrase in the lettered boxes.

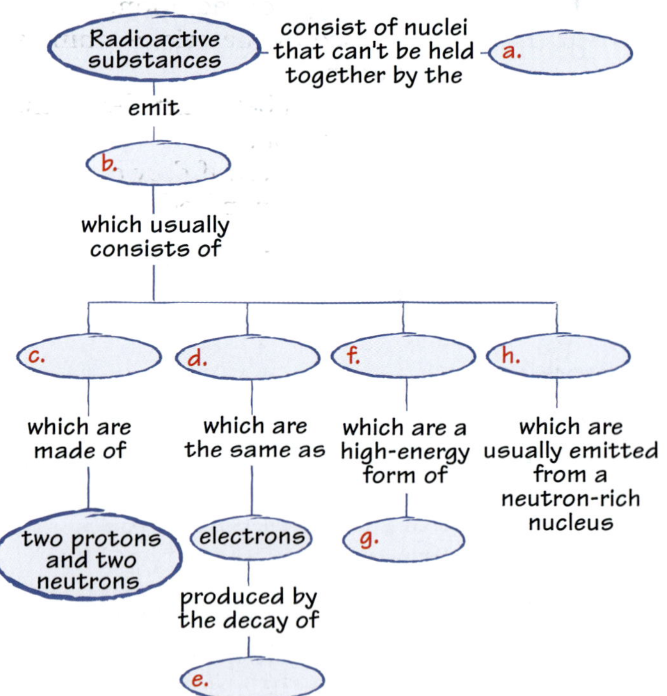

Standardized Test Prep

Understanding Concepts

***Directions (1–3):* For *each* question, write on a separate sheet of paper the letter of the correct answer.**

1 How can nuclear power plants produce substantial amounts of energy while consuming very little fuel?
- **A.** Radioactive isotopes release a large amount of chemical energy.
- **B.** When large atoms break apart, some of their mass is converted to energy.
- **C.** The bonds between uranium atoms are very strong and release energy when they are broken.
- **D.** A significant amount of energy is released when two atoms come together to form one larger atom.

2 Why can alpha particles be used safely in home smoke detectors?
- **F.** They are not a type of radiation.
- **G.** They are stopped by material as thin as a sheet of paper.
- **H.** They combine with beta particles in the air to form a neutron.
- **I.** They are harmless even if they come in contact with the human body.

3 When an atom emits a beta particle, how does its mass change?
- **A.** −4
- **B.** −1
- **C.** 0
- **D.** +1

***Directions (4):* Write a short response to the question.**

4 The nuclei of atoms are made of protons and neutrons. Every atomic nucleus larger than that of hydrogen has at least two positively charged protons. Why do the nuclei remain intact instead of being broken apart by the repulsion of their electric charges?

Test TIP

Try to figure out the answer to a question before you look at the choices. Then compare your answer with each answer choice. Choose the answer that most closely matches your own.

Reading Skills

***Directions (5):* Read the passage below. Then answer the question.**

Radioactive isotopes are often used as "tracers" to follow the path of an element through a chemical reaction. For example, using radiotracers, chemists have determined that the oxygen atoms in O_2 that are produced by a green plant during photosynthesis come from the oxygen in water and not the oxygen in carbon dioxide.

5 How could you design an experiment to determine whether the source of the oxygen produced by photosynthesis is carbon dioxide molecules or water molecules?

Interpreting Graphics

***Directions (6):* Base your answer to question 6 on the illustration below.**

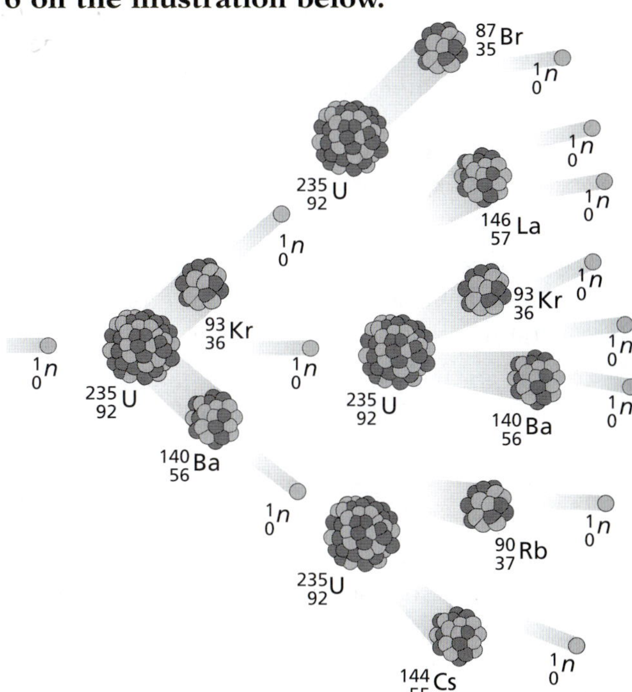

6 What process is represented by the illustration?
- **F.** alpha decay
- **G.** nuclear chain reaction
- **H.** radioactivity
- **I.** nuclear fusion

Skills Practice Lab

Simulating Nuclear Decay Reactions

Introduction

In this lab you will simulate the decay of lead-210 into its isotope lead-206. This decay of lead-210 into its isotope lead-206 occurs in a multistep process. Lead-210, $^{210}_{82}Pb$, first decays into bismuth-210, $^{210}_{83}Bi$, which decays into polonium-210, $^{210}_{84}Po$, which finally decays into the isotope lead-206, $^{206}_{82}Pb$.

Objectives

- USING SCIENTIFIC METHODS ***Simulate*** the decay of radioactive isotopes by throwing a set of dice, and observe the results.
- ***Graph*** the results to identify patterns in the amounts of isotopes present.

Materials

10 dice
large paper cup with plastic lid
roll of masking tape
scissors

Procedure

1. On a sheet of paper, prepare a table as shown below. Leave room to add extra rows at the bottom, if necessary.

Throw #	# of dice representing each Isotope $^{210}_{82}Pb$	$^{210}_{83}Bi$	$^{210}_{84}Po$	$^{206}_{82}Pb$
0 (start)	10	0	0	0
1				
2				
3				
4				

2. Place all 10 dice in the cup. Each die represents an atom of $^{210}_{82}Pb$, a radioactive isotope.
3. Put the lid on the cup, and shake it a few times. Then remove the lid, and spill the dice. In this simulation, each throw represents a *half-life.*
4. All the dice that land with 1, 2, or 3 up represent atoms of $^{210}_{82}Pb$ that have decayed into $^{210}_{83}Bi$. The remaining dice still represent $^{210}_{82}Pb$ atoms. Separate the two sets of dice. Count the dice, and record the results in your data table.
5. To keep track of the dice representing the decayed atoms, you will make a small mark on them. On a die, the faces with *1, 2,* and *3* share a corner. With a pencil, draw a small circle around this shared corner, and this die represents the $^{210}_{83}Bi$ atoms.
6. Put all the dice back in the cup, shake them and roll them again. In a decay process, there are two possibilities: some atoms decay and some do not. See the diagram below to track your results.

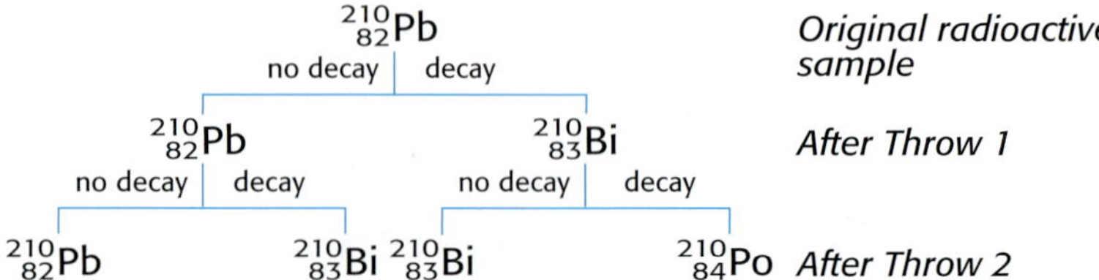

Isotope type	Decays into	Signs of decay	Identifying the atoms in column 2
$^{210}_{82}Pb$	$^{210}_{83}Bi$	Unmarked dice land on *1, 2,* or *3*	Mark $^{210}_{83}Bi$ by drawing a circle around the corner where faces *1, 2,* and *3* meet.
$^{210}_{83}Bi$	$^{210}_{84}Po$	Dice with one loop land on *1, 2,* or *3*	Draw a circle around the corner where faces *4, 5,* and *6* meet.
$^{210}_{84}Po$	$^{206}_{82}Pb$	Dice with two loops land on *1, 2,* or *3*	Put a small piece of masking tape over the two circles.
$^{206}_{82}Pb$	Decay ends		

7. After the second throw, we have three types of atoms. Sort the dice into three sets.
   a. The first set consists of dice with a circle drawn on them that landed with *1, 2,* or *3* facing up. These represent $^{210}_{83}Bi$ atoms that have decayed into $^{210}_{84}Po$.
   b. The second set consists of two types of dice: the dice with one circle that did not land on *1, 2,* or *3* (undecayed $^{210}_{83}Bi$) and the unmarked dice that landed with *1, 2,* or *3* facing up (representing the decay of original $^{210}_{82}Pb$ into $^{210}_{83}Bi$).
   c. The third set includes unmarked dice that did not land with *1, 2,* or *3* facing up. These represent the original undecayed $^{210}_{82}Pb$ atoms.
8. After each throw, do the following: separate the different types of atoms in groups, count the atoms in each group, record your data in your table, and mark the dice to identify each isotope. Use the table above as a guide.
9. For your third throw, put all the dice back into the cup. After the third throw, some of the $^{210}_{84}Po$ will decay into the stable isotope $^{206}_{82}Pb$. Use the table above and step 8 to figure out what else happens after the third throw.
10. Continue throwing the dice until all the dice have decayed into $^{206}_{82}Pb$, which is a stable isotope. Hence, these dice will remain unchanged in all future throws.

Analysis

1. Write nuclear decay equations for the nuclear reactions modeled in this lab.
2. In your lab report, prepare a graph like the one shown at right. Using a different color or symbol for each atom, plot the data for all four atoms on the same graph.
3. What do your results suggest about how the amounts of $^{210}_{82}Pb$ and $^{206}_{82}Pb$ on Earth are changing over time?

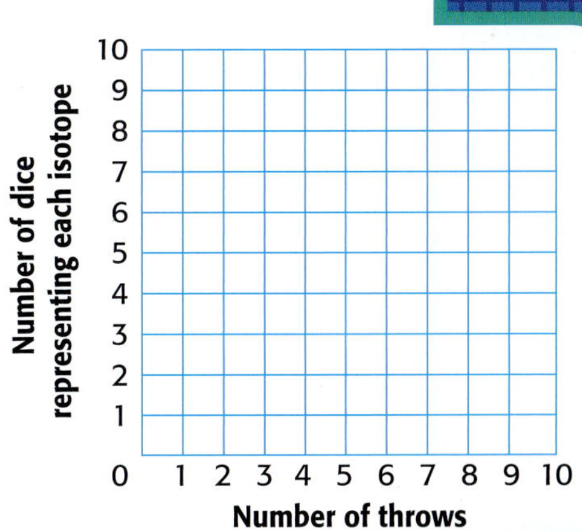

Conclusions

4. $^{210}_{82}Pb$ is continually produced through a series of nuclear decays that begin with $^{238}_{92}U$. Does this information cause you to modify your answer to item 3? Explain why.

CareerLink

Science Reporter

Science reporters are usually among the first people to hear about scientific discoveries. News organizations hire science reporters to explain these discoveries to the general public in a clear, understandable, and entertaining way. To learn more about science reporting as a career, read the interview with science reporter Corinna Wu, who writes for Science News magazine, in Washington, D.C.

Corinna Wu describes scientific research and discovery in the articles she writes.

"I think writing is something you can learn—it's a craft. Lots of people talk about talents, but I think it's something you can do if you work at it."

What does a science reporter do?

I write and report news and feature articles for a weekly science news magazine. That entails finding news stories— generally about research. I have to call the researchers and ask them questions about how they did their work and the significance of the work. Then I write a short article explaining the research to ordinary people.

What is your favorite part of your work?

I like learning about a new subject every week. I get to ask all the stupid questions I was afraid to ask in school.

How did you become interested in science reporting as a career?

After college, I had a summer internship at NASA, at the Johnson Space Center in Houston, Texas, doing materials research there. I had lots of time to read space news magazines. It was at that time that I realized, "Hey, people write this stuff."

What kinds of skills are important for a science reporter?

One thing that is really important is to really love writing. If you don't like to write already, it's pretty hard to make yourself do it every day. It helps to have a creative bent, too. It also helps to enjoy explaining things. Science writing by nature is explanatory, more so than other kinds of journalism.

You have a science background. How does that help you do your job?

I majored in chemistry as an undergraduate and got a master's degree in materials science. I find that I draw on that academic background a lot, in terms of understanding the research.

Do you think a science reporter needs a science background?

Ideally, you should be studying science while writing on the side. But if you have to do one or the other, I'd do science first. It's harder to pick up the science later. Science builds on itself. It takes years to really get a grasp of it.

Why do you think science reporting is important?

Science and technology are becoming part of our everyday lives. It's important for people to keep up on research in these areas. There is an element of education in everything you write.

What advice do you have for students who are interested in science reporting?

Read as much as you can—newspapers, magazines, books. Nothing beats getting real experience writing. If you have a newspaper or magazine at school, get involved in that. You draw on academic experiences—you don't know when they will become useful.

www.scilinks.org
Topic: Science Writer
SciLinks code: **HK4125**
SCILINKS. Maintained by the National Science Teachers Association

Musical Metal

Science catches up with the shimmering sound of steel drums

By CORINNA WU

More than half a century ago in Trinidad, a teenage Elliot "Ellie" Mannette hammered 14 bumps into the steel bottom of an upside-down, 55-gallon oil barrel. Each raised section, when struck, resounded with a clear note.

Mannette entered a contest and brought along the new creation. "All the others played small drums," he says, "and I showed up with my big drum. Everyone was surprised."

That humble, street-band instrument would evolve into the modern Caribbean steel drum, or steelpan, loved around the world for its bright, shimmering tones.

Mannette, who turns 71 next month, today lives in Morgantown, W.Va., where he has served as an artist-in-residence at West Virginia University for about 5 years. An acknowledged master craftsman, Mannette is also training a group of a dozen apprentices in the art of making and tuning steel drums.

Mannette has always worked intuitively. Now, with Mannette's help, some scientists who are themselves fans of the steelpan have begun to study this intriguing instrument in hopes of divining the technical secrets of its celestial sound. At the University of Texas at El Paso (UTEP), materials scientists and musicians have teamed up to analyze the metallurgy of the drum, connecting what they see under their microscopes with what they hear with their ears.

Lawrence E. Murr, director of UTEP's Materials Research Institute, first encountered steel drums as many people have—on a cruise to the Caribbean. "I'm a metallurgist of sorts, so I got interested in how they work," he says. "I just fell in love with the music. It's a very special sound. I vowed I would get hold of a drum and cut the notes out and look at them."

A step toward doing just that came in 1996 at a cocktail party, where Murr learned that a UTEP music professor, Larry White, had just received a grant to purchase a set of steel drums.

"When we finally got together," Murr says, White "thought I was crazy because I said, 'I really want to take the drums apart to know what makes them tick.'"

Murr recalls White's reaction: "'Not my drums!'"

Luckily, White agreed to work with Murr—as long as he didn't cut up his new set of steelpans. Searching around for steel drum experts, Murr quickly found Mannette, who provided the team with some old drums they could cut apart and analyze. Mannette "was real excited [about the project]," Murr says, "because he was always interested in having somebody do legitimate science on the steel drum."

Mannette would like to see materials scientists determine what kind of steel allows him to make the most beautiful-sounding drum. Oil barrels made by different manufacturers have different steel compositions and, therefore, different properties. Right now, says Mannette, "I have no control over the composition. The ideal steel might be very different. We just don't know what it might be."

Soon, White and Murr assembled a group of music and engineering students interested in learning more about the instrument. White took Murr's engineering students into his classes to teach them how to read music and play the drums. Meanwhile, the engineers began the task of examining the metal up close.

They studied the microscopic structure of the hammered steel in samples taken from actual drums and tested idealized single-note disks cut from sheets of stainless steel. What they have found has amazed them, Murr says. "The more research we do, the more we realize that [Mannette's] intuition was fortuitous."

The design and processing methods that Mannette pioneered, and that steelpan makers have used ever since the 1940s, turn out to be perfectly suited for producing the drum's complex, rich sound. The researchers will publish their latest results in an upcoming issue of the JOURNAL OF MATERIALS SCIENCE.

When Mannette was a youth, discarded barrels were abundant in oil-rich Trinidad, so he and his compatriots shaped them to make music. Drums are still made mostly by hand using many of Mannette's original techniques.

To form a steelpan, the drum maker first "sinks the head" by hitting the bottom of the barrel with a sledgehammer, making it concave like a bowl. "If you don't do it correctly, it breaks," says Murr. Then, the note-making surfaces are hammered up from underneath, forming raised sections on the bowl's surface. Often, the side of the barrel is cut to make it shorter.

A tenor, or lead, drum can have as many as 32 striking surfaces arranged in a circular pattern. A bass drum might have only three. Other drums in a typical band include what are called guitars and cellos (each with 8 or 9 striking surfaces), which cover the midrange. The drummer strikes the notes with mallets, usually aluminum tubes covered with a piece of rubber.

Grooves or a line of holes bordering the raised surfaces help to isolate them from each other. Nevertheless, hitting one note causes some excitation of neighboring

A steelpan held upside-down over a fire turns blue from oxidization. Heat ages the steel, modifying the drum's sound.

A conventional pattern for a tenor drum contains 29 notes arranged in circles of fifths—each note is a musical fifth above or below its neighbors. The notes in the innermost ring are one octave higher than those in the middle ring, which are themselves one octave higher than the notes in the outermost ring.

236 SCIENCE NEWS, VOL. 154 OCTOBER 10, 1998

notes, an effect that contributes to the instrument's intricate sound. "Because the notes are patterned onto the same drum head, the vibrational modes of one note will sympathetically vibrate with another," Murr explains.

Thomas D. Rossing, a physicist at Northern Illinois University in DeKalb, has examined the acoustic properties of steel drums with a technique called holographic interferometry. He excites one note electromagnetically at one of its fundamental frequencies, then uses the interferometer to visualize which areas of the playing surface reverberate. "At amplitudes typical of a performance, almost the entire drum vibrates and radiates sound," he report- ed in the March 1996 PHYSICS TOD[...] Such extensive influence of one note [...] others is unusual in a musical ins[...] ment.

Through their metallurgical stu[...] the UTEP researchers tried to draw [...] nections between the structure [...] steel and the musical quality of the [...] They learned that drum makers [...] ciously take advantage of the pro[...]

"Science is a strong tool, a strong way of looking at the world. I feel that trying to introduce people to that way of looking at the world is very important."

—Corinna Wu

CHAPTER 10

Motion

Chapter Preview

Focus ACTIVITY

Background A skier such as the one shown here is obviously in motion, very fast motion. In fact, skiers have set world records by reaching speeds of over 240 km/h. So, it is easy to understand that a skier coming down a mountain is very much in motion. But what is motion? What is the correct way to describe motion?

To describe motion in the language of science, you need to answer questions such as the following. Does an object make patterns with its motion? How fast does the object move? In what direction does the object move? Does its speed change? Does the object change its direction? Does it repeat its motion? Do you need to compare the motion to another object in motion or to an object standing still? Is motion a relative term?

Activity 1 Choose a windup or battery-operated toy. You will also need a meterstick, a stopwatch, paper, and a pencil. Measure and record time, distance, direction, and any pattern of the toy's motion. Record your findings.

Activity 2 Use the same windup or battery-operated toy you used for Activity 1. After putting the toy into motion, set it on a toy truck or train. Then, put that toy truck or train in motion. Measure and record the distance traveled by the toy on the truck or train and the corresponding time interval. Repeat this activity several times and record all of your findings.

How is an athlete's speed calculated? When instruments report the speed, they do so by measuring both distance and time in small increments and then dividing the distance by the time.

internet connect

www.scilinks.org

Topic: Motion SciLinks code: HK4091

SCILINKS. Maintained by the National Science Teachers Association

Pre-Reading Questions

1. What are some of the ways that objects move?
2. How can you tell when something is moving?

SECTION 1

Measuring Motion

KEY TERMS

motion
displacement
speed
velocity

OBJECTIVES

- **Explain** the relationship between motion and a frame of reference.
- **Relate** speed to distance and time.
- **Distinguish** between speed and velocity.
- **Solve** problems related to time, distance, displacement, speed, and velocity.

We are surrounded by moving things. From a car moving in a straight line to a satellite traveling in a circle around Earth, objects move in many ways. In everyday life, **motion** is so common that it seems very simple. But understanding and describing motion scientifically requires some advanced concepts. To begin, how do we know when an object is moving?

motion an object's change in position relative to a reference point

Observing Motion

You may think that the motion of an object is easy to detect—just observe the object. But you actually must observe the object in relation to another object that stays in place, called a *stationary* object. The stationary object is a *reference point,* sometimes called a *reference frame.* Earth is a common reference point. In ***Figure 1,*** a mountain is used as a reference point.

When an object changes position in comparison to a reference point, the object is in motion. You can describe the direction of an object in motion with a reference direction. Typical reference directions are north, south, east, west, up, or down.

Figure 1

During the time required to take these two photographs, the hot-air balloon changed position compared with a stationary reference point—the mountain. Therefore, the balloon was in motion.

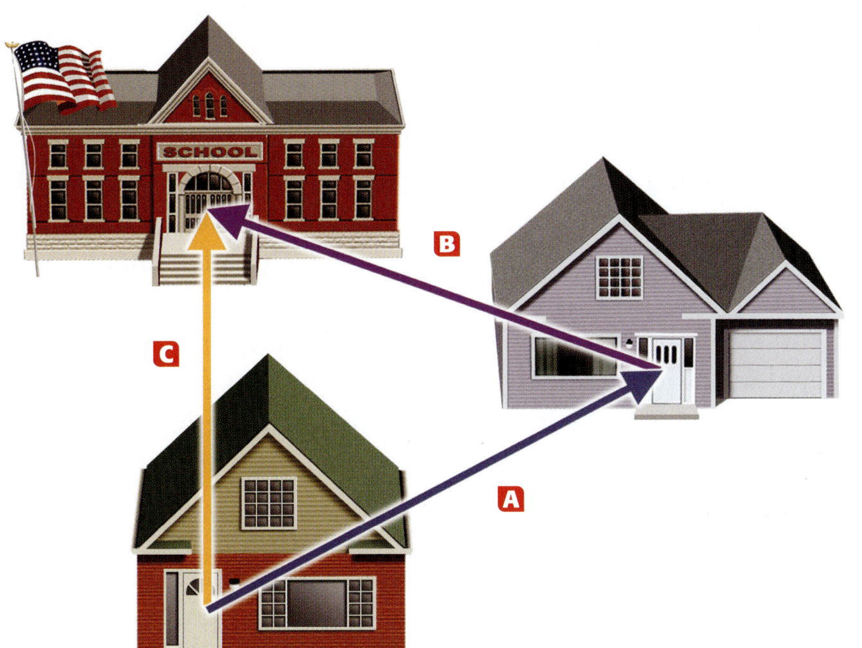

Figure 2

A student walks from his house to his friend's house (A), and then from his friend's house to the school (B). Line (A) plus line (B) equals the total distance he traveled. Line (C) is the displacement he traveled.

Distance measures the path taken

In addition to direction, you also need to know how far an object moves if you want to accurately describe its motion. To measure distance, you measure the actual path you took. If you started at your home and wandered around your neighborhood for a while by changing directions a few times, a string that followed your path would be as long as the distance you traveled.

Displacement is the change of an object's position

If you stretched a string in a straight line from your home directly to your final destination, the length of that string would be your **displacement.** This concept is illustrated in ***Figure 2*** above. In that illustration, the total of line (A) plus line (B) represents the actual distance traveled. Line (C) represents displacement, which is the change in position.

There are two differences between distance and displacement: straightness and direction. Distance can be a straight line, but it doesn't have to be. Displacement must be a straight line. So, displacement is shorter than the actual distance traveled unless the actual distance traveled is a straight line from the initial position to the final position.

Also, displacement must be in a particular direction. The distance between your home and school may be twelve blocks, but that information doesn't indicate whether you are going toward or away from school. Displacement must always indicate the direction, such as twelve blocks *toward school.*

displacement the change in position of an object

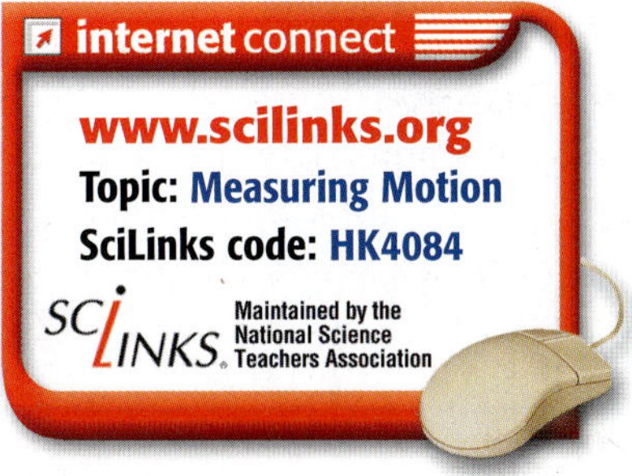

Speed and Velocity

As has been stated, an object is moving if its position changes against some background that stays the same. In ***Figure 3,*** a horse is seen galloping against the background of stationary trees. The change in position as compared to a reference frame or reference point is measured in terms of an object's displacement from a fixed point.

You know from everyday experience that some objects move faster than others. **Speed** describes how fast an object moves. ***Figure 3*** shows speeds for some familiar things. A speeding race car moves faster than a galloping horse. But how do we determine speed?

speed the distance traveled divided by the time interval during which the motion occurred

Speed measurements involve distance and time

To find speed, you must measure two quantities: the distance traveled by an object and the time it took to travel that distance. Notice that all the speeds shown in ***Figure 3*** are expressed as a distance unit divided by a time unit. The SI unit for speed is meters per second (m/s). Speed is sometimes expressed in other units, such as kilometers per hour (km/h) or miles per hour (mi/h). The captions for ***Figure 3*** express speed in all three of these units of measurement.

When an object covers equal distances in equal amounts of time, it is moving at a *constant speed.* For example, if a race car has a constant speed of 96 m/s, the race car travels a distance of 96 meters every second, as shown in ***Table 1.*** So, the term *constant speed* means that the speed does not change. As you probably know, most objects do not move with constant speed.

Table 1
Distance-Time Values for a Race Car

Time (s)	Distance (m)
0	0
1	96
2	192
3	288
4	384

Figure 3
We encounter a wide range of speeds in our everyday life.

1.4 m/s
5.0 km/h
3.1 mi/h
Walking person

7.3 m/s
26 km/h
16 mi/h
Wheelchair racer

19 m/s
68 km/h
42 mi/h
Galloping horse

Speed can be studied with graphs and equations

You can investigate the relationship between distance and time in many ways. You can plot a graph with distance on the vertical axis and time on the horizontal axis, you can use mathematical equations and calculations, or you can combine these two approaches. Whatever method you use, your measurements are always either distances or displacements and time intervals during which the distances or displacements occur.

Speed can be determined from a distance-time graph

In a distance-time graph the distance covered by an object is noted at regular intervals of time, as shown on the line graph in ***Figure 4.*** Line graphs are usually made with the *x*-axis (horizontal axis) representing the independent variable and the *y*-axis (vertical axis) representing the dependent variable.

On our graph, time is the independent variable because time will pass whether distance is traveled or not. Distance is the dependent variable because the distance traveled depends upon the amount of time the object is moving. So, time is plotted on the *x*-axis and distance is plotted on the *y*-axis.

For a race car moving at a constant speed, the distance-time graph is a straight line. The speed of the race car can be found by calculating the slope of the line. The slope of any distance-time graph gives the speed of the object.

Suppose all objects in ***Figure 3*** are moving at a constant speed. The distance-time graph of each object is drawn in ***Figure 4.*** Notice that the distance-time graph for a faster moving object is steeper than the graph for a slower moving object. An object at rest, such as a parked car, has a speed of 0 m/s. Its position does not change as time goes by. So, the distance-time graph of a resting object is a flat line with a slope of zero.

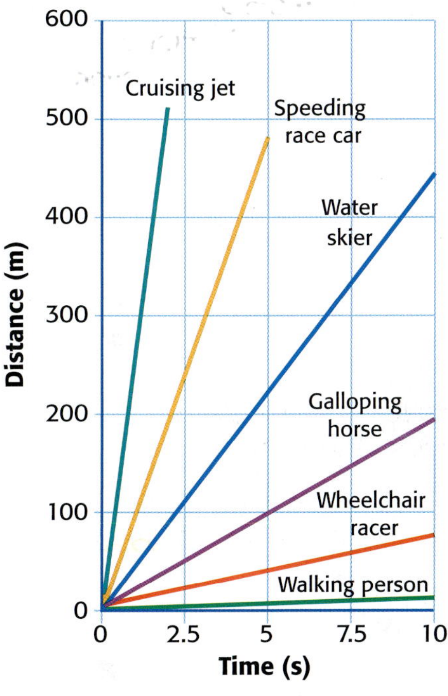

Figure 4

When an object's motion is graphed by plotting distance on the *y*-axis and time on the *x*-axis, the slope of the graph is speed.

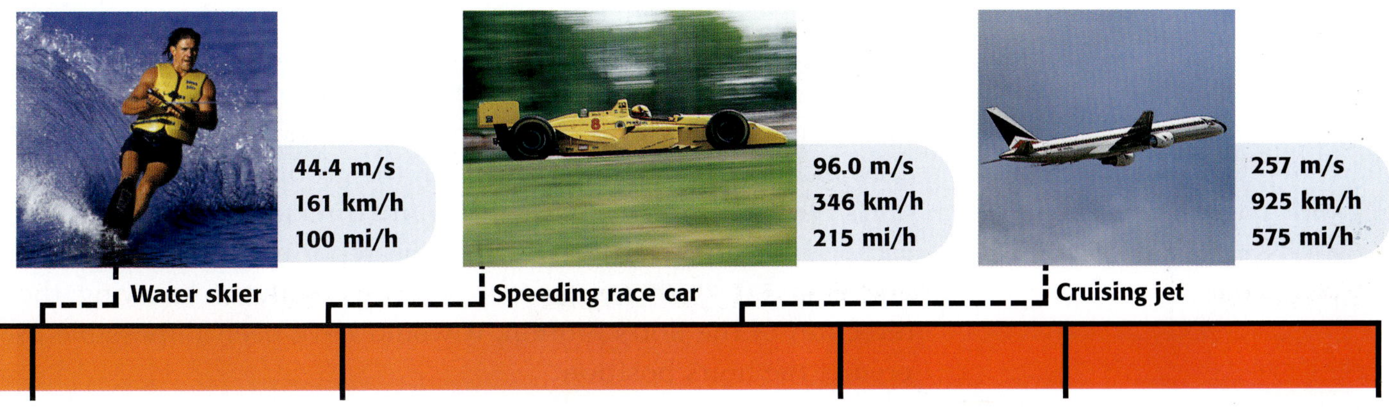

Average speed is calculated as distance divided by time

Most objects do not move at a constant speed. The speed of an object can change from one instant to another. One way to describe the motion of an object moving at changing speeds is to use *average speed.* Average speed is simply the distance traveled by an object divided by the time the object takes to travel that distance. Average speed can also be expressed as a simple mathematical formula.

Figure 5

A wheelchair racer's speed can be determined by timing the racer on a set course.

Equation for Average Speed

$$speed = \frac{distance}{time} \qquad v = \frac{d}{t}$$

Suppose a wheelchair racer, such as the one shown in ***Figure 5,*** finishes a 132 m race in 18 s. By inserting the time and distance measurements into the formula, you can calculate the racer's average speed.

$$v = \frac{d}{t} = \frac{132 \text{ m}}{18 \text{ s}} = 7.3 \text{ m/s}$$

The racer's average speed over the entire distance is 7.3 m/s. But the racer probably did not travel at this speed for the whole race. For instance, the racer's pace may have been faster near the start of the race and slower near the end as the racer became tired.

Instantaneous speed is the speed at a given point in time

You could find the racer's speed at any given point in time by measuring the distance traveled in a shorter time interval. The smaller the time interval, the more accurate the measurement of speed would be. Speed measured in an infinitely small time interval is called *instantaneous speed.* Although it is impossible to measure an infinitely small time interval, some devices measure speed over very small time intervals. For practical purposes, a car's speedometer gives the instantaneous speed of the car.

Velocity describes both speed and direction

velocity the speed of an object in a particular direction

Sometimes, describing the speed of an object is not enough. You may also need to know the direction in which the object is moving. In 1997, a 200 kg (450 lb) lion escaped from a zoo in Florida. The lion was located by searchers in a helicopter. The helicopter crew was able to guide searchers on the ground by reporting the lion's **velocity,** which is its speed *and* direction of motion. The escaped lion's velocity may have been reported as 4.5 m/s *to the north* or 2.0 km/h *toward the highway.* Without knowing the direction of the lion's motion, it would have been impossible to predict the lion's position.

The direction of motion can be described in various ways, such as east, west, south, or north of a fixed point. Or, it can be an angle from a fixed line. Also, direction can be described as positive or negative along the line of motion. So, if a body is moving in one direction, it has positive velocity. If it is moving in the opposite direction, it has negative velocity. In this book, velocity is considered to be positive in the direction of motion.

Math Skills

Velocity Metal stakes are sometimes placed in glaciers to help measure a glacier's movement. For several days in 1936, Alaska's Black Rapids glacier surged as swiftly as 89 meters per day down the valley. Find the glacier's velocity in m/s. Remember to include direction.

1 List the given and the unknown values.

Given: *time,* $t = 1$ day

displacement, $d = 89$ m down the valley

Unknown: *velocity,* $v = ?$ (m/s and direction)

2 Perform any necessary conversions.

To find the velocity in meters per second, the value for time must be in seconds.

$$t = 1 \text{ day} = 24 \text{ h} \times \frac{60 \text{ min}}{1 \text{ h}} \times \frac{60 \text{ s}}{1 \text{ min}}$$

$$t = 86\,400 \text{ s} = 8.64 \times 10^4 \text{ s}$$

3 Write the equation for speed.

$$\text{speed} = \frac{\textit{displacement}}{\textit{time}} = \frac{d}{t}$$

4 Insert the known values into the equation, and solve.

$$v = \frac{d}{t} = \frac{89 \text{ m}}{8.64 \times 10^4 \text{ s}} \text{ (For velocity, include direction.)}$$

$$v = 1.0 \times 10^{-3} \text{ m/s down the valley}$$

Practice

Velocity

1. Find the velocity in m/s of a swimmer who swims 110 m toward the shore in 72 s.
2. Find the velocity in m/s of a baseball thrown 38 m from third base to first base in 1.7 s.
3. Calculate the displacement in meters a cyclist would travel in 5.00 h at an average velocity of 12.0 km/h to the southwest.

- When a problem requires you to calculate velocity, you can use the speed equation. Remember to specify direction.
- The speed equation can also be rearranged to isolate distance or displacement on the left side of the equation in the following way.

$$v = \frac{d}{t}$$

Multiply both sides by t

$$v \times t = \frac{d}{t} \times t$$

$$vt = d$$

$$d = vt$$

You will need to use this form of the equation in Practice Problem 3. Remember to specify direction when you are asked for a displacement.

Figure 6

Determining Resultant Velocity

Person's resultant velocity

15 m/s east + 1 m/s east = 16 m/s east

A When you have two velocities that are in the same direction, add them together to find the resultant velocity, which is in the direction of the two velocities.

Person's resultant velocity

15 m/s east + (−1 m/s west) = 14 m/s east

B When you have two velocities that are in opposite directions, add the positive velocity to the negative velocity to find the resultant velocity, which is in the direction of the larger velocity.

Combine velocities to determine resultant velocities

If you are riding in a bus traveling east at 15 m/s, you and all the other passengers are traveling at a velocity of 15 m/s east. But suppose you stand up and walk down the bus's aisle while it is moving. Are you still moving at the same velocity as the bus? No! ***Figure 6*** shows how you can combine velocities to determine the *resultant velocity.*

SECTION 1 REVIEW

SUMMARY

- When an object changes position in comparison to a stationary reference point, the object is in motion.
- The average speed of an object is defined as the distance the object travels divided by the time of travel.
- The distance-time graph of an object moving at constant speed is a straight line. The slope of the line is the object's speed.
- The velocity of an object consists of both its speed and its direction of motion.

1. **Describe** the measurements necessary to find the average speed of a high school track athlete.
2. **Determine** the unit of a caterpillar's speed if you measure the distance in centimeters (cm) and the time it takes to travel that distance in minutes (min).
3. **Identify** the following measurements as speed or velocity.
   a. 88 km/h
   b. 19 m/s to the west
   c. 18 m/s down
   d. 10 m/s
4. **Critical Thinking** Imagine that you could ride a baseball that is hit high enough and far enough for a home run. Using the baseball as a reference frame, what does the Earth appear to do?

Math Skills

5. How much time does it take for a student running at an average speed of 5.00 m/s to cover a distance of 2.00 km?

SECTION 2

Acceleration

OBJECTIVES

- **Describe** the concept of acceleration as a change in velocity.
- **Explain** why circular motion is continuous acceleration even when the speed does not change.
- **Calculate** acceleration as the rate at which velocity changes.
- **Graph** acceleration on a velocity-time graph.

KEY TERMS
acceleration

When you increase speed, your velocity changes. Your velocity also changes if you decrease speed or if your motion changes direction. For example, your velocity changes when you turn a corner. Any time you change velocity, you are accelerating. Any change in velocity is called **acceleration.**

acceleration the rate at which velocity changes over time; an object accelerates if its speed, direction, or both change

Acceleration and Motion

Imagine that you are a race car driver. You press on the accelerator. The car goes forward, moving faster and faster each second. Like velocity, acceleration has direction. When the car is speeding up, it is accelerating positively. Positive acceleration is in the same direction as the motion and increases velocity.

Acceleration can be a change in speed

Suppose you are facing south on your bike and you start moving and speed up as you go. Every second, your southward velocity increases, as shown in ***Figure 7.*** After 1 s, your velocity is 1 m/s south. After 2 s, your velocity is 2 m/s south. Your velocity after 5 s is 5 m/s south. Your acceleration can be expressed as an increase of one meter per second per second (1 m/s/s) or 1 m/s^2 south.

Figure 7
You are accelerating whenever your speed changes. This cyclist's speed increases by 1 m/s every second.

Figure 8

These skaters accelerate when changing direction, even if their speed doesn't change.

Acceleration can also be a change in direction

Besides being a change in speed, acceleration can also be a change in direction. The skaters in ***Figure 8*** are accelerating because they are changing direction. Why is changing direction considered to be an acceleration? Acceleration is defined as the rate at which velocity changes over time. Velocity includes both speed and direction, so an object accelerates if its speed, direction, or both change. This idea leads to the seemingly strange but correct conclusion that you can constantly accelerate while never speeding up or slowing down.

If you travel at a constant speed in a circle, even though your speed is never changing, your direction is always changing. So, you are always accelerating. The moon is constantly accelerating in its orbit around Earth. A motorcyclist who rides around the inside of a large barrel is constantly accelerating. When you ride a Ferris wheel at an amusement park, you are accelerating. All these examples have one thing in common—change in direction as the cause of acceleration.

Uniform circular motion is constant acceleration

Are you surprised to find out that as you stand on Earth you are accelerating? After all, you are not changing speed, and you are not changing direction—or are you? In fact, you are traveling in a circle as Earth revolves. An object traveling in a circular motion is always changing its direction. As a result, its velocity is always changing, even if its speed does not change. Thus, acceleration is occurring. The acceleration that occurs in uniform circular motion is known as centripetal acceleration. Another example of *centripetal acceleration* is shown in ***Figure 9.***

Figure 9

The blades of these windmills are constantly changing direction as they travel in a circle. So, centripetal acceleration is occurring.

Calculating Acceleration

To find the acceleration of an object moving in a straight line, you need to measure the object's velocity at different times. The average acceleration over a given time interval can be calculated by dividing the change in the object's velocity by the time in which the change occurs. The change in an object's velocity is symbolized by Δv.

Acceleration Equation (for straight-line motion)

$$acceleration = \frac{final\ velocity - initial\ velocity}{time} \qquad a = \frac{\Delta v}{t}$$

If the acceleration is small, the velocity is increasing very gradually. If the acceleration has a greater value, the velocity is increasing more rapidly. For example, a human can accelerate at about 2 m/s^2. On the other hand, a sports car that goes from 0 km/h to 96 km/h (60 mi/h) in 3.7 s has an acceleration of 7.2 m/s^2.

Because we use only positive velocity in this book, a positive acceleration always means the object's velocity is increasing—the object is speeding up. Negative acceleration means the object's velocity is decreasing—the object is slowing down.

INTEGRATING

MATHEMATICS

In the seventeenth century, both Sir Isaac Newton and Gottfried Leibniz studied acceleration and other rates of change. Independently, each created calculus, a branch of math that allows for describing rates of change of a quantity like velocity.

Acceleration is the rate at which velocity changes

People often use the word *accelerate* to mean "speed up," but in science it describes any change in velocity. Imagine that you are skating down the sidewalk. You see a large rock in your path. You slow down and swerve to avoid the rock. A friend says, "That was great acceleration. I'm amazed that you could slow down and turn so quickly!" You accelerated because your velocity changed. The velocity decreased in speed, and you changed directions. So, your velocity changed in two different ways.

The student in ***Figure 10*** is accelerating to a stop. Suppose this student was originally going at 20 m/s and stopped in 0.50 s. The change in velocity is 0 m/s − 20 m/s = −20 m/s, which is negative because the student is slowing down. The student's acceleration is

$$\frac{0\ m/s - 20\ m/s}{0.50\ s} = -40\ m/s^2$$

Figure 10

The rate of velocity change is acceleration, whether it is direction or speed that changes.

When you press on the gas pedal in a car, you speed up. Your acceleration is in the direction of the motion and therefore is positive. When you press on the brake pedal, your acceleration is opposite the direction of motion. You slow down, and your acceleration is negative. When you turn the steering wheel, your velocity changes because you are changing direction.

Disc Two, Module 9:
Speed and Acceleration
Use the Interactive Tutor to learn more about these topics.

Math Skills

Acceleration A flowerpot falls off a second-story windowsill. The flowerpot starts from rest and hits the sidewalk 1.5 s later with a velocity of 14.7 m/s. Find the average acceleration of the flowerpot.

1 List the given and unknown values.

Given: *time*, $t = 1.5$ s

initial velocity, $v_i = 0$ m/s

final velocity, $v_f = 14.7$ m/s down

Unknown: *acceleration*, $a = ?$ m/s^2 (and direction)

2 Write the equation for acceleration.

$$acceleration = \frac{final\ velocity - initial\ velocity}{time} = \frac{v_f - v_i}{t}$$

3 Insert the known values into the equation, and solve.

$$a = \frac{v_f - v_i}{t} = \frac{14.7 \text{ m/s} - 0 \text{ m/s}}{1.5 \text{ s}}$$

$$a = \frac{14.7 \text{ m/s}}{1.5 \text{ s}} = 9.8 \text{ m/s}^2 \text{ down}$$

Practice HINT

- When a problem asks you to calculate acceleration, you can use the acceleration equation.

$$a = \frac{\Delta v}{t}$$

To solve for other variables, rearrange it as follows.

- To isolate t, first multiply both sides by t.

$$a \times t = \frac{\Delta v}{t} \times t$$

$$\Delta v = at$$

Next divide both sides by a.

$$\frac{\Delta v}{a} = \frac{at}{a}$$

$$t = \frac{\Delta v}{a}$$

You will need to use this form of the equation in Practice Problem 4.

- In Practice Problem 5, isolate final velocity.

$$v_f = v_i + at$$

Practice

Acceleration

1. Natalie accelerates her skateboard along a straight path from 0 m/s to 4.0 m/s in 2.5 s. Find her average acceleration.
2. A turtle swimming in a straight line toward shore has a speed of 0.50 m/s. After 4.0 s, its speed is 0.80 m/s. What is the turtle's average acceleration?
3. Find the average acceleration of a northbound subway train that slows down from 12 m/s to 9.6 m/s in 0.8 s.
4. Marisa's car accelerates at an average rate of 2.6 m/s^2. Calculate how long it takes her car to speed up from 24.6 m/s to 26.8 m/s.
5. A cyclist travels at a constant velocity of 4.5 m/s westward, and then speeds up with a steady acceleration of 2.3 m/s^2. Calculate the cyclist's speed after accelerating for 5.0 s.

Acceleration can be determined from a velocity-time graph

You have learned that an object's speed can be determined from a distance-time graph of its motion. You can also make a velocity-time graph by plotting velocity on the vertical axis and time on the horizontal axis.

A straight line on a velocity-time graph means that the velocity changes by the same amount over each time interval. This is called *constant acceleration*. The slope of a line on a velocity-time graph gives you the value of the acceleration. A line with a positive slope represents an object that is speeding up. A line with a negative slope represents an object that is slowing down. A straight horizontal line represents an object that has an unchanging velocity and therefore has no acceleration.

The bicyclists in ***Figure 11A*** are riding in a straight line at a constant speed of 13.00 m/s, as shown by the data in ***Table 2.*** ***Figure 11B*** is a distance-time graph for the cyclists. Because the velocity is constant, the graph is a straight line. The slope of the line equals the cyclists' velocity. ***Figure 11C*** is a velocity-time graph for the same cyclists. The slope of this line represents the cyclists' acceleration. In this case, the slope is zero (a horizontal line) because the acceleration is zero.

Did You Know?

The faster a car goes, the longer it takes a given braking force to bring the car to a stop. *Braking distance* describes how far a car travels between the moment the brakes are applied and the moment the car stops. As a car's speed increases, so does its braking distance. For example, when a car's speed is doubled, its braking distance is four times as long.

Figure 11

A When you ride your bike straight ahead at constant speed, you are not accelerating, because neither your velocity nor your direction changes.

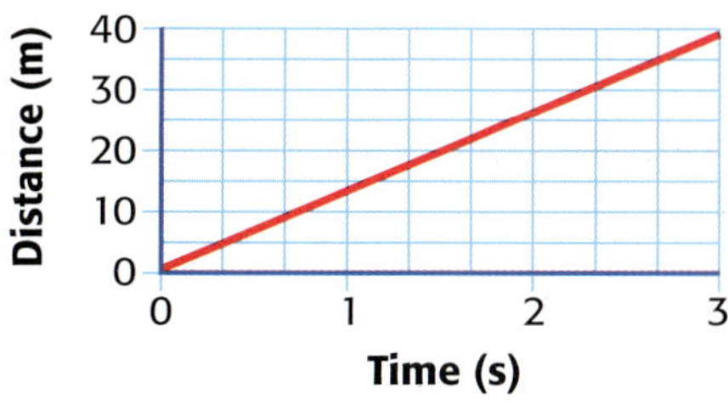

B If you plot the distance traveled against the time it takes, the resulting graph is a straight line with a slope of 13.00 m/s.

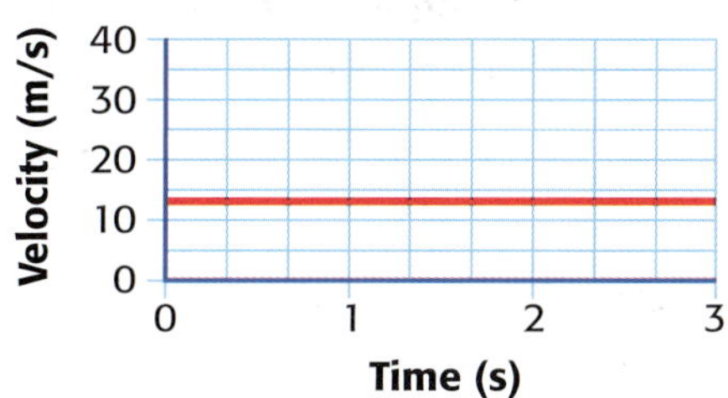

C Plotting the velocity against time results in a horizontal line because the velocity does not change. The acceleration is 0 m/s^2.

Table 2
Data for a Bicycle with Constant Speed

Time (s)	Speed (m/s)
0	13.00
1	13.00
2	13.00
3	13.00
4	13.00

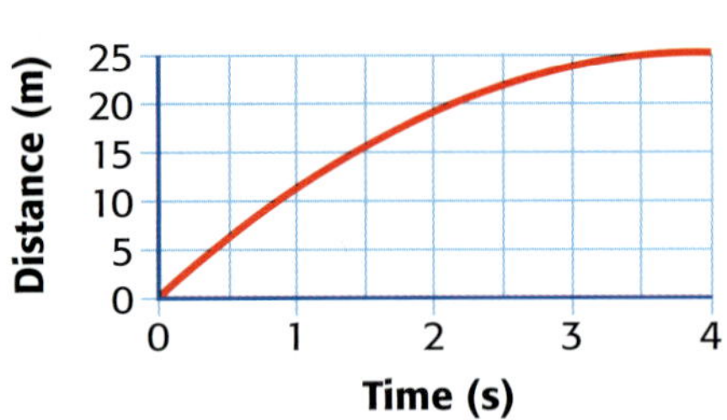

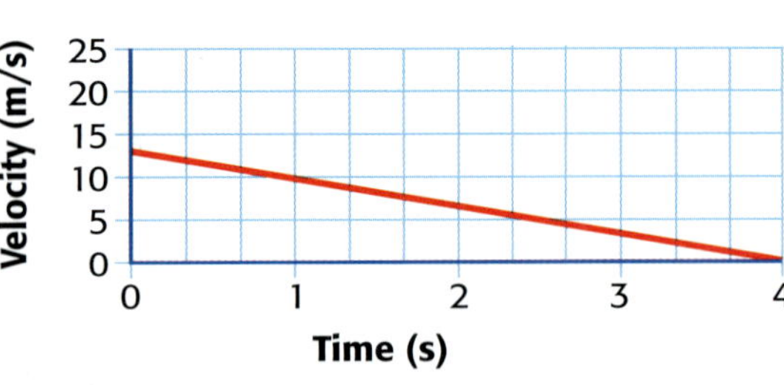

Figure 12

A When you slow down, your velocity changes. Your acceleration is negative because you are decreasing your velocity.

B If you plot the distance you travel against the time it takes you, the distance you travel each second becomes shorter and shorter until you finally stop.

C Plotting the velocity against time results in a line that has a negative slope, which means the acceleration is negative.

Table 3
Data for a Slowing Bicycle

Time (s)	Speed (m/s)
0	13.00
1	9.75
2	6.50
3	3.25
4	0

The rider in ***Figure 12A*** is slowing down from 13.00 m/s to 3.25 m/s over a period of 3.00 s, as shown by the data in ***Table 3.*** You can find out the rate at which velocity changes by calculating the acceleration.

$$a = \frac{3.25 \text{ m/s} - 13.00 \text{ m/s}}{3.00 \text{ s}} = -3.25 \text{ m/s}^2$$

The rider's velocity decreases by 3.25 m/s each second. The acceleration has a negative sign because the rider is slowing down. ***Figure 12B*** is a distance-time graph of the rider's motion, and ***Figure 12C*** is a velocity-time graph.

SECTION 2 REVIEW

SUMMARY

- Acceleration is a change in an object's velocity. Accelerating means speeding up, slowing down, or changing direction.
- For straight-line motion, average acceleration is defined as the change in an object's velocity per unit of time.
- Circular motion is acceleration because of the constant change of direction.
- A velocity-time graph can be used to determine acceleration.

1. **Identify** the straight-line accelerations below as either speeding up or slowing down.
   a. 5.7 m/s^2
   b. -9.8 m/s^2
   c. -2.43 m/s^2
   d. 9.8 m/s^2
2. **Critical Thinking** Joshua skates in a straight line at a constant speed for one minute, then begins going in circles at the same rate of speed, and then finally begins to increase speed. When is he accelerating? Explain your answer.

Math Skills

3. What is the final speed of a skater who accelerates at a rate of 2.0 m/s^2 from rest for 3.5 s?
4. Graph the velocity of a car accelerating at a uniform rate from 7.0 m/s to 12.0 m/s in 2.0 s. Calculate the acceleration.

SECTION 3

Motion and Force

OBJECTIVES

- **Explain** the effects of unbalanced forces on the motion of objects.
- **Compare and contrast** static and kinetic friction.
- **Describe** how friction may be either harmful or helpful.
- **Identify** ways in which friction can be reduced or increased.

KEY TERMS

force
friction
static friction
kinetic friction

You often hear the word **force** in everyday conversation: "That storm had a lot of force!" "Our basketball team is a force to be reckoned with." But what exactly is a force? In science, force is defined as anything that changes the state of rest or motion of an object. This section will explore how forces change motions.

force an action exerted on a body in order to change the body's state of rest or motion; force has magnitude and direction

Balanced and Unbalanced Forces

When you throw or catch a ball, you exert a force to change the ball's velocity. What causes an object to change its velocity, or accelerate? Usually, many forces are acting on an object at any given time. The *net force* is the combination of all of the forces acting on the object. Whenever there is a net force acting on an object, the object accelerates in the direction of the net force. An object will not accelerate if the net force acting on it is zero.

Balanced forces do not change motion

When the forces applied to an object produce a net force of zero, the forces are balanced. *Balanced forces* do not cause an object at rest to start moving. Furthermore, balanced forces do not cause a change in the motion of a moving object.

Many objects have only balanced forces acting on them. For example, a light hanging from the ceiling does not move up or down, because an elastic force due to tension pulls the light up and balances the force of gravity pulling the light down. A hat resting on your head is also an example of balanced forces. In ***Figure 13,*** the opposing forces on the piano are balanced. Therefore, the piano remains at rest.

Figure 13
The forces applied by these two students balance each other, so the piano does not move.

Figure 14
When two opposite forces acting on the same object are unequal, the forces are unbalanced. A change in motion occurs in the direction of the greater force.

Unbalanced forces do not cancel completely

In ***Figure 14,*** another student pushes on one side of the piano. In this case, there are two students pushing against the piano on one side and only one student pushing against the piano on the other side. If the students all have the same mass and are all pushing with the same force, there is an *unbalanced force:* two students pushing against one student. Because the net force on the piano is greater than zero, the piano will begin to accelerate in the direction of the greater force.

What happens if forces act in different directions that are not opposite each other? In this situation, the combination of forces acts like a single force on the object, which causes acceleration in a direction that combines the directions of the applied forces. If you push eastward on a box, and your friend pushes northward, the box will accelerate in a northeasterly direction.

VOCABULARY Skills Tip

The word force *comes from the Latin word* fortis, *which means "strength." The word* fortress *comes from the same root.*

The Force of Friction

Imagine a car that is rolling along a flat, evenly paved street. Experience tells you that the car will keep slowing down until it eventually stops. This steady change in the car's speed gives you a clue that a force must be acting on the car. The unbalanced force that acts against the car's direction of motion is **friction.**

Friction occurs because the surface of any object is rough. Even surfaces that look or feel very smooth are actually covered with microscopic hills and valleys. When two surfaces are in contact, the hills and valleys of one surface stick to the hills and valleys of the other surface.

friction a force that opposes motion between two surfaces that are in contact

Friction opposes the applied force

Because of friction, a constant force must be applied to a car just to keep it moving. The force pushing the car forward must be greater than the force of friction opposing the car's motion, as shown in ***Figure 15A.*** Once the car reaches its desired speed, the car will maintain this speed if the forces acting on the car are balanced, as shown in ***Figure 15B.***

Friction also affects objects that aren't moving. For example, when a truck is parked on a hill with its brakes set, as shown in ***Figure 15C,*** friction opposes the force of gravity along the hill and prevents the truck from rolling away.

Static friction is greater than kinetic friction

The friction between surfaces that are stationary is called **static friction.** The friction between moving surfaces is called **kinetic friction.** Because of forces between molecules of the two surfaces, the force required to make a stationary object start moving is usually greater than the force necessary to keep it moving. In other words, static friction is usually greater than kinetic friction.

static friction the force that resists the initiation of sliding motion between two surfaces that are in contact and at rest

kinetic friction the force that opposes the movement of two surfaces that are in contact and are sliding over each other

Not all kinetic friction is the same

There are different kinds of kinetic friction. The type of friction depends on the motion and the nature of the objects. For example, when objects slide past each other, the friction that occurs is called *sliding friction.* If a round object rolls over a flat surface, the friction is called *rolling friction.* Rolling friction is usually less than sliding friction.

Figure 15

Frictional Forces and Acceleration

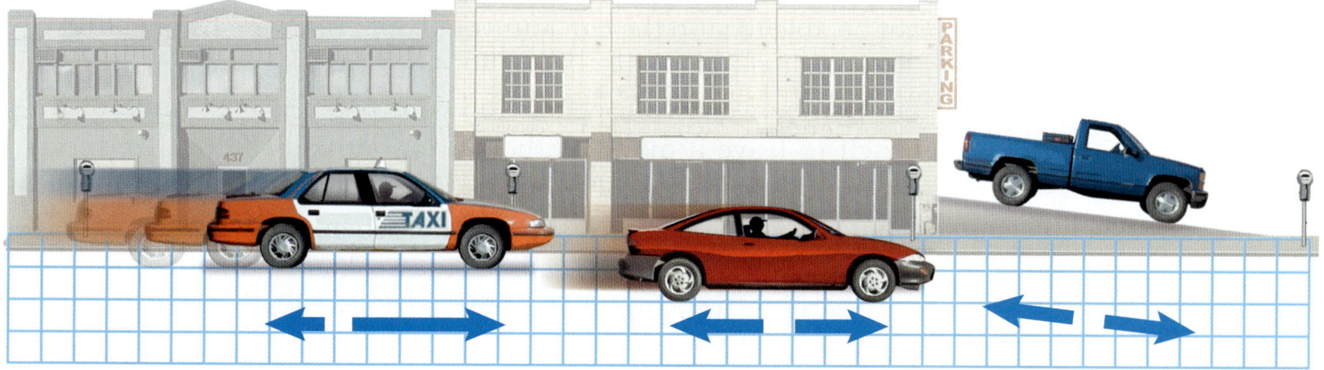

Unbalanced forces: acceleration

A When a car is accelerating, the forces are unbalanced. The force moving the car forward is greater than the opposing force of friction.

Balanced forces: constant speed

B When a car is cruising at constant speed, the force moving the car forward is balanced by the force of friction.

Balanced forces: no motion

C This truck does not roll. The force of friction between the brakes and the wheels balances the force of gravity.

Figure 16

With the need for better fuel efficiency and increased speed, car designs have been changed to reduce air resistance. Modern cars are much more aerodynamic than cars of earlier eras.

Air resistance also opposes motion

Any object moving through a fluid such as air encounters friction between the air and the surface of the moving object. That friction is called *fluid friction.* Air slides past a car as it moves, which causes fluid friction. Fluid friction can be minimized by very smooth surfaces.

In addition to fluid friction, another factor involved in air resistance is the displacement of air. For example, as a car moves, it must push air out of the way. The car must displace a certain volume of air for each car length that it moves. Air resistance to the car's motion increases as the car travels faster, because more air must be moved each second. This effect is very different from kinetic friction. The amount of air moved depends on the shape of the car. Designing the shape of the car so that less air must be displaced, as shown in **Figure 16,** is called *streamlining.*

Friction and Motion

Without friction, the tires of a car would not be able to push against the ground and move the car forward, the brakes would not be able to stop the car, and you would not even be able to grip the door handle to get inside! Without friction, a car is useless. Friction between your pencil and your paper is necessary for the pencil to leave a mark. Without friction, balls and other sports equipment would slip from your fingers when you tried to pick them up, and you would slip and fall when you tried to walk.

However, friction can cause some problems, too. In a car, friction between moving engine parts increases their temperature and causes the parts to wear down. Motor oil must be regularly added to the engine to keep it from overheating due to friction, and engine parts need to be changed as they wear out.

Harmful friction can be reduced

Because friction can be both harmful and helpful, it is sometimes desirable to reduce or increase friction. One way to reduce harmful friction is to use *lubricants*. Lubricants are substances that are applied to surfaces to reduce the friction between them. Some examples of common lubricants are motor oil, wax, and grease. ***Figure 17*** shows why lubricants are important to maintaining car parts.

Lubricants are usually liquids, but they can be solids or gases, too. An example of a lubricant gas is the air that comes out of the tiny holes of an air-hockey table.

Friction can also be reduced by replacing sliding friction with rolling friction. Ball bearings are placed between the wheels and axles of in-line skates and bicycles to reduce friction and thereby make the wheels turn more easily.

Another way to reduce friction is to make the surfaces smoother. For example, sliding across rough wood on a park bench can be uncomfortable if there is a large amount of friction between your legs and the bench. Rubbing the bench with sandpaper makes it smoother and therefore more comfortable for sitting, because the friction between the bench and your legs is reduced.

Competitive swimmers and bikers reduce the amount of fluid friction by wearing clothes that fit closely. Even their headgear is designed to decrease fluid friction in both the air and the water.

Figure 17

Motor oil is used as a lubricant in car engines. Without oil, engine parts would wear down quickly, like the connecting rod shown on the right of this photograph.

Helpful friction can be increased

One way to increase helpful friction is to make surfaces rougher. For example, sand scattered on icy roads keeps cars from skidding. Baseball players sometimes wear textured batting gloves to increase the friction between their hands and the bat so that the bat does not slide or fly out of their hands.

Another way to increase friction is to increase the force pushing the surfaces together. For example, you can ensure that your magazine will not blow away at the park by putting a heavy rock on it. The added mass of the rock increases the friction between the magazine and the ground or park bench. If you are sanding a piece of wood, you can sand the wood faster by pressing harder on the sandpaper. ***Figure 18*** gives another example of a way to increase helpful friction.

Figure 18

No one enjoys cleaning pans with baked-on food! To make the chore pass quickly, press down on the pan with the scrubber to increase friction.

Figure 19

Without friction, a car cannot be controlled.

Cars could not move without friction

What causes a car to move? A car's wheels turn, and they push against the road. The road pushes back on the car and causes the car to accelerate. Without friction between the tires and the road, the tires would not be able to push against the road, and the car would not experience a net force. Friction, therefore, causes the acceleration (whether speeding up, slowing down, or changing direction).

Water, snow, and ice provide less friction between the road and the car than usual. Normally, as a car moves slowly over water on the road, the water is pushed out from under the tires. However, if the car moves too quickly, the water becomes trapped and cannot be pushed out from under the tires. The water trapped between the tires and the road may lift the car off the road, as shown in ***Figure 19.*** This is called *hydroplaning*. When hydroplaning occurs, there is very little friction between the tires and the water, and the car becomes difficult to control. This dangerous situation is an example of the need for friction.

SECTION 3 REVIEW

SUMMARY

- Objects subjected to balanced forces either do not move or move at constant velocity.
- An unbalanced force must be present to cause any change in an object's state of motion or rest.
- Friction is a force that opposes motion between the surfaces of objects moving, or attempting to move, past each other.
- Static friction opposes motion between two stationary surfaces. Kinetic friction opposes motion between two surfaces that are moving past one another.
- Friction can be helpful or harmful. There are many ways to decrease or increase friction.

1. **Describe** a situation in which unbalanced forces are acting on an object. What is the net force on the object, and how does the net force change the motion of the object?
2. **Identify** the type of friction in each situation described below.
   - **a.** Two students are pushing a box that is at rest.
   - **b.** The box pushed by the students is now sliding.
   - **c.** The students put rollers under the box and push it forward.
3. **Explain** why friction is necessary to drive a car on a road. How could you increase friction on an icy road?
4. **Describe** three different ways to decrease the force of friction between two surfaces that are moving past each other.
5. **Critical Thinking** When you wrap a sandwich in plastic food wrap to protect it, you must first unroll the plastic wrap from the container, and then wrap the plastic around the sandwich. In both steps you encounter friction. In each step, is friction helpful or harmful? Explain your answer.
6. **Critical Thinking** The force pulling a truck downhill is 2000 N. What is the size of the static friction acting on the truck if the truck doesn't move?

Graphing Skills

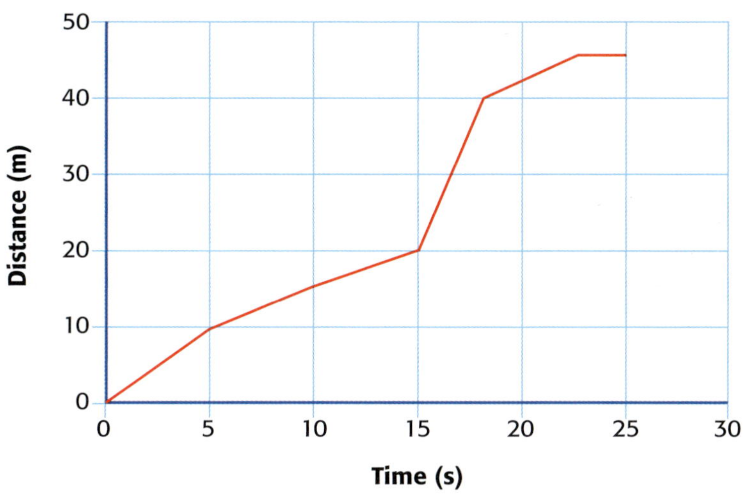

Examine the above graph, and answer the following questions. (See Appendix A for help in interpreting a graph.)

1. Does the graph indicate an increase or decrease of the quantities? Explain your answer.
2. Identify the independent and dependent variables. What is the relationship between the two variables?
3. What information about the runner's speed can be determined from the graph? Is the speed constant during the run?
4. What is the runner's maximum speed? During what time interval does the runner reach this speed? What is the runner's minimum speed?
5. What is the total distance traveled by the runner? What trend suggests that this is the total distance run even when the graph is continued beyond the 25.0 s mark?
6. How is this graph similar to any graph showing distance traveled in a single direction over a given time interval?
7. Construct a graph best suited for the information in the table below. Assuming all measurements are made in 7.0 s, which car has the greatest acceleration? If the time interval for car B is 8.0 s instead of 7.0 s, which car has the greatest acceleration?

Car type	Maximum speed (m/s)
A	23.3
B	28.0
C	26.2

CHAPTER 10 REVIEW

Chapter Highlights

Before you begin, review the summaries of the key ideas of each section, found at the end of each section. The vocabulary terms are listed on the first page of each section.

UNDERSTANDING CONCEPTS

1. If you jog for 1 h and travel 10 km, 10 km/h describes your
a. momentum.
b. average speed.
c. displacement.
d. acceleration.

2. __________ is a speed in a certain direction.
a. Acceleration
b. Friction
c. Momentum
d. Velocity

3. An object's speed is a measure of
a. how fast the object is moving.
b. the object's direction.
c. the object's displacement per unit of time.
d. All of the above

4. A car travels a distance of 210 mi in exactly 4 h. The driver calculates that he traveled 52.5 mi/h. Which of the following terms most nearly describes his calculation?
a. average speed
b. instantaneous speed
c. instantaneous acceleration
d. displacement

5. Which of the quantities below represents a velocity?
a. 25 m/s
b. 10 km/min
c. 15 mi/h eastward
d. 3 mi/h

6. Which of the following is *not* accelerating?
a. a ball being juggled
b. a woman walking at 2.5 m/s along a straight road
c. a satellite circling Earth
d. a braking cyclist

7. At the end of a game, a basketball player on the winning team throws the basketball straight up as high as he can throw it. At the top of its path, the basketball's velocity is
a. 0 m/s.
b. 10 m/s up.
c. 10 m/s down.
d. Not enough information is given to determine its velocity.

8. Which one of the following is *not* caused by a net force?
a. starting up a bicycle that was previously not moving
b. changing a bicycle's speed while it is moving in a straight line
c. changing a bicycle's direction while it is moving at constant speed
d. keeping a bicycle going in a straight line at constant speed

9. A book is sitting still on your desk. Which of the following best describes this situation?
a. There are no forces acting on the book.
b. The book is moving compared to the reference frame.
c. There are balanced forces acting on the book.
d. There are unbalanced forces acting on the book.

USING VOCABULARY

10. State whether 30 m/s westward represents a *speed,* a *velocity,* or both.

11. Why is identifying the *reference frame* important in describing motion?

12. What is the difference between *distance* and *displacement*?

13. What is *uniform circular motion*?

14. How are *friction* and *air resistance* alike? How are they different?

15. How do *static friction* and *kinetic friction* differ from each other?

BUILDING MATH SKILLS

16. **Interpreting Data** Bob straps on his in-line skates and pushes down a hill. His velocity changes from 0 m/s at the start to 4.5 m/s exactly 15 s later. What is Bob's average acceleration?

17. **Interpreting Data** A baseball is hit straight up at an initial velocity of 30 m/s. If the ball has a negative acceleration of about 10 m/s^2, how long does the ball take to reach the top of its path?

18. **Velocity** Heather and Matthew take 45 s to walk eastward along a straight road to a store 72 m away. What is their average velocity?

19. **Velocity** Simpson drives his car with an average velocity of 85 km/h eastward. How long will it take him to drive 560 km on a perfectly straight highway?

20. **Acceleration** A driver is traveling eastward on a dirt road when she spots a pothole ahead. She slows her car from 14.0 m/s to 5.5 m/s in 6.0 s. What is the car's acceleration?

21. **Acceleration** How long will it take a cyclist with a forward acceleration of −0.50 m/s^2 to bring a bicycle with an initial forward velocity of 13.5 m/s to a complete stop?

BUILDING GRAPHING SKILLS

22. **Graphing** The following graphs describe the motion of four different balls—*a, b, c,* and *d.* Use the graphs to determine whether each ball is accelerating, sitting still, or moving at a constant velocity.

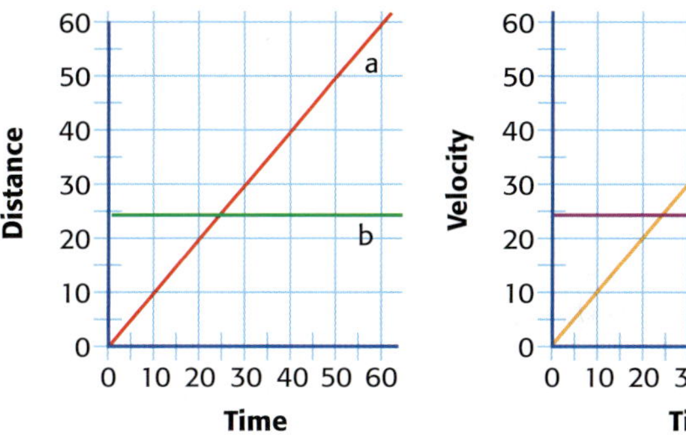

23. **Graphing** A rock is dropped from a bridge, and the distance it travels and the speed at which it is falling are measured every second until it hits the water. The data are shown in the chart below. Make two graphs of the data, a distance-time graph and a velocity-time graph. Use your graphs to answer the questions below.

Time	Distance traveled	Downward speed
0 s	0 m	0 m/s
1 s	5 m	10 m/s
2 s	20 m	20 m/s
3 s	45 m	30 m/s

a. Why is the distance-time graph curved?
b. Why is the velocity-time graph a straight line?
c. Use the velocity-time graph to figure out the rock's acceleration.

CHAPTER 10 REVIEW

THINKING CRITICALLY

24. Drawing Conclusions What can you conclude about the forces acting on an object traveling in uniform circular motion?

25. Applying Knowledge When you drive, you will sometimes have to decide in a brief moment whether to stop for a yellow light. Discuss the variables you must consider in making your decision. Use the concepts of force, acceleration, and velocity in your discussion.

DEVELOPING LIFE/WORK SKILLS

26. Working Cooperatively For one day, write down a brief description of the different kinds of motions you see. Work with a group to generate a common list of the different kinds of motions observed. What reference points did you use to detect the motion? How did these reference points help you determine motion? Compare your list with those from other groups in your class.

27. Applying Information Visit a local hardware store or interview a carpenter to investigate various textures of sandpaper. Write a report describing the kinds of surfaces for which various sandpapers are appropriate, and how they are used. What is a "grit number?" Explain how to choose the *best* grit number for a particular wood surface. Incorporate information about friction from this chapter.

INTEGRATING CONCEPTS

28. Connection to Physical Education A track athlete ran the 50 m dash. She ran 4 m/s during the first 25 m and 5 m/s during the last 25 m. What was her average speed? How long did it take her to run the 50 m dash?

29. Creative Thinking What are some of the ways that competitive swimmers can decrease the amount of friction or drag between themselves and the water they are swimming through? How does each method work to decrease friction?

30. Concept Mapping Copy the unfinished concept map below onto a sheet of paper. Complete the map by writing the correct word or phrase in the lettered boxes.

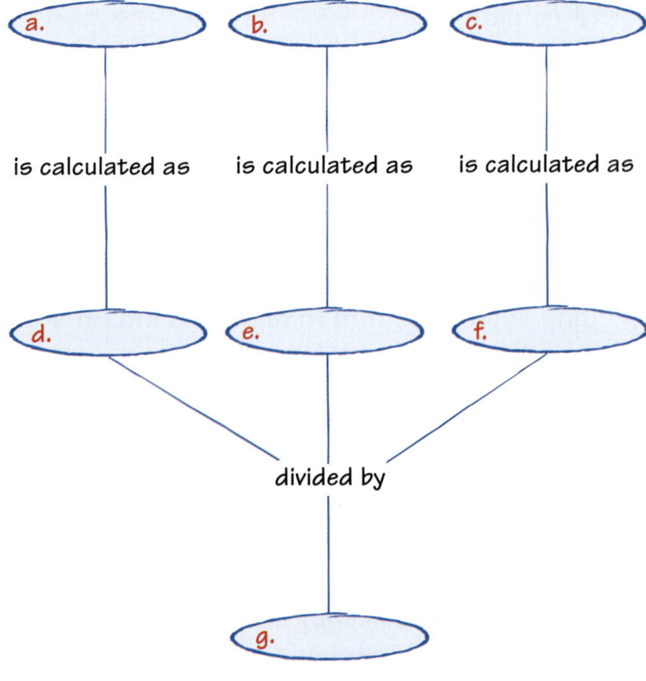

Standardized Test Prep

Understanding Concepts

***Directions (1–3):* For *each* question, write on a separate sheet of paper the letter of the correct answer.**

1 A bicyclist traveling at 10 m/s applies her brakes, reducing her velocity to 5 m/s. If it takes 2 seconds to slow the bike, what is the acceleration during that period?

A. -5 m/s^2 **C.** 0 m/s^2
B. -2.5 m/s^2 **D.** 2.5 m/s^2

2 What happens to a moving object when the forces acting on it are exactly balanced?

F. The object gradually slows and stops moving due to friction.
G. The object moves at a constant speed, neither speeding up nor slowing down.
H. The object accelerates because there is no friction to oppose forces acting on it.
I. The object accelerates because the force of gravity is stronger than friction.

3 For which of the following is the velocity constant?

A. a baseball traveling away from a bat after a hit
B. a bicyclist on an oval track moving at a constant speed of 15 km/h
C. a helicopter hovering motionless above a fixed point on the ground
D. a canoe being carried down a winding river by a steady current

***Directions (4–5):* For *each* question, write a short response.**

4 When describing the motion of an object, why do you need a reference point?

5 A jet airplane must use a substantial amount of fuel to keep flying at a constant velocity. What two forces would change the velocity of the plane if the engines were shut off?

When several questions refer to the same graph or table, answer the questions you are most sure of first.

Reading Skills

***Directions (6):* Read the passage below. Then answer the question.**

Some boats used in calm waters actually float on a cushion of air. A fan blows air below the hull of the craft, while another fan pushes air backward, propelling the boat forward. If the downward fan is turned off, the boat stops moving. The rear-facing fan cannot cause the boat to move until the other fan is turned on again.

6 Demonstrate why the rear-facing fan can accelerate the boat when it is on a cushion of air, but not when it is in contact with the surface of the water.

Interpreting Graphics

***Directions (7–8):* Base your answers to questions 7 and 8 on the graph below, which shows distance (m) versus time (s).**

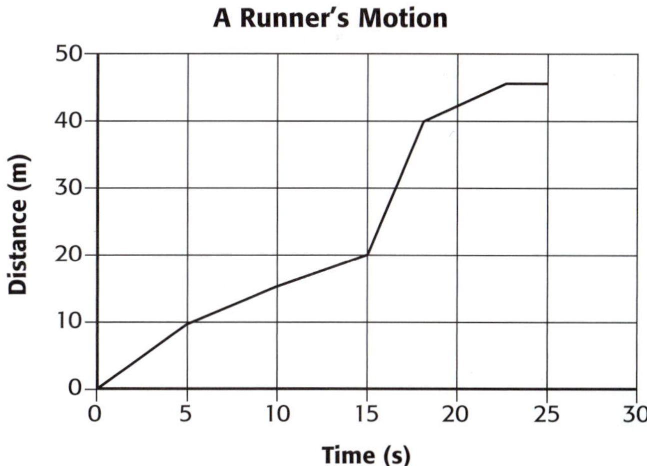

7 What is the average speed of the runner whose motion is plotted on the graph?

F. 1.0 m/s **H.** 2.0 m/s
G. 1.8 m/s **I.** 4.5 m/s

8 During which interval is the runner's average speed the greatest?

A. 0 s to 5 s
B. 5 s to 10 s
C. 15 s to 20 s
D. 20 s to 25 s

Skills Practice Lab

Introduction

In this experiment, you will investigate three types of friction—static, sliding, and rolling—to determine which is the largest force and which is the smallest force.

Objectives

- USING SCIENTIFIC METHODS ***Form a hypothesis*** to predict which type of friction force—static, sliding, or rolling—will be greatest and which will be smallest.
- ***Measure*** the static, sliding, and, rolling friction when pulling a textbook across a table.
- ***Calculate*** average values from multiple trials.
- ***Compare*** results to initial predictions.

Materials

scissors
spring scale
string
textbook (covered)
wooden or metal rods (4)

Static, Sliding, and Rolling Friction

Procedure

Preparing for Your Experiment

1. Which type of friction do you think is the largest force: static, sliding, or rolling? Which is the smallest?
2. Form a hypothesis by writing a short paragraph that answers the question above. Explain your reasoning.
3. Prepare a data table like the one shown at right. **SAFETY CAUTION** Secure loose clothing and remove dangling jewelry. Don't wear open-toed shoes or sandals in the lab. Use knives and other sharp instruments with extreme care. Never cut objects while holding them in your hands. Place objects on a suitable work surface for cutting.

Collecting Data and Testing the Hypothesis

4. Cut a piece of string, and tie it in a loop that fits inside a textbook. Hook the string to the spring scale as shown.
5. To measure the static friction between the book and the table, pull the spring scale very slowly. Gradually increase the force with which you pull on the spring scale until the book starts to slide across the table. Pull very gently. If you pull too hard, the book will start lurching, and you will not get accurate results.
6. Practice pulling the book as in step 5 several times. On a smooth trial, note the largest force that appears on the scale *before* the book starts to move. Record this result in your data table as *static friction.*
7. Repeat step 6 two times, and record the results in your data table.
8. After the textbook begins to move, you can determine the sliding friction. Start pulling the book as in step 5. Once the book starts to slide, continue applying just enough force to keep the book sliding at a slow, constant speed. Practice this several times. On a smooth trial, note the force that appears on the scale as the book is sliding at a slow, constant speed. Record this force in your data table as *sliding friction.*

	Static friction (N)	Sliding friction (N)	Rolling friction (N)
Trial 1			
Trial 2			
Trial 3			
Average			

9. Repeat step 8 two times, and record the results in your data table.
10. Place two or three rods under the textbook to act as rollers. Make sure the rods are evenly spaced. Place another rod in front of the book so that the book will roll onto it. Pull the spring scale slowly so that the book rolls across the rods at a slow, constant speed. Practice this several times, repositioning the rods each time. On a smooth trial, note the force that appears on the scale as the book is moving at a slow, constant speed. Record this force in your data table as *rolling friction*.
11. Repeat step 10 two times, and record the results in your data table.

Analysis

1. **Organizing Data** For each type of friction, add the results of the three trials and divide by three to get an average. Record these averages in your data table.
2. **Analyzing Data** Which of the three types of friction was the largest force on average?
3. **Analyzing Data** Which of the three types of friction was the smallest force on average?

Conclusions

4. **Evaluating Results** Did your answers to Analysis questions 2 and 3 agree with the hypotheses you made before collecting data? If not, explain how your results differed from what you predicted.
5. **Applying Conclusions** Imagine that you are an engineer at a construction site. You are planning to drag a heavy load of building materials on a pallet by using a cable attached to a truck. When will the force exerted by the cable be greatest, before the pallet starts moving or while it is moving? How could you reduce the amount of force needed to move the pallet?
6. **Evaluating Methods** In each trial, the force that you measured was actually the force that you were exerting on the spring scale, which was in turn exerted on the book. Why could you assume that this was equal to the force of friction in each case?

Forces

Chapter Preview

1 **Laws of Motion**
   - Newton's First Law
   - Newton's Second Law

2 **Gravity**
   - Law of Universal Gravitation
   - Free Fall and Weight
   - Free Fall and Motion
   - Projectile Motion and Gravity

3 **Newton's Third Law**
   - Action and Reaction Forces
   - Momentum

Background When you kick a soccer ball, you are applying force to the ball. At the same time, the ball is also applying force to your foot. Force is involved in soccer in many ways. Soccer players have to know what force to apply to the ball. They must be able to anticipate the effects of force so that they will know where the ball is going and how to react. They sometimes experience force in the form of collisions with other players.

Another illustration of force in soccer is a change in the ball's direction. Soccer players need to know how to use force to kick the ball in a new direction or to continue to kick it in the same direction it had been going.

Activity 1 Hold this textbook at arm's length in front of your shoulders. Move the book from left to right and back again. Repeat these actions with a piece of paper. What differences do you notice between the effort needed to change the direction of the paper and the effort needed to change the direction of the textbook? Why would there be a difference?

Activity 2 You can investigate Earth's pull on objects by using a stopwatch, a board, and two balls of different masses. Set one end of the board on a chair and the other end on the floor. Time each ball as it rolls down the board. Then, several more times, roll both balls down the board at different angles by using books under one end of the board and changing the number of books to change the angle. Does the heavier ball move faster, move more slowly, or take the same amount of time as the lighter one? What factors do you think may have affected the motion of the two balls?

Soccer gives us many examples of the use of force.

Pre-Reading Questions

1. How is force used in other sports, such as basketball, baseball, and hockey? Give examples.
2. Give as many examples as you can think of about how force is involved in driving a car.

SECTION 1

Laws of Motion

KEY TERMS
inertia

OBJECTIVES

- **Identify** the law that says that objects change their motion only when a net force is applied.
- **Relate** the first law of motion to important applications, such as seat belt safety issues.
- **Calculate** force, mass, and acceleration by using Newton's second law.

Every motion you observe or experience is related to a force. Sir Isaac Newton described the relationship between motion and force in three laws that we now call Newton's laws of motion. Newton's laws apply to a wide range of motion—a caterpillar crawling on a leaf, a person riding a bicycle, or a rocket blasting off into space.

inertia the tendency of an object to resist being moved or, if the object is moving, to resist a change in speed or direction until an outside force acts on the object

Newton's First Law

If you slide your book across a rough surface, such as carpet, the book will soon come to rest. On a smooth surface, such as ice, the book will slide much farther before stopping. Because there is less frictional force between the ice and the book, the force must act over a longer time before the book comes to a stop. Without friction, the book would keep sliding forever. This is an example of Newton's first law, which is stated as follows.

An object at rest remains at rest and an object in motion maintains its velocity unless it experiences an unbalanced force.

In a moving car, you experience the effect described by Newton's first law. As the car stops, your body continues forward, as the crash-test dummies in ***Figure 1*** do. Seat belts and other safety features are designed to counteract this effect.

Figure 1
Crash-test dummies, used by car manufacturers to test cars in crash situations, continue to travel forward when the car comes to a sudden stop, in accordance with Newton's first law.

Objects tend to maintain their state of motion

Inertia is the tendency of an object at rest to remain at rest or, if moving, to continue moving at a constant velocity. All objects resist changes in motion, so all objects have inertia. An object with a small mass, such as a baseball, can be accelerated with a small force. But a much larger force is required to accelerate a car, which has a relatively large mass.

Inertia is related to an object's mass

Newton's first law of motion is often summed up in one sentence: Matter resists any change in motion. An object at rest will remain at rest until something makes it move. Likewise, a moving object stays in motion at the same velocity unless a force acts on it to change its speed or direction. Since this property of matter is called inertia, Newton's first law is sometimes called the *law of inertia*.

Mass is a measure of inertia. An object with a small mass has less inertia than an object with a large mass. Therefore, it is easier to change the motion of an object with a small mass. For example, a softball has less mass and less inertia than a bowling ball does. Because the softball has a small amount of inertia, it is easy to pitch, and the softball's direction will change easily when it is hit with a bat. Imagine how difficult playing softball with a bowling ball would be! The bowling ball would be hard to pitch, and changing its direction with a bat would be very difficult.

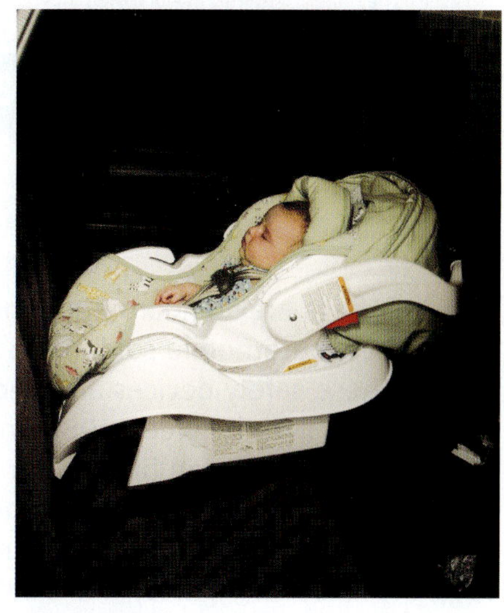

Figure 2

During an abrupt stop, this baby would continue to move forward. The backward-facing car seat distributes the force that holds the baby in the car.

Seat belts and car seats provide protection

Because of inertia, you slide toward the side of a car when the driver makes a sharp turn. Inertia is also why it is impossible for a plane, car, or bicycle to stop instantaneously. There is always a time lag between the moment the brakes are applied and the moment the vehicle comes to rest.

When the car you are riding in comes to a stop, your seat belt and the friction between you and the seat stop your forward motion. They provide the unbalanced rearward force needed to bring you to a stop as the car stops.

Babies are placed in special backward-facing car seats, as shown in ***Figure 2.*** With this type of car seat, the force that is needed to bring the baby to a stop is safely spread out over the baby's entire body.

Newton's First Law

1. Set an index card over a glass. Put a coin on top of the card.
2. With your thumb and forefinger, quickly flick the card sideways off the glass. Observe what happens to the coin. Does the coin move with the index card?
3. Try again, but this time slowly pull the card sideways and observe what happens to the coin.
4. Use Newton's first law of motion to explain your results.

Should a Car's Air Bags Be Disconnected?

Air bags are standard equipment in every new automobile sold in the United States. These safety devices are credited with saving almost 1700 lives between 1986 and 1996. However, air bags have also been blamed for the deaths of 36 children and 20 adults during the same period. In response to public concern about the safety of air bags, the National Highway Traffic Safety Administration has proposed that drivers be allowed to disconnect the air bags on their vehicles.

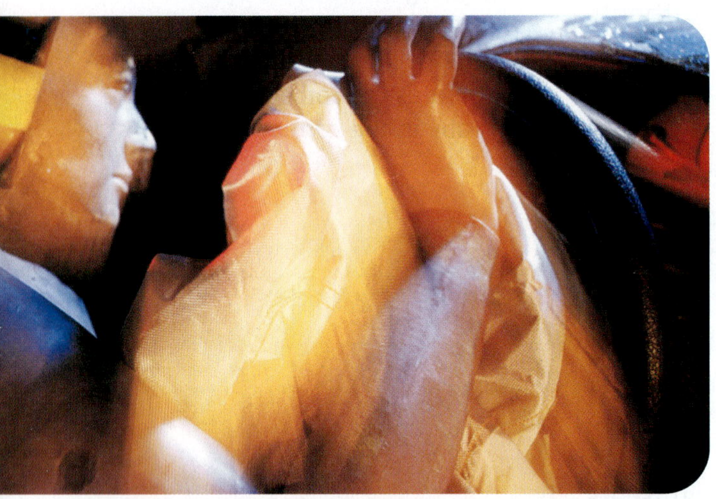

In a collision, air bags explode from a compartment to cushion the passenger's upper body and head.

How Do Air Bags Work?

When a car equipped with air bags comes to an abrupt stop, sensors in the car detect the sudden change in speed (negative acceleration) and trigger a chemical reaction inside the air bags. This reaction very quickly produces nitrogen gas, which causes the bags to inflate and explode out of their storage compartments in a fraction of a second. The inflated air bags cushion the head and upper body of the driver and the passenger in the front seat, who keep moving forward at the time of impact because of their inertia. Also, the inflated air bags increase the amount of time over which the stopping forces act. So, as the riders move forward, the air bags absorb the impact.

What Are the Risks?

Because an air bag inflates suddenly and with great force, it can cause serious head and neck injuries in some circumstances. Seat belts reduce this risk by holding passengers against the seat backs. This allows the air bag to inflate before the passenger's head comes into contact with it. In fact, most of the people killed by air bags either were not using seat belts or had not adjusted the seat belts properly.

Two groups of people are at risk for injury by air bags even with seat belts on: drivers shorter than about 157 cm (5 ft 2 in.) and infants riding next to the driver in a rear-facing safety seat.

Alternatives to Disconnecting Air Bags

Always wearing a seat belt and placing child safety seats in the back seat of the car are two easy ways to reduce the risk of injury from air bags. Shorter drivers can buy pedal extenders that allow them to sit farther back and still safely reach the pedals. Some vehicles without a back seat have a switch that can deactivate the passenger-side air bag. Automobile manufacturers are also working on air bags that inflate less forcefully.

Your Choice

1. **Critical Thinking** Are air bags useful if your car is struck from behind by another vehicle?
2. **Locating Information** Research "smart" air-bag systems, and prepare a report.

Newton's Second Law

Newton's first law describes what happens when the net force acting on an object is zero: the object either remains at rest or continues moving at a constant velocity. What happens when the net force is not zero? Newton's second law describes the effect of an unbalanced force on the motion of an object.

Force equals mass times acceleration

Newton's second law, which describes the relationship between mass, force, and acceleration, can be stated as follows.

The unbalanced force acting on an object equals the object's mass times its acceleration.

Mathematically, Newton's second law can be written as follows.

Newton's Second Law

$$force = mass \times acceleration$$

$$F = ma$$

Consider the difference between pushing an empty shopping cart and pushing the same cart filled with groceries, as shown in ***Figure 3***. If you push with the same amount of force in each situation, the empty cart will have a greater acceleration because it has a smaller mass than the full cart does. The same amount of force produces different accelerations because the masses are different. If the masses are the same, a greater force produces a greater acceleration, as shown in ***Figure 4*** on the next page.

Figure 3

Because the full cart has a larger mass than the empty cart does, the same force gives the empty cart a greater acceleration.

Figure 4

A A small force on an object causes a small acceleration.

B A larger force on the object causes a larger acceleration.

Force is measured in newtons

Newton's second law can be used to derive the SI unit of force, the newton (N). One newton is the force that can give a mass of 1 kg an acceleration of 1 m/s^2, expressed as follows.

$$1 \text{ N} = 1 \text{ kg} \times 1 \text{ m/s}^2$$

The pound (lb) is sometimes used as a unit of force. One newton is equivalent to 0.225 lb. Conversely, 1 lb is equal to 4.448 N.

Math Skills

Newton's Second Law Zookeepers lift a stretcher that holds a sedated lion. The total mass of the lion and stretcher is 175 kg, and the upward acceleration of the lion and stretcher is 0.657 m/s^2. What is the unbalanced force necessary to produce this acceleration of the lion and the stretcher?

1 List the given and unknown values.

Given: *mass,* $m = 175$ kg

acceleration, $a = 0.657 \text{ m/s}^2$

Unknown: *force,* $F = ?$ N

2 Write the equation for Newton's second law.

force = *mass* × *acceleration*

$F = ma$

3 Insert the known values into the equation, and solve.

$F = 175 \text{ kg} \times 0.657 \text{ m/s}^2$

$F = 115 \text{ kg} \times \text{m/s}^2 = 115 \text{ N}$

Sir Isaac Newton (1642–1727) was a central figure in the Scientific Revolution during the seventeenth century. He was born in 1642, the same year that Galileo died.

Practice

Newton's Second Law

1. What is the net force necessary for a 1.6×10^3 kg automobile to accelerate forward at 2.0 m/s^2?
2. A baseball accelerates downward at 9.8 m/s^2. If the gravitational force is the only force acting on the baseball and is 1.4 N, what is the baseball's mass?
3. A sailboat and its crew have a combined mass of 655 kg. Ignoring frictional forces, if the sailboat experiences a net force of 895 N pushing it forward, what is the sailboat's acceleration?

- When a problem requires you to calculate the unbalanced force on an object, you can use Newton's second law ($F = ma$).
- The equation for Newton's second law can be rearranged to isolate mass on the left side as follows.

$$F = ma$$

Divide both sides by a.

$$\frac{F}{a} = \frac{m\cancel{a}}{\cancel{a}}$$

$$m = \frac{F}{a}$$

You will need this form in Practice Problem 2.

- In Practice Problem 3, you will need to rearrange the equation to isolate acceleration on the left.

Newton's second law can also be stated as follows:

The acceleration of an object is proportional to the net force on the object and inversely proportional to the object's mass.

Therefore, the second law can be written as follows.

$$acceleration = \frac{force}{mass}$$

$$a = \frac{F}{m}$$

SECTION 1 REVIEW

SUMMARY

- An object at rest remains at rest and an object in motion maintains a constant velocity unless it experiences an unbalanced force (Newton's first law).
- Inertia is the property of matter that resists change in motion.
- Properly used seat belts protect passengers.
- The unbalanced force acting on an object equals the object's mass times its acceleration, or $F = ma$ (Newton's second law).

1. **State** Newton's first law of motion in your own words, and give an example that demonstrates that law.
2. **Explain** how the law of inertia relates to seat belt safety.
3. **Critical Thinking** Using Newton's laws, predict what will happen in the following situations:
   a. A car traveling on an icy road comes to a sharp bend.
   b. A car traveling on an icy road has to stop quickly.

Math Skills

4. What is the acceleration of a boy on a skateboard if the unbalanced forward force on the boy is 15 N? The total mass of the boy and the skateboard is 58 kg.
5. What force is necessary to accelerate a 1250 kg car at a rate of 40 m/s^2?
6. What is the mass of an object if a force of 34 N produces an acceleration of 4 m/s^2?

SECTION 2

Gravity

KEY TERMS

free fall
terminal velocity
projectile motion

OBJECTIVES

- **Explain** that gravitational force becomes stronger as the masses increase and rapidly becomes weaker as the distance between the masses increases, $F = G\frac{m_1m_2}{d^2}$
- **Evaluate** the concept that free-fall acceleration near Earth's surface is independent of the mass of the falling object.
- **Demonstrate** mathematically how free-fall acceleration relates to weight.
- **Describe** orbital motion as a combination of two motions.

Have you ever seen a videotape of the first astronauts on the moon? When they tried to walk on the lunar surface, they bounced all over the place! Why did the astronauts—who were wearing heavy spacesuits—bounce so easily on the moon, as shown in ***Figure 5***?

Law of Universal Gravitation

For thousands of years, two of the most puzzling scientific questions were "Why do objects fall toward Earth?" and "What keeps the planets in motion in the sky?" A British scientist, Sir Isaac Newton (1642–1727), realized that they were two parts of the same question. Newton generalized his observations on gravity in a law now known as the *law of universal gravitation.* The law states that all objects in the universe attract each other through gravitational force.

Figure 5

Because gravity is less on the moon than on Earth, the Apollo astronauts bounced as they walked on the moon's surface.

Universal Gravitation Equation

$$F = G\frac{m_1m_2}{d^2}$$

This equation says that the gravitational force increases as one or both masses increase. It also says that the gravitational force decreases as the distance between the masses increases. In fact, because distance is squared in the equation, even a small increase in distance can cause a large decrease in force. The symbol G in the equation represents a constant.

All matter is affected by gravity

Whether two objects are very large or very small, there is a gravitational force between them. When something is very large, such as Earth, the force is easy to detect. However, we do not notice that something as small as a toothpick exerts gravitational force. Yet no matter how small or how large the objects are, every object exerts a gravitational force, as illustrated by both parts of ***Figure 6.*** The force of gravity between two masses is easier to understand if you consider it in two parts: (1) the size of the masses and (2) the distance between them. So, these two ideas will be considered separately.

INTEGRATING

BIOLOGY

Gravity plays a role in your body. Blood pressure, for example, is affected by gravity. Therefore, your blood pressure will be greater in the lower part of your body than in the upper part. Doctors and nurses take your blood pressure on your arm at the level of your heart to see what the blood pressure is likely to be at your heart.

Gravitational force increases as mass increases

Gravity is given as the reason why an apple falls down from a tree. When an apple breaks its stem, it falls down because the gravitational force between Earth and the apple is much greater than the gravitational force between the apple and the tree.

Imagine an elephant and a cat. Because an elephant has a larger mass than a cat does, the gravitational force between an elephant and Earth is greater than the gravitational force between a cat and Earth. That is why a cat is much easier to pick up than an elephant! There is also gravitational force between the cat and the elephant, but it is very small because the cat's mass and the elephant's mass are so much smaller than Earth's mass. The gravitational force between most objects around you is relatively very small.

Figure 6

The arrows indicate the gravitational force between objects. The length of the arrows indicates the strength of the force.

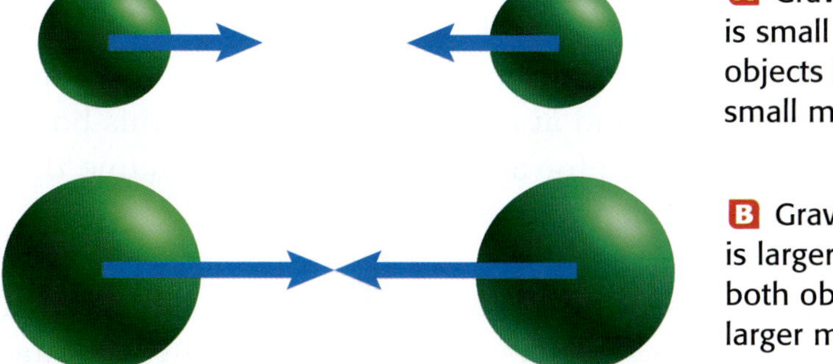

A Gravitational force is small between objects that have small masses.

B Gravitational force is larger when one or both objects have larger masses.

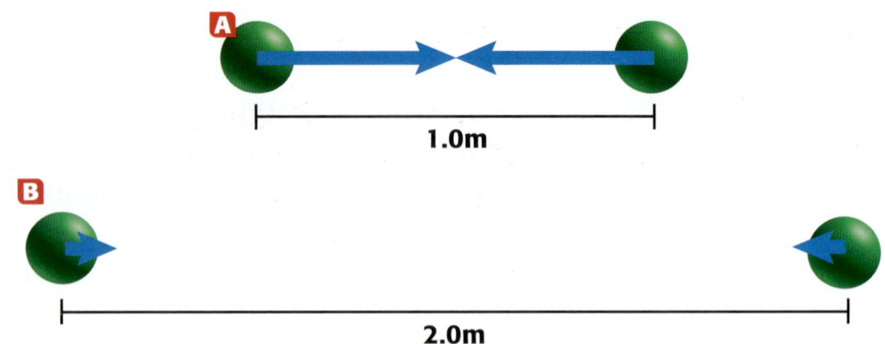

Figure 7

A Gravitational force rapidly becomes stronger as the distance between two objects decreases.

B Gravitational force rapidly becomes weaker as the distance between two objects increases.

Gravitational force decreases as distance increases

Gravitational force also depends on the distance between two objects, as shown in ***Figure 7.*** The force of gravity changes as the distance between the balls changes. If the distance between the two balls is doubled, the gravitational force between them decreases to one-fourth its original value. If the original distance is tripled, the gravitational force decreases to one-ninth its original value. Gravitational force is weaker than other types of forces, even though it holds the planets, stars, and galaxies together.

free fall the motion of a body when only the force of gravity is acting on the body

Free Fall and Weight

When gravity is the only force acting on an object, the object is said to be in **free fall.** The free-fall acceleration of an object is directed toward the center of Earth. Because free-fall acceleration results from gravity, it is often abbreviated as the letter g. Near Earth's surface, g is approximately 9.8 m/s^2.

Free-fall acceleration near Earth's surface is constant

In the absence of air resistance, all objects near Earth's surface accelerate at the same rate, regardless of their mass. As shown in ***Figure 8,*** the feather and the apple, dropped from the same height, would hit the ground at the same moment. In this book, we disregard air resistance for all calculations. We assume that all objects on Earth accelerate at exactly 9.8 m/s^2.

Why do all objects have the same free-fall acceleration? Newton's second law shows that acceleration depends on both force and mass. A heavier object experiences a greater gravitational force than a lighter object does. But a heavier object is also harder to accelerate because it has more mass. The extra mass of the heavy object exactly compensates for the additional gravitational force.

Figure 8

In a vacuum, a feather and an apple fall with the same acceleration because both are in free fall.

Weight is equal to mass times free-fall acceleration

The force on an object due to gravity is called its *weight*. On Earth, your weight is simply the amount of gravitational force exerted on you by Earth. If you know the free-fall acceleration, g, acting on a body, you can use $F = ma$ (Newton's second law) to calculate the body's weight. Weight equals mass times free-fall acceleration. Mathematically, this is expressed as follows.

$$weight = mass \times free\text{-}fall\ acceleration$$
$$w = mg$$

Note that because weight is a force, the SI unit of weight is the newton. For example, a small apple weighs about 1 N. A 1.0 kg book has a weight of 1.0 kg $\times$ 9.8 m/s^2 = 9.8 N.

You may have seen pictures of astronauts floating in the air, as shown in ***Figure 9.*** Does this mean that they don't experience gravity? In orbit, astronauts, the space shuttle, and all objects on board experience free fall because of Earth's gravity. In fact, the astronauts and their surroundings all accelerate at the same rate. Therefore, the floor of the shuttle does not push up against the astronauts and the astronauts appear to be floating. This situation is referred to as *apparent weightlessness*.

Figure 9
In the low-gravity environment of the orbiting space shuttle, astronauts experience apparent weightlessness.

Weight is different from mass

Mass and weight are easy to confuse. Although mass and weight are directly proportional to one another, they are not the same. Mass is a measure of the amount of matter in an object. Weight is the gravitational force an object experiences because of its mass.

The weight of an object depends on gravity, so a change in an object's location will change the object's weight. For example, on Earth, a 66 kg astronaut weighs 66 kg $\times$ 9.8 m/s^2 = 650 N (about 150 lb), but on the moon's surface, where g is only 1.6 m/s^2, the astronaut would weigh 66 kg $\times$ 1.6 m/s^2, which equals 110 N (about 24 lb). The astronaut's mass remains the same everywhere, but the weight changes as the gravitational force acting on the astronaut changes in each place.

Weight influences shape

Gravitational force influences the shapes of living things. On land, large animals must have strong skeletons to support their mass against the force of gravity. The trunks of trees serve the same function. For organisms that live in water, however, the downward force of gravity is balanced by the upward force of the water. For many of these creatures, strong skeletons are unnecessary. Because a jellyfish has no skeleton, it can drift gracefully through the water but collapses if it washes up on the beach.

INTEGRATING

SPACE SCIENCE
Planets in our solar system have different masses and different diameters. Therefore, each has its own unique value for g. Find the weight of a 58 kg person on the following planets:

Earth, where g = 9.8 m/s^2

Venus, where g = 8.9 m/s^2

Mars, where g = 3.7 m/s^2

Neptune, where g = 11.0 m/s^2

Figure 10

When a skydiver reaches terminal velocity, the force of gravity is balanced by air resistance.

Velocity is constant when air resistance balances weight

Both air resistance and gravity act on objects moving through Earth's atmosphere. A falling object stops accelerating when the force of air resistance becomes equal to the gravitational force on the object (the weight of the object), as shown in ***Figure 10.*** This happens because the air resistance acts in the opposite direction to the weight. When these two forces are equal, the object stops accelerating and reaches its maximum velocity, which is called the **terminal velocity.**

When skydivers start a jump, their parachutes are closed, and they are accelerated toward Earth by the force of gravity. As their velocity increases, the force they experience because of air resistance increases. When air resistance and the force of gravity are equal, skydivers reach a terminal velocity of about 320 km/h (200 mi/h). But when they open the parachute, air resistance increases greatly. For a while, this increased air resistance slows them down. Eventually, they reach a new terminal velocity of several kilometers per hour, which allows them to land safely.

terminal velocity the constant velocity of a falling object when the force of air resistance is equal in magnitude and opposite in direction to the force of gravity

Free Fall and Motion

Skydivers are often described as being in free fall before they open their parachutes. However, that is an incorrect description, because air resistance is always acting on the skydiver. An object is in free fall only if gravity is pulling it down and no other forces are acting on it. Because air resistance is a force, free fall can occur only where there is no air—in a vacuum (a place in which there is no matter) or in space. Thus, a skydiver falling to Earth is not in free fall.

Because there is no air resistance in space, objects in space are in free fall. Consider a group of astronauts riding in a spacecraft. When they are in space, gravity is the only force acting on the spacecraft and the astronauts. As a result, the spacecraft and the astronauts are in free fall. They all fall at the same rate of acceleration, no matter how great or small their individual masses are.

Orbiting objects are in free fall

Why do astronauts appear to float inside a space shuttle? Is it because they are "weightless" in space? You may have heard that objects are weightless in space, but this is not true. It is impossible to be weightless anywhere in the universe.

As you learned earlier in this section, weight—a measure of gravitational force—depends on the masses of objects and the distances between them. If you traveled in space far away from all the stars and planets, the gravitational force acting on you would be almost undetectable because the distance between you and other objects would be great. But you would still have mass, and so would all the other objects in the universe. Therefore, gravity would still attract you to other objects—even if just slightly—so you would still have weight.

Astronauts "float" in orbiting spaceships, not because they are weightless but because they are in free fall. The moon stays in orbit around Earth, as in ***Figure 11,*** and the planets stay in orbit around the sun, all because of free fall. To better understand why these objects continue to orbit and do not fall to Earth, you need to learn more about what orbiting means.

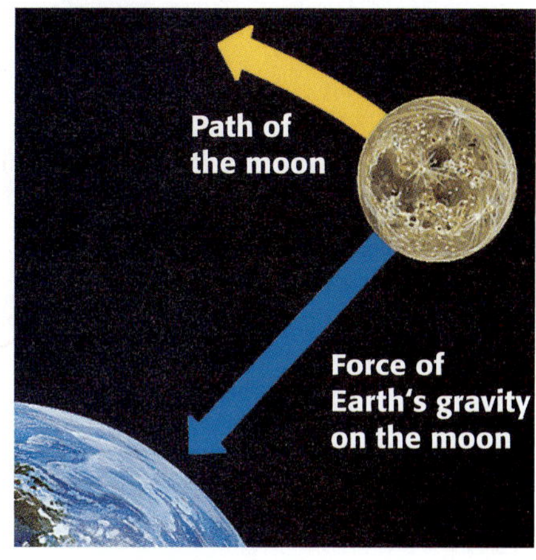

Figure 11

The moon stays in orbit around Earth because Earth's gravitational force provides a pull on the moon.

Two motions combine to cause orbiting

An object is said to be orbiting when it is traveling in a circular or nearly circular path around another object. When a spaceship orbits Earth, it is moving forward but it is also in free fall toward Earth. ***Figure 12*** shows how these two motions combine to cause orbiting.

Figure 12

How an Orbit Is Formed

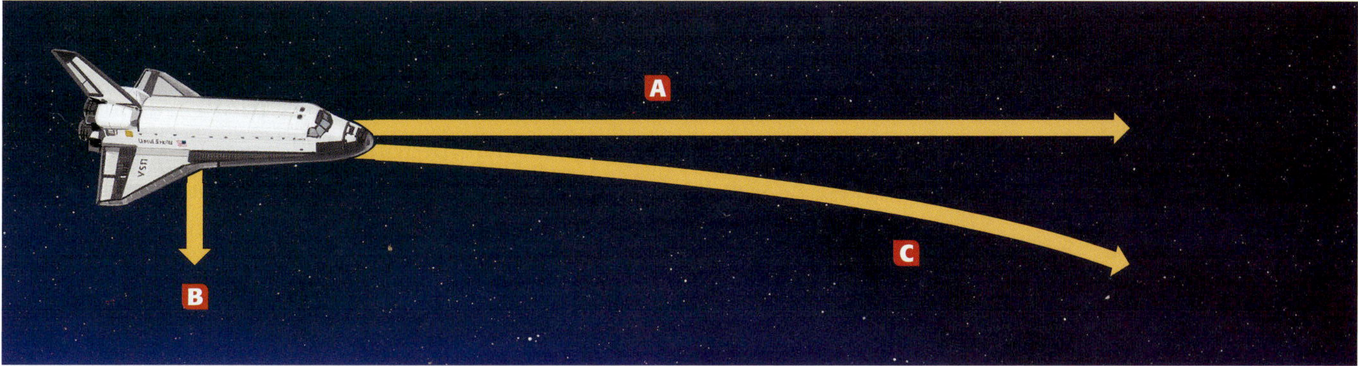

A The shuttle moves forward at a constant speed. This would be its path if there were no gravitational pull from Earth.

B The shuttle is in free fall because gravity pulls it toward Earth. This would be its path if it were not traveling forward.

C When the forward motion combines with free fall, the shuttle follows the curve of Earth's surface. This is known as *orbiting.*

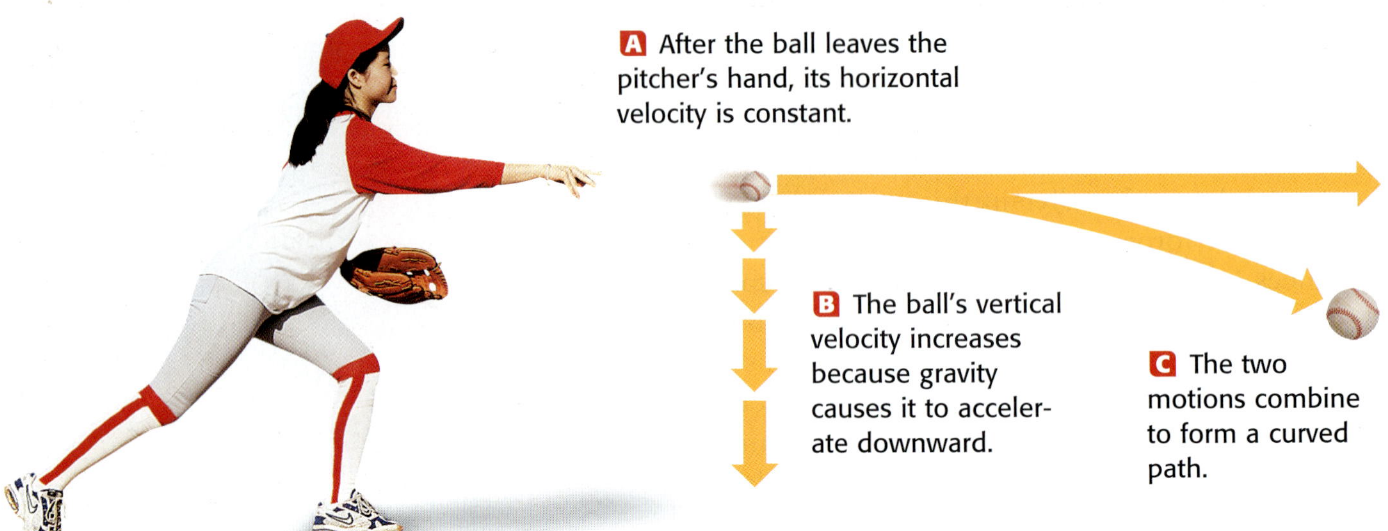

Figure 13

Two motions combine to form projectile motion.

▶ **projectile motion** the curved path that an object follows when thrown, launched, or otherwise projected near the surface of Earth; the motion of objects that are moving in two dimensions under the influence of gravity

Projectile Motion and Gravity

The orbit of the space shuttle around Earth is an example of **projectile motion.** Projectile motion is the curved path an object follows when thrown, launched, or otherwise projected near the surface of Earth. The motions of leaping frogs, thrown balls, and arrows shot from a bow are all examples of projectile motion. Projectile motion has two components—horizontal and vertical. The two components are independent; that is, they have no effect on each other. In other words, the downward acceleration due to gravity does not change a projectile's horizontal motion, and the horizontal motion does not affect the downward motion. When the two motions are combined, they form a curved path, as shown in ***Figure 13.***

Projectile motion has some horizontal motion

When you throw a ball, your hand and arm exert a force on the ball that makes the ball move forward. This force gives the ball its horizontal motion. Horizontal motion is motion that is perpendicular (90°) to Earth's gravitational field.

After you have thrown the ball, there are no horizontal forces acting against the ball (if you ignore air resistance). Therefore, there are no forces to change the ball's horizontal motion. So, the horizontal velocity of the ball is constant after the ball leaves your hand, as shown in ***Figure 13.***

Ignoring air resistance allows you to simplify projectile motion so that you can understand the horizontal and then the vertical components of projectile motion. Then, you can put them together to understand projectile motion as a whole.

Projectile motion also has some vertical motion

In addition to horizontal motion, vertical motion is involved in the movement of a ball that has been thrown. If it were not, the ball would continue moving in a straight line, never falling. Again imagine that you are throwing the ball as in ***Figure 13.*** When you let go of the ball, gravity pulls it downward, which gives the ball vertical motion. Vertical motion is motion in the direction in which the force of Earth's gravity acts.

In the absence of air resistance, gravity on Earth pulls downward with an acceleration of 9.8 m/s^2 on objects that are in projectile motion, just as it does on all falling objects. ***Figure 14*** shows that the downward accelerations of a thrown object and of a falling object are identical.

Because objects in projectile motion accelerate downward, you should always aim above a target if you want to hit it with a thrown or propelled object. This is why archers point their arrows above the bull's eye on a target. If they aimed an arrow directly at a bull's eye, the arrow would strike below the center of the target rather than the middle.

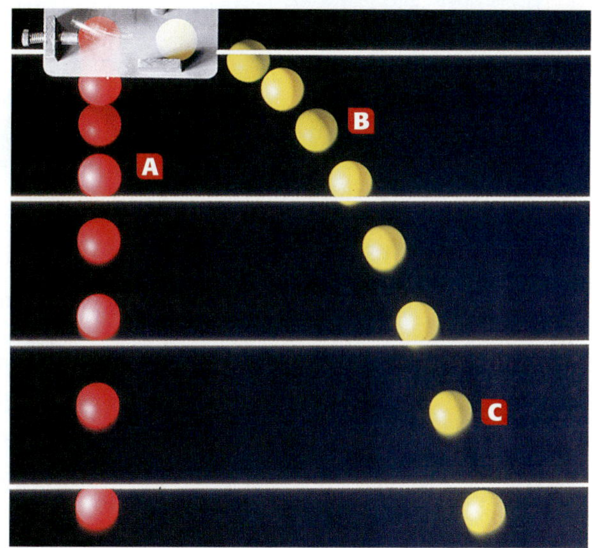

Figure 14

A The red ball was dropped without a horizontal push.

B The yellow ball was given a horizontal push off the ledge at the same time it was dropped. It follows a projectile-motion path.

C The two balls have the same acceleration downward because of gravity. The horizontal motion of the yellow ball does not affect its vertical motion.

SECTION 2 REVIEW

SUMMARY

- Gravitational force between two masses strengthens as the masses become more massive and rapidly weakens as the distance between them increases.
- Gravitational acceleration results from gravitational force, is constant, and does not depend on mass.
- Mathematically, *weight* = *mass* × *free-fall acceleration,* or $w = mg$.
- Projectile motion is a combination of a downward free-fall motion and a forward horizontal motion.

1. **State** the law of universal gravitation, and use examples to explain the effect of changing mass and changing distance on gravitational force.
2. **Explain** why your weight would be less on the moon than on Earth even though your mass would not change. Use the law of universal gravitation in your explanation.
3. **Describe** the difference between mass and weight.
4. **Name** the two components that make up orbital motion, and explain how they do so.
5. **Critical Thinking** Using Newton's second law, explain why the gravitational acceleration of any object near Earth is the same no matter what the mass of the object is.

Math Skills

6. The force between a planet and a spacecraft is 1 million newtons. What will the force be if the spacecraft moves to half its original distance from the planet?

SECTION 3

Newton's Third Law

KEY TERMS
momentum

OBJECTIVES

- **Explain** that when one object exerts a force on a second object, the second object exerts a force equal in size and opposite in direction on the first object.
- **Show** that all forces come in pairs commonly called *action* and *reaction pairs.*
- **Recognize** that all moving objects have momentum.

When you kick a soccer ball, as shown in ***Figure 15,*** you notice the effect of the force exerted by your foot on the ball. The ball experiences a change in motion. Is this the only force present? Do you feel a force on your foot? In fact, the soccer ball exerts an equal and opposite force on your foot. The force exerted on the ball by your foot is called the *action force,* and the force exerted on your foot by the ball is called the *reaction force.*

Action and Reaction Forces

Notice that the action and reaction forces are applied to different objects. These forces are equal and opposite. The action force acts on the ball, and the reaction force acts on the foot. This is an example of Newton's third law of motion, also called the *law of action and reaction.*

For every action force, there is an equal and opposite reaction force.

Figure 15
According to Newton's third law, the soccer ball and the foot exert equal and opposite forces on one another.

Forces always occur in pairs

Newton's third law can be stated as follows: All forces act in pairs. Whenever a force is exerted, another force occurs that is equal in size and opposite in direction. Action and reaction force pairs occur even when there is no motion. For example, when you sit on a chair, your weight pushes down on the chair. This is the action force. The chair pushing back up with a force equal to your weight is the reaction force.

Figure 16

A The action force is the swimmer pushing the water backward.

B The reaction force is the water pushing the swimmer forward.

Force pairs do not act on the same object

Newton's third law indicates that forces always occur in pairs. In other words, every force is part of an action and reaction force pair. Although the forces are equal and opposite, they do not cancel one another because they are acting on different objects. In the example shown in ***Figure 16,*** the swimmer's hands and feet exert the action force on the water. The water exerts the reaction force on the swimmer's hands and feet. In this and all other examples, the action and reaction forces do not act on the same object. Also note that action and reaction forces always occur at the same time.

Equal forces don't always have equal effects

Another example of an action-reaction force pair is shown in ***Figure 17.*** If you drop a ball, the force of gravity pulls the ball toward Earth. This force is the action force exerted by Earth on the ball. But the force of gravity also pulls Earth toward the ball. That force is the reaction force exerted by the ball on Earth.

It's easy to see the effect of the action force—the ball falls to Earth. Why don't you notice the effect of the reaction force—Earth being pulled upward? Remember Newton's second law: an object's acceleration is found by dividing the force applied to the object by the object's mass. The force applied to Earth is equal to the force applied to the ball. However, Earth's mass is much larger than the ball's mass, so Earth's acceleration is much smaller than the ball's acceleration.

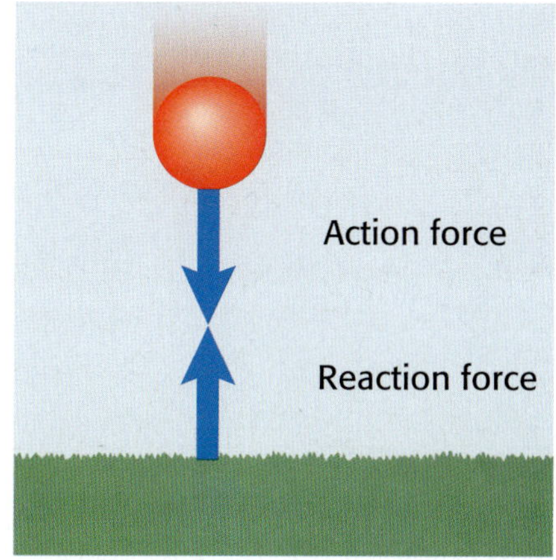

Figure 17

The two forces of gravity between Earth and a falling object are an example of a force pair.

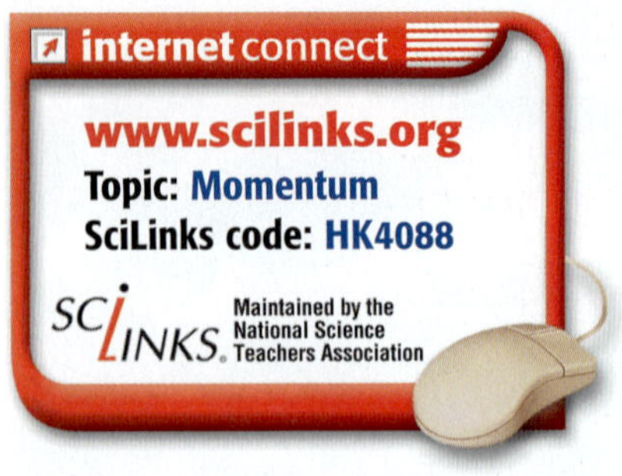

Momentum

If a compact car and a large truck are traveling with the same velocity and the same braking force is applied to each, the truck takes more time to stop than the car does. Likewise, a fast-moving car takes more time to stop than a slow-moving car with the same mass does. The truck and the fast-moving car have more **momentum** than the compact car and the slow-moving car do. Momentum is a property of all moving objects, which is equal to the product of the mass and the velocity of the object.

momentum a quantity defined as the product of the mass and velocity of an object

Moving objects have momentum

For movement along a straight line, momentum is calculated by multiplying an object's mass by its velocity. The SI unit for momentum is kilograms times meters per second (kg•m/s).

Momentum Equation

$$momentum = mass \times velocity$$

$$p = mv$$

The momentum equation shows that for a given velocity, the more mass an object has, the greater its momentum is. A massive semi truck on the highway, for example, has much more momentum than a sports car traveling at the same velocity has. The momentum equation also shows that the faster an object is moving, the greater its momentum is. For instance, a fast-moving train has much more momentum than a slow-moving train with the same mass has. If an object is not moving, its momentum is zero.

Like velocity, momentum has direction. An object's momentum is in the same direction as its velocity. The momentum of the bowling ball shown in ***Figure 18*** is directed toward the pins.

Figure 18

Because of the large mass and high speed of this bowling ball, it has a lot of momentum and is able to knock over the pins easily.

Math Skills

Momentum Calculate the momentum of a 6.00 kg bowling ball moving at 10.0 m/s down the alley toward the pins.

1 List the given and unknown values.

Given: *mass*, $m = 6.00$ kg

velocity, $v = 10.0$ m/s down the alley

Unknown: *momentum*, $p = ?$ kg • m/s (and direction)

2 Write the equation for momentum.

$momentum = mass \times velocity, p = mv$

3 Insert the known values into the equation, and solve.

$p = mv = 6.00 \text{ kg} \times 10.0 \text{ m/s}$

$p = 60.0$ kg • m/s down the alley

- When a problem requires that you calculate velocity when you know momentum and mass, you can use the momentum equation.
- You may rearrange the equation to isolate velocity on the left side, as follows: $v = \frac{p}{m}$. You will need this form of the momentum equation for Practice Problem 2.

Practice

Momentum

1. Calculate the momentum of the following objects.
   a. a 75 kg speed skater moving forward at 16 m/s
   b. a 135 kg ostrich running north at 16.2 m/s
   c. a 5.0 kg baby on a train moving eastward at 72 m/s
   d. a seated 48.5 kg passenger on a train that is stopped
2. Calculate the velocity of a 0.8 kg kitten with a momentum of 5 kg • m/s forward.

Force is related to change in momentum

To catch a baseball, you must apply a force on the ball to make it stop moving. When you force an object to change its motion, you force it to change its momentum. In fact, you are actually changing the momentum of the ball over a period of time.

As the time period of the momentum's change becomes longer, the force needed to cause this change in momentum becomes smaller. So, if you pull your glove back while you are catching the ball, as in ***Figure 19,*** you are extending the time for changing the ball's momentum. Extending the time causes the ball to put less force on your hand. As a result, the sting to your hand is reduced.

As another example, when pole-vaulters, high jumpers, and gymnasts land after jumping, they move in the direction of the motion. This motion extends the time of the momentum change. As a result, the impact force decreases.

Figure 19

Moving the glove back during the catch increases the time of the momentum's change and decreases the impact force.

Figure 20

A The cue ball is moving forward with momentum. The billiard ball's momentum is zero.

B When the cue ball hits the billiard ball, the action force makes the billiard ball move forward. The reaction force stops the cue ball.

C Because the cue ball's momentum was transferred to the billiard ball, the cue ball's momentum after the collision is zero.

Momentum is conserved in collisions

Imagine that two cars of different masses traveling with different velocities collide head on. Can you predict what will happen after the collision? The momentum of the cars after the collision can be predicted. This prediction can be made because, in the absence of outside influences, momentum is conserved. Some momentum may be transferred from one vehicle to the other, but the total momentum remains the same. This principle is known as the law of conservation of momentum.

The total amount of momentum in an isolated system is conserved.

The total momentum of the two cars before a collision is the same as the total momentum after the collision. This law applies whether the cars bounce off each other or stick together. In some cases, cars bounce off each other to move in opposite directions. If the cars stick together after a collision, the cars will continue in the direction of the car that originally had the greater momentum.

Momentum is transferred

When a moving object hits a second object, some or all of the momentum of the first object is transferred to the second object. If only some of the momentum is transferred, the rest of the momentum stays with the first object.

Imagine you hit a billiard ball with a cue ball so that the billiard ball starts moving and the cue ball stops, as shown in ***Figure 20.*** The cue ball had a certain amount of momentum before the collision. During the collision, all of the cue ball's momentum was transferred to the billiard ball. After the collision, the billiard ball moved away with the same amount of momentum the cue ball had originally. This example illustrates the law of conservation of momentum. Any time two or more objects interact, they may exchange momentum, but the total momentum stays the same.

Newton's third law can explain conservation of momentum. In the example of the billiard ball, the cue ball hit the billiard ball with a certain force. This force was the action force. The reaction force was the equal but opposite force exerted by the billiard ball on the cue ball. The action force made the billiard ball start moving, and the reaction force made the cue ball stop moving.

Conservation of momentum explains rocket propulsion

Newton's third law and the conservation of momentum are used in rocketry. Rockets have many different sizes and designs, but the basic principle remains the same. The push of the hot gases through the nozzle is matched by an equal push in the opposite direction on the combustion (burning) chamber, which accelerates the rocket forward, as shown in **Figure 21.**

Many people wrongly believe that rockets work because the hot gases flowing out the nozzle push against the atmosphere. If this were true, rockets couldn't travel in outer space where there is no atmosphere. What really happens is that momentum is conserved. Together, the rocket and fuel form a system. When the fuel is pushed out the back, they remain a system. The change in the fuel's momentum must be matched by a change in the rocket's momentum in the opposite direction for the overall momentum to stay the same. This example shows the conservation of momentum. Also, the upward force on the rocket and the downward force on the fuel are an action-reaction pair.

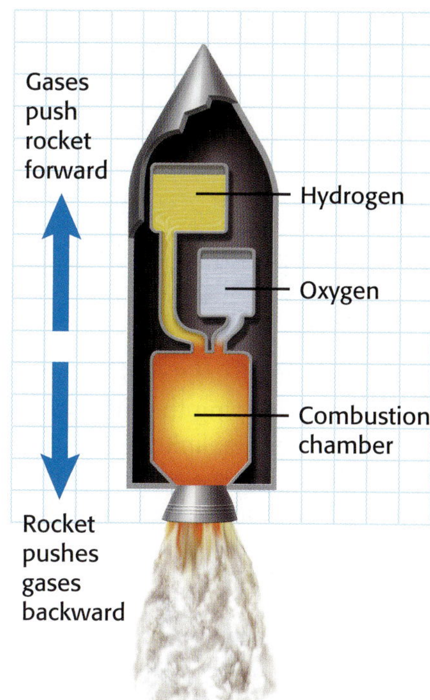

Figure 21
All forces occur in action-reaction pairs. In this case, the upward push on the rocket equals the downward push on the exhaust gases.

Action and reaction force pairs are everywhere

Figure 22 gives more examples of action-reaction pairs. In each example, notice which object exerts the action force and which object exerts the reaction force. Even though we are concentrating on just the action and reaction force pairs, there are other forces at work, each of which is also part of an action-reaction pair. For example, when the bat and ball exert action and reaction forces, the bat does not fly toward the catcher, because the batter is exerting yet another force on the bat.

Figure 22
Examples of Third Law Forces

A The rabbit's legs exert a force on Earth. Earth exerts an equal force on the rabbit's legs, which causes the rabbit to accelerate upward.

B The bat exerts a force on the ball, which sends the ball into the outfield. The ball exerts an equal force on the bat.

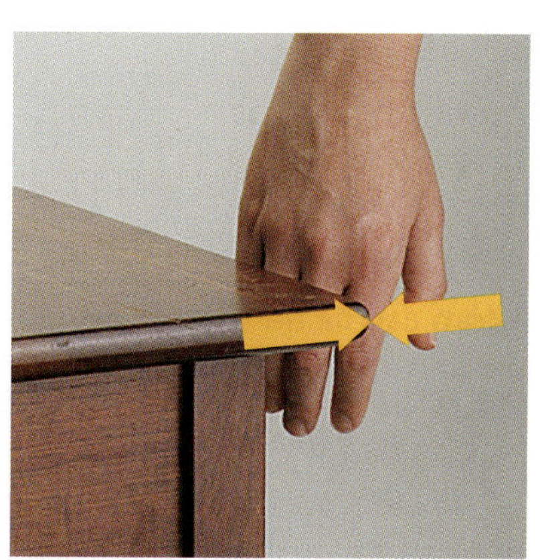

C When your hand hits the table with a force, the table's force on your hand is equal in size and opposite in direction.

How are action and reaction forces related?

Materials ✔ 2 spring scales ✔ 2 kg mass

1. Hang the 2 kg mass from one of the spring scales.
2. Observe the reading on the spring scale.
3. While keeping the mass connected to the first spring scale, link the two scales together. The first spring scale and the mass should hang from the second spring scale, as shown in the figure at right.
4. Observe the readings on each spring scale.

Analysis

1. What are the action and reaction forces involved in the spring scale–mass system you have constructed?
2. How did the readings on the two spring scales in step 4 compare? Explain how this is an example of Newton's third law.

SECTION 3 REVIEW

SUMMARY

- When one object exerts an action force on a second object, the second object exerts a reaction force on the first object. Forces always occur in action-reaction force pairs.
- Action-reaction force pairs are equal in size and opposite in direction.
- Every moving object has momentum, which is the product of the object's mass and velocity.
- Momentum can be transferred in collisions, but the total momentum before and after a collision is the same. This is the law of conservation of momentum.
- Rocket propulsion can be explained in terms of conservation of momentum.

1. **State** Newton's third law of motion, and give an example that shows how this law works.
2. **List** three examples of action-reaction force pairs that are not mentioned in the chapter.
3. **Define** momentum, and explain what the law of conservation of momentum means.
4. **Explain** why, when a soccer ball is kicked, the action and reaction forces don't cancel each other.
   a. The force of the player's foot on the ball is greater than the force of the ball on the player's foot.
   b. They act on two different objects.
   c. The reaction force happens after the action force.
5. **Critical Thinking** The forces exerted by Earth and a skier become an action-reaction force pair when the skier pushes the ski poles against Earth. Explain why the skier accelerates while Earth does not seem to move at all. (**Hint:** Think about the math equation for Newton's second law of motion for each of the forces.)

Math Skills

6. **Calculate** the momentum of a 1.0 kg ball traveling eastward at 12 m/s.

Math Skills

Algebraic Rearrangements

A car's engine exerts a force of 1.5×10^4 N in the forward direction, while friction exerts an opposing force of 9.0×10^3 N. If the car's mass is 1.5×10^3 kg, what is the magnitude and direction of the car's net acceleration?

1 List all given and unknown values.

Given: *forward force,* $F_1 = 1.5 \times 10^4$ N
opposing force, $F_2 = 9.0 \times 10^3$ N
mass, $m = 1.5 \times 10^3$ kg

Unknown: acceleration (m/s^2)

2 Write down the equation for force, and rearrange it for calculating the acceleration.

$$F = ma$$

$$a = \frac{F}{m}$$

3 Solve for acceleration.

The net acceleration must be obtained from the net force, which is the overall, unbalanced force acting on the car.

$F_{net} = F_1 - F_2$, so

$$ma_{net} = F_1 - F_2$$

The net acceleration is therefore

$$a_{net} = \frac{(F_1 - F_2)}{m} = \frac{(1.5 \times 10^4 \text{ N} - 9.0 \times 10^3 \text{ N})}{1.5 \times 10^3 \text{ kg}} = \frac{6.0 \times 10^3 \text{ N}}{1.5 \times 10^3 \text{ kg}} = 4.0 \text{ m/s}^2$$

The net acceleration is 4.0 m/s^2, and like the net force, it is in the forward direction.

Practice

Following the example above, calculate the following:

1. A car has a mass of 1.50×10^3 kg. If the net force acting on the car is 6.75×10^3 N to the east, what is the car's acceleration?
2. A bicyclist decelerates with a force of 3.5×10^2 N. If the bicyclist and bicycle have a total mass of 1.0×10^2 kg, what is the acceleration?
3. Roberto and Laura are studying across from each other at a wide table. Laura slides a 2.2 kg book toward Roberto with a force of 11.0 N straight ahead. If the force of friction opposing the movement is 8.4 N, what is the magnitude and direction of the book's acceleration?

CHAPTER 11 REVIEW

Chapter Highlights

Before you begin, review the summaries of the key ideas of each section, found at the end of each section. The vocabulary terms are listed on the first page of each section.

UNDERSTANDING CONCEPTS

1. Newton's first law of motion states that an object
- **a.** at rest remains at rest unless it experiences an unbalanced force.
- **b.** in motion maintains its velocity unless it experiences an unbalanced force.
- **c.** will tend to maintain its motion unless it experiences an unbalanced force.
- **d.** All of the above

2. The first law of motion applies to
- **a.** only objects that are moving.
- **b.** only objects that are not moving.
- **c.** all objects, whether moving or not.
- **d.** no object, whether moving or not.

3. A measure of inertia is an object's
- **a.** mass.
- **b.** weight.
- **c.** velocity.
- **d.** acceleration.

4. Automobile seat belts are necessary for safety because of a passenger's
- **a.** weight.
- **b.** inertia.
- **c.** speed.
- **d.** gravity.

5. Suppose you are pushing a car with a certain net force. If you then push with twice the net force, the car's acceleration
- **a.** becomes four times as much.
- **b.** becomes two times as much.
- **c.** stays the same.
- **d.** becomes half as much.

6. Any change in an object's velocity is caused by
- **a.** the object's mass.
- **b.** the object's direction.
- **c.** a balanced force.
- **d.** an unbalanced force.

7. An object's acceleration is
- **a.** directly proportional to the net force.
- **b.** inversely proportional to the object's mass.
- **c.** in the same direction as the net force.
- **d.** All of the above

8. Gravitational force between two masses ____________ as the masses increase and rapidly ____________ as the distance between the masses increases.
- **a.** strengthens, strengthens
- **b.** weakens, weakens
- **c.** weakens, strengthens
- **d.** strengthens, weakens

9. An example of action-reaction forces is
- **a.** air escaping from a toy balloon.
- **b.** a rocket traveling through the air.
- **c.** a ball bouncing off a wall.
- **d.** All of the above

10. A baseball player catches a line-drive hit. If the reaction force is the force of the player's glove stopping the ball, the action force is
- **a.** the force of the player's hand on the glove.
- **b.** the force applied by the player's arm.
- **c.** the force of the ball pushing on the glove.
- **d.** the force of the player's shoes on the dirt.

USING VOCABULARY

11. What is inertia, and why is it important in the laws of motion?

12. What is the unit of measure of force, and how is it related to other measurement units?

13. What is the difference between *free fall* and *weightlessness*?

14. A wrestler weighs in for the first match on the moon. Will the athlete weigh more or less on the moon than he does on Earth? Explain your answer by using the terms *weight, mass, force,* and *gravity.*

15. Describe a skydiver's jump from the airplane to the ground. In your answer, use the terms *air resistance, gravity,* and *terminal velocity.*

16. Give an example of *projectile motion,* and explain how the example demonstrates that a vertical force does not influence horizontal motion.

BUILDING MATH SKILLS

17. Force The net force acting on a 5 kg discus is 50 N. What is the acceleration of the discus?

18. Force A block pushed with a force of 13.5 N accelerates at 6.5 m/s^2 to the left. What is the mass of the block?

19. Force A student tests the second law of motion by accelerating a block of ice at a rate of 3.5 m/s^2. If the ice has a mass of 12.5 kg, what force must the student apply to the ice?

20. Weight A bag of sugar has a mass of 2.26 kg. What is its weight in newtons on the moon, where the acceleration due to gravity is one-sixth of that on Earth? (**Hint:** On Earth, $g = 9.8$ m/s^2.)

21. Momentum Calculate the momentum of the following objects:

a. a 65 kg skateboarder moving forward at the rate of 3.0 m/s

b. a 20.0 kg toddler in a car traveling west at the rate of 22 m/s

c. a 16 kg penguin at rest

BUILDING GRAPHING SKILLS

22. Graphing An experiment is done with a lab cart. Varying forces are applied to the cart and measured while the cart is accelerating. These forces are all in the direction of the movement of the cart, such as pushes to make the cart accelerate. Each push is made after the cart has stopped from the previous push. The following data were obtained in the experiment.

Trial	Acceleration	Applied force
1	0.70 m/s^2	0.35 N
2	1.70 m/s^2	0.85 N
3	2.70 m/s^2	1.35 N
4	3.70 m/s^2	1.85 N
5	4.70 m/s^2	2.35 N

Graph the data in the table. Place acceleration on the x-axis and applied force on the y-axis. Because $F = ma$ and therefore $m = \frac{F}{a}$, what does the line on the graph represent? Use your graph to determine the mass of the lab cart.

THINKING CRITICALLY

23. Critical Thinking What happens to the gravitational force between two objects if their masses do not change but the distance between them becomes four times as much?

24. Critical Thinking There is no gravity in outer space. Write a paragraph explaining whether this statement is true or false.

25. Problem Solving How will acceleration change if the mass being accelerated is multiplied by three but the net force is cut in half?

26. Applying Knowledge For each pair, determine whether the objects have the same momentum. If the objects have different momentums, determine which object has more momentum.

a. a car and train that have the same velocity
b. a moving ball and a still bat
c. two identical balls moving at the same speed in the same direction
d. two identical balls moving at the same speed in opposite directions

DEVELOPING LIFE/WORK SKILLS

27. Locating Information Use the library and/or the Internet to find out about the physiological effects of free fall. Also find out how astronauts counter the effects of living in a free-fall environment, sometimes called *microgravity.* Use your information to propose a minimum acceleration for a space shuttle to Mars that would minimize physiological problems for the crew, both during flight and upon return to Earth's atmosphere.

28. Interpreting Data At home, use a garden hose to investigate the laws of projectile motion. Design experiments to investigate how the angle of the hose affects the range of the water stream. (Assume that the initial speed of water is constant.) How can you make the water reach the maximum range? How can you make the water reach the highest point? What is the shape of the water stream at each angle? Present your results to the rest of the class, and discuss the conclusions with regard to projectile motion and its components.

internet connect

www.scilinks.org
Topic: Rocket Technology **SciLinks code:** HK4123

SCILINKS. Maintained by the National Science Teachers Association

29. Working Cooperatively Read the following arguments about rocket propulsion. With a small group, determine which of the following statements is correct. Use a diagram to explain your answer.

a. Rockets cannot travel in space because there is nothing for the gas exiting the rocket to push against.
b. Rockets can travel because gas exerts an unbalanced force on the front of the rocket. This net force causes the acceleration.
c. Argument b cannot be true. The action and reaction forces will be equal and opposite. Therefore, the forces will balance, and no movement will be possible.

INTEGRATING CONCEPTS

30. Connection to Social Studies Research Galileo's work on falling bodies. What did he want to demonstrate? What theories did he try to refute?

31. Concept Mapping Copy the concept map below onto a sheet of paper. Write the correct phrase in each lettered box.

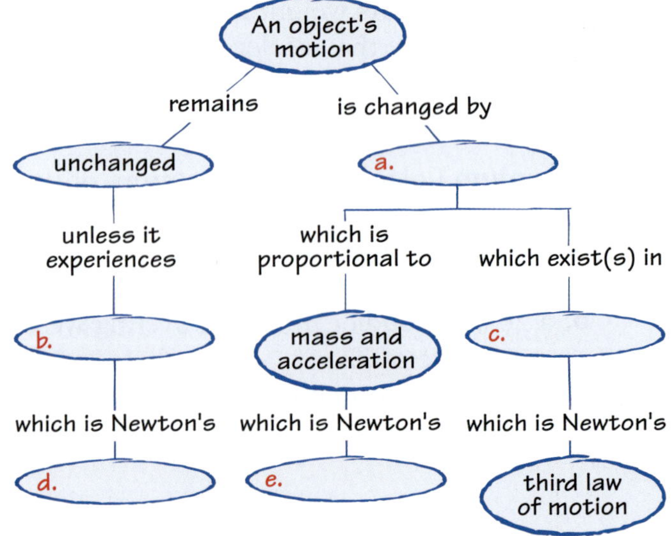

Standardized Test Prep

Understanding Concepts

***Directions (1–3):* For *each* question, write on a separate sheet of paper the letter of the correct answer.**

1 What is the net force on a 2.0 kg weight hanging motionless on a string?
- **A.** 0.0 N
- **B.** 2.0 N
- **C.** 9.8 N
- **D.** 19.6 N

2 What is the source of the force that causes a jet airplane to accelerate forward?
- **F.** gravitational pull
- **G.** air pressure on the wings
- **H.** exhaust gases pushing against the engine
- **I.** exhaust gases pushing against the atmosphere

3 Why does a skydiver not accelerate downward after reaching terminal velocity?
- **A.** The force of gravity is inactive on the skydiver at terminal velocity.
- **B.** Air resistance exceeds the force of gravity.
- **C.** Air resistance balances the force of gravity.
- **D.** The force of gravity decreases as the skydiver descends.

***Directions (4–5):* For *each* question, write a short response.**

4 The ancient Greek scientist, Aristotle, claimed that the speed of a falling object depends on its weight. But you can disprove his hypothesis by dropping a pen and a baseball simultaneously and observing when they hit the floor.

Why do falling objects not act as Aristotle thought they would?

For questions requiring an extended response, make an outline listing the key points of your response before you begin writing.

5 Analyze why you would weigh less on the surface of Mars, even though your body remains exactly the same size and shape.

Reading Skills

***Directions (6):* Read the passage below. Then answer the question.**

The United States Air Force trains astronauts in a large jet airplane, which is known as the "Vomit Comet" because many people get airsick during its flight. The plane accelerates upward and then falls back toward Earth, in the form of an arc. At the peak of its flight, the passengers seem to float inside the plane, and objects around them appear to be unaffected by gravity for about 20 seconds during each arc.

6 Describe the forces that are acting on the passengers as the plane begins its acceleration upward towards the top of the arc.

Interpreting Graphics

***Directions (7):* Base your answer to question 7 on the illustration below.**

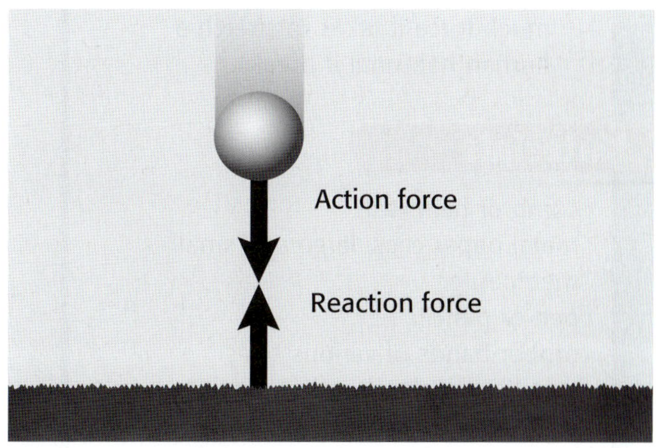

7 When a ball is falling toward Earth, what is the reaction force to the pull of gravity on the ball?
- **F.** air pressure pushing up on the ball
- **G.** force of the ground against the ball
- **H.** upward pull of the ball on Earth
- **I.** pull of gravity on the ball toward Earth

Skills Practice Lab

Introduction

How can you use a rubber band to measure the force necessary to break a human hair?

Objectives

- USING SCIENTIFIC METHODS ***Design*** an experiment to test a hypothesis.
- ***Build*** and calibrate an instrument that measures force.
- ***Use*** your instrument to measure how much force it takes to stretch a human hair until it breaks.

Materials

comb or hairbrush
metal paper clips, large and small
metric ruler
pen or pencil
rubber bands of various sizes
standard hooked masses ranging from 10 to 200 g

Measuring Forces

Procedure

Testing the Strength of a Human Hair

1. Obtain a rubber band and a paper clip.
2. Carefully straighten the paper clip so that it forms a double hook. Cut the rubber band and tie one end to the ring stand and the other end to one of the paper clip hooks. Let the paper clip dangle.
3. In your lab report, prepare a table as shown below.
4. Measure the length of the rubber band. Record this length in ***Table 1.***
5. Hang a hooked mass from the lower paper clip hook. Supporting the mass with your hand, allow the rubber band to stretch downward slowly. Then remove your hand carefully so the rubber band does not move.
6. Measure the stretched rubber band's length. Record the mass that is attached and the rubber band's length in ***Table 1.*** Calculate the change in length by subtracting your initial reading of the rubber band's length from the new length.
7. Repeat steps 5 and 6 three more times using different masses each time.
8. Convert each mass (in grams) to kilograms using the following equation.

   $$mass \text{ (in kg)} = mass \text{ (in g)} \div 1000$$

   Record your answers in ***Table 1.***
9. Calculate the force (weight) of each mass in newtons using the following equation.

   $$force \text{ (in N)} = mass \text{ (in kg)} \times 9.8 \text{ m/s}^2$$

   Record your answers in ***Table 1.***

Table 1 **Calibration**

Rubber-band length (cm)	Change in length (cm)	Mass on hook (g)	Mass on hook (kg)	Force (N)
	0	0	0	0

Designing Your Experiment

10. With your lab partner(s), devise a plan to measure the force required to break a human hair using the instrument you just calibrated. How will you attach the hair to your instrument? How will you apply force to the hair?
11. In your lab report, list each step you will perform in your experiment.
12. Have your teacher approve your plan before you carry out your experiment.

Performing Your Experiment

13. After your teacher approves your plan, gently run a comb or brush through a group member's hair several times until you find a loose hair at least 10 cm long that you can test.
14. In your lab report, prepare a data table similar to the one shown at right to record your experimental data.
15. Perform your experiment on three different hairs from the same person. Record the maximum rubber-band length before the hair snaps for each trial in Table 2.

Table 2 **Experimentation**

Trial	Rubber-band length (cm)	Force (N)
Hair 1		
Hair 2		
Hair 3		

▶ Analysis

1. Plot your calibration data in your lab report in the form of a graph like the one shown at right. On your graph draw the line or smooth curve that fits the points best.
2. Use the graph and the length of the rubber band for each trial of your experiment to determine the force that was necessary to break each of the three hairs. Record your answers in ***Table 2***.

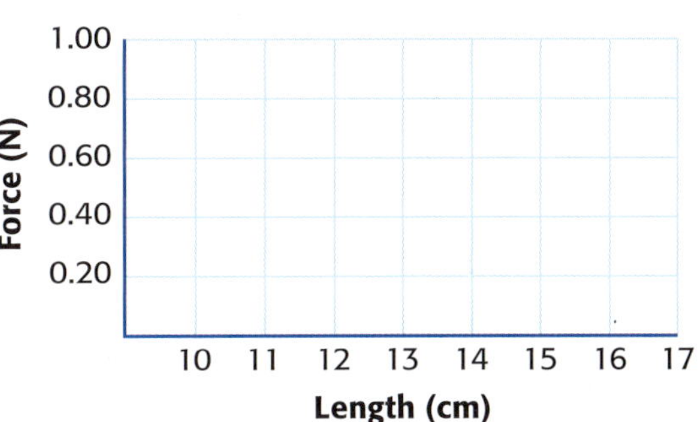

▶ Conclusions

3. Suppose someone tells you that your results are flawed because you measured length and not force. How can you show that your results are valid?

viewpoints

Should Bicycle Helmets Be Required by Law?

In some communities, bicyclists are required by law to wear a helmet and can be ticketed if they do not. Few people dispute the fact that bicycle helmets can save lives when used properly.

But others say that it is a matter of private rights and that the government should not interfere. Should it be up to bicyclists to decide whether or not to wear a helmet and to suffer any consequences?

But are the consequences limited to the rider? Who will pay when the rider gets hurt? Should the rider bear the cost of an injury that could have been prevented?

Is this an issue of public health or private rights? What do you think?

Require Bicycle Helmets

> FROM: Chad A., Rochester, MN

More and more people are getting head injuries every year because they do not wear a helmet. Nowadays helmets look so cool—I wouldn't be ashamed to wear one.

> FROM: Laurel R., Coral Springs, FL

I believe that this is a public issue only for people under the age of 12. Children 12 and under still need guidance and direction about safety, and they are usually the ones riding their bicycles out in the road or in traffic. Often they don't pay attention to cars or other motor vehicles around them.

> FROM: Jocelyn B., Chicago, IL

They should treat helmets the same way they treat seat belts. I was in a tragic bike accident when I was 7. I was jerked off my bike, and I slid on the glass-laden concrete. To make a long story short, I think there should be a helmet law because people just don't know the danger.

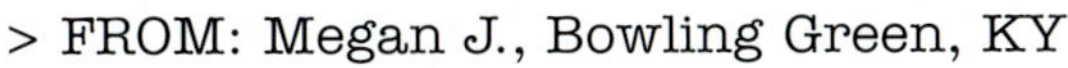

> FROM: Megan J., Bowling Green, KY

Although wearing a bicycle helmet can be considered a matter of public health, the rider is the one at risk. It is a personal choice, no matter what the public says.

> FROM: Melissa F., Houston, TX

Bicycle helmets shouldn't be required by law. Helmets are usually a little over $20, and if you have five kids, the helmets alone cost $100. You'd still have to buy the bikes.

Don't Require Bicycle Helmets

> FROM: Heather R., Rochester, MN

It has to do with private rights. The police have more serious issues to deal with, like violent crimes. Bicycle riders should choose whether or not they want to risk their life by riding without a helmet.

Your Turn

1. **Critiquing Viewpoints** Select one of the statements on this page that you agree with. Identify and explain at least one weak point in the statement. What would you say to respond to someone who brought up this weak point as a reason you were wrong?
2. **Critiquing Viewpoints** Select one of the statements on this page that you disagree with. Identify and explain at least one strong point in the statement. What would you say to respond to someone who brought up this point as a reason they were right?
3. **Creative Thinking** Suppose you live in a community that does not have a bicycle helmet law. Design a campaign to persuade people to wear helmets, even though it isn't required by law. Your campaign could include brochures, posters, and newspaper ads.
4. **Acquiring and Evaluating Data** When a rider falls off a bicycle, the rider continues moving at the speed of the bicycle until the rider strikes the pavement and slows down rapidly. For bicycle speeds ranging from 5.0 m/s to 25.0 m/s, calculate what acceleration would be required to stop the rider in just 0.50 s. How large is the force that must be applied to a 50.0 kg rider to cause this acceleration? Organize your data and results in a series of charts or graphs.

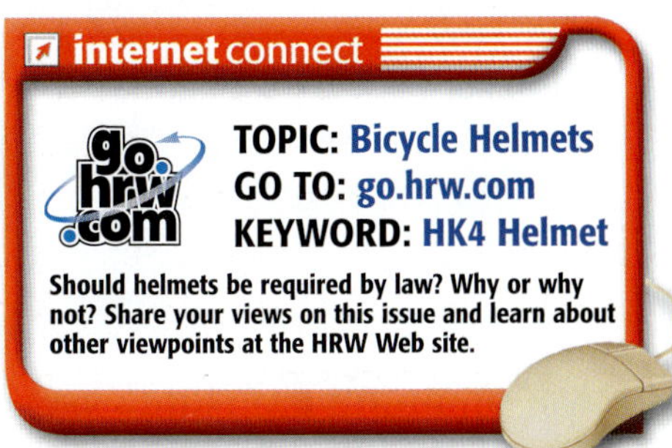

CHAPTER 12

Work and Energy

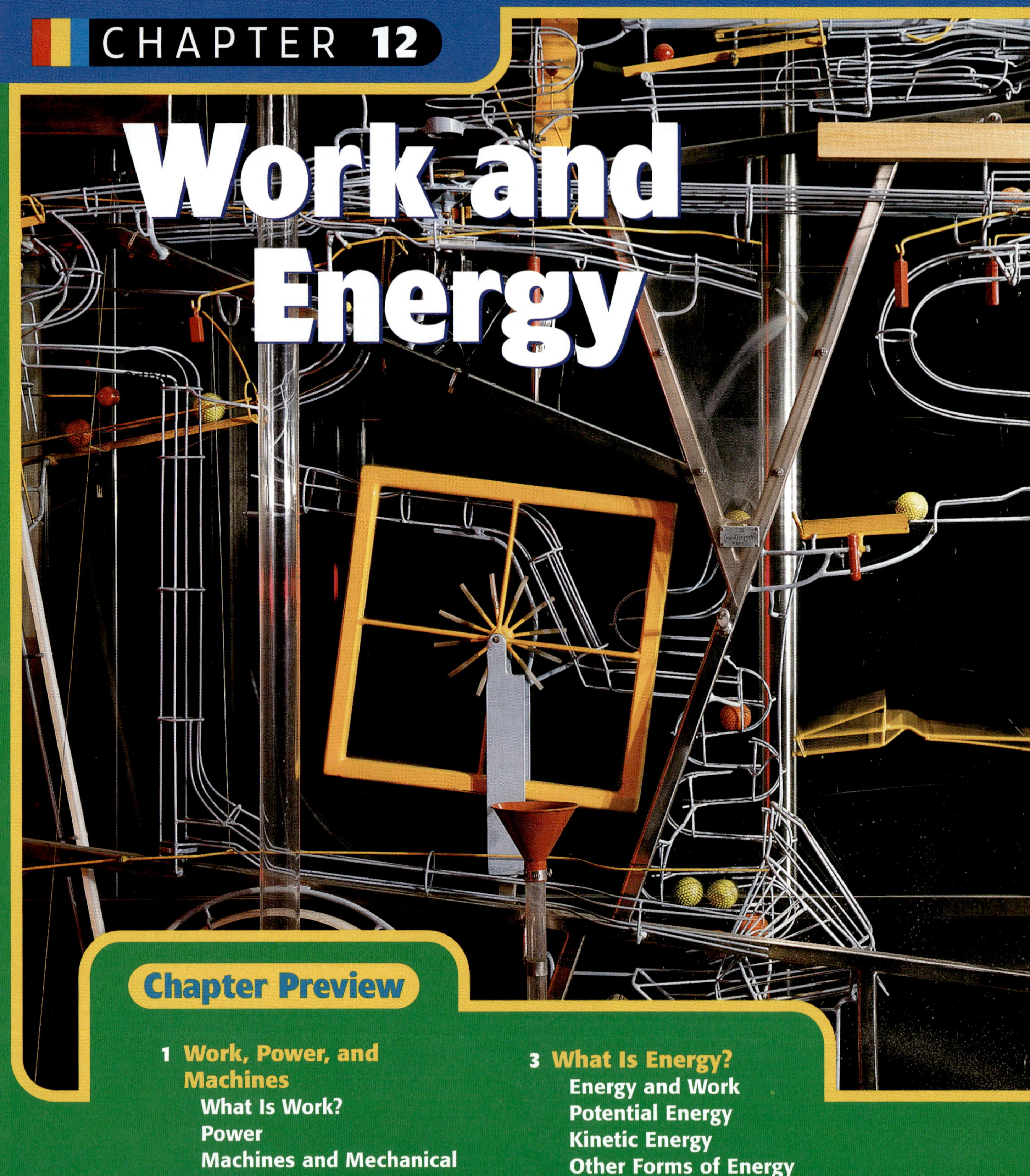

Chapter Preview

1 **Work, Power, and Machines**
- What Is Work?
- Power
- Machines and Mechanical Advantage

2 **Simple Machines**
- The Lever Family
- The Inclined Plane Family
- Compound Machines

3 **What Is Energy?**
- Energy and Work
- Potential Energy
- Kinetic Energy
- Other Forms of Energy

4 **Conservation of Energy**
- Energy Transformations
- The Law of Conservation of Energy
- Efficiency of Machines

Kinetic sculptures are sculptures that have moving parts. The changes in the motion of different parts of a kinetic sculpture can be explained in terms of forces or in terms of energy transformations.

Focus ACTIVITY

Background The collection of tubes, tracks, balls, and blocks of wood shown at left is an audio-kinetic sculpture. A conveyor belt lifts the balls to a point high on the track, and the balls wind their way down as they are pulled by the force of gravity and pushed by various other forces. They twist through spirals, drop straight down tubes, and sometimes go up and around loops as if on a roller coaster. Along the way, the balls trip levers and bounce off elastic membranes. The sculpture uses the energy of the falling balls to produce sounds in wood blocks and metal tubes.

This kinetic sculpture can be considered a machine or a collection of many small machines. Other kinetic sculptures may incorporate simple machines such as levers, wheels, and screws. The American artist Alexander Calder, shown at left, is well known for his hanging mobiles that move in response to air currents.

This chapter introduces the basic principles of energy that explain the motions and interactions of machines.

Activity 1 Look around your kitchen or garage. What kinds of tools or utensils do you see? How do these tools help with different kinds of projects? For each tool, consider where force is applied to the tool and how the tool may apply force to another object. Is the force transferred to another part of the tool? Is the force that the tool can exert on an object larger or smaller than the force exerted on the tool?

Activity 2 Any piece of artwork that moves is a kinetic sculpture. Design one of your own. Some ideas for materials include hangers, rubber bands, string, wood and metal scraps, and old toys.

Pre-Reading Questions

1. How would you define work and energy? Do these words have the same meaning in everyday speech and in science?
2. What different types of energy do you know about?

SECTION 1

Work, Power, and Machines

KEY TERM

work
power
mechanical advantage

OBJECTIVES

- **Define** *work* and *power*.
- **Calculate** the work done on an object and the rate at which work is done.
- **Use** the concept of mechanical advantage to explain how machines make doing work easier.
- **Calculate** the mechanical advantage of various machines.

If you needed to change a flat tire, you would probably use a car jack to lift the car. Machines—from complex ones such as a car to relatively simple ones such as a car jack, a hammer, or a ramp—help people get things done every day.

What Is Work?

work the transfer of energy to a body by the application of a force that causes the body to move in the direction of the force

Imagine trying to lift the front of a car without using a jack. You could exert a lot of force without moving the car at all. Exerting all that force might seem like hard work. In science, however, the word **work** has a very specific meaning.

Work is done only when force causes a change in the position or the motion of an object in the direction of the applied force. Work is calculated by multiplying the force by the distance over which the force is applied. We will always assume that the force used to calculate work is acting along the line of motion of the object.

Work Equation

$$work = force \times distance$$
$$W = F \times d$$

In the case of trying to lift the car, you might apply a large force, but if the distance that the car moves is equal to zero, the work done on the car is also equal to zero.

However, once the car moves even a small amount, you have done some work on it. You could calculate how much by multiplying the force you have applied by the distance the car moves.

The weightlifter in ***Figure 1*** is applying a force to the barbell as she holds it overhead, but the barbell is not moving. Is she doing any work on the barbell?

Figure 1
As this weightlifter holds the barbell over her head, is she doing any work on the barbell?

Work is measured in joules

Because work is calculated as force times distance, it is measured in units of newtons times meters, N•m. These units are also called *joules* (J). In terms of SI base units, a joule is equivalent to 1 kg•m^2/s^2.

$$1\ \text{N}\bullet\text{m} = 1\ \text{J} = 1\ \text{kg}\bullet\text{m}^2/\text{s}^2$$

Because these units are all equal, you can choose whichever unit is easiest for solving a particular problem. Substituting equivalent units will often help you cancel out other units in a problem.

You do about 1 J of work when you slowly lift an apple, which weighs about 1 N, from your arm's length down at your side to the top of your head, a distance of about 1 m.

Disc Two, Module 10: **Work**
Use the Interactive Tutor to learn more about this topic.

Math Skills

Work Imagine a father playing with his daughter by lifting her repeatedly in the air. How much work does he do with each lift, assuming he lifts her 2.0 m and exerts an average force of 190 N?

1 List the given and unknown values.

Given: *force*, F = 190 N

distance, d = 2.0 m

Unknown: *work*, W = ? J

2 Write the equation for work.

work = *force* × *distance* $W = F \times d$

3 Insert the known values into the equation, and solve.

$W = 190\ \text{N} \times 2.0\ \text{m} = 380\ \text{N}\bullet\text{m} = 380\ \text{J}$

Practice

Work

1. A crane uses an average force of 5200 N to lift a girder 25 m. How much work does the crane do on the girder?
2. An apple weighing 1 N falls through a distance of 1 m. How much work is done on the apple by the force of gravity?
3. The brakes on a bicycle apply 125 N of frictional force to the wheels as the bicycle travels 14.0 m. How much work have the brakes done on the bicycle?
4. While rowing in a race, John uses his arms to exert a force of 165 N per stroke while pulling the oar 0.800 m. How much work does he do in 30 strokes?
5. A mechanic uses a hydraulic lift to raise a 1200 kg car 0.5 m off the ground. How much work does the lift do on the car?

▶ In order to use the work equation, you must use units of newtons for force and units of meters for distance. Practice Problem 5 gives a mass in kilograms instead of a weight in newtons. To convert from mass to force (weight), use the definition of weight:

$$w = mg$$

where m is the mass in kilograms and g = 9.8 m/s^2. Then plug the value for weight into the work equation as the force.

Power

Running up a flight of stairs doesn't require more work than walking up slowly does, but it is more exhausting. The amount of time it takes to do work is an important factor when considering work and machines. The quantity that measures work in relation to time is **power.** Power is the rate at which work is done, that is, how much work is done in a given amount of time.

power a quantity that measures the rate at which work is done or energy is transformed

Power Equation

$$power = \frac{work}{time} \qquad P = \frac{W}{t}$$

Running takes less time than walking does. How does reducing the time in this equation affect the power if the amount of work stays the same?

Power is measured in watts

Power is measured in SI units called *watts* (W). A watt is the amount of power required to do 1 J of work in 1 s, about as much power as you need to lift an apple over your head in 1 s. Do not confuse the abbreviation for watts, W, with the symbol for work, *W*. You can tell which one is meant by the context in which it appears and by whether it is in italics.

What is your power output when you climb the stairs?

Materials ✔ *flight of stairs* ✔ *stopwatch* ✔ *meterstick*

1. Determine your weight in newtons. If your school has a scale that reads in kilograms, multiply your mass in kilograms by 9.8 m/s^2 to determine your weight in newtons. If your school has a scale that weighs in pounds, multiply your weight by a factor of 4.45 N/lb.
2. Divide into pairs. Have your partner use the stopwatch to time how long it takes you to walk quickly up the stairs. Record the time. Then switch roles and repeat.
3. Measure the height of one step in meters. Multiply the number of steps by the height of one step to get the total height of the stairway.
4. Multiply your weight in newtons by the height of the stairs in meters to get the work you did in joules. Recall the work equation: *work* = *force* × *distance,* or $W = F \times d$.
5. To get your power in watts, divide the work done in joules by the time in seconds that it took you to climb the stairs.

Analysis

1. How would your power output change if you walked up the stairs faster?
2. What would your power output be if you climbed the same stairs in the same amount of time while carrying a stack of books weighing 20 N?
3. Why did you use your weight as the force in the work equation?

Math Skills

Power It takes 100 kJ of work to lift an elevator 18 m. If this is done in 20 s, what is the average power of the elevator during the process?

1 List the given and unknown values.

Given: *work,* $W = 100 \text{ kJ} = 1 \times 10^5 \text{ J}$

time, $t = 20 \text{ s}$

The distance of 18 m will not be needed to calculate power.

Unknown: *power,* $P = ?\ \text{W}$

2 Write the equation for power.

$$power = \frac{work}{time} \qquad P = \frac{W}{t}$$

3 Insert the known values into the equation, and solve.

$$P = \frac{1 \times 10^5 \text{ J}}{20 \text{ s}} = 5 \times 10^3 \text{ J/s}$$

$$P = 5 \times 10^3 \text{ W}$$

$$P = 5 \text{ kW}$$

Did You Know?

Another common unit of power is horsepower (hp). This originally referred to the average power output of a draft horse. One horsepower equals 746 W. With that much power, a horse could raise a load of 746 apples, weighing 1 N each, by 1 m every second.

Practice

Power

1. While rowing across the lake during a race, John does 3960 J of work on the oars in 60.0 s. What is his power output in watts?
2. Every second, a certain coal-fired power plant produces enough electricity to do 9×10^8 J (900 MJ) of work. What is the power output of this power plant in units of watts (or in units of megawatts)?
3. Using a jack, a mechanic does 5350 J of work to lift a car 0.500 m in 50.0 s. What is the mechanic's power output?
4. Suppose you are moving a 300 N box of books. Calculate your power output in the following situations:
   a. You exert a force of 60.0 N to push the box across the floor 12.0 m in 20.0 s.
   b. You lift the box 1 m onto a truck in 3 s.
5. Anna walks up the stairs on her way to class. She weighs 565 N and the stairs go up 3.25 m vertically.
   a. Calculate her power output if she climbs the stairs in 12.6 s.
   b. What is her power output if she climbs the stairs in 10.5 s?

▶ In order to calculate power in Practice Problems 4 and 5, you must first use the work equation to calculate the work done in each case.

Machines and Mechanical Advantage

Figure 2

A jack makes it easier to lift a car by multiplying the input force and spreading the work out over a large distance.

Which is easier, lifting a car yourself or using a jack as shown in ***Figure 2?*** Which requires more work? Using a jack is obviously easier. But you may be surprised to learn that using a jack requires the same amount of work. The jack makes the work easier by allowing you to apply less force at any given moment.

Machines multiply and redirect forces

Machines help us do work by redistributing the work that we put into them. Machines can change the direction of an input force. Machines can also increase or decrease force by changing the distance over which the force is applied. This process is often called multiplying the force.

Different forces can do the same amount of work

Compare the amount of work required to lift a box straight onto the bed of a truck, as shown in ***Figure 3A,*** with the amount of work required to push the same box up a ramp, as shown in ***Figure 3B.*** When the mover lifts straight up, he must apply 225 N of force for a short distance. Using the ramp, he can apply a smaller force over a longer distance. But the work done is about the same in both cases.

Both a car jack and a loading ramp make doing work easier by increasing the distance over which force is applied. As a result, the force required at any point is reduced. Therefore, a machine allows the same amount of work to be done by either decreasing the distance while increasing the force or by decreasing the force while increasing the distance.

Figure 3

A When lifting a box straight up, a mover applies a large force over a short distance.

B Using a ramp to lift the box, the mover applies a smaller force over a longer distance.

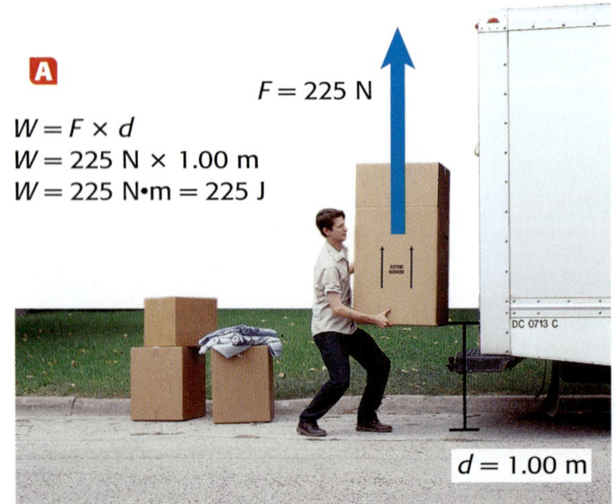

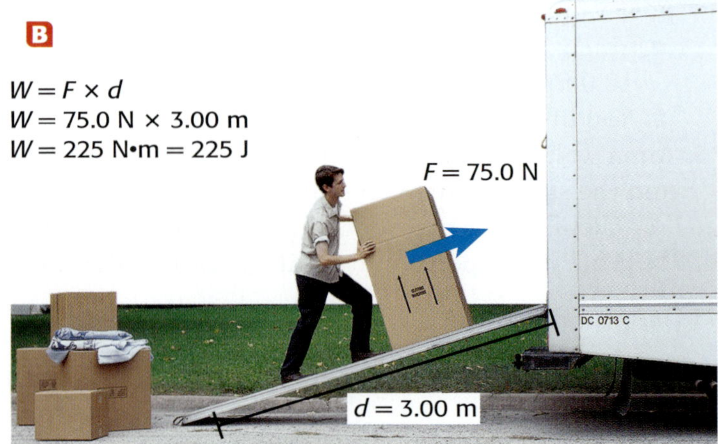

Mechanical advantage tells how much a machine multiplies force or increases distance

A ramp makes doing work easier by increasing the distance over which force is applied. But how long should the ramp be? An extremely long ramp would allow the mover to use very little force, but he would have to push the box a long distance. A very short ramp, on the other hand, would be too steep and would not help him very much.

To solve problems like this, scientists and engineers use a number that describes how much the force or distance is multiplied by a machine. This number is called the **mechanical advantage,** and it is defined as the ratio between the output force and the input force. It is also equal to the ratio between the input distance and the output distance if friction is ignored.

Mechanical Advantage Equation

$$\textit{mechanical advantage} = \frac{\textit{output force}}{\textit{input force}} = \frac{\textit{input distance}}{\textit{output distance}}$$

mechanical advantage a quantity that measures how much a machine multiplies force or distance

A machine with a mechanical advantage greater than 1 multiplies the input force. Such a machine can help you move or lift heavy objects, such as a car or a box of books. A machine with a mechanical advantage of less than 1 does not multiply force, but increases distance and speed. When you swing a baseball bat, your arms and the bat together form a machine that increases speed without multiplying force.

Math Skills

Mechanical Advantage Calculate the mechanical advantage of a ramp that is 5.0 m long and 1.5 m high.

1 List the given and unknown values.

Given: *input distance* = 5.0 m

output distance = 1.5 m

Unknown: *mechanical advantage* = ?

2 Write the equation for mechanical advantage.

Because the information we are given involves only distance, we only need part of the full equation:

$$\textit{mechanical advantage} = \frac{\textit{input distance}}{\textit{output distance}}$$

3 Insert the known values into the equation, and solve.

$$\textit{mechanical advantage} = \frac{5.0\ \cancel{m}}{1.5\ \cancel{m}} = 3.3$$

INTEGRATING BIOLOGY

You may not do any work on a car if you try to lift it without a jack, but your body will still get tired from the effort because you are doing work on the muscles inside your body.

When you try to lift something, your muscles contract over and over in response to a series of electrical impulses from your brain. With each contraction, a tiny bit of work is done on the muscles. In just a few seconds, this can add up to thousands of contractions and a significant amount of work.

- The mechanical advantage equation can be rearranged to isolate any of the variables on the left.
- For practice problem 4, you will need to rearrange the equation to isolate output force on the left.
- For practice problem 5, you will need to rearrange to isolate output distance. When rearranging, use only the part of the full equation that you need.

Practice

Mechanical Advantage

1. Calculate the mechanical advantage of a ramp that is 6.0 m long and 1.5 m high.
2. Determine the mechanical advantage of an automobile jack that lifts a 9900 N car with an input force of 150 N.
3. A sailor uses a rope and pulley to raise a sail weighing 140 N. The sailor pulls down with a force of 140 N on the rope. What is the mechanical advantage of the pulley?
4. Alex pulls on the handle of a claw hammer with a force of 15 N. If the hammer has a mechanical advantage of 5.2, how much force is exerted on a nail in the claw?
5. While rowing in a race, John pulls the handle of an oar 0.80 m on each stroke. If the oar has a mechanical advantage of 1.5, how far does the blade of the oar move through the water on each stroke?

SECTION 1 REVIEW

SUMMARY

- Work is done when a force causes an object to move. This meaning is different from the everyday meaning of *work*.
- Work is equal to force times distance. The most commonly used SI unit for work is joules.
- Power is the rate at which work is done. The SI unit for power is watts.
- Machines help people by redistributing the work put into them. They can change either the size or the direction of the input force.
- The mechanical advantage of a machine describes how much the machine multiplies force or increases distance.

1. Define work and power. How are work and power related to each other?
2. Determine if work is being done in these situations:
   a. lifting a spoonful of soup to your mouth
   b. holding a stack of books motionless over your head
   c. letting a pencil fall to the ground
3. **Describe** how a ramp can make lifting a box easier without changing the amount of work being done.
4. **Critical Thinking** A short ramp and a long ramp both reach a height of 1 m. Which has a greater mechanical advantage?

Math Skills

5. How much work in joules is done by a person who uses a force of 25 N to move a desk 3.0 m?
6. A bus driver applies a force of 55.0 N to the steering wheel, which in turn applies 132 N of force on the steering column. What is the mechanical advantage of the steering wheel?
7. A student who weighs 400 N climbs a 3 m ladder in 4 s.
   a. How much work does the student do?
   b. What is the student's power output?
8. An outboard engine on a boat can do 1.0×10^6 J of work in 50.0 s. Calculate its power in watts. Convert your answer to horsepower (1 hp = 746 W).

SECTION 2

Simple Machines

OBJECTIVES

- **Name** and describe the six types of simple machines.
- **Discuss** the mechanical advantage of different types of simple machines.
- **Recognize** simple machines within compound machines.

KEY TERMS
simple machines
compound machines

The most basic machines of all are called **simple machines.** Other machines are either modifications of simple machines or combinations of several simple machines. ***Figure 4*** shows examples of the six types of simple machines. Simple machines are divided into two families, the lever family and the inclined plane family.

simple machine one of the six basic types of machines, which are the basis for all other forms of machines

The Lever Family

To understand how levers do work, imagine using a claw hammer to pull out a nail. As you pull on the handle of the hammer, the head turns around the point where it meets the wood. The force you apply to the handle is transferred to the claw on the other end of the hammer. The claw then does work on the nail.

Figure 4
The Six Simple Machines

Figure 5

The Three Classes of Levers

A All **first-class levers** have a fulcrum located between the points of application of the input and output forces.

B In a **second-class lever,** the fulcrum is at one end of the arm and the input force is applied to the other end. The wheel of a wheelbarrow is a fulcrum.

C **Third-class levers** multiply distance rather than force. As a result, they have a mechanical advantage of less than 1. The human body contains many third-class levers.

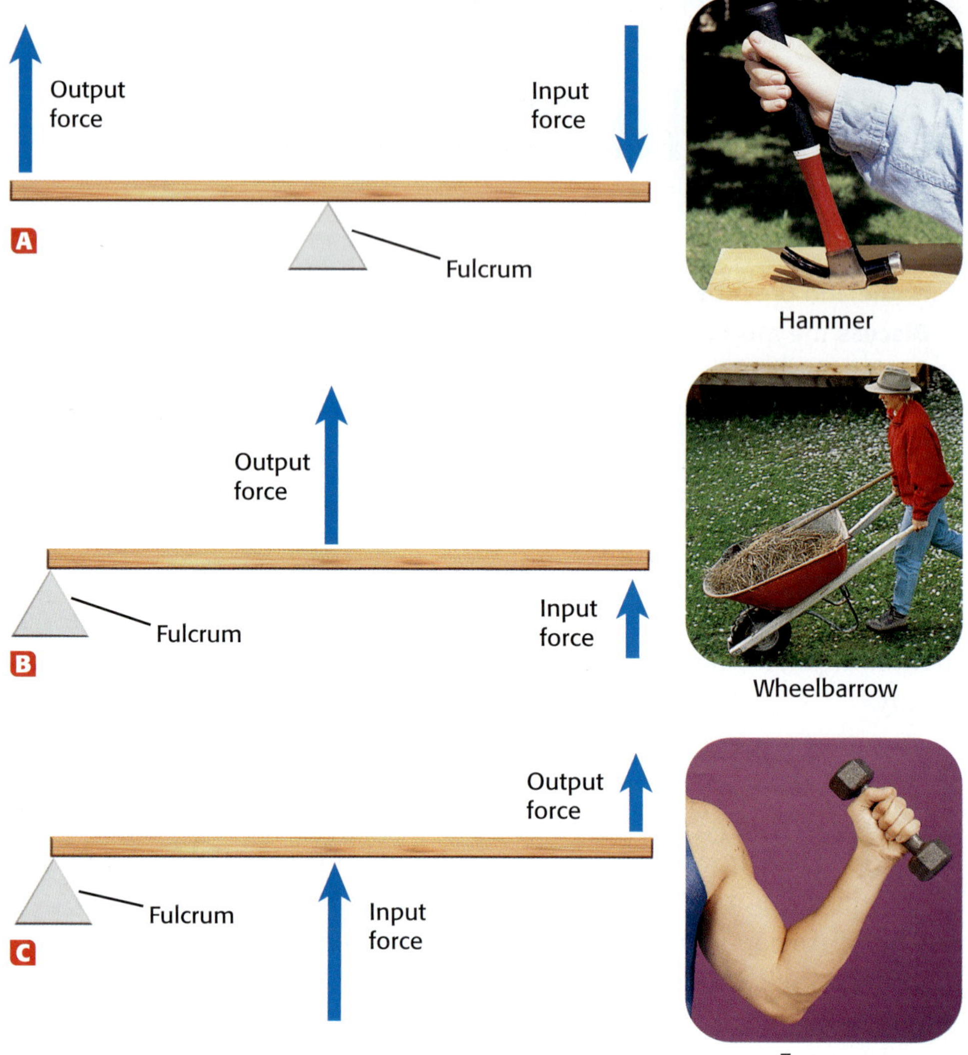

Levers are divided into three classes

All levers have a rigid *arm* that turns around a point called the *fulcrum*. Force is transferred from one part of the arm to another. In that way, the original input force can be multiplied or redirected into an output force. Levers are divided into three classes depending on the location of the fulcrum and of the input and output forces.

Figure 5A shows a claw hammer as an example of a first-class lever. First-class levers are the most common type. A pair of pliers is made of two first-class levers joined together.

Figure 5B shows a wheelbarrow as an example of a second-class lever. Other examples of second-class levers include nutcrackers and hinged doors.

Figure 5C shows the human forearm as an example of a third-class lever. The biceps muscle, which is attached to the bone near the elbow, contracts a short distance to move the hand a large distance.

Pulleys are modified levers

You may have used pulleys to lift things, as when raising a flag to the top of a flagpole or hoisting a sail on a boat. A pulley is another type of simple machine in the lever family.

Figure 6A shows how a pulley is like a lever. The point in the middle of a pulley is like the fulcrum of a lever. The rest of the pulley behaves like the rigid arm of a first-class lever. Because the distance from the fulcrum is the same on both sides of a pulley, a single, fixed pulley has a mechanical advantage of 1.

Using moving pulleys or more than one pulley at a time can increase the mechanical advantage, as shown in ***Figure 6B*** and ***Figure 6C.*** Multiple pulleys are sometimes put together in a single unit called a *block and tackle*.

Figure 6

The Mechanical Advantage of Pulleys

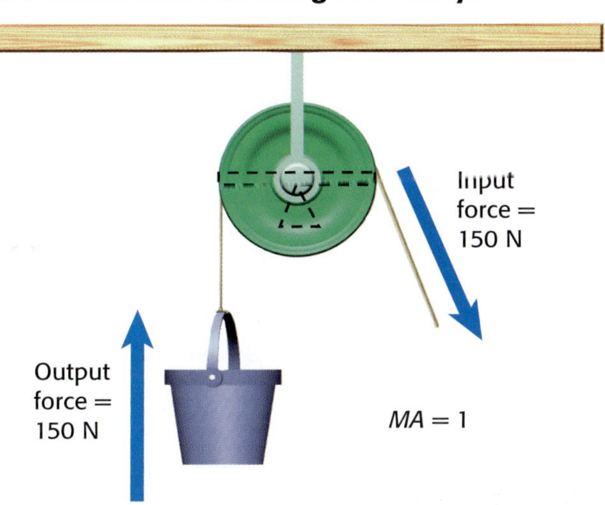

A Lifting a 150 N weight with a single, fixed pulley, the weight must be fully supported by the rope on each side of the pulley. This type of pulley has a mechanical advantage of 1.

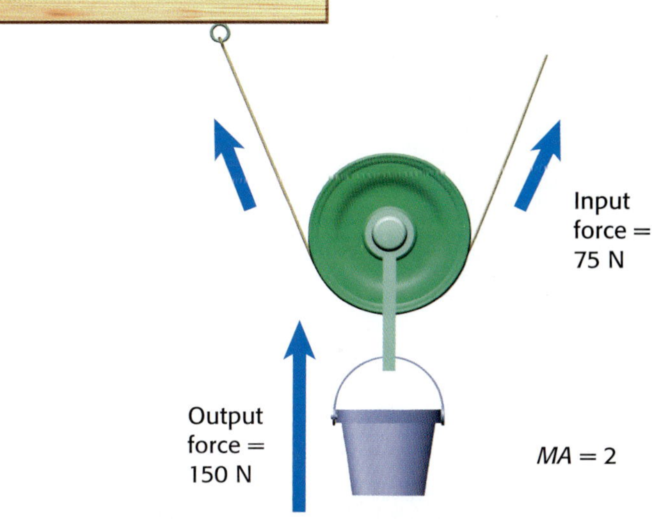

B Using a moving pulley, the 150 N force is shared by two sections of rope pulling upward. The input force on the right side of the pulley has to support only half of the weight. This pulley system has a mechanical advantage of 2.

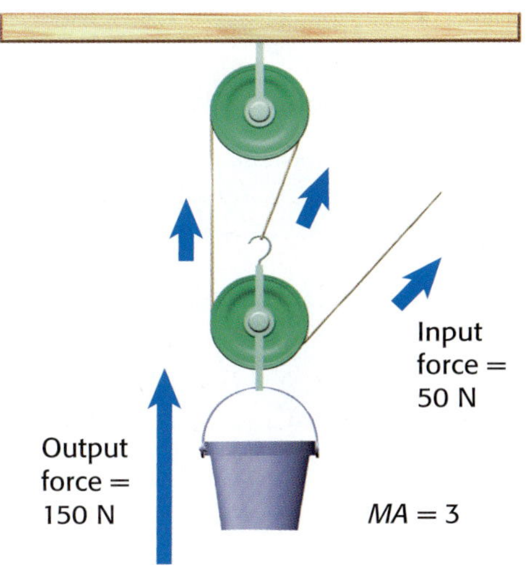

C In this arrangement of multiple pulleys, all of the sections of rope pull up against the downward force of the weight. This gives an even higher mechanical advantage.

Figure 7
How is a wheel and axle like a lever? How is it different from a pulley?

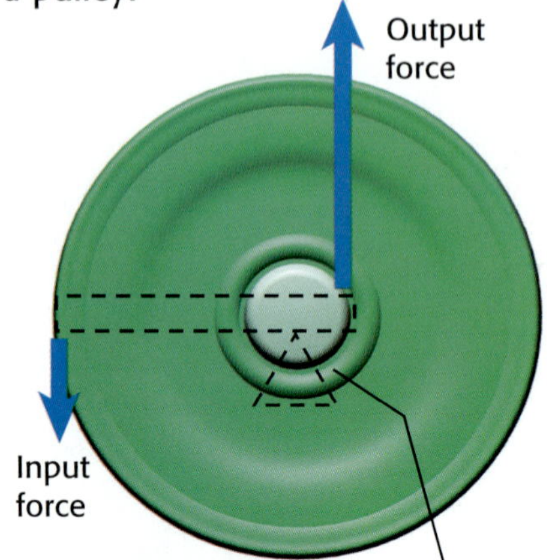

A wheel and axle is a lever or pulley connected to a shaft

The steering wheel of a car is another kind of simple machine: a wheel and axle. A wheel and axle is made of a lever or a pulley (the wheel) connected to a shaft (the axle), as shown in **Figure 7.** When the wheel is turned, the axle also turns. When a small input force is applied to the steering wheel, the force is multiplied to become a large output force applied to the steering column, which turns the front wheels of the car. Screwdrivers and cranks are other common wheel-and-axle machines.

The Inclined Plane Family

Earlier we showed how pushing an object up a ramp requires less force than lifting the same object straight up. A loading ramp is another type of simple machine, an inclined plane.

Inclined planes multiply and redirect force

When you push an object up a ramp, you apply a force to the object in a direction parallel to the ramp. The ramp then redirects this force to lift the object upward. This is why the output force of the ramp is shown in **Figure 8A** as an arrow pointing straight up. The output force is the force needed to lift the object straight up.

An inclined plane turns a small input force into a large output force by spreading the work out over a large distance. Pushing something up a long ramp that climbs gradually is easier than pushing something up a short, steep ramp.

Quick ACTIVITY

A Simple Inclined Plane

1. Make an inclined plane out of a board and a stack of books.
2. Tie a string to an object that is heavy but has low friction, such as a metal toy car or a roll of wire. Use the string to pull the object up the plane.
3. Still using the string, try to lift the object straight up through the same distance.
4. Which action required more force? In which case did you do more work?

Figure 8 **The Inclined Plane Family**

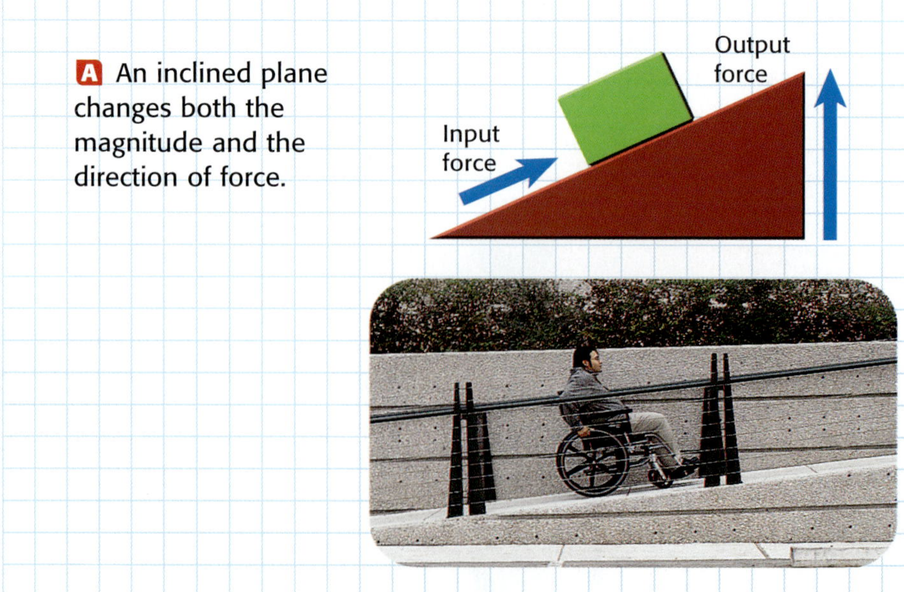

A An inclined plane changes both the magnitude and the direction of force.

A wedge is a modified inclined plane

When an ax blade or a splitting wedge hits a piece of wood, it pushes through the wood and breaks it apart, as shown in ***Figure 8B.*** An ax blade is an example of a wedge, another kind of simple machine in the inclined plane family. A wedge functions like two inclined planes back to back. Using a wedge is like pushing a ramp instead of pushing an object up the ramp. A wedge turns a single downward force into two forces directed out to the sides. Some types of wedges, such as nails, are used as fasteners.

A screw is an inclined plane wrapped around a cylinder

A type of simple machine that you probably use often is a screw. The threads on a screw look like a spiral inclined plane. In fact, a screw is an inclined plane wrapped around a cylinder, as shown in ***Figure 8C.*** Like pushing an object up a ramp, tightening a screw with gently sloping threads requires a small force acting over a large distance. Tightening a screw with steeper threads requires more force. Jar lids are screws that people use every day. Spiral staircases are also common screws.

Connection to SOCIAL STUDIES

The ancient Egyptians built dozens of large stone pyramids as tombs for the bodies of kings and queens. The largest of these is the pyramid of Khufu at Giza, also called the Great Pyramid. It is made of more than 2 million blocks of stone. These blocks have an average weight of 2.5 tons, and the largest blocks weigh 15 tons. How did the Egyptians get these huge stones onto the pyramid?

Making the Connection

1. The Great Pyramid is about 140 m tall. How much work would be required to raise an average-sized pyramid block to this height? (2.5 tons = 2.2×10^4 N)
2. If the Egyptians used ramps with a mechanical advantage of 3, then an average block could be moved with a force of 7.3×10^3 N. If one person can pull with a force of 525 N, how many people would it take to pull an average block up such a ramp?

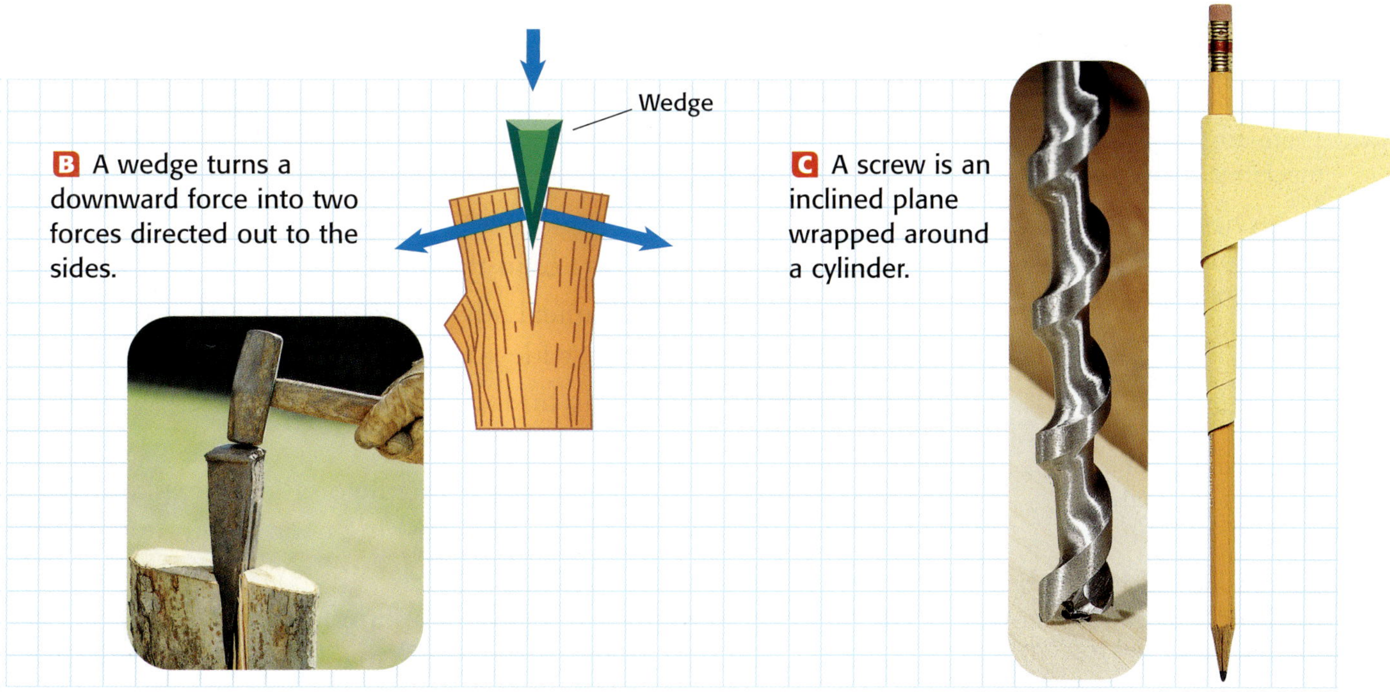

B A wedge turns a downward force into two forces directed out to the sides.

C A screw is an inclined plane wrapped around a cylinder.

Compound Machines

compound machine a machine made of more than one simple machine

Many devices that you use every day are made of more than one simple machine. A machine that combines two or more simple machines is called a **compound machine.** A pair of scissors, for example, uses two first class levers joined at a common fulcrum; each lever arm has a wedge that cuts into the paper. Most car jacks use a lever in combination with a large screw.

Of course, many machines are much more complex than these. How many simple machines can you identify in the bicycle shown in ***Figure 9?*** How many can you identify in a car?

Figure 9

A bicycle is made of many simple machines.

SECTION 2 REVIEW

SUMMARY

- The most basic machines are called simple machines. There are six types of simple machines in two families.
- Levers have a rigid arm and a fulcrum. There are three classes of levers.
- Pulleys and wheel-and-axle machines are also in the lever family.
- The inclined plane family includes inclined planes, wedges, and screws.
- Compound machines are made of two or more simple machines.

1. **List** the six types of simple machines.
2. **Identify** the kind of simple machine represented by each of these examples:
   a. a drill bit **b.** a skateboard ramp **c.** a boat oar
3. **Describe** how a lever can increase the force without changing the amount of work being done.
4. **Explain** why pulleys are in the lever family.
5. **Compare** the mechanical advantage of a long, thin wedge with that of a short, wide wedge. Which is greater?
6. **Critical Thinking** Can an inclined plane have a mechanical advantage of less than 1?
7. **Critical Thinking** Using the principle of a lever, explain why it is easier to open a door by pushing near the knob than by pushing near the hinges. What class of lever is a door?
8. **Creative Thinking** Choose a compound machine that you use every day, and identify the simple machines that it contains.

SECTION 3

What Is Energy?

OBJECTIVES

- **Explain** the relationship between energy and work.
- **Define** *potential energy* and *kinetic energy.*
- **Calculate** kinetic energy and gravitational potential energy.
- **Distinguish** between mechanical and nonmechanical energy.

KEY TERMS

potential energy
kinetic energy
mechanical energy

The world around you is full of energy. When you see a flash of lightning and hear a thunderclap, you are observing light and sound energy. When you ride a bicycle, you have energy just because you are moving. Even things that are sitting still have energy waiting to be released. We use other forms of energy, like nuclear energy and electrical energy, to power things in our world, from submarines to flashlights. Without energy, living organisms could not survive. Our bodies use a great deal of energy every day just to stay alive.

Energy and Work

When you stretch a slingshot, as shown in ***Figure 10,*** you are doing work, and you transfer energy to the elastic band. When the elastic band snaps back, it may in turn transfer that energy again by doing work on a stone in the slingshot. Whenever work is done, energy is transformed or transferred to another system. In fact, one way to define energy is as the ability to do work.

Figure 10
A stretched slingshot has the ability to do work.

Energy is measured in joules

While work is done only when an object experiences a change in its position or motion, energy can be present in an object or a system when nothing is happening at all. But energy can be observed only when it is transferred from one object or system to another, as when a slingshot transfers the energy from its elastic band to a stone in the sling.

The amount of energy transferred from the slingshot can be measured by how much work is done on the stone. Because energy is a measure of the ability to do work, energy and work are expressed in the same units—joules.

Potential Energy

Stretching a rubber band requires work. If you then release the stretched rubber band, it will fly away from your hand. The energy used to stretch the rubber band is stored as potential energy so that it can do work at a later time. But where is the energy between the time you do work on the rubber band and the time you release it?

Figure 11

This apple has gravitational potential energy. The energy results from the gravitational attraction between the apple and Earth.

Potential energy is stored energy

A stretched rubber band stores energy in a form called **potential energy.** Potential energy is sometimes called energy of position because it results from the relative positions of objects in a system. The rubber band has potential energy because the two ends of the band are far away from each other. The energy stored in any type of stretched or compressed elastic material, such as a spring or a bungee cord, is called *elastic potential energy.*

The apple in ***Figure 11*** will fall if the stem breaks off the branch. The energy that could potentially do work on the apple results from its position above the ground. This type of stored energy is called *gravitational potential energy.* Any system of two or more objects separated by a distance contains gravitational potential energy resulting from the gravitational attraction between the objects.

potential energy the energy that an object has because of the position, shape, or condition of the object

Gravitational potential energy depends on both mass and height

An apple at the top of the tree has more gravitational potential energy with respect to the Earth than a similar apple on a lower branch. But if two apples of different masses are at the same height, the heavier apple has more gravitational potential energy than the lighter one.

Because it results from the force of gravity, gravitational potential energy depends both on the mass of the objects in a system and on the distance between them.

Gravitational Potential Energy Equation

$$grav.\ PE = mass \times free\text{-}fall\ acceleration \times height$$

$$PE = mgh$$

In this equation, notice that *mg* is the weight of the object in newtons, which is the same as the force on the object due to gravity. So this equation is really just a calculation of force times distance, like the work equation.

Height can be relative

The height used in the equation for gravitational potential energy is usually measured from the ground. However, in some cases, a relative height might be more important. For example, if an apple were in a position to fall into a bird's nest on a lower branch, the apple's height above the nest could be used to calculate the apple's potential energy relative to the nest.

Math Skills

Gravitational Potential Energy A 65 kg rock climber ascends a cliff. What is the climber's gravitational potential energy at a point 35 m above the base of the cliff?

1 List the given and unknown values.

Given: *mass,* $m = 65$ kg

height, $h = 35$ m

free-fall acceleration, $g = 9.8\ \text{m/s}^2$

Unknown: *gravitational potential energy,* $PE = ?$ J

2 Write the equation for gravitational potential energy.

$PE = mgh$

3 Insert the known values into the equation, and solve.

$PE = (65\ \text{kg})(9.8\ \text{m/s}^2)(35\ \text{m})$

$PE = 2.2 \times 10^4\ \text{kg}\bullet\text{m}^2/\text{s}^2 = 2.2 \times 10^4\ \text{J}$

Practice

Gravitational Potential Energy

1. Calculate the gravitational potential energy in the following systems:
   a. a car with a mass of 1200 kg at the top of a 42 m high hill
   b. a 65 kg climber on top of Mount Everest (8800 m high)
   c. a 0.52 kg bird flying at an altitude of 550 m
2. Lake Mead, the reservoir above Hoover Dam, has a surface area of approximately 640 km^2. The top 1 m of water in the lake weighs about 6.3×10^{12} N. The dam holds that top layer of water 220 m above the river below. Calculate the gravitational potential energy of the top 1 m of water in Lake Mead.
3. A science student holds a 55 g egg out a window. Just before the student releases the egg, the egg has 8.0 J of gravitational potential energy with respect to the ground. How far is the student's arm from the ground in meters? (**Hint:** Convert the mass to kilograms before solving.)
4. A diver has 3400 J of gravitational potential energy after stepping up onto a diving platform that is 6.0 m above the water. What is the diver's mass in kilograms?

- The gravitational potential energy equation can be rearranged to isolate height on the left.

  $mgh = PE$

  Divide both sides by mg, and cancel.

  $$\frac{\cancel{mg}h}{\cancel{mg}} = \frac{PE}{mg}$$

  $$h = \frac{PE}{mg}$$

- You will need this version of the equation for practice problem 3.
- For practice problem 4, you will need to rearrange the equation to isolate mass on the left. When solving these problems, use $g = 9.8\ \text{m/s}^2$.

Kinetic Energy

Once an apple starts to fall from the branch of a tree, as in ***Figure 12A,*** it has the ability to do work. Because the apple is moving, it can do work when it hits the ground or lands on the head of someone under the tree. The energy that an object has because it is in motion is called **kinetic energy.**

kinetic energy the energy of a moving object due to the object's motion

Kinetic energy depends on mass and speed

A falling apple can do more work than a cherry falling at the same speed. That is because the kinetic energy of an object depends on the object's mass.

An apple that is moving at 10 m/s can do more work than an apple moving at 1 m/s can. As an apple falls, it accelerates. The kinetic energy of the apple increases as it speeds up. In fact, the kinetic energy of a moving object depends on the square of the object's speed.

VOCABULARY Skills Tip

Kinetic *comes from the Greek word* kinetikos, *which means "motion."*

Kinetic Energy Equation

$$\textit{kinetic energy} = \frac{1}{2} \times \textit{mass} \times \textit{speed squared}$$

$$KE = \frac{1}{2}mv^2$$

Figure 12B shows a graph of kinetic energy versus speed for a falling apple that weighs 1.0 N. Notice that kinetic energy is expressed in joules. Because kinetic energy is calculated using both mass and speed squared, the base units are kg•m^2/s^2, which are equivalent to joules.

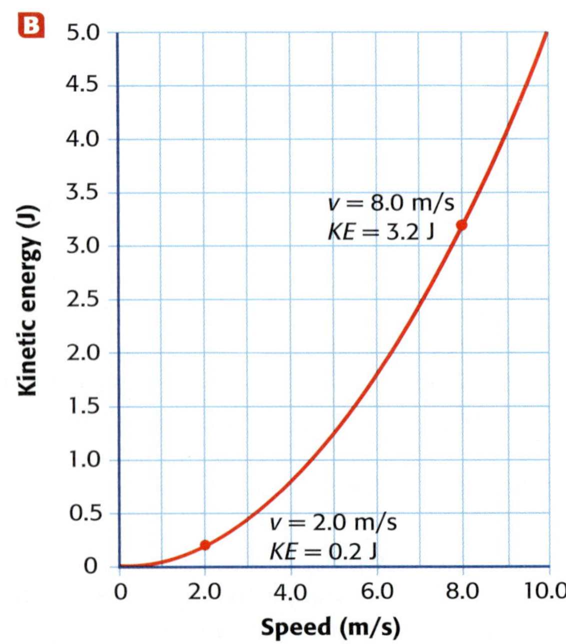

Figure 12

A A falling apple can do work on the ground underneath—or on someone's head.

B A small increase in the speed of an apple results in a large increase in kinetic energy.

Kinetic energy depends on speed more than mass

The line on the graph of kinetic energy versus speed curves sharply upward as speed increases. At one point, the speed is 2.0 m/s and the kinetic energy is 0.20 J. At another point, the speed has increased four times to 8.0 m/s. But the kinetic energy has increased 16 times, to 3.2 J. In the kinetic energy equation, speed is squared, so a small increase in speed produces a large increase in kinetic energy.

You may have heard that car crashes are much more dangerous at speeds above the speed limit. The kinetic energy equation provides a scientific reason for that fact. Because a car has much more kinetic energy at higher speeds, it can do much more work—which means much more damage—in a collision.

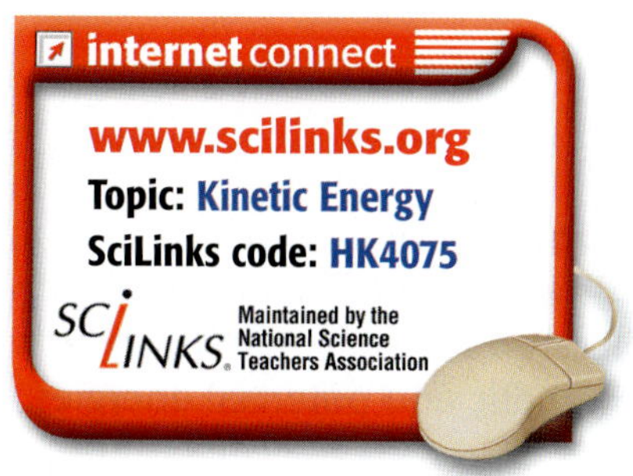

Math Skills

Kinetic Energy What is the kinetic energy of a 44 kg cheetah running at 31 m/s?

1 List the given and unknown values.

Given: *mass,* $m = 44$ kg

speed, $v = 31$ m/s

Unknown: *kinetic energy,* $KE = ?$ J

2 Write the equation for kinetic energy.

$$kinetic\ energy = \frac{1}{2} \times mass \times speed\ squared$$

$$KE = \frac{1}{2}mv^2$$

3 Insert the known values into the equation, and solve.

$$KE = \frac{1}{2}(44\ \text{kg})(31\ \text{m/s})^2$$

$$KE = 2.1 \times 10^4\ \text{kg}\bullet\text{m}^2/\text{s}^2 = 2.1 \times 10^4\ \text{J}$$

Practice

Kinetic Energy

1. Calculate the kinetic energy in joules of a 1500 kg car moving at the following speeds:
   a. 29 m/s
   b. 18 m/s
   c. 42 km/h (**Hint:** Convert the speed to meters per second before substituting into the equation.)
2. A 35 kg child has 190 J of kinetic energy after sledding down a hill. What is the child's speed in meters per second at the bottom of the hill?
3. A bowling ball traveling 2.0 m/s has 16 J of kinetic energy. What is the mass of the bowling ball in kilograms?

- The kinetic energy equation can be rearranged to isolate speed on the left.

$$\frac{1}{2}mv^2 = KE$$

Multiply both sides by $\frac{2}{m}$.

$$\left(\frac{2}{m}\right) \times \frac{1}{2}mv^2 = \left(\frac{2}{m}\right) \times KE$$

$$v^2 = \frac{2KE}{m}$$

Take the square root of each side.

$$\sqrt{v^2} = \sqrt{\frac{2KE}{m}}$$

$$v = \sqrt{\frac{2KE}{m}}$$

You will need this version of the equation for Practice Problem 2.

- For Practice Problem 3, you will need to use the equation rearranged with mass isolated on the left:

$$m = \frac{2KE}{v^2}$$

Other Forms of Energy

mechanical energy the amount of work an object can do because of the object's kinetic and potential energies

Apples have potential energy when they are hanging on a branch above the ground, and they have kinetic and potential energy when they are falling. The sum of the potential energy and the kinetic energy in a system is called **mechanical energy.** Mechanical energy can also be thought of as the amount of work an object can do because of the object's kinetic and potential energies.

Apples can also give you energy when you eat them. What kind of energy is that? In almost every system, there are hidden forms of energy that are related to the motion and arrangement of atoms that make up the objects in the system.

Energy that lies at the level of atoms and that does not affect motion on a large scale is sometimes called *nonmechanical energy*. However, a close look at the different forms of energy in a system usually reveals that they are in most cases just special forms of kinetic or potential energy.

Atoms and molecules have kinetic energy

You have learned that atoms and molecules are constantly in motion. Therefore, these tiny particles have kinetic energy. Like a bowling ball hitting pins, kinetic energy is transferred between particles through collisions. The average kinetic energy of particles in an object increases as the object gets hotter and decreases as it cools down. In another chapter, you will learn more about how the kinetic energy of particles relates to heat and temperature.

Figure 13 shows the motion of atoms in two parts of an iron object at different temperatures. In both parts, the iron atoms inside the object are vibrating. The atoms in the hotter part of the object are vibrating more rapidly than the atoms in the cooler part, so they have greater kinetic energy.

Figure 13
The atoms in a hot object, such as a horseshoe, have kinetic energy. The kinetic energy is related to the object's temperature.

If a scientist wanted to analyze the motion of a horseshoe in a game of "horseshoes," the motion of particles inside the shoes would not be important. For the sake of that study, the energy due to the motion of the atoms would be considered nonmechanical energy.

However, if the same scientist wanted to study the change in the properties of iron when heated in a blacksmith's shop, the motion of the atoms would become significant to the study, and the kinetic energy of the particles within the horseshoe would then be viewed as mechanical energy.

Chemical reactions involve potential energy

In a chemical reaction, bonds between atoms break apart. When the atoms bond together again in a new pattern, a different substance is formed. Both the formation of bonds and the breaking of bonds involve changes in energy. The amount of *chemical energy* associated with a substance depends in part on the relative positions of the atoms it contains.

Because chemical energy depends on position, it is a kind of potential energy. Reactions that release energy involve a decrease in the potential energy within substances. For example, when a match burns, as shown in ***Figure 14,*** the release of stored energy from the match head produces light and a small explosion of hot gas.

Figure 14
When a match burns, the chemical energy stored inside the head of the match is released, producing light and a small explosion of hot gas.

Living things get energy from the sun

Where do you get the energy you need to live? It comes in the form of chemical energy stored in the food you eat. But where did that energy come from? When you eat a meal, you are eating either plants or animals, or both. Animals also eat plants or other animals, or both. At the bottom of the food chain are plants and algae that derive their energy directly from sunlight.

Plants use *photosynthesis* to turn the energy in sunlight into chemical energy. This energy is stored in sugars and other organic molecules that make up cells in living tissue. When your body needs energy, some of these organic molecules are broken down through *respiration*. Respiration releases the energy your body needs to live and do work.

The Energy in Food

We get energy from the food we eat. This energy is often measured by another unit, the Calorie. One Calorie is equivalent to 4186 J.

Applying Information

1. Look at the nutrition label on this "energy bar." How many Calories of energy does the bar contain?
2. Calculate how many joules of energy the bar contains by multiplying the number of Calories by the conversion factor of 4186 J/Cal.
3. An average person needs to take in about 10 million joules of energy every day. How many energy bars would you have to eat to get this much energy?

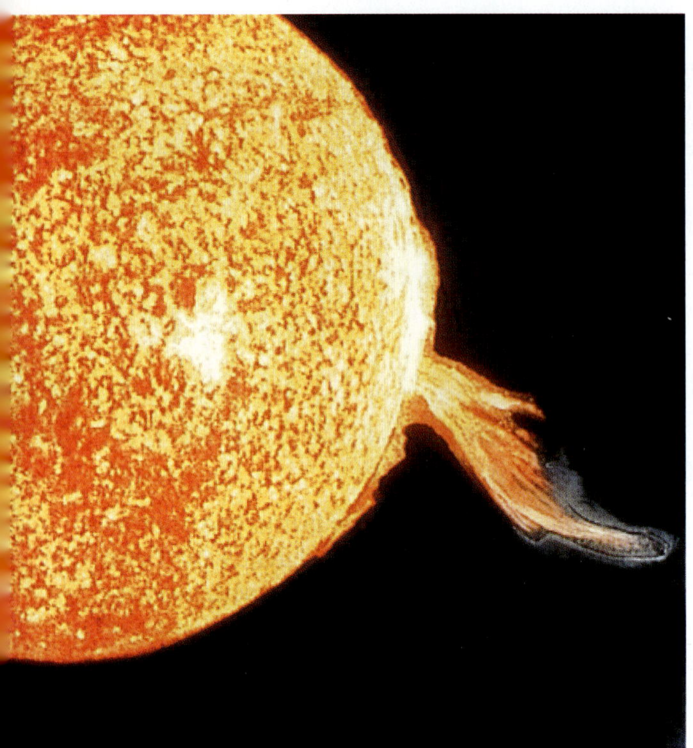

Figure 15

The nuclei of atoms contain enormous amounts of energy. The sun is fueled by nuclear fusion reactions in its core.

The sun gets energy from nuclear reactions

The sun, shown in ***Figure 15,*** not only gives energy to living things but also keeps our whole planet warm and bright. And the energy that reaches Earth from the sun is only a small portion of the sun's total energy output. How does the sun produce so much energy?

The sun's energy comes from nuclear fusion, a type of reaction in which light atomic nuclei combine to form a heavier nucleus. Nuclear power plants use a different process, called nuclear fission, to release nuclear energy. In fission, a single heavy nucleus is split into two or more lighter nuclei. In both fusion and fission, small quantities of mass are converted into large quantities of energy.

You have learned that mass is converted to energy during nuclear reactions. This nuclear energy is a kind of potential energy stored by the forces holding subatomic particles together in the nuclei of atoms.

Electricity is a form of energy

The lights and appliances in your home are powered by another form of energy, electricity. Electricity results from the flow of charged particles through wires or other conducting materials. Moving electrons can increase the temperature of a wire and cause it to glow, as in a light bulb. Moving electrons also create magnetic fields, which can do work to power a motor or other devices. The lightning shown in ***Figure 16*** is caused by electrons traveling through the air between the ground and a thundercloud.

Figure 16

Electrical energy is derived from the flow of charged particles, as in a bolt of lightning or in a wire. We can harness electricity to power appliances in our homes.

Light can carry energy across empty space

An asphalt surface on a bright summer day is hotter where light is shining directly on it than it is in the shade. Light energy travels from the sun to Earth across empty space in the form of *electromagnetic waves.*

A beam of white light can be separated into a color spectrum, as shown in **Figure 17.** Light toward the blue end of the spectrum carries more energy than light toward the red end.

Figure 17

Light is made of electromagnetic waves that carry energy across empty space.

SECTION 3 REVIEW

SUMMARY

- Energy is the ability to do work.
- Like work, energy is measured in joules.
- Potential energy is stored energy.
- Elastic potential energy is stored in any stretched or compressed elastic material.
- The gravitational potential energy of an object is determined by its mass, its height, and *g*, the free-fall acceleration due to gravity. $PE = mgh$.
- An object's kinetic energy, or energy of motion, is determined by its mass and speed. $KE = \frac{1}{2}mv^2$.
- Potential energy and kinetic energy are forms of mechanical energy.
- In addition to mechanical energy, most systems contain nonmechanical energy.
- Nonmechanical energy does not usually affect systems on a large scale.

1. **List** three different forms of energy.
2. **Explain** how energy is different from work.
3. **Explain** the difference between potential energy and kinetic energy.
4. **Determine** what form or forms of energy apply to each of the following situations, and specify whether each form is mechanical or nonmechanical:
   - **a.** a Frisbee flying though the air
   - **b.** a hot cup of soup
   - **c.** a wound clock spring
   - **d.** sunlight
   - **e.** a boulder sitting at the top of a cliff
5. **Critical Thinking** Water storage tanks are usually built on towers or placed on hilltops. Why?
6. **Creative Thinking** Name one situation in which gravitational potential energy might be useful, and name one situation where it might be dangerous.

Math Skills

7. Calculate the gravitational potential energy of a 93.0 kg sky diver who is 550 m above the ground.
8. What is the kinetic energy in joules of a 0.02 kg bullet traveling 300 m/s?
9. Calculate the kinetic or potential energy in joules for each of the following situations:
   - **a.** a 2.5 kg book held 2.0 m above the ground
   - **b.** a 15 g snowball moving through the air at 3.5 m/s
   - **c.** a 35 kg child sitting at the top of a slide that is 3.5 m above the ground
   - **d.** an 8500 kg airplane flying at 220 km/h

SECTION 4

Conservation of Energy

KEY TERM
efficiency

OBJECTIVES

- **Identify** and describe transformations of energy.
- **Explain** the law of conservation of energy.
- **Discuss** where energy goes when it seems to disappear.
- **Analyze** the efficiency of machines.

Imagine you are sitting in the front car of a roller coaster, such as the one shown in ***Figure 18.*** The car is pulled slowly up the first hill by a conveyor belt. When you reach the crest of the hill, you are barely moving. Then you go over the edge and start to race downward, speeding faster and faster until you reach the bottom of the hill. The wheels are roaring along the track. You continue to travel up and down through a series of smaller humps, twists, and turns. Finally, you climb another hill almost as big as the first, drop down again, and then coast to the end of the ride.

Figure 18

The tallest roller coaster in the world is the Fujiyama, in Fujikyu Highland Park, Japan. It spans 70 m from its highest to lowest points.

Energy Transformations

In the course of a roller coaster ride, energy changes form many times. You may not have noticed the conveyor belt at the beginning, but in terms of energy it is the most important part of the ride. All of the energy required for the entire ride comes from work done by the conveyor belt as it lifts the cars and the passengers up the first hill.

The energy from that initial work is stored as gravitational potential energy at the top of the first hill. After that, the energy goes through a series of transformations, or changes, turning into kinetic energy and turning back into potential energy. A small quantity of this energy is transferred as heat to the wheels and as vibrations that produce a roaring sound in the air. But whatever form the energy takes during the ride, it is all there from the very beginning.

Figure 19

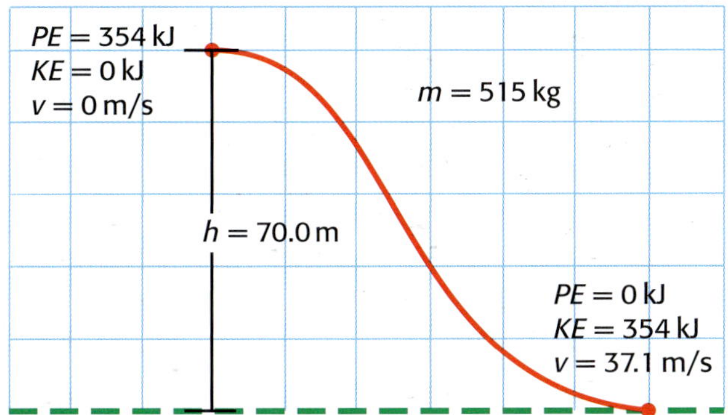

A As a car goes down a hill on a roller coaster, potential energy changes to kinetic energy.

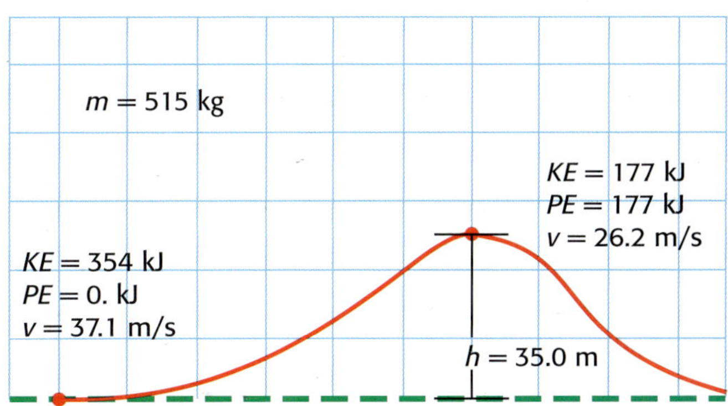

B At the top of this small hill, half the kinetic energy has become potential energy. The rest of the kinetic energy carries the car over the crest of the hill at high speed.

Potential energy can become kinetic energy

Almost all of the energy of a car on a roller coaster is potential energy at the top of a tall hill. The potential energy gradually changes to kinetic energy as the car accelerates downward. At the bottom of the lowest hill, the car has a maximum of kinetic energy and a minimum of potential energy.

Figure 19A shows the potential energy and kinetic energy of a car at the top and the bottom of the biggest hill on the Fujiyama roller coaster. Notice that the system has the same amount of energy, 354 kJ, whether the car is at the top or the bottom of the hill. That is because all of the gravitational potential energy at the top changes to kinetic energy as the car goes down the hill. When the car reaches the lowest point, the system has no potential energy because the car cannot go any lower.

Kinetic energy can become potential energy

When the car is at the lowest point on the roller coaster, it has no more potential energy, but it has a lot of kinetic energy. This kinetic energy can do the work to carry the car up another hill. As the car climbs the hill, the car slows down, decreasing its kinetic energy. Where does that energy go? Most of it turns back into potential energy as the height of the car increases.

At the top of a smaller hill, the car will still have some kinetic energy, along with some potential energy, as shown in ***Figure 19B.*** The kinetic energy will carry the car forward over the crest of the hill. Of course, the car could not climb a hill taller than the first one without an extra boost. The car does not have enough energy.

Energy transformations explain the flight of a ball

The relationship between potential energy and kinetic energy can explain motion in many different situations. Let's look at some other examples.

A tennis player tosses a 0.05 kg tennis ball into the air to set up for a serve, as shown in ***Figure 20.*** He gives the ball 0.5 J of kinetic energy, and it travels straight up. As the ball rises higher, the kinetic energy is converted to potential energy. The ball will keep rising until all the kinetic energy is gone. At its highest point, the ball has 0.5 J of potential energy. As the ball falls down again, the potential energy changes back to kinetic energy.

Imagine that a tennis trainer wants to know how high the ball will go when it is given 0.5 J of initial kinetic energy by a tennis player. The trainer could make a series of calculations using force and acceleration, but in this case using the concept of energy transformations is easier. The trainer knows that the ball's initial kinetic energy is 0.5 J and that its mass is 0.05 kg. To find out how high the ball will go, the trainer has to find the point where the potential energy equals its initial kinetic energy, 0.5 J. Using the equation for gravitational potential energy, the height turns out to be 1 m above the point that the tennis player releases the ball.

internet connect

www.scilinks.org
Topic: Energy Transformations
SciLinks code: HK4049

SCILINKS. Maintained by the National Science Teachers Association

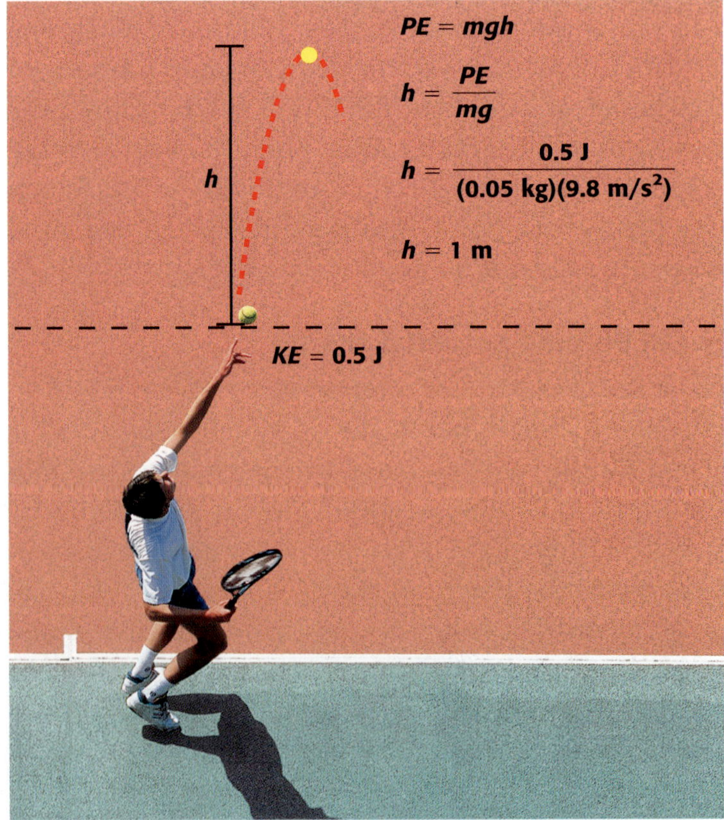

Figure 20
The kinetic energy of the ball at the bottom of its path equals the potential energy at the top of the path.

Energy transformations explain a bouncing ball

Before a serve, a tennis player usually bounces the ball a few times while building concentration. The motion of a bouncing ball can also be explained using energy principles. As the tennis player throws the ball down, he adds kinetic energy to the potential energy the ball has at the height of her hand. The kinetic energy of the ball then increases steadily as the ball falls because the potential energy is changing to kinetic energy.

When the ball hits the ground, there is a sudden energy transformation as the kinetic energy of the ball changes to elastic potential energy stored in the compressed tennis ball. The elastic potential energy then quickly changes back to kinetic energy as the ball bounces upward.

If all of the kinetic energy in the ball changed to elastic potential energy, and that elastic potential energy all changed back to kinetic energy during the bounce, the ball would bounce up to the tennis player's hand. Its speed on return would be exactly the same as the speed at which it was thrown down. If the ball were dropped instead of thrown down, it would bounce up to the same height from which it was dropped.

Quick ACTIVITY

Energy Transfer

1. Flex a piece of thick wire or part of a coat hanger back and forth about 10 times with your hands. Are you doing work?
2. After flexing the wire, cautiously touch the part of the wire where you bent it. Does the wire feel hot? What happened to the energy you put into it?

Mechanical energy can change to other forms of energy

If changes from kinetic energy to potential energy and back again were always complete, then balls would always bounce back to the same height they were dropped from and cars on roller coasters would keep gliding forever. But that is not the way things really happen.

When a ball bounces on the ground, not all of the kinetic energy changes to elastic potential energy. Some of the kinetic energy compresses the air around the ball, making a sound, and some of the kinetic energy makes the ball, the air, and the ground slightly hotter. Because these other forms of energy are not directly due to the motion or position of the ball, they can be considered nonmechanical energy. With each bounce, the ball loses some mechanical energy, as shown in ***Figure 21.***

Likewise, a car on a roller coaster cannot keep moving up and down the track forever. The total mechanical energy of a car on a roller coaster constantly decreases due to friction and air resistance. This energy does not just disappear though. Some of it increases the temperature of the track, the car's wheels, and the air. Some of the energy compresses the air, making a roaring sound. Often, when energy seems to disappear, it has really just changed to a nonmechanical form.

Figure 21

With each bounce of a tennis ball, some of the mechanical energy changes to nonmechanical energy.

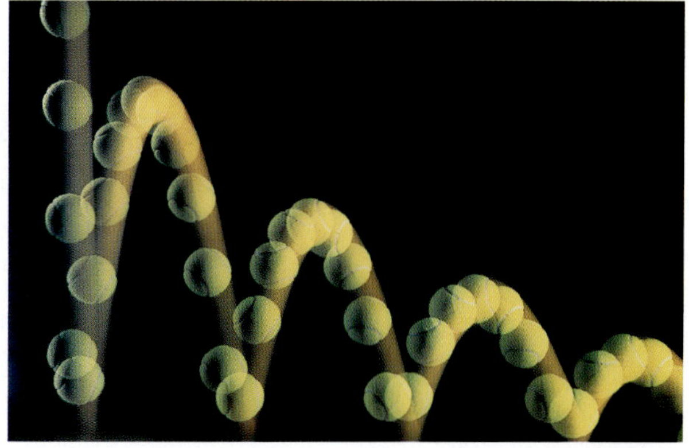

The Law of Conservation of Energy

In our study of machines, we saw that the work done on a machine is equal to the work that it can do. Similarly, in our study of the roller coaster, we found that the energy present at the beginning of the ride is present throughout the ride and at the end of the ride, although the energy continually changes form.

This simple observation is based on one of the most important principles in all of science—the law of conservation of energy. Here is the law in its simplest form.

Energy cannot be created or destroyed.

In a mechanical system such as a swinging pendulum, the energy in the system at any time can be calculated by adding the kinetic and potential energy to get the total mechanical energy.

Energy doesn't appear or disappear

Energy cannot be created from nothing. Imagine a girl jumping on a trampoline. If her second bounce is higher than her first bounce, we must conclude that she added energy to her bounce by pushing with her legs. Whenever the total energy in a system increases, it must be due to energy that enters the system.

Because mechanical energy can change to nonmechanical energy due to friction, air resistance, and other factors, tracing the flow of energy in a system can be difficult. Some of the energy may leak out of the system into the surrounding environment, as when the roller coaster produces sound. But none of the energy disappears; it just changes form.

The first law of thermodynamics describes energy conservation

Energy can be transferred as work or as heat. For example, when you do work to lift a ball, you give the ball potential energy. When you sand wood, the wood gets warm, and energy is transferred as heat. For any system, the net change in energy equals the energy transferred as work and as heat. When there is no energy transferred as heat or as work, energy is conserved. This form of the law of energy conservation is called the first law of thermodynamics.

Scientists study energy systems

Energy has many different forms and can be found almost everywhere. Accounting for all of the energy in a given situation can be complicated. To make studying a situation easier, scientists often limit their view to a small area or a small number of objects. These boundaries define a system.

INTEGRATING

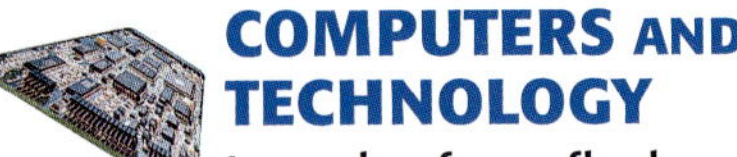

COMPUTERS AND TECHNOLOGY

In order for a flashlight to work, there must be a supply of energy.

A flashlight battery contains different chemicals that can react with each other to release energy. When the flashlight is turned on, chemical potential energy changes to electrical energy, and electrons begin to flow through a wire attached to the battery. Inside the bulb, the wire filament begins to glow, and the energy is transformed into light energy.

After the flashlight has been used for a certain amount of time, the battery will run out of energy. It will have to be replaced or recharged.

Systems may be open or closed

A system might include a gas burner and a pot of water. A scientist could study the flow of energy from the burner into the pot and ignore the small amount of energy going into the pot from the lights in the room, from a hand touching the pot, and so on.

When the flow of energy into and out of a system is small enough that it can be ignored, the system is called a *closed system*. Most systems are *open systems,* which exchange energy with the space that surrounds them. Earth is an open system, as shown in **Figure 22.** Is your body an open or closed system?

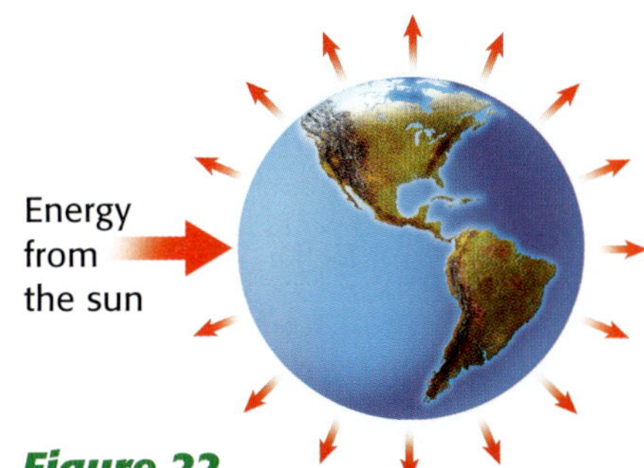

Figure 22
Earth is an open system because it receives energy from the sun and radiates some of its own energy out into space.

Is energy conserved in a pendulum?

Materials
- 1–1.5 m length of string
- pencil with an eraser
- meterstick
- level
- pendulum bob
- nail or hook in the wall above a chalkboard

1. Hang the pendulum bob from the string in front of a chalkboard. On the board, draw the diagram as shown in the photograph at right. Use the meterstick and the level to make sure the horizontal line is parallel to the ground.
2. Pull the pendulum ball back to the "X." Make sure everyone is out of the way; then release the pendulum and observe its motion. How high does the pendulum swing on the other side?
3. Let the pendulum swing back and forth several times. How many swings does the pendulum make before the ball noticeably fails to reach its original height?
4. Stop the pendulum and hold it again at the "X" marked on the board. Have another student place the eraser end of a pencil on the intersection of the horizontal and vertical lines. Make sure everyone is out of the way again, especially the student holding the pencil.
5. Release the pendulum again. This time its motion will be altered halfway through the swing as the string hits the pencil. How high does the pendulum swing now? Why?
6. Try placing the pencil at different heights along the vertical line. How does this affect the motion of the pendulum? If you put the pencil down close enough to the arc of the pendulum, the pendulum will do a loop around it. Why does that happen?

Analysis

1. Use the law of conservation of energy to explain your observations in steps 2–6.
2. If you let the pendulum swing long enough, it will start to slow down, and it won't rise to the line any more. That suggests that the system has lost energy. Has it? Where did the energy go?

Efficiency of Machines

Figure 23
Like all machines, the pulleys on a sailboat are less than 100 percent efficient.

If you use a pulley to raise a sail on a sailboat like the one in ***Figure 23,*** you have to do work against the forces of friction in the pulley. You also have to lift the added weight of the rope and the hook attached to the sail. As a result, only some of the energy that you transfer to the pulley is available to raise the sail.

Not all of the work done by a machine is useful work

Because of friction and other factors, only some of the work done by a machine is applied to the task at hand; the machine also does some incidental work that does not serve any intended purpose. In other words, there is a difference between the total work done by a machine and the *useful* work done by the machine, that is, work that the machine is designed or intended to do.

Although all of the work done on a machine has some effect on the output work that the machine does, the output work might not be in the form that you expect. In lifting a sail, for example, some of the work available to lift the sail, which would be useful work, is transferred away as heat that warms the pulley because of friction. This warming is not a desired effect. The amount of useful work might decrease slightly more if the pulley squeaks, because some energy is "lost" as it dissipates into forces that vibrate the pulley and the air to produce the squeaking sound.

Efficiency is the ratio of useful work out to work in

The **efficiency** of a machine is a measure of how much useful work it can do. Efficiency is defined as the ratio of useful work output to total work input.

Efficiency Equation

$$efficiency = \frac{useful\ work\ output}{work\ input}$$

efficiency a quantity, usually expressed as a percentage, that measures the ratio of useful work output to work input

Efficiency is usually expressed as a percentage. To change an answer found using the efficiency equation into a percentage, just multiply the answer by 100 and add the percent sign, "%."

A machine with 100 percent efficiency would produce exactly as much useful work as the work done on the machine. Because every machine has some friction, no machine has 100 percent efficiency. The useful work output of a machine never equals—and certainly cannot exceed—the work input.

Perpetual motion machines are impossible

Figure 24 shows a machine designed to keep on going forever without any input of energy. These theoretical machines are called *perpetual motion machines.* Many clever inventors have devoted a lot of time and effort to designing such machines. If such a perpetual motion machine could exist, it would require a complete absence of friction and air resistance.

Figure 24
Theoretically, a perpetual motion machine could keep going forever without any energy loss or energy input.

Math Skills

Efficiency A sailor uses a rope and an old, squeaky pulley to raise a sail that weighs 140 N. He finds that he must do 180 J of work on the rope in order to raise the sail by 1 m (doing 140 J of work on the sail). What is the efficiency of the pulley? Express your answer as a percentage.

1 List the given and unknown values.

Given: *work input* = 180 J

useful work output = 140 J

Unknown: *efficiency* = ? %

2 Write the equation for efficiency.

$$efficiency = \frac{useful\ work\ output}{work\ input}$$

3 Insert the known values into the equation, and solve.

$$efficiency = \frac{140\ \text{J}}{180\ \text{J}} = 0.78$$

To express this as a percentage, multiply by 100 and add the percent sign, "%."

$efficiency = 0.78 \times 100 = 78\%$

Practice

Efficiency

1. Alice and Jim calculate that they must do 1800 J of work to push a piano up a ramp. However, because they must also overcome friction, they actually must do 2400 J of work. What is the efficiency of the ramp?
2. It takes 1200 J of work to lift the car high enough to change a tire. How much work must be done by the person operating the jack if the jack is 25 percent efficient?
3. A windmill has an efficiency of 37.5 percent. If a gust of wind does 125 J of work on the blades of the windmill, how much output work can the windmill do as a result of the gust?

- The efficiency equation can be rearranged to isolate any of the variables on the left
- For practice problem 2, you will need to rearrange the equation to isolate work input on the left side.
- For practice problem 3, you will need to rearrange to isolate useful work output.
- When using these rearranged forms to solve the problems, you will have to plug in values for efficiency. When doing so, do not use a percentage, but rather convert the percentage to a decimal by dropping the percent sign and dividing by 100.

Machines need energy input

Because energy always leaks out of a system, every machine needs at least a small amount of energy input to keep going. Unfortunately, that means that perpetual motion machines are impossible. But new technologies, from magnetic trains to high speed microprocessors, reduce the amount of energy leaking from systems so that energy can be used as efficiently as possible.

SECTION 4 REVIEW

SUMMARY

- Energy readily changes from one form to another.
- In a mechanical system, potential energy can become kinetic energy, and kinetic energy can become potential energy.
- Mechanical energy can change to nonmechanical energy as a result of friction, air resistance, or other means.
- Energy cannot be created or destroyed, although it may change form. This is called the law of conservation of energy.
- A machine cannot do more work than the work required to operate the machine. Because of friction, the work output of a machine is always somewhat less than the work input.
- The efficiency of a machine is the ratio of the useful work performed by the machine to the work required to operate the machine.

1. **List** three situations in which potential energy becomes kinetic energy and three situations in which kinetic energy becomes potential energy.
2. **State** the law of conservation of energy in your own words. Give an example of a situation in which the law of conservation of energy is demonstrated.
3. **Describe** the rise and fall of a basketball using the concepts of kinetic energy and potential energy.
4. **Explain** why machines are not 100 percent efficient.
5. **Applying Knowledge** Use the concepts of kinetic energy and potential energy to describe the motion of a child on a swing. Why does the child need a push from time to time?
6. **Creative Thinking** Using what you have learned about energy transformations, explain why the driver of a car has to continuously apply pressure to the gas pedal in order to keep the car cruising at a steady speed, even on a flat road. Does this situation violate the law of conservation of energy? Explain.

Math Skills

7. **Efficiency** When you do 100 J of work on the handle of a bicycle pump, it does 40 J of work pushing the air into the tire. What is the efficiency of the pump?
8. **Efficiency and Power** A river does 6500 J of work on a water wheel every second. The wheel's efficiency is 12 percent.
   - **a.** How much work in joules can the axle of the wheel do in a second?
   - **b.** What is the power output of the wheel?
9. **Efficiency and Work** John is using a pulley to lift the sail on his sailboat. The sail weighs 150 N and he must lift it 4.0 m.
   - **a.** How much work must be done on the sail?
   - **b.** If the pulley is 50 percent efficient, how much work must John do on the rope in order to lift the sail?

Graphing Skills

Total Mechanical Energy of a Bouncing Ball

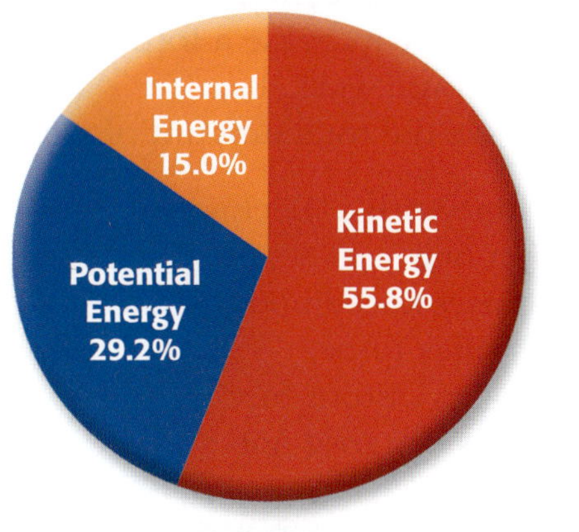

t = 0.75 s

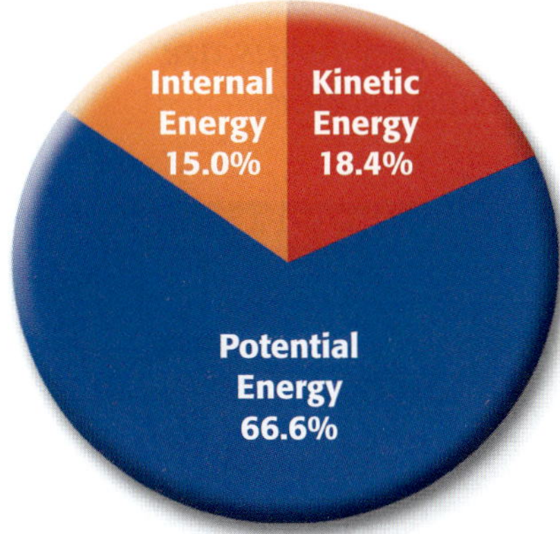

t = 1.5 s

Examine the graphs above and answer the following questions.

1. What type of graphs are these?
2. Identify the information provided by each graph.
3. Does the total mechanical energy change between 0.75 s and 1.5 s? What does change in this time interval?
4. Assume that the internal energy of the ball increases only when it bounces off the floor. What can you tell about the number of times the ball has bounced between 0.75 s and 1.5 s?
5. In which graph is the ball moving fastest? In which is the ball higher above the ground? Explain your answers.
6. Suppose you are asked to design a ball that bounces to nearly the same height as that from which it is dropped. In terms of energy, what property would this ball require?
7. Construct the type of graph best suited for the data given in the table below. Is mechanical energy conserved in this process? Explain your answer.

Time (s)	Potential energy (J)	Kinetic energy (J)	Internal energy (J)
0	30.0	0	0
0.50	15.0	12.0	3.0
1.00	5.0	20.0	5.0
1.50	0	24.0	6.0

CHAPTER 12 REVIEW

Chapter Highlights

Before you begin, review the summaries of the key ideas of each section, found at the end of each section. The key vocabulary terms are listed on the first page of each section.

UNDERSTANDING CONCEPTS

1. ________ is defined as force acting over a distance.
a. Power
b. Energy
c. Work
d. Potential energy

2. The quantity that measures how much a machine multiplies force is called
a. mechanical advantage.
b. leverage.
c. efficiency.
d. power.

3. The unit that represents 1 J of work done each second is the
a. power.
b. newton.
c. watt.
d. mechanical advantage.

4. Which of the following situations does *not* involve potential energy being changed into kinetic energy?
a. an apple falling from a tree
b. shooting a dart from a spring-loaded gun
c. pulling back on the string of a bow
d. a creek flowing downstream

5. ________ is determined by both mass and velocity.
a. Work
b. Power
c. Potential energy
d. Kinetic energy

6. Energy that does not involve the large-scale motion or position of objects in a system is called
a. potential energy.
b. mechanical energy.
c. nonmechanical energy.
d. conserved energy.

7. Which of the following can a machine not do?
a. change the direction of a force
b. multiply or increase a force
c. redistribute work
d. increase the total amount of work done

8. A machine with a mechanical advantage of less than one
a. increases speed and distance.
b. multiplies force.
c. increases output force.
d. reduces distance and speed.

USING VOCABULARY

9. Write one sentence using *work* in the scientific sense, and write another sentence using it in a different, nonscientific sense. Explain the difference in the meaning of *work* in the two sentences.

WRITING SKILL

10. A can opener is a *compound machine.* Name three *simple machines* that it contains.

11. For each of the following, state whether the system contains primarily *kinetic energy* or *potential energy:*
a. a stone in a stretched slingshot
b. a speeding race car
c. water above a hydroelectric dam

12. How is *energy* related to *work, force,* and *power?*

13. List several examples of how *electrical energy* and *light energy* are useful to you.

BUILDING MATH SKILLS

14. You and two friends apply a force of 425 N to push a piano up a 2.0 m long ramp.

a. Work How much work in joules has been done when you reach the top of the ramp?

b. Power If you make it to the top in 5.0 s, what is your power output in watts?

c. Mechanical Advantage If lifting the piano straight up would require 1700 N of force, what is the mechanical advantage of the ramp?

15. A crane uses a block and tackle to lift a 2200 N flagstone to a height of 25 m.

a. Work How much work is done on the flagstone?

b. Efficiency In the process, the crane's hydraulic motor does 110 kJ of work on the cable in the block and tackle. What is the efficiency of the block and tackle?

c. Potential Energy What is the potential energy of the flagstone when it is 25 m above the ground?

THINKING CRITICALLY

16. Critical Thinking Use the law of conservation of energy to explain why the work output of a machine can never exceed the work input.

17. Applying Knowledge If a bumper car triples its speed, how much more work can it do on a bumper car at rest? (**Hint:** Use the equation for kinetic energy.)

18. Critical Thinking You are attempting to move a large rock using a long lever. Will the work you do on the lever be greater than, the same as, or less than the work done by the lever on the rock? Explain your answer.

19. Interpreting Graphics The diagram below shows five different points on a roller coaster.

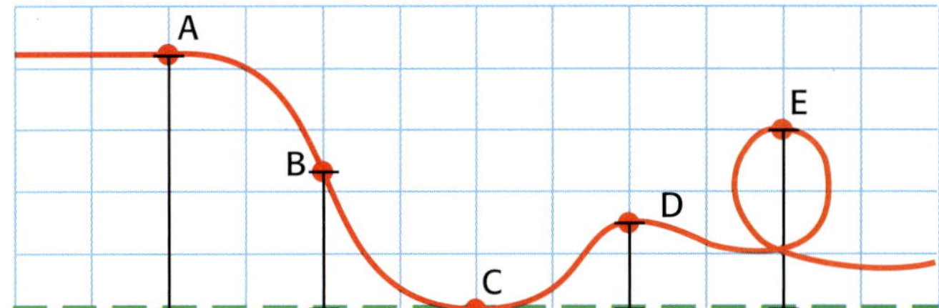

a. List the points in order from the point where the car would have the greatest potential energy to the point where it would have the least potential energy.

b. Now list the points in order from the point where the car would have the greatest kinetic energy to the point where it would have the least kinetic energy.

c. How are your two lists related to each other?

20. Applying Knowledge If a machine cannot multiply the amount of work, then what is the advantage of using a machine?

21. Applying Knowledge You are designing a roller coaster in which a car will be pulled to the top of a hill and then will be released to roll freely down the hill toward the top of the next hill. The next hill is twice as high. Will your design be successful?

22. Applying Knowledge In two or three sentences, explain the force-distance trade-off that occurs when a machine is used to make work easier. Use the lever as an example of one type of trade-off.

23. Applying Knowledge Why do you think that levers have a greater mechanical efficiency than other simple machines do?

DEVELOPING LIFE/WORK SKILLS

24. Applying Knowledge You are trying to pry the lid off a paint can with a screwdriver, but the lid will not budge. Should you try using a shorter screwdriver or a longer screwdriver? Explain.

25. Designing Systems Imagine you are trying to move a piano into a second-floor apartment. It will not fit through the stairwell, but it will fit through a large window 3.0 m off the ground. The piano weighs 1740 N and you can exert only 290 N of force. Design a system of machines you could use to lift the piano to the window.

26. Teaching Others Prepare a poster or a series of models of common machines that explains their uses and how they work. Include a diagram next to each sample labeling parts of each machine. Add your own examples of machines to the following list: nail clipper, wheelbarrow, can opener, nutcracker, electric drill, screwdriver, tweezers, and a key in a lock.

27. Designing Systems Many mountain roads are built so that they zigzag up a mountain rather than go straight up toward the peak. Discuss the advantage of such a design from the viewpoint of energy conservation and power. Think of a winding road as a series of inclined planes.

INTEGRATING CONCEPTS

28. Connection to Sports A baseball pitcher applies a force to the ball as his arm moves a distance of 1.0 m. Using a radar gun, the coach finds that the ball has a speed of 18 m/s after it is released. A baseball has a mass of 0.15 kg. Calculate the average force that the pitcher applied to the ball. (**Hint:** You will need to use both the kinetic energy equation and the work equation.)

29. Concept Mapping Copy the unfinished concept map below onto a sheet of paper. Complete the map by writing the correct word or phrase in the lettered boxes.

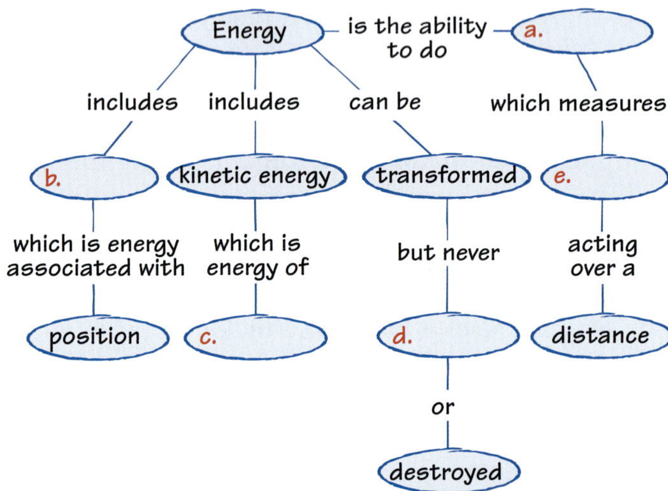

30. Connection to Earth Science Many fuels come from fossilized plant and animal matter. How is the energy stored in these fuels? How do you think that energy got into the fuels in the first place?

31. Connection to Biology When lifting an object using the biceps muscle, the forearm acts as a lever with the fulcrum at the elbow. The input work is provided by the biceps muscle pulling up on the bone. Assume that the muscle is attached 1.0 cm from the elbow and that the total length of the forearm from elbow to palm is 32 cm. How much force must the biceps exert to lift an object weighing 12 N? What class of lever is the forearm in this example?

internet connect

www.scilinks.org

Topic: Energy and Sports SciLinks code: HK4047

SCILINKS. Maintained by the National Science Teachers Association

Standardized Test Prep

Understanding Concepts

Directions (1–3): **For *each* question, write on a separate sheet of paper the letter of the correct answer.**

1 What causes the force of acceleration of a Space Shuttle booster rocket?
- **A.** exhaust gases pushing against the ground
- **B.** exhaust gases pushing against the atmosphere
- **C.** exhaust gases pushing against the rocket itself
- **D.** exhaust gases pushing against other gas molecules in the rocket

2 Which of the following is true about an object in orbit?
- **F.** It is beyond Earth's gravity.
- **G.** Its velocity does not change.
- **H.** It is constantly falling toward Earth.
- **I.** Its forward acceleration comes from air pressure.

3 Which of these statements describes the law of conservation of energy?
- **A.** No machine is 100% efficient.
- **B.** Energy is neither created nor destroyed.
- **C.** The energy resources of Earth are limited.
- **D.** The energy of a system is always decreasing.

Directions (4): **Write a short response to the question.**

4 A coal-burning power plant produces electrical energy with an efficiency of 30%. If the chemical energy produced by burning one kilogram of coal is 25,000,000 joules (J), how many joules of electrical energy are produced by the combustion of one gram of coal?

Test questions may not be arranged in order of increasing difficulty. If you are unable to answer a question, mark it and move on to another question.

Reading Skills

Directions (5): **Read the passage below. Then answer the question.**

When astronauts first landed on the moon, cameras sent back pictures of them jumping. They were able to jump much higher than on Earth even though they were wearing very heavy space suits. Muscles generate the same amount of force on Earth, on the moon, or in space.

5 Analyze why the astronauts could jump higher on the moon without exerting any additional force.

Interpreting Graphics

Directions (6–7): **Base your answers to questions 6 and 7 on the illustration below, which shows the mechanical advantage of pulleys.**

Mechanical Advantage of a Pulley System

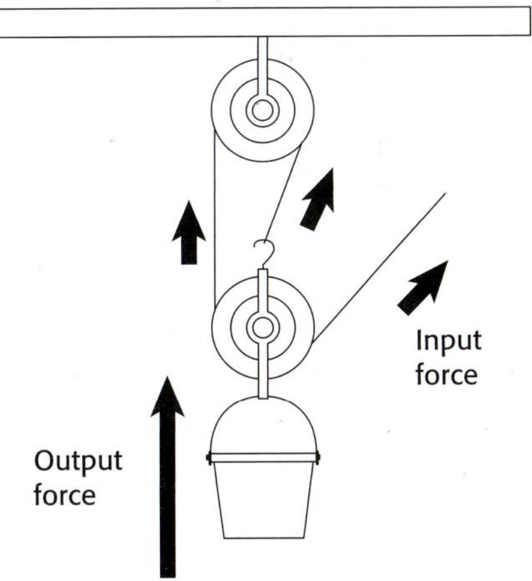

6 If the input force on this pulley system is 100 N, what is the output force?
- **F.** 100 N
- **G.** 200 N
- **H.** 300 N
- **I.** 400 N

7 How could the amount of force required to raise the bucket be decreased even more?
- **A.** Add additional pulleys.
- **B.** Increase the length of the rope.
- **C.** Thread the rope through the pulleys in opposite order.
- **D.** Increase the amount of force on the free end of the rope.

Skills Practice Lab

Introduction

Raised objects have gravitational potential energy. Moving objects have kinetic energy. How are these two quantities related in a system that involves a ball rolling down a ramp?

Objectives

- ***Measure*** the height, distance traveled, and time interval for a ball rolling down a ramp.
- ***Calculate*** the ball's potential energy at the top of the ramp and its kinetic energy at the bottom of the ramp.
- USING SCIENTIFIC METHODS ***Analyze the results*** to find the relationship between potential energy and kinetic energy.

Materials

balance
board, at least 90 cm (3 ft) long
box
golf ball, racquet ball, or handball
masking tape
meterstick
stack of books, at least 60 cm (2 ft) high
stopwatch

Determining Energy for a Rolling Ball

Procedure

Preparing for Your Experiment

1. On a blank sheet of paper, prepare a table like the one shown below.

Table 1 **Potential Energy and Kinetic Energy**

	Height 1	Height 2	Height 3
Mass of ball (kg)			
Length of ramp (m)			
Height of ramp (m)			
Time ball traveled, first trial (s)			
Time ball traveled, second trial (s)			
Time ball traveled, third trial (s)			
Average time ball traveled (s)			
Final speed of ball (m/s)			
Final kinetic energy of ball (J)			
Initial potential energy of ball (J)			

2. Measure the mass of the ball, and record it in your table.
3. Place a strip of masking tape across the board close to one end, and measure the distance from the tape to the opposite end of the board. Record this distance in the row labeled "Length of ramp."
4. Make a catch box by cutting out one side of a box.
5. Make a stack of books approximately 30 cm high. Build a ramp by setting the taped end of the board on top of the books, as shown in the photograph on the next page. Place the other end in the catch box. Measure the vertical height of the ramp at the tape, and record this value in your table as "Height of ramp."

Making Time Measurements

6. Place the ball on the ramp at the tape. Release the ball, and measure how long it takes the ball to travel to the bottom of the ramp. Record the time in your table.
7. Repeat step 6 two more times and record the results in your table. After three trials, calculate the average travel time and record it in your table.
8. Repeat steps 5–7 with a stack of books approximately 45 cm high, and repeat the steps again with a stack approximately 60 cm high.

Analysis

1. Calculate the average speed of the ball using the following equation:

$$average\ speed = \frac{length\ of\ ramp}{average\ time\ ball\ traveled}$$

2. Multiply average speed by 2 to obtain the final speed of the ball, and record the final speed.
3. Calculate and record the final kinetic energy of the ball by using the following equation:

$$KE = \frac{1}{2} \times mass\ of\ ball \times (final\ speed)^2$$

$$KE = \frac{1}{2}mv^2$$

4. Calculate and record the initial potential energy of the ball by using the following equation:

$$grav.\ PE = mass\ of\ ball \times (9.8\ \mathrm{m/s^2}) \times height\ of\ ramp$$

$$PE = mgh$$

Conclusions

5. For each of the three heights, compare the ball's potential energy at the top of the ramp with its kinetic energy at the bottom of the ramp.
6. How did the ball's potential and kinetic energy change as the height of the ramp was increased?
7. Suppose you perform this experiment and find that your kinetic energy values are always just a little less than your potential energy values. Does that mean you did the experiment wrong? Why or why not?

CareerLink

Civil Engineer

In a sense, civil engineering has been around since people started to build structures. Civil engineers plan and design public projects, such as roads, bridges, and dams, and private projects, such as office buildings. To learn more about civil engineering as a career, read the profile of civil engineer Grace Pierce, who works at Traffic Systems, Inc., in Orlando, Florida.

"I get to help in projects that provide a better quality of life for people. It's a good feeling."

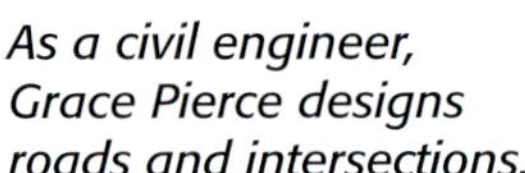

As a civil engineer, Grace Pierce designs roads and intersections.

What do you do as a civil engineer?

I'm a transportation engineer with a bachelor's degree in civil engineering. I do a lot of transportation studies, transportation planning, and engineering—anything to do with moving cars. Right now, my clients are about a 50-50 mix of private and public.

What part of your job do you like best?

Transportation planning. On the planning side, you get to be involved in developments that are going to impact the community . . . being able to tap into my creative sense to help my clients get what they want.

What do you find most rewarding about your job?

Civil engineering in civil projects. They are very rewarding because I get to see my input on a very fast time scale.

What kinds of skills do you think a good civil engineer needs?

You need a good solid academic background. You need communication skills and writing ability. Communication is key. You should get involved in activities or clubs like Toastmasters, which can help you with your presentation skills. You should get involved with your community.

What part of your education do you think was most important?

Two years before graduation, I was given the opportunity to meet with the owner of a company who gave me a good preview of what he did. It's really important to get out there and get the professional experience as well as the academic experience before you graduate.

You didn't enter college immediately after high school. Did you have to do anything differently from a younger student?

I went to school as an older student. I didn't go back to college until age 27. I knew that because I was competing with younger folks, I really had to hustle.

What advice do you have for anyone interested in civil engineering?

Have a vision. Have a goal, whatever that might be, and envision yourself in that arena. Work as hard as you can to realize that vision. Find out what you want to do, and find someone who can mentor you. Use every resource available to you in high school and college, including professors and people in the community. And in the process, have fun. It doesn't have to be dreary.

"I think my industry is going toward the 'smart' movement of vehicles and people. The future is intelligent transportation systems using automated systems."

—Grace Pierce

CHAPTER 13

Heat and Temperature

Chapter Preview

Unlike visible light, infrared radiation from the fire passes through the smoke, making an otherwise invisible fire easy to see and locate. In infrared images, the high-temperature fire is brighter than its cooler surroundings.

Background The fire started at night. By the time firefighters arrived the next morning, the forest was filled with thick smoke. The firefighters knew the fire was raging, but they had to see through the smoke to find the fire's location.

Fortunately, firefighters have instruments that detect infrared radiation, which is a form of light that is invisible to the eye. It is given off by hot objects, such as burning wood. Infrared radiation passes through the smoke and is picked up by infrared detectors. The images formed by these instruments are converted into pictures. From these pictures, the fire's location can be determined, and the firefighters can fight the fire.

Activity 1 Use a prism to separate a beam of sunlight into its component colors, and project these onto a sheet of paper. Use a thermometer to record the temperature of the air in the room, and then place the thermometer bulb in each colored band for 3 minutes. Record the final temperature of each colored band. Place the thermometer on the dark side of the red band, where infrared radiation is found, for 3 minutes. How do the final temperature readings differ? Do your results suggest why infrared radiation is associated with hot objects?

Activity 2 Obtain several cups that are the same size but are made of different materials (glass, metal, ceramic, plastic foam). Fill one cup with hot tap water. Measure the time it takes for the outside of the cup to feel hot (about 35°C). Repeat this for each cup. List the cups by their materials, with the one that warms fastest listed first. Note any differences such as cup thickness, cup volume, or changes in the temperature of your hand.

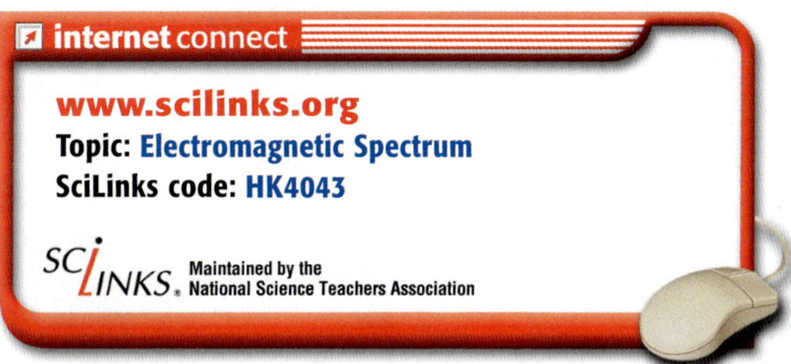

Pre-Reading Questions

1. Write a paragraph summarizing what you know about heat as energy.
2. List three ways that temperature has affected you recently.

SECTION 1

Temperature

KEY TERMS
temperature
thermometer
absolute zero
heat

OBJECTIVES

- **Define** *temperature* in terms of the average kinetic energy of atoms or molecules.
- **Convert** temperature readings between the Fahrenheit, Celsius, and Kelvin scales.
- **Recognize** heat as a form of energy transfer.

temperature a measure of how hot (or cold) something is; specifically, a measure of the average kinetic energy of the particles in an object

People use **temperature** readings, such as those shown in ***Figure 1,*** to make a wide variety of decisions every day. You check the temperature of the outdoor air to decide what to wear. The temperature of a roasting turkey is monitored to see if it is properly cooked. A nurse monitors the condition of a patient by checking the patient's body temperature. But what exactly is it that you, the cook, and the nurse are measuring? What does the temperature indicate?

Temperature and Energy

When you touch the hood of an automobile, you sense how hot or cold it is. In everyday life, we associate this sensation of hot or cold with the temperature of an object. However, this sensation serves only as a rough indicator of temperature. The Quick Activity on the next page illustrates this point.

Figure 1
Many decisions are made based on temperature.

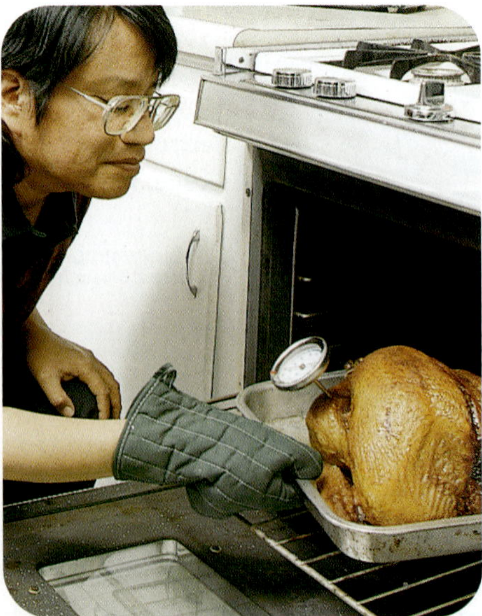
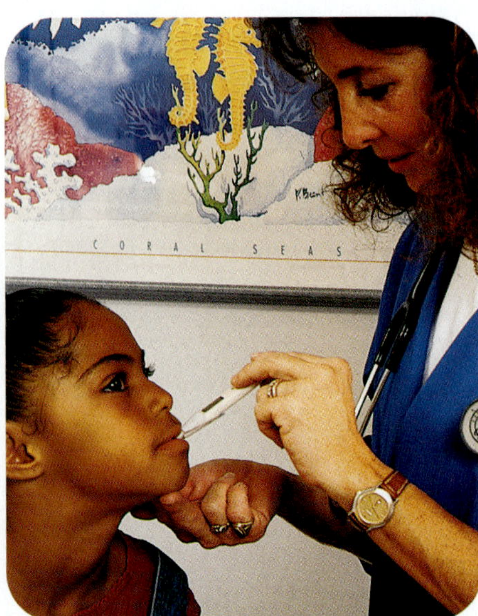

Sensing Hot and Cold

For this exercise you will need three bowls.

1. Put an equal amount of water in all three bowls. In the first bowl, put some cold tap water. Put some hot tap water in the second bowl. Then, mix equal amounts of hot and cold tap water in the third bowl.
2. Place one hand in the hot water and the other hand in the cold water. Leave them there for 15 s.
3. Place both hands in the third bowl, which contains the mixture of hot and cold water. How does the water temperature feel to each hand? Explain.

As you know, all particles in a substance are constantly moving. Like all moving objects, each particle has kinetic energy. If we average the kinetic energy of all the particles in an object, it turns out that this average kinetic energy is proportional to the temperature of the object.

In other words, as the average kinetic energy of an object increases, its temperature will increase. Compared to a cool car hood, the particles in a hot hood move faster because they have more kinetic energy. But how do we measure the temperature of an object? It is impossible to find the kinetic energy of every particle in an object and calculate its average. Actually, nature provides a very simple way to measure temperature directly.

Common thermometers rely on expansion

Icicles forming on trees, flowers wilting in the sun, and the red glow of a stove-top burner are all indicators of certain temperature ranges. You feel these temperatures as hot or cold. How you sense hot and cold depends not only on an object's temperature but also on other factors, such as the temperature of your skin.

To measure temperature, we rely on a simple physical property of substances: most objects expand when their temperatures increase. Ordinary **thermometers** are based on this principle and use liquid substances such as mercury or colored alcohol that expand as their temperature increases and contract as their temperature falls, because of energy exchange.

For example, the thermometer shown in ***Figure 2*** can measure the temperature of air on a sunny day. As the temperature rises, the particles in the liquid inside the thermometer gain kinetic energy and move faster. With this increased motion, the particles in the liquid move farther apart causing it to expand and rise up the narrow tube.

thermometer an instrument that measures and indicates temperature

Figure 2

A liquid thermometer uses the expansion of a liquid, alcohol or mercury, to indicate changes in temperature.

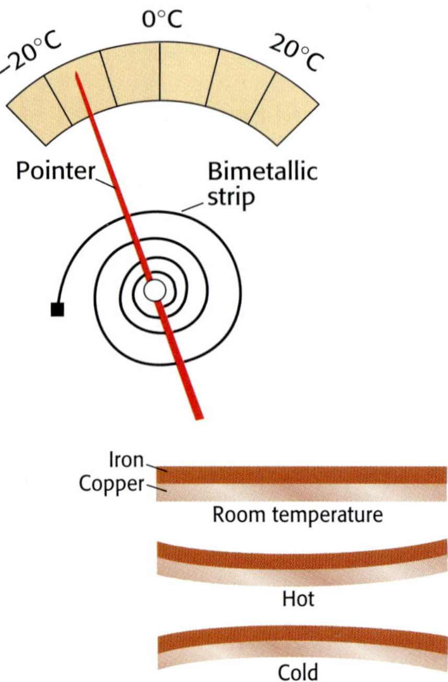

Figure 3

A refrigerator thermometer uses the bending of a strip made from two metals to indicate the correct temperature.

Thermometers can use different methods

Liquid thermometers can measure only temperatures within a certain range. This is because below a certain temperature, the liquid used in the thermometer freezes. Also, above a certain temperature the liquid boils. Therefore, different types of thermometers are designed to measure extreme temperatures.

A refrigerator thermometer is based on the expansion of metal, as shown in ***Figure 3.*** The thermometer contains a coil made from two different metal strips pressed together. Both strips expand and contract at different rates as the temperature changes. As the temperature falls, the coil unwinds moving the pointer to the correct temperature. As the temperature rises, the coil winds up moving the pointer in the opposite direction.

A digital thermometer, shown in ***Figure 4,*** is designed to measure temperature by noting the change in current. Changes in temperature also cause electric current to change.

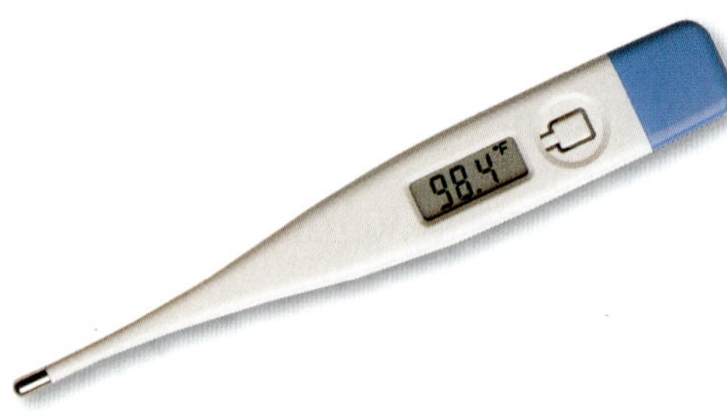

Figure 4

A digital thermometer uses changes in electricity to measure temperature.

Fahrenheit and Celsius are common scales used for measuring temperatures

The units on the Fahrenheit scale are called degrees Fahrenheit, or °F. On the Fahrenheit scale, water freezes at 32°F and boils at 212°F.

Most countries other than the United States use the Celsius (or centigrade) scale. This scale is widely used in science. The Celsius scale gives a value of 0°C to the freezing point of water and a value of 100°C to the boiling point of water at standard atmospheric pressure. The difference between these two points is divided into 100 equal parts, called degrees Celsius, or °C.

A degree Celsius is 1.8 times as large as a degree Fahrenheit. Also, the temperature at which water freezes differs for the two scales by 32 degrees. To convert from one scale to the other, use one of the following formulas.

Conversion Equations

$$\text{Fahrenheit temperature} = \left(1.8 \times \text{Celsius temperature}\right) + 32.0$$

$$T_F = 1.8t + 32.0$$

$$\text{Celsius temperature} = \frac{(\text{Fahrenheit temperature} - 32.0)}{1.8}$$

$$t = \frac{(T_F - 32.0)}{1.8}$$

The Kelvin scale is based on absolute zero

You have probably heard of negative temperatures, such as those reported on extremely cold winter days in the northern United States and Canada. Remember that temperature is a measure of the average kinetic energy of the particles in an object. Even far below 0°C these particles are moving and therefore have some kinetic energy. But how low can the temperature fall? Physically, the lowest possible temperature is –273.16°C. This temperature is referred to as **absolute zero**. At absolute zero the energy of an object is zero. That is, the energy of the object cannot be any lower.

Temperature Values on Different Scales

Fahrenheit scale (°F): 220, 210, 200, 190, 180, 170, 160, 150, 140, 130, 120, 110, 100, 90, 80, 70, 60, 50, 40, 30, 20, 10, 0, –10, –20, –30, –40

Celsius scale (°C): 100, 90, 80, 70, 60, 50, 40, 30, 20, 10, 0, –10, –20, –30, –40

Kelvin scale (K): 370, 360, 350, 340, 330, 320, 310, 300, 290, 280, 270, 260, 250, 240, 230

Examples: Water boils; Summer day in desert; Human body temperature; Warm room; Cool room; Cold room; Water freezes; Winter day in plains; Winter day in tundra

Figure 5

Temperature on the Celsius scale can be converted to both Fahrenheit and Kelvin scales. Note that all Kelvin temperatures are positive.

Absolute zero is the basis for another temperature scale called the Kelvin scale. On this scale, 0 kelvin, or 0 K, is absolute zero. Since the lowest possible temperature is assigned a zero value, there are no negative temperature values on the Kelvin scale. The Kelvin scale is used in many fields of science, especially those involving low temperatures. The three temperature scales are compared in ***Figure 5.***

In magnitude, a unit of kelvin is equal to a degree on the Celsius scale. Therefore, the temperature of any object in kelvins can be found by simply adding 273 to the object's temperature in degrees Celsius. The equation for this conversion is given below.

absolute zero the temperature at which molecular energy is at a minimum (0 K on the Kelvin scale or –273.16°C on the Celsius scale)

Celsius-Kelvin Conversion Equation

$$\text{Kelvin temperature} = \text{Celsius temperature} + 273$$

$$T = t + 273$$

INTEGRATING

SPACE SCIENCE

From cold deep space to hot stars, astronomers measure a wide range of temperatures of objects in the universe. All objects produce different types of electromagnetic waves depending on their temperature. By identifying the distribution of wavelengths an object radiates, astronomers can estimate the object's temperature.

Light (an electromagnetic wave) received from the sun indicates that the temperature of its surface is 6000 K. If you think that is hot, try the center of the sun, where the temperature increases to 15 000 000 K!

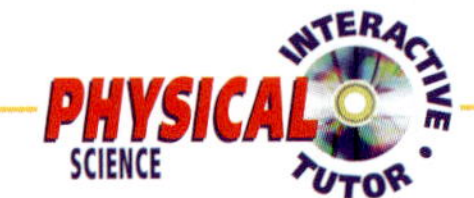

Disc One, Module 7: **Heat**
Use the Interactive Tutor to learn more about these topics.

Math Skills

Temperature Scale Conversion The highest atmospheric temperature ever recorded on Earth was 57.8°C. Express this temperature both in degrees Fahrenheit and in kelvins.

1 List the given and unknown values.

Given: $t = 57.8°C$

Unknown: $T_F = ?°F$, $T = ?K$

2 Write down the equations for temperature conversions.

$T_F = 1.8t + 32.0$

$T = t + 273$

3 Insert the known values into the equations, and solve.

$T_F = (1.8 \times 57.8) + 32.0 = 104 + 32.0 = 136°F$

$T = 57.8 + 273 = 331\ K$

Practice

Temperature Scale Conversion

1. Express these temperatures in degrees Fahrenheit and in kelvins.
   a. the boiling point of liquid hydrogen (–252.87°C)
   b. the temperature of a winter day at the North Pole (–40.0°C)
   c. the melting point of gold (1064°C)
2. Make the necessary conversions to complete the table below.

Example	Temp. (°C)	Temp. (°F)	Temp. (K)
Air in a typical living room	21	?	?
Metal in a running car engine	?	?	388
Liquid nitrogen	–200	?	?
Air on a summer day in the desert	?	110	?

3. Use **Figure 5** to determine which of the following is a likely temperature for ice cubes in a freezer.
   a. – 20°C
   b. – 4°F
   c. 253 K
   d. all of the above
4. Use **Figure 5** to determine which of the following is the nearest value for normal human body temperature.
   a. 50°C
   b. 75°F
   c. 310 K
   d. all of the above

Relating Temperature to Energy Transfer

When you touch a piece of ice, it feels very cold. When you step into a hot bath, the water feels very hot. Clasping your hands together usually produces neither sensation. These three cases can be explained by comparing the temperatures of the two objects that are making contact with each other.

The feeling associated with temperature difference results from energy transfer

Imagine that you are holding a piece of ice. The temperature of ice is lower than the temperature of your hand; therefore, the molecules in the ice move slowly compared with the molecules in your hand. As the molecules on the surface of your hand collide with those on the surface of the ice, energy is transferred to the ice. As a result, the molecules in the ice speed up and their kinetic energy increases. This causes the ice to melt.

How do temperature and energy relate?

Materials

- glass beaker
- tongs
- 2 pieces of string, 20 cm each
- thermometer
- clock
- electric hot plate
- graduated cylinder
- 40 identical small metal washers
- 2 plastic-foam cups

1. Tie 10 washers on one piece of string and 30 washers on another piece of string.
2. Fill the beaker two-thirds full with water, lower the washers in, and set the beaker on the hot plate.
3. Heat the water to boiling.
4. While the water heats, put exactly 50 mL of cool water in each plastic-foam cup.
5. Use a thermometer to measure and record the initial temperature of water in each cup.
6. When the water in the beaker has boiled for about 3 minutes, use tongs to remove the group of 30 washers. Gently shake any water off the washers back into the beaker, and quickly place the washers into one of the plastic-foam cups.
7. Observe the change in temperature of the cup's water. Record the highest temperature reached.
8. Repeat steps 6 and 7 by placing the10 washers in the other plastic-foam cup.

Analysis

1. Which cup had the higher final temperature?
2. Both cups had the same starting temperature. Both sets of washers started at 100°C. Why did one cup reach a higher final temperature?

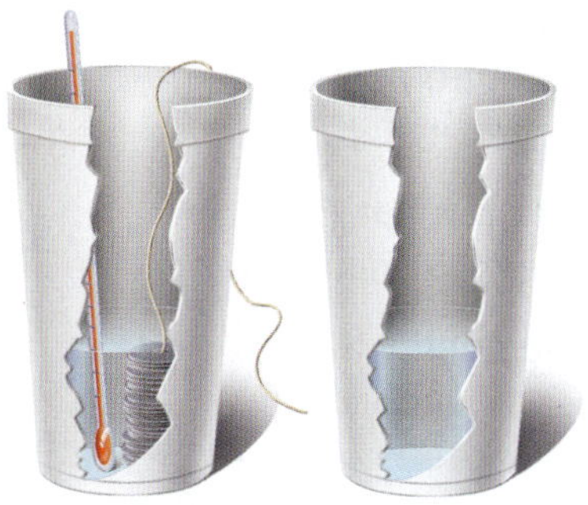

Temperature changes indicate an energy transfer

The energy transferred between the particles of two objects due to a temperature difference between the two objects is called **heat.** This transfer of energy always takes place from a substance at a higher temperature to a substance at a lower temperature. For example, if you hold a glass of ice water in your hands, energy will be transferred as heat from your hand to the glass. However, if you hold a very hot cup of water, energy will be transferred as heat from the cup to your hand.

heat the energy transferred between objects that are at different temperatures

Because temperature is an indicator of the average kinetic energy of internal particles, you can use temperature to predict which way energy will be transferred. Internal kinetic energy will be transferred as heat from the warmer object to the cooler object. So, when this energy is transferred from the hot water in the cup to your skin, the temperature of the water falls while the temperature of your skin rises.

When both your skin and the cup in your hand approach the same temperature, less energy is transferred from the cup to your skin. To continue the transfer of energy, enough energy must be added to the water as heat to keep the water's temperature higher than the skin's temperature. The greater the difference in the temperatures of the two objects is, the greater the amount of energy that will be transferred as heat is.

INTEGRATING

HEALTH

Food supplies the human body with energy. An active 120 lb teenager on a typical diet takes in and expends about 2400 Calories (4.187×10^7 J) per day, or 48.5 J/s. Much of this energy is eventually transferred away as heat, which is why a full classroom feels hotter toward the end of class.

SECTION 1 REVIEW

SUMMARY

- Temperature is a measure of the average kinetic energy of an object's particles.
- On the Celsius temperature scale, water freezes at 0° and boils at 100°.
- A kelvin is the same size as a degree Celsius. The lowest temperature possible—absolute zero—is 0 K.
- At absolute zero, particle kinetic energy is minimal.
- Heat is the energy transferred between objects with different temperatures.

1. **Define** *absolute zero* in terms of kinetic energy of particles.
2. **Predict** which molecules will move faster on average: water molecules in hot soup or water molecules in iced lemonade.
3. **Predict** whether a greater amount of energy will be transferred as heat between 1 kg of water at 10°C and a freezer at –15°C or between 1 kg of water at 60°C and an oven at 65°C.
4. **Critical Thinking** Determine which of the following has a higher temperature and which contains a larger amount of total kinetic energy: a cup of boiling water or Lake Michigan.

Math Skills

5. Convert the temperature of the air in an air-conditioned room, 20.0°C, to equivalent values on the Fahrenheit and Kelvin temperature scales.
6. Convert the coldest outdoor temperature ever recorded, –128.6°F, to equivalent Celsius and Kelvin temperatures.

SECTION 2

Energy Transfer

OBJECTIVES

- **Investigate** and demonstrate how energy is transferred by conduction, convection, and radiation.
- **Identify** and distinguish between conductors and insulators.
- **Solve** problems involving specific heat.

KEY TERMS

thermal conduction
convection
convection current
radiation
specific heat

While water is being heated for your morning shower, your breakfast food is cooking. In the freezer, water in ice trays becomes solid after the freezer cools the water to 0°C. Outside, the morning dew evaporates soon after light from the rising sun strikes it. These are all examples of energy transfers from one object to another.

Methods of Energy Transfer

The transfer of heat energy from a hot object can occur in three ways. Roasting marshmallows around a campfire, as shown in ***Figure 6,*** provides an opportunity to experience each of these three ways.

Figure 6 **Ways of Transferring Energy**

A Conduction transfers energy as heat along the wire and into the hand.

B Embers swirl upward in the convection currents that are created as warmed air above the fire rises.

C Electromagnetic waves emitted by the hot campfire transfer energy by radiation.

Figure 7

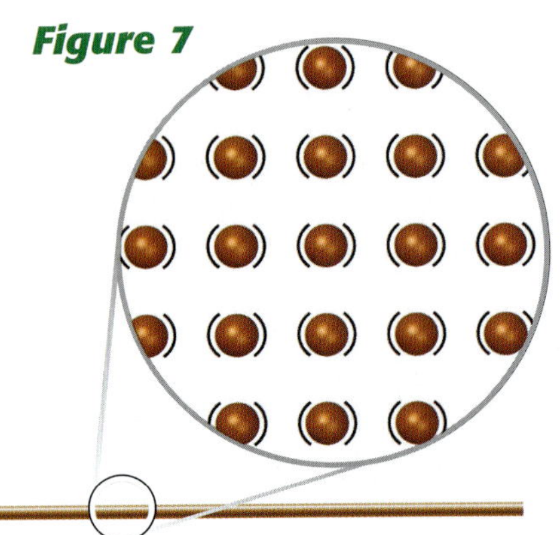

A Before conduction takes place, the average kinetic energy of the particles in the metal wire is the same throughout.

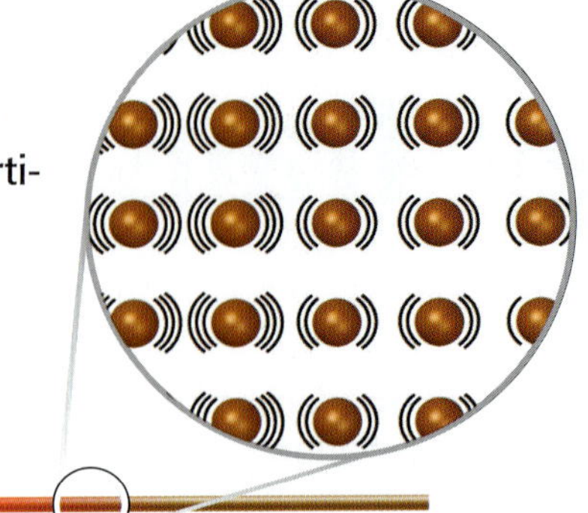

B During conduction, the rapidly moving particles in the wire transfer some of their energy to slowly moving particles nearby.

Conduction involves objects in direct contact

Imagine you place a marshmallow on one end of a wire made from a metal coat hanger. Then you hold the other end of the wire while letting the marshmallow cook in the campfire flame. Soon, the end of the wire you are holding will get warmer. This is an example of energy transfer by **thermal conduction.**

thermal conduction the transfer of energy as heat through a material

convection the movement of matter due to differences in density that are caused by temperature variations

Conduction is one of the methods of energy transfer. Conduction takes place when two objects that are in contact are at unequal temperatures. It also takes place between particles within an object. In the case of the wire in the campfire, the rapidly moving air molecules close to the flame collide with the atoms at the end of the wire. The energy transferred to the atoms in the wire causes them to vibrate rapidly. As shown in ***Figure 7,*** these rapidly vibrating atoms collide with slowly vibrating atoms, transferring energy as heat all along the wire. The energy is then transferred to you as the wire's atoms collide with the molecules in your skin, creating a hot sensation in your hand.

Convection results from the movement of warm fluids

While roasting your marshmallow, you may notice that tiny glowing embers from the fire rise and begin to swirl, as shown in ***Figure 6.*** They are following the movement of air away from the fire. The air close to the fire becomes hot and expands so that there is more space between the air particles. As a result, the air becomes less dense and moves upward, carrying its extra energy with it, as shown in ***Figure 8.*** The rising warm air is replaced by cooler, denser air. The cooler air then becomes hot by the fire until it also expands and rises. Eventually, the rising hot air cools, contracts, becomes denser, and sinks. This is an example of energy transfer by **convection.**

Convection involves the movement of the heated substance itself. This is possible only if the substance is a fluid—either a liquid or a gas—because particles within solids are not as free to move.

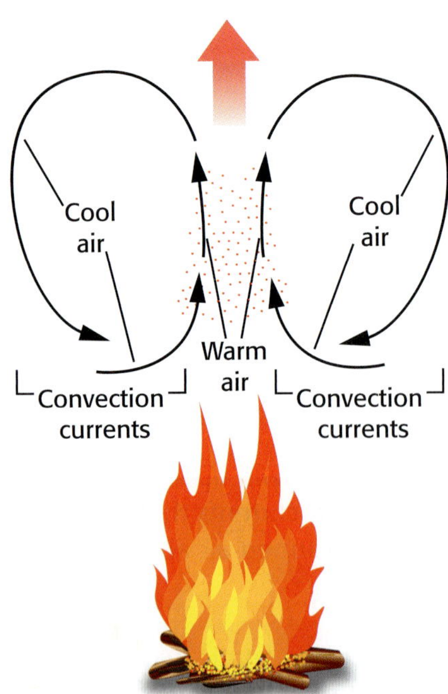

Figure 8

During convection, energy is carried away by a heated fluid that expands and rises above cooler, denser fluids.

Heated fluids have convection currents

The cycle of a heated fluid that rises and then cools and falls is called a **convection current.** When a pan of water is heated, the molecules of water at the bottom of the pan gradually rise and heat the molecules toward the top. The proper heating and cooling of a room requires the use of convection currents. Warm air expands and rises from vents near the floor. It cools and contracts near the ceiling and then sinks back to the floor. Eventually, the temperature of all the air in the room is increased by convection currents.

convection current the vertical movement of air currents due to temperature variations

radiation the energy that is transferred as electromagnetic waves, such as visible light and infrared waves

Radiation does not require physical contact between objects

As you stand close to a campfire, you can feel its warmth. This warmth can be felt even when you are not in the path of a convection current. The energy that is transferred as heat from the fire in this case is in the form of *electromagnetic waves,* which include infrared radiation, visible light, and ultraviolet rays. The energy that is transferred as electromagnetic waves is called **radiation.** You will learn more about electromagnetic radiation later.

When you stand near a fire, your skin absorbs the energy radiated by the fire. As the molecules in your skin absorb this energy, the average kinetic energy of these molecules—and thus the temperature of your skin—increases. A hot object radiates more energy than a cool object, as shown in ***Figure 9.***

Radiation differs from conduction and convection in that it does not involve the movement of matter. Radiation is therefore the only method of energy transfer that can take place in a vacuum, such as outer space. Much of the energy we receive from the sun is transferred by radiation.

Quick ACTIVITY

Convection

Light a candle. Carefully observe the motion of the tiny soot particles in smoke. They move because of convection currents.

Figure 9

Changes in Radiated Energy

A Before surgery, as seen in the infrared photo, the fingers are cooler than the rest of the hand. This results from poor blood flow in this patient's fingers.

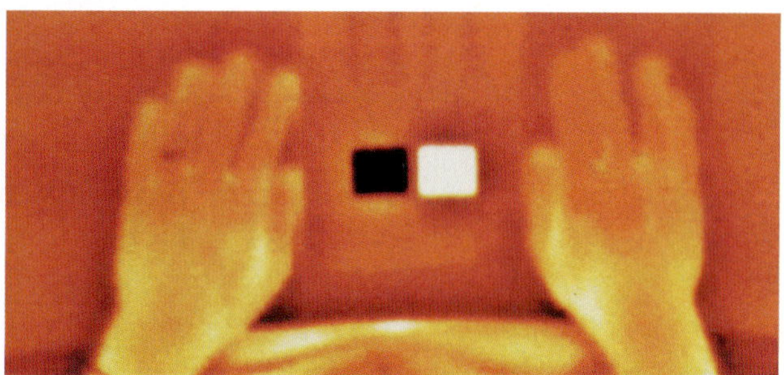

B After surgery, the blood flow has been restored, so the temperature of the fingers increases. The amount of energy they radiate also increases.

What color absorbs more radiation?

Materials

- *empty soup can, painted black inside and out, label removed*
- *empty soup can, label removed*
- *2 thermometers*
- *clock*
- *graduated cylinder*
- *bright lamp or sunlight*

1. Prepare a data table with three columns and at least seven rows. Label the first column "Time," the second column "Temperature of painted can (°C)," and the third column "Temperature of unpainted can (°C)."
2. Pour 50 mL of cool water into each can.
3. Place a thermometer in each can, and record the temperature of the water in each can at the start. Leave the thermometers in the cans. Aim the lamp at the cans, or place them in sunlight.
4. Record the temperature of the water in each can every 3 minutes for at least 15 minutes.

Analysis

1. Prepare a graph. Label the *x*-axis "Time" and the *y*-axis "Temperature." Plot your data for each can of water.
2. Which color absorbed more radiation?
3. Which variables in the lab were controlled (unchanged throughout the experiment)? For each of the following variables, explain your answer.
   a. starting temperature of water in cans
   b. volume of water in cans
   c. distance of cans from light
   d. size of cans
4. Use your results to explain why panels used for solar heating are often painted black.
5. Based on your results, what color would you want your car to be in the winter? in the summer? Justify your answer.

Conductors and Insulators

When you are cooking, the pan must conduct energy to heat the food, but the handle must be insulated from the heat so that you can hold it. If you are using conduction to increase the temperature of a substance, you must use materials through which energy can be quickly transferred as heat. Cooking pans are usually made of metal because energy is passed quickly between the particles in most metals. Any material through which energy can be easily transferred as heat is called a *conductor*.

Many people try to avoid wasting energy. It is most often wasted by energy transfer through the roof or the walls of your home. You can reduce this energy transfer by using poor conductors, called *insulators* or *insulation*. Insulation in the attic or walls of homes helps to prevent unwanted energy transfer.

Energy transfers through particle collisions

Gases are extremely poor conductors because their particles are far apart, and transfer of energy is less likely to occur. The particles in liquids are more closely packed. However, while liquids conduct better than gases, they are not effective conductors.

Some solids, such as rubber and wood, conduct energy about as well as liquids. So, rubber and wood are good insulators. Some solids are better conductors than other solids. Metals, such as copper and silver, conduct energy as heat very well. Metals, in general, are better conductors than nonmetals.

Examples of conductors and insulators are shown in ***Figure 10.*** The skillet is made of iron, a good conductor, so energy is transferred effectively as heat to the food. Wood is an insulator, so the energy from the hot skillet won't reach your hand through the wooden spoon or the wooden handle.

Figure 10

The skillet conducts energy from the stove element to the food. The wooden spoon and handle insulate the hands from the energy of the skillet.

Conductors and Insulators

For this activity you will need several flatware utensils. Each one should be made of a different material, such as stainless steel, aluminum, and plastic. You will also need a bowl and ice cubes.

1. Place the ice cubes in the bowl. Position the utensils in the bowl so that an equal length of each utensil lies under the ice.
2. Check the utensils' temperature by briefly touching each utensil at the same distance from the ice every 20 s. Which utensil becomes colder first? What variables might affect your results?

Figure 11

The spoon's temperature increases rapidly because of the spoon's low specific heat.

Specific Heat

You have probably noticed that a metal spoon, like the one shown in ***Figure 11,*** becomes hot when it is placed in a cup of hot liquid. You have also probably noticed that a spoon made of a different material, such as plastic, does not become hot as quickly. The difference between the final temperatures of the two spoons depends on whether they are good conductors or good insulators. But what makes a substance a good or poor conductor depends in part on how much energy a substance requires to change its temperature by a certain degree.

Specific heat describes how much energy is required to raise an object's temperature

Not all substances behave the same when they absorb heat energy. For example, a metal spoon left in a metal pot becomes hot seconds after the pot is placed on a hot stovetop burner. This is because a few joules of energy are enough to raise the spoon's temperature substantially. However, if an amount of water with the same mass as the spoon is placed in the same pot, that same amount of energy will produce a much smaller temperature change in the water.

specific heat the quantity of heat required to raise a unit mass of homogenous material 1 K or 1°C in a specified way given constant pressure and volume

For all substances, **specific heat** is a characteristic physical property, which is denoted by c. In this book, we will think of specific heat of any substance as the amount of energy required to raise 1 kg of that substance by 1 K.

Some values for specific heat are given in ***Table 1.*** They are in units of J/kg•K, meaning that each is the amount of energy in J needed to raise the temperature of 1 kg of the substance by exactly 1 K.

Table 1 **Specific Heats at 25°C**

Substance	c (J/kg•K)	Substance	c (J/kg•K)
Water (liquid)	4186	Copper	385
Steam	1870	Gold	129
Ammonia (gas)	2060	Iron	449
Ethanol (liquid)	2440	Mercury	140
Aluminum	897	Lead	129
Carbon (graphite)	709	Silver	234

On a hot summer day, the temperature of the water in a swimming pool remains much lower than the air temperature and the temperature of the concrete around the pool. This is due to water's relatively high specific heat as well as the large mass of water in the pool. Similarly, at night, the concrete and the air cool off quickly, while the water changes temperature only slightly.

Specific heat can be used in calculations

Because specific heat is a ratio, it can be used to predict the effects of larger temperature changes for masses other than 1 kg. For example, if it takes 4186 J to raise the temperature of 1 kg of water by 1 K, twice as much energy, 8372 J, will be required to raise the temperature of 2 kg of water by 1 K. But about 25 120 J will be required to raise the temperature of the 2 kg of water by 3 K. This relationship is summed up in the equation below.

Specific Heat Equation

energy = (specific heat) × (mass) × (temperature change)

$$\text{energy} = cm\Delta t$$

Specific heat can change slightly with changing pressure and volume. However, problems and questions in this chapter will assume that specific heat does not change.

INTEGRATING

EARTH SCIENCE

Sea breezes result from both convection currents in the coastal air and differences in the specific heats of water and sand or soil. During the day, the temperature of the land increases more than the temperature of the ocean water, which has a larger specific heat. As a result, the temperature of the air over land increases more than the temperature of air over the ocean. This causes the warm air over the land to rise and the cool ocean air to move inland to replace the rising warm air. At night, the temperature of the dry land drops below that of the ocean, and the direction of the breezes is reversed.

Math Skills

Specific Heat How much energy must be transferred as heat to the 420 kg of water in a bathtub in order to raise the water's temperature from 25°C to 37°C?

1 List the given and unknown values.

Given: Δt = 37°C − 25°C = Δ12°C = Δ12 K

ΔT = 12 K

m = 420 kg

c = 4186 J/kg•K

Unknown: energy = ? J

2 Write down the specific heat equation from this page.

$$\text{energy} = cm\Delta t$$

3 Substitute the specific heat, mass, and temperature change values, and solve.

$$\text{energy} = \left(\frac{4186\ \text{J}}{\text{kg}\bullet\text{K}}\right) \times (420\ \text{kg}) \times (12\ \text{K})$$

$$\text{energy} = 21\ 000\ 000\ \text{J} = 2.1 \times 10^4\ \text{kJ}$$

- To rearrange the equation to isolate temperature change, divide both sides of the equation by *cm*.

$$\frac{\text{energy}}{cm} = \left(\frac{\cancel{cm}}{\cancel{cm}}\right)\Delta t$$

$$\Delta t = \frac{\text{energy}}{cm}$$

- Use this version of the equation for Practice Problem 4.
- For Practice Problems 5 and 6, you will need to isolate *m* and *c*.

Practice

Specific Heat

1. How much energy is needed to increase the temperature of 755 g of iron from 283 K to 403 K?
2. How much energy must a refrigerator absorb from 225 g of water so that the temperature of the water will drop from 35°C to 5°C?
3. A 144 kg park bench made of iron sits in the sun, and its temperature increases from 25°C to 35°C. How many kilojoules of energy does the bench absorb?
4. An aluminum baking sheet with a mass of 225 g absorbs 2.4×10^4 J from an oven. If its temperature was initially 25°C, what will its new temperature be?
5. What mass of water is required to absorb 4.7×10^5 J of energy from a car engine while the temperature increases from 298 K to 355 K?
6. A vanadium bolt gives up 1124 J of energy as its temperature drops 25 K. If the bolt's mass is 93 g, what is its specific heat?

SECTION 2 REVIEW

SUMMARY

- Conduction is the transfer of energy as heat between particles as they collide within a substance or between objects in contact.
- Convection currents are the movement of gases and liquids as they become heated, expand, and rise, then cool, contract, and fall.
- Radiation is energy transfer by electromagnetic waves.
- Conductors are materials through which energy is easily transferred as heat.
- Insulators are materials that conduct energy poorly.
- Specific heat is the energy required to heat 1 kg of a substance by 1 K.

1. **Describe** how energy is transferred by conduction, convection, and radiation.
2. **Predict** whether the hottest part of a room will be near the ceiling, in the center, or near the floor, given that there is a hot-air vent near the floor. Explain your reasoning.

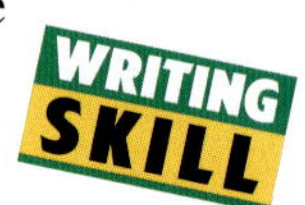

3. **Explain** why there are temperature differences on the moon's surface, even though there is no atmosphere present.
4. **Critical Thinking** Explain why cookies baked near the turned-up edges of a cookie sheet receive more energy than those baked near the center.

Math Skills

5. When a shiny chunk of metal with a mass of 1.32 kg absorbs 3250 J of energy, the temperature of the metal increases from 273 K to 292 K. Is this metal likely to be silver, lead, or aluminum?
6. A 0.400 kg sample of glass requires 3190 J for its temperature to increase from 273 K to 308 K. What is the specific heat for this type of glass?

SECTION 3

Using Heat

OBJECTIVES

- **Describe** the concepts of different heating and cooling systems.
- **Compare** different heating and cooling systems in terms of their transfer of usable energy.
- **Explain** how a heat engine uses heat energy to do work.

refrigerant
heat engine

Heating a house in the winter, cooling an office building in the summer, or preserving food throughout the year is possible because of machines that transfer energy as heat from one place to another. An example of one of these machines, an air conditioner, is shown in ***Figure 12.*** An air conditioner does work to remove energy as heat from the warm air inside a room and then transfers the energy to the warmer air outside the room. An air conditioner can do this because of two principles about energy that you have already studied.

The first principle is that the total energy used in any process—whether that energy is transferred as a result of work, heat, or both—is conserved. This principle of conservation of energy is called the first law of thermodynamics.

The second principle is that the energy transferred as heat always moves from an object at a higher temperature to an object at a lower temperature.

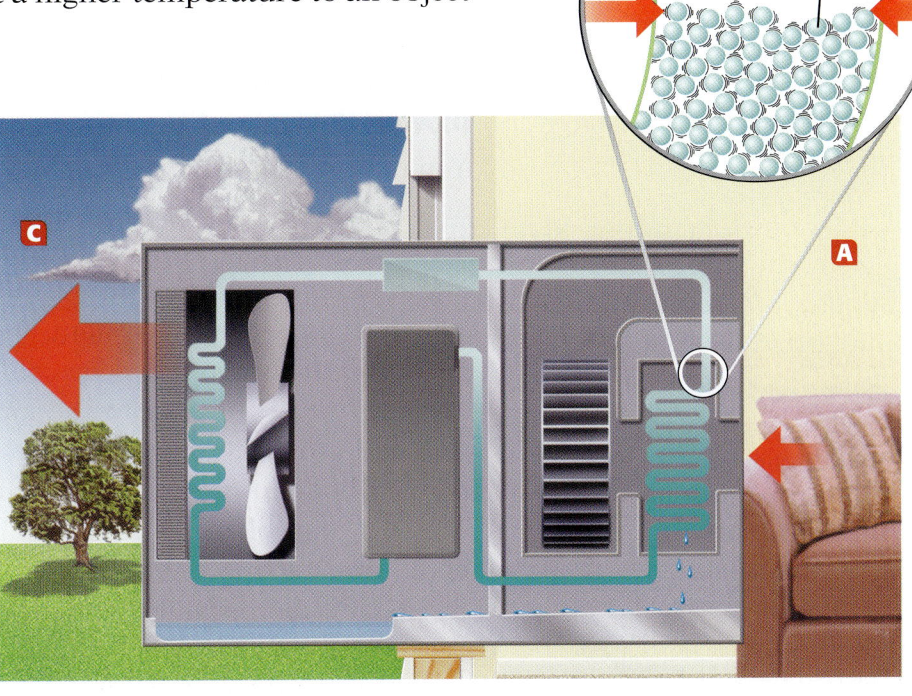

Figure 12

A A substance that easily evaporates and condenses is used in air conditioners to transfer energy from a room to the air outside.

B When the liquid evaporates, it absorbs energy from the surrounding air, thereby cooling it.

C Outside, the air conditioner causes the gas to condense, releasing energy.

Connection to SOCIAL STUDIES

In 1769, a Scottish engineer named James Watt patented a new design that made steam engines more efficient. During the next 50 years, the improved steam engines were used to power trains and ships. Previously, transportation had depended on the work done by horses or the wind.

Watt's new steam engines were used in machines and factories of the industrial revolution. In 1784, Watt used steam coils to heat his office. This was the first practical use of steam for heating.

Making the Connection

1. Old steam-powered riverboats are popular tourist attractions in many cities. Make a list of at least three other instances in which the energy in steam is used for practical purposes.
2. What devices in older buildings function like the steam coils Watt used for heating his office?

Heating Systems

People generally feel and work their best when the temperature of the air around them is in the range of 21°C–25°C (70°F–77°F). To raise the indoor temperature on colder days, energy must be transferred into a room's air by a *heating system*. Most heating systems use a source of energy to raise the temperature of a substance such as air or water.

Work can increase average kinetic energy

When you rub your hands together, they become warmer. The energy you transfer to your hands by work is transferred to the molecules of your hands, and their temperature increases. Processes that involve energy transfer by work are called mechanical processes.

Another example of a mechanical heating process is a device used in the past by certain American Indian tribes to start fires. The device consists of a bow with a loop in the bowstring that holds a pointed stick. The sharp end of the stick is placed in a small indentation in a stone. A small pile of wood shavings is then put around the place where the stick and stone make contact. A person then does work to move the bow back and forth. This energy is transferred to the stick, which turns rapidly. The friction between the stick and stone causes the temperature to rise until the shavings are set on fire.

Some of the energy from food is transferred as heat to blood moving throughout the human body

You may not think of yourself as a heating system. But unless you are sick, your body maintains a temperature of about 37°C (98.6°F), whether you are in a place that is cool or hot. Maintaining this temperature in cool air requires your body to function like a heating system.

If you are surrounded by cold air, energy will be transferred as heat from your skin to the air, and the temperature of your skin will drop. To compensate, stored nutrients are broken down by your body to provide energy, and this energy is transferred as heat to your blood. The warm blood circulates through your body, transferring energy as heat to your skin and increasing your skin's temperature. In this way your body can maintain a constant temperature.

Heated water or air transfers energy as heat in central heating systems

Most modern homes and large buildings have a central heating system. As is the case with your body, when the building is surrounded by cold air, energy is transferred as heat from the building to the outside air. The temperature of the building begins to drop.

A central heating system has a furnace that burns coal, fuel oil, or natural gas. The energy released in the furnace is transferred as heat to water, steam, or air, as shown in ***Figure 13.*** The steam, hot water, or hot air is then moved to each room through pipes or ducts. Because the temperature of the pipe is higher than that of the air, energy is transferred as heat to the air in the room.

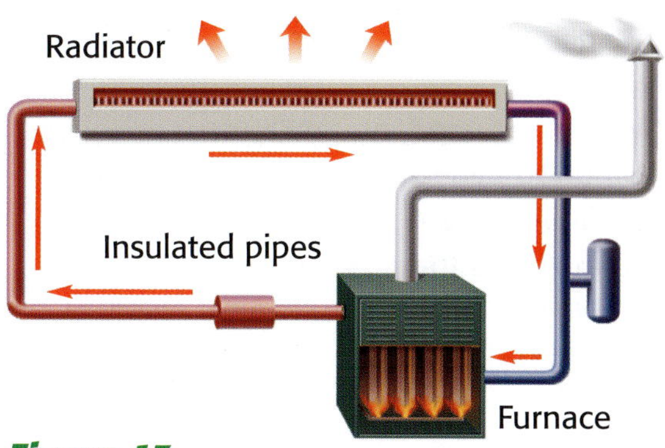

Figure 13

Hot-water, steam, and hot-air systems heat buildings by circulating heated fluids to each room.

Solar heating systems also use warmed air or water

Cold-blooded animals, such as lizards and turtles, increase their body temperature by using external sources, such as the sun. You may have seen these animals sitting motionless on rocks on sunny days, as shown in ***Figure 14.*** During such behavior, called basking, energy is absorbed by the reptile's skin through conduction from the warmer air and rocks and by radiation from sunlight. This absorbed energy is then transferred as heat to the reptile's blood. As the blood circulates, it transfers this energy to all parts of the reptile's body.

Solar heating systems, such as the one illustrated in ***Figure 15,*** use an approach similar to that of a basking reptile. A solar collector uses panels to gather energy radiated from the sun. This energy is used to heat water. The hot water is then moved throughout the house by the same methods other hot-water systems use.

Figure 14

Reptiles bask in the sun to raise their body temperature.

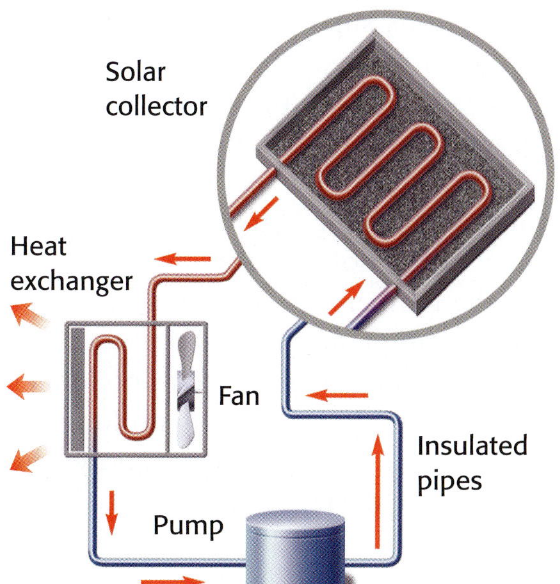

Figure 15

An active solar heating system moves solar-heated water through pipes and a heat exchanger.

Figure 16

A In a passive solar heating system, energy from sunlight is absorbed in a rooftop panel.

B Pipes carry the hot fluid that exchanges heat energy with the air in each room.

The warm water can also be pumped through a device called a heat exchanger, which transfers energy from the water to a mass of air by conduction and radiation. The warmed air is then blown through ducts as with other warm-air heating systems.

Both of these types of solar heating systems are called active solar heating systems. They require extra energy from another source, such as electricity, in order to move the heated water or air around.

Passive solar heating systems, as shown in ***Figure 16,*** require no extra energy to move the hot fluids through the pipe. In this type of system, energy transfer is accomplished by radiation and convection currents created in heated water or air. In warm, sunny climates, passive solar heating systems are easy to construct and maintain and are clean and inexpensive to operate.

Usable energy decreases in all energy transfers

When energy can be easily transformed and transferred to accomplish a task, such as heating a room, we say that the energy is in a usable form. After this transfer, the same amount of energy is present, according to the law of conservation of energy. Yet less of it is in a form that can be used.

The energy used to increase the temperature of the water in a hot-water tank should ideally stay in the hot water. However, it is impossible to keep some energy from being transferred as heat to parts of the hot-water tank and its surroundings. The amount of usable energy decreases even in the most efficient heating systems.

Due to conduction and radiation, some energy is lost to the tank's surroundings, such as the air and nearby walls. Cold water in the pipes that feed into the water heater also draws energy from some of the hot water in the tank. When energy from electricity is used to heat water in the hot-water heater, some of the energy is used to increase the temperature of the electrical wire, the metal cover of the water heater, and the air around the water heater. All of these portions of the total energy can no longer be used to heat the water. Therefore, that energy is no longer in a usable form. In general, the amount of usable energy always decreases whenever energy is transferred or transformed.

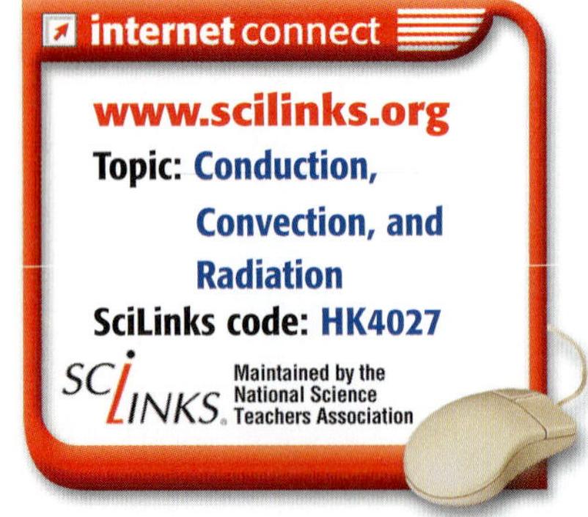

Insulation minimizes undesirable energy transfers

During winter, some of the energy from the warm air inside a building is lost to the cold outside air. Similarly, during the summer, energy from warm air outside seeps into an air-conditioned building, raising the temperature of the cool inside air. Good insulation can reduce, but not entirely eliminate, the unwanted transfer of energy to and from the building's surroundings. As shown in **Figure 17,** insulation material is placed in the walls and attics of homes and other buildings to reduce the unwanted transfer of energy as heat.

A standard rating system has been developed to measure the effectiveness of insulation materials. This rating, called the *R-value,* is determined by the type of material used and the material's thickness. *R*-values for several common building and insulating materials of a given thickness are listed in **Table 2.** The greater the *R*-value, the greater the material's ability to decrease unwanted energy transfers.

Figure 17

Insulating materials, such as fiberglass and cellulose, are used in most buildings to reduce the loss of heat energy.

Cooling Systems

If you quickly let the air out of a compressed-air tank like the one used by scuba divers, the air from the tank and the tank's nozzle feel slightly cooler than they did before the air was released. This is because the molecules in the air lose some of their kinetic energy as the air's pressure and volume change and the temperature of the air decreases. This process is a simple example of a *cooling system.* In all cooling systems, energy is transferred as heat from one substance to another, leaving the first substance with less energy and thus a lower temperature.

Table 2 **R-Values for Some Common Building Materials**

Substance	*R*-value
Drywall, 1.3 cm (0.50 in.)	0.45
Wood shingles, (overlapping)	0.87
Flat glass, 0.318 cm (0.125 in.)	0.89
Hardwood siding, 2.54 cm (1.00 in.)	0.91
Vertical air space, 8.9 cm (3.5 in.)	1.01
Insulating glass, 0.64 cm (0.25 in.)	1.54
Cellulose fiber, 2.54 cm (1.00 in.)	3.70
Brick, 10.2 cm (4.00 in.)	4.00
Fiberglass batting, 8.9 cm (3.5 in.)	10.90

Cooling systems often use evaporation to transfer energy from their surroundings

In the case of a refrigerator, the temperature of the air and food inside is lowered. But because the first law of thermodynamics requires energy to be conserved, the energy inside the refrigerator must be transferred to the air outside the refrigerator. If you place your hand near the rear or base of a refrigerator, you will feel warm air being discharged. Much of the energy in this air was removed from inside the refrigerator.

Hidden in the back wall of a refrigerator is a set of coiled pipes through which a substance called a **refrigerant** flows, as shown in ***Figure 18.*** During each operating cycle of the refrigerator, the refrigerant evaporates into a gas and then condenses back into a liquid.

refrigerant a material used to cool an area or an object to a temperature that is lower than the temperature of the environment

Recall from the beginning of this section that evaporation produces a cooling effect. Changes of state always involve the transfer of relatively large amounts of energy. In liquids that are good refrigerants, evaporation occurs at a much lower temperature than that of the air inside the refrigerator. When the liquid refrigerant is in a set of pipes near the inside of the refrigerator, heat energy is transferred from the air to the refrigerant. This exchange causes the air and food to cool.

INTEGRATING

BIOLOGY

In hot regions, the ears of many mammals serve as cooling systems. Larger ears provide more area for energy to be transferred from blood to the surrounding air, helping the animals to maintain their body temperature. Rabbits and foxes that live in the desert have much longer ears than rabbits and foxes that live in temperate or arctic climates.

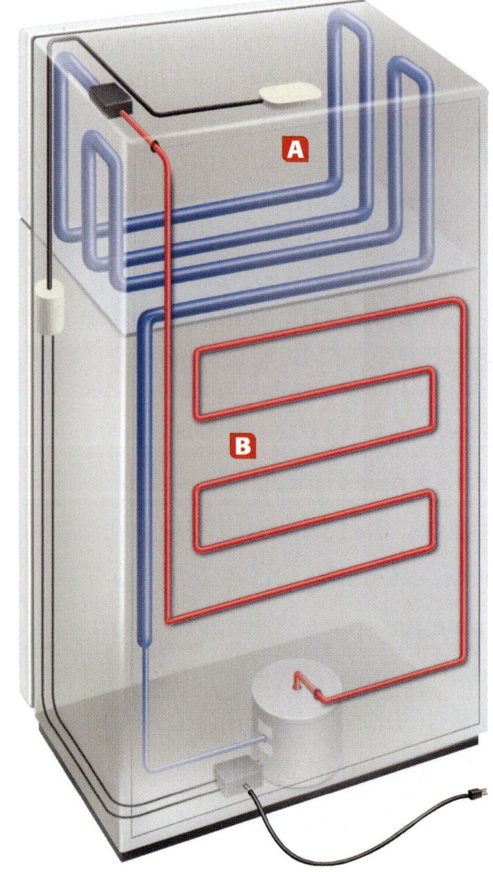

Figure 18

A Liquid refrigerant flowing through the pipes inside a refrigerator cools the compartment by evaporation.

B Energy is removed by the outside coils as the warmed refrigerant vapor cools and condenses back into a liquid.

Condensation transfers energy to the surroundings

The refrigerant has become a gas by absorbing energy. This gas moves to the section of coils outside the refrigerator, where electrical energy is used to power a compressor. Pressure is used to condense the refrigerant back into a liquid. Because condensation involves transferring heat energy from the vapor, the temperature of the air outside the refrigerator increases. This explains why the outside coils stay warm.

Air-conditioning systems in homes and buildings use the same process that refrigerators use. As air near the evaporation coils is cooled, a fan blows this air through ducts into the rooms and hallways. Convection currents in the room then allow the cool air to circulate as displaced warmer air flows into return ducts.

Heat pumps can transfer energy to or from rooms

Heat pumps use the evaporation and condensation of a refrigerant to provide heating in the winter and cooling in the summer. A heat pump is a refrigeration unit in which the cooling cycle can be reversed.

As shown in ***Figure 19A,*** the liquid refrigerant travels through the outdoor coils during the winter and absorbs enough energy from the outside air to evaporate. Work is done on the gas by a compressor, increasing the refrigerant's energy. Then the refrigerant moves through the coils inside the house, as shown in ***Figure 19B.*** The hot gas transfers heat energy to the air inside the house. This process warms the air while cooling the refrigerant gas enough for it to condense back into a liquid.

In the summer, the refrigerant is pumped in the opposite direction, so that the heat pump functions like a refrigerator or an air conditioner. The liquid refrigerant absorbs energy from the air inside the house as it evaporates. The hot refrigerant gas is then moved to the coils, which are outside the house. The refrigerant then condenses, transferring energy as heat to the outside air.

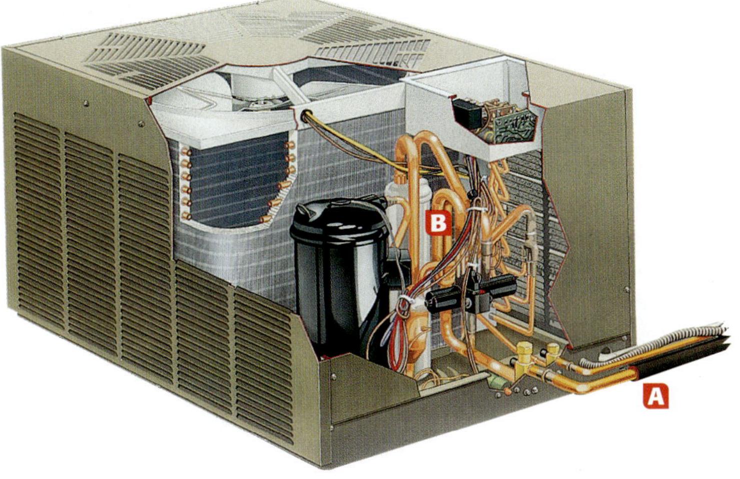

Figure 19

A Liquid refrigerant evaporates in the outdoor coils as energy is transferred from the air.

B The hot refrigerant gas moves through the coils into the indoor portion of the pump, where the refrigerant condenses back into a liquid and transfers energy as heat into the room.

heat engine a machine that transforms heat into mechanical energy, or work

Heat Engines

Heat engines convert potential chemical energy and internal kinetic energy to mechanical energy by using the process of combustion. The two main types of heat engines—internal combustion engines and external combustion engines—are named for where combustion takes place (inside the engine or outside the engine). Examples of internal engines are the engines in cars and trucks. An example of an external engine is a steam engine.

Internal combustion engines burn fuel inside the engine

In an internal combustion engine, fuel burns in cylinders within the engine. There are pistons inside the cylinders, as shown in ***Figure 20.*** Up and down movements, or strokes, of the pistons cause the crankshaft to turn. The motion of the crankshaft is transferred to the wheels of the car or truck, for example.

An automobile engine is a four-stroke engine, because four strokes take place for each cycle of the piston. The four strokes are called *intake, compression, power,* and *exhaust* strokes.

Figure 21 illustrates the four-stroke cycle of the pistons in an engine with a carburetor. A *carburetor* is another part of the engine, in which gasoline liquid becomes vaporized.

Some engines have fuel injectors instead of carburetors. In fuel-injected engines, only air enters the cylinder during the intake stroke. During the compression stroke, fuel vapor is injected directly into the compressed air in the cylinder. The other steps are the same as in an engine with a carburetor.

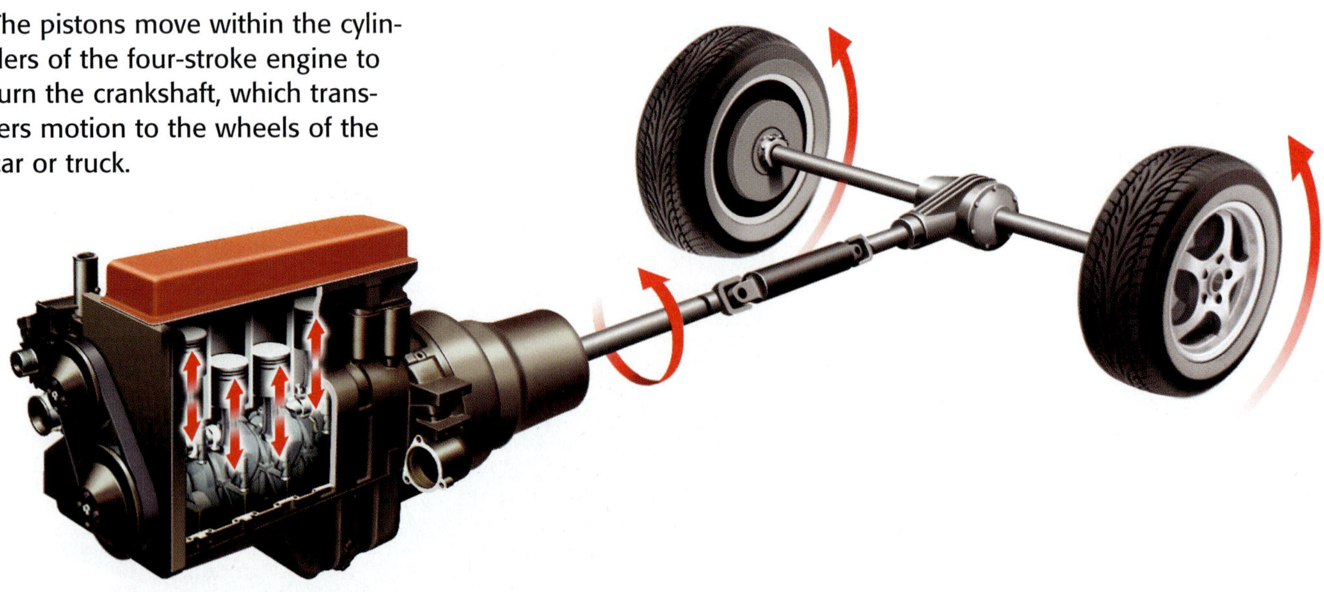

Figure 20

The pistons move within the cylinders of the four-stroke engine to turn the crankshaft, which transfers motion to the wheels of the car or truck.

Not all internal combustion engines work alike

Diesel engines are also internal combustion engines, but they work differently. A diesel engine has no spark plugs. Instead, the fuel-air mixture is compressed so much that it becomes hot enough to ignite without a spark from a spark plug.

In an internal combustion engine, only part of the potential chemical energy is converted to mechanical energy. As engine parts move, friction and other forces cause much of the energy to be lost to the atmosphere as heat. In fact, an internal combustion engine becomes so hot that a cooling system is used to cool the engine.

Internal combustion engines vary in number of pistons

Most motorcycle engines have two cylinders. Automobile engines usually have four, six, or eight cylinders. Because of the four-stroke cycle, a four-piston engine can run efficiently with each piston at a different stroke of the cycle. However, engines with six or eight cylinders have more power than four-piston engines.

Figure 21

A In the *intake* stroke, a mixture of fuel vapor and air is brought into the cylinder from the carburetor as the piston moves downward.

B In the *compression* stroke, the piston moves up and compresses the fuel-air mixture.

C At the beginning of the *power* stroke, a spark from the spark plug ignites the compressed mixture and causes the mixture to expand quickly and move the piston down to turn the crankshaft.

D The *exhaust* stroke takes place when the piston moves up again and forces the waste products to move out of the exhaust valve.

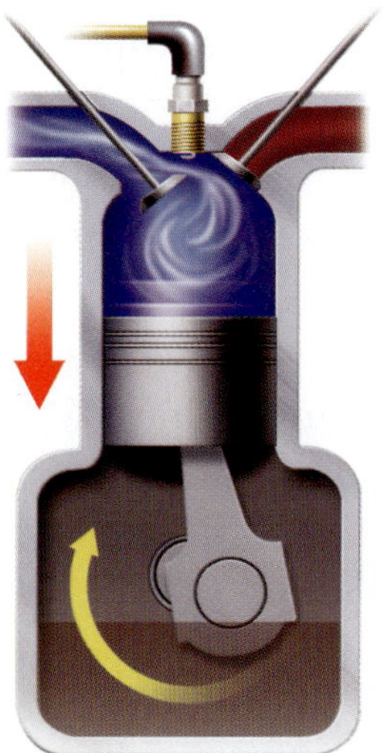

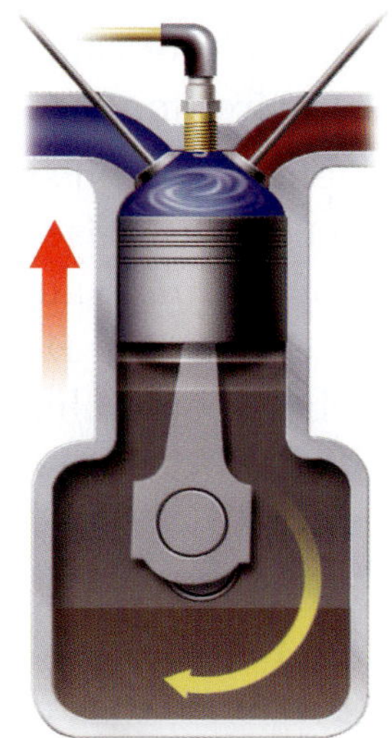

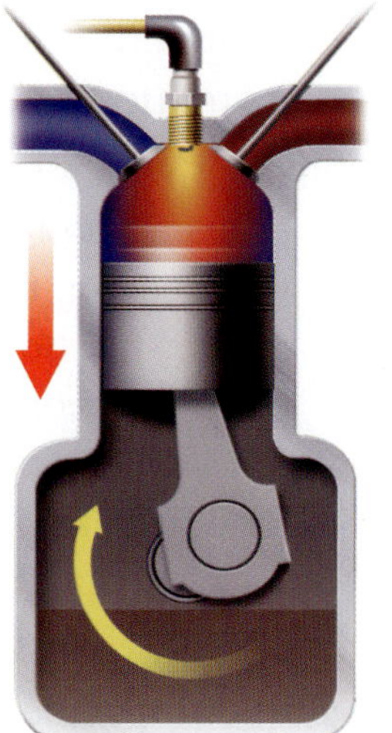

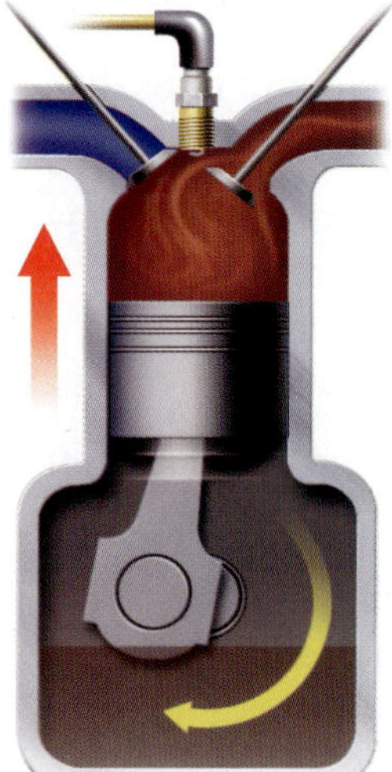

Buying Appliances Most major appliances, including those that involve the transfer of energy as heat, are required by law to have an *Energyguide* label attached to them.

The label indicates the average amount of energy used by the appliance in a year. It also gives the average cost of using the appliance based on a national average of cost per energy unit.

The *Energyguide* label provides consumers a way to compare various brands and models of appliances.

Applying Information

1. Use the *Energyguide* label shown to find how much energy the appliance uses each hour.
2. What is the daily operating cost of the appliance?

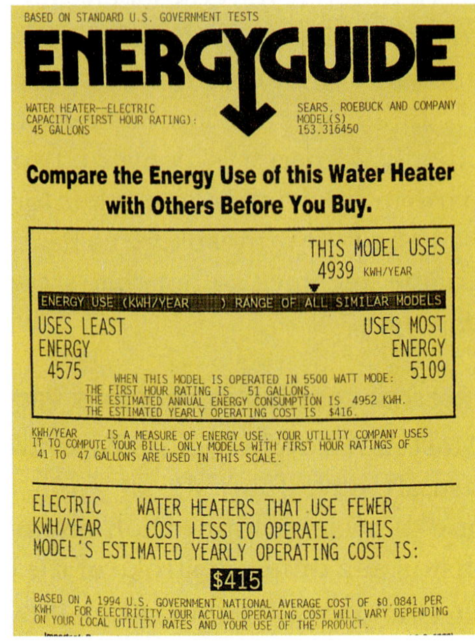

SECTION 3 REVIEW

SUMMARY

- Heating and cooling systems regulate temperature by transferring energy.
- Usable energy decreases during any process in which energy is transferred.
- The total amount of energy, both usable and unusable, is constant in any process.
- In heating systems, energy is transferred to a fluid, which then transfers its energy to the air in rooms.
- Refrigerators and air conditioners use the evaporation of a refrigerant for cooling.
- Heat engines use heat to do work.

1. **Explain** how evaporation is a cooling process.
2. **List** one type of home heating system, and describe how it transfers energy to warm the air inside the rooms.
3. **Describe** how energy changes from a usable form to a less usable form in a building's heating system.
4. **Compare** the advantages and disadvantages of using a solar heating system in your geographical area.
5. **Search** the Internet to find information on how *R*-values of insulation affect the environment.
6. **Critical Thinking** Water has a high specific heat, meaning it takes a good deal of energy to raise its temperature. For this reason, the cost of heating water may be a large part of a monthly household energy bill. Describe two ways the people in your household could change their routines, without sacrificing results, in order to save money and energy by using less hot water.
7. **Critical Thinking** Draw and describe each of the strokes of an automobile engine. Explain how the spark-plug ignition of compressed gas results in work done by the engine.

Math Skills

Order of Operations

A plate with a temperature of 95.0°C is placed in a vat of water with a temperature of 26.0°C. The equilibrium temperature of the plate and water is 28.2°C. The mass of the plate is 1.5 kg, and the mass of the water is 3.0 kg. What is the plate's specific heat? To calculate this, first calculate the energy transferred as heat to the water. Then use energy conservation, and rearrange the equation to calculate the plate's specific heat.

1 List all the given and unknown values.

Use this step to perform the first operation, which is calculating the temperature change.

Given: temperature change of plate (Δt_{plate}) = 95.0°C − 28.2°C = Δ66.8°C = Δ66.8 K

temperature change of water (Δt_{water}) = 28.2°C − 26.0°C = Δ2.2°C = Δ2.2 K

mass of plate (m_{plate}) = 1.5 kg

mass of water (m_{water}) = 3.0 kg

specific heat of water (c_{water}) = 4186 J/kg•K

Unknown: specific heat of plate (c_{plate}) (J/kg•K)

2 Write down the specific heat equation, and then rearrange it to calculate the specific heat of the plate.

$$energy = cm\Delta t = c_{water}m_{water}\Delta t_{water}$$

$$c_{plate} = \frac{energy}{m_{plate}\Delta t_{plate}}$$

3 Solve for energy, and then calculate the specific heat of the plate.

$$energy = \left(\frac{4186\ J}{kg \bullet K}\right) \times (3.0\ kg) \times (2.2\ K) = 2.8 \times 10^4\ J$$

$$c_{plate} = \frac{2.8 \times 10^4\ J}{(1.5\ kg) \times (\Delta 66.8\ K)} = \frac{2.8 \times 10^4\ J}{1.0 \times 10^2\ kg \bullet K} = 280\ J/kg \bullet K$$

Practice

Follow the example above to calculate the following:

1. Suppose in the example problem that the water's initial temperature was 29.0°C and that the equilibrium temperature of the plate and water was 35.0°C. Assuming that the plate's properties are the same as those in the example, what would the mass of the water be?

Chapter Highlights

Before you begin, review the summaries of the key ideas of each section, found at the end of each section. The vocabulary terms are listed on the first page of each section.

UNDERSTANDING CONCEPTS

1. Temperature is proportional to the average kinetic energy of particles in an object. Thus an increase in temperature results in a(n)
a. increase in mass.
b. decrease in average kinetic energy.
c. increase in average kinetic energy.
d. decrease in mass.

2. The temperature at which the particles of a substance have no more kinetic energy to transfer is
a. −273 K.
b. 0 K.
c. 0°C.
d. 273 K.

3. The type of energy transfer that takes place between objects in direct contact is
a. conduction.
b. convection.
c. contraction.
d. radiation.

4. Which type of energy transfer can occur in empty space?
a. convection
b. contraction
c. conduction
d. radiation

5. An *R*-value is a rating for materials used as
a. conduction.
b. convection.
c. insulation.
d. condensation.

6. Which of the following would be an example of a very good conductor of heat energy?
a. liquid
b. wood
c. air
d. metal

7. Which of the following would be an example of a very good insulator?
a. metal
b. air
c. wood
d. liquid

8. The amount of usable energy decreases when
a. systems are used only for heating.
b. systems are used only for cooling.
c. systems are used for heating or cooling.
d. the heating or cooling system's design allows loss of heat energy.

9. A refrigerant in a cooling system cools the surrounding air
a. as it evaporates.
b. as it condenses.
c. both as it evaporates and as it condenses.
d. when it neither evaporates nor condenses.

10. Solar heating systems are classified as
a. positive and negative.
b. active and passive.
c. AC and DC.
d. active and indirect.

USING VOCABULARY

11. How would a *thermometer* that measures temperatures using the Kelvin scale differ from one that measures temperatures using the Celsius scale?

12. Explain how *convection currents* form downdrafts in deserts near tall mountain ranges, as shown in the figure below.

13. Use the differences between a *conductor* and an *insulator* and the concept of *specific heat* to explain whether you would rather drink a hot beverage from a metal cup or from a china cup.

14. If you wear dark clothing on a sunny day, the clothing will become hot after a while. Use the concept of *radiation* to explain this.

15. Describe how a *heat engine* works, including the four strokes of the heat-engine cycle.

BUILDING MATH SKILLS

16. **Temperature Scale Conversion** A piece of dry ice, solid CO_2, has a temperature of -100°C. What is its temperature in kelvins and in degrees Fahrenheit?

17. **Temperature Scale Conversion** The temperature in deep space is thought to be around 3 K. What is 3 K in degrees Celsius? in degrees Fahrenheit?

18. **Specific Heat** How much energy would be absorbed by 550 g of copper when it is heated from 24°C to 45°C? (**Hint:** Refer to **Table 1** on p. 432.)

BUILDING GRAPHING SKILLS

19. **Interpreting Graphics** Graph the Celsius-Fahrenheit conversion equation, plotting Celsius temperature along the x-axis and Fahrenheit temperature on the y-axis. Use an x-axis range from –100°C to 100°C, then use the graph to find the following values:
    a. the Fahrenheit temperature equal to 77°C
    b. the Fahrenheit temperature equal to -40°C
    c. the Celsius temperature equal to 23°F
    d. the Celsius temperature equal to -17°F

THINKING CRITICALLY

20. **Applying Knowledge** Explain how the common thermometer works by expansion. What expands, and how does that expansion indicate the temperature?

21. **Applying Knowledge** If two objects that have different temperatures come into contact with each other, what can you say about their temperatures after several minutes of contact?

22. **Critical Thinking** Search the Internet to find two types of heat engines, and answer the following questions about each of them. Does the engine take in heat energy and convert it to mechanical energy? Or, does the engine take in another form of energy and convert it to mechanical energy? If it was another form, what type of energy is taken in, and why do you think the engines are called heat engines?

23. **Creative Thinking** Why do the metal shades of desk lamps have small holes at the top?

24. **Creative Thinking** If you bite into a piece of hot apple pie, the pie filling might burn your mouth while the crust, at the same temperature, will not. Explain why.

25. **Applying Technology** Glass can conduct some energy. Double-pane windows consist of two plates of glass separated by a small layer of insulating air. Explain why a double-pane window prevents more energy from escaping your house than a single-pane window.

26. **Understanding Systems** Explain why window unit air conditioners always have the back part of the air conditioner hanging outside. Why is it that the entire air-conditioner cannot be in the room?

27. **Making Decisions** If the only factor considered were specific heat, which would make a better coolant for automobile engines: water or ethanol? Explain your answer.

28. **Critical Thinking** Explain why a refrigerant must have a very low boiling point. Why is it important that the refrigerant evaporates?

DEVELOPING LIFE/WORK SKILLS

29. **Working Cooperatively** Read the following statements, and discuss with a group of classmates which statement is correct. Explain your answer.
    - **a.** Energy is lost when water is boiled.
    - **b.** The energy used to boil water is still present, but it is no longer in a usable form unless you use work or heat to make it usable.

30. **Allocating Resources** In one southern state the projected yearly costs for heating a home were \$463 using a heat pump, \$508 using a natural-gas furnace, and \$1220 using electric radiators. Contact your local utility company to determine the projected costs for the three different systems in your area. Make a table comparing the costs of the three systems.

31. **Interpreting and Communicating** Suppose that an internal combustion engine has a 25% efficiency, meaning that 25% of the energy put into the engine is converted to usable energy. Search the Internet for alternative energy sources that would have a greater efficiency than you found from an internal combustion engine. Report which alternative energy source you would recommend. Explain why you would recommend that energy source.

32. **Interpreting and Communicating** In a store, look at actual ENERGYGUIDE labels attached to three different models of one brand of any appliance you choose. From the information provided on the labels, compare those three models. Report to the class which of the three models you found to be the most energy efficient, according to the information on the ENERGYGUIDE labels.

INTEGRATING CONCEPTS

33. **Connection to Social Studies** WRITING SKILL Research the work of Benjamin Thompson. What was the prevailing theory of heat during Thompson's time? What observations led to Thompson's theory?

34. **Concept Mapping** Copy the unfinished concept map below onto a sheet of paper. Complete the map by writing the correct word or phrase in the lettered boxes.

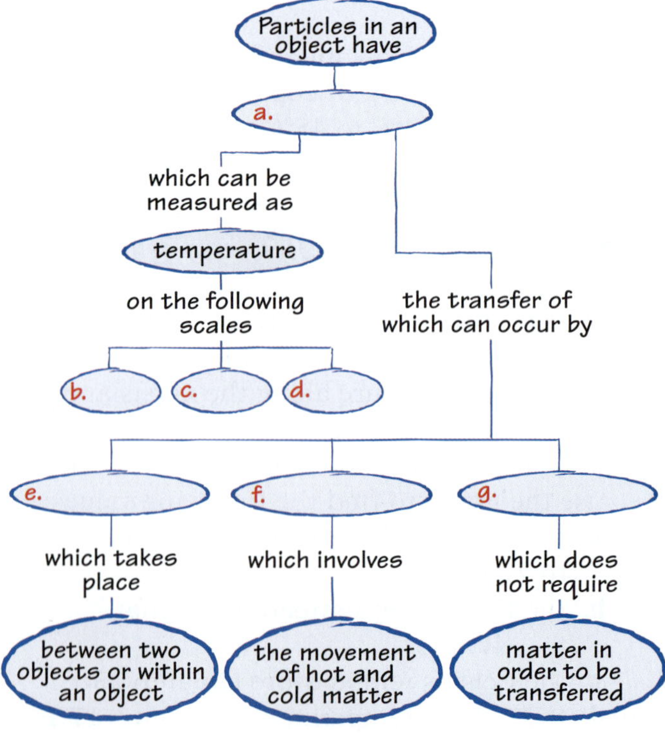

Standardized Test Prep

Understanding Concepts

***Directions (1–3):* For *each* question, write on a separate sheet of paper the letter of the correct answer.**

1. What happens to the energy that is lost when an engine is less than 100% efficient?
   A. It is destroyed during combustion.
   B. It is converted to heat and transferred to the environment.
   C. It is converted to matter in the form of gases that enter the atmosphere.
   D. It is lost as friction between the tires of the vehicle and the surface of the road.

2. What change occurs in matter when its temperature is increased?
   F. The specific heat of the material increases.
   G. Atoms and molecules in the material move faster.
   H. The attraction between atoms and molecules increases.
   I. The frequency of collisions between atoms and molecules decreases.

3. What transfer method carries energy from the sun to Earth?
   A. conduction
   B. convection
   C. insulation
   D. radiation

***Directions (4–5):* For *each* question, write a short response.**

4. Why does the temperature of hot chocolate decrease faster if you place a metal spoon in the liquid?

5. Determine why you can't cool your kitchen on a hot day by opening the refrigerator to let the cold air escape into the room.

Test TIP

If you find a particular question difficult, put a light pencil mark beside it and keep working. (Do not write in this book). As you answer other questions, you may find information that helps you answer the difficult question.

Reading Skills

***Directions (6):* Read the passage below. Then answer the question.**

The specific heat of water is very high compared to that of the soil and rock that make up land surfaces. In areas near a large body of water, the water does not heat as quickly as the land during the summer and does not cool as quickly as the land during the winter. This causes the climate in coastal areas to be generally milder than inland areas at the same latitude. For example, San Francisco has cooler summers and warmer winters than Sacramento, less than 150 km to the east.

6. How does the specific heat of water affect its ability to moderate coastal temperatures?

Interpreting Graphics

***Directions (7):* Base your answer to question 7 on the illustration below.**

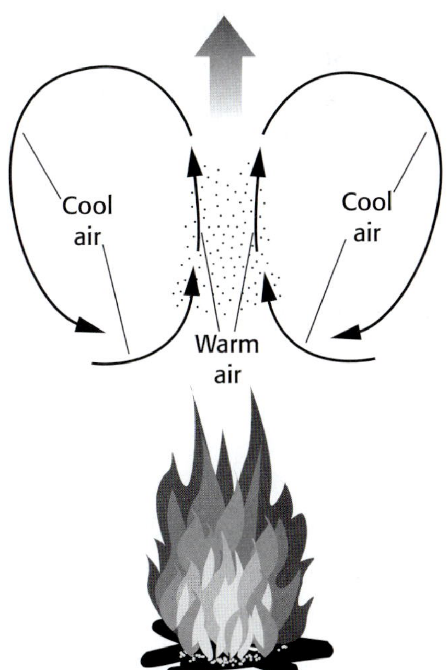

7. What form of heat transfer is represented by this illustration?
   F. conduction
   G. convection
   H. insulation
   I. radiation

Skills Practice Lab

Introduction

How can you determine whether the thickness of a metal wire affects its ability to conduct energy as heat?

Objectives

- USING SCIENTIFIC METHODS ***Develop*** a plan to measure how quickly energy is transferred as heat through a metal wire.
- ***Compare*** the speed of heat conduction in metal wires of different thicknesses.

Materials

candle
candle holder
clothespin
lighter or matches
metal wires of different thicknesses, each about 30 cm long (3)
metric ruler
stopwatch

Investigating Conduction of Heat

Procedure

Demonstrating Conduction in Wires

1. Obtain three wires of different thicknesses. Clip a clothespin on one end of one of the wires. Lay the wire and attached clothespin on the lab table.
2. Light the candle and place it in the holder.

   SAFETY CAUTION Tie back long hair and confine loose clothing. Never reach across an open flame. Always use the clothespin to hold the wire as you heat it and move it to avoid burning yourself. Remember that the wires will be hot for some time after they are removed from the flame.
3. Hold the lighted candle in its holder above the middle of the wire, and tilt the candle slightly so that some of the melted wax drips onto the middle of the wire.
4. Wait a couple of minutes for the wire and dripped wax to cool completely. The dripped wax will harden and form a small ball. Using the clothespin to hold the wire, place the other end of the wire in the candle's flame. When the ball of wax melts, remove the wire from the flame, and place it on the lab table. Think about what caused the wax on the wire to melt.

Designing Your Experiment

5. With your lab partner(s), decide how you will use the materials available in the lab to compare the speed of conduction in three wires of different thicknesses. Form a hypothesis about whether a thick wire will conduct energy more quickly or more slowly than a thin wire.
6. In your lab report, list each step you will perform in your experiment.
7. Have your teacher approve your plan before you carry out your experiment.

Performing Your Experiment

8. After your teacher approves your plan, you can carry out your experiment.
9. Prepare a data table in your lab report that is similar to the one shown below.
10. Record in your table how many seconds it takes for the ball of wax on each wire to melt. Perform three trials for each wire, allowing the wires to cool to room temperature between trials.

Conductivity Data

	Wire diameter (mm)	Time to melt wax (s) Trial 1	Trial 2	Trial 3	Average time
Wire 1					
Wire 2					
Wire 3					

Analysis

1. Find the diameter of each wire you tested. If the diameter is listed in inches, convert it to millimeters by multiplying by 25.4. If the diameter is listed in mils, convert it to millimeters by multiplying by 0.0254. In your data table, record the diameter of each wire in millimeters.
2. Calculate the average time required to melt the ball of wax for each wire. Record your answers in your data table.
3. Plot your data in your lab report in the form of a graph like the one shown. On your graph, draw the line or smooth curve that fits the points best.
4. **Reaching Conclusions** Based on your graph, does a thick wire or a thin wire conduct energy more quickly?
5. When roasting a large cut of meat, some cooks insert a metal skewer into the meat to make the inside cook more quickly. If you were roasting meat, would you insert a thick skewer or a thin skewer? Why?

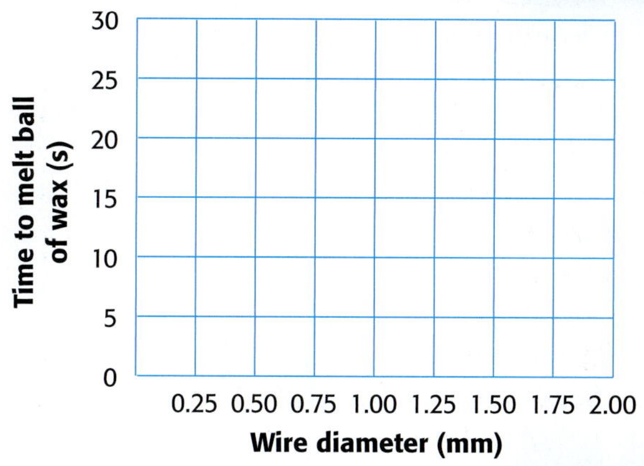

Conclusions

6. Suppose someone tells you that your conclusion is valid only for the particular metal you tested. How could you show that your conclusion is valid for other metals as well?

CHAPTER 14

Waves

Chapter Preview

Background The energy in an ocean wave can lift a surfboard up into the air and carry the surfer into shore. Ocean waves get most of their energy from the wind. A wave may start as a small ripple in a calm sea, then build up as the wind pushes it along. Waves that start on the coast of northern Canada may be very large by the time they reach a beach in the Hawaiian Islands.

The winds that create ocean waves are caused by convection currents in the atmosphere, which are driven by energy from the sun. Energy travels across empty space from the sun to Earth—in the form of light waves.

Waves are all around us. As you read this book, you are depending on light waves. Light bounces off the pages and into your eyes. When you talk with a friend you are depending on sound waves traveling through the air. Sometimes the waves can be gentle, such as those that rock a canoe in a pond. Other times waves can be very destructive, such as those created by earthquakes.

Activity 1 Fill a long, rectangular pan with water. Experiment with making waves in different ways. Try making waves by sticking the end of a pencil into the water, by moving a wide stick or board back and forth, and by striking the side of the pan. Place wooden blocks or other obstacles into the pan, and watch how the waves change when they encounter the obstacles.

Activity 2 With some of your classmates, practice the "wave" as is often performed by fans at football games. How does it resemble an ocean wave? How does it differ from other forms of motion?

A surfer takes advantage of the energy in ocean waves. Energy travels from the sun to Earth in the form of waves.

Pre-Reading Questions

1. What things do you do every day that depend on waves? What kinds of waves do you think are involved?
2. What properties do you think these different kinds of waves have in common?

SECTION 1

Types of Waves

KEY TERMS

wave
medium
mechanical wave
electromagnetic wave
transverse wave
longitudinal wave

OBJECTIVES

- **Recognize** that waves transfer energy.
- **Distinguish** between mechanical waves and electromagnetic waves.
- **Explain** the relationship between particle vibration and wave motion.
- **Distinguish** between transverse waves and longitudinal waves.

When a stone is thrown into a pond, it creates ripples on the surface of the water, as shown in ***Figure 1***. If there is a leaf floating on the water, the leaf will bob up and down and back and forth as each ripple, or wave, disturbs it. But after the waves pass, the leaf will almost return to its original position on the water.

What Is a Wave?

wave a periodic disturbance in a solid, liquid, or gas as energy is transmitted through a medium

Like the leaf, individual drops of water do not travel outward with a wave. They move only slightly from their resting place as each ripple passes by. If drops of water do not move very far as a wave passes, and neither does a leaf on the surface of the water, then what moves along with the wave? Energy does. A wave is not just the movement of matter from one place to another. A **wave** is a disturbance that carries energy through matter or space.

Figure 1
A stone thrown into a pond creates waves.

Most waves travel through a medium

The waves in a pond are disturbances traveling through water. Sound also travels as a wave. The sound from a stereo is a pattern of changes in the air between the stereo speakers and your ears. Earthquakes create waves, called *seismic waves,* that travel through Earth.

In each of these examples, the waves involve the movement of some kind of matter. The matter through which a wave travels is called the **medium.** In the example of the pond, the water is the medium. For sound from a stereo, air is the medium. And in earthquakes, Earth itself is the medium.

Waves that require a medium are called **mechanical waves.** Almost all waves are mechanical waves, with one important exception: light waves.

Connection to ENGINEERING

If you have ever been hit by an ocean wave at the beach, you know these waves carry a lot of energy. Could this energy be put to good use?

Research is currently underway to find ways to harness the energy of ocean waves. Some small floating navigation buoys, which shine lights to help ships find their way in the dark, obtain energy solely from the waves. A few larger systems are in place that harness wave energy to provide electricity for small coastal communities.

Making the Connection

1. In a library or on the Internet, research different types of devices that harness wave energy. How much power do some of these devices provide? Is that a lot of power?
2. Design a device of your own to capture the energy from ocean waves. The device should take the motion of waves and convert it into a motion that could be used to drive a machine, such as a pump or a wheel.

Light does not require a medium

Light can travel from the sun to Earth across the empty space between them. This is possible because light waves do not need a medium through which to travel. Instead, light waves consist of changing electric and magnetic fields in space. For that reason, light waves are also called **electromagnetic waves.**

Visible light waves are just one example of a wide range of electromagnetic waves. Radio waves, such as those that carry signals to your radio or television, are also electromagnetic waves. Other kinds of electromagnetic waves will be introduced in Section 2. In this book, the terms *light* and *light wave* may refer to any electromagnetic wave, not just visible light.

medium a physical environment in which phenomena occur

mechanical wave a wave that requires a medium through which to travel

electromagnetic wave a wave that consists of oscillating electric and magnetic fields, which radiate outward at the speed of light

Waves transfer energy

Energy is the ability to exert a force over a certain distance. It is also known as the ability to do *work.* We know that waves carry energy because they can do work. For example, water waves can do work on a leaf, on a boat, or on a beach. Sound waves can do work on your eardrum. Light waves can do work on your eye or on photographic film.

A wave caused by dropping a stone in a pond might carry enough energy to move a leaf up and down several centimeters. The bigger the wave is, the more energy it carries. A cruise ship moving through water in the ocean could create waves big enough to move a fishing boat up and down a few meters.

Figure 2
This portrait of a tsunami was created by the Japanese artist Hokusai in 1830.

Figure 2 shows a woodblock print of a *tsunami,* a huge ocean wave caused by earthquakes. A tsunami may be as high as 30 m when it reaches shore, taller than a 10-story building. Such waves carry enough energy to cause a lot of damage to coastal towns and shorelines. Normal-sized ocean waves do work on the shore, too, breaking up rocks into tiny pieces to form sandy beaches.

Energy may spread out as a wave travels

If you stand next to the speakers at a rock concert, the sound waves may damage your ears. Likewise, if you look at a bright light bulb from too close, the light may damage your eyes. But if you are 100 m away, the sound of the rock band or the light from the bulb is harmless. Why?

Think about waves created when a stone falls into a pond. The waves spread out in circles that get bigger as the waves move farther from the center. Each of these circles, called a *wave front,* has the same amount of total energy. But as the circles get larger, the energy spreads out over a larger area.

When sound waves travel in air, the waves spread out in spheres, as shown in ***Figure 3.*** These spheres are similar to the circular ripples on a pond. As they travel outward, the spherical wave fronts get bigger, so the energy in the waves spreads out over a larger area. This is why large amplifiers and speakers are needed to fill a concert hall with sound, even though the same music can sound just as loud if it is played on a portable radio and listened to with a small pair of headphones.

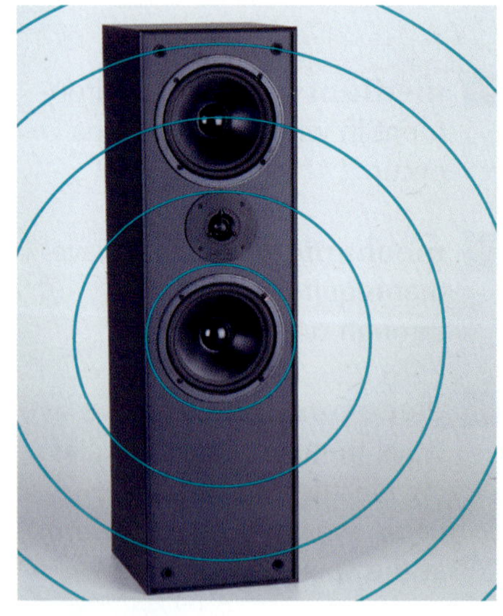

Figure 3
Sound waves from a stereo speaker spread out in spherical wave fronts.

Vibrations and Waves

When a singer sings a note, vocal cords in the singer's throat move back and forth. That motion makes the air in the throat vibrate, creating sound waves that eventually reach your ears. The vibration of the air in your ears causes your eardrums to vibrate. The motion of the eardrum triggers a series of electrical pulses to your brain, and your brain interprets them as sounds.

Waves are related to vibrations. Most waves are caused by a vibrating object. Electromagnetic waves may be caused by vibrating charged particles. In a mechanical wave, the particles in the medium also vibrate as the wave passes through the medium.

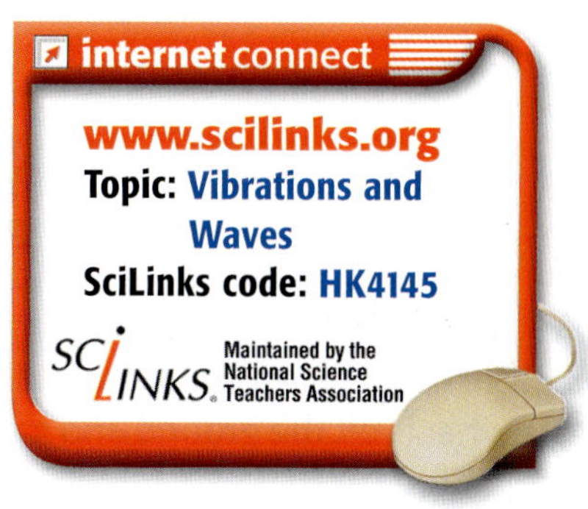

Vibrations involve transformations of energy

Figure 4 shows a mass hanging on a spring. If the mass is pulled down slightly and released, it will begin to move up and down around its original resting position. This vibration involves transformations of energy, much like those in a swinging pendulum.

When the mass is pulled away from its resting place, the mass-spring system gains elastic potential energy. The spring exerts a force that pulls the mass back to its original position.

As the spring moves back toward the original position, the potential energy in the system changes to kinetic energy. The mass moves beyond its original resting position to the other side.

At the top of its motion, the mass has lost all its kinetic energy. But the system now has both elastic potential energy and gravitational potential energy. The mass moves downward again, past the resting position, and back to the beginning of the cycle.

Figure 4

When a mass hanging on a spring is disturbed from rest, it starts to vibrate up and down around its original position.

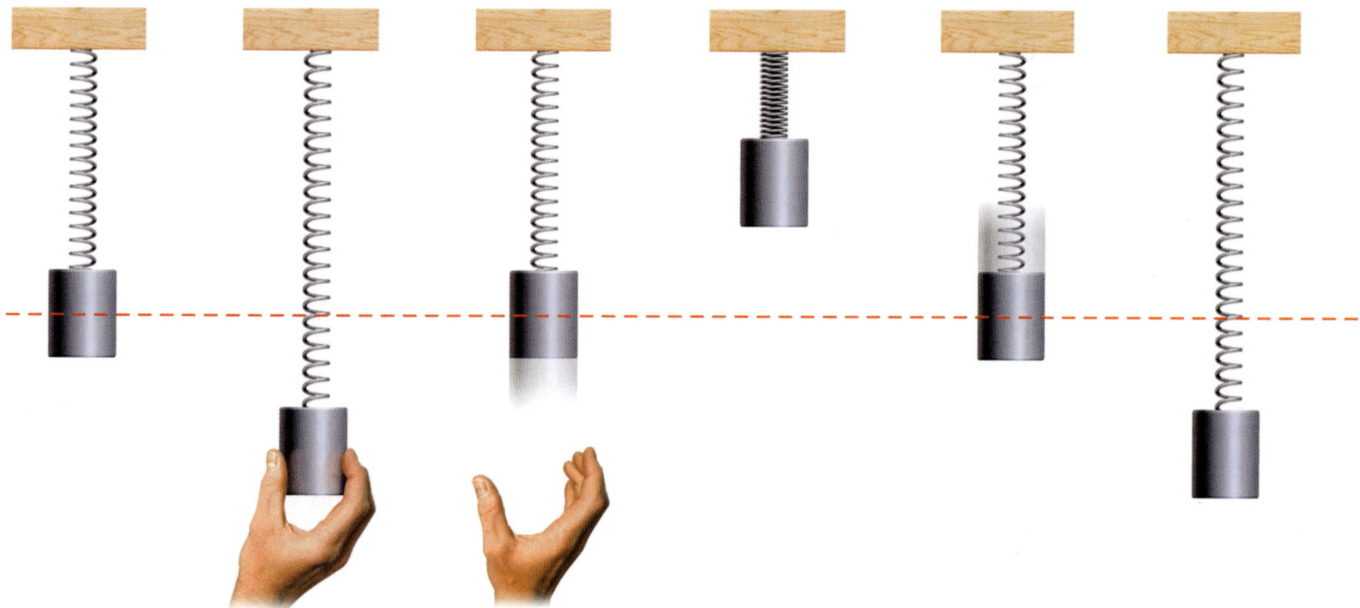

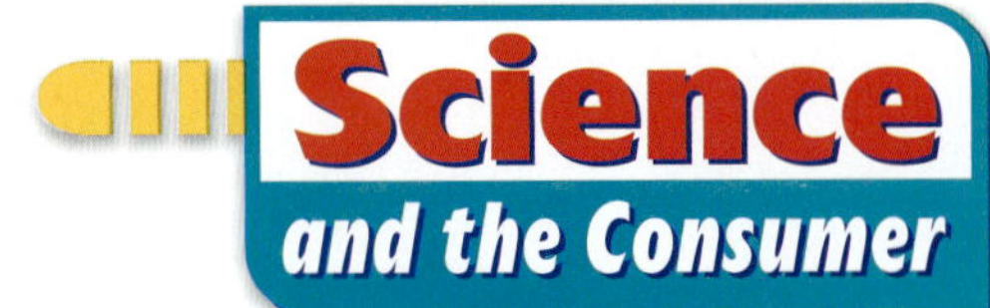

Shock Absorbers: Why Are They Important?

Bumps in the road are certainly a nuisance, but without strategic use of damping devices, they could also be very dangerous. To control a car going 100 km/h (60 mi/h), a driver needs all the wheels of the vehicle on the ground. Bumps in the road lift the wheels off the ground and may rob the driver of control of the car.

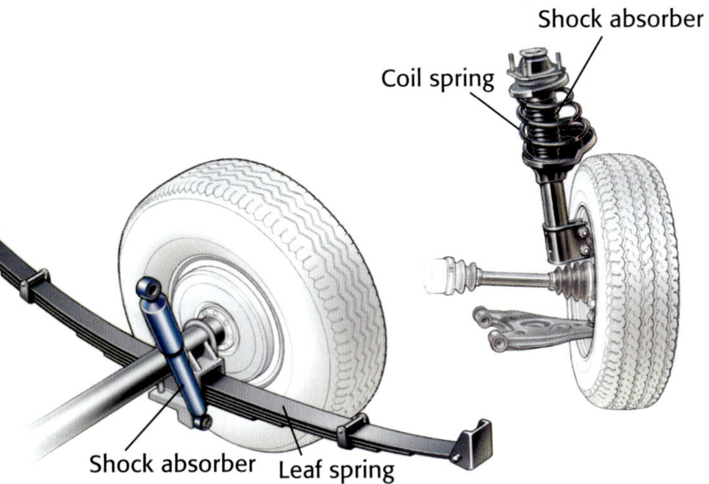

Springs Absorb Energy

To solve this problem, cars are fitted with springs at each wheel. When the wheel of a car goes over a bump, the spring absorbs kinetic energy so that the energy is not transferred to the rest of the car. The energy becomes elastic potential energy in the spring, which then allows the spring to push the wheel back down onto the road.

Springs Alone Prolong Vibrations

Once a spring is set in motion, it tends to continue vibrating up and down in simple harmonic motion. This can create an uncomfortable ride, and it may also affect the driver's control of the car. One way to cut down on unwanted vibrations is to use stiff springs that compress only a few centimeters with thousands of newtons of force. However, the stiffer the spring is, the rougher the ride is and the more likely the wheels are to come off the road.

Shock Absorbers Dampen Vibrations

Modern automobiles are fitted with devices known as shock absorbers that absorb energy without prolonging vibrations. Shock absorbers are fluid-filled tubes that turn the simple harmonic motion of the springs into a damped harmonic motion. In a damped harmonic motion, each cycle of stretch and compression of the spring is much smaller than the previous cycle. Modern auto suspensions are set up so that all a spring's energy is absorbed by the shock absorbers in just one up-and-down cycle.

Shock Absorbers and Springs Come in Different Arrangements

Different types of springs and shock absorbers are combined to give a wide variety of responses. For example, many passenger cars have coil springs with shock absorbers parallel to the springs, or even inside the springs, as shown at near left. Some larger vehicles have heavy-duty leaf springs made of stacks of steel strips. Leaf springs are stiffer than coil springs, but they can bear heavier loads. In this type of suspension system, the shock absorber is perpendicular to the spring, as shown at far left.

The stiffness of the spring can affect steering response time, traction, and the general feel of the car. Because of the variety of combinations, your driving experiences can range from the luxurious "floating-on-air" ride of a limousine to the bone-rattling feel of a true sports car.

Your Choice

1. **Making Decisions** If you were going to haul heavy loads, would you look for a vehicle with coil springs or leaf springs? Why?
2. **Critical Thinking** How do shock absorbers stop an automobile from continually bouncing?

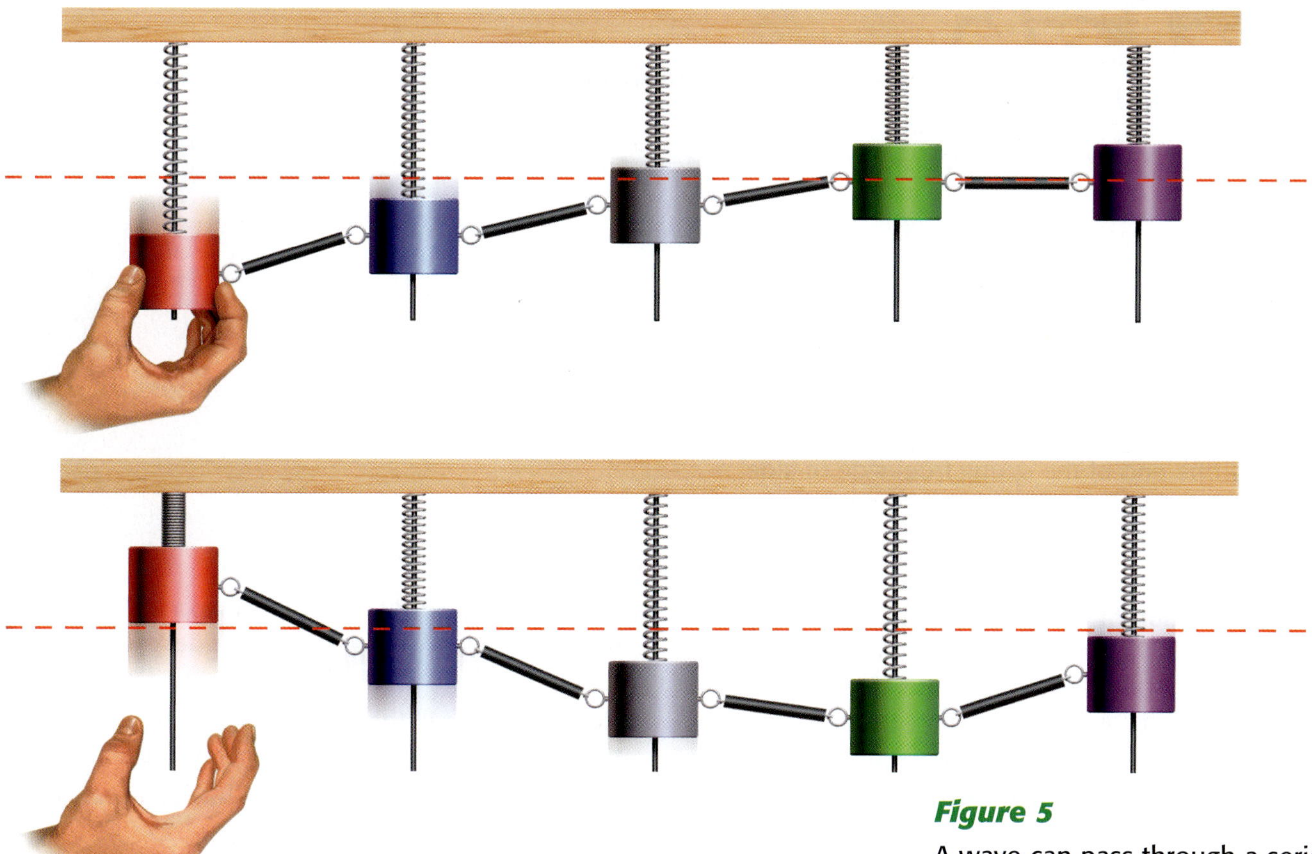

Figure 5

A wave can pass through a series of masses on springs. The masses act like the particles in a medium.

Whenever the spring is expanded or compressed, it is exerting a force that pushes the mass back almost to the original resting position. As a result, the mass will continue to bounce up and down. This type of vibration is called *simple harmonic motion*.

A wave can pass through a series of vibrating objects

Imagine a series of masses and springs tied together in a row, as shown in ***Figure 5.*** If you pull down on a mass at the end of the row, that mass will begin to vibrate up and down. As the mass on the end moves, it pulls on the mass next to it, causing that mass to vibrate. The energy in the vibration of the first mass, which is a combination of kinetic energy and elastic potential energy, is transferred to the mass-spring system next to it. In this way, the disturbance that started with the first mass travels down the row. This disturbance is a wave that carries energy from one end of the row to the other.

If the first mass were not connected to the other masses, it would keep vibrating up and down on its own. However, because it transfers its energy to the second mass, it slows down and then returns to its resting position. A vibration that fades out as energy is transferred from one object to another is called *damped harmonic motion*.

Quick Lab

How do particles move in a medium?

Materials ✓ *long, flexible spring* ✓ *colored ribbon*

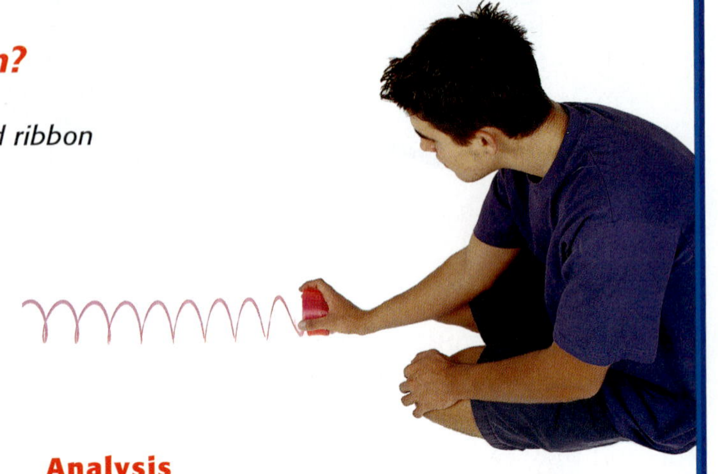

1. Have two people each grab an end of the spring and stretch it out along a smooth floor. Have another person tie a small piece of colored ribbon to a coil near the middle of the spring.
2. Swing one end of the spring from side to side. This will start a wave traveling along the spring. Observe the motion of the ribbon as the wave passes by.
3. Take a section of the spring and bunch it together as shown in the figure at right. Release the spring. This will create a different kind of wave traveling along the spring. Observe the motion of the ribbon as this wave passes by.

Analysis

1. How would you describe the motion of the ribbon in step 2? How would you describe its motion in step 3?
2. How can you tell that energy is passing along the spring? Where does that energy come from?

The motion of particles in a medium is like the motion of masses on springs

If you tie one end of a rope to a doorknob, pull it straight, and then rapidly move your hand up and down once, you will generate a single wave along the rope, as shown in ***Figure 6.*** A small ribbon tied to the middle of the rope can help you visualize the motion of a single particle of matter in the rope.

As the wave approaches, the ribbon moves up in the air, away from its resting position. As the wave passes farther along the rope, the ribbon drops below its resting position. Finally, after the wave passes by, the ribbon returns to its original starting point. Like the ribbon, each part of the rope moves up and down as the wave passes by.

The motion of each part of the rope is like the vibrating motion of a mass hanging on a spring. As one part of the rope moves, it pulls on the part next to it, transferring energy. In this way, a wave passes along the length of the rope.

Figure 6

As this wave passes along a rope, the ribbon moves up and down while the wave moves to the right.

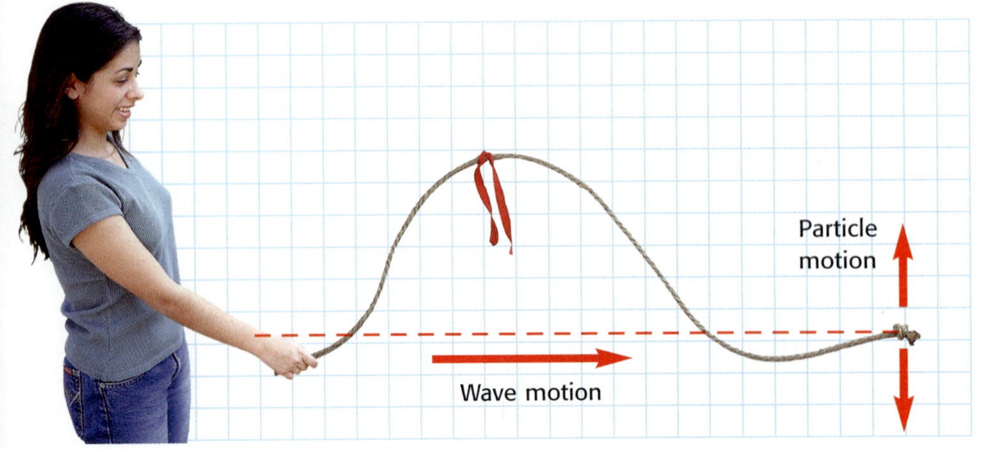

Transverse and Longitudinal Waves

Particles in a medium can vibrate either up and down or back and forth. Waves are often classified by the direction that the particles in the medium move as a wave passes by.

Quick ACTIVITY

Polarization

Polarizing filters block all light except those waves that oscillate in a certain direction. Look through two polarizing filters at once. Then rotate one by 90° and look again. What do you observe?

Transverse waves have perpendicular motion

When a crowd does "the wave" at a sporting event, people in the crowd stand up and raise their hands into the air as the wave reaches their part of the stadium. The wave travels around the stadium in a circle, but the people move straight up and down. This is similar to the wave in the rope. Each particle in the rope moves straight up and down as the wave passes by from left to right.

In these cases, the motion of the particles in the medium (in the stadium, the people in the crowd) is perpendicular to the motion of the wave as a whole. Waves in which the motion of the particles is perpendicular to the motion of the wave as a whole are called **transverse waves.**

Light waves are another example of transverse waves. The fluctuating electric and magnetic fields that make up a light wave are perpendicular to one another and are also perpendicular to the direction the light travels.

transverse wave a wave in which the particles of the medium move perpendicular to the direction the wave is traveling

longitudinal wave a wave in which the particles of the medium vibrate parallel to the direction of wave motion

Longitudinal waves have parallel motion

Suppose you stretch out a long, flexible spring on a table or a smooth floor, grab one end, and move your hand back and forth, directly toward and directly away from the other end of the spring. You would see a wave travel along the spring as it bunches up in some spots and stretches in others, as shown in ***Figure 7.***

As a wave passes along the spring, a ribbon tied to one of the coils of the spring will move back and forth, parallel to the direction that the wave travels. Waves that cause the particles in a medium to vibrate parallel to the direction of wave motion are called **longitudinal waves.**

Sound waves are an example of longitudinal waves that we encounter every day. Sound waves traveling in air compress and expand the air in bands. As sound waves pass by molecules in the air move backward and forward parallel to the direction that the sound travels.

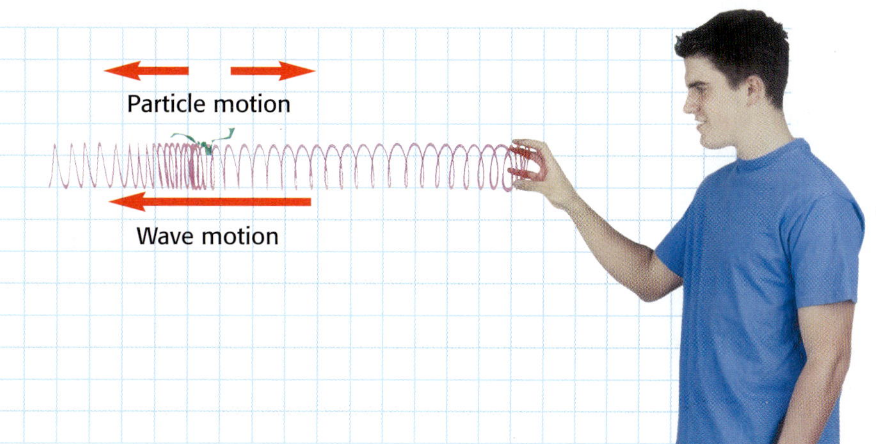

Figure 7

As a longitudinal wave passes along this spring, the ribbon tied to the coils moves back and forth, parallel to the direction the wave is traveling.

In a surface wave, particles move in circles

Waves on the ocean or in a swimming pool are not simply transverse waves or longitudinal waves. Water waves are an example of *surface waves.* Surface waves occur at the boundary between two different mediums, such as between water and air. The particles in a surface wave move both perpendicularly and parallel to the direction that the wave travels.

Follow the motion of the beach ball in ***Figure 8*** as a wave passes by traveling from left to right. At first, the ball is in a trough. As the crest approaches, the ball moves to the left and upward. When the ball is very near the crest, it starts to move to the right. Once the crest has passed, the ball starts to fall back downward, then to the left. The up and down motions combine with the side to side motions to produce a circular motion overall.

The beach ball helps to make the motion of the wave more visible. Particles near the surface of the water also move in a similar circular pattern.

Figure 8

Ocean waves are surface waves at the boundary between air and water.

SECTION 1 REVIEW

SUMMARY

- A wave is a disturbance that carries energy through a medium or through space.
- Mechanical waves require a medium through which to travel. Light waves, also called electromagnetic waves, do not require a medium.
- Particles in a medium may vibrate perpendicularly to or parallel to the direction a wave is traveling.

1. **Identify** the medium for the following waves:
   a. ripples on a pond
   b. the sound waves from a stereo speaker
   c. seismic waves
2. **Name** the one kind of wave that does not require a medium.
3. **Describe** the motion of a mass vibrating on a spring. How does this relate to wave motion?
4. **Explain** the difference between transverse waves and longitudinal waves. Give an example of each type.
5. **Describe** the motion of a water molecule on the surface of the ocean as a wave passes by.
6. **Critical Thinking** Describe a situation that demonstrates that water waves carry energy.

Characteristics of Waves

OBJECTIVES

- **Identify** the crest, trough, amplitude, and wavelength of a wave.
- **Define** the terms *frequency* and *period.*
- **Solve** problems involving wave speed, frequency, and wavelength.
- **Describe** the Doppler effect.

KEY TERMS

crest
trough
amplitude
wavelength
period
frequency
Doppler effect

If you have spent any time at the beach or on a boat, you have probably observed many properties of waves. Sometimes the waves are very large; other times they are smaller. Sometimes they are close together, and sometimes they are farther apart. How can these differences be described and measured in more detail?

Wave Properties

The simplest transverse waves have somewhat similar shapes no matter how big they are or what medium they travel through. An ideal transverse wave has the shape of a *sine curve,* such as the curve on the graph in ***Figure 9A.*** A sine curve looks like an S lying on its side. Sine curves can be used to represent waves and to describe their properties.

Waves that have the shape of a sine curve, such as those on the rope in ***Figure 9B,*** are called *sine waves.* Although many waves, such as water waves, are not ideal sine waves, they can still be modeled with the graph of a sine curve.

Figure 9

A A sine curve can be used to demonstrate the characteristics of waves.

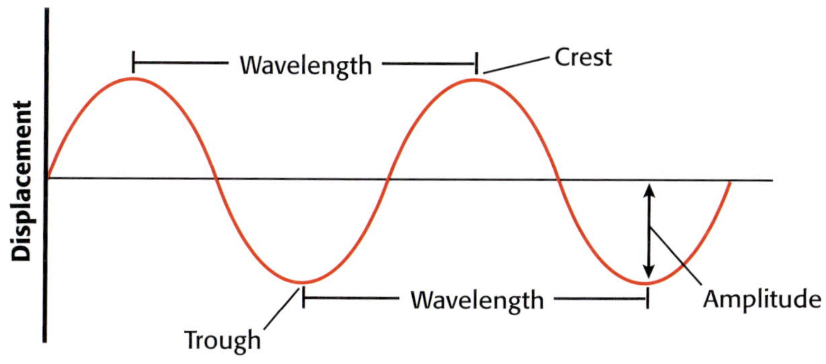

B This transverse wave on a rope is a simple sine wave.

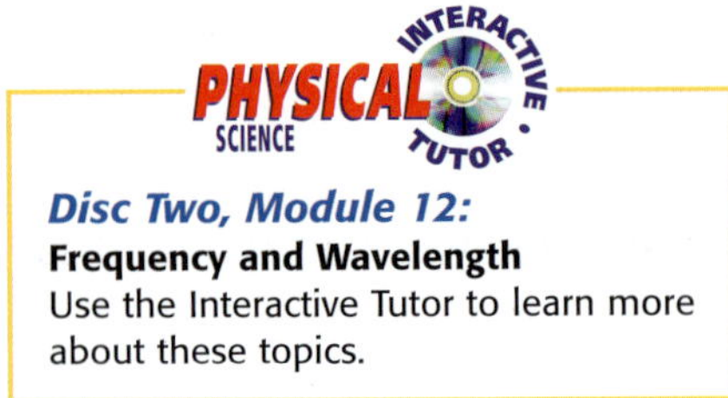

Disc Two, Module 12:
Frequency and Wavelength
Use the Interactive Tutor to learn more about these topics.

Amplitude measures the amount of particle vibration

The highest points of a transverse wave are called **crests.** The lowest parts of a transverse wave are called **troughs.** The greatest distance that particles are displaced from their normal resting positions because of a wave is called the **amplitude.** The amplitude is also half the vertical distance between a crest and a trough. Larger waves have bigger amplitudes and carry more energy.

But what about longitudinal waves? These waves do not have crests and troughs because they cause particles to move back and forth instead of up and down. If you make a longitudinal wave in a spring, you will see a moving pattern of areas where the coils are bunched up alternating with areas where the coils are stretched out. The crowded areas are called *compressions.* The stretched-out areas are called *rarefactions.* ***Figure 10A*** illustrates these properties of a longitudinal wave.

Figure 10B shows a graph of a longitudinal wave. Density of the medium is plotted on the vertical axis; the horizontal axis represents the distance along the spring. The result is a sine curve. The amplitude of a longitudinal wave is the maximum deviation from the normal density or pressure of the medium, which is shown by the high and low points on the graph.

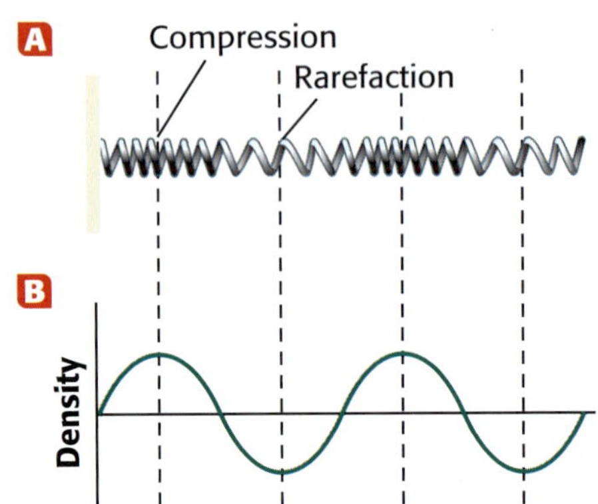

Figure 10

A A longitudinal wave has compressions and rarefactions.

B The high and low points of this sine curve correspond to compressions and rarefactions in the spring.

Wavelength measures the distance between two equivalent parts of a wave

The crests of ocean waves at a beach may be separated by several meters, while ripples in a pond may be only a few centimeters apart. Crests of a light wave may be separated by only billionths of a meter.

The distance from one crest of a wave to the next crest, or from one trough to the next trough, is called the **wavelength.** In a longitudinal wave, the wavelength is the distance between two compressions or between two rarefactions. The wavelength is the distance between any two successive identical parts of a wave.

Not all waves have a single wavelength that is easy to measure. Most sound waves have a very complicated shape, so the wavelength may be difficult to determine. If the source of a wave vibrates in an irregular way, the wavelength may change over time.

When used in equations, wavelength is represented by the Greek letter lambda, λ. Because wavelength is a distance measurement, it is expressed in the SI unit meters.

- **crest** the highest point of a wave
- **trough** the lowest point of a wave
- **amplitude** the maximum distance that the particles of a wave's medium vibrate from their rest position
- **wavelength** the distance from any point on a wave to an identical point on the next wave

The period measures how long it takes for waves to pass by

If you swim out into the ocean until your feet can no longer touch the bottom, your body will be free to move up and down as waves come into shore. As your body rises and falls, you can count off the number of seconds between two successive wave crests.

The time required for one full wavelength of a wave to pass a certain point is called the **period** of the wave. The period is also the time required for one complete vibration of a particle in a medium—or of a swimmer in the ocean. In equations, the period is represented by the symbol T. Because the period is a time measurement, it is expressed in the SI unit seconds.

period the time that it takes a complete cycle or wave oscillation to occur

frequency the number of cycles or vibrations per unit of time

Frequency measures the rate of vibrations

While swimming in the ocean or floating in an inner tube, as shown in ***Figure 11,*** you could also count the number of crests that pass by in a certain time, say in 1 minute. The **frequency** of a wave is the number of full wavelengths that pass a point in a given time interval. The frequency of a wave also measures how rapidly vibrations occur in the medium, at the source of the wave, or both.

Figure 11

A person floating in an inner tube can determine the period and frequency of the waves by counting off the number of seconds between wave crests.

The symbol for frequency is f. The SI unit for measuring frequency is hertz (Hz), named after Heinrich Hertz, who in 1888 became the first person to experimentally demonstrate the existence of electromagnetic waves. Hertz units measure the number of vibrations per second. One vibration per second is 1 Hz, two vibrations per second is 2 Hz, and so on. You can hear sounds with frequencies as low as 20 Hz and as high as 20 000 Hz. When you hear a sound at 20 000 Hz, there are 20 000 compressions hitting your ear every second.

The frequency and period of a wave are related. If more vibrations are made in a second, each one takes a shorter amount of time. In other words, the frequency is the inverse of the period.

Frequency-Period Equation

$$\textit{frequency} = \frac{1}{\textit{period}} \qquad f = \frac{1}{T}$$

In the inner tube example, a wave crest passes the inner tube every 2 s, so the period is 2 s. The frequency can be found by using the frequency-period equation above. Because 0.5 (1/2) is the inverse of 2, the frequency is 0.5 Hz, or half a wave per second.

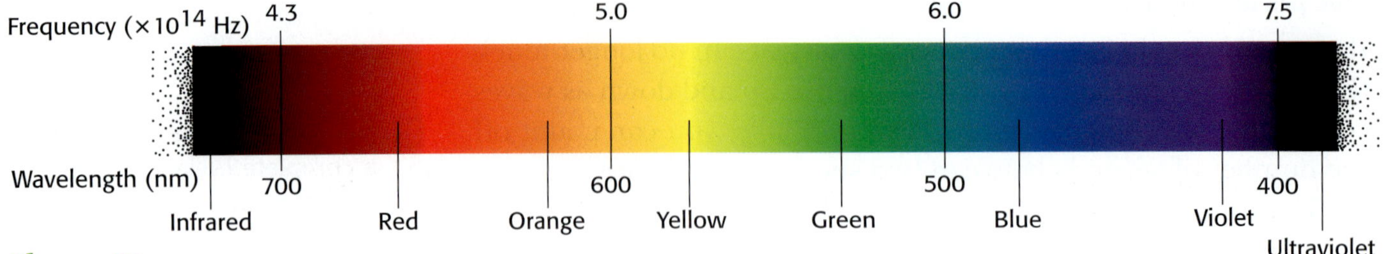

Figure 12

The part of the electromagnetic spectrum that we can see is called visible light.

Light comes in a wide range of frequencies and wavelengths

Our eyes can detect light with frequencies ranging from about 4.3×10^{14} Hz to 7.5×10^{14} Hz. Light in this range is called *visible light*. The differences in frequency in visible light account for the different colors we see, as shown in ***Figure 12.***

Electromagnetic waves also exist at other frequencies that we cannot see directly. The full range of light at different frequencies and wavelengths is called the *electromagnetic spectrum*. ***Table 1*** lists several different parts of the electromagnetic spectrum, along with some real-world applications of the different kinds of waves.

Table 1 **The Electromagnetic Spectrum**

Type of wave	Range of frequency and wavelength	Applications
Radio wave	$f < 1 \times 10^9$ Hz $\lambda > 30$ cm	AM and FM radio; television broadcasting; radar; aircraft navigation
Microwave	1×10^9 Hz $< f < 3 \times 10^{11}$ Hz 30 cm $> \lambda >$ 1 mm	Atomic and molecular research; microwave ovens
Infrared (IR) wave	3×10^{11} Hz $< f < 4.3 \times 10^{14}$ Hz 1 mm $> \lambda >$ 700 nm	Infrared photography; remote-control devices; heat radiation
Visible light	4.3×10^{14} Hz $< f < 7.5 \times 10^{14}$ Hz 700 nm (red) $> \lambda >$ 400 nm (violet)	Visible-light photography; optical microscopes; optical telescopes
Ultraviolet (UV) light	7.5×10^{14} Hz $< f < 5 \times 10^{15}$ Hz 400 nm $> \lambda >$ 60 nm	Sterilizing medical instruments; identifying fluorescent minerals
X ray	5×10^{15} Hz $< f < 3 \times 10^{21}$ Hz 60 nm $> \lambda > 1 \times 10^{-4}$ nm	Medical examination of bones, teeth, and organs; cancer treatments
Gamma ray	3×10^{18} Hz $< f < 3 \times 10^{22}$ Hz 0.1 nm $> \lambda > 1 \times 10^{-5}$ nm	Food irradiation; studies of structural flaws in thick materials

Wave Speed

Imagine watching as water waves move past a post at a pier such as the one in **Figure 13.** If you count the number of crests passing the post for 10 s, you can determine the frequency of the waves by dividing the number of crests you count by 10 s. If you measure the distance between crests, you can find the wavelength of the wave. But how fast are the water waves moving?

Figure 13

By observing the frequency and wavelength of waves passing a pier, you can calculate the speed of the waves.

Wave speed equals frequency times wavelength

The speed of a moving object is found by dividing the distance the object travels by the time it takes to travel that distance. Speed can be calculated using the speed equation:

$$speed = \frac{distance}{time}$$

$$v = \frac{d}{t}$$

If SI units are used for measuring distance and time, speed is expressed as meters per second (m/s). The *wave speed* is simply how fast a wave moves. Finding the speed of a wave is just like finding the speed of a moving object: you need to measure how far the wave travels in a certain amount of time.

For a wave, it is most convenient to use the wavelength as the distance traveled. The amount of time it takes the wave to travel a distance of one wavelength is the period. Substituting these into the speed equation gives an equation that can be used to calculate the speed of a wave.

$$speed = \frac{wavelength}{period}$$

$$v = \frac{\lambda}{T}$$

Because the period is the inverse of the frequency, dividing by the period is equivalent to multiplying by the frequency. Therefore, the speed of a wave can also be calculated by multiplying the wavelength by the frequency.

Wave Speed Equation

$$wave\ speed = frequency \times wavelength$$

$$v = f \times \lambda$$

Suppose that waves passing by a post at a pier have a wavelength of 10 m, and two waves pass by in 5 s. The period is therefore 2.5 s, and the frequency is the inverse of 2.5 s, or 0.4 Hz. The waves in this case travel with a wave speed of 4 m/s.

INTEGRATING

EARTH SCIENCE

Earthquakes create waves, called *seismic waves,* that travel through Earth. There are two main types of seismic waves, *P waves* (primary waves) and *S waves* (secondary waves).

P waves travel faster than S waves, so the P waves arrive at a given location first. P waves are longitudinal waves and can travel through solids and liquids.

S waves move more slowly than P waves but also carry more energy. S waves are transverse waves and can travel through only solids.

- When a problem requires you to calculate wave speed, you can use the wave speed equation on the previous page.
- The wave speed equation can also be rearranged to isolate frequency on the left in the following way:

$$v = f \times \lambda$$

Divide both sides by λ.

$$\frac{v}{\lambda} = \frac{f \times \cancel{\lambda}}{\cancel{\lambda}}$$

$$f = \frac{v}{\lambda}$$

You will need to use this form of the equation in Practice Problem 3.

- In Practice Problem 4, you will need to rearrange the equation to isolate wavelength on the left.

Math Skills

Wave Speed The string of a piano that produces the note middle C vibrates with a frequency of 264 Hz. If the sound waves produced by this string have a wavelength in air of 1.30 m, what is the speed of sound in air?

1 List the given and unknown values.

Given: *frequency,* $f = 264$ Hz

wavelength, $\lambda = 1.30$ m

Unknown: *wave speed,* $v = ?$ m/s

2 Write the equation for wave speed.

$$v = f \times \lambda$$

3 Insert the known values into the equation, and solve.

$$v = 264 \text{ Hz} \times 1.30 \text{ m} = 264 \text{ s}^{-1} \times 1.30 \text{ m}$$

$$v = 343 \text{ m/s}$$

Practice

Wave Speed

1. The average wavelength in a series of ocean waves is 15.0 m. A wave crest arrives at the shore on average every 10.0 s, so the frequency is 0.100 Hz. What is the average speed of the waves?
2. An FM radio station broadcasts electromagnetic waves at a frequency of 94.5 MHz (9.45×10^7 Hz). These radio waves have a wavelength of 3.17 m. What is the speed of the waves?
3. Green light has a wavelength of 5.20×10^{-7} m. The speed of light is 3.00×10^8 m/s. Calculate the frequency of green light waves with this wavelength.
4. The speed of sound in air is about 340 m/s. What is the wavelength of a sound wave with a frequency of 220 Hz (on a piano, the A below middle C)?

The speed of a wave depends on the medium

Sound waves can travel through air. If they couldn't, you would not be able to have a conversation with a friend or hear music from a radio across the room. Because sound travels very fast in air (about 340 m/s), you don't notice a time delay in most normal situations.

If you swim with your head underwater, you may hear certain sounds very clearly. Sound waves travel better—and three to four times faster—in water than in air. Dolphins, such as those in ***Figure 14,*** use sound waves to communicate with one another over long distances underwater. Sound waves travel even faster in solids than in air or in water. Sound waves have speeds 15 to 20 times faster in rock or metal than in air.

If someone strikes a long steel rail with a hammer at one end and you listen for the sound at the other end, you might hear two bangs. The first sound comes through the steel rail itself and reaches you shortly before the second sound, which travels through the air.

The speed of a wave depends on the medium. In a given medium, though, the speed of waves is constant; it does not depend on the frequency of the wave. No matter how fast you shake your hand up and down to create waves on a rope, the waves will travel the same speed. Shaking your hand faster just increases the frequency and decreases the wavelength.

Figure 14
Dolphins use sound waves to communicate with one another. Sound travels three to four times faster in water than in air.

Kinetic theory explains differences in wave speed

The arrangement of particles in a medium determines how well waves travel through it. The different states of matter are due to different degrees of organization at the particle level.

In gases, the molecules are far apart and move around randomly. A molecule must travel through a lot of empty space before it bumps into another molecule. Waves don't travel as fast in gases.

In liquids, such as water, the molecules are much closer together. But they are also free to slide past one another. As a result, vibrations are transferred more quickly from one molecule to the next than they are in a gas. This situation can be compared to vibrating masses on springs that are so close together that the masses rub against each other.

In a solid, molecules are not only closer together but also tightly bound to each other. The effect is like having vibrating masses that are glued together. When one mass starts to vibrate, all the others start to vibrate almost immediately. As a result, waves travel very quickly through most solids.

Light has a finite speed

When you flip a light switch, light seems to fill the room instantly. However, light does take time to travel from place to place. All electromagnetic waves in empty space travel at the same speed, the speed of light, which is 3.00×10^8 m/s (186 000 mi/s). The speed of light in empty space is a constant that is often represented by the symbol c. Light travels slower when it has to pass through a medium such as air or water.

Quick ACTIVITY

Wave Speed

1. Place a rectangular pan on a level surface, and fill the pan with water to a depth of about 2 cm.
2. Cut a wooden dowel (3 cm in diameter or thicker) to a length slightly less than the width of the pan, and place the dowel in one end of the pan.
3. Move or roll the dowel slowly back and forth, and observe the length of the wave generated.
4. Now move the dowel back and forth faster (increased frequency). How does that affect the wavelength?
5. Do the waves always travel the same speed in the pan?

The Doppler Effect

Imagine that you are standing on a corner as an ambulance rushes by. As the ambulance passes, the sound of the siren changes from a high pitch to a lower pitch. Why? Do the sound waves produced by the siren change as the ambulance goes by? How does the motion of the ambulance affect the sound?

Pitch is determined by the frequency of sound waves

The *pitch* of a sound, how high or low it is, is determined by the frequency at which sound waves strike the eardrum in your ear. A higher-pitched sound is caused by sound waves of higher frequency. As you know from the wave speed equation, frequency and wavelength are also related to the speed of a wave.

Suppose you could see the sound waves from the ambulance siren when the ambulance is at rest. You would see the sound waves traveling out from the siren in circular wave fronts, as shown in ***Figure 15A.*** The distance between two successive wave fronts shows the wavelength of the sound waves. When the sound waves reach your ears, they have a frequency equal to the number of wave fronts that strike your eardrum each second. That frequency determines the pitch of the sound that you hear.

Figure 15

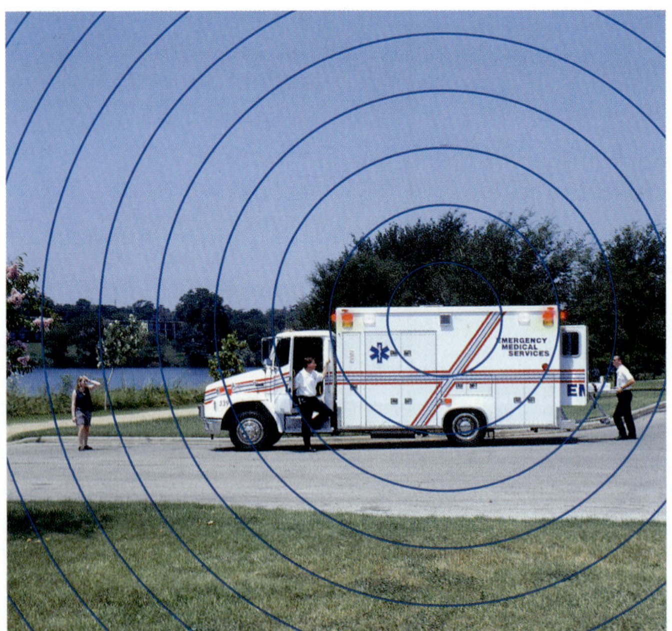

A When an ambulance is not moving, the sound waves produced by the siren spread out in circles. The frequency of the waves is the same at any location.

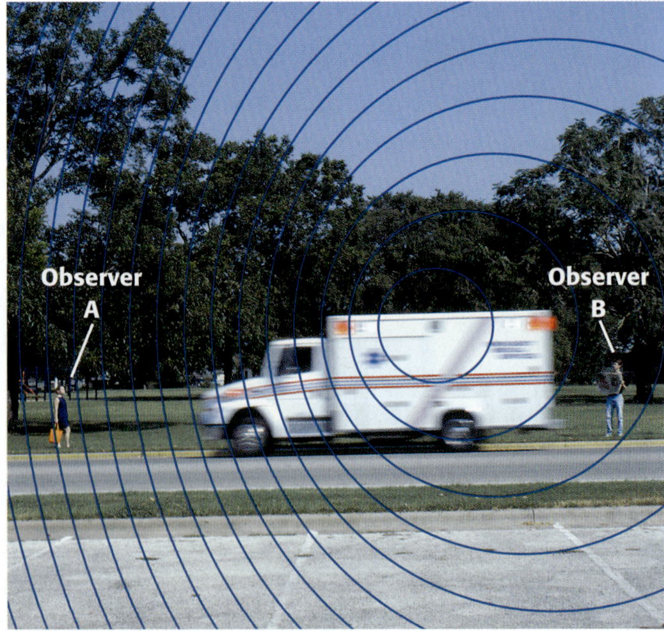

B When an ambulance is moving, the sound waves produced by the siren are closer together in front and farther apart behind. Observer A hears a higher-pitched sound than Observer B hears.

Frequency changes when the source of waves is moving

If the ambulance is moving toward you, the sound waves from the siren are compressed in the direction of motion, as shown in ***Figure 15B.*** Between the time that one sound wave and the next sound wave are emitted by the siren, the ambulance moves a short distance. This shortens the distance between wave fronts, while the wave speed remains the same. As a result, the sound waves reach your ear at a higher frequency.

Because the waves now have a higher frequency, you hear a higher-pitched sound than you would if the ambulance were at rest. Similarly, if the ambulance were moving away from you, the frequency at which the waves reached your ear would be less than if the ambulance were at rest, and you would hear the sound of the siren at a lower pitch. This change in the observed frequency of a wave resulting from the motion of the source or observer is called the **Doppler effect.** The Doppler effect occurs for light and other types of waves as well.

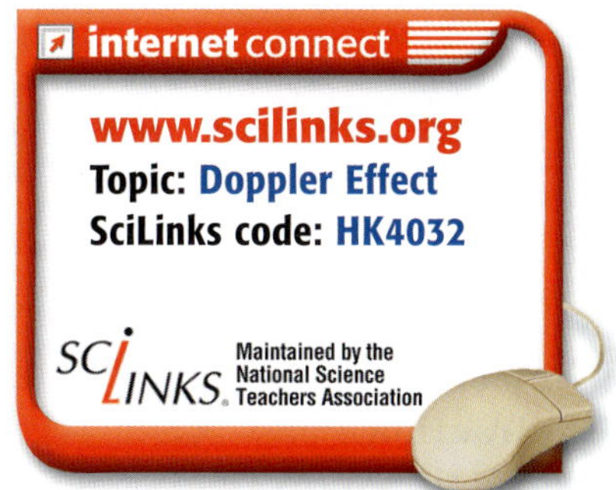

Doppler effect an observed change in the frequency of a wave when the source or observer is moving

SECTION 2 REVIEW

SUMMARY

- The highest points of a transverse wave are called crests; the lowest parts are called troughs.
- The amplitude of a transverse wave is half the vertical distance between a crest and a trough.
- The wavelength is the distance between two identical parts of a wave.
- The period of a wave is the time it takes a wavelength to pass a certain point.
- The frequency of a wave is the number of vibrations that occur in a given amount of time. (1 Hz = 1 vibration/s)
- The speed of a wave equals the frequency times the wavelength. ($v = f \times \lambda$)

1. **Draw** a sine curve, and label a crest, a trough, and the amplitude.
2. **State** the SI units used for wavelength, period, frequency, and wave speed.
3. **Describe** how the frequency and period of a wave are related.
4. **Explain** why sound waves travel faster in liquids or solids than in air.
5. **Critical Thinking** What happens to the wavelength of a wave when the frequency of the wave is doubled but the wave speed stays the same?
6. **Critical Thinking** Imagine you are waiting for a train to pass at a railroad crossing. Will the train whistle have a higher pitch as the train approaches you or after it has passed you by?

Practice

7. A wave along a guitar string has a frequency of 440 Hz and a wavelength of 1.5 m. What is the speed of the wave?
8. The speed of sound in air is about 340 m/s. What is the wavelength of sound waves produced by a guitar string vibrating at 440 Hz?
9. The speed of light is 3×10^8 m/s. What is the frequency of microwaves with a wavelength of 1 cm?

SECTION 3

Wave Interactions

KEY TERMS

reflection
diffraction
refraction
interference
constructive interference
destructive interference
standing wave

OBJECTIVES

- **Describe** how waves behave when they meet an obstacle or pass into another medium.
- **Explain** what happens when two waves interfere.
- **Distinguish** between constructive interference and destructive interference.
- **Explain** how standing waves are formed.

When waves are simply moving through a medium or through space, they may move in straight lines like waves on the ocean, spread out in circles like ripples on a pond, or spread out in spheres like sound waves in air. But what happens when a wave meets an object or another wave in the medium? And what happens when a wave passes into another medium?

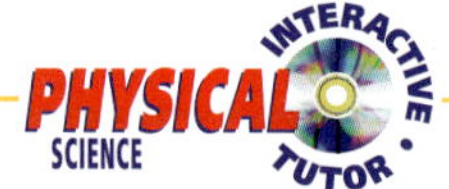

Disc Two, Module 13: **Reflection**
Use the Interactive Tutor to learn more about this topic.

Reflection, Diffraction, and Refraction

You probably already know what happens when light waves strike a shiny surface: they reflect off the surface. Other waves reflect, too. ***Figure 16*** shows two ways that a wave on a rope may be reflected. **Reflection** is simply the bouncing back of a wave when it meets a surface or boundary.

reflection the bouncing back of a ray of light, sound, or heat when the ray hits a surface that it does not go through

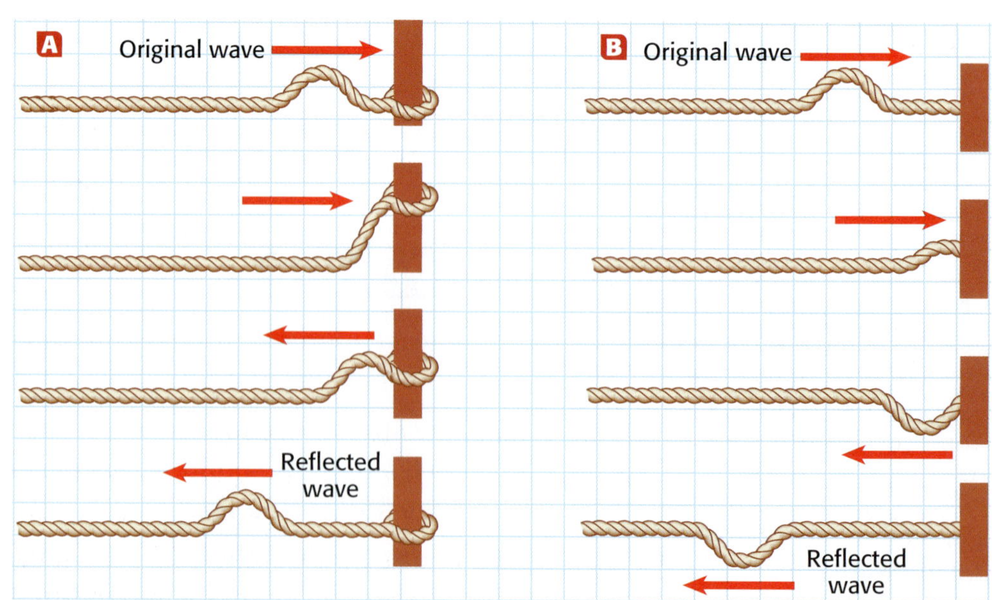

Figure 16
A If the end of a rope is free to slide up and down a post, a wave on the rope will reflect from the end.
B If the end of the rope is fixed, the reflected wave is turned upside down.

Waves reflect at a free boundary

Figure 16A shows the reflection of a single wave traveling on a rope. The end of the rope is free to move up and down on a post. When the wave reaches the post, the loop on the end moves up and then back down. This is just what would happen if someone were shaking that end of the rope to create a new wave. The reflected wave in this case is exactly like the original wave except that the reflected wave is traveling in the opposite direction to the direction of the original wave.

internet connect

www.scilinks.org
Topic: Reflection, Refraction, Diffraction
SciLinks code: HK4119

SCILINKS. Maintained by the National Science Teachers Association

At a fixed boundary, waves reflect and turn upside down

Figure 16B shows a slightly different situation. In this case, the end of the rope is not free to move because it is attached to a wall. When the wave reaches the wall, the rope exerts an upward force on the wall. The wall is too heavy to move, but it exerts an equal and opposite downward force on the rope, following Newton's third law. The force exerted by the wall causes another wave to start traveling down the rope. This reflected wave travels in the opposite direction and is turned upside down.

diffraction a change in the direction of a wave when the wave finds an obstacle or an edge, such as an opening

Diffraction is the bending of waves around an edge

If you stand outside the doorway of a classroom, you may be able to hear the sound of voices inside the room. But if the sound waves cannot travel in a straight line to your ear, how are you able to hear the voices?

When waves pass the edge of an object or pass through an opening, such as an open window or a door, they spread out as if a new wave were created there. In effect, the waves seem to bend around an object or opening. This bending of waves as they pass an edge is called **diffraction.**

Figure 17A shows waves passing around a block in a tank of water. Before they reach the block, the waves travel in a straight line. After they pass the block, the waves near the edge bend and spread out into the space behind the block. Diffraction is the reason that shadows never have perfectly sharp edges.

The tank in ***Figure 17B*** contains two blocks placed end to end with a small gap in between. In this case, waves bend around two edges and spread out as they pass through the opening. Sound waves passing through a door behave the same way. Because sound waves spread out into the space beyond the door, a person near the door on the outside can hear sounds from inside the room.

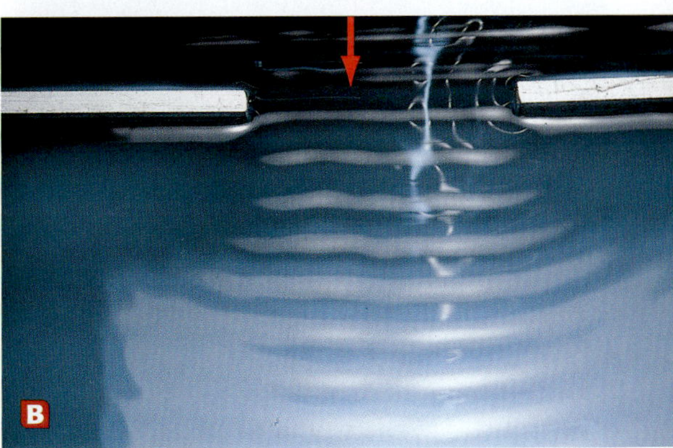

Figure 17

A Waves bend when they pass the edge of an obstacle.

B When they pass through an opening, waves bend around both edges.

Figure 18

Because light waves bend when they pass from one medium to another, this spoon looks like it is in two pieces.

Waves can also bend by refraction

Figure 18 shows a spoon in a glass of water. Why does the spoon look like it is broken into two pieces? This strange sight results from light waves bending, but not because of diffraction. This time, the waves are bending because of **refraction.** Refraction is the bending of waves when they pass from one medium into another. All waves are refracted when they pass from one medium to another at an angle.

Light waves from the top of the spoon handle pass straight through the air and the glass from the spoon to your eyes. But the light waves from the rest of the spoon start out in the water, then pass into the glass, then into the air. Each time the waves enter a new medium, they bend slightly because of a change in speed. By the time those waves reach your eyes, they are coming from a different angle than the waves from the top of the spoon handle. But your eyes just see that one set of light waves are coming from one direction, and another set of waves are coming from a different direction. As a result, the spoon appears to be broken.

refraction the bending of a wavefront as the wavefront passes between two substances in which the speed of the wave differs

interference the combination of two or more waves of the same frequency that results in a single wave

Interference

What would happen if you and another person tried to walk through the exact same place at the same time? You would run into each other. Material objects, such as a human body, cannot share space with other material objects. More than one wave, however, can exist in the same place at the same time.

Waves in the same place combine to produce a single wave

When several waves are in the same location, the waves combine to produce a single, new wave that is different from the original waves. This is called **interference.** *Figure 19* shows interference occurring as water waves pass through each other. Once the waves have passed through each other and moved on, they return to their original shape.

You can show the interference of two waves by drawing one wave on top of another on a graph, as in *Figure 20.* The resulting wave can be found by adding the height of the waves at each point. Crests are considered positive, and troughs are considered negative. This method of adding waves is sometimes known as the *principle of superposition.*

Figure 19

Water waves passing through each other produce interference patterns.

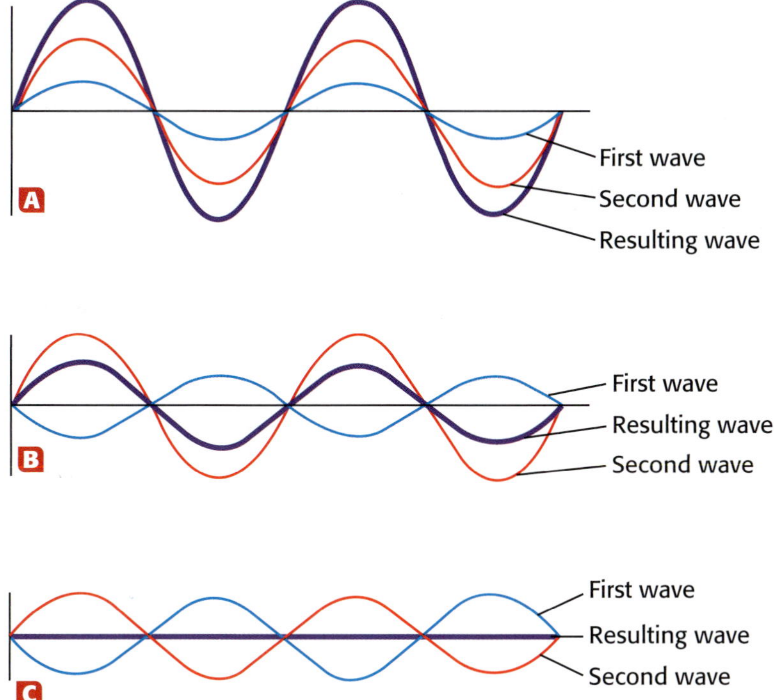

Figure 20

Constructive and Destructive Interference

A When two waves line up so their crests overlap, they add together to make a larger wave.

B When the crest of a large wave overlaps with the trough of a smaller wave, subtraction occurs.

C Two waves of the same size may completely cancel each other out.

Constructive interference increases amplitude

When the crest of one wave overlaps the crest of another wave, the waves reinforce each other, as shown in ***Figure 20A.*** Think about what happens at the particle level. Suppose the crest of one wave would move a particle up 4 cm from its original position, and another wave crest would move the particle up 3 cm.

When both waves hit at the same time, the particle moves up 4 cm due to one wave and 3 cm due to the other for a total of 7 cm. The result is a wave whose amplitude is the sum of the amplitudes of the two individual waves. This is called **constructive interference.**

Disc Two, Module 14: **Refraction**
Use the Interactive Tutor to learn more about this topic.

constructive interference any interference in which waves combine so that the resulting wave is bigger than the original waves

Destructive interference decreases amplitude

When the crest of one wave meets the trough of another wave, the resulting wave has a smaller amplitude than the larger of the two waves, as shown in ***Figure 20B.*** This is called **destructive interference.**

To understand how this works, imagine again a single particle. Suppose the crest of one wave would move the particle up 4 cm, and the trough of another wave would move it down 3 cm. If the waves hit the particle at the same time, the particle would move in response to both waves, and the new wave would have an amplitude of just 1 cm. When destructive interference occurs between two waves that have the same amplitude, the waves may completely cancel each other out, as shown in ***Figure 20C.***

destructive interference any interference in which waves combine so that the resulting wave is smaller than the largest of the original waves

Interference of light waves creates colorful displays

Figure 21

The colorful swirls on a bubble result from the constructive interference of some colors and the destructive interference of other colors.

The interference of light waves often produces colorful displays. You can see a rainbow of colors when oil is spilled onto a watery surface. Soap bubbles, like the ones shown in ***Figure 21,*** have reds, blues, and yellows on their surfaces. The colors in these examples are not due to pigments or dyes. Instead, they are due to the interference of light.

When you look at a soap bubble, some light waves bounce off the outside of the bubble and travel directly to your eye. Other light waves travel into the thin shell of the bubble, bounce off the inner side of the bubble's shell, then travel back through the shell, into the air and to your eye. Those waves travel farther than the waves reflected directly off the outside of the bubble. At times the two sets of waves are out of step with each other. The two sets of waves interfere constructively at some frequencies (colors) and destructively at other frequencies (colors). The result is a swirling rainbow effect.

Interference of sound waves produces beats

The sound waves from two tuning forks of slightly different frequencies will interfere with each other as shown in ***Figure 22A.*** Because the frequencies of the tuning forks are different, the compressions arrive at your ear at different rates.

When the compressions from the two tuning forks arrive at your ear at the same time, constructive interference occurs, and the sound is louder. A short time later, the compression from one and the rarefaction from the other arrive together. When this happens, destructive interference occurs, and a softer sound is heard. After a short time, the compressions again arrive at the same time, and again a loud sound is heard. Overall, you hear a series of loud and soft sounds called *beats*.

Figure 22

A When two waves of slightly different frequencies interfere with each other, they produce beats.

B A piano tuner can listen for beats to tell if a string is out of tune.

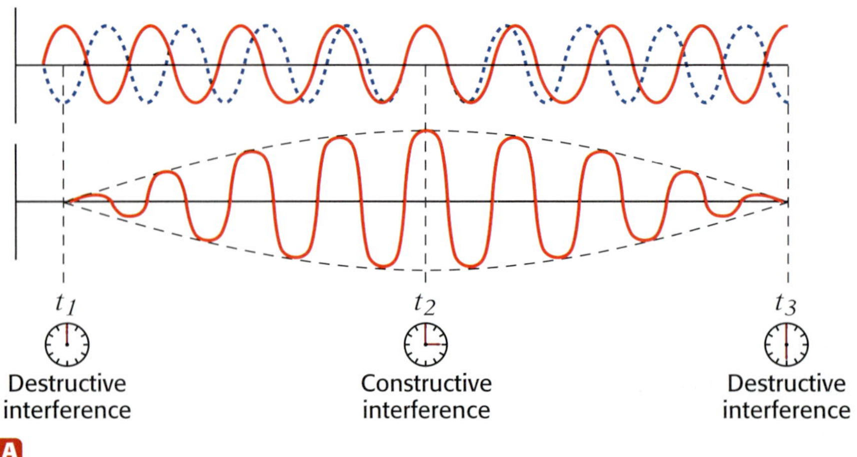

Figure 22B shows a piano tuner tuning a string. Piano tuners listen for beats between a tuning fork of known frequency and a string on a piano. By adjusting the tension in the string, the tuner can change the pitch (frequency) of the string's vibration. When no beats are heard, the string is vibrating with the same frequency as the tuning fork. In that case, the string is said to be in tune.

Standing Waves

Waves can also interfere in another way. Suppose you send a wave through a rope tied to a wall at the other end. The wave is reflected from the wall and travels back along the rope. If you continue to send waves down the rope, the waves that you make will interfere with those waves that reflect off the wall and travel back toward you.

Interference can cause standing waves

Standing waves can form when a wave is reflected at the boundary of a medium. In a standing wave, interference of the original wave with the reflected wave causes the medium to vibrate in a stationary pattern that resembles a loop or a series of loops. Although it appears as if the wave is standing still, in reality waves are traveling in both directions.

Connection to ARCHITECTURE

You might have experienced destructive interference in an auditorium or a concert hall. As sound waves reflect from the walls, there are places, known as *dead spots,* where the waves interfere destructively and cancel out.

Dead spots are produced by the interference of sound waves coming directly from the stage and waves reflected off the walls. For this reason, architects design concert halls so that the dimensions are not simple multiples of each other. They also try to avoid smooth, parallel walls in the design. Irregularities in the wall and ceiling contribute to reducing the direct reflections of waves and the possible resulting interference.

Making the Connection

1. With a friend, go to a square or rectangular room with walls made of brick, cinder block, or concrete. Have one person talk or sing loudly while the other person moves around the room to locate dead spots.
2. Draw an overhead view of the room, and mark the locations of the dead spots. Why do you think the dead spots are in those places?
3. Write a short paragraph explaining how the room could be changed to reduce or eliminate the dead spots.

Standing waves have nodes and antinodes

Each loop of a standing wave is separated from the next loop by points that have no vibration, called *nodes.* Nodes lie at the points where the crests of the original waves meet the troughs of the reflected waves, causing complete destructive interference.

One of the nodes on a fixed rope lies at the point of reflection, where the rope cannot vibrate. Another node is near your hand. If you shake the rope up and down at the right frequency, you can create standing waves with several nodes along the length of the string.

Midway between the nodes lie points of maximum vibration, called *antinodes.* Antinodes form where the crests of the original waves line up with the crests of the reflected waves so that complete constructive interference occurs.

standing wave a pattern of vibration that simulates a wave that is standing still

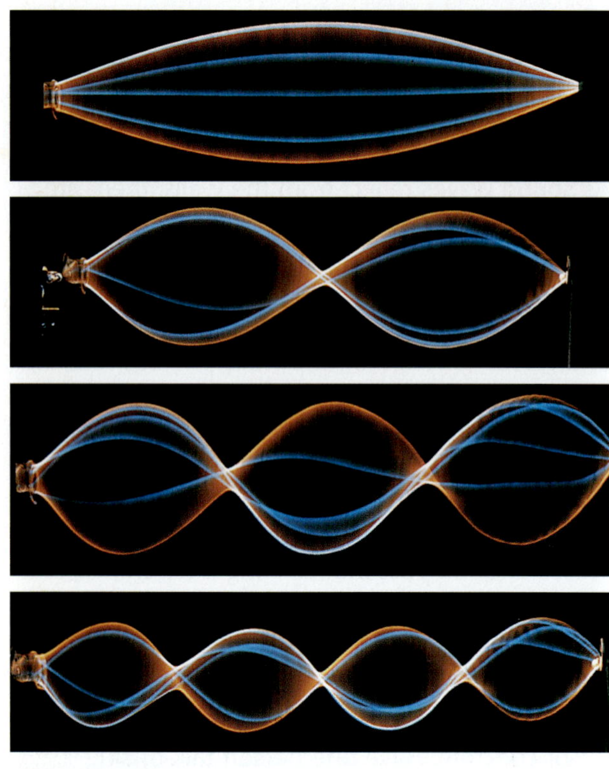

Figure 23

These photos of standing waves were captured using a strobe light that flashes different colors at different times.

Standing waves can have only certain wavelengths

Figure 23 shows several different possible standing waves on a string fixed at both ends. Only a few waves with specific wavelengths can form standing waves in any given string.

The simplest standing waves occur when the wavelength of the waves is twice the length of the string. In that case, it just looks like the entire string is shaking up and down. The only nodes are on the two ends of the string.

If the string vibrates with a higher frequency, the wavelength becomes shorter. At a certain frequency, the wavelength is exactly equal to the length of the string. In the middle of the string, complete destructive interference occurs, producing a node.

In general, standing waves can exist whenever a multiple of half-wavelengths will fit exactly in the length of the string. It is even possible for standing waves of more than one wavelength to exist on a string at the same time.

SECTION 3 REVIEW

SUMMARY

- Waves bouncing off a surface is called reflection.
- Diffraction is the bending of waves as they pass an edge or corner.
- Refraction is the bending of waves as they pass from one medium to another.
- Interference results when two waves exist in the same place and combine to make a single wave.
- Interference may cause standing waves.

1. **Describe** what may happen when ripples on a pond encounter a large rock in the water.
2. **Explain** why you can hear two people talking even after they walk around a corner.
3. **Name** the conditions required for two waves to interfere constructively.
4. **Explain** why colors appear on the surface of a soap bubble.
5. **Draw** a standing wave, and label the nodes and antinodes.
6. **Critical Thinking** What conditions are required for two waves on a rope to interfere completely destructively?
7. **Critical Thinking** Imagine that you and a friend are trying to tune the lowest strings on two different guitars to the same pitch. Explain how you could use beats to determine if the strings are tuned to the same frequency.
8. **Critical Thinking** Determine the longest possible wavelength of a standing wave on a string that is 2 m long.

Graphing Skills

Interpreting Graphs

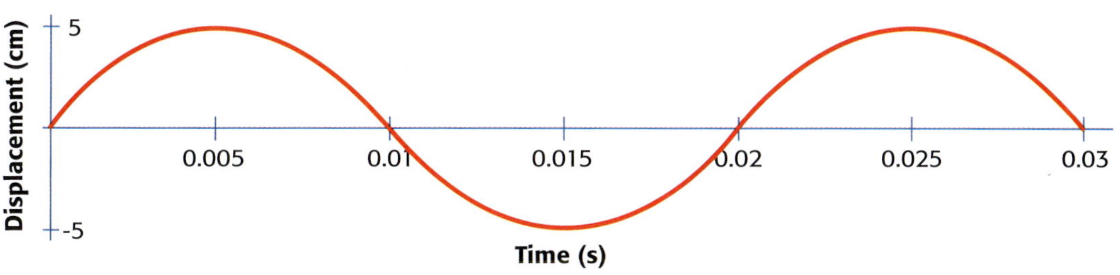

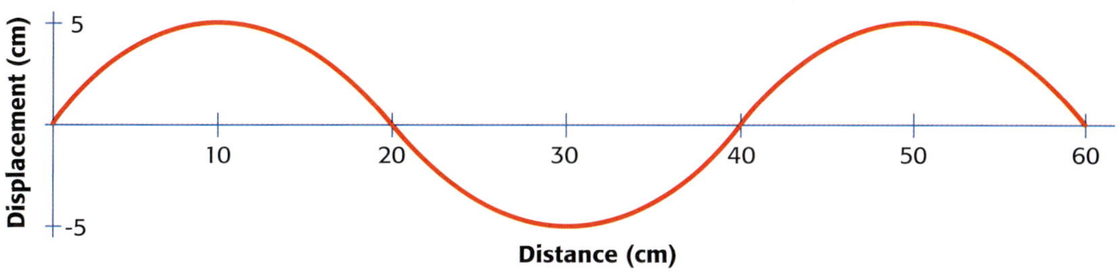

The graphs above show the behavior of a single transverse wave. Study the graphs, and answer the following questions.

1. What types of graphs are these?
2. What variable is described in the *x*-axis of the first graph? What variable is described in the *x*-axis of the second graph?
3. What information about the wave is indicated by the first graph? What information is indicated by the second graph?
4. Determine from the graphs the period, amplitude, and wavelength of the wave.
5. Using the frequency-period equation, calculate the frequency of the wave. Use the wave speed equation to calculate the speed of the wave.
6. Why are both graphs needed to provide complete information about the wave?
7. Plot the data given in the table to the right. From the graph, calculate the wavelength and amplitude of the wave.

x-axis (cm)	*y*-axis (cm)
0	0.93
0.25	2.43
0.50	3.00
0.75	2.43
1.00	0.93
1.25	−0.93
1.50	−2.43
1.75	−3.00
2.00	−2.43
2.25	−0.93
2.50	0.93
2.75	2.43
3.00	3.00

CHAPTER 14 REVIEW

Chapter Highlights

Before you begin, review the summaries of the key ideas of each section, found at the end of each section. The key vocabulary terms are listed on the first page of each section.

UNDERSTANDING CONCEPTS

1. A wave is a disturbance that transmits
- **a.** matter.
- **b.** particles.
- **c.** energy.
- **d.** a medium.

2. The speed of a wave depends on the
- **a.** medium.
- **b.** frequency.
- **c.** amplitude.
- **d.** wavelength.

3. Most waves are caused by
- **a.** velocity.
- **b.** amplitude.
- **c.** a vibration.
- **d.** earthquakes.

4. A sound wave is an example of
- **a.** an electromagnetic wave.
- **b.** a transverse wave.
- **c.** a longitudinal wave.
- **d.** a surface wave.

5. In an ocean wave, the molecules of water
- **a.** move perpendicular to the direction of wave travel.
- **b.** move parallel to the direction of wave travel.
- **c.** move in circles.
- **d.** don't move at all.

6. Half the vertical distance between the crest and trough of a wave is called the
- **a.** frequency.
- **b.** crest.
- **c.** wavelength.
- **d.** amplitude.

7. The number of waves passing a given point per unit of time is called the
- **a.** frequency.
- **c.** wavelength.
- **b.** wave speed.
- **d.** amplitude.

8. The combining of waves as they meet is known as
- **a.** a crest.
- **c.** interference.
- **b.** noise.
- **d.** the Doppler effect.

9. The Greek letter λ is often used to represent a wave's
- **a.** period.
- **c.** frequency.
- **b.** wavelength.
- **d.** amplitude.

USING VOCABULARY

10. How would you describe the *amplitude* of a wave using the words *crest* and *trough*?

11. Explain the difference between waves bending due to *refraction* and *diffraction*.

12. Imagine you are shaking the end of a rope to create a series of waves. What will you observe if you begin shaking the rope more quickly? Use the terms *wave speed, frequency,* and *wavelength* in your answer.

13. Describe the changes in *elastic potential energy* and *kinetic energy* that occur when a mass vibrates on a spring.

14. Use the *kinetic theory* to explain the difference in *wave speed* in solids, liquids, and gases.

15. Why is the reflection of a wave at a *free boundary* different from reflection at a *fixed boundary*?

16. How do *beats* help determine whether two sound waves are of the same *frequency?* Use the terms *constructive interference* and *destructive interference* in your answer.

17. How is an *electromagnetic wave* different from a *mechanical wave*?

18. You have a long metal rod and a hammer. How would you hit the metal rod to create a *longitudinal wave*? How would you hit it to create a *transverse wave*?

19. Draw a picture of a *standing wave*, and label a *node* and an *antinode*.

BUILDING MATH SKILLS

20. **Wave Speed** Ocean waves are hitting a beach at a rate of 2.0 Hz. The distance between wave crests is 1.5 m. Calculate the speed of the waves.

21. **Wavelength** The frequency of radio waves range from about 3.00×10^5 Hz to 3.00×10^7 Hz. What is the range of wavelengths of these waves? Use 3.00×10^8 m/s as the speed of electromagnetic waves.

22. **Frequency** The note A above middle C on a piano emits a sound wave with wavelength 0.77 m. What is the frequency of the wave? Use 340 m/s as the speed of sound in air.

BUILDING GRAPHING SKILLS

23. **Graphing** Draw a sine curve, and label a crest, a trough, and the amplitude.

24. **Interpreting Graphics** The wave shown in the figure below has a frequency of 25.0 Hz. Find the following values for this wave:
    a. amplitude
    b. wavelength
    c. speed
    d. period

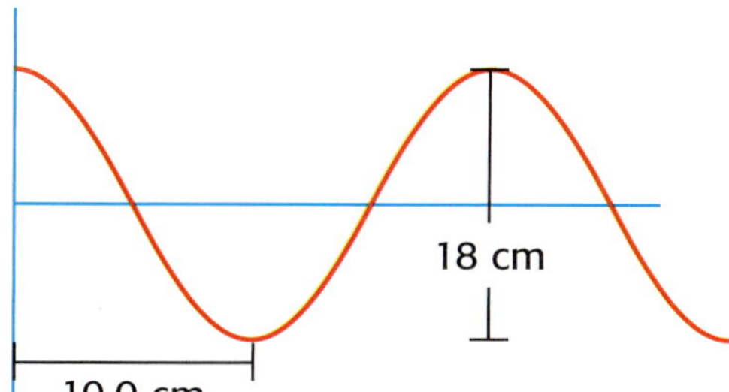

THINKING CRITICALLY

25. **Understanding Systems** A friend standing 2 m away strikes two tuning forks at the same time, one at a frequency of 256 Hz and the other at 240 Hz. Which sound will reach your ear first? Explain.

26. **Applying Knowledge** When you are watching a baseball game, you may hear the crack of the bat a short time after you see the batter hit the ball. Why does this happen? (**Hint:** Consider the relationship between the speed of sound and the speed of light.)

27. **Understanding Systems** You are standing on a street corner, and you hear a fire truck approaching. Does the pitch of the siren stay constant, increase, or decrease as it approaches you? Explain.

28. **Applying Knowledge** If you yell or clap your hands while standing at the edge of a large rock canyon, you may hear an echo a few seconds later. Explain why this happens.

29. **Interpreting Graphics** Draw the wave that results from interference between the two waves shown below.

a. 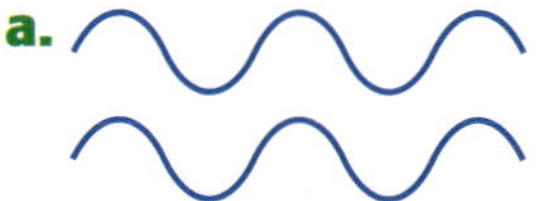

b. 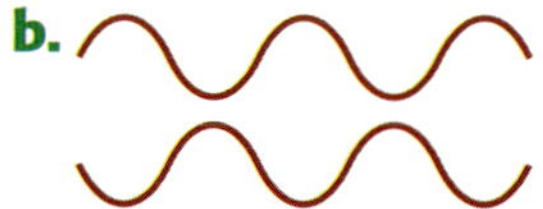

DEVELOPING LIFE/WORK SKILLS

30. **Applying Knowledge** Describe how you interact with waves during a typical school day. Document the types of waves you encounter. Document also how often you interact with each type of wave. Decide whether one type of wave is more important in your life than the other types of waves.

31. **Applying Technology** With your teacher's help, use a microphone and an oscilloscope or a CBL™ interface to obtain an image of a sound. Determine the frequency and wavelength of the sound. COMPUTER SKILL

32. **Making Decisions** A new car is advertised as having antinoise technology. The manufacturer claims that inside the car any sounds are negated. Evaluate the possibility of such a claim. What would have to be created to cause destructive interference with any sound in the car? Do you believe that the manufacturer is correct in its statement?

33. **Working Cooperatively** Work with other classmates to research architectural acoustics that would affect a restaurant. Investigate acoustics problems in places where many people gather. How do odd-shaped ceilings, decorative panels, and glass windows affect echoes? Prepare a model of your school cafeteria showing what changes you would make to reduce the level of noise.

34. **Applying Knowledge** A piano tuner listens to a tuning fork vibrating at 440 Hz to tune the string of a piano. He hears beats between the tuning fork and the piano string. Is the string in tune? Explain your answer.

INTEGRATING CONCEPTS

35. **Connection to Space Science** The Doppler effect occurs for light waves as well as for sound waves. Research some of the ways in which the Doppler effect has helped astronomers understand the motion of distant galaxies and other objects in deep space.

36. **Connection to Earth Science** What is the medium for seismic waves?

37. **Connection to Architecture** Explore and describe research on earthquake-proof buildings and materials. Evaluate the impact of this research on society in terms of building codes and architectural styles in earthquake-prone areas such as Los Angeles, San Francisco, and Tokyo.

38. **Concept Mapping** Copy the unfinished concept map below onto a sheet of paper. Complete the map by writing the correct word or phrase in the lettered boxes.

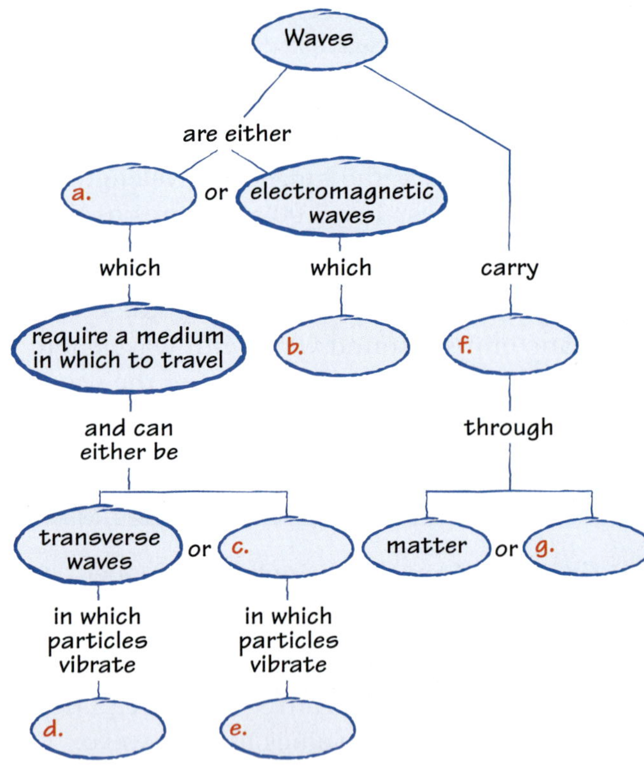

Standardized Test Prep

Understanding Concepts

***Directions (1–4):* For *each* question, write on a separate sheet of paper the letter of the correct answer.**

1 Which of the following waves can be transmitted without a medium?
- **A.** electromagnetic
- **B.** longitudinal
- **C.** mechanical
- **D.** transverse

2 How do longitudinal waves carry energy from a source?
- **F.** Particles vibrate outward from the source of the wave.
- **G.** Particles vibrate parallel to the direction of the wave.
- **H.** Particles vibrate perpendicular to the direction of the wave.
- **I.** Particles vibrate both parallel and perpendicular to the direction of the wave.

3 What is measured by the amplitude of a wave?
- **A.** the amount of vibration of particles
- **B.** the direction of vibration of particles
- **C.** the rate of vibration of particles
- **D.** the wavelength of vibration of particles

4 Which combination of wave interactions can cause a standing wave?
- **F.** diffraction and interference
- **G.** diffraction and reflection
- **H.** reflection and interference
- **I.** reflection and refraction

***Directions (5):* Write a short response to the question.**

5 Why do astronauts on the moon need a radio transmitter to carry on a conversation with each other?

Allow a few minutes at the end of the test-taking period to check for mistakes made in marking answers.

Reading Skills

***Directions (6–7):* Read the passage below. Then answer the questions.**

The Doppler Effect applies to light as well as sound. Astronomers have used this fact to measure the speed of objects in space as they move away from Earth. They know the frequency and wavelength of the light as it leaves a star because the energy transitions in atoms are the same throughout the universe. When the light reaches Earth, it has a different frequency from when it left the star.

6 Assess how the knowledge that light always travels at the same speed is essential for determining the speed at which a distant galaxy and Earth are moving apart.

7 Astronomers have observed that the wavelength of light reaching Earth from one edge of the sun is slightly different than from the other edge. What can be concluded about the sun based on this observation?

Interpreting Graphics

***Directions (8–9):* Base your answers to questions 8 and 9 on the illustration below.**

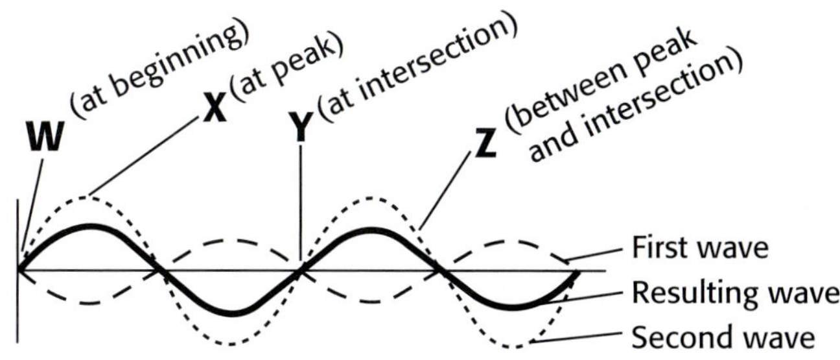

8 What wave phenomenon is demonstrated in this illustration?
- **A.** diffraction
- **B.** interference
- **C.** reflection
- **D.** refraction

9 Which of the points on the illustration indicates an antinode?
- **F.** *W*
- **G.** *X*
- **H.** *Y*
- **I.** *Z*

Skills Practice Lab

Modeling Transverse Waves

Introduction

When a transverse wave model is created with a sand pendulum, what wave characteristics can you measure?

Objectives

- ***Create*** sine curves by pulling paper under a sand pendulum.
- ***Measure*** the amplitude, wavelength, and period of transverse waves using sine curves as models.
- USING SCIENTIFIC METHODS ***Form a hypothesis*** about how changes to the experiment may change the amplitude and wavelength.
- ***Calculate*** frequency and wave speed using your measurements.

Materials

colored sand
masking tape
meterstick
nail
paper or plastic-foam cup
ring stand or other support
rolls of white paper, about 30 cm wide
stopwatch
string and scissors

Procedure

Making Sine Curves with a Sand Pendulum

1. Review the discussion in Section 2 on the use of sine curves to represent transverse waves.
2. On a blank sheet of paper, prepare a table like the one shown at right.
3. Use a nail to puncture a small hole in the bottom of a paper cup. Also punch two holes on opposite sides of the cup near the rim. Tie strings of equal length through the upper holes. Make a pendulum by tying the strings from the cup to a ring stand or other support. Clamp the stand down at the end of a table, as shown in the photograph at right. Cover the bottom hole with a piece of tape, then fill the cup with sand. **SAFETY CAUTION** Wear gloves while handling the nails and punching holes.
4. Unroll some of the paper, and mark off a length of 1 m using two dotted lines. Then roll the paper back up, and position the paper under the pendulum, as shown in the photograph at right.
5. Remove the tape over the hole. Start the pendulum swinging as your lab partner pulls the paper perpendicular to the cup's swing. Another lab partner should loosely hold the paper roll. Try to pull the paper in a straight line with a constant speed. The sand should trace a sine curve on the paper, as in the photograph at right.
6. As your partner pulls the paper under the pendulum, start the stopwatch when the sand trace reaches the first dotted line marking the length of 1 m. When the sand trace reaches the second dotted line, stop the watch. Record the time in your table.
7. When you are finished making a curve, stop the pendulum and cover the hole in the bottom of the cup. Be careful not to jostle the paper; if you do, your trace may be erased. You may want to tape the paper down.

Length along paper = 1 m	Time (s)	Average wavelength (m)	Twice average amplitude (m)
Curve 1			
Curve 2			
Curve 3			

8. For the part of the curve between the dotted lines, measure the distance from the first crest to the last crest, then divide that distance by the total number of crests. Record your answer in the table under "Average wavelength."
9. For the same part of the curve, measure the vertical distance between the first crest and the first trough, between the second crest and the second trough, and so on. Add the distances together, then divide by the number of distances you measured. Record your answer in the table under "Twice average amplitude."

Designing Your Experiment

10. With your lab partners, form a hypothesis about how to make two additional sine curve traces, one with a different average wavelength than the first trace and one with a different average amplitude.
11. In your lab report, write down your plan for changing these two factors. Before you carry out your experiment, your teacher must approve your plan.

Performing Your Experiment

12. After your teacher approves your plan, carry out your experiment. For each curve, measure and record the time, the average wavelength, and the average amplitude.
13. After each trace, return the sand to the cup and roll the paper back up.

Analysis

1. For each of your three curves, calculate the average speed at which the paper was pulled by dividing the length of 1 m by the time measurement. This is equivalent to the speed of the wave that the curve models or represents.
2. For each curve, use the wave speed equation to calculate average frequency.

$$\text{average frequency} = \frac{\text{average wave speed}}{\text{average wavelength}} \qquad f = \frac{v}{\lambda}$$

Conclusions

3. What factor did you change to alter the average wavelength of the curve? Did your plan work? If so, did the wavelength increase or decrease?
4. What factor did you change to alter the average amplitude? Did your plan work?

CareerLink

Ultrasonographer

Most people have seen a sonogram showing an unborn baby inside its mother's womb. Ultrasound technologists make these images with an ultrasound machine, which sends harmless, high-frequency sound waves into the body. Ultrasonographers work in hospitals, clinics, and doctors' offices. Besides checking on the health of unborn babies, ultrasonographers use their tools to help diagnose cancer, heart disease, and other health problems. To find out more about this career, read this interview with Estela Zavala, a registered diagnostic medical sonographer who works at Austin Radiological Association in Austin, Texas.

"Ultrasound is a helpful diagnostic tool that allows you to see inside the body without the use of X rays."

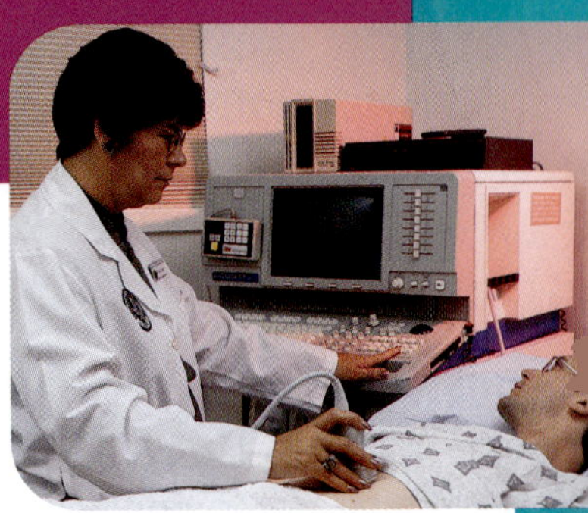

Estela Zavala uses an ultrasound machine to check this man's kidneys.

What does an ultrasonographer do?

We scan various organs of the body with an ultrasound machine to see if there are any abnormalities. For example, we can check a gallbladder to see if there are any stones in it. We already know what healthy organs look like, so anything unusual shows up in these pictures. This can help a doctor make a diagnosis.

How does the ultrasound machine make pictures?

The machine creates high-frequency sound waves. When the sound waves reflect off of the organs in the body, the waves strike a piezoelectric crystal in the detector. Piezoelectric crystals can convert the pressure energy from the ultrasound wave into an electrical signal. The ultrasound system processes the signal to create an image.

What part of your job do you find most satisfying?

I like helping people find out what is wrong with them in a noninvasive way. Before ultrasound, invasive surgery was often the only option.

What is challenging about your job?

The technology is constantly changing. We are using ultrasound in more ways than ever before. For example, we can now create images of veins and arteries.

What skills does an ultrasonographer need?

First you need excellent hand-eye coordination, so you can move the equipment over the parts of the body you need to image. You also have to know a lot about all of the organs in the body. It is very important to be able to work quickly, because sometimes patients are uncomfortable.

How much training and education did you receive before becoming an ultrasonographer?

After graduating from high school, I went to an X-ray school to be licensed as an X-ray technologist. A medical background like this is necessary for entering ultrasound training. First I went to an intensive 1-month training program, which involved 2 weeks of hands-on work and 2 weeks of classwork. After that, I worked for a licensed radiologist for about a year. Finally, I attended an accredited year-long ultrasound program at a local community college before becoming fully licensed.

What part of your education do you think was the most valuable?

The best part was the on-the-job training that was involved. You need to do a lot of ultrasounds before you can become proficient.

Would you recommend ultrasound technology as a career to students?

Yes, I would recommend it. Just remember that you must have some medical experience first, such as being a nurse or an X-ray technician, if you want to continue into other areas of radiology, like ultrasound.

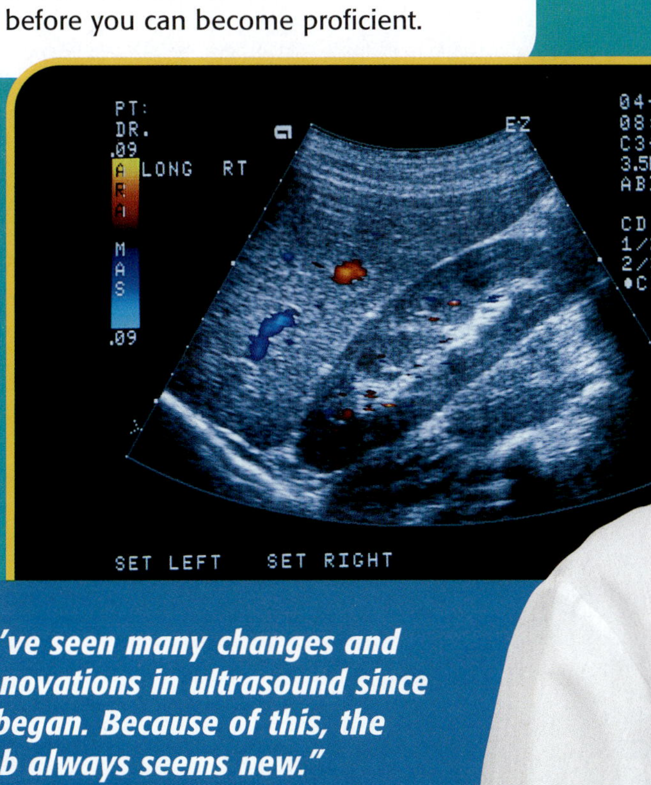

"I've seen many changes and innovations in ultrasound since I began. Because of this, the job always seems new."
—Estela Zavala

HAPTER 15

Sound and Light

Chapter Preview

Whether in a Colorado canyon or on a busy street in New York City, the air is filled with sound and light.

Focus ACTIVITY

Background Imagine that you are walking through a canyon at sunset. As the light of the sun fades, you see the first stars of the night. Your footsteps make an echo that bounces around the canyon walls. As you approach your destination, you hear the sounds of people talking around a campfire.

Now imagine that you are walking down a street in a big city. You see the flash of neon signs and the colors of street lights. You hear the sound of cars, and you hear music from a car radio. Through the open door of a restaurant, you hear dishes clanking and people laughing.

Sound and light carry information about the world around us. This chapter will focus on the behavior of sound waves and light waves. You will learn how sound is produced, how mirrors and lenses work, how we see and hear, and how sound and light are used in different applications, ranging from music to medicine.

Activity 1 Stand outside in front of a large wall, and clap your hands. Do you hear an echo? How much time passes between the time you clap your hands and the time you hear the echo? Use this estimated time to estimate the distance to the wall. You will need two other pieces of information: the speed of sound in air, about 340 m/s, and the speed equation, $v = d/t$.

Activity 2 Find a crosswalk with a crossing signal. Watch as the signal changes from "Walk" to "Don't Walk" and back again. Does the crossing signal ever produce a sound? If so, why? If not, why would it be a good idea for the signal to produce a sound?

Pre-Reading Questions

1. How do you hear sounds? Are there sounds you can't hear?
2. Does a reflection of an object look exactly like the object? Why or why not?
3. How high is the speed of light? How would you measure it?

SECTION 1

Sound

KEY TERMS

sound wave
pitch
infrasound
ultrasound
resonance
sonar

OBJECTIVES

- **Recognize** what factors affect the speed of sound.
- **Relate** loudness and pitch to properties of sound waves.
- **Explain** how harmonics and resonance affect the sound from musical instruments.
- **Describe** the function of the ear.
- **Explain** how sonar and ultrasound imaging work.

When you listen to your favorite musical group, you hear a variety of sounds. You may hear the steady beat of a drum, the twang of guitar strings, the wail of a saxophone, chords from a keyboard, or human voices.

Although these sounds all come from different sources, they are all longitudinal waves produced by vibrating objects. How does a musical instrument or a stereo speaker make sound waves in the air? What happens when those waves reach your ears? Why does a guitar sound different from a violin?

sound wave a longitudinal wave that is caused by vibrations and that travels through a material medium

Properties of Sound

When a drummer hits a drum, the head of the drum vibrates up and down, as shown in ***Figure 1A.*** Each time the drumhead moves upward, it compresses the air above it. As the head moves back down again, it leaves a small region of air that has a lower pressure. As this happens over and over, the drumhead creates a series of compressions and rarefactions in the air, as shown in ***Figure 1B.***

The **sound waves** from a drum are longitudinal waves, in which the particles of air vibrate in the same direction the wave travels. Sound waves are caused by vibrations, and carry energy through a medium. Sound waves in air spread out in all directions away from the source. When sound waves from the drum reach your ears, the waves cause your eardrums to vibrate. Other sounds are produced in different ways from the sound waves produced by a drum, but in all cases a vibrating object sets the medium around it in motion.

Figure 1

A The head of a drum vibrates up and down when it is struck by the drummer's hand.
B The vibrations of the drumhead create sound waves in the air.

Table 1 **Speed of Sound in Various Mediums**

Medium	Speed of sound (m/s)	Medium	Speed of sound (m/s)
Gases		**Liquids at 25°C**	
Air (0°C)	331	Water	1490
Air (25°C)	346	Sea water	1530
Air (100°C)	386	**Solids**	
Helium (0°C)	972	Copper	3813
Hydrogen (0°C)	1290	Iron	5000
Oxygen (0°C)	317	Rubber	54

The speed of sound depends on the medium

If you stand a few feet away from a drummer, it may seem that you hear the sound from the drum at the same time that the drummer's hand strikes the drum head. Sound waves travel very fast, but not infinitely fast. The speed of sound in air at room temperature is about 346 m/s (760 mi/h).

Table 1 shows the speed of sound in various materials and at various temperatures. The speed of sound in a particular medium depends on how well the particles can transmit the compressions and rarefactions of sound waves. In a gas, such as air, the speed of sound depends on how often the molecules of the gas collide with one another. At higher temperatures, the molecules move around faster and collide more frequently. An increase in temperature of 10°C increases the speed of sound in a gas by about 6 m/s.

Sound waves travel faster through liquids and solids than through gases. In a liquid or solid the particles are much closer together than in a gas, so the vibrations are transferred more rapidly from one particle to the next. However, some solids, such as rubber, dampen vibrations so that sound does not travel well. Materials like rubber can be used for soundproofing.

Loudness is determined by intensity

How do the sound waves change when you increase the volume on your stereo or television? The loudness of a sound depends partly on the energy contained in the sound waves. The *intensity* of a sound wave describes the rate at which a sound wave transmits energy through a given area of the medium. Intensity depends on the amplitude of the sound wave as well as your distance from the source of the waves. *Loudness* depends on the intensity of the sound wave. The greater the intensity of a sound, the louder the sound will seem.

Quick ACTIVITY

Sound in Different Mediums

1. Tie a spoon or other utensil to the middle of a 1–2 m length of string.
2. Wrap the loose ends of the string around your index fingers and place your fingers against your ears.
3. Swing the spoon so that it strikes a tabletop, and compare the volume and quality of the sound received with those received when you listen to the sound directly through the air.
4. Does sound travel better through the string or through the air?

Relative Intensities of Common Sounds

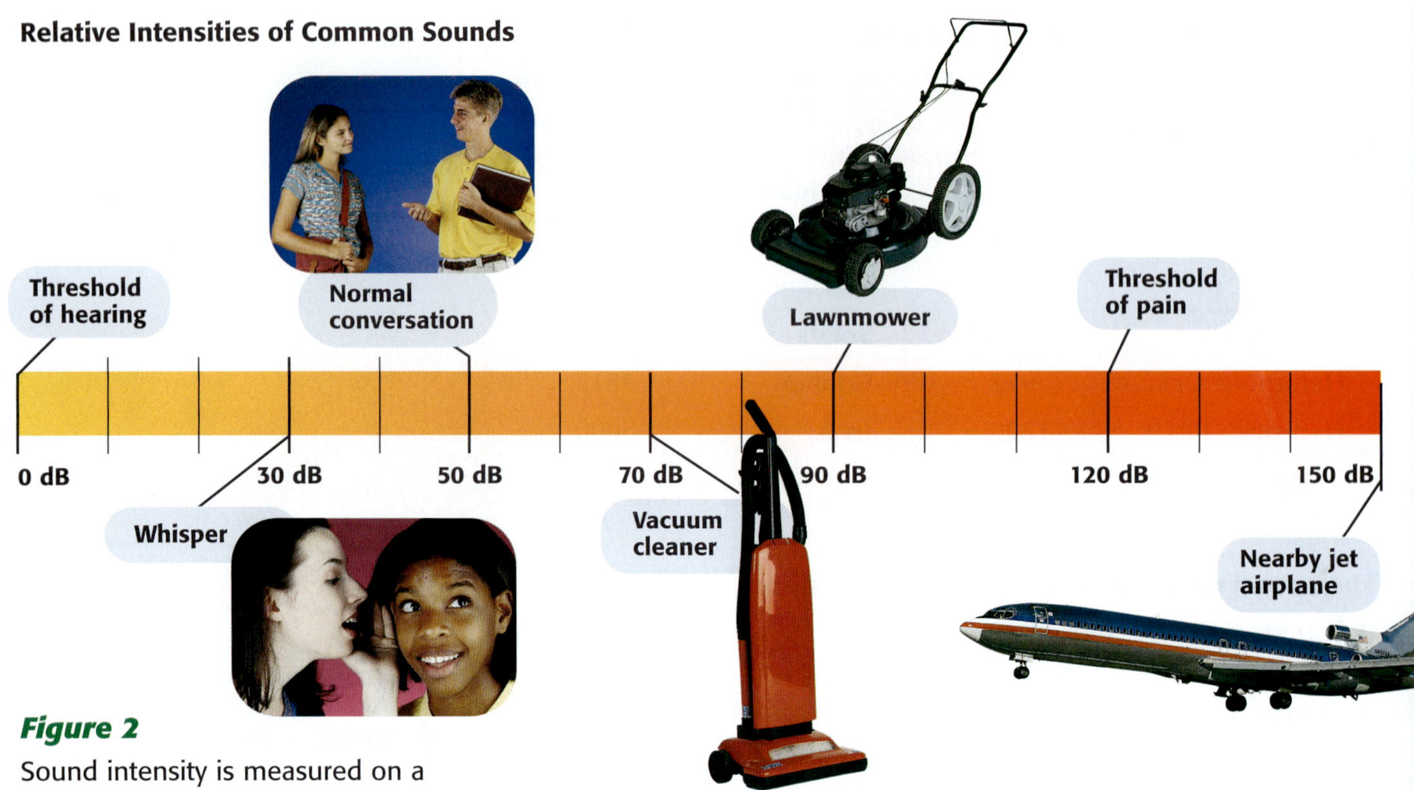

Figure 2

Sound intensity is measured on a logarithmic scale of decibels.

However, a sound with twice the intensity of another sound does not seem twice as loud. Humans perceive loudness on a logarithmic scale. This means that a sound seems twice as loud when its intensity is 10 times the intensity of another sound.

The *relative intensity* of sounds is found by comparing the intensity of a sound with the intensity of the quietest sound a person can hear, the threshold of hearing. Relative intensity is measured in units called *decibels*, dB. A difference in intensity of 10 dB means a sound seems about twice as loud. ***Figure 2*** shows some common sounds and their decibel levels.

The quietest sound a human can hear is 0 dB. A sound of 120 dB is at the threshold of pain. Sounds louder than this can hurt your ears and give you headaches. Extensive exposure to sounds above 120 dB can cause permanent deafness.

pitch a measure of how high or low a sound is perceived to be depending on the frequency of the sound wave

Quick ACTIVITY

Frequency and Pitch

1. Hold one end of a flexible metal or plastic ruler on a desk with about half of the ruler hanging off the edge. Bend the free end of the ruler and then release it. Can you hear a sound?
2. Try changing the position of the ruler so that less hangs over the edge. How does that change the sound produced?

Pitch is determined by frequency

The **pitch** of a sound is related to the frequency of sound waves. A high-pitched note is made by something vibrating very rapidly, like a violin string or the air in a flute. A low-pitched sound is made by something vibrating more slowly, like a cello string or the air in a tuba.

In other words, a high-pitched sound corresponds to a high frequency, and a low-pitched sound corresponds to a low frequency. Trained musicians are capable of detecting subtle differences in frequency, even as slight as a change of 2 Hz.

Ranges of Hearing for Various Mammals

150 000 Hz
Dolphin
46 000 Hz
Human
20 000 Hz
12 000 Hz
6 Hz
20 Hz
40 Hz
70 Hz
Elephant
Dog

Figure 3

Humans can hear sounds ranging from 20 Hz to about 20 000 Hz, but many other animals can hear sounds well into the infrasound and ultrasound ranges.

Humans hear sound waves in a limited frequency range

The human ear can hear sounds from sources that vibrate as slowly as 20 vibrations per second (20 Hz) and as rapidly as 20 000 Hz. Any sound with a frequency below the range of human hearing is known as **infrasound;** any sound with a frequency above human hearing range is known as **ultrasound.** Many animals can hear frequencies of sound outside the range of human hearing, as shown in ***Figure 3.***

infrasound slow vibrations of frequencies lower than 20 Hz

ultrasound any sound wave with frequencies higher than 20 000 Hz

Musical Instruments

Musical instruments, from deep bassoons to twangy banjos, come in a wide variety of shapes and sizes and produce a wide variety of sounds. But musical instruments can be grouped into a small number of categories based on how they make sound. Most instruments produce sound through the vibration of strings, air columns, or membranes.

Musical instruments rely on standing waves

When you pluck the string of a guitar, particles in the string start to vibrate. Waves travel out to the ends of the string, and then reflect back toward the middle. These vibrations cause a standing wave on the string, as shown in ***Figure 4.*** The two ends of the strings are nodes, and the middle of the string is an antinode.

Figure 4

Vibrations on a guitar string produce standing waves on the string. These standing waves in turn produce sound waves in the air.

Figure 5

Colored dust lies along the nodes of the standing waves on the head of this drum.

By placing your finger on the string somewhere along the neck of the guitar, you can change the pitch of the sound. This happens because a shorter length of string vibrates more rapidly. In other words, the standing wave has a higher frequency.

Standing waves can exist only at certain wavelengths on a string. The primary standing wave on a vibrating string has a wavelength that is twice the length of the string. The frequency of this wave, which is also the frequency of the string's vibrations, is called the *fundamental frequency*.

All musical instruments use standing waves to produce sound. In a flute, standing waves are formed in the column of air inside the flute. The wavelength and frequency of the standing waves can be changed by opening or closing holes in the flute body, which changes the length of the air column. Standing waves also form on the head of a drum, as shown in ***Figure 5.***

Harmonics give every instrument a unique sound

If you play notes of the same pitch on a tuning fork and a clarinet, the two notes will sound different from each other. If you listen carefully, you may be able to hear that the clarinet is actually producing sounds at several different pitches, while the tuning fork produces a pure tone of only one pitch.

A tuning fork vibrates only at its fundamental frequency. The air column in a clarinet, however, vibrates at its fundamental frequency and at certain whole-number multiples of that frequency, called *harmonics*. ***Figure 6*** shows the harmonics present in a tuning fork and a clarinet when each sounds the note A-natural.

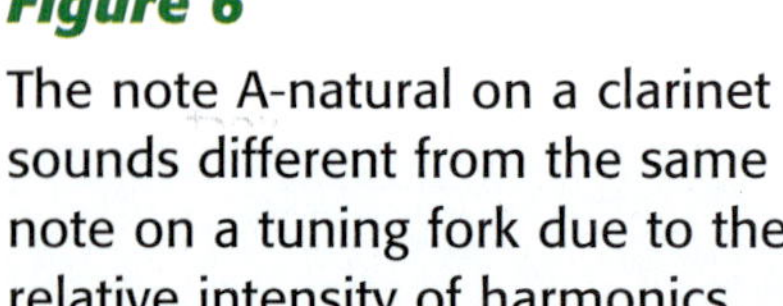

Figure 6

The note A-natural on a clarinet sounds different from the same note on a tuning fork due to the relative intensity of harmonics.

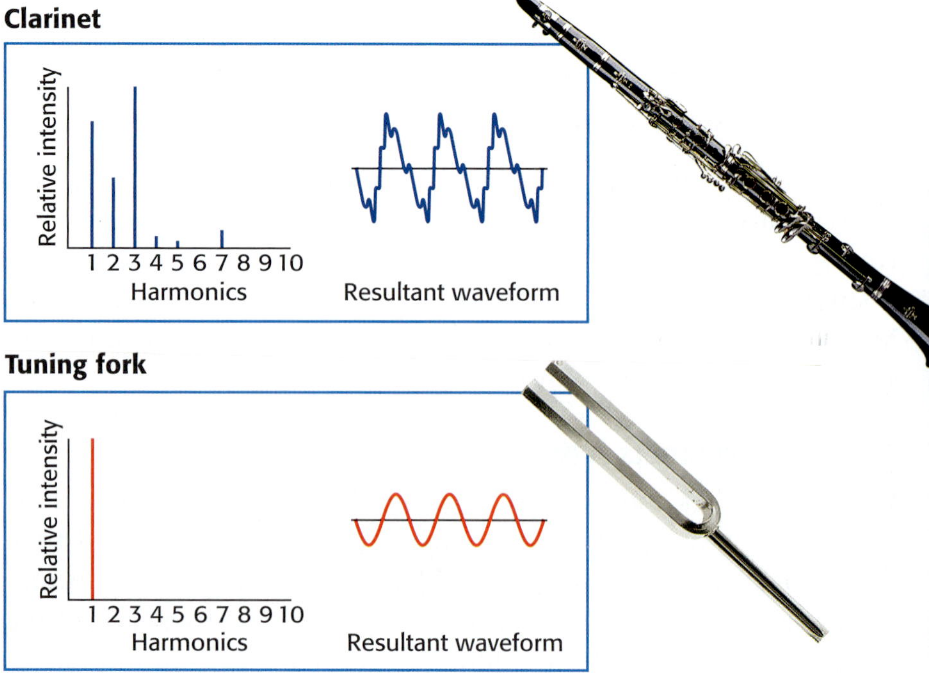

In the clarinet, several harmonics combine to make a complex wave. Note, however, that this wave still has a primary frequency that is the same as the frequency of the wave produced by the tuning fork. This is the fundamental frequency, which makes the note sound a certain pitch. Every musical instrument has a characteristic sound quality resulting from the mixture of harmonics.

Instruments use resonance to amplify sound

When you pluck a guitar string, you can feel that the bridge and the body of the guitar also vibrate. These vibrations, which are a response to the vibrating string, are called *forced vibrations*. The body of the guitar is more likely to vibrate at certain specific frequencies called *natural frequencies*.

The sound produced by the guitar will be loudest when the forced vibrations cause the body of the guitar to vibrate at a natural frequency. This effect is called **resonance.** When resonance occurs, the sound is amplified because both the string and the guitar itself are vibrating at the same frequency.

resonance a phenomenon that occurs when two objects naturally vibrate at the same frequency

Quick Lab

How can you amplify the sound of a tuning fork?

Materials

- *tuning forks of various frequencies*
- *rubber block for activating forks*
- *various objects made of metal and wood*

1. Activate a tuning fork by striking the tongs of the fork against a rubber block.
2. Touch the base of the tuning fork to different wood or metal objects, as shown in the figure at right. Listen for any changes in the sound of the tuning fork.
3. Activate the fork again, but now try touching the end of the tuning fork to the ends of other tuning forks (make sure that the tines of the forks are free to vibrate, not touching anything). Can you make another tuning fork start vibrating in this way?
4. If you find two tuning forks that resonate with each other, try activating one and holding it near the tongs of the other one. Can you make the second fork vibrate without touching it?

Analysis

1. What are some characteristics of the objects that helped to amplify the sound of the tuning fork in step 2?
2. What is the relationship between the frequencies of tuning forks that resonate with each other in steps 3 and 4?

The natural frequency of an object depends on its shape, size, and mass, as well as the material it is made of. Complex objects such as a guitar have many natural frequencies, so they resonate well at many different pitches. However, some musical instruments, such as an electric guitar, do not resonate well and must be amplified electronically.

Hearing and the Ear

The head of a drum or the strings and body of a guitar vibrate to create sound waves in air. But how do you hear these waves and interpret them as different sounds?

The human ear is a very sensitive organ that senses vibrations in the air, amplifies them, and then transmits signals to the brain. In some ways, the process of hearing is the reverse of the process by which a drum head makes a sound. In the ear, sound waves cause membranes to vibrate.

Vibrations pass through three regions in the ear

Your ear is divided into three regions—outer, middle, and inner—as shown in ***Figure 7.*** Sound waves are funneled through the fleshy part of your outer ear and down the ear canal. The ear canal ends at the eardrum, a thin, flat piece of tissue.

When sound waves strike the eardrum, they cause the eardrum to vibrate. These vibrations pass from the eardrum through the three small bones of the middle ear—known as the hammer, the anvil, and the stirrup. When the vibrations reach the stirrup, the stirrup strikes a membrane at the opening of the inner ear, sending waves through the spiral-shaped cochlea.

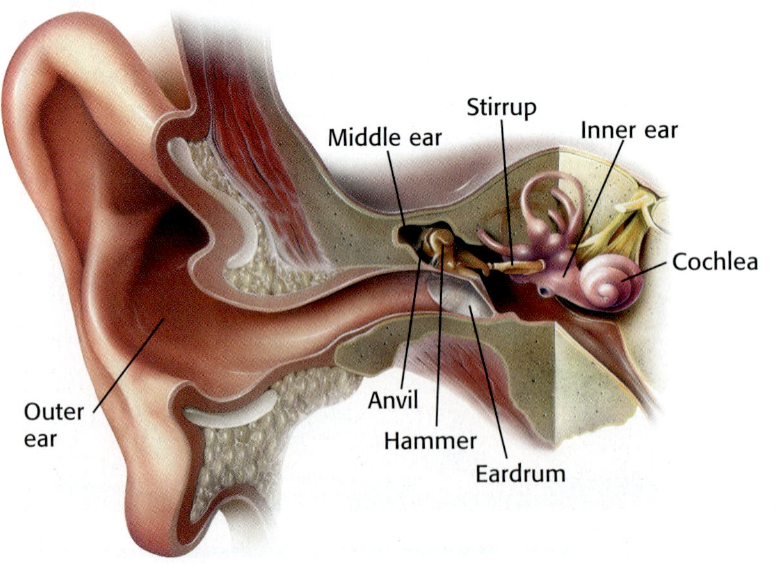

Figure 7
Sound waves are transmitted as vibrations through the ear. Vibrations in the cochlea stimulate nerves that send impulses to the brain.

Resonance occurs in the inner ear

The cochlea contains a long, flexible membrane called the *basilar membrane*. Different parts of the basilar membrane vibrate at different natural frequencies. As waves pass through the cochlea, they resonate with specific parts of the basilar membrane.

A wave of a particular frequency causes only a small portion of the basilar membrane to vibrate. Hair cells near that part of the membrane then stimulate nerve fibers that send an impulse to the brain. The brain interprets this impulse as a sound with a specific frequency.

Ultrasound and Sonar

If you shout over the edge of a rock canyon, you may hear the sound reflected back to you in an echo. Like all waves, sound waves can be reflected. The reflection of sound waves can be used to determine distances and to create maps and images.

Figure 8

Bats use ultrasound echoes to navigate in flight.

Sonar is used for underwater location

How can a person on a ship measure the distance to the ocean floor, which may be thousands of meters from the surface of the water? One way is to use **sonar.**

sonar **so**und **n**avigation **a**nd **r**anging, a system that uses acoustic signals and echo returns to determine the location of objects or to communicate

A sonar system determines distance by measuring the time it takes for sound waves to be reflected back from a surface. A sonar device on a ship sends a pulse of sound downward, and measures the time, t, that it takes for the sound to be reflected back from the ocean floor. Using the average speed of the sound waves in water, v, one can calculate the distance, d, by using a form of the speed equation that solves for distance.

$$d = vt$$

If a school of fish or a submarine passes under the ship, the sound pulse will be reflected back much sooner.

Ultrasound waves—sound waves with frequencies above 20 000 Hz—work particularly well in sonar systems because they can be focused into narrow beams and can be directed more easily than other sound waves. Bats, like the one in ***Figure 8,*** use reflected ultrasound waves to navigate in flight and to locate insects for food.

Ultrasound imaging is used in medicine

The echoes of very high frequency ultrasound waves, between 1 million and 15 million Hz, are used to produce computerized images called *sonograms*. Using sonograms, doctors can safely view organs inside the body without having to perform surgery. Sonograms can be used to diagnose problems, to guide surgical procedures, or even to view unborn fetuses, as shown in ***Figure 9.***

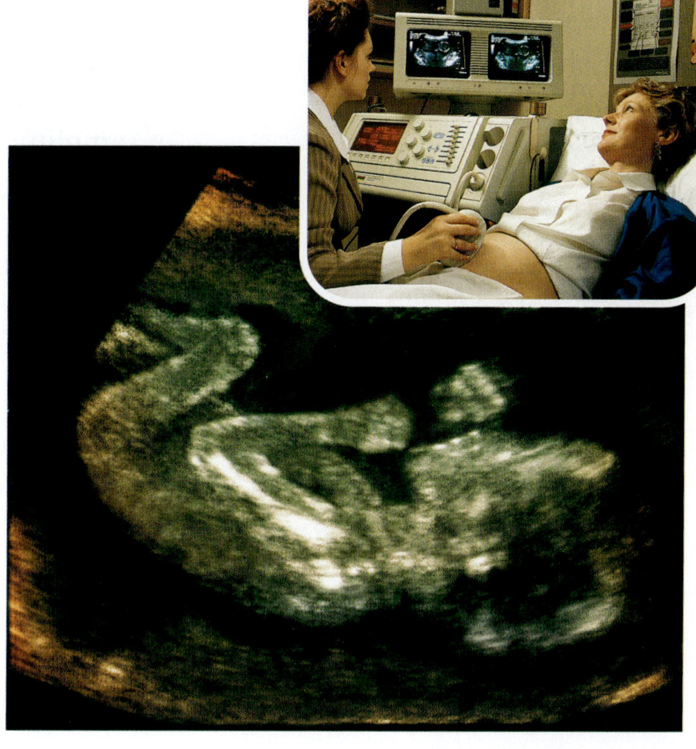

Figure 9

An image of an unborn fetus can be generated from reflected ultrasound waves.

Some ultrasound waves are reflected at boundaries

At high frequencies, ultrasound waves can travel through most materials. But some sound waves are reflected when they pass from one type of material into another. How much sound is reflected depends on the density of the materials at each boundary. The reflected sound waves from different boundary surfaces are compiled into a sonogram by a computer and displayed on a screen.

The advantage of using sound to see inside the human body is that it doesn't harm living cells as X rays may do. However, to see details, the wavelengths of the ultrasound must be slightly smaller than the smallest parts of the object being viewed. The higher the frequency of waves in a given medium are, the shorter the wavelength will be. Sound waves with a frequency of 15 million Hz have a wavelength of less than 1 mm when they pass through soft tissue.

SECTION 1 REVIEW

SUMMARY

- The speed of sound waves depends on temperature, density, and other properties of the medium.
- Pitch is determined by the frequency of sound waves.
- Infrasound and ultrasound lie beyond the range of human hearing.
- The loudness of a sound depends on intensity. Relative intensity is measured in decibels (dB).
- Musical instruments use standing waves and resonance to produce sound.
- The ear converts vibrations in the air into nerve impulses to the brain.
- Reflection of sound or ultrasound waves can be used to determine distances or to create sonograms.

1. **Identify** two factors that affect the speed of sound.
2. **Explain** why sound travels faster in water than in air.
3. **Distinguish** between infrasound and ultrasound waves.
4. **Determine** which of the following must change when pitch gets higher.
   a. amplitude
   b. frequency
   c. wavelength
   d. intensity
   e. speed of the sound waves
5. **Determine** which of the following must change when a sound gets louder.
   a. amplitude
   b. frequency
   c. wavelength
   d. intensity
   e. speed of the sound waves
6. **Explain** why the note middle C played on a piano sounds different from the same note played on a violin.
7. **Explain** why an acoustic guitar generally sounds louder than an electric guitar without an electronic amplifier.
8. **Describe** the process through which sound waves in the air are translated into nerve impulses to the brain.
9. **Critical Thinking** Why are sonograms made with ultrasound waves instead of audible sound waves?
10. **Creative Thinking** Why do most pianos contain a large *sounding board* underneath the strings? (**Hint:** The piano would be harder to hear without it.)

SECTION 2

The Nature of Light

OBJECTIVES

- **Recognize** that light has both wave and particle characteristics.
- **Relate** the energy of light to the frequency of electromagnetic waves.
- **Describe** different parts of the electromagnetic spectrum.
- **Explain** how electromagnetic waves are used in communication, medicine, and other areas.

KEY TERMS

photon
intensity
radar

Most of us see and feel light almost every moment of our lives, from the first rays of dawn to the warm glow of a campfire. Even people who cannot see can feel the warmth of the sun on their skin, which is an effect of infrared light. We are very familiar with light, but how much do we understand about what light really is?

Waves and Particles

It is difficult to describe all of the properties of light with a single scientific model. The two most commonly used models describe light either as a wave or as a stream of particles.

Light produces interference patterns like water waves

In 1801, the English scientist Thomas Young devised an experiment to test the nature of light. He passed a beam of light through two narrow openings and then onto a screen on the other side. He found that the light produced a striped pattern on the screen, like the pattern in ***Figure 10A.*** This pattern is similar to the pattern caused by water waves interfering in a ripple tank, as shown in ***Figure 10B.***

Figure 10

A Light passed through two small openings produces light and dark bands on a screen.

B Two water waves in a ripple tank also produce an interference pattern with light and dark bands.

Figure 11

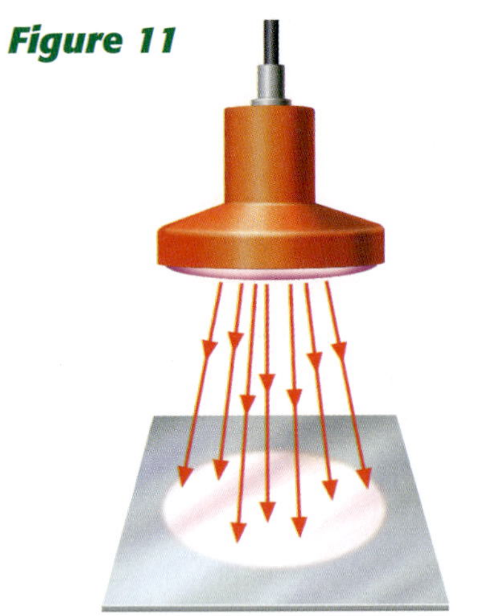

A Bright red light cannot knock electrons off this metal plate.

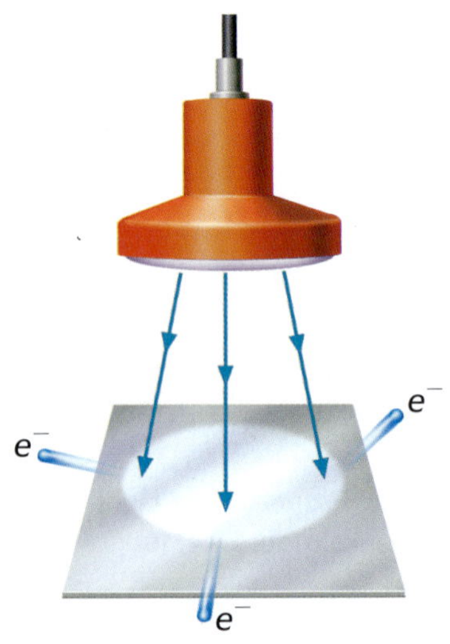

B Dim blue light can knock electrons off the plate. The wave model of light cannot explain this effect, but the particle model can.

Light can be modeled as a wave

Because the light in Young's experiment produced interference patterns, Young concluded that light must consist of waves. The model of light as a wave is still used today to explain many of the basic properties of light and its behavior.

This model describes light as transverse waves that do not require a medium in which to travel. Light waves are also called electromagnetic waves because they consist of changing electric and magnetic fields. The transverse waves produced by these fields can be described by their amplitude, wavelength, and frequency.

The wave model of light explains much of the observed behavior of light. For example, light waves may reflect when they meet a mirror, refract when they pass through a lens, or diffract when they pass through a narrow opening. Light waves also interfere with one another, and they can even form standing waves.

The wave model of light cannot explain some observations

In the early part of the 20th century, physicists began to realize that some observations could not be explained with the wave model of light. For example, when light strikes a piece of metal, electrons may fly off the metal's surface. Experiments show that in some cases, dim blue light may knock some electrons off a metal plate, while very bright red light cannot knock off any electrons, as shown in ***Figure 11.***

According to the wave model, very bright red light should have more energy than dim blue light because the waves in bright light should have greater amplitude. But this does not explain how the blue light can knock electrons off the plate while the red light cannot.

Light can be modeled as a stream of particles

One way to explain the effects of light striking a metal plate is to assume that the energy of the light is contained in small packets. A packet of blue light carries more energy than a packet of red light, enough to knock an electron off the plate. Bright red light contains many packets, but no single one has enough energy to knock an electron off the plate.

In the particle model of light, these packets are called **photons,** and a beam of light is considered to be a stream of photons. Photons are considered particles, but they are not like ordinary particles of matter. Photons do not have mass; they are more like little bundles of energy. But unlike the energy in a wave, the energy in a photon is located in a particular place.

photon a unit or quantum of light

The model of light used depends on the situation

Light can be modeled as either waves or particles; so which explanation is correct? The success of any scientific theory depends on how well it can explain different observations. Some effects, such as the interference of light, are more easily explained with the wave model. Other cases, like light knocking electrons off a metal plate, are explained better by the particle model. The particle model also easily explains how light can travel across empty space without a medium.

Most scientists currently accept both the wave model and the particle model of light, and use one or the other depending on the situation that they are studying. Some believe that light has a "dual nature," so that it actually has different characteristics depending on the situation. In many cases, using either the wave model or the particle model of light gives good results.

Figure 12

The energy of photons of light is related to the frequency of electromagnetic waves.

Wave frequency	Photon energy
2.25×10^{14} Hz	1.5×10^{-19} J
4.5×10^{14} Hz	3.0×10^{-19} J
9.0×10^{14} Hz	6.0×10^{-19} J

The energy of light is proportional to frequency

Whether modeled as a particle or as a wave, light is also a form of energy. Each photon of light can be thought of as carrying a small amount of energy. The amount of this energy is proportional to the frequency of the corresponding electromagnetic wave, as shown in ***Figure 12.***

A photon of red light, for example, carries an amount of energy that corresponds to the frequency of waves in red light, 4.5×10^{14} Hz. A photon with twice as much energy corresponds to a wave with twice the frequency, which lies in the ultraviolet range of the electromagnetic spectrum. Likewise, a photon with half as much energy, which would be a photon of infrared light, corresponds to a wave with half the frequency.

The speed of light depends on the medium

In a vacuum, all light travels at the same speed, called *c*. The speed of light is very large, 3×10^8 m/s (about 186 000 mi/s). Light is the fastest signal in the universe. Nothing can travel faster than the speed of light.

Light also travels through transparent mediums, such as air, water, and glass. When light passes through a medium, it travels slower than it does in a vacuum. ***Table 2*** shows the speed of light in several different mediums.

Table 2 **Speed of Light in Various Mediums**

Medium	Speed of light ($\times 10^8$ m/s)
Vacuum	2.997925
Air	2.997047
Ice	2.29
Water	2.25
Quartz (SiO_2)	2.05
Glass	1.97
Diamond	1.24

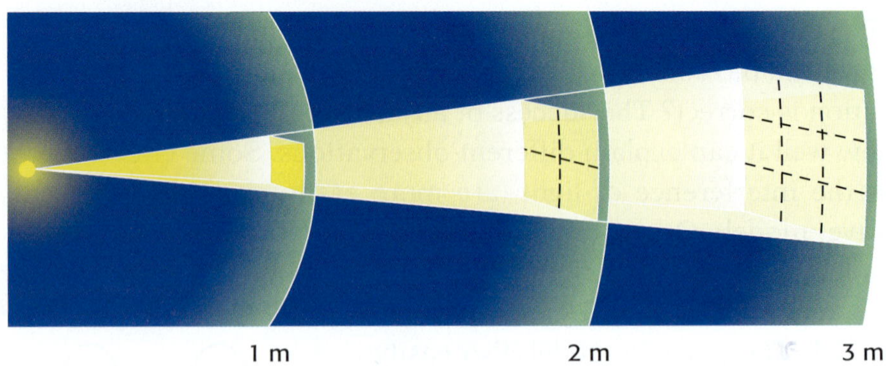

Figure 13

Less light falls on each unit square as the distance from the source increases.

The brightness of light depends on intensity

You have probably noticed that it is easier to read near a lamp with a 100 W bulb than near a lamp with a 60 W bulb. That is because a 100 W bulb is brighter than a 60 W bulb. The quantity that measures the amount of light illuminating a surface is called **intensity,** and it depends on the amount of light—the number of photons, or power—that passes through a certain area of space.

intensity the rate at which energy flows through a given area of space

Like the intensity of sound, the intensity of light from a light source decreases as the light spreads out in spherical wave fronts. Imagine a series of spheres centered around a source of light, as shown in ***Figure 13.*** As light spreads out from the source, the number of photons or power passing through a given area on a sphere, say 1 cm^2, decreases. An observer farther from the light source will therefore see the light as dimmer than will an observer closer to the light source.

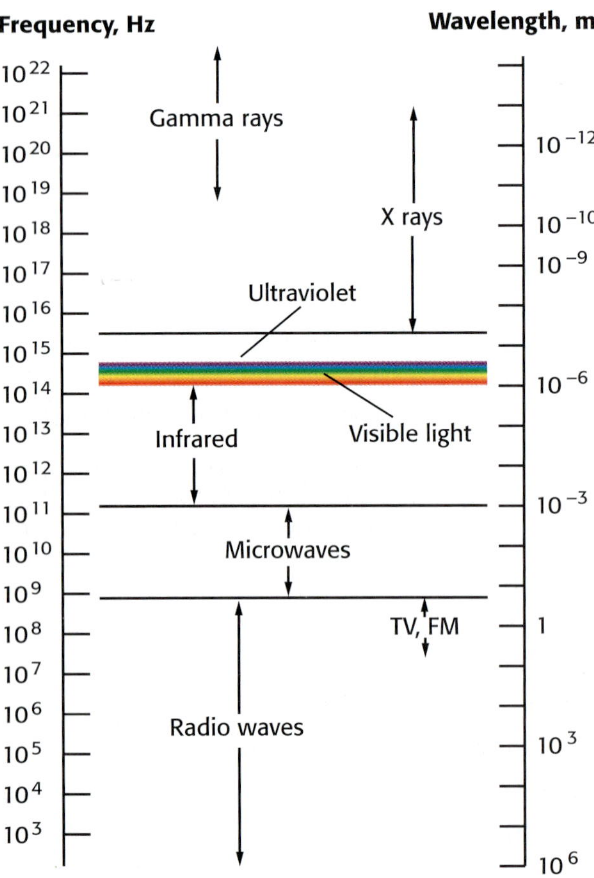

Figure 14

The electromagnetic spectrum includes all possible kinds of light.

The Electromagnetic Spectrum

Light fills the air and space around us. Our eyes can detect light waves ranging from 400 nm (violet light) to 700 nm (red light). But the visible spectrum is only one small part of the entire electromagnetic spectrum, shown in ***Figure 14.*** We live in a sea of electromagnetic waves, ranging from the sun's ultraviolet light to radio waves transmitted by television and radio stations.

The electromagnetic spectrum consists of light at all possible energies, frequencies, and wavelengths. Although all electromagnetic waves are similar in certain ways, each part of the electromagnetic spectrum also has unique properties. Many modern technologies, from radar guns to cancer treatments, take advantage of the different properties of electromagnetic waves.

Sunlight contains ultraviolet light

The invisible light that lies just beyond violet light falls into the *ultraviolet* (UV) portion of the spectrum. Ultraviolet light has higher energy and shorter wavelengths than visible light does. Nine percent of the energy emitted by the sun is UV light. Because of its high energy, some UV light can pass through thin layers of clouds, causing you to sunburn even on overcast days.

X rays and gamma rays are used in medicine

Beyond the ultraviolet part of the spectrum lie waves known as *X rays,* which have even higher energy and shorter wavelengths than ultraviolet waves. X rays have wavelengths less than 10^{-8} m. The highest energy electromagnetic waves are gamma rays, which have wavelengths as short as 10^{-14} m.

An X-ray image at the doctor's office is made by passing X rays through the body. Most of them pass right through, but a few are absorbed by bones and other tissues. The X rays that pass through the body to a photographic plate produce an image such as the one in ***Figure 15.***

X rays are useful tools for doctors, but they can also be dangerous. Both X rays and gamma rays have very high energies, so they may kill living cells or turn them into cancer cells. However, gamma rays can also be used to treat cancer by killing the diseased cells.

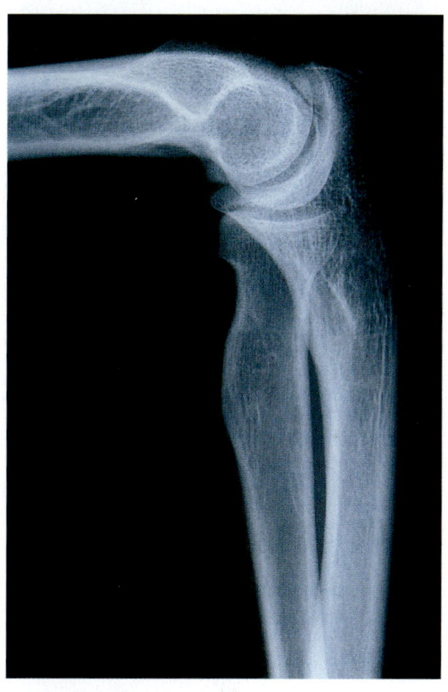

Figure 15

X-ray images are negatives. Dark areas show where the rays passed through, while bright areas show denser structures in the body.

REAL WORLD APPLICATIONS

Sun Protection Short-term exposure to UV light can cause sunburn; prolonged or repeated exposure may lead to skin cancer. To protect your skin, you should shield it from UV light whenever you are outdoors by covering your body with clothing, wearing a hat, and using a sunscreen.

Sunscreen products contain a chemical that blocks some or all UV light, preventing it from penetrating your skin. The Skin Protection Factor (SPF) of sunscreens varies as shown in the table at right.

Applying Knowledge

1. A friend is taking an antibiotic, and his doctor tells him to avoid UV light while on the medication. What SPF factor should he use, and why?
2. You and another friend decide to go hiking on a cloudy day. Your friend claims that she does not need any sunscreen because the sun is not out. What is wrong with her reasoning?

SPF factor	Effect on skin
None	Offers no protection from damage by UV
4 to 6	Offers some protection if you tan easily
7 to 8	Offers extra protection but still permits tanning
9 to 10	Offers excellent protection if you burn easily but would still like to get a bit of a tan
15	Offers total protection from burning
22	Totally blocks UV

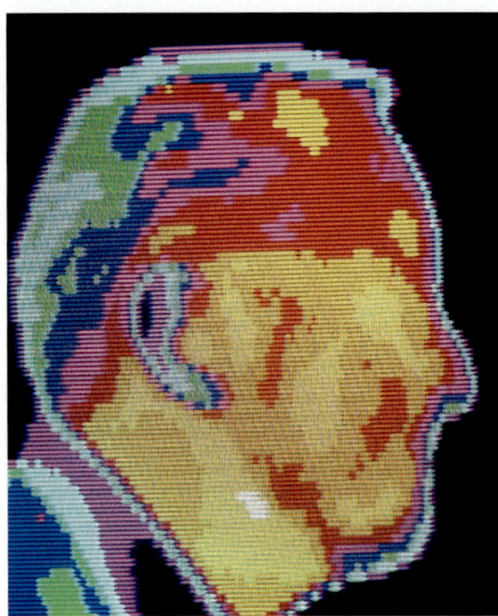

Figure 16

An infrared camera reveals the temperatures of different parts of an object.

Infrared light can be felt as warmth

Electromagnetic waves with wavelengths slightly longer than red light fall into the *infrared* (IR) portion of the spectrum. Infrared light from the sun, or from a heat lamp, warms you. Infrared light is used to keep food warm. You might have noticed reddish lamps above food in a cafeteria. The energy provided by the infrared light is just enough to keep the food hot without continuing to cook it.

Devices and photographic film that are sensitive to infrared light can reveal images of objects like the one in ***Figure 16.*** An infrared sensor can be used to measure the heat that objects radiate and then create images that show temperature variations. By detecting infrared radiation, areas of different temperature can be mapped. Remote sensors on weather satellites that record infrared light can track the movement of clouds and record temperature changes in the atmosphere.

Microwaves are used in cooking and communication

Electromagnetic waves with wavelengths in the range of centimeters, longer than infrared waves, are known as *microwaves*. The most familiar application of microwaves today is in cooking.

Microwave ovens in the United States use microwaves with a frequency of 2450 MHz (12.2 cm wavelength). Microwaves are reflected by metals and are easily transmitted through air, glass, paper, and plastic. However, water, fat, and sugar all absorb microwaves. Microwaves can travel about 3–5 cm into most foods.

As microwaves penetrate deeper into food, they are absorbed along with their energy. The rapidly changing electric field of the microwaves causes water and other molecules to vibrate. The food warms up as the energy of these vibrations is delivered to other parts of the food.

Microwaves are also used to carry telecommunication signals. Most mobile phones use microwaves to transmit information, and space probes transmit signals back to Earth with microwaves.

Did You Know?

Because microwaves reflect off the inside walls of a microwave oven, they may form standing waves. Food lying at the antinodes, where the vibrations are at a maximum, gets cooked more than food lying at the nodes, where there are no vibrations. For that reason, most microwave ovens rotate food items to ensure even heating.

Radio waves are used in communications and radar

Electromagnetic waves longer than microwaves are classified as *radio waves*. Radio waves have wavelengths that range from tenths of a meter to millions of meters. This portion of the electromagnetic spectrum includes TV signals, AM and FM radio signals, and other radio waves.

Air-traffic control towers at airports use **radar** to determine the locations of aircraft. Antennas at the control tower emit radio waves, or sometimes microwaves, out in all directions.

radar **ra**dio **d**etection **a**nd **r**anging, a system that uses reflected radio waves to determine the velocity and location of objects

When the signal reaches an airplane, a transmitter on the plane sends another radio signal back to the control tower. This signal gives the plane's location and elevation above the ground.

At shorter range, the original signal sent by the antenna may reflect off the plane and back to a receiver at the control tower. A computer then calculates the distance to the plane using the time delay between the original signal and the reflected signal. The locations of various aircraft around the airport are displayed on a screen like the one shown in ***Figure 17.***

Radar is also used by police to monitor the speed of vehicles. A radar gun fires a radar signal of known frequency at a moving vehicle and then measures the frequency of the reflected waves. Because the vehicle is moving, the reflected waves will have a different frequency, according to the Doppler effect. A computer chip converts the difference in frequency into a speed and shows the result on a digital display.

Figure 17

The radar system in an air traffic control tower uses reflected radio waves to monitor the location and speed of airplanes.

SECTION 2 REVIEW

SUMMARY

- Light can be modeled as electromagnetic waves or as a stream of particles called photons.
- The energy of a photon is proportional to the frequency of the corresponding light wave.
- The speed of light in a vacuum, c, is 3.0×10^8 m/s. Light travels more slowly in a medium.
- The electromagnetic spectrum includes light at all possible values of energy, frequency, and wavelength.

1. **State** one piece of evidence supporting the wave model of light and one piece of evidence supporting the particle model of light.
2. **Name** the regions of the electromagnetic spectrum from the shortest wavelengths to the longest wavelengths.
3. **Determine** which photons have greater energy, those associated with microwaves or those associated with visible light.
4. **Determine** which band of the electromagnetic spectrum has the following:
   - **a.** the lowest frequency
   - **b.** the shortest wavelength
   - **c.** the greatest energy
   - **d.** the least energy
5. **Critical Thinking** You and a friend are looking at the stars, and you notice two stars close together, one bright and one fairly dim. Your friend comments that the bright star must emit much more light than the dimmer star. Is he necessarily right? Explain your answer.

SECTION 3

Reflection and Color

KEY TERMS

light ray
virtual image
real image

OBJECTIVES

- **Describe** how light reflects off smooth and rough surfaces.
- **Explain** the law of reflection.
- **Show** how mirrors form real and virtual images.
- **Explain** why objects appear to be different colors.
- **Describe** how colors may be added or subtracted.

You may be used to thinking about light bulbs, candles, and the sun as objects that send light to your eyes. But everything else that you see, including this textbook, also sends light to your eyes. Otherwise, you would not be able to see them.

Of course, there is a difference between the light from the sun and the light from a book. The sun emits its own light. The light that comes from a book is created by the sun or a lamp, then bounces off the pages of the book to your eyes.

light ray a line in space that matches the direction of the flow of radiant energy

Reflection of Light

Every object reflects some light and absorbs some light. Mirrors, such as those on the solar collector in ***Figure 18,*** reflect almost all incoming light. Because mirrors reflect light, it is possible for you to see an image of yourself in a mirror.

Figure 18

This solar collector in the French Pyrenees uses mirrors to reflect and focus light into a huge furnace, which can reach temperatures of 3000°C.

Light can be modeled as a ray

It is useful to use another model for light, the **light ray,** to describe reflection, refraction, and many other effects of light at the scale of everyday experience. A light ray is an imaginary line running in the direction that the light travels. It is the same as the direction of wave travel in the wave model of light or the path of photons in the particle model of light.

Light rays do not represent a full picture of the complex nature of light but are a good approximation of light in many cases. The study of light in cases in which light behaves like a ray is called *geometrical optics*. Using light rays, one can trace the path of light in geometrical drawings called *ray diagrams*.

Figure 19

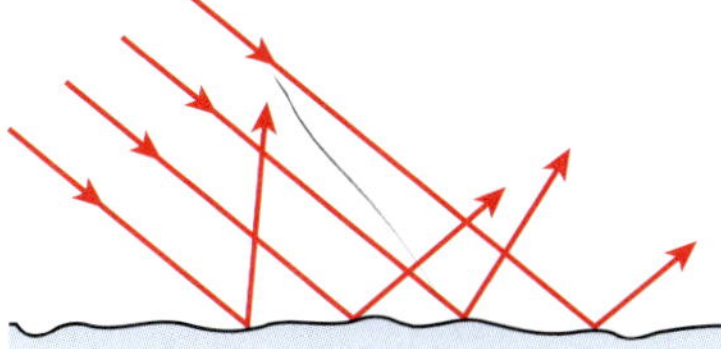

A Light rays reflected from a rough surface are reflected in many directions.

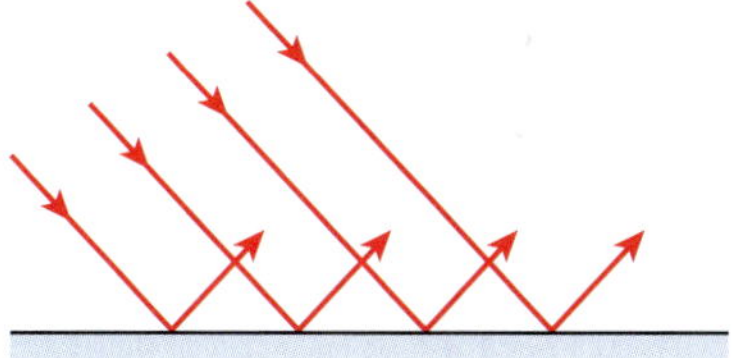

B Light rays reflected from a smooth surface are reflected in the same direction.

internet connect

www.scilinks.org
Topic: Reflection
SciLinks code: HK4118

SCILINKS. Maintained by the National Science Teachers Association

Rough surfaces reflect light rays in many directions

Many of the surfaces that we see every day, such as paper, wood, cloth, and skin, reflect light but do not appear shiny. When a beam of light is reflected, the path of each light ray in the beam changes from its initial direction to another direction. If a surface is rough, light striking the surface will be reflected at all angles, as shown in ***Figure 19A.*** Such reflection of light into random directions is called *diffuse reflection*.

Smooth surfaces reflect light rays in one direction

When light hits a smooth surface, such as a polished mirror, it does not reflect diffusely. Instead, all the light hitting a mirror from one direction is reflected together into a single new direction, as shown in ***Figure 19B.***

The new direction of the light rays is related to the old direction in a definite way. The angle of the light rays reflecting off the surface, called the *angle of reflection,* is the same as the angle of the light rays striking the surface, called the *angle of incidence.* This is called the *law of reflection.*

The angle of incidence equals the angle of reflection.

Both of these angles are measured from a line perpendicular to the surface at the point where the light hits the mirror. This line is called the *normal.* ***Figure 20*** is a ray diagram that illustrates the law of reflection.

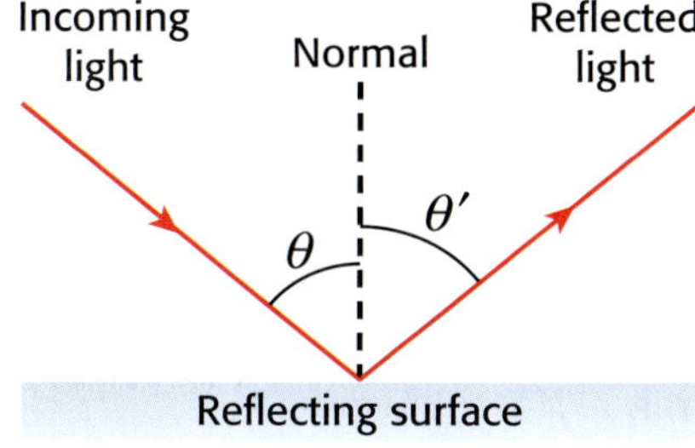

Figure 20

When light hits a smooth surface, the angle of incidence (θ) equals the angle of reflection (θ').

INTEGRATING

SPACE SCIENCE

There are two primary types of telescopes, refracting and reflecting. Refracting telescopes use glass lenses to focus light into an image at the eyepiece; reflecting telescopes use curved mirrors to focus light.

The lens of a refracting telescope cannot be very large, because the weight of the glass would cause the lens to bend out of shape. Curved mirrors are thinner and lighter than lenses, so they are stable at larger diameters.

The largest refracting telescope, at the Yerkes Observatory in Wisconsin, has a lens that is 1 m in diameter. The Mauna Kea Observatory in Hawaii houses four of the largest reflecting telescopes. Two of them have single mirrors that are over 8 m in diameter, and two use multiple mirrors for a total diameter of 10 m.

Mirrors

When you look into a mirror, you see an image of yourself that appears to be behind the mirror, as in ***Figure 21A.*** It is like seeing a twin or copy of yourself standing on the other side of the glass, although flipped from left to right. You also see a whole room, a whole world of space beyond the mirror, even if the mirror is placed against a wall. How is this possible?

Flat mirrors form virtual images by reflection

The ray diagram in ***Figure 21B*** shows the path of light rays striking a flat mirror. When a light ray is reflected by a flat mirror, the angle it is reflected is equal to the angle of incidence, as described by the law of reflection. Some of the light rays reflect off the mirror into your eyes.

virtual image an image that forms at a location from which light rays appear to come but do not actually come

However, your eyes do not know where the light rays have been. They simply sense light coming from certain directions, and your brain interprets the light as if it traveled in straight lines from an object to your eyes. As a result, you perceive an image of yourself behind the mirror.

Of course, there is not really a copy of yourself behind the mirror. If someone else looked behind the mirror, they would not see you, an image, or any source of light. The image that you see results from the apparent path of the light rays, not an actual path. An image of this type is called a **virtual image.** The virtual image appears to be as far behind the mirror as you are in front of the mirror.

Figure 21

A A virtual image appears behind a flat mirror.

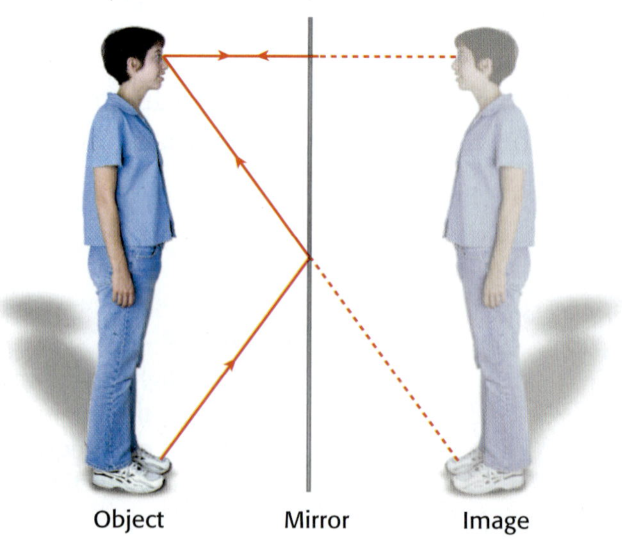

B A ray diagram shows where the light actually travels as well as where you perceive that it has come from.

Curved mirrors can distort images

If you have ever been to the "fun house" at a carnival, you may have seen a curved mirror like the one in ***Figure 22.*** Your image in a curved mirror does not look exactly like you. Parts of the image may be spread out, making you look wide or tall. Other parts may be compressed, making you look thin or short. How does such a mirror work?

Curved mirrors still create images by reflecting light according to the law of reflection. But because the surface is not flat, the line perpendicular to the mirror (the normal) points in different directions for different parts of the mirror.

Where the mirror bulges out, two light rays that start out parallel are reflected into different directions, making an image that is stretched out. Mirrors that bulge out are called *convex mirrors*.

Similarly, parts of the mirror that are indented reflect two parallel rays in toward one another, making an image that is compressed. Indented mirrors are called *concave mirrors*.

Figure 22

A curved mirror produces a distorted image.

Concave mirrors can create real images

Concave mirrors are used to focus reflected light. A concave mirror can form one of two kinds of images. It may form a virtual image behind the mirror or a **real image** in front of the mirror. A real image results when light rays from a single point of an object are focused onto a single point or small area.

real image an image of an object formed by light rays that actually come together at a specific location

If a piece of paper is placed at the point where the light rays come together, the real image appears on the paper. If you tried this with a virtual image, say by placing a piece of paper behind a mirror, you would not see the image on the paper. That is the primary difference between a real and a virtual image. With a real image, light rays really exist at the point where the image appears; a virtual image appears to exist in a certain place, but there are no light rays there.

Telescopes use curved surfaces to focus light

Many reflecting telescopes use curved mirrors to reflect and focus light from distant stars and planets. Radio telescopes, such as the one in ***Figure 23,*** gather radio waves from extremely distant objects, such as galaxies and quasars.

Different materials will reflect certain wavelengths of light and will allow other wavelengths to pass through them. Because radio waves reflect off almost any solid surface, these telescopes do not need to use mirrors. Instead, parallel radio waves bounce off a curved dish, which focuses the waves onto another, smaller curved surface poised above the dish. The waves are then directed into a receiver at the center of the dish.

Figure 23

A radio telescope dish reflects and focuses radio waves into the receiver at the center of the dish.

Seeing Colors

The different wavelengths of visible light correspond to many of the colors that you perceive. When you see light with a wavelength of about 550 nm, your brain interprets it as *green*. If the light comes from the direction of a leaf, then you may think, "That leaf is green."

A leaf does not emit light on its own; in the darkness of night, you may not be able to see the leaf at all. So where does the green light come from?

Objects have color because they reflect certain wavelengths

If you pass the light from the sun through a prism, the prism separates the light into a rainbow of colors. White light from the sun actually contains light from all the visible wavelengths of the electromagnetic spectrum.

When white light strikes a leaf, as shown in ***Figure 24A,*** the leaf reflects light with a wavelength of about 550 nm, corresponding to the color green. The leaf absorbs light at other wavelengths. When the light reflected from the leaf enters your eyes, your brain interprets it as *green*. Transparent objects such as color filters work in a similar way. A green filter transmits green light and absorbs other colors.

Likewise, the petals of a rose reflect red light and absorb other colors, so the petals appear to be red. If you view a rose and its leaves under red light, as shown in ***Figure 24B,*** the petals will still appear red but the leaves will appear black. Why?

Figure 24

A Rose in White and Red Light

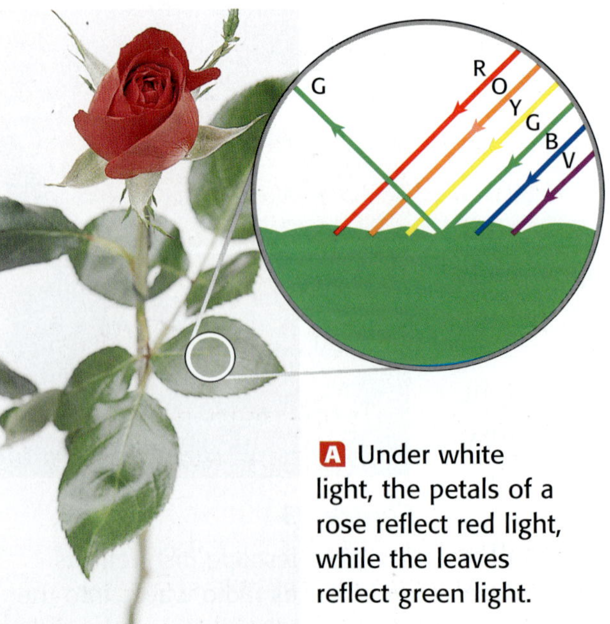

A Under white light, the petals of a rose reflect red light, while the leaves reflect green light.

B Under red light, the petals still look red, but the leaves look black because there is no green light for them to reflect.

Figure 25

A Red, green, and blue lights can combine to produce yellow, magenta, cyan, or white.

B Yellow, magenta, and cyan filters can be combined to produce red, green, blue, or black.

Colors may add or subtract to produce other colors

Televisions and computer monitors display many different colors by combining light of the *additive primary colors,* red, green, and blue. Adding light of two of these colors together can produce the secondary colors yellow, cyan, and magenta, as shown in ***Figure 25A.*** Mixing all three additive primary colors makes white.

In the reverse process, pigments, paints, or filters of the *subtractive primary colors*, yellow, cyan, and magenta, can be combined to create red, green, and blue as shown in ***Figure 25B.*** If filters or pigments of all three colors are combined in equal proportions, all the light is absorbed, leaving black. Black is not really a color at all; it is the absence of color.

SECTION 3 REVIEW

SUMMARY

- Light is reflected when it strikes a boundary between two different mediums.
- When light reflects off a surface, the angle of reflection equals the angle of incidence.
- Mirrors form images according to the law of reflection.
- The color of an object depends on the wavelengths of light that the object reflects.

1. **List** three examples of the diffuse reflection of light.
2. **Describe** the law of reflection in your own words.
3. **Draw** a diagram to illustrate the law of reflection.
4. **Discuss** how a plane mirror forms a virtual image.
5. **Discuss** the difference, in terms of reflection, between objects that appear blue and objects that appear yellow.
6. **Explain** why a plant may look green in sunlight but black under red light.
7. **Critical Thinking** A friend says that only mirrors and other shiny surfaces reflect light. Explain what is wrong with this reasoning.
8. **Creative Thinking** A convex mirror can be used to see around a corner at the intersection of hallways. Draw a simple ray diagram illustrating how this works.

SECTION 4

Refraction, Lenses, and Prisms

KEY TERMS

total internal reflection
lens
magnification
prism
dispersion

OBJECTIVES

- **Describe** how light is refracted as it passes between mediums.
- **Explain** how fiber optics use total internal reflection.
- **Explain** how converging and diverging lenses work.
- **Describe** the function of the eye.
- **Describe** how prisms disperse light and how rainbows form.

Light travels in a straight line through empty space. But in our everyday experience, we encounter light passing through various mediums, such as the air, windows, a glass of water, or a pair of eyeglasses. Under these circumstances, the direction of a light wave may be changed by refraction.

Figure 26
Light refracts when it passes from one medium into another.

Refraction of Light

Light waves bend, or refract, when they pass from one medium to another. If light travels from one transparent medium to another at any angle other than straight on, the light changes direction when it meets the boundary, as shown in **Figure 26.** Light bends when it changes mediums because the speed of light is different in each medium.

Imagine pushing a lawn mower at an angle from a sidewalk onto grass, as in **Figure 27.** The wheel that enters the grass first will slow down due to friction. If you keep pushing on the lawn mower, the wheel on the grass will act like a moving pivot, and the lawn mower will turn to a different angle.

Figure 27
This lawn mower changes direction as it passes from the sidewalk onto the grass.

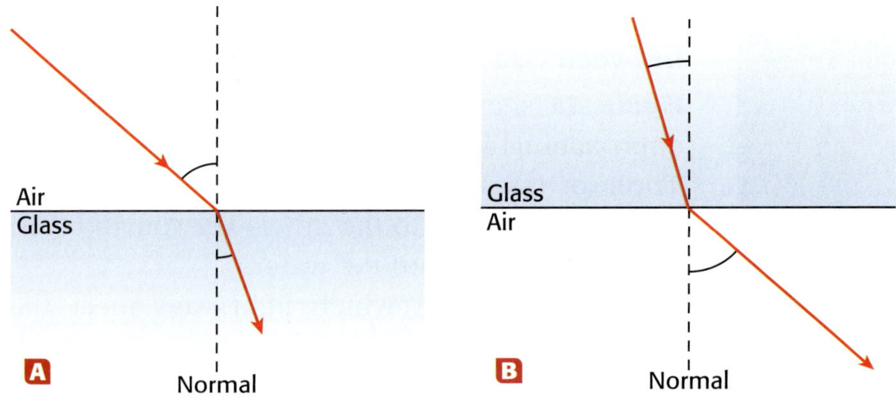

Figure 28

A When the light ray moves from air into glass, its path is bent toward the normal.

B When the light ray passes from glass into air, its path is bent away from the normal.

When light moves from a material in which its speed is higher to a material in which its speed is lower, such as from air to glass, the ray is bent toward the normal, as shown in ***Figure 28A.*** This is like the lawnmower moving from the sidewalk onto the grass. If light moves from a material in which its speed is lower to one in which its speed is higher, the ray is bent away from the normal, as shown in ***Figure 28B.***

Refraction makes objects appear to be in different positions

When a cat looks at a fish underwater, the cat perceives the fish as closer than it actually is, as shown in the ray diagram in ***Figure 29A.*** On the other hand, when the fish looks at the cat above the surface, the fish perceives the cat as farther than it really is, as shown in ***Figure 29B.***

The misplaced images that the cat and the fish see are virtual images like the images that form behind a mirror. The light rays that pass from the fish to the cat bend away from the normal when they pass from water to air. But the cat's brain doesn't know that. It interprets the light as if it traveled in a straight line, and sees a virtual image. Similarly, the light from the cat to the fish bends toward the normal, again causing the fish to see a virtual image.

Refraction in the atmosphere creates mirages

Have you ever been on a straight road on a hot, dry summer day and seen what looks like water on the road? If so, then you may have seen a *mirage*. A mirage is a virtual image caused by refraction of light in the atmosphere.

Light travels at slightly different speeds in air of different temperatures. Therefore, when light from the sky passes into the layer of hot air just above the asphalt on a road, it refracts, bending upward away from the road. Because you see an image of the sky coming from the direction of the road, your mind may assume that there is water on the road causing a reflection.

Figure 29

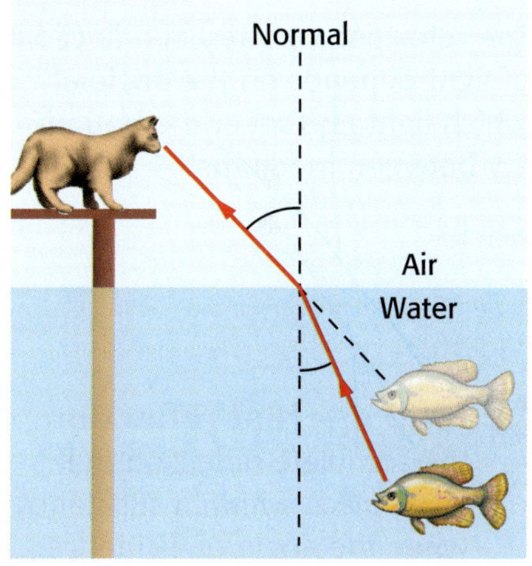

A To the cat on the pier, the fish appears to be closer than it really is.

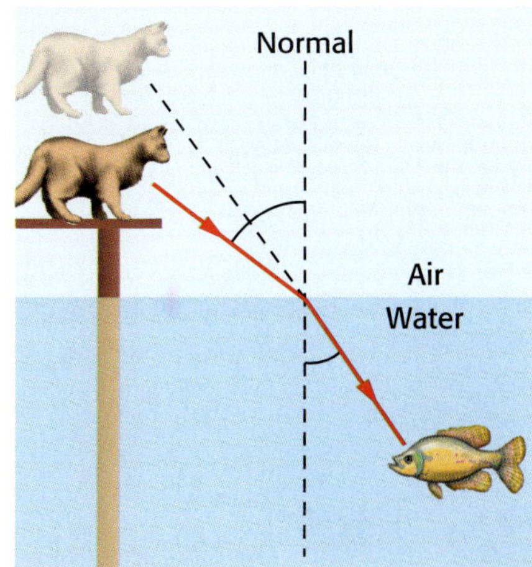

B To the fish, the cat seems to be farther from the surface than it actually is.

Figure 30

The refraction or internal reflection of light depends on the angle at which light rays meet the boundary between mediums.

Light can be reflected at the boundary between two transparent mediums

Figure 30 shows four different beams of light approaching a boundary between air and water. Three of the beams are refracted as they pass from one medium to the other. The fourth beam is reflected back into the water.

If the angle at which light rays meet the boundary between two mediums becomes small enough, the rays will be reflected as if the boundary were a mirror. This angle is called the *critical angle,* and this type of reflection is called **total internal reflection.**

total internal reflection the complete reflection that takes place within a substance when the angle of incidence of light striking the surface boundary is less than the critical angle

Fiber optics use total internal reflection

Fiber-optic cables are made by fusing bundles of transparent fibers together, as shown in ***Figure 31A.*** Light inside a fiber in a fiber-optic cable bounces off of the walls of the fiber due to total internal reflection, as shown in ***Figure 31B.***

If the fibers are arranged in the same pattern at both ends of the cable, the light that enters one end can produce a clear image at the other end. Fiber-optic cables of that sort are used to produce images of internal organs during surgical procedures.

Because fiber-optic cables can carry many different frequencies at once, they transmit computer data or signals for telephone calls more efficiently than standard metal wires. Many long-distance phone calls are now transmitted over optical fibers.

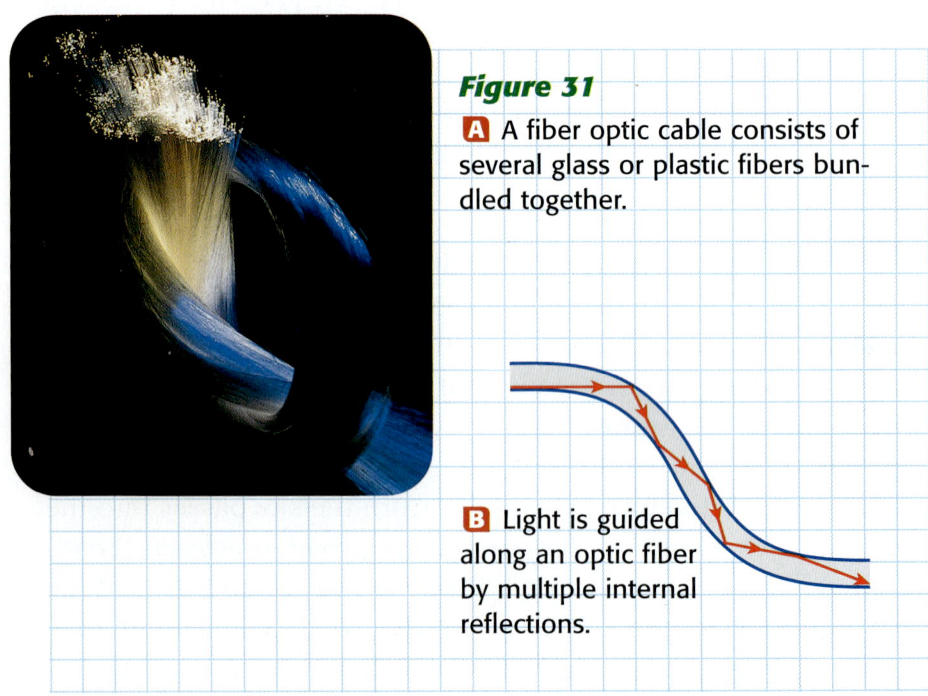

Figure 31

A A fiber optic cable consists of several glass or plastic fibers bundled together.

B Light is guided along an optic fiber by multiple internal reflections.

Figure 32

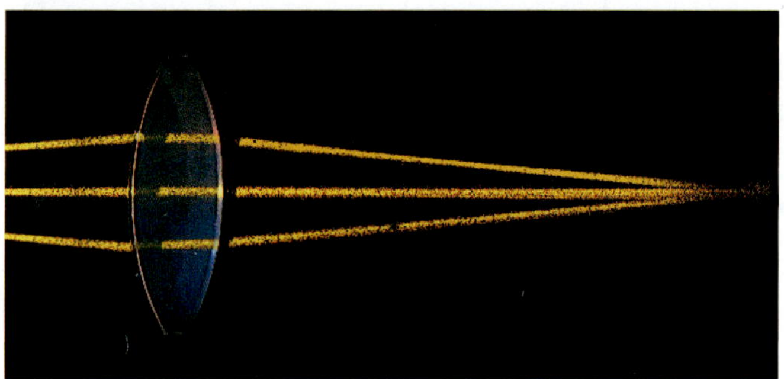

A When rays of light pass through a converging lens (thicker at the middle), they are bent inward.

B When they pass through a diverging lens (thicker at the ends), they are bent outward.

Lenses

You are probably already very familiar with one common application of the refraction of light: lenses. From cameras to microscopes, eyeglasses to the human eye, lenses change the way we see the world.

lens a transparent object that refracts light waves such that they converge or diverge to create an image

magnification a change in the size of an image compared with the size of an object

Lenses rely on refraction

Light traveling at an angle through a flat piece of glass is refracted twice—once when it enters the glass and again when it reenters the air. The light ray that exits the glass is still parallel to the original light ray, but it has shifted to one side.

On the other hand, when light passes through a curved piece of glass, a **lens,** there is a change in the direction of the light rays. This is because each light ray strikes the surface of a curved object at a slightly different angle.

A *converging lens,* as shown in ***Figure 32A,*** bends light inward. A lens that bends light outward is a *diverging lens,* as shown in ***Figure 32B.***

A converging lens can create either a virtual image or a real image, depending on the distance from the lens to the object. A diverging lens, however, can only create a virtual image.

Lenses can magnify images

A magnifying glass is a familiar example of a converging lens. A magnifying glass reveals details that you would not normally be able to see, such as the pistils of the flower in ***Figure 33.*** The large image of the flower that you see through the lens is a virtual image. **Magnification** is any change in the size of an image compared with the size of the object. Magnification usually produces an image larger than the object, but not always.

Figure 33
A magnifying glass makes a large virtual image of a small object.

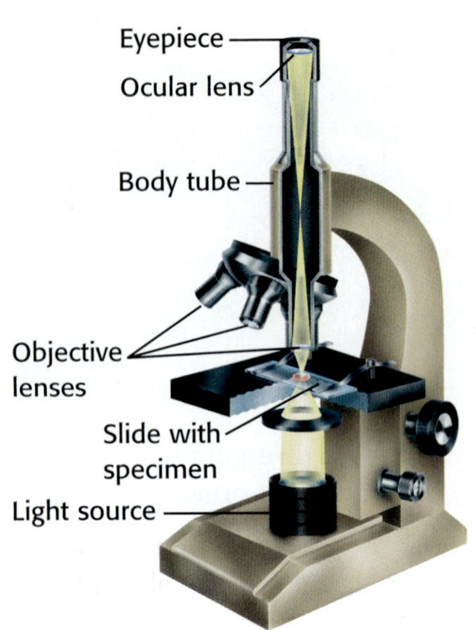

Figure 34

A compound microscope uses several lens to produce a highly magnified image.

If you hold a magnifying glass over a piece of paper in bright sunlight, you can see a real image of the sun on the paper. By adjusting the height of the lens above the paper, you can focus the light rays together into a small area, called the *focal point.* At the focal point, the image of the sun may contain enough energy to set the paper on fire.

Microscopes and refracting telescopes use multiple lenses

A compound microscope uses multiple lenses to provide greater magnification than a magnifying glass. ***Figure 34*** illustrates a basic compound microscope. The objective lens first forms a large real image of the object. The eyepiece then acts like a magnifying glass and creates an even larger virtual image that you see when you peer through the microscope.

Section 3 explained how reflecting telescopes use curved mirrors to create images of distant objects such as planets and galaxies. Refracting telescopes work more like a microscope, focusing light through several lenses. Light first passes through a large lens at the top of the telescope, then through another lens at the eyepiece. The eyepiece focuses an image onto your eye.

The eye depends on refraction and lenses

The refraction of light by lenses is not just used in microscopes and telescopes. Without refraction, you could not see at all.

The operation of the human eye, shown in ***Figure 35,*** is in many ways similar to that of a simple camera. Light enters a camera through a large lens, which focuses the light into an image on the film at the back of the camera.

Figure 35

The cornea and lens refract light onto the retina at the back of the eye.

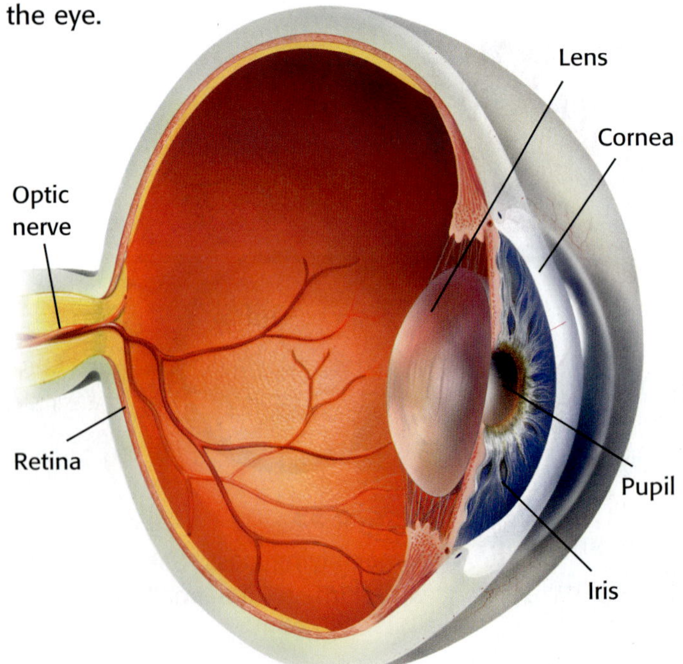

Light first enters the eye through a transparent tissue called the cornea. The cornea is responsible for 70 percent of the refraction of light in the eye. After the cornea, light passes through the pupil, a hole in the colorful iris.

From there, light travels through the lens, which is composed of glassy fibers situated behind the iris. The curvature of the lens determines how much further the lens refracts light. Muscles can adjust the curvature of the lens until an image is focused on the back layer of the eye, the retina.

The retina is composed of tiny structures, called rods and cones, that are sensitive to light. When light strikes the rods and cones, signals are sent to the brain where they are interpreted as images.

Cones are concentrated in the center of the retina, while rods are mostly located on the outer edges. The cones are responsible for color vision, but they only respond to bright light. That is why you cannot see color in very dim light. The rods are more sensitive to dim light, but cannot resolve details very well. That is why you can glimpse faint movements or see very dim stars out of the corners of your eyes.

internet connect

www.scilinks.org
Topic: Refraction
SciLinks code: HK4120

SCILINKS. Maintained by the National Science Teachers Association

Dispersion and Prisms

A **prism,** like the one in ***Figure 36,*** can separate white light into its component colors. Water droplets in the air can also do this, producing a rainbow. But why does the light separate into different colors?

prism in optics, a system that consists of two or more plane surfaces of a transparent solid at an angle with each other

Different colors of light are refracted differently

Although light waves of all wavelengths travel at the same speed (3.0×10^8 m/s) in a vacuum, when a light wave travels through a medium the speed of the light wave *does* depend on its wavelength. In the visible spectrum, violet light travels the slowest and red light travels the fastest.

Because violet light travels slower than red light, violet light refracts more than red light when it passes from one medium to another. When white light passes from air to the glass in the prism, violet bends the most, red the least, and the rest of the visible spectrum appears in between. This effect, in which light separates into different colors because of differences in wave speed, is called **dispersion.**

dispersion in optics, the process of separating a wave (such as white light) of different frequencies into its individual component waves (the different colors)

Figure 36

A prism separates white light into its component colors. Notice that violet light is bent more than red light.

Figure 37

Sunlight is dispersed and internally reflected by water droplets to form a rainbow.

Rainbows are caused by dispersion and internal reflection

Rainbows, like the one in ***Figure 37,*** may form any time water droplets are in the air. When sunlight strikes a droplet of water, the light is dispersed into different colors as it passes from the air into the water. Some of the light then reflects off the back surface of the droplet by total internal reflection. The light disperses further when it passes out of the water back into the air.

When light finally leaves the droplet, violet light emerges at an angle of 40 degrees, red light at 42 degrees, with the other colors in between. We see light from many droplets as arcs of color, forming a rainbow. Red light comes from droplets higher in the air and violet light comes from lower droplets.

SECTION 4 REVIEW

SUMMARY

- Light may refract when it passes from one medium to another.
- Light rays may also be reflected at a boundary between mediums.
- Lenses form real or virtual images by refraction.
- Converging lenses cause light rays to converge to a point. Diverging lenses cause light rays to spread apart, or diverge.
- A prism disperses white light into a color spectrum.

1. **Explain** why a lawn mower turns when pushed at an angle from a sidewalk onto the grass.
2. **Draw** a ray diagram showing the path of light when it travels from air into glass.
3. **Explain** how light can bend around corners inside an optical fiber.
4. **Explain** how a simple magnifying glass works.
5. **Describe** the path of light from the time it enters the eye to the time it reaches the retina.
6. **Critical Thinking** Which color of visible light travels the slowest through a glass prism?
7. **Critical Thinking** A spoon partially immersed in a glass of water may appear to be in two pieces. Is the image of the spoon in the water a real image or a virtual image?
8. **Creative Thinking** If light traveled at the same speed in raindrops as it does in air, could rainbows exist? Explain.

Math Skills

Fractions

The intensity of light at a distance *r* from a source with power output *P* is described by the following equation:

$$intensity = \frac{power}{4\pi(distance)^2} = \frac{P}{4\pi r^2}$$

What is the intensity of a 100.0 W light bulb at a distance of 5.00 m?

1 List all given and unknown values.

Given: power (*P*), 100.0 W

distance (*r*), 5.00 m

Unknown: intensity (W/m^2)

2 Write down the equation for intensity.

$$intensity = \frac{P}{4\pi r^2}$$

3 Solve for intensity.

$$intensity = \frac{100.0 \text{ W}}{4 \times \pi \times (5.00 \text{ m})^2}$$

$$intensity = \frac{100.0 \text{ W}}{4 \times 3.14 \times 25 \text{ m}^2}$$

$$intensity = \frac{100.0 \text{ W}}{314 \text{ m}^2} = 0.318 \text{ W/m}^2$$

Because a watt (W) is the amount of power required to do 1 joule (J) of work in 1 s, 0.318 J of energy pass through each square meter of area at a distance of 5.00 m from the light bulb each second.

Practice

Follow the example above to answer the following questions.

1. What is the intensity of the 100.0 W light bulb in the example above at a distance of 1.00 m from the light bulb? How many times greater is this intensity than the intensity at 5.00 m?
2. The total power output of the sun is 3.85×10^{26} W. What is the intensity of sunlight at a distance of 1.50×10^{11} m (the average distance of Earth from the sun)?
3. When the sun is directly above the clouds that form the "surface" of Saturn, the intensity of sunlight is 15.0 W/m^2. What is the distance from the sun to Saturn? How many times farther is this than the distance between the sun and Earth?

CHAPTER 15 REVIEW

Chapter Highlights

Before you begin, review the summaries of the key ideas of each section, found at the end of each section. The key vocabulary terms are listed on the first page of each section.

UNDERSTANDING CONCEPTS

1. The speed of sound depends on
- **a.** the temperature of the medium.
- **b.** the density of the medium.
- **c.** how well the particles of the medium transfer energy.
- **d.** All of the above

2. Relative intensity is measured in units abbreviated as
- **a.** dB.
- **b.** Hz.
- **c.** J.
- **d.** V.

3. A flat mirror forms an image that is
- **a.** smaller than the object.
- **b.** larger than the object.
- **c.** virtual.
- **d.** real.

4. The wave interaction most important for echolocation is
- **a.** reflection.
- **b.** interference.
- **c.** diffraction.
- **d.** resonance.

5. Light can be modeled as
- **a.** electromagnetic waves.
- **b.** a stream of particles called photons.
- **c.** rays that travel in straight lines.
- **d.** All of the above

6. The energy of a photon is proportional to
- **a.** amplitude.
- **b.** wavelength.
- **c.** frequency.
- **d.** the speed of light.

7. Which of the following wavelengths of visible light bends the most when passing through a prism?
- **a.** red
- **b.** yellow
- **c.** green
- **d.** blue

USING VOCABULARY

8. How is the loudness of a sound related to *amplitude* and *intensity*?

9. How is the *pitch* of a sound related to its *frequency*?

10. Explain how a guitar produces sound. Use the following terms in your answer: *standing waves, resonance.*

11. Why does a clarinet sound different from a tuning fork, even when played at the same pitch? Use these terms in your answer: *fundamental frequency, harmonics.*

12. Describe *infrasonic* and *ultrasonic* waves, and explain why humans cannot hear them.

13. Describe the anatomy of the ear, and explain how the ear senses vibrations. Use the terms *outer ear, middle ear,* and *inner ear.*

14. Define *sonar* and *radar*. State their differences and their similarities, and describe a situation in which each technique would be useful.

15. Explain the difference between a *virtual image* and a *real image*. Give an example of each type of image.

16. Explain why a leaf may appear green in white light but black in red light. Use the following terms in your answer: *wavelength, reflection.*

17. What is the difference between a *converging lens* and a *diverging lens*?

18. Draw a figure that illustrates what happens when light rays hit a rough surface and a smooth surface. Explain how your illustration demonstrates *diffuse reflection* and the *law of reflection.*

BUILDING GRAPHING SKILLS

19. **Graphing** As a ship travels across a lake, a sonar device on the ship sends out pulses of ultrasound and detects the reflected pulses. The table below gives the ship's distance from the shore and the time for each pulse to return to the ship. Construct a graph of the depth of the lake as a function of distance from the shore.

Distance from shore (m)	Time to receive pulse ($\times 10^{-2}$ s)
100	1.7
120	2.0
140	2.6
150	3.1
170	3.2
200	4.1
220	3.7
250	4.4
270	5.0
300	4.6

BUILDING MATH SKILLS

You may use the following for items 20–23:

- the wave speed equation, $v = f \times \lambda$
- a rearranged form of the speed equation, $d = vt$
- the average speed of sound in water or soft tissue, 1500 m/s
- the speed of light, 3.0×10^8 m/s

20. **Sound Waves** Calculate the wavelength of ultrasound used in medical imaging if the frequency is 15 MHz.

21. **Sonar** Calculate the distance to the bottom of a lake when a ship using sonar receives the reflection of a pulse in 0.055 s.

22. **Electromagnetic Waves** Calculate the wavelength of radio waves from an AM radio station broadcasting at 1200 kHz.

23. **Electromagnetic Waves** Waves composing green light have a wavelength of about 550 nm. What is their frequency?

THINKING CRITICALLY

24. **Understanding Systems** By listening to an orchestra, how can you determine that the speed of sound is the same for all frequencies?

25. **Thinking Critically** Sonar devices on ships use a narrow ultrasonic beam for determining depth. A wider beam is used to locate fish. Why?

26. **Aquiring and Evaluating Data** A guitar has six strings, each tuned to a different pitch. Research what pitches the strings are normally tuned to and what frequencies correspond to each pitch. Then calculate the wavelength of the sound waves that each string produces. Assume the speed of sound in air is 340 m/s.

27. **Creative Thinking** Imagine laying this page flat on a table, then standing a mirror upright at the top of the page. Using the law of reflection, draw the image of each of the following letters of the alphabet in the mirror.

A B C F W T

28. **Understanding Systems** The glass in greenhouses is transparent to certain wavelengths and opaque to others. Research this type of glass, and write a paragraph explaining why it is an ideal material for greenhouses.

WRITING SKILL

CHAPTER 15 REVIEW

29. **Applying Knowledge** Why is white light not dispersed into a spectrum when it passes through a flat pane of glass like a window?

30. **Interpreting Graphics** Examine the chart of the electromagnetic spectrum in ***Figure 14.*** Which type of electromagnetic wave has the shortest wavelength? Which has the highest frequency? How does wavelength change as frequency increases?

DEVELOPING LIFE/WORK SKILLS

31. **Teaching Others** Your aunt is scheduled for an ultrasound examination of her gall bladder and she is worried that it will be painful. All she knows is that the examination has something to do with sound. How would you explain the procedure to her?

32. **Applying Technology** Meteorologists use Doppler radar to measure the speed of approaching storms and the velocity of the swirling air in tornadoes. Research this application of radar, and write a short paragraph describing how it works. **WRITING SKILL**

INTEGRATING CONCEPTS

33. **Connection to Health** Research the effect of UV light on skin. Are all wavelengths of UV light harmful to your skin? What problems can too much exposure to UV light cause? Is UV light also harmful to your eyes? If so, how can you protect your eyes?

34. **Connection to Biology** While most people can see all the colors of the spectrum, people with *colorblindness* are unable to see at least one of the primary colors. What part of the eye do you think is malfunctioning in colorblind people?

35. **Connection to Fine Arts** Describe how you can make red, green, blue, and black paint with a paint set containing only yellow, magenta, and cyan paint.

36. **Connection to Space Science** Telescopes can produce images in several different regions of the electromagnetic spectrum. Research photos of areas of the galaxy taken with infrared light, microwaves, and radio waves. What features are revealed by infrared light that are hidden in visible light? What kinds of objects are often studied with radio telescopes?

37. **Concept Mapping** Copy the unfinished concept map below onto a sheet of paper. Complete the map by writing the correct word or phrase in the lettered boxes.

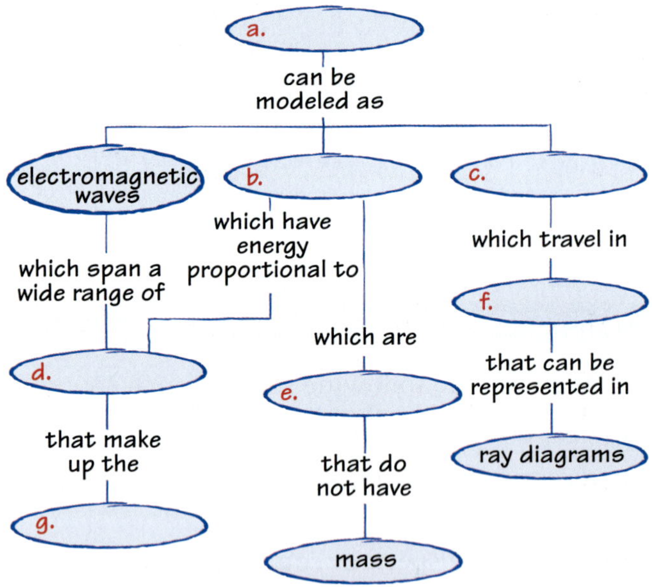

Standardized Test Prep

Understanding Concepts

***Directions (1–3):* For *each* question, write on a separate sheet of paper the letter of the correct answer.**

1 Which of these regions of the electromagnetic spectrum has the highest energy?

A. gamma rays
B. infrared
C. radio waves
D. ultraviolet

2 Why are X-rays used instead of microwaves to make images of bones inside your body?

F. Microwaves are more hazardous than X-rays because of their higher energy.
G. Microwaves have a wavelength that is too short to be absorbed by bone as are X-rays.
H. Microwaves do not have enough intensity to pass through soft tissues but X-rays do.
I. X-rays have shorter wavelengths so they pass through soft tissues, but microwaves are absorbed.

3 Why can you hear someone standing around the corner of a building but not see them?

A. Sound waves diffract around the corner, but light waves do not.
B. Sound waves interfere around the corner, but light waves do not.
C. Sound waves reflect around the corner, but light waves do not.
D. Sound waves refract around the corner, but light waves do not.

***Directions (4):* Write a short response to the question.**

4 In the early 20th century, physicists observed that a dim blue light can knock electrons off a metal plate but even a very bright red light cannot. Explain how this observation led to a model of light that includes photons.

Test TIP

Carefully read the instructions, the question, and the answer options before choosing an answer.

Reading Skills

***Directions (5–6):* Read the passage below. Then answer the questions.**

Many remote control devices, such as television remotes and wireless computer keyboards, use infrared light. A controller sends signal information to a sensor on the television or computer that responds to radiation of a particular wavelength. A universal remote control is designed to send signals at different wavelengths, so that it can be used with several different appliances, such as a television and a DVD player.

5 Demonstrate how you can have many different electronic devices that can be operated with remote controls in the same room, but each one only responds to its own control unit.

6 Explain why a television remote control can be used across a room from the television, but it will not work around a corner or if someone is standing between the remote control and the television.

Interpreting Graphics

***Directions (7):* Base your answer to question 7 on the illustration below.**

Light Transmission Around Bends in an Optic Fiber

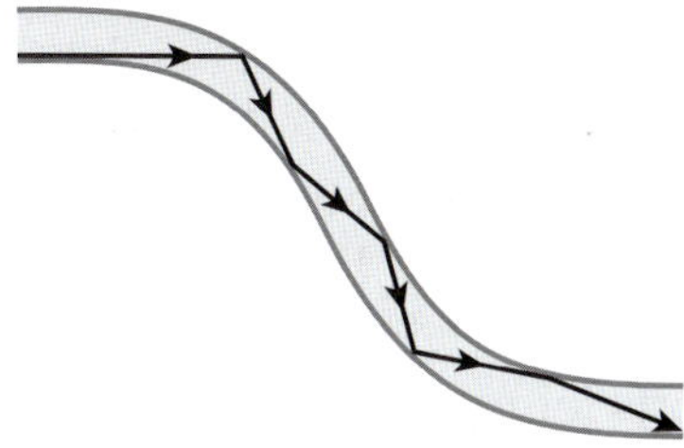

7 The transmission of light through an optic fiber, as illustrated, uses what process?

F. diffraction
G. interference
H. reflection
I. refraction

Skills Practice Lab

Introduction

How can you find the focal length of a lens and verify the value?

Objectives

- ▶ ***Observe*** images formed by a convex lens.
- ▶ ***Measure*** the distance of objects and images from the lens.
- ▶ USING SCIENTIFIC METHODS ***Analyze*** your results to determine the focal length of the lens.

Materials

cardboard screen, 10 cm × 20 cm
convex lens, 10 cm to 15 cm focal length
lens holder
light box with light bulb
meterstick
screen holder
supports for meterstick

Forming Images with Lenses

▶ Procedure

Preparing for Your Experiment

1. The shape of a lens determines the size, position, and types of images that it may form. When parallel rays of light from a distant object pass through a converging lens, they come together to form an image at a point called the focal point. The distance from this point to the lens is called the focal length. In this experiment, you will find the focal length of a lens, and then verify this value by forming images, measuring distances, and using the lens formula,

$$\frac{1}{d_o} + \frac{1}{d_i} = \frac{1}{f}$$

where d_o = *object distance*,
d_i = *image distance*, and
f = *focal length*.

2. On a clean sheet of paper, make a table like the one shown at right.
3. Set up the equipment as illustrated in the figure below. Make sure the lens and screen are securely fastened to the meterstick.

Determining Focal Length

4. Stand about 1 m from a window, and point the meterstick at a tree, parked car, or similar object. Slide the screen holder along the meterstick until a clear image of the distant object forms on the screen. Measure the distance between the lens and the screen in centimeters. This distance is very close to the focal length of the lens you are using. Record this value at the top of your data table.

Focal length of lens, f: ______ cm	Object distance, d_o (cm)	Image distance, d_i (cm)	$\frac{1}{d_o}$	$\frac{1}{d_i}$	$\frac{1}{d_o}+\frac{1}{d_i}$	$\frac{1}{f}$	Size of object (mm)	Size of image (mm)
Trial 1								
Trial 2								
Trial 3								

Forming Images

5. Set up the equipment as illustrated in the figure at right. Again, make sure that all components are securely fastened.

6. Place the lens more than twice the focal length from the light box. For example, if the lens has a focal length of 10 cm, place the lens 25 or 30 cm from the light.
7. Move the screen along the meterstick until you get a good image. Record the distance from the light to the lens, d_o, and the distance from the lens to the screen, d_i, in centimeters as Trial 1 in your data table. Also record the height of the object and of the image in millimeters. The object in this case may be either the filament of the light bulb or a cut-out shape in the light box.
8. For Trial 2, place the lens exactly twice the focal length from the object. Slide the screen along the stick until a good image is formed, as in step 7. Record the distances from the screen and the sizes of the object and image as you did in step 7.
9. For Trial 3, place the lens at a distance from the object that is greater than the focal length but less than twice the focal length. Adjust the screen, and record the measurements as you did in step 7.

Analysis

1. Perform the calculations needed to complete your data table.
2. How does $\frac{1}{d_o}+\frac{1}{d_i}$ compare with $\frac{1}{f}$ in each of the three trials?

Conclusions

3. If the object distance is greater than the image distance, how will the size of the image compare with the size of the object?

Science in ACTION

Holography

Have you ever been watching TV or looking at a magazine and seen something that made you think, "Wait a minute—is that real?" Sometimes, special effects and images made with computers are so lifelike that you can't believe your eyes. But even the most realistic TV images or photographs can't fool you into thinking that they are real, solid objects. Images on a movie screen have height and width but no depth. Therefore, these images always appear flat. Solid objects, however, are three-dimensional, which means they have height, width, and depth. Holograms are three-dimensional images so real that many people try to reach out and pick them up!

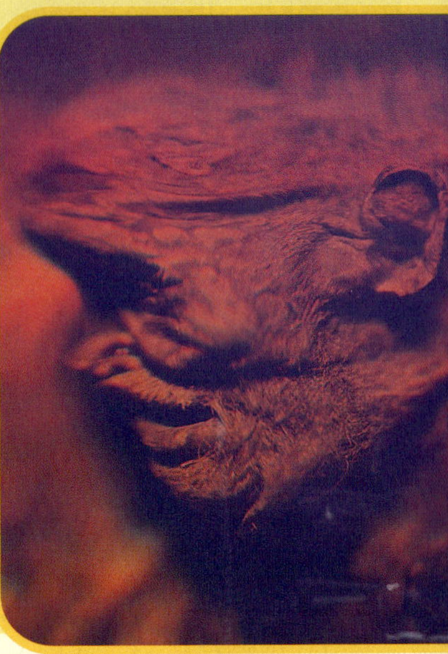

"Lindow Man" lived about 2300 years ago. This hologram allows researchers anywhere in the world to study his form.

Laser light helps capture the information required to form a three-dimensional image on holographic film.

The Science of Holograms

To create a hologram, a person places an object behind or near a sheet of transparent holographic film. Laser light is shown through the film and onto the object. The light reflects off the object and back onto the film, where it meets the original light beam. Like regular photographic film, the holographic film records the light's wavelength (which determines color) and amplitude (which determines intensity, or brightness). But holographic film also captures the interference pattern created by the colliding light beams. After the film is developed and light is shown on the holographic film, tiny reflectors in the film bounce back light at exactly the same directions at which it originally came from the object. The result is a three-dimensional image that appears to float in space. Amazingly, holographic images are so complete that the viewer can view the image from different angles and see different sides of the image, just like a solid object can be viewed.

This full-color hologram is brighter and more realistic thanks to recent advances in holographic film and techniques.

Putting Holograms to Work

Although simple holograms printed on reflective plastic are a common security device on credit cards, holograms that truly appear three-dimensional are not yet widely used. But with recent advances in holographic film, high-definition holograms may soon appear in some unexpected places. Holographic "clones" of art or cultural artifacts may one day be displayed in museums to avoid risk to the originals. Because holographic film contains no pigments or dyes, they do not fade over time and can therefore be used as a permanent three-dimensional record of rare and fragile objects, such as a specimen of a nearly extinct insect. The technology also exists to create hologram-like images of moving objects—including people—that appear to move through thin air.

Science and You

1. **Applying Knowledge** Why don't images on a TV screen or in photographs appear as real as solid objects?
2. **Applying Knowledge** What two characteristics of light does regular photographic film capture?
3. **Applying Knowledge** What third characteristic of light captured by holographic film gives the holographic image depth?
4. **Critical Thinking** Why do you think some people may object to using holographic images in museums in place of originals?
5. **Critical Thinking** Can you think of a practical application for holographic images not mentioned here? Write a short paragraph explaining how a particular problem or challenge could be solved by using a hologram.

CHAPTER 16

Electricity

Chapter Preview

Electricity arcs across the fusion chamber at Sandia National Laboratory in the large photo above. Video games and all other electrical appliances use the movement of electrons to operate.

Background A race car rounds a curve and speeds to the finish line in first place. Afterward, the screen darkens and the driver's score is displayed. Video games are complex pieces of electrical equipment with a detailed video display and computer chips that use electric power supplied by a power plant miles away. And in turn, that energy comes from burning fossil fuels, falling water, the wind, or nuclear fission.

At the Sandia National Laboratory, in New Mexico, powerful electrical arcs are generated in a split second when scientists fire a fusion device. Each electrical arc is similar to a bolt of lightning. A huge number of electrons move across the chamber with each arc. Although they cannot be seen, electrons move inside all electrical devices, including video games. Electricity is involved in many interactions between everyday objects, and is a vital part of the natural world and of every living organism.

Activity 1 Use the bulb and battery from a flashlight, and some wire or aluminum foil to make the light bulb light up. Try connecting the light bulb to the battery in several different ways. What works? What doesn't?

Activity 2 Find your electric meter at home. Observe how the horizontal gear moves and the numbers on the dials change. If you have an electric clothes dryer or air conditioner, observe the dials on the meter when one of these appliances is operating. Compare this with the rate of movement of the dials when all the electrical appliances and lights are turned off. Based on your results, what do you think the electric meter measures?

internet connect

www.scilinks.org
Topic: Applications of the Electric Spark
SciLinks code: HK4008

SCILINKS® Maintained by the National Science Teachers Association

Pre-Reading Questions

1. Why are power outages more common during thunderstorms?
2. Make a list of all the electrical devices in your home. What do they all have in common? How do they differ?

SECTION 1

Electric Charge and Force

KEY TERMS

electric charge
electrical conductor
electrical insulator
electric force
electric field

OBJECTIVES

- **Indicate** which pairs of charges will repel and which will attract.
- **Explain** what factors affect the strength of the electric force.
- **Describe** the characteristics of the electric field due to a charge.

Disc Two, Module 15:
Force Between Charges
Use the Interactive Tutor to learn more about this topic.

When you speak into a telephone, the microphone in the handset changes your sound waves into electric signals. Light shines in your room when you flip a switch. And if you step on a pin with bare feet, your nerves send messages back and forth between your brain and your muscles so that you react quickly. These messages are carried by electric pulses moving through your nerve cells.

Electric Charge

electric charge an electrical property of matter that creates electric and magnetic forces and interactions

You have probably been shocked from touching a doorknob after walking across a rug on a dry day. This happens because your body picks up **electric charge** as your shoes move across the carpet. Although you may not notice these charges when they are spread throughout your body, you notice them as they pass from your finger to the metal doorknob. You experience this movement of charges as a shock.

Like charges repel, and opposite charges attract

One way to observe charge is to rub a balloon back and forth across your hair. You may find that the balloon is attracted to your hair, as shown in ***Figure 1A.*** If you rub two balloons across your hair and then gently bring them near each other, as shown in ***Figure 1B,*** the balloons will push away from, or repel, each other.

Figure 1

A If you rub a balloon across your hair on a dry day, the balloon and your hair become charged and are attracted to each other.

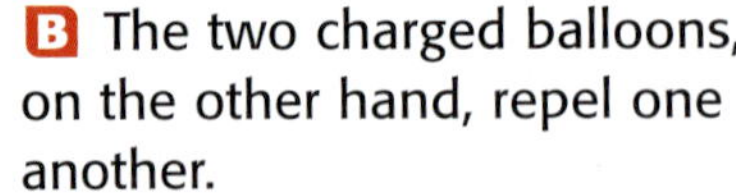

B The two charged balloons, on the other hand, repel one another.

After this experiment, the balloons and your hair have some kind of charge on them. Your hair is attracted to both balloons, yet the two balloons are repelled by each other. This means there must be two types of charges—the type on the balloons and the type on your hair.

The two balloons must have the same kind of charge because each became charged in the same way. Because the two charged balloons repel each other, we see that like charges repel. However, a rubbed balloon and your hair, which did not become charged in the same way, are attracted to one another. This is because unlike charges attract.

The two types of charges are called *positive* and *negative*. When you rub a balloon on your hair, the charge on your hair is positive and the charge on the balloon is negative. When there is an equal amount of positive and negative charges on an object, it has no net charge.

Connection to SOCIAL STUDIES

Benjamin Franklin (1706–1790) first suggested the terms *positive* and *negative* for the two different types of charge.

At the age of 40, Franklin was a successful printer and journalist. He saw some experiments on electricity and was so fascinated by them that he began to devote much of his time to experimenting.

Franklin was the first person to realize that lightning is a huge electric discharge, or spark. He invented the first lightning rod, for which he became famous. He also flew a kite into thunderclouds—at great risk to his life—to collect charge from them.

During and after the Revolutionary War, Franklin gained fame as a politician and statesman.

Making the Connection

1. Franklin is credited with many famous inventions besides his groundbreaking electricity experiments. Prepare a presentation in the form of a skit, story, or computer program about his work on fire departments, public libraries, or post offices.
2. One of Franklin's other technological achievements was the invention of the Franklin stove. Research this stove, and write a brochure explaining the benefits of this stove to prospective customers of Franklin's time. WRITING SKILL

An object's electric charge depends on the imbalance of its protons and electrons

All matter, including you, is made up of atoms. Atoms in turn are made up of even smaller building blocks—electrons, protons, and neutrons. Electrons are negatively charged, protons are positively charged, and neutrons are neutral (no charge).

Objects are made up of an enormous number of neutrons, protons, and electrons. Whenever there is an imbalance in the number of protons and electrons in an atom, molecule, or other object, it has a net electric charge. The difference in the numbers of protons and electrons determines an object's electric charge. Negatively charged objects have more electrons than protons. Positively charged objects have fewer electrons than protons.

The SI unit of electric charge is the *coulomb,* C. The electron and proton have exactly the same amount of charge, 1.6×10^{-19} C. Because they are oppositely charged, a proton has a charge of $+1.6 \times 10^{-19}$ C, and an electron has a charge of -1.6×10^{-19} C. An object with a total charge of -1.0 C has 6.25×10^{18} excess electrons. Because the amount of electric charge on an object depends on the numbers of protons and electrons, the net electric charge of a charged object is always a multiple of 1.6×10^{-19} C.

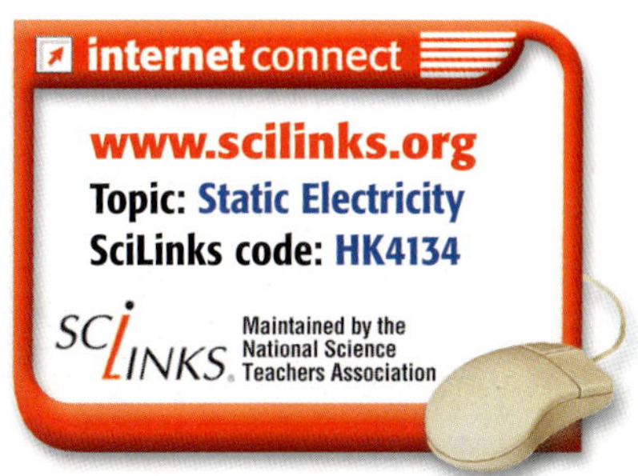

Figure 2

Appliance cords are made of metal wire surrounded by plastic. Electric charges move easily through the wire, but the plastic insulation prevents them from leaking into the surroundings.

electrical conductor a material in which charges can move freely and that can carry an electric current

electrical insulator a material that does not transfer current easily

Conductors allow charges to flow; insulators do not

Have you ever noticed that the electric cords attached to appliances, such as the stereo shown in ***Figure 2,*** are plastic? These cords are not plastic all the way through, however. The center of an electric cord is made of thin copper wires twisted together. Cords are layered like this because of the electric properties of each material.

Materials like the metal in cords are called **conductors.** Conductors allow electric charges to move relatively freely. The plastic in the cord, however, does not allow electric charges to move freely. Materials that do not transfer charge easily are called **insulators.** Cardboard, glass, silk, and plastic are insulators.

Charges in the electric cord attached to an appliance can move through the conducting center but cannot escape through the surrounding insulator. This design makes the appliances more efficient and helps protect people from dangerous electric shock.

INTEGRATING

BIOLOGY

Atoms or molecules with a net electric charge are known as *ions.* All living cells contain ions. Most cells also need to be bathed in solutions of ions to stay alive. As a result, most living things are fairly good conductors.

Dry skin can be a good insulator. But if your skin gets wet it becomes a conductor, and charge can move through your body more easily. So there is a greatly increased risk of electrocution when your skin is wet.

Objects can be charged by the transfer of electrons

Protons and neutrons are relatively fixed in the nucleus of the atom, but the outermost electrons can be easily transferred from one atom to another. When different materials are rubbed together, electrons can be transferred from one material to the other. The direction in which the electrons are transferred depends on the materials.

For example, when you slide across a fabric car seat, some electrons are transferred between your clothes and the car seat. Depending on the types of materials involved, the electrons can be transferred from your clothes to the seat or from the seat to your clothes. One material gains electrons and becomes negatively charged, and the other loses electrons and becomes positively charged. This is an example of *charging by friction.*

Figure 3

A When a negative rod touches a neutral doorknob, electrons move from the rod to the doorknob.

B The transfer of electrons to the metal doorknob gives the doorknob a net negative charge.

Objects can also be charged without friction. One way to charge a neutral object without friction is by touching it with a charged object. As shown in **Figure 3A,** when the negatively charged rubber rod touches a neutral object, like the doorknob, some electrons move from the rod to the doorknob. The doorknob then has a net negative charge, as shown in **Figure 3B.** The rubber rod still has a negative charge, but the charge is smaller. If a positively charged rod touches a neutral doorknob, electrons move into the rod from the neutral doorknob, giving the doorknob a positive charge. Objects charged in this manner are said to be charged by *contact.*

Charges move within uncharged objects

The charges in a neutral conductor can be redistributed without contacting a charged object. If you just bring a negatively charged rubber rod close to the doorknob, the movable electrons in the doorknob will be repelled. Because the doorknob is a conductor, the electrons will move away from the rod. As a result, the portion of the doorknob closest to the negatively charged rod will have an excess of positive charge. The portion farthest from the rod will have a negative charge. But the doorknob will be neutral. Although the total charge on the doorknob will be zero, the opposite sides will have an *induced* charge, as shown in **Figure 4.**

Figure 4

A negatively charged rod brought near a metal doorknob induces a positive charge on the side of the doorknob closest to the rod and a negative charge on the side farthest from the rod.

Figure 5

The negatively charged comb induces a positive charge on the surface of the tissue paper closest to the comb, so the comb and the paper are attracted to each other.

electric force the force of attraction or repulsion between objects due to charge

How can the negatively charged comb in ***Figure 5*** pick up pieces of neutral tissue paper? The electrons in tissue paper cannot move about freely because the paper is an insulator. But when a charged object is brought near an insulator, the positions of the electrons within the individual molecules of the insulator change slightly. One side of a molecule will be slightly more positive or negative than the other side. This *polarization* of the atoms or molecules of an insulator produces an induced charge on the surface of the insulator. The surface of the tissue paper nearest the comb has an induced positive charge. The surface farthest from the comb has an induced negative charge.

Quick ACTIVITY

Charging Objects

1. Rub two air-filled balloons vigorously on a piece of wool.
2. Hold your balloons near each other.
3. Now try to attach one balloon to the wall.
4. Turn on a faucet, and hold a balloon near the stream of tap water.
5. Explain what happens to the charges in the balloons, wool, water, and wall.

Electric Force

The attraction of tissue paper to a negatively charged comb and the repulsion of the two balloons are examples of **electric force.** It is also the reason clothes sometimes cling to each other when you take them out of the dryer. Such pushes and pulls between charges are all around you. For example, a table feels solid, even though its atoms contain mostly empty space. The electric force between the electrons in the table's atoms and your hand is strong enough to prevent your hand from going through the table. In fact, the electric force at the atomic and molecular level is responsible for most of the common forces we can observe, such as the force of a spring and the force of friction.

The electric force is also responsible for effects that we can't see; it is part of what holds an atom together. The bonding of atoms to form molecules is also due to the electric force. The electric force plays a part in the interactions among molecules, such as the proteins and other building blocks of our bodies. Without the electric force, life itself would be impossible.

Electric force depends on charge and distance

The electric force between two charged objects varies depending on the amount of charge on each object and the distance between them. The electric force between two objects is proportional to the product of the charges on the objects. If the charge on one object is doubled, the electric force between the objects will also be doubled.

The electric force is also inversely proportional to the square of the distance between two objects. For example, if the distance between two small charges is doubled, the electric force between them decreases to one-fourth its original value. If the distance between two small charges is quadrupled, the electric force between them decreases to one-sixteenth its original value.

Electric force acts through a field

As described earlier, electric force does not require that objects touch. How do charges interact over a distance? One way to model this property of charges is with the concept of an **electric field.** A charged particle produces an electric field in the space around it. Another charged particle in that field will experience an electric force. This force is due to the electric field associated with the first charged particle.

electric field a region in space around a charged object that causes a stationary charged object to experience an electric force

One way to show an electric field is by drawing *electric field lines*. Electric field lines point in the direction of the electric force on a positive charge. Because two positive charges repel one another, the electric field lines around a positive charge point outward, as shown in ***Figure 6A.*** In contrast, the electric field lines around a negative charge point inward, as shown in ***Figure 6B.*** Regardless of the charge, electric field lines never cross one another.

Figure 6

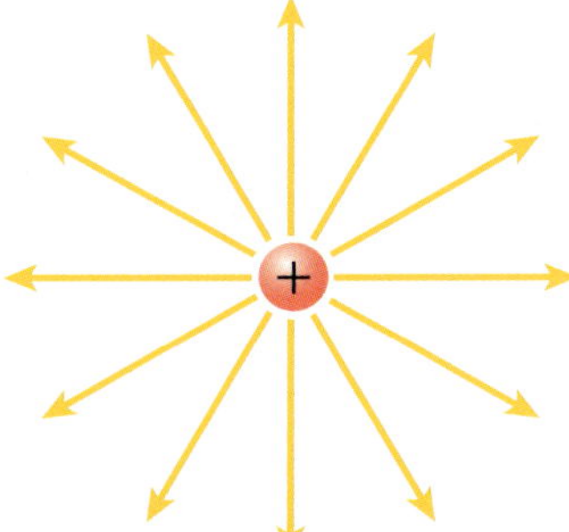

A The electric field lines show that a positive charge placed in the electric field due to a positive charge would be pushed away.

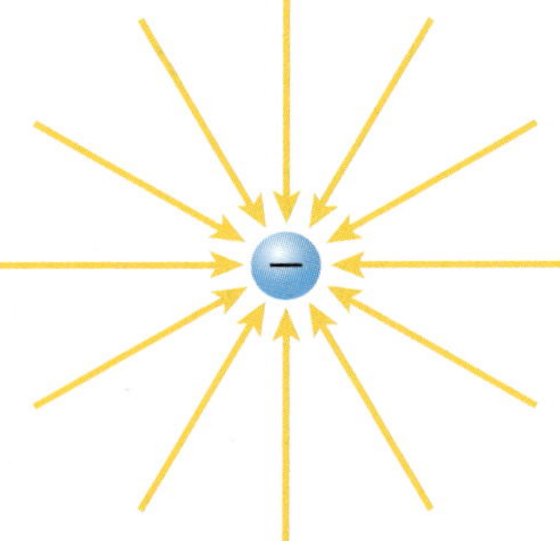

B A positive charge placed in the electric field due to a negative charge would be pulled in.

Did You Know?

Electric force and gravitational force both depend on a physical property of objects—charge and mass, respectively—and the distance between the objects. They have the same mathematical form. But gravitational force is attractive, while electric force is both attractive and repulsive. Also, the electric force between two charged particles separated by a given distance is much greater than the gravitational force between the particles.

Figure 7

A The electric field lines for two positive charges show the repulsion between the charges.

B Half the field lines starting on the positive charge end on the negative charge because the positive charge is twice as great as the negative charge.

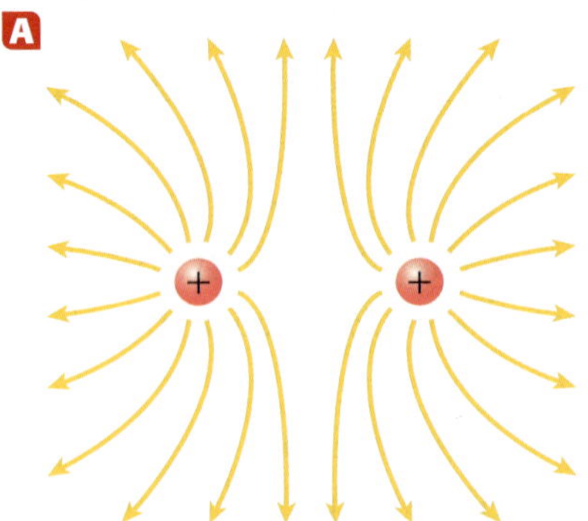

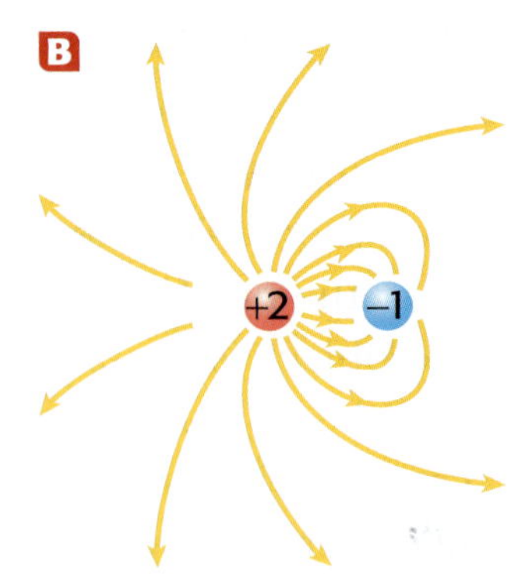

You can see from ***Figure 7*** that the electric field between two charges can be represented using these rules. The field lines in ***Figure 7A*** point away from the positive charges, showing that the positive charges repel each other. Field lines show not only the direction of an electric field but also the relative strength due to a given charge. As shown in ***Figure 7B,*** there are twice as many field lines pointing outward from the +2 charge as there are ending on the −1 charge. More lines are drawn for greater charges to indicate greater force.

SECTION 1 REVIEW

SUMMARY

- There are two types of electric charge, positive and negative.
- Like charges repel; unlike charges attract.
- The electric force between two charged objects is proportional to the product of the charges and inversely proportional to the square of the distance between the objects.
- Electric force acts through electric fields.
- Electric fields surround charged objects. Any charged object that enters an electric field experiences an electric force.

1. **Identify** the electric charge of each of the following atomic particles: a proton, a neutron, and an electron.
2. **Describe** the interaction between two like charges. Is the interaction the same between two unlike charges?
3. **Diagram** what will happen if a positively charged rod is brought near the following objects:
   a. a metal washer **b.** a plastic disk
4. **Categorize** the following as conductors or insulators:
   a. copper wire
   b. your body when your skin is wet
   c. a plastic comb
5. **Explain** how the electric force between two positive charges changes if
   a. the distance between the charges is tripled.
   b. the amount of one charge is doubled.
6. **Critical Thinking** What missing electric charge would produce the electric field shown at right?

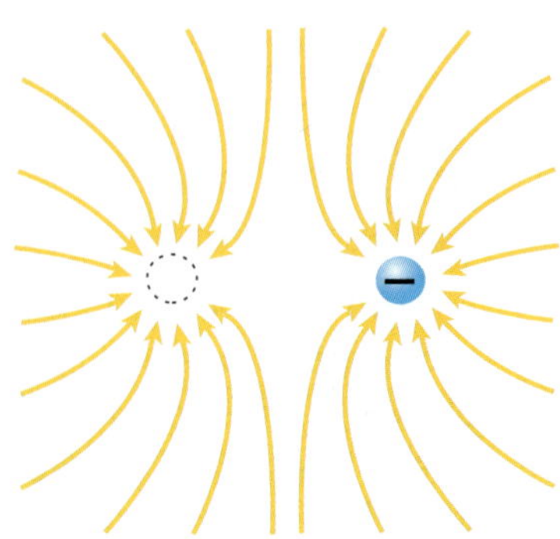

SECTION 2

Current

OBJECTIVES

- **Describe** how batteries are sources of voltage.
- **Explain** how a potential difference produces a current in a conductor.
- **Define** *resistance.*
- **Calculate** the resistance, current, or voltage, given the other two quantities.
- **Distinguish** between conductors, superconductors, semiconductors, and insulators.

KEY TERMS

electrical potential energy
potential difference
cell
current
resistance

When you wake up in the morning, you reach up and turn on the light switch. The light bulb is powered by moving charges. How do charges move through a light bulb? And what causes the charges to move?

Disc Two, Module 8:
Batteries and Cells
Use the Interactive Tutor to learn more about these topics.

Voltage and Current

Gravitational potential energy depends on the relative position of the ball, as shown in ***Figure 8A.*** A ball rolling downhill moves from a position of higher gravitational potential energy to one of lower gravitational potential energy. An electric charge also has potential energy—**electrical potential energy**—that depends on its position in an electric field.

electrical potential energy the ability to move an electric charge from one point to another

Just as a ball will roll downhill, a negative charge will move away from another negative charge. This is because of the first negative charge's electric field. The electrical potential energy of the moving charge decreases, as shown in ***Figure 8B,*** because the electric field does work on the charge.

A

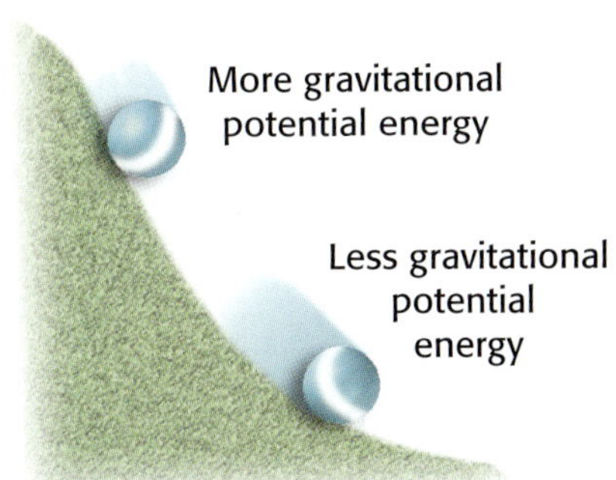

B

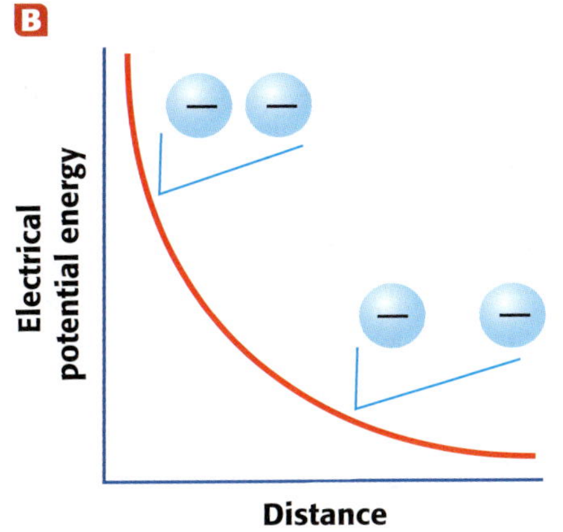

Figure 8

A The gravitational potential energy of a ball decreases as it rolls downhill.

B The electrical potential energy between two negative charges decreases as the distance between them increases.

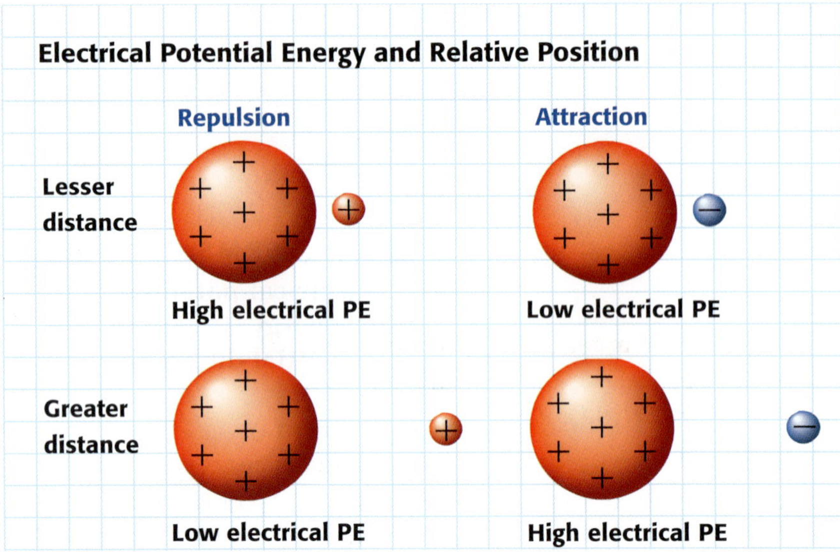

Figure 9
The electrical potential energy of a charge depends on its position in an electric field.

You can do work on a ball to move it uphill. This will increase the ball's gravitational potential energy. In the same way, a force can push a charge in the opposite direction of the electric force. This increases the electrical potential energy associated with the charge's relative position. **Figure 9** shows how the electrical potential energy depends on the distance between two charged objects for both an attractive and a repulsive electric force.

Potential difference is measured in volts

Usually, it is more practical to consider the **potential difference** than electrical potential energy. Potential difference is the change in the electrical potential energy of a charged particle divided by its charge. This change occurs as a charge moves from one place to another in an electric field.

The SI unit for potential difference is the *volt,* V, which is equivalent to one joule per coulomb (1 J/C). For this reason, potential difference is often called *voltage.*

potential difference between any two points, the work that must be done against electric forces to move a unit charge from one point to the other

cell a device that is a source of electric current because of a potential difference, or voltage, between the terminals

There is a voltage across the terminals of a battery

The voltage across the two *terminals* of a battery can range from about 1.5 V for a small battery to about 12 V for a car battery, as shown in **Figure 10.** Most common batteries are an electric **cell**—or a combination of connected electric cells—that convert chemical energy into electrical energy. One terminal is positive, and the other is negative. A summary of various types of electric cells is given in **Table 1.**

Electrochemical cells contain an *electrolyte,* a solution that conducts electricity, and two *electrodes,* each a different conducting material. These cells can be dry cells or wet cells. Dry cells, such as those used in flashlights, contain a paste-like electrolyte. Wet cells, such as those used in almost all car batteries, contain a liquid electrolyte. An average cell has a potential difference of 1.5 V between the positive and negative terminals.

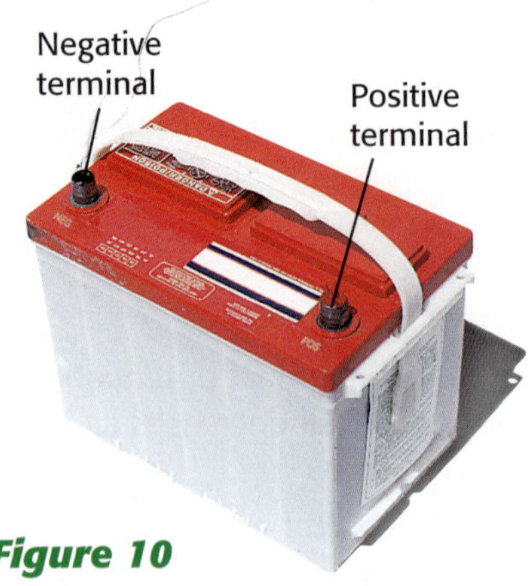

Figure 10
For a typical car battery, there is a voltage of 12 V across the negative (black) terminal and the positive (red) terminal.

A voltage sets charges in motion

When a flashlight is switched on, the terminals of the battery are connected through the light bulb. Electrons move through the light bulb from the negative terminal to the positive terminal.

Table 1 Types of Electric Cells

Electrical cell	Basic principle	Uses
Electrochemical	Electrons are transferred between different metals immersed in an electrolyte.	Common batteries, automobile batteries
Photoelectric and photovoltaic	Electrons are released from a metal when struck by light of sufficient energy.	Artificial satellites, calculators, streetlights
Thermoelectric	Two different metals are joined together, and the junctions are held at different temperatures, causing electrons to flow.	Thermostats for furnaces and ovens
Piezoelectric	Opposite surfaces of certain crystals become electrically charged when under pressure.	Crystal microphones and headsets, computer keypads, record cartridge

When charges are accelerated by an electric field to move to a position of lower potential energy, an electric **current** is produced. Current is the rate at which these charges move through a conductor. The SI unit of current is the *ampere,* A. One ampere, or *amp,* equals 1 C of charge moving past a point in 1 second.

current the rate that electric charges move through a conductor

A battery is a *direct current* source because the charges always move from one terminal to the other in the same direction. Current can be made up of positive, negative, or a combination of both positive and negative charges. In metals, moving electrons make up the current. In gases and many chemical solutions, current is the result of both positive and negative charges in motion.

In our bodies, current is mostly positive charge movement. Nerve signals are in the form of a changing voltage across the nerve cell membrane. **Figure 11A** shows that a resting cell has more negative charges on the inside than on the outside. **Figure 11B** shows how a nerve impulse moves along the cell membrane. As one end of the cell is stimulated, channels nearby in the cell membrane open, allowing Na^+ ions to enter. Later, potassium channels open, and K^+ ions exit the cell, restoring the original voltage across the cell membrane.

Figure 11

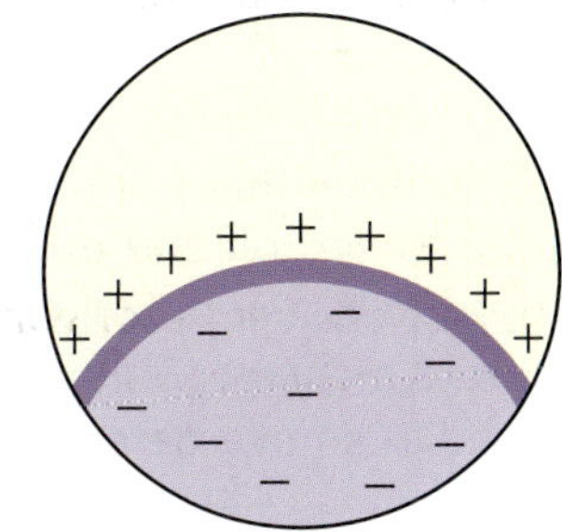

A A resting nerve cell is more negatively charged than its surroundings.

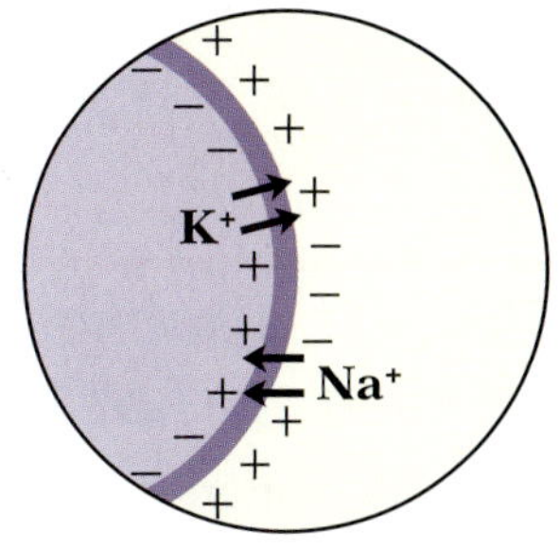

B As a nerve impulse moves along the cell membrane, the voltage across it changes.

Conventional current is defined as movement of positive charge

A negative charge moving in one direction has the same effect as a positive charge moving in the opposite direction. *Conventional current* is defined as the current made of positive charge that would have the same effect as the actual motion of charge in the material. *In this book, the direction of current will always be given as the direction of positive charge movement that is equivalent to the actual motion of charges in the material.* So the direction of current in a wire is opposite the direction that electrons move in that wire.

Which Is the Best Type of Battery?

"Heavy-duty," "long-lasting alkaline," and "environmentally friendly rechargeable" are some of the labels that manufacturers put on batteries. But how do you know which type to use?

The answer depends on how you will use the battery. Some batteries are used continuously, but others are turned off and on frequently, such as those used in a stereo. Still other batteries must be able to hold a charge without being used, such as those used in smoke detectors and flashlights.

Heavy-Duty Batteries Are Inexpensive

In terms of price, a heavy-duty battery typically costs the least but lasts only about 30 percent as long as an alkaline battery. This makes heavy-duty batteries impractical for most uses and an unnecessary source of landfill clutter.

Regular Alkaline Batteries Are Expensive but Long Lasting

Regular alkaline batteries are more expensive but have longer lives, lasting up to 6 hours with continuous use and up to 18 hours with intermittent use. They hold a full charge for years, making them good for use in flashlights and similar devices. They are less of an environmental problem than they previously were because manufacturers have stopped using mercury in them. However, because they are single-use batteries, they also end up in landfills very quickly.

Rechargeable Batteries Don't Clutter Landfills

Rechargeable batteries are the most expensive to purchase initially. If recycled, however, they are the most economical in the long run and are the most environmentally sound choice. The most common rechargeable cells are either NiCads—containing nickel, Ni, and cadmium, Cd, metals—or alkaline. Either type of rechargeable battery can be recharged hundreds of times. Although rechargeable batteries last only about half as long on one charge as regular alkaline batteries, the energy to recharge them costs pennies. Rechargeable NiCads lose about 1% of their stored energy each day they are not used and should therefore never be used in smoke detectors or flashlights.

Your Choice

1. **Making Decisions** Which type of battery would you use in a portable stereo? Explain your reasoning.
2. **Critical Thinking** Why is it important not to use NiCads in smoke detectors?
3. **Locating Information** Use library resources or the Internet to learn more about batteries used in gasoline-powered and electric cars. Prepare a summary of the types of rechargeable car batteries available.

Using a Lemon as a Cell

Because lemons are very acidic, their juice can act as an electrolyte. If various metals are inserted into a lemon to act as electrodes, the lemon can be used as an electrochemical cell.

SAFETY CAUTION Handle the wires only where they are insulated.

1. Using a knife, make two parallel cuts 6 cm apart along the middle of a juicy lemon. Insert a copper strip into one of the cuts and a zinc strip the same size into the other.
2. Cut two equal lengths of insulated copper wire. Use wire strippers to remove the insulation from both ends of each wire. Connect one end of each wire to one of the terminals of a galvanometer.
3. Touch the free end of one wire to the copper strip in the lemon. Touch the free end of the other wire to the zinc strip, as shown in the figure at right. Record the galvanometer reading for the zinc-copper cell.
4. Replace the strips of copper and zinc with equally sized strips of different metals. Record the galvanometer readings for each pair of electrodes. Which pair of electrodes resulted in the largest current?
5. Construct a table of your results.

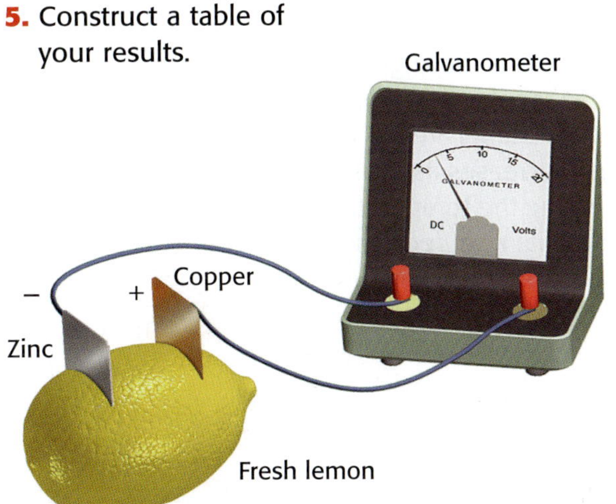

Electrical Resistance

Most electrical appliances you plug into an outlet are designed for the same voltage: 120 V. But light bulbs come in many varieties, from dim 40 W bulbs to bright 100 W bulbs. These bulbs shine differently because they have different amounts of current in them. The difference in current between these bulbs is due to their **resistance.** Resistance is caused by internal friction, which slows the movement of charges through a conducting material. Because it is difficult to measure the internal friction directly, resistance is defined by a relationship between the voltage across a conductor and the current through it.

resistance the opposition posed by a material or a device to the flow of current

The resistance of the *filament* of a light bulb, as shown in ***Figure 12,*** determines how bright the bulb is. The filament of a dim 40 W light bulb has a higher resistance than the filament of a bright 100 W light bulb.

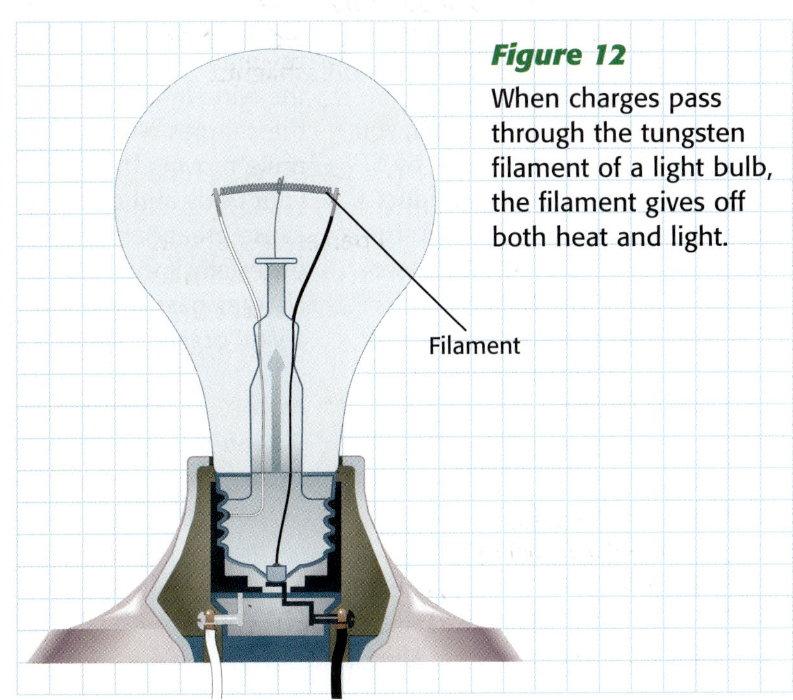

Figure 12 When charges pass through the tungsten filament of a light bulb, the filament gives off both heat and light.

Resistance can be calculated from current and voltage

You have probably noticed that electrical devices such as televisions or stereos become warm after they have been on for a while. As moving electrons collide with the atoms of the material, some of their kinetic energy is transferred to the atoms. This energy transfer causes the atoms to vibrate, and the material warms up. In most materials, some of the kinetic energy of electrons is lost as heat.

A conductor's resistance indicates how much the motion of charges within it is resisted because of collisions. Resistance is found by dividing the voltage across the conductor by the current.

Resistance Equation

$$resistance = \frac{voltage}{current} \qquad R = \frac{V}{I}$$

The SI unit of resistance is the *ohm*, Ω, which is equal to volts per ampere. If a voltage across a conductor of 1 V produces a current of 1 A, then the resistance of the conductor is 1 Ω.

A *resistor* is a special type of conductor used to control current. Every resistor is designed to have a specific resistance. For example, for any applied voltage, the current in a 10 Ω resistor is half the current in a 5 Ω resistor.

Did You Know?

Resistance depends on the material used as well as the material's length, cross-sectional area, and temperature. Longer pieces of a material have greater resistance. Increasing the cross-sectional area of a material decreases its resistance. Lowering the temperature of a material also decreases its resistance.

The Danger of Electric Shock

If you are in contact with the ground or with water, you can receive an electric shock by touching an uninsulated conducting, or "live," wire. An electric shock from such a wire can result in serious burns or even death.

The degree of damage to your body by an electric shock depends on several factors. Large currents are more dangerous than smaller currents. A current of 0.1 A is often fatal. But the amount of time you are exposed to the current also matters. If the current is larger than about 0.01 A, the muscles in the hand touching the wire contract, and you may be unable to let go of the wire. In this case, the charges will continue moving through your body and can cause great damage, especially if the charges pass through a vital organ, such as the heart.

Current (A)	Effect
0.001	Slight tingle
0.005	Pain
0.010	Muscle spasms
0.015	Loss of muscle control
0.070	Probably fatal (if contact is more than 1 second)

Applying Information

1. You can use the definition of *resistance* to calculate the amount of current that would be in a body, given the voltage and resistance. Using the table above as a reference, determine the effect of touching the terminals of a 24 V battery. Assume that your body is dry and has a resistance of 100 000 Ω.
2. If your skin is moist, your body's resistance is only about 1000 Ω. How would touching the terminals of a 24 V battery affect your body if your skin is moist?

Math Skills

Resistance The headlights of a typical car are powered by a 12 V battery. What is the resistance of the headlights if they draw 3.0 A of current when turned on?

1 List the given and unknown values.

Given: *current,* $I = 3.0$ A

voltage, $V = 12$ V

Unknown: *resistance,* $R = ?\ \Omega$

2 Write the equation for resistance.

$$resistance = \frac{voltage}{current} \qquad R = \frac{V}{I}$$

3 Insert the known values into the equation, and solve.

$$R = \frac{V}{I} = \frac{12\ \text{V}}{3.0\ \text{A}}$$

$$R = 4.0\ \Omega$$

Practice

Resistance

1. Find the resistance of a portable lantern that uses a 24 V power supply and draws a current of 0.80 A.
2. The current in a resistor is 0.50 A when connected across a voltage of 120 V. What is its resistance?
3. The current in a handheld video game is 0.50 A. If the resistance of the game's circuitry is 12 Ω, what is the voltage produced by the battery?
4. A 1.5 V battery is connected to a small light bulb with a resistance of 3.5 Ω. What is the current in the bulb?

Practice HINT

- When a problem requires you to calculate the resistance of an object, you can use the resistance equation as shown on the previous page.
- The resistance equation can also be rearranged to isolate voltage on the left in the following way:

$$R = \frac{V}{I}$$

Multiply both sides by I.

$$IR = \frac{VI}{I}$$

$$V = IR$$

You will need this version of the equation for Practice Problem 3.

- For Practice Problem 4, you will need to rearrange the equation to isolate current on the left.

Conductors have low resistances

Whether or not charges will move in a material depends partly on how tightly electrons are held in the atoms of the material. A good conductor is any material in which electrons can flow easily under the influence of an electric field. Metals, like the copper found in wires, are some of the best conductors because electrons can move freely throughout them. Certain metals, conducting alloys, or carbon are used in resistors.

When you flip the switch on a flashlight, the light seems to come on immediately. But the electrons don't travel that rapidly. The electric field is directed through the conductor at almost the speed of light when a voltage source is connected to the conductor. Electrons everywhere throughout the conductor simultaneously experience a force due to the electric field and move in the opposite direction of the field lines. This is why the light comes on so quickly in a flashlight.

Some materials become superconductors below a certain temperature

Certain metals and compounds have zero resistance when their temperature falls below a certain temperature called the *critical temperature*. These types of materials are called *superconductors*. The critical temperature varies among materials, from less than −272°C (−458°F) to as high as −123°C (−189°F).

Metals such as niobium, tin, and mercury and some metallic compounds containing barium, copper, and oxygen become superconductors below their respective critical temperatures. Superconductors have been used in electrical devices such as filters, powerful magnets, and Maglev high-speed express trains.

Figure 13

Most electrical devices contain conductors, insulators, and semiconductors.

Semiconductors are intermediate to conductors and insulators

Semiconductors belong to a third class of materials with electrical properties between those of insulators and conductors. In their pure state, semiconductors are insulators. The controlled addition of specific atoms of other materials as impurities dramatically increases a semiconductor's ability to conduct electric charge. Silicon and germanium are two common semiconductors. Complex electrical devices, like the computer board shown in **Figure 13,** are made of conductors, insulators, and semiconductors.

Quick Lab

How can materials be classified by resistance?

Materials

- 6 V battery
- flashlight bulb in base holder
- 2 wire leads with alligator clips
- 2 metal hooks
- block of wood
- glass stirring rod
- iron nail
- wooden dowel
- copper wire
- piece of chalk
- strip of cardboard
- plastic utensil
- aluminum nail
- brass key
- strip of cork

1. Construct a conductivity tester, as shown in the diagram.
2. Test the conductivity of various materials by laying the objects one at a time across the hooks of the conductivity tester.

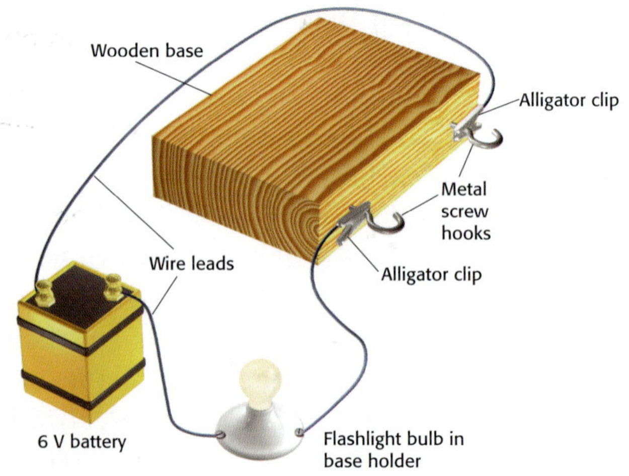

Analysis

1. What happens to the conductivity tester if a material is a good conductor?
2. Which materials were good conductors?
3. Which materials were poor conductors?
4. Explain the results in terms of resistance.

Insulators have high resistance

Insulators have high resistance to charge movement. So insulating materials are used to prevent electric current from leaking. For example, plastic coating around the copper wire of an electric cord keeps the current from escaping into the floor or your body.

Sometimes it is important to provide a pathway for current to leave a charged object. So a conducting wire is run between the charged object and the ground, thereby *grounding* the object. Grounding is an important part of electrical safety.

Many electrical sockets are wired with three connections: two current-carrying wires and the ground wire. If there is any charge buildup, or if the live wire contacts an appliance, the ground wire conducts the charge to Earth. The excess charge can spread over the planet safely.

SECTION 2 REVIEW

SUMMARY

- A charged object has electrical potential energy due to its position in an electric field.
- Potential difference, or voltage, is the difference in electrical potential energy per unit charge.
- A voltage causes charges to move, producing a current.
- Current is the rate of charge movement.
- Electrical resistance can be calculated by dividing voltage by current.
- Conductors are materials in which electrons flow easily.
- Superconductors have no resistance below their critical temperature.
- Insulators are materials with high resistance.

1. **Describe** the motion of charges through a flashlight, from one terminal of a battery to the other.
2. **Identify** which of the following could produce current:
   a. a wire connected across a battery's terminals
   b. two electrodes in a solution of positive and negative ions
   c. a salt crystal, whose ions cannot move
   d. a sugar-water mixture
3. **Predict** which way charges are likely to move between two positions of different electrical potential energy, one high and one low.
   a. from low to high
   b. from high to low
   c. back and forth between high and low
4. **Define** resistance, and state the quantities needed to calculate an object's resistance.
5. **Classify** the following materials as conductors or insulators: wood, paper clip, glass, air, paper, plastic, steel nail, rubber.
6. **Critical Thinking** Recent discoveries have led some scientists to hope that a material will be found that is superconducting at room temperature. Why would such a material be useful?

Math Skills

7. If the current in a certain resistor is 6.2 A and the voltage across the resistor is 110 V, what is its resistance?
8. If the voltage across a flashlight bulb is 3 V and the bulb's resistance is 6 Ω, what is the current through the bulb?

SECTION 3

Circuits

KEY TERMS

electric circuit
schematic diagram
series
parallel
electrical energy
fuse
circuit breaker

OBJECTIVES

- **Use** schematic diagrams to represent circuits.
- **Distinguish** between series and parallel circuits.
- **Calculate** electric power using voltage and current.
- **Explain** how fuses and circuit breakers are used to prevent circuit overload.

Disc Two, Module 16:
Frequency and Wavelength
Use the Interactive Tutor to learn more about these topics.

electric circuit a set of electrical components connected such that they provide one or more complete paths for the movement of charges

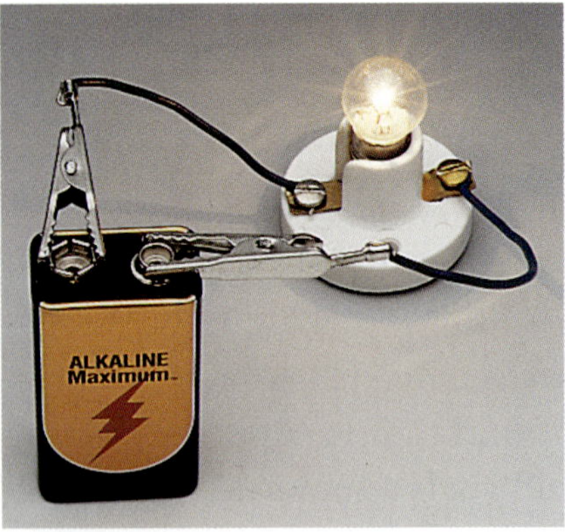

Figure 14
When this battery is connected to a light bulb, the voltage across the battery generates a current that lights the bulb.

Think about how you would get the bulb shown in ***Figure 14*** to light up. Would the bulb light if the bulb were not fully screwed into the socket? How about if one of the clips were removed from the battery?

What Are Circuits?

When a wire connects the terminals of the battery to the light bulb, as shown in ***Figure 14,*** charges that built up on one terminal of the battery have a path to follow to reach the opposite charges on the other terminal. Because there are charges moving uniformly, a current exists. This current causes the filament inside the light bulb to give off heat and light.

An electric circuit is a path through which charges can be conducted

Together, the bulb, battery, and wires form an **electric circuit.** In the circuit shown in ***Figure 14,*** the path from one battery terminal to the other is complete. Because of the voltage of the battery, electrons move through the wires and bulb from the negative terminal to the positive terminal. Then the battery adds energy to the charges as they move within the battery from the positive terminal back to the negative one.

In other words, there is a closed-loop path for electrons to follow. The conducting path produced when the light bulb is connected across the battery's terminals is called a *closed circuit.* Without a complete path, there is no charge flow and therefore no current. This is called an *open circuit.*

The inside of the battery is part of the closed path of current through the circuit. The voltage source, whether a battery or an outlet, is always part of the conducting path of a closed circuit.

Switches interrupt the flow of charges in a circuit

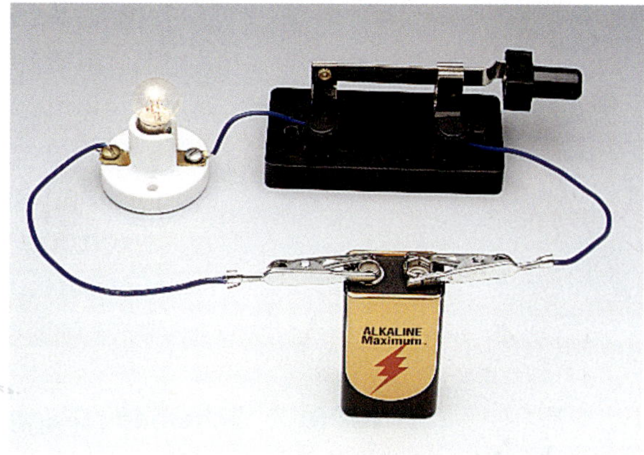

Figure 15

When added to the circuit, a switch can be used to open and close the circuit.

If a device called a *switch* is added to the circuit, as shown in ***Figure 15,*** you can use the switch to open and close the circuit. You have used a switch many times. The switches on your wall at home are used to turn lights on and off. Although they look different from the switch in ***Figure 15,*** their function is the same. When you flip a switch at home, you either close or open the circuit to turn a light on or off.

The switch shown in ***Figure 15*** is called a knife switch. The metal bar is a conductor. When the bar is touching both sides of the switch, as shown in ***Figure 15,*** the circuit is closed. Electrons can move through the bar to reach the other side of the switch and light the bulb. If the metal bar on the switch is lifted, the circuit is open. Then there is no current, and the bulb does not glow.

Schematic diagrams are used to represent circuits

Suppose you wanted to describe to someone the contents and connections in the photo of the light bulb and battery in ***Figure 15.*** How might you draw each element? Could you use the same representations of the elements to draw a bigger circuit?

A diagram that depicts the construction of an electrical circuit or apparatus is called a **schematic diagram.** ***Figure 16*** shows how the battery and light bulb can be drawn as a schematic diagram. The symbols that are used in this figure can be used to describe any other circuit with a battery and one or more bulbs. All electrical devices, from toasters to computers, can be described using schematic diagrams. Because schematic diagrams use standard symbols, they can be read by people all over the world.

schematic diagram a graphical representation of a circuit that uses lines to represent wires and different symbols to represent components

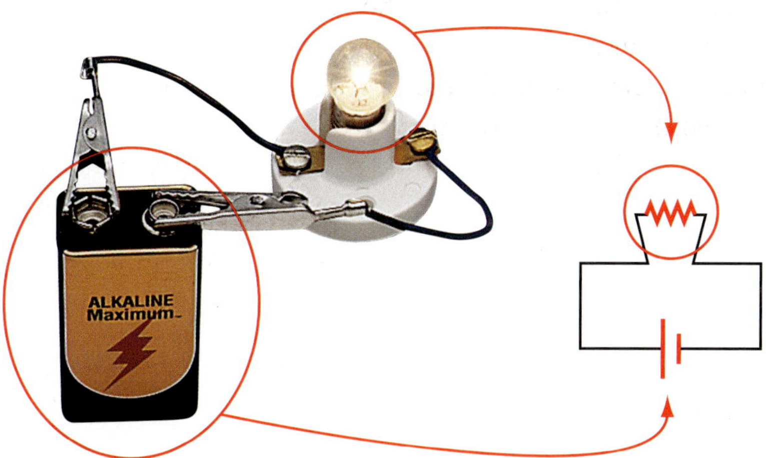

Figure 16

The connections between the light bulb and battery can be represented by symbols. This type of illustration is called a schematic diagram.

As shown in ***Table 2,*** each element used in a piece of electrical equipment is represented by a symbol that reflects the element's construction or function. For example, the schematic-diagram symbol that represents an open switch resembles the open-knife switch shown in the corresponding photograph. Any circuit can be drawn using a combination of these and other, more complex schematic diagram symbols.

Table 2 **Schematic Diagram Symbols**

Component	Symbol used in this book	Explanation
Wire or conductor		Wires that connect elements are conductors.
Resistor		Resistors are shown as wires with multiple bends, indicating resistance to a straight path.
Bulb or lamp		The winding of the filament indirectly indicates that the light bulb is a resistor, something that impedes the movement of electrons or the flow of charge.
Battery or other direct current source	+ –	The difference in line height indicates a voltage between positive and negative terminals of the battery. The taller line represents the positive terminal of the battery.
Switch Open Closed	Open Closed	The small circles indicate the two places where the switch makes contact with the wires. Most switches work by breaking only one of the contacts, not both.

Series and Parallel Circuits

Section 2 showed that the current in a circuit depends on voltage and the resistance of the device in the circuit. What happens when there are two or more devices connected to a battery?

Series circuits have a single path for current

When appliances or other devices are connected in a **series** circuit, as shown in ***Figure 17A,*** they form a single pathway for charges to flow. Charges cannot build up or disappear at a point in a circuit. For this reason, the amount of charge that enters one device in a given time interval equals the amount of charge that exits that device in the same amount of time. Because there is only one path for a charge to follow when devices are connected in series, the current in each device is the same. Even though the current in each device is the same, the resistances may be different. Therefore, the voltage across each device in a series circuit can be different.

If one element along the path in a series circuit is removed, the circuit will not work. For example, if either of the light bulbs in ***Figure 17A*** were removed, the other one would not glow. The series circuit would be open. Several kinds of breaks may interrupt a series circuit. The opening of a switch, the burning out of a light bulb, a cut wire, or any other interruption can cause the whole circuit to fail.

Parallel circuits have multiple paths for current

When devices are connected in **parallel,** rather than in series, the voltage across each device is the same. The current in each device does not have to be the same. Instead, the sum of the currents in all of the devices equals the total current. A simple parallel circuit is shown in ***Figure 17B.*** The two lights are connected to the same points. The electrons leaving one end of the battery can pass through either bulb before returning to the other terminal. If one bulb has less resistance, more charge moves through that bulb because the bulb offers less opposition to the movement of charges.

Even if one of the bulbs in the circuit shown in ***Figure 17B*** were removed, charges would still move through the other loop. Thus, a break in any one path in a parallel circuit does not interrupt the flow of electric charge in the other paths.

Quick ACTIVITY

Series and Parallel Circuits

1. Connect two flashlight bulbs, a battery, wires, and a switch so that both bulbs light up.
2. Make a diagram of your circuit. Is it a series or a parallel circuit?
3. Now make the other type of circuit. Compare the brightness of the bulbs in the two types of circuits.

series the components of a circuit that form a single path for current

parallel a circuit in which all of the components are connected to each other side by side

Figure 17

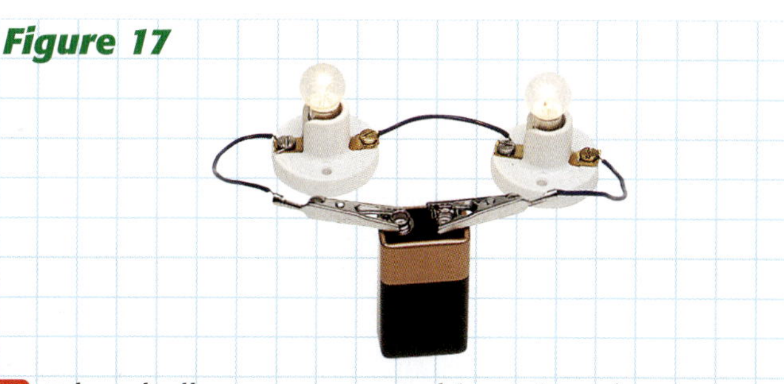

A When bulbs are connected in series, charges must pass through both light bulbs to complete the circuit.

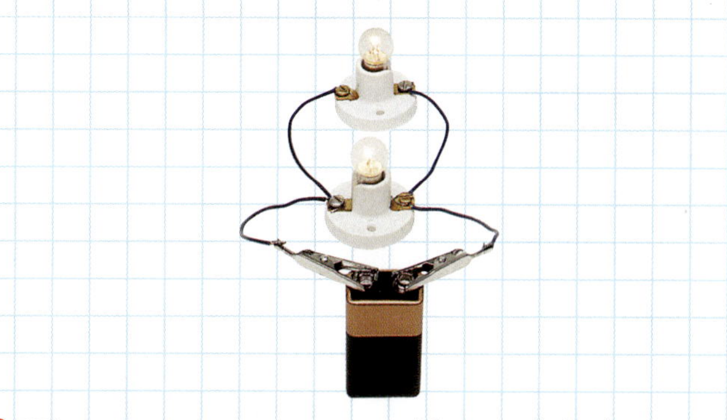

B When devices are connected in parallel, charges have more than one path to follow. The circuit can be complete even if one light bulb burns out.

Electric Power and Electrical Energy

electrical energy the energy that is associated with charged particles because of their positions

Many of the devices you use on a daily basis, such as the toaster shown in ***Figure 18,*** require **electrical energy** to run. The energy for these devices may come from a battery or from a power plant miles away.

Figure 18

Household appliances use electrical energy to do useful work. Some of that energy is lost as heat.

Electric power is the rate at which electrical energy is used in a circuit

When a charge moves in a circuit, it loses energy. This energy is transformed into useful work, such as the turning of a motor, and is lost as heat in a circuit. The rate at which electrical work is done is called *electric power.* Electric power is the product of total current (I) in and voltage (V) across a circuit.

Electric Power Equation

$$power = current \times voltage$$
$$P = IV$$

The SI unit for power is the watt (W). A watt is equivalent to 1 A × 1 V. Light bulbs are rated in terms of watts. For example, a typical desk lamp uses a 60 W bulb. A typical hair dryer is rated at about 1800 W.

If you combine the electric power equation above with the equation $V = IR$, the power lost, or *dissipated,* by a resistor can be calculated.

$$P = I^2R = \frac{V^2}{R}$$

Math Skills

Electric Power When a hair dryer is plugged into a 120 V outlet, it has a 9.1 A current in it. What is the hair dryer's power rating?

1 List the given and unknown values.

Given: *voltage,* $V = 120$ V

current, $I = 9.1$ A

Unknown: *electric power,* $P = ?$ W

2 Write the equation for electric power.

$$power = current \times voltage$$
$$P = IV$$

3 Insert the known values into the equation, and solve.

$$P = (9.1 \text{ A})(120 \text{ V})$$
$$P = 1.1 \times 10^3 \text{ W}$$

VOCABULARY Skills Tip

The SI unit of power, the watt, *was named after the Scottish inventor James Watt in honor of his important work on steam engines.*

Practice

Electric Power

1. An electric space heater requires 29 A of 120 V current to adequately warm a room. What is the power rating of the heater?
2. A graphing calculator uses a 6.0 V battery and draws 2.6×10^{-3} A of current. What is the power rating of the calculator?
3. A color television has a power rating of 320 W. How much current is in the television when it is connected across 120 V?
4. The operating voltage for a light bulb is 120 V. The power rating of the bulb is 75 W. Find the current in the bulb.
5. The current in the heating element of an electric iron is 5.0 A. If the iron dissipates 590 W of power, what is the voltage across it?

Practice HINT

- When a problem requires you to calculate power, you can use the power equation as shown on the previous page.
- The electric power equation can also be rearranged to isolate current on the left in the following way:

$$P = IV$$

Divide both sides by V.

$$\frac{P}{V} = \frac{IV}{V}$$

$$I = \frac{P}{V}$$

You will need this version of the equation for Practice Problems 3 and 4.

- For Practice Problem 5, you will need to rearrange the equation to isolate voltage on the left.

Electric companies measure energy consumed in kilowatt-hours

Power companies charge for energy used in the home, not power. The unit of energy that electric companies use to track consumption of energy is the kilowatt-hour (kW•h). One kilowatt-hour is the energy delivered in 1 hour at the rate of 1 kW. In SI units, 1 kW•h = 3.6×10^6 J.

Depending on where you live, the cost of energy ranges from 5 to 20 cents per kilowatt-hour. All homes and businesses have an electric meter, like the one shown in ***Figure 19.*** Electric meters are used by an electric company to determine how much electrical energy is consumed over a certain time interval.

Figure 19

An electric meter, such as the one shown here, records the amount of energy consumed.

Fuses and Circuit Breakers

When too many appliances, lights, CD players, televisions, and other devices are connected across a 120 V outlet, the overall resistance of the circuit is lowered. That means the electrical wires carry more than a safe level of current. When this happens, the circuit is said to be *overloaded.* The high currents in overloaded circuits can cause fires.

Worn insulation on wires can also be a fire hazard. If a wire's insulation wears down, two wires may touch, creating an alternative pathway for current. This is called a *short circuit.* The decreased resistance greatly increases the current in the circuit. Short circuits can be very dangerous. Grounding appliances reduces the risk of electric shock from a short circuit.

fuse an electrical device that contains a metal strip that melts when current in the circuit becomes too great

circuit breaker a switch that opens a circuit automatically when the current exceeds a certain value

Fuses melt to prevent circuit overloads

To prevent overloading in circuits, **fuses** are connected in series along the supply path. A fuse is a ribbon of wire with a low melting point. If the current in the line becomes too large, the fuse melts and the circuit is opened.

Fuses "blow out" when the current in the circuit reaches a certain level. For example, a 20 A fuse will melt if the current in the circuit exceeds 20 A. A blown fuse is a sign that a short circuit or a circuit overload may exist somewhere in your home. It is best to find out what made a fuse blow out before replacing it.

Circuit breakers open circuits with high current

Many homes are equipped with **circuit breakers** instead of fuses. A circuit breaker uses a magnet or *bimetallic strip,* a strip with two different metals welded together, that responds to current overload by opening the circuit. The circuit breaker acts as a switch. As with blown fuses, it is wise to determine why the circuit breaker opened the circuit. Unlike fuses, circuit breakers can be reset by turning the switch back on.

SECTION 3 REVIEW

SUMMARY

- An electric circuit is a path charges can move along.
- In a series circuit, devices are connected along a single pathway. A break anywhere along the path will stop the current.
- In a parallel circuit, two or more paths are connected to the voltage source. A break along one path will not stop the movement of charges in the other paths.
- Electric power supplied to a circuit or dissipated in a circuit is calculated as the product of the current and voltage.
- Circuit breakers and fuses protect circuits from current overloads.

1. **Identify** the types of elements in the schematic diagram at right and the number of each type.

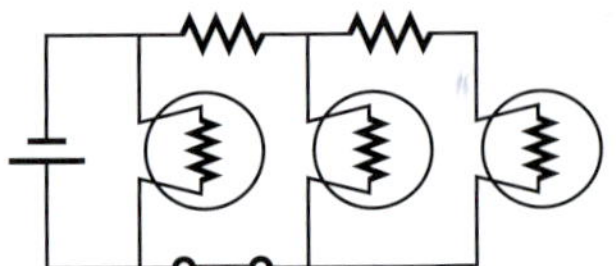

2. **Describe** the advantage of using a parallel arrangement of decorative lights rather than a series arrangement.
3. **Draw** a schematic diagram with four lights in parallel.
4. **Draw** a schematic diagram of a circuit with two light bulbs in which you could turn off either light and still have a complete circuit. (**Hint:** You will need to use two switches.)
5. **Contrast** how a fuse and a circuit breaker work to prevent overloading in circuits.
6. **Critical Thinking** Predict whether a fuse will work successfully if it is connected in parallel with the device it is supposed to protect.

Math Skills

7. When a VCR is connected across a 120 V outlet, the VCR has a 9.5 A current in it. What is the power rating of the VCR?
8. A 40 W light bulb and a 75 W light bulb are in parallel across a 120 V outlet. Which bulb has the greater current?

Graphing Skills

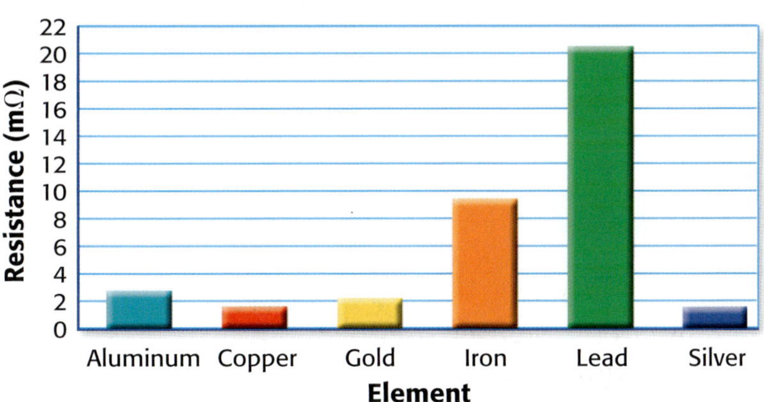

(All wire samples are 0.1 cm^2 in area and 1.0 m in length. Resistances are measured at 20.0°C.)

Examine the graph above and answer the following questions (See Appendix A for help interpreting a graph.)

1. What type of graph is this?
2. What variables are shown in this graph?
3. Identify the dependent variable. What is the relationship between the two variables?
4. The information provided by the graph is restricted to certain conditions. What are those conditions? How would the data vary if these conditions changed?
5. Which element listed would make the poorest conductor? Which listed element conducts electricity best?
6. Suppose aluminum, copper, iron, and silver cost \$0.50, \$0.95, \$0.18, and \$135 per kilogram, respectively. Based on this information and the graph above, which element would you choose as a conductor of electricity over a long distance? Explain your answer.
7. Use the data in the table below to construct the type of graph best suited for the data. How does carbon's electrical behavior differ from that of most conducting metals?

Temperature (°C)	Resistance of Carbon Wire (1.0 m long; 1 cm^2 in area) (Ω)
0	0.354
200	0.318
400	0.284
600	0.248
800	0.214

CHAPTER 16 REVIEW

Chapter Highlights

Before you begin, review the summaries of the key ideas of each section, found at the end of each section. The key vocabulary terms are listed on the first page of each section.

UNDERSTANDING CONCEPTS

1. The electric force between two objects depends on all of the following except
  a. the distance between the objects.
  b. the electric charge of the first object.
  c. how the two objects became electrically charged.
  d. the electric charge of the second object.

2. If two charges attract each other,
  a. both charges must be positive.
  b. both charges must be negative.
  c. the charges must be different.
  d. the charges must be the same.

3. In the figure below,
  a. the positive charge is greater than the negative charge.
  b. the negative charge is greater than the positive charge.
  c. both charges are positive.
  d. both charges are negative.

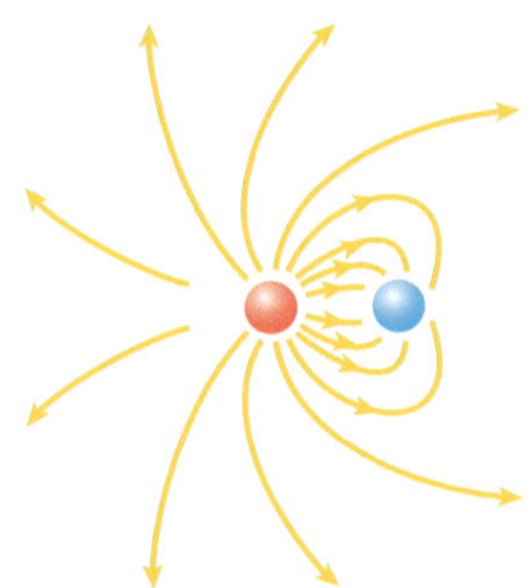

4. The __________ is the change in the electrical potential energy of a charged particle per unit charge.
  a. circuit
  b. voltage
  c. induction
  d. power

5. In order to produce a current in a cell, the terminals must
  a. have a potential difference.
  b. be exposed to light.
  c. be in a liquid.
  d. be at two different temperatures.

6. An electric current does not exist in a(n)
  a. closed circuit.
  b. series circuit.
  c. parallel circuit.
  d. open circuit.

7. Which of the following can help prevent a circuit from overloading?
  a. a fuse
  b. a switch
  c. a circuit breaker
  d. both (a) and (c)

8. Which of the following schematic diagrams represent circuits that cannot have current in them as drawn?

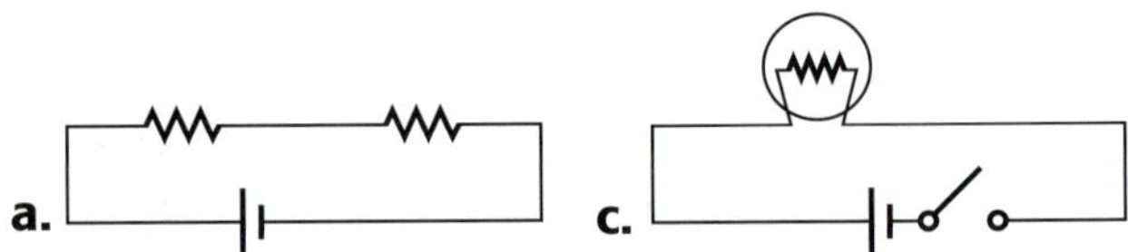

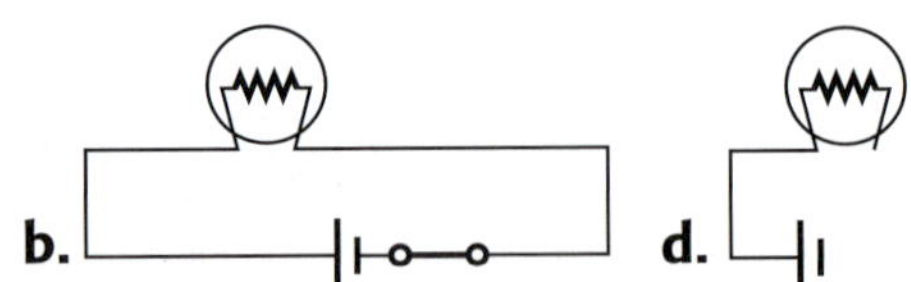

USING VOCABULARY

9. Explain the energy changes involved when a positive charge moves because of a nearby, negatively charged object. Use the terms *electrical potential energy, work,* and *kinetic energy* in your answer.

10. What causes *resistance* in an electric circuit? How is resistance measured?

11. How do charges move through an insulated wire connected across a battery? Use the terms *potential difference, current, conductor,* and *insulator* in your answer.

12. How would you *ground* an electrical appliance?

13. Contrast the movement of charges in a *series circuit* and in a *parallel circuit.* Use a diagram to aid in your explanation.

14. If a string of lights goes out when one of the bulbs is removed, are the lights probably connected in a *series circuit* or a *parallel circuit*? Explain your answer.

15. What is *electric power*? Do electric meters measure electric power? If not, what do they measure?

16. Explain the difference between a *fuse* and a *circuit breaker.* If you were designing a circuit for a reading lamp, would you include a fuse, a circuit breaker, or neither? Explain your answer.

BUILDING MATH SKILLS

17. **Electric Force** The electric force is proportional to the product of the charges and inversely proportional to the square of the distance between them. If q_1 and q_2 are the charges on two objects, and d is the distance between them, which of the following represents the electric force, F, between them?

 a. $F \propto \frac{q_1 q_2}{d}$ **c.** $F \propto \frac{d^2}{q_1 q_2}$

 b. $F \propto \frac{q_1 q_2}{d^2}$ **d.** $F \propto \frac{(q_1 q_2)^2}{d}$

18. **Resistance** A potential difference of 12 V produces a current of 0.30 A in a piece of copper wire. What is the resistance of the copper wire?

19. **Resistance** What is the voltage across a 75 Ω resistor with 1.6 A of current?

20. **Resistance** A nickel wire with a resistance of 25 Ω is connected across the terminals of a 3.0 V flashlight battery. How much current is in the wire?

21. **Power** A portable cassette player uses 3.0 V (two 1.5 V batteries in series) and has 0.33 A of current. What is its power rating?

22. **Power** Find the current in a 2.4 W flashlight bulb powered by a 1.5 V battery.

BUILDING GRAPHING SKILLS

23. **Interpreting Graphs** The graph below shows how electrical potential energy changes as the distance between two charges changes. Is the second charge positive or negative?

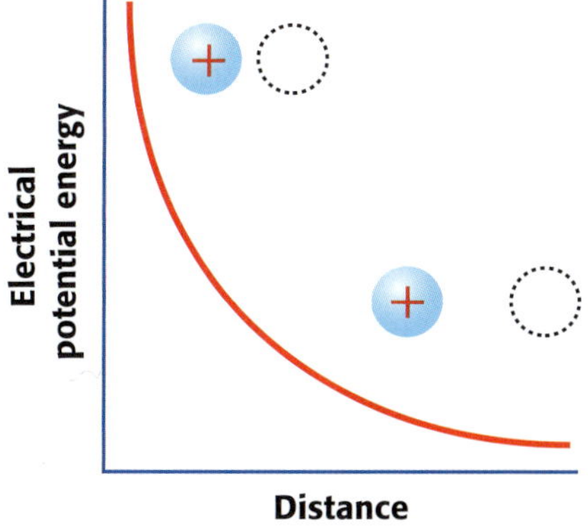

THINKING CRITICALLY

24. **Understanding Systems** Why is charge usually transferred by electrons? Which materials transfer electrons most easily? In what situations can positive charge move?

25. Problem Solving Humid air is a better electrical conductor because it has a higher water content than dry air. Do you expect shocks from static electricity to be worse as the humidity increases or as it decreases? Explain your answer.

26. Understanding Systems The gravitational force is always attractive, while the electric force is both attractive and repulsive. What accounts for this difference?

27. Designing Systems How many ways can you connect three light bulbs in a circuit with a battery? Draw a schematic diagram of each circuit.

28. Applying Knowledge At a given voltage, which light bulb has the greater resistance, a 200 W light bulb or a 75 W light bulb?

DEVELOPING LIFE/WORK SKILLS

29. Interpreting and Communicating COMPUTER SKILL A metal can is placed on a wooden table. If a positively charged ball suspended by a thread is brought close to the can, the ball will swing toward the can, make contact, then move away. Explain why this happens, and predict what will happen to the ball next. Use presentation software or a drawing program to make diagrams showing the charges on the ball and on the can at each phase.

30. Working Cooperatively With a small group of classmates, make a chart about electrical safety in the home and outdoors. Use what you have learned in this chapter and information from your local fire department. Include how to prevent electric shock.

INTEGRATING CONCEPTS

31. Concept Mapping Copy the unfinished concept map below onto a sheet of paper. Complete the map by writing the correct word or phrase in the lettered boxes.

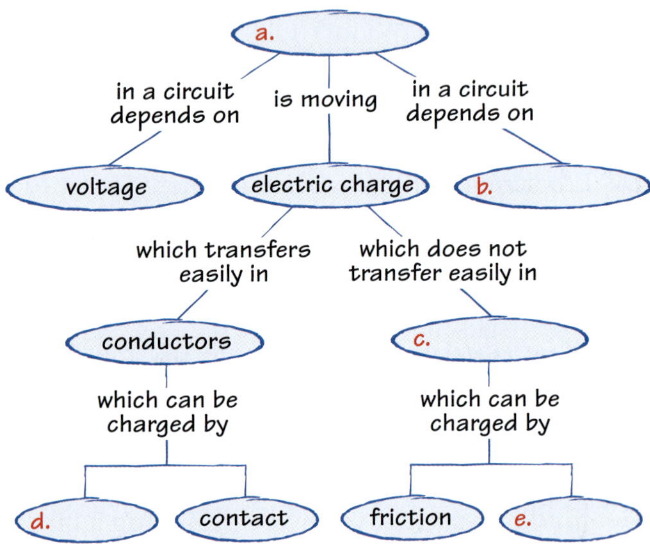

32. Connection to Engineering Research one of the four types of electrical cells. Write a report describing how it works.

33. Connection to Environmental Science Research how an *electrostatic precipitator* removes smoke and dust particles from the polluting emissions of fuel-burning industries. Find out what industries in your community use a precipitator. What are the advantages and costs of using this device? What alternatives are available? Summarize your findings in a brochure, poster, or chart.

Standardized Test Prep

Understanding Concepts

***Directions (1–3):* For *each* question, write on a separate sheet of paper the letter of the correct answer.**

1 A 12-volt battery is connected to a light bulb that has a resistance of 240 ohms. Calculate the amount of current in amperes drawn by the circuit.

A. 0.05 A
B. 0.5 A
C. 2.0 A
D. 20.0 A

2 Which of the following statements is true?

F. Electrical forces exist between any two neutral particles.
G. Electrical forces exist between any two charged particles.
H. Electrical forces exist only between particles with the same charge.
I. Electrical forces exist only between particles with opposite charges.

3 What happens to an object that is charged by induction?

A. It acquires excess electrons.
B. It remains electrically neutral.
C. It acquires a net charge from the object that is inducing the charge.
D. A current exists between it and the object that is inducing the charge.

***Directions (4–5):* For *each* question, write a short response.**

4 A stream of water is deflected when a negatively charged rod is held close to it. Use the concept of induced charge to explain what happens.

5 How does a fuse protect a circuit from overloading?

Test TIP

Using a graph to answer a question, read the graph's title and the labels on the graph's axes. For graphs that show a change in some variable over time, keep in mind that the steepness and direction of a curve indicate the relative rate of change at a given point in time.

Reading Skills

***Directions (6):* Read the passage below. Then answer the question.**

In 1909 Robert Millikan measured the charge on an electron in what is known as the oil-drop experiment. He sprayed oil droplets into a chamber. Two plates with opposite charges produced an electric field. Some of the drops acquired a negative charge. The field was adjusted so there was an upward force equal to the downward pull of gravity. From the strength of this force, Millikan could calculate the amount of the electric charge on the drop.

6 Analyze how the electric field could cause an oil drop to float inside the chamber.

Interpreting Graphics

***Directions (7–8):* Base your answers to questions 7 and 8 on the graph below.**

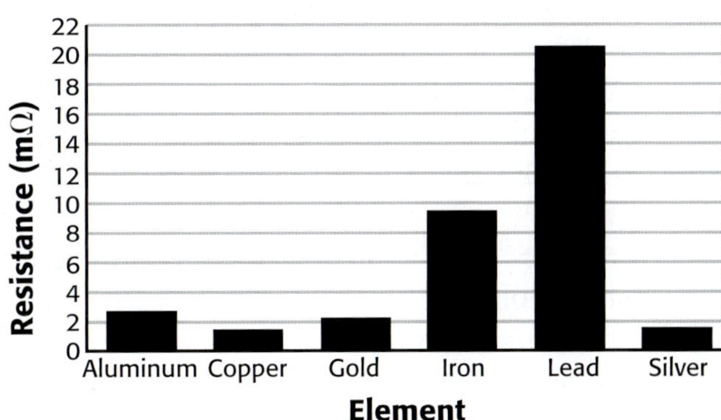

7 Which metal would be the best choice for a power line, based on electrical resistance?

F. aluminum
G. iron
H. lead
I. silver

8 Which metal would most likely be the best substitute for the tungsten filament in an incandescent light bulb based on resistance?

A. aluminum
B. iron
C. lead
D. silver

Skills Practice Lab

Introduction

How can you show how the current that flows through an electric circuit depends on voltage and resistance?

Objectives

- ***Construct*** parallel and series circuits.
- USING SCIENTIFIC METHODS ***Predict*** voltage and current by using the resistance law.
- ***Measure*** voltage, current, and resistance.

Materials

battery holder
connecting wires (3)
dry-cell battery
masking tape
multimeter
resistors (2)

Constructing Electric Circuits

▶ Procedure

1. In this laboratory exercise, you will use an instrument called a multimeter to measure voltage, current, and resistance. Your teacher will demonstrate how to use the multimeter to make each type of measurement.
2. As you read the steps listed below, refer to the diagrams for help making the measurements. Write down your predictions and measurements in your lab notebook. **SAFETY CAUTION** Handle the wires only where they are insulated.

Circuits with a Single Resistor

3. Measure the resistance in ohms of one of the resistors. Write the resistance on a small piece of masking tape, and tape it to the resistor. Repeat for the other resistor.
4. Use the resistance equation to predict the current in amps that will be in a circuit consisting of one of the resistors and one battery. (**Hint:** You must rearrange the equation to solve for current.)
5. Test your prediction by building the circuit. Do the same for the other resistor.

Circuits with Two Resistors in Series

6. Measure the total resistance across both resistors when they are connected in series.

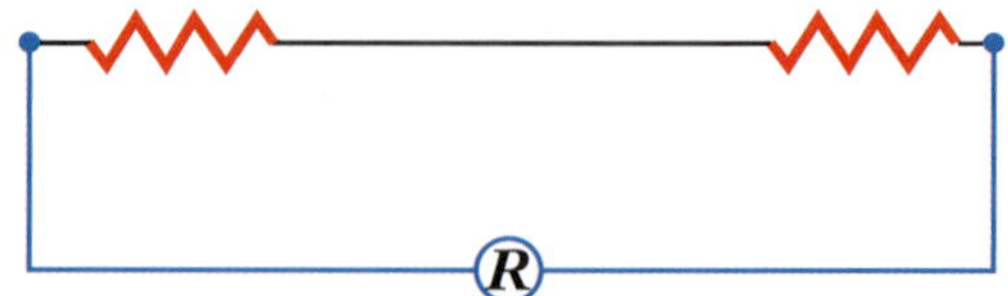

7. Using the total resistance you measured, predict the current that will be in a circuit consisting of one battery and both resistors in series. Test your prediction.

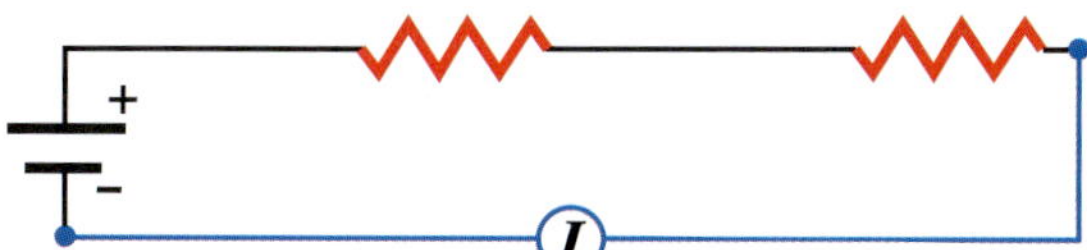

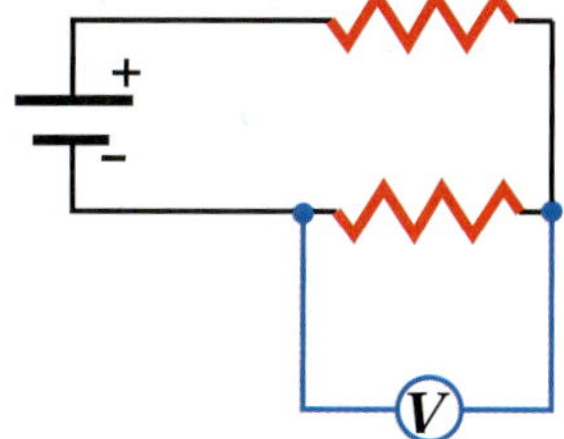

8. Using the current you measured, predict the voltage across each resistor in the circuit you just built. Test your prediction.

Circuits with Two Resistors in Parallel

9. Measure the total resistance across both resistors when they are connected in parallel.
10. Using the total resistance you measured, predict the total current that will be in an entire circuit consisting of one battery and both resistors in parallel. Test your prediction.
11. Predict the current that will be in each resistor individually in the circuit you just built. Test your prediction.

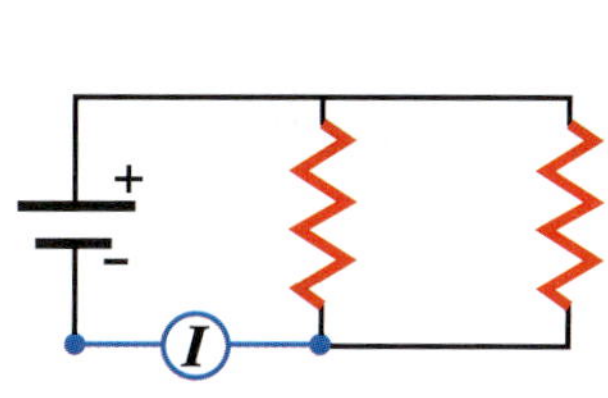

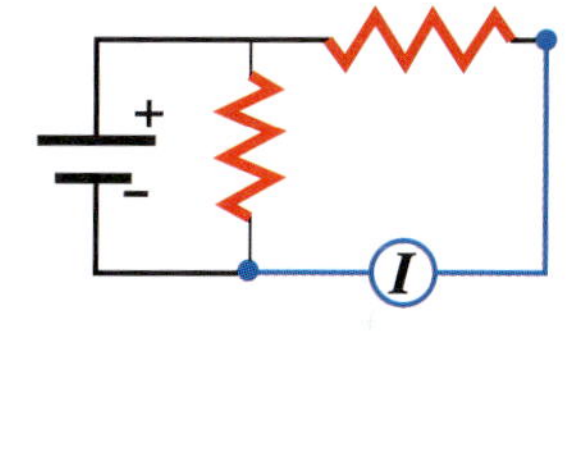

Analysis

1. If you have a circuit consisting of one battery and one resistor, what happens to the current if you double the resistance?
2. What happens to the current if you add a second, identical battery in series with the first battery?
3. What happens to the current if you add a second resistor in parallel with the first resistor?
4. **Reaching Conclusions** Suppose you have a circuit consisting of one battery plus a 10 Ω resistor and a 5 Ω resistor in series. Which resistor will have the greater voltage across it?
5. **Reaching Conclusions** Suppose you have a circuit consisting of one battery plus a 10 Ω resistor and a 5 Ω resistor in parallel. Which resistor will have more current in it?

Conclusions

6. Suppose someone tells you that you can make the battery in a circuit last longer by adding more resistors in parallel. Is that correct? Explain your reasoning.

CareerLink

Physicist

Physicists are scientists who are trying to understand the fundamental rules of the universe. Physicists pursue these questions at universities, private corporations, and government agencies. To learn more about physics as a career, read the interview with physicist Robert Martinez, who works at the University of Texas in Austin, Texas.

What kinds of problems are you studying?

We're working on a technique that will allow us to study single molecules. We could look at, say, molecules on the surface of a cell. What we're doing is building a kind of microscope for optical spectroscopy, which is a way to find out the colors of molecules. Studying the colors of molecules can tell us what those molecules are made of.

How does this allow you to identify molecules?

Atoms act as little beams, and the bonds act as little springs. By exciting them with light, we can get them to vibrate and give off different colors of light. It's a little bit like listening to a musical instrument and telling from the overtones that a piano is different from a trumpet or a clarinet.

Robert Martinez uses a microscope that he has developed to identify single molecules.

"I think of our current project a little bit like the nineteenth century explorers did. They didn't know what they would find on the other side of the ridge or the other side of the ocean, but they had to go look."

What facets of your work do you find most interesting?

The thing that I like about what we're doing is that it's very practical, very hands-on. Also, the opportunity exists to explore whole new areas of physics and chemistry that no one has explored before. What we are doing has the promise of giving us new tools—new "eyes"—to look at important problems.

What qualities do you think a physicist needs?

You've got to be innately curious about how the world works, and you've got to think it's understandable and you are capable of understanding it. You've got to be courageous. You've got to be good at math.

Can you remember any experiences that were particularly valuable for you?

When I was growing up, my dad was a pipe fitter for the city of Los Angeles, and I got to be his apprentice. I got a lot of practical experience that way. I think it's important to take the lawn mower engine apart, take the toaster apart—unplug it first—and see how it works.

Which part of your education was most important?

I liked graduate school a great deal. When I started in research, I had an adviser who was very hands off. What I got was the freedom to go as high as I could or to fall on my face. It was a place where I could stretch out and use things I had under my belt but didn't get to use in the classroom. Outside of school, my dad was my best teacher. He was very bright and had a lot of practical experience.

What advice would you give someone interested in physics?

If it interests you at all, stick with it. If you have doubts, try to talk to people who know what physicists do and know about physics training. The number of people with physics training far exceed the number of people who work as physicists. A good fraction of engineering is physics, for instance.

internet connect

www.scilinks.org
Topic: Physicist
SciLinks code: HK4105

SCILINKS. Maintained by the National Science Teachers Association

"I think that children are born scientists. It's just a matter of keeping your eyes open—keeping your curiosity alive."
—Robert Martinez

CHAPTER 17

Magnetism

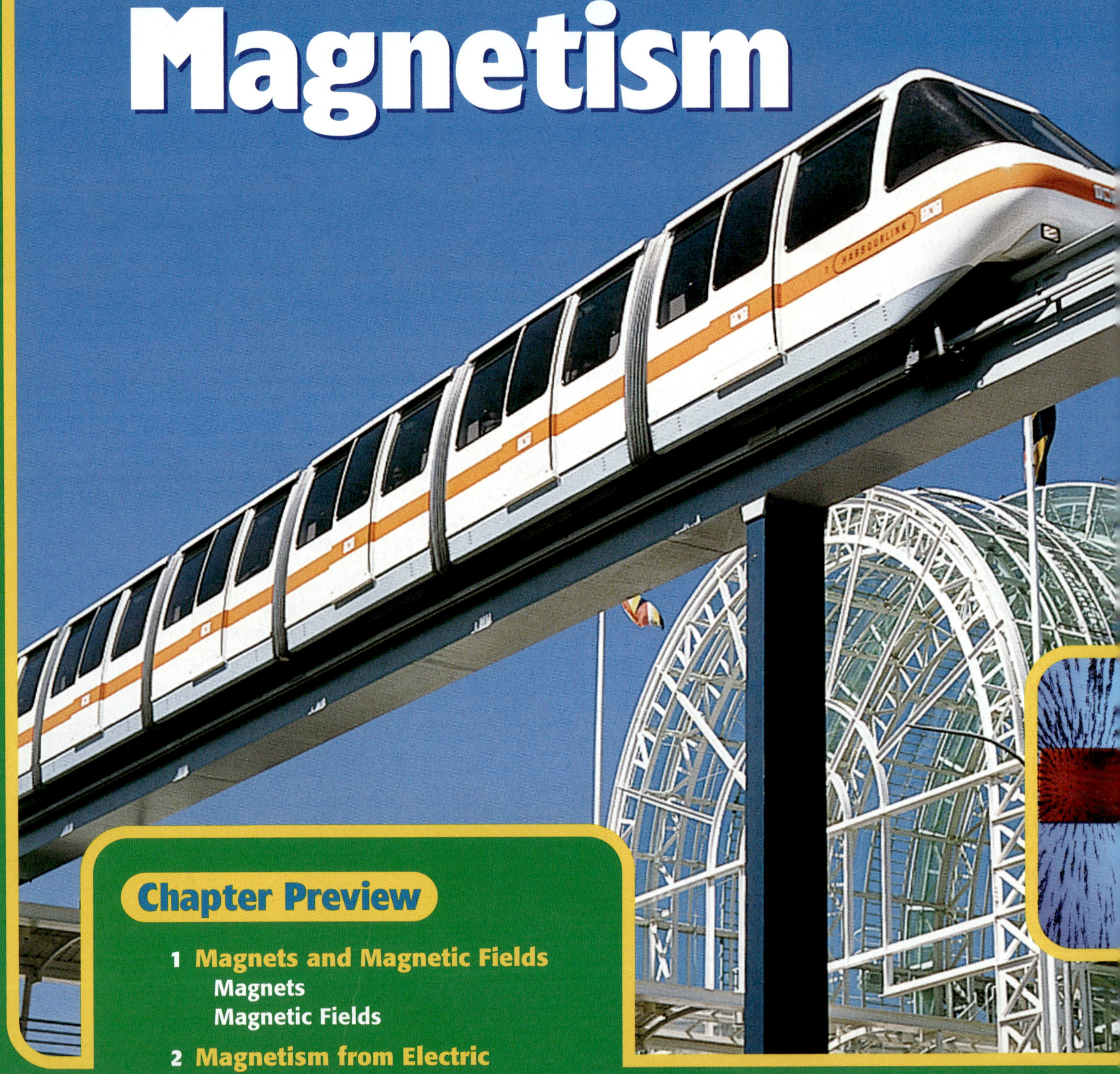

Chapter Preview

Focus ACTIVITY

Background Just as a magnet exerts a force on the iron filings in the small photo at left, a modern type of train called a *Maglev* train is levitated and accelerated by magnets. A Maglev train uses magnetic forces to lift the train off the track, reducing the friction and allowing the train to move faster. These trains, in fact, have reached speeds of more than 500 km/h (310 mi/h).

In addition to enabling the train to reach high speeds, the lack of contact with the track provides a smoother, quieter ride. With improvements in the technologies that produce the magnetic forces used in levitation, these trains may become more common in high-speed transportation.

Activity 1 You can see levitation in action with two ring-shaped magnets and a pencil. Drop one of the ring magnets over the tip of the pencil so that it rests on your hand. Now drop the other magnet over the tip of the pencil. If the magnets are oriented correctly, the second ring will levitate above the other. If the magnets attract, remove the second ring, flip it over, and again drop it over the tip of the pencil.

The magnetic force exerted on the levitating magnet is equal to the magnet's weight. Use a scale to find the magnet's mass; then use the weight equation $w = mg$ to calculate the magnetic force necessary to levitate this magnet.

Activity 2 Place two bar magnets flat on a table with the N poles about 2 cm apart. Cover the magnets with a sheet of plain paper. Sprinkle iron filings on the paper. Tap the paper gently until the filings line up. Make a sketch showing the orientation of the filings. Where does the magnetic force seem to be the strongest?

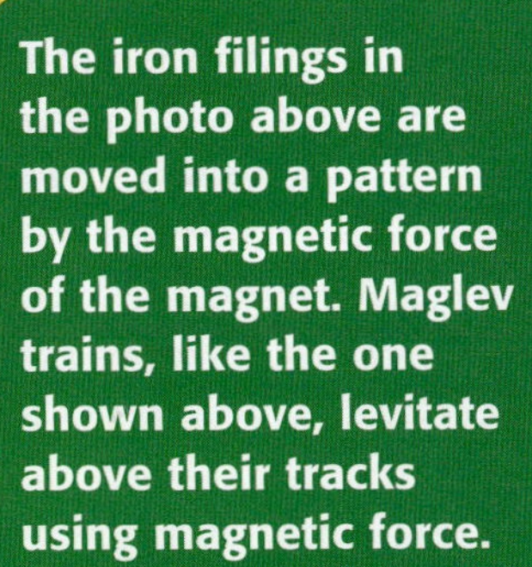

The iron filings in the photo above are moved into a pattern by the magnetic force of the magnet. Maglev trains, like the one shown above, levitate above their tracks using magnetic force.

Pre-Reading Questions

1. Magnets can exert a force on objects without touching the objects. What other forces behave the same way? Do all these forces attract the same kinds of objects?
2. Do all parts of a bar magnet attract a paperclip equally? Why or why not?

SECTION 1

Magnets and Magnetic Fields

KEY TERMS
magnetic pole
magnetic field

OBJECTIVES

- **Recognize** that like magnetic poles repel and unlike poles attract.
- **Describe** the magnetic field around a permanent magnet.
- **Explain** how compasses work.
- **Describe** the orientation of Earth's magnetic field.

You may think of magnets as devices used to attach papers or photos to a refrigerator door. But magnets are involved in many different devices, such as alarm systems like the one shown in ***Figure 1.*** This type of alarm system uses the simple magnetic attraction between a piece of iron and a magnet to alert homeowners that a window or door has been opened.

When the window is closed, as shown in ***Figure 1A,*** the iron switch is attracted to the magnet. This attraction keeps the electrical contacts in the switch closed, which completes the circuit. Thus, a current is in the system when it is turned on. When the window slides open, as shown in ***Figure 1B,*** the magnet is no longer close enough to the iron to attract it strongly. The spring pulls the switch open, which breaks the circuit, and sounds the alarm.

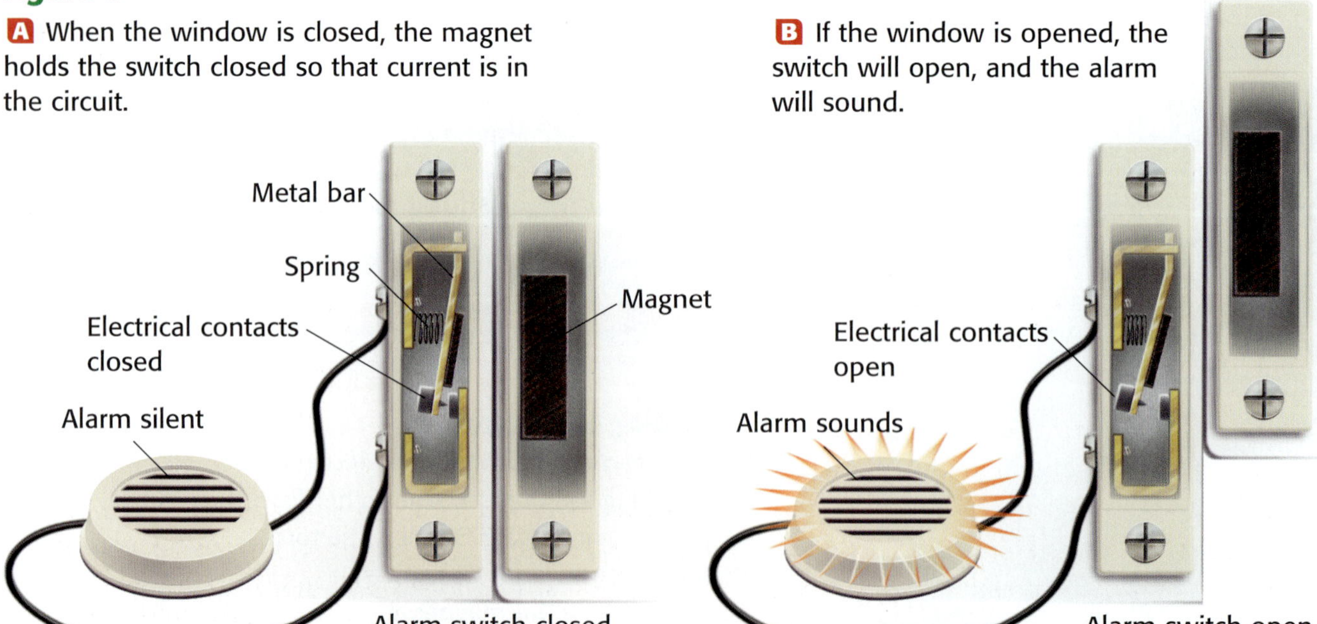

Figure 1

A When the window is closed, the magnet holds the switch closed so that current is in the circuit.

B If the window is opened, the switch will open, and the alarm will sound.

Magnets

Magnets got their name from the region of Magnesia, which is now part of modern-day Greece. The first naturally occurring magnetic rocks, called *lodestones,* were found in this region almost 3000 years ago. A lodestone, shown in **Figure 2,** is composed of an iron-based material called *magnetite.*

Figure 2

A naturally occurring magnetic rock, called a lodestone, will attract a variety of iron objects.

Some materials can be made into permanent magnets

Some substances, such as lodestones, are magnetic all the time. These types of magnets are called *permanent magnets.* You can change any piece of iron, such as a nail, into a permanent magnet by stroking it several times with a permanent magnet. A slower method is to place the piece of iron near a strong magnet. Eventually the iron will become magnetic and will remain magnetic even when the original magnet is removed.

Although a magnetized piece of iron is called a "permanent" magnet, its magnetism can be weakened or even removed. Possible ways to do this are to heat or hammer the piece of iron. Even when this is done, some materials retain their magnetism longer than others.

Scientists classify materials as either magnetically *hard* or magnetically *soft.* Iron is a soft magnetic material. Although a piece of iron is easily magnetized, it also tends to lose its magnetic properties easily. In contrast, hard magnetic materials, such as cobalt and nickel, are more difficult to magnetize. Once magnetized, however, they don't lose their magnetism easily.

Magnets exert magnetic forces on each other

As shown in **Figure 3,** a magnet lowered into a bucket of nails will often pick up several nails. As soon as a nail touches the magnet, the nail acts as a magnet and attracts other nails. More than one nail is lifted because each nail in the chain becomes temporarily magnetized and exerts a *magnetic force* on the nail below it. This ability disappears when the chain of nails is no longer touching the magnet, although the nails may become slightly magnetized after they have been in contact with the permanent magnet. In contrast, the aluminum bucket is not attracted to the magnet at all.

There is a limit to how long the chain of nails can be. The length of the chain depends on the ability of the nails to become magnetized and the strength of the magnet. The farther from the magnet each nail is, the smaller its magnetic force. Eventually, the magnetic force between the two lowest nails is not strong enough to overcome the force of gravity, and the bottom nail falls.

Figure 3

When a magnet is lowered into a bucket of nails, it can pick up a chain of nails. Each nail is temporarily magnetized by the nail above it.

magnetic pole one of two points, such as the ends of a magnet, that have opposing magnetic qualities

The word pole *is used in physics for two related opposites that are separated by some distance along an axis. The word* polar, *used in chemistry, has the same origin.*

Like poles repel, and opposite poles attract

As you know, the closer two like electrical charges are brought together, the more they repel each other. The closer two opposite charges are brought together, the more they attract each other. A similar situation exists for **magnetic poles.**

Magnets have a pair of poles, a north pole and a south pole. The poles of magnets exert a force on one another. Two like poles, such as two south poles, repel each other. Two unlike poles, however, attract each other. Thus, the north pole of one magnet will attract the south pole of another magnet. Also, the north pole of one magnet repels the north pole of another magnet.

It is impossible to isolate a south magnetic pole from a north magnetic pole. If a magnet is cut, each piece will still have two poles. No matter how small the pieces of a magnet are, each piece still has both a north and a south pole.

Magnetic Fields

Try moving the south pole of one magnet toward the south pole of another that is free to move. As you do this, the magnet you are not touching will move away. A force is being exerted on the second magnet even though it never touches the magnet in your hand. The force is acting at a distance. This may seem unusual, but you are already familiar with other forces that act at a distance. Gravitational forces and the force between electric charges also act at a distance.

Quick ACTIVITY

Test Your Knowledge of Magnetic Poles

1. Tape the ends of a bar magnet so that its pole markings are covered.
2. Tie a piece of string to the center of the magnet and suspend it from a support stand, as shown in the figure at right.
3. Use another bar magnet to determine which pole of the hanging magnet is the north pole and which is the south pole. What happens when you bring one pole of your magnet near each end of the hanging magnet?
4. Now try to identify the poles of the hanging magnet using the other pole of your magnet.
5. After you have decided the identity of each pole, remove the tape to check. Can you determine which are north poles and which are south poles if you cover the poles on both magnets?

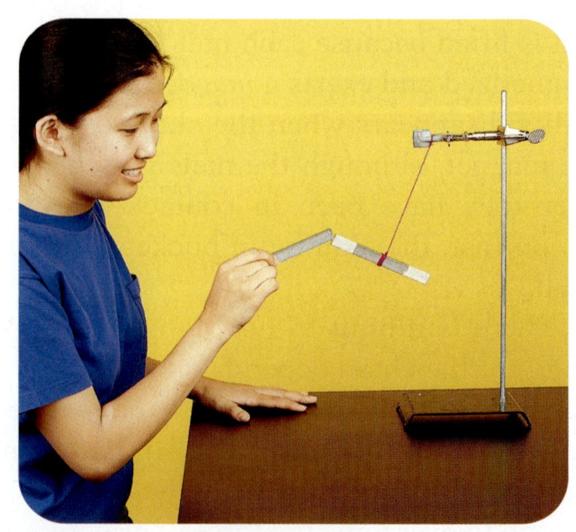

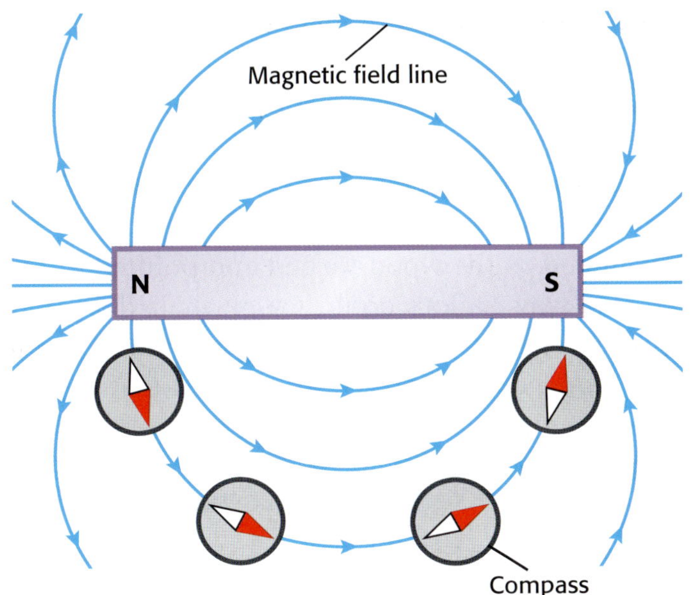

Figure 4

The magnetic field of a bar magnet can be traced with a compass. Note that the north pole of each compass points in the direction of the field lines from the magnet's north pole to its south pole.

Magnets are sources of magnetic fields

Magnetic force is a field force. When magnets repel or attract each other, it is due to the interaction of their **magnetic fields.**

magnetic field a region where a magnetic force can be detected

All magnets produce a magnetic field. Some magnetic fields are stronger than others. The strength of the magnetic field depends on the material from which the magnet is made and the degree to which it has been magnetized.

Electric field lines are used to represent an electric field. Similarly, magnetic field lines are used to represent the magnetic field of a bar magnet, as shown in ***Figure 4.*** These field lines all form closed loops. ***Figure 4*** shows only the field near the magnet. The field also exists within the magnet and farther away from the magnet. The magnetic field, however, gets weaker with distance from the magnet. As with electric field lines, magnetic field lines that are close together indicate a strong magnetic field. Field lines that are farther apart indicate a weaker field. Knowing this, you can tell from ***Figure 4*** that a magnet's field is strongest near its poles.

Compasses can track magnetic fields

One way to analyze a magnetic field's direction is to use a compass, as shown in ***Figure 4.*** A compass is a magnet suspended on top of a pivot so that the magnet can rotate freely. You can make a simple compass by hanging a bar magnet from a support with a string tied to the magnet's midpoint.

Connection to SOCIAL STUDIES

With the invention of iron and steel ships in the late 1800s, it became necessary to develop a new type of compass. The *gyrocompass,* a device containing a spinning loop, was the solution. Because of inertia, the gyrocompass always points toward Earth's geographic North Pole, regardless of which way the ship turns.

Making the Connection

1. Why does the metal hull of a ship affect the function of magnetic compasses?
2. A gyrocompass contains a device called a gyroscope. Research gyroscopes, and briefly explain how they work.

A compass aligns with Earth's magnetic field just as iron filings align with the field of a bar magnet. The compass points in a direction that lies along, or is tangent to, the magnetic field line at that point.

The first compasses were made using lodestones. A lodestone was placed on a small plank of wood and floated in calm water. Sailors then watched as the wood turned and pointed toward the north star. In this way, sailors could gauge their direction even during the day, when stars were not visible. Later, sailors found that a steel or iron needle rubbed with lodestone acted in the same manner.

Quick ACTIVITY

Magnetic Field of a File Cabinet

1. Stand in front of a metal file cabinet, and hold a compass face up and parallel to the ground.
2. Move the compass from the top of the file cabinet to the bottom, and check to see if the direction of the compass needle changes. If the compass needle changes direction, the file cabinet is magnetized.
3. Can you explain what might have caused the file cabinet to become magnetized? Remember that Earth's magnetic field not only points horizontal to Earth but also points up and down.

Earth's magnetic field is like that of a bar magnet

A compass can be used to determine direction because Earth acts like a giant bar magnet. As shown in ***Figure 5,*** Earth's magnetic field has both direction and strength. If you were to move northward along Earth's surface with a compass whose needle could point up and down, the needle of the compass would slowly tilt forward. At a point in northeastern Canada, the needle would point straight down. This point is one of Earth's magnetic poles. There is an opposite magnetic pole in Antarctica.

The source of Earth's magnetism is a topic of scientific debate. Although Earth's core is made mostly of iron, the iron in the core is too hot to retain any magnetic properties. Instead, many researchers believe that the circulation of ions or electrons in the liquid layer of Earth's core may be the source of the magnetism. Others believe it is due to a combination of several factors.

Earth's magnetic field has changed direction throughout geologic time. Evidence of more than 20 reversals in the last 5 million years is preserved in the magnetization of sea-floor rocks.

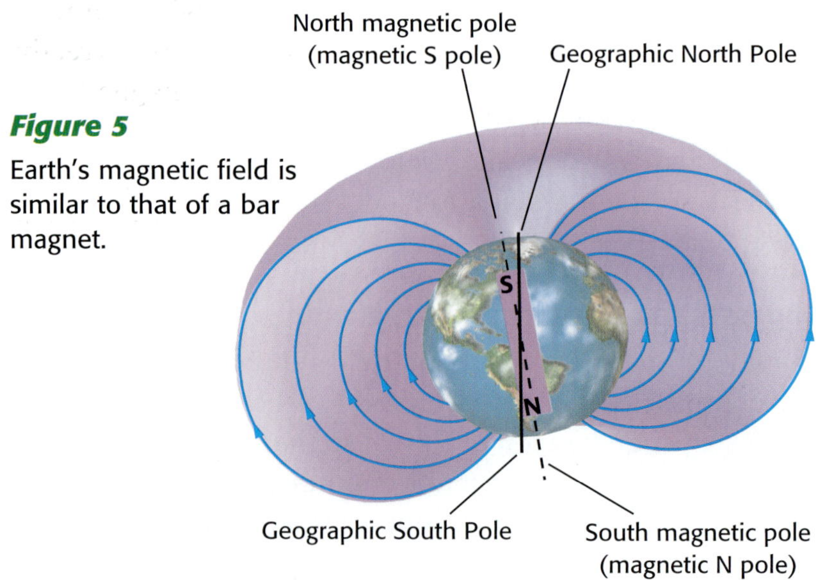

Figure 5
Earth's magnetic field is similar to that of a bar magnet.

Earth's magnetic poles are not the same as its geographic poles

One of the interesting things about Earth's magnetic poles, as shown in ***Figure 5,*** is that they are not in the same place as the geographic poles. Another important feature of Earth's magnetic poles is the orientation of their magnetic field. Earth's magnetic field points from the geographic South Pole to the geographic North Pole. This orientation is similar to a bar magnet, like the one shown in ***Figure 5.*** The magnetic pole in Antarctica is actually a magnetic N pole, and the magnetic pole in northern Canada is actually a magnetic S pole.

For historical reasons, the poles of magnets are named for the geographic pole they point toward. Thus, the end of the magnet labeled *N* is a "north-seeking" pole, and the end of the magnet labeled *S* is a "south-seeking" pole.

Did You Know?

For years scientists have speculated that some birds, such as geese and pigeons, use Earth's magnetic field to guide their migrations. Magnetic particles that seem to have a navigational role have been found in tissues from migrating animals such as birds, bees, and fish.

SECTION 1 REVIEW

SUMMARY

- All magnets have two poles that cannot be isolated.
- Like poles repel each other, and unlike poles attract each other.
- The magnetic force is the force due to interacting magnetic fields.
- The magnetic field of a magnet is strongest near its poles and gets weaker with distance.
- The direction of a magnetic field can be traced using a compass.
- Earth's magnetic field has both north and south poles.
- Earth's magnetic poles are not at the same location as the geographic poles. The magnetic N pole is in Antarctica, and the magnetic S pole is in northern Canada.

1. **Determine** whether the magnets will attract or repel each other in each of the following cases.

   a. S N   N S

   b. S N   S N

   c. N S / S N

2. **State** how many poles each piece of a magnet will have when you break it in half.
3. **Identify** which of the compass-needle orientations in the figure below correctly describe the direction of the bar magnet's magnetic field.

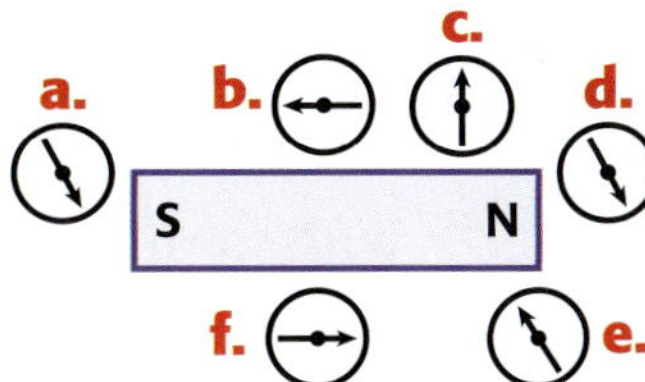

4. **Describe** the direction a compass needle would point if you were in Australia.
5. **Critical Thinking** The north pole of a magnet is attracted to the geographic North Pole, yet like poles repel. Explain why.

SECTION 2

Magnetism from Electric Currents

KEY TERMS

solenoid
electromagnet
galvanometer
electric motor

OBJECTIVES

- **Describe** how magnetism is produced by electric currents.
- **Interpret** the magnetic field of a solenoid and of an electromagnet.
- **Explain** the magnetic properties of a material in terms of magnetic domains.
- **Explain** how galvanometers and electric motors work.

During the eighteenth century, people noticed that a bolt of lightning could momentarily change the direction of a compass needle. They also noticed that iron pans sometimes became magnetized during lightning storms. These observations suggested a relationship between electricity and magnetism, but it wasn't until 1820 that the relationship was understood.

Figure 6
The iron filings show that the magnetic field of a current-carrying wire forms concentric circles around the wire.

Magnetism from Electric Currents

In 1820, a Danish science teacher named Hans Christian Oersted first experimented with the effects of an electric current on the needle of a compass. He found that magnetism is produced by moving electric charges.

Electric currents produce magnetic fields

The experiment shown in ***Figure 6*** uses iron filings to demonstrate that a current-carrying wire creates a magnetic field. Because of this field, the iron filings make a distinct pattern around the wire.

If pieces of iron are free to move, they will align with a magnetic field. The pattern of the filings in ***Figure 6*** suggests that the magnetic field around a current-carrying wire forms concentric circles around the wire. If you were to bring a compass close to a current-carrying wire, as Oersted did, you would find that the needle points in a direction tangent to the circles of iron filings. When the current stops flowing, the magnetic field disappears.

Use the right-hand rule to find the direction of the magnetic field produced by a current

Is the direction of the wire's magnetic field clockwise or counterclockwise? Repeated measurements have shown an easy way to predict the direction of the field; this method is called the *right-hand rule*. The right-hand rule is explained below.

If you imagine holding the wire in your right hand with your thumb pointing in the direction of the positive current, the direction your fingers would curl is in the direction of the magnetic field.

Figure 7 illustrates the right-hand rule. Pretend the wire is grasped with the right hand with the thumb pointing upward, in the direction of the current. When the hand holds the wire, the fingers encircle the wire with the fingertips pointing in the direction of the magnetic field, counterclockwise in this case. If the current were toward the bottom of the page, the thumb would point downward, and the magnetic field would point clockwise. *Remember—never grasp or touch an uninsulated wire. You could be electrocuted.*

The magnetic field of a coil of wire resembles that of a bar magnet

As Oersted demonstrated, the magnetic field of a current-carrying wire exerts a force on a compass needle. This force causes the needle to turn in the direction of the wire's magnetic field. However, this force is very weak. One way to increase the force is to increase the current in the wire, but large currents can be fire hazards. A safer way to create a strong magnetic field that will provide a greater force is to wrap the wire into a coil, as shown in ***Figure 8.*** This device is called a **solenoid.**

In a solenoid, the magnetic field of each loop of wire adds to the strength of the magnetic field of the loop next to it. The result is a strong magnetic field similar to the magnetic field produced by a bar magnet. A solenoid even has a north and south pole, just like a magnet.

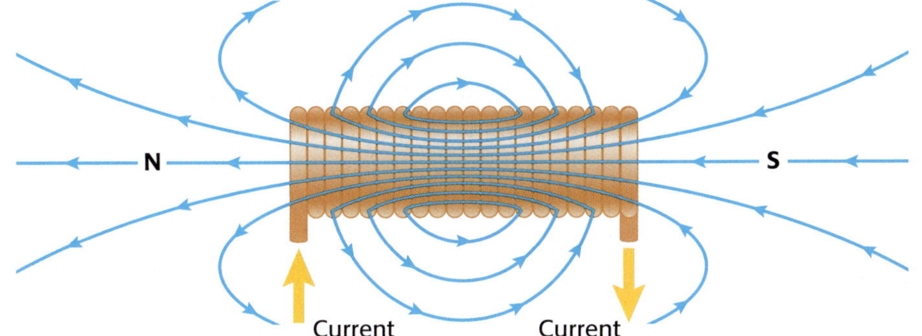

Figure 8

The magnetic field of a solenoid resembles the magnetic field of a bar magnet.

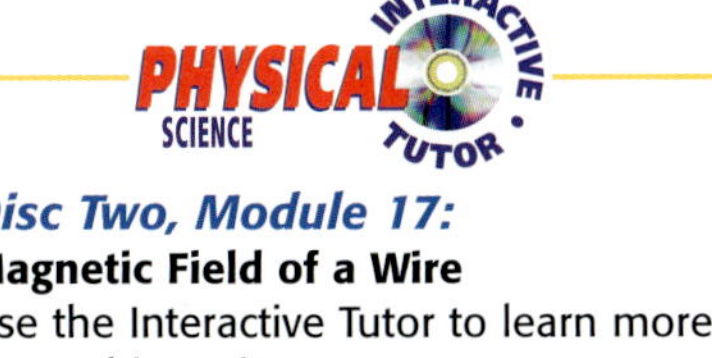

Disc Two, Module 17:
Magnetic Field of a Wire
Use the Interactive Tutor to learn more about this topic.

Figure 7

Use the right-hand rule to find the direction of the magnetic field around a current-carrying wire.

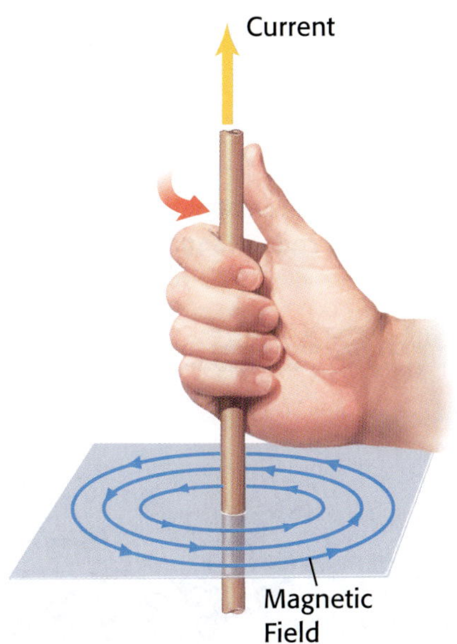

solenoid a coil of wire with an electric current in it

The strength of the magnetic field of a solenoid depends on the number of loops of wire and the amount of current in the wire. In particular, more loops or more current can create a stronger magnetic field.

The strength of a solenoid's magnetic field can be increased by inserting a rod made of iron (or some other potentially magnetic metal) through the center of the coils. The resulting device is called an **electromagnet.** The magnetic field of the solenoid causes the rod to become a magnet as well. The magnetic field of the rod then adds to the coil's field, creating a stronger magnet than the solenoid alone.

electromagnet a coil that has a soft iron core and that acts as a magnet when an electric current is in the coil

Magnetism can be caused by moving charges

The movement of charges causes all magnetism. The magnetic field of a bar magnet is an example.

But what charges are moving in a bar magnet? Negatively charged electrons moving around the nuclei of all atoms make magnetic fields. Atomic nuclei also have magnetic fields because protons move within the nucleus. Each electron has a property called *electron spin,* which also produces a tiny magnetic field.

In most cases the various sources of magnetic fields in an element cancel out and leave the atom essentially nonmagnetic. However, in some materials such as iron, nickel, and cobalt, not all of the fields cancel. Thus, each atom in those metals has its own magnetic field.

How can you make an electromagnet?

Materials
- D-cell
- compass
- 1 m length of insulated wire
- large iron or steel nail

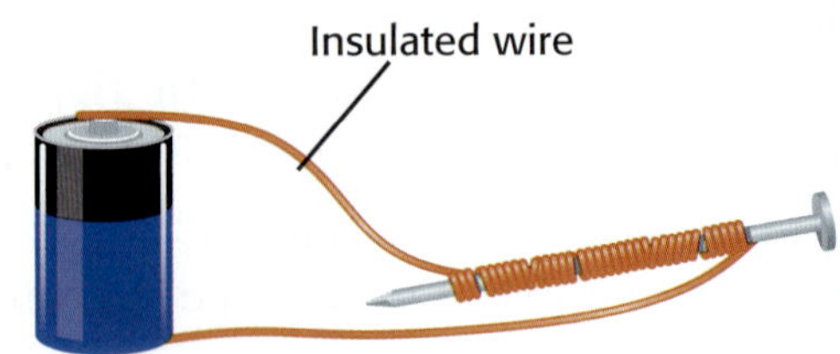

1. Wind the wire around the nail, as shown at right. Remove the insulation from the ends. Hold the insulated wire with the ends against the terminals.
2. Move the compass toward the nail to determine whether the nail is magnetized. If it is magnetized, the compass needle will spin to align with the nail's magnetic field.
3. Switch connections to the cell so the current is reversed. Again bring the compass toward the same part of the nail.

Analysis

1. What type of device have you produced? Explain your answer.
2. What happens to the direction of the compass needle after you reverse the direction of the current? Why does this happen?
3. After detaching the coil from the cell, what can you do to make the nail nonmagnetic?

Figure 9

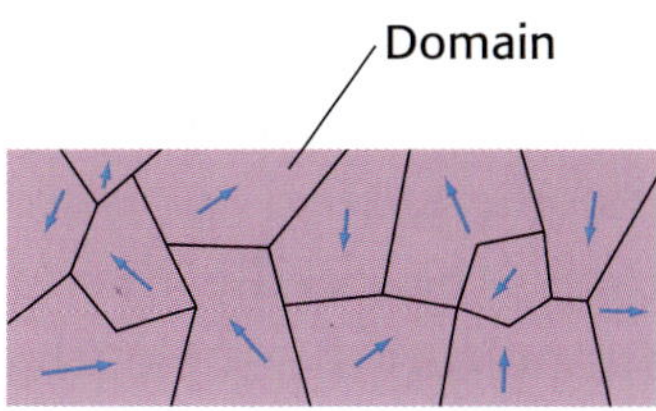

A When a potentially magnetic substance is unmagnetized, its domains are randomly oriented.

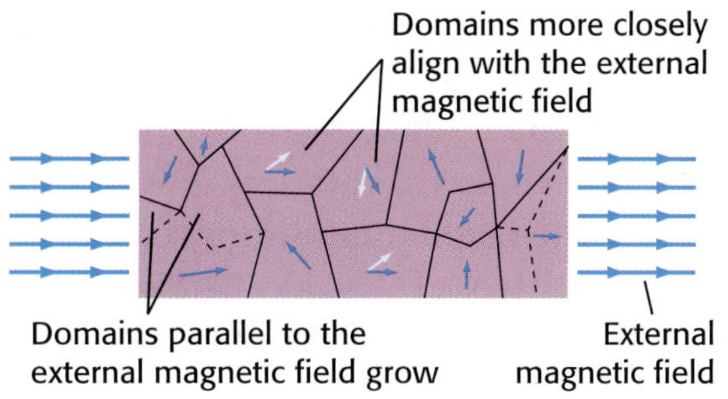

B When in an external magnetic field, the direction of the domains becomes more uniform, and the material becomes magnetized.

Just as a compass needle rotates to align with a magnetic field, magnetic atoms rotate to align with the magnetic fields of nearby atoms. The result is small regions within the material called *domains*. The magnetic fields of atoms in a domain point in the same direction.

As shown in **Figure 9A,** the magnetic fields of the domains inside an unmagnetized piece of iron are not aligned. When a strong magnet is brought nearby, the domains line up more closely with the magnetic field, as shown in **Figure 9B.** The result of this reorientation is an overall magnetization of the iron.

galvanometer an instrument that detects, measures, and determines the direction of a small electric current

Electromagnetic Devices

Many modern devices make use of the magnetic field produced by coils of current-carrying wire. Devices as different as hair dryers and stereo speakers function because of the magnetic field produced by these current-carrying conductors.

Galvanometers detect current

Galvanometers are devices used to measure current in *ammeters* and voltage in *voltmeters.* The basic construction of a galvanometer is shown in **Figure 10.** In all cases, a galvanometer detects current, or the movement of charges in a circuit.

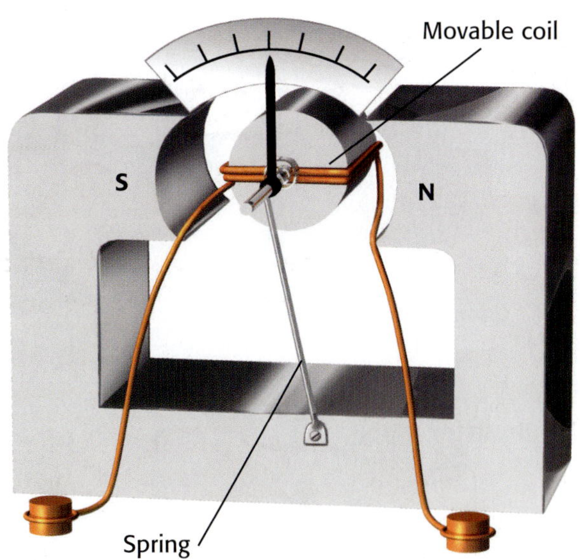

Figure 10

When there is current in the coil of a galvanometer, magnetic repulsion between the coil and the magnet causes the coil to twist.

A galvanometer consists of a coil of insulated wire wrapped around an iron core that can rotate between the poles of a permanent magnet. When the galvanometer is attached to a circuit, a current will exist in the coil of wire. The coil and iron core will act as an electromagnet and produce a magnetic field. This magnetic field will interact with the magnetic field of the surrounding permanent magnet. The resulting forces will turn the core.

As stated earlier in this section, the greater the current in the electromagnet, the stronger its magnetic field. If the core's magnetic field is strong, the force on the core will be great, and the core will rotate through a large angle. A needle extends upward from the core to a scale. As the core rotates, the needle moves across the scale. The greater the movement across the scale, the larger the current.

Electric motors convert electrical energy to mechanical energy

electric motor a device that converts electrical energy into mechanical energy

Electric motors are another type of device that uses magnetic force to cause motion. ***Figure 11*** is an illustration of a simple direct current, or DC, motor.

As shown by the arrow in ***Figure 11,*** the coil of wire in a motor turns when a current is in the wire. But unlike the coil in a galvanometer, the coil in an electric motor keeps spinning. If the coil is attached to a shaft, it can do work. The end of the shaft is connected to some other device, such as a propeller or wheel. This design is often used in mechanical toys.

A device called a *commutator* is used to make the current change direction every time the flat coil makes a half revolution. This commutator is two half rings of metal. Devices called *brushes* connect the wires to the commutator. Because of the slits in the commutator, charges must move through the coil of wire to reach the opposite half of the ring. As the coil and commutator spin, the current in the coil changes direction every time the brushes come in contact with a different side of the ring.

So the magnetic field of the coil changes direction as the coil spins. In this way, the coil is repelled by both the north and south poles of the magnet surrounding it. Because the current keeps reversing, the loop rotates in one direction. If the current did not keep changing direction, the loop would just bounce back and forth in the magnetic field until the force of friction caused it to come to rest.

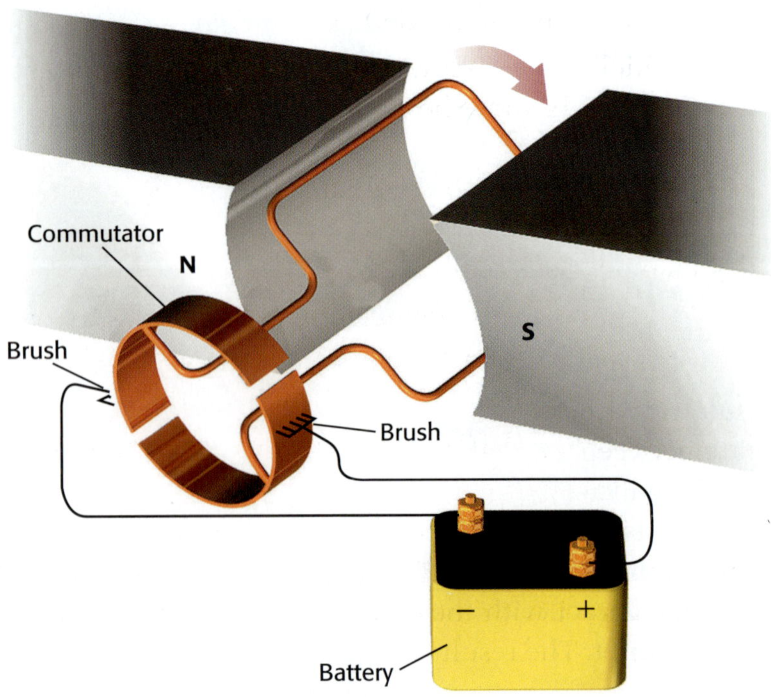

Figure 11

In an electric motor, the current in the coil produces a magnetic field that interacts with the magnetic field of the surrounding magnet, causing the coil to turn.

Stereo speakers use magnetic force to produce sound

Motion caused by magnetic force can even be used to produce sound waves. This is how most stereo speakers work. The speaker shown in ***Figure 12*** consists of a permanent magnet and a coil of wire attached to a flexible paper cone. When a current is in the coil, a magnetic field is produced. This field interacts with the field of the permanent magnet, causing the coil and cone to move in one direction. When the current reverses direction, the magnetic force on the coil also reverses direction. As a result, the cone accelerates in the opposite direction.

This alternating force on the speaker cone makes it vibrate. Varying the magnitude of the current changes how much the cone vibrates. These vibrations produce sound waves. In this way, an electric signal is converted to a sound wave.

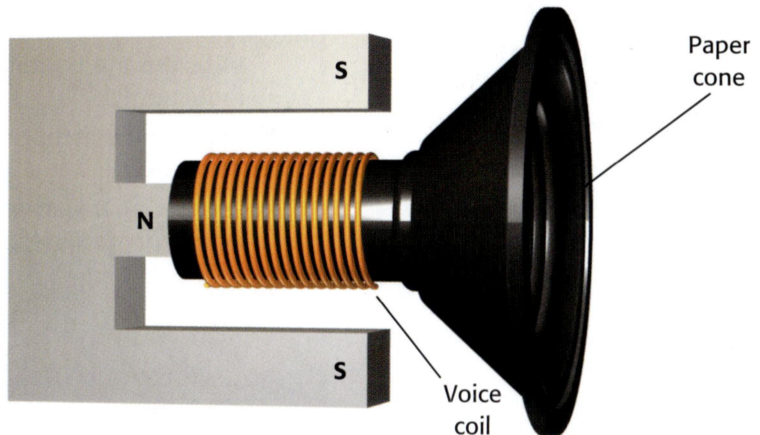

Figure 12

In a speaker, when the direction of the current in the coil of wire changes, the paper cone attached to the coil moves, producing sound waves.

SECTION 2 REVIEW

SUMMARY

- A magnetic field is produced around a current-carrying wire.
- A current-carrying solenoid has a magnetic field similar to that of a bar magnet.
- An electromagnet consists of a current-carrying solenoid with an iron core.
- A domain is a group of atoms whose magnetic fields are aligned.
- Galvanometers measure the current in a circuit using the magnetic field produced by a current in a coil.
- Electric motors convert electrical energy to mechanical energy.

1. **Describe** the shape of the magnetic field produced by a straight current-carrying wire.
2. **Determine** the direction in which a compass needle will point when held above a wire with positive charges moving west. (**Hint:** Use the right-hand rule.)
3. **Identify** which of the following would have the strongest magnetic field. Assume the current in each is the same.
   - **a.** a straight wire
   - **b.** an electromagnet with 30 coils
   - **c.** a solenoid with 20 coils
   - **d.** a solenoid with 30 coils
4. **Explain** why a very strong magnet attracts both poles of a weak magnet. Use the concept of magnetic domains in your explanation.
5. **Predict** whether a solenoid suspended by a string could be used as a compass.
6. **Critical Thinking** A friend claims to have built a motor by attaching a shaft to the core of a galvanometer and removing the spring. Can this motor rotate through a full rotation? Explain your answer.

SECTION 3

Electric Currents from Magnetism

KEY TERMS

electromagnetic induction
generator
alternating current
transformer

OBJECTIVES

- **Describe** the conditions required for electromagnetic induction.
- **Apply** the concept of electromagnetic induction to generators.
- **Explain** how transformers increase or decrease voltage across power lines.

Can you have current in a wire without a battery or some other source of voltage? In 1831, Michael Faraday discovered that a current can be produced by pushing a magnet through a coil of wire. In other words, moving a magnet in and out of a coil of wire causes charges in the wire to move. This process is called **electromagnetic induction.**

electromagnetic induction the process of creating a current in a circuit by changing a magnetic field

Electromagnetic Induction and Faraday's Law

Electromagnetic induction is so fundamental that it has become one of the laws of physics—*Faraday's law.* Faraday's law states the following:

An electric current can be produced in a circuit by a changing magnetic field.

Consider the loop of wire moving between the two magnetic poles in ***Figure 13.*** As the loop moves in and out of the magnetic field of the magnet, a current is *induced* in the circuit. As long as the wire continues to move in or out of the field in a direction that is not parallel to the field, an induced current will exist in the circuit.

Rotating the circuit or changing the strength of the magnetic field will also induce a current in the circuit. In each case, there is a changing magnetic field passing through the loop. You can predict whether a current will be induced using the concept of magnetic field lines. A current will be induced if the number of field lines that pass through the loop changes.

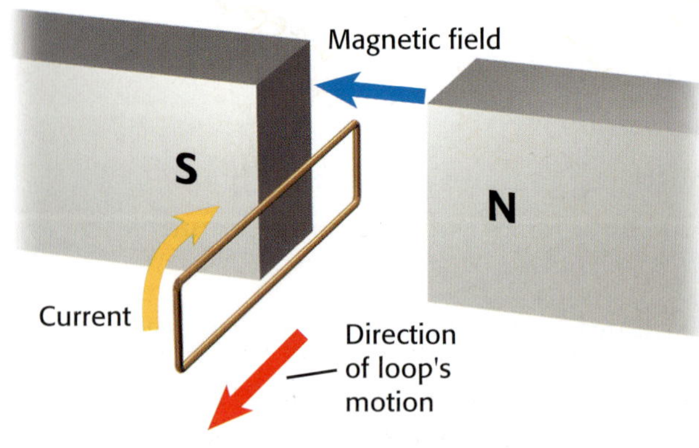

Figure 13
When the loop moves in or out of the magnetic field, a current is induced in the wire.

It would seem that electromagnetic induction creates energy from nothing, but this is not true. Electromagnetic induction does not violate the law of conservation of energy. Pushing a loop through a magnetic field requires work. The greater the magnetic field, the stronger the force required to push the loop through the field. The energy required for this work comes from an outside source, such as your muscles pushing the loop through the magnetic field. So while electrical energy is produced by electromagnetic induction, energy is required to move the loop.

Moving electric charges experience a magnetic force when in a magnetic field

When studying electromagnetic induction, it is helpful to imagine the individual charges in a wire. A charged particle moving in a magnetic field will experience a force due to the magnetic field. Experiments have shown that this magnetic force is zero when the charge moves along or opposite the direction of the magnetic field lines. The force is at its maximum value when the charge moves perpendicular to the field. As the angle between the charge's direction and the direction of the magnetic field decreases, the force on the charge decreases.

INTEGRATING

BIOLOGY

Many types of bacteria contain magnetic particles of iron oxide and iron sulfide. These particles are encased in a membrane within the cell, forming a magnetosome. The magnetosomes in a bacterium spread out in a line and align with Earth's magnetic field. In this way, as the cell uses its flagella to swim, it travels along a north-south axis. Recently, magnetite crystals have been found in human brain cells, but the role these particles play remains uncertain.

Quick Lab

Can you demonstrate electromagnetic induction?

Materials

- ✓ galvanometer
- ✓ solenoid
- ✓ 2 insulated wire leads
- ✓ 2 bar magnets

1. Set up the apparatus as shown in the photo at right. With this arrangement, current induced in the solenoid will pass through the galvanometer.
2. Holding one of the bar magnets, insert its north pole into the solenoid while observing the galvanometer needle. What happens?
3. Pull the magnet out of the solenoid, and record the movement of the galvanometer needle.
4. Turn the magnet around, and move the south pole in and out of the solenoid. What happens?
5. Vary the speed of the magnet. What happens if you do not move the magnet at all?
6. Try again using two magnets alongside each other with north poles and south poles together. How does the amount of current induced depend on the strength of the magnetic field?

Analysis

1. What evidence did you find that current is induced by a changing magnetic field?
2. Compare the current induced by a south pole with that induced by a north pole.
3. What two observations did you make that show that more current is induced if the magnetic field changes rapidly?

Figure 14

A When the wire in a circuit moves perpendicular to a magnetic field, the current induced in the wire is at a maximum.
B When the wire moves parallel to a magnetic field, there is zero current induced in the wire.

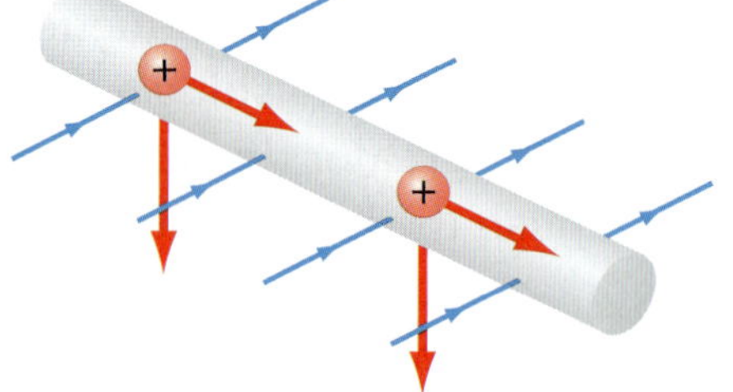

A Maximum current when the wire moves perpendicular to the magnetic field

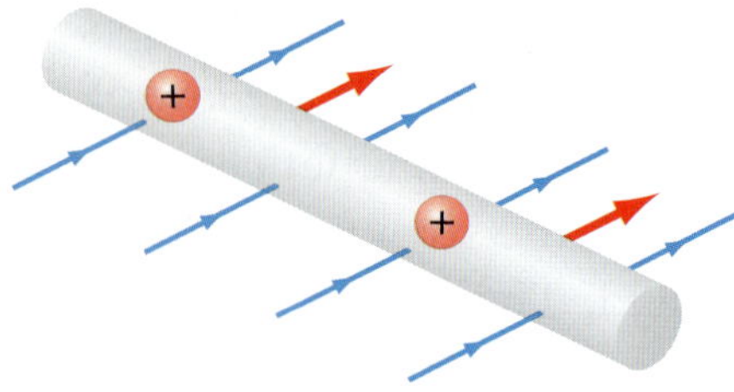

B Zero current when the wire moves parallel to the magnetic field

Now apply this concept to current. Imagine the wire in a circuit as a tube full of charges, as shown in ***Figure 14.*** When the wire is moving perpendicular to a magnetic field, the force on the charges is at a maximum. In this case, there will be a current in the wire and circuit, as shown in ***Figure 14A.*** When a wire is moving parallel to the field, as in ***Figure 14B,*** no current is induced in the wire. Because the charges are moving parallel to the field, they experience no magnetic force.

Generators convert mechanical energy to electrical energy

generator a machine that converts mechanical energy into electrical energy

alternating current an electric current that changes direction at regular intervals (abbreviation, AC)

Generators are similar to motors except that they convert mechanical energy to electrical energy. If you expend energy to do work on a simple generator, like the one in ***Figure 15,*** the loop of wire inside turns within a magnetic field and current is produced. For each half rotation of the loop, the current produced by the generator reverses direction.

This type of generator is therefore called an **alternating current,** or *AC,* generator. The generators that produce the electrical energy that you use at home are alternating current generators. The current supplied by the outlets in your home and in most of the world is alternating current.

As can be seen by the glowing light bulb in ***Figure 15,*** the coil turning in the magnetic field of the magnet creates a current. The magnitude and direction of the current that results from the coil's rotation vary depending on the orientation of the loop in the field.

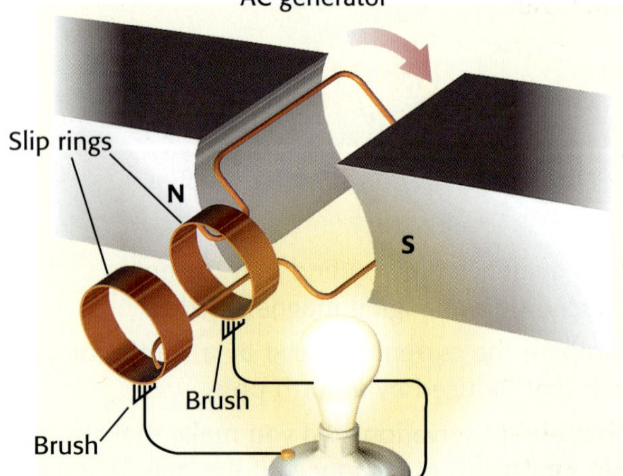

Figure 15

In an alternating current generator, the mechanical energy of the loop's rotation is converted to electrical energy when a current is induced in the wire. The current lights the light bulb.

Table 1 **Induced Current in a Generator**

Position of loop	Amount of current	Graph of current versus angle of rotation
Magnetic field	Zero current	Current; 0° 90° 180° 270° 360° Rotation angle
Magnetic field	Maximum current	Current; 0° 90° 180° 270° 360° Rotation angle
Magnetic field	Zero current	Current; 0° 90° 180° 270° 360° Rotation angle
Magnetic field	Maximum current (opposite direction)	Current; 0° 90° 180° 270° 360° Rotation angle
Magnetic field	Zero current	Current; 0° 90° 180° 270° 360° Rotation angle

Table 1 shows how the magnitude of the current produced by an AC generator varies with time. When the loop is perpendicular to the field, the current is zero. Recall that a charge moving parallel to a magnetic field experiences no magnetic force. This is the case here. The charges in the wire experience no magnetic force, so no current is induced in the wire.

As the loop continues to turn, the current increases until it reaches a maximum. When the loop is parallel to the field, charges on either side of the wire move perpendicular to the magnetic field. Thus, the charges experience the maximum magnetic force, and the current is large. Current decreases as the loop rotates, reaching zero when it is again perpendicular to the magnetic field. As the loop continues to rotate, the direction of the current reverses.

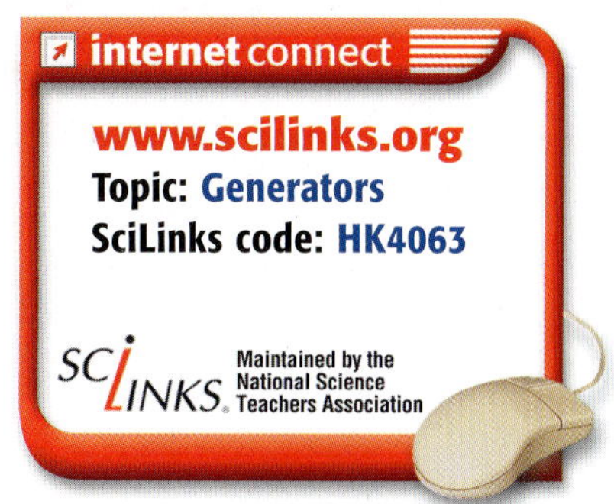

Generators produce the electrical energy you use in your home

Large power plants use generators to convert mechanical energy to electrical energy. The mechanical energy used in a commercial power plant comes from a variety of sources. One of the most common sources is running water. Dams are built to harness the kinetic energy of falling water. Water is forced through small channels at the top of the dam. As the water falls to the base of the dam, it turns the blades of large turbine fans. The fans are attached to a core wrapped with many loops of wire that rotate within a strong magnetic field. The end result is electrical energy.

Coal power plants use the heat from burning coal to make steam that eventually turns the blades of the turbines. Other sources of energy are nuclear fission, wind, hot water from geysers (geothermal), and solar power.

Some mechanical energy is always lost as heat, and the available electrical energy is reduced due to resistance in the wires of the generator. Many power plants are not very efficient. More efficient and safer methods of producing energy are continually being sought.

Did You Know?

Although the light from a fluorescent light bulb appears to be constant, the current in the bulb actually varies, changing direction 60 times each second. The light appears to be steady because the changes are too rapid for our eyes to perceive.

Electricity and magnetism are two aspects of a single electromagnetic force

So far you've read that a moving charge produces a magnetic field and that a changing magnetic field causes an electric charge to move. The energy that results from these two forces is called electromagnetic energy.

Light is a form of electromagnetic energy. Visible light travels as electromagnetic waves, or *EM* waves, as do other forms of radiation, such as radio signals and X rays. These waves are also called *EMF* (electromagnetic frequency) waves. As shown in ***Figure 16,*** EM waves are made up of oscillating electric and magnetic fields that are perpendicular to each other. This is true of any type of EM wave, regardless of the frequency.

Both the electric and magnetic fields in an EM wave are perpendicular to the direction the wave travels. So EM waves are transverse waves. As the wave moves along, the changing electric field generates the magnetic field. The changing magnetic field generates the electric field. Each field regenerates the other, allowing EM waves to travel through empty space.

Figure 16

An electromagnetic wave consists of electric and magnetic field waves at right angles to each other.

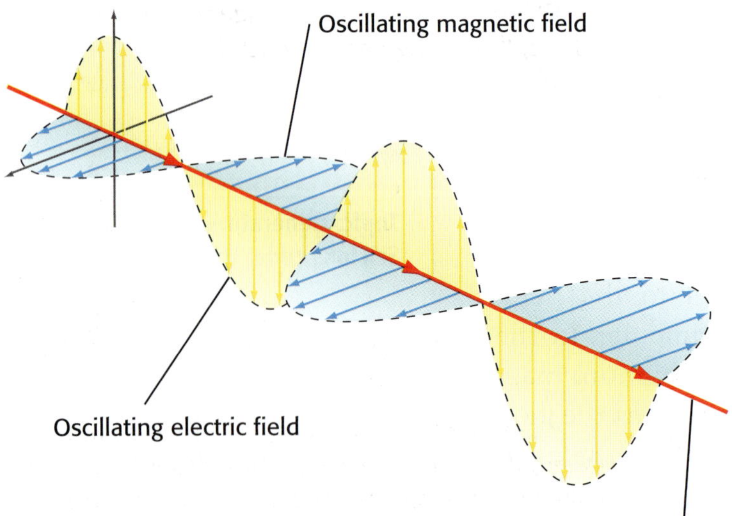

Figure 17

A transformer uses the alternating current in the primary circuit to induce an alternating current in the secondary circuit.

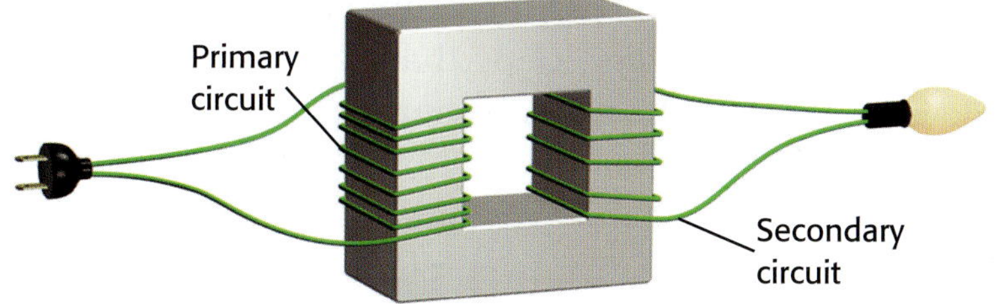

transformer a device that increases or decreases the voltage of alternating current

Transformers

You may have seen metal cylinders on power line poles in your neighborhood. These cylinders hold EM devices called **transformers.** **Figure 17** is a simple representation of a transformer. Two wires are coiled around opposite sides of a closed iron loop. In this transformer, one wire is attached to a source of alternating current, such as a power outlet in your home. The other wire is attached to an appliance, such as a lamp.

When there is current in the primary wire, this current creates a changing magnetic field that magnetizes the iron core. The changing magnetic field of the iron core then induces a current in the secondary coil. The direction of the current in the secondary coil changes every time the direction of the current in the primary coil changes.

Transformers can increase or decrease voltage

The voltage induced in the secondary coil of a transformer depends on the number of loops, or *turns,* in the coil. As shown in **Figure 18A,** both the primary and secondary wires are coiled only once around the iron core. If the incoming current has a voltage of 5 V, then the voltage measured in the other circuit will be close to 5 V. When the number of turns in the two coils is equal, the voltage induced in the secondary coil is about the same as the voltage in the primary coil.

In **Figure 18B,** two secondary coils with just one turn each are placed on the iron core. In this case, a voltage of slightly less than 5 V is induced in each coil. If these turns are joined together to form one coil with two turns, as shown in **Figure 18C,** the voltmeter will measure an induced voltage of slightly less than twice as much as the voltage produced by one coil.

Figure 18

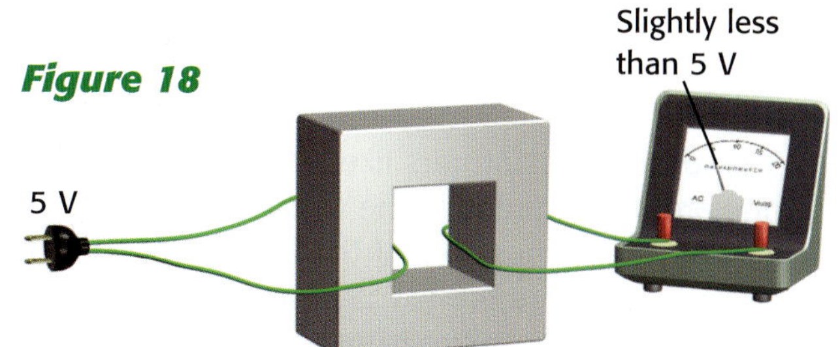

A When the primary and secondary circuits in a transformer each have one turn, the voltage across each is about equal.

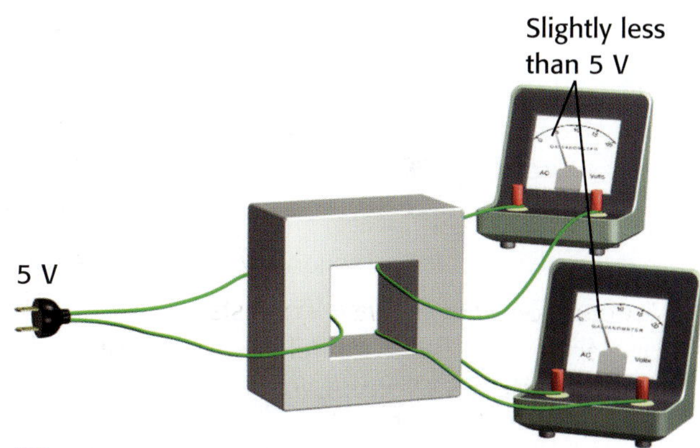

B When an additional secondary circuit is added, the voltage across each is again about equal.

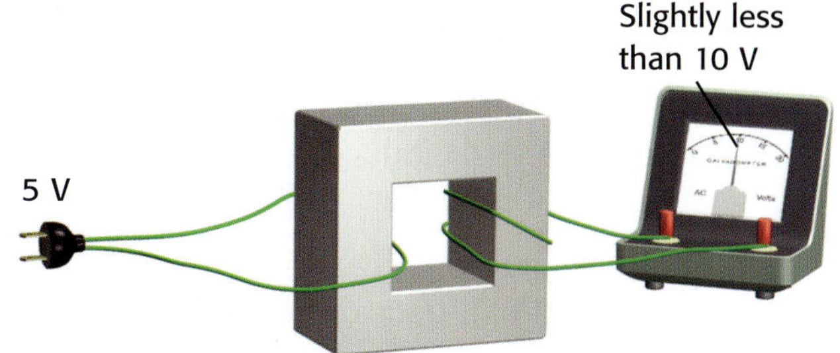

C When the two secondary circuits are combined, the secondary circuit has about twice the voltage of the primary circuit. Actual transformers may have thousands of turns.

Figure 19

Step-down transformers like this one are used to reduce the voltage across power lines so that the electrical energy supplied to homes and businesses is safer to use.

Thus, the voltage across the secondary coil is about twice as large as the voltage across the primary coil. This device is called a *step-up transformer* because the voltage across the secondary coil is greater than the voltage across the primary coil.

If the secondary coil has fewer loops than the primary coil, then the voltage is lowered by the transformer. This type of transformer is called a *step-down transformer*.

Step-up and step-down transformers are used in the transmission of electrical energy from power plants to homes and businesses. A step-up transformer is used at or near the power plant to increase the voltage of the current to about 120 000 V. At this high voltage, less energy is lost due to the resistance of the transmission wires. A step-down transformer, like the one shown in ***Figure 19,*** is then used near your home to reduce the voltage of the current to about 120 V. This lower voltage is much safer. Many appliances in the United States operate at 120 V.

SECTION 3 REVIEW

SUMMARY

- A current is produced in a circuit by a changing magnetic field.
- In a generator, mechanical energy is converted to electrical energy by a conducting loop turning in a magnetic field.
- Electromagnetic waves consist of magnetic and electric fields oscillating at right angles to each other.
- In a transformer, the magnetic field produced by a primary coil induces a current in a secondary coil.
- The voltage across the secondary coil of a transformer is proportional to the number of loops, or turns, it has relative to the number of turns in the primary coil.

1. **Identify** which of the following will *not* increase the current induced in a wire loop moving through a magnetic field.
   a. increasing the strength of the magnetic field
   b. increasing the speed of the wire
   c. rotating the loop until it is perpendicular to the field
2. **Explain** how hydroelectrical power plants use moving water to produce electricity.
3. **Determine** whether the following statement describes a step-up transformer or a step-down transformer: The primary coil has 7000 turns, and the secondary coil has 500 turns.
4. **Predict** the movement of the needle of a galvanometer attached to a coil of wire for each of the following actions. Assume that the north pole of a bar magnet has been inserted into the coil, causing the needle to deflect to the right.
   a. pulling the magnet out of the coil
   b. letting the magnet rest in the coil
   c. thrusting the south pole of the magnet into the coil
5. **Critical Thinking** A spacecraft orbiting Earth has a coil of wire in it. An astronaut measures a small current in the coil, even though there is no battery connected to it and there are no magnets on the spacecraft. What is causing the current?

Study Skills

Interpreting Scientific Illustrations

Illustrations, figures, and photographs can be useful for understanding a scientific concept that is difficult to visualize. In the case of magnetism, keeping track of the directions of field lines and currents can be made easier with proper understanding of illustrations and their relation to the *right-hand rule*.

1 Determine what the figure is trying to show.

We'll use ***Figure 20A*** below, which shows how an electric current is induced in a wire loop moved out of a magnetic field. The caption reads, "When the loop moves in or out of the magnetic field, a current is induced in the wire." Examine the directions of the arrows in the figure, as these indicate the relationship between the loop's motion, the magnetic field, and the induced current.

2 Examine the illustration's labels and art to learn general information.

Note that the red arrow indicates the direction in which the loop is moved. Take your right hand, palm outstretched and thumb extended out, and point the thumb in the direction of the loop's motion. Now move your hand to align your fingers with the direction of the magnetic field, which is indicated by the blue arrow. (Do not curl your fingers.) The direction of the current will be out of the palm of your hand, along whichever part of the wire loop is still in the magnetic field. As this is the far, short end of the loop, the current points downward in that part of the wire, and so the current moves around the loop in the direction of the yellow arrows.

Figure 20

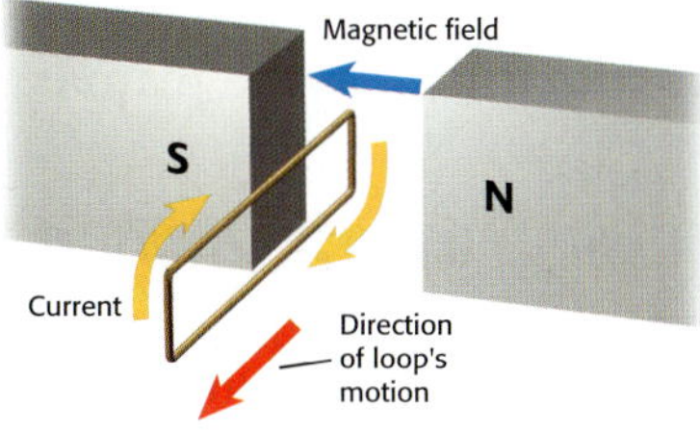

A When the loop moves in or out of the magnetic field, a current is induced in the wire.

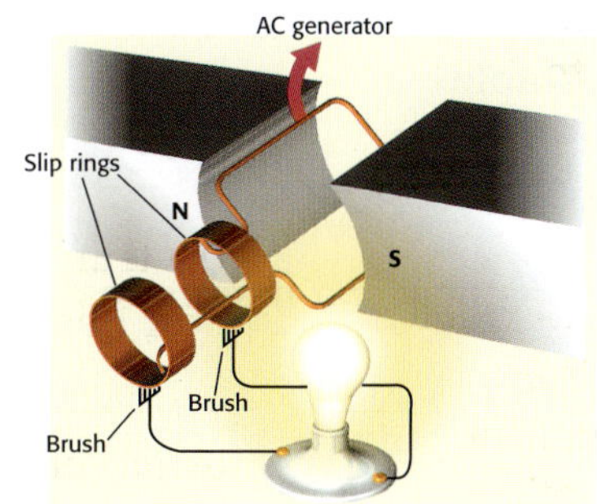

B In an alternating current generator, the mechanical energy of the loop's rotation is converted into electrical energy.

Practice

1. Apply the right-hand rule to the generator shown in ***Figure 20B.*** In what direction is the current flowing?
2. Does the current in ***Figure 20B*** always flow in this direction? If not, why not?

CHAPTER 17 REVIEW

Chapter Highlights

Before you begin, review the summaries of the key ideas of each section, found at the end of each section. The key vocabulary terms are listed on the first page of each section.

UNDERSTANDING CONCEPTS

1. If the poles of two magnets repel each other,
- **a.** both poles must be south poles.
- **b.** both poles must be north poles.
- **c.** one pole is a south pole and the other is a north pole.
- **d.** the poles are the same type.

2. The part of a magnet where the magnetic field and forces are strongest is called a magnetic
- **a.** field.
- **b.** pole.
- **c.** attraction.
- **d.** repulsion.

3. A _______ magnetic material is easy to magnetize but loses its magnetism easily.
- **a.** hard
- **b.** magnetically unstable
- **c.** soft
- **d.** No such material exists.

4. An object's ability to generate a magnetic field depends on its
- **a.** size.
- **b.** location.
- **c.** composition.
- **d.** direction.

5. A compass held directly below a current-carrying wire with a positive current moving north will point
- **a.** east.
- **b.** north.
- **c.** south.
- **d.** west.

6. An electric motor uses an electromagnet to change
- **a.** mechanical energy to electrical energy.
- **b.** magnetic fields in the motor.
- **c.** magnetic poles in the motor.
- **d.** electrical energy to mechanical energy.

7. An electric generator is a device that can convert
- **a.** nuclear energy to electrical energy.
- **b.** wind energy to electrical energy.
- **c.** energy from burning coal to electrical energy.
- **d.** All of the above.

8. The process of producing an electric current by moving a magnet in and out of a coil of wire is called
- **a.** magnetic deduction.
- **b.** electromagnetic induction.
- **c.** magnetic reduction.
- **d.** magnetic production.

9. In a transformer, the voltage of a current will be increased if the secondary circuit
- **a.** has more turns than the primary circuit.
- **b.** has fewer turns than the primary circuit.
- **c.** has the same number of turns as the primary circuit.
- **d.** is parallel to the primary circuit.

USING VOCABULARY

10. Use the terms *magnetic pole* and *magnetic field* to explain why the N pole of a compass points toward northern Canada.

11. Write a paragraph explaining some of the advantages and disadvantages of using a magnetic compass to determine direction. Use the terms *magnetic pole* and *magnetic field* in your answer. WRITING SKILL

12. What happens to the magnetic *domains* in a material when it is placed in a strong magnetic field?

13. How does a *galvanometer* measure electric current? How is it similar to an *electric motor*? How does it differ?

14. What is the purpose of a *commutator* in an *electric motor*?

15. Use the terms *generator* and *electromagnetic induction* to explain how *electrical energy* can be generated using the *kinetic energy* of falling water.

BUILDING GRAPHING SKILLS

16. Graphing The figure below is a graph of current versus rotation angle for the output of an alternating-current generator.

- **a.** At what point(s) does the generator produce no current?
- **b.** Is less or more current being produced at point *B* than at points *C* and *E*?
- **c.** Is less or more current being produced at point *D* than at points *C* and *E*?
- **d.** What does the negative value for the current at *D* signify?

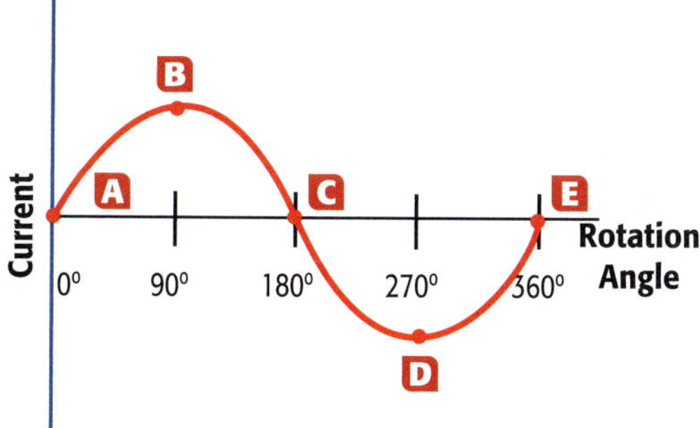

17. Interpreting Graphics If the coil of the generator referred to in item 16 were like the one shown in ***Table 1,*** what would the coil orientation be relative to the magnetic field in order to produce the maximum current at *B*?

THINKING CRITICALLY

18. Problem Solving How could you use a compass with a magnetized needle to determine if a steel nail were magnetized?

19. Understanding Systems Fire doors are doors that can slow the spread of fire from room to room when they are closed. In some buildings, fire doors are held open by electromagnets. Explain why electromagnets are used instead of permanent magnets.

20. Understanding Systems Transformers are usually used to raise or lower the voltage across an alternating-current circuit. Could a transformer be used in a direct-current circuit? How about if the direct current were pulsating (turning on and off)?

21. Understanding Systems Which of the following might be the purpose of the device shown below?

- **a.** to measure the amount of voltage across the wire
- **b.** to determine the direction of the current in the wire
- **c.** to find the resistance of the wire

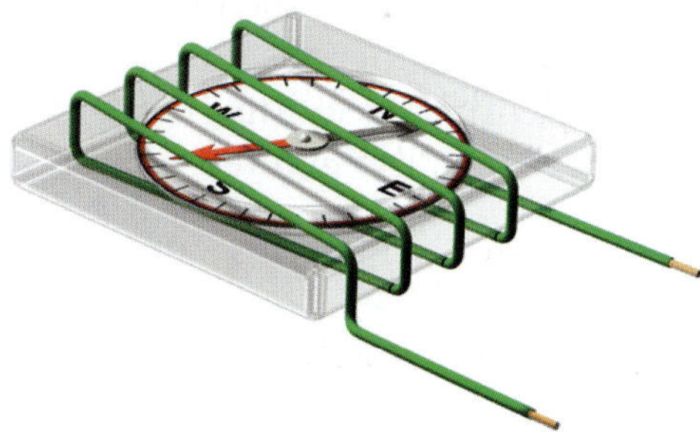

22. Problem Solving You have two iron bars and a ball of string in your possession; one bar is magnetized, and one is not magnetized. How can you determine which bar is magnetized?

DEVELOPING LIFE/WORK SKILLS

23. Applying Technology Use your imagination and your knowledge of electromagnetism to invent a useful electromagnetic device. Use a computer-drawing program to make sketches of your invention, and write a description of how it works.

COMPUTER SKILL

CHAPTER 17 REVIEW

24. Interpreting and Communicating Research one of the following electromagnetic devices: a hair dryer, a doorbell, and a tape recorder. Write a half-page description of how electromagnetism is used in the device, using diagrams where appropriate. WRITING SKILL

25. Applying Knowledge What do adapters do to voltage and current? Examine the input/output information on several adapters to find out. Do they contain step-up or step-down transformers?

26. Researching Information A transformer is needed to plug American appliances into wall sockets in other countries. Research how these transformers work. Why are they necessary?

INTEGRATING CONCEPTS

27. Concept Mapping Copy the unfinished concept map below onto a sheet of paper. Complete the map by writing the correct word or phrase in the lettered boxes.

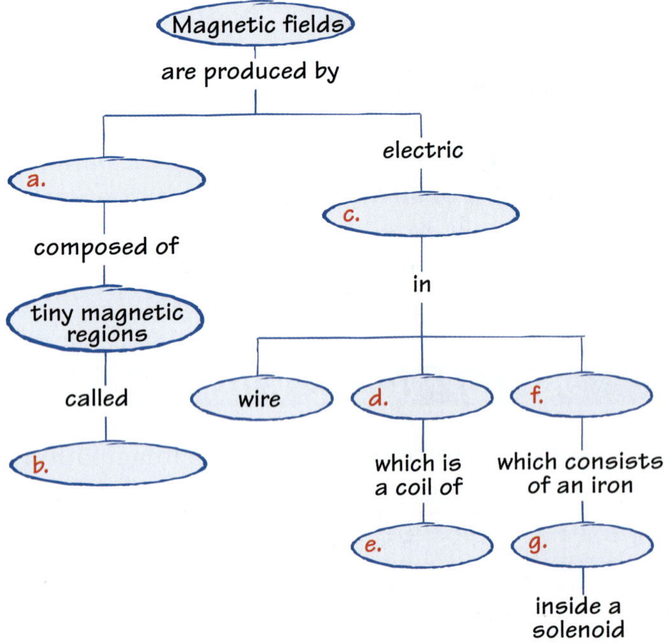

28. Concept Mapping Create your own concept map by using the content in one of the sections of this chapter. Write three propositions from your completed concept map.

29. Connection to Social Studies Why was the discovery of lodestones in Greece important to navigators hundreds of years later?

30. Connection to Health Some studies indicate that magnetic fields produced by power lines may contribute to leukemia among children who grow up near high-voltage power lines. Research the history of scientific studies of the connection between leukemia and power lines. What experiments show that growing up near power lines increases risk of leukemia? What evidence is there that there is no relation between leukemia and the magnetic fields produced by power lines?

31. Connection to Physics Find out how electromagnetism is used in containing nuclear fusion reactions. Write a report on your findings. WRITING SKILL

32. Connection to Fine Arts Electric guitars use electromagnetic induction to produce sound. Research electric guitars to find out how they work, and draw a diagram that illustrates the process electric guitars use to create sound. What other musical instruments could be modified to work the same way?

Standardized Test Prep

Understanding Concepts

***Directions (1–3):* For *each* question, write on a separate sheet of paper the letter of the correct answer.**

1 How many coil turns are needed on the secondary coil of a step-down transformer that reduces voltage from 2 400 volts to 120 volts if the primary coil has 1,000 turns?

A. 1 **C.** 50
B. 20 **D.** 120

2 What conditions are necessary to induce an electric current?

F. A conductor must move past a stationary magnetic field.
G. A magnetic field must move past a stationary conductor.
H. A conductor and a magnetic field must move relative to one another.
I. A magnetic field and a conductor must move together relative to a stationary point.

3 What is the result of cutting a bar magnet in half?

A. two unmagnetized bars
B. two magnets with north poles only
C. two smaller magnets with both north and south poles
D. one magnet with north poles only and one magnet with south poles only

***Directions (4–5):* For each question, write a short response.**

4 Light is a form of electromagnetic energy. Explain how the effect of electric and magnetic fields on each other produces a light wave.

5 Differentiate between an alternating electric current and a direct electric current.

Test TIP

When using an illustration that has labels to answer a question, read the labels carefully, and then check that the answer you choose matches your interpretation of the labels.

Reading Skills

***Directions (6):* Read the passage below. Then answer the question.**

A type of train that is in development uses the force of magnetism to propel it forward. It is known as a magnetic levitation or maglev train, because magnetic forces are also used to reduce friction. Instead of wheels, the train has large magnets that float above magnets in the track. Alternating electromagnetic fields drive the train forward or slow it down using magnetic attraction and repulsion. Because there is very little friction to overcome, maglev trains move rapidly while consuming less energy than traditional vehicles.

6 How does the design of the maglev train reduce friction and consume less fuel?

Interpreting Graphics

***Directions (7):* Base your answer to question 7 on the illustration below, which shows the magnetic fields of an electric motor.**

A Simple Motor

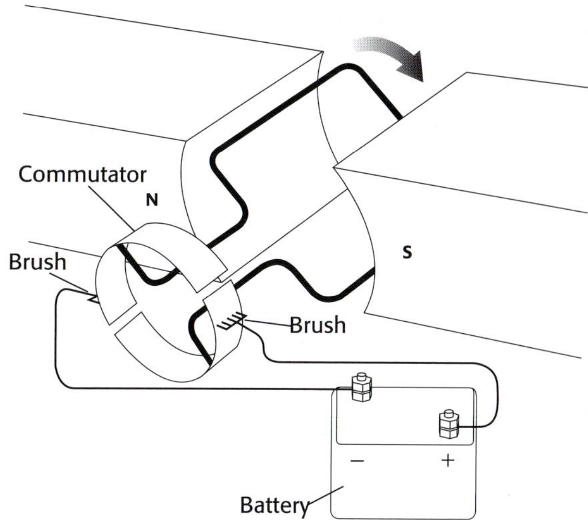

7 What is the purpose of the commutator in this electric motor?

F. constant direction of electron flow
G. alternation of the coil magnetic field
H. production of mechanical energy
I. production of a magnetic field

Skills Practice Lab

Making a Better Electromagnet

Introduction

How can you build the strongest electromagnet from a selection of batteries, wires, and metal rods?

Objectives

- ***Build*** several electromagnets.
- ***Determine*** how many paper clips each electromagnet can lift.
- USING SCIENTIFIC METHODS ***Analyze your results*** to identify the features of a strong electromagnet.

Materials

battery holders (2)
D-cell batteries (2)
electrical tape
extra insulated wire
metal rods (1 each of iron, tin, aluminum, and nickel)
small paper clips (1 box)
thick insulated wire, 1 m
thin insulated wire, 1 m
wire stripper

▶ Procedure

Building an Electromagnet

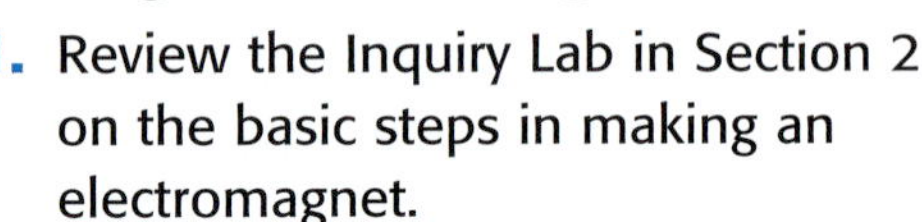

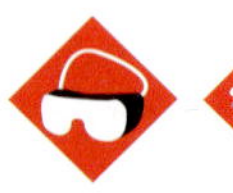

1. Review the Inquiry Lab in Section 2 on the basic steps in making an electromagnet.
2. On a blank sheet of paper, prepare a table like the one shown at right.
3. Wind the thin wire around the thickest metal core. Carefully pull the core out of the center of the thin wire coil. Repeat the above steps with the thick wire. You now have two wire coils that can be used to make electromagnets.
   SAFETY CAUTION Handle the wires only where they are insulated.

Designing Your Experiment

4. With your lab partners, decide how you will determine what features combine to make a strong electromagnet. Think about the following before you predict the features that the strongest electromagnet would have.
   a. Which metal rod would make the best core?
   b. Which of the two wires would make a stronger electromagnet?
   c. How many coils should the electromagnet have?
   d. Should the batteries be connected in series or in parallel?

Electromagnet number	Wire (thick or thin)	# of coils	Core (iron, tin, alum., or nickel)	Batteries (series or parallel)	# of paper clips lifted
1					
2					
3					
4					
5					
6					

5. In your lab report, list each step you will perform in your experiment.
6. Before you carry out your experiment, your teacher must approve your plan.

Performing Your Experiment

7. After your teacher approves your plan, carry out your experiment. You should test all four metal rods, both thicknesses of wire, and both series and parallel battery connections. Count the number of coils of wire in each electromagnet you build.
8. Record your results in your data table.

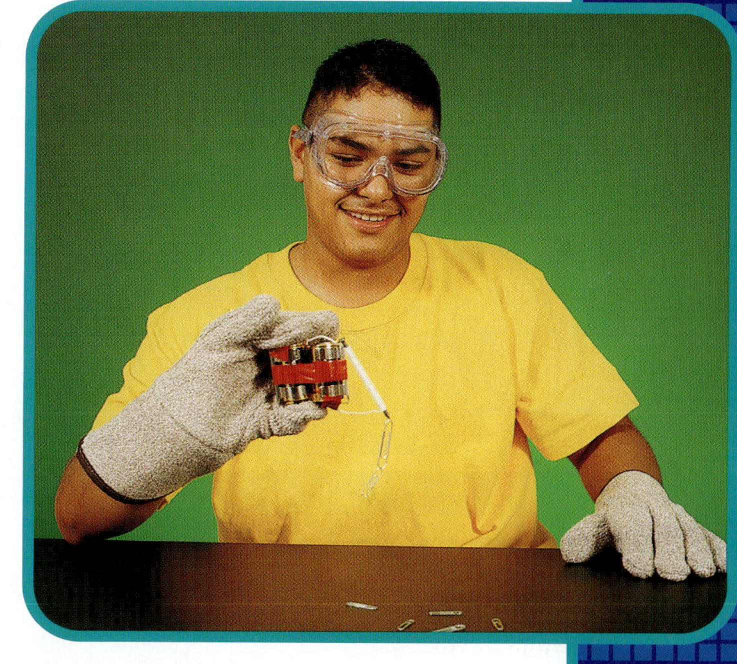

Analysis

1. Did the thick wire or the thin wire make a stronger electromagnet? How can you explain this result?
2. Which metal cores made the strongest electromagnets? Why?
3. Could your electromagnet pick up more paper clips when the batteries were connected in series or in parallel? Explain why.
4. What combination of wire, metal core, and battery connection made the strongest electromagnet?

Conclusions

5. Suppose someone tells you that your conclusion is invalid because each time you tested a magnet on the paper clips, the paper clips themselves became more and more magnetized. How could you show that your conclusion is valid?

Communication Technology

Chapter Preview

Improvements in communications satellites (left) make it possible for more telephone, radio, and television signals to travel from one place to another. These advancements, in both satellites and other communication equipment, are largely the result of improvements in the speed and storage capacity of modern computers.

Background When you write a letter, you assume that the recipient can read and understand what you have written. But how would you send a message to intelligent life on another planet?

NASA had to consider this question in the early 1970s when it began sending spacecraft to the outer regions of the solar system. Like bottles drifting on an ocean, these probes would eventually drift out of the solar system into deep space. With messages attached to these spacecraft, any extraterrestrial beings that might discover a craft could learn where the craft came from if they could understand the message.

When the *Voyager 1* and *2* spacecraft were launched, large gold-plated copper disks were sent with them. Each disk was a large phonograph record consisting of sounds of nature, music from various nations, and greetings in all modern languages.

Activity 1 Suppose you are chosen to develop a visual message to be sent with a probe into deep space. Make a list of information you think would be most important to convey to intelligent extraterrestrial beings. What assumptions have you made about the receivers of this information?

Activity 2 On a piece of plain paper, draw the design for the space message you developed in Activity 1. Share your design with your classmates. See if they understand what you tried to communicate. Are there parts of your design that your classmates have trouble understanding? What might you do to remedy this?

Pre-Reading Questions

1. Give examples of situations in which observing written communication may save someone's life.
2. List three specific ways in which communications have changed in your lifetime.

SECTION 1

Signals and Telecommunication

KEY TERMS

signal
code
telecommunication
analog signal
digital signal
optical fiber

OBJECTIVES

- **Distinguish** between signals and codes.
- **Define** and give an example of telecommunication.
- **Compare** analog signals with digital signals.
- **Describe** two advantages of optical fibers over metal wires for transmitting signals.
- **Describe** how microwave relays transmit signals using Earth-based stations and communications satellites.

You communicate with people every day. Each time you talk to a friend, wave goodbye or hello, or give someone a "thumbs up," you are sending and receiving information. Even actions such as shaking someone's hand and frowning are forms of communication.

Signals and Codes

All of the different forms of communication just mentioned use **signals.** A signal is any sign or event that conveys information. People often use nonverbal signals along with words to communicate. Some signals, such as those shown in ***Figure 1,*** are so common that almost everyone in the United States recognizes their meaning. Signals can be sent in the form of gestures, flags, lights, shapes, colors, or even electric current.

signal anything that serves to direct, guide, or warn

Figure 1

A A handshake indicates friendship or good will.

B A green light means "go."

C A football referee's raised hands tell the crowd and the score-keeper that the kick was good.

Codes are used to send signals

In a baseball game, the catcher often sends signals to the pitcher. These signals can tell the pitcher what type of pitch to throw. For the catcher's signals to be understood by the pitcher, the two players must work out the meaning of the signals, or **code,** before the game starts.

code a set of rules used to interpret data that convey information

You hear and use codes every day, perhaps without even being aware of it. The language you speak is a code. Not everybody in the world understands it. An idea or message can be represented in different languages using very different symbols. The phrase "thank you" in English, for instance, is expressed as *gracias* in Spanish, شكران in Arabic, and 谢谢 in Chinese.

Some codes are used by particular groups. For example, chemists around the world use Au, Pb, and O as symbols for the elements gold, lead, and oxygen, respectively. Also, all mathematicians recognize =, −, and + as symbols that mean "equals", "minus", and "plus."

In addition to signals and codes, communication requires a sender and a receiver. A sender transmits, or sends, a message to a receiver.

Signals are sent in many different forms

Signals such as waving or speaking can be received only if the person at the other end can see or hear the signal. As a result, these signals cannot be sent very far. To send a message over long distances, the signal needs to be converted into a form that can travel long distances easily. Both electricity and electromagnetic waves offer excellent ways to send such signals.

The first step in using electricity to send sound is to convert the sound into an electric current. This electrical signal is produced by using a microphone. The microphone matches the changes in sound waves with comparable changes in electric current. You can imagine the microphone making a copy of the sound in the form of electricity. Next, this electrical signal travels along a wire over longer distances. At the other end, the electrical signal is amplified and converted back into sound by using a speaker.

Connection to SOCIAL STUDIES

In 1837, an American named Samuel Morse received a patent on a device called the electric telegraph. The telegraph uses a code made of a series of pulses of electric current to send messages. A machine at the other end marks a paper tape—a dot in response to a short pulse and a dash in response to a long pulse. Morse code, as shown below, represents letters and numbers as a series of dashes and dots.

A •–	**N** –•	**1** •––––
B –•••	**O** –––	**2** ••–––
C –•–•	**P** •––•	**3** •••––
D –••	**Q** ––•–	**4** ••••–
E •	**R** •–•	**5** •••••
F ••–•	**S** •••	**6** –••••
G ––•	**T** –	**7** ––•••
H ••••	**U** ••–	**8** –––••
I ••	**V** •••–	**9** ––––•
J •–––	**W** •––	**0** –––––
K –•–	**X** –••–	
L •–••	**Y** –•––	
M ––	**Z** ––••	

Making the Connection

1. Write a simple sentence, such as "I am here."
2. Translate it into Morse code, and using sounds, tapping, or a flashlight, send it to a partner.
3. Have your partner write down the code and try to translate the message using Morse code.

A transducer converts signals

A speaker is a type of *transducer,* which is a device that converts a signal from one form to another. A speaker converts an incoming electrical signal into sound. After the conversion, the original sound is heard once again. Two types of transducers, a speaker and a microphone, are shown in ***Figure 2.*** The microphone is a transducer that converts a sound signal into an electrical signal.

Telecommunication

telecommunication the sending of visible or audible information by electromagnetic means

Not long after the discovery of electric current, people tried to find ways of using electricity to send messages over long distances. In 1844, the first telegraph line provided a faster way to send messages between Baltimore and Washington, D.C. More telegraph lines were then installed. By 1861, messages could be sent rapidly between the West Coast and the East Coast.

About 30 years after the first electric telegraph service was provided, the telephone was developed. In another 25 years, the wireless telegraph was invented. With wireless technology, a telegraph message could be sent by radio waves without the use of wires and cables. Sending and receiving signals by using electromagnetic means is referred to as **telecommunication.**

Figure 2

Transducer

A The sound waves are converted into an electrical signal by the microphone.

B The signal travels in the form of an electric current through a wire.

Current

Time

Transducer

C In the speaker, the signal is amplified and converted back into sound.

Figure 3

This weight scale is an analog device. The spring inside the scale stretches continuously in proportion to the weight.

internet connect

www.scilinks.org
Topic: Analog/Digital Signals
SciLinks code: HK4005

SCILINKS. Maintained by the National Science Teachers Association

An analog signal varies continuously within a range

What do a thermometer, a speedometer, and a spring scale have in common? They are analog devices, which means that their readings change continuously as the quantity they are measuring—temperature, wheel rotation, or weight—changes. A reading given by each of these measuring devices is an **analog signal.**

analog signal a signal whose properties, such as amplitude and frequency, can change continuously in a given range

digital signal a signal that can be represented as a sequence of discrete values

An example of an analog device is shown in ***Figure 3.*** As the weight on the scale increases, the needle moves in one direction. As the weight decreases, the needle moves in the opposite direction. The position of the needle on this scale can have any possible value between 0 and 20.0 lb (0 N and 89 N).

The audio signal from the microphone in ***Figure 2*** is an analog signal in the form of a changing electric current. Analog signals consisting of radio waves can be used to transmit picture, sound, and telephone messages.

Digital signals consist of separate bits of information

Unlike an analog signal, which can change continuously, a **digital signal** consists of only discrete, or fixed, values. The binary number system consists of two discrete values, 0 and 1. The combination for a lock, shown in ***Figure 4,*** is in a digital form. It is composed of discrete values, or digits, each of which can have one of six values—1, 2, 3, 4, 5, or 6.

A simple type of digital signal uses a flashing light. Sailors sometimes use a flashing *signal lamp* to send Morse code for ship-to-ship and ship-to-shore communication. Morse code, which was developed by Samuel Morse for transmitting information by telegraph, uses three "digits": a short interval between clicks, a long interval between clicks, and no click at all.

Figure 4

The code to open this lock is in a digital form, consisting of a series of whole numbers.

A binary digital signal consists of a series of zeros and ones

Most digital signals use *binary digital code,* which consists of two values, usually represented as 0 and 1. Each binary digit is called a bit. In electrical form, 0 and 1 are represented by the two states of an electric current: *off* (no current present) and *on* (current present). Information such as numbers, words, music, and pictures can be represented in binary code. ***Figure 5*** shows a binary digital code that is used to represent the English alphabet.

Most modern telecommunication systems transmit and store data in binary digital code. A compact disc (CD) player, shown in ***Figure 6,*** uses a laser beam to read the music that is digitally stored on the disc.

Figure 5

The English alphabet can be represented by combinations of the binary digits 1 and 0.

On (1) Off (0) On (1) Off (0) On (1) Off (0)

0 1 0 0 0 0 1 1 | 0 1 0 0 0 0 0 1 | 0 1 0 1 0 1 0 0

C | A | T

Alphabetic Characters and Their Binary Codes

A 01000001	**H** 01001000	**O** 01001111	**V** 01010110
B 01000010	**I** 01001001	**P** 01010000	**W** 01010111
C 01000011	**J** 01001010	**Q** 01010001	**X** 01011000
D 01000100	**K** 01001011	**R** 01010010	**Y** 01011001
E 01000101	**L** 01001100	**S** 01010011	**Z** 01011010
F 01000110	**M** 01001101	**T** 01010100	
G 01000111	**N** 01001110	**U** 01010101	

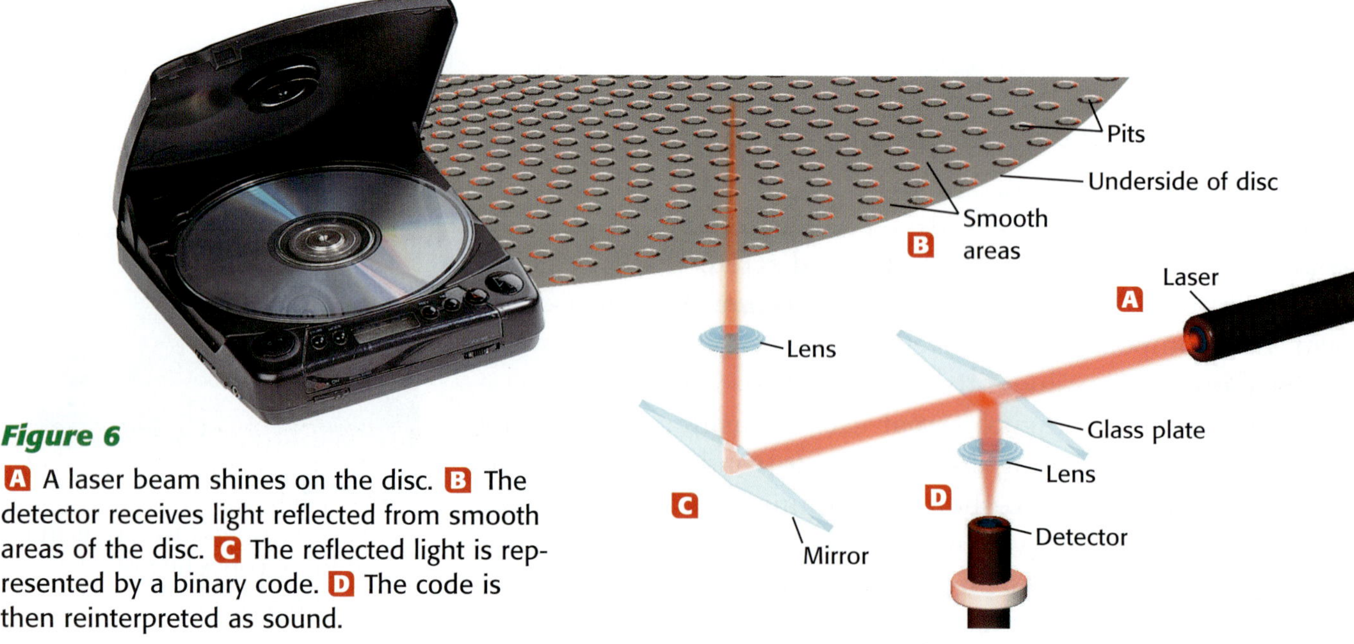

Figure 6

A A laser beam shines on the disc. **B** The detector receives light reflected from smooth areas of the disc. **C** The reflected light is represented by a binary code. **D** The code is then reinterpreted as sound.

Sound can be stored digitally

Sound is a wave of compressions (high air pressure) and rarefactions (low air pressure). Therefore, a sound can be described by noting the air pressure changes. The air pressure is measured in numbers and represented in binary digits.

How is the air pressure measured in numbers? This process is indirect. First, a microphone is used to convert the sound into an analog signal as a changing electric current. Then, an electronic device measures this changing current in numbers or digits at regular intervals. In fact, for CD sound recordings, the current is measured 44 100 times every second! The air pressure measurement is converted into binary digits in terms of 16 bits. For instance, 0000000010000010 is the digital representation of air pressure at a particular moment. This conversion process is basically the same for creating digital signals from analog signals. This conversion also occurs in a digital telephone.

Figure 7
The world's first wrist-wear audio player can be used with a computer to download MP3 music files.

Digital signals can be sent quickly and accurately

Digital signals have many advantages over analog signals. Some digital "switches," consisting of electronic components, can be turned on and off up to a billion times per second. This allows a digital signal to send a lot of data in a small amount of time to receivers such as the audio player in ***Figure 7.***

Noise and static have less effect on digital transmissions. Most digital signals include codes that constantly check the pattern of the received signal and correct any errors that may occur in the signal. By contrast, analog signals must be received, amplified, and retransmitted several times by components along the transmission route. Each time, the signal can get a little more distorted.

Telecommunication Today

Many telecommunication devices, such as telephones, transmit signals along metal wires. But, other ways are more efficient. Metal wires are being replaced with glass fibers that carry signals using pulses of light. Radio waves also carry signals. A call may at times involve sending a signal by way of a communication satellite.

Optical fibers are more efficient than metal wires

A thin glass or plastic fiber, called an **optical fiber,** can be used to carry a beam of light. The light is reflected by the inside walls of the fiber, so it does not escape. Instead of carrying signals that are coded into electric currents, these fibers carry signals that are represented by pulses of light emitted by a laser.

optical fiber a transparent thread of plastic or glass that transmits light

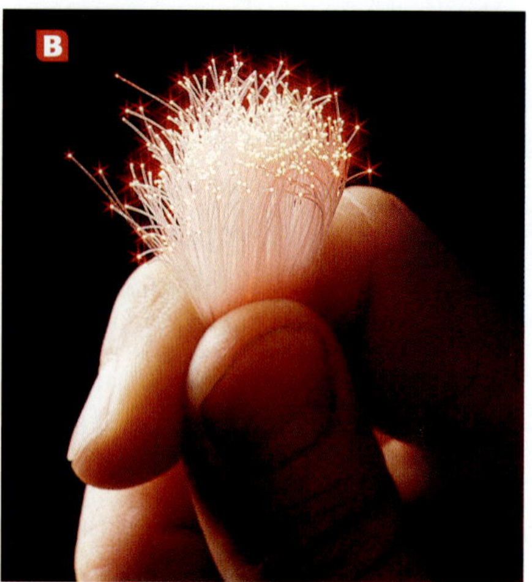

Figure 8

A single standard metal-wire cable **A** is much thicker than an optical-fiber cable **B**, yet it carries much less information than an optical fiber does.

Many telephone lines now in use in the United States consist of optical fibers. The optical-fiber system is lighter and smaller than the wire-cable system, as shown in ***Figure 8,*** making it much easier to put in place. A standard metal-wire cable, which is about 7.6 cm in diameter, can carry up to 1000 coded conversations at one time. A single optical fiber can carry 11 000 conversations at once using the present coding system.

As the use of the Internet and telephones dramatically increases, telephone companies are busy expanding fiber-optic networks. The materials used to make the optical fibers are so pure that a half-mile-thick slab made from them would transmit as much light as a clean windowpane.

Figure 9

A microwave relay tower picks up a signal, amplifies it, and relays it to the next tower.

Relay systems make it possible to send messages across the world

If you've traveled around the United States, you may have noticed tall steel towers with triangular or cone-shaped boxes and perhaps some dish-shaped antennas. These are microwave relay towers. They use microwave frequencies to transmit and relay signals over land.

As shown in ***Figure 9,*** a tower picks up a signal transmitted by another tower, amplifies the signal, and retransmits it toward the next tower. The next tower repeats the process, passing the signal along until it reaches its destination. Microwave transmission is often used to connect distant places with telephone signals.

Microwave towers should be tall

Microwaves are a form of electromagnetic waves. For the microwave signals to be sent from one tower to the next as in **Figure 10,** each tower must be almost visible from the top of the other. A tower built high in the Rocky Mountains would be able to relay signals for 80 to 160 km. However, a tower built in the plains can relay only a little farther than the horizon, or about 40 km.

Microwave transmission allows you to make telephone calls across land without wires or fiber-optic networks. But how could you call a friend who lives across the ocean in Australia?

In the past, your call would have been carried by one of the cables that run along the ocean floor between continents. Because there are so many telephones, online computers, and fax machines today, the demand is too much for these cables. Communication satellites that orbit Earth help send these messages.

Figure 10

A microwave relay tower picks up a signal, amplifies it, and relays it to the next tower.

Communications satellites receive and transmit electromagnetic waves

These satellites use solar power to generate electricity. This allows them to operate receivers, transmitters, and antennas. These satellites receive and send microwaves just like the towers described earlier. Because they are so high above the ground, these satellites can relay signals between telephone exchanges thousands of kilometers apart.

A satellite receives a microwave signal, called an *uplink,* from a ground station on Earth. The satellite then processes and transmits a *downlink* signal to another ground station. To keep the signals separate, the uplink signal consists of electromagnetic waves with a frequency of around 6 GHz (gigahertz, or 10^9 cycles per second), while the downlink signal typically has a lower frequency of about 4 GHz.

The transmitting antenna of a communications satellite must be aimed so that it covers the largest land area without the signal becoming too weak. This area is called a *satellite footprint* and increases as the distance between the satellite and Earth's surface increases. With several such satellites, a signal from one location can be transmitted and received anywhere in the world.

Many communications satellites have geostationary orbits

If you live in an area where people receive television signals from satellites by using dish-shaped antennas, you may have noticed that the dish always points in one direction. If a satellite orbits Earth, its position would change. Why does the dish not have to be moved in order to stay pointed at the orbiting satellite?

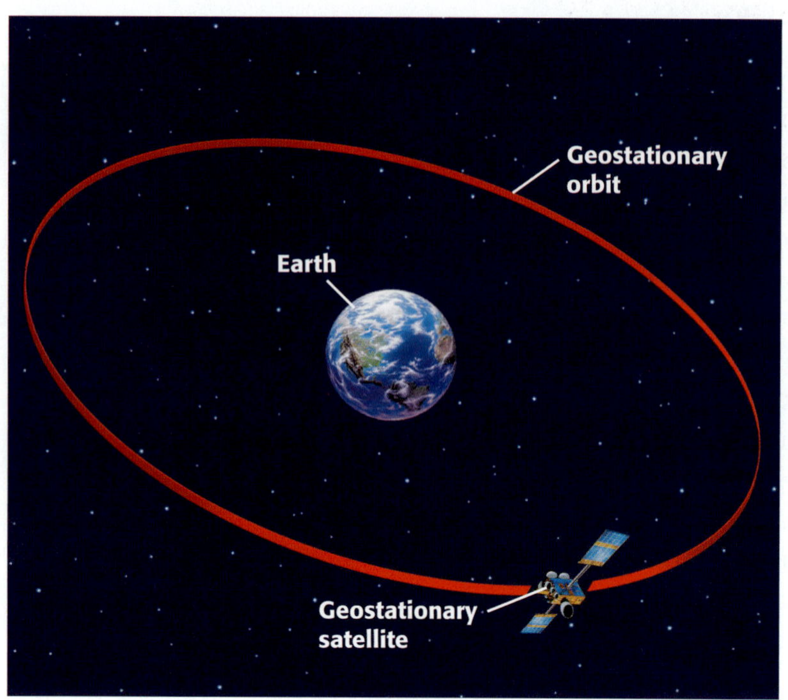

The answer is that these satellites orbit Earth every 24 hours, the same amount of time it takes for Earth to rotate once. Therefore the position of the satellite relative to the ground doesn't change. The orbit of this type of satellite is called a *geostationary orbit,* or a *geosynchronous orbit.* To be in a geostationary orbit, a satellite must be 35 880 km directly over Earth's equator and have a speed of 11 050 km/h, as shown in **Figure 11.**

Figure 11
A geostationary satellite appears to stay in a fixed position above the same spot on Earth. Once a dish is aimed at one of these satellites, it does not have to be moved again.

SECTION 1 REVIEW

SUMMARY

- A signal conveys a message that can be sent using gestures, shapes, colors, electricity, or light.
- An analog signal varies continuously.
- A digital signal represents information in the form of discrete digits.
- A two-number code, called a binary digital code, represents the signal conditions of "on" or "off" by either a 1 or a 0.
- Telecommunication sends a signal long distances by means of electricity or light.
- Satellites are used to relay microwave signals around the world.

1. **List** five examples of telecommunication.
2. **Explain** why talking to your friend on the telephone is an example of telecommunication but talking to her face to face is not an example of telecommunication.
3. **Describe** how a sound is translated into an analog signal.
4. **Indicate** which of the following are analog signals and which are digital:
   a. music recorded on a compact disc
   b. speed displayed by the needle on a speedometer dial
   c. time displayed on a clock with three or four numerals
   d. time displayed on a clock with hands and a circular dial
5. **Discuss** two advantages of optical fibers over metal wires as media for carrying signals.
6. **Explain** how communications satellites transmit messages around the world.
7. **Explain** what a geostationary orbit is and why many communications satellites are put in geostationary orbits.
8. **Critical Thinking** Explain why a taller microwave relay tower on Earth's surface has a longer transmission range than a shorter relay tower has.

SECTION 2

Telephone, Radio, and Television

OBJECTIVES

- **Describe** how a telephone converts sound waves to electric current during a phone call.
- **Distinguish** between physical transmission and atmospheric transmission for telephone, radio, and television signals.
- **Explain** how radio and television signals are broadcast using electromagnetic waves.
- **Explain** how radio and television signals are received and changed into sound and pictures.

KEY TERMS

atmospheric transmission
carrier
modulate
cathode-ray tube
pixel

What sort of information do communication satellites relay around the world? Some information is vital business information, and some is secret government and military communication. Much of the information, however, consists of radio and television programming and telephone conversations.

Telephones

When you talk on the telephone, the sound waves of your voice are converted to an electrical signal by a transducer, a microphone in the mouthpiece of the telephone. As you hear the voice from the earpiece, a speaker, another transducer, is changing an electrical signal back into sound waves.

The electret microphone vibrates with sound waves, creating an analog signal

Most newer telephones use an *electret microphone.* In this type of microphone, an electrically charged membrane is mounted over an *electret,* which is a material that has a constant electric charge. The membrane vibrates up and down with the sound waves of your voice, as shown in ***Figure 12.***

This motion causes a changing electric field so that an analog electrical signal that corresponds to your voice is produced. This signal is then transmitted as variations in an electric current between your telephone and the telephone of the person to whom you are talking.

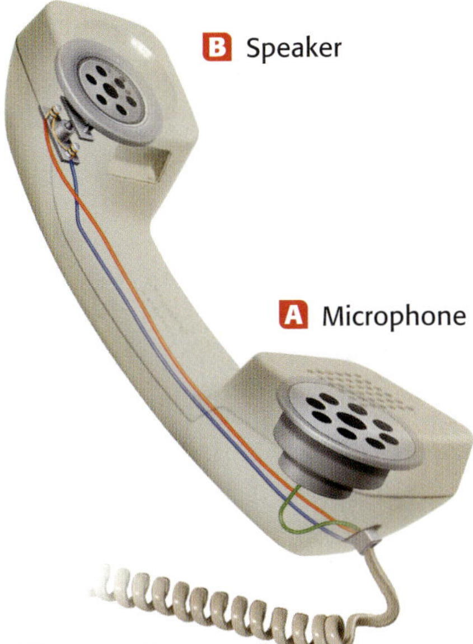

Figure 12

The sound waves from your voice are transformed by the microphone **A** into an analog electrical signal. A speaker **B** converts the analog electrical signal back to sound waves.

The movement of the speaker cone converts the analog signal back into sound waves

When you get a telephone call, the electrical signal enters your telephone. The incoming electrical signal travels through a coil of wire that is fastened to a thin membrane called a *speaker cone*.

The wire coil is placed in a constant magnetic field and can move back and forth. The varying electric current of the incoming signal creates a varying magnetic field that interacts with the constant magnetic field. This causes the coil to move back and forth, which in turn causes the speaker cone to move in the same way. The movement of the speaker cone creates sound waves in the air that match the sound of your caller's voice. Speakers in radios, televisions, and stereo systems work the same way.

INTEGRATING

BIOLOGY

Biologists have discovered that information is transmitted through the human body by the nervous system. The nervous system contains billions of nerve cells that form bundles of cordlike fibers. Nerve signals, known as *impulses,* can travel along nerve fibers at speeds ranging from about 1 m/s to 90 m/s. Nerve signals are relayed through the body by a combination of electrical and chemical processes.

Telephone messages are sent through a medium in physical transmission

Telephone messages can be voice calls, faxes, or computer data. But how do the messages arrive at the right place? When you make a call, the signal is sent along wires to a local station. Telephone wires arrive at and leave the station in bundles called cables that are strung along poles or run underground. The station's switching equipment detects the number called.

If you are calling someone who lives nearby, such as a neighbor, the switching equipment sends the signal down wires that connect your phone through the station to your neighbor's phone. When the signal reaches your neighbor's phone, the phone rings. When your neighbor picks up the phone, the circuit is completed.

Sometimes telephone conversations travel a short distance by wire and then are carried by light through fiber-optic cables. In this case, the varying current is fed to a laser *diode,* a device used to convert alternating current, causing the laser light to brighten and dim. In this way, the electrical signal is converted into a light or optical signal. This light passes through an optical fiber to its destination, where a sensor changes light back to an electrical signal. Transmission of signals by wires or optical fibers is called *physical transmission*.

Messages traveling longer distances are sent by atmospheric transmission

Long-distance calls may be transmitted over wire or fiber-optic cables, or they may be sent through the atmosphere using microwave radiation. The transfer of information by means of electromagnetic waves through the atmosphere or space is called **atmospheric transmission.** The use of microwaves for telephone signals is one example of atmospheric transmission.

atmospheric transmission the passage of an electromagnetic wave signal through the atmosphere between a transmitter and a receiver

Computers help route calls

When you make a call, computers are used to find the most direct form of routing. Either physical or atmospheric transmission or a combination of the two may be used for long-distance calls, as shown in **Figure 13.** If the telephone system is very busy, computers may route your call indirectly through a combination of cables and microwave links. Your call to someone 100 mi away could actually travel for thousands of miles.

Cellular phones transmit messages in the form of electromagnetic waves

A cellular phone is just a small radio transmitter/receiver, or *transceiver.* Cellular phones communicate with one of an array of antennas mounted on towers or tall buildings. The area covered by each antenna is called a *cell.*

As the user moves from one cell to another, the phone switches to communicate with the next antenna. As long as the telephone is not too far from a cellular antenna, the user can make and receive calls.

A cordless phone is also a radiowave transceiver. The phone communicates with its base station, which is also a transceiver. The base station is connected to a standard phone line.

Figure 13

Your telephone call **A** arrives at a local switching station **B**. Depending on its destination, the call is routed through a wire cable **C**, fiber-optic cable **D**, microwave towers **E**, or communication satellites **F**. The telephone signal then arrives at another switching station **G** where it travels to your friend's house, and the phone rings.

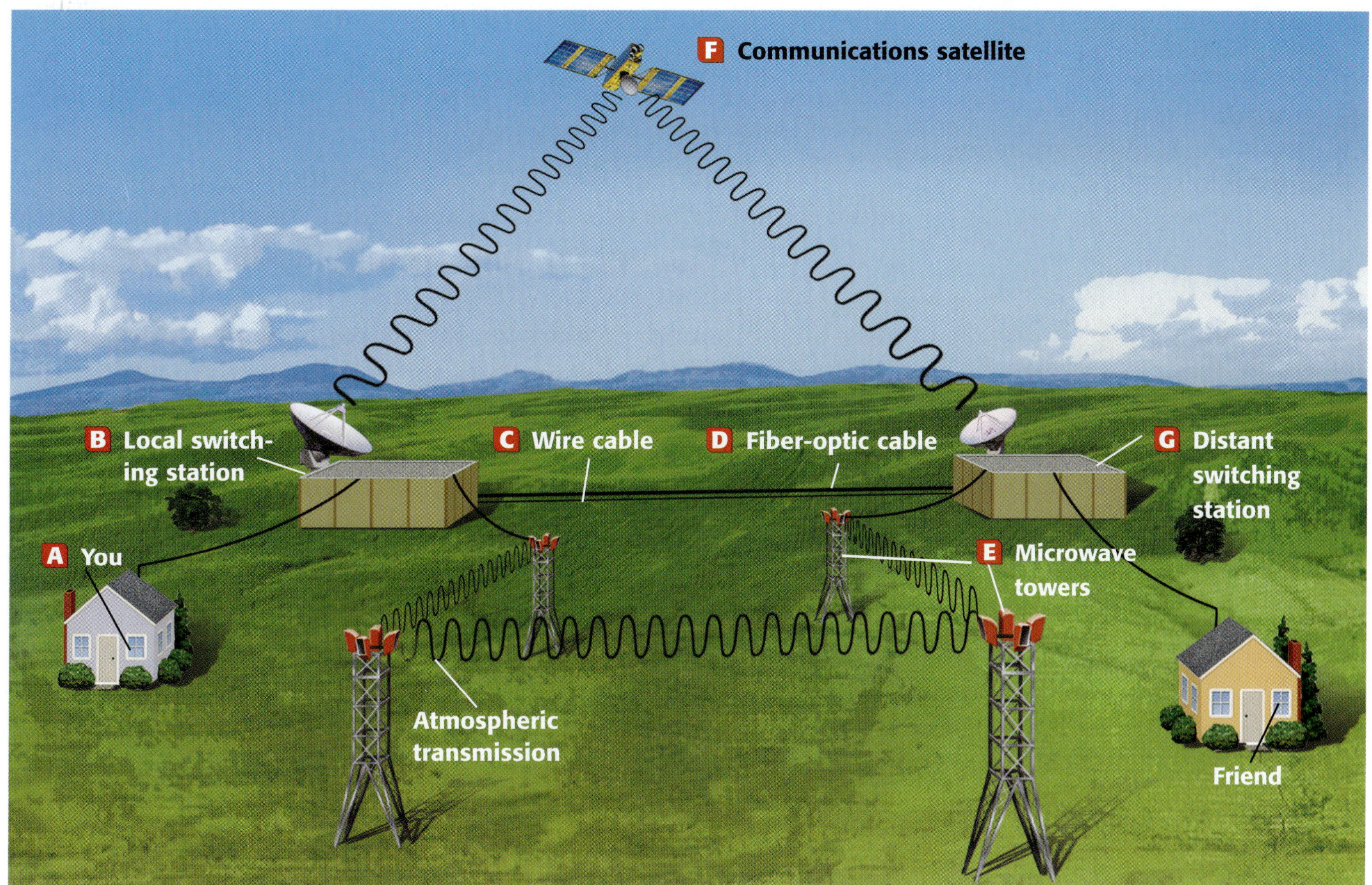

Radio and Television

Figure 14

Morse code was a method of transmitting communication signals before the time of radio waves.

The first long-distance transmission of a signal using radio waves was made across the English Channel in 1899. At the time, the signals were sent in Morse code, as in ***Figure 14.*** For the next 20 years, all radio transmissions were sent this way. It was not until 1918 that voice messages could be sent over the air using radio waves. In 1920, the first commercial radio station, KDKA, in Pittsburgh, Pennsylvania, went on the air, broadcasting sound signals by means of radio waves.

Sound waves are converted to electromagnetic waves for radio broadcast

A radio signal begins as a sound, or audio, signal that is first converted into a varying electric current from a microphone, tape deck, or CD player. This varying current is the analog of the sound waves from a voice or music source, as shown in ***Figure 15A.***

A microphone is capable of producing only a weak signal, which has to be amplified, or increased in power, using an electronic device called an amplifier.

Now the signal is ready to be broadcast using a transmitter at the radio station. The visible part of the transmitter is an antenna, and the transmitter also contains different electric circuits including an oscillator. The oscillator produces a **carrier,** which is a signal of constant frequency and amplitude, as shown in ***Figure 15B.*** The numbers you see on your radio dial correspond to the carrier wave's frequency.

carrier a wave that can be modulated to send a signal

modulate to change a wave's amplitude or frequency in order to send a signal

You can imagine the carrier wave as the wave on which the audio signal to be broadcasted will ride. The audio signal contains the sound information in the frequency range of the human voice, from about 100 to 3000 Hz. Also, the change in the loudness of the sound appears in the signal in terms of changing amplitude. The sound signal and the carrier signal meet in a specialized circuit in the transmitter. Here they combine and the audio signal changes, or **modulates,** the carrier wave. The result is a signal of constant frequency with an amplitude that is shaped by the audio signal, as shown in ***Figure 15C.***

Figure 15

Amplitude Modulation
An audio signal carrying sound information modulates a carrier wave.

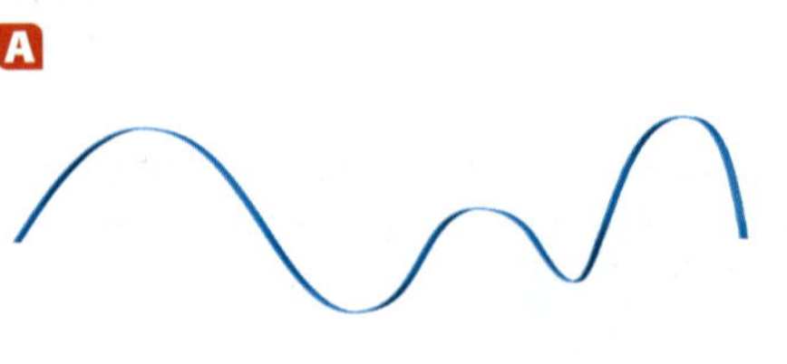

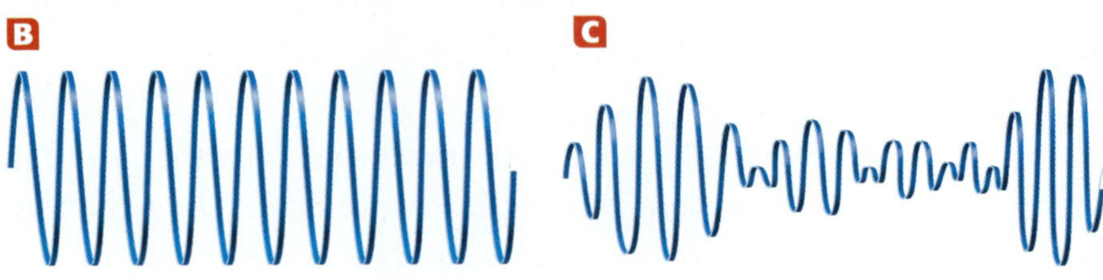

Modulation can be either AM or FM

Most broadcast carrier waves are modulated either by *amplitude modulation* (AM) or by *frequency modulation* (FM). In amplitude modulation, the audio signal increases and decreases the amplitude of the carrier wave in a pattern that matches the audio signal. In frequency modulation, the audio signal affects the frequency of the carrier wave, changing it in a pattern that matches the audio signal.

The modulated signal generated in the transmitter causes electric charges to move up and down along the length of the antenna. The resulting motion of the charges produces radio waves corresponding to the modulated signal.

The path that radio waves follow depends on the transmission frequency. Higher frequency transmissions can follow only a simple straight line. This is called *line-of-sight transmission.* To receive a signal from an FM radio station, which can broadcast at frequencies between 88 and 108 MHz, your radio must be located no farther than just over the horizon from the broadcasting antenna (usually about 40 to 80 km).

You can receive AM stations that are much farther than 80 km away. AM frequencies between 540 and 1700 kHz can travel as *ground waves,* which can follow the curvature of the Earth for some distance, unlike line-of-sight transmissions.

In regions where broadcast signals cannot be received, such as in mountain valleys, television signals are conveyed through cables. Microwave links from satellites or microwave towers are fed by cable to local stations. From there, they are sent out by either broadcast or cable.

Radio stations use sky waves to broadcast long distances

Another way AM radio stations can broadcast farther is by using *sky waves.* Sky waves spread out from the antenna into the sky and are reflected in the upper atmosphere, which contains charged particles. Sky waves are reflected back to Earth by these particles.

Some radio broadcasting uses sky waves to reach distant locations around the world. Certain powerful AM signals that use sky waves can be received thousands of miles away. These stations are often limited to using sky waves at night, when stations that have interfering signals may be off the air.

Radio receivers convert electromagnetic waves back into sound

The antenna of your radio receiver works as a transducer. When radio waves strike it, they produce very weak electric currents that match the original radio signal. But radio waves from many stations with different frequencies are striking the antenna. Fortunately, each station broadcasts with a different carrier frequency. Like the girl in ***Figure 16,*** you have to adjust the antenna circuit with a *tuner* so that the radio responds to only the frequency of the station you want to hear.

Figure 16

Even when the antenna is hidden, it is responding to radio waves.

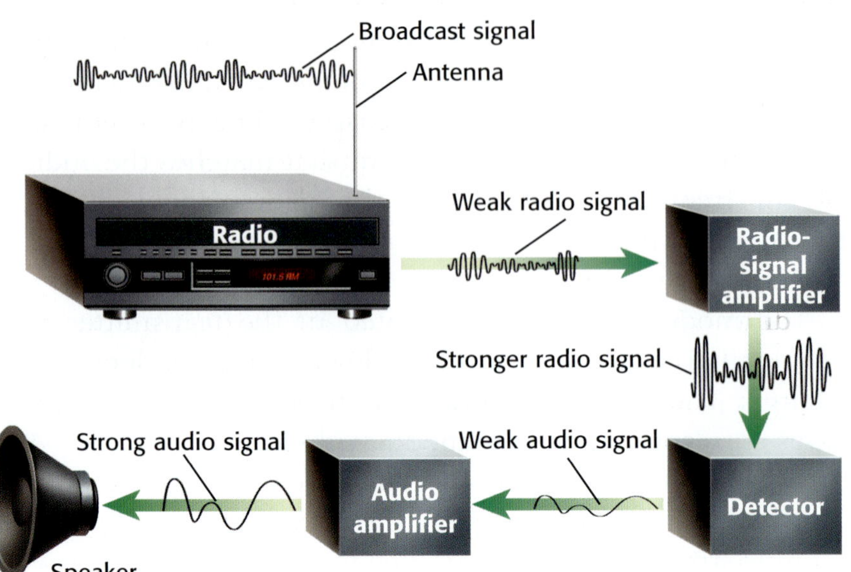

Figure 17

After the detector removes the audio signal from the carrier wave, the signal is amplified and sent to a speaker. (Note that the amplifiers and detector shown as boxes correspond to different circuits that are part of the radio.)

Next the modulated signal from the antenna is sent to a detector, as shown in **Figure 17.** The carrier wave has a very high frequency compared with the original electrical signal, so the two can be separated easily. The electrical signal then goes to an amplifier, which increases the signal's power. Finally, the amplified signal is sent to a speaker, where the sound that was originally broadcast is recreated.

Television sets convert electromagnetic waves back into images and sound

Television signals are also received by an antenna. By selecting a channel, you tune the television to the carrier frequency of the station of your choice. The carrier wave is passed to a detector that separates the audio and video electrical signals from the carrier. The audio electrical signals are sent to an audio amplifier and speaker, just as in a radio. The video electrical signal, which contains the color and brightness information, is used to create an image on the face of a picture tube.

cathode-ray tube a tube that uses an electron beam to create a display on a phosphorescent screen

The picture tube of a black-and-white television is a large **cathode-ray tube,** or CRT. A CRT makes a beam (ray) of electrons from a negatively charged cathode. The beam is directed toward the face of the tube that is covered with *phosphors,* which glow when an electron beam strikes them. Electromagnets arranged around the neck of the tube deflect the beam, causing it to move across the phosphor-coated face. The moving beam lights up the phosphors in a pattern that recreates the shot taken by the television camera. Each pass of the beam is called a *scan line.* In the United States, each complete image is made up of 525 scan lines.

Color picture tubes produce electron beams

Color picture tubes in some televisions, like the one shown in ***Figure 18,*** produce three electron beams, one for each of the primary colors of light: red, blue, and green. The phosphors on the face of the tube are arranged in groups of three dots, one of each color. Each group of three dots is a **pixel,** the smallest piece of an electronically produced picture.

To make sure the beam for red strikes only red phosphors, two different approaches can be used. In one, a screen with holes, called a *shadow mask,* lies just behind the face of the tube. The beam for each color passes through a hole in the shadow mask at an angle so that the beam strikes only the phosphor dot that glows the correct color. Another approach in some televisions use a single electron beam deflected toward the phosphor of the correct color by a charged wire grid.

pixel the smallest element of a display image

VOCABULARY *Skills Tip*

The term pixel *is derived from the phrase* **pic**ture **el**ement.

Figure 18

A The video signals modulating the television carrier waves are detected and are then used to control the electron beams in the cathode-ray tube. The sound signal is amplified and sent to a speaker, while video signals vary the intensity of the three electron beams.

B Electromagnets sweep the beams across the face of the screen. The intensity of each beam determines how bright the phosphor dots light up.

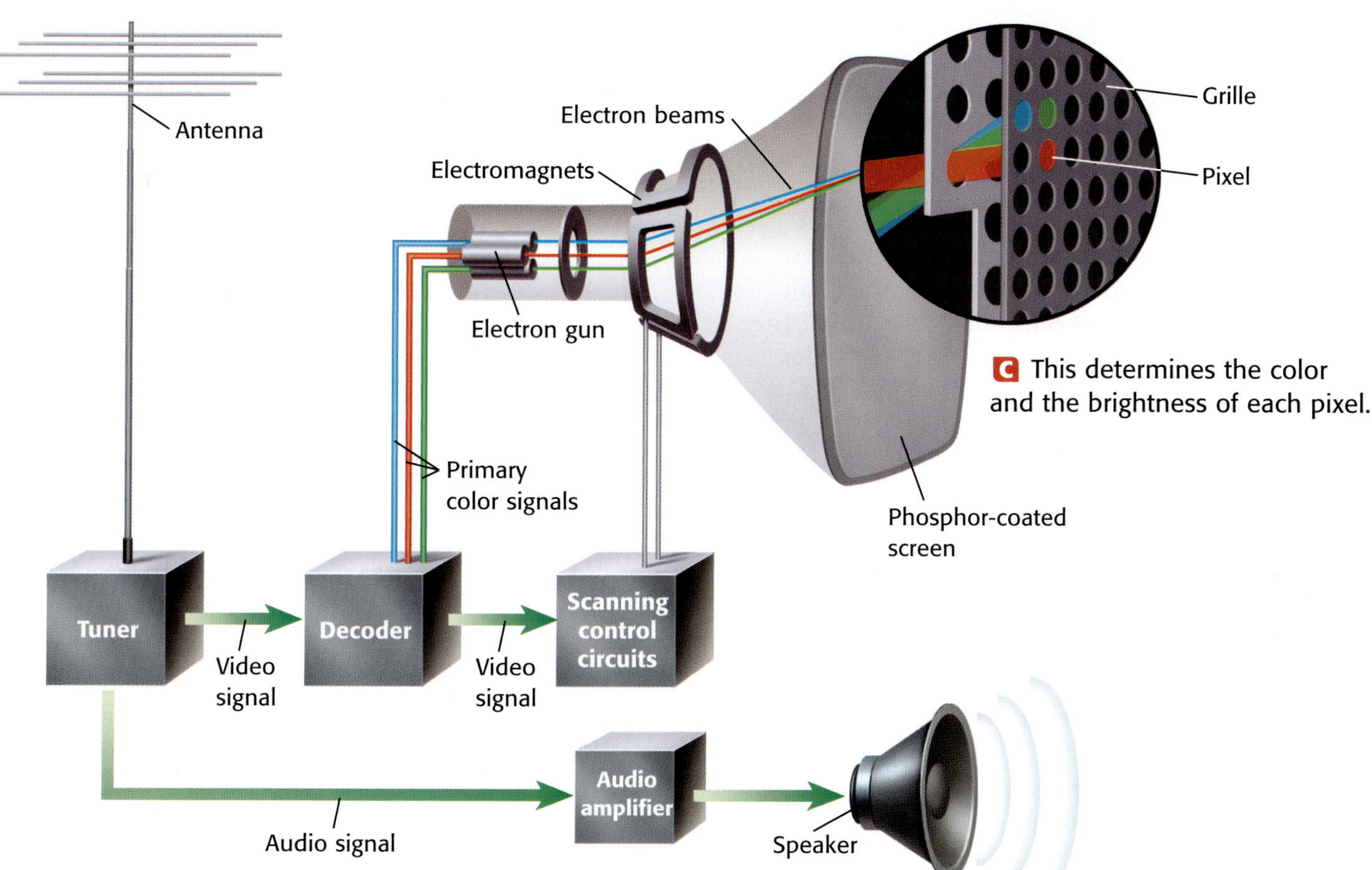

C This determines the color and the brightness of each pixel.

TV by the Numbers: High-Definition Digital TV

After 2005, new television shows may have a much different look than the ones broadcast before 2005. That's because the Federal Communications Commission (FCC) required that all television stations in the United States to broadcast only digital, high-definition television, called HDTV for short, by 2006.

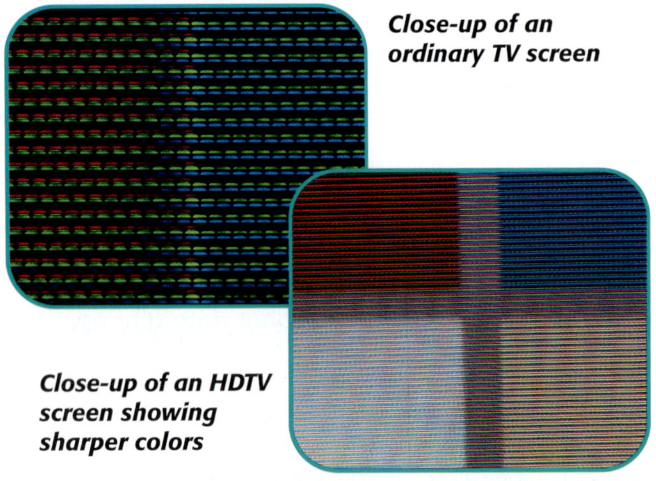

Close-up of an ordinary TV screen

Close-up of an HDTV screen showing sharper colors

Comparing HDTV with Ordinary TV

The HDTV picture looks very detailed and sharp compared with an ordinary television picture. You can even see the faces of fans at a sports event. The picture has a width-to-height ratio of 16:9, similar to many movies that you see in a theater. Some displays are large flat screens that hang on the wall like a painting or mirror. HDTV sound is clear, digital sound, like that recorded on a CD.

However, you won't have to throw out your old television set in 2006. A converter box will let your old TV show pictures that are broadcast in HDTV. However, the picture won't look any better than if it is a regular broadcast.

History of HDTV

The development of HDTV began in the early 1980s when engineers realized that newer microprocessors would be able to both send and decode data fast enough to transmit a detailed television picture digitally. In 1988, 23 different HDTV systems were proposed to the FCC. In 1993, several companies joined the Massachusetts Institute of Technology in what was called the Grand Alliance. Its purpose was to create HDTV standards for broadcasters. In 1996, the FCC approved an entirely digital system, and by late 1998, the first commercial HDTV receivers were on sale at prices between $10 000 and $20 000.

HDTV Technology

HDTV achieves its sharp picture by using almost 1200 scan lines, compared with 525 on analog TV. The digital signal can also be continuously checked for accuracy, so the picture remains clear.

The movie industry is very interested in HDTV. It will be able to release new HDTV tapes and discs of movies already released on other video formats. Another possibility is that some movies can be released to pay-per-view HDTV at the same time they are released in theaters. The HDTV picture and sound quality should be so good that some people may prefer to stay at home to watch a new movie.

Your Choice

1. **Making Decisions** What effect do you think HDTV will have on movie theaters, especially if studios make movies available on HDTV for the same price as a theater ticket? Explain whether you think people will still want to go to theaters.
2. **Critical Thinking** When home VCRs were introduced in the mid-1970s, they cost about $2500. By 1980, the price was about $600. By 1985, the price was about $450. By the mid-1990s, you could buy a good-quality VCR for about $250. Check the current price of an HDTV, and use the VCR example to project what one might cost in 5 years.

How do red, blue, and green TV phosphors produce other colors?

Materials
- ✔ *three adjustable flashlights with bright halogen bulbs*
- ✔ *several pieces of red, blue, and green cellophane*
- ✔ *white paper*

1. Adjust the focus of each flashlight so that it produces a circle of light about 15 cm in diameter on a white sheet of paper. Turn off the flashlights.
2. Place a piece of red cellophane over the lens of one flashlight, green cellophane over the lens of another, and blue over the lens of the third.
3. Turn on the flashlights, and shine the three beams on white paper so the circles of light overlap slightly.
4. Adjust the distance between the flashlights and the paper until the area where all three circles overlap appears white. Add more cellophane if necessary.

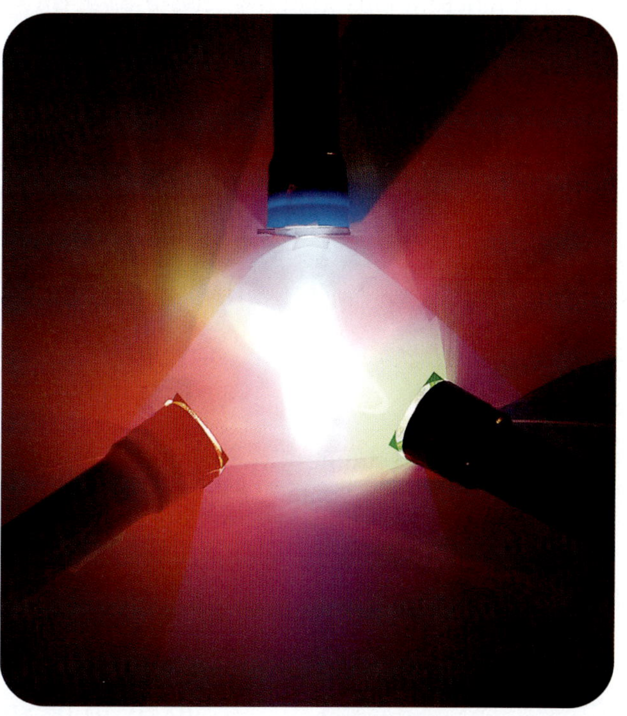

Analysis

1. Describe the three colors formed where two of the beams overlap.
2. What combinations of light produced the colors yellow and cyan?

SECTION 2 REVIEW

SUMMARY

- Telephones change sound to electrical signals and electrical signals to sound.
- Signals can be sent by physical transmission or by atmospheric transmission.
- Signals modulate carrier waves by amplitude modulation (AM) and frequency modulation (FM).
- Television converts electromagnetic waves.

1. **Describe** how telephones convert sound to electrical signals and electrical signals to sound.
2. **List** three ways that telephone signals can travel.
3. **Identify** which have a higher frequency—AM or FM signals.
4. **Describe** the function of phosphors in a cathode-ray tube.
5. **Describe** how a radio receiver converts a broadcast signal into sound waves.
6. **Describe** how television sets convert electromagnetic waves into images and sound.
7. **Critical Thinking** Why do you think there is increasing interest in using fiber-optic cables to provide homes with cable television service?

SECTION 3

Computers and the Internet

KEY TERMS

computer
random-access memory
read-only memory
hardware
software
operating system
Internet

OBJECTIVES

- **Describe** a computer, and list its four basic functions.
- **Describe** the binary nature of computer data and the use of logic gates.
- **Distinguish** between hardware and software, and give examples of each.
- **Explain** how the Internet works.
- **Define** how technological tools are applied to address personal and societal needs.

Did you heat a bagel in the microwave for breakfast? Have you ever inserted a card in a slot to pay your fare on a bus or subway? Maybe you rode to school in a car. Did you stop for a traffic light? Was the temperature in your classroom comfortable? Did a clerk scan a bar code on an item you bought at the store?

All of these situations involve computers or the use of computers to function. The computer that controls traffic lights may be large and complex, while the one in the microwave oven is likely to be small and simple.

computer an electronic device that can accept data and instructions, follow the instructions, and output the results

Computers

A **computer** is a machine that can receive data, perform high-speed calculations or logical operations, and output the results. Although computers operate automatically, they do only what they are programmed to do. Computers respond to commands that humans give them, even though they sometimes may appear to "think" on their own.

Computers have been changing greatly since the 1940s

The first electronic computer was the Electronic Numerical Integrator and Computer (ENIAC), shown in ***Figure 19.*** It was developed during World War II. ENIAC was as big as a house and weighed 30 tons. Its 18 000 vacuum tubes consumed 180 000 W of electric power. During the late 1940s, computers began to be used in business and industry. As they became smaller, faster, and cheaper, their use in offices and homes dramatically increased.

Figure 19
ENIAC, the world's first practical digital computer, like the one shown here, used 18 000 vacuum tubes. The modern microprocessor has thousands of times ENIAC's computing power.

Today computers are so common that we hardly notice them. Try to imagine what computer developers in the 1940s would think if they could see a modern personal computer, or PC, which fits on a desk and computes thousands of times faster than the earlier cumbersome computers like ENIAC.

Computers carry out four functions

Digital computers perform four basic functions: input, storage, processing, and output. The input function can be carried out using any number of devices, as shown in ***Figure 20.*** When you use a personal computer, you can use a keyboard or a mouse to input data and instructions for the computer. You may use a mouse to draw or select text in a document.

Other input devices include a scanner, which can enter drawings or photographs. A modem connected to a telephone line can be both an input and an output device.

Microphones, musical instruments, and cameras can be used as input devices. Once the data are processed, the result, or output, may be displayed on a monitor. You can also send output to a printer. Sound output goes to speakers or to a recording device. Both input and output data can be stored in storage devices.

Figure 20
A computer can receive data from many devices, store information on a hard drive, process data as needed, and store results or send them to an output device.

INTEGRATING

PHYSICS

All PCs are digital computers, but analog computers also exist. An example of an analog computer in a car is the gasoline gauge, whose needle moves in response to a voltage sent from a sensor in the gas tank.

VOCABULARY Skills Tip

Most disks used for computer work today are not actually floppy. The name floppy disk *originally referred to a larger disk that was encased in softer, plastic sleeves.*

Computer input is in the form of binary code

All input devices provide data to the computer in the form of binary code. For example, a keyboard contains a small processor that detects which key is pressed and sends the computer a binary code that represents the character you typed. Devices such as temperature sensors, pressure sensors, and light sensors provide information in the form of varying voltage. This information is analog; that is, it changes continuously over the range of the quantity being measured. Such information must be passed through an analog-to-digital converter (A to D converter) before the data can be used by a computer.

Computers process binary data, including numbers, letters, and other symbols, in groups of eight *bits*. Each bit can have only one of two values, usually represented as 1 and 0. A group of eight bits is called a *byte*.

As shown in **Figure 5,** when you type the capital letter *W*, the computer receives the data byte 01010111. The lowercase letter *e* is received as 01100101. So, if you type the word *We*, the computer recognizes the word as 0101011101100101, a combination of the *W* and *e* bytes.

Computers must have a means of storing data

Both input and output data can be stored on long-term storage devices, such as the *hard-disk drive,* sometimes called the hard drive. Hard-drive storage capacity has increased very rapidly. From 1999 to 2001, available storage increased from approximately 20 to 80 billion bytes (gigabytes or Gigs). Hard drives are so called to distinguish them from disk drives that use removable "floppy" disks and drives that use compact discs (CDs). Floppy disks can be removed from one computer and used in another.

Quick ACTIVITY

How Fast Are Digital Computers?

1. With a partner, time how long it takes for each of you to solve problems involving adding, subtracting, multiplying, and dividing large numbers. Do each problem first by hand and then with the help of a hand-held calculator, which is a form of digital computer. Solve at least five problems using each method.
2. Find the average amount of time spent doing the problems by hand and with a calculator. Compare the two averages, and discuss your results.

Figure 21

The head of the hard drive moves over the surface of the disk, reading and recording data in narrow tracks.

Both hard drives and floppy drives use disks coated with a magnetizable substance. Disks of this type are generally referred to as *magnetic media.* A small read-write head, similar to the record-play head in a cassette tape recorder, transfers data to and from the disk, as shown in ***Figure 21.*** Each data bit consists of a very small area that is magnetized in one direction for 0 and in the opposite direction for 1. These magnetized areas are arranged in tracks around the disk. When data are being read, the disk spins and the head detects the magnetic direction of each area that passes. When data are being recorded, or "written" on the disk, a current passes through a small coil of wire in the head. The direction of the current at any time creates a magnetic field in one direction or the other. This magnetic field allows the head to record information on the disks in bits of 0s and 1s.

On a disk, the time required to access (read or write) data depends on where the information is stored on the disk and the position of the read-write head.

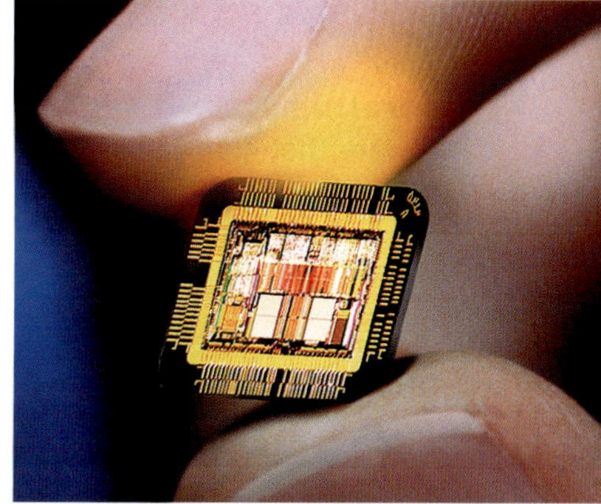

Figure 22

This chip is covered with tiny transistors that function as two-position switches. This feature allows the computer to operate as a binary machine.

Random-access memory is used for short-term storage of data and instructions

For working memory, the computer needs to be able to access data quickly. This type of memory is contained on microchips, tiny integrated circuits, as shown in ***Figure 22,*** and is called **random-access memory,** or RAM.

random-access memory a storage device that allows a computer user to write and read data; it is the amount of data that the memory chips can hold at one time (abbreviation, RAM)

Each RAM microchip is covered with millions of tiny transistors, electronic devices that transfer current across resistors. Like a light switch, each transistor can be placed in one of two electrical states: *on* or *off.* Each transistor represents either a 0 or a 1 and can thus store one data bit. This memory is called random-access because any of the data stored in RAM can be accessed at the same time. Unlike accessing data stored on the disk, accessing information in RAM doesn't depend on location.

Read-only memory is for long-term storage of operating instructions

read-only memory a memory device that contains data that can be read but cannot be changed (abbreviation, ROM)

hardware the parts or pieces of equipment that make up a computer

software a set of instructions or commands that tells a computer what to do; a computer program

operating system the software that controls a computer's activities

Another type of memory is called **read-only memory,** or ROM. The information in ROM is permanently stored when the chip is manufactured. As a result, it can be read but not changed. When you first turn on a computer, instructions that are stored in ROM set up the computer so that it is ready to receive input data from the keyboard or the hard drive.

Optical storage devices can be more permanent than magnetic disks

Information can also be stored on *compact discs* (CDs) and *digital versatile discs* (DVDs). These discs are called optical media because the information on them is read by a laser light. When they are used to store computer data, they are referred to as CD-ROMs and DVD-ROMs because the data they hold are permanently recorded on them.

Operating systems control hardware

All of the physical components of a computer are called **hardware.** The hardware of the computer can compute and store data only if we provide it with the necessary instructions. These instructions are called computer programs, or **software.**

When a computer is turned on, one of the first programs executed by the computer is the **operating system,** or OS. The OS coordinates the computer hardware—memory, keyboard, disks, printer, mouse, and monitor. It also handles the transfer of computer files to and from disks and organizes the files. The operating system provides the environment in which other computer programs run. These other programs are called applications. Applications include word processors, drawing programs, spreadsheet programs, and programs to organize and manipulate large amounts of information, such as a store's inventory or polling data. Applications also include computer games and programs that allow you to browse the Internet, as this section will explain.

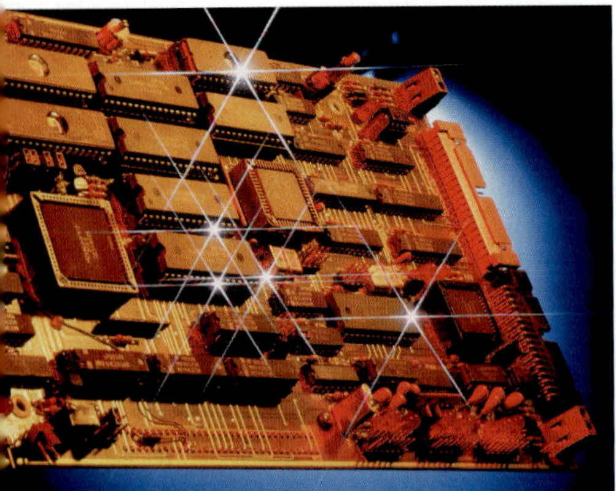

Figure 23

The motherboard is like the nervous system of a computer. It contains the CPU, memory chips, and logic circuits.

The processing function is the primary operation of a computer

The processing function is where computing actually takes place. Computing or data processing is carried out by the *central processing unit,* or CPU. The CPU of a personal computer usually consists of one microchip, which is not much larger than a postage stamp. The CPU is one of the many chips located on the motherboard, as shown in ***Figure 23.***

Chips have many components

This chip, or microprocessor, consists of millions of tiny electronic parts, including resistors, transistors, and capacitors (devices for storing electric charges), most of which act as switches. These components form huge numbers of circuits on the surface of the chip.

Logic circuits in the CPU make decisions

The heart of the CPU is an *arithmetic/logic unit,* or ALU, which performs calculations and logic decisions. The CPU also contains temporary data storage units, called *registers,* which hold results from previous calculations and other data waiting to be processed. A control section coordinates all of the processor activities. Finally, there are conductors that connect the various parts of the CPU to one another and to the rest of the computer.

When you start a program, the program first loads into random-access memory. Next the CPU performs a "fetch" operation, which brings in the first program instruction. Then it carries out that instruction and fetches the next instruction. The CPU proceeds in this fashion, fetching new instructions and obtaining data from the keyboard, mouse, disk, or other input device. Then it processes the data and creates output that is sent to the monitor or printer.

The CPU's logic gates can be built up to evaluate data and make decisions

As with memory chips, transistors in the CPU act as switches. The switches can operate as devices called *logic gates.* Just as a real gate can be open or shut, a logic gate can open or close a circuit depending on the condition of two inputs. One kind of logic gate, called an AND gate, closes the circuit and allows current to pass only when both inputs are in the "on" position.

You could use a similar device to alert you when it is both cold and raining so that you would know how to dress. You could connect moisture and temperature sensors to an AND gate and arrange to have it close a circuit and ring a bell. The bell would ring only when the temperature fell below 40°F and it was raining. If it were cold but dry, the bell would not ring. Similarly, the bell would not ring if it were warm but raining.

Connection to ARCHITECTURE

Architects, industrial designers, and engineers often use computer-aided design (CAD) to model new products. With CAD, you can construct a visual model of an object. Then you can rotate it to see how it looks from different positions, and you can make parts of the model transparent so that you can see how it fits together. You can test the model by subjecting it to computer-simulated wind, rain, heat, cold, and other real-world conditions.

Making the Connection

1. Suppose you are designing a bridge that will replace an old bridge across a river in a large city. What real-world conditions would you need to simulate to test your model?
2. What factors would you consider when trying to design a house that will absorb and use solar energy?

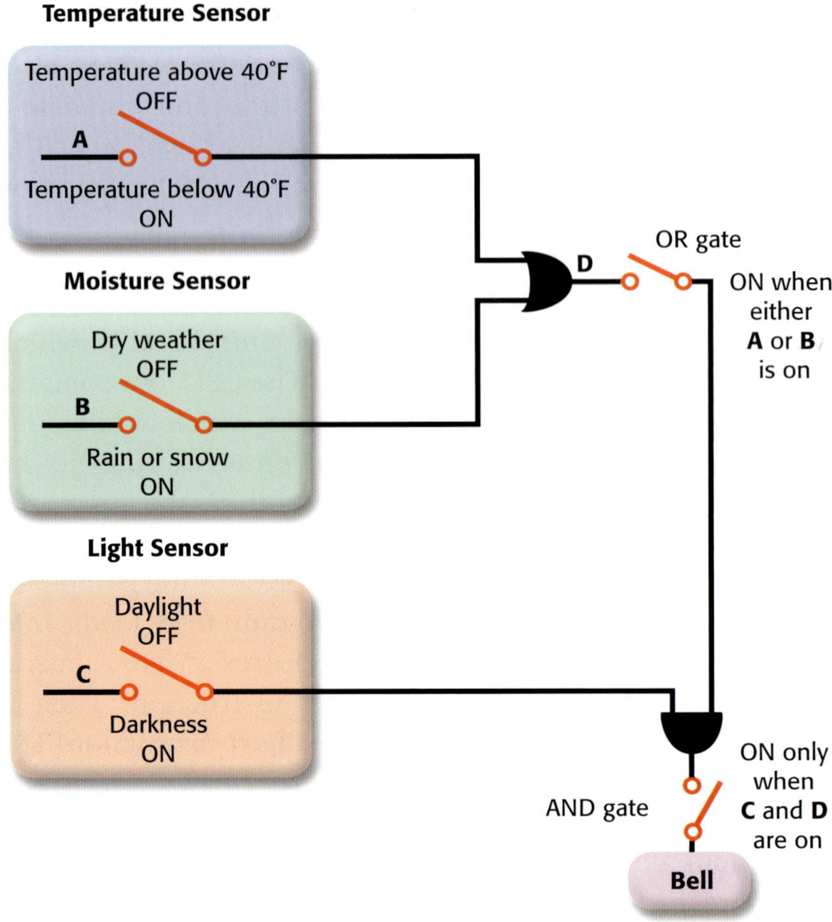

Figure 24

This logic system evaluates three variables—temperature, moisture, and light—in order to make a decision.

If you use a type of logic gate called an OR gate, as shown in ***Figure 24,*** the bell will ring when it is cold or raining. If you want the bell to ring when it is cold or when it is raining, but only if it is dark outside, you can use an OR gate followed by an AND gate.

Figure 25

LANs have given schools, businesses, and government great communication possibilities.

Computer Networks and the Internet

As the use of desktop personal computers became common in the 1980s, people looked for ways to link all of the computers within a single business, university, or government agency. The development of local area networks, or LANs, was the solution. In a LAN, as in ***Figure 25,*** all PCs are connected by cables to a central computer called a *server.* A server consists of a computer with lots of memory and several hard-disk drives for storing huge amounts of information.

This system allows workers to share data files that are stored on the server. One can also send a document to another person on the network. Soon after LANs were established, people were exchanging memos and documents over the network. This type of communication is called electronic mail, or E-mail.

The Internet is a worldwide network of computers

As the number of powerful computers increased, especially in government and universities, the U.S. Department of Defense wanted to connect them in a nationwide network. However, the department's computer experts worried about setting up a network that depended on only a few computers. If anything went wrong, the entire network would stop working.

Instead, a network in which every computer could communicate with every other computer was created. If part of the network were destroyed, the remainder would still be able to transmit information. This was the beginning of the **Internet.**

Because many companies had set up internal networks that used the same communication methods as the Defense Department's network, it was easy for them to connect to the network by telephone lines. Many other governments and corporations around the world joined to form a worldwide network that we now call the Internet, which is really a network of other networks.

If you have used the Internet, you are probably most familiar with the part known as the *World Wide Web,* or WWW, or just the Web. The Web was created in Europe in 1989 as a way for scientists to use the Internet to share data and other information.

The Web was mostly a resource for scientific information. It has since exploded into a vast number of sites created by individuals, government agencies, companies, and other groups. The Web is meeting many needs of individuals and of society.

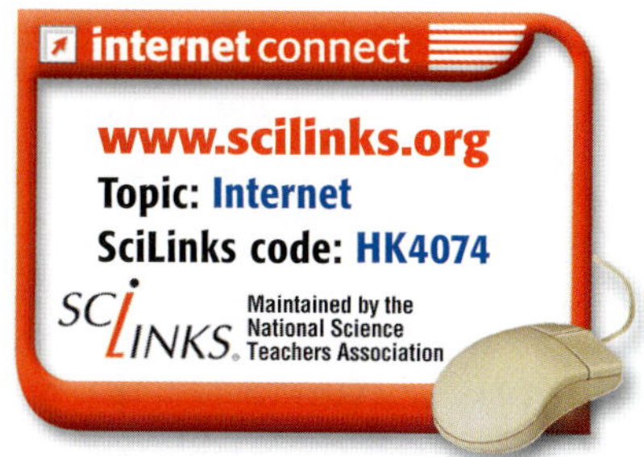

Internet a large computer network that connects many local and smaller networks all over the world

Using a Search Engine

Search engines provide a way to find specific information in the vast amount of information that is available on the Internet. Finding information successfully depends on several things, one of which is picking appropriate keywords for your search.

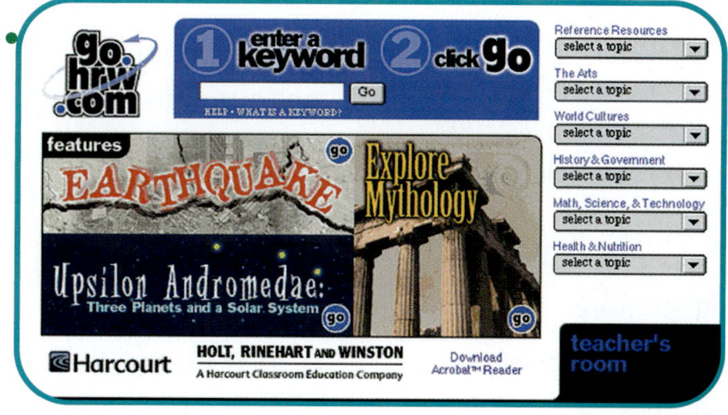

Applying Information

1. Pick a science topic that interests you. Write down a few keywords that you think will occur in information about the topic.
2. Use an Internet search engine to find three Web sites that have information on the topic. Experiment with keywords until you find the kinds of sites you want.
3. Try the same keywords on other search engines. Do they all find the same sites?
4. How did the results differ? Can you detect whether an engine specializes in certain types of information?

Figure 26

The Internet opens doors of opportunity in mere seconds.

You need three things to use the Internet

To use the Internet, as in ***Figure 26,*** you need a computer with a modem to connect the computer to a telephone line. The word *modem* is short for modulator/demodulator, a device that codes the output data of your computer and uses it to modulate a carrier wave that is transmitted over telephone lines. The modem also extracts data from an incoming carrier wave and sends that data to your computer.

Next you need a software program called an Internet, or Web, browser. This program interprets signals received from the Internet and shows the results on your monitor. It also changes your input into signals that can be sent out.

Finally, you need a telephone connection to an Internet service provider, or ISP. An ISP is usually a company that connects the modem signal of your computer to the Internet for a monthly fee.

Internet communication uses transmission pathways like those used to relay television, radio, and telephone signals. With the Internet system, you can communicate with a Web site anywhere on Earth in just seconds.

SECTION 3 REVIEW

SUMMARY

- Computers perform four functions: input, storage, processing, and output.
- Input is in the form of binary code, grouped in eight bits called a *byte.*
- The physical components of computers are called hardware.
- Programs and instructions are called software.
- Computing activity takes place in a central processing unit, which also carries out logic functions.
- The Internet is a worldwide network of computers that can store and transmit vast amounts of data.

1. **List** three computer input devices and three output devices.
2. **Describe** the four main functions of a digital computer.
3. **Explain** how data are stored on and read from a magnetic hard-disk drive.
4. **Indicate** how ROM and RAM differ.
5. **Distinguish** between the ways that optical media and magnetic media function.
6. **Identify** which of the following components are part of a computer's hardware and which are part of its software.
   - **a.** a CPU microchip
   - **b.** a program to calculate when a car needs an oil change
   - **c.** the instructions for the computer clock to be displayed
   - **d.** RAM memory
7. **Explain** the purpose of an operating system.
8. **Compare** AND gates with OR gates.
9. **Restate** the three things, in addition to a computer, that you need to use the Internet.
10. **Creative Thinking** Describe how technological tools might be used in the future both for personal needs and for the needs of society.

Study Skills

Pattern Puzzle

Pattern puzzles help you remember information in the correct order and can help you understand scientific processes.

1 Write down the steps of a process in your own words.

We'll use the chapter's description of how a computer's four functions apply to a typed sentence. In your own words, write these steps on a sheet of notebook paper, one step per line.

- Words are typed on a keyboard (input).
- The input words are sent as digital data bytes to a central processing unit (CPU).
- The CPU stores data bytes in a file on the hard-disk drive.
- The words are taken from the stored file and are displayed as output on a monitor.

2 Cut the sheet of paper into thin strips with one step per strip. Shuffle the strips so that they are out of sequence.

- The CPU stores data bytes in a file on the hard disk drive.
- The words are taken from the stored file and displayed as output on a monitor.
- The input words are sent as digital data bytes to a central processing unit (CPU).
- Words are typed on a keyboard (input).

3 Place the strips in the correct sequence. Confirm the order of the process by checking your text or class notes.

- Words are typed on a keyboard (input).
- The input words are sent as digital data bytes to a central processing unit (CPU).
- The CPU stores data bytes in a file on a hard-disk drive.
- The words are taken from the stored file and are displayed as output on a monitor.

Practice

Use concepts from the chapter to properly arrange the following pattern puzzle:

- The call undergoes atmospheric transmission by microwaves.
- The call is received at a switching station and sent to its final destination.
- A telephone call is transmitted by wire cable to the local switching station.
- The microwaves are amplified and relayed between transmission towers.

CHAPTER 18 REVIEW

Chapter Highlights

Before you begin, review the summaries of key ideas of each section, found at the end of each section. The vocabulary terms are listed on the first page of each section.

UNDERSTANDING CONCEPTS

1. A __________ is necessary in order to interpret a signal.
a. CPU
b. modulation
c. operating system
d. code

2. A microphone uses a transducer to
a. convert digital signals into analog signals.
b. convert sound waves into an electric current.
c. convert a digital signal into an analog signal.
d. amplify a sound wave.

3. The up-and-down movement of electrons in the wire of a transmitting antenna produces __________ waves.
a. electromagnetic
b. visible light
c. sound
d. television

4. Telephone signals sent down wires rely on
a. electromagnetic waves.
b. digital signals.
c. electric current.
d. atmospheric transmission.

5. If the __________ is adjusted, a radio can receive a certain station.
a. amplifier voltage
b. speaker circuit
c. tuner circuit
d. carrier frequency

6. FM radio waves do *not* rely on
a. line-of-sight transmission.
b. carrier waves.
c. amplitude modulation.
d. a transducer.

7. Memory in a computer that is permanent and cannot be added to is called
a. RAM.
b. ROM.
c. CPU.
d. CRT.

USING VOCABULARY

8. How does telecommunication differ from ordinary communication?

9. Describe the differences between *analog signals* and *digital signals*.

10. How does *physical transmission* differ from *atmospheric transmission*?

11. Which of the following diagrams correctly represents the path of a light beam through an *optical fiber*? Explain your choice. How is a binary digital signal sent through an optical fiber?

a.
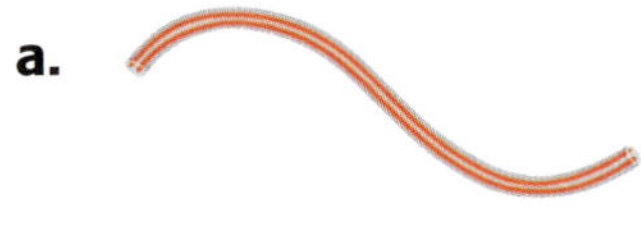

b.
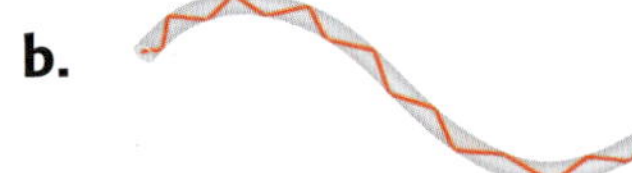

12. Describe how a television converts a television signal into sounds and images that you can hear and see. Use the terms *cathode-ray tube, phosphor, scan line,* and *shadow mask* in your answer.

13. List three parts of a computer's CPU, and explain the functions of those three parts.

14. List two examples of computer *hardware* that are input devices. List two examples of computer hardware that are output devices.

15. RAM stands for *random-access memory.* Why is this kind of computer memory called *random access*?

BUILDING GRAPHING SKILLS

16. Graphing In 1965, an engineer named Moore stated that the number of transistors on integrated-circuit chips would double every 18 to 24 months. This idea became known as Moore's law. The data in the table below show the actual numbers of transistors on the CPU chips that have been introduced since 1972. Make a graph with "Years" on the x-axis and "Number of transistors" on the y-axis. Describe the shape of the graph. Does your graph support Moore's law? Does the projected value for the year 2010 seem realistic?

Year	Microprocessor	Number of transistors
1972	4004	2300
1973	8008	3500
1974	8080	6000
1978	8086	29 000
1982	80286	134 000
1986	80386	275 000
1989	80486	1,200,000
1993	Pentium	3,100,000
1996	Pentium Pro	5,500,000
1997	Pentium II	7,500,000
1999	Pentium III	9,500,000
2010	?	800,000,000 (estimated)

THINKING CRITICALLY

17. Applying Knowledge Your basketball team and coach have a meeting in which you decide that certain hand gestures and finger positions will convey certain messages such as pass, stall, or play zone defense, etc. Use this example to explain the difference between a signal and a code.

18. Interpreting Graphics Identify the diagram that represents each of the following:

a. a carrier wave
b. an audio signal
c. an amplitude-modulated carrier

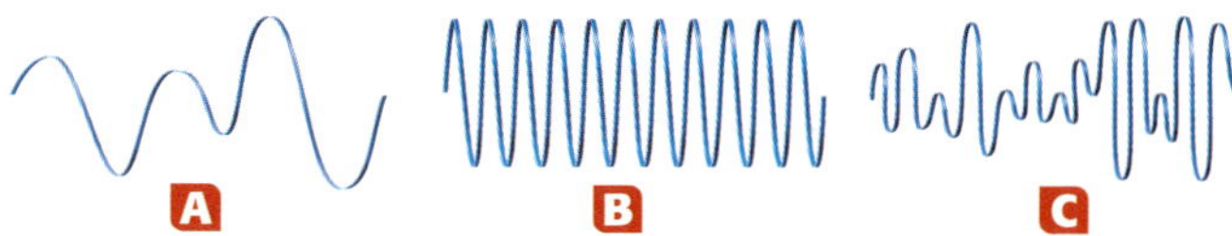

19. Applying Knowledge Use words or draw a diagram to explain why an FM radio signal can be received farther away as the height of the transmitting tower is increased. Also explain why you can receive more-distant television stations by using a higher television antenna.

20. Problem Solving Suppose you want a light to come on automatically when someone comes to your door but only if it is dark outside. You have a proximity sensor, which is a device that closes an electric circuit when a person comes close to the door. What other sensor and what kind of logic gate do you need?

21. Applying Knowledge Suppose you are attempting to connect your computer to the World Wide Web, but it is not working. List two possible reasons why your computer is not able to connect, and explain how you could check for each one.

DEVELOPING LIFE/WORK SKILLS

22. Applying Technology What computer-input device would work best in each of the following situations? Justify your choices.

a. You want to use a picture from a magazine in a report for history class.
b. You want to play a computer game in which you fly a plane.
c. You want to compose an E-mail message and send it to a friend.

23. Interpreting and Communicating ENIAC was among the world's first digital computers. At your library or on the Internet, research the construction and early uses of ENIAC. Write a paragraph that summarizes your findings.

24. Researching and Communicating Microchips consist of many components. At your library or on the Internet, research the construction and functions of microchips. Communicate those findings in a written report or in a sketch with labels and captions. When you report your findings, explain why you chose the method of communication that you used.

25. Working Cooperatively Working with a group of classmates, research the achievements of the following people in the fields of communication and computer technology. Construct a classroom display that includes a picture of each person along with a summary of his or her contributions to the advancement of communication and computer technology.

a. Edwin Armstrong
b. Grace Murray Hopper
c. An Wang
d. Lewis Latimer
e. Vladimir Zworykin
f. John W. Mauchly

INTEGRATING CONCEPTS

26. Connection to Fine Arts Many animated motion pictures and television shows are now produced with the help of computers. Research the development of computer animation and special effects over the last several years. When were the first computerized special effects used in a motion picture? Based on your findings, what advances in computer effects and animation do you predict will occur in the next 10 years?

27. Connection to Social Studies Internet access has led to problems involving free speech and privacy. Should there be controls to prevent the spread of potentially dangerous or offensive information? Should others have free access to information about you? Research specific examples of these problems and find out what laws have been passed to address them. What arguments are made for and against free speech? An important fact to consider is that the Internet is not limited to one country.

28. Concept Mapping Copy the unfinished concept map below onto a sheet of paper. Complete the map by writing the correct word or phrase in each of the lettered boxes.

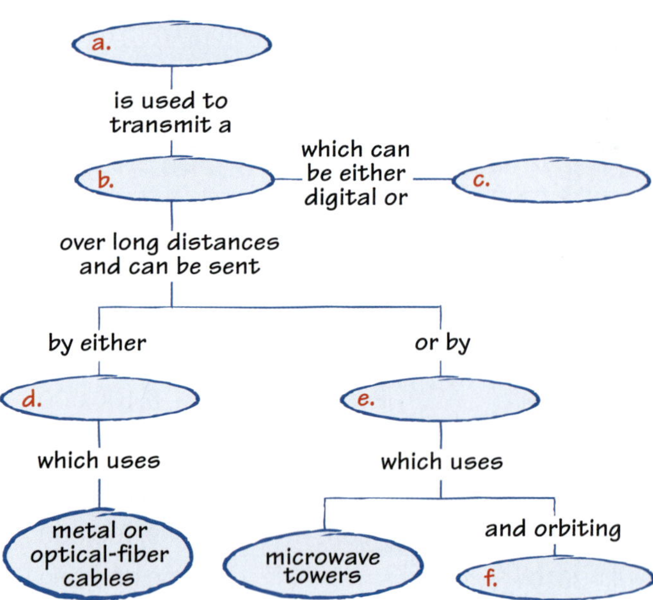

Standardized Test Prep

Understanding Concepts

***Directions (1–4):* For *each* question, write on a separate sheet of paper the letter of the correct answer.**

1. What type of communication system is a series of microwave towers?
   A. optical
   B. physical transmission
   C. relay
   D. satellite

2. What type of carrier is produced by varying electric and magnetic fields in a radio oscillator?
   F. electromagnetic waves
   G. microwaves
   H. sound waves
   I. sky waves

3. Digital versatile discs (DVD) are an example of what type of storage device?
   A. hard-disk drive
   B. magnetic medium
   C. optical medium
   D. random-access memory

4. What is the purpose of RAM in a computer?
   F. "fetch" operations
   G. long-term storage
   H. processing instructions
   I. working memory

***Directions (5–6):* For *each* question, write a short response.**

5. Differentiate between the two ways a broadcasting station can modulate a signal during a radio transmission.

6. The electromagnetic waves used for radio and telephone communication are in the radio and microwave part of the electromagnetic spectrum. Why are these waves better for atmospheric communication than the wavelengths in the visible or ultraviolet parts of the spectrum?

Test *TIP*

For short-response and essay questions, be sure to answer the prompt as fully as possible. Include major steps, important facts, descriptive examples, and supporting details in your response.

Reading Skills

***Directions (7):* Read the passage below. Then answer the question.**

The World Wide Web (WWW) began as a concept at CERN, a major European research organization, in the early 1990s. Researchers there wanted to allow users of the growing network of computers around the world to set up "servers" — computers that act as nodes for transferring information to anyone with access to the network. A key part of this development was a "user-friendly" language that could be learned easily by someone who wanted to write a document. Once it was easy for people to use the web, its popularity grew. Since 1992, the web has grown from 50 servers to tens of millions of servers.

7. Evaluate how the usefulness of the web depends on the availability of inexpensive, small computers, and how it has helped expand communication technologies.

Interpreting Graphics

***Directions (8):* Base your answer to question 8 on the illustration below.**

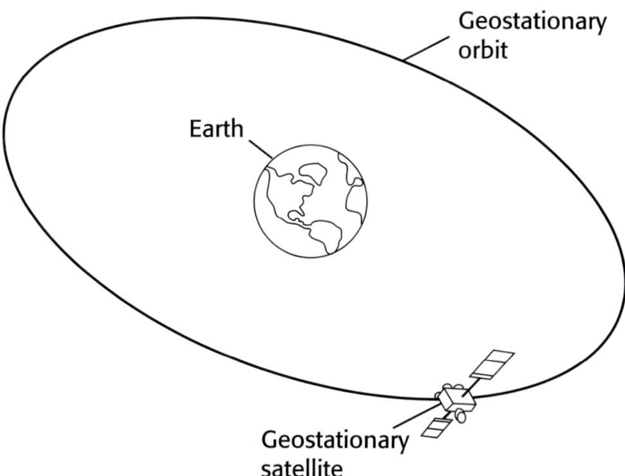

8. The satellite is in a very high orbit above Earth. Why doesn't a satellite dish antenna have to move to follow this satellite?

Skills Practice Lab

Introduction

Can you determine the speed of sound in air?

Objectives

- USING SCIENTIFIC METHODS ***Observe*** the reinforcement of sound in a column of air.
- ***Determine*** the speed of sound in air by calculating the wavelength of sound at a known frequency.

Materials

glass cylinder, tall
glass tube, about 4 cm in diameter and 50 cm in length
meterstick
rubber stopper, large
thermometer
tuning forks of known frequency (2)
wood dowel or wire handle for stopper

Determining the Speed of Sound

Procedure

1. The speed of sound is equal to the product of frequency and wavelength. The frequency is known in this experiment, and the wavelength will be determined.
2. If you hold a vibrating tuning fork above a column of air, the note or sound produced by the fork is strongly reinforced when the air column in the glass tube is just the right length. This reinforcement is called *resonance,* and the length is called the *resonant length*. The resonant length of a closed tube is about one-fourth the wavelength of the note produced by the fork.
3. On a paper, copy ***Table 1*** at right.

Determining the Speed of Sound

SAFETY CAUTION Make sure the tuning fork does not touch the glass tube or cylinder, as the glass may shatter from the vibrations.

4. Set up the equipment as shown in the figure at right.
5. Record the frequency of the tuning fork as the number of vibrations per second (vps) in your ***Table 1.***
6. Make the tuning fork vibrate by striking it with a large rubber stopper mounted on a dowel or heavy wire.
7. Hold the tube in a cylinder nearly full of water, as illustrated in the figure.
8. Hold the vibrating fork over the open end of the tube. Adjust the air column by moving the tube up and down until you find the point where the resonance causes the loudest sound. Then hold the tube in place while your partner measures the distance from the top of the glass tube to the surface of the water (which is the part of the tube sticking out of water). Record this length to the nearest millimeter as Trial 1 in ***Table 1.***
9. Repeat steps 6–8 two more times using the same tuning fork, and record your data in ***Table 1.***
10. Using a different tuning fork, repeat steps 4 through 8.

Table 1 **Data Needed to Determine the Speed of Sound in Air**

	Tuning fork 1	Tuning fork 2
Vibration rate of fork (vps)		
Length of tube above water (mm), Trial 1		
Length of tube above water (mm), Trial 2		
Length of tube above water (mm), Trial 3		

Analysis

1. On a clean sheet of paper, make a table like the one shown below.
2. Measure the inside diameter of your tube and record this measurement in your ***Table 2.*** The reflection of sound at the open end of a tube occurs at a point about 0.4 of its diameter above the end of the tube. Calculate this value and record it in ***Table 2.*** This distance is added to the length to get the resonant length. Record the resonant length in ***Table 2.***
3. Complete the calculations shown in ***Table 2.***
4. Measure the air temperature, and calculate the speed of sound using the information shown below. Record your answer in ***Table 2.***

   Speed of sound = 332 m/s at 0°C + 0.6 m/s for every degree above 0°C

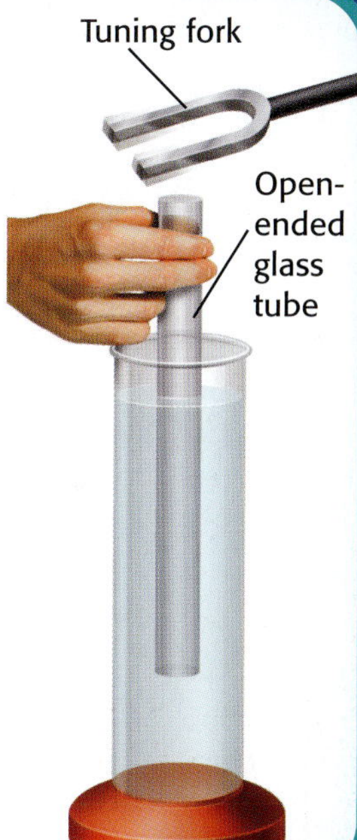

Table 2 **Calculating the Speed of Sound**

	Tuning fork 1	Tuning fork 2
Average measured length of air column (mm)		
Inside diameter (mm)		
Inside diameter × 0.4 (mm)		
Resonant length		
Wavelength of sound (mm), 4 × resonant length		
Wavelength of sound (m), wavelength of sound (mm) × $\frac{1}{1000}$		
Speed of sound (m/s), wavelength × vibration rate of fork		
Speed of sound (m/s), calculated from step 4		

Conclusions

5. Should the speed of sound determined with the two tuning forks be the same?
6. How does the value for the speed of sound you calculated compare with the speed of sound you determined by measuring the air column?
7. How could you determine the frequency of a tuning fork that had an unknown value?

Science in ACTION

Is there life outside our solar system?

Although the great distances make travel to other solar systems in today's spacecraft impossible, can we 'hear' evidence of intelligent life in the universe? A unique organization of scientists known as the Search for Extra-Terrestrial Intelligence (SETI) is working to answer that question.

Will this Roswell, NM, "Alien Parking" sign become a common sight?

History of SETI

In 1959, two young physicists named Philip Morrison and Giuseppe Cocconi noticed that because radio waves travel at the speed of light and require little power, they were the perfect way to communicate across the vastness of space. Morrison and Cocconi reasoned that if intelligent civilizations did exist somewhere in the universe, it would be possible to use radio telescopes to eavesdrop on their radio transmissions, or even detect a signal deliberately sent into space. They even proposed an exact frequency to start the search: 1420 MHz, the emission frequency of the hydrogen atom, the most common element in the universe.

The Search Is On

The very next year, the first attempts were made to listen in on a handful of nearby stars. Although modest, these early attempts paved the way for much broader investigations. Today, SETI uses some of the world's biggest radio telescopes, including the mammoth Arecibo dish in Puerto Rico, to monitor millions of radio channels over an ever-expanding area of the universe. Likewise, the SETI organization has grown to hundreds of astronomers, physicists, and communications specialists from all over the world. SETI now also includes scientists from the relatively new discipline of astrobiology, the study of the conditions and environments necessary for life on other planets.

This 305 m–diameter aluminum dish at the Arecibo Observatory in Puerto Rico receives signals from outer space.

The Allen Telescope Array, designed by astronomers and engineers with SETI and the University of California–Berkeley, is a significant step in the exploration of the cosmos in the search for extraterrestrial intelligence.

The Future of SETI

It's now known that many millions of stars in the universe are orbited by planets, and there is growing evidence that water, an essential ingredient of life, exists on other planets. Based on these and other discoveries, SETI received funding to build the first large-scale radio telescope dedicated to this research. The Allen Telescope Array will consist of approximately 350 small satellite dishes linked together to make a collecting area equal to a 100-meter telescope. SETI scientists are optimistic that this new telescope will eventually help them search more than 1 million stars. SETI will also look for new kinds of alien evidence and will use conventional optical telescopes in California to search the night sky for flashes of light (such as from high-powered lasers) signaling us from other solar systems. Although SETI has not yet found a confirmed extra-terrestrial signal, improved technologies and greater interest from the public continue to support SETI in their search for proof that we are not alone.

Science and You

1. **Understanding Concepts** Most SETI researchers monitor radio frequencies in the microwave range of the electromagnetic spectrum because it is almost free of natural interference. Why is this a good idea?
2. **Critical Thinking** Explain one possible flaw in concentrating on radio transmissions for evidence of alien life.
3. **Acquiring and Evaluating** A unique project called SETI@Home uses the power of thousands of personal computers in homes, schools, and offices around the world to process the enormous amount of data gathered by SETI. Using the Internet, research the SETI@Home project and write a short paper explaining how the project works and why it's a good idea to utilize personal computers to process scientific data. If you like, ask your teacher for permission to use a computer at school for SETI@Home.

CHAPTER 19

The Solar System

Chapter Preview

This artist's composite shows the nine planets of our solar system and four of Jupiter's moons. Other objects, such as the comet above, whirl through our dynamic solar system.

Focus ACTIVITY

Background How do you describe to people where you live? If they live nearby, just naming your neighborhood may be enough. What if the people lived very far away? You may have to tell them the name of the town, state, country, or continent. But what if they lived outside of our solar system? You may have to explain to them that you live on Earth, the third planet from the sun and one of thousands of celestial bodies that orbit around an average star in the Milky Way galaxy.

Our solar system contains a vast diversity of objects—from small, rocky asteroids to huge, gas giant planets. So far, we have discovered life as we know it only in one place—Earth. Could there be other life in our solar system or on planets around other stars? This is a big question for the 21st century. Learning about life means understanding what makes our planet special and exploring the characteristics of the other bodies in the solar system.

Activity 1 Make a list of 20 items you would take on a camping trip. Add a spacesuit and oxygen, and examine your list to see if it has what you need to survive on Mars for a month. Explain what items you would eliminate from your list and what items would you add?

Activity 2 Go outside on a clear evening at dusk, and look up at the sky. Spend 20 min counting stars as they become visible. Describe the first stars you see. How many did you count in 20 min? Do you see any lights in the sky that might not be stars? If so, what do you think they might be, and how would you find out what they are?

internet connect

www.scilinks.org
Topic: Comets, Asteroids, and Meteoroids
SciLinks code: HK4024
SCILINKS. Maintained by the National Science Teachers Association

Pre-Reading Questions

1. How is the moon different from a planet such as Earth?
2. When you look up at the sky, how can you tell the difference between stars and planets?

SECTION 1

Sun, Earth, and Moon

KEY TERMS

planet
solar system
satellite
phase
eclipse

OBJECTIVES

- **Recognize** Earth as one of many planets that orbit the sun.
- **Explain** how gravity works within the solar system.
- **Describe** eclipses and phases of the moon.
- **List** two characteristics of the moon, and show how the moon affects Earth's tides.

planet any of the nine primary bodies that orbit the sun; a similar body that orbits another star

You know the sun, moon, and stars appear to rise and set each day because Earth spins on its axis. The stars that are visible at night revolve throughout the year as Earth orbits the sun. These two motions affect our view of the sky.

The View from Earth

Like ancient viewers of the sky, you can go outside and watch stars cross the sky on any clear night. Over time, you may notice one of the brighter objects changing its position and crossing the paths of stars. The Greeks called these objects *planets,* which means "wanderers." We now think of a **planet** as any large object that orbits the sun or another star. Five planets (in addition to Earth) are visible to the unaided eye: Mercury, Venus, Mars, Jupiter, and Saturn.

The sun is our closest star

There are billions of stars, but one is special to us. It took thousands of years for scientists to realize that the sun is a star. Because the sun is so close to us, it is very bright. As you see in ***Figure 1,*** our atmosphere scatters the sun's light and makes the daytime sky so bright that we can't see the other stars. The sun is an average star, not particularly hot or cool, and of average size. Its diameter is 1.4 million kilometers, about 110 times the diameter of Earth. Its mass is over 300 000 times the mass of Earth.

The solar system is the sun, planets, and other objects that orbit the sun. The system includes objects of all sizes—large planets, small satellites, asteroids, comets, gas, and dust. Astronomers are discovering that many other stars in our galaxy have planets, but we don't know any system as well as we know our own.

Figure 1

People on Earth are very familiar with one star–the sun.

Everything revolves around the sun

As the largest member of our solar system, the sun is not just the object that all the planets orbit. It is also the source of heat and light for the entire system. As Earth spins on its axis every 24 h, we see the sun rise and set. Many patterns of human life such as rising in the morning, eating meals at certain times throughout the day, and sleeping at night follow the sun's cycle. Most animals have patterns of activity and sleep. But unlike us, animals don't have school, television, or electric lights to interrupt their patterns.

As each year progresses, you can watch the growing seasons of plants change. Some plants, such as the morning glories in ***Figure 2,*** are very sensitive to light and move to face the sun as it rises and travels across the daytime sky.

Heat from the sun is a main cause of weather patterns on Earth. Another type of weather, space weather, is caused by energetic particles that leave the sun during solar flares and storms. When these particles reach Earth, they can zap communication satellites and cause blackouts.

Figure 2

The sun is important to all life on Earth. These morning glories turn their faces to the morning sun.

Planets and distant stars are visible in the night sky

Ancient peoples looked at the night sky and saw patterns that reminded them of their myths. When we pick out the shapes of constellations, we use some of the same patterns the Greeks saw and named. These ancient scientists also watched the five bright planets wander in regular paths among the stars. ***Figure 3*** shows Saturn wandering through the constellation Leo, which is named for its lionlike shape. By watching the sky for many years, the ancient Greeks calculated that the stars were more distant than the planets were. Over a thousand years later, after the invention of the telescope, people found other objects in the night sky, including many faint stars and three more planets: Uranus, Neptune, and Pluto.

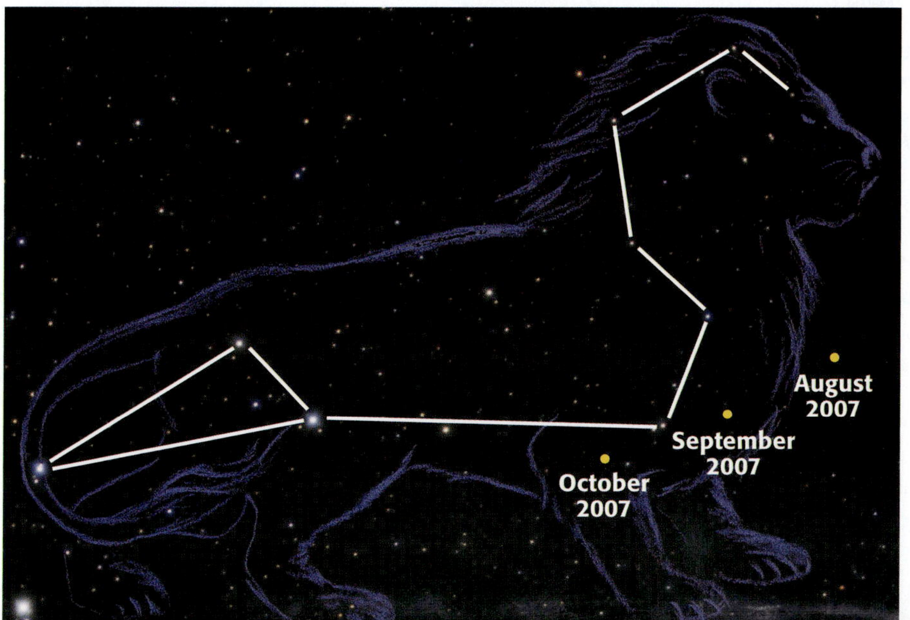

Figure 3

The planet Saturn moves against the background of stars in the constellation Leo.

Earth is a part of a solar system

A school system has parts such as students, teachers, and administrators, which all interact according to a set of rules. The solar system also has its parts and its own set of rules. The **solar system** is the sun and all of the objects that orbit it. The sun is the most important part of our system and makes up 99% of the total mass of the solar system. The nine planets and their moons make up most of the remaining 1%. The solar system has many other smaller objects—meteoroids, asteroids, comets, gas, and dust. Although smaller objects don't have much mass, they help us understand how the solar system is organized.

solar system the sun and all of the planets and other bodies that travel around it

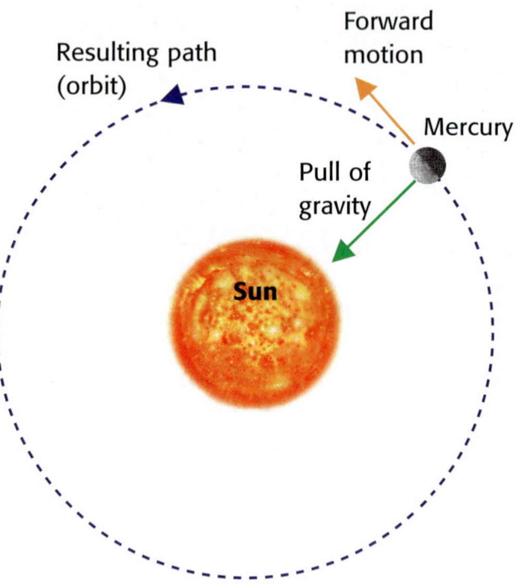

Figure 4

The pull of gravity causes Mercury to fall toward the sun, changing what would be a straight line into a curved orbit.

Gravity holds the solar system together

The force of gravity between two objects depends upon their masses and the distance between them. The greater the mass, the larger the gravitational force an object exerts on another if they are equally distant. The closer two objects are to each other, the stronger the gravitational pull is between them. The sun exerts the largest force in the solar system because its mass is so large. ***Figure 4*** shows the pull of the sun, which keeps Mercury in its orbit. Imagine swinging a ball on a string. If you let go of the string, the ball flies off in a straight line. Without the sun's pull, Mercury and all the other planets would similarly shoot off into space. Gravity is also the force that keeps moons orbiting around planets. You experience gravity as the force that keeps you on Earth. Every object in the solar system pulls on every other object. Even though Jupiter is more massive than Earth, you don't notice its pull on you because it is too far away.

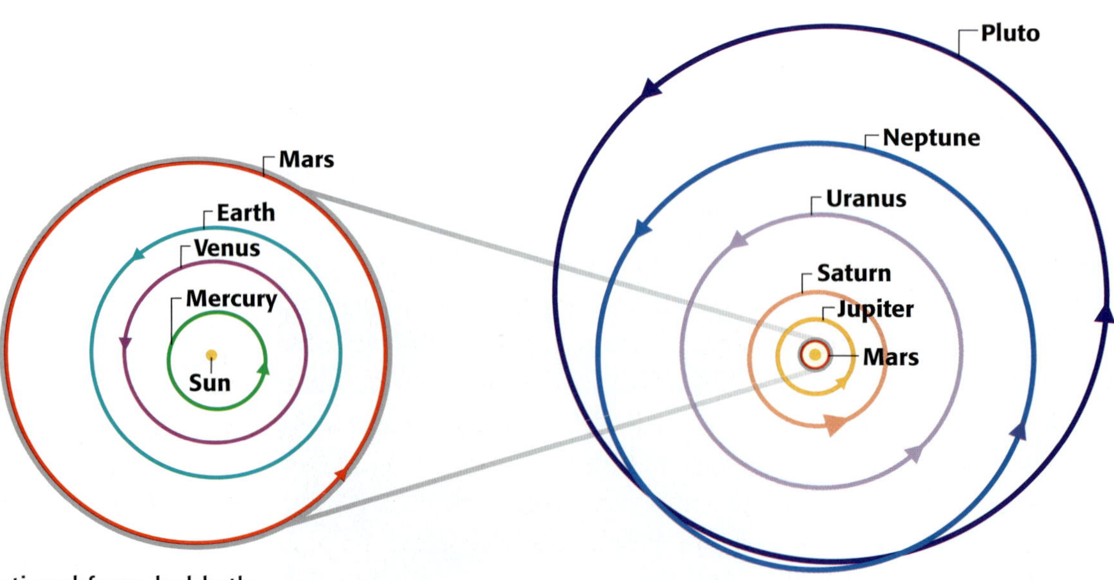

Figure 5

The sun's gravitational force holds the planets in almost circular orbits.

Nine planets orbit the sun

Planets can be seen because their surfaces or atmospheres reflect sunlight. A planet's distance from the sun determines how long the planet takes to orbit the sun. ***Figure 5*** shows the orbits of the planets in order of distance from the sun. Mercury, the closest, takes 88 days to orbit the sun, which is the shortest time of all the planets. Earth takes one year, or 365.25 days. Pluto, the most distant planet, takes 248 years or over 90 000 days. For part of its orbit, Pluto is closer to the sun than Neptune is, but its average distance from the sun is the farthest.

A **satellite** is an object in orbit around a body that has a larger mass. The moon is Earth's satellite because Earth has the larger mass. ***Figure 6*** shows the relative diameters of the planets. The four closest to the sun are small and rocky and have few or no satellites. The next four are large and gaseous and have many satellites. Pluto has one satellite.

Figure 6

The planets in the solar system are shown in relative scale. The sun's diameter is almost 10 times larger than Jupiter's. Distances between the planets are not shown to scale.

satellite a natural or artificial body that revolves around a planet

Satellites orbit planets

All of the planets in our solar system have moons except Mercury and Venus. Currently, we know of 135 natural satellites, or moons, orbiting the planets in our solar system. In 1970, we only knew of 33. Space missions have discovered many small satellites, and more could be found in the future. The smallest satellites are less than 3 km in diameter, while the largest, including Jupiter's Ganymede and Saturn's Titan, are larger than the planet Mercury. All satellites are held in their orbits by the gravitational forces of their planets. Like planets, satellites reflect sunlight. A few satellites have atmospheres, but most do not.

Figure 7

The moon has dark maria and light highlands and craters.

The Moon

The moon does not orbit the sun directly; it orbits Earth at a distance of 384 000 km. The moon's surface is covered with craters, mostly caused by asteroid collisions early in the history of the solar system. The *maria*, or large, dark patches on the moon, shown in ***Figure 7,*** are seas of lava that flowed out of the moon's interior, filled the impact craters, and cooled to solid rock.

The moon has phases because it orbits Earth

The moon appears to have different shapes throughout the month that are called **phases.** The relative positions of Earth, the moon, and the sun determine the phases of the moon, as shown in ***Figure 8.*** At any given time, the sun illuminates half the moon's surface, just as at any given time it is day on one half of Earth and night on the other half. As the moon revolves around Earth, the illuminated portion of the side of the moon facing Earth changes. When the moon is full, the half that is facing you is lit. When the moon is new, the side that is facing you is dark, so you can't see it. Quarter phases occur when you can see half of the sunlit side. The time from one full moon to the next is 29.5 days, or about one calendar month.

phase the change in the illuminated area of one celestial body as seen from another celestial body; phases of the moon are caused by the positions of Earth, the sun, and the moon

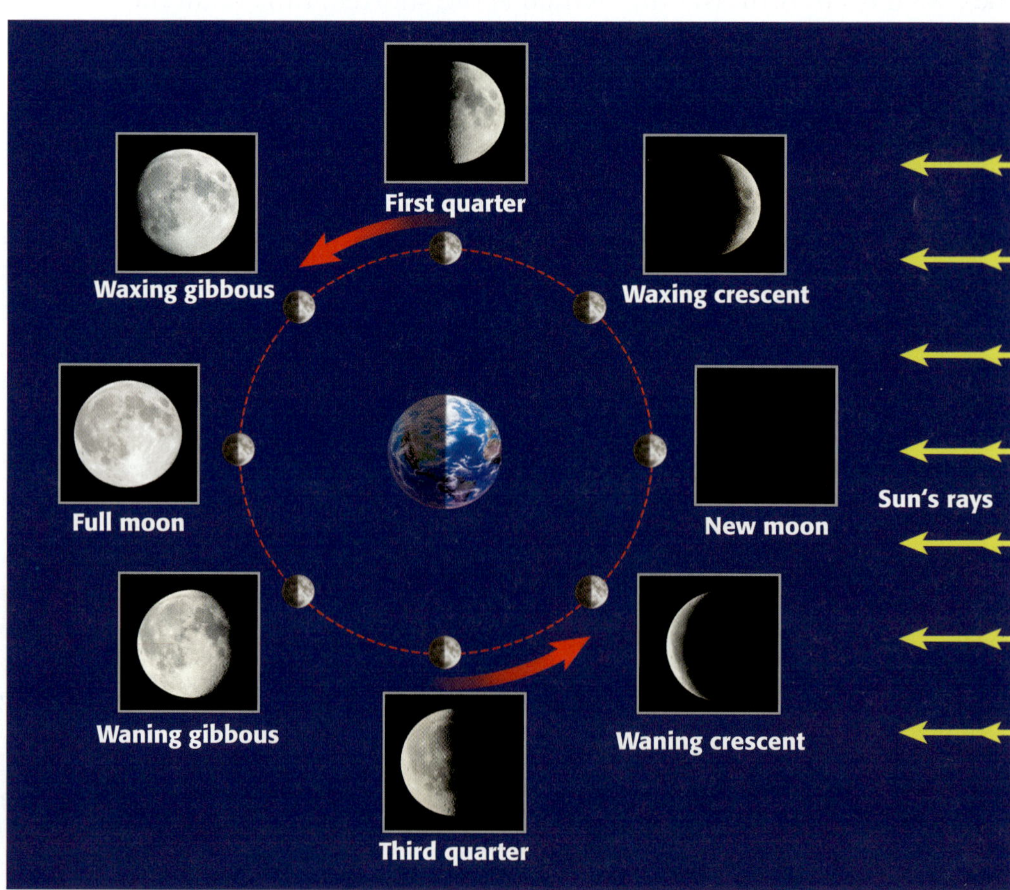

Figure 8

As the moon changes position relative to Earth and the sun, it goes through different phases. (The figure is not to scale.)

Figure 9

Eclipses occur when Earth, the sun, and the moon are in a line. **A** shows a solar eclipse, and **B** shows a lunar eclipse.

Phases of the moon are not caused by Earth's shadow

The relative sizes of and distance between Earth and the moon are not shown to scale in ***Figure 8.*** Earth and the moon may seem to make shadows that fall on each other all the time. But Earth, which has a diameter that is four times the diameter of the moon, is a distance of 30 Earth-diameters from the moon. Therefore, the moon's shadow is so small that it hits only a small part of Earth even when Earth, the moon, and the sun line up exactly.

Eclipses occur when Earth, the moon, and the sun line up

While exploring Jamaica in 1504, Christopher Columbus impressed the native people by consulting a table of astronomical observations and predicting that the sky would darken. The event he predicted was an **eclipse.** Eclipses can be predicted and can happen when Earth, the sun, and the moon are in a straight line. An eclipse occurs when one object moves into the shadow cast by another object.

eclipse an event in which the shadow of one celestial body falls on another

During a new moon, the moon may cast a shadow onto Earth, as shown in ***Figure 9A.*** Observers within that small shadow on Earth see the sky turn dark as the moon blocks out the sun. This event is called a solar eclipse. On the other hand, when the moon is full, it may pass into the shadow of Earth, as shown in ***Figure 9B.*** All the observers on the nightside of Earth can see the full moon darken as the moon passes through Earth's shadow. This event is called a lunar eclipse. Because the moon's orbit is slightly tilted compared with Earth's orbit around the sun, the moon is usually slightly above or below the line between Earth and the sun. So, eclipses are relatively rare.

The moon affects Earth's tides

Figure 10

The gravitational pull of the moon is the main cause of tides on Earth.

Coastal areas on Earth, such as the one shown in ***Figure 10,*** have two high tides and two low tides each day. Even though tides are affected by Earth's landscape, tides are mainly a result of the gravitational influence of the moon. The moon's gravitational pull is strongest on the side of Earth nearest the moon. On the side near the moon, the water and land is pulled toward the moon, which creates a bulge. The movement of water is more noticeable than the movement of land because water is more changeable. The pull of the moon is weaker on the side of Earth that is farthest from the moon.

Earth rotates and so one area on Earth will have two maximum, or high, tides and two minimum, or low, tides in one day. Because the moon is also orbiting Earth, the times of these tides change throughout the month.

The sun has a minor effect on tides. When the sun is on the same side of Earth as the moon, the gravitational forces are at their strongest, and tides are at their highest for the month.

SECTION 1 REVIEW

SUMMARY

- The sun and the nine planets make up our solar system.
- Planets are visible because they reflect sunlight.
- Gravity holds the solar system together and keeps planets in orbit around the sun.
- The moon's surface has meteor-impact craters and maria from lava flows.
- Eclipses and phases of the moon are caused by the relative positions of Earth, the sun, and the moon.
- Tides are caused by differences in the pull of the moon's gravity on different areas of Earth.

1. **Identify** what makes planets and satellites shine.
2. **Explain** how gravity keeps planets in orbit around the sun.
3. **Predict** which satellite experiences the larger gravitational force if two satellites have the same mass, but one is twice as far away from the planet as the other.
4. **Explain** what happens during a lunar eclipse. What phase is the moon in during a lunar eclipse?
5. **Describe** two features of the moon, and explain how they formed.
6. **Explain** what causes tides.
7. **Describe** the positions of the sun, Earth, and the moon during a full moon and during a quarter phase.
8. **Critical Thinking** At what phase of the moon will tides be the highest? Explain.
9. **Critical Thinking** Examine ***Figure 8*** closely. If the moon were a crescent as seen from Earth, what would Earth look like to an astronaut on the moon?
10. **Critical Thinking** The Greeks thought that there were five planets visible with the unaided eye: Mercury, Venus, Mars, Jupiter, and Saturn. What other planet is visible with the unaided eye?

SECTION 2

The Inner and Outer Planets

OBJECTIVES

- **Identify** the planets of the solar system and their features.
- **Distinguish** between the inner and outer planets and their relative distances from the sun.
- **State** two characteristics that allow Earth to sustain life.
- **Describe** two characteristics of a gas giant.

KEY TERMS

terrestrial planet
hydrosphere
asteroid
gas giant

The solar system has inner planets close to the sun and more-distant outer planets, too. The inner ones are called **terrestrial planets** because they are rocky like Earth. They receive more of the sun's energy and have higher temperatures than the outer planets do.

terrestrial planet one of the highly dense planets nearest to the sun; Mercury, Venus, Earth, and Mars

The Inner Planets

Figure 11 shows the orbits of the terrestrial planets: Mercury, Venus, Earth, and Mars. They are small and have solid, rocky surfaces. Using telescopes, satellites, and surface probes, scientists can study the geologic features of these planets.

Figure 11 The four terrestrial inner planets—Mercury, Venus, Earth, and Mars—are closest to the sun.

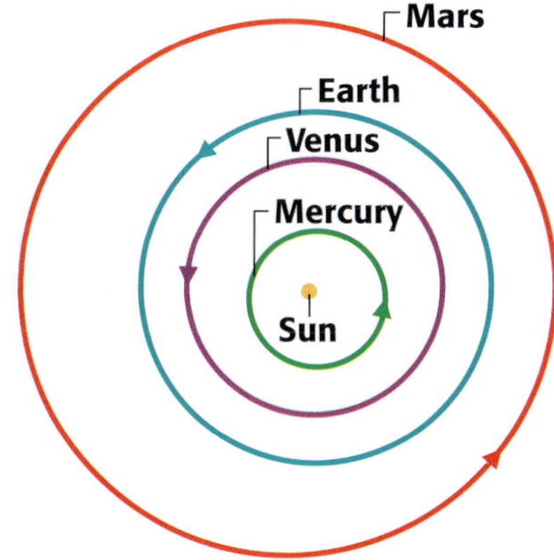

Mercury has extreme temperatures

Until we sent space missions, such as *Mariner 10,* to investigate Mercury, we did not know much about it. The photograph in ***Figure 12*** shows that Mercury, much like Earth's moon, is pocked with craters. Because Mercury has such a small orbit around the sun, it is never very far from the sun. The best times to observe Mercury are just before sunrise or just after sunset, but even then it is difficult to see, even with a telescope.

Figure 12 Mercury is pocked with craters.

Connection to SOCIAL STUDIES

All civilizations in the world have used the motions of celestial objects to keep time. Most calendars are based on Earth's orbit around the sun and have a 365-day year. Some cultures, such as the Chinese, based their calendars on the moon. The Maya of ancient Mexico had several sophisticated calendars. One was based on the sun, just as ours is today, but their special interest was Venus. They carefully observed and measured the 584 days it takes for Venus to return to the same place in the sky and calculated that five of these cycles took eight of the 365-day years. The huge Aztec calendar stone shown below shows the Aztec's belief in the cyclical nature of change in the cosmos.

Making the Connection

1. Why are more calendars based on the sun than on other celestial objects?
2. The Egyptians built pyramids that were aligned with celestial objects. What does this tell you about their interests?

Distances in the solar system are often measured in terms of the distance from Earth to the sun, which is one astronomical unit (AU), or 150 million km. Mercury is 0.4 AU from the sun. Mercury is so close to the sun that its surface temperature is over 670 K, which is hot enough to melt tin. The temperature on Mercury's night side drops to 103 K, which is far below the freezing point of water. Mercury spins slowly on its axis. A day on Mercury is 176 Earth days. Mercury's year is 0.24 Earth years. As a result, during two of its years Mercury experiences only one day! Mercury is not a likely place to find life because it has almost no atmosphere and no water.

Thick clouds on Venus cause a runaway greenhouse effect

Venus is 0.7 AU from the sun. It is only seen near sunset or sunrise and is called either the morning star or the evening star. From Earth, Venus shows phases. Photos taken by *Mariner 10* show thick layers of clouds made mostly of carbon dioxide. These cloud layers make Venus very reflective.

Radar maps that measure the surface of Venus through the clouds, like the map shown in **Figure 13,** indicate that the surface of Venus has mountains and plains. Venus spins in the opposite direction from the other planets and the sun. One day on Venus is 117 Earth days long, and one year on Venus is 0.6 Earth years long.

Figure 13

The Magellan spacecraft used radar to measure the surface below Venus' clouds. Brown and yellow show high ground, and green and blue show low ground.

Venus does not provide an environment that can support life. Venus is hot, and its atmosphere contains large amounts of sulfuric acid. In addition, the atmospheric pressure at the surface of Venus is more than 90 times the pressure on Earth. Venus' thick atmosphere prevents the release of energy by radiation, creating a "runaway" greenhouse effect that keeps the surface temperature of Venus over 700 K. A greenhouse effect occurs when radiation from the sun is trapped and heat builds up, as in a greenhouse on Earth. The "runaway" greenhouse effect that is taking place on Venus means that the more heat is built up, the more efficient the atmosphere becomes at trapping radiation. This effect causes unrelenting high temperatures.

Earth has ideal conditions for living creatures

Earth, our home, is the third planet from the sun. We measure other planets in the solar system in relation to Earth. Earth rotates on its axis in one Earth day. It revolves around the sun at a distance of 1 AU in one Earth year. It has a mass of one Earth mass.

Earth is the only planet we know that sustains life. It is also the only planet that has large amounts of liquid water on its surface. Water floats when it freezes, so life can continue under the ice. Other substances, such as carbon dioxide, freeze from the bottom up. All the water on Earth's surface, both liquid and frozen, is called the **hydrosphere.** The continents and the hydrosphere hold an amazing diversity of life, as shown in ***Figure 14.*** Because water takes a long time to heat or cool, the hydrosphere moderates the temperature of Earth. One example of this effect is that areas near coasts seldom have temperatures as cold as inland areas on a continent.

Figure 14

Oceans on Earth host a vast diversity of life.

The atmosphere protects Earth from radiation and sustains life

Earth, shown in ***Figure 15,*** has an atmosphere composed of 78% nitrogen, 21% oxygen, and 1% carbon dioxide and other gases. Like the hydrosphere, the atmosphere helps moderate temperatures between day and night. The greenhouse effect traps heat in the atmosphere, so Earth's surface doesn't freeze at night. Compare Earth with Mercury, a planet that doesn't have an atmosphere to protect it. Mercury is extremely hot during the day, and it gets very cold at night.

hydrosphere the portion of Earth that is water

Earth's atmosphere protects us from some harmful ultraviolet radiation and high-energy particles from the sun. The radiation and particles are blocked in our upper atmosphere before they can damage life on Earth. The atmosphere also protects us from space debris, which can be leftover portions of artificial satellites or small rocks from space. As they speed through the atmosphere toward Earth's surface, these objects heat up and vaporize or shatter. Only very large objects can survive the trip through Earth's atmosphere.

Earth's original atmosphere changed over time as gases were released from volcanoes and by plants during photosynthesis. Earth is the only planet we know of that has enough oxygen in its atmosphere to sustain complex life as we know it.

Figure 15

A photo of Earth taken from space shows clouds, oceans, and land.

Figure 16

The small *Sojourner* robot rover from the *Pathfinder* mission to Mars moved on the surface to examine rocks; this rock was named *Yogi.*

Many missions have been sent to Mars

Although humans have yet to visit Mars, many probes have landed on its surface. *Viking 1* and *2* each sent a lander to the surface in 1976. In 1997, the *Pathfinder* mission reached Mars and deployed a rover named *Sojourner,* shown in ***Figure 16,*** which explored the surface using robotic navigation systems.

Figure 17 shows a white region at the poles of Mars. This is one of the polar icecaps of carbon dioxide that contain small amounts of frozen water. People who dream of colonizing Mars hope to harvest water from the ice caps. Features on other parts of the planet suggest that water used to flow across the surface as a liquid. Mars has a very thin atmosphere, composed mostly of carbon dioxide. Mars is 1.5 AU from the sun and has two small satellites, Phobos and Deimos. Mars's mass is 11% of Earth's. It orbits the sun in 1.9 Earth years and its day is 24.7 Earth hours. Mars is very cold; its surface temperature ranges from 144 K to 300 K.

Figure 17

The *Viking I* and *II* probes took many images of Mars to make this composite. Note the polar ice caps.

Mars has the largest volcanoes in the solar system

Orbiting space missions detected some of Mars's unique features. The Martian volcano Olympus Mons is the largest mountain in the solar system. It is almost three times the height of Mount Everest. The Martian volcanoes grew from lava flows. Because Mars has low gravity, the weight of the lava was lower than on other planets, and volcanoes could grow very large.

Like the moon, Mars has many impact craters. Its thin atmosphere doesn't burn up objects from space, and so they often impact the surface. The surface of Mars is red from iron oxide. It has frequent dust storms stronger than those in the Sahara desert. These dust storms form large red dunes.

The asteroid belt divides the inner and outer planets

Between Mars and Jupiter lie hundreds of smaller, rocky objects that range in diameter from 3 km to 700 km. These objects are called **asteroids,** or minor planets. There are probably thousands of other asteroids too small to see from Earth. ***Figure 18*** shows the asteroid Ida as photographed in 1993. Most asteroids remain between Mars and Jupiter, but some wander away from this region. Some pass close to the sun and sometimes cross Earth's orbit. The odds of a large asteroid hitting Earth are fortunately very small, but many research programs are keeping track of them. Some pieces of asteroids have hit Earth as meteorites. As a portion of the rock burns up in the atmosphere it makes a bright streak in the sky, which we call a meteor.

Figure 18

Asteroid Ida was photographed by the Galileo spacecraft. It is 58 km long.

The Outer Planets

Figure 19 shows the orbits of the planets most distant from the sun: are Jupiter, Saturn, Uranus, Neptune, and Pluto. Except for Pluto, the outer planets are much larger than the inner planets and have thick, gaseous atmospheres, many satellites, and rings. These large planets are called the **gas giants.**

Because the gas giants have no solid surface, a spaceship cannot land on them. However, the *Pioneer* missions, launched in 1972 and 1973, the *Voyager 1* and *2* missions, launched in 1977, and the *Galileo* spacecraft, launched in 1989, flew to the large outer planets. *Galileo* even dropped a probe into the atmosphere of Jupiter in 1995. A mission called *New Horizons* is planned to investigate Pluto before the year 2020.

asteroid a small, rocky object that orbits the sun, usually in a band between the orbits of Jupiter and Mars

gas giant a planet that has a deep, massive atmosphere, such as Jupiter, Saturn, Uranus, or Neptune

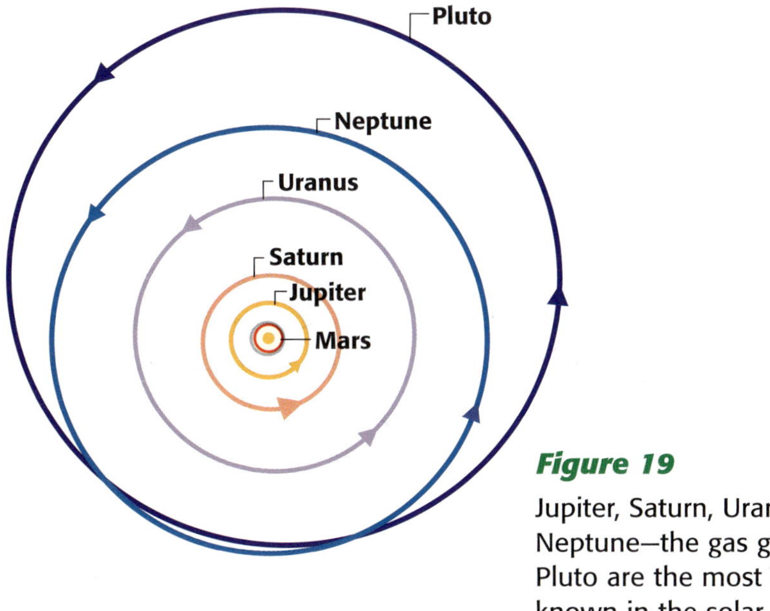

Figure 19

Jupiter, Saturn, Uranus, and Neptune—the gas giants—and little Pluto are the most distant planets known in the solar system.

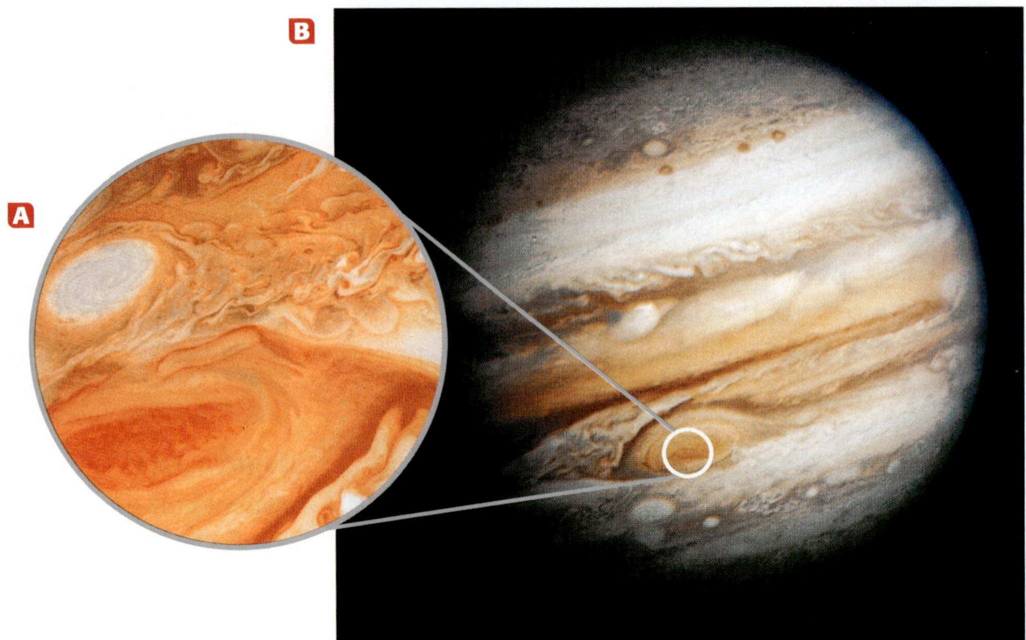

Figure 20

A The Great Red Spot is a huge, hurricane-like storm on Jupiter. **B** Jupiter is the largest planet in the solar system.

Jupiter is the largest planet in the solar system

Jupiter, shown in ***Figure 20B,*** is the first planet beyond the asteroid belt. Jupiter is big enough to hold 1300 Earths. If it were 80 times more massive than it is, it could have become a star. At a distance of 5 AU, Jupiter takes about 12 Earth years (y) to orbit the sun. A day on Jupiter is less than 10 Earth hours long. Images of Jupiter's atmosphere show swirling clouds of hydrogen, helium, methane, and ammonia. Complex features in Jupiter's atmosphere appear to be jet streams and huge storms. One of these storms, the Great Red Spot, shown in ***Figure 20A,*** is a huge hurricane that measures over twice the diameter of Earth. The Great Red Spot has existed for hundreds of years.

In 1610, Galileo discovered the four largest of Jupiter's 61 satellites, which he named Io, Europa, Ganymede, and Callisto. Using binoculars or a small telescope, you can see them near Jupiter. Io has a thin atmosphere and active volcanoes. Europa may have liquid water under its icy surface.

All the gas giant planets have rings and satellites

Although the vast rings of Saturn were recognized in 1659, it took modern technology to discover the thin, faint rings around the other gas giants. Uranus' rings were not discovered until 1977. Space missions have discovered most of the satellites known in the solar system. Jupiter has 61, Saturn has 31, Uranus has 26, and Neptune has 13. Most are cratered, and many have interesting surface features. Some satellites are thought to have thin atmospheres.

Saturn has the most extensive ring system

Saturn is 95 times the mass of the Earth and takes over 29 y to orbit the sun. A day on Saturn is 10.7 h. Like Jupiter, it is a gas giant and rotates fastest at the equator and slower near the poles. In addition to its many satellites, Saturn has a spectacular system of rings, as shown in ***Figure 21.***

These rings are narrow bands of tiny particles of dust, rock, and ice. There is a range of sizes of the particles which measure from millimeters to meters. Most are probably the size of a large snowball on Earth. Competing gravitational forces from Saturn and its many satellites hold the particles in place around the planet. The rings are rather thin in comparison to their diameter. Many are only 10 or 20 m thick and stretch around the entire planet. Scientists aren't sure exactly how the rings formed. One hypothesis is that they came from a smashed satellite. Others believe the rings formed from leftover material when Saturn and its satellites formed long ago.

Did You Know?

The density of Saturn is so low that it would float in water—if you could find a big enough bathtub.

Saturn may still be forming

Saturn radiates three times more energy than it receives from the sun. Scientists believe helium in Saturn's outer layers is condensing and falling inward. As the helium nears the central core, it heats up. Think about pumping air into a bicycle tire. As you pump, the air inside the tire compresses, which causes the tire to heat up. Eventually, for both the tire and Saturn, the extra energy is radiated away. When Saturn uses up its atmospheric helium, this process will stop and Saturn will reach a state of equilibrium. Until then, Saturn is considered to still be forming.

A

Figure 21

A This photo shows a close-up view of the structure of Saturn's rings, made of thousands of small rocks and ice.

B You can see the shadow of the rings on Saturn's surface if you look closely.

Figure 22

A Methane in the atmosphere of Uranus gives it a blue color.

B The Great Dark Spot is a huge storm in Neptune's blue atmosphere.

Uranus and Neptune are blue giants

Beyond Saturn lie the planets Uranus and Neptune, which are shown in ***Figure 22A*** and ***Figure 22B.*** These two gas giants are similar to each other in size and color. Although they are smaller than Saturn and Jupiter, they are still large enough to hold thick, gaseous atmospheres composed of hydrogen, helium, and methane. The methane gives both planets a bluish color.

William Herschel discovered Uranus by accident in 1781. He wanted to name it after King George III, but another astronomer suggested that it be given a name from mythology, as the other planets were. Uranus is 14 Earth masses, and it takes approximately 84 y to orbit the sun at its distance of 19 AU.

After Uranus was discovered, astronomers used what they knew about gravity to guide their search for other planets. Because every mass attracts every other mass, changes in the expected orbit of Uranus could be used to predict the existence and position of other planets. Predicted independently by John Adams and Urbain Leverrier, Neptune was discovered in 1846 by Johann Galle. It is 17 Earth masses, and takes approximately 164 y to orbit the sun at a distance of 30 AU.

Uranus and Neptune are far away from the sun. The gas in their upper atmospheres is very cold, about 58 K. A day on Uranus is 17 h, but its pole is tilted over on its side at a 98° angle. Because of this tilt, Uranus has the most extreme seasons in the solar system. The few clouds in the atmosphere of Uranus show wind speeds of 200 to 500 km/h. A day on Neptune is 16 h. Neptune also has storm systems similar to Jupiter's.

Deep Space Exploration

Deep space missions help astronomers get much closer to and take more detailed images of objects in our solar system.

Ion power was tested on a probe called *Deep Space 1.* Ions are charged particles much like those that make your clothes stick when they come out of the dryer. Ions made from the element xenon race out of the probe at a speed of 100 000 km/h. Each one that is pushed out propels the probe forward, just as a balloon moves forward when some of its air is released. This new propulsion lets probes travel into very deep space.

Applying Information

1. Why do probes get better images than those taken from telescopes on Earth?
2. What direction will the probe go when the ion engine is on? What determines its speed?

Pluto is an oddball planet

After the discovery of Neptune, American astronomer Percival Lowell used fluctuations in Neptune's orbit to predict yet another planet. In 1930, Clyde Tombaugh found a planet very close to where Lowell had predicted one might be. This new planet Pluto, shown in ***Figure 23*** with its satellite Charon, is not like the other outer planets. It has only a thin, gaseous atmosphere and a solid, icy surface. Pluto orbits the sun in a long ellipse and its orbit is at a different angle than the rest of the solar system. For these reasons, some scientists believe Pluto was captured by the gravity of the sun some time after the formation of the solar system.

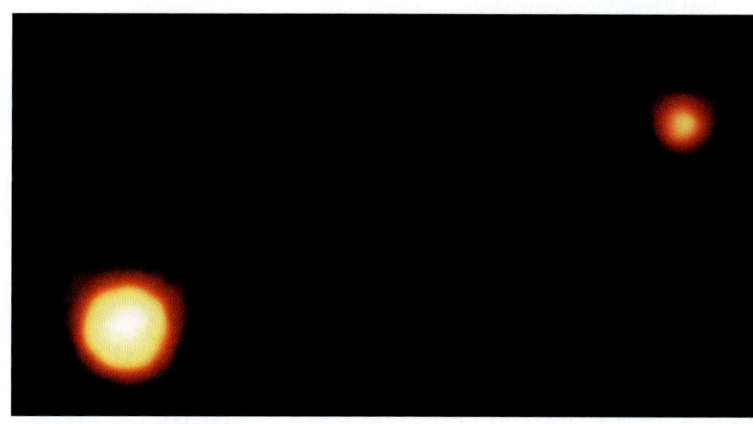

Figure 23

Pluto's satellite, Charon, has a diameter almost half as large as Pluto. Pluto was discovered in 1930, and Charon was discovered in 1978.

Pluto isn't always the farthest planet in the solar system. Its orbit sometimes cuts inside the orbit of Neptune. Pluto's average distance from the sun is almost 40 AU. It takes 248 y to complete one orbit. Its mass is only 0.002 Earth's mass, closer to the mass of a satellite than that of a planet. Some scientists even refuse to classify it as a planet. They think Pluto might be an ejected satellite of Neptune or simply a leftover piece of debris from when the solar system formed.

SECTION 2 REVIEW

SUMMARY

- The solar system has the planets Mercury, Venus, Earth, Mars, Jupiter, Saturn, Uranus, Neptune, and Pluto.
- The inner planets are relatively close to the sun and have few satellites.
- Earth sustains life. It has water, an atmosphere, and oxygen.
- The inner and outer planets are separated by the asteroid belt.
- The gas giants are farther from the sun, are relatively cold, and have rings and many satellites.

1. **List** the planets in order of distance from the sun.
2. **Describe** one feature of each inner planet.
3. **Explain** why the surface of Venus is hotter than the surface of Mercury.
4. **Describe** one feature of each outer planet.
5. **Compare** the terrestrial planets with the gas giants.
6. **Explain** why most satellites and planets have many craters.
7. **Describe** how the hydrosphere and atmosphere help make Earth a good place for life as we know it.
8. **Explain** why distance from the sun is an important factor for a planet to support life.
9. **Critical Thinking** Why are space missions needed to learn about other planets?
10. **Critical Thinking** What characteristics would a planet around another star need to sustain life as we know it?

SECTION 3

Formation of the Solar System

KEY TERMS

nebula
nebular model
accretion
comet

OBJECTIVES

- **Contrast** ancient models of the solar system with the current model.
- **Estimate** the age of our solar system.
- **Summarize** two points of the nebular model, and describe how it can explain astronomical observations.
- **Explain** how scientists think the moon was formed.

The oldest record of human interest in astronomy was found in Nabta, Egypt. Scientists and historians believe a group of stones were specially arranged 6000 to 7000 years ago to line up with the sun on the longest day of the year, called the summer solstice. How ancient people in Egypt used this ancient observatory and how they understood the sky remains a mystery.

Astronomy—The Original Science

Historians believe that many ancient peoples watched the changing sky. ***Figure 24*** shows Stonehenge, a structure thousands of years old, that was probably used for keeping time. Its stones are also aligned with the summer and winter solstices.

Some ancient peoples used stories or myths to explain star movements. Eventually, mathematical tools began to be used to make models of observed astronomical objects. But ancient curiosity was the beginning of astronomy. Ancient questions about the universe gave rise to science and led to the scientific method which is used throughout the sciences today.

Figure 24
Stonehenge, located in England, is one of the world's oldest observatories.

The first model put Earth in the center

Like many people who came before them, the ancient Greeks observed the sky to keep track of time. But they took a new approach in trying to understand Earth's place in the universe. They used logic and mathematics, especially geometry. The Greek philosopher Aristotle explained the phases of the moon and eclipses by using a model of the solar system with Earth in the center. His *geocentric* or "Earth-centered" model is shown in ***Figure 25.***

This model was expanded by Ptolemy in 140 CE. Ptolemy thought that the sun, moon, and planets orbited Earth in perfect circles. His theory described what we see in day-to-day life, including motions of the sun and planets. Because it predicted many astronomical events well, Ptolemy's model was used for over a thousand years.

Figure 25

Before Copernicus, people believed Earth was in the center of the universe.

Copernicus moved the sun to the center

In 1543, Nicolaus Copernicus proposed a *heliocentric,* or "sun-centered," model. He realized that many adjustments used to make Ptolemy's model work would not be needed in a model in which the sun was in the center. In this new model, Earth and the other planets orbit the sun in perfect circles. Although Copernicus's model was not perfect, it explained the motion of the planets more simply than Ptolemy's model did. In 1605, Johannes Kepler improved the model by proposing that the orbits around the sun are ellipses, or ovals, rather than circles.

Newton explained it all

The heliocentric model was useful for time keeping and for navigation. However, no one had explained why planets orbited the sun in elliptical orbits. In 1687, Isaac Newton explained that the force that keeps the planets in orbit around the sun, and satellites in orbit around planets is gravity. His theory states that the gravitational force that keeps planets in orbit around the sun is the same force we experience when things fall to Earth. His theory also states that every object in the universe exerts a gravitational force on every other object. Newton was the first to propose that everything in the universe follows the same rules and acts in a predictable way. All classical physics, including much of astronomy, is built on this assumption.

Did You Know?

The astronomer Johannes Kepler proposed that planets orbit the sun in elliptical paths. However, some scientists continued to believe that Earth was the center of the solar system until Isaac Newton showed that elliptical orbits could be predicted using his laws of motion.

Figure 26

A The young solar nebula begins to collapse because of gravity.

B The solar nebula begins to rotate, flatten, and get warmer near its center.

C Planetesimals begin to form within the swirling disk.

The Nebular Model

According to dating of rocks, scientists believe the solar system is approximately 4.6 billion years old. Scientists trying to build a good model to explain how the solar system formed started with the following questions: Why are the planets so far away from each other? Why are they almost in the same plane? Why are their orbits nearly circular? Why do they orbit in the same direction? Why are the terrestrial planets different from the gas giants? A good model would also have to explain the presence and behavior of objects such as satellites, comets, and asteroids.

The solar system may have begun as a nebula

A **nebula** is a large cloud of dust and gas in space. The most widely accepted model of the formation of the solar system is the **nebular model.** According to the nebular model, the sun, like every star, formed from a cloud of gas and dust that collapsed because of gravity, as shown in ***Figure 26A.***

nebula a large cloud of dust and gas in interstellar space; a region in space where stars are born or where stars explode at the end of their lives

nebular model a model for the formation of the solar system in which the sun and planets condense from a cloud (or nebula) of gas and dust

The nebula then formed a rotating disk

As this cloud collapsed, it formed into a flat, rotating disk, as shown in ***Figure 26B.*** In the center, where the material became denser and hotter, a star began to form. As the cloud collapsed, it spun faster and faster, just as ice skaters spin faster when they pull their arms in. Because spinning bodies tend to change shape as they collapse, the nebula flattened. Scientists find this model helpful because objects that form out of a disk will lie in the same plane, have almost circular orbits, and orbit in the same direction as the material in the center.

D Because of their greater gravitational attraction, the largest planetesimals begin to collect the dust and gas of the solar nebula.

E Smaller planetesimals collide with the larger ones, and the planets begin to grow.

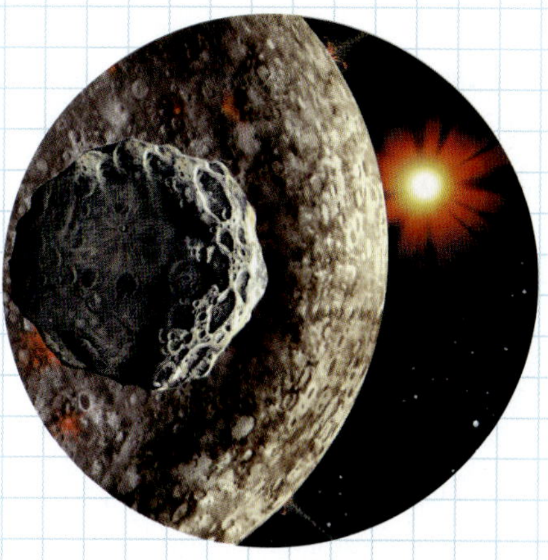

F The remaining dust and gas are gradually removed from the solar nebula, which leaves planets around the sun—a new solar system.

Planets formed by the accretion of matter in the disk

As in ***Figure 26C,*** *planetesimals*, or particles that become planets, began to form in the disk. They formed mostly through the process of **accretion,** which is when small particles collide and stick together. As shown in ***Figure 26D,*** these planetesimals grew bigger as they collected more material. ***Figure 26E*** shows the planets beginning to grow. Each planet swept up material in its region of the disk, which explains why the planetary orbits are separate from each other.

The nebular theory explains why the terrestrial planets are different from the gas giants. The gas and dust close to the sun did not join together easily. Radiation from the newly formed sun exerted pressure on the rest of the gas and dust in the disk. The planets near the sun lost their lighter materials, leaving behind rocky planets. Colder gas and dust in the outer part of the disk joined easily and became the gas giants. These planets were large enough and cold enough to hold light nebular gases, such as hydrogen and helium, in their atmospheres.

The nebular model also explains smaller rocks in space

Satellites may have formed around gas giants in the same way planets formed around the sun. Another possibility is that planetesimals were captured by the gravitational pull of the gas giants. Some smaller satellites may have broken off from larger ones. Most satellites orbit planets in the same direction that the planets orbit the sun. ***Figure 26F*** shows the solar system as it looks today. Asteroids and other small rocks are most likely leftover planetesimals from solar-system formation.

accretion the accumulation of matter

Quick ACTIVITY

Estimating 4.6 Billion

1. Find a small box, and measure its length, width, and height
2. Multiply the height by the width by the length to find the volume of the box.
3. Fill half the box with popcorn kernels.
4. Count the number of kernels in the box, and multiply that number by two.
5. Divide 4 600 000 000 by the total number from step 4.
6. How big would your box need to be to hold 4.6 billion popcorn kernels?
7. If you have time, estimate the weight of 4.6 billion kernels.

Figure 27

The many pieces of comet Shoemaker-Levy 9 hit Jupiter.

Rocks in Space

There are many types of small bodies in our solar system, including satellites, asteroids, meteoroids, and comets. Satellites orbit planets, and most asteroids can be found between Mars and Jupiter. Meteoroids are small pieces of rock that enter Earth's atmosphere. Most meteoroids burn up in the atmosphere, and we see them as meteors streaking through the night sky. If a meteoroid survives the atmosphere and hits the ground, it is called a meteorite. **Comets** are probably composed of leftover material from when the solar system formed.

Comets may give us clues to the origin of the solar system

By studying comets, scientists have gained important information about the material that made the solar system. Comets are composed of dust and of ice made from methane, ammonia, carbon dioxide, and water. In 1994, pieces of the comet Shoemaker-Levy 9 plowed into the planet Jupiter, as shown in ***Figure 27.*** The comet had been pulled into many pieces by Jupiter's gravity. The impacts showed that the comet also contained silicon, magnesium, and iron. We will learn more about comets in 2006 when the *Stardust* mission returns to Earth with comet samples.

Comets have long tails and icy centers

comet a small body of ice, rock, and cosmic dust loosely packed together that follows an elliptical orbit and that gives off gas and dust in the form of a tail as it passes close to the sun

Because of their composition, comets are sometimes called "dirty snowballs." When a comet passes near the sun, solar radiation heats the ice so the comet gives off gases in the form of a long tail. Some comets, such as the one in ***Figure 28,*** have two tails—an ion tail made of charged particles that is blown by the solar wind and a dust tail that follows the comet's orbit.

A comet's orbit is usually very long. Although some of the comet is lost with each passage by the sun, the icy center, or nucleus, continues its journey around the sun. When its tail eventually disappears, a comet becomes more difficult to see. It will brighten only when it passes by the sun again.

Figure 28

In this photo, you can see the two tails of Comet Hale-Bopp. The blue streak is the ion tail, and the white streak is the dust tail.

Where do comets come from?

During the formation of our solar system, some planetesimals did not join together. These leftovers strayed far from the sun. The gravitational force of the gas giants pulled on these small pieces, and over hundreds of millions of years they moved into distant orbits. These far-flung pieces make up the Oort cloud of comets, shown in ***Figure 29,*** which may be up to 100 000 AU wide and extend in all directions. Planetesimals that remained in the nebular disk formed the Kuiper belt beyond the orbit of Neptune. Some scientists believe that Pluto may simply be the largest object in the Kuiper belt.

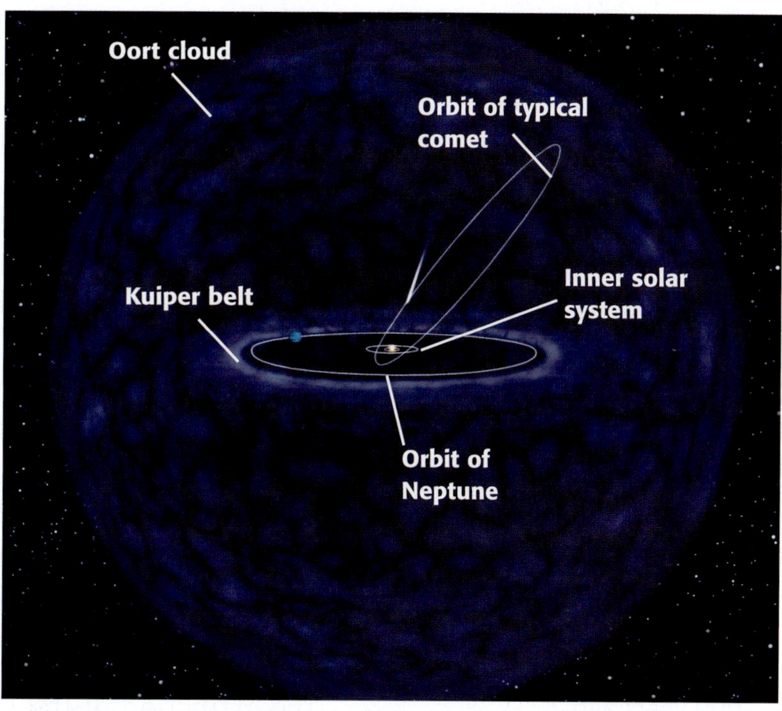

Figure 29

Comets come from the Kuiper belt, a disk-shaped region beyond the orbit of Neptune, and the Oort cloud, a spherical region in the outer solar system beyond the orbit of Pluto.

Halley's comet is one of the most famous comets. It travels in a highly elliptical orbit that brings it near the sun every 76 years. It appears in Earth's sky once every 76 years. Compared with the rest of the solar system it orbits backward, which suggests that its orbit was probably greatly altered by a planet's gravity.

Asteroids can be made of many different elements

We can study asteroids by studying meteorites. Meteor showers can occur when Earth passes through a comet tail, but larger rocks that make it through our atmosphere come from asteroids. As shown in ***Figure 30,*** there are three major types of asteroids. Stony meteorites include carbon-rich specimens that contain organic materials and water. Metallic meteorites are made of iron and nickel. Stony-iron meteorites are a combination of the two types. Most meteorites that have been collected are stony and have compositions like those of the inner planets and the moon.

Figure 30

There are three major types of meteorites.

Meteorites sometimes strike Earth

Figure 31

Barringer Crater in Arizona is due to an impact that happened over 50 000 years ago.

Most meteoroids were once part of asteroids, although a few came from Mars or from our moon. Objects less than 10 m across usually burn up in the atmosphere. ***Figure 31*** shows Barringer Crater, which was made by the impact of a meteoroid that probably weighed 200 000 metric tons (200 000 000 kg). The crater is over 1 km wide and 175 m deep. As you recall, when a meteoroid strikes Earth, it is called a meteorite. Twenty-five metric tons (25 000 kg) of iron meteorite fragments have been found. The rest vaporized on impact, or were scattered, broken by erosion, or buried. Earth has nearly 100 craters larger than 0.1 km. Many craters look like circular lake basins. Erosion and volcanic activity can erase traces of the craters, but new technologies, including satellite photos, can help locate them. From this data, scientists estimate that a large-scale collision happens only once every few hundred thousand years.

Many scientists believe that an asteroid or comet that was 10 to 15 km wide struck Earth about 65 million years ago caused the extinction of the dinosaurs. The energy released was probably as much as the energy of 10 million hydrogen bombs. Large amounts of dust may have swirled into Earth's atmosphere and darkened the sky for years. Plants died, and eventually the dinosaurs, which depended on plants for food, died. Today, government programs track asteroids that come near Earth.

Artificial satellites Sputnik 1 in 1957 was the first of thousands of artificial satellites launched into Earth orbit. Satellites today are used for weather monitoring, communications, espionage, and monitoring changes in oceans and land-use on Earth. Astronomers use satellites to look out into space. Most satellites are only a few hundred kilometers above Earth's surface. To get a satellite to orbit Earth requires a vehicle such as the space shuttle. Rockets, which are also used to launch satellites, follow Newton's third law of motion: for every action force, there is an equal and opposite reaction force. Rockets throw gas out the bottom end of the rocket that, in turn, gives motion in the opposite direction and pushes the rocket upward.

Applying Information

1. There are over 2000 satellites orbiting Earth. Why don't they run into each other?
2. If a satellite breaks apart, what happens to the pieces?
3. To set up a communications network that would reach all of Earth, would you need more than one satellite? Explain.

How the Moon Formed

Before the moon's composition was known, there were several theories for how it formed. Some thought a separate body was captured by Earth's gravity. If this theory were true, the moon's composition would be very different from Earth's. Others thought the moon formed at the same time as Earth, which would mean its composition would be identical to Earth's. When the moon's composition was learned to be similar to Earth's, but not identical, a third theory emerged about how the moon was formed.

Earth collided with a large body

When Earth was still forming, it was *molten,* or heated to an almost liquid state. The heavy material was sinking to the center to form the core, and the lighter material floated to form the mantle and crust. A Mars-sized body struck Earth at an angle and was deflected, as shown in ***Figure 32A.*** At impact, a large part of Earth's mantle was blasted into space.

The ejected material clumped together

The debris began to clump together to form the moon, as shown in ***Figure 32B.*** The debris consisted of the iron core of the body mantle material from Earth and from the impacting body. The iron core became the core of the moon. This theory explains why moon rocks brought back to Earth from the *Apollo* mission share some characteristics of Earth's mantle.

The moon began to orbit Earth

Figure 32C shows the material that formed the moon revolving around Earth because of Earth's gravitational pull. After the moon cooled, impacts created basins on the surface. Lava flooded the basins to make the maria. Smaller impacts made craters on the lunar surface. Today, lava flows on the moon have essentially ceased.

Some scientists doubt this theory because it involves a "unique" event. A unique event has only happened a few times in history. But, the moon itself is unique. It is the only large satellite around a terrestrial planet, and except for Charon, it is the largest moon with respect to its planet.

Figure 32

A **Impact** A large body collided with Earth and blasted part of the mantle into space.

B **Ejection** The resulting debris began to revolve around Earth.

C **Formation** The material began to join together to form the moon.

Other Stars Have Planets

Astronomers have discovered over 90 planets by measuring the small gravitational effects they have on their parent stars. As a planet orbits its star, it causes the star to wobble back and forth. Imagine an adult and a child on a seesaw. The adult sits very close to the center and doesn't move much. The child sits away from the center and moves up and down much farther than the adult. The massive star is like the adult, and the small planet like the child. We have no images of these newly discovered planets. Because planets shine by reflected starlight, they are too faint to see. Astronomers use special techniques and technology such as the Keck telescopes, shown in ***Figure 33,*** to observe the movements of the parent star over time.

Figure 33

The Keck telescopes and others like them help astronomers find planets outside our solar system.

Almost all of the newly discovered planets have masses close to the mass of Jupiter or Saturn. Many of them have noncircular orbits that bring them close to 1 AU from their star. Only a few are in systems that have more than one planet. Modern detection methods favor finding large planets. Although many are around stars like our sun, these systems are not like our solar system.

SECTION 3 REVIEW

SUMMARY

- The sun is in the center of the solar system. Most planets are in the same plane and orbit in the same direction that the sun rotates.
- The solar system is approximately 4.6 billion years old.
- In the nebular model, a disk formed from a cloud of gas and dust. Planets formed by accretion of matter in the disk.
- The moon may have formed after a Mars-sized object struck Earth.

1. **Explain** how our current model of the solar system differs from Ptolemy's model.
2. **State** the approximate age of the solar system.
3. **Describe** two steps of solar system formation.
4. **Describe** how comets change when they near the sun.
5. **List** the three types of meteorites.
6. **Explain** why the study of comets, asteroids, and meteoroids is important to understand the formation of the solar system.
7. **Contrast** the theory of the formation of our moon with how satellites may have formed around the gas giants.
8. **Critical Thinking** Do you think the government should spend money on programs to search for asteroids that may strike Earth? Explain.
9. **Critical Thinking** Do you think planets like Earth exist around other stars? Do you think they may contain life? Explain.

Study Skills

Concept Mapping

Concept mapping is an effective tool for helping you organize the important material in a chapter. It also is a means for checking your understanding of key terms and concepts.

1 Select a main concept for the map.

We will use *planets* as the main concept of this map.

2 List all the important concepts.

We'll use the terms: *planets, satellites, phases,* and *eclipses.*

3 Build the map by placing the concepts according to their importance under the main concept and adding linking words to give meaning to the arrangement of concepts.

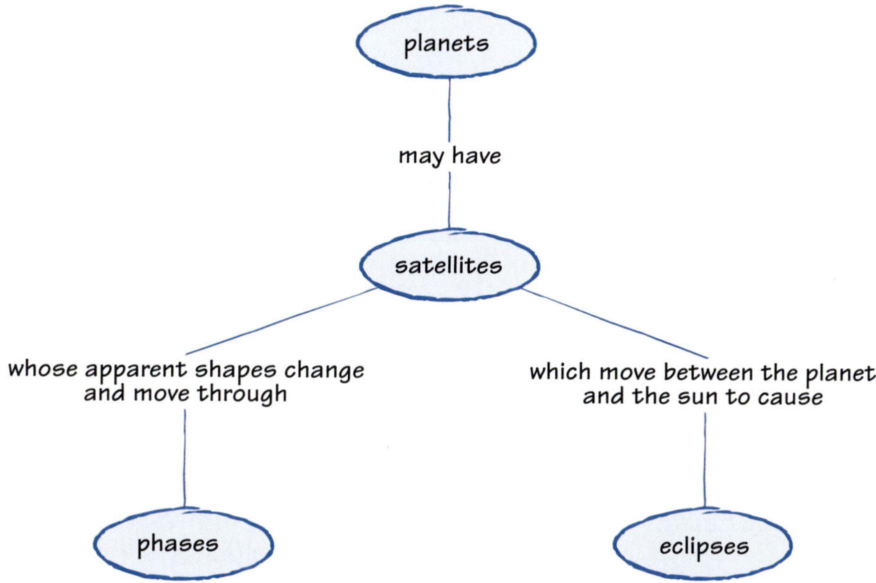

From this completed concept map we can write the following propositions:

Planets may have satellites whose apparent shapes change and move through phases.

Planets may have satellites, which move between the planet and the sun to cause eclipses.

Practice

1. Draw your own concept map by using the main topic *outer planets.*
2. Write three propositions from your completed concept map.

CHAPTER 19 REVIEW

Chapter Highlights

Before you begin, review the summaries of the key ideas of each section, found at the end of each section. The key vocabulary terms are listed on the first page of each section.

UNDERSTANDING CONCEPTS

1. Which outer planet is not a gas giant?
a. Jupiter **c.** Saturn
b. Neptune **d.** Pluto

2. Earth is gravitationally attracted to
a. Mercury. **c.** the sun.
b. the moon. **d.** All of the above.

3. Meteor showers occur when
a. Earth passes through the orbit of a comet.
b. a large asteroid comes near Earth.
c. Earth enters the asteroid belt.
d. Earth enters the Oort cloud.

4. The current theory states that our moon formed when
a. a Jupiter-sized object collided with Earth.
b. a Mars-sized object collided with Earth.
c. planetesimals came together in a disk around the Earth.
d. Earth's gravity captured a stray object in space, and it began to orbit Earth.

5. The planet Jupiter has a day that is
a. longer than one Earth day.
b. shorter than one Earth day.
c. equal to one Earth day.
d. equal to one Jupiter year.

6. The theory that the sun and planets formed out of the same cloud of gas and dust is called the _____ theory.
a. big bang **c.** nebular
b. planetary **d.** nuclear

7. Which planet has the hottest surface?
a. Mercury **c.** Earth
b. Venus **d.** Mars

8. The center of our solar system is
a. Earth. **c.** the sun.
b. the moon. **d.** the Oort cloud.

9. Most calendars are based on
a. Earth's orbit of sun.
b. Moon's orbit of Earth.
c. Jupiter's orbit of sun.
d. Venus' position in sky.

10. The solar system is about _____ years old.
a. 0.5 million **c.** 0.5 billion
b. 4.6 million **d.** 4.6 billion

11. Planets near other stars are found by
a. making images of the planet and the star.
b. detecting the temperature of the planet.
c. detecting the atmosphere of the planet.
d. detecting the gravitational effect of the planet.

USING VOCABULARY

12. Arrange the following from the largest to smallest in mass: *terrestrial planet, satellite, meteorite, sun,* and *solar system.*

13. Name two distinguishing characteristics of a *satellite.*

14. WRITING SKILL Write a paragraph explaining the origin of the solar system according to the nebular theory. Use the following terms: *planet, accretion, nebula,* and *nebular model.*

15. Describe the arrangement of the sun, the moon, and Earth during a *solar eclipse* and a *lunar eclipse.*

16. Name the three major types of *meteorites.*

17. List the names of the *terrestrial planets* in order of distance from the sun.

18. List the names of the *gas giant* planets in order of mass.

19. Explain why Earth has ideal conditions for life by using the terms *AU, atmosphere,* and *hydrosphere*.

20. Describe the difference between an *asteroid* and a *satellite,* and explain where most *asteroids* in our solar system are found.

21. Sketch two different *phases* of the moon, and describe the arrangement of the sun, Earth, and the moon that causes them.

22. Describe two different models of the solar system using the terms *heliocentric* and *geocentric*. Which model do we use today?

BUILDING MATH SKILLS

23. **Applying Technology** The free-fall acceleration, g, near the surface of a planet is given by the equation below.

$$g = \left(6.67 \times 10^{-11} \frac{m^3}{kg \bullet s^2}\right) \times \frac{\textit{(planet mass)}}{\textit{(planet radius)}^2}$$

Use this equation to create a spreadsheet that will calculate the free-fall acceleration near the surface of each of the planets in the table below.

Name	Mass (kg)	Radius (m)
Mercury	3.3×10^{23}	2.4 million
Venus	4.9×10^{24}	6.1 million
Earth	6.0×10^{24}	6.4 million
Mars	6.4×10^{23}	3.4 million

24. **Applying Technology** Add a column to the spreadsheet you created in item 23 to record the weight on each of the inner planets of a person who has a mass of 70 kg. Calculate the weight using the equation *weight = mass × acceleration*. Which of the planets has gravity most like Earth's?

BUILDING GRAPHING SKILLS

25. **Graphing** The table below shows the average distance from the sun for each planet and its orbital period. Plot the data in a graph and explain why you used that kind of graph.

Planet	Distance (AU)	Period (y)
Mercury	0.4	0.2
Venus	0.7	0.6
Earth	1.0	1
Mars	1.5	2
Jupiter	5.2	12
Saturn	9.6	29
Uranus	19.2	84
Neptune	30	164
Pluto	39	248

26. **Graphing** Halley's comet has a period of 76 years. Using your graph from item 25, determine its average distance from the sun.

THINKING CRITICALLY

27. **Critical Thinking** How can Venus be the third brightest object in the sky when it doesn't produce any visible light of its own?

28. **Understanding Systems** Imagine that you are an astronaut on Mars. You look into the sky and see Deimos directly overhead. It is in full phase. What time of day is it on Mars?

29. **Applying Knowledge** The moon rotates at the same rate as it revolves, so one side never faces Earth. Is the far side of the moon always dark? Explain your answer.

30. **Applying Knowledge** The moon is constantly moving in the sky, but the times of tides are different every day. How much time is between high tide and low tide?

CHAPTER 19 REVIEW

31. **Critical Thinking** The moon and Earth both average 1 AU from the sun. The moon is covered with craters. Earth has very few craters. Explain this difference.

32. **Applying Knowledge** If Mars were the same distance from the sun as Earth is, how would it be different than it is today?

33. **Critical Thinking** Pluto rotates on its axis in 6.387 days. Charon orbits Pluto in 6.387 days. Explain how Charon would look from the surface of Pluto.

DEVELOPING LIFE/WORK SKILLS

34. **Interpreting and Communicating** In your library or on the Internet, research the size of Jupiter and its satellites and the distances between different objects in the Jupiter system. Create a poster, booklet, computer presentation, or other presentation that can be used to teach fifth-graders about making and comparing scale models of the Jupiter system.

35. **Working Cooperatively** Working in teams, research the question "Should astronauts go to Mars?" Consider the financial costs and the technical challenges for the development of the mission as well as the psychological challenges for the astronauts.

36. **Applying Technology** Use a computer-art program to illustrate how a comet looks at different parts of its elliptical orbit.

INTEGRATING CONCEPTS

37. **Connection to Music** In 1914 to 1916, the composer Gustav Holst composed *The Planets,* a symphonic suite that portrays each of the planets according to its role in mythology. Listen to a recording of *The Planets.* Write a paragraph describing which parts of the music seem to match scientific facts about the planets and which do not. Why do you think Pluto is missing from *The Planets*?

38. **Connection to Art** Many artists have used astronomical themes or objects in their works. Two examples are Vermeer's 1668 painting *The Astronomer* and Alexander Calder's 1940s mobile entitled *Constellation.* Examine one of these works, and describe how the work relates to astronomy, or create a work of art that relates your feelings about the solar system.

39. **Concept Mapping** Copy the unfinished concept map below onto a sheet of paper. Complete the map by writing the correct word or phrase in the lettered boxes.

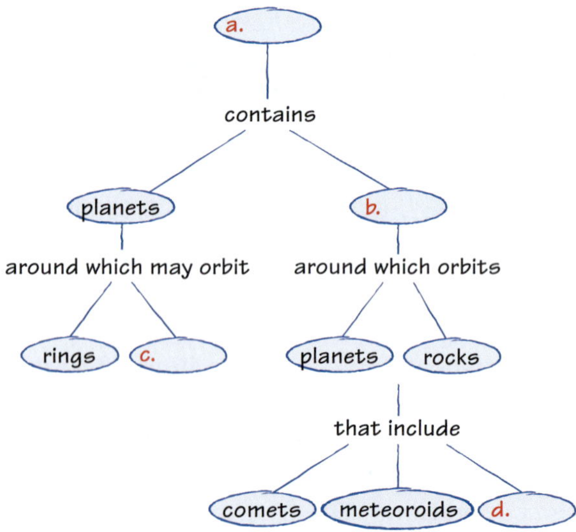

Standardized Test Prep

Understanding Concepts

Directions (1–4): **For *each* question, write on a separate sheet of paper the letter of the correct answer.**

1. A total eclipse can occur only during which of these conditions?
   A. full moon
   B. new moon
   C. rising moon
   D. setting moon

2. Which of these observations is explained by the nebular theory?
   F. Jupiter's moon Io has volcanoes.
   G. The orbit of Halley's comet around the sun is very elongated.
   H. The surface temperature is much higher on Venus than on Earth.
   I. Except for Pluto, the planets revolve around the sun in the same plane.

3. What evidence caused scientists to hypothesize that the moon was originally part of Earth that was broken off by a collision?
   A. distance between Earth and the moon
   B. relative sizes of Earth and the moon
   C. discovery of large impact craters on Earth
   D. composition of samples of rock taken on the moon

4. What are the main components of a comet?
   F. iron, nickel
   G. hydrogen, helium
   H. rocks, iron, nickel
   I. methane, ammonia, carbon dioxide, water

Directions (5): **Write a short response to the question.**

5. The mass of Jupiter is about 1600 times as large as the mass of the moon. Assess why the moon causes tides in the oceans of Earth while Jupiter causes no noticeable tides.

Test TIP

If you are unsure of the correct answer to a multiple-choice question, start by crossing out answers that you know are wrong.

Reading Skills

Directions (6): **Read the passage below. Then answer the question.**

During a lunar eclipse, the shadow of Earth blocks sunlight from the moon. Usually, the moon is still visible, glowing with a dim reddish color. This color is due to the filtering effect of Earth's atmosphere on light. Shorter wavelengths, on the blue end of the spectrum, are scattered, but the longer red wavelengths tend to refract. This means that the atmosphere acts as a lens, focusing some of the red light from the sun into the shadow. The moon reflects some of the red light back toward Earth, causing the moon to appear red.

6. Why does red light but not blue light reach the surface of the moon during an eclipse?

Interpreting Graphics

Directions (7): **Base your answer to question 7 on the illustration below.**

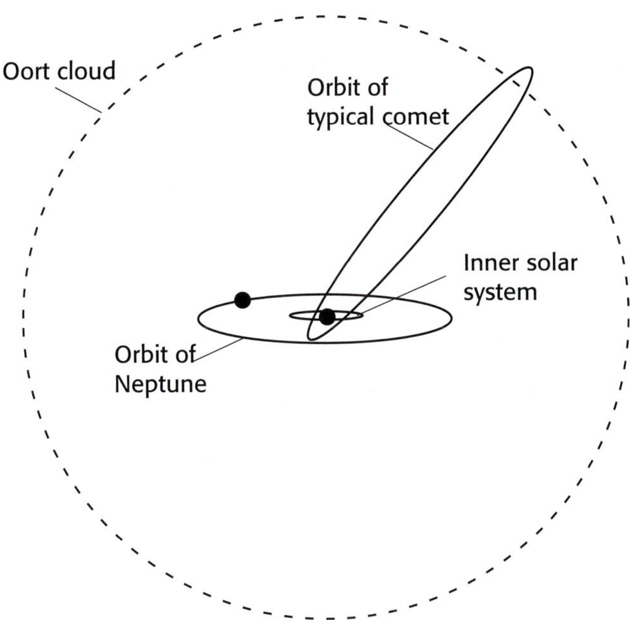

7. Comets can be observed only during a small portion of their orbit around the sun. Why is it hard to detect them most of the time?

Skills Practice Lab

Estimating the Size and Power Output of the Sun

Introduction

The sun is 1.496×10^{11} m from Earth. How can you use this distance and a few simple measurements to find the size and power output of the sun?

Objectives

- **Construct** devices for observing and measuring properties of the sun.
- **Measure** an image of the sun, and temperatures in sunlight and in light from a light bulb.
- USING SCIENTIFIC METHODS **Analyze the results** by calculating the size of the sun and the power output of the sun.

Materials

aluminum foil and pin
black paint or magic marker
Celsius thermometer
glass jar with a hole in the lid
index card
lamp with a 100 W bulb
masking tape
meterstick
modeling clay
shoe box
scissors
2×8 cm sheet of very thin metal

Procedure

1. Construct a solar viewer in the following way.
   a. Cut a round hole in one end of the shoe box.
   b. Tape a piece of aluminum foil over the hole. Use the pin to make a tiny hole in the center of the foil.
   c. Tape the index card inside the shoebox on the end opposite the hole.
2. Construct a solar collector in the following way.
   a. Gently fit the sheet metal around the bulb of the thermometer. Bend the edges out so that they form "wings," as shown at right. Paint the wings black. SAFETY CAUTION **Thermometers are fragile.** Do not squeeze the bulb of the thermometer or let the thermometer strike any solid objects.

   b. Slide the top of the thermometer through the hole in the lid of the jar. Use modeling clay and masking tape to hold the thermometer in place.
   c. Place the lid on the jar. Adjust the thermometer so the metal wings are centered.
3. Place the lamp on one end of a table that is not in direct sunlight. Remove any shade or reflector from the lamp.

Measurements with the Solar Viewer

4. Stand in direct sunlight, with your back to the sun, and position the solar viewer so that an image of the sun appears on the index card. SAFETY CAUTION **Never look directly at the sun.** Permanent eye damage or even blindness may result.
5. Carefully measure and record the diameter of the image of the sun. Also measure and record the distance from the image to the pinhole.

Measurements with the Solar Collector

6. Place the solar collector in sunlight. Tilt the jar so that the sun shines directly on the metal wings. Watch the temperature reading rise until it reaches a maximum value. Record that value. Place the collector in the shade to cool.
7. Now place the solar collector about 30 cm from the lamp on the table. Tilt the jar so that the light shines directly on the metal wings. Watch the temperature reading rise until it reaches a stable value.
8. Move the collector toward the lamp in 2 cm increments. At each position, let the collector sit until the temperature reading stabilizes. When you find a point where the reading on the thermometer matches the reading you observed in step 6, measure and record the distance from the solar collector to the light bulb.

Analysis

1. The ratio of the sun's actual diameter to its distance from Earth is the same as the ratio of the diameter of the sun's image to the distance from the pinhole to the image.

$$\frac{\textit{diameter of the sun, } S}{\textit{Earth} - \textit{sun distance, } D} = \frac{\textit{diameter of image, } i}{\textit{pinhole} - \textit{image distance, } d}$$

Solving for the sun's diameter, S, gives the following equation.

$$S = \frac{D}{d} \times i$$

Substitute your measured values, and $D = 1.5 \times 10^{11}$ m, into this equation to calculate the value of *S*. Remember to convert all distance measurements to units of meters.

2. The ratio of the power output of the sun to the sun's distance from Earth squared is the same as the ratio of the power output of the light bulb to the solar collector's distance from the bulb squared.

$$\frac{\textit{power of sun, } P}{(\textit{earth} - \textit{sun distance, } D)^2} = \frac{\textit{power of light bulb, } b}{(\textit{bulb} - \textit{collector distance, } d)^2}$$

Solving for the sun's power output, *P*, gives the following equation.

$$P = \frac{D^2}{d^2} \times b$$

Substitute your measured distance for *d*, the known wattage of the bulb for *b*, and $D = 1.5 \times 10^{11}$ m, into this equation to calculate the value of *P* in watts. Remember to convert all distance measurements to units of meters.

Conclusions

3. How does your *S* compare with the accepted diameter of the sun, 1.392×10^9 m?
4. How does your *P* compare with the accepted power output of the sun, 3.85×10^{26} W?

Science in
ACTION

Mining the Moon

On December 14, 1972, the crew of Apollo 17 climbed from the surface of the moon back on board the spacecraft for the return to Earth. Since then, NASA has turned its attention to more-distant goals and no one has set foot on the moon. But today, a rare isotope of helium known as helium-3 is fueling new interest in returning to the moon—and not just for scientific discovery.

A helium-3 mining camp on the moon might look something like this artist's rendition.

Energy from the moon

Here on Earth, helium-3 is used for fuel in the latest generation of fusion power plants. Unlike traditional fusion the fusion of helium-3 emits very little radiation. Therefore, it is considered the ultimate clean and safe energy source. But helium-3 is very rare on Earth, and our supply will soon be exhausted. The energy industry and others are now pointing to the moon as a potential source of this precious fuel, because huge amounts of helium-3 exist in the moon's powdery surface. Some argue that using relatively simple technologies we could harvest the moon's helium-3 and send it back to Earth for a safe, reliable energy source that would last many centuries. But is the moon's helium-3 worth the costs and risks of getting it to Earth?

This false-color mosaic shows differences in the moon's composition.

The challenges of lunar mining

Extreme temperatures, solar radiation, the lack of atmosphere, and the constant barrage of small meteorites make the moon a dangerous place to live and work. Advocates for moon mining argue that much of the mining work could be carried out by robots, which would reduce the risk to human life. Also, the knowledge gained by building a permanent mining outpost on the moon would be valuable to any future manned space missions. So, how do we fund an expensive lunar mining program? Plans to minimize costs range from the practical (such as gathering solar energy on the moon to power mining equipment) to the highly imaginative (such as using huge slingshots to launch packages of helium-3 to orbiting spacecraft for transport). Some space entrepreneurs envision the moon as a destination for tourists who would pay high fees to bounce across the Sea of Tranquility and climb lunar mountains. The money gathered from these enterprises could be used to fund mining and other space-related industry. Although moon mining may be many years off, some people are already looking ahead to mining other space resources, including precious metals and rare-earth elements from asteroids that pass near Earth.

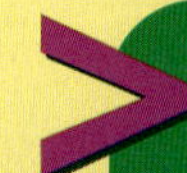

Science and You

1. **Applying Knowledge** Why is helium-3 such a valuable resource?
2. **Applying Knowledge** Name two major challenges to mining the moon.
3. **Understanding Concepts** Why do you think NASA has not sent astronauts to the moon since 1972? Give two reasons.
4. **Critical Thinking** In 1998, the unmanned spacecraft Lunar Prospector gathered evidence that large amounts of frozen water exist in deep craters on the moon. Do you think the presence of frozen water on the moon could help lunar mining efforts?
5. **Critical Thinking** The United Nations has declared that no country can lay claim to the moon or the resources that exists there. However, the rule does not apply to private companies. Do you think private companies should be allowed to "own" mining rights on the moon? Explain.

CHAPTER 20

The Universe

Chapter Preview

Focus ACTIVITY

Background Optical telescopes take pictures of objects by collecting visible light. Visible light is only a small part of the electromagnetic spectrum. Radio waves have longer wavelengths than the light waves that allow us to see with our eyes. In 1932, scientists discovered that astronomical objects emit radio waves. Radio telescopes are sophisticated systems that collect the radio waves emitted by astronomical objects. One of the largest radio telescopes is the Very Large Array in New Mexico. It is composed of 27 dish antennas that work together as a single instrument. Unlike your radio at home, a radio telescope does not convert radio waves to sound. The radio waves are processed by a computer to form a picture such as the image of the Crab Nebula shown below. When scientists combine the data coming from the 27 radio telescopes, the data are as precise as if they had come from an antenna 36 km in diameter!

Activity 1 Examine the photograph of the Very Large Array. Look at the sky behind the antennas—do you see star trails due to the rotation of Earth? Knowing that Earth rotates once every 24 h, estimate how many degrees a star travels in the night sky in 1 h. (**Hint:** One rotation is 360°.)

Activity 2 Turn to Appendix B, and locate the star maps. Pick a constellation and brainstorm how it got its name. You may need to look up the name in a dictionary to find out what the name means in its original language. Write a few paragraphs that explain your hypothesis.

internet connect

www.scilinks.org

Topic: Radioastronomy **SciLinks code:** HK4116

SCILINKS. Maintained by the National Science Teachers Association

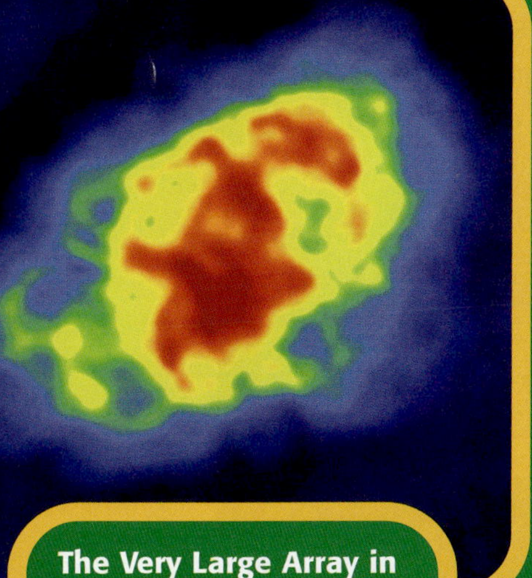

The Very Large Array in New Mexico can make detailed images of astronomical objects such as the Crab Nebula, which scientists think is the remains of a supernova explosion.

Pre-Reading Questions

1. Name as many celestial objects as you can think of. Which objects are outside our solar system?
2. Where would you find information about the locations of the objects that you named in question 1?

SECTION 1

The Life and Death of Stars

KEY TERMS

star
light-year
red giant
white dwarf
supernova
black hole

OBJECTIVES

- **Describe** the basic structure and properties of stars.
- **Explain** how the surface temperature of a star is measured.
- **Recognize** that all normal stars are powered by fusion reactions that form elements.
- **Identify** the stages in the evolution of stars.

On a clear night, you can see about 6000 stars. People have observed stars for thousands of years, but only in the last 100 years have we begun to understand the life of stars.

star a large celestial body that is composed of gas and that emits light; the sun is a typical star

light-year the distance that light travels in one year; about 9.5 trillion kilometers

What Are Stars?

Stars are huge spheres of very hot gas that emit light and other radiation. The nearest star to Earth is the sun. Ancient Greek scientists thought that the stars were attached to a large, invisible sphere. The Greeks also grouped stars into shapes and patterns called constellations. Today, we still use constellations to group stars, such as those in the constellation Orion, shown in ***Figure 1.*** Since ancient times, we have learned that stars are located at different distances from Earth. We use the unit **light-year** (ly) to describe a star's distance from Earth. One light-year is the distance that light travels in one year, or 9.5×10^{15} m.

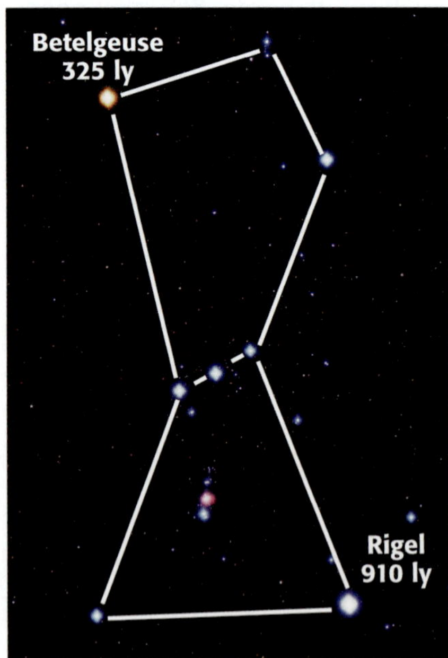

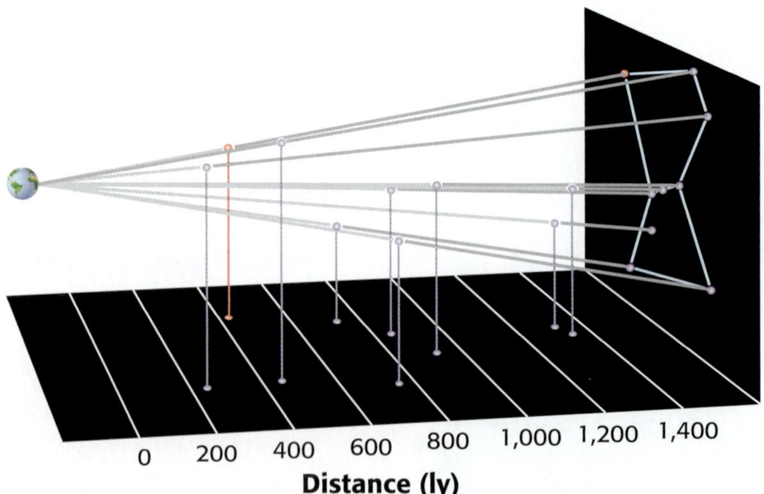

Figure 1

A The stars in the constellation Orion looked like the shape of a hunter to the ancient Greeks.

B The stars in Orion, which appear close together when viewed from Earth, are located at different distances from us and from each other.

Stars are driven by nuclear fusion reactions

A star is a huge sphere of very hot hydrogen and helium gas that emits light. A star is held together by the enormous gravitational forces that result from its own mass. Inside the core, or middle, of a star, these forces create a harsh environment. The pressure is more than a billion times the atmospheric pressure on Earth. The temperature is hotter than 15 million kelvins, and the density is more than 13 times the density of lead.

Nuclear fusion takes place in the core. Fusion combines the nuclei of hydrogen atoms into helium. Positively charged particles, such as the nuclei of hydrogen atoms, normally repel each other, but inside a star, where the temperature and pressure are very high, these particles collide at high speeds. When they collide, they fuse together to form new nuclei called *deuterons,* which have one proton and one neutron. Next, two deuterons collide to form the nucleus of a helium atom. When two particles fuse, energy is released. The energy from these fusion reactions creates outward pressure that balances the inward pull of gravity.

Using a Star Chart

Locate the following stars on the star chart in Appendix B: Betelgeuse, Rigel, Sirius, Capella, and Aldebaran. Name the constellation to which each star belongs. Which of these stars appears closest in the sky to Polaris, the North Star?

Energy moves slowly through the layers of a star

Figure 2 shows the layers of the sun. Other stars have similar structures, although the temperatures and depths of the layers may differ. Energy moves through the layers of a star by a combination of radiation and convection. During convection, rising hot gas moves upward, away from the star's center, and cooler, denser gas sinks toward the center. During radiation, energy is transferred to individual atoms. The atoms absorb the energy and then transfer it to other atoms in random directions. Atoms near the star's surface radiate energy into space.

The energy from a nuclear fusion reaction may take millions of years to work its way through a star. When the energy finally reaches the surface, it is released into space as radiation and light.

Once light leaves the surface of a star, it radiates across space at the speed of light in a vacuum, 3×10^8 m/s. At this speed, it takes light from the sun about eight minutes to reach Earth.

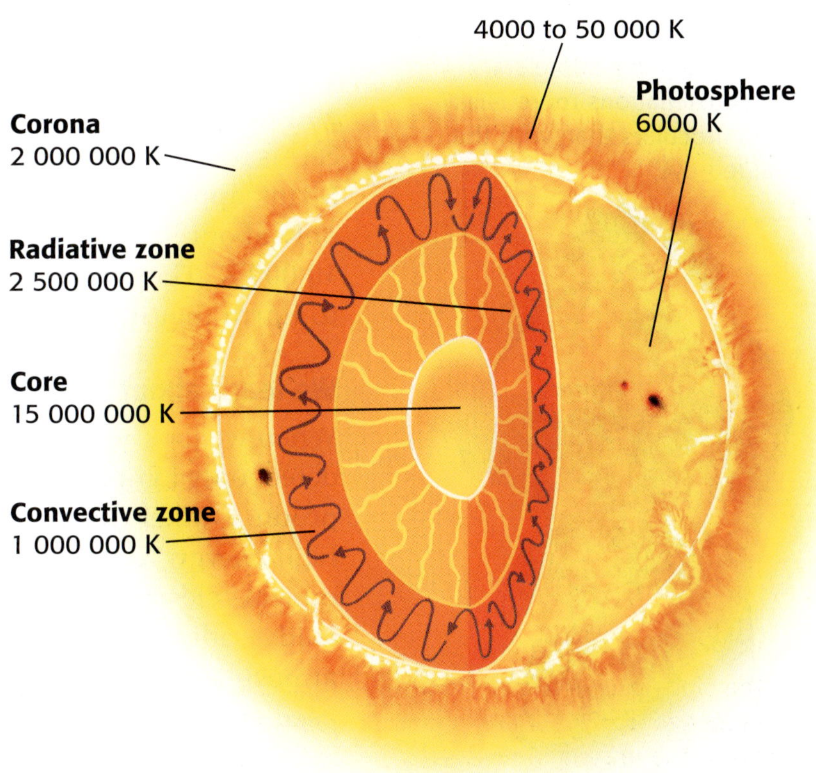

Figure 2

Energy released by fusion reactions in the core slowly works its way through the layers of the sun by the forces of radiation and convection.

Figure 3

Sirius is the brightest star in the night sky, and it is shown on the mouth of the larger dog on this star chart that dates back to 1725.

Studying Stars

Although the ancient Greeks noticed that stars had color and divided stars by their apparent brightness, astronomers did not really begin to learn about the nature of stars until after the invention of the optical telescope.

Why do some stars appear brighter than others?

The brightness of a star depends on the star's temperature, size, and distance from Earth. The brightest star in the night sky is Sirius in the constellation Canis Major, which is shown in ***Figure 3.*** Sirius appears so bright because it is relatively close to Earth, only about 9 ly away. The surface temperature of Sirius is about 10 000 K. The sun's surface is only 6000 K, but the sun is so close to Earth that it dominates the sky during the day.

Figure 4

You can observe some stars and constellations more easily with binoculars than with the unaided eye.

We learn about stars by studying light

When we look with our eyes or use binoculars, as in ***Figure 4,*** we detect only light in the visible part of the spectrum. But stars also produce other wavelengths of electromagnetic radiation, from high-energy X rays to low-energy radio waves. Scientists use optical telescopes to study visible light and radio telescopes to study radio waves emitted from astronomical objects. Earth's atmosphere blocks other wavelengths, so telescopes in space are used to study a wider range of the electromagnetic spectrum.

A star's color is related to its temperature

When light from a glowing hot object passes through a prism, it generates a spectrum of many colors. This spectrum changes with temperature in a definite way: hotter objects glow with light that is more intense and that has shorter wavelengths (closer to the blue end of the spectrum), while the light from cooler objects has greater intensity and longer wavelengths (closer to red).

Although the light from a glowing object contains many colors, the color that we see when we look directly at a hot object is determined mainly by the wavelength at which the object emits the most light. ***Figure 5*** is a graph that shows the intensity, or brightness, of light at different wavelengths for three stars. The sun appears yellow because the peak wavelength of the sun is near the color yellow. Yellow also corresponds to a temperature near 6000 K. Hot stars emit more energy at every wavelength than cooler stars do.

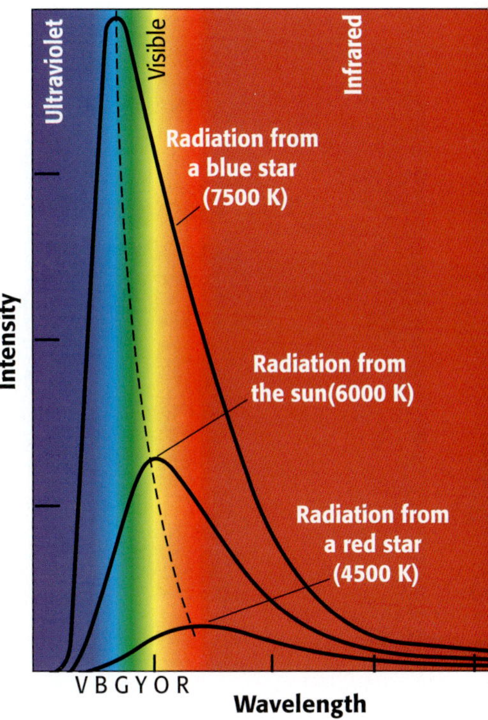

Figure 5

This graph shows the intensity of light at different wavelengths for the sun and two other stars.

Spectral lines reveal the composition of stars

How do we know what stars are made of? The spectra of most stars have dark lines. These dark lines are caused by gases in the outer layers of the stars that absorb the light at these wavelengths. The temperature of these outer layers determines which gases produce spectral lines. For example, cool hydrogen has no spectral lines. Because each element produces a unique pattern of spectral lines, astronomers can match the dark lines in starlight to the known lines of elements found on Earth. ***Figure 6*** shows how the spectral lines of both hydrogen and helium can be found in a star's spectrum.

Astronomers have analyzed more than 20 000 lines in the sun's spectrum to find the composition of its atmosphere. Like the composition of most stars of its age, the sun's mass is 71% hydrogen, 27% helium, and 2% other elements.

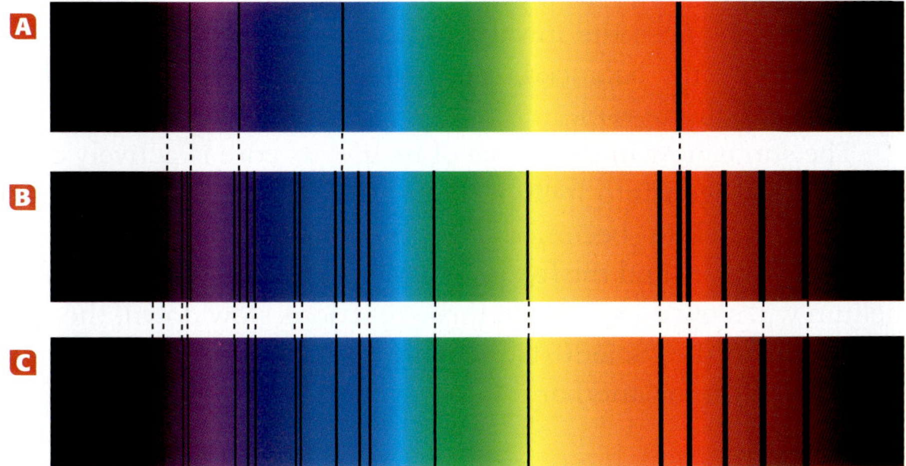

Figure 6

When light is passed through hydrogen gas A, or helium gas C, then through a slit and prism, dark lines appear in the spectrum. If both hydrogen and helium are present, both sets of lines appear B.

The Fate of Stars

Figure 7

New stars are constantly being formed in clouds of gas and dust such as these columns in the Eagle Nebula.

Figure 7 shows stars being formed in a cloud of gas and dust called a *nebula*. Stars are born, go through different stages of development, and eventually die. Stars appear different from one another in part because they are at different stages in their life cycles. Nearly 90% of all stars in our galaxy, including the sun, are in midlife, still converting hydrogen into helium in their interiors.

Some stars, such as Rigel, are younger than the sun, while others, such as Betelgeuse, are farther along in their life cycles. Some objects in the universe are remnants of very old stars that died long ago. But how do stars form? And how do they keep on shining for billions of years?

The sun formed from a cloud of gas and dust

About 5 billion years ago, in an arm of the Milky Way galaxy, a thin, invisible cloud of gas and dust collapsed inward, pulled by the force of the cloud's own gravity. As the cloud fell together, it began to spin. The smaller the cloud became, the faster it spun. About 30 million years after the cloud started to collapse, the center of the cloud reached a temperature of 15 million kelvins.

Electrons were then stripped from hydrogen atoms to leave hydrogen nuclei, which are positively charged protons. Recall that positively charged particles repel each other. But at very high temperatures, protons may get as close to each other as 10^{-15} m. At such a small distance, the strong nuclear force overpowers the electrical repulsion. Through this process of nuclear fusion, the protons combine to form helium. Scientists think that once this process of nuclear fusion started in the core of the cloud, the star we call the sun turned on.

The sun now has a balance of inward and outward forces

The fusion reactions in the core of the sun produce an outward force that balances the inward force due to gravity. With these two forces evenly balanced, the sun has maintained an equilibrium for 5 billion years.

The sun is now in the prime of its life; its core is actively converting hydrogen into helium. Over time, the percentage of the core that is helium becomes larger. Eventually, the core will run out of hydrogen, and the fusion reactions that turn hydrogen into helium will slow down. When these reactions slow down, the sun will begin to die. Scientists estimate that the sun can continue nuclear fusion for another 5 billion years.

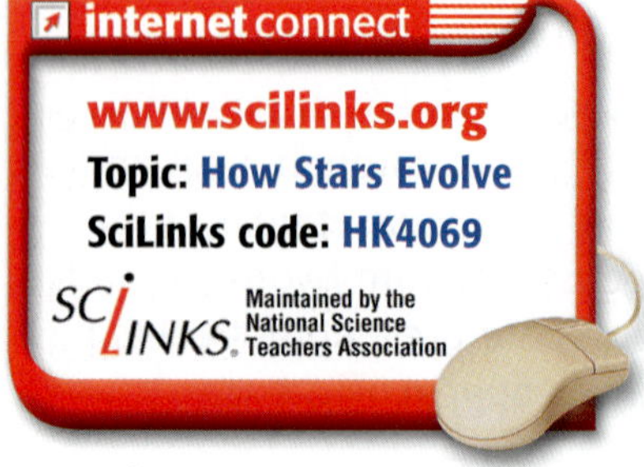

The sun will become a red giant before it dies

As fusion slows, the pressure in the core of the sun will drop and the core will contract, which will cause the core temperature to rise. The sun's outer layers will expand, and the sun will become a **red giant** like the one shown in ***Figure 8.*** The star is red because its surface is cooler, but the core is hot enough to convert helium into carbon and oxygen.

After about 100 million years, the core of the red giant sun will run out of helium and will contract further, which will cause the outer layers to expand again. At this point, the temperature at the core is not high enough to fuse these heavier elements. The outer layers will continue to expand out from the core and will eventually leave the star. The remnant will become a **white dwarf,** a small and very dense star about the size of Earth. White dwarfs no longer fuse elements, so they slowly cool. Stars with a mass of 1.4 solar masses or smaller will have a similar life cycle. Most stars in our galaxy will end as white dwarfs.

Figure 8

When the sun becomes a red giant, it will expand out past Earth's orbit

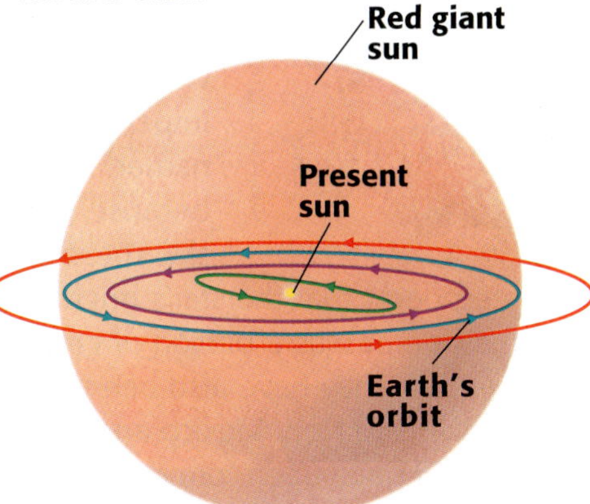

Supergiant stars explode in supernovas

Massive stars evolve faster than smaller stars do. They also develop hotter cores that create heavier elements through fusion. Forming an iron core signals the beginning of a supergiant star's violent death because fusing iron atoms to make heavier elements requires adding rather than releasing energy. When a core becomes mostly iron, fusion stops. When fusion stops, there is no longer any outward pressure to balance the gravitational force. The core collapses because of its own gravity and then rebounds with a shock wave that violently blows the star's outer layers away from the core. The resulting huge, bright explosion is called a Type II **supernova,** shown in ***Figure 9.*** Elements heavier than iron (such as gold and lead) form during a supernova. A Type I supernova occurs when a white dwarf in a binary system (a system composed of two stars) collects enough mass from its companion to exceed 1.4 solar masses.

red giant a large, reddish star late in its life cycle

white dwarf a small, hot, dim star that is the leftover center of an old star

supernova a gigantic explosion in which a massive star collapses and throws its outer layers into space; plural *supernovae*

Figure 9

Supernova 1987A, a Type II supernova, was the first supernova visible to the unaided eye in 400 years. The first image shows what the original star looked like before the explosion.

Connection to SOCIAL STUDIES

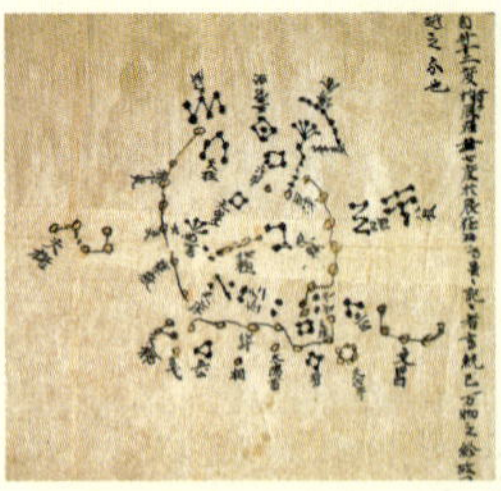

On July 4, 1054, a bright supernova appeared in the constellation Taurus. It was visible for three weeks. Imperial Chinese astronomers named it a "guest" star because it was new to the sky. These astronomers told the emperor that the star's brightness meant that the emperor was a person of great worth. This supernova may have also been observed by Native Americans in New Mexico and Arizona where rock paintings have been found. Later, the remnants of this supernova gained the name "Crab Nebula."

After a Type II supernova, either a neutron star or a black hole forms

Figure 10 shows a nebular remnant of a supernova. If the core that remains after a supernova has a mass of 1.4 to 3 solar masses, the remnant can become a *neutron star*. Neutron stars are only a few kilometers in diameter, but they are very massive. A neutron star is as dense as matter in the nucleus of an atom, about 10^{17} kg/m^3. A thimbleful of a neutron star would weigh more than 100 million tons on Earth. Neutron stars can be detected as *pulsars,* or sources of pulsating radio waves.

If the leftover core has a mass that is greater than three solar masses, it will collapse to form an even stranger object—a **black hole,** which consists of matter so massive and compressed that nothing, not even light, can escape its gravity. Because no light can escape, a black hole cannot be seen directly. Black holes have a powerful gravitational pull, so they can be detected indirectly by observing the radiation of light and X rays from objects that revolve rapidly around them.

black hole an object so massive and dense that not even light can escape its gravity

Figure 10

The Crab Nebula is the remains of a supernova seen by Chinese observers in the year 1054.

The H-R diagram shows how stars evolve

In 1911, Ejnar Hertzsprung compared the temperature and brightness of stars and carefully plotted his data on a graph. In 1913, Henry Norris Russell made similar plots. Together, the two graphs form the Hertzsprung-Russell diagram, or H-R diagram, which is shown in **Figure 11.** The vertical axis indicates brightness. Absolute magnitude indicates how bright stars would be if they were all the same distance from Earth. The horizontal axis indicates surface temperature of the stars, with hotter temperatures on the left.

When stars are born, they appear as *protostars* on a diagonal line called the *main sequence.* Most stars are main sequence stars. None of them are old enough to have evolved off the main sequence. The position of a star on the main sequence depends on the initial mass of the star. As stars age and pass through different stages in their life cycles, their positions on the H-R diagram change. Because most stars spend most of their lives in midlife, more stars appear on the main sequence than on other parts of the H-R diagram. Red giant stars are both cool and bright, so they appear in the upper right. White dwarf stars are both faint and hot, so they appear in the lower left.

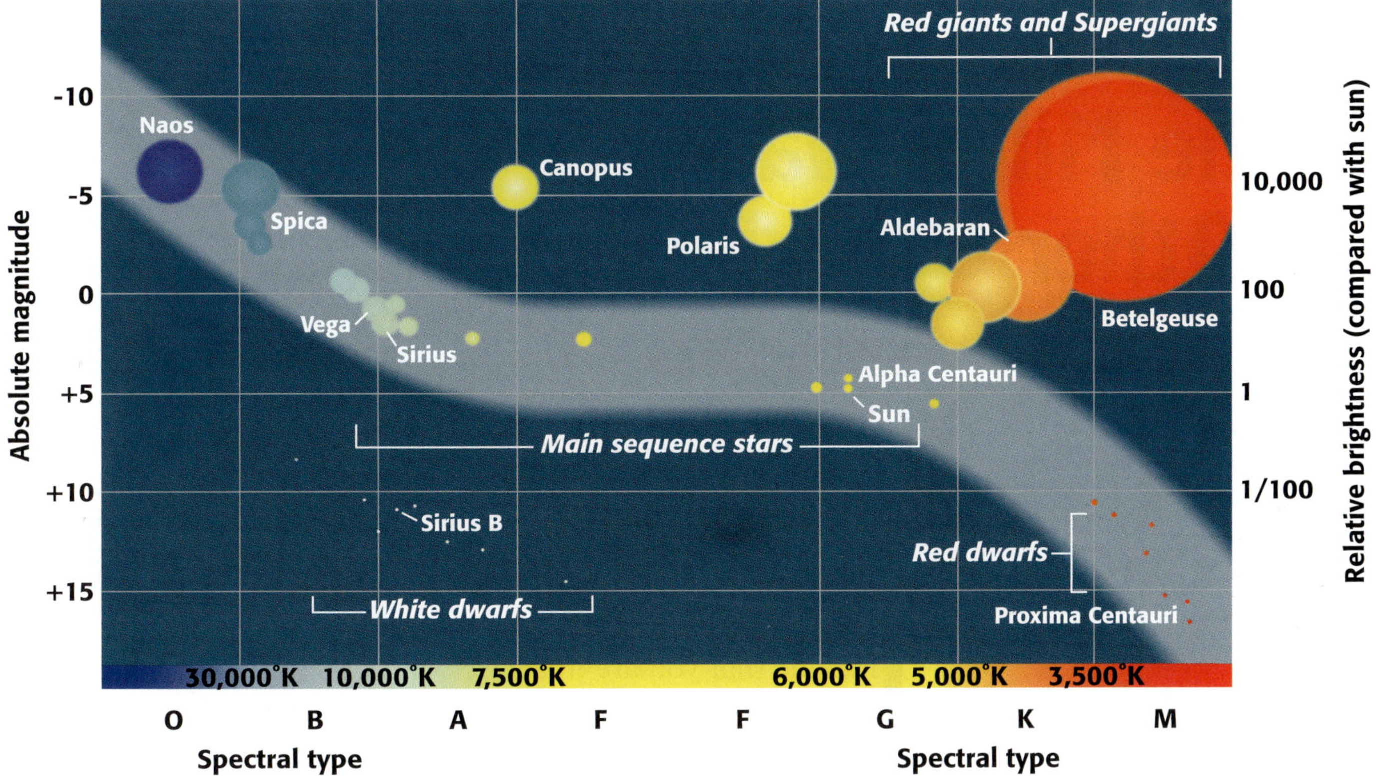

Our sun went from a protostar to a main sequence star in tens of millions of years. It will stay on the main sequence for about 10 billion years. As it becomes a red giant, it will become brighter, cooler, and redder; it will move up and to the right on the H-R diagram for about 100 million years. The sun will become a white dwarf, in the lower left, about 50 million years later.

Figure 11
The H-R diagram is a tool that astronomers use to help them understand how stars change over time.

SECTION 1 REVIEW

SUMMARY

- Stars are spheres of gas that produce energy by fusion.
- The composition of stars is measured using spectra.
- In most stars, outward pressure balances the inward pull of the star's gravity.
- Stars smaller than 1.4 solar masses become red giants and then white dwarfs.
- Massive stars become supergiants and explode in supernovae to become neutron stars or black holes.

1. **Determine** the distance between Polaris and Earth in meters. Polaris is 431 ly from Earth. The speed of light is 3.0×10^8 m/s.
2. **Arrange** the following from smallest to largest: sun, supernova, red giant, and white dwarf.
3. **Describe** the stages in the life of a star of 1 solar mass and in the life of a star of 20 solar masses.
4. **Critical Thinking** Which of the following elements is not likely to be formed in the sun at some time during its life?
   a. helium
   b. carbon
   c. oxygen
   d. iron
5. **Critical Thinking** You and a friend are looking at the stars, and your friend says, "Stars must be shrinking because gravity is constantly pulling their particles together." Explain what is wrong with this reasoning.

SECTION 2

The Milky Way and Other Galaxies

KEY TERMS

galaxy
cluster
interstellar matter
quasar

OBJECTIVES

- **Define** galaxy, and identify Earth's home galaxy.
- **Describe** two characteristics of a spiral galaxy.
- **Distinguish** between the three types of galaxies.
- **Describe** two aspects of a quasar, and identify the tools scientists use to study quasars.

Imagine that you are in a special space ship that allows you to leave Earth, travel through the solar system to nearby stars, and explore all of space. What do you imagine you will see beyond our solar system?

galaxy a collection of stars, dust, and gas bound together by gravity

Galaxies

While the nearest stars are a few light-years away, the nearest galaxy to our own is millions of light-years from Earth. A **galaxy** is a collection of millions or billions of stars. The deeper scientists look into space, the more galaxies they find. There may be more than 100 billion galaxies. If you counted 1000 galaxies per night, it would take 275 000 years to count all of them.

Figure 12
The Andromeda Galaxy is 2.2 million ly from Earth. From a dark location, this galaxy is visible to the unaided eye as a faint blur.

Galaxies contain millions or billions of stars

Galaxies, such as the Andromeda Galaxy shown in ***Figure 12,*** contain millions to billions of stars bound together by gravity. Because stars age at different rates, a galaxy may contain many types of stars. Young stars are often found near the nebular gas and dust where they were born. Older stars may be throughout the galaxy or in regions that contain no gas and dust. Although galaxies contain many stars, scientists do not expect to be able to observe stellar systems within other galaxies. The distances to other galaxies are so large that searches for other planets focus on nearby stars, usually within our own galaxy.

Gravity holds galaxies together in clusters

Without gravity, everything in space might be a veil of gas spread out through space. With gravity, clouds of gas come together and collapse to form stars. After the first stars in a galaxy age, throwing off gas and dust or becoming supernovae, new stars form. The gas, dust, and stars collapse into galaxies because of gravity.

Galaxies are not spread out evenly through space. They are grouped together in **clusters** like the one shown in ***Figure 13.*** The members of a cluster of galaxies are bound together by gravity. The Milky Way galaxy and the Andromeda galaxy are two of the largest members of the Local Group, a cluster of more than 30 galaxies. New members of the Local Group are being discovered as new telescopes, such as the Hubble Space Telescope shown in ***Figure 14,*** become available to astronomers.

Clusters of galaxies can form even larger groups called *superclusters*. A typical supercluster contains thousands of galaxies containing trillions of stars in individual clusters. Superclusters can be as large as 100 million ly across. They are the largest structures in the universe.

Figure 13

The Hercules Cluster of galaxies is 650 million ly from Earth.

cluster a group of stars or galaxies bound by gravity

Figure 14

A Edwin Hubble used the telescopes at Mount Wilson Observatory in California to explore galaxies beyond the Milky Way galaxy.

B The *Hubble Space Telescope,* shown here being launched from the space shuttle, now probes the depths of the universe from its orbit above Earth.

Types of Galaxies

Edwin Hubble divided all galaxies into three major types: spiral, elliptical, and irregular. All three types have many stars, but they have different structures. Spiral galaxies have spiral arms made of gas, dust, and stars. Elliptical galaxies have little gas or dust. Irregular galaxies do not have a particular shape.

Figure 15

When we see the band of light called the *Milky Way,* we are looking along the plane of our galaxy, the Milky Way galaxy.

We live in the Milky Way galaxy

If you live away from bright outdoor lights, you may be able to see the Milky Way, a faint, narrow band of light and dark patches across the sky. This band, shown in ***Figure 15,*** consists of stars, gas, and dust in our galaxy, the Milky Way galaxy.

Most of the objects you can see in the night sky are part of the Milky Way galaxy. Because our solar system is inside the Milky Way galaxy, we cannot see all of it at once. But scientists can use astronomical data to piece together a picture of the Milky Way galaxy, such as the one shown in ***Figure 16.*** Our solar system is located within a spiral arm, about 26 000 ly from the center, or about half of the distance to the edge.

The Milky Way is a spiral galaxy

Our galaxy is a huge spiraling disk of stars, gas, and dust. Like most spiral galaxies, the Milky Way galaxy has a huge bulge in the center. The nucleus of the galaxy is very dense and has many old stars. The gas and dust have been used up to form stars. Many astronomers think that a large black hole is at the very center of our galaxy. Spiral galaxies, such as Messier 74 (M74), which is shown in ***Figure 17A,*** have gas and dust between the stars. This gas and dust is called **interstellar matter.** Clouds of interstellar matter provide materials that allow new stars to form. Because hot young stars are blue, the spiral arms often appear bluish. Because old stars are often red, the bulge in the middle appears reddish. The arms have both old and new stars as well as gas and dust.

interstellar matter the gas and dust located between the stars in a galaxy

Figure 16

An idea of what the Milky Way galaxy might look like from the outside can be pieced together from astronomical data.

Figure 17

A Seen from above, the Milky Way galaxy might look like this spiral galaxy, named *Messier 74.*

B Unlike the Milky Way galaxy, elliptical galaxies such as *Messier 87* do not have spiral arms.

C The Magellanic Cloud is a large irregular galaxy that is easily seen in the Southern Hemisphere.

Elliptical galaxies have no spiral arms

Elliptical galaxies have no spiral arms and are spherical or egg shaped. They contain mostly older stars and have little interstellar matter. Older stars are red, so elliptical galaxies, such as M87 in **Figure 17B** often have a reddish color. Elliptical galaxies are found in a wide range of sizes. Giant elliptical galaxies contain trillions of stars and can be up to 200 000 ly in diameter. Dwarf elliptical galaxies contain a few million stars and are much smaller.

A spiral galaxy can be recognized even when it is tilted at an angle, but because an elliptical galaxy has no regular features, scientists have trouble knowing whether an elliptical galaxy is head-on or sideways in relation to Earth.

All other galaxies are irregular galaxies

Edwin Hubble named the third category irregular galaxies because they lack regular shapes and do not have a well-defined structure. Some irregular galaxies contain little interstellar matter, while others have large amounts and contain mostly young blue stars. **Figure 17C** shows the large irregular galaxy that is nearest to the Milky Way, the Large Magellanic Cloud. This galaxy is a part of the Local Group of galaxies.

There are many more dwarf irregular galaxies than large ones. Dwarf galaxies are often found near larger galaxies. Some irregular galaxies may be oddly shaped because the gravitational influence of nearby galaxies distorts their spiral arms.

Did You Know?

Many new technologies have come out of the space program. A company has recently starting selling a jacket made out of the same material that NASA uses to insulate spacecraft. The material, called *aerogel,* can withstand temperatures from −45°C to 1650°C (−50°F to 3000°F), and keeps the person inside the jacket very warm even in the coldest weather.

Figure 18

This quasar, which is named 3C273, has a powerful jet shooting from it and produces more energy than the sun.

How Galaxies Evolve

When scientists observe distant galaxies, they are looking back in time. When astronomers observe a galaxy that is 1 billion ly away, they are observing light that left the galaxy one billion years ago. Scientists do not know what such a galaxy is doing now, but by studying closer galaxies that might be similar to ancient ones, they can slowly piece together the puzzle of how galaxies change over time.

Quasars may be infant galaxies

When astronomers first detected radio waves in space, they had difficulty finding stars that accompanied some of the radio sources. In 1960, a faint object was finally matched with a strong radio signal. This object was the first **quasar,** or quasi-stellar object, named for its starlike appearance, as shown in ***Figure 18.*** On further study, scientists discovered that quasars are the most distant and most radiant objects in space. One explanation for the strong radiation is that each quasar has a huge central black hole (about a billion solar masses) and a large disk of gas and dust around it. Friction in the disk releases energy into space at many wavelengths, especially radio waves. Optical telescopes show quasars embedded in faint galaxies. Quasars may be the central parts of distant galaxies, seen as they were when very young.

quasar quasi-stellar radio sources; very luminous objects that produce energy at a high rate and that are thought to be the most distant objects in the universe

Radio Telescopes and Cell Phones

Electromagnetic radiation comes in many wavelengths. Radio telescopes detect radio waves from space. Radio waves are especially important in studying distant objects such as quasars and the interstellar matter within galaxies. But just as optical telescopes are affected by light pollution, radio telescopes are affected by unwanted radio signals. Cell phones can easily drown out the distant signals of many galaxies. For this reason, cell phones are banned near many radio telescopes, such as the Arecibo in Puerto Rico.

Applying Information

1. Why do cell phones affect telescopes more than phones that use wires do?
2. What other sorts of pollution may affect radio telescopes? Where might you build a radio telescope to avoid radio pollution?

Galaxies change over time

All stars change over time. Massive stars explode in supernovae, and lower-mass stars become red giants and, eventually, white dwarfs. Because gas, dust, and stars make up galaxies, entire galaxies also change over time. As galaxies consume their gas and dust, they become unable to make new stars. Many galaxies in the Hubble Deep Field, shown in ***Figure 19,*** are blue, indicating that we are viewing them when they were young, before they used their stores of gas and dust.

Galaxies also change as a result of collisions. Stars within a galaxy are far apart and can easily pass each other if two galaxies collide. But as galaxies approach each other, the mutual gravitational attraction changes their shapes. While the stars rarely hit each other, the collision of gas and dust sets off rapid bursts of new star formation. Scientists are trying to discover why elliptical galaxies do not contain young stars and how they used up their gas and dust. One possibility is that gas and dust were stripped away in collisions that also stripped away many of the younger stars.

Figure 19

The Hubble Deep Field project discovered many faint and very distant galaxies.

SECTION 2 REVIEW

SUMMARY

- A galaxy is a collection of millions or billions of stars bound together by gravity.
- Our solar system lies in a spiral arm in the Milky Way galaxy.
- Spiral galaxies have a bulge near the center and spiral arms made of gas, dust, and stars.
- Elliptical galaxies have little gas and dust and a spherical or oval shape.
- Irregular galaxies have no regular shape.
- Quasars are stellar in appearance but emit large amounts of radiation, especially radiowaves.

1. **List** the types of galaxies and describe one important feature of each type.
2. **Explain** why the Milky Way appears as a narrow band of light in the night sky.
3. **Draw** a sketch of the Milky Way galaxy. Label the nucleus and the central bulge, and indicate the position of our solar system.
4. **Compare** the colors of spiral galaxies with the colors of elliptical galaxies.
5. **Describe** how quasars got their name.
6. **Arrange** these structures from largest to smallest: solar system, sun, spiral galaxy, dwarf elliptical galaxy, and cluster of galaxies.
7. **Explain** how scientists know that elliptical galaxies do not contain many young stars?
8. **Critical Thinking** Why do stars rarely collide during galactic collisions?

SECTION 3

Origin of the Universe

KEY TERMS

universe
red shift
blue shift
big bang theory

OBJECTIVES

- **Describe** the basic structure of the universe.
- **Describe** red shift, and explain what it tells scientists about our universe.
- **State** the main features of the big bang theory, and explain the evidence supporting the expansion of the universe.
- **Explain** how scientists are using tools and models to hypothesize what may happen to the universe in the future.

Just imagine the following: colliding galaxies that rip stars from each other, a dead star so dense that one thimbleful of its matter would weigh more than 100 million tons on Earth, a volcano on Mars that is nearly three times taller than Mount Everest and that has a base larger than Louisiana. All of these things are part of the universe.

universe the sum of all space, matter, and energy that exist, that have existed in the past, and that will exist in the future

What Is the Universe?

By the term **universe,** scientists mean everything physical that exists in space and time. The universe consists of all space, matter, and energy that exists—now, in the past, and in the future. There is only one observable universe. ***Figure 20*** shows objects in the universe and their relative sizes.

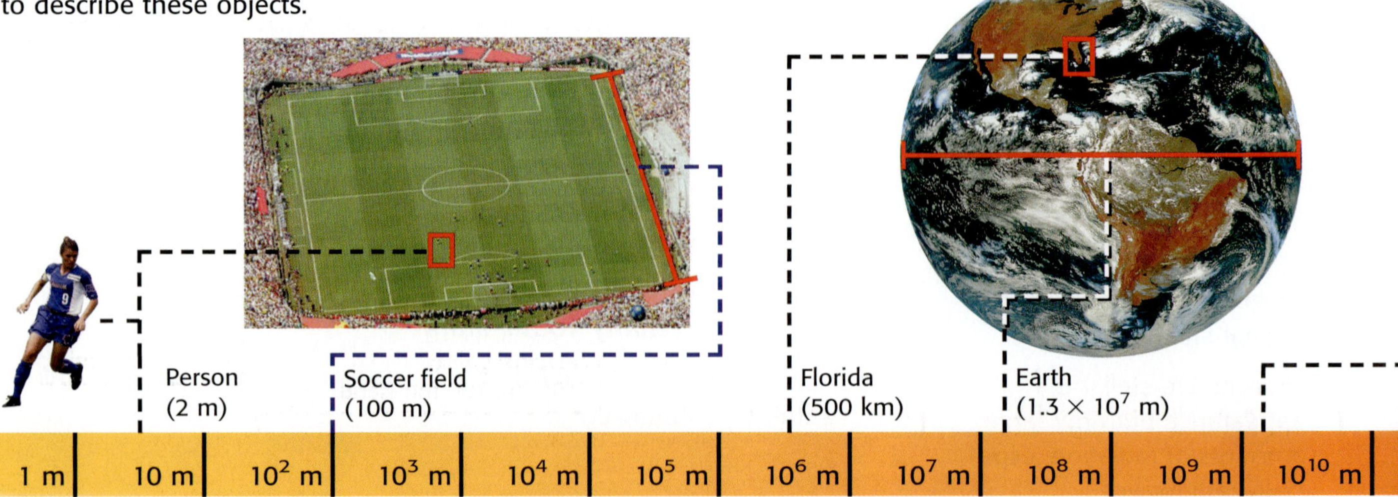

Figure 20
The sizes of astronomical objects are so great that measuring units such as the light-year are needed to describe these objects.

You are part of the universe, as is Earth and everything on it. With the unaided eye, we can see about 6000 stars, 5 of the planets, our moon, and several nebulae, star clusters, and galaxies. As shown in ***Figure 20,*** huge distances are involved in studying the universe. Perhaps you can imagine the size of a soccer field, your city, your country, or even Earth, but the comparisons become difficult as we imagine objects on scales beyond Earth, such as the solar system. The solar system is only a small part of our galaxy, which is but one of many galaxies in one of many clusters of galaxies.

We see the universe now as it was in the past

Astronomers need large units of measure to express distances. As you recall, a light-year is the distance that light travels in one year, or 9.5×10^{15} m. This distance is so long that driving it in a car moving at highway speed would take more than 10 million years. Remember that while a year is a unit of time, a light-year is a unit of distance.

It takes time for light to travel in space. The farther away an object is, the older the light that we get from that object is. When we say the sun is 8 light-minutes away, we are not only expressing its distance, but also the fact that we see it as it was eight minutes ago. We never see it as it really is, right now. The same is true for stars, planets (Pluto is more than 5 light-hours away), galaxies, or clusters of galaxies. When we see very distant objects, we see them as they were when they were younger. Astronomers can compare how galaxies age by looking at many galaxies at different distances, and therefore at different ages.

Did You Know?

Because light travels at a constant speed of 3×10^8 m/s, we can measure how long it takes starlight to reach Earth. Light from Sirius travels 8 years and 7 months. If you look at Altair (in the constellation Aquila), you see light that left the star 16 years and 9 months ago. You could even find a star whose light left the year you were born.

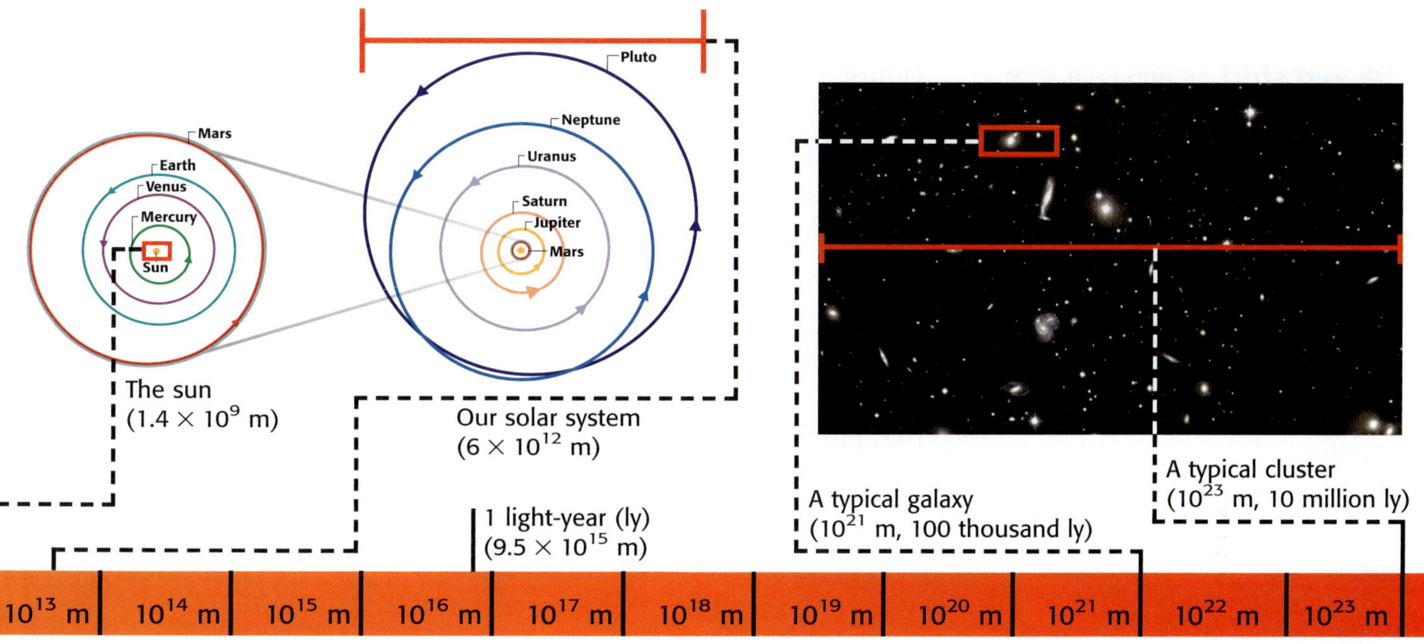

Figure 21

Astronaut Bruce McCandless maneuvers through space in a suit specially designed to allow him to propel himself. His spacesuit also protects him from the conditions of space.

Most of the universe is empty space

Despite the variety of objects in the universe, such as interstellar matter, stars, and galaxies, there is almost nothing between objects. ***Figure 21*** shows an astronaut in a suit designed to help a person survive in space. It is extremely hot facing the sun in space, and it is very cold facing away from it. Space is a vacuum with no air and no air pressure. The suit provides the insulation, breathable air, and air pressure that the human body needs to survive. In this case, the astronaut is bathed in particles streaming from the sun. Farther out, there is so little between stars that the space can truly be called "empty."

What Happened at the Beginning?

How the universe came to be is an age-old question. Ancient cultures had myths to explain the origin of the universe. Today, scientists study stars and galaxies for clues by using new tools and techniques. Scientists interested in the early history of our universe use large telescopes to study the most distant objects, whose light was emitted billions of years ago.

The universe is expanding

In 1929, Edwin Hubble announced that the universe is expanding. Hubble based his conclusion on observations of the spectral lines in light from other galaxies. He found that these spectral lines were almost always shifted toward the red end of the spectrum. This effect, called **red shift,** can be explained by the Doppler effect. The Doppler effect states that when an object is moving away from us, waves emitted from the object stretch out. The faster a light source moves away, the more that light stretches to longer wavelengths and shifts toward the red end of the spectrum, as shown in ***Figure 22.***

When an object is approaching us, the shift is toward shorter wavelengths at the spectrum's blue end and is called **blue shift.** ***Table 1*** shows the distance, velocity, and frequency shift of several galaxies. Hubble found that most galaxies have red shifts and that galaxies that are farther away have greater red shifts. Hubble explained this by proposing that almost every galaxy is moving away from Earth. Therefore, galaxies are also moving away from each other, and the universe is expanding.

red shift an apparent shift toward longer wavelengths of light caused when a luminous object moves away from the observer

blue shift an apparent shift toward shorter wavelengths of light caused when a luminious object moves toward the observer

Table 1 **Velocity, Frequency Shift, and Distance from Earth of Several Galaxies**

Name of galaxy	Type	Velocity (km/s)	Red shift or blue shift	Distance (ly)
Andromeda galaxy (M31)	spiral	–10	blue	2.4×10^6
Barnard's galaxy (NGC 6822)	irregular	15	red	2.2×10^6
NGC 55 (in Sculptor)	spiral	115	red	1.0×10^7
Sunflower galaxy (M 63)	spiral	550	red	3.6×10^7
Virgo A (M87)	elliptical	822	red	7.2×10^7
Fornax A (NGC 1316)	spiral	1713	red	9.8×10^7

Expansion implies that the universe was once smaller

Although galaxies that are close to each other are gravitationally attracted to each other, galaxies are moving away from each other in general. Imagine time running backward, like a movie being rewound. If every galaxy normally moves away from every other galaxy, then as time goes backward, the galaxies move closer together. Long ago, the entire universe might have been contained in an extremely small space, effectively a point.

If time moves forward again from that point, all of the matter in the universe appears to expand rapidly outward like a gigantic explosion. Scientists call this hypothetical explosion the *big bang*. If the expansion has been constant since the big bang, we can estimate the age of the universe. Velocity is equal to distance divided by time. The velocities of galaxies can be measured by using red shift and the Doppler effect, but the distances to these faint objects are difficult to measure. Using estimates for distance and velocity, scientists have estimated that the age of the universe is between 10 and 20 billion years.

INTEGRATING

CHEMISTRY

One of the major discoveries of the 1800s was that spectral lines found in chemistry labs were also found in celestial objects. This discovery showed that objects act predictably everywhere in the universe and allowed scientists to identify elements found in space as identical to elements found on Earth. Astronomers began to study how atoms react in conditions that differed from those on Earth.

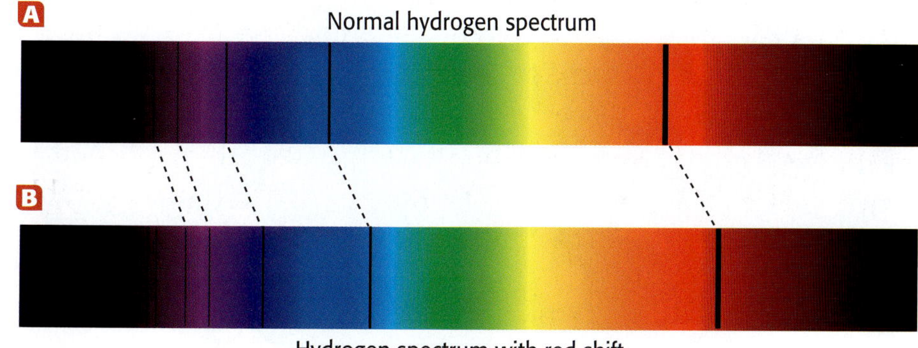

Figure 22

A The spectral lines of hydrogen gas can be seen and measured in a laboratory.

B When this pattern appears in starlight, we know that the star contains hydrogen. In this case, the lines show a red shift, suggesting that the star is moving away from us.

Did the universe start with a big bang?

Although scientists have proposed several different theories to explain the expansion of the universe, the most complete and widely accepted is the big bang theory. The **big bang theory** states that the universe began with a gigantic explosion 10 billion to 20 billion years ago. *In this book, we will assume that the universe is 15 billion years old.*

According to this theory, nothing existed before the big bang. There was no time and no space. But out of this nothingness came the vast system of space, time, matter, and energy that now makes up the universe. The explosion released all of the matter and energy that still exist in the universe today.

big bang theory the theory that all matter and energy in the universe was compressed into an extremely small volume that 10 to 20 billion years ago exploded and began expanding in all directions

Cosmic background radiation supports the big bang theory

In 1965, Arno Penzias and Robert Wilson were making adjustments to a new radio antenna that they had built. They could not explain a steady but very dim signal from all over the sky in the form of radiation at microwave wavelengths. They realized that the signal they were receiving was the *cosmic background radiation* predicted by the big bang theory.

Imagine the changes in color that occur as the burner on an electric stove cools off. First, the hot burner glows yellow or white. As the burner cools, it becomes dimmer and glows red. It may still be rather hot when it finally looks black. The color you see corresponds to the wavelength at which the burner radiates the most light. In outer space, the burner would cool until it reached the temperature of space.

Many scientists believe that the microwaves detected by Penzias and Wilson are dim remains of the radiation produced during the big bang. Using maps of cosmic background radiation, such as the one shown in **Figure 23,** scientists have found that the universe has an overall temperature of about 2.7 K.

Quick ACTIVITY

Modeling the Expanding Universe

1. Inflate a round balloon to about half full, and then pinch it closed to keep the air inside.
2. Use a marker to draw several dots close together on the balloon. Mark one of the dots with an *M* to indicate the Milky Way galaxy.
3. Now continue inflating the balloon. How do the dots move relative to each other?
4. How is this inflating balloon a good model for the expanding universe?
5. In what ways might this balloon not be a good model for the expanding universe?

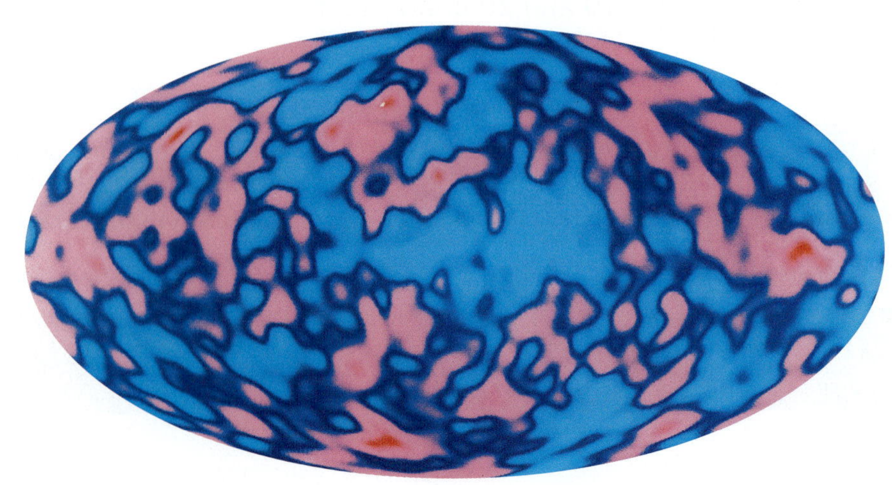

Figure 23

The colors in this computerized map of cosmic background radiation across the entire sky represent slight differences in temperature above and below 2.7 K.

Figure 24

This timeline shows major events in the evolution of the universe. The first 1 million (10^6) years are based on the big bang theory.

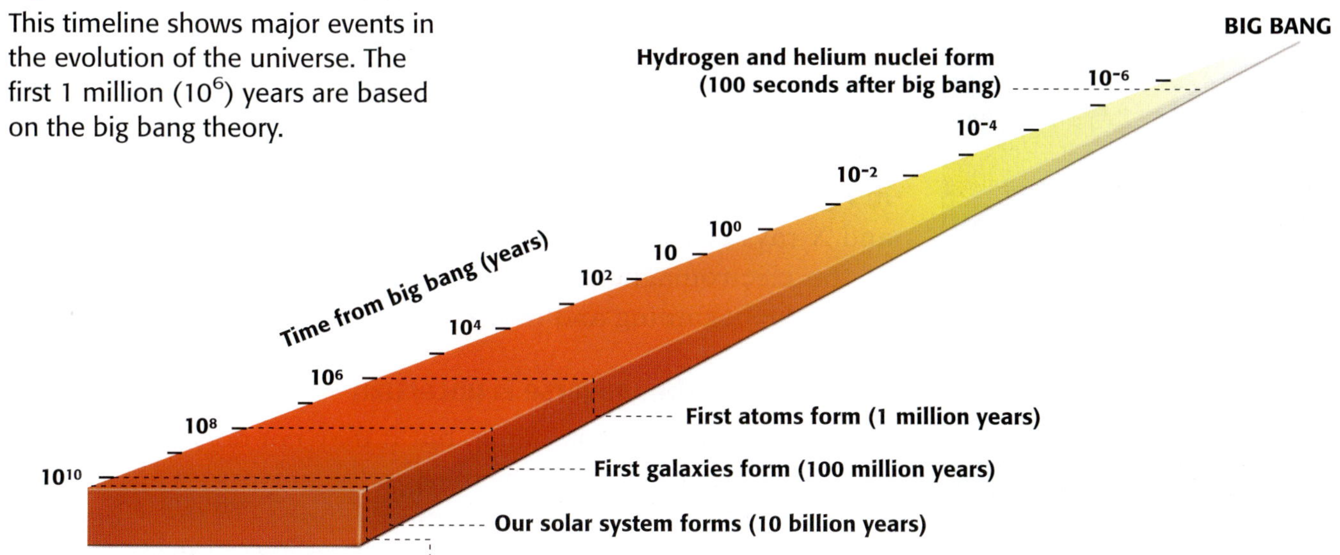

Radiation dominated the early universe

According to the big bang theory, expansion cooled the universe enough for matter such as protons, neutrons, and electrons to form from the radiation within a few seconds after the big bang. Hydrogen and helium nuclei and other particles were present, but the temperature was still too high for entire atoms to form and remain stable. The universe was dominated by radiation, which immediately overcame the attraction between electrons and nuclei. ***Figure 24*** shows key points in the evolution of the universe as predicted by the big bang theory. Note that the timeline uses a logarithmic scale, so the last 5 billion years can be found in a small area near the end.

Figure 25

Helium is found in stars, but heavier elements, such as lead, are the result of supernovae.

Processes in stars lead to bigger atoms

In a million years, the universe had expanded and cooled enough for hydrogen and helium atoms to form. Hydrogen comprised 75% of the matter, and helium comprised 25%. Hydrogen fuels stars and acts as a building block for other elements. Once hydrogen atoms formed, stars and galaxies began to form, too. Our solar system is thought to be 4.6 billion years old, forming 10 billion years after the big bang.

All elements other than hydrogen and helium form in stars. Nuclear fusion in stars produces helium and elements up to the atomic number of iron. Heavier elements form during supernovae. ***Figure 25*** shows helium and lead that were produced in a star. The lead is in the form of galena, or lead sulfide.

Predicting the Future of the Universe

Scientists use their ever-increasing knowledge to hypothesize what might happen in the future. They depend on a mixture of theory and precise observations of very faint objects. These observations depend on technology, such as the telescopes shown in ***Figure 26.*** New space telescopes that collect infrared radiation and X rays are being built and launched. Data in these regions of the electromagnetic spectrum may provide important clues about the beginning and future of the universe.

Figure 26

Astronomers observe the universe by using modern telescopes, such as the telescopes at the Cerro Tololo Inter-American Observatory in Chile.

The future of the universe is uncertain

The universe is still expanding, but it may not do so forever. The combined gravity of all of the mass in the universe is also pulling the universe inward, in the direction opposite to the expansion. The competition between these two forces leaves three possible outcomes for the universe:

1. The universe will keep expanding forever.
2. The expansion of the universe will gradually slow down, and the universe will approach a limit in size.
3. The universe will stop expanding and start to fall back in on itself.

The fate of the universe depends on mass

Figure 27 shows three possible fates of the universe. Which one occurs depends on the amount of matter in the universe. If there is not enough mass, the gravitational force will be too weak to stop the expansion, so the universe will keep expanding forever. If there is just the right amount of mass, the expansion will continually slow down but will never stop completely. If there is more mass than this right amount, gravity will eventually overcome the expansion and the universe will start to contract. Eventually, a contracting universe could collapse back to a single point in a "big crunch." As things drew closer to each other, galaxies and stars would collide. The universe would become extremely hot and very small. At this point, the universe may end, or another big bang may start the cycle all over again.

It is hard to predict what will happen in this very distant future. Much of the mass in the universe is very difficult to detect, so we do not yet know the total mass of the universe.

Figure 27

There are three possible fates for the universe.

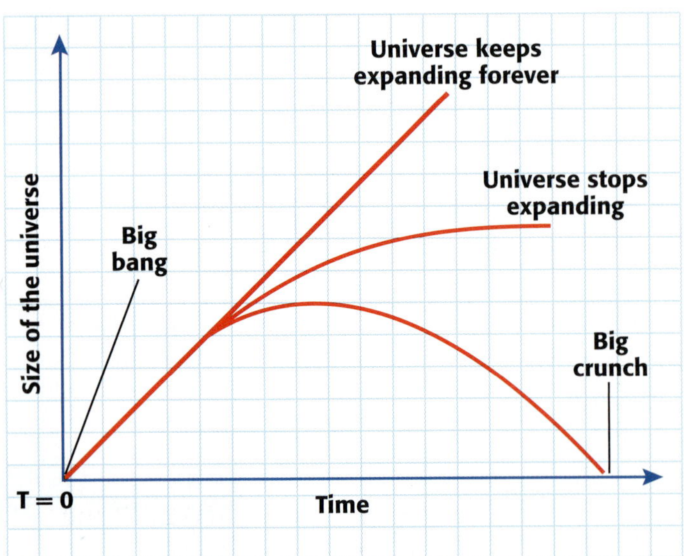

New technology helps scientists test theories

Predictions of the future of the universe rest on theories of the past. Scientists test theories by making observations to see whether the theories make accurate predictions. If observations do not agree with theory, new theories are needed. To make these important observations, very powerful telescopes and other sensitive equipment are needed.

One example of new, more sensitive technology is the Chandra X-Ray Observatory, shown in ***Figure 28A.*** The presence of X rays indicates matter at temperatures of more than one million degrees. The Crab Nebula emits radiation at many wavelengths, including X rays, as shown in ***Figure 28B.*** Compare this image with the visible light picture in ***Figure 10*** and the radio image on the first page of this chapter. Observations in each wavelength region tell us something about the Crab Nebula and about supernovae and their release of elements in general.

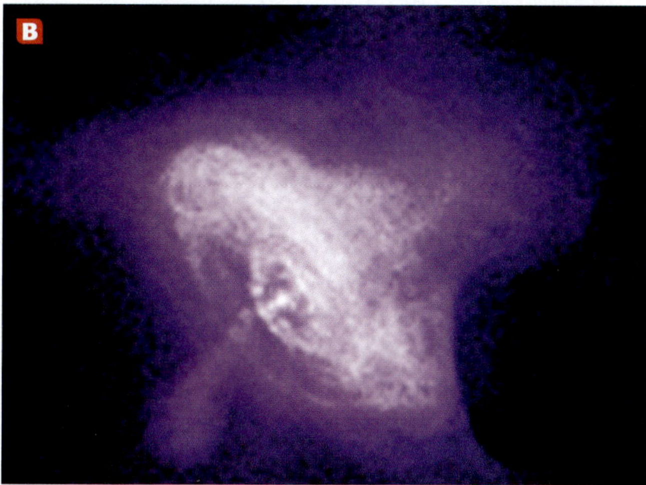

Figure 28

A The Chandra X-Ray Observatory collects information from matter at very high temperatures.

B The Chandra X-Ray Observatory created this image of the Crab Nebula.

There is debate about dark matter

Astronomers estimate the mass of the universe by measuring stars, galaxies, and matter in the interstellar medium. But observations of gravitational interactions between galaxies, such as the interaction shown in ***Figure 29*** indicate that there is more matter than what is visible. Some scientists call this undetectable matter *dark matter*. Dark matter may be planets, black holes, or brown dwarfs. Brown dwarfs are starlike objects that lack enough mass to begin fusion. Dark matter could also be exotic atomic particles that no one knows how to observe. As much as 90% of the universe may be composed of dark matter. What it is, where it is, and how to detect it remain a mystery.

Figure 29

Spiral galaxies NCG 2207 and IC 2163 are colliding.

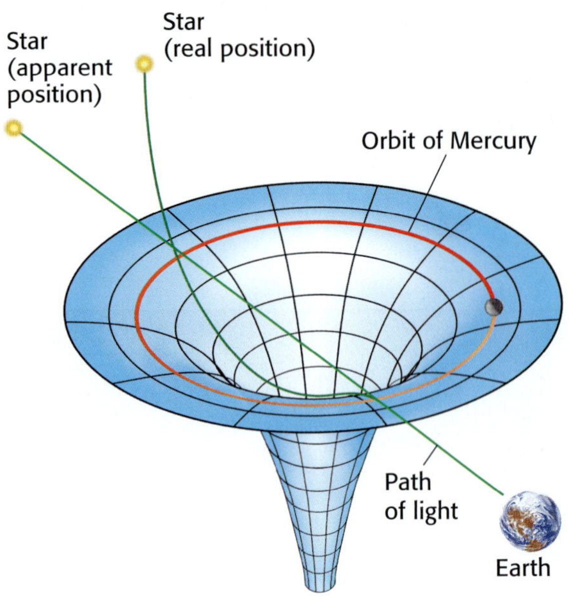

Figure 30

According to Einstein's theory of relativity, the mass of the sun curves the space near the sun.

Scientists use mathematics to build better models

People easily accept Newton's theory of gravity because it corresponds to our experiences of the world. Newton wrote his theory in a mathematical form that can be applied to many circumstances on Earth and in space. In 1916, Albert Einstein expanded on Newton's theories by developing the general theory of relativity, which he also expressed in a mathematical form. Einstein's theory is hard to understand, in part because its effects are only noticeable at a very large scale.

According to Einstein's theory, mass curves space, much in the same way that your body curves a mattress when you sit on it. In 1919, observations of a total solar eclipse showed that Einstein was correct. Stars in the direction of the sun, which could be seen only during the eclipse, were in slightly different positions than expected. The mass of the sun had curved space, causing light to come from a slightly different location, as shown in ***Figure 30.*** Larger masses, such as galaxies, will distort space even more. In this way, a mathematical model was tested and supported by observation.

SECTION 3 REVIEW

SUMMARY

- The universe is all of the space, matter, and energy that exist, have existed, and will exist.
- The big bang theory states that the universe began 10 billion to 20 billion years ago as an explosion.
- The discovery of cosmic background radiation supports the big bang theory.
- Red shift shows that most galaxies are moving away from each other and that the universe is expanding.
- Astronomers use mathematical models and observations to discern the past and future of the universe.

1. **Define** the word *universe,* and list three things that are found in the universe.
2. **Define** the terms *red shift* and *blue shift.*
3. **Describe** the evidence that the universe is expanding.
4. **Explain** why the microwave background radiation is now less than 3 K even though the universe was originally very hot.
5. **Compare** the features that you see in the three images of the Crab Nebula in this chapter. Make a list of similarities and a list of differences.
6. **Critical Thinking** Why didn't the first stars to form have solar systems with Earth-like planets and satellites?
7. **Critical Thinking** If an object is moving away from us at a high speed and is observed in the radio region of the spectrum, what does red shift mean? Explain.
8. **Critical Thinking** Why is it unlikely that dark matter is composed mostly of stars?

Graphing Skills

Bar Graphs

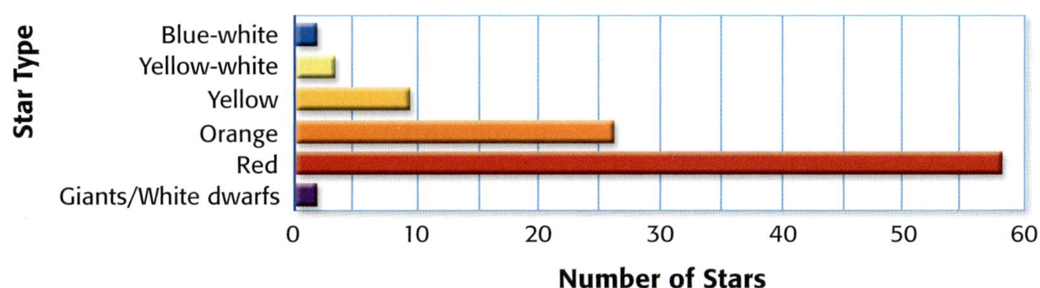

Stars have different colors depending on their masses and ages. The graph above indicates the colors and types of the 100 stars nearest Earth (within 26 ly). Examine the graph and answer the following questions. (See Appendix A for help interpreting a graph.)

1. What variables are shown in this graph?
2. What is the most common type of star nearest Earth? What stars are least common?
3. Most stars are main sequence stars. The more massive a main sequence star is, the greater its surface temperature and brightness. Using the graph and H-R diagram, what can you conclude about the brightness, temperature, and mass of the stars nearest Earth? Which form most easily: stars with large or small masses?
4. If you were to construct a similar graph from a list of the 100 brightest stars as seen from Earth, the number of red and orange main sequence stars would decrease and the number of giant stars would increase. What can you conclude from this information?
5. Construct a graph best suited for the information listed below. How many elliptical galaxies are among the nearest (within 26 million ly) to Earth?

Galaxy Type	Percentage among 190 nearest galaxies
Elliptical	10.0
Spiral	38.4
Irregular	51.6

6. Beyond 26 million ly, the number of irregular galaxies does not increase as much as the numbers of the other types of galaxies. What can you conclude from this information?

CHAPTER 20 REVIEW

Chapter Highlights

Before you begin, review the summaries of the key ideas of each section, found at the end of each section. The key vocabulary terms are listed on the first page of each section.

UNDERSTANDING CONCEPTS

1. What are the three basic types of galaxies?
   a. spiral, elliptical, and irregular
   b. closed, elliptical, and open
   c. spiral, quasar, and pulsar
   d. open, binary, and globular

2. A pattern of stars seen from Earth is a
   a. galaxy. **c.** Milky Way.
   b. nebula. **d.** constellation.

3. By studying starlight, astronomers may learn
   a. the elements that are in the star.
   b. the surface temperature of the star.
   c. the speed at which the star is moving toward or away from Earth.
   d. All of the above

4. A light-year is a unit of
   a. time. **c.** temperature.
   b. mass. **d.** distance.

5. A star like the sun will end its life as a
   a. pulsar. **c.** white dwarf.
   b. black hole. **d.** supernova.

6. What kind of galaxy is the Milky Way galaxy?
   a. elliptical **c.** cluster
   b. spiral **d.** irregular

7. Giant elliptical galaxies have _____ of stars.
   a. dozens **c.** hundreds
   b. thousands **d.** millions

8. A Type II supernova explodes when it begins to fuse _____ in its core.
   a. hydrogen **c.** helium
   b. carbon **d.** iron

9. Which of the following is a possible age of the universe, according to the big bang theory?
   a. 4.6 million years **c.** 4.6 billion years
   b. 15 million years **d.** 15 billion years

10. Dark matter is detected because it
    a. is bright. **c.** is dark.
    b. has gravity. **d.** is hot.

11. According to Einstein's theory of relativity, space is curved by a great _____ nearby.
    a. mass **c.** vacuum
    b. comet **d.** satellite

USING VOCABULARY

12. Arrange the following from largest to smallest: *dwarf elliptical galaxy, spiral galaxy, pulsar, red giant,* and *cluster of galaxies.*

13. Describe *nuclear fusion,* and identify in which part of a star it takes place.

14. Write a paragraph that explains the origin of the universe as presented in this chapter. Use the following terms: *big bang theory, red shift, galaxy, interstellar matter,* and *star.*

15. Describe the arrangement of the components of the Milky Way galaxy. Use the terms *interstellar matter, stars, bulge,* and *spiral arms.*

16. Explain the current theory of what a *quasar* is.

17. Write a paragraph that describes how the mass of a star determines the death of the star. Include the terms *star, white dwarf, supernova, neutron star,* and *black hole.* WRITING SKILL

18. Describe the difference between *blue shift* and *red shift.*

19. Explain what makes up a *cluster,* and approximate how large a cluster may be.

BUILDING MATH SKILLS

20. Using Graphics The figure below shows the intensity of radiation at different wavelengths for three stars. Draw the curve for a star whose surface temperature is 20 000 K.

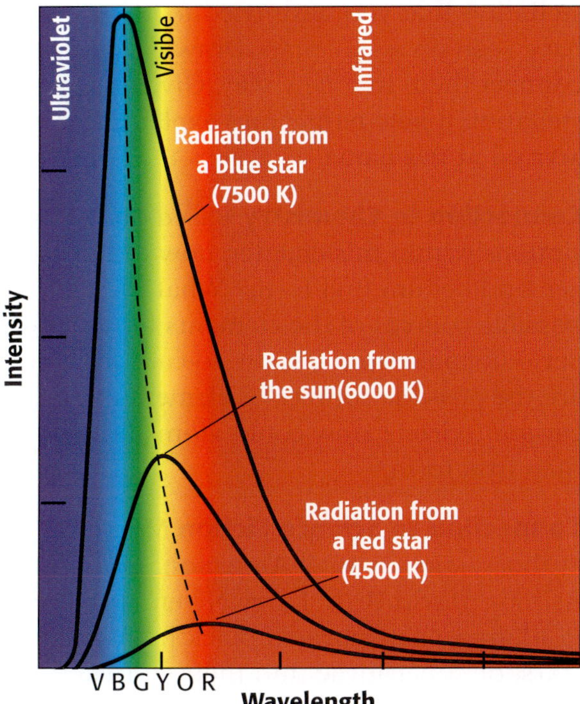

BUILDING GRAPHING SKILLS

21. Graphing Graph the following data. Put distance on the horizontal axis.

Object	Distance (thousand ly)	Velocity (km/s)
Andromeda galaxy	224	−10
Centaurus A	2116	251
M66	3680	593
M49	6746	822
Fornax A	9200	1713

22. Estimate the distance between Earth and a galaxy whose velocity is 2000 km/s.

23. The Andromeda galaxy has a negative value for velocity. What does this mean physically?

THINKING CRITICALLY

24. Critical Thinking Why are most of the stars in the Milky Way galaxy red?

25. Critical Thinking Name two ways that two stars that are the same distance from Earth can have different brightnesses.

26. Understanding Systems What keeps a star from collapsing under its own weight?

27. Applying Knowledge If Edwin Hubble had observed that the spectral lines from every galaxy were blue shifted, what might he have concluded about the universe? What could we conclude about the fate of the universe?

28. Critical Thinking Where in a galaxy would a black hole most likely be?

29. Applying Knowledge Could a black hole consume an entire galaxy? Explain your answer in a paragraph. Use concepts you learned in the chapter.

COMPUTER SKILL

DEVELOPING LIFE/WORK SKILLS

30. Interpreting and Communicating Research how astronomers find distances to stars and galaxies. Make a poster or presentation that describes at least three methods.

31. Working Cooperatively Working in teams, research how ancient cultures around the world explained the Milky Way. Present your findings to the class.

32. Applying Technology Use a computer art program to illustrate different types of galaxies.

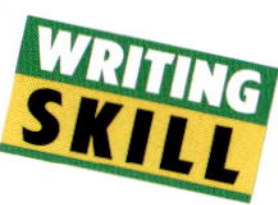

33. Communicating Effectively Write an article for your school newspaper in which you explain why developing theories about the future of the universe is important. WRITING SKILL

INTEGRATING CONCEPTS

34. Concept Mapping Copy the unfinished concept map below onto a sheet of paper. Complete the map by writing the correct word or phrase in the lettered boxes.

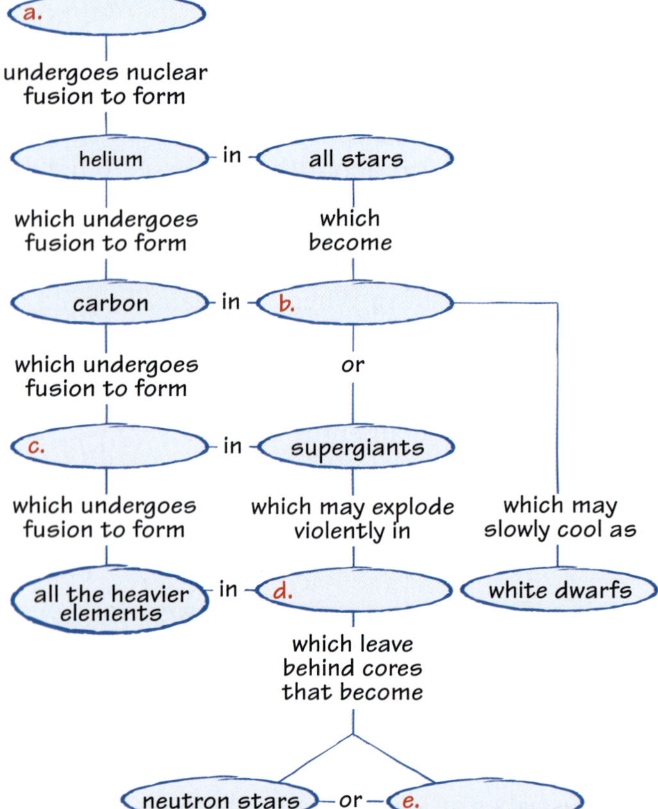

35. Connection to Literature Robert Frost wrote a poem entitled "Fire and Ice" that begins "Some say the world will end in fire, Some say in ice." Explain how these lines relate to possible fates of the universe.

36. Connection to Literature In *Following the Equator,* Mark Twain wrote, "Constellations have always been troublesome things to name. If you give one of them a fanciful name, it will always refuse to live up to it; it will always persist in not resembling the thing it has been named for." Choose a constellation that you have tried to observe or have seen on a star map. Draw the stars and connect them in a new way. Give the constellation a new name, and explain how you arrived at the name.

37. Connection to Chemistry Based on the descriptions within this chapter, how did hydrogen and helium first form? What are the possible sources of the elements found on the periodic table from lithium to carbon? What are the possible sources of elements from carbon to iron? How could atoms heavier than iron form?

38. Connection to Science Fiction Many authors, such as Poul Anderson, Isaac Asimov, David Brin, Larry Niven, and Fred Pohl, have incorporated black holes, neutron stars, or supernovae into their stories. Read one of their stories and compare the author's use of scientific concepts with information that you learned in this chapter.

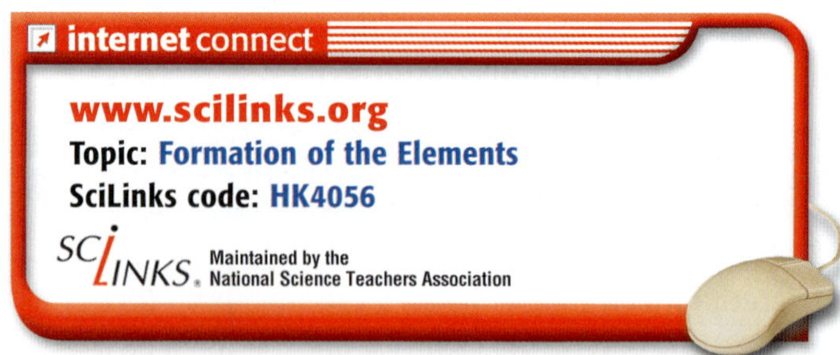

Standardized Test Prep

Understanding Concepts

***Directions (1–2):* For *each* question, write on a separate sheet of paper the letter of the correct answer.**

1 Light travels 9.5×10^{15} meters in one year. Express the distance between the sun and its nearest neighbor, Alpha Centauri—4.1×10^{16} meters—in terms of light-years.

A. 0.43 **C.** 4.3
B. 2.2 **D.** 22.0

2 Toward which end of the spectrum is the light of a receding galaxy shifted?

F. blue **H.** red
G. green **I.** yellow

***Directions (3):* Write a short response to the question.**

3 A star, such as the sun, in the middle of the main sequence, remains at equilibrium for billions of years before it changes. What forces keep the star from shrinking or expanding during that period?

Reading Skills

***Directions (4):* Read the passage below. Then answer the question.**

When a very large star collapses, it can form a black hole. Inside a black hole, mass is so dense that even light cannot reach the escape velocity of its gravitational field. A black hole with a mass ten times as great as the sun would have a radius of only about 30 kilometers. Matter that strikes a black hole becomes part of its mass. Black holes are detected by their gravitational effects on matter around them.

4 Why can black holes only be observed by their effects and not by direct observation through a large telescope?

When using a diagram to answer questions, carefully study each part of the figure as well as any lines or labels used to indicate parts of the figure.

Interpreting Graphics

***Directions (5-8):* Base your answers to questions 5 through 8 on the illustration below.**

H-R Diagram

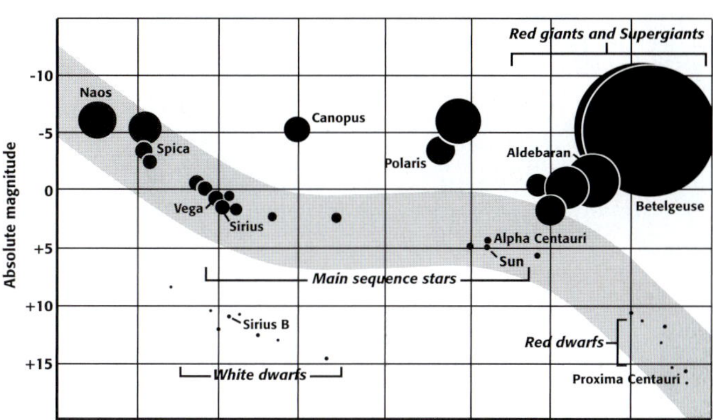

5 Which of these stars is most likely to become a white dwarf in the near future?

A. Betelgeuse
B. Sirius
C. Proxima Centauri
D. Alpha Centauri

6 Why does Sirius appear brighter in the night sky than Betelgeuse?

F. Sirius is a brighter star than Betelgeuse.
G. Betelgeuse is farther from Earth than Sirius.
H. Betelgeuse is cooler than Sirius, so it does not emit as much light.
I. Sirius has a smaller diameter, so it is a more concentrated light source.

7 Which type of star would more likely be found in the arms of the Milky Way than in its core?

A. red giants
B. white dwarfs
C. green main sequence stars
D. yellow main sequence stars

8 Which of these stars would appear to be brightest if all of them were observed from the same distance?

F. Aldebaran **H.** Sun
G. Canopus **I.** Vega

Skills Practice Lab

Investigating Different Types of Galaxies

Introduction

Galaxies are of many sizes and types. How can you tell the differences in type among galaxies by simple measurements of their images?

Objectives

- ***Recognize*** the orientation of galaxies.
- ***Classify*** galaxies according to type.
- ***Measure*** the diameters of galaxies.
- USING SCIENTIFIC METHODS ***Analyze the results*** by calculating the ratio of spiral galaxies to elliptical galaxies within a cluster.

Materials

magnifying glass
metric ruler, clear plastic
photograph of a galaxy cluster

Procedure

Preparing for Your Experiment

1. Examine the photographs of galaxies in this chapter. Make sketches of what each galaxy might look like if you rotated it from a "top-down" view to a "side" view.
2. Examine the large photograph of the Hercules Cluster of galaxies in ***Figure 31*** on the next page. Your teacher may also provide you with a larger version of the photograph. The photograph contains both stars that are between us and the cluster and galaxies that are within the cluster. Write your criteria for distinguishing between a nearby star and a galaxy.

Classifying Galaxies

3. Set up a classification system that divides different galaxies into categories. Ignore the individual identity of stars. You should have at least three different types of galaxies. Discuss in your group what types you will use, and what characteristics define each type.
4. Find at least one example of each type in the photograph and write down the coordinates of each example. Compare your examples with others in your group.
5. Classify each galaxy you see in the photograph, and note the coordinates of each galaxy. If necessary, use a magnifying glass to view the picture more clearly. If you can identify something as a galaxy but are unclear of its type, classify it as "uncertain" galaxy.

Measuring Galaxies

6. Locate the largest and smallest galaxy for each of your classification types.
7. Measure the sizes of these galaxies in millimeters. This process may be easier to do if you use a magnifying glass and a clear ruler.

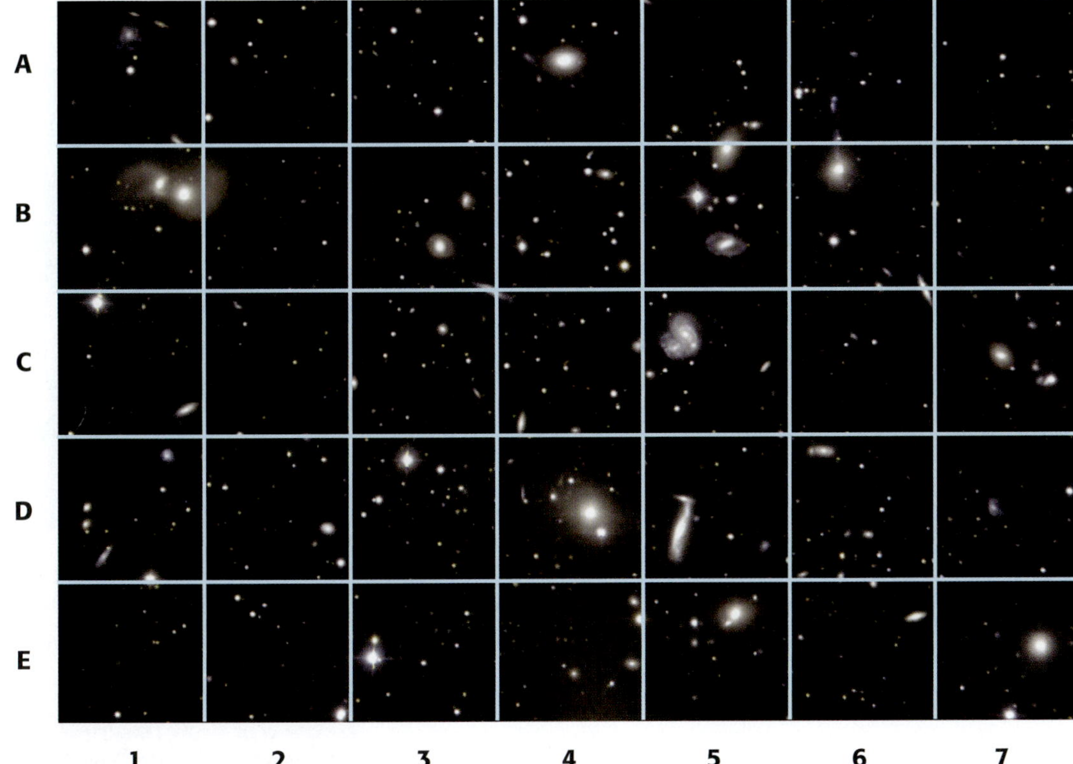

Figure 31
The Hercules Cluster

Analysis

1. Count how many galaxies you have of each type. Add up the totals for all types to get the total number of galaxies observed.
2. Calculate the ratio of each type to the other types by dividing the total of one type by the total number of galaxies observed. For example if you have 33 of type A and 100 total galaxies, then the ratio would be 33 divided by 100, or about one-third.
3. Make a table showing the types of galaxies, their total numbers, and their calculated ratios.

Conclusions

4. What type of galaxy is most common in this cluster?
5. Which of your classification types typically has larger galaxies?
6. Do you think there may be smaller galaxies that you missed seeing? Explain.
7. Which type of galaxy is easiest to confuse with foreground stars?
8. All the galaxies in a cluster are about the same distance from Earth. Therefore, differences in cluster size are due to differences in the sizes of the galaxies. If the largest spiral you measured was the same size as the Milky Way galaxy, estimate the total diameter of this cluster of galaxies.

CareerLink

Joanne Cohn, Cosmologist

Cosmologists study the origin, evolution, and future of the universe. They use observations and scientific theory to try to answer some of science's most fundamental questions: How old is the universe? What happened during the Big Bang? What are Black Holes? Is the universe expanding? And if so, how fast? Read on to hear from Joanne Cohn, a cosmologist at the University of California in Berkeley, California.

Joanne Cohn is a cosmologist at the University of California in Berkeley, California.

"I'm still amazed that the laws of physics that we use on Earth can help us measure and describe the entire known universe!"

What does a cosmologist do?

A cosmologist studies the universe as a physical system. To study a system, you want to know what it is made of, and that's one of the important questions in the field today—what is the universe filled with? We want to know what ingredients make up our universe so we can understand various scenarios, like how matter assembles into large collapsed objects such as galaxies, how light travels through what is out there to us, and how light is given off by stars. It is very much like a detective story, where you try to figure out the players (types of matter in the universe) and the story (how they interacted in the past to get where they are today).

Why do you think your work is important?

My work is important to people who want to know what the universe is made of and how it is evolving. The universe contains us and all physical phenomena we know about, so it is of interest to people who want to know what is out there and what is happening and what has happened.

What question about the universe are you most interested in answering?

I'm interested in knowing how gravity from a galaxy changes the way light rays that travel near it behave. Light that travels near a galaxy is deflected and 'lensed' by the galaxy, and it's possible to use this lensing to learn about the matter in the galaxy.

What kinds of tools and models do you use in your work?

I use theoretical descriptions of how gravity and other physical forces work, and then use computers to make calculations and simulations. I also use simple models of galaxy shapes as a starting point for comparisons with real observations from galaxies.

What's the most challenging part of your job?

The field moves very fast, so you always feel like you'd like to be faster to make sure you can finish things that you started before someone else does it first. Also, you want to calculate things very carefully and thoroughly, and this often means being bogged down in details like finding a '2' somewhere in a calculation that doesn't quite work.

What kinds of skills and qualities are important for a cosmologist?

The most important skills are physics and math skills, being able to do calculations and make models. Writing and speaking skills are also important because you need to be able to communicate your results, and write papers for the scientific community.

What advice do you have for students who are interested in cosmology?

Get involved in either astronomy or physics as a college student, and start learning about independent science research to find out if you like it.

"I really feel like an explorer, finding out what is happening out there in the universe."

—Joanne Cohn

CHAPTER 21

Planet Earth

Chapter Preview

Crater Lake, in Oregon, sits within the top of a collapsed volcano.

Focus ACTIVITY

Background Crater Lake is the deepest lake in the United States, measuring 589 m (1932 ft) at its deepest point. The lake is inside a volcano called Mount Mazama. As Mount Mazama erupted around 6800 years ago, the molten rock and volcanic ash that helped to support the cone of the volcano were ejected. The top then collapsed, creating a big hole. As the hole filled with rainwater and melted snow, Crater Lake was formed. A secondary eruption produced a small volcanic cone, which rose above the water's surface and became Wizard Island, the small island seen in the photo at left.

Activity 1 Imagine you are an early explorer who has just discovered Crater Lake. Examine the photos at left, and describe what you see, explaining how the lake may have formed. When you are finished, write down possible weaknesses for your explanation. Share your results with your class.

Activity 2 Collect a handful of rocks of different sizes. Examine them using a magnifying glass, and make notes about each rock's shape and surface texture. Place the rocks in a plastic container with a tight-fitting lid, add enough water to cover the rocks, and close the container. Shake the container 100 times, and drain the water into a glass jar. Examine the rocks and the water carefully, and report any changes in either. If you have time, repeat shaking the container another 100 times, and write down your observations. What forces does this activity mimic?

Pre-Reading Questions

1. Think about the area where you live, and try to describe what it looked like one year ago. What part of the landscape has changed in a year? Brainstorm on what changes may take place over 100 years.
2. Have the continents always looked exactly as they do today? If not, what happened?

SECTION 1

Earth's Interior and Plate Tectonics

KEY TERMS

crust
mantle
core
lithosphere
plate tectonics
magma
subduction
fault

OBJECTIVES

- **Identify** Earth's different geologic layers.
- **Explain** how the presence of magnetic bands on the ocean floor supports the theory of plate tectonics.
- **Describe** the movement of Earth's lithosphere using the theory of plate tectonics.
- **Identify** the three types of plate boundaries and the principal structures that form at each of these boundaries.

You know from experience that Earth's surface is solid. You walk on it every day. You may have even dug into it and found that it is often more solid once you dig and reach rock. However, Earth is not solid all the way to the center.

crust the thin and solid outermost layer of Earth above the mantle

mantle the layer of rock between Earth's crust and core

What Is Earth's Interior Like?

Figure 1 shows Earth's major compositional layers. We live on the topmost layer of Earth—the **crust.** Because the crust is relatively cool, it is made up of hard, solid rock. The crust beneath the ocean is called oceanic crust and has an average thickness of 5–8 km (3.1–4.9 mi). Continental crust is less dense and thicker, with an average thickness of about 20–40 km (12–25 mi). The continental crust is deepest beneath high mountains, where it commonly reaches depths of 70 km or more.

Beneath the crust lies the **mantle,** a layer of rock that is denser than the crust. Almost 2900 km (1800 mi) thick, the mantle makes up about 80% of Earth's volume. Because humans have never drilled all the way to the mantle, we do not know for sure what it is like. However, geologic events, such as earthquakes and volcanoes, provide evidence of the mantle's consistency.

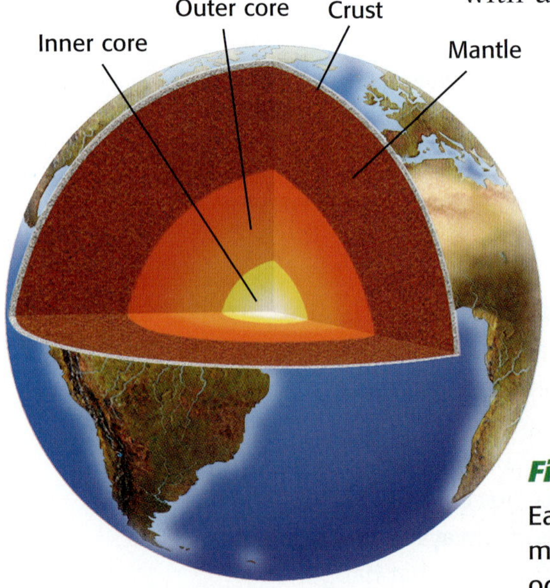

Figure 1

Earth is composed of an inner core, an outer core, a mantle, and a crust. Though it is difficult to see, the oceanic crust is thinner than the continental crust.

For the most part, the mantle is solid. The outermost part is also rigid, like the crust. Deeper than a few hundred kilometers, however, it is extremely hot, and said to be "plastic"—soft and easily deformed, like a piece of gum.

The center of Earth, the **core,** is believed to be composed mainly of iron and nickel. It has two layers. The *inner core,* which is solid metal, is surrounded by the liquid metal *outer core.*

core the center part of Earth below the mantle

Earth's interior gets warmer with depth

If you have ever been in a cave, you may have noticed that the temperature in the cave was cool. That's because the air and rocks beneath Earth's surface are shielded from the warming effects of the sun. However, if you were to travel far beneath the surface, such as into a deep mine, you would find that the temperature becomes uncomfortably hot. South African gold mines, for instance, reach depths of up to 3 km (2 mi), and their temperatures approach 50°C (120°F). The high temperatures in these mines are caused not by the sun but by energy that comes from Earth's interior.

Geologists believe the mantle is much hotter than the crust, as shown in ***Figure 2.*** These high temperatures cause the rocks in the mantle to behave plastically. This is the reason for the inner mantle's deformable, gumlike consistency.

The core is hotter still. On Earth's surface, the metals contained in the core would boil at the temperatures shown in ***Figure 2.*** Iron boils at 2750°C (4982°F), and nickel boils at 2732°C (4950°F). But in the outer core, these metals remain liquid because the pressure due to the weight of the mantle and crust is so great that the substances in the outer core are prevented from changing to their gaseous form. Similarly, pressure in the inner core is so great that the atoms are forced together as a solid despite the intense heat.

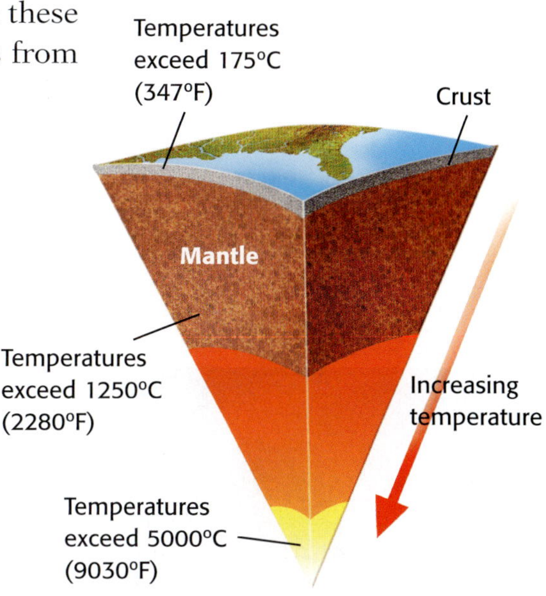

Figure 2

Temperatures in Earth's interior increase with depth. Temperatures near the center of the core can be as hot as the surface of the sun.

Radioactive elements contribute to Earth's high internal temperature

Earth's interior contains radioactive isotopes. These radioactive isotopes (mainly those of uranium, thorium, and potassium) are quite rare. Their nuclei break up, releasing energy as they become more stable. Because Earth is so large, it contains enough atoms of these elements to produce a huge quantity of energy. This energy is one of the major factors contributing to Earth's high internal temperature.

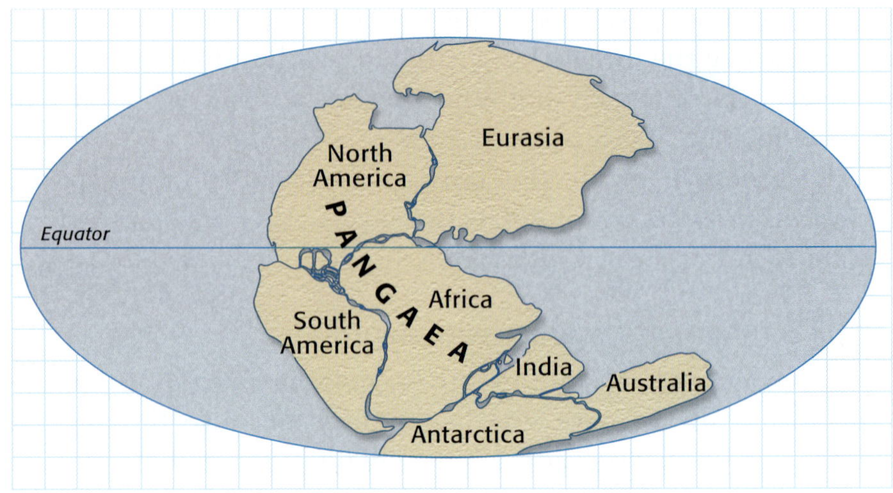

Figure 3
This map shows Pangaea as Alfred Wegener envisioned it.

Plate Tectonics

Around 1915, a German scientist named Alfred Wegener noticed that the eastern coast of South America and the western coast of Africa appeared to fit together like pieces of a puzzle. By studying maps, Wegener found that several other continents' coastlines also seemed to fit together. He pieced all the continents together to form a supercontinent that he called *Pangaea* (pan GEE uh). ***Figure 3*** shows what Pangaea might have looked like approximately 200 million years ago.

Using fossil evidence, Wegener showed that 200 million years ago the same kinds of animals lived on continents that are now oceans apart. He argued that the animals could not have evolved on separate continents. ***Figure 4*** shows the fossil of a Mesosaurus found in Brazil. Identical fossils were found in western Africa, giving scientists strong evidence for a past connection between the continents.

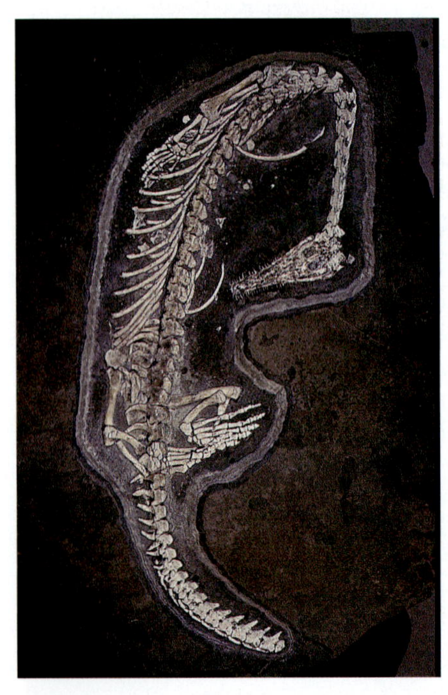

Figure 4
These Mesosaurus bones were discovered in Sao Paulo, Brazil.

Evidence for Wegener's ideas came later

The evidence for *continental drift* or the theory that Earth's surface is made up of large moving plates, was compelling. However, scientists did not have an explanation of how continents could move. Wegener's theory was ignored until the mid-1960s, when structures discovered on the ocean floor gave evidence of a mechanism for the slow movement of continents, or continental drift.

In the 1960s, evidence was discovered in the middle of the oceans that helped explain the mechanisms of continental drift. New technology provided images of "bands" of rock on the ocean floor with alternating magnetic polarities, like the bands illustrated in ***Figure 6.*** These bands differ from one another in the alignment of the magnetic minerals in the rocks they contain.

Alignment of oceanic rocks supports the theory of moving plates

As molten rock pours out onto the ocean floor, as shown in ***Figure 5,*** iron minerals such as magnetite align themselves parallel to Earth's magnetic field, just as compass needles do. After the rocks cool to about 550°C (1020°F), the alignment of these magnetic regions in the iron minerals becomes fixed like the stripes shown in ***Figure 6.*** The result is a permanent record of Earth's magnetic field as it was just before the rock cooled.

So why are there differently oriented magnetic bands of rock? Earth's magnetic field has reversed direction many times during its history, with the north magnetic pole becoming the south magnetic pole and the south magnetic pole becoming the north magnetic pole. This occurs on average once every 200 000 years. This process is recorded in the rocks as bands. These magnetic bands are symmetrical on either side of the Mid-Atlantic Ridge. The rocks are youngest near the center of the ridge. The farther away from the ridge you go, the older the rocks appear. This suggests that the crust was moving away from the plate boundary.

lithosphere the solid, outer layer of Earth, that consists of the crust and the rigid upper mantle

plate tectonics the theory that explains how the outer parts of Earth change through time, and that explains the relationships between continental drift, sea-floor spreading, seismic activity, and volcanic activity

Earth has plates that move over the mantle

The **lithosphere** is approximately 100 km (60 mi) thick and is made up of the crust and the upper portion of the mantle. The lithosphere is made up of about seven large pieces (and several smaller pieces) called *tectonic plates*. The word *tectonic* refers to the structure of the crust of a planet. The continents are embedded into these plates, which fit together like pieces of a puzzle and move in relation to one another. The theory describing the movement of plates is called **plate tectonics.**

Tectonic plates move at speeds ranging from 1 to 16 cm (0.4 to 6.3 in) per year. Although this speed may seem slow, tectonic plates have moved a considerable distance because they have been moving for hundreds of millions or billions of years.

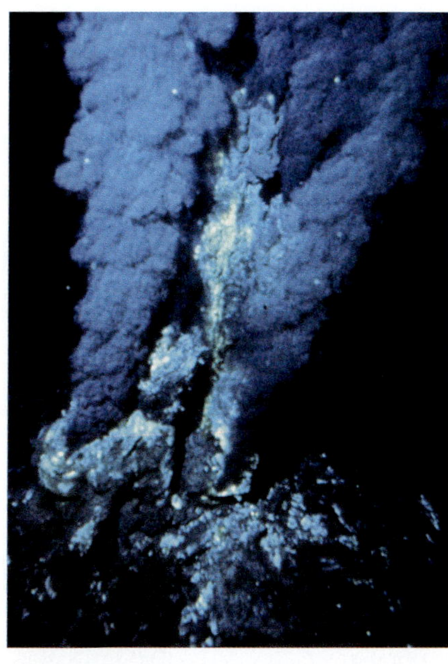

Figure 5

Hydrothermal vents are driven by heat from the eruption of fresh lava on the sea floor.

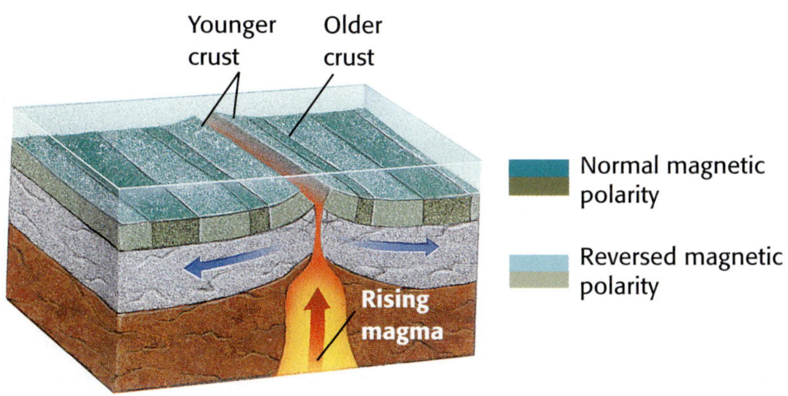

Figure 6

The stripes illustrate Earth's alternating magnetic field. Light stripes represent when Earth's polarity was the same way it is today, while the darker stripes show reversed polarity.

Convection and plate tectonics

1. Fill a shallow pan with water until it is 3 cm from the top.
2. Heat the water over low heat for 30 s. Add a few drops of food coloring to the pan, and watch what happens.
3. Turn off the heat, and place 5 cardboard pieces as close together as possible in the center of the pan.
4. Turn on the heat, and sketch the movement of the cardboard.
5. What do the water and the cardboard pieces represent? What did you observe in step 2?
6. How was the movement in step 4 like continental drift? How could you make a more accurate model of plate tectonics?

VOCABULARY Skills Tip

The word tectonic *originates from the Greek word* tektonikos, *meaning "construction." In everyday usage, the word* tectonics *also relates to architecture.*

It is unknown exactly why tectonic plates move

Figure 7 shows the edges of Earth's tectonic plates. The arrows indicate the direction of each plate's movement. Note that plate boundaries do not always coincide with continental boundaries. Some plates move toward each other, some move away from each other, and still others move alongside each other. One hypothesis suggests that plate movement results from convection currents in the *asthenosphere,* the hot, plastic portion of the mantle. The plates of the lithosphere "float" on top of the asthenosphere.

Some scientists believe that the plates are pieces of the lithosphere that are being moved around by convection currents. The soft rock in the asthenosphere circulates by convection, similar to the way mushy oatmeal circulates as it boils, and this slow movement of rock might push the plates of the lithosphere along. Other scientists believe that the forces generated by convection currents are not sufficient to move the plates, and that instead plates are driven by the force of gravity acting on their own weight.

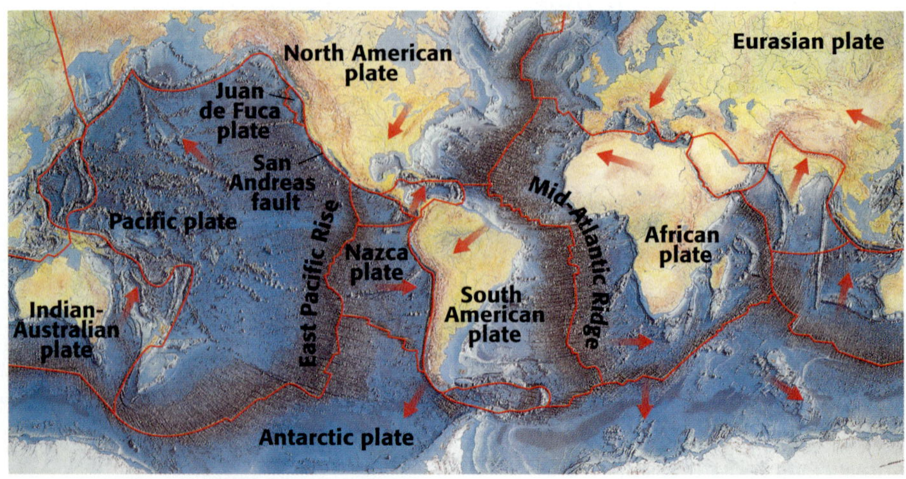

Figure 7

Earth's lithosphere is made up of several large tectonic plates. Plate boundaries are marked in red, and arrows indicate plate movement.

Plate Boundaries

The theory of plate tectonics helps scientists study and sometimes predict volcanic eruptions and has provided information on earthquakes. Volcanoes and earthquakes, such as the one that caused the damage shown in ***Figure 8,*** often occur where tectonic plates come together. At these plate boundaries, many other dramatic geological features, such as mountains and rift valleys, can occur.

Figure 8

An earthquake, which occurred in 1999, damaged this running track in Taiwan.

Mid-oceanic ridges result from divergent boundaries

A *divergent boundary* occurs where two plates move apart, creating a gap between them. When this happens, hot rock rises from the asthenosphere and cools, forming new lithospheric rock. The two diverging plates then pull the newly formed lithosphere away from the gap. The drop in pressure also causes the rising asthenosphere to partially melt, forming **magma,** which separates to form new oceanic crust.

Mid-oceanic ridges are mountain ranges at divergent boundaries in oceanic crust. Unlike most mountains on land, which are formed by the bending and folding of continental crust, mid-oceanic ridges are mountain ranges created by magma rising to Earth's surface and cooling. ***Figure 9B*** shows how a mid-oceanic ridge forms. As the plates move apart, magma rises from between the diverging plates and fills the gap. The new oceanic crust forms a large valley, called a *rift valley,* surrounded by high mountains. The most studied mid-oceanic ridge is called the Mid-Atlantic Ridge which is shown in ***Figure 9A.*** This ridge runs roughly down the center of the Atlantic Ocean from the Arctic Ocean to an area off the southern tip of South America.

magma liquid rock produced under Earth's surface

Figure 9

A When divergent boundaries occur in the oceanic crust they form a mid-oceanic ridge.
B Tectonic plates move apart at divergent boundaries, forming rift valleys and mountain systems.

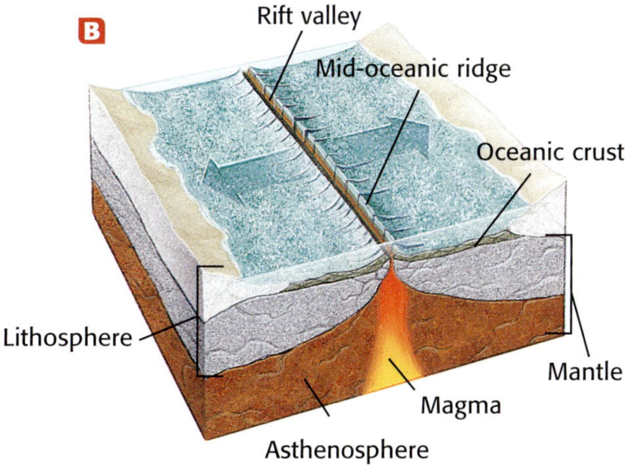

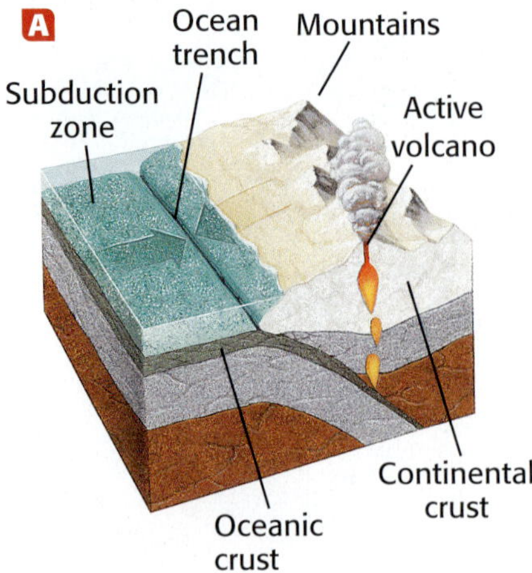

Figure 10

A Ocean trenches, volcanoes, and mountains, such as those shown in B form near the boundary where oceanic and continental plates collide.

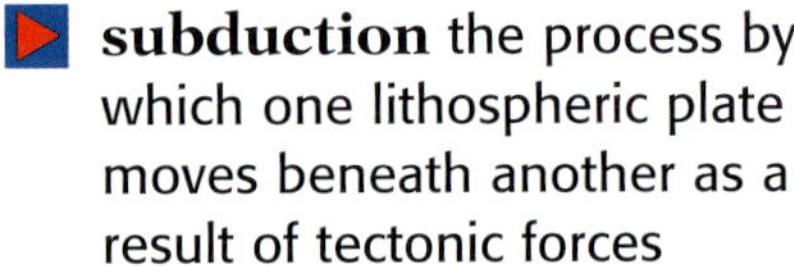

subduction the process by which one lithospheric plate moves beneath another as a result of tectonic forces

Oceanic plates dive beneath continental plates at convergent boundaries

Knowing that lithosphere is being created, you may wonder why Earth isn't expanding. The reason is that while new lithosphere is formed at divergent boundaries, older lithosphere is destroyed at *convergent boundaries*. The Andes Mountains, which are shown in ***Figure 10B,*** formed along a convergent boundary between an oceanic plate and the South American continental plate. The oceanic plate, which is denser, dives beneath the continental plate and drags the oceanic crust along with it. This process is called **subduction.** As shown in ***Figure 10A,*** ocean trenches, mountains, and volcanoes are formed at *subduction zones*.

Ocean trenches form along the boundary between two oceanic plates or between an oceanic plate and a continental plate. These trenches can be very deep. The deepest is the Mariana Trench in the Pacific Ocean. Located off the coast of Asia, the deepest point in the trench is more than 11 km (6.8 mi) beneath the ocean surface. The Peru-Chile Trench is associated with the formation of the Andes Mountains and is more than 7 km (4.3 mi) deep.

Subduction of ocean crust generates volcanoes

Chains of often-explosive volcanic mountains form on the overriding plate at subduction zones—where oceanic crust meets continental crust. As the water-bearing rocks and sediments of the oceanic plate are heated by surrounding mantle, they release water into the overlying mantle. Water is very effective at lowering the melting point of rock at high presure and so magma is formed and rises into the crust. The magma cools, and the accumulation of low-density magnetic rock over time forms a chain of high mountains and plateaus.

Volcanic mountains also form at convergent boundaries. Magma rises to the surface and cools, forming new rock. These volcanoes are formed far inland from their associated oceanic trenches. Aconcagua (ah kawng KAH gwah), the tallest mountain in the Western Hemisphere, is a volcanic mountain in the Andes. At a height of 6959 m (22 831 ft), the peak of Aconcagua is more than 13.8 km (8.6 mi) above the bottom of the Peru-Chile Trench.

Colliding tectonic plates create mountains

The Himalayas, shown in ***Figure 11,*** are the tallest mountains. They formed during the collision between the continental tectonic plate containing India and the Eurasian continental plate. They continue to grow in both width and height as the two plates continue to collide. Mount Everest, the highest mountain in the world, is part of this range. Mount Everest's peak is 8850 m (29 034 ft) above sea level.

Figure 11

The Himalayas are still growing today as the tectonic plate containing Asia and the plate containing India continue to collide.

Transform fault boundaries can crack Earth

Plate movement can cause breaks in the lithosphere. Once a break occurs, rock in the lithosphere continues to move, scraping past nearby rock. The crack where rock moves is called a **fault.** Faults can occur in any area where forces are great enough to break rock. When rock moves horizontally at faults along plate boundaries, the boundary is called a *transform fault boundary* as shown in ***Figure 12A.***

Plate movement at transform fault boundaries is one cause of earthquakes. You may have heard of earthquakes along the San Andreas fault which is shown in ***Figure 12B,*** and which runs from Mexico through California and out to sea north of San Francisco. Transform fault boundaries occur in many places across Earth, including the ocean floor.

fault a crack in Earth created when rocks on either side of a break move

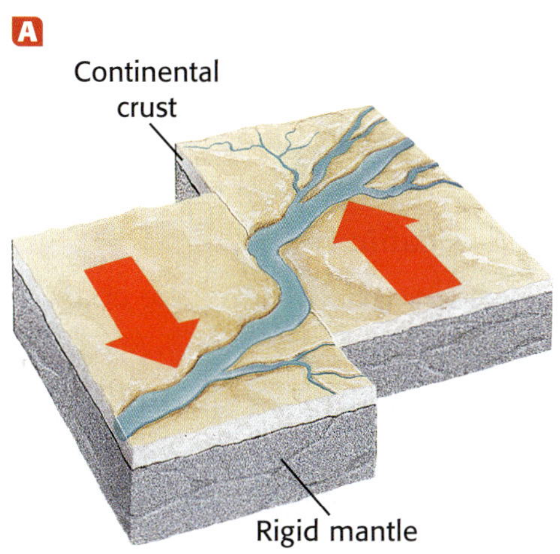

Figure 12

A The change in the course of the river and the fault results from plate movement.

B The San Andreas fault system is over 800 mi long.

Can you model tectonic plate boundaries with clay?

Materials
- ✓ ruler
- ✓ plastic knife
- ✓ paper
- ✓ lab apron
- ✓ scissors
- ✓ 2–3 lb modeling clay
- ✓ rolling pin or rod

Procedure

1. Use a ruler to draw two 10 cm × 20 cm rectangles on your paper, and cut them out.
2. Use a rolling pin to flatten two pieces of clay until they are each about 1 cm thick. Place a paper rectangle on each piece of clay. Using the plastic knife, trim each piece of clay along the edges to match the shape of the paper.
3. Flip the two clay rectangles so that the paper is at the bottom, and place them side by side on a flat surface. Slowly push the models toward each other until the edges of the clay begin to buckle and rise off the table.
4. Turn the models around so that the unbuckled edges are touching. Place one hand on each. Slide one clay toward you and the other away from you. Apply only slight pressure toward the seam where the two pieces of clay touch.

Analysis

1. What type of plate boundary are you demonstrating with the model in step 3?
2. What type of plate boundary are you demonstrating in step 4?
3. Compare the appearances of the facing edges of the models in the two processes. How do you think similar processes might affect Earth's surface?

SECTION 1 REVIEW

SUMMARY

- The layers of Earth are the crust, mantle, and core.
- Earth's outer layer is broken into several tectonic plates, which ride on top of the mantle beneath.
- The alignment of iron in oceanic rocks supports the theory of plate tectonics.
- Plates spread apart at divergent boundaries, collide at convergent boundaries, and slide past each other at transform fault boundaries.

1. **Explain** why the inner core remains a solid even though it is very hot.
2. **Describe** how the gap is filled when two tectonic plates move away from each other.
3. **Determine** whether each of the following is likely to occur at convergent or divergent boundaries:
   - **a.** rift valley
   - **b.** continental mountains
   - **c.** mid-oceanic ridge
   - **d.** ocean trench
4. **Explain** how magnetic bands provide evidence that tectonic plates are moving apart at mid-oceanic ridges.
5. **Predict** what type of plate boundary exists along the coastline near Japan's volcanic mountain ranges.
6. **Critical Thinking** The oldest continental rocks are 4 billion years old, whereas the oldest sea-floor rocks are 200 million years old. Explain the difference in these ages.

SECTION 2

Earthquakes and Volcanoes

OBJECTIVES

- **Identify** the causes of earthquakes.
- **Distinguish** between primary, secondary, and surface waves in earthquakes.
- **Describe** how earthquakes are measured and rated.
- **Explain** how and where volcanoes occur.
- **Describe** the different types of common volcanoes.

KEY TERMS

focus
epicenter
surface waves
seismology
Richter scale
vent

Imagine rubbing two rough-sided rocks back and forth against each other. The movement won't be smooth. Instead, the rocks will create a vibration that is transferred to your hands. The same thing happens when rocks slide past one another at a fault. The resulting vibrations are called earthquakes.

What Are Earthquakes?

Compare the occurrence of earthquakes, shown as red dots in ***Figure 13,*** with the plate boundaries, marked by black lines. Each red dot marks the occurrence of an earthquake sometime between 1985 and 1995. You can see that earthquakes occur mostly at the boundaries of tectonic plates, where the plates shift with respect to one another.

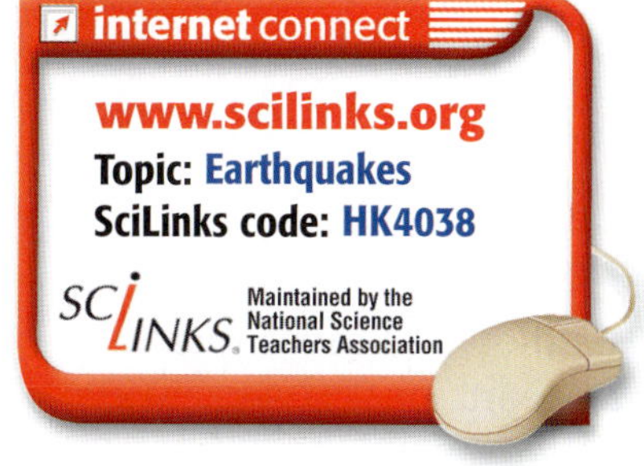

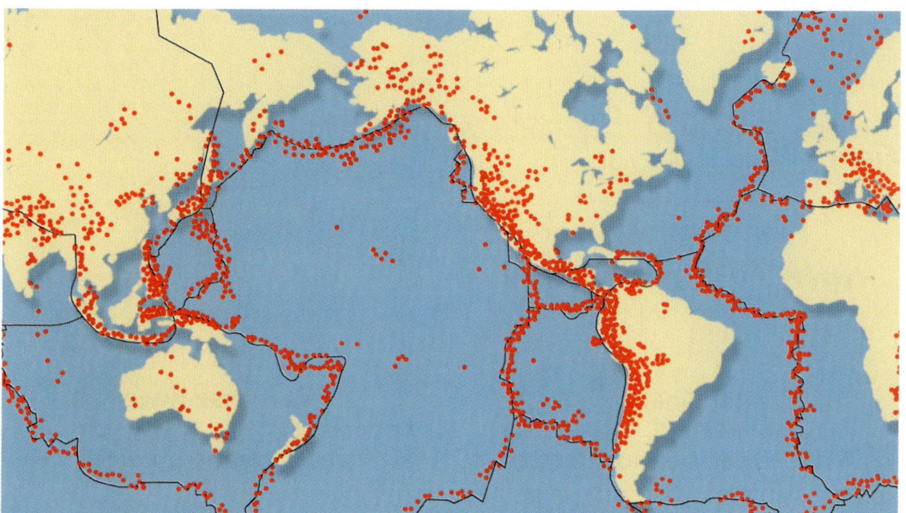

Figure 13
Each red dot in this illustration marks the occurrence of a moderate to large earthquake sometime between 1985 and 1995.

focus the area along a fault at which the first motion of an earthquake occurs

epicenter the point on Earth's surface directly above an earthquake's focus

Earthquakes occur at plate boundaries

As plates move, their edges experience immense pressure. Eventually, the stress becomes so great that it breaks rock along a fault line. Energy is released as *seismic waves*. As the seismic waves travel through Earth, they create the shaking that we experience during an earthquake.

The exact point inside Earth where an earthquake originates is called the **focus.** Earthquake waves travel in all directions from the focus, which is often located far below Earth's surface. The point on the surface immediately above the focus is called the **epicenter,** as shown in ***Figure 14A.*** Because the epicenter is the point on Earth's surface that is closest to the focus, the damage there is usually greatest although damage can occur many miles from the epicenter, as shown in ***Figure 14B.***

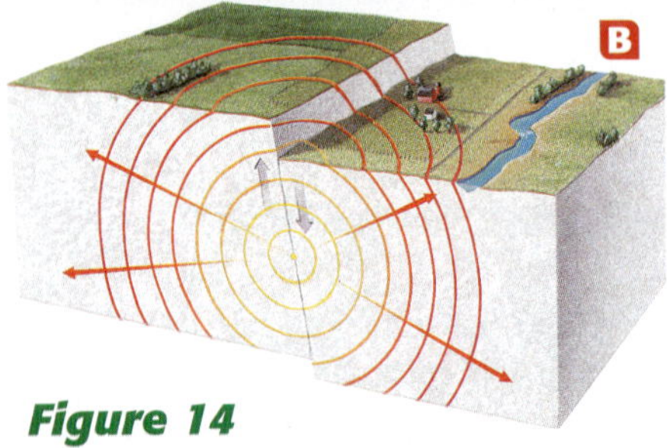

Figure 14

A Earthquakes cause rock to break apart.

B The epicenter of an earthquake is the point on the surface directly above the focus.

Energy from earthquakes is transferred by waves

The energy released by an earthquake is measured as shock waves. Earthquakes generate three types of waves. *Longitudinal* waves originate from an earthquake's focus. Longitudinal waves move faster through rock than other waves do and are the first waves to reach recording stations. For this reason, longitudinal waves are also called *primary*, or *P waves*.

A longitudinal wave travels by compressing Earth's crust in front of it and stretching the crust in back of it. You can simulate longitudinal waves by compressing a portion of a spring and then releasing it, as shown in ***Figure 15A.*** Energy will travel through the coil as a longitudinal wave.

The second type of wave is a *transverse wave*. Transverse waves move more slowly than longitudinal waves. Thus, these slower waves are called *secondary* or *S waves*. The motion of a transverse wave is similar to that of the wave created when a rope is shaken up and down, as shown in ***Figure 15B.***

Figure 15

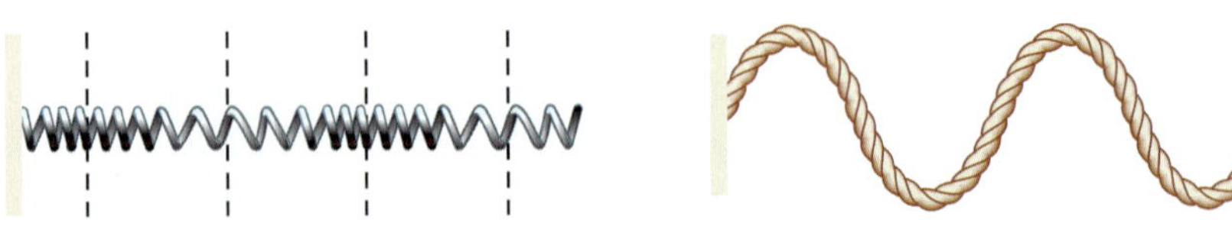

Longitudinal wave

Transverse wave

A P waves can be modeled by compressing and releasing a spring.

B S waves can be modeled by shaking a rope.

Waves move through Earth and along its surface

Both P waves and S waves spread out from the focus in all directions, like light from a light bulb. In contrast, the third type of wave moves only across Earth's surface. These waves, called **surface waves,** are the result of Earth's entire mass shaking like a bell that has been rung. Earth's surface bends and reshapes as it shakes. The resulting rolling motion of Earth's surface is a combination of up-and-down motion and back-and-forth motion. In this type of wave, points on Earth's surface have a circular motion, like the movement of ocean waves far from shore.

Surface waves, such as the ones shown in ***Figure 16,*** cause more destruction than either P waves or S waves. P waves and S waves shake buildings back and forth or up and down at relatively high frequencies. But the rolling action of surface waves, with their longer wavelengths, can cause buildings to collapse.

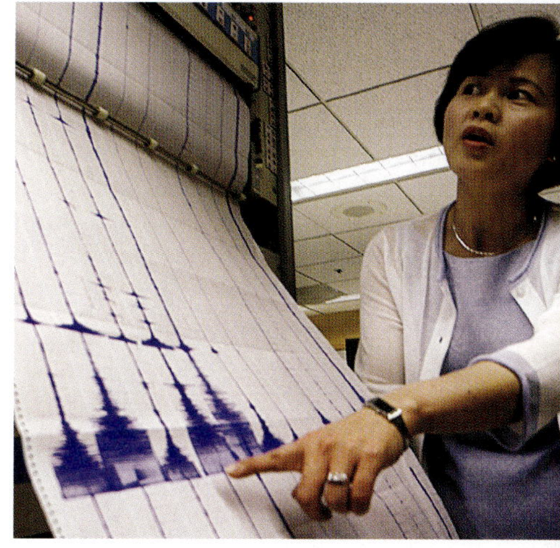

Figure 16

A seismologist points out a surface wave that was measured during a large earthquake.

Measuring Earthquakes

Because energy from earthquakes is transferred by waves, scientists can measure the waves to learn about earthquakes, and about the interior of the Earth through which the waves travel. Scientists hope that learning more will give them tools to predict earthquakes and save lives.

surface wave a seismic wave that can move only through solids

seismology the study of earthquakes including their origin, propagation, energy, and prediction

Seismologists detect and measure earthquakes

Seismology is the study of earthquakes. Seismologists use sensitive machines called *seismographs* to record data about earthquakes, including P waves, S waves, and surface waves. Seismographs use inertia to measure ground motion during an earthquake. Examine the seismograph in ***Figure 17.*** A stationary pendulum hangs from a support fastened to Earth as a drum of paper turns beneath the pendulum with a pen at its tip. When Earth does not shake, the seismograph records an almost straight line. If Earth shakes, the base of the seismograph moves, but the pendulum is protected from Earth's movement by the string. The pendulum draws zigzag lines on the paper that indicate an earthquake has occurred. Records of seismic activity are called seismograms. ***Figure 17*** shows a typical seismogram.

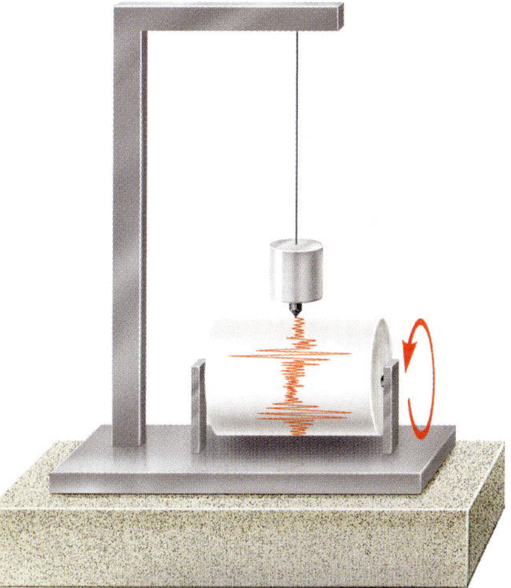

Figure 17

When the ground shakes, the pendulum remains still while a rotating drum of paper records Earth's movement.

Three seismograph stations are necessary to locate the epicenter of an earthquake

There are more than 1000 seismograph stations across the world. At each station, three seismographs are used to measure different motions: north to south, east to west, and up and down. P waves, the first to be recorded by seismographs, make a series of small, zigzag lines. S waves arrive later, appearing as larger, more ragged lines. Surface waves arrive last and make the largest lines. The difference in time between the arrival of P waves and the arrival of S waves enables seismologists to calculate the distance between the seismograph station and the earthquake's epicenter. When the distances from three seismograph stations are calculated, three circles can be drawn on a map as shown in ***Figure 18.*** Each circle has the geographic locations of a seismograph station as its center, with the radius being the distance to the epicenter. Therefore, the epicenter can be found by finding where all three circles intersect.

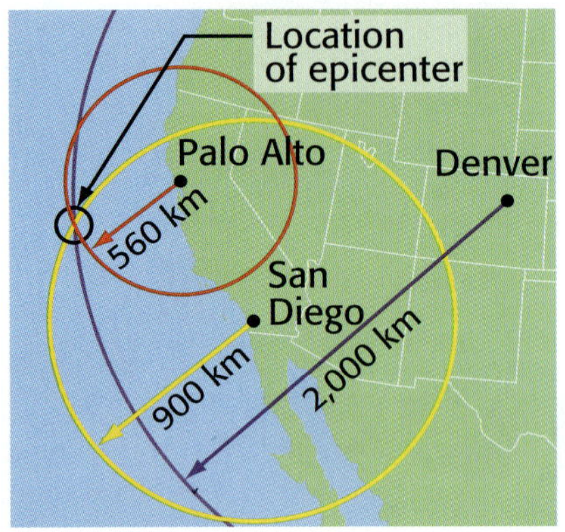

Figure 18

The point where the three circles intersect is the epicenter of the earthquake.

Geologists use seismographs to investigate Earth's interior

Seismologists have found that S waves do not reach seismographs on the side of Earth's core opposite the focus, as shown in ***Figure 19.*** This is evidence that part of the core is liquid because S waves, which are transverse waves, cannot travel through a liquid.

By comparing seismograms recorded during earthquakes, seismologists have noticed that the velocity of seismic waves varies depending on where the waves are measured. Waves change speed and direction whenever the density of the material they are traveling through changes. The differences in velocity suggest that Earth's interior consists of several layers of different densities. By comparing data, scientists have constructed the model of Earth's interior described in Section 1.

P waves
S waves
Epicenter
No direct
P waves
Liquid
outer
core
Solid
inner
core
Mantle
105°
140°
No direct
S waves
No direct
P waves

Figure 19

No direct S waves can be detected more than 105° from the epicenter. No direct P waves can be detected between 105° and 140° from the epicenter.

Table 1 **Earthquake Magnitude, Effects, and Frequency**

Magnitude (Richter scale)	Characteristic effects of shallow earthquakes	Estimated number of earthquakes recorded each year
2.0 to 3.4	Not felt but recorded	More than 150,000
3.5 to 4.2	Felt by a few people in the affected area	30,000
4.3 to 4.8	Felt by most people in the affected area	4800
4.9 to 5.4	Felt by everyone in the affected area	1400
5.5 to 6.1	Moderate to slight damage	500
6.2 to 6.9	Widespread damage to most structures	100
7.0 to 7.3	Serious damage	15
7.4 to 7.9	Great damage	4
8.0 to 8.9	Very great damage	Occur infrequently
9.0	Would be felt in most parts of the Earth	Possible but never recorded
10.0	Would be felt all over the Earth	Possible but never recorded

The Richter scale is a measure of the magnitude of earthquakes

The **Richter scale** is a measure of the energy released by an earthquake. The 1964 Alaskan earthquake, with a magnitude of 8.4, is the largest earthquake of recent times. Each step on the Richter scale represents a 30-fold increase in the energy released. So an earthquake of magnitude 8 releases 30^4, or 810,000, times as much energy as one of magnitude 4! ***Table 1*** summarizes the effects and number of earthquakes with varying magnitudes. Notice that low magnitude earthquakes occur frequently.

Richter scale a scale that expresses the magnitude of an earthquake

The Richter scale cannot predict how severe an earthquake will be. The amount of damage depends on several factors, such as the distance between populated areas and the epicenter, and the type of construction used in area buildings. The Armenian earthquake of 1988 and the San Francisco earthquake of 1989 both had a magnitude of 7 on the Richter scale. In Armenia, there was devastating property damage, and more than 25,000 people died. In contrast, only 70 people died in San Francisco.

Why was there such a big difference between the effects of these two earthquakes? The focus of the Armenian earthquake was 5 km down, but in San Francisco it was 19 km down. The deeper the focus, the less the effects will be felt at the surface.

Also, the rock in San Francisco is harder than that of Armenia. Softer rock breaks apart and changes position more easily than rigid rock. The difference in fatalities was mainly due to building construction. Other factors that determine how destructive an earthquake will be are the time of day that the event occurs, soil composition, and how saturated the ground is.

Did You Know?

The effect of an earthquake on Earth's surface is called the earthquake's intensity. The modified Mercalli scale is the most commonly used intensity scale. An earthquake is assigned a lower number if people felt the quake but it didn't cause much damage. Earthquakes that cause structural damage are assigned a higher number. The scale has been used to develop intensity maps for planners, building officials, and insurance companies.

Scientists are trying to predict earthquakes

In the past, people would try to predict earthquakes by watching animals for strange behavior. Today, scientists are trying to measure changes in Earth's crust that can signal an earthquake. Scientists might someday be able to warn people of an impending earthquake and save lives by learning to observe rock for signs of stress and strain. The random nature of earthquake rupture makes prediction extremely difficult, but finding a reliable system could save tens of thousands of lives in the future.

Volcanoes

vent an opening at the surface of Earth through which volcanic material passes

A volcano is any opening in Earth's crust through which magma has reached Earth's surface. These openings are called **vents.** Volcanoes often form hills or mountains as materials pour or explode from the vent, as shown in ***Figure 20.*** Volcanoes release molten rock, ash, and a variety of gases that result from melting in the mantle or in the crust.

Volcanoes generally have one central vent, but they can also have several smaller vents. Magma from inside a volcano can reach Earth's surface through any of these vents. When magma reaches the surface, its physical behavior changes, and it is called *lava.*

Figure 20

Volcanoes build up into hills or mountains as lava and ash explode from openings in Earth called vents.

Shield volcanoes have mild eruptions

Magma rich in iron and magnesium is very fluid and forms lava that tends to flow great distances. The eruptions are usually mild and can occur several times. The buildup of this kind of lava produces a gently sloping mountain, called a *shield volcano.* Shield volcanoes are some of the largest volcanoes. Mauna Loa, in Hawaii, is a shield volcano, as shown in ***Figure 21A.*** Mauna Loa's summit is more than 4000 m (13 000 ft) above sea level and more than 9020 m (29 500 ft) above the sea floor.

Composite volcanoes have trapped gas

Composite volcanoes are made up of alternating layers of ash, cinders, and lava. Their magma is rich in silica and therefore is much more viscous than the magma of a shield volcano. Gases are trapped in the magma, causing eruptions that alternate between flows and explosive activity that produces cinders and ash. Composite volcanoes are typically thousands of meters high, with much steeper slopes than shield volcanoes. Japan's Mount Fuji, shown in ***Figure 21B,*** is a composite volcano. Mount St. Helens, Mount Rainier, Mount Hood, and Mount Shasta, all in the western United States, are also composite volcanoes.

Cinder cones are the most abundant volcano

Cinder cones are the smallest and most abundant volcanoes. When large amounts of gas are trapped in magma, violent eruptions occur—vast quantities of hot ash and lava are thrown from the vent. These particles then fall to the ground around the vent, forming the cone. Cinder cones tend to be active for only a short time and then become dormant. As shown in **Figure 21C,** Parícutin (pah REE koo teen), in Mexico, is a cinder cone. Parícutin erupted in 1943. After 2 years, the volcano's cone had grown to a height of 450 m (1480 ft). The eruptions finally ended in 1952. Volcanoes form not only on land but also under the oceans. In shallow water, volcanoes can erupt violently, forming clouds of ash and steam. An underwater volcano is called a *seamount* and looks like a composite volcano.

Figure 21
The type of volcano that forms depends largely on the makeup of the magma. Differences in the fluidity of the magma determine the type of eruption that occurs.

Types of Volcanoes

A Shield volcano

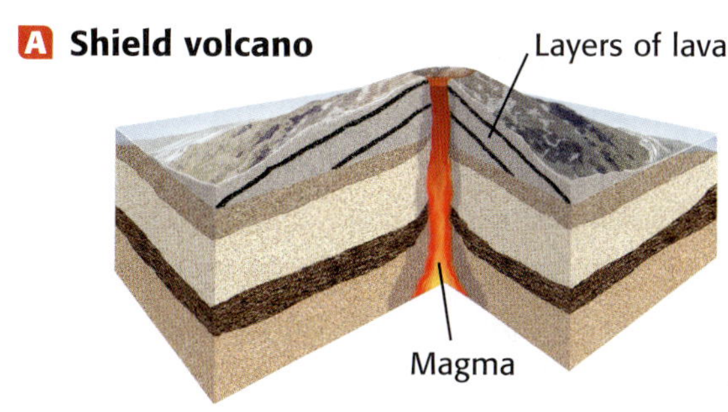

Mauna Loa, Hawaii

B Composite volcano

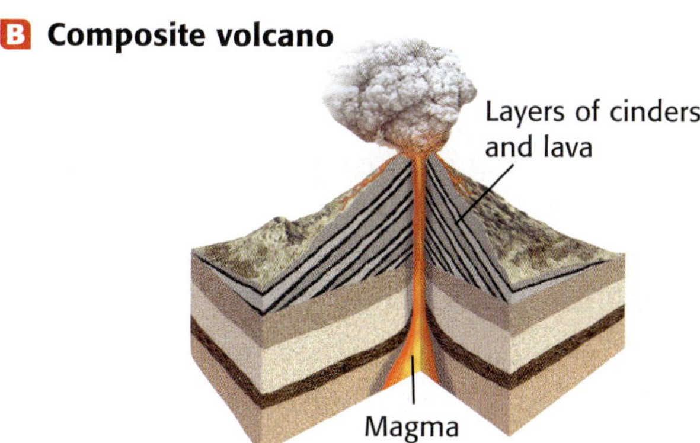

Mount Fuji, Japan

C Cinder cone

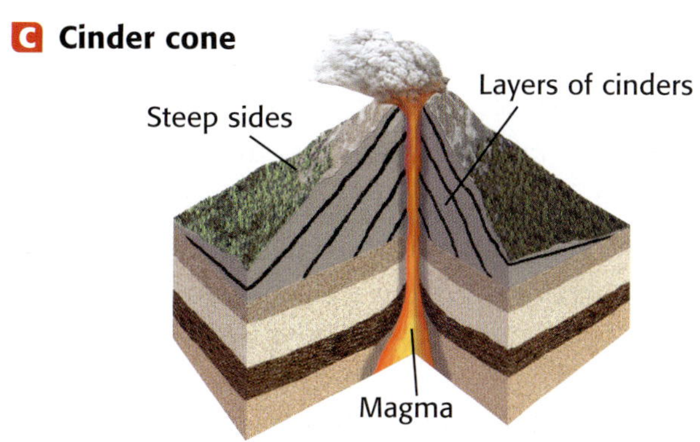

Parícutin, Mexico

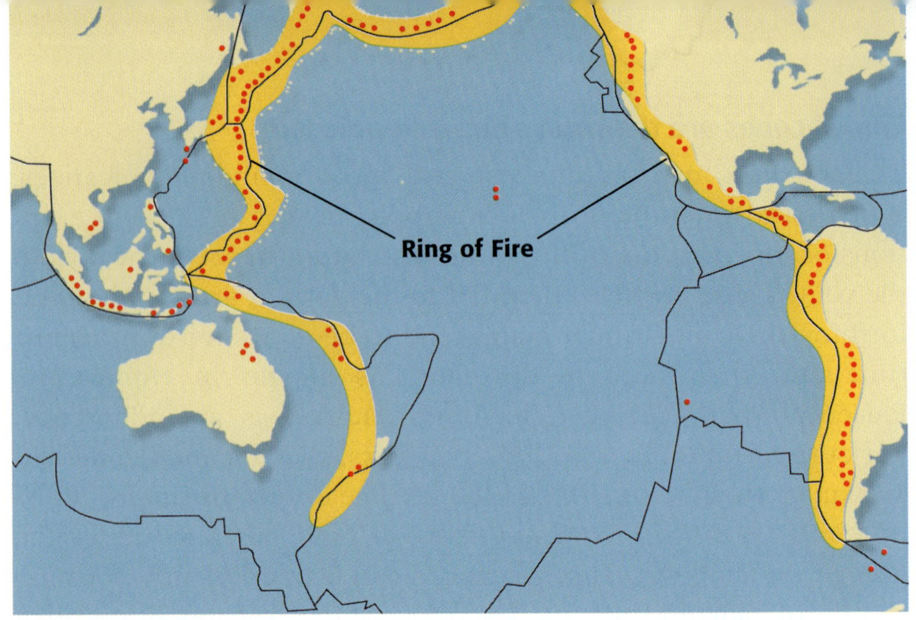

Figure 22
Seventy-five percent of the active volcanoes on Earth occur along the edges of the Pacific Ocean. Together these volcanoes form the Ring of Fire.

Most volcanoes occur at convergent plate boundaries

Like earthquakes, volcanoes are linked to plate movement. Volcanoes are common all around the edges of the Pacific Ocean, where oceanic tectonic plates collide with continental plates. In fact, 75% of the active volcanoes on Earth are located in these areas. As seen in ***Figure 22,*** the volcanoes around the Pacific Ocean lie in a zone known as the Ring of Fire.

As a plate sinks at a convergent boundary, it causes melting in the mantle and magma rises to the surface. The volcanoes that result form the edges of the Ring of Fire. These volcanoes tend to erupt cooler, less-fluid lava and clouds of ash and gases. The high-viscosity lava makes it difficult for the gases to escape. Gas pressure builds up, causing explosive eruptions.

Underwater volcanoes occur at divergent plate boundaries

As plates move apart at divergent boundaries, magma rises to fill in the gap. This magma creates the volcanic mountains that form the ridges around a central rift valley.

The volcanic island of Iceland, in the North Atlantic Ocean, is on the Mid-Atlantic Ridge. The island is continuously expanding from its center; the eastern and western sides of the island are growing outward in opposite directions. As a result, a great deal of geologic activity, such as volcanoes and hot springs, occurs on the island.

Connection to SOCIAL STUDIES

Mount St. Helens, in the Cascade Range in Washington, erupted explosively on May 18, 1980. Sixty people and thousands of animals were killed, and 10 million trees were blown down by the air blast created by the explosion. During the eruption, the north side of the mountain was blown away. Gas and ash were ejected upward, forming a column more than 19.2 km (11.9 mi) high. The ash was reported to have fallen as far east as central Montana.

Since the May 18 explosion, Mount St. Helens has had several minor eruptions. As a result, a small volcanic cone is now visible in the original volcano's crater.

Making the Connection

1. What might have caused the eruption of Mount St. Helens to be so explosive?
2. The force of the blast didn't push the ashes all the way to Montana. What other natural force might have transported the ashes that far?

Volcanoes occur at hot spots

Some volcanoes occur in the middle of plates. They occur because mushroom-shaped trails of hot rock, called *mantle plumes,* rise from deep inside the mantle, melt as they rise, and erupt from volcanoes at *hot spots* at the surface.

When mantle plumes form below oceanic plates, lava and ash build up on the ocean floor. If the resulting volcanoes grow large enough, they break through the water's surface and become islands. As the oceanic plate continues moving, however, the mantle plume does not move along with it. The plume continues to rise under the moving oceanic plate, and a new volcano is formed at a different point. A "trail" in the form of a chain of extinct volcanic islands is left behind.

The Hawaiian Islands lie in a line that roughly corresponds to the motion of the Pacific plate. The island of Hawaii is the most recently formed in the chain, and contains the active volcanoes situated over the mantle plume. Volcanic activity produces fertile soil which helps tropical plants, like those shown in **Figure 23,** grow.

Figure 23
Tropical plants often grow on the fertile ground that results from volcanoes.

SECTION 2 REVIEW

SUMMARY

- Earthquakes occur as a result of sudden movement within Earth's lithosphere.
- P waves are longitudinal waves, and they travel the fastest.
- S waves are transverse waves, and they travel more slowly.
- Surface waves travel the slowest. They result from Earth's vibrating like a bell.
- Volcanoes are formed when magma rises and penetrates the surface of Earth.
- The three types of volcanoes are shield volcanoes, cinder cones, and composite volcanoes.

1. **Identify** which type of seismic wave is described in each of the following:
   - **a.** cannot travel through the core
   - **b.** cause the most damage to buildings
   - **c.** are the first waves to reach seismograph stations
2. **Select** which of the following describes a shield volcano:
   - **a.** formed from violent eruptions
   - **b.** has gently sloping sides
   - **c.** formed from hot ash
   - **d.** has steep sides
3. **Identify** whether volcanoes are likely to form at the following locations:
   - **a.** hot spot
   - **b.** transform fault boundary
   - **c.** divergent plate boundary
   - **d.** convergent boundary between continental and oceanic plates
4. **Differentiate** between the focus and the epicenter of an earthquake.
5. **Explain** how a mid-oceanic ridge is formed.
6. **Explain** why Iceland is a good place to use hydrothermal power, which is power produced from heated water.
7. **Critical Thinking** Are quiet eruptions or explosive eruptions more likely to increase the height of a volcano? Why?

SECTION 3

Minerals and Rocks

KEY TERMS
mineral
igneous rock
weathering
sedimentary rock
metamorphic rock

OBJECTIVES
- **Identify** the three types of rock.
- **Explain** the properties of each type of rock based on physical and chemical conditions under which the rock formed.
- **Describe** the rock cycle and how rocks change form.
- **Explain** how the relative and absolute ages of rocks are determined.

Devils Tower, in Wyoming, shown in ***Figure 24,*** rises 264 m (867 ft) above its base. According to an American Indian legend, the tower's jagged columns were formed by a giant bear scraping its claws across the rock. The tower is actually the solidified core of a volcano. Over millions of years, the surrounding softer rock was worn away by the Belle Fourche River finally exposing the core. Volcanic pipes, which are similar to volcanic cores, can be a source of diamonds. They contain solidified magma that extends from the mantle to Earth's surface.

mineral a natural, usually inorganic solid that has a characteristic chemical composition, an orderly internal structure, and a characteristic set of physical properties

Figure 24
Devils Tower, in northeastern Wyoming, is the solidified core of a volcano.

Structure and Origins of Rocks

All rocks are composed of **minerals.** Minerals are naturally occurring, nonliving substances that have a composition that can be expressed by a chemical formula. Minerals also have a definite internal structure. Quartz, for example, is a mineral made of silicon dioxide, SiO_2. It is composed of crystals, as are most minerals. Coal, on the other hand, is not a mineral because it is formed from decomposed plant matter. *Granite* is not a mineral either; it is a rock composed of different minerals.

There are about 3500 known minerals in Earth's crust. However, no more than 20 of these are commonly found in rocks. Together, these 20 or so minerals make up more than 95% of all the rocks in Earth's crust. Some of the most common of these *rock-forming minerals* are feldspar, pyroxene, mica, olivine, dolomite, quartz, amphibole, and calcite.

Each combination of rock-forming minerals results in a rock with a unique set of properties. Rocks may be porous, granular, or smooth; they may be soft or hard and have different densities or colors. The appearance and characteristics of a rock reflect its mineral composition and the way it formed.

Figure 25

A Notice the coarse-grained texture of this sample of granite, an intrusive igneous rock.

B Obsidian, an extrusive igneous rock, cools much more quickly than granite.

Molten rock cools to form igneous rock

When molten rock cools and solidifies it forms **igneous rock.** Nearly all igneous rocks are made of crystals of various minerals, such as those shown in the granite in ***Figure 25A.*** As the rock cools, the minerals in the rock crystallize and grow. In general, the more quickly the rock cools, the less the crystals grow. For instance, obsidian, a smooth stone used by early American Indians to make tools, is similar to granite in composition, but it cools much more quickly. As a result, obsidian has either very small crystals or no crystals at all and is mostly glass. ***Figure 25B*** shows a piece of obsidian.

Obsidian is categorized as an *extrusive* igneous rock because it cools on Earth's surface. *Basalt,* a fine-grained, dark-colored rock, is the most common extrusive igneous rock. Granite, on the other hand, is called an *intrusive* igneous rock because it forms from magma that cools while trapped beneath Earth's surface. Because the magma is insulated by the surrounding rocks, it takes a very long time to cool—sometimes millions of years. Because of this long cooling period, the crystals in intrusive igneous rocks are larger than those in extrusive igneous rocks. The crystals of granite, for example, are easy to see with the naked eye. They are much lighter in color than those of basalt. Both rocks contain feldspar, but granite also has quartz, while basalt has pyroxene.

igneous rock rock that forms when magma cools and solidifies

Connection to SOCIAL STUDIES

Throughout history, humans have used rocks and minerals to fashion tools. During the Stone Age, the Bronze Age, and the Iron Age people used stone, bronze, and iron, respectively, to make tools and weapons. The industrial revolution began when humans learned to burn coal to run machinery. After humans learned to extract oil from Earth's crust, gasoline-powered vehicles were invented, and we entered the automobile age.

Making the Connection

1. Research minerals that have been mined for their iron content. Where are the mines that were first used to harvest these minerals?
2. Scientists have divided the Stone Age into three phases—Paleolithic, Mesolithic, and Neolithic—on the basis of toolmaking techniques. Research these phases, and distinguish between the techniques used in each.

Remains of older rocks and organisms form sedimentary rocks

Figure 26

Sedimentary rock can have many distinct layers.

Even very hard rock with large crystals will break down over thousands of years. The process by which rocks are broken down is called **weathering.** Pieces of rock fall down hillsides due to gravity or get washed down by wind and rain. Rivers then carry the pieces down into deltas, lakes, or the sea. Chemical processes also knock pieces of rock away. The action of physical and chemical weathering eventually breaks the pieces into pebbles, sand, and even smaller pieces.

As pieces of rock accumulate, they can form another type of rock— **sedimentary rock.** Think of sedimentary rocks like those shown in ***Figure 26*** as recycled rocks. The sediment they are made of contains fragments of older rocks and, in some cases, fossils.

Loose sediment forms rock in two ways

There are two ways sediment can become rock; and both require precipitation. In one, layers of sediment get compressed from weight above, forming rock. In the second way, minerals dissolved in water seep between bits of sediment and "glue" them together. In ***Figure 27A,*** the bits of rock in the conglomerate are fused together with material containing mostly quartz.

Sedimentary rocks are named according to the size of the fragments they contain. As mentioned, a rock made of pebbles is called a conglomerate. A rock made of sand is called sandstone. A rock made of fine mud is usually called mudstone, but if it is flaky and breaks easily into layers, it is called shale. Limestone, another kind of sedimentary rock, is often made of the fossils of organisms that lived in the water, as shown in ***Figure 27B.*** Sometimes the fossilized skeletons are so small or are broken up into such small fragments that they can't be seen with the naked eye. Places where limestone is found were once beneath water.

weathering the natural process by which atmospheric and environmental agents, such as wind, rain, and temperature changes, disintegrate and decompose rocks

sedimentary rock a rock formed from compressed or cemented layers of sediment

Figure 27

A Conglomerate rock is composed of rounded, pebble-sized fragments of weathered rock.

B Limestone is made mostly of fossils of sea creatures.

Rocks that undergo pressure and heating without melting form metamorphic rock

Heat and pressure within Earth cause changes in the texture and mineral content of rocks. These changes produce **metamorphic rocks.** The word *metamorphic* comes from the Greek word *metamorphosis,* which means "to change form."

Limestone, a sedimentary rock, will turn into marble, a metamorphic rock, under the effects of heat and pressure. Marble is a stone used in buildings, such as the Taj Mahal, in India. ***Figure 28*** is a photo of the exterior of the Taj Mahal. Notice the swirling, colored bands that make marble so attractive. These bands are the result of impurities that existed in the limestone before it was transformed into marble.

Rocks may be changed, or *metamorphosed,* in two ways: by heat alone or, more commonly, by a combination of heat and pressure. In both cases, the solid rock undergoes a chemical change over millions of years, without melting. As a result, new minerals form in the rocks. The texture of the rocks is changed too, and any fossils in sedimentary rocks are transformed and destroyed.

The most common types of metamorphic rock are formed by heat and pressure deep in the crust. *Slate* forms in this way. It metamorphoses from mudstone or shale, as shown in ***Figure 29.*** Slate is a hard rock that can be split very easily along planes in the rock, creating large, flat surfaces.

Figure 28

The Taj Mahal, in India, is made of marble, a metamorphic rock often used in buildings.

metamorphic rock a rock that forms from other rocks as a result of intense heat, pressure, or chemical processes

Figure 29

A Mudstone is composed of silt- or clay-sized particles. Its characteristics can be seen in some examples of slate.

B Slate is a metamorphic rock that is transformed under heat and pressure from sedimentary shale rocks.

Figure 30

The rock cycle illustrates the changes that sedimentary, igneous, and metamorphic rocks undergo.

Old rocks in the rock cycle form new rocks

So far, you have seen some examples of one type of rock becoming another. For instance, limestone exposed to heat and pressure becomes marble. Exposed rocks are weathered, forming sediments. These sediments may be cemented together to make sedimentary rock. The various types of rock are all a part of one rock system. The sequence of events in which rocks can be weathered, melted, altered, and formed is described by the *rock cycle*.

Figure 30 illustrates the stages of the rock cycle. Regardless of which path is taken, rock formation occurs very slowly, often over tens of thousands to millions of years.

As magma or lava (F) cools underground, it forms igneous rock (E), such as granite. If the granite is heated and put under pressure, it may become metamorphic rock (D); if it is exposed at the surface of Earth, it may be weathered and become sand (B, C). The sand may be transported, deposited, and cemented to become the sedimentary rock (A) sandstone. As more time passes, several other layers of sediment are deposited above the sandstone. With enough heat and pressure, the sandstone becomes a metamorphic rock (D). This metamorphic rock (D) may then be forced deep within Earth, where it melts, forming magma (F).

internet connect

www.scilinks.org
Topic: Rock types
SciLinks code: HK4122

SCILINKS. Maintained by the National Science Teachers Association

How Old Are Rocks?

Rocks form and change over millions of years. It is difficult to know the exact time when a rock formed. To determine the age of rocks on a geological time scale, several techniques have been developed.

The relative age of rocks can be determined using the principle of superposition

Think about your hamper of dirty clothes at home. If you don't disturb the stack of clothes in the hamper, you can tell the relative time the clothes were placed in the hamper. In other words, you may not know how long ago you placed a particular red shirt in the hamper, but you can tell that the shirts above the red shirt were placed there more recently. In a similar manner, the *relative age* of rocks can be determined using the *principle of superposition.* The principle of superposition states the following:

Assuming no disturbance in the position of the rock layers, the oldest will be on the bottom, and the youngest will be on top.

The principle of superposition is useful in studying the sequence of life on Earth. For instance, the cliffside in ***Figure 31*** shows several sedimentary layers stacked on top of one another. The layers on the bottom are older than the layers above them.

Although the various layers of sedimentary rock are most visible in cliffsides and canyon walls, you would also find layering if you dug down anywhere there is sedimentary rock. By applying the principle of superposition, scientists know that fossils in the upper layers are the remains of animals that lived more recently than the animals that were fossilized in lower layers.

Figure 31
According to the principle of superposition, the layers of sedimentary rock on top are the most recent layers if the rocks have not been disturbed.

Radioactive dating can determine a more exact, or absolute, age of rocks

The chapter on nuclear changes showed that the nuclei of some isotopes decay, emitting energy at a fairly constant rate. These isotopes are said to be radioactive. The radioactive elements that make up minerals in rocks decay over billions of years. Physicists have determined the rate at which these elements decay, and geologists can use this data to determine the age of rocks. They measure both the amount of the original radioactive material left undecayed in the rock and the amount of the product of the radioactive material's decay. The amount of time that passed since the rock formed can be calculated from this ratio.

Many different isotopes can be analyzed when rocks are dated. Some of the most reliable are isotopes of potassium, argon, rubidium, strontium, uranium, and lead.

While the principle of superposition gives only the relative age of rocks, radioactive dating gives the *absolute age* of a rock.

Did You Know?

Radioactive dating is not always accurate. For instance, as heat and pressure are applied to a rock and water flows through it, soluble radioactive materials can escape from the minerals in the rock. Because there is often no method for measuring how much radioactive material is lost, it is difficult to accurately date some older rocks that have been heated and put under pressure or that are partly weathered.

SECTION 3 REVIEW

SUMMARY

- Igneous rocks are formed from cooling molten rock.
- Sedimentary rocks form by the deposition of pieces of other rocks and the remains of living organisms.
- Metamorphic rocks form after exposure to heat and/or pressure for an extended time.
- Rocks can change type, as described by the rock cycle.
- The relative age of rock can be determined using the principle of superposition. Unless the layers are disturbed, the layers on the bottom are the oldest.
- Radioactive dating is used to determine the absolute age of rocks.

1. **Modify** the following false statement to make it a true statement: Fossils are found in igneous rock.
2. **Explain** how the principle of superposition is used by geologists to compare the ages of rocks.
3. **Determine** the type of rock that will form in each of the following scenarios:
   - **a.** Lava pours onto the ocean floor and cools.
   - **b.** Minerals cement small pieces of sand together.
   - **c.** Mudstone is subjected to great heat and pressure over a long period of time.
4. **Explain** why a construction worker who uses a jackhammer on a rock does not produce a metamorphic rock.
5. **Identify** what type of rock might have a lot of holes in it due to the formation of gas bubbles. Explain your answer.
6. **Critical Thinking** A paleontologist who is researching extinctions notices that certain fossils are never found above a layer of sediment containing the radioactive isotope rubidium-87 or below another layer containing the same isotope. To determine when these animals became extinct, should the paleontologist use relative dating, absolute dating, or a combination of the two? Explain your answer.

SECTION 4

Weathering and Erosion

OBJECTIVES

- **Distinguish** between chemical and physical weathering.
- **Explain** how chemical weathering can form underground caves in limestone.
- **Describe** the importance of water to chemical weathering.
- **Identify** three different physical elements that can cause erosion.

KEY TERMS

acid precipitation
erosion
deposition

Compared to the destructive power of an earthquake or a volcano, the force exerted by a river may seem small. But, over time, forces such as water and wind can make vast changes in the landscape. Parunaweep Canyon, shown in ***Figure 32,*** is one of the most magnificent examples of how water can shape Earth's surface.

Physical Weathering

There are two types of weathering processes: physical and chemical. Physical, or mechanical, weathering breaks rocks into smaller pieces but does not alter their chemical compositions. Erosion by water or wind are examples of physical weathering. Chemical weathering breaks down rock by changing its chemical composition.

Ice can break rocks

Ice can play a part in the physical or mechanical weathering of rock. A common kind of mechanical weathering is called *frost wedging.* This occurs when water seeps into cracks or joints in rock and then freezes. When the water freezes, its volume increases by about 10%, pushing the rock apart. Every time the ice thaws and refreezes, it wedges farther into the rock, and the crack in the rock widens and deepens. This process eventually breaks off pieces of the rock or splits the rock apart.

Plants can also break rocks

The roots of plants can also act as wedges as the roots grow into cracks in the rocks. As the plant grows, the roots exert a constant pressure on the rock. The crack continues to deepen and widen, eventually causing a piece of the rock to break off.

Figure 32
Parunaweep Canyon, in Zion National Park, Utah, is a striking example of the effect of water on Earth's surface.

Chemical Weathering

Figure 33 shows the sedimentary layers in Badlands National Park, in South Dakota. They appear red because they contain hematite. Hematite, Fe_2O_3, is one of the most common minerals and is formed as iron reacts with oxygen in an oxidation reaction. When certain elements, especially metals, react with oxygen, they become oxides and their properties change. When these elements are in minerals, oxidation can cause the mineral to decompose or form new minerals. This is an example of *chemical weathering*. The results of chemical weathering are not as easy to see as those of physical weathering, but chemical weathering can have a great effect on the landscape over millions of years.

Figure 33

Red sedimentary layers in Badlands National Park contain iron that has reacted with oxygen to form hematite.

Carbon dioxide can cause chemical weathering

Another common type of chemical weathering occurs when carbon dioxide from the air dissolves in rainwater. The result is water that contains carbonic acid, H_2CO_3. Although carbonic acid is a weak acid, it reacts with some minerals. As the slightly acidic water seeps into the ground, it can weather rock underground.

For example, calcite, the major mineral in limestone, reacts with carbonic acid to form calcium bicarbonate. Because the calcium bicarbonate is dissolved in water, the decomposed rock is carried away in the water, leaving underground pockets. The cave shown in ***Figure 34*** resulted from the weathering action of carbonic acid on calcite in underground layers of limestone.

Figure 34

Carbonic acid dissolved the calcite in the sedimentary rock limestone to produce this underground cavern.

Water plays a key role in chemical weathering

Minerals react chemically with water. This reaction changes the physical properties of minerals, and often changes entire landscapes. Other times, minerals dissolve completely into water and are carried to a new location. Often minerals are transported to lower layers of rock. This process is called *leaching*. Some mineral ore deposits, like those mined for aluminum, are deposited by leaching.

Water can also carry dissolved oxygen that reacts with minerals that contain metals such as iron. This type of chemical weathering is called *oxidation*. When oxygen combines with the iron found in rock, it forms iron oxide, or rust. The red color of soil in some areas of the southeastern United States is mainly caused by the oxidation of minerals containing iron.

acid precipitation precipitation, such as rain, sleet, or snow, that contains a high concentration of acids, often because of pollution in the atmosphere

Acid precipitation can slowly dissolve minerals

Rain and other forms of precipitation have a slightly acidic pH, around 5.7, because they contain carbonic acid. When fossil fuels, especially coal, are burned, sulfur dioxide and nitrogen oxides are released and may react with water in clouds to form nitric acid, or nitrous acid, and sulfuric acid. These clouds form precipitation that falls to Earth as **acid precipitation.** The pH value of rainwater in some northeastern United States cities between 1940 and 1990 averaged between 4 and 5. In some individual cases, the pH dropped below 4, to levels nearly as acidic as vinegar.

Acid precipitation causes damage to both living organisms and inorganic matter. Acid rain can erode metal and rock, such as the statue in Brooklyn, New York, shown in ***Figure 35.*** Marble and limestone dissolve relatively rapidly even in weak acid.

In 1990, the Acid Rain Control Program was added to the Clean Air Act of 1970. According to the program, power plants and factories were given 10 years to decrease the release of sulfur dioxide to about half the amount they emitted in 1980. The acidity of rain has been greatly reduced since power plants have installed *scrubbers* that remove the sulfur oxide gases.

Figure 35

Acid precipitation weathers stone structures, such as this marble statue in Brooklyn, New York.

Figure 36

Deltas, such as this one in New Zealand, are formed by deposition.

Erosion

Erosion is the removal and transportation of weathered and non-weathered materials by running water, wind, waves, ice, underground water, and gravity.

Water erosion shapes Earth's surface

Water is the most effective physical weathering agent. Have you ever seen a murky river? Muddy rivers carry sediment in their water. As sediment moves along with the water, it scrapes the riverbanks and the river bottom. As the water continues to scour the surface, it carries the new sediment away. This process of loosening and moving sediments is known as **erosion.**

There is a direct relationship between the velocity of the water and the size and amount of sediment it can carry. Quickly moving rivers can carry away a lot of sediment, and create extraordinary canyons.

As a river becomes wider or deepens, it flows more slowly and cannot carry as much sediment. As a result, sediment is deposited on the floor of these calmer portions of the river or stream. The process of depositing sediment is called **deposition.** Rivers eventually flow into large bodies of water, such as seas and oceans, where the sediment is deposited along the continental shores. As rivers slow at the continental boundary, large deposits of sediment are laid down. These areas, called deltas, often have rich, fertile soils, making them excellent agricultural areas. ***Figure 36*** shows the Greenstone River delta, in New Zealand.

erosion a process in which the materials of the Earth's surface are loosened, dissolved, or worn away and transported from one place to another by a natural agent, such as wind, water, ice, or gravity

deposition the process in which material is laid down

Oceans also shape Earth

The oceans also have a dramatic effect on Earth's landscape. On seashores, the waves crash onto land, creating tall cliffs and jagged coastlines. The Cliffs of Moher, in western Ireland, shown in ***Figure 37,*** reach heights of 204 m (669 ft) above the water. The cliffs were formed partially by the force of waves in the Atlantic Ocean eroding the rocky shale and sandstone coast.

Figure 37

The action of waves slowly tearing away at the rocky coast formed the Cliffs of Moher.

Glaciers erode mountains

Large masses of ice, such as the glacier shown in ***Figure 38A,*** can exert tremendous forces on rocks. The constantly moving ice mass carves the surface it rests on, often creating U-shaped valleys, such as the one shown in ***Figure 38B.*** The weight of the ice and the forward movement of the glacier cause the mass to act like a huge scouring pad. Immense boulders that are carried by the ice scrape across other rocks, grinding them to a fine powder. Glacial meltwater streams carry the fine sediment away from the glacier and deposit it along the banks and floors of streams or at the bottom of glacier-formed lakes.

Figure 38

A Tustamena Glacier, in Alaska, has slowly pushed its way through these mountains.

B Glaciers are capable of carving out large U-shaped valleys, such as this valley in Alaska.

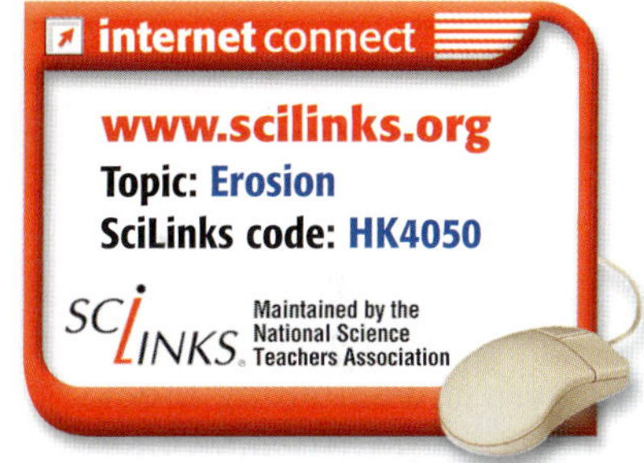

Wind can also shape the landscape

Just as water or glaciers can carry rocks along, scraping other rocks as they pass, wind can also weather the Earth's surfaces. Have you ever been in a dust storm and felt your skin "burn" from the swirling dust? This happens because fast-moving wind can carry sediment, just as water can. Wind that carries sediment creates a sandblaster effect, smoothing Earth's surface and eroding the landscape.

The sandstone arches of Arches National Park, in Utah, are formed partly by wind erosion. Look at ***Figure 39.*** Can you guess how these arches might have formed? Geologists have struggled to find a good explanation for the formation of arches.

The land in and around Arches National Park is part of the Colorado Plateau, an area that was under a saltwater sea more than 300 million years ago. As this sea evaporated, it deposited a thick layer of salt that has since been covered by many layers of sedimentary rock. The salt layer deforms more easily than rock layers. As the salt layers warped and deformed over the years, they created surface depressions and bulges. Arches formed where the overlying sedimentary rocks were pushed upward by the salt.

Figure 39

This sandstone arch in Arches National Park, in Utah, was created as high-speed winds weathered the terrain.

Figure 40

Fins are formed when sandstone is pushed upward, and cracks are slowly eroded. Wind, water, and ice erode the fins until they collapse or form arches.

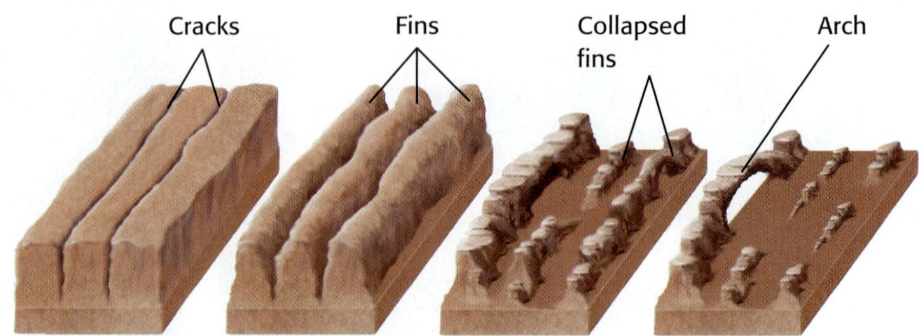

Figure 40 shows how one theory explains the formation of arches. As land is pushed upward in places, small surface cracks form. These cracks are eroded by water, ice, and wind until narrow free-standing rock formations, called *fins,* are formed. When these fins are exposed along their sides, the wind wears away at the cement that holds the sediment together, causing large pieces of the rock to fall away. Some fins collapse completely; others that are more sturdy and balanced form arches.

SECTION 4 REVIEW

SUMMARY

- Physical weathering breaks down rock by water erosion, ice wedging, wind abrasion, glacial abrasion, and other forces.
- In chemical weathering, rock is altered as minerals in rock react chemically.
- Carbonic acid acts as a chemical weathering agent and is responsible for the formation of underground limestone caves.
- Water plays an important role in shaping Earth's landscape.
- Acid precipitation can weather rock and harm living organisms.

1. **List** two agents of physical weathering that might occur in the mountains in northern Montana.
2. **Explain** how the wind may be involved in the formation of sandstone arches.
3. **Distinguish** between physical weathering, chemical weathering, and erosion in the following examples:
   - **a.** Rock changes color as it is oxidized.
   - **b.** Rock shatters as it freezes.
   - **c.** Wind erodes the sides of the Egyptian pyramids in Giza.
   - **d.** An underground cavern is formed as water drips in from Earth's surface.
4. **Explain** why the following statement is incorrect: Acid precipitation is any precipitation that has a pH less than 7.
5. **Predict** which will experience more weathering, a rock in the Sonora Desert, in southern Arizona, or a rock on a beach in North Carolina.
6. **Critical Thinking** On many coastlines, erosion is wearing the beach away and threatening to destroy homes. How would you prevent this destruction?

Study Skills

Concept Mapping

Concept mapping is an important study guide and a good way to check your understanding of key terms and concepts.

1 Select a main concept for the map.

We will use tectonic plates as the main concept of this map.

2 List all the important concepts.

We'll use the terms: lithosphere, divergent boundaries, convergent boundaries, and transform fault boundaries.

3 Build the map by placing the concepts according to their importance under the main concept, tectonic plates, and add linking words to give meaning to the arrangement of concepts.

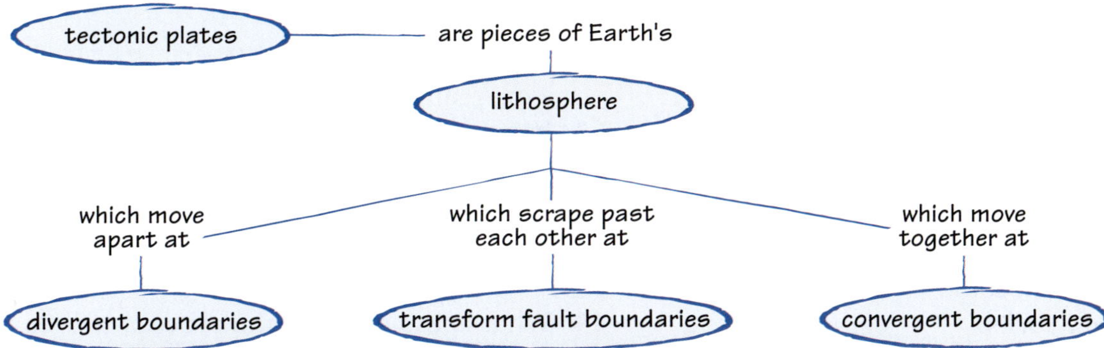

From this completed concept map we can write the following propositions:

Tectonic plates are pieces of Earth's lithosphere which move apart at divergent boundaries.

Tectonic plates scrape past each other at transform fault boundaries.

Tectonic plates move together at convergent boundaries.

Practice

1. Add on to the concept map using the words *earthquake, volcano,* and *fault,* as well as the appropriate linking words.
2. Use as the main concept erosion and create your own concept map.
3. Write two propositions from your completed concept map.

CHAPTER 21 REVIEW

Chapter Highlights

Before you begin, review the summaries of the key ideas of each section, found at the end of each section. The key vocabulary terms are listed on the first page of each section.

UNDERSTANDING CONCEPTS

1. Vibrations in Earth caused by sudden movements of rock are called
a. epicenters.
b. earthquakes.
c. faults.
d. volcanoes.

2. Using the difference in the time it takes for P waves and S waves to arrive at three different seismograph stations, seismologists can find an earthquake's
a. epicenter.
b. surface waves.
c. fault zone.
d. intensity.

3. The Richter scale expresses an earthquake's
a. damage.
b. location.
c. duration.
d. magnitude.

4. High pressure and high temperature cause igneous rocks to become
a. sedimentary rocks.
b. limestone.
c. metamorphic rocks.
d. clay.

5. _______ rock is formed from magma.
a. Igneous
b. Metamorphic
c. Sedimentary
d. Schist

6. Underground caves in limestone can be formed by a reaction including
a. sulfuric acid.
b. hematite.
c. ice crystals.
d. carbonic acid.

7. Which of the following parts of Earth's interior is liquid?
a. inner core
b. crust
c. outer core
d. mantle

8. The most common type of volcano is the
a. cinder cone.
b. composite volcano.
c. shield volcano.
d. giant volcano.

9. Which one of these forces shapes Earth's surface?
a. glaciers
b. oceans
c. winds
d. all of the above

USING VOCABULARY

10. Using the terms *crust, mantle,* and *core,* describe Earth's internal structure.

11. Explain the difference between the relative and the absolute age of a rock.

12. Use the terms *focus, epicenter, P waves, S waves,* and *surface waves* to describe what happens during an earthquake.

13. In what type of rock—igneous, sedimentary, or metamorphic—are you most likely to find a fossil?

14. What is the name of the process of breaking down rock?

15. Explain how deltas form at the continental boundary using the terms *erosion* and *deposition.*

16. Explain what role water plays in chemical weathering and in physical weathering.

17. Restate the theory of plate tectonics using the terms *plate tectonics, lithosphere,* and *continental drift.*

18. Explain why earthquakes happen near faults.

19. Describe the Richter Scale, including information on its purpose and what kind of phenomena it describes.

20. What kind of rock are marble and slate?

21. Describe how wind can erode rock and shape Earth's surface, and list two other elements that can cause erosion.

22. Describe the difference between a divergent and convergent plate boundary. Name the features found near each type of boundary.

BUILDING MATH SKILLS

23. **Graphing** Examine the graph in the figure below, and answer the questions that follow.

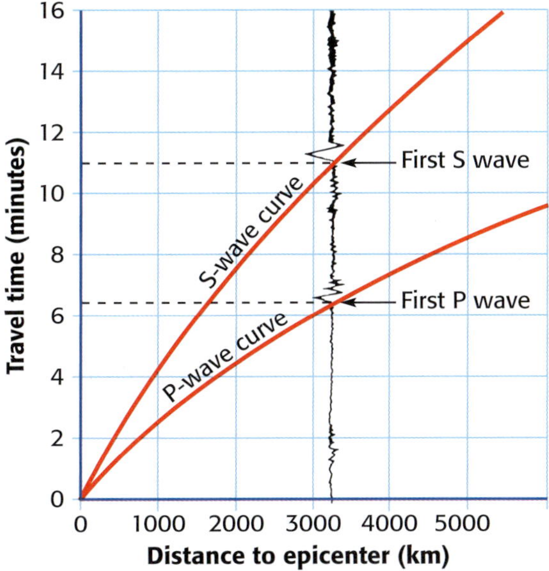

a. Approximately how far, in kilometers, was the epicenter of the earthquake from the seismograph that recorded the seismogram shown here?
b. When did the first P wave reach the seismograph?
c. When did the first S wave reach the seismograph?
d. What is the difference in travel time between the two waves?

THINKING CRITICALLY

24. **Critical Thinking** Why are mathematics and theory the only practical ways to determine the temperature of Earth's core?

25. **Applying Knowledge** Is a tall building more likely to be damaged by an earthquake if it is on a mountain of granite or in a valley of sediment? Explain.

26. **Applying Knowledge** You are on a field trip to the top of a mountain. Your teacher tells you that the rocks are metamorphic. What can you tell about the geologic history of the area?

27. **Problem Solving** Imagine you are on a dinosaur dig and your team finds two sets of dinosaur bones entwined as if they died while engaged in battle. You know one of the dinosaurs lived 180 million to 120 million years ago and the other lived 130 million to 115 million years ago. What can you say about the age of the rock the dinosaur fossils were found in?

28. **Interpreting Diagrams** The figure below shows a cross-sectional diagram of a portion of a plate boundary. It shows plates, the ocean, mountains, and rivers. The mouths of the rivers reach the shore, where they deposit sediments. Using the diagram, answer the following questions:
   a. What type of plate boundary is shown? How do you know?
   b. What type of physical weathering processes are probably acting on the mountains?
   c. What type of land-shaping processes are occurring on and near the beach?
   d. What forces might have formed this coastal mountain range?

CHAPTER 21 REVIEW

DEVELOPING LIFE/WORK SKILLS

29. Making Decisions Pretend you are the superintendent of the Washington State Police Department. Seismologists in the area of Mount St. Helens predict that the volcano will erupt in one week. Write a report describing the evacuation procedures. In your report, describe the area you will evacuate and a plan for how people will be contacted. WRITING SKILL

30. Applying Technology Sonar is the best method for identifying features under water. Sound waves are emitted from one device, and the time it takes for the wave to bounce off an object and return is calculated by another. This information is used to determine how far away a feature is. Draw a graph that could be made by a ship's sonar device as it tracks the ocean bottom from the shoreline to a deep ocean trench and farther out to sea.

31. Applying Technology Use a computer drawing program to create cutaway diagrams of a fault before, during, and after an earthquake.

32. Acquiring and Evaluating Data Mount Mazama exploded with a great deal of force. Go to the library and research Mount Mazama. How big was the eruption? How might the eruption have affected Earth's global climate?

INTEGRATING CONCEPTS

33. Connection to Biology Charles Darwin, known for his theory of evolution by natural selection, was the first to explain how atolls (AT ahls) form. What are atolls? What was his explanation?

34. Connection to Social Studies The Grand Canyon is one of the most geologically informative and beautiful sites in the United States. Read about the people who have lived along the Colorado River and in the Grand Canyon. How do we know Paleo-Indians lived there? Who were the Anasazi? Who was John Wesley Powell? Write a one-page essay about the history of these people and this region. WRITING SKILL

35. Concept Mapping Copy the unfinished concept map on this page onto a sheet of paper. Complete the map by writing the correct word or phrase in the lettered boxes.

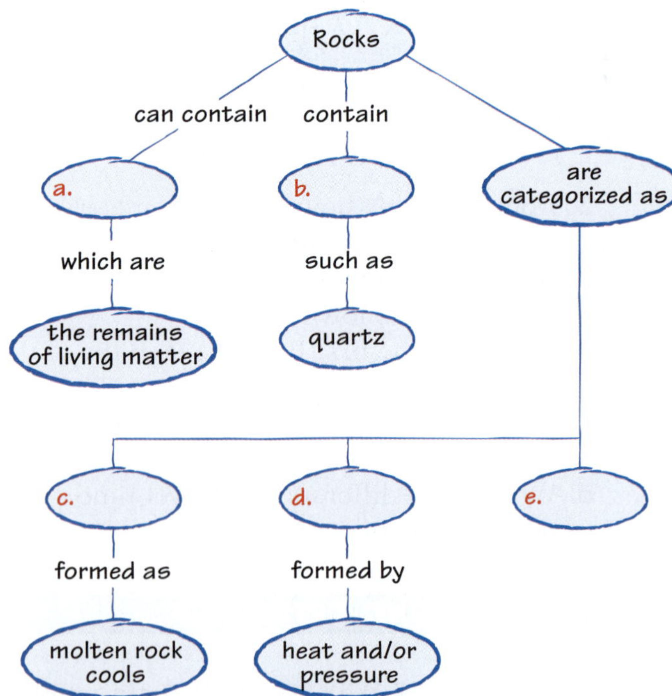

Standardized Test Prep

Understanding Concepts

***Directions (1–4):* For *each* question, write on a separate sheet of paper the letter of the correct answer.**

1 Which of these occurs where two tectonic plates move away from each other?
- **A.** convergent boundary
- **B.** divergent boundary
- **C.** ocean trench
- **D.** subduction zone

2 What causes earthquakes along the San Andreas fault in California?
- **F.** subduction of the Pacific plate by the North American plate
- **G.** collision between the Pacific plate and the North American plate
- **H.** divergent movement of the Pacific plate and the North American plate
- **I.** horizontal movement along the boundary of the Pacific plate and the North American plate

3 How can the absolute age of a layer of rock be determined?
- **A.** by the principle of superposition
- **B.** by the ratio of radioisotopes
- **C.** by the amount of weathering that has shaped the rock
- **D.** by analysis of the types of minerals that make up the rock

4 Which of the following is an example of chemical weathering of rock?
- **F.** deposition
- **G.** erosion
- **H.** frost wedging
- **I.** leaching

***Directions (5):* Write a short response to the question.**

5 Both S waves and P waves travel from the site of an earthquake. How does the difference in the way these waves travel reveal information about the structure of Earth's interior?

Test TIP

When possible, highlight or underline numbers or words critical to the understanding of a question.

Reading Skills

***Directions (6):* Read the passage below. Then answer the question.**

In 1912 Alfred Wegener first proposed the theory that all of the continents formed when one giant continent broke apart. Wegener used the shape of the continents, the distribution of fossils, and similarity of rocks at different parts of the world as evidence.

Wegener's Continental Drift theory was not immediately accepted by scientists. Some wondered about, but could not find, forces that would be strong enough to move such large masses of solid rock over great distances. In the middle of the 20th century, evidence from ocean floor exploration provided new evidence that continents move. The theory of plate tectonics, which explains how land masses move, not across the ocean floor, but across the Earth's mantle, is now widely accepted.

6 Why do most scientists now accept the idea of moving continents, even though earlier scientists did not?

Interpreting Graphics

***Directions (7):* Base your answer to question 7 on the illustration below.**

Cross-section of a Volcano

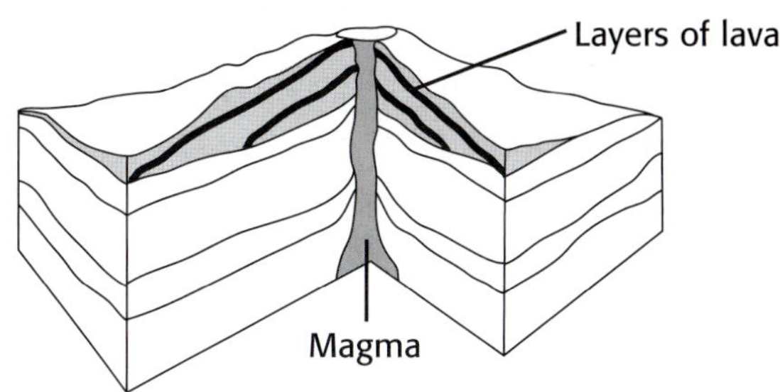

7 What type of volcano is illustrated here?
- **A.** cinder cone
- **B.** composite
- **C.** seamount
- **D.** shield

Skills Practice Lab

Introduction

During an earthquake, seismic waves travel through Earth in all directions from the earthquake's focus. How can you find the location of the epicenter by studying seismic waves?

Objectives

- ***Calculate*** the distance from an earthquake's epicenter to surrounding seismographs.
- ***Find*** the location of the earthquake's epicenter.
- USING SCIENTIFIC METHODS ***Draw conclusions*** by explaining the relationship between seismic waves and the location of an earthquake's epicenter.

Materials

calculator
drawing compass
ruler
tracing paper

Analyzing Seismic Waves

Procedure

Preparing for Your Experiment

1. In this lab, you will examine seismograms showing two kinds of seismic waves: primary waves (P waves) and secondary waves (S waves).
2. P waves have an average speed of 6.1 km/s. S waves have an average speed of 4.1 km/s.
   a. How long does it take P waves to travel 100 km?
   b. How long does it take S waves to travel 100 km?

   (**Hint:** You will need to use the equation for velocity and rearrange it to solve for time.)
3. Because S waves travel more slowly than P waves, S waves will reach a seismograph after P waves arrive. This difference in arrival times is known as the lag time.
4. Use the time intervals found in step 2 to calculate the lag time you would expect from a seismograph located exactly 100 km from the epicenter of an earthquake.

Measuring the Lag Time from Seismographic Records

5. On a blank sheet of paper, prepare a table like the one shown below.

City	Lag time(s)	Distance to epicenter
Austin, TX		
Portland, OR		
Bismarck, ND		

6. The illustration at the top of the next page shows the records produced by seismographs in three cities following an earthquake.
7. Using the time scale at the bottom of the illustration, measure the lag time for each city. Be sure to measure from the start of the P wave to the start of the S wave. Enter your measurements in your table.

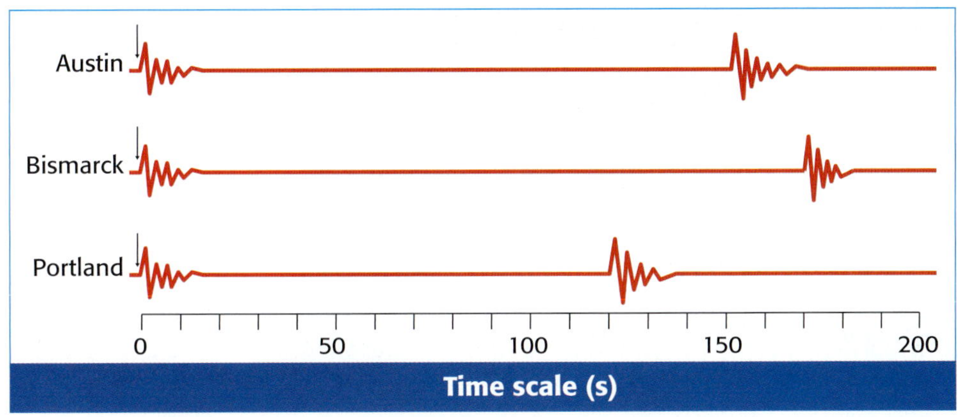

8. Using the lag time you found in step 4 and the formula below, calculate the distance from each city to the epicenter of the earthquake. Enter your results in your table.

distance = (measured lag time ÷ lag time for 100 km) × 100 km

Analysis

1. Trace the map at the bottom of this page on a blank sheet of paper. Using the scale below your map, adjust the drawing compass so that it will draw a circle whose radius equals the distance from the epicenter of the earthquake to Austin. Then put the point of the compass on Austin, and draw a circle on your map. How is the location of the epicenter related to the circle?
2. Repeat the process in item 1 using the distance from Portland to the epicenter. This time put the point of the compass on Portland, and draw the circle. Where do the two circles intersect? The epicenter is one of these two sites.
3. **Reaching Conclusions** Repeat the process once more for Bismarck, and find that city's distance from the epicenter. The epicenter is located at the site where all three circles intersect. What city is closest to that site?

Conclusions

4. Why is it necessary to use seismographs in three different locations to find the epicenter of an earthquake?
5. Would it be possible to use this method for locating an earthquake's epicenter if earthquakes produced only one kind of seismic wave? Explain your answer.
6. Someone tells you that the best way to determine the epicenter is to find a seismograph where the P and S waves occur at the same time. What is wrong with this reasoning?

CareerLink

Paleontologist

Paleontologists are life's historians. They study fossils and other evidence to understand how and why life has changed during Earth's history. Most paleontologists work for universities, government agencies, or private industry. To learn more about paleontology as a career, read this interview with paleontologist Geerat Vermeij, who works in the Department of Geology at the University of California, Davis.

"I think one needs to be able to recognize puzzles and then think about ways of solving them."

Vermeij is a world-renowned expert on living and fossil mollusks, but he has never seen one. Born blind, he has learned to scrutinize specimens with his hands.

Describe your work as a paleontologist.

I study the history of life and how life has changed from its beginning to today. I'm interested in long-term trends and long-term patterns. My work involves everything from field studies of how living organisms live and work to a lot of work in museum collections. I work especially on shell-bearing mollusks, but I have thought about and written about all of life.

What questions are you particularly interested in?

How enemies have influenced the evolution of plants and animals. I study arms races (evolutionary competitions) over geological time. And I study how the physical history of Earth has affected evolution.

What is your favorite part of your work?

That's hard to say. I enjoy doing the research and writing. I'd say it was a combination of working with specimens, reading for background, and writing (scientific) papers and popular books. I have written four books.

What qualities make a good paleontologist?

First and foremost, hard work. The second thing is you need to know a lot. You have to have a lot of information at hand to put what you observe into context. And you need to be a good observer.

What skills does a paleontologist need?

To me, the curiosity to learn a lot is essential. You have to have the ability to understand and do science and to communicate it.

What attracted you to a career in paleontology?

It's a love of natural history in general and shells in particular that led inexorably to my career. As long as I can remember, I have been interested in natural history. I knew pretty much what I wanted to be from the age of 10.

What education and experiences have been most useful to you?

I think it was very good for me to start early. I started school when I was just shy of my fourth birthday. I started reading the scientific literature in high school.

What advice do you have for students who are interested in paleontology?

People should work on their interests and not let them slide. They should pursue their interests outside of school. If they live near a museum, for example, getting involved in the museum's activities, getting to know the people there, and so forth is a good idea.

Why do you think paleontology is important, and did that influence your choice of career?

It gives us a window on life and the past, which like history in general, can provide lessons on what we are doing to the Earth. It gives us perspective on crises and opportunities. The main reason people should pursue interests is for their own sake. I just love the things I work on. It can be utilitarian, but that's not the rationale for my work.

"I hope that in 15 years' time people will be asking questions that today are inconceivable. The road ahead is not marked."
—Geerat Vermeij

CHAPTER 22

The Atmosphere

Chapter Preview

Background Like many other weather phenomena, rainbows are caused by water in Earth's atmosphere. Rainbows are visible when the air is filled with water droplets. Sunlight striking the droplets passes through their front surface and is partially reflected back toward the viewer from the back of the droplet.

But why do we see the rainbow of colors? A rainbow occurs when sunlight is bent as it passes from air to water and back to air again.

Activity 1 Look at the two rainbows in the smaller photo at left. One of these rainbows, called a secondary rainbow, results when light is reflected a second time in the raindrops. The second reflection causes the order of the colors to be reversed. Compare the order of the colors in the two rainbows with that of the rainbow in the photo of the irrigation trucks. Can you tell which rainbow is the secondary rainbow? How?

Activity 2 Rainbows are most commonly seen as arches because the ends of the rainbow disappear at the horizon. But if an observer is at an elevated vantage point, such as on an airplane or at the rim of a canyon, a complete circular rainbow can be seen.

You can create a circular rainbow in your yard. On a warm, clear day when the sun is overhead, turn on a water hose and spray water into the air above you. If the mist is fine enough, you should be able to create a rainbow that encircles your body.

Rainbows can be seen when the air is filled with water droplets.

Pre-Reading Questions

1. What would Earth be like without an atmosphere?
2. How do scuba divers breathe under water?

SECTION 1

Characteristics of the Atmosphere

KEY TERMS

troposphere
temperature inversion
stratosphere
ozone
mesosphere
thermosphere
greenhouse effect

OBJECTIVES

- **Identify** the primary layers of the atmosphere.
- **Describe** how the atmosphere has evolved over time.
- **Describe** how the oxygen–carbon dioxide cycle works, and explain its importance to living organisms.
- **Discuss** the recent changes in Earth's atmosphere.

If you were to see Earth's atmosphere from space, it would look like a thin blue halo of light around Earth. This fragile envelope provides the air we breathe, regulates global temperature, and filters out dangerous solar radiation.

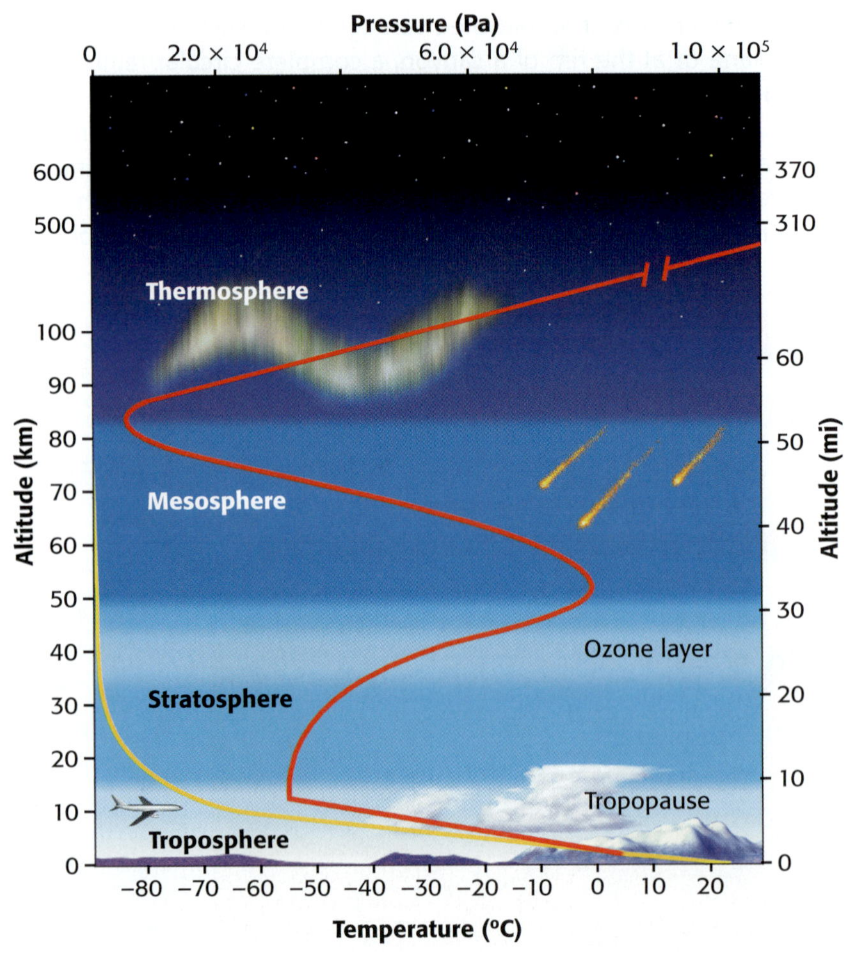

Layers of the Atmosphere

Without the atmosphere, you would have no oxygen to breathe. The atmosphere, however, does not contain oxygen alone. Earth's atmosphere consists of a variety of gases. The two main gases in the atmosphere are nitrogen (about 78%) and oxygen (about 21%). The remaining elements exist only in very small amounts and are called *trace gases.*

The atmosphere has several layers. These layers differ in temperature, density, and amount of certain gases present. ***Figure 1*** shows the position and relative thicknesses of Earth's atmospheric layers.

Figure 1

The layers of the atmosphere are marked by differences in temperature and pressure. Red indicates temperature. Yellow indicates pressure.

Almost all weather occurs in the troposphere

You live in the layer closest to Earth's surface. This layer is called the **troposphere.** Clouds, wind, rain, and snow occur mostly in the troposphere.

The troposphere is the densest of the atmospheric layers. Consider the weight of all the other gas layers pressing down on the gases in the troposphere. The weight causes the gas molecules to squeeze together into a smaller volume. The result is a greater density than exists in higher layers of the atmosphere.

troposphere the lowest layer of the atmosphere, in which temperature drops at a constant rate as altitude increases

temperature inversion the atmospheric condition in which warm air traps cooler air near Earth's surface

The troposphere gets cooler with increasing altitude

If you were to climb a mountain, you would notice that the air is much colder at the top of the mountain than it is at the base. The air closest to the mountain's base is warmed by the ground and oceans, which absorb solar energy during the day and heat the atmosphere by radiation and conduction. Air at higher altitudes is less dense and is not as close to those sources of heat. As you travel higher into the troposphere, the temperature decreases by about 6°C for every kilometer of altitude.

At the top of the troposphere, the temperature stops decreasing. The boundary where this occurs is called the *tropopause.* The low temperature (–55°C) at the tropopause keeps the water vapor and clouds in the troposphere. This is the reason that clouds, rain and snow are restricted to the troposphere. The tropopause acts like a lid on the water and water vapor in the troposphere. The altitude of the tropopause is different at different places on Earth. At the poles, it occurs at about 8 km (5 mi). Near the equator, it rises to nearly 18 km (11 mi).

VOCABULARY Skills Tip

The names of all of Earth's atmospheric layers end in the root word sphere, *implying their spherical shape.*

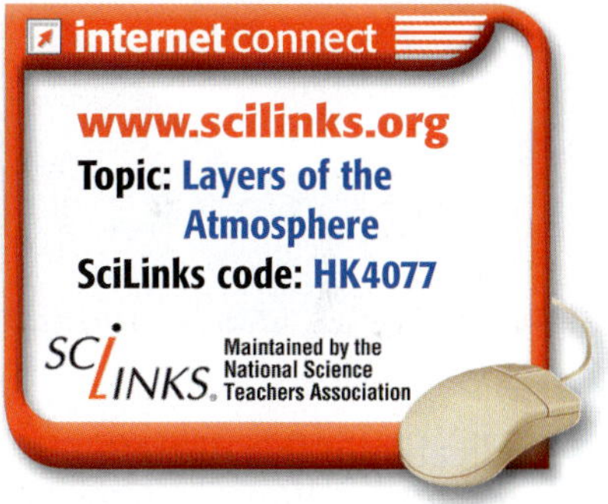

Cold air can become trapped beneath warm air

Although the troposphere is generally warmer close to Earth's surface, cool air sometimes gets trapped beneath the warm air. This is called a **temperature inversion.**

When a temperature inversion occurs, cooler air cannot rise and the air can become thick with pollution. This is true especially in areas surrounded by mountains, which also prevent the polluted air from escaping. The Los Angeles Basin in California is often filled with a brown haze as shown in **Figure 2.** Cool air from the Pacific Ocean blows into the basin, becomes trapped by the overriding warm air, and fills with pollutants.

Figure 2

A temperature inversion traps polluted air in the Los Angeles Basin, in California.

As long as a temperature inversion remains, trapped pollutants cannot escape. A person breathing these toxins can become ill. While these conditions exist, it is not healthy for people to exercise outside because they inhale a greater amount of pollutants as they breathe heavily.

stratosphere the upper layer of the atmosphere, which lies immediately above the troposphere and extends from 10 km to about 50 km above Earth's surface

ozone a gas molecule that is made up of three oxygen atoms

The stratosphere gets *warmer* with increasing altitude

In 1892, unmanned balloons were built that could record temperatures in the **stratosphere,** the layer above the tropopause. Later, humans further explored this cold, low-pressure layer by using balloons and airplanes with enclosed, heated cabins such as the WB-57F shown in **Figure 3.** These explorers found that the temperature in the lower stratosphere remains fairly constant, staying around –55°C (–67°F) from near the tropopause to an altitude of about 25 km (about 16 mi). At 25 km, the temperature begins to increase with altitude until it reaches about 0°C (32°F).

Figure 3

A heated cabin in this aircraft allows its pilot to do high-altitude atmospheric research, such as collecting air and particle samples after a volcanic eruption.

The stratosphere extends to about 50 km (31 mi). In addition to getting warmer instead of cooler, the stratosphere differs from the troposphere in composition, weather, and density. Unlike the troposphere, the stratosphere has little water vapor—the gaseous form of water because water vapor cannot get through the cold tropopause. Because of this lack of water vapor, the stratosphere contains few clouds and no storms.

The increase in temperature in the upper stratosphere occurs in the atmospheric layer known as the *ozone layer.* The ozone layer is warmer because it contains a form of oxygen called **ozone** that absorbs solar radiation. Whereas the oxygen we breathe is a molecule that consists of two oxygen atoms, as shown in **Figure 4A,** ozone molecules have three oxygen atoms, as shown in **Figure 4B.** Ozone is important because it absorbs much of the sun's ultraviolet radiation. The ozone layer shields life on Earth's surface from ultraviolet-radiation damage. Ozone will be discussed later in this section.

Figure 4

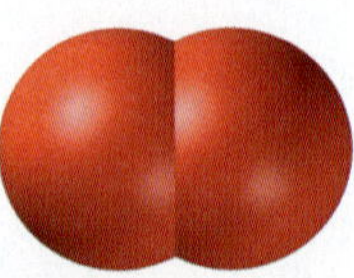

A Oxygen molecules have two atoms of oxygen.

B Ozone molecules have three atoms of oxygen.

The mesosphere and thermosphere exhibit extremes of temperature

Temperature begins to fall again in the **mesosphere.** As in the troposphere, temperatures in the mesosphere, 50–80 km (31–50 mi) above Earth's surface, decrease with increasing altitude. Near the top of this layer, temperatures fall to below –80°C (–112°F), the coldest temperature in Earth's atmosphere.

Beyond the mesosphere, temperatures begin to rise again. This layer, at an altitude of about 80–480 km (50–298 mi), is called the **thermosphere.** The main gases are still nitrogen and oxygen, but the molecules are very far apart. This may lead you to think that the thermosphere is very cold, but it is actually very hot. Temperatures in this layer average around 980°C (1796°F) because the small amount of molecular oxygen in the thermosphere heats up as it absorbs intense solar radiation.

The outermost portion of the thermosphere, at about 480 km, is known as the *exosphere*. In the exosphere, some gases escape from the gravitational pull of Earth and exit into space. In addition, gases in space are captured by Earth's gravity and added to Earth's atmosphere.

mesosphere the coldest layer of the atmosphere, between the stratosphere and the mesopause

thermosphere the uppermost layer of the atmosphere, in which temperature increases as altitude increases

The ionosphere is used in radio communication

When solar energy is absorbed in the lower thermosphere and upper mesosphere, electrically charged ions are formed. The area where this occurs is sometimes called the *ionosphere*.

Electrons in the ionosphere reflect radio waves, as shown in ***Figure 5,*** allowing them to be received over long distances. Without the ionosphere, most radio signals would travel directly into space, and only locations very close to a transmitter could receive the signals.

Because these ions require solar radiation in order to form, their number in the lower layers of the ionosphere decreases at night. This means the radio waves can travel higher into the atmosphere before being reflected. As a result, the radio waves return to Earth's surface farther from their source than they do in the daytime, as shown at right.

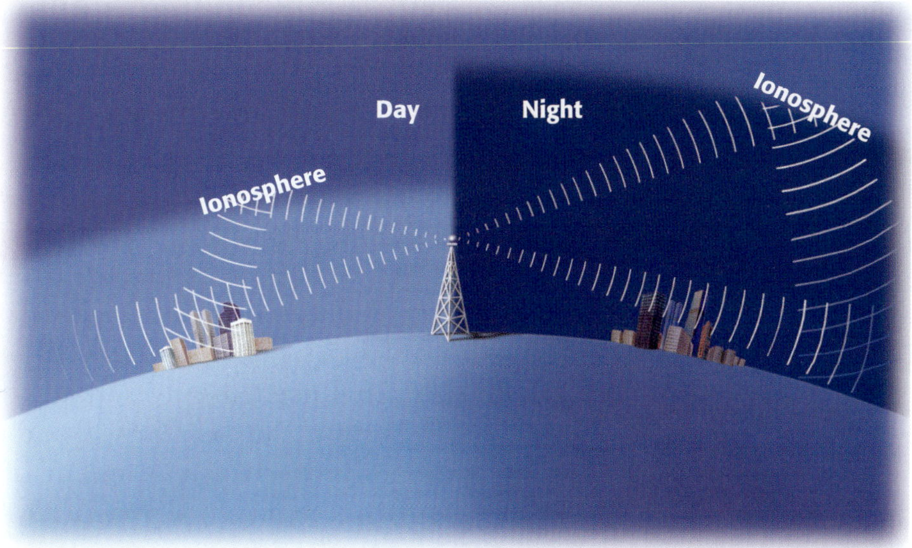

Figure 5

Radio waves can be received from far away because they are reflected by the ionosphere. At night, when ion density decreases in the lower atmosphere, transmissions can be received farther away.

Figure 6

Auroras, such as this one seen above mountains in Alaska, occur in the ionosphere.

The ionosphere is where auroras take place

The ionosphere is also where colorful light displays called *auroras* can be seen encircling Earth's magnetic poles. Auroras form when energetic ions from the sun hit atoms and molecules in the ionosphere, causing photons to be emitted. The *aurora borealis,* shown in **Figure 6,** appears in the sky above the Northern magnetic pole. A similar phenomenon, the *aurora australis,* is observed in the south, above Antarctica.

Figure 7

A Early in Earth's existence, the atmosphere contained mostly carbon dioxide, nitrogen, and a few other trace gases.

B As Earth changed, so did the gases in the atmosphere.

Changes in Earth's Atmosphere

When Earth began to solidify about 4.4 billion years ago, volcanic eruptions released a variety of gases. This process, called *outgassing,* created an atmosphere of gases, some of which would be poisonous to us today. As shown in **Figure 7A,** these gases included hydrogen, H_2, water vapor, H_2O, ammonia, NH_3, methane, CH_4, carbon monoxide, CO, carbon dioxide, CO_2, and nitrogen, N_2, but not oxygen, O_2.

Photosynthetic plants contribute oxygen to the atmosphere

Amazingly, life-forms evolved that were comfortable in this early atmosphere. Bacteria and other single-celled organisms lived in the oceans. Around 2.5 billion years ago, some cells evolved a method of capturing energy from the sun and converting it to sugar that could be used as a food source. This process, called *photosynthesis,* also produced oxygen as a byproduct. These organisms needed only sunlight, water, and carbon dioxide for their survival, so they thrived and multiplied in this environment. Gradually, the oxygen content of the atmosphere increased to about 20%, as shown in **Figure 7B.** About 350 million years ago, the concentration of oxygen reached a level similar to what it is today.

Animals produce carbon dioxide necessary for photosynthesis

As *aerobic*, or oxygen-breathing, organisms evolved, they joined plants in a balance that led to our present atmosphere. The steps of the oxygen–carbon dioxide cycle describe this balance. These steps are summarized in ***Figure 8,*** which shows a simple depiction of the series of chemical reactions that take place. Plants need carbon dioxide, CO_2, for photosynthesis and food production. Oxygen, O_2, is then released as a waste product of photosynthesis. Animals breathe oxygen during a process called *respiration* and release carbon dioxide as waste. The carbon dioxide they exhale is then used by plants and other photosynthetic organisms, and the process is repeated.

VOCABULARY *Skills Tip*

The word ozone *comes from the Greek word* ozein, *which means "to smell." Ozone gas has a strong odor. You may have smelled ozone after a thunderstorm when atmospheric oxygen was converted to ozone by the electrical energy of lightning.*

Man-made chemicals can deplete the ozone layer

Recall that the stratosphere contains a layer of ozone molecules. Ozone is formed when the sun's ultraviolet rays strike molecules of O_2. The energy splits the molecules, and the single atoms of oxygen bond with O_2 molecules to make O_3, ozone. These O_3 molecules in turn absorb much of the sun's damaging ultraviolet radiation. Without the ozone layer, ultraviolet rays would cause serious damage to the cells of living things. Thus, scientists were concerned when they found lower than expected concentrations of ozone in the stratosphere in 1985.

Ozone destruction was caused mainly by chemicals known as chlorofluorocarbons, or CFCs. CFCs were widely used in the last 65 years of the twentieth century as refrigerants and in spray cans. Persuaded by evidence of a connection between CFCs and ozone destruction, most industrialized countries stopped production of CFCs on January 1, 1996. These bans have drastically decreased the amount of CFCs entering the stratosphere.

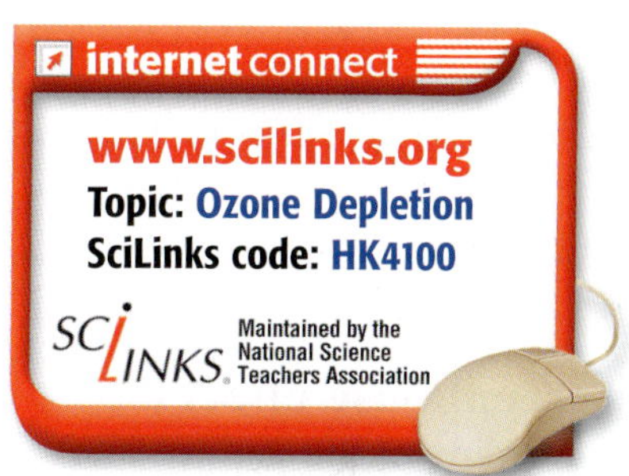

Figure 8

In the oxygen–carbon dioxide cycle, plants produce oxygen, which is used by animals for respiration. Animals produce carbon dioxide, which is used by plants for photosynthesis.

Figure 9

The greenhouse effect is a process in which atmospheric gases trap some of the energy from the sun in the troposphere.

A Solar radiation warms Earth's surface and is radiated back into the atmosphere as heat radiation.

B Greenhouse gases, such as CO_2 and H_2O, receive this heat radiation and radiate some of it back toward Earth's surface.

C CO_2 is added to the air in the burning of fossil fuels and in forest fires, possibly causing global warming.

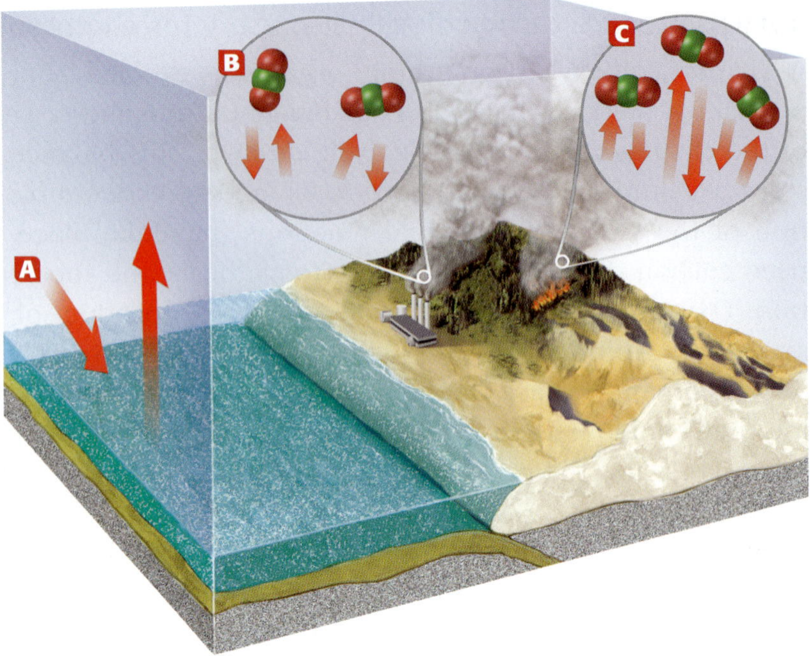

The greenhouse effect keeps Earth warm

Have you ever been in a greenhouse or opened a car on a sunny day? It is surprisingly warm inside. Although some greenhouses are heated, much of the warmth results from the sun's energy entering and becoming trapped inside the glass or plastic walls of the greenhouse.

Unlike a greenhouse, Earth's atmosphere has no walls, but certain atmospheric gases act like glass walls by keeping Earth much warmer than it would be without an atmosphere. As shown in ***Figure 9,*** energy released from the sun as radiation is absorbed by Earth's surface. Then some of this energy is transferred back toward space as radiation. Carbon dioxide, water vapor, and other gases absorb some of this energy, making the atmosphere warmer. The warm atmosphere releases some of this energy in the form of radiation, some of which is directed back toward Earth's surface. This effect is called the **greenhouse effect.**

greenhouse effect the warming of the surface and lower atmosphere of Earth that occurs when carbon dioxide, water vapor, and other gases in the air absorb and reradiate infrared radiation

Quick ACTIVITY

The Greenhouse Effect

1. Pour 500 mL of water into two identical glass jars. (If the jars are small, use 200 mL of water and fewer ice cubes.)
2. Add five ice cubes and a thermometer to each jar, and wrap one jar in a resealable plastic bag.
3. Put both jars in the sun or under lamps.
4. Record the temperature of the water in each jar every five minutes, and record your observations.
5. Make a line graph from your results.
6. Which jar warmed up faster? Explain why.

Increased levels of carbon dioxide may lead to global warming

Without the greenhouse effect, Earth would have a colder average temperature than it does. But too much of the greenhouse effect can cause problems. If too much heat is trapped, the global temperature will rise. This *global warming* could cause the icecaps to melt, ocean levels to rise, and droughts to occur in some areas.

Carbon dioxide occurs naturally and is necessary for plant photosynthesis. In the last 100 years, the burning of coal, oil, and gas for power plants, machinery, and cars has added excess carbon dioxide to the air. Recently, scientists have hypothesized that this increase in the amount of carbon dioxide is the reason the troposphere's average temperature has risen 0.5°C in the past 100 years. Whether carbon dioxide is responsible for global warming and what to do about it continues to be debated around the world.

SECTION 1 REVIEW

SUMMARY

- The layers of Earth's atmosphere are the troposphere, stratosphere, mesosphere, and thermosphere.
- The oxygen–carbon dioxide cycle produces the oxygen we breathe. Plants release oxygen. Animals breathe this oxygen and release carbon dioxide, which is used by plants.
- The ozone layer protects life on Earth by absorbing much of the ultraviolet radiation entering Earth's atmosphere.
- CFCs are linked to the deterioration of the ozone layer. For this reason, their use has been banned in most countries.
- The addition of CO_2 to the atmosphere by the burning of fossil fuels may cause global warming. This issue continues to be debated.

1. **Identify** the two atmospheric layers that contain air as warm as 25°C.
2. **Identify** which characteristic is true of the ionosphere.
   a. It gets warmer with altitude.
   b. It is used in radio communication.
   c. It is where auroras take place.
   d. It exhibits extremes in temperature.
3. **Identify** which of the following gases is most abundant in Earth's atmosphere today.
   a. argon
   b. nitrogen
   c. oxygen
   d. carbon dioxide
4. **Compare** Earth's early atmosphere with its present one.
5. **Describe** the role that plants play in the oxygen–carbon dioxide cycle.
6. **Explain** why the following statement is incorrect:

   Global warming could cause oceans to rise, so the greenhouse effect must be eliminated completely.
7. **Predict** how much colder it is at the top of Mount Everest, which is almost 9 km above sea level, than it is at the Indian coastline. (**Hint:** The temperature in the troposphere decreases by 6°C/km.)
8. **Critical Thinking** In 1982, Larry Walters rose to an altitude of approximately 4900 m on a lawn chair attached to 45 helium-filled weather balloons. Give two reasons why Walters's efforts were dangerous.

SECTION 2

Water and Wind

KEY TERMS

water cycle
transpiration
precipitation
humidity
dew point
barometric pressure
Coriolis effect

OBJECTIVES

- **Describe** the three phases of the water cycle.
- **Explain** how temperature and humidity are related.
- **Identify** various cloud types by their appearance and the altitudes at which they typically occur.
- **Use** the concept of pressure gradients to explain how winds are created, and explain how Earth's rotation affects their direction.

You come in contact with water throughout every day, not just when you drink it or when you shower or wash your hands. You experience water in the air because water exists as an invisible gas in the air. It also exists in air as a liquid, suspended in the atmosphere as clouds or fog, or falling as rain or snow. All of this water in the atmosphere affects the weather on Earth.

The Water Cycle

Water is continuously being moved through the troposphere in a process described by the **water cycle.** ***Figure 10*** shows the main processes that take place in the water cycle.

The major part of the water cycle occurs between the oceans and the continents. Solar energy strikes ocean water, causing water molecules to escape from the liquid and rise as gaseous water vapor. This process is known as evaporation.

water cycle the continuous movement of water from the ocean to the atmosphere to the land and back to the ocean

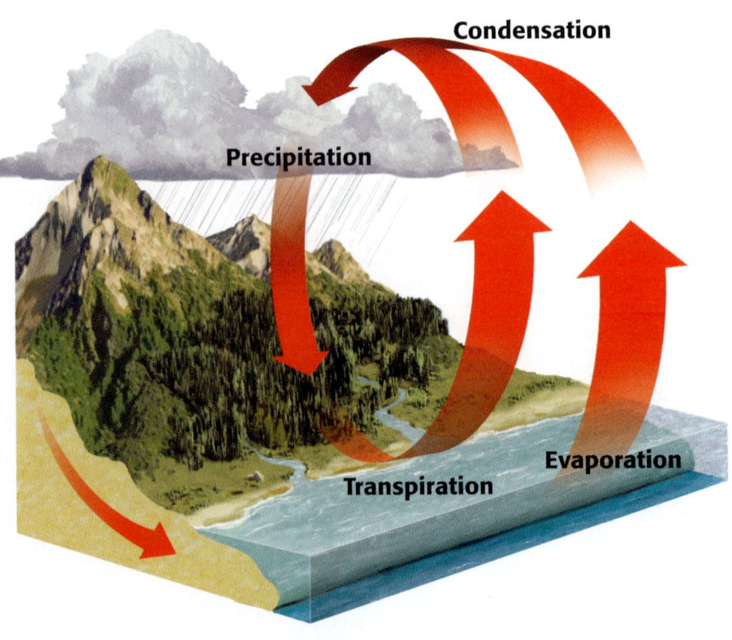

Figure 10
Evaporation, transpiration, condensation, and precipitation make up the continuous process called the water cycle.

Evaporated water vapor condenses to form precipitation

Figure 11

This frog depends on the humidity in its environment.

Evaporation occurs when sunlight strikes water in lakes, rivers, and the soil. Additional water travels to the air through **transpiration.** During transpiration, plants lose moisture through small pores in their leaves. While transpiration may seem insignificant, the addition of water vapor to the atmosphere can be large. For example, a 1 km^2 cornfield typically transpires 3 40 0000 L (900 000 gal) of water per day.

In the atmosphere, water vapor rises until the air is cool enough to condense the vapor into tiny droplets of water. We observe these droplets as clouds. As clouds cool and condense more vapor, they often release their moisture in the form of **precipitation.** Most precipitation falls as rain, snow, hail, or sleet. Precipitation can occur over land or water. When precipitation falls on land, it stays on the surface until it evaporates, flows into a larger body of water, or is absorbed into the ground to become *ground water.*

transpiration the process by which plants release water vapor into the air through stomata

precipitation any form of water that falls to Earth's surface from the clouds

humidity the amount of water vapor in the air

Air contains varying quantities of water vapor

You have probably noticed that air doesn't always feel the same. Sometimes it is thick and moist, while at other times it is crisp and dry. The air around you contains varying amounts of water vapor, and you experience the effects of changing **humidity,** or the quantity of moisture in the atmosphere. Some animals depend on this humidity as shown in ***Figure 11.***

Relative humidity is the actual quantity of water vapor present in the air compared with the maximum quantity of water vapor that can be present at that particular temperature. In weather forecasts, the relative humidity is usually given as a percentage. A relative humidity of 85% means that the air contains 85 percent of the water that it can contain at that temperature. Air that has a relative humidity of 100% is said to be *saturated.*

Warmer temperatures evaporate more water

As illustrated in ***Figure 12,*** the temperature of the air determines the air's maximum water vapor content. At warm temperatures, molecules move very quickly and are farther apart. Thus, the water is more likely to exist as a gas. As the temperature decreases, the water molecules slow down. At these slower speeds, the attractive forces between water molecules have a greater effect, and the molecules may condense into a liquid.

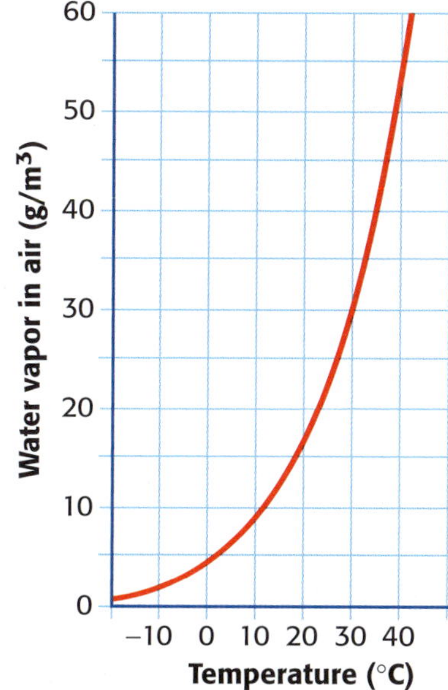

Figure 12

Warm air can hold more water vapor than cold air can.

Water vapor becomes liquid at dew point

The exact temperature at which water vapor molecules slow enough to form liquid water is called the **dew point.** Dew point depends on humidity. When the humidity is high, there are more molecules of water in the air and it is easier for them to form liquid water. So the higher the humidity is, the higher the dew point is. In fact, we can measure humidity by finding the dew point. You may have seen drops of water, or condensation, on a glass of ice water. The cold surface of the glass provides a place where the dew point is reached, and water shifts from gas to liquid.

dew point the temperature at which air or a gas begins to condense to a liquid

Clouds form as warm, moist air rises

You may know from walking through fog—a low-lying cloud—that clouds are wet. Clouds are formed when warm air rises and water vapor condenses into tiny droplets of liquid as it cools. This process usually occurs in the troposphere. Clouds are made up of tiny droplets of liquid water and, at higher altitudes, small ice crystals. Depending on where clouds form, they can have many different shapes and characteristics.

Figure 13

Clouds are classified by their form and the altitude at which they occur.

Cloud names describe their shape and altitude

Figure 13 shows the different kinds of clouds that can occur. Cloud names describe both their appearance and the altitude at which they occur. Different types are named using combinations of the three root words *cirrus, stratus,* and *cumulus.*

Cirrus clouds are thin and wispy, and they occur at high altitudes—between 6 km and 11 km (3.7–6.8 mi) above Earth. Stratus clouds are sheetlike and layered. These clouds typically form at lower altitudes—less than 6 km. Cumulus clouds are white and fluffy with somewhat flat bottoms. The flat base is the point at which rising air begins to condense. Cumulus clouds form at various altitudes—anywhere from about 500 m to about 12 km (7.5 mi) above Earth.

Cloud names reflect combined characteristics

Cloud names reflect the combined characteristics of each cloud type. *Cirrostratus* clouds are high, layered clouds that form a thin white veil over the sky. *Altostratus* and *altocumulus* clouds are simply stratus and cumulus clouds that occur at middle altitudes. When a cloud name includes the root *nimbo* or *nimbus,* the cloud is the type that produces precipitation. Cumulonimbus clouds are towering rain clouds that often produce thunderstorms. Nimbostratus clouds are large, gray clouds that often produce steady precipitation.

You may have seen a halo around the sun or moon. This halo results from the refraction of light as it passes through ice crystals in cirrostratus clouds. Sometimes the presence of a halo is the only way to tell that a very thin, transparent layer of cirrostratus clouds is present.

Quick ACTIVITY

Measuring Rainfall

1. Set an empty soup can outside in the open, away from any source of runoff. At the same time each day, use a metric ruler to measure the amount of rain or other precipitation that has accumulated in the can.
2. Record your measurements. Keep a record of the precipitation in your area for a week.
3. Listen to or read local weather reports to see if your measurements are close to those given in the reports.

Air Pressure

The term **barometric pressure** is often used in weather reports in the newspaper and on television. Changes in barometric pressure often accompany changes in the weather. Falling pressure may indicate a large air mass is leaving the area, while rising pressure can mean an air mass is moving in. The barometric pressure, also called *atmospheric pressure* or *air pressure,* is the pressure that results from the weight of a column of air extending from the top of the thermosphere to the point of measurement.

Instruments used to measure air pressure are called barometers. ***Figure 14A*** is a photo of a *mercury barometer,* and ***Figure 14B*** shows an *aneroid barometer.* Aneroid barometers do not contain liquid and are more portable than mercury barometers, but mercury barometers are more accurate.

barometric pressure the pressure due to the weight of the atmosphere; also called air pressure or atmospheric pressure

A **Mercury barometer**

B

Figure 14

A Mercury barometers measure the weight of the air, which is also called *barometric pressure.*

B Aneroid barometers do not contain liquid and are less accurate than mercury barometers.

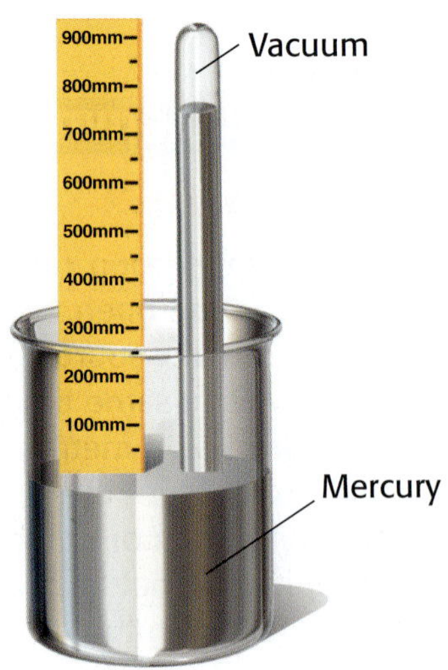

Figure 15

The height of the mercury in the tube of a mercury barometer indicates the barometric pressure in millimeters.

INTEGRATING

HEALTH

Just as air exerts pressure on the objects around it, blood in your body exerts pressure against the walls of your arteries. To measure a person's blood pressure, a cuff is wrapped around the upper arm and a stethoscope is placed over the arteries of the forearm. Air is pumped into the cuff until the pressure exerted by the cuff stops the flow of blood.

The doctor or nurse then listens to the person's pulse as air is let out slowly until the pressure in the cuff is less than the blood pressure when the heart contracts. This pressure is called the *systolic* pressure.

More air is released until the pulsing of the heart is no longer audible. The pressure at this point, called the *diastolic* pressure, is the blood pressure when the heart relaxes.

Barometers measure air pressure

Figure 15 shows how a simple mercury barometer works. The mercury barometer contains a long tube that is open at one end and closed at the other. The tube is filled with mercury and then inverted into a small container of mercury. Some but not all of the mercury spills out of the tube and into the container. The atmosphere exerts a pressure on the mercury in the container, holding some of the mercury in the tube to a height above the mercury in the container. Any change in the height of the column of mercury means that the atmosphere's pressure has changed.

At sea level, the barometric pressure of air at 0°C is around 760 mm of mercury. This amount of pressure is defined as 1 atmosphere (1 atm) of pressure. The SI unit for pressure is the pascal (Pa), which is equivalent to one newton per square meter.

Aneroid barometers are more commonly used. The word *aneroid* means "without liquid." This type of barometer contains a sealed metal chamber from which part of the air has been removed. When the air pressure changes, the chamber expands or contracts, moving a needle on a dial.

Wind

Have you ever seen a movie in which an airplane window gets broken? When the window breaks, all the loose objects in the plane are pushed out the window. Although it is unlikely that an airplane window would actually break, the portrayal of objects flying out the window is correct.

Differences in pressure create winds

Commercial airplanes fly very high in the troposphere, between 10 km and 13 km above Earth. At this altitude, the air is not very dense and the atmospheric pressure is very low. However, because of pressurization by pumps, the pressure inside the airplane is relatively high—similar to the air pressure at Earth's surface.

If an airplane window were to break, the dense air in the plane's cabin would spread out into the less-dense air outside the cabin. The airflow produced in this situation would push loose objects out the window.

Just as a difference in air pressure would create airflow from inside the airplane to the outside, differences in pressure in the atmosphere can cause wind. When air pressure varies from one place to another, a pressure gradient exists. The air in a *pressure gradient* moves from areas of high pressure to areas of low pressure. This movement of air from a high-pressure area to a low-pressure area is called wind.

Earth's rotation affects the direction of winds

The direction in which wind moves is influenced by Earth's rotation. The effect of Earth's rotation on the direction of wind is described by the **Coriolis effect.** To understand how the Coriolis effect works, you must first understand that points at different latitudes on Earth move at different speeds as Earth rotates. Consider two houses at different latitudes. A house located on the equator travels faster than a house located near one of the poles. Can you see why this must be true? Earth goes through one full rotation in 24 hours. During this time, the house at the equator must travel the distance of Earth's circumference. Closer to the poles, a circle of latitude is smaller. Therefore, the house closer to the pole moves through a shorter distance in the same amount of time. Thus, this house moves more slowly.

Imagine a cannonball in a cannon at the equator. The cannonball is moving along with Earth as it rotates. The cannonball's speed at this time is a little greater than 1610 km/h (1000 mi/h) to the east—the speed at which all points on the equator move because of Earth's rotation. When the cannonball is fired to the north, it continues to move east at about 1610 km/hr. As the cannonball moves farther north, however, the portion of Earth beneath the cannonball is moving more slowly. The result is a flight path like the one shown in ***Figure 16*** where the cannonball's path appears to curve eastward.

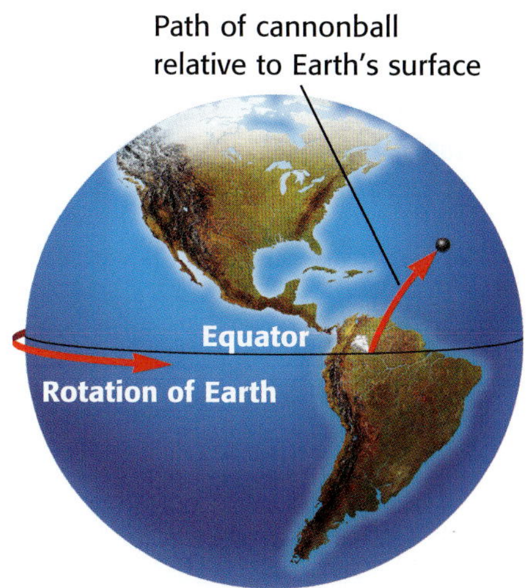

Figure 16

Because of Earth's rotation, a cannonball fired directly north from the equator will curve to the east relative to Earth's surface.

Coriolis effect the curving of the path of a moving object from an otherwise straight path due to Earth's rotation

Predictable air circulation forms wind patterns

The movement of winds is analogous to the cannonball's movement. When moving north in the Northern Hemisphere, winds curve to the right. Conversely, winds moving south in the Southern Hemisphere curve to the left. Next consider air moving south from the North Pole. The wind would lag behind the rotation of Earth and travel west, or to the left on the figure at right because it has a slower speed than the spinning Earth. Similarly, wind moving north from the South Pole would travel west, or to the left, because of its slower speed.

In summary, *winds in the Northern Hemisphere curve clockwise, and winds in the Southern Hemisphere curve counterclockwise.* The resulting circulation patterns are so regular that meteorologists have named them as shown in ***Figure 17.***

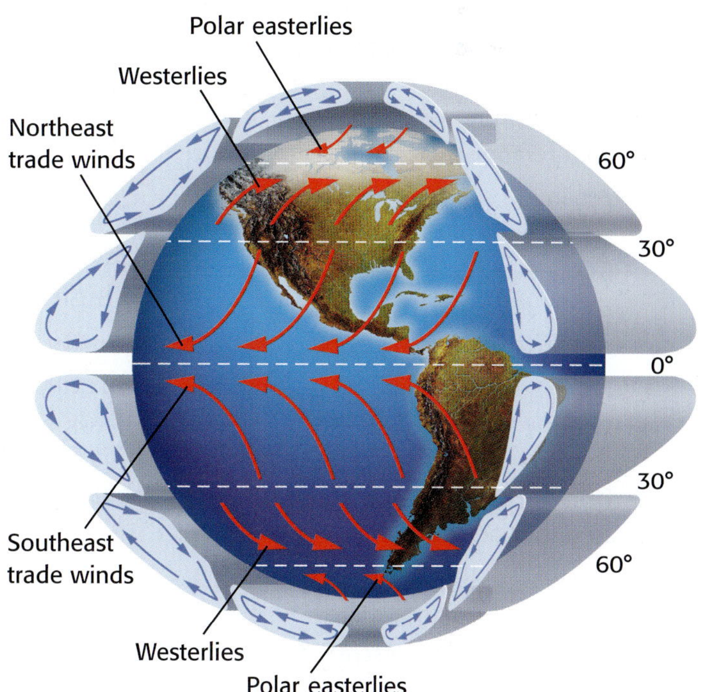

Figure 17

Both the Northern Hemisphere and the Southern Hemisphere have three wind belts.

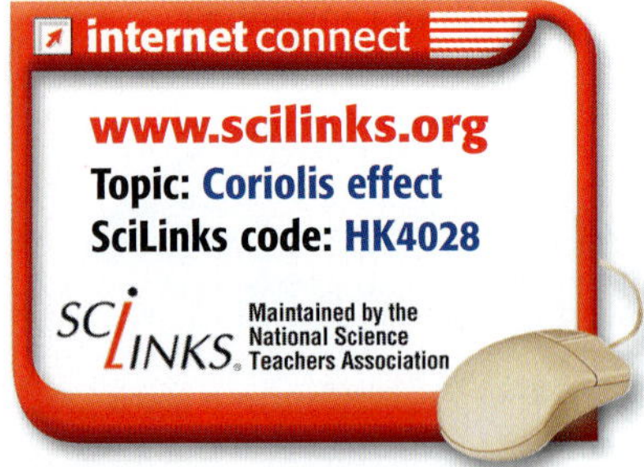

Global wind patterns form circulation cells

Note that the wind patterns shown in ***Figure 17*** move in vertical loops. Because temperatures at the equator tend to be warmer than at other latitudes, the air there rises and creates a low-pressure belt. As this warm air rises, it moves toward the poles.

In the Northern Hemisphere, much of the northward-moving air sinks at about 30° latitude, forming a high pressure area near Earth's surface. Flowing from a high-pressure area to a low-pressure area, air flows both north and south. At about 60° latitude, air flowing along the surface from the polar high and the high pressure band at 30° converge. As these air masses converge, air rises, forming a low-pressure belt.

A similar circulation pattern, in which rising warm air is coupled with sinking cold air, occurs in the Southern Hemisphere. Thus, air in each of the hemispheres completes three loops, called *cells*.

SECTION 2 REVIEW

SUMMARY

- In the water cycle, water from oceans and lakes evaporates and rises in the atmosphere. After it cools and condenses, the water falls back to Earth as precipitation.
- Warm air can contain more water vapor than cold air.
- Clouds are classified according to their appearance and the altitude at which they occur. ***Figure 13*** summarizes the various types of clouds.
- Wind is caused by the air in a pressure gradient moving from a high-pressure area to a low-pressure area.
- Earth's rotation affects the direction of winds. This phenomenon is described by the Coriolis effect.

1. **Identify** which one of the following processes is not a step in the water cycle:
   a. evaporation **c.** photosynthesis
   b. condensation **d.** precipitation
2. **Determine** whether wind moving north from the equator will curve eastward or westward due to the Coriolis effect.
3. **Distinguish** between humidity and relative humidity.
4. **Select** which one of the following describes a cumulus cloud:
   a. sheetlike
   b. fluffy, white, and flat-bottomed
   c. wispy and feathery
   d. high altitude
5. **Identify** which one of the following statements describes a mercury barometer:
   a. less accurate than an aneroid barometer
   b. contains a chamber that has a lot of water inside
   c. the height of the mercury in the tube indicates the barometric pressure
   d. more commonly used than aneroid barometers
6. **Predict** which of the following would be a more humid area: the Sahara Desert on a cold night or the Florida coast on a warm day.
7. **Critical Thinking** Which has a lower pressure, the air in your lungs as you inhale or the air outside your body?

SECTION 3

Weather and Climate

OBJECTIVES

- **Describe** the formation of cold fronts and warm fronts.
- **Describe** various severe weather situations, including thunderstorms, tornadoes, and hurricanes.
- **Distinguish** between climate and weather.
- **Identify** factors that affect Earth's climate.

KEY TERMS

air mass
front
climate
topography

How is a weather forecast made? *Meteorologists,* people who study weather, gather data about weather conditions in different areas. By using weather maps, meteorologists can try to predict weather by tracking the movement of air pockets called **air masses.** Interactions between air masses have predictable effects on the weather in a given location.

air mass a large body of air where temperature and moisture content are similar throughout

Fronts and Severe Weather

You have probably heard about *cold fronts* and *warm fronts*. A **front** is the place where a cold air mass and a warm air mass meet. Examine the weather map in ***Figure 18A.*** Cold fronts are shown as a blue line with blue triangles. Warm fronts are shown as a red line with red semicircles. Clouds, rain, and sometimes snow can occur at fronts. When fronts move through an area, the result is usually precipitation, as shown in ***Figure 18B,*** and a change in wind direction and temperature.

front the boundary between air masses of different densities and usually different temperatures

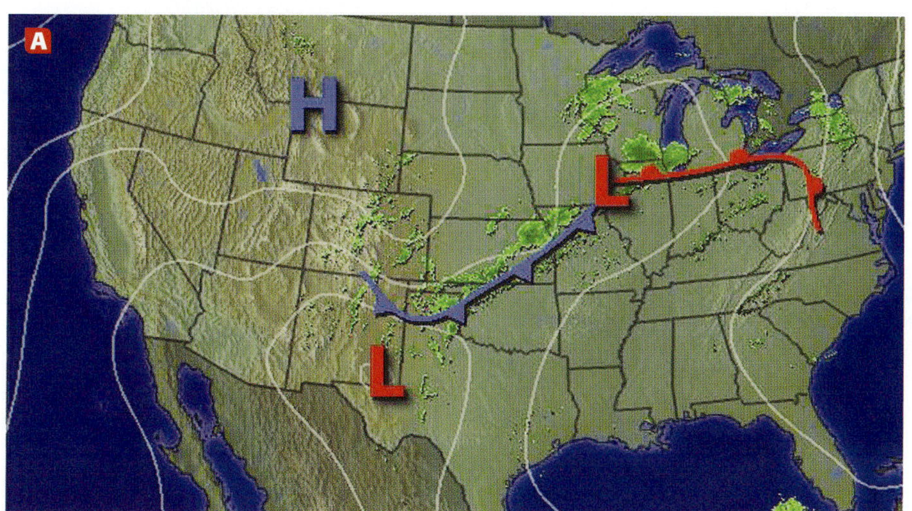

Figure 18
A Weather maps can give you a large-scale view of the weather.
B People also experience weather on a very local level.

INTEGRATING

PHYSICS

Large bodies of water regulate local climates because water has a high specific heat. Even though Minneapolis, Minnesota, and Portland, Oregon, are at about the same latitude, they have very different climates. The difference is caused by the Pacific Ocean. During winter months, the ocean does not get as cold as the surrounding air. As a result, Pacific winds warm the Oregon coastline.

In summertime, the Pacific Ocean does not get as warm as the surrounding air, and Pacific winds cool Portland.

There are three types of fronts

In a warm front, a mass of warm air moves toward and over a slower mass of cold air, as shown in ***Figure 19A.*** As the warm air is pushed up over the cool air, it cools and forms clouds.

Cirrus and cirrostratus clouds can be seen high in the sky as a warm front approaches. As time passes, lower-lying clouds move overhead. Often, nimbostratus clouds release steady rain or snow for one to two days.

With a cold front, the forward edge of a mass of cold air moves under a slower mass of warm air and pushes it up, as shown in ***Figure 19B.*** Note that the front edge of the cold front is steeper than that of the warm front shown in ***Figure 19A.*** Because of this steep edge, warm air rises quickly, forming cumulonimbus clouds. High winds, thunderstorms, and sometimes tornadoes accompany this type of front.

A *stationary front* occurs when two air masses meet but neither is displaced. Instead, the air masses move side by side along the front. The weather conditions near a stationary front are similar to those near a warm front.

Figure 19

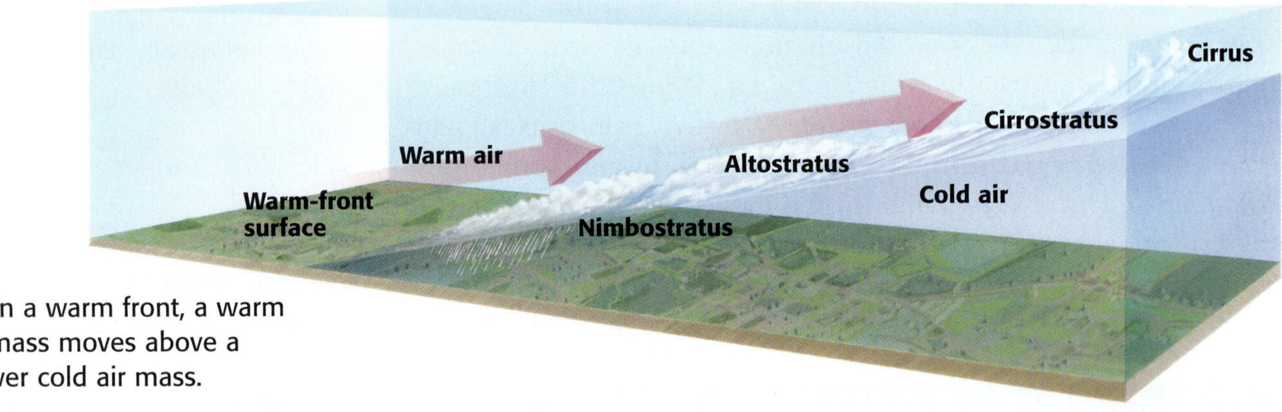

A In a warm front, a warm air mass moves above a slower cold air mass.

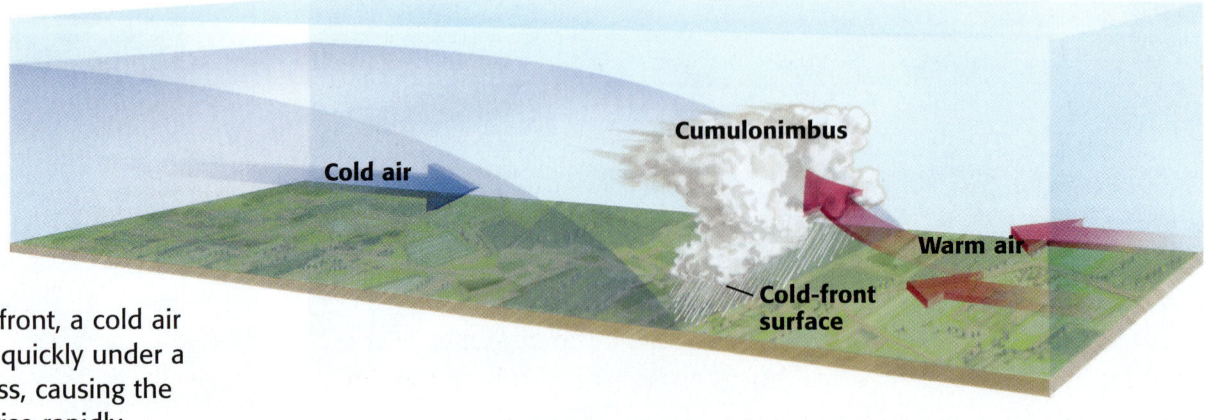

B In a cold front, a cold air mass moves quickly under a warm air mass, causing the warm air to rise rapidly.

Calculating the Distance to a Thunderstorm How can you tell if lightning is close by? The distance can be determined by counting the seconds between the lightning flash and the sound of thunder. This time lag occurs because light travels faster than sound. Count the seconds between the flash of lightning and the thunder, and use the following calculation:

time (s)/3 = distance (km)
time (s)/5 = distance (mi)

Applying Information

1. You see lightning and begin counting. When you reach the count of 3, you hear thunder. How far away was the lightning?
2. At 3:37:45 P.M., you see lightning strike. You hear thunder at 3:38:03 P.M. How many miles away did the lightning strike?

Lightning is a discharge of atmospheric electrical energy

Lightning is a big spark. Water droplets and ice crystals in thunderclouds build up electrical charges. Often, sparks jump between clouds or between clouds and Earth to equalize the charge. Thunderstorms can be exciting, but they can also be very dangerous if lightning strikes the ground near you. Lightning superheats the air so fast that the air expands faster than the speed of sound. The shockwave created is thunder.

Tornadoes are funnels of high-speed wind

Tornadoes like the one shown in ***Figure 20*** are high-speed, rotating winds. Tornadic winds are the most violent winds on Earth with speeds thought to be as great as 500 km/h (about 310 mi/h). Tornadoes occur most commonly in the United States, especially in the Midwest and along the Gulf of Mexico. They occur during spring and early summer, and typically form along a front between cool, dry air and warm, humid air. As warm air rises, more air rushes in to replace it. This air sometimes begins to rotate as it rises and can spawn a tornado.

Typically a tornado begins as a column of water droplets, called a *funnel cloud,* that reaches down from dark storm clouds with heavy rain and lightning. As the funnel reaches the ground, it begins sucking objects upward. The rotating winds on the outer edge of a tornado can tear apart homes and trees. Tornadoes are too fast and unpredictable to attempt to outrun, even if you are in a car. If you see a tornado, move to a storm cellar or basement, or lie flat under a table at the center of a room with few windows. If you are outside, lie in a ditch or low-lying area, and cover your head with your hands.

Figure 20

A tornado such as this one in Pampa, Texas, is seen as a rapidly spinning funnel cloud.

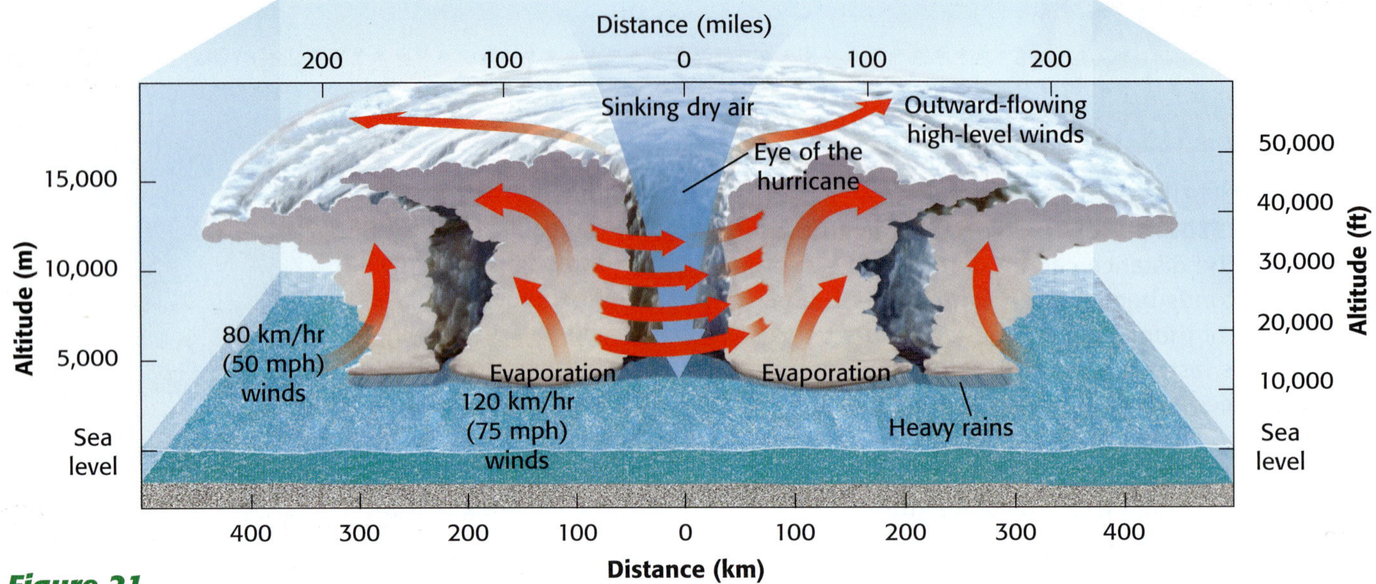

Figure 21

Hurricanes are nearly circular in shape and rotate around a center called the eye as shown in this cross section.

Hurricanes are large storm systems

Hurricanes are similar to thunderstorms but are much larger. These storms are called *hurricanes* in North America and the Caribbean, *cyclones* in the Indian Ocean, and *typhoons* in the western Pacific. In the Northern Hemisphere, hurricanes occur in late summer and early fall, when the oceans are warmest. As the warm water evaporates and the water vapor rises, intense low-pressure areas called *tropical depressions* form. These tropical depressions can build strength and become hurricanes. As shown in ***Figure 21,*** hurricanes are large circulating masses of clouds, wind, and rain with diameters of about 600 km (373 mi).

Hurricanes are powered by the energy released as water vapor condenses to form clouds. As the vapor condenses, it releases heat into the air, the air heats and expands, and the pressure inside the clouds decreases. Warm, moist air continues to rise and condense, releasing more energy. This rising air creates fierce winds, shown by the red arrows in ***Figure 21.*** The storm gradually weakens as it moves over land or cool water.

Although hurricanes move fairly slowly, they are extremely powerful. Winds in a hurricane reach speeds from 118 km/h (73 mi/h) to greater than 250 km/h (155 mi/h). The eye of the hurricane is very calm. This can be very dangerous because people often believe the storm has passed and leave the protective cover of their homes only to be caught in the storm again.

climate the average weather conditions in an area over a long period of time

Did You Know?

In the Northern Hemisphere, the winds and clouds in a hurricane rotate counterclockwise around the center, or eye, of the hurricane. In the Southern Hemisphere, hurricanes rotate clockwise. The direction of rotation is caused by Earth's rotation as described by the Coriolis effect.

Climate

Weather changes day to day, but **climate** does not change. Climate is the *average* weather of a region, often measured over many years.

Temperatures tend to be higher close to the equator

Figure 22 shows sunlight striking Earth. Rays striking farther from the equator spread out over a greater area and are less concentrated than rays that strike the equator. At the poles, rays pass parallel to Earth's surface and do not warm the atmosphere as much. Hence, the poles are very cold. Earth is not always oriented so that the equator is perpendicular to incoming solar radiation. However, the equator is close to perpendicular throughout the year. Because of this, areas close to the equator have warmer climates.

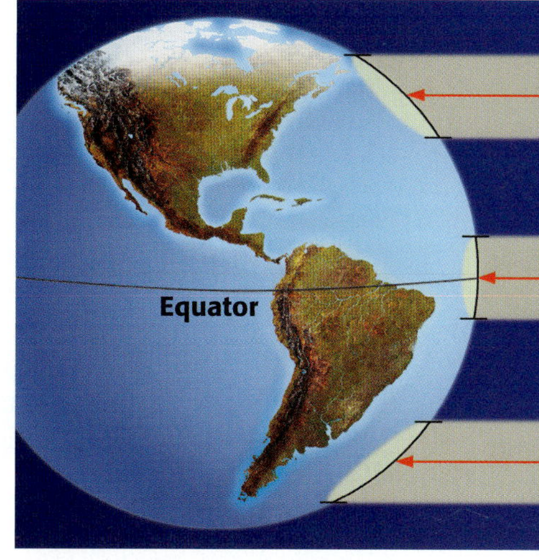

Figure 22

Solar energy is more concentrated at the equator than at the poles because Earth's surface is curved.

Earth's tilt and rotation account for our seasons

In summer months, the days are longer and warmer. In winter months, the days are shorter and colder. Why do we experience these differing conditions? Earth's orbit is an ellipse, and you might expect that summer is when Earth is closest to the sun. This is not true. In fact, Earth is farthest from the sun on July 4 and closest to the sun about January 3. Earth's seasons are actually caused by the tilt of Earth on its axis. As shown in ***Figure 23,*** Earth's axis is tilted 23.5° from the perpendicular to the plane of the planet's orbit about the sun. Because of this tilt, the sun seems to rise to different heights in different seasons.

When the North Pole is tilted toward the sun, as in position *A* in ***Figure 23,*** the sun rises higher in the Northern Hemisphere than when the North Pole is pointed away from the sun. The days become longer and the temperature increases. This is summer in the Northern Hemisphere and winter in the Southern Hemisphere. Our longest day of the year is the *summer solstice,* which occurs around June 21.

When the South Pole is tilted toward the sun, as in position *C* in ***Figure 23,*** the sun rises higher in the Southern Hemisphere. It is summer in the Southern Hemisphere and winter in the Northern Hemisphere. Our shortest day of the year occurs on December 21, which is called the *winter solstice.*

At positions *B* and *D,* Earth's axis is tilted neither away from nor toward the sun. Day and night are of equal length all over Earth. The day on which this happens is called an equinox. Position *D* corresponds to the *vernal* (spring) *equinox,* which occurs around March 21. Position *B* occurs about September 22 and is called the *autumnal* (fall) *equinox.*

Figure 23

This illustration (not to scale) shows that Earth's axis is tilted 23.5° from the perpendicular to the orbital plane. The direction of tilt of Earth's axis remains the same throughout Earth's orbit.

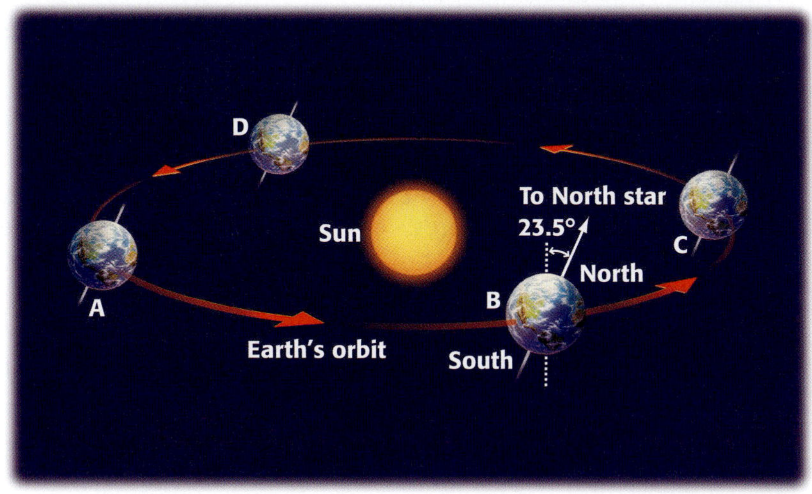

topography the configuration of a land surface, including its relief

Earth's surface features affect climate

The rise and fall of a land surface is called **topography.** Variations in Earth's topography affect the climate of a region. Mountains can have a profound effect on the climate of an area. As air rises over a mountain, it cools, and clouds form. When mountains are near oceans, as shown in ***Figure 24,*** the air is so humid that the clouds cannot hold all of the water vapor, and precipitation results. On the other side of the mountain, cool, dry air warms as it descends. Deserts often form and are said to lie in a rain shadow. Broad flat surfaces, such as the Great Plains, do not stop wind flow. Winds can come from several directions and merge on the plains. This mixing of wind produces thunderstorms and even tornadoes.

Figure 24

Air passing over a mountain loses moisture as it rises and cools. This dry air warms as it descends.

Global climate changes over time

From the early atmosphere to the many ice ages, Earth's climate has varied greatly over time. Many factors, such as the movement of the continents and slight changes in Earth's tilt, have produced these changes. The greenhouse effect may increase and temperatures could rise. Volcanic eruptions may produce gases that reflect solar energy, causing cooling. Because of all these factors, Earth's climate is likely to continue to change over the millennia to come.

SECTION 3 REVIEW

SUMMARY

- A warm front forms as warm air moves over slower cold air. A cold front forms as cold air moves under slower warm air.
- Lightning is a discharge of electrical energy.
- Tornadoes are high-speed rotating winds that form around rising warm air.
- Hurricanes are large storm systems that have high-speed winds and very low pressures.
- Climate is the average weather of a region over time.
- Some factors that affect climate are latitude, seasons, and topography.

1. **Determine** whether each of the following statements describes a warm front or a cold front:
   - **a.** A warm air mass moves above a slower cold air mass.
   - **b.** It is characterized by high winds and thunderstorms.
   - **c.** A cold air mass moves quickly under a slower-moving warm air mass.
   - **d.** It is characterized by steady rain.
2. **Distinguish** between thunder and lightning.
3. **Identify** which of the following would not have an effect on the climate of a nearby region:
   - **a.** a mountain range
   - **b.** the equator
   - **c.** a thunderstorm
   - **d.** the Atlantic Ocean
4. **Determine** whether a tornado is more likely to form along a cold front or a warm front.
5. **Critical Thinking** Grapes grow well in areas where the climate is generally mild. Would you recommend planting grapes on the California coast or on the plains of North Dakota? Explain your answer.

Math Skills

Percentages

Relative humidity is the amount of water vapor in the air divided by the maximum amount of water vapor that can remain in air at the same temperature. Relative humidity is usually expressed as a percentage. If air at 35°C can contain 40.0 g/m^3 of water vapor, what is the amount of water vapor actually present if the relative humidity is 65%?

1 List all given and unknown values.

Given: relative humidity, 65%

maximum amount of water in air, 40.0 g/m^3

Unknown: actual amount of water in air (g/m^3)

2 Write down the equation for relative humidity, and rearrange it so you can calculate the actual amount of water in the air.

$$relative\ humidity = \frac{actual\ water\ in\ air}{maximum\ water\ in\ air} \times 100$$

$$actual\ water\ in\ air = \frac{relative\ humidity \times maximum\ water\ in\ air}{100}$$

3 Solve for the actual amount of water in the air.

$$actual\ water\ in\ air = \frac{65 \times 40.0\ g/m^3}{100} = 26\ g/m^3$$

Therefore, 26 g of water vapor is actually present in each cubic meter of air at a temperature of 35°C.

Practice

Following the example above, calculate the following:

1. If the maximum amount of water vapor in air at 15°C is 12.5 g/m^3, what is the actual amount of water vapor in the air if the relative humidity is 85.0%?
2. If, at a relative humidity of 60.0%, the actual amount of water vapor in air at 30°C is 18.0 g/m^3, what is the maximum amount of water vapor in the air?
3. If the maximum amount of water vapor in air at 20°C is 17.0 g/m^3, and the actual amount of water vapor in the air is 14.0 g/m^3, what is the relative humidity?

CHAPTER 22 REVIEW

Chapter Highlights

Before you begin, review the summaries of the key ideas of each section, found at the end of each section. The key vocabulary terms are listed on the first page of each section.

UNDERSTANDING CONCEPTS

1. Almost all the water vapor in the atmosphere is in the
a. exosphere. **b.** ionosphere. **c.** stratopause. **d.** troposphere.

2. CFCs, chemicals that are used as refrigerants and propellants in spray cans, are partly to blame for the reduction of ________ in the stratosphere.
a. carbon dioxide **b.** oxygen **c.** ozone **d.** clouds

3. Clouds form when water vapor in the air condenses as
a. the air is heated. **b.** the air is cooled. **c.** snow falls. **d.** snow forms.

4. When air temperature drops, the air's ability to contain water vapor is
a. slightly higher. **b.** much higher. **c.** about the same. **d.** lower.

5. Winds in the Northern Hemisphere curve clockwise because of
a. CO_2. **b.** climate. **c.** the Coriolis effect. **d.** CFCs.

6. Cumulonimbus and nimbostratus clouds both
a. appear white and fluffy.
b. produce precipitation.
c. occur at high altitudes.
d. look thin and wispy.

7. When a moving warm air mass encounters a mountain range, it
a. stops moving. **b.** slows and sinks. **c.** rises and cools. **d.** reverses direction.

8. Electrons in the ________ reflect radio waves.
a. mesosphere **b.** ionosphere **c.** radiosphere **d.** mesosphere

9. Which one of the following is not a part of the water cycle?
a. precipitation **b.** condensation **c.** transpiration **d.** humidity

10. ________ are created when air masses of different temperatures meet.
a. Wind storms **b.** Weather systems **c.** Air masses **d.** Fronts

USING VOCABULARY

11. Explain how carbon dioxide in the atmosphere relates to the *greenhouse effect.*

12. How is *ozone* formed?

13. Describe the *water cycle* using the terms *precipitation, condensation, transpiration,* and *evaporation.*

14. Using the terms *humidity* and *dew point,* explain why you might find small droplets of water on your lawn in the morning.

15. Describe the formation of a warm *front.*

16. Explain the difference between *weather* and *climate.*

17. Describe the relationship between air temperature and *humidity*.

18. Define *barometric pressure,* and describe how it affects weather.

19. Distinguish between a *tornado* and a *funnel cloud.*

20. Explain how a storm becomes a hurricane using the terms *hurricane, tropical depression,* and *winds.*

21. Write a paragraph which discusses how seasons change using the terms *tilt, rotation, solstice,* and *equinox.* Explain the differences between seasons in the Northern Hemisphere and seasons in the Southern Hemisphere. WRITING SKILL

22. Describe two factors that can cause global changes in *climate.*

23. Explain *respiration* and its role in photosynthesis.

BUILDING MATH SKILLS

24. **Climatography** Visual aids called climatographs are used to display information about the climate of a specific region. Using the climatograph for Moscow, Idaho, in the figure below, answer the following questions:
    - **a.** What was the average temperature in Moscow during August?
    - **b.** What was the total precipitation in the Moscow area for the month of January?
    - **c.** What was the approximate total precipitation for the year?

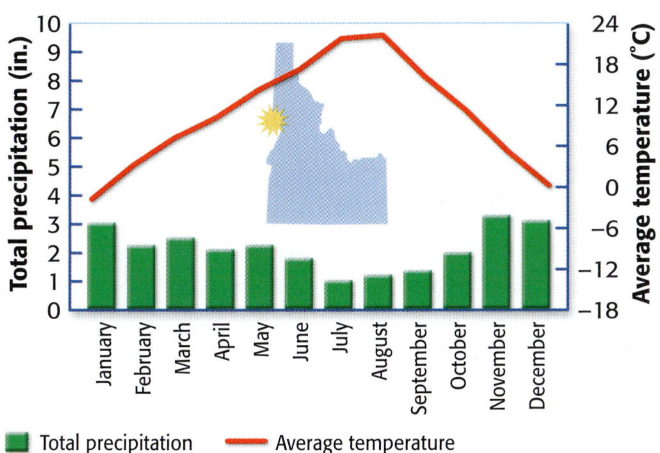

BUILDING GRAPHING SKILLS

25. Research the average rainfall in your city, area, or state for each month of the year. Using this data, create two different kinds of graphs. Decide which graph is better for clearly representing the information. Include both of your graphs with a short paragraph explaining which one you would use in a presentation.

THINKING CRITICALLY

26. **Creative Thinking** Describe how your life would be changed if global temperatures were to increase by several degrees.

27. **Critical Thinking** Is it safe to be on the street in an automobile during a tornado? Explain your answer.

28. **Acquiring and Evaluating Data** Find out the local high and low temperatures for each day of a 2 week period. Using a computer spreadsheet program, graph the data and find the average high and low temperatures. COMPUTER SKILL

29. **Acquiring and Evaluating Data** Research the debate concerning global warming. What evidence supports global warming, and what evidence calls it into question? Write one paragraph describing each side of the debate. Then, write a third paragraph examining the limitations of the scientific data and describing how scientists are trying to predict what will happen in the future. WRITING SKILL

30. **Critical Thinking** What evidence do scientists have that Earth's climate has changed over time? How can this evidence help scientists study changes our climate is making now?

31. **Interpreting Graphics** Use the weather map shown below to name three states that have a cold front moving through them. Predict what kind of weather they can expect.

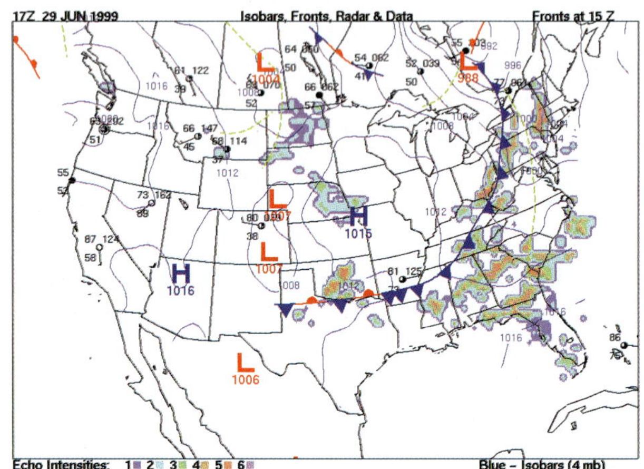

DataStreme Project, American Meteorological Society

DEVELOPING LIFE/WORK SKILLS

32. **Working Cooperatively** Obtain a week's worth of local or national weather maps from the paper or the Internet. In a small group, prepare a weather forecast. Interpret the daily weather, and follow any trends. Explain pressure areas and the resulting fronts, any precipitation, and average temperatures. Have a volunteer from your group present the forecast to the class.

33. **Acquiring and Evaluating Data** WRITING SKILL Contact or research a news source, and find out about the satellites it uses to predict the weather. Write a short paragraph describing how satellites help predict the weather and climate.

INTEGRATING CONCEPTS

34. **Concept Mapping** Copy the unfinished concept map below onto a sheet of paper. Complete the map by writing the correct word or phrase in the lettered boxes.

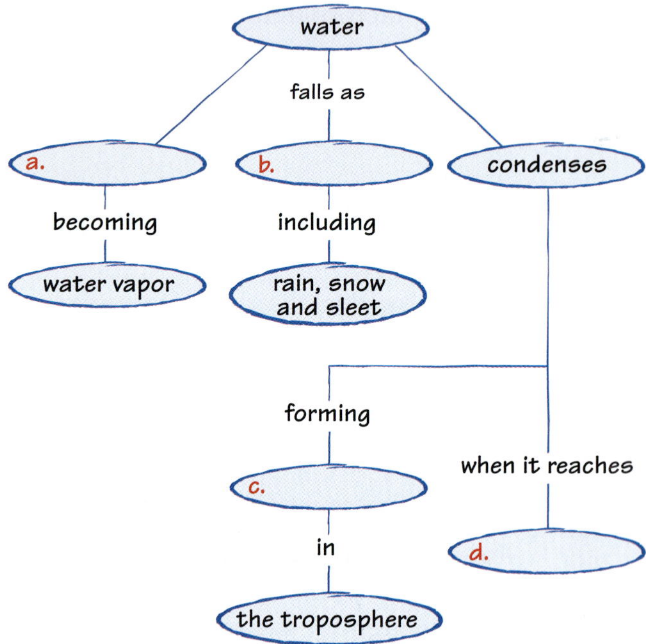

35. **Concept Mapping** Create your own concept map using one or two sections of this chapter. Copy your concept map on a piece of paper, leaving some cells blank. Swap concept maps with members of your small group, and discuss any difficulties that may arise.

36. **Connection to Chemistry** Research the effects of methane on the atmosphere. How is methane produced? What are some sources of methane in the atmosphere? What is its effect on global warming? Can we eliminate methane from the atmosphere?

Standardized Test Prep

Understanding Concepts

***Directions (1–3):* For *each* question, write on a separate sheet of paper the letter of the correct answer.**

1 During a temperature inversion, which of these can trap polluted air close to the ground?

A. acid rain
B. ocean breezes
C. thunder clouds
D. warm air layer

2 What is the main substance added to the atmosphere by the combustion of fossil fuels that may contribute to global warming?

F. carbon dioxide
G. CFCs
H. oxygen
I. petroleum

3 What causes the seasonal variations in climate that occur on most of Earth's surface?

A. the variations in distance from the sun
B. the difference in the amount of solar energy striking the equator and the poles
C. the variations in solar energy due to the tilt of Earth's axis relative to the orbital plane
D. the redistribution of energy around the surface of Earth by ocean currents and winds

***Directions (4–5):* For *each* question, write a short response.**

4 Even though animals use oxygen in the atmosphere, the amount of oxygen available remains constant. Analyze how the carbon dioxide-oxygen cycle maintains the ratio of gases needed for life to exist on Earth.

5 In general, climates are cooler near the poles and warmer near the equator. Given this observation, why are some mountains near the equator covered with snow year-round?

Test TIP

Slow, deep breathing may help you relax. If you suffer from test anxiety, focus on your breathing in order to calm down.

Reading Skills

***Directions (6):* Read the passage below. Then answer the question.**

The climate and weather inside a city are often very different from that of surrounding rural areas. Buildings and pavement absorb more energy from the sun, and activities such as transportation and industry produce additional heat. The temperature in a city can be as much as 10°C higher than the temperature outside of the city. This heat contributes to increased smog and changes precipitation patterns. As people have become aware of these "heat islands," they are taking measures to reduce the heat island effect, such as using light colored roofs to reflect heat, and planting trees and other plants to absorb solar energy.

6 How could planting gardens on the roofs of buildings in cities help reduce the effect of heat islands?

Interpreting Graphics

***Directions (7):* Base your answer to question 7 on the illustration below.**

7 Which of the following results from the situation shown in the illustration?

F. coastal rains as warm air rises
G. inland rains as cool air descends
H. rain on both sides of the mountain
I. dry climate on both sides of the mountain

Skills Practice Lab

Measuring Temperature Effects

Introduction

Air rises or sinks in Earth's atmosphere due to differences in buoyancy related to changes in the density of air that are caused by differences in temperature. How can you determine the effect of temperature on the buoyancy of air?

Objectives

- Measure the volume of a constant mass of air at different temperatures.
- USING SCIENTIFIC METHODS ***Draw conclusions*** by inferring changes in buoyancy and density from changes in volume.

Materials

400 mL beaker
60 mL disposable syringe
glycerin
hot and cold tap water
ice
petroleum jelly
thermometer

Procedure

Preparing for Your Experiment

1. On a blank sheet of paper, prepare a table like the one shown below.

Temp. (°C)	Pull volume (mL)	Push volume (mL)	Average volume (mL)

2. Measure the air temperature in the room, and record the temperature in your data table.
3. Remove the cap from the tip of the syringe, and move the plunger. If the plunger does not move smoothly and easily, lubricate the inside wall of the syringe with a few drops of glycerin.
4. Adjust the position of the plunger until the syringe is about two-thirds full of air. Add a dab of petroleum jelly to the tip of the syringe, and replace the cap.

Measuring the Volume of Air

5. Gently pull on the plunger, and then release it. When the plunger stops, read the volume of air inside the syringe. Record the volume in your data table in the column labeled "Pull volume."
6. With your finger on the cap, gently push on the plunger and then release it. When the plunger stops, read the volume of air inside the syringe. Record the volume in your data table in the column labeled "Push volume."
   SAFETY CAUTION Do not point the syringe at anyone while you push on the plunger. Wear safety goggles.

Designing Your Experiment

7. With your lab partners, decide how you will use the materials available in the lab to determine the effect of temperature on air density. Test at least two temperatures below room temperature and two temperatures above room temperature. It is important that the mass of air inside the syringe does not change during your experiment. How can you ensure that the mass of air remains constant?
8. In your lab report, list each step you will perform in your experiment.
9. Before you carry out your experiment, your teacher must approve your plan.

Performing Your Experiment

10. After your teacher approves your plan, carry out your experiment.
11. Record your results in your data table.
    SAFETY CAUTION Use care when working with hot water; it can cause severe burns.

Analysis

1. At each temperature you tested, calculate the average volume by adding the pull volume and push volume and dividing the sum by 2. Record the result in your data table.
2. Plot your data in your lab report in the form of a graph set up like the one at right. Draw a straight line on the graph that fits the data points best.

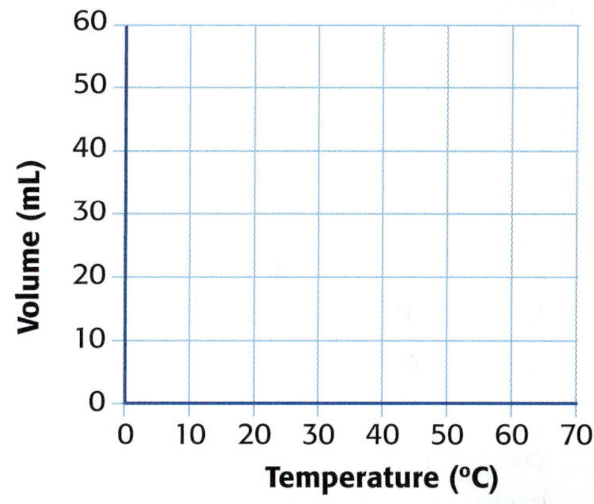

3. **Reaching Conclusions** How does the volume of a constant mass of air change as the temperature of the air increases? For the mass of air you used in your experiment, how much would the volume change if the temperature increased from 10°C to 60°C?
4. **Reaching Conclusions** Recall that the density of a substance equals the substance's mass divided by its volume. Do your results indicate that the density of air increases or decreases as the temperature of the air increases? Explain.
5. **Reaching Conclusions** Based on your results, would a body of air become more or less buoyant as it becomes colder than the surrounding air?

Conclusions

6. Suppose someone tells you that your conclusions are invalid because some of your data points lie above or below the best-fit line you drew. How could you show that your conclusions are valid?

viewpoints

Should Laws Require Zero-Emission Cars?

California has proposed laws to increase the number of zero-emission vehicles in the state. These vehicles emit no pollution or greenhouse gases. Automobile companies are developing electric cars and other technologies to meet these requirements.

Often these cars are substantially more expensive than gasoline-burning models. Is the pollution situation so desperate that this is necessary? Or is this a case of laws interfering with the car market?

> FROM: Sheneah T., Chicago, IL

As technology advances, we will be able to make better cars that won't depend on gas as much. If we were to cut down on the amount of pollution, this would make our environment better to live in. This goes back to an issue of public health. If cars emit less pollution, we would have fewer cases of respiratory disorders and a much cleaner environment.

Require These Cars Now

> FROM: Megan B., Houston, TX

A law requiring zero-emission vehicles is probably the best way to prevent air pollution. The various ways companies are changing cars to be more environmentally safe just isn't cutting it. Why do we spend tens of thousands of dollars for fun but not to help save the world?

> FROM: Kathryn W., Rochester, MN

I think the government should definitely get involved in these issues. The laws can be changed later, if needed, but we can't go back in time and fix the problem.

> FROM: Margo K., Coral Springs, FL

Although zero-emission vehicles are better for the environment, there are many expenses that come along with them. I disagree with the law because of the cost of the new vehicles. Rather than making zero-emission vehicles mandatory, if the idea is spread, people will act upon it.

Don't Require These Cars Now

> FROM: Marianne C., Bowling Green, KY

Not everyone will be able to afford these expensive cars. I don't think people should be obligated to buy cars to save the planet. People should do other things instead, like planting trees or carpooling.

> FROM: Amar T., Palos Park, IL

From a car enthusiast's point of view, I feel that no state should make zero-emission cars mandatory for three main reasons: First, at this time zero-emission cars do not perform as well as cars with an internal-combustion engine. Second, zero-emission cars, like electrical cars, have small cruising ranges, and their fuel cells take up too much space. Finally, they are more expensive than gasoline-burning cars.

Your Turn

1. **Critiquing Viewpoints** Select one of the statements on this page that you agree with. Identify and explain at least one weak point in the statement. What would you say to respond to someone who brought up this weak point as a reason you were wrong?
2. **Critiquing Viewpoints** Select one of the statements on this page that you disagree with. Identify and explain at least one strong point in the statement. What would you say to respond to someone who brought up this point as a reason they were right?
3. **Interpreting and Communicating** Imagine that you work for an advertising firm that has been hired to promote an expensive new zero-emission vehicle. Create an advertisement or brochure for the car that tries to persuade people to buy the new car.
4. **Understanding Systems** Other critics of such laws point out that zero-emission cars do not end the pollution entirely. Some toxic waste is made when these cars are manufactured. Write a paragraph in which you outline a method for deciding whether the pollution emitted by a regular car is worse for the environment than the waste made in making a zero-emission vehicle.

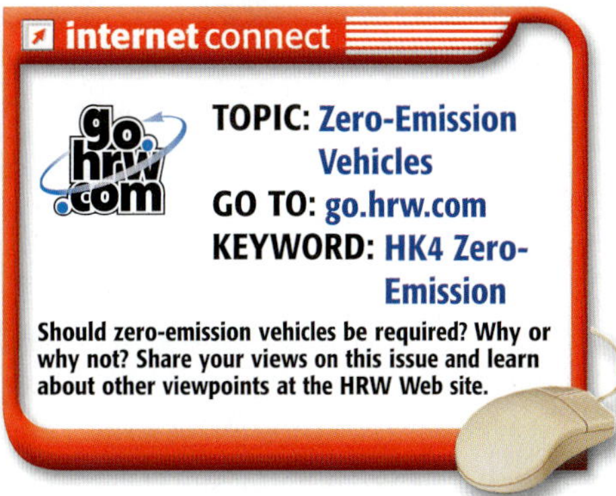

internet connect

TOPIC: Zero-Emission Vehicles
GO TO: go.hrw.com
KEYWORD: HK4 Zero-Emission

Should zero-emission vehicles be required? Why or why not? Share your views on this issue and learn about other viewpoints at the HRW Web site.

CHAPTER 23

Using Natural Resources

Chapter Preview

1 **Organisms and Their Environment**
- What Is an Ecosystem?
- Changes in Ecosystems
- Evaluating Changes in Ecosystems

2 **Energy and Resources**
- The Search for Resources
- Alternative Sources of Energy
- The Efficiency of Energy Conversion

3 **Pollution and Recycling**
- What Causes Pollution?
- Air Pollution
- Water Pollution
- Pollution on Land
- Reducing Pollution

The World Solar Challenge is held each year to raise awareness of alternative energy sources. Drivers travel 3000 km across Australia using solar-powered cars.

Focus ACTIVITY

Background The engines are started. The drivers check their gauges one last time. The flag rises, then falls. They're off!

Is this a typical race? Not quite. These race cars are powered by solar energy. Not a drop of gasoline is needed to make them run. Teams of college students designed and built the cars to compete in an annual event called Sunrayce.

Sunrayce began in 1990, and its goal is to raise awareness of alternative energy sources, such as the sun. Each summer, students travel more than 2093 km (1300 mi) across the United States in these solar-powered cars.

Solar-powered cars must be lightweight and efficient. Although the average race speed is about 35 mi/h, the cars can reach top speeds of 65 mi/h. Each car is powered by solar cells. These cells, which are made of thin layers of silicon, capture the sun's energy and store it in batteries.

Activity 1 Obtain a solar cell from an electronics store or your school's science lab. Using the solar cell, a low-wattage light bulb, and two pieces of insulated electrical wire, create a current in the cell and the bulb. Place the end of one wire on the metal bottom of the bulb and the end of the other wire on the side of the bulb. Place the other end of both wires on the solar cell. In your own words, describe the movement of charges between the cell and the bulb.

Activity 2 Make a list of the energy sources you use at home. Find out from your parents which source of energy costs the most per month. Make a pie chart showing your results. Call your local power company to find out what type of resource is used to generate electrical power.

Pre-Reading Questions

1. Where does energy come from?
2. What can be done to reduce pollution?

SECTION 1

Organisms and Their Environment

KEY TERMS

ecosystem
community
succession

OBJECTIVES

- **Explain** the structure of an ecosystem.
- **Describe** the effects one species can have on an ecosystem.
- **Discuss** two ways natural forces can change ecosystems.
- **Discuss** two ways humans can change ecosystems.

Should money be spent drilling for oil in the wilderness of Alaska, or would the money be better spent promoting solar power? Should a nearby swamp be drained to provide parking for a mall in your town, or is the swamp best left alone? No matter how you feel about these issues, you need to know how they will affect the world around you.

ecosystem a community of organisms and their abiotic environment

We humans, like all other living things, fill our needs by using natural resources. These resources are taken from the world around us. Every action taken, whether it is someone draining a swamp or a bird catching prey, affects all the other living things in the **ecosystem,** as shown in ***Figure 1.***

To evaluate the effects of your decisions on the issues that cause change in your environment, you must first understand how the many parts of an ecosystem relate to one another.

internet connect
www.scilinks.org
Topic: Ecosystem Factors
SciLinks code: HK4040
SCILINKS Maintained by the National Science Teachers Association

Figure 1

Each living and nonliving element in this desert ecosystem directly affects the others.

What Is an Ecosystem?

Consider a squirrel in a city park. The squirrel gathers and stores food. It lives in a tree and drinks water from a sun-dappled pond. The soil, trees, sunshine, and water are natural resources found within the city park. The city park itself is an ecosystem.

Living elements in an ecosystem can include plants, animals, and people. Nonliving elements include sunlight, air, soil, water, and temperature. Cycles of energy and matter are at the base of an ecosystem. The interrelated elements within a desert ecosystem are shown in ***Figure 1.*** The cactuses, sagebrush, lizards, snakes, scorpions, and birds interact with one another and with their surroundings to make a stable, balanced ecosystem.

internet connect
www.scilinks.org
Topic: Ecosystems
SciLinks code: HK4041
SCILINKS Maintained by the National Science Teachers Association

Not all ecosystems are the same size

Ecosystems can be large or small. The entire planet is one big ecosystem containing all the living and nonliving things on Earth—the land and water, the organisms, and the atmosphere. A shallow forest pool no bigger than a rain puddle is also an example of an ecosystem. This ecosystem is made up of water, mud, bacteria, mosquitoes, air, and larvae all living together.

community a group of species that live in the same habitat and interact with each other

Living things are adapted to their ecosystem

Living things are found almost everywhere: on land, in the air, and in water. Each organism has adapted to factors in its environment, such as temperature, humidity, and the other living things around it. For instance, polar bears are adapted to cold, wet places, and camels are adapted to hot, dry places. Neither animal could survive in the other's environment.

Ecosystems are divided into communities

All of the interacting animals and plants living in one area within an ecosystem form a **community.** There can be several communities in an ecosystem. The animals and plants of the tundra make up one community. The seals, fish, and algae of the nearby ocean make up another. Polar bears belong to *both* communities. ***Figure 2*** shows the different divisions within an ecosystem.

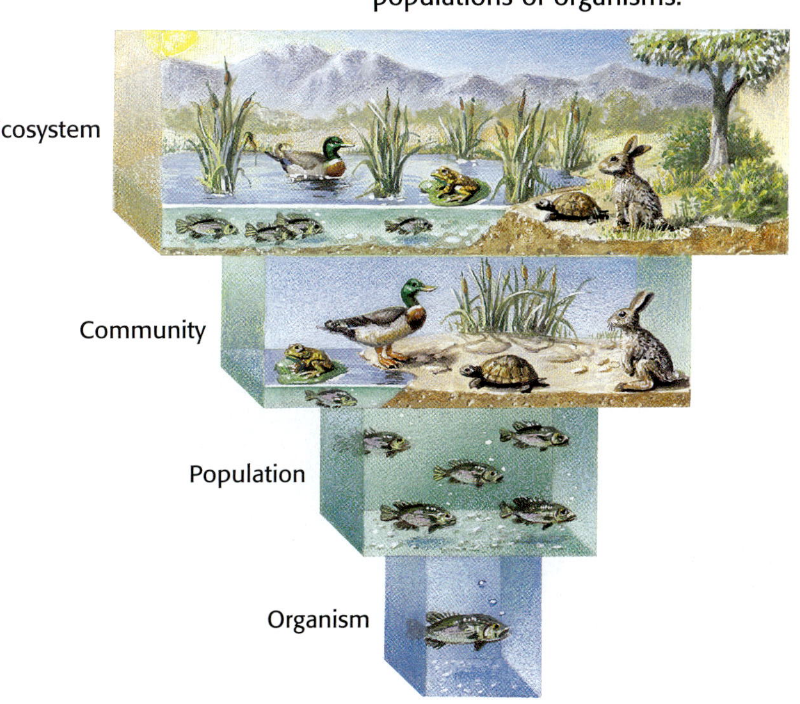

Figure 2

Ecosystems are made up of communities that contain different populations of organisms.

Figure 3

The living and nonliving elements of this aquarium ecosystem help to keep it balanced.

Changes in Ecosystems

Sunlight, water, air, soil, animals, plants—the elements that make up an ecosystem are numerous. Each element is balanced with the others so that the ecosystem can be maintained over a long period of time.

Look at the aquarium shown in ***Figure 3***. The amount of salt in the water and the temperature of the water are at the right levels. The fish, snails, and plants all have sufficient space and food. In short, there are enough resources for every living thing in the aquarium ecosystem. The ecosystem is balanced.

Balanced ecosystems remain stable

When an ecosystem is balanced, the population sizes of the different species do not change much relative to one another. Overall, there is a natural balance between those that eat and those that are eaten. Other factors, such as disease or food shortage, prevent populations from growing too much. If the balance within an ecosystem is disturbed, change results.

The graph in ***Figure 4*** is based on a Canadian study of the snowshoe hare and its predator, the lynx. What happened to the lynx population when there were fewer snowshoe hares?

When the prey population of a particular place decreases, there is less food for the predators. As a result, some of the predators die. On the other hand, if the prey population increases, more predators may move into the area. A variety of factors, including population change, can affect the balance in an ecosystem. What happens when one factor changes?

Figure 4

The population of snowshoe hares directly affects the population of lynxes.

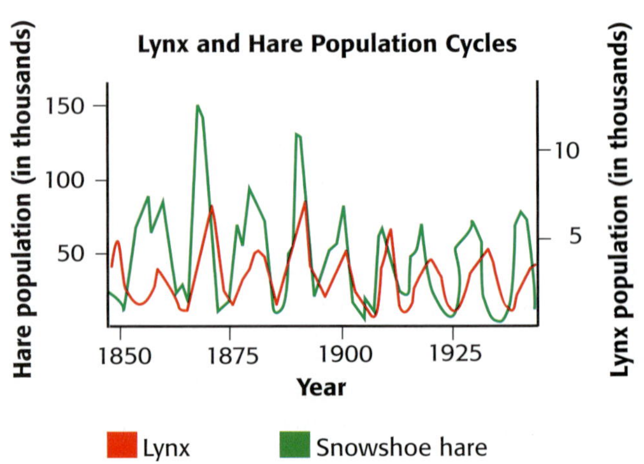

A change in one feature can affect the whole system

Throughout the 1990s, researchers closely watched a piece of land in Central America that was once a tropical rain forest. After the trees were logged, a species of wild pig vanished from the forest because the pigs no longer had enough food and shelter. Three species of frogs disappeared soon thereafter. Was this related to the loss of the wild pigs?

The pigs wallowed in mud, forming puddles that the frogs used for breeding. Suddenly there were no puddles, and the frogs had to find another place to breed. A change in one factor of an ecosystem can affect all the living and nonliving elements within the system.

The key to understanding ecosystems can be summed up in one word: *interrelatedness*. The elements that make up an ecosystem function together to keep the entire system stable. If something changes, time and natural forces often work to return the ecosystem to its previous state.

Ecosystems tend to gradually return to their original conditions

Yellowstone National Park is one of the largest tourist attractions in the United States. The park, located in northwestern Wyoming and southern Montana, covers about 2.2 million acres (3,472 mi^2) of land and is known for its active geysers and hot springs. Wildfire has had a role in the dynamics of this area for thousands of years, since long before it was a park.

But during the summer of 1988, large areas of the park were burned to the ground by fires, as shown in ***Figure 5A.*** The fires, which were started by lightning and careless human activity, spread quickly through the open forest during this particularly dry summer and left nearly a third of the park blackened with ash. Firefighters are often unsuccessful in putting out these fires. Frequently, it is rain or snow that eventually put the fires out.

The following spring, the appearance of the "dead" forest began to change. Large numbers of small, green plants began to flourish and replace areas that had been covered with fallen trees. Year after year, gradual developments took place in the recovering area, as shown in ***Figure 5B.***

Figure 5

A Yellowstone National Park has been plagued with a series of uncontrollable fires. In fact, nearly all of Yellowstone's plant communities have burned at one time or another.

B The following spring, new plant life flourished in the recovering park.

Figure 6

Different views of Glacier Bay, Alaska, show the types of change that took place over 200 years, as glaciers receded.

In time, a complex ecosystem will develop. This process, shown in ***Figure 6,*** is known as **succession.** The end product is a stable but complicated community where birth, death, growth, and decay take place continuously. This will keep the ecosystem stable if no major disruptions occur.

succession the replacement of one type of community by another at a single location over a period of time

Evaluating Changes in Ecosystems

Ecosystems undergo both short-term and long-term changes. Short-term changes are usually easily reversed, but long-term changes can take many years to be reversed, and sometimes may never be reversed at all.

Short-term ecosystem changes include the seasons

During autumn, many trees and shrubs lose their leaves. In the winter, many birds migrate to warmer places. Other animals hibernate by lowering their metabolism. These animals can sleep through the winter in snug burrows or caves. In spring, the migrating birds return, animals come out of hibernation, buds open, and seeds begin to sprout. As ***Figure 7*** shows, an ecosystem can appear quite different during different times of the year.

Figure 7

This area of forest looks quite different in the spring than it does in the winter.

Changes in climate cause long-term ecosystem changes

Figure 8
Icy glaciers covered much of North America and parts of Europe and Asia during the last ice age (approximately 20 000 years ago).

In your lifetime, the climate where you live probably hasn't changed much. Some years may be colder than others, but average monthly temperatures do not vary greatly from year to year. Throughout Earth's geologic history, there have been periods known as ice ages, when icy glaciers covered much of the continents. ***Figure 8*** shows the size of the glacier that covered much of North America during the last ice age. This period ended roughly 11 500 years ago.

During ice ages, temperatures are much colder than usual. These cold spells alternate with warmer periods. Scientists hypothesize that ice ages are caused by a variety of factors, including plate tectonics, changes in the tilt of Earth's axis, changes in the shape of Earth's orbit around the sun, and changes in the speed and pattern of the ocean's circulation.

The combined effect of these changes in Earth's position in space is difficult to predict. One thing we do know is that these changes cause temperature differences in ecosystems.

Long-term changes in ecosystems can also be caused by events such as volcanic eruptions. At other times, many small factors act together to cause change. In these cases, it may be hard to know how much each factor adds to the change. One example of this is the many and varied factors affecting global temperature change.

Why do seasons occur?

✔ *globe* ✔ *unshaded lamp*

1. Place the lamp on a table, and turn the lamp on.
2. Stand about 2 m from the table, and hold the globe at arm's length, pointing it toward the lamp.
3. Tilt the globe slightly so that the bottom half—the Southern Hemisphere—is illuminated by the lamp.
4. Keeping the axis of Earth's rotation pointing in the same direction, walk halfway around the table.

Analysis

1. What part of the globe is lit by the lamp's light now? What season does this represent in this part of Earth?
2. Would there be any seasonal changes if the Earth's axis were not tilted? Explain your answer.
3. In addition to experiencing seasonal changes, ecosystems also experience short-term changes as day changes into night. What movement of Earth causes night and day to occur?

Figure 9

Clearing trees, driving cars, constructing buildings, and farming are just a few human activities that cause changes in ecosystems.

Changes can be caused by human activity

Physical factors are not the only things that cause changes in ecosystems. People also alter the environment in a variety of ways, as shown in ***Figure 9.*** Activities such as logging, driving cars, growing crops, and constructing roads and buildings change the environment.

All of those activities have some benefits, but they also cause some problems. The benefits of some human activities, such as building dams, are numerous. For instance, the El Chocon Cerros Colorados project brought much-needed flood control to the foothills of the Andes Mountains in Argentina. Formerly, the rivers that flowed down from the mountains flooded twice each year. At other times the region was too dry to grow crops. The construction of a system of dams stopped this cycle. Excess water is now stored in large reservoirs behind the dams. This water is used for irrigation which allows farmers to grow crops year-round. In addition, the dam is used to generate hydroelectric power for much of the country.

Such large dams, however, can cause problems. Without the floods, rivers no longer deposit rich soil, so most farmers use chemical fertilizers on their crops instead. Runoff from these fertilizers can contaminate ground water and streams, making water supplies unsafe for humans and other living things.

Many of the adverse effects of dams constructed before the 1970s were not foreseen by their developers. Today scientists and engineers have a better understanding of how ecosystems work. Often, major projects such as constructing a dam must undergo an environmental analysis before construction begins. If the project is likely to destroy an entire ecosystem, it may have to be redesigned, relocated, or canceled altogether.

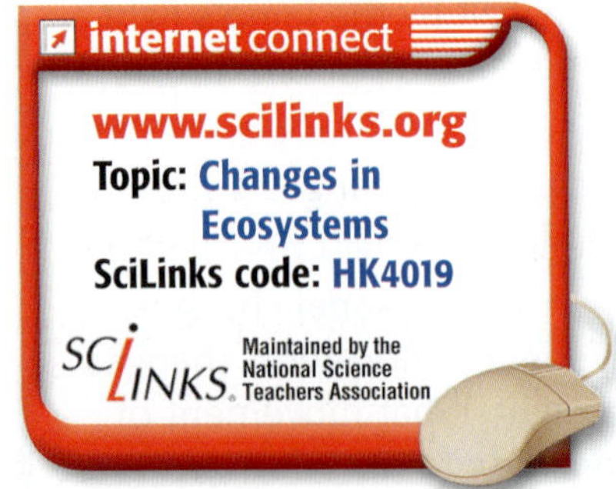

Changes can be caused by introduction of nonnative species

Some species move from one ecosystem to another on their own. Animals may migrate to new areas, and seeds can be carried by wind or water to different places. Humans often influence the spread of nonnative species to other ecosystems, sometimes accidentally and sometimes on purpose.

Starlings, for instance, were purposely brought to the United States. In the 1800s, a few dozen European starlings were released in New York City. The birds rapidly multiplied, and today there are millions of them across the United States.

Both starlings and native North American bluebirds nest in holes in tree trunks and fence posts, as shown in ***Figure 10.*** As a result, the two species compete for shelter. The bluebirds nearly lost the battle. Concerned citizens launched a multistate effort to build and distribute bird boxes. These boxes, specially designed with small entrances, provided nesting places for the bluebirds and kept the larger starlings out.

There are other ways in which unwanted organisms may be introduced to an ecosystem. For instance, small insects can be carried across borders accidentally. Often they are hidden in crates of fruit and vegetables.

In its new environment, the nonnative species may have no natural enemies to keep its numbers in check. As a result, its members can quickly multiply and modify an ecosystem. The new competing species may wipe out an existing native species and cause change in the ecosystem.

Figure 10
Starlings compete with bluebirds for nesting sites in the holes of tree trunks or fence posts.

SECTION 1 REVIEW

SUMMARY

- Living and nonliving elements form an ecosystem.
- The elements of an ecosystem maintain a balance. One change can affect an entire ecosystem.
- A disturbed ecosystem may return to its original state.
- Ecosystem changes can be short-term or long-term.
- Climatic changes, human activities, and nonnative species introduction can cause changes in ecosystems.

1. **List** two factors that keep populations stable.
2. **Analyze** the following statement: An ecosystem is like a fine-tuned car.
3. **Describe** how the loss of one species in a pond can affect other species.
4. **Define** *succession*.
5. **Predict** how a thunderstorm could lead to a long-term change in an ecosystem.
6. **List** two changes in the Earth's position in space that can affect climatic change in ecosystems.
7. **Critical Thinking** Describe a common human activity that can disrupt an ecosystem. Propose a solution to the problem.
8. **Critical Thinking** List several ways nonnative plants may be introduced to an environment.

SECTION 2

Energy and Resources

KEY TERMS

fossil fuel
nonrenewable resource
renewable resource
geothermal energy

OBJECTIVES

- **Identify** different sources of energy used by living things, and trace each source back to the sun.
- **Describe** the advantages and disadvantages of several energy sources.
- **Describe** the types of conversion processes necessary for different energy sources to produce electricity.
- **Identify** how efficient different conversion processes are.

You probably use more energy than you think you do. Energy is needed to light streets and homes, heat water and buildings, cook food, power vehicles, run appliances, and make the products you use every day. Where does all this energy come from?

The Search for Resources

We rely on natural resources to meet our basic needs for food and shelter. We also depend on natural resources to provide the energy and raw materials needed at home, at work, and for growing food. ***Figure 11*** compares the patterns of energy use in the United States with the patterns of energy use worldwide.

How Energy Is Used in the United States

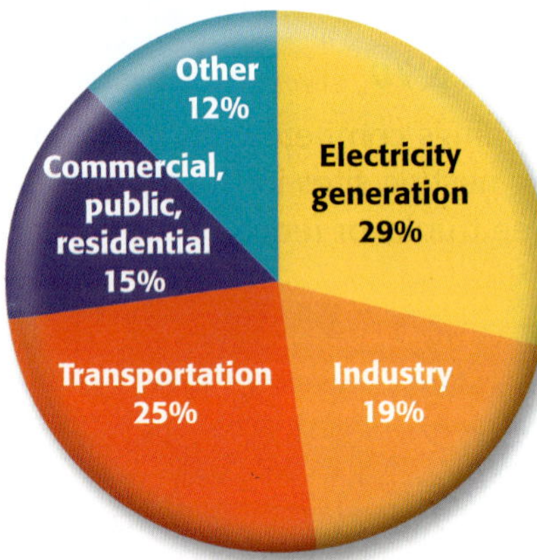

How Energy Is Used Worldwide

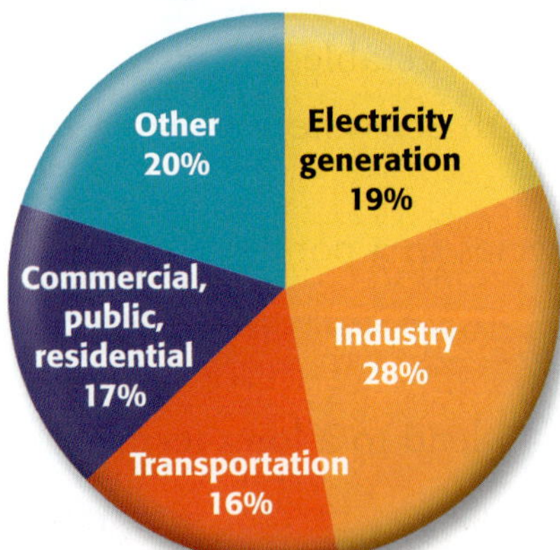

Source: Worldwatch Institute and U.S. Department of Commerce

Figure 11

These pie charts show how energy use in the United States compares with energy use worldwide. (Worldwide calculations include the United States.)

The sun is the source of energy

Almost all energy comes from the sun. The sun sends out energy as radiation of various wavelengths.

Plants convert energy from the sun into chemical energy

Plants use some of the energy from sunlight to change the simple molecules of carbon dioxide and water into oxygen and more complex molecules of simple sugars. This process is called photosynthesis. It allows plants to change the sun's energy into stored chemical energy.

Some animals eat plants to obtain energy. Through a series of chemical reactions, the animals are able to convert the sugars in plants back to carbon dioxide and water. This process, which also produces energy, is known as cellular respiration. This cycle of energy transfer repeats itself continuously in nature. ***Figure 12*** shows the interrelatedness of organisms processing and moving carbon dioxide through an ecosystem.

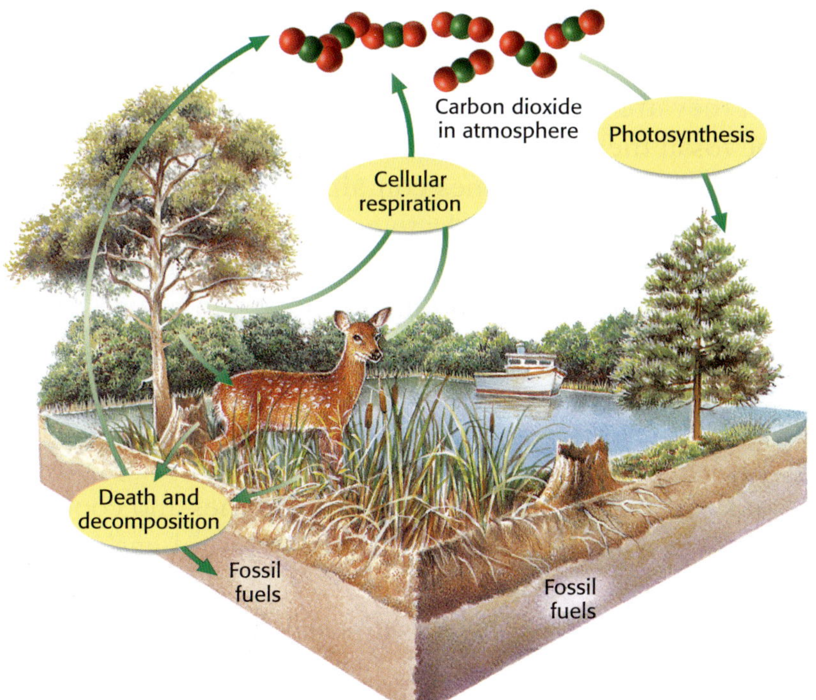

Figure 12

Carbon dioxide is a product of cellular respiration.

Fossil fuels form deep underground

Most living things cannot decompose and release their stored energy without air. For example, microscopic plants and animals living in the ocean die and are buried under layers of sediment where they are not in contact with air. Without air, the organic chemicals in the remains of the living things cannot combine with oxygen and change back to carbon dioxide and water. Instead, pressure and heat from the settled rock above the remains cause different chemical reactions. These reactions turn the organic chemicals into substances that contain mainly carbon and hydrogen, as shown in ***Figure 13.*** These substances are known as **fossil fuels.**

fossil fuel a nonrenewable energy resource formed from the remains of organisms that lived long ago; examples include oil, coal, and natural gas

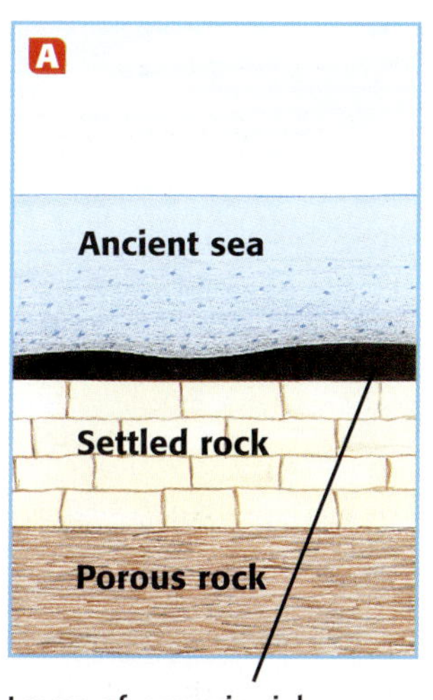

Figure 13

A Microscopic plants and animals collect in layers of mud forming an organic rich ooze.
B This organic rich layer is underlain and overlain by settled rock. Heat and pressure "cook" the ooze, causing oil to form.
C Geologic forces cause the rock layers to bend. The oil is forced out of its original layer, migrates into porous rocks, and is trapped.

Fossil fuels can be solids, liquids, or gases

Although substances such as natural gas, oil, and coal seem very different, they are all made of carbon and hydrogen molecules.

Some fossil fuels are mixtures of liquids and gases. Liquid oil and natural gas are sometimes contained in porous rocks. Wells must be drilled into these rocks to reach the fossil fuels.

Oil is a mixture of many different substances. It comes out of the ground as a tarlike black liquid. Before it can be used, it must be purified and separated. Refineries separate oil into gasoline, kerosene, diesel fuel, and other products. Oil formed in shallow oceans, as did natural gas.

Natural gas is made mostly of methane, a colorless, odorless, poisonous gas. It is often used for heating homes and cooking, as shown in ***Figure 14.*** In the United States, natural gas makes up 22% of the fossil fuels used.

Coal is a solid fossil fuel composed mainly of carbon. It formed in ancient swamps when the remains of large, fernlike plants were buried under layers of sediment.

Figure 14

Natural gas can provide the energy needed to prepare food.

Methane (CH_4)

The supply of fossil fuels is limited

When fossil fuels are burned, they form carbon dioxide and water and release energy. This energy is the energy of the sun that was trapped in plants hundreds of millions of years ago. Because fossil fuels take so long to form, they are considered **nonrenewable resources.** They are now being used by humans much faster than natural processes can replace them.

nonrenewable resource a substance that is consumed faster than it forms and therefore can not be replaced within a human life span

Figure 15A shows that the vast majority of the world's energy needs are met by the burning of fossil fuels. ***Figure 15B*** shows the estimated reserves of the world's supply of fossil fuels. If oil and natural gas use continue at current rates, the reserves may run out during your lifetime. What alternative sources of energy will provide the energy needed for everyday activities?

Figure 15

Although 84% of the world's energy is supplied by fossil fuels, oil and natural-gas reserves will soon run out.

A World Energy Sources

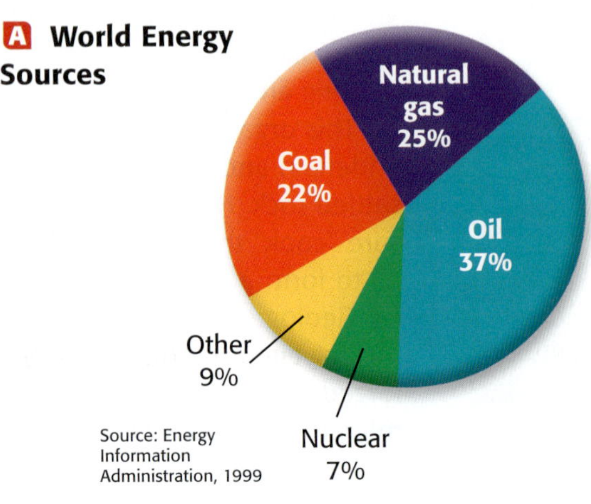

B World Energy Reserves

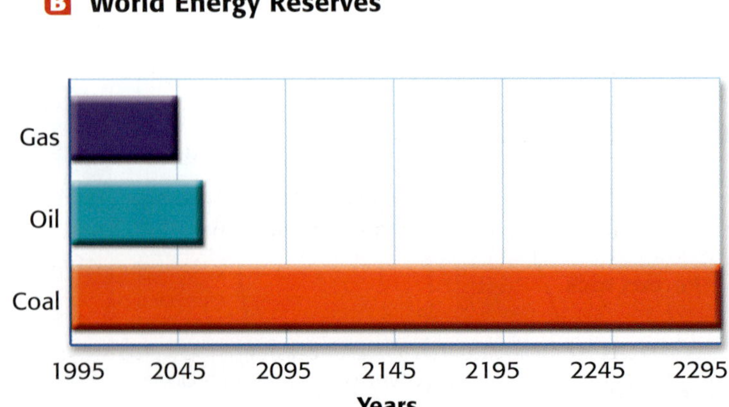

Alternative Sources of Energy

Fossils fuels are not the only energy source around. We can harness energy from the sun, wind, water, and Earth. We can even obtain energy from atoms. The more these alternative sources of energy are used, the less we will rely on fossil fuels.

Another advantage of using alternative sources of energy is that many are **renewable resources.** This means they can be replaced by natural processes in a relatively short amount of time.

renewable resource a natural resource that can be replaced at the same rate as it is consumed, such as food production by photosynthesis

Solar power plants and solar cells can make electricity from sunlight

Every day, the sun makes more energy than is used to supply electricity to the United States for a year. But harnessing the sun's energy to supply electricity is not simple. Some parts of Earth do not get as much sunlight as other parts. Even when there is enough sunlight, tools are needed to convert the sun's energy and change it into a useful form.

In the 1990s, the first solar power plant capable of storing energy as heat was opened in the Mojave Desert, in California. The solar panels of the power plant shown in ***Figure 16*** store the sun's heat and use it for energy.

Another tool used to harness the sun's energy is a solar cell, shown in ***Figure 17.*** Solar cells are able to produce electricity from sunlight. Although their use has been limited, the level of efficiency of these devices has greatly improved over the last two decades.

Figure 16

The Mojave Desert in California is home to the first solar power plant capable of storing heat.

The energy in wind can be used by windmills

Energy from the sun is a contributing factor in the production of another renewable energy resource —wind energy. Wind energy actually comes from the sun. Different places on Earth receive different amounts of sunlight, which causes variations in temperature. These temperature differences cause the movement of air, known as wind.

Wind is one of the oldest sources of renewable energy used by humans. It has been used to sail ships for thousands of years. As with other sources of energy, the use of wind energy has advantages and disadvantages. It can be unreliable. Even in exceptionally windy areas, wind doesn't blow steadily all the time. This can cause differences in the amount of power generated. However, the use of windmills is becoming increasingly popular in some areas because of their low cost.

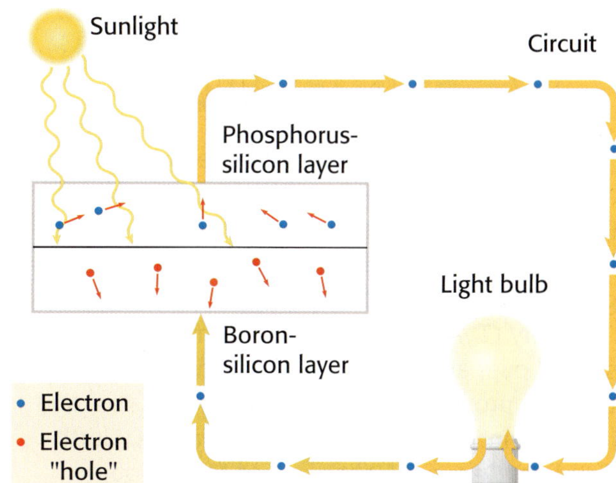

Figure 17

Solar cells convert sunlight directly into electricity.

Figure 18

The spinning blades of a windmill are connected to a generator. When the blades spin faster, the generator produces more energy.

Windmills have been used for over 1000 years. Today wind farms generate electrical power, as seen in **Figure 18.**

Moving water produces energy

Falling water releases a lot of energy, but even the energy produced from water depends on sunlight. For example, the water in oceans evaporates as sunlight transfers energy by heat. This water rises into the atmosphere, falls back down later as rain or snow, and flows downhill into creeks and rivers. Once the water is in the creeks and rivers, it flows back to the ocean, and the cycle begins again.

In hydroelectric power plants, dams are built on fast-moving rivers to create large holding places for water. **Figure 19** illustrates how the stored water pours through turbines, making them spin. The turbines are connected to generators that produce hydroelectric power, another type of renewable resource.

Dams have already been built on most of the world's big rivers, so the potential for increasing the use of this energy source is limited.

geothermal energy the energy produced by heat with the Earth

Connection to SOCIAL STUDIES

To aid the nation's economic recovery following the Great Depression, President Franklin D. Roosevelt proposed a series of projects aimed at increasing employment and serving the public good. One such project was the Tennessee Valley Authority (TVA), a connected system of 40 dams spread over an area of 106 000 km^2. The TVA system still provides electricity to homes, farms, and factories in Tennessee, Kentucky, Virginia, North Carolina, Georgia, Alabama, and Mississippi.

Making the Connection

Go to your local library and find a map showing the area that the TVA covers. Draw your own map showing all 40 dams.

Geothermal energy taps Earth's warmth

Under Earth's crust, reservoirs of steam or hot water produce **geothermal energy.** These holding pools usually lie near beds of molten magma, which heat the steam or water. Wells are drilled into the reservoirs, and the steam or hot water rises to the surface, where it is used to turn turbines to generate electrical power.

Figure 19
The incoming water causes the turbines in a dam to turn. The turbines run a generator that produces electricity.

Geothermal energy is a major source of electricity in volcanically active areas such as New Zealand, Iceland, and parts of California. Geothermal plants, such as the one shown in ***Figure 20,*** are common in these places. This type of energy works best when the beds of molten rock lie very close to Earth's surface. However, not many areas have magma beds close to the surface, so widespread use of this resource is unlikely.

Atoms produce nuclear energy

Atomic reactions produce a type of alternative energy resource called nuclear energy. Chain reactions involving nuclear fission produce a great deal of energy. This energy can be transferred as heat to water in a nuclear reactor. The heated water or steam can then be used to turn a turbine and generate electricity. Nuclear energy does not release pollutants into the air like the burning of fossil fuels does. However, harnessing nuclear energy produces highly radioactive waste.

Nuclear energy has seen limited use in the United States. It currently provides only 8% of our energy. Scientists working with nuclear fusion hope that it will someday be a useful and renewable resource. But so far, more energy is needed to sustain a fusion reaction than is produced by the reaction.

Figure 20
This geothermal plant in New Zealand produces electricity.

The Efficiency of Energy Conversion

Regardless of which energy resource we use, some usable energy is lost each time energy is converted to another form.

Energy is wasted when input is greater than output

In a coal-fired power plant, chemical energy is released when coal burns with oxygen in the air in a combustion reaction. This heat energy is transferred to water, which forms steam. Some energy is lost in this conversion. In order to obtain a high pressure, the steam is heated, and more energy is lost. The steam must be at a high pressure to provide the force to turn the huge steam turbines. This changes the energy into kinetic energy of the moving turbines.

The spinning turbines are connected to coils of large generators. These coils carry current and act as large electromagnets. As they spin, they generate a high voltage in the fixed coils surrounding them. The energy is now in the form of electrical potential energy. This causes a current that carries the electricity to local consumers through a cable. ***Figure 21*** shows a coal-fired power plant and a diagram of how electricity is produced in a typical power station.

A large power station might be rated at 1000 MW. This means that it delivers 1 billion J of energy every second. But three times the fuel, equal to 3 billion J, is needed because two-thirds of the energy input is wasted. Most power stations that use fossil fuels for energy are only 30 to 40% efficient, though newer models recycle waste heat, which increases efficiency.

Figure 21

This power plant converts coal into electrical energy.

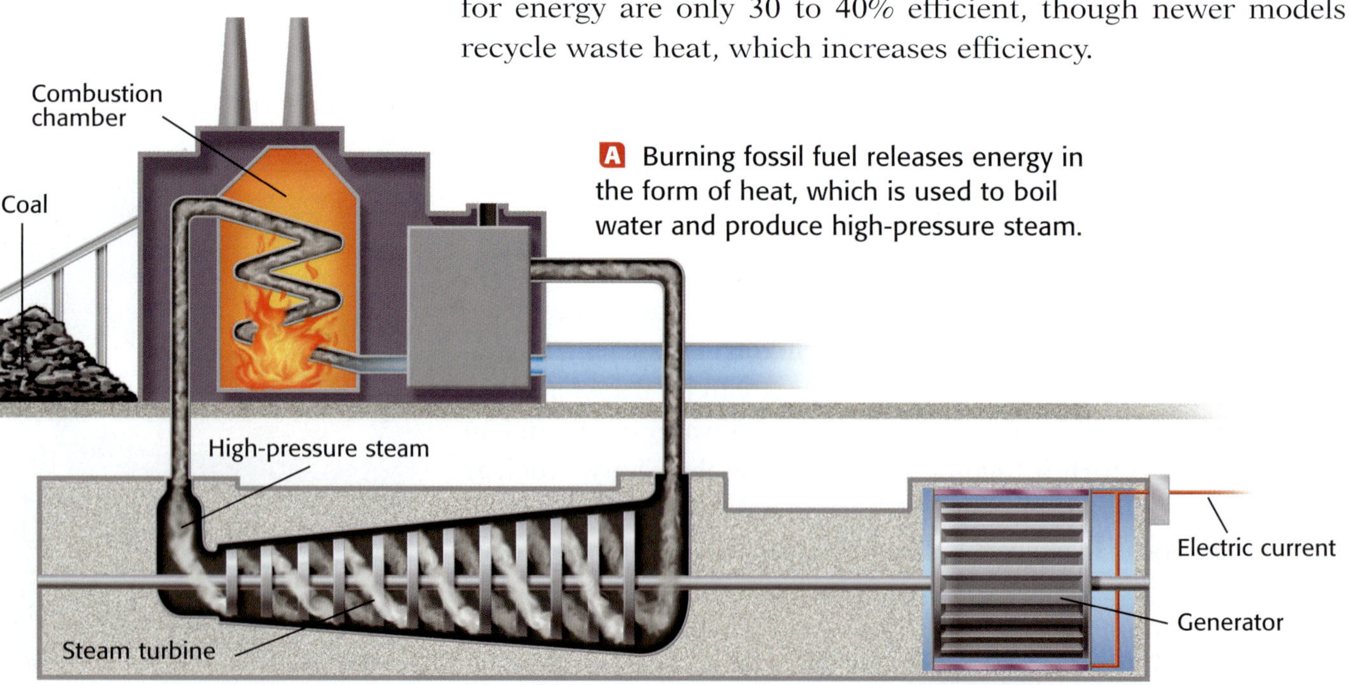

A Burning fossil fuel releases energy in the form of heat, which is used to boil water and produce high-pressure steam.

B The steam is directed against the blades of a turbine, which is set into motion.

C The turbine is connected to an electric generator. The turbine sets the generator in motion, generating electricity.

Wasted energy can be used

Some wasted energy occurs in the production of all types of energy sources. Nuclear power stations are roughly as efficient, or inefficient, as fossil-fuel power plants are. Both types of power plants produce waste. Even wind-powered plants have some inefficiency because of the energy conversions involved.

There are ways to make use of some of this wasted energy. For example, although the water from power stations is not hot enough to make electricity, it can be used to heat homes. In Germany, most towns have their own small power station. Rather than dump the warm water into a river, it is piped to people's homes to keep them heated. These are called combined heat and power schemes. They reduce wasted energy and make electricity less expensive.

SECTION 2 REVIEW

SUMMARY

- Most of the energy used in the world comes from fossil fuels, which are nonrenewable resources.
- Energy from the sun produces solar energy and wind energy.
- Hydroelectric power can be generated from large reservoirs of water. Moving water produces energy.
- Geothermal energy is generated from underground reservoirs in volcanically active areas.
- The use of nuclear energy has been limited in the U.S.
- Energy is lost each time it is converted to another form. Some wasted energy has the potential for use.

1. **List** five possible ways that you might use electricity during lunch.
2. **Describe** the cycle of energy transfer among organisms. Name the process that plants use to convert energy from the sun into chemical energy.
3. **Compare** the amount of energy used in the United States with the amount used worldwide. Write a paragraph explaining the social and economic reasons for the difference.

4. **Describe** some advantages and disadvantages of solar energy.
5. **Explain** in a paragraph the energy conversions that occur when a drop of rain falls on a mountain, rolls downhill, passes through a hydroelectric plant, and turns a turbine to generate electricity. WRITING SKILL
6. **Predict** which of the following will be more efficient in terms of capturing the most energy. Justify your answer.
   - **a.** burning paper to boil water to make steam to turn a turbine
   - **b.** using wind to generate electricity
7. **Critical Thinking** A classmate says that geothermal power is perfectly efficient because it never runs out. What's wrong with this reasoning?

Sun-Warmed Houses

Specially designed houses make use of the sun's heat in two different ways—passive solar heating and active solar heating.

How Does Passive Solar Heating Work?

In passive solar heating, no special devices are used. The house is simply built to take advantage of the sun's energy. For example, passive solar houses have large windows that face south, enabling them to receive a lot of sunlight throughout the day. Many have glass-enclosed fronts called sunspaces, which work to trap solar energy like glass in a greenhouse. During the winter, the energy that enters the sunspace keeps the room comfortably warm during the day. The floor is made of tiles that absorb heat and then radiate it out into the room throughout the evening.

How Is Energy Conserved in Passive Solar Heating?

The rest of the house still has to be heated in winter, but heating costs are generally much lower than they ordinarily would be. Some of the energy that would normally escape through an outside wall is kept inside because the sunspace acts as a good insulator.

Homes that take advantage of solar heating generally have lower electric bills.

On the north side of passive solar houses, there are only small windows in order to reduce energy loss. Also, the walls are built to be good insulators. Once the house is warm, its walls and furnishings act as a large "heat store," keeping the warmth inside.

How Does Active Solar Heating Work?

In active solar heating, houses use solar heaters—active solar-energy devices—to heat water or air. In solar heaters, a flat-plate collector is placed on the roof to gather sunlight. The collector is a flat box covered with glass or plastic. The bottom of the box is often painted black because dark colors absorb radiation better than light colors do. The collector gathers and traps heat, warming the air or water inside. The heated air or water flows into an insulated storage tank. Electric pumps or fans circulate the heated air or water throughout the house. Because they can store solar energy, active solar heating systems work 24 hours a day. However, during long periods of cloudy days, backup heating systems are necessary.

Your Choice

1. **Making Decisions** A house that uses fossil fuels for energy might cost its owners $1000 in heating expenses during the winter. An energy-efficient house could reduce this cost by 50 percent, but it might cost $10 000 more to build. Do you think the energy savings are worth the added construction cost? Explain your reasoning.
2. **Critical Thinking** What problem might people who live in houses with sunspaces have in the summer? How could they solve this problem?

SECTION 3

Pollution and Recycling

OBJECTIVES

- **Identify** several pollutants caused by fossil fuel use.
- **Compare** the economic and environmental impacts of using various energy sources.
- **Describe** types of pollution in air, in water, and on land.
- **Identify** ways to reduce, reuse, and recycle.

KEY TERMS

pollution
global warming
eutrophication
recycling

Think about the items in your classroom. You can probably identify ordinary items such as desks, lights, chalk, paper, pencils, backpacks, books, doors, and windows. Your classroom contains many products, all made from natural resources.

Making each product required energy. And the manufacture of nearly all of the products caused some kind of **pollution.** Whenever natural resources generate energy or become products, other things are usually made in the process. If these things are not used, they may be thrown out and cause pollution. Pollution is the contamination of the air, the water, or the soil, as shown in ***Figure 22.***

pollution an undesirable change in the natural environment that is caused by the introduction of substances that are harmful to living organisms, or by excessive wastes, heat, noise, or radiation

What Causes Pollution?

When you think of pollution, you may think of litter, such as that cluttering the water in ***Figure 22A.*** Or you may think of smog, the clouds of dust, smoke, and chemicals shown in ***Figure 22B.***

Pollution can be as invisible as a colorless, odorless gas or as obvious as bad-smelling trash left by the side of the road. Most forms of pollution have several common features. Understanding these features will help you make better choices.

Figure 22

A Trash polluted the water off the coast of Oahu, Hawaii.
B Contaminants polluted the air in Mexico City.

Table 1 Air Pollutants

Pollutant	Description	Primary Sources	Effects
Carbon monoxide	CO is an odorless, colorless, poisonous gas.	It is produced by the incomplete burning of fossil fuels. Cars, trucks, buses, small engines, and some industrial processes are the major sources of CO.	◆ Interferes with the blood's ability to carry oxygen ◆ Slows reflexes and causes drowsiness ◆ Can cause death in high concentrations ◆ Can cause headaches and stress on the heart ◆ Can hamper the growth and development of the fetus
Nitrogen oxides (NO_x)	When combustion (burning) temperatures are greater than 538°C (1000°F), nitrogen and oxygen combine to form nitrogen oxides.	NO_x compounds come from the burning of fuels in vehicles, power plants, and industrial boilers.	◆ Can make the body vulnerable to respiratory infection, lung disease, and possibly cancer ◆ Contribute to the brownish haze often seen over congested areas and to acid rain ◆ Can cause metal corrosion and the fading and deterioration of fabrics
Sulfur dioxide (SO_2)	SO_2 is produced by chemical interactions between sulfur and oxygen.	SO_2 comes from the burning of fossil fuels. It is released from refineries, smelters, paper mills, and chemical plants.	◆ Contributes to acid rain ◆ Can harm plant life and irritate the respiratory systems of humans and animals
Volatile organic compounds (VOCs)	VOCs are organic chemicals that vaporize readily and produce toxic fumes. They include gasoline and paint thinner.	Cars are a major source of VOCs. They also come from solvents, paints, glues, and burning fuels.	◆ Contribute to the formation of smog ◆ Cause serious health problems, such as cancer ◆ May harm plants
Particulate matter (particulates or PM)	Particulates are tiny particles of liquid or solid matter. Some examples are smoke, dust, and acid droplets.	Construction, agriculture, forestry, and fires produce particulates. Industrial processes and motor vehicles that burn fossil fuels also produce particulates.	◆ Form clouds that reduce visibility and cause a variety of respiratory problems ◆ Are linked to cancer ◆ Corrode metals, erode buildings and sculptures, and soil fabrics

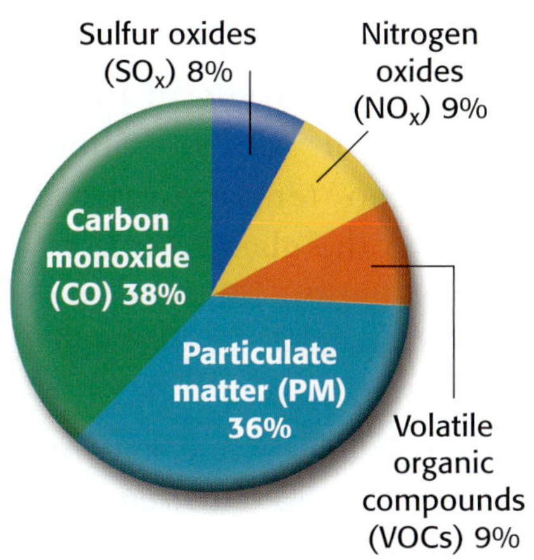

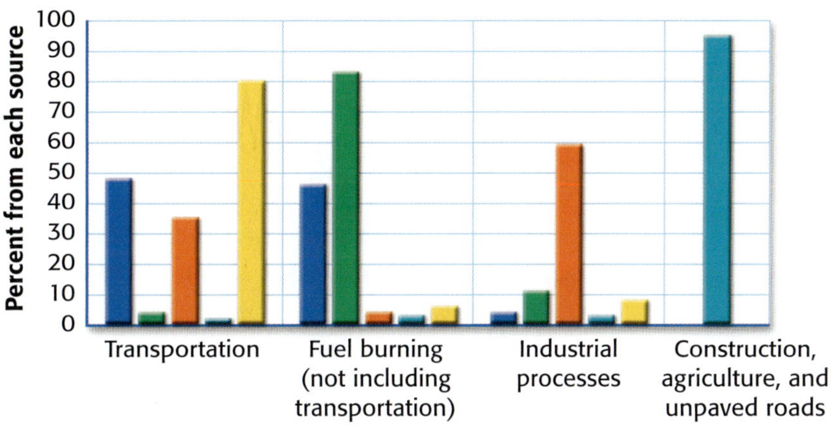

Figure 23

Carbon monoxide, produced mainly from the burning of fossil fuels, is the major air pollutant in the United States.

Some pollution has natural causes

Pollution can be caused by natural processes. For example, following an explosive volcanic eruption, dust and ash can be spread throughout the air. This can make it hard for some people to breathe. The dust and ash can also cover leaves of trees and plants, preventing them from absorbing sunlight.

Manmade pollution is more common

Most pollution is caused by human activities. Many chemical reactions can be used to make new materials or to release energy. But most chemical reactions produce two or more products. If the other products are not reused properly or recycled, they can add to the pollution problem.

Air Pollution

Air pollution comes in many forms, from individual molecules to clumps of dust and other matter, called particulates. ***Figure 23*** shows major air pollutants and sources of air pollutants in the United States. ***Table 1*** describes these different forms of pollution.

Combustion of fuels produces most air pollution

As you have learned, most of the energy we use to drive cars, heat and light buildings, and power machinery comes from the burning of fossil fuels. The burning process is known as combustion.

During combustion, the fuel, which contains carbon and hydrogen, reacts with oxygen to release energy. Along with this desirable product, two other products are formed: carbon dioxide gas and water vapor. These combustion products escape into the air as invisible gases. The reaction for burning methane from natural gas is shown below.

$$CH_4 + 2O_2 \longrightarrow CO_2 + 2H_2O$$

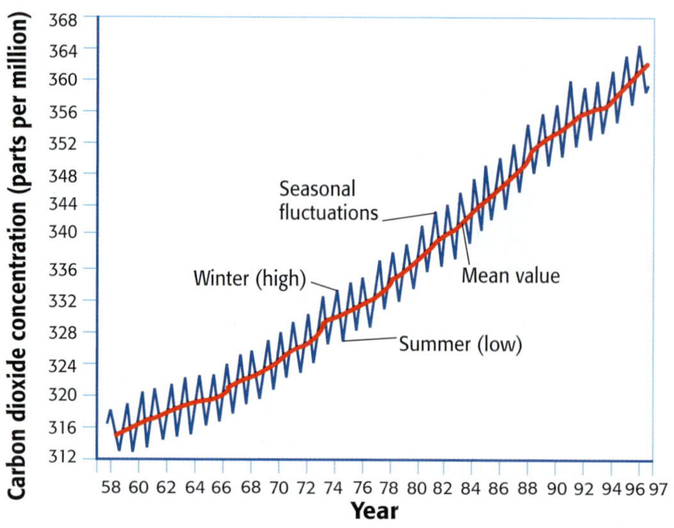

Figure 24

This graph shows an increase in atmospheric carbon dioxide from 1958 to 1997.

Carbon dioxide is a greenhouse gas

Carbon dioxide is found naturally in Earth's atmosphere. It is one of the greenhouse gases, which help keep temperatures on Earth balanced. Just as the glass of a greenhouse garden traps radiation that keeps the inside warm, greenhouse gases in the atmosphere trap radiation that keeps Earth warm. Without the greenhouse effect, temperatures on Earth would be roughly 33°C lower.

Humans release about twenty-one billion tons of carbon dioxide into the air every year. ***Figure 24*** shows how the amount of atmospheric carbon dioxide has changed since 1958. Some scientists hypothesize that by 2100 the amount of carbon dioxide in the atmosphere will be twice its level in 1880. Some records indicate that the average temperature of Earth is already showing a small increase. In the past 100 years, the average temperature in the United States has increased by about 0.7°C. It is estimated that if the level of atmospheric carbon dioxide doubles, global temperatures would increase by about 0.7°C. This **global warming** may not sound like a lot, but it could drastically affect Earth's climate. Weather patterns could change, bringing droughts to some areas and floods to others. Other scientists point out that ice ages and warming periods occurred in the past without large human sources of CO_2.

global warming a gradual increase in the average global temperatures that is due to a higher concentration of gases such as carbon dioxide in the atmosphere

Combustion releases other pollutants

The burning of fossil fuels also releases sulfur dioxide and nitrogen dioxide. Once released, these gases react with other atmospheric gases and with water. Chemical reactions like these can make rain, sleet, or snow acidic. Normal precipitation is slightly acidic, with a pH of roughly 5.6. Acid precipitation typically has a pH of between 4 and 5—a very great difference.

Acid precipitation can harm or even kill aquatic life. It can also leach out nutrients from soil and damage large areas of forests. In addition, it can corrode metals and damage buildings by eroding stonework.

Figure 25

This coal-burning power plant provides power, but it also produces sulfur dioxide and nitrogen dioxide.

Air pollution can cause breathing problems

When nitrogen oxide compounds in car exhaust react with sunlight, they can produce a cloud of chemicals called photochemical smog. The result is a brown haze that can make eyes sting and cause severe headaches and breathing difficulties.

Ozone is one of the harmful chemicals in photochemical smog. High up in the atmosphere, ozone blocks harmful ultraviolet radiation. Close to Earth's surface, however, ozone is a pollutant. It can cause problems for people who suffer from asthma or other conditions affecting the throat and lungs.

Photochemical smog is most common in sunny, densely populated cities, such as Los Angeles and Tokyo. In Tokyo, many people wear masks to protect themselves from the polluted air, and companies supply fresh-air dispensers to their employees. The smog also damages plants. Decreased yields of citrus fruits, such as oranges and lemons, may be linked to photochemical smog in areas not far from Los Angeles. To combat the problem, many cities have made concerted efforts to expand public transportation systems and to encourage people to carpool. These efforts help reduce the number of vehicles on the road and thus the amount of pollutants released into the air.

Quick ACTIVITY

Observing Air Pollution

1. Cut off a piece of masking tape about 8 cm long.
2. Place the sticky side of the tape against an outside wall, and press gently.
3. Remove the tape, and hold it against a sheet of white paper.
4. Did the tape pick up dust? If so, what might be the source of the dust?
5. Repeat the experiment on other walls in different places, and compare the amounts of dust observed.
6. Suggest reasons why some walls appear to have more dust than others.

Water Pollution

All living things need water to survive. In fact, the bodies of most organisms, including humans, are made up mostly of water. Many people believe that water is our most valuable natural resource. Unpolluted water is even more important to aquatic organisms, which spend their entire life in a liquid environment.

On July 6, 1988, a load of aluminum sulfate was accidentally tipped into the water supply in Camelford, England. Before the problem was discovered, people became ill.

Accidents are responsible for some water pollution but not all. Most water pollution can be traced to industrial waste, agricultural fertilizers, and everyday human activities. A bucket of dirty, soapy water dumped down a kitchen drain can eventually make its way into the water supply. Flushing toilets, washing cars, and pouring chemicals down drains are actions that can contribute to water pollution.

In many countries, water is cleaned at water-purification plants before it is piped to consumers. But because many chemicals dissolve easily in water, it's difficult to remove all of the impurities from the water.

Figure 26

The plastic six-pack ring around the neck of this herring gull is one example of how water pollution can affect the environment.

Figure 27
This algal bloom is the result of an abundance of nitrates in the water.

Pesticides and fertilizers often end up polluting water

Most modern farms use chemical fertilizers. These fertilizers can get washed away by rain and end up in streams, rivers, lakes, ponds, or oceans. The fertilizers may contain nitrate ions, which encourage the growth of bacteria and algae.

Fed on the nitrates, the bacteria and algae grow so fast that they use up most of the oxygen in the water. The result is an algal bloom, such as the one shown in ***Figure 27.*** Fish and other aquatic wildlife suffer from the reduced oxygen and die. This process, known as **eutrophication,** is made worse if hot water from power stations or factories is discharged into the river or lake. The extra warmth makes the bacteria and algae multiply even faster.

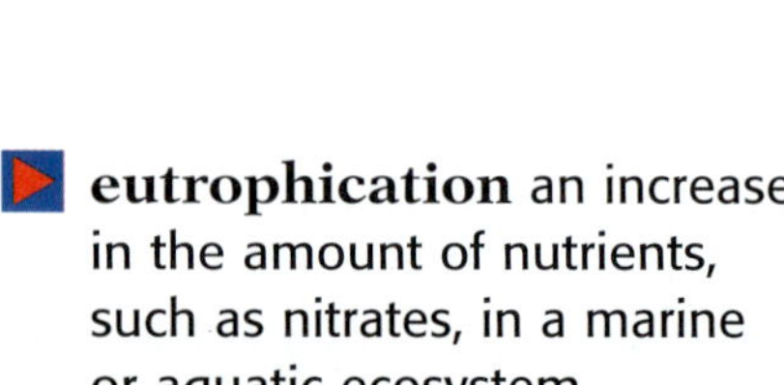

eutrophication an increase in the amount of nutrients, such as nitrates, in a marine or aquatic ecosystem

Animals on land and in water can be affected by another group of chemicals that eventually make their way into bodies of water. These chemicals, called pesticides, are used to control crop-damaging pests.

Like fertilizers, pesticides can be washed by rain into streams, rivers, lakes, or ponds. There they are ingested by fish and other aquatic animals. As larger animals eat the fish, the chemicals are passed along the food chain. In the 1970s, a pesticide called DDT was widely used to control mosquitoes and other insects, leading to the eradication of malaria in the United States. DDT caused the eggs of fish-eating pelicans and other fish-eating birds to become thin and fragile. The pelicans nearly became extinct before the use of DDT was banned in the United States.

Pollution on Land

Pollution that affects our land has many sources. In some cases, the source is obvious, as when trash is dumped illegally by a roadside. In other cases, the source is not so obvious. For example, dirt near many highways contains an unusually high amount of lead. This lead originally came from car exhaust. The lead was part of a compound added to gasoline to help car engines run more smoothly. Leaded gasoline was banned in the 1970s, but there are still greater amounts of lead in soil near busy highways.

Contaminants in soil are hard to remove

A common type of land-based pollution occurs when hazardous chemicals soak into the soil. For example, in 1983, the entire town of Times Beach, Missouri, was bought by the U.S. Environmental Protection Agency. The town's soil was contaminated by a highly toxic chemical compound called dioxin.

Exposure to dioxin, a chemical produced in the paper-making process, had been linked to an increased risk of cancer. The soil in the town had become contaminated because the waste oil used to keep the dust on the town's roads down contained small amounts of dioxin. After the roads were repeatedly sprayed over several years, the dioxin levels became very high. This resulted in the deaths of some livestock and other animals and it also adversely affected the health of some of the town's residents.

Dioxin, like many land-based pollutants, does not dissolve well in water. It does not break down easily. It is therefore very difficult to remove it from the soil. The EPA bought the town because it was less expensive than cleaning the entire town's soil.

How can oil spills be cleaned up?

Materials
- cleaning materials
- cold water
- cooking oil
- rectangular baking pan

1. Fill the pan halfway with cold water.
2. Pour a small amount of cooking oil into the water.
3. Try to clean up the "oil spill" using at least four different cleaning materials.

Analysis

1. Evaluate the effectiveness of each material. Which worked best? Explain why.
2. Did any of the materials "pollute" the water with particles or residue? How might you clean up this pollution?

Figure 28
Many landfills are closing because of a lack of space.

Landfill space is running out

Even when trash is taken to a landfill, like the one shown in ***Figure 28,*** and disposed of legally, it can still cause pollution. Each time an item is placed in a landfill, there is less space remaining for other materials. In some regions of the United States, landfills are closing because they are full. Few new landfills are opening.

Currently, each person in the United States throws away almost a half ton of garbage every year. If current trends continue, parts of the United States will soon run out of landfill space.

Reducing Pollution

The are many ways to reduce or limit pollution. Government regulation is one way. In the United States there are several laws that encourage clean water supplies and discourage the pollution of air, soil, and water. Countries may also work together to combat the problem. For instance, in December 1997, international representatives met in Kyoto, Japan, to negotiate an agreement to reduce greenhouse-gas emissions.

Choosing alternatives often involves trade-offs

Even greater improvements in the pollution problem come when individuals, communities, and companies make careful choices. For example, to reduce the air pollution caused by the burning of fossil fuels, people can make an effort to use alternative energy sources. Individuals can make a difference by conserving energy. However, even nonpolluting sources of energy, such as wind, solar, and hydroelectric power, require large amounts of land and are potentially disruptive to ecosystems.

Small-scale sources of energy, such as disposable batteries, have an environmental impact too. These batteries contain mercury and other potentially toxic chemicals. In the United States alone, more than 2 billion disposable batteries are discarded every year. The toxic chemicals can leak into the ground, polluting water supplies and soil.

Reducing the use of energy and products can cut down on pollution

Because of the trade-offs involved, many people believe that the best solution to the problem of pollution is to reduce our overall consumption. If less energy is used, less pollution is generated. Turning off lights and lowering thermostats are two simple ways to conserve energy. Carpooling or buying a car with higher-than-average gas mileage is another way to conserve energy.

INTEGRATING

BIOLOGY

When trash is buried at a landfill, microorganisms called aerobes use oxygen in the dirt to slowly decompose food, paper, and other biodegradable garbage. This process causes soil temperatures to rise, killing off the aerobes.

Anaerobes, microorganisms that thrive in oxygen-free environments, continue the long task of decomposing the refuse. But generally, anaerobes break down trash even more slowly than aerobes do. Nonbiodegradable trash, such as plastics, glass, and metals, stays essentially intact in landfills.

Recycling Codes: How Are Plastics Sorted?

More than half of the states in the United States have enacted laws that require plastic products to be labeled with numerical codes that identify the type of plastic used in them. These codes are shown in the table below. Used plastic products can be sorted by these codes and properly recycled or processed. Only codes 1 and 2 are widely accepted for recycling. Codes 3 and 6 are rarely recycled. Knowing what the numerical codes mean will give you an idea of how successfully a given plastic product can be recycled. This may affect your decision to buy or not buy particular items.

Your Choice

1. **Making Decisions** Find out what types of plastic are recycled in your area. With this in mind, will you change your buying habits?
2. **Critical Thinking** How can consumers influence what types of plastic are recycled?

internet connect

www.scilinks.org

Topic: Recycling Plastics SciLinks code: HK4117

SciLINKS. Maintained by the National Science Teachers Association

Recycling Codes for Plastic Products

Recycling code	Type of plastic	Physical properties	Example	Uses for recycled products
1	Polyethylene terephthalate (PET)	Tough, rigid; can be a fiber or a plastic; solvent resistant; sinks in water	Soda bottles, clothing, electrical insulation, automobile parts	Backpacks, sleeping bags, carpet, new bottles, clothing
2	High density polyethylene (HDPE)	Rough surface; stiff plastic; resistant to cracking	Milk containers, bleach bottles, toys, grocery bags	Furniture, toys, trash cans, picnic tables, park benches, fences
3	Polyvinyl chloride (PVC)	Elastomer or flexible plastic; tough; poor crystallization; unstable to light or heat; sinks in H_2O	Pipe, vinyl siding, automobile parts, clear bottles for cooking oil	Toys, playground equipment
4	Low density polyethylene (LDPE)	Moderately crystalline, flexible plastic; solvent resistant; floats on water	Trash bags, dry-cleaning bags, frozen-food and meat packaging	Trash cans, trash bags, compost containers
5	Polypropylene (PP)	Rigid, very strong; fiber or flexible plastic; lightweight; heat-and stress-resistant	Heat-proof containers, rope, appliance parts, outdoor carpet, luggage, diapers, automobile parts	Brooms, brushes, ice scrapers, battery cable, insulation, rope
6	Polystyrene (P/S, PS)	Somewhat brittle, rigid plastic; resistant to acids and bases but not to organic solvents; sinks in H_2O, unless it is a foam	Fast-food containers, toys, videotape reels, electrical insulation, plastic utensils, disposable drinking cups, CD jewel cases	Insulated clothing, egg cartons, thermal insulation

Figure 29

This recycling plant in New York City helps reduce the amount of waste going into landfills.

Some people conserve water by reusing rinse water from dishes and laundry to water gardens and lawns. This way, they use less water, so less energy is required to purify it and pump it to them. In addition, the water they use does not enter the sewer system. This reduces the amount of energy used by the water-treatment plant.

Recycling is the final way to prevent pollution

After you have tried to reduce how much you use and are successfully reusing it as much as possible, there's still one more thing you can do. When something is worn out and is no longer useful, instead of throwing it away, you can try **recycling.**

Recycling allows materials to be used again to make other products rather than being thrown away. ***Figure 29*** shows a recycling plant in New York City. Such plants commonly recycle paper products such as cardboard and newspapers; metal products such as copper, aluminum, and tin; and plastics such as detergent bottles and shopping bags.

Recycling these materials can make a huge difference in the amount of waste that ends up in a landfill. Paper products alone take up 41 percent of landfill space. Yet we currently recycle less than 30 percent of our paper.

recycling the process of recovering valuable or useful materials from waste or scrap, or reusing some items

SECTION 3 REVIEW

SUMMARY

- Pollution can be caused by natural events and by human activities.
- Acid rain is caused when sulfur dioxide and nitrogen oxides react with moisture in the air.
- Government regulation and recycling can lessen the pollution of air, water, and soil.
- Making an effort to reduce the energy products you use can cut down on pollution.

1. **List** an activity related to home, work, and growing food that can lead to water pollution.
2. **Distinguish** between the greenhouse effect and global warming.
3. **Explain** how riding a bike can reduce photochemical smog.
4. **Define** *eutrophication*. Explain how it occurs.
5. **Name** an alternative energy source, and describe one benefit and one drawback.
6. **Analyze** all of the possible polluting steps in the making of a pencil. Write a paragraph describing each step.

7. **Critical Thinking** Do you think recycling should be mandatory? Explain your reasoning.

Study Skills

Researching Information

Researching information is essential to learning more, including the latest information, about a topic. It is therefore important to know how to use resources, and to be able to decide for yourself if the information you receive is reliable.

1 Begin research at your library using general reference materials.

We'll research the topic "global warming." Begin by using general references, such as a recent edition of *The New Encyclopaedia Britannica,* which may be found at most libraries. Start with a broader topic, such as "Climate and Weather," to find information specific to your research.

2 Review articles written in periodicals.

Using *The Reader's Guide to Periodical Literature,* which may be found at your library, look up the topic for a given year. Note whether it is cross-referenced to another topic, and if there are subtopics listed underneath. For instance, if you want to know about the relationship between solar activity and climate, you would look under "Climate-Solar Relationships," which would refer you to "Sun and Meteorology." The citation "The Sun-Climate Connection, S. L. Baliurus and W. Soon, Sky and Telescope, v 92, p. 38–41, D' 96," indicates that the article may be found in volume 92 (December 1996) of *Sky and Telescope* magazine.

3 Search the Internet.

Because of the wide range of quality and reliability of on-line sites, it is best to use sites maintained by scientific organizations. Among these are the large sites for the National Aeronautic and Space Administration (www.nasa.gov) and the National Oceanic and Atmospheric Administration (www.noaa.gov). Also available for research are websites for scientific periodicals, like *Scientific American* (www.sciam.com) and *Science* (www.scienceonline.org).

Practice

Use information from the chapter and the example above as a starting point to answer the questions below:

1. Research factors that affect the reflection and absorption of sunlight on Earth. Approximately how much solar energy is transferred to Earth's atmosphere through evaporation and condensation of water?
2. Research articles that suggest a connection between changes in solar activity and climate change on Earth. Use these to explain the Maunder Minimum and the "Little" Ice Age.

CHAPTER 23 REVIEW

Chapter Highlights

Before you begin, review the summaries of key ideas of each section, found at the end of each section. The vocabulary terms are listed on the first page of each section.

UNDERSTANDING CONCEPTS

1. Choose the list that is ordered from largest to smallest.
- **a.** population, organism, community, ecosystem
- **b.** organism, population, ecosystem, community
- **c.** ecosystem, community, population, organism
- **d.** ecosystem, population, community, organism

2. Starlings are an example of
- **a.** a non-native species introduced into the U.S.
- **b.** a climatic ecosystem change.
- **c.** a species that migrated to the U.S. on their own.
- **d.** a species threatened by ecosystem change.

3. When fossil fuels are burned, they form carbon dioxide and
- **a.** water.
- **b.** oxygen.
- **c.** hydrocarbons.
- **d.** carbohydrates.

4. Fossil fuels are made mostly out of what elements?
- **a.** carbon and hydrogen
- **b.** carbon and calcium
- **c.** calcium and hydrogen
- **d.** potassium and chlorine

5. In power stations, ______ of the energy input is wasted.
- **a.** one-third
- **b.** one-half
- **c.** two-thirds
- **d.** all

6. Which of the following is not true of recycling?
- **a.** Recycling does not affect the amount of waste that ends up in a landfill.
- **b.** Recycling reduces litter.
- **c.** Recycling reduces energy usage.
- **d.** Recycled materials can be used to make other products.

7. The major air pollutant in the U.S. is
- **a.** sulfur oxides.
- **b.** carbon monoxide.
- **c.** nitrogen oxides.
- **d.** particulate matter.

8. Atomic reactions can produce an alternative source of energy called
- **a.** fossil fuels.
- **b.** solar energy.
- **c.** geothermal energy.
- **d.** nuclear energy.

USING VOCABULARY

9. Describe how *interrelatedness* is crucial to the concept of ecosystems.

10. Compare hydroelectric power with geothermal energy. List advantages and disadvantages of each.

11. Driving cars releases pollutants into the atmosphere. State how these pollutants can lead to *acid precipitation.*

12. A forest *ecosystem* is wiped out by disease. Using the concept of *succession,* explain how the forest might recover.

13. Most energy on Earth comes from the sun. Describe how the burning of *fossil fuels* releases stored energy from the sun.

14. Is land a *renewable* or *nonrenewable* resource? Explain your reasoning.

15. Name one of the *greenhouse gases* and state its relationship to *global warming.*

16. Describe the process of *eutrophication.* List several sources of nitrates and name several consequences of *eutrophication.*

BUILDING MATH SKILLS

17. **Estimating** The world population in 1999 was approximately 5.8 billion. That number is expected to double in 40 years. Assuming a steady growth rate, estimate the world population in the years 2019, 2039, 2059, and 2079. Write a paragraph explaining how population changes might affect an ecosystem.

18. **Calculating** Each person in the United States produces roughly 2 kg (4.4 lb) of garbage per day. How long would it take you to fill a dump truck with a 16 000 lb capacity? If each person recycled one-half of his or her trash, how much less garbage would each person produce in one year?

THINKING CRITICALLY

19. **Applying Knowledge** A factory is situated along the banks of a river. A large city is located farther upstream. On the outskirts of the city, farmers grow corn and wheat. Researchers are finding dead fish in the river. Write several paragraphs explaining the steps you would take to determine the cause. WRITING SKILL

20. **Creative Thinking** In political and environmental circles, the phrase NIMBY stands for "Not In My Backyard." Judging from what you have learned about natural resources and pollution, what do you think this phrase means? Would you apply this sentiment to anything in your life?

21. **Applying Knowledge** Have you ever had fish as pets? If so, you probably know that if you change the water without taking certain precautions the fish are likely to die. Knowing what you know about balanced ecosystems, why would this happen?

22. **Acquiring and Evaluating Data** The United States has a lot of space in comparison to certain other countries, like Japan. Using a search engine on the Internet, research what countries like Switzerland and Japan do instead of using landfills.

23. **Applying Knowledge** What does the phrase "virgin forest" mean? Using environmental texts from the library, determine whether there are any virgin forests in the U.S. What does one look like?

DEVELOPING LIFE/WORK SKILLS

24. **Teaching Others** Using a desktop-publishing program, work in groups of three or four students to design a brochure to encourage recycling or energy conservation at your school. As a group, decide beforehand who your audience will be—do you want to reach younger students, your peers, or the school administration? List the benefits and possible drawbacks in your brochure. Explain how costs can be reduced without hindering the school's operation. COMPUTER SKILL WRITING SKILL

25. **Applying Technology** Research recent developments and advancements in solar-power technology. Then write a brief report analyzing the feasibility of the technology. Share your results with the class. WRITING SKILL

26. Allocating Resources Three people live in the same neighborhood and work at the same office. One person spends $20 per week, one spends $25 per week, and one spends $30 per week for gasoline and parking. They work 51 weeks per year. If they formed a car pool, how much could each person save annually? Using a spreadsheet program, create a spreadsheet that will calculate how much each person would save in 5 years. (**Hint:** Assume that each person drives a total of 17 weeks.)

COMPUTER SKILL

27. Acquiring and Evaluating Data Go to your local library and research any nonnative species that have been introduced into your area. What positive and negative effects have resulted from their arrival?

28. Acquiring and Evaluating Data Research the 1986 Safe Drinking Water Act and the 1987 Clean Water Act. What incentives are in place to encourage clean water supplies?

INTEGRATING CONCEPTS

29. Connection to Health Sunscreens, which protect people from ultraviolet rays, have different sun protection factors (SPFs). For someone who burns after 10 minutes in the sun, a sunscreen with an SPF of 8 would give that person 80 minutes of protection. If the same person wanted to stay in the sun for 2.5 hours without reapplying sunscreen, what SPF should he or she use?

internet connect

www.scilinks.org

Topic: Global Warming SciLinks code: HK4065

SCILINKS. Maintained by the National Science Teachers Association

30. Connection to Social Studies Research a particular region of the world other than the area where you live. Find out which energy resource is used to meet the energy needs of this particular region.

31. Connection to Social Studies One of the purported causes of global warming is the burning of fossil fuels. As a group, discuss how building energy-efficient houses might help counteract this effect. What incentives would you suggest to encourage people to make their homes more efficient? How would you judge if they're worth the cost?

32. Connection to History Human-caused environmental pollution has occurred throughout history. Research a historical example of environmental pollution, and write a short essay about it. Also research and include information about a historic conservation effort.

WRITING SKILL

33. Mapping Concepts Copy the unfinished concept map below onto a sheet of paper. Complete the map by writing the correct word or phrase in the lettered boxes.

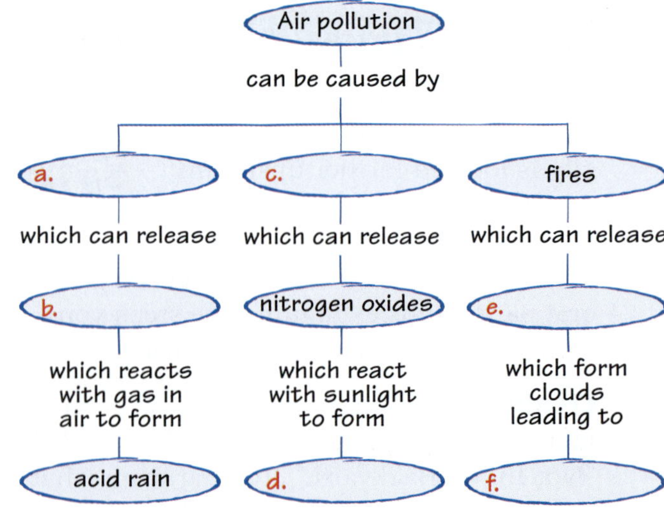

Standardized Test Prep

Understanding Concepts

Directions (1–3): **For *each* question, write on a separate sheet of paper the letter of the correct answer.**

1 What greenhouse gas is produced by combustion of fossil fuels?
A. carbon dioxide
B. carbon monoxide
C. helium
D. methane

2 Why are coal, oil, and natural gas known as fossil fuels?
F. They are nonrenewable sources of energy.
G. They are generally found in deposits where fossils are found.
H. They have been used as energy sources since prehistoric times.
I. They were formed by the decomposition of ancient plants and animals.

3 Within an ecosystem, what factor distinguishes a community?
A. All organisms are of the same species.
B. The plants and animals of a community live close together.
C. All of the plants and animals in a community interact in some way.
D. The organisms in a community have adapted to live in the ecosystem.

Directions (4–5): **For *each* question, write a short response.**

4 Changes in an ecosystem, such as cutting a forest, can have unexpected consequences. Deduce how cutting the trees in a forest can affect other plants and animals, even some that live far from the forest.

5 The population of predators is related to the amount of prey available as food. How does the balance of populations change, and how is balance restored, if the prey population suddenly decreases?

Test TIP

When answering an extended-response question, first make an outline of what you plan to write.

Reading Skills

Directions (6): **Read the passage below. Then answer the question.**

In 1883 the volcano on Krakatoa Island in the South Pacific erupted with one of the most violent explosions ever witnessed. All living things on islands many kilometers away were destroyed. Most of the island itself disappeared, and what remained was covered with sterile ash. Over the next 50 years scientists studied the recovery of life on Krakatoa. Within a year, they discovered a species of spider. By 1886 the ground was covered with algae, ferns, and flowering plants. A survey in 1933 found a fully functioning rainforest with birds, bats, snakes, even crocodiles.

6 Differentiate between the ecosystem on Krakatoa after this recovery and the ecosystem before the eruption.

Interpreting Graphics

Directions (7): **Base your answer to question 7 on the graph below, which shows carbon dioxide concentration from 1958 to 1997.**

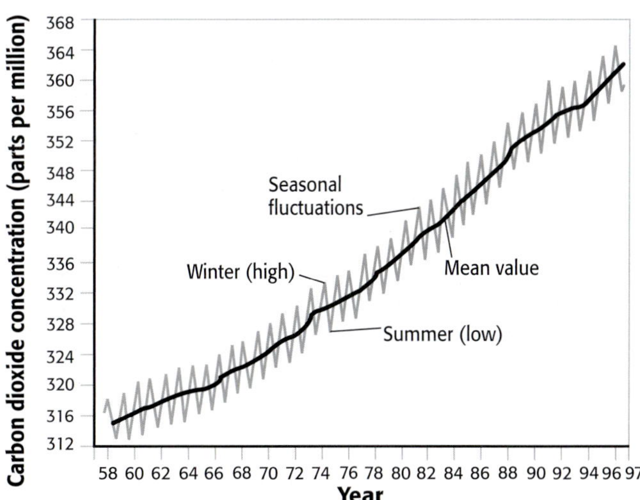

7 This data supports the conclusion that
F. fossil fuel use has raised CO_2 levels
G. CO_2 concentration increases in summer
H. CO_2 concentration has increased over several decades
I. the increase in CO_2 level has caused global warming

Skills Practice Lab

Changing the Form of a Fuel

Introduction

Can you use your familiarity with products used in or near the home to help you identify some of the products of destructive distillation?

Objectives

- USING SCIENTIFIC METHODS ***Observe*** the process of destructive distillation.
- ***Analyze*** the amounts of products produced, and try to identify the products.

Materials

2 test tubes
one-hole stopper
two-hole stopper
bent glass tubing with fire-polished ends
20-cm long rubber tubing
gas burner
ringstand and 2 buret clamps
2 widemouth bottles
2 glass plates, 7 × 7 cm square
gas-collecting trough
pieces of wood splints
graduated cylinder
balance

Procedure

Preparing for Your Experiment

Destructive distillation is the process of heating a material such as wood or coal in the absence of air. The material that is driven off as a gas is called volatile matter. When cooled, some of the matter remains as a gas. Much of the matter condenses to form a mixture of liquids. These liquids can be distilled to yield a number of different products. In this investigation, you (or your teacher) will heat wood to temperatures high enough to cause the wood to break down into different components, which you will try to identify.

1. On a clean sheet of paper, make a table like the one shown below.
2. Label your glassware as shown in the illustration on the next page.
3. Using the balance, determine the mass of test tube A. Record the value in your table.
4. Using the graduated cylinder, determine the volume of gas bottles 1 and 2. Record the values in your table.
5. Determine the mass of test tube B. Record the value in your table. Dry test tube B before setting up your equipment.

Data Table
Mass of test tube A (g)
Mass of test tube A with wood (g)
Mass of wood (g)
Mass of test tube A with solid residue (g)
Mass of solid residue (g)
Volume of gas bottle 1 (mL)
Volume of gas bottle 2 (mL)
Volume of gas produced (mL)
Mass of test tube B (g)
Mass of liquid produced (g)
Volume of liquid produced (mL)

Destructive Distillation of Wood   

SAFETY CAUTION Wear protective gloves when inserting the glass tubing through the stoppers. Rub glycerin on the tubing and the inside of the stopper holes before pushing the tubing through the stoppers. Rotate the tubing slowly, and push gently. If you have difficulty, ask your teacher for help.

6. Set up the equipment as illustrated below.
7. The gas bottle in the pan should be completely filled with water. Insert the delivery tube into the gas bottle.

SAFETY CAUTION Protect clothing, hair, and eyes when using a gas burner. The gases formed in the destructive distillation of wood are combustible.

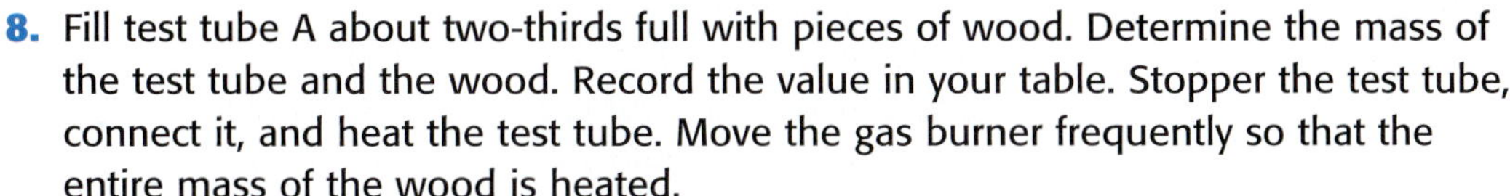

8. Fill test tube A about two-thirds full with pieces of wood. Determine the mass of the test tube and the wood. Record the value in your table. Stopper the test tube, connect it, and heat the test tube. Move the gas burner frequently so that the entire mass of the wood is heated.
9. When all the water is driven from the gas bottle, place a glass plate over the mouth of the bottle, and remove the bottle from the pan. Set the gas bottle upright on the table, leaving it covered with the glass plate.
10. Place another water-filled bottle in the pan as before, and reinsert the gas delivery tube. Keep heating until the gas stops coming from test tube A.

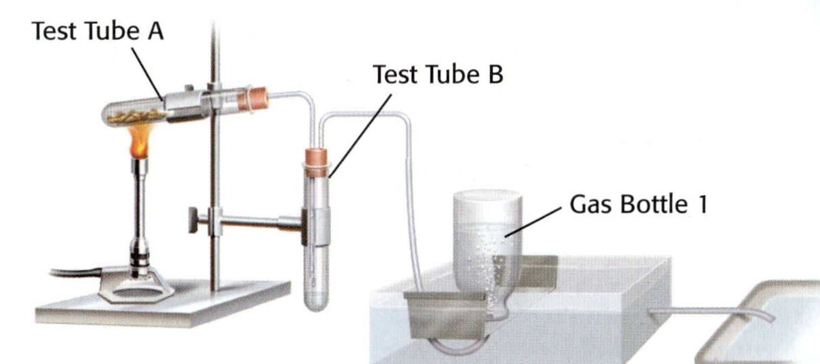

Analysis

1. How much gas was produced? How much gas was produced for 1 g of wood?
2. What happens when a burning splint is thrust into the gas?
3. Describe the contents of test tube B. What was the mass of the liquid produced? What was the volume? What about for 1 g of wood?
4. What does the solid material remaining in test tube A look like?
5. How much solid material was left? How much solid material remains for each 1 g of original wood?
6. Using insulated tongs, hold a piece of the solid material in the gas burner flame. How does it burn?

Conclusions

7. Why would you expect charcoal to give off little or no flame when it is burned?
8. Why is this type of distillation called destructive?
9. What do you think the liquids can be used for?

Science in ACTION

This fuel cell car looks futuristic, but alternatives to gas-burning vehicles are already available.

Cars of the Future

Nearly every engine in the world, from a lawnmower engine to the engines of a Boeing 747 airplane, depends on a petroleum-based product, such as gasoline, for fuel. But the world's supply of petroleum is limited. Emissions from gas-burning engines are a major cause of air pollution. Despite these problems, few better alternatives to gas engines have been developed until recently.

Traffic jams such as this are a major cause of air pollution.

Electric versus Hybrid

Because electric cars run on battery power, they do not release pollutants into the atmosphere. Although these zero-emission vehicles first hit the streets more than 100 years ago, they never became popular because they lacked power. Also, electric cars require frequent recharging. So how do we continue to use cars while conserving resources? The answer may be to use hybrid cars.

Hybrid cars use a combination of batteries and an efficient engine. Although hybrid cars need gasoline, they are more fuel-efficient than gas-powered cars. Hybrids are also convenient for drivers because the cars never need recharging. When the car brakes, the electric motor produces electricity and recharges the batteries.

The rapeseed plant is a source of cooking oil and is used in a process to make cleaner-burning diesel fuel.

Fuel Cells Burn Alternative Fuels

Alternative fuel sources may also be used to power our cars in the future. A fuel cell converts the energy of a chemical reaction into electricity that powers the car. Fuel cells are efficient because they contain no moving parts and do not lose heat. A typical car engine loses 80% of its energy as heat. Fuel cells are already being used in industry and on our space shuttles, and car makers are hurrying to make fuel cells for cars. Some people hope that in addition to reducing our use of petroleum and reducing emissions, fuel cells may also reduce groundwater pollution caused by discarded car batteries and spilled oil and gas.

Plants May Power Cars in the Future

Scientists are also looking to plant and animal materials, or *biomass,* as a potential source of fuel. The most common way to get energy from biomass is to burn it to make heat much like burning wood in a fireplace. But biomass can also be converted into liquid fuels for specially adapted car engines. Cars of the future may run on used vegetable oil from fast-food restaurants!

Science and You

1. **Applying Knowledge** Describe the difference between an electric car and a hybrid car.
2. **Understanding Concepts** Describe two advantages that electric cars have over gas-powered cars.
3. **Critical Thinking** Many advances in alternative energy have come from NASA. Why do you think NASA and the space program is interested in alternative energy?
4. **Critical Thinking** Do you think wood and other organic materials could be recycled from landfills and used as biomass? Explain.
5. **Making Decisions** Electric cars rely on electricity produced by power plants that burn fossil fuels. Would you buy an electric car to help save natural resources? Explain.

Reference Section

APPENDIX A
Reading and Study Skills
Math Skills Refresher
Graphing Skills
Lab Skills
APPENDIX B
Useful Data
APPENDIX C
Problem Bank
APPENDIX D
Selected Answers
to Problems
APPENDIX B
The World: Physical
Figure B-3
PACIFIC
OCEAN

Reading and Study Skills

As a science student, you are expected to understand the information you read in this textbook and hear from your teacher. To be successful, you also need to be able to organize the information you receive and to take good notes. This appendix is designed to help you learn these skills, which will help you become a more successful student.

The first section, which contains reading skills and study skills, is followed by sections on graphing skills, a math refresher, and lab skills. At the end of every chapter in this book, there is a skills practice page. The skills practice pages are designed to help you develop your skills. If you have difficulty in one particular area, such as graphing skills, this appendix is an excellent resource for extra explanation and practice.

Recognizing Key Words

To begin improving your understanding of what you read, you need to know how to recognize key words in a sentence and key ideas in a paragraph. Finding the key ideas or words may be difficult for several reasons. First, you may not understand what a key idea is. A key idea is the idea that the author is trying to help you understand. When you are reading, ask yourself what the author is trying to tell you in the paragraph or sentence. The answer to that question is often the key idea.

The second reason that finding the key word or idea may be difficult is that its location within a paragraph or sentence often changes. Sometimes the key idea appears at the beginning of a sentence, and sometimes it is in the middle or at the end. To recognize key words in a sentence, ask yourself the following question about every word in a sentence.

If this word was taken out of the sentence, would I still understand what the sentence is trying to say?

Consider the following example.

Find the key words in the following sentence.

You are to report to the counselor's office at 4:00 P.M., and don't forget to take your books with you.

Key words: you, report, counselor's office, 4:00 P.M., take, books.

If you communicated the key words to someone, he or she would understand what to do.

Practice

Identify the key words in the following sentences.

1. Claude Monet is considered by many to be one of the most influential impressionist painters that ever lived.
2. Please go to the store and pick up a container of milk, some butter, and maple syrup, so we can eat breakfast soon.
3. Venus, the second planet from the sun, appears close to the sun and is called both *the morning star* and *the evening star.*

Recognizing Key Ideas in a Paragraph

Recognizing key ideas in a sentence is much like recognizing key words in a paragraph. As you're reading, ask yourself whether you would still understand what the author is trying to say if the sentence was taken out of the paragraph.

Recognizing key ideas in a paragraph is very important to your success as a science student. It is usually the key ideas within a section or chapter that you are held accountable for and that will appear on tests and quizzes.

If you cannot identify the key ideas within a paragraph, it is important to reread the paragraph. After you have reread the section, try to identify particular sentences or parts of sentences that do not directly address the subject of the paragraph. Reread the paragraph again, and omit the less important passages. Then, ask yourself again if you understand what the author is trying to say. Repeat this process until you feel confident that you understand what the passage is trying to convey.

This process may take time in the beginning, but recognizing key ideas is an important skill to acquire if you want to become a good student. As you build your scientific vocabulary and become more familiar with this and other study skills, recognizing key ideas will become easier.

Consider the following example.

Some household products should never be combined because they react to produce harmful substances. Ammonia and bleach react to produce a poisonous substance called *chloramine,* NH_2Cl. Also, vinegar and bleach react to produce chlorine gas, Cl_2, another poisonous substance. To be safe, you should never combine household products.

Key idea: Household products react to produce poisonous substances, so you should never combine them.

The key idea is the most important information. In this paragraph, the specific examples of household chemicals were not a part of the key idea. They help explain the concept, but they can be left out of the summarzed key idea.

Practice

Identify the key idea in the following paragraph.

1. Soaps have traditionally been made from animal fats or vegetable oils. Soap can dissolve in both oil and water. Soaps are emulsifiers that let oil and water mix and keep the oil and water from separating. When you wash your face with soap, the oil on your face is suspended in the soapy water. The water you use to rinse your face with carries the soap and unwanted oil away to leave your face clean.

Outlining

Outlining is one of the most widely used methods for taking notes. Taking good notes is a skill that is very important for understanding, comprehension, and achieving success on tests. The information in the chapters of *Holt Science Spectrum* is organized in a way to help you easily outline the key ideas in a chapter or section. Outlines you make from the key ideas can help you prepare for tests and can be used to check your comprehension of the chapter.

Most outlines follow the same structure. Main ideas or topics are listed first and usually follow a roman numeral. We will use the chapter titled "Chemical Reactions" as an example. The main topic is on the first page of the chapter and is the title of the section that is written in green. Because the section title is the main topic, we list it first along with the roman numeral I.

I. The Nature of Chemical Reactions

After we write the main topic, we will add major points that provide information about the main topic. These major points appear in red type under the section title. The two major points that we will add to our outline follow the letters A and B.

I. The Nature of Chemical Reactions
- A. Chemical Reactions Change Substances
- B. Energy and Reactions

The next step in outlining is to fill in the subpoints that describe or explain the major points. In this book, these subpoints will appear as sentences in blue type. We add the subpoints to our outline under the major points that they explain. The subpoints should follow numerals.

I. The Nature of Chemical Reactions
- A. Chemical Reactions Change Substances
  1. Production of gas and change of color are signs of a chemical reaction.
  2. Chemical reactions rearrange atoms.
- B. Energy and Reactions
  1. Energy must be added to break bonds.
  2. Forming bonds releases energy.
  3. Energy is conserved in chemical reactions.
  4. Reactions that release energy are exothermic.
  5. Reactions that absorb energy are endothermic.

The last step in outlining is to add the supporting details for the subpoints. In this book, these details will appear in the body of the text under the details subpoint. We add the details to our outline under the subpoints that they explain. Details should follow lowercase letters.

I. The Nature of Chemical Reactions
- A. Chemical Reactions Change Substances
  1. Production of gas and change of color are signs of a chemical reaction.
     - a. An example of a change caused by a chemical reaction is seen in the process of baking bread. The dough rises because gas is produced, and the dough turns brown during baking.

2. Chemical reactions rearrange atoms.
   a. Reactants contain the same types of atoms as products but they are often rearranged.
   b. Atoms are neither created nor destroyed.
   c. Atoms are rearranged as bonds are broken and formed.

Remember that the major topics are always listed next to a roman numeral. The major points are listed under the main topics and follow a capital letter. Major points are followed by subpoints, which follow a numeral. Finally, supporting details are under subpoints and follow a lowercase letter.

Outlining Guidelines

I. The main topic is listed here.
   A. Major points, which provide information about the main topic are listed here.
      1. Subpoints, which provide information about or describe the major points are listed here.
         a. Supporting details of the subpoints are listed here.

Practice

1. Build an outline using the following topics, ideas, and supporting details taken from the chapter entitled "Planet Earth."
   A. Physical Weathering
   c. Acid precipitation causes damage to both living organisms and inorganic matter such as statues.
   1. Ice can break rocks.
   I. Weathering and Erosion
   a. Frost wegding occurs when water seeps into crack in rock and then freezes.
   2. Plants can also break rocks.
   B. Chemical Weathering
   1. Carbon dioxide can cause chemical weathering.
   2. Water plays a key role in chemical weathering.
   3. Acid precipitation can slowly dissolve minerals.
   a. Carbon dioxide from the air dissolves in rainwater to create carbonic acid.
   b. Carbonic acid reacts with minerals in rocks and then washes away carrying the rock with it.
   a. When fossil fuels, especially coal, are burned sulfur dioxide and nitrogen oxides are released into the air.
   2. Acid precipitation occurs when sulfur dioxide and nitrogen oxides in the air react with water in clouds to form weak acids that fall to Earth.
   a. Water reacts chemically with many minerals.
   b. Leaching occurs when water dissolves or reacts with minerals in rocks and then is transported to lower layers or rock.
2. Pick a section of one of the chapters in this book, and write an outline.

APPENDIX A

Power Notes

Power notes help you organize the concepts you are studying by distinguishing main ideas from details and providing a framework of important concepts. Power notes are easier to use than outlines because their structure is simpler. You assign a power of *1* to each main idea and a *2, 3,* or *4* to each detail. You can use power notes to organize ideas while reading your text or to reorganize your class notes to study.

Start with a few boldfaced vocabulary terms. Later you can strengthen your notes by expanding these into more-detailed phrases. Use the following general format to help you structure your power notes.

Power 1 Main idea
  Power 2 Detail or support for power 1
    Power 3 Detail or support for power 2
      Power 4 Detail or support for power 3

1. Pick a Power 1 word.

We'll use the term *atom* found in the chapter on Atoms and The Periodic Table of your textbook.

Power 1 Atom

2. Using the text, select some Power 2 words to support your Power 1 word.

We'll use the terms *nucleus* and *electron cloud,* which are two parts of an atom.

Power 1 Atom
  Power 2 Nucleus
  Power 2 Electron Cloud

3. Select some Power 3 words to support your Power 2 words.

We'll use the terms *positive charge* and *negative charge,* two terms that describe the Power 2 words.

Power 1 Atom
  Power 2 Nucleus
    Power 3 Positive charge
  Power 2 Electron cloud
    Power 3 Negative charge

4. Continue to add powers to support and detail the main idea as necessary.

If you have a main idea that needs a lot of support, add as many powers as needed to describe the idea. You can use power notes to organize the material in an entire section or chapter of your textbook to study for classroom quizzes and tests.

Power 1 Atom
  Power 2 Nucleus
    Power 3 Positive charge
    Power 3 Protons
      Power 4 Positive charge
    Power 3 Neutrons
      Power 4 No charge
  Power 2 Electron cloud
    Power 3 Negative charge

Practice

1. Use the chapter entitled "Atoms and The Periodic Table" and the power notes structure below to organize the following terms: *electron lost, electron gained, ionization, anion, cation, negative charge,* and *positive charge.*

Power 1 ______________________
  Power 2 ______________________
    Power 3 ______________________
    Power 3 ______________________
  Power 2 ______________________
    Power 3 ______________________
    Power 3 ______________________

Two-column Notes

Two-column notes can be used to learn and review definitions of vocabulary terms or details of specific concepts. The two-column-note strategy is simple: write the term, main idea, or concept in the left-hand column. Then write the definition, example, or detail on the right.

One strategy for using two-column notes is to organize main ideas and their details. The main ideas from your reading are written in the left-hand column of your paper and can be written as questions, key words, or a combination of both. Key words can include boldface terms as well as any other terms you may have trouble remembering. Questions may include those the author has asked or any questions your teacher may have asked during class. Details describing these main ideas are then written in the right-hand column of your paper.

1. Identify the main ideas.
The main ideas for each chapter are listed in the section objectives. However, you decide which ideas to include in your notes. The table below shows some of the main ideas from the objectives in the first section of the chapter entitled Introduction to Science.

2. Divide a blank sheet of paper into two columns, and write the main ideas in the left-hand column.
Do not copy ideas from the book or waste time writing in complete sentences. Summarize your ideas using quick phrases that are easy to understand and remember. Decide how many details you need for each main idea, and include that number to help you to focus on the necessary information.

3. Write the detail notes in the right-hand column.
Be sure you list as many details as you designated in the main-idea column.

The two-column method of review is perfect for preparing for quizzes or tests. Just cover the information in the right-hand column with a sheet of paper, and after reciting what you know, uncover the notes to check your answers.

Practice

1. Make your own two-column notes using the periodic table. Include in the details the symbol and the atomic number of each of the following elements.
   a. neon **b.** lead **c.** calcium **d.** copper **e.** oxygen **f.** sodium

Main idea	Detail notes	
▶ Scientific theory (4 characteristic properties)	▶ tested experimentally ▶ possible explanation	▶ explains natural event ▶ used to predict
▶ Scientific law (3 characteristic properties)	▶ tested experimentally ▶ summary of an observation	▶ can be disproved
▶ Models (4 characteristic properties)	▶ represents an object or event ▶ physical	▶ computer ▶ mathematical

APPENDIX A

Pattern Puzzles

You can use pattern puzzles to help you remember information in the correct order. Pattern puzzles are not just a tool for memorization. They can also help you better understand a variety of scientific processes, from the steps in solving a mathematical conversion to the procedure for writing a lab report.

1. Write down the steps of a process in your own words.

We'll use the Math Skills feature on converting amount to mass from the chapter entitled "Atoms and The Periodic Table." On a sheet of paper, write down one step per line, and do not number the steps. Also, do not copy straight from your text. Writing the steps in your own words helps you check your understanding of the process. You may want to divide the longer steps into two or three shorter steps.

- List the given and unknown information.
- Look at the periodic table to determine the molar mass of the substance.
- Write the correct conversion factor to convert moles to grams.
- Multiply the amount of substance by the conversion factor.
- Solve the equation and check your answer.

2. Cut the sheet of paper into strips with only one step per strip of paper.

Shuffle the strips of paper so that they are out of sequence.

- Look at the periodic table to determine the mola mass of the substance.
- Solve the equation and check your answer.
- List the given and unknown information.
- Multiply the amount of substance by the conversion factor.
- Write the correct conversion factor to convert moles to grams.

3. Place the strips in their proper sequence. Confirm the order of the process by checking your text or your class notes.

- List the given and unknown information.

- Look at the periodic table to determine the molar mass of the substance.

- Write the correct conversion factor to convert moles to grams.

- Multiply the amount of substance by the conversion factor.

- Solve the equation and check your answer.

Pattern puzzles can be used to help you prepare for a laboratory experiment. That way it will be easier for you to remember what you need to do when you get into the lab, especially if your teacher gives pre-lab quizzes.

You'll want to use pattern puzzles if your teacher is planning a lab practical exam to test whether you know how to operate laboratory equipment. That way you can study and prepare for such a test even though you don't have a complete set of lab equipment at home.

Pattern puzzles work very well with problem-solving. If you work a pattern puzzle for a given problem type several times first, you will find it much easier to work on the different practice problems assigned in your homework.

Pattern puzzles are especially helpful when you are studying for tests. It is a good idea to make the puzzles on a regular basis so that when test time comes you won't be rushing to make them. Bind each puzzle using paper clips, or store the puzzles in individual envelopes. Before tests, use your puzzles to practice and to review.

Pattern puzzles are also a good way to study with others. You and a classmate can take turns creating your own pattern puzzles and putting each other's puzzles in the correct sequence. Studying with a classmate in this way will help make studying fun and allow you and your classmate to help each other.

Practice

1. Write the following sentences describing the process of making pattern puzzles in the correct order.
   - Place the strips in their proper sequence.
   - Write down the steps of the process in your own words.
   - Shuffle the strips of paper.
   - Choose a multiple-step process from your text.
   - Using your text, confirm the order of the process.
   - Cut the paper into strips so that there is one step per strip.

APPENDIX A

KWL Notes

The KWL strategy is a helpful way to learn. It is different from the other learning strategies you have seen in this appendix. KWL stands for "what I **K**now—what I **W**ant to know—what I **L**earned." KWL prompts you to brainstorm about the subject matter before you read the assigned pages. This strategy helps you relate your new ideas and concepts with those you have already learned. This allows you to understand and apply new knowledge more easily. The objectives at the beginning of each section in your text are ideal for using the KWL strategy. Just read and follow the instructions in the example below.

1. **Read the section objectives.**
   You may also want to scan headings, boldface terms, and illustrations in the section. We'll use a few of the objectives from the first section of the chapter entitled Matter.
   - Explain the relationship between matter, atoms, and elements.
   - Distinguish between elements and compounds.
   - Categorize materials as pure substances or mixtures.

2. **Divide a sheet of paper into three columns, and label the columns "What I know," "What I want to know," and "What I learned."**

3. **Brainstorm about what you know about the information in the objectives, and write these ideas in the first column.**
   It is not necessary to write complete sentences. What's most important is to get as many ideas out as possible. In this way, you will already be thinking about the topic being covered. That will help you learn new information, because it will be easier for you to link it to recently-remembered knowledge.

4. **Think about what you want to know about the information in the objectives, and write these ideas in the second column.**
   You should want to know the information you will be tested over, so include information from both the section objectives and any other objectives your teacher has given you.

5. **While reading the section, or after you have read it, use the third column to write down what you learned.**
   While reading, pay close attention to any information about the topics you wrote in the "What I want to know" column. If you do not find all of the answers you are looking for, you may need to reread the section or find a second source for the information. Be sure to ask your teacher if you still cannot find the information after reading the section a second time.

What I know	What I want to know	What I learned

What I know	What I want to know	What I learned
▶ atoms are very small particles ▶ oxygen is an element ▶ elements are listed on the periodic table	▶ Explain the relationship between matter, atoms, and elements.	▶ matter is anything that occupies space ▶ atoms are the smallest particles with properties of an element ▶ elements cannot be broken down into simpler substances with the same properties ▶ atoms and elements are matter
▶ compounds are made of elements	▶ Distinguish between elements and compounds.	▶ elements combine chemically to make compounds ▶ compounds can be broken down into elements
▶ mixtures are combinations of more than one substance ▶ pure substances have only one component	▶ Categorize materials as pure substances or mixtures.	▶ pure substances have fixed compositions and definite properties ▶ mixtures are combinations of more than one pure substance ▶ elements and compounds are pure substances ▶ grape juice is a mixture

6. It is also important to review your brainstormed ideas when you have completed reading the section.

Compare your ideas in the first column with the information you wrote down in the third column. If you find that some of your brainstormed ideas are incorrect, cross them out. It is extremely important to identify and correct any misconceptions you had before you begin studying for your test.

Your completed KWL notes can make learning science much easier. First of all, this system of note-taking makes gaps in your knowledge easier to spot. That way you can focus on looking for the content you need easier, whether you look in the textbook or ask your teacher.

If you've identified the objectives clearly, the ideas you are studying the most are the ones that will matter most.

Practice

1. Use column 3 from the table above to identify and correct any misconceptions in the following brainstorm list.
   a. Physically mixing elements will form a compound.
   b. Diamond is a compound.
   c. Sodium chloride is an element.
   d. Lemonade is a pure substance.

Concept Maps

Making concept maps can help you decide what material in a chapter is important and how best to learn that material. A concept map presents key ideas, meanings, and relationships for the concepts being studied. It can be thought of as a visual road map of the chapter.

Concept maps can begin with vocabulary terms. Vocabulary terms are generally labels for concepts, and concepts are generally nouns. Concepts are linked using linking words to form propositions. A proposition is a phrase that gives meaning to the concept. For example, "matter is changed by energy" is a proposition.

1. **Select a main concept for the map.**

   We will use *matter* as the main concept for this map.

2. **List all the important concepts.**

   We'll use some of the terms in the second section of the chapter entitled "Matter."

   energy
   chemical property
   physical property
   density
   chemical change
   physical change
   reactivity

3. **Build the map by placing the concepts according to their importance under the main concept, and adding linking words to give meaning to the arrangement of concepts.**

   One way of arranging the concepts is shown in ***Map A.*** When adding the links, be sure that each proposition makes sense. To distinguish concepts from links, place your concepts in circles, ovals, or rectangles. Then add cross-links with lines connecting concepts across the map. ***Map B*** on the next page is a finished map covering the main ideas found in the vocabulary list in Step 1.

Practice mapping by making concept maps about topics you know. For example, if you know a lot about a particular sport, such as basketball, you can use that topic to make a practice map. By perfecting your skills with information that you know very well, you will begin to feel more confident about making maps from the information in a chapter.

Map A

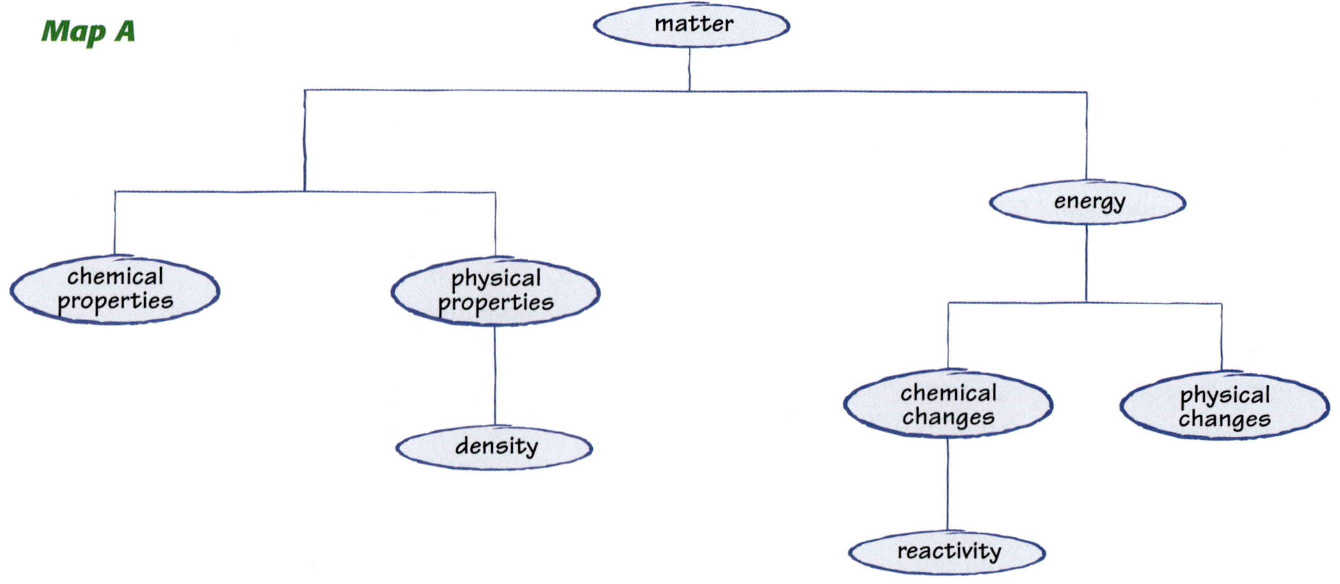

Making maps might seem difficult at first, but the process gets you to think about the meanings and relationships among concepts. If you do not understand those relationships, you can get help early on.

In addition, many people find it easier to study by looking at a concept map, rather than flipping through a chapter full of text because concept mapping is a visual way to organize the information in a chapter. Not only does it isolate the key concepts in a chapter, it also makes the relationships and linkages among those ideas easy to see and understand.

One useful strategy is to trade concept maps with a classmate. Everybody organizes information slightly differently, and something they may have done may help you understand the content better.

Remember, although concept mapping may take a little extra time, the time you spend mapping will pay off when it is time to review for a test or final exam.

Practice

1. Classify each of the following as either a concept or linking word(s).
   - **a.** compound
   - **b.** is classified as
   - **c.** forms
   - **d.** is described by
   - **e.** element
   - **f.** reacts with
   - **g.** pure substance
   - **h.** defines
2. Write three propositions from the information in ***Map B.***

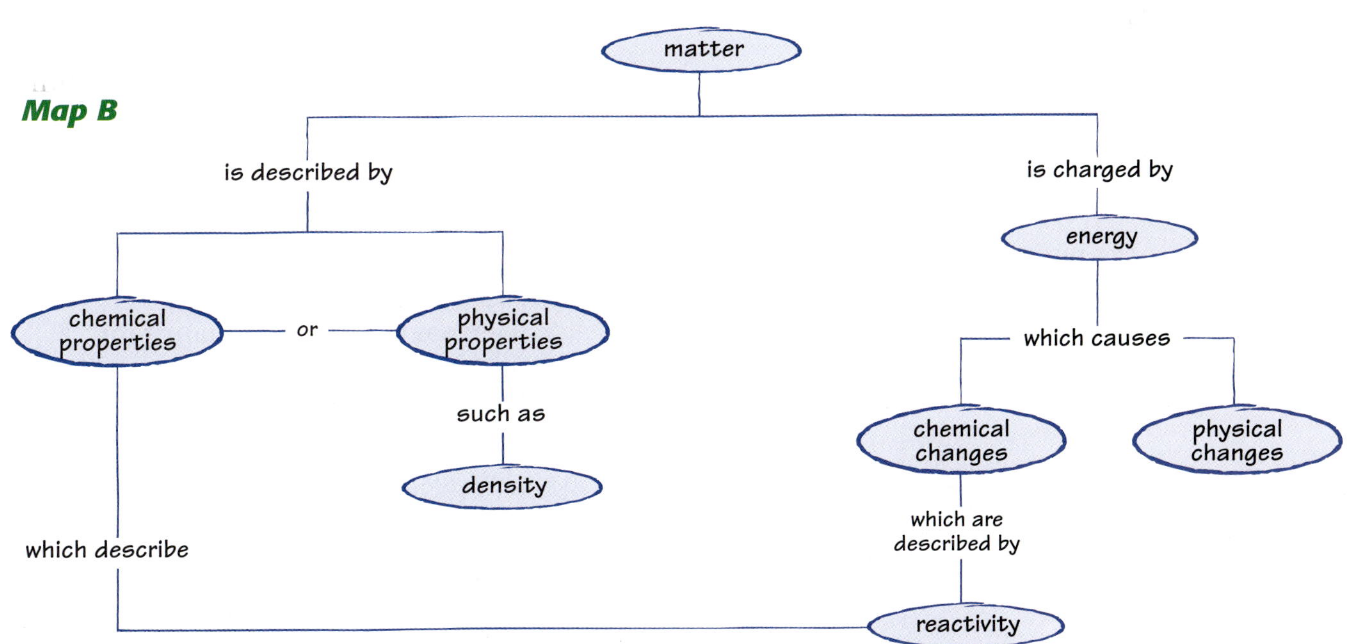

Process Flow Chart

A process flow chart is a special kind of concept map used for processes. The steps in a process almost always occur in the same order, so a process flow chart helps you to remember what order the steps occur in.

Unlike regular concept maps, process flow charts do not contain linking words. Instead, the arrows represent the next step in a process.

Examine the following process flow chart that shows the steps that occurred when the moon formed.

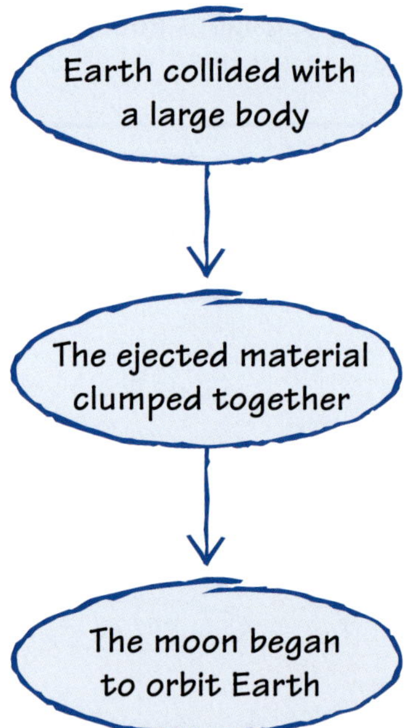

Another kind of process flow chart can be used to show the relationship between steps in a cycle, such as the one shown below that illustrates the steps of the water cycle.

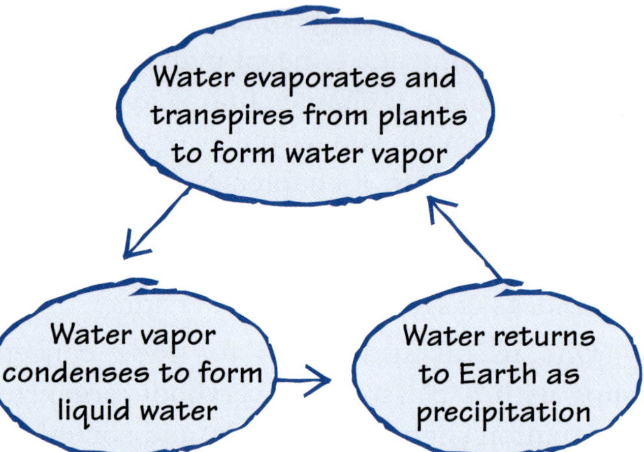

Notice that process flow charts that represent cycles have no beginnings or endings.

Practice

1. Create a process flow chart using the following scrambled steps.
   - As the water falls, it turns blades on a turbine fan
   - Dams are built to harness energy
   - As the loops turn, electrical current (or energy) is produced
   - Water is forced through small channels at the top of the dam
   - The fans are attached to a core that is wrapped with many loops of wire
   - The loops of wire rotate within a strong magnetic field
2. Use a cycle discussed in this book, and create your own process flow chart.

Interpreting Scientific Illustrations

Illustrations, figures, and photographs can be very useful when you are trying to understand a scientific idea. Many illustrations are included in this book to help you visualize relationships that are hard to visualize or understand. Some ideas or things are illustrated because they shown are too small or too large for you to see. Others are illustrated to help you remember relationships. The illustration on the right appears in the chapter entitled "Sound and Light."

When you are looking at a scientific illustration, refer to the text and remind yourself what the figure shows. The text that appears before the figure begins with the title "Objects have color because they reflect certain wavelengths of light." The title tells you the topic of the illustration.

Most figures have captions and labels that can also help you understand what the figure shows. First, examine the labels, and make sure that you understand what is being illustrated. Next, read the caption carefully, and restate it in your own words. If you can restate the caption you have a good idea of what the figure shows.

Figure 24

A Rose in White and Red Light

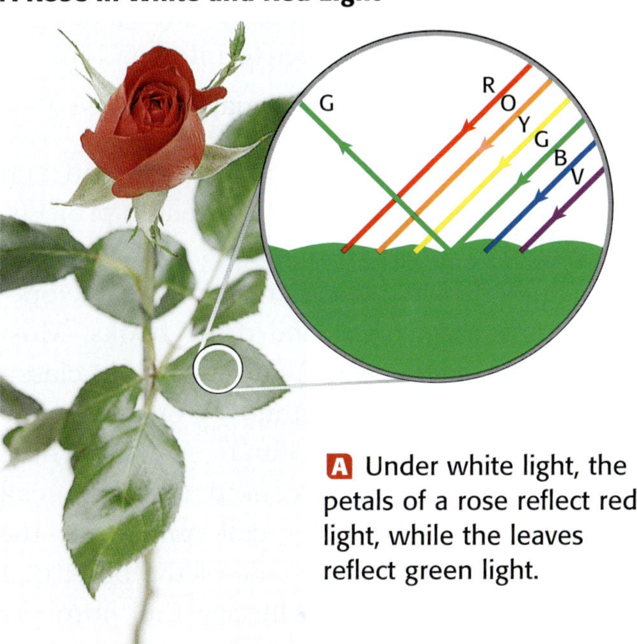

A Under white light, the petals of a rose reflect red light, while the leaves reflect green light.

B Under red light, the petals still look red, but the leaves look black because there is no green light for them to reflect.

Practice

1. Look at Figure 24A. Write your own labels for Figure 24B by using labels similar to labels on Figure 24.
2. After you have examined the figure carefully, restate the captions in your own words.

APPENDIX A

Researching Information

Many resources are available to help you research information. A wide variety of printed materials, such as newspapers, magazines, and books are available. The Internet is also becoming an important resource for information.

Using your library or media center

Printed materials are divided into fiction and nonfiction. For most scientific research projects, you will use nonfiction materials. These materials include newspapers, dictionaries, encyclopedias, some magazines, and other books. Most libraries and media centers use two main classification systems—the Library of Congress system and the Dewey decimal system. These classification systems are used to assign call numbers to the books. A call number is the series of numbers on the side of the book that help you to find it in the library. Call numbers are also listed in the card catalog or in the database your library uses to help you find books. ***Table 1*** shows a simplified Library of Congress system, which is used in most large libraries. ***Table 2*** shows a simplified Dewey decimal system. This system is often used in smaller libraries such as school libraries.

Practice

1. What system does your school library use to classify books?
2. Where are the encyclopedias in your school library?
3. Does your school library use a card catalog or a computer database to help you search for books?
4. List three nonfiction magazines that your school library has subscriptions to.
5. Name the title and call number for a book on science.

Table 1
Library of Congress classification system

Letter on book binding	Subject
A	General works
B	Philosophy, Psychology, and Religion
C–F	History
G–H	Geography and Social Sciences (e.g., Anthropology)
J	Political Science
K	Law
L	Education
M	Music
N	Fine Arts
P	Literature
Q	Science
R	Medicine
S	Agriculture
T	Technology
U–V	Military and Naval Science
Z	Bibliography and Library Science

Table 2
Dewey decimal system

Number on book binding	Subject
000–099	General works
100–199	Philosophy and Psychology
200–299	Religion
300–399	Social Sciences
400–499	Language
500–599	Pure Sciences
600–699	Technology
700–799	Arts
800–899	Literature
900–999	History

Using the Internet

Most research you do on a computer will involve the Internet and the World Wide Web. The Internet serves a variety of purposes but not all of these purposes involve providing accurate information, so it is important to be skeptical of information you get from the Internet.

To begin researching information on the Internet, you may want to begin with a search engine. A search engine is a Web site where you can search for other Web sites by subject or keyword. There are many different search engines that specialize in different kinds of information. When you are beginning a research project, find the address of a search engine and type that address into the address line like the one shown below.

For example, use the search engine **www.scirus.com**. *Scirus* is a search engine that specializes in scientific information. After typing **www.scirus.com** into the address line, push the return or enter key. Spelling and punctuation become very important when you are trying to find a Web site. Because there are so many Web sites on the World Wide Web, misspellings may take you to a different site than you intended. The first page of the search engine will look something like this:

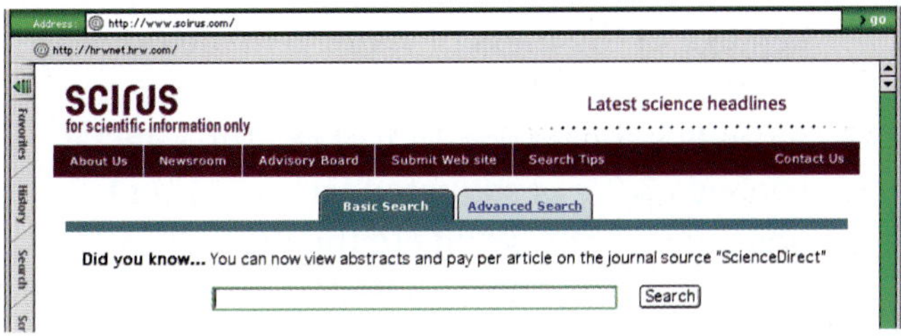

To search for information on black holes, enter the keyword "black hole" into the search line and hit the return or enter key. This process results in a search all the Web sites that are in the database for the keyword black holes and produces a list like the one shown below.

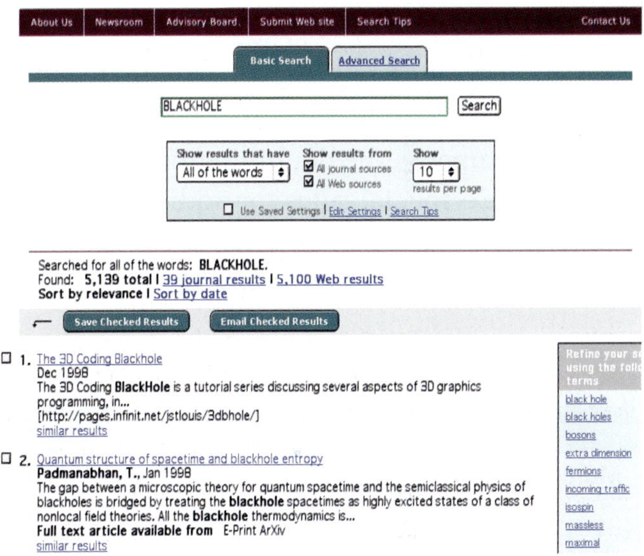

You should browse this list and pick Web sites that most closely fit your specific research topic. Another good search engine is **www.firstgov.gov**, which searches all government databases and Web sites. Government sites are a good source of reliable information.

Practice

1. Use an Internet search engine to search for Web sites about tectonic plates. List three Web sites, and discuss how reliable you think each one may be.
2. If you were looking for information about federal nutrition guidelines, where would you start? Explain your answer.
3. Why should you double check information you find through the Internet?

Math Skills Refresher

Fractions

Fractions represent numbers that are less than one. In other words, fractions are a way of numerically representing a part of a whole. For example, if you have a pizza with 8 slices, and you eat 2 of the slices, you have 6 out of the 8 slices, or $\frac{6}{8}$, of the pizza left. The top number in the fraction is called the numerator. The bottom number is the denominator.

There are special rules for adding, subtracting, multiplying, and dividing fractions. These rules are summarized in ***Table 3.***

Table 3 **Basic Operations for Fractions**

	Rule and example
Multiplication	$\left(\frac{a}{b}\right)\left(\frac{c}{d}\right) = \frac{ac}{bd}$ $\quad \left(\frac{2}{3}\right)\left(\frac{4}{5}\right) = \frac{8}{15}$
Division	$\frac{a}{b} \div \frac{c}{d} = \frac{\left(\frac{a}{b}\right)}{\left(\frac{c}{d}\right)} = \frac{ad}{bc}$ $\frac{2}{3} \div \frac{4}{5} = \frac{\left(\frac{2}{3}\right)}{\left(\frac{4}{5}\right)} = \frac{(2)(5)}{(3)(4)} = \frac{10}{12}$
Addition and subtraction	$\frac{a}{b} \pm \frac{c}{d} = \frac{ad \pm bc}{bd}$ $\frac{2}{3} - \frac{4}{5} = \frac{(2)(5) - (3)(4)}{(3)(5)} = -\frac{2}{15}$

Practice

1. Perform the following calculations:
   - **a.** $\frac{7}{8} + \frac{1}{3} =$
   - **b.** $\frac{7}{8} \times \frac{1}{3} =$
   - **c.** $\frac{7}{8} \div \frac{1}{3} =$
   - **d.** $\frac{7}{8} - \frac{1}{3} =$

Percentages

Percentages are no different from other fractions, except that in a percentage, the whole (or the number in the denominator) is considered to be 100. Any percentage, $x\%$, can be read as x out of 100. For example, if you have completed 50% of an assignment, you have completed $\frac{50}{100}$ or $\frac{1}{2}$ of the assignment.

Percentages can be calculated by dividing the part by the whole. When your calculator solves a division problem that is less than 1, it gives you a decimal value instead of a fraction. For example, 0.45 can be written as the fraction $\frac{45}{100}$. This is equal to 45%. An easy way to calculate percentages is to divide the part by the whole, then multiply by 100. This multiplication moves the decimal point two positions to the right, giving you the number that would be over 100 in a fraction. Try this example.

You scored 73 out of 92 problems on your last exam. What was your percentage score?

First divide the part by the whole to get a decimal value: $\frac{73}{92}$. Note that 0.7935 is equal to $\frac{79.35}{100}$.

Then multiply by 100 to yield the percentage: $0.7935 \times 100 = 79.35\%$.

Practice

1. Oxygen in water has a mass of 16.00 g. The water has a total mass of 18.01 g. What percentage of the mass of water is made up of oxygen?
2. A candy bar contains 14 g of fat. The total fat contains 3.0 g of saturated fat and 11 g of unsaturated fats. What are the percentages of saturated and unsaturated fat in the candy bar?

Exponents

An exponent is a number that is superscripted to the right of another number. The best way to explain how an exponent works is with an example. In the value 5^4, 4 is the exponent on 5. The number with its exponent means that 5 is multiplied by itself 4 times.

$$5^4 = 5 \times 5 \times 5 \times 5 = 625$$

You will frequently hear exponents referred to as powers. Using this terminology, the above equation could be read as *five to the fourth power equals 625.* Keep in mind that any number raised to the zero power is equal to one. Also, any number raised to the first power is equal to itself: $5^1 = 5$.

Just as there are special rules for dealing with fractions, there are special rules for dealing with exponents. These rules are summarized in ***Table 4.***

You probably recognize the symbol for a square root, $\sqrt{\ }$. This means that a number times itself equals the value inside the square root. It is also possible to have roots other than the square root. For example, $\sqrt[3]{x}$ means that some number, n, times itself three times equals the number x, or $n \times n \times n = x$. We can turn our example of $5^4 = 625$ around to solve for the fourth root of 625.

$$\sqrt[4]{625} = 5$$

Taking the nth root of a number is the same as raising that number to the power of $1/n$. Therefore, $\sqrt[4]{625} = 625^{1/4}$.

A scientific calculator is a must for solving most problems involving exponents and roots. Many calculators have dedicated keys for squares and square roots. But what about different powers, such as cubes and cube roots? Most scientific calculators have a key shaped like a caret, ^. If you type in "5^4," when you hit the equals sign or the enter key, the calculator will determine that $5^4 = 625$, and display that answer.

For roots, you enter the decimal equivalent of the fractional exponent. For example, to solve the problem of the fourth root of 625, instead of entering one-fourth as the exponent, enter "625^0.25," because 0.25 is equal to one-fourth.

Table 4 **Rules for dealing with exponents**

	Rule	Example
Zero power	$x^0 = 1$	$7^0 = 1$
First power	$x^1 = x$	$6^1 = 6$
Multiplication	$(x^n)(x^m) = x^{(n+m)}$	$(x^2)(x^4) = x^{(2+4)} = x^6$
Division	$\frac{x^n}{x^m} = x^{(n-m)}$	$\frac{x^8}{x^2} = x^{(8-2)} = x^6$
Exponents that are fractions	$x^{1/n} = \sqrt[n]{x}$	$4^{1/3} = \sqrt[3]{4} = 1.5874$
Exponents raised to a power	$(x^n)^m = x^{nm}$	$(5^2)^3 = 5^6 = 15\,625$

Practice

1. Perform the following calculations:
   - **a.** $9^1 =$
   - **b.** $(3^3)^5 =$
   - **c.** $\frac{2^8}{2^2} =$
   - **d.** $(14^2)(14^3) =$
   - **e.** $11^0 =$
   - **f.** $6^{1/6} =$

APPENDIX A

Order of Operations

Use this phrase to remember the correct order for long mathematical problems: *Please Excuse My Dear Aunt Sally.* This phrase stands for *Parentheses, Exponents, Multiplication, Division, Addition, Subtraction.* These rules can be summarized in **Table 5.**

Table 5 Order of Operations

Step	Operation
1	Simplify groups inside parentheses. Start with innermost group and work out.
2	Simplify all exponents.
3	Perform multiplication and division in order from left to right.
4	Perform addition and subtraction in order from left to right.

Look at the following example:

$$4^3 + 2 \times [8 - (3 - 1)] = ?$$

First simplify the operations inside parentheses. Begin with the innermost parentheses:

$$(3 - 1) = 2$$
$$4^3 + 2 \times [8 - 2] = ?$$

Then move on to the next-outer parentheses:

$$[8 - 2] = 6$$
$$4^3 + 2 \times 6 = ?$$

Now, simplify all exponents:

$$4^3 = 64$$
$$64 + 2 \times 6 = ?$$

The next step is to perform multiplication:

$$2 \times 6 = 12$$
$$64 + 12 = ?$$

Finally, solve the addition problem:

$$64 + 12 = 76$$

Practice

1. $2^3 \div 2 + 4 \times (9 - 2^2) =$
2. $\dfrac{2 \times (6 - 3) + 8}{4 \times 2 - 6} =$

Geometry

Quite often, a useful way to model the objects and substances studied in science is to consider them in terms of their shapes. For example, many of the properties of a wheel can be understood by pretending that the wheel is a perfect circle.

For this reason, being able to calculate the area or the volume of certain shapes is a useful skill in science. **Table 6** provides equations for the area and volume of several geometric shapes.

Table 6 Geometric Areas and Volumes

Geometric Shape	Useful Equations
Rectangle	Area = lw
Circle	Area = πr^2 Circumference = $2\pi r$
Triangle	Area = $\frac{1}{2}bh$
Sphere	Surface area = $4\pi r^2$ volume = $\frac{4}{3}\pi r^3$
Cylinder	Volume = $\pi r^2 h$
Rectangular box	Surface area = $2(lh + lw + hw)$ volume = lwh

Practice

1. What is the volume of a cylinder with a diameter of 14 cm and a height of 8 cm?
2. Calculate the surface area of a 4 cm cube.
3. Will a sphere with a volume of 76 cm^3 fit in a rectangular box that is 7 cm × 4 cm × 10 cm?

Algebraic Rearrangements

Algebraic equations contain *constants* and variables. Constants are simply numbers, such as 2, 5, and 7. Variables are represented by letters such as x, y, z, a, b, and c. Variables are unspecified quantities and are also called the unknowns.

Often, you will need to determine the value of a variable, but all you will be given will be an equation expressed in terms of algebraic expressions instead of a simple equation expressed in numbers only.

An algebraic expression contains one or more of the four basic mathematical operations: addition, subtraction, multiplication, and division. Constants, variables, or terms made up of both constants and variables can be involved in the basic operations.

The key to figuring out the value of a variable in an algebraic equation is that the quantity described on one side of the equals sign is equal to the quantity described on the other side of the equals sign.

If you are trying to determine the value of a variable in an algebraic expression, you would like to be able to rewrite the equation as a simple one that tells you exactly what x (or some other variable) equals.

But how do you get from a more complicated equation to a simple one?

Again, the key lies in the fact that both sides of the equation are equal. That means if you do the same operation on either side of the equation, the results will still be equal.

Look at the following simple problem:

$$8x = 32$$

If we wish to solve for x, we can multiply or divide each side of the equation by the same factor. You can add, subtract, multiply, or divide anything to or from one side of an equation as long as you do the same thing to the other side of the equation. In this case, if we divide both sides by 8, we have:

$$\frac{8x}{8} = \frac{32}{8}$$

The 8s on the left side of the equation cancel each other out, and the fraction $\frac{32}{8}$ can be reduced to give the whole number, 4. Therefore, $x = 4$.

Next consider the following equation:

$$x + 2 = 8$$

Remember, we can add or subtract the same quantity from each side. If we subtract 2 from each side, we get

$$x + 2 - 2 = 8 - 2$$
$$x + 0 = 6$$
$$x = 6$$

Now consider one more equation:

$$\frac{x}{5} = 9$$

If we multiply each side by 5, the 5 originally on the left side of the equation cancels out. We are left with x on the left by itself and 45 on the right:

$$x = 45$$

In all cases, *whatever operation is performed on the left side of the equals sign must also be performed on the right side.*

Practice

1. Rearrange each of the following equations to give the value of the variable indicated with a letter.

a. $8x - 32 = 128$

b. $6 - 5(4a + 3) = 26$

c. $-3(y - 2) + 4 = 29$

d. $-2(3m + 5) = 14$

e. $\left[8\frac{(8 + 2z)}{32}\right] + 2 = 5$

f. $\frac{(6b + 3)}{3} - 9 = 2$

APPENDIX A

Scientific Notation

Many quantities that scientists deal with have very large or very small values. For example, about 3 000 000 000 000 000 000 electrons' worth of charge pass through a standard light bulb in one second, and the ink required to make the dot over an *i* in this textbook has a mass of about 0.000 000 001 kg.

Obviously, it is very cumbersome to read, write, and keep track of numbers like these. We avoid this problem by using a method dealing with powers of the number 10.

Study the positive powers of ten shown in the chapter entitled Introduction to Science. You should be able to check those numbers using what you know about exponents. The number of zeros corresponds to the exponent on 10. The number for 10^4 is 10 000; it has 4 zeros.

But how can we use the powers of 10 to simplify large numbers such as the number of electron-sized charges passing through a light bulb? This large number is equal to 3×1 000 000 000 000 000 000. The factor of 10 has 18 zeros. Therefore, it can be rewritten as 10^{18}. This means that 3 000 000 000 000 000 000 can be expressed as 3×10^{18}.

That explains how to simplify really large numbers, but what about really small numbers, like 0.000 000 001 kg? Negative exponents can be used to simplify numbers that are less than 1.

Next, study the negative powers of 10. The exponent on 10 equals the number of decimal places you must move the decimal point to the right so that there is one digit just to the left of the decimal point. Using the mass of the ink in the dot on an i, the decimal point has to be moved 9 decimal places to the right for the numeral 1 to be just to the left of the decimal point. The mass of the ink, 0.000 000 001 kg, can be rewritten as 1×10^{-9} kg.

Numbers that are expressed as some power of 10 multiplied by another number with only one digit to the left of the decimal point are said to be written in scientific notation. For example, 5943 000 000 is 5.943×10^9 when expressed in scientific notation. The number 0.000 0832 is 8.32×10^{-5} when expressed in scientific notation.

When a number is expressed in scientific notation, it is easy to determine the order of magnitude of the number. The order of magnitude is the power of ten that the number would be rounded to. For example, in the number 5.943×10^9, the order of magnitude is 10^{10}, because 5.943 rounds to another 10, and 10 times 10^9 is 10^{10}. For numbers less than 5, the order of magnitude is just the power of ten when the number is written in scientific notation.

The order of magnitude can be used to help quickly estimate your answers. Simply perform the operations required, but instead of using numbers, use the orders of magnitude. Your final answer should be within two orders of magnitude of your estimate.

Practice

1. Rewrite the following values using scientific notation:

a. 12 300 000 m/s
b. 0.000 000 000 0045 kg
c. 0.000 0653 m
d. 55 432 000 000 000 s
e. 273.15 K
f. 0.000 627 14 kg

SI

One of the most important parts of scientific research is being able to communicate your findings to other scientists. Today, scientists need to be able to communicate with other scientists all around the world. They need a common language in which to report data. If you do an experiment in which all of your measurements are in pounds, and you want to compare your results to a French scientist whose measurements are in grams, you will need to convert all of your measurements. For this reason, *Le Système International d'Unités,* or SI system was devised in 1960.

You are probably accustomed to measuring distance in inches, feet, and miles. Most of the world, however, measures distance in centimeters (abbreviated cm), meters (abbreviated m), and kilometers (abbreviated km). The meter is the official SI unit for measuring distance.

Notice that centi*meter* and kilo*meter* each contain the word *meter.* When dealing with SI units, you frequently use the base unit, in this case the meter, and add a prefix to indicate that the quantity you are measuring is a multiple of that unit. Most SI prefixes indicate multiples of 10. For example, the centimeter is 1/100 of a meter. Any SI unit with the prefix *centi-* will be 1/100 of the base unit. A centigram is 1/100 of a gram.

Table 7 Some SI Units

Quantity	Unit name	Abbreviation
Length	meter	m
Mass	kilogram	kg
Time	second	s
Temperature	kelvin	K
Amount of substance	mole	mol
Electric current	ampere	A
Pressure	pascal	Pa
Volume	meters^3	m^3

Table 8 Some SI Prefixes

Prefix	Abbreviation	Exponential factor
Giga-	G	10^9
Mega-	M	10^6
Kilo-	k	10^3
Hecto-	h	10^2
Deka-	da	10^1
Deci-	d	10^{-1}
Centi-	c	10^{-2}
Milli-	m	10^{-3}
Micro-	μ	10^{-6}
Nano-	n	10^{-9}
Pico-	p	10^{-12}
Femto-	f	10^{-15}

What about the *kilo*meter? The prefix *kilo-* indicates that the unit is 1000 times the base unit. A kilometer is equal to 1000 meters. Multiples of 10 make dealing with SI values much easier than values such as feet or gallons. If you wish to convert from feet to miles, you must remember a large conversion factor, 1.893939×10^{-4} miles/foot. If you wish to convert from kilometers to meters, you need only look at the prefix to know that you will multiply by 1000.

Table 7 lists the SI units. **Table 8** gives the possible prefixes and their meaning. When working with a prefix, simply take the unit abbreviation and add the prefix abbreviation to the front of the unit. For example, the abbreviation for kilometer is written km.

Practice

1. Convert each value to the requested units.

a. 0.035 m to decimeters

b. 5.24 m^3 to centimeters^3

c. 13450 g to kilograms

APPENDIX A

Significant Figures

The following list can be used to review how to determine the number of significant figures in a reported value. After you have reviewed the rules, use ***Table 9*** to check your understanding of the rules. Cover up the second column of the table, and try to determine how many significant figures each number has. If you get confused, refer to the rule given.

Table 9 **Significant Figures**

Measurement	Number of significant figures	Rule
12 345	5	1
2400 cm	2	3
305 kg	3	2
2350. cm	4	4
234.005 K	6	2
12.340	5	6
0.001	1	5
0.002 450	4	5 and 6

Rules for Determining the Number of Significant Figures in a Measurement:

1. All nonzero digits are significant. **Example:** 1246 has four significant figures (shown in red).
2. Any zeros between significant digits are also significant. 1206 has four significant figures.
3. If the value does not contain a decimal point, any zeros to the right of a nonzero digit are not significant. 1200 has only two significant figures.
4. Any zeros to the right of a significant digit and to the left of a decimal point are significant. 1200. has four significant figures.
5. If a value has no significant digits to the left of a decimal point, any zeros to the right of the decimal point, and to the left of a significant digit, are not significant. **Example:** 0.0012 has only two significant figures.
6. If a measurement is reported that ends with zeros to the right of a decimal point, those zeros are significant. **Example:** 0.1200 has four significant figures.

If you are adding or subtracting two measurements, your answer can only have as many decimal positions as the value with the least number of decimal places. The final answer in the following problem has five significant figures. It has been rounded to two decimal places because 0.04 g only has two decimal places.

$$\begin{array}{r} 134.050 \text{ g} \\ -\ 0.04 \text{ g} \\ \hline 134.01 \text{ g} \end{array}$$

When multiplying or dividing measurements, your final answer can only have as many significant figures as the value with the least number of significant figures. Examine the following multiplication problem.

$$\begin{array}{r} 12.0 \text{ cm}^2 \\ \times\, 0.04 \text{ cm} \\ \hline 0.5 \text{ cm}^3 \end{array}$$

The final answer has been rounded to one significant figure because 0.04 cm has only one. When performing both types of operations (addition/subtraction vs. multiplication/division), complete one type, round, perform the other type, round, perform the other type, and round the result.

Practice

1. Determine the number of significant figures in each of the following measurements:
   a. 65.04 mL
   b. 564.00 m
   c. 0.007504 kg
   d. 1210 K
2. Perform each of the following calculations, and report your answer with the correct number of significant figures and units:
   a. 0.004 dm + 0.12508 dm
   b. 340 m ÷ 0.1257 s
   c. 40.1 kg × 0.2453 m^2
   d. 1.03 g − 0.0456 g

Graphing Skills

Line Graphs

In laboratory experiments, you will usually be controlling one variable and seeing how it affects another variable. Line graphs can show these relations clearly. For example, you might perform an experiment in which you measure the growth of a plant over time to determine the rate of the plant's growth. In this experiment, you are controlling the time intervals at which the plant height is measured. Therefore, time is called the *independent variable*. The height of the plant is the *dependent variable*. **Table 10** gives some sample data for an experiment to measure the rate of plant growth.

The independent variable is plotted on the x-axis. This axis will be labeled *Time (days)*, and will have a range from 0 days to 35 days. Be sure to properly label your axis including the units on the values.

The dependent variable is plotted on the y-axis. This axis will be labeled *Plant Height (cm)* and will have a range from 0 cm to 5 cm.

Think of your graph as a grid with lines running horizontally from the y-axis, and vertically from the x-axis. To plot a point, find the x (in this example time) value on the x axis. Follow the vertical line from the x axis until it intersects the horizontal line from the y-axis at the corresponding y (in this case height) value. At the intersection of these two lines, place your point. **Figure 3** shows what a line graph of the data in **Table 10** might look like.

Table 10 Experimental Data for Plant Growth versus Time

Time (days)	Plant height (cm)
0	1.43
7	2.16
14	2.67
21	3.25
28	4.04
35	4.67

Figure 3

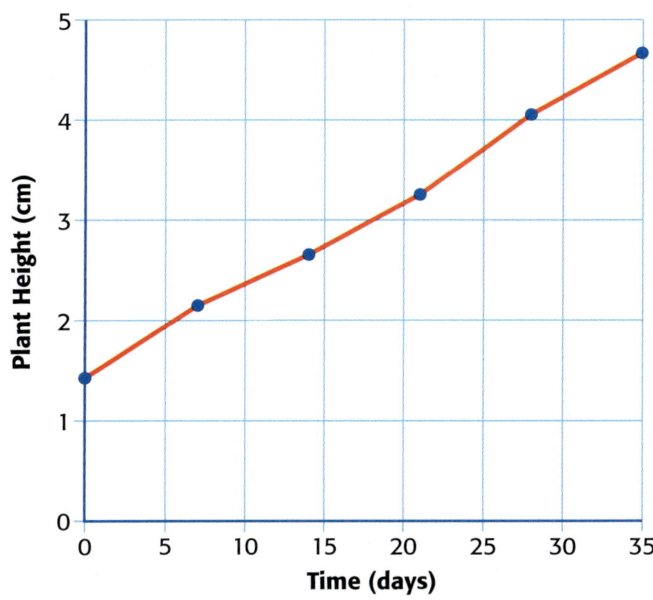

Practice

1. What does the line in **Figure 3** show, and what can you conclude about the plants used in the experiment?
2. Create a line graph of the following data.

Number of Days	Plant height (cm)
0	1.46
7	2.67
14	3.89
21	4.82

3. Compare the graph you made with **Figure 3.** What can you conclude about the two different groups of plants?

APPENDIX A

Scatter Plots

Some experiments or groups of data are best represented in a graph that is similar to a line graph and that is called a scatter plot. As in a line graph, the data points are plotted on the graph by using values on an x-axis and a y-axis. Scatter plots are often used to find trends in data. Instead of connecting the data points with a line, a trend can be represented by a best-fit line. A best-fit line is a line that represents all of the data points without necessarily going through all of them. To find a best-fit line, pick a line that is equidistant from as many data points as possible. Examine the graph below.

Figure 4

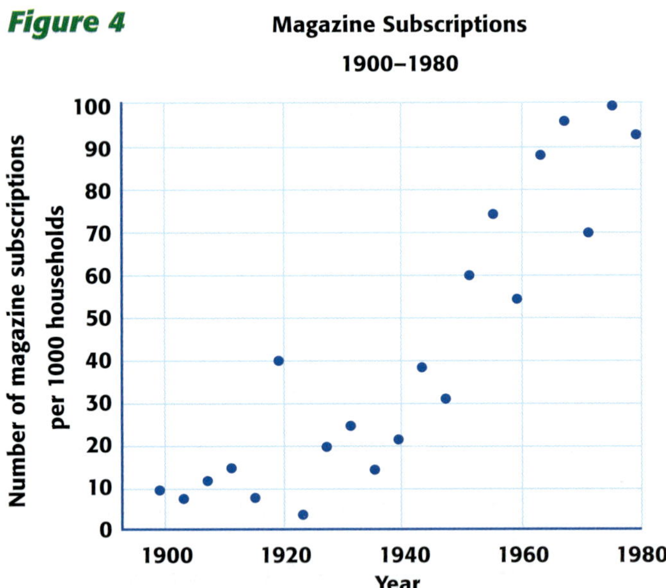

If we connected all of the data points with lines, the lines would create a zigzag pattern that would not tell us much about our data. But if we find a best-fit line, we can see a trend more clearly. Furthermore, if we pick two points on the best-fit line, we can estimate its slope. Examine the dotted lines on ***Figure 5.***

The points can be estimated as 18 magazine subscriptions per 100 households in 1920, and 42 magazine subscriptions per 100 households in 1940. If we subtract 1920 from 1940, and 18 subscriptions from 42 subscriptions (using the point slope formula), we see that the line shows a trend of an increase of 24 subscriptions per 1000 households acres every 20 years. Scatter plots can also be used when there are two or more trends within one group of data or when there is no distinct trend at all.

Figure 5

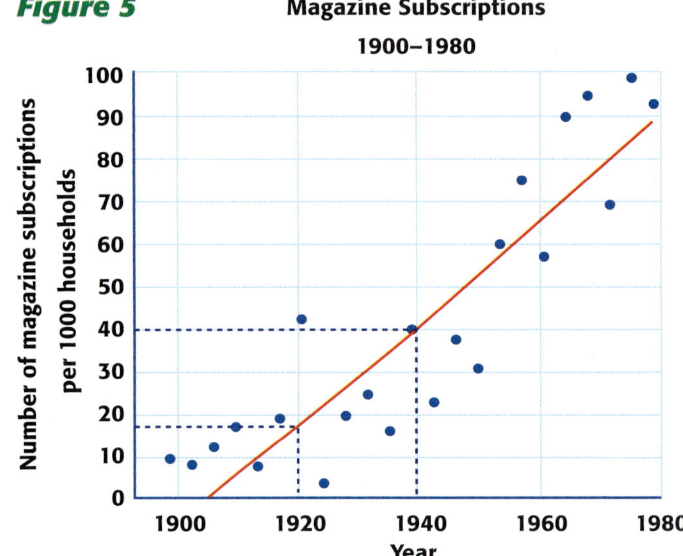

Practice

1. Copy the graph below, and draw a best-fit line.

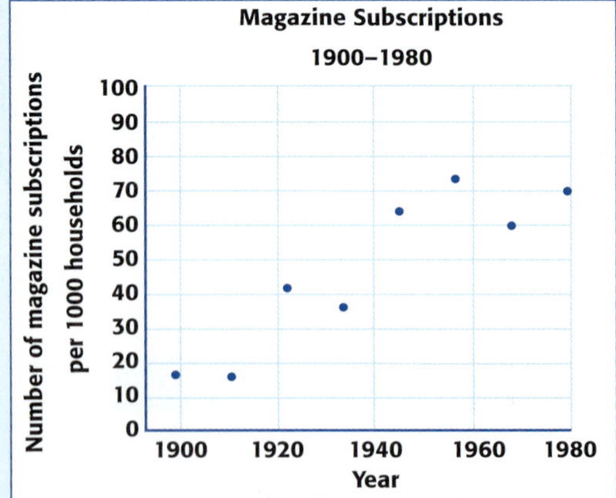

2. What does that line represent?
3. If these were the data from a different city than the data in ***Figure 5,*** what conclusions could you draw about the two cities?

Bar Graphs

Figure 6

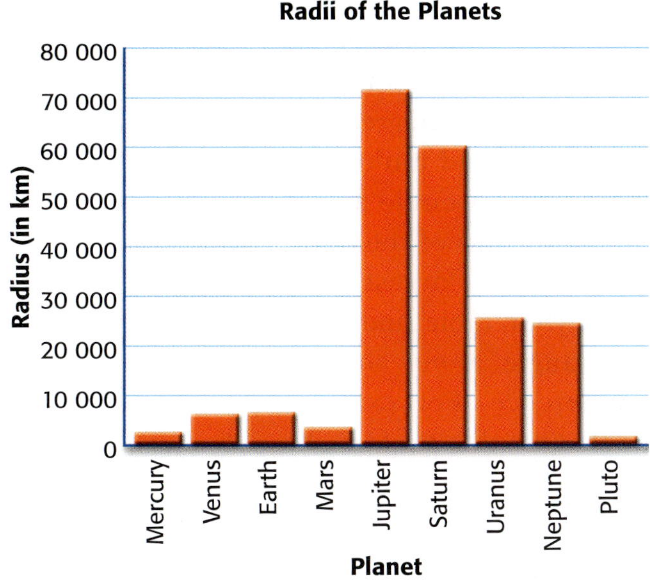

Bar graphs make it easy to compare data quickly. We can see from ***Figure 6*** that Jupiter has the largest radius, and that Pluto has the smallest radius. We can also quickly arrange the planets in order of size.

Bar graphs can also be used to identify trends, especially trends among differing quantities. Examine ***Figure 7*** below.

Figure 7

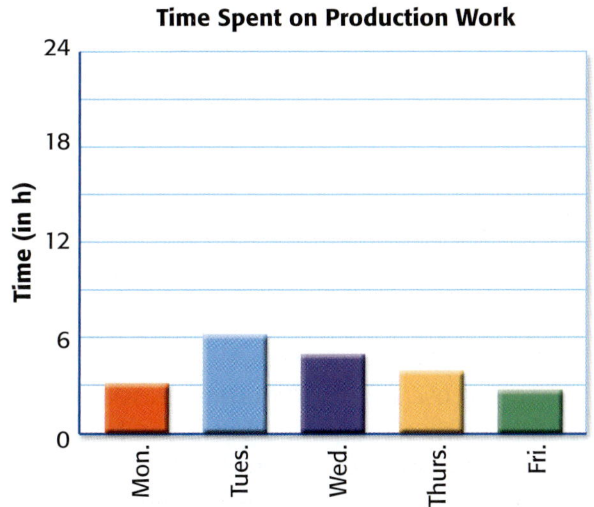

The data are represented accurately, but it is not easy to draw conclusions quickly. Remember that when you are creating a graph, you want the graph to be as clear as possible. If we graph the exact same data on a graph with slightly different axes, as shown in ***Figure 8,*** it may be much easier to draw conclusions.

Figure 8

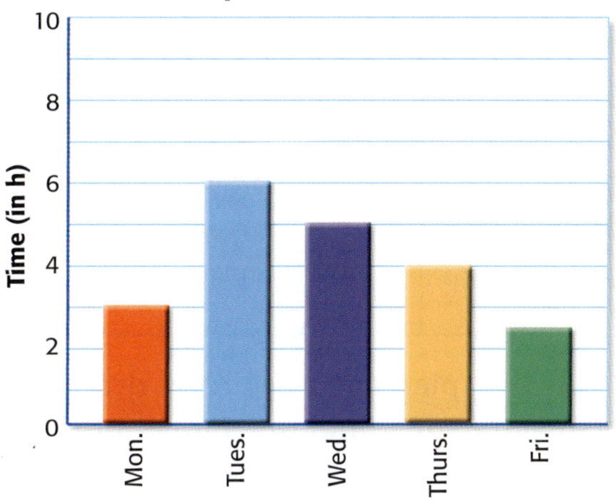

Practice

1. What day of the week is most productive, according to ***Figure 8?***
2. What day of the week is least productive?
3. Using the following data, create a clear and easily readable bar graph.

Fiscal period	Money spent (in millions)
First quarter	89
Second quarter	56
Third quarter	72
Fourth quarter	41

Pie Charts

Pie charts are an easy way to visualize how parts make up a whole. Frequently, pie charts are made from percentage data such as the data in ***Table 11.***

Table 11 **Elemental Composition of Earth's Crust**

Element	Percentage of Earth's Crust
Oxygen	46%
Silicon	28%
Aluminum	8%
Iron	6%
Calcium	4%
Sodium	2%
Magnesium	2%
Potassium	2%
Titanium	1%
All remaining elements	1%

To create a pie chart, begin by drawing a circle. Imagine dividing the circle into 100 equal parts. Because 50 parts would be half of the circle, we know that 46% will be slightly less than half of the pie. We shade a piece that is less than half, and label it "Oxygen." Continue this process until the entire pie graph has been filled. Each element should be a different color to make the chart easy to read as in ***Figure 9.***

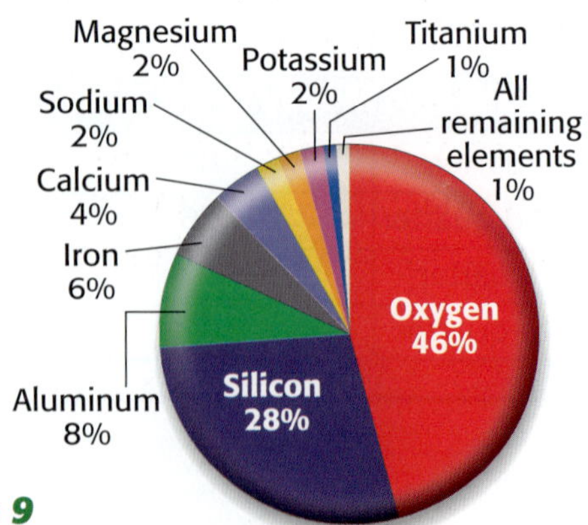

Figure 9

Another way to construct a pie chart involves using a protractor. This method is especially helpful when your data can't be converted into simple fractions. First, convert the percentages to degrees by dividing each number by 100 and multiplying that result by 360. Next, draw a circle and make a vertical mark across the top of the circle. Using a protractor, measure the largest angle from your table and mark this angle along the circumference. For example, 32.9% would be 118° because 32.9/100 = .329 and .329 × 360 = 118.

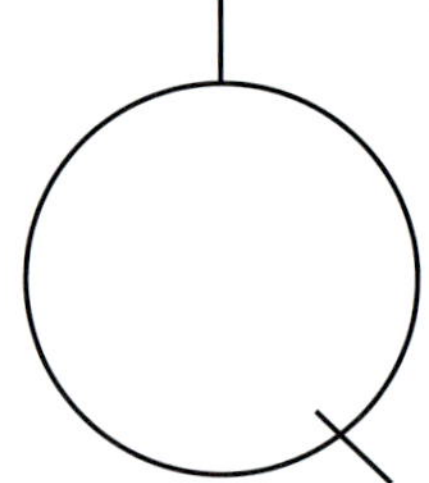

Next, measure a second angle from the second mark to make a third mark along the circumference. Continue this process until all of your slices are measured. Draw lines from the marks to the center of the circle, and label each slice.

Practice

1. Use the data below to create a pie chart.

Kind of land use	Percentage of total land
Grassland and rangeland	29
Wilderness and parks	9
Urban	2
Wetlands and deserts	3
Forest	30
Cropland	17

2. If humans use half of forests and grasslands, plus all of croplands and urban areas, how much of the total land is used by humans?

Lab Skills

Making Measurements in the Laboratory

Reading a balance for mass

When a balance is required for determining mass, you will probably use a centigram balance like the one shown in ***Figure 10.*** The centigram balance is sensitive to 0.01 g. This means that your mass readings should all be recorded to the nearest 0.01 g.

Before using the balance, always check to see if the pointer is resting at zero. If the pointer is not at zero, check the slider weights. If all the slider weights are at zero, turn the zero adjust knob until the pointer rests at zero. The zero adjust knob is usually located at the far left end of the balance beam as shown in ***Figure 10.*** Note: The balance will not adjust to zero if the movable pan has been removed.

Figure 10

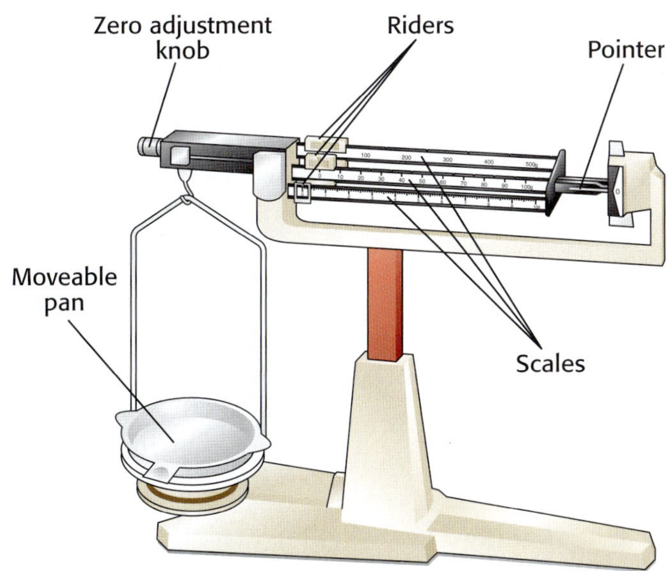

In many experiments you will be asked to obtain a specified mass of a solid. When measuring the mass of a chemical, place a piece of weighing paper on the balance pan. **Never place chemicals or hot objects directly on the balance pan.** They can permanently damage the surface of the balance pan and affect the accuracy of later measurements.

Determine the mass of the paper by adjusting the weights on the various scales. Record the mass of the weighing paper to the nearest 0.01 g. Then add the mass you wish to obtain by sliding over the appropriate weights on the balance. For example, if your weighing paper has a mass of 0.15 g, and you wish to obtain 13 g of table salt, the balance begins at 0.15 g. You then need to add 13 g to this mass. Do this by sliding the 10-gram scale to 10 and the 1-gram scale to 3. The balance is no longer balanced.

Slowly add the solid onto the weighing paper until the balance is once again balanced. Do not waste time trying to obtain *exactly* 13.00 g of a solid. Instead, read the mass when the pointer swings close to zero. Remember, you must read the final mass on the balance and subtract the mass of the weighing paper (0.15 g) from it to find the mass of the solid to two decimal places, as is appropriate for measurements that are made by using a centigram balance.

Measuring temperature with a thermometer

A thermometer is used to measure temperature. Examine your thermometer and the temperature range for the Celsius scale. You will probably be using an alcohol or a digital thermometer in your laboratory.

Mercury thermometers are hazardous and will probably not be available in your school laboratory, although you may still have a mercury fever thermometer at home. **If a mercury thermometer should ever break, immediately notify your teacher or parent. Your teacher or parent will clean up the spill. Do not touch the mercury.**

Alcohol thermometers, like mercury thermometers, have a column of liquid that rises in a glass cylinder depending on the temperature at the tip of the thermometer. One caution concerning alcohol thermometers is that they can burst at very high temperatures. Never let the thermometer be exposed to temperatures well above its range.

When working with any thermometer, it is especially important to pay close attention to the precision of the instrument. Most alcohol thermometers are marked in intervals of 1°C. The intervals are usually so close together that it is impossible to estimate temperature values measured with such a thermometer to any more precision than a half a degree, 0.5°C. Thus, if you are using this type of thermometer, it would be impossible to actually measure a temperature like 25.15°C.

It is also very important to keep your eye at about the same level as the colored fluid in the thermometer. If you are looking at the thermometer from below, the reading you see will appear a degree or two higher than it really is. Similarly, if you look at the thermometer from above, the reading will seem to be a degree or two lower than it really is.

Reading a graduated cylinder for volume

Many different types of laboratory glassware, from beakers to flasks contain markings indicating volume. However, these markings are merely approximate, and they are not consistently checked when the beaker or flask was made.

For truly accurate volume measurements, you should use a graduated cylinder, like the one shown in ***Figure 11.*** When a graduated cylinder is made, its accuracy is checked and rechecked. You will also notice that a graduated cylinder is marked in smaller increments than beakers are (usually individual milliliters, although some graduated cylinders are even more precise).

Most liquids have a concave surface that forms in a test tube or graduated cylinder. This concave surface is called a meniscus. When measuring the volume of a liquid, you must consider the meniscus, like the one labeled ***Figure 11.*** Always measure the volume from the bottom of the meniscus. The markings on a graduated cylinder are designed to take into account the little bits of water that extend up along the walls slightly above the marking lines.

It may be difficult to read a volume measurement, so if you need to, hold a piece of white paper behind the graduated cylinder. This should make the meniscus level easier to see.

Figure 11

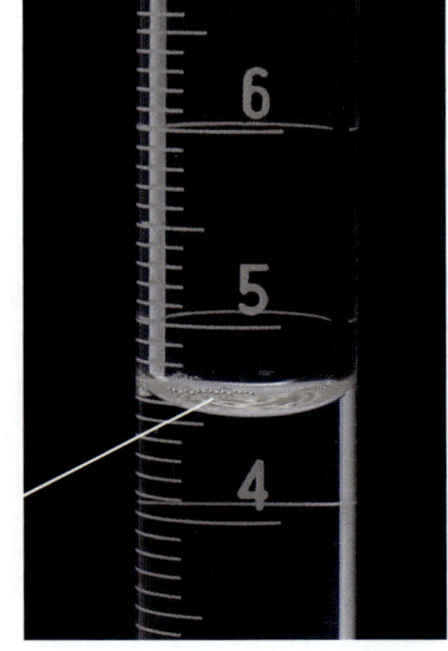

Meniscus, 4.5 mL

How to Write a Laboratory Report

In many of the laboratory investigations that you will be doing, you will be trying to support a hypothesis or answer a question by performing experiments following the scientific method. You will frequently be asked to summarize your experiments in a laboratory report. Laboratory reports should contain the following parts:

Title

This is the name of the experiment you are doing. If you are performing an experiment from a laboratory manual, the title will be the same as the title of the experiment.

Hypothesis

The hypothesis is what you think will happen during the investigation. It is often written as an "If . . . then" statement. When you conduct your experiment, you will be changing one condition, or variable, and observing and measuring the effect of this change. The condition that you are changing is called the *independent* variable and should follow the "If . . ." statement. The effect that you expect to observe is called the *dependent* variable and should follow the ". . . then" statement. For example, look at the following hypothesis:

If salamanders are reared in acidic water, then more salamanders will develop abnormally.

"If salamander are reared in acidic water" is the independent variable—salamanders normally live in nearly neutral water and you are changing this to acidic water. "Then more salamanders will develop abnormally" is the dependent variable—this is the change that you expect to observe and measure.

Materials

List of all the equipment and other supplies you will need to complete the experiment. If the investigation is taken from a laboratory manual, the materials are generally listed for you, but you will need to recopy them into your lab report. It is important that your lab report be complete enough for someone to use it to retest your results.

Procedure

The procedure is a step-by-step explanation of exactly what you did in the experiment. Investigations from laboratory manuals will have the procedure carefully written out for you, but you must write the procedure in your lab report EXACTLY as you performed it. This will not necessarily be an exact copy of the procedure in your laboratory manual.

Data

Your data are your observations. Data can include measurements, so it is important to record the correct units. They are often recorded in the form of tables, graphs, and drawings.

Analyses and Conclusions

This part of the report explains what you have learned. You should evaluate your hypothesis and explain any errors you made in the investigation. Keep in mind that not all hypotheses will be correct. Sometimes you will disprove your original hypothesis, rather than prove it. You simply need to explain why things did not work out the way you thought they would. In laboratory manual investigations, there will be questions to guide you in analyzing your data. You should use these questions as a basis for your conclusions.

APPENDIX B

Table 1 **SI Base Units**

Quantity	Unit	Abbreviation
Length	meter	m
Mass	kilogram	kg
Time	second	s
Temperature	kelvin	K
Electric current	ampere	A
Amount of substance	mole	mol
Luminous intensity	candela	cd

Table 2 **Other Commonly Used Units**

Quantity	Unit	Abbreviation	Conversion
Electric charge	coulomb	C	1 A•s
Temperature	degree Celsius	°C	1 K
Frequency	hertz	Hz	1/s
Work and energy	joule	J	$1\ \frac{kg \cdot m^2}{s^2} = 1\ N \cdot m$
Force	newton	N	$1\ \frac{kg \cdot m}{s^2}$
Pressure	pascal	Pa	$1\ \frac{kg}{m \cdot s^2} = 1\ \frac{N}{m^2}$
Angular displacement	radian	rad	(unitless)
Electric potential difference	volt	V	$1\ \frac{kg \cdot m^2}{A \cdot s^3} = 1\ \frac{J}{C}$
Power	watt	W	$1\ \frac{kg \cdot m^2}{s^3} = 1\ \frac{J}{s}$
Resistance	ohm	Ω	$1\ \frac{kg \cdot m^2}{A^2 \cdot s^3} = 1\ \frac{V}{A}$

Table 3 Densities of Various Materials

Material	Density (g/cm^3)	Material	Density (g/cm^3)
Air, dry	1.293×10^{-3}	Ice	0.917
Aluminum	2.70	Iron	7.86
Bone	1.7–2.0	Lead	11.3
Brick, common	1.9	Mercury	13.5336
Butter	0.86–0.87	Paper	0.7–1.15
Carbon (diamond)	3.5155	Rock salt	2.18
Carbon (graphite)	2.2670	Silver	10.5
Copper	8.96	Sodium	0.97
Cork	0.22–0.26	Stainless steel	8.02
Ethanol	0.783	Steel	7.8
Gasoline	0.7	Sugar	1.59
Gold	19.3	Water (at 25°C)	0.997 05
Helium	1.78×10^{-4}	Water (ice)	0.917

Table 4 Specific Heats

Material	*c* (J/kg•K)	Material	*c* (J/kg•K)
Acetic acid (CH_3COOH)	2070	Lead (Pb)	129
Air	1007	Magnetite (Fe_3O_4)	619
Aluminum (Al)	897	Mercury (Hg)	140
Calcium (Ca)	647	Methane (CH_4)	2200
Calcium carbonate ($CaCO_3$)	818	Neon (Ne)	1030
Carbon (C, diamond)	487	Nickel (Ni)	444
Carbon (C, graphite)	709	Nitrogen (N_2)	1040
Carbon dioxide (CO_2)	843	Oxygen (O_2)	918
Copper (Cu)	385	Platinum (Pt)	133
Ethanol (CH_3CH_2OH)	2440	Silver (Ag)	234
Gold (Au)	129	Sodium (Na)	1228
Helium (He)	5193	Sodium chloride (NaCl)	864
Hematite (Fe_2O_3)	650	Tin (Sn)	228
Hydrogen (H_2)	14 304	Tungsten (W)	132
Hydrogen peroxide (H_2O_2)	2620	Water (H_2O)	4186
Iron (Fe)	449	Zinc (Zn)	388

Values at 25°C and 1 atm pressure

Figure 1 Periodic Table of the Elements

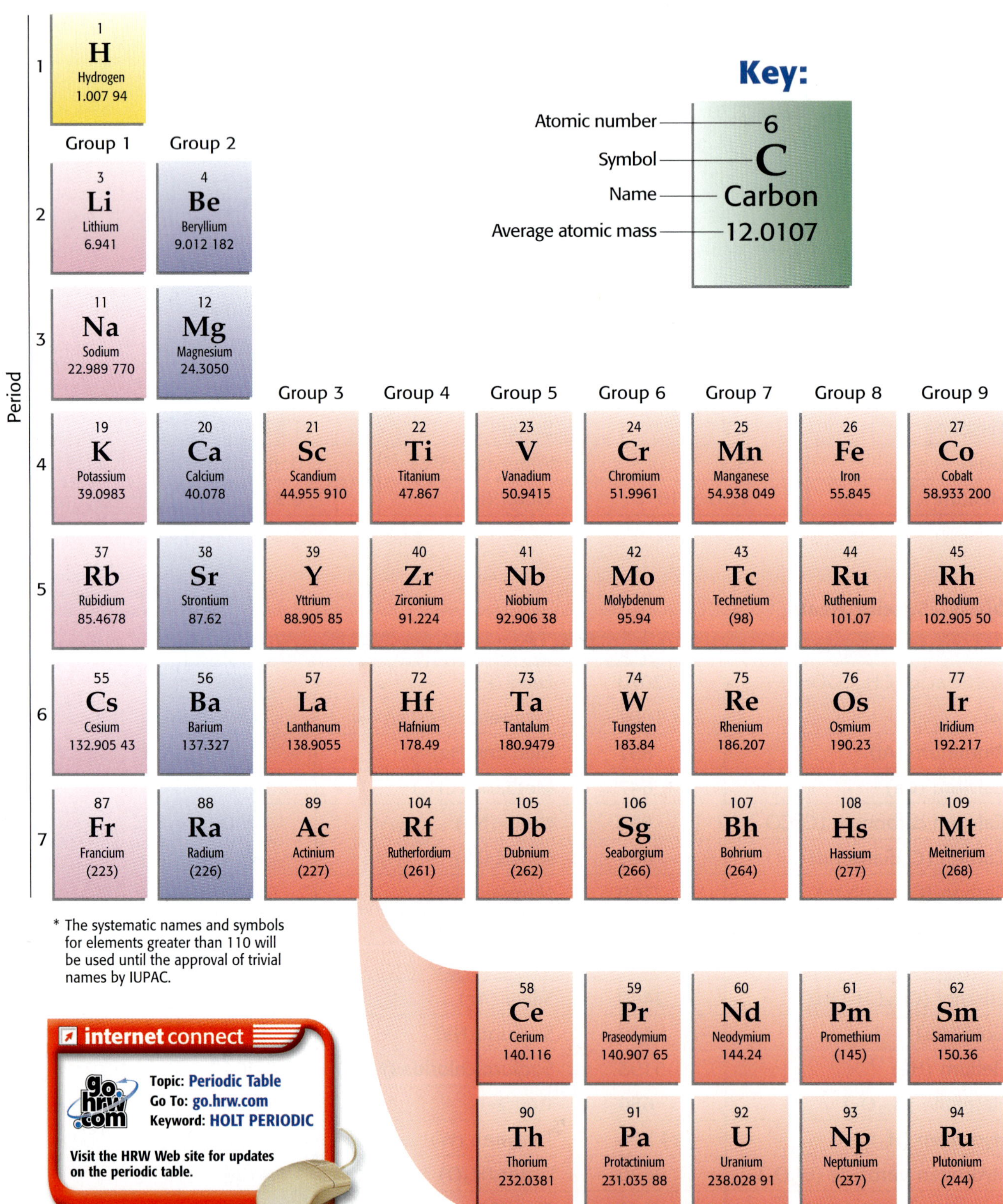

Period	Group 1	Group 2	Group 3	Group 4	Group 5	Group 6	Group 7	Group 8	Group 9
1	1 H Hydrogen 1.007 94								
2	3 Li Lithium 6.941	4 Be Beryllium 9.012 182							
3	11 Na Sodium 22.989 770	12 Mg Magnesium 24.3050							
4	19 K Potassium 39.0983	20 Ca Calcium 40.078	21 Sc Scandium 44.955 910	22 Ti Titanium 47.867	23 V Vanadium 50.9415	24 Cr Chromium 51.9961	25 Mn Manganese 54.938 049	26 Fe Iron 55.845	27 Co Cobalt 58.933 200
5	37 Rb Rubidium 85.4678	38 Sr Strontium 87.62	39 Y Yttrium 88.905 85	40 Zr Zirconium 91.224	41 Nb Niobium 92.906 38	42 Mo Molybdenum 95.94	43 Tc Technetium (98)	44 Ru Ruthenium 101.07	45 Rh Rhodium 102.905 50
6	55 Cs Cesium 132.905 43	56 Ba Barium 137.327	57 La Lanthanum 138.9055	72 Hf Hafnium 178.49	73 Ta Tantalum 180.9479	74 W Tungsten 183.84	75 Re Rhenium 186.207	76 Os Osmium 190.23	77 Ir Iridium 192.217
7	87 Fr Francium (223)	88 Ra Radium (226)	89 Ac Actinium (227)	104 Rf Rutherfordium (261)	105 Db Dubnium (262)	106 Sg Seaborgium (266)	107 Bh Bohrium (264)	108 Hs Hassium (277)	109 Mt Meitnerium (268)

58 Ce Cerium 140.116	59 Pr Praseodymium 140.907 65	60 Nd Neodymium 144.24	61 Pm Promethium (145)	62 Sm Samarium 150.36
90 Th Thorium 232.0381	91 Pa Protactinium 231.035 88	92 U Uranium 238.028 91	93 Np Neptunium (237)	94 Pu Plutonium (244)

* The systematic names and symbols for elements greater than 110 will be used until the approval of trivial names by IUPAC.

- Hydrogen
- Semiconductors (also known as *metalloids*)

Metals

- Alkali metals
- Alkaline-earth metals
- Transition metals
- Other metals

Nonmetals

- Halogens
- Noble gases
- Other nonmetals

Group 10	Group 11	Group 12	Group 13	Group 14	Group 15	Group 16	Group 17	Group 18
								2 **He** Helium 4.002 602
			5 **B** Boron 10.811	6 **C** Carbon 12.0107	7 **N** Nitrogen 14.0067	8 **O** Oxygen 15.9994	9 **F** Fluorine 18.998 4032	10 **Ne** Neon 20.1797
			13 **Al** Aluminum 26.981 538	14 **Si** Silicon 28.0855	15 **P** Phosphorus 30.973 761	16 **S** Sulfur 32.065	17 **Cl** Chlorine 35.453	18 **Ar** Argon 39.948
28 **Ni** Nickel 58.6934	29 **Cu** Copper 63.546	30 **Zn** Zinc 65.409	31 **Ga** Gallium 69.723	32 **Ge** Germanium 72.64	33 **As** Arsenic 74.921 60	34 **Se** Selenium 78.96	35 **Br** Bromine 79.904	36 **Kr** Krypton 83.798
46 **Pd** Palladium 106.42	47 **Ag** Silver 107.8682	48 **Cd** Cadmium 112.411	49 **In** Indium 114.818	50 **Sn** Tin 118.710	51 **Sb** Antimony 121.760	52 **Te** Tellurium 127.60	53 **I** Iodine 126.904 47	54 **Xe** Xenon 131.293
78 **Pt** Platinum 195.078	79 **Au** Gold 196.966 55	80 **Hg** Mercury 200.59	81 **Tl** Thallium 204.3833	82 **Pb** Lead 207.2	83 **Bi** Bismuth 208.980 38	84 **Po** Polonium (209)	85 **At** Astatine (210)	86 **Rn** Radon (222)
110 **Ds** Darmstadtium (281)	111 **Uuu*** Unununium (272)	112 **Uub*** Ununbium (285)	113 **Uut*** Ununtrium (284)	114 **Uuq*** Ununquadium (289)	115 **Uup*** Ununpentium (288)			

A team at Lawrence Berkeley National Laboratories reported the discovery of elements 116 and 118 in June 1999. The same team retracted the discovery in July 2001. The discovery of elements 113, 114, and 115 has been reported but not confirmed.

63 **Eu** Europium 151.964	64 **Gd** Gadolinium 157.25	65 **Tb** Terbium 158.925 34	66 **Dy** Dysprosium 162.500	67 **Ho** Holmium 164.930 32	68 **Er** Erbium 167.259	69 **Tm** Thulium 168.934 21	70 **Yb** Ytterbium 173.04	71 **Lu** Lutetium 174.967
95 **Am** Americium (243)	96 **Cm** Curium (247)	97 **Bk** Berkelium (247)	98 **Cf** Californium (251)	99 **Es** Einsteinium (252)	100 **Fm** Fermium (257)	101 **Md** Mendelevium (258)	102 **No** Nobelium (259)	103 **Lr** Lawrencium (262)

The atomic masses listed in this table reflect the precision of current measurements. (Values listed in parentheses are the mass numbers of those radioactive elements' most stable or most common isotopes.)

APPENDIX B

Figure 2 **The Electromagnetic Spectrum**

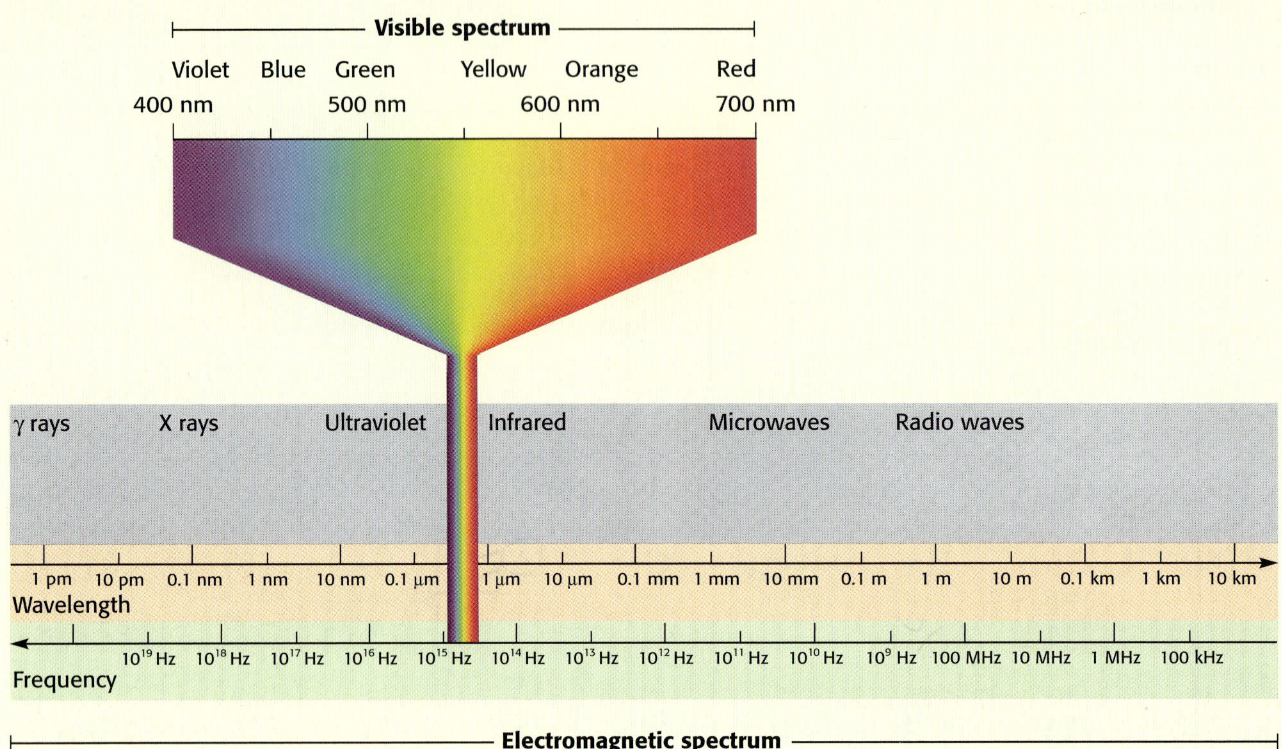

Table 5 **Properties of the Planets**

Planet	Diameter (km)	Average surface temperature (°C)	Number of moons	Atmosphere
Mercury	4879	167	0	Essentially none
Venus	12 104	464	0	Thick: carbon dioxide, nitrogen
Earth	12 756	15	1	Nitrogen, oxygen
Mars	6794	−63	2	Thin: carbon dioxide
Jupiter	142 984	−108	61	Hydrogen, helium, ammonia, methane
Saturn	120 536	−139	31	Hydrogen, helium, ammonia, methane
Uranus	51 118	−197	26	Hydrogen, helium, methane
Neptune	49 528	−201	13	Hydrogen, helium, methane
Pluto	2390	−223	1	Very thin: nitrogen, methane

Figure 3 Sky Maps for the Northern Hemisphere

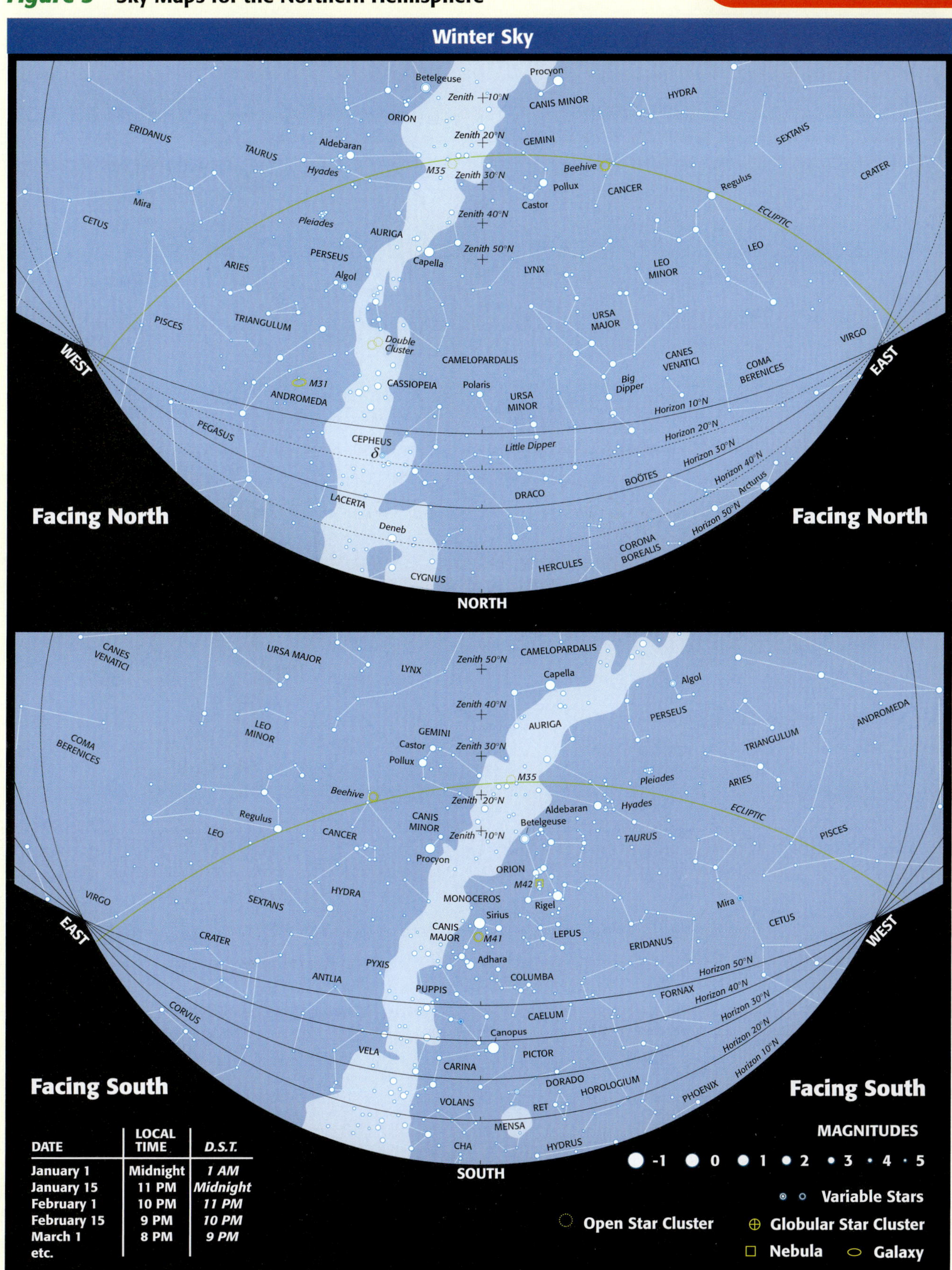

DATE	LOCAL TIME	D.S.T.
January 1	Midnight	*1 AM*
January 15	11 PM	*Midnight*
February 1	10 PM	*11 PM*
February 15	9 PM	*10 PM*
March 1	8 PM	*9 PM*
etc.		

Figure 4 **The World: Physical**

ARCTIC OCEAN
80°N
KARA SEA
LAPTEV SEA
EAST SIBERIAN SEA
Yenisei River
Lena River
Kolyma River
Ob River
URAL MOUNTAINS
Volga River
Lake Baikal
60°N
SEA OF OKHOTSK
KAMCHATKA PENINSULA
Amur River
Sakhalin Island
Balqash Lake
ARAL SEA
ALTAY MOUNTAINS
CASPIAN SEA
BLACK SEA
GOBI
ASIA
Hokkaido
SEA OF JAPAN
Honshu
40°N
Huang He
Tigris River
Euphrates River
Shikoku
Kyushu
Indus River
Chang River
EAST CHINA SEA
HIMALAYAS
PERSIAN GULF
THAR DESERT
Ganges River
Mekong River
Nile River
RED SEA
ARABIAN PENINSULA
Taiwan
Tropic of Cancer
20°N
ARABIAN SEA
BAY OF BENGAL
SOUTH CHINA SEA
Philippine Islands
PACIFIC OCEAN
RICA
Sri Lanka
STRAIT OF MALACCA
MALAY PENINSULA
Borneo
Equator
0°
Sumatra
Celebes
New Guinea
Solomon Islands
Lake Tanganyika
Lake Victoria
Java
INDIAN OCEAN
CORAL SEA
MOZAMBIQUE CHANNEL
Madagascar
New Hebrides
Fiji Islands
GREAT SANDY DESERT
KALAHARI DESERT
New Caledonia
20°S
AUSTRALIA
Tropic of Capricorn
GREAT VICTORIA DESERT
Darling River
GREAT DIVIDING RANGE
North Island
TASMAN SEA
NEW ZEALAND
Tasmania
South Island
60°S
40°E
60°E
80°E
100°E
120°E
140°E
160°E
CTICA
Europe
DENMARK STRAIT
Iceland
North Cape
KJELEN MTS.
BARENTS SEA
KARA SEA
URAL MTS.
0 250 500 750 Miles
0 250 500 750 Kilometers
Projection: Mollweide
60°N
NORTH SEA
BALTIC SEA
British Isles
Volga River
Rhine River
50°N
ATLANTIC OCEAN
Danube River
ALPS
BAY OF BISCAY
BLACK SEA
40°N
MEDITERRANEAN SEA
STRAIT OF GIBRALTAR
Crete
Tigris R.
Euphrates R.

Figure 5 Map of Natural Resources in the United States

Coal
Natural gas
Petroleum
Iron ore
Silver
Gold
Copper
Uranium

SCALE
0 250 500 Miles
0 250 500 Kilometers
Projection: Albers Equal Area

Figure 6 Typical Weather Map

H
H
1020
1016
1020
1016
1012
26 158
23 6
53 208
35 3
57 213
38
56 201
35
61 218
35
61 181
39
62 172
37
63 183
40

Table 6 **International Weather Symbols**

Current Weather			
Hail	Light drizzle	Light rain	Light snow
Freezing rain	Steady, light drizzle	Steady, light rain	Steady, light snow
Smoke	Intermittent, moderate drizzle	Intermittent, moderate rain	Intermittent, moderate snow
Tornado	Steady, moderate drizzle	Steady, moderate rain	Steady, moderate snow
Dust storms	Intermittent, heavy drizzle	Intermittent, heavy rain	Intermittent, heavy snow
Fog	Steady, heavy drizzle	Steady, heavy rain	Steady, heavy snow
Thunder-storm			
Lightning			
Hurricane			
Cloud Coverage			
Clear	Scattered	Four-eighths covered	Seven-eighths covered
One-eighth Coverage	Three-eighths covered	Five-eighths covered	Overcast
Clouds			
Low:	Stratus	Cumulus	Cumulonimbus calvus
	Stratocumulus	Cumulus congestus	Cumulonimbus with anvil
Middle:	Altostratus	Altocumulus	Altocumulus castellanus
High:	Cirrus	Cirrostratus	Cirrocumulus
Wind Speed (in km/h)			
Calm	4-13	24-33	
1-3	14-23	34-40	

APPENDIX C Problem Bank

Conversions

1. Earth's moon has a radius of 1738 km. Write this measurement in megameters.
2. Convert each of the following values as indicated:
   a. 113 g to milligrams
   b. 700 pm to nanometers
   c. 101.1 kPa to pascals
   d. 13 MA to amperes
3. Maryland has 49 890 m of coastline. What is this length in centimeters?
4. In 1997 Andy Green, a Royal Air Force pilot, broke the land speed record in Black Rock Desert, Nevada. His car averaged 341.11 m/s. The speed of sound in Black Rock at the time that he broke the record was determined to be 0.33584 km/s. Did Andy Green break the sound barrier?
5. The mass of the planet Pluto is 12 500 000 000 000 000 000 000 kg. What is the mass of Pluto in gigagrams?

Writing Scientific Notation

6. Express each of the following values in scientific notation:
   a. 110.45 m
   b. 0.000 003 45 s
   c. 132 948 kg
   d. 0.034 3900 cm
7. In 1998, the population of the United States was about 270 000 000 people. Write the estimated population in scientific notation.
8. In 1997, 70 294 601 airplanes either took off or landed at Chicago's O'Hare airport. What is the number of arrivals and departures at O'Hare given in scientific notation?
9. The planet Saturn has a mass of 568 000 000 000 000 000 000 000 000 kg. Express the mass of Saturn in scientific notation.
10. Approximately four-and-a-half million automobiles were imported into the United States last year. Write this number in scientific notation.

Using Scientific Notation

11. Perform the following calculations involving numbers that have been written in scientific notation:
    a. $3.02 \times 10^{-3} + 4.11 \times 10^{-2}$
    b. $(6.022 \times 10^{23}) \div (1.04 \times 10^{4})$
    c. $(1.00 \times 10^{2}) \times (3.01 \times 10^{3})$
    d. $6.626 \times 10^{34} - 5.442 \times 10^{32}$
12. Mount Everest, the tallest mountain on Earth, is 8.850×10^{3} m high. The Mariana Trench is the deepest point of any ocean on Earth. It is 1.0924×10^{4} m deep. What is the vertical distance from the highest mountain on Earth to the deepest ocean trench on Earth?
13. In 1950 Americans consumed nearly 1.4048×10^{9} kg of poultry. In 1997, Americans consumed 1.2369×10^{10} kg of poultry. By what factor did America's poultry consumption increase between 1950 and 1997?
14. The following data were obtained for the number of immigrants admitted to the United States in major Texas cities in 1996. What is the total number of immigrants admitted in these Texas cities for that year?

City	Number of immigrants admitted
Houston	2.1387×10^{4}
Dallas	1.5915×10^{4}
El Paso	8.701×10^{3}
Ft. Worth/Arlington	6.274×10^{3}

15. The surface area of the Pacific Ocean is 1.66×10^{14} m^2. The average depth of the Pacific Ocean is 3.9395×10^{3} m. If you could calculate the volume of the Pacific by simply multiplying the surface area by the average depth, what would the volume of the Pacific Ocean be?

Significant Figures

16. Determine the number of significant figures in each of the following values:
a. 0.026 48 kg
b. 47.10 g
c. 1 625 000 J
d. 29.02 cm

17. Solve the following addition problems, and round each answer to the correct number of significant figures:
a. 0.00241 g + 0.0123 g
b. 24.10 cm + 3.050 cm
c. 0.367 L + 2.51 L + 1.6004 L

18. Solve the following multiplication or division problems, and round each answer to the correct number of significant figures:
a. 129 g ÷ 29.20 cm^3
b. 120 mm × 355 mm × 12.1 mm
c. 45.4 g ÷ (0.012 cm × 0.444 cm × 0.221 cm)

19. Determine the volume of a cube whose width is 32.1 cm. Round your answer to the correct number of significant figures.

20. Solve the following subtraction problems, and round each answer to the correct number of significant figures:
a. 1.23 cm^3 − 0.044 cm^3
b. 89.00 kg − 0.1 kg
c. 780 mm − 64 mm

Density

21. Sugar has a density of 1.59 g/cm^3. What mass of sugar fits into a 140 cm^3 bowl?

22. The continent of North America has an area of 2.4346×10^{13} m^2. When North America had a population of 3.01×10^8 people, what was its population density?

23. The average density of Earth is 5.515 g/cm^3. The average density of Earth's moon is 3.34 g/cm^3. What is the difference in mass between 10.0 cm^3 of Earth and 10.0 cm^3 of Earth's moon?

24. A rubber balloon has a mass of 0.45 g, and can hold 1.78×10^{-3} m^3 of helium. If the density of helium is 0.178 kg/m^3, what is the balloon's total mass?

25. What is the density of a 0.996 g piece of graphite with a volume of 0.44 cm^3?

Pascal's Principle

26. A 6.50×10^{-3} m^2 piston compresses gas in a cylinder with a surface area of 9.75×10^{-2} m^2. What is the force on the cylinder walls if 50.0 N are applied to the piston?

27. A hydraulic lift raises a 1.0×10^4 N car on a 0.30 m^2 piston. If the compressor piston has an area of 0.015 m^2, what minimum force is needed to lift the car?

28. Air is blown into a trombone with a force of 3.5 N. A trombone's bore has a radius of 0.65 cm at the mouthpiece and 8.9 cm at the bell, where the air exits. What is the force on the exiting air?

29. A toy consists of a short, water-filled cylinder and a 28 cm^2 piston with a small hole in its center. A 4.5 N force applied to the piston causes water to flow through the hole with a force of 1.14×10^{-2} N. What is the area of the hole?

30. The air inside an automobile tire exerts a force that is 1.42×10^5 N greater than the force exerted by the outside air. The net force of air flowing through a hole in the tire is 2.72 N. If the tire's area is 0.656 m^2, what is the area of the hole?

Boyle's Law

31. A piston compresses gas in a 3.5 L cylinder to a volume of 2.1 L. If the gas pressure is initially 150 kPa, what is its pressure after it is compressed?

32. During a drive to the mountains, a tire's volume increases from 15.0 L to 15.5 L. If the pressure on the tire is initially 101.3 kPa, what is the final pressure?

33. An air-filled balloon has a volume of 0.250 L at 101 kPa. When immersed in a pool of mercury, the balloon's volume is 0.108 L. What pressure is exerted by the mercury on the balloon?

34. A toy balloon contains 0.75 L of helium at a pressure of 101 kPa. The balloon rises until the pressure on the balloon is 85 kPa. What is the balloon's volume?

35. An air bubble with a volume of 1.3 cm^3 forms underwater, where the pressure is 750 kPa. What is the bubble's volume when the pressure is 125 kPa?

Conversion Factors

36. Give the correct factor to convert between each of the following values:
    a. 4 reams of paper $\rightarrow$ 2000 sheets of paper
    b. 2.5 mol of gallium, Ga $\rightarrow$ 170 g of Ga
    c. 1.00 cm^3 of water $\rightarrow$ 0.997 g of water
    d. 1.35×10^{34} atoms of silver, Ag $\rightarrow 2.24 \times 10^{10}$ mol of silver

37. A Calorie, as reported on nutritional labels, is equal to 4.184 kJ. A carbonated beverage contains about 150 Calories. What is the energy content in joules?

38. a. The density of gold is 19.3 g/cm^3. What is the mass of a bar of gold with dimensions of 10.0 cm $\times$ 26.0 cm $\times$ 8.0 cm?
    b. Gold is priced by the ounce. One gram is equal to 0.0353 oz. If the price of gold is $253.50 per ounce, what is the value of the bar described in part (a)?

39. How many atoms of copper are there in a piece of copper tube that contains 34.5 mol of copper, Cu? (**Hint:** There are 6.022×10^{23} atoms in one mole.)

40. In February of 1962 John Glenn orbited Earth three times in 4 hours and 55 minutes. How long did it take him to make one revolution around Earth? In June of 1983 Sally Ride became the first U.S. woman in space. Her mission lasted 146 hours, 24 minutes. If each revolution of Sally Ride's mission took the same amount of time as each revolution of John Glenn's mission, how many times did Ride orbit Earth?

Converting Amount to Mass

41. Determine the mass in grams of each of the following:
    a. 67.9 mol of silicon, Si
    b. 1.45×10^{-4} mol of cadmium, Cd
    c. 0.045 mol of gold, Au
    d. 3.900 mol of tungsten, W

42. Fullerenes, also known as buckyballs, are a form of elemental carbon. One variety of fullerene has 60 carbon atoms in each molecule. What is the molar mass of 1 mol of this 60-carbon atom molecule? What is the mass of 5.23×10^{-2} mol of this fullerene?

43. An experiment requires 2.0 mol of cadmium, Cd, and 2.0 mol of sulfur, S. What mass of each element is required?

44. If there are 6.02×10^{27} mol of iron, Fe, in a portion of Earth's crust, what is the mass of iron present?

45. a. A certain molecule of polyester contains 1.00×10^5 carbon atoms. What is the mass of carbon in 1 mol of this polyester?
    b. The same polyester molecule contains 4.00×10^4 oxygen atoms. What is the mass of oxygen in 1 mol?

Converting Mass to Amount

46. Imagine that you find a jar full of diamonds. You measure the mass of the diamonds and find that they have a mass of 45.4 g. Determine the amount of carbon in the diamonds.

47. A tungsten, W, filament in a light bulb has a mass of 2.0 mg. Calculate the amount of tungsten in this filament.

48. One liter of sea water contains 1.05×10^4 mg of sodium. How much sodium is in one liter of sea water?

49. Every kilogram of Earth's crust contains 282 g of silicon. How many moles of silicon are present in 2 kg of Earth's crust?

50. Chlorine rarely occurs in nature as Cl atoms. It usually occurs as gaseous Cl_2 molecules, molecules made up of two chlorine atoms joined together. What is the molar mass of gaseous Cl_2? Calculate the amount of chlorine molecules found in 4.30 g of chlorine gas.

Writing Ionic Formulas

51. Write the ionic formula for the salt made from potassium and bromine.

52. Calcium chloride is used by the canning industry to make the skin of fruit such as tomatoes more firm. What is the ionic formula for calcium chloride?

53. Write the ionic formulas formed by each of the following pairs:

a. lithium and oxygen

b. magnesium and oxygen

c. sodium and chlorine

d. magnesium and nitrogen

54. The active ingredient in most toothpaste is sodium fluoride. Write the ionic formula for this cavity-fighting compound.

55. What is the formula for the ionic compound formed from strontium and iodine?

Balancing Chemical Equations

56. Iron, Fe, combines with oxygen gas, O_2, to form iron(III) oxide. Balance the following equation for the synthesis of iron(III) oxide.

$$Fe + O_2 \rightarrow Fe_2O_3$$

57. Iron is often produced from iron ore by treating it with carbon monoxide in a blast furnace. Balance the equation for the production of iron.

$$Fe_2O_3 + CO \rightarrow Fe + CO_2$$

58. Zinc sulfide can be used as a white pigment. Balance the following equation for synthesizing zinc sulfide.

$$Na_2S + Zn(NO_3)_2 \rightarrow ZnS + NaNO_3$$

59. Kerosene, $C_{14}H_{30}$, is often used as a heating fuel or a jet fuel. When kerosene burns in oxygen, O_2, it produces carbon dioxide, CO_2, and water, H_2O. Write the balanced chemical equation for the reaction of kerosene and oxygen.

60. Plants use the process of photosynthesis to convert carbon dioxide and water into glucose and oxygen. This process helps remove carbon dioxide from the atmosphere. Balance the following equation for the production of glucose and oxygen from carbon dioxide and water.

$$CO_2 + H_2O \rightarrow C_6H_{12}O_6 + O_2$$

Molarity

61. Calculate the molarity of a hydrochloric acid (HCl) solution if 1.32 mol HCl are dissolved in water to form 5.28 L of solution.

62. Calculate the molarity of a potassium chloride (KCl) solution if 23.5 g of solute are dissolved in water to form 0.42 L of solution.

63. How many moles of sucrose, $C_{12}H_{22}O_{11}$, are needed to make 1.5 L of a 0.30 M sugar solution?

64. A 0.350 M solution of silver bromide, AgBr, in water, has a volume of 0.750 L. What is the mass of the solute?

65. A 0.67 M solution is made by dissolving 0.45 kg of copper(II) sulfate, $CuSO_4$, in water. What is the volume of the solution?

Determining pH

66. Calculate the pH of a 0.001 M solution of HCl, a strong acid.

67. A solution of HBr, a strong acid, has a concentration of 1.0×10^{-5} M. What is the pH of this solution?

68. What is the pH of a solution that has a hydronium ion concentration of 1.0×10^{-10} M?

69. A solution of HI, a strong acid, has a pH of 2. What is the concentration of the solution?

70. A solution has a pH of 11. What is the concentration of hydronium ions?

Nuclear Decay

71. Complete the following equations of nuclear decay by β-emission.

a. $^{40}_{19}K \longrightarrow {}^{40}_{20}___ + {}^{0}_{-1}e$

b. $^{234}_{90}Th \longrightarrow {}^{234}_{91}___ + {}^{0}_{-1}e$

72. Carbon-14 decays by β-emission. What element is formed when carbon loses a β-particle?

73. Which type of emission would result in each of the following nuclear changes?

a. $^{15}_{6}C \longrightarrow {}^{15}_{7}N$

b. $^{147}_{62}Sm \longrightarrow {}^{143}_{60}Nd$

74. Uranium-238 decays by α-emission. What element is formed when a uranium atom loses an α-particle?

75. Complete the following equation for the decay of radon-222.

$$^{222}_{86}Rn \longrightarrow {}^{218}_{84}___ + {}^{4}_{2}He$$

Half-life

76. The half-life of thorium-232, $^{232}_{90}Th$, is 1.4×10^{10} years. How much of a 50.0 g sample of thorium-232 will remain as thorium after 4.2×10^{10} years?

77. Radium, used in radiation treatment for cancer, has a half-life of 1.60×10^3 years. If you begin with a 0.25 g sample, what mass of radium will remain after 8.00×10^3 years?

78. The half-life of iodine-131 is 8.04 days. How long will it take for the mass of iodine present to drop to 1/16?

79. What is the half-life of an element if 1/8 of a sample remains after 12 years?

80. The half life of cobalt-60 is 10.47 minutes. What fraction of a sample will remain after 52.35 minutes?

Velocity

81. Amy Van Dyken broke the world record for a 50.0 m swim using the butterfly stroke in 1996. She swam 50.0 m in 26.55 seconds. What was her average velocity assuming that she swam the 50.0 m in a perfectly straight line?

82. If Amy Van Dyken swam her record-breaking 50 m by swimming to one end of the pool, then turning around and swimming back to her starting position, what would her average velocity be?

83. When Andy Green broke the land speed record, his vehicle was traveling across a flat portion of the desert with a forward velocity of 341.11 m/s. How long would it take him at that velocity to travel 4.500 km?

84. If a car moves along a perfectly straight road at a velocity of 24 m/s, how far will the car go in 35 minutes?

85. If you travel southeast from one city to another city that is 314 km away, and the trip takes you 4.00 hours, what is your average velocity?

Acceleration

86. While driving at an average velocity of 15.6 m/s down the road, a driver slams on the brakes to avoid hitting a squirrel. The car stops completely in 4.2 seconds. What is the average acceleration of the car?

87. A sports car is advertised as being able to go from 0 to 60 in 6.00 seconds. If 60 mi/h is equal to 27 m/s, what is the sports car's average acceleration?

88. If a bicycle has an average acceleration of $-0.44\ m/s^2$, and its initial forward velocity is 8.2 m/s, how long will it take the cyclist to bring the bicycle to a complete stop?

89. An airliner has an airborne velocity of 232 m/s. What is the plane's average acceleration if it takes the plane 15 minutes to reach its airborne velocity?

90. A school bus can accelerate from a complete stop at $1.3\ m/s^2$. How long will it take the bus to reach a velocity of 12.1 m/s?

Newton's Second Law

91. A peach falls from a tree with an acceleration of $9.8\ m/s^2$. The peach has a mass of 7.4 g. How much force acts on the peach? (**Hint:** Convert g to kg.)

92. A group of people push a car from a resting position with a force of 1.99×10^3 N. The car and its driver have a mass of 831 kg. What is the acceleration of the car?

93. If the space shuttle accelerates upward at $35\ m/s^2$, what net force will a 59 kg astronaut experience?

94. A soccer ball is pushed with a force of 15.2 N. The soccer ball has a mass of 2.45 kg. What is the ball's acceleration?

95. A person steps off a diving board and falls into a pool with an acceleration of $9.8\ m/s^2$. The downward force acting on the person is 637 N. What is the mass of the person?

Momentum

96. **a.** A 703 kg car is traveling with a velocity of 20.1 m/s forward. What is the momentum of the car?

    b. If a 315 kg trailer is attached to the car, what is the new combined momentum?

97. You are traveling west on your bicycle at 4.2 m/s, and you and your bike have a combined mass of 75 kg. What is the momentum of you and your bicycle?

98. A runner, who has a mass of 52 kg, has a momentum of 218 kg · m/s along a trail. What is the runner's velocity?

99. A commercial airplane travels at a velocity of 234 m/s north. The plane seats 253 people. If the average person on the plane has a mass of 68 kg, what is the momentum of the passengers on the plane?

100. A bowling ball has a mass of 5.44 kg. It is moving down the lane at 2.1 m/s when it strikes the pins. What is the momentum with which the ball hits the pins?

Work

101. A car breaks down 2.1 m from the shoulder of the road. 1.99×10^3 N of force is used to push the car off the road. How much work has been done on the car?

102. Pulling a boat forward into a docking slip requires 1570 J of work. The boat must be pulled a total distance of 5.3 m. What is the force with which the boat is pulled?

103. A box with a mass of 3.2 kg is pushed 0.667 m across a floor with an acceleration of 3.2 m/s^2. How much work is done on the box?

104. A book is pushed a distance of 0.78 m by a force that gives the book an acceleration of 1.54 m/s^2. If 1.56 J of work is done on the book, what is the book's mass?

105. A 227 kg object is moved a distance of 2.4 m by a force. If 686 J of work is done on the object, what is the object's acceleration?

Power

106. A student does 686 J of work on an object in 3.1 seconds. What is the power output of the student?

107. How much energy is wasted by a 60 W bulb if the bulb is left on over an 8 hour night?

108. A nuclear reactor is designed with a capacity of 1.02×10^8 kW. How much energy, in megajoules, should the reactor be able to generate in a day?

109. An electric mixer uses 350 W. If 8.75×10^3 J of work are done by the mixer, how long has the mixer run?

110. A team of horses is hitched to a cart. The team pulls with a force of 471 N. The cart travels 2.3 km in 20 minutes. Calculate the power delivered by the horses.

Mechanical Advantage

111. A roofer needs to get a stack of shingles onto a roof. Pulling the shingles up manually uses 1549 N of force. The roofer decides that it would be easier to use a system of pulleys to raise the shingles. Using the pulleys, 446 N are required to lift the shingles. What is the mechanical advantage of the system of pulleys?

112. A dam used to make hydroelectric power opens and closes its gates with a lever. The gate weighs 660 N. The lever has a mechanical advantage of 6. Calculate the input force on the lever needed to lift the gate.

113. A crane has a mechanical advantage of 27. An input force of 8650 N is used by the crane to lift a pile of steel girders. What is the weight of the girders?

114. What is the mechanical advantage of a first-class lever if the fulcrum is exactly in the center of the lever? How would the mechanical advantage change if the fulcrum were moved 10 cm closer to the input force?

115. A student pedals a unicycle to school. The pedals on the unicycle have a radius of 8.0 cm. The student travels 1.6 km to school. During the journey, the pedals make 750 revolutions. What is the mechanical advantage of the unicycle?

Gravitational Potential Energy

116. A pear is hanging from a pear tree. The pear is 3.5 m above the ground and has a mass of 0.14 kg. What is the pear's gravitational potential energy?

117. A person in an airplane has a mass of 74 kg and has 6.6 MJ of gravitational potential energy. What is the altitude of the plane?

118. A high jumper jumps 2.04 m. If the jumper has a mass of 67 kg, what is his gravitational potential energy at the highest point in the jump?

119. A cat sits on the top of a fence that is 2.0 m high. The cat has a gravitational potential energy of 88.9 J. What is the mass of the cat?

120. A frog with a mass of 0.23 kg hops up in the air. At the highest point in the hop, the frog has a gravitational potential energy of 0.744 J. How high can it hop?

Kinetic Energy

121. A sprinter runs at a forward velocity of 10.9 m/s. If the sprinter has a mass of 72.5 kg, what is the sprinter's kinetic energy?

122. A car having a mass of 654 kg has a kinetic energy of 73.4 kJ. What is the car's speed?

123. A tennis ball with a mass of 51 g has a velocity of 9.7 m/s. What is the kinetic energy of the tennis ball?

124. A rock is rolling down a hill with a velocity of 4.67 m/s. It has a kinetic energy of 18.9 kJ. What is the mass of the rock?

125. Calculate the kinetic energy of an airliner with a mass of 7.6×10^4 kg that is flying at a speed of 524 km/h.

Efficiency

126. If a machine has an efficiency of 26.7%, how much energy is lost if 40.5 kJ of work is done on the machine?

127. What is the efficiency of a machine if 55.3 J of work are done on the machine, but only 14.3 J of work are done by the machine?

128. A microwave oven uses 89 kJ in one minute. The microwave has an output of 54 kJ per minute. What is the efficiency of the microwave?

129. A coal-burning power plant has an efficiency of 42%. If 4.99 MJ of energy are used by the power plant, how much useful energy is generated by the power plant?

130. A swimmer does 45 kJ of work while swimming. If the swimmer is wasting 42 kJ of energy while swimming, what is the efficiency for the activity?

Temperature Conversions

131. A normal body temperature is 98.6°F. What is this temperature in degrees Celsius?

132. Convert the following temperatures to the Kelvin scale.

a. 214°F

b. 1.00×10^2°C

c. 27°C

d. 32°F

133. What are the freezing point and boiling point of water in the Celsius, Fahrenheit, and Kelvin scales?

134. What is absolute zero in the Celsius scale?

135. If it is 315 K outside, is it hot or cold?

Specific Heat

See **Appendix B** for a table of specific heats.

136. How much energy is required to raise the temperature of 5.0 g of silver from 298 K to 334 K? (**Hint:** Convert g to kg.)

137. During an experiment, 45 J of energy is transferred to 5.3 g of water. If the water began at 27°C, what is the final temperature of the water?

138. During an experiment, a piece of aluminum foil is heated from 27°C to 98°C. If the foil absorbed 344 J of energy, what is the mass of the foil?

139. If a piece of graphite and a diamond have the same mass and are placed on the same burner, which object will heat up faster? Why?

140. The iron ore hematite is heated until its temperature has risen by 153°C. If the piece of hematite has a mass of 34 kg, how much energy was required to raise the temperature this much?

Wave Speed

141. The speed of light in a vacuum is 3.0×10^8 m/s. A red laser beam has a wavelength of 698 nm. How long, in picoseconds, will it take for one wavelength of the laser light to pass by a fixed point?

142. Two people are standing on opposite ends of a field. The field is 92 m long. One person speaks. It takes 270 ms for the person across the field to hear them. What is the speed of sound?

143. A water wave has a speed of 1.3 m/s. A person sitting on a pier observes that it takes 1.2 s for a full wavelength to pass the edge of the pier. What is the wavelength of the water wave?

144. Jupiter is 7.79×10^8 km from the sun. How long does it take the sun's light to reach Jupiter?

145. A green laser has a wavelength of 508 nm. What is the frequency of this laser light?

Resistance

146. What is the resistance of a wire that has a current of 1.4 A in it when it is connected to a 6.0 V battery?

147. An electric space heater is plugged into a 120 V outlet. A current of 12.0 A is in the coils in the space heater. What is the resistance of the coils?

148. A graphing calculator needs 7.78×10^{-3} A of current to function. The resistance in the calculator is 1150 Ω. What is the voltage required to operate the calculator?

149. A steam iron has a current of 9.17 A when plugged into a 120 V outlet. What is the resistance in the steam iron?

150. An electric clothes dryer requires a potential difference of 240 V. The power cord that runs between the electrical outlet and the dryer supports a current of 30 A. What is the resistance in this power cord?

Electric Power

151. A flashlight uses a 3.0 V battery. The bulb has a current of 0.50 A. What is the electric power used by the flashlight?

152. What is the current in a 60 W light bulb when it is plugged into a 120 V outlet?

153. A student takes her hair dryer to Europe. In the United States, her hair dryer uses 1200 W of power when connected to a 120 V outlet. In Europe, the outlet has a potential difference of 240 V. When she uses her hair dryer in Europe, she notices that it gets very hot, and starts to smell as though it is burning. Determine the current in the hair dryer in the United States. Then calculate the resistance in the hair dryer. Calculate the current and the power in the hair dryer in Europe to explain why the hair dryer heats up when plugged into the European outlet.

154. A portable stereo requires a 12 V battery. It uses 43 W of power. Calculate the current in the stereo.

155. A microwave oven has a current of 12.3 A when operated using a 120 V outlet. How much power does the microwave use?

Selected Answers to Problems

Chapter 1 Introduction to Science

Math Skills
Practice, page 17

2. 3500 ms
4. 0.0025 kg
6. 2.8 mol
8. 3000 ng

Math Skills
Practice, page 23

2. a. 4500 g
b. 0.006 05 m
c. 3 115 000 km
d. 0.000 000 0199 cm

Math Skills
Practice, page 24

2. a. 4.8×10^2 L/s
b. 6.9 g/cm^3
c. 5.5×10^5 cm^2
d. 8.3 10^{-1} cm^3

Math Skills
Practice, page 25

2. 1.6×10^2 cm^3
4. 2.3 m/s

Section 3 Review
Math Skills, page 26

6. a. 9.20×10^7 m^2
b. 9.66×10^{-5} cm^2
c. 6.70 g/cm^3

Chapter Review
Building Math Skills, page 28–29

14. See pie chart below

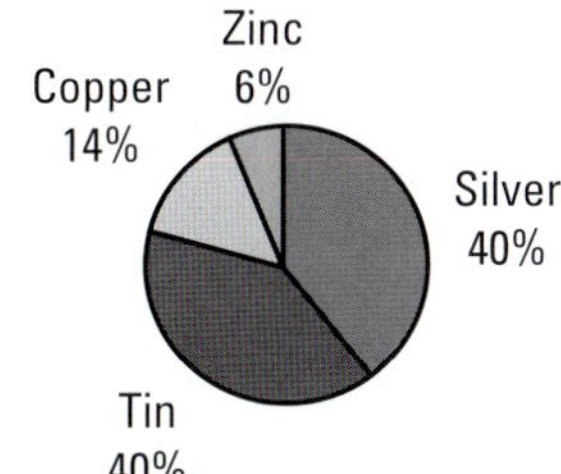

16. a. 2.6×10^{14} A•s
b. 6.42×10^{-7} m^3/s

Chapter 2 Matter

Math Skills
Practice, page 48

2. $D = \frac{163 \text{ g}}{50.0 \text{ cm}^3}$

$D = \frac{3.26 \text{ g}}{\text{cm}^3}$

Section 2 Review
Math Skills, page 52

6. $D = \frac{0.36 \text{ g}}{2500 \text{ cm}^3}$

$D = \frac{1.4 \times 10^{-4} \text{g}}{\text{cm}^3}$

Chapter 3 States of Matter

Section 2 Review
Math Skills, page 86

8. a. 15 N
b. It will sink because its weight is greater than the buoyant force acting on it.

Math Skills
Practice, page 91

2. $V_2 = \frac{P_1V_1}{P_2}$

$V_2 = \frac{(0.500 \text{ atm})(300 \text{ mL})}{0.750 \text{ atm}}$

$V_2 = 200 \text{ mL}$

4. $V_2 = \frac{P_1V_1}{P_2}$

$V_2 = \frac{(0.947 \text{ atm})(150 \text{ mL})}{1.000 \text{ atm}}$

$V_2 = 140 \text{ mL}$

Chapter 4 Atoms and the Periodic Table

Math Skills
Practice, page 132

2. 10 extra eggs

Math Skills
Practice, page 133

2. 72.1 g Ca
4. 203 g Cu

APPENDIX D

Section 4 Review
Math Skills, page 134

6. 94 g Pt
8. 0.39 mol Si

Chapter 5
The Structure of Matter

Math Skills
Practice, page 161

2. $BeCl_2$
4. $Co(OH)_3$

Section 3 Review
Math Skills, page 164

6. The total charge of the compound must be zero. Each of the two cyanide ions has a charge of 1–. The charge of the cadmium ion must be 2+ to add to the 2 × (1–) charge from the cyanide ions to equal zero.

Chapter 6
Chemical Reactions

Math Skills
Practice, page 213

2. 322 g

Chapter Review
Building Math Skills, p. 215

14. $2HgO \rightarrow 2Hg + O_2$
18. 450 g

Chapter 7
Solutions

Section 3 Review
Math Skills, page 244

6. 6. 0.5 M
8. 0.373 M

Chapter Review
Building Math Skills, page 247

18. moles $ZnBr_2$=

$$\frac{\text{mass } ZnBr_2}{\text{molar mass } ZnBr_2} =$$

$$\frac{12.5 \text{ g } ZnBr_2}{225 \text{ g } ZnBr_2/\text{mol } ZnBr_2} =$$

0.0556 mol $ZnBr_2$

$$\frac{0.0556 \text{ mol } ZnBr_2}{0.250 \text{ L}} =$$

0.222 M $ZnBr_2$

Chapter 8
Acids, Bases, and Salts

Math Skills
Practice, page 262

2. pH = 2
   pOH = 12

Chapter Review
Building Math Skills, page 277

20. Because HCl is a strong acid, the concentration of hydronium ions in the solution is the same as the molar concentration of HCl.
    0.10 mol HCl/100.0 L =
    0.0010 mol/L =
    1×10^{-3} M H_3O^+
    pH = −(−3) = 3

Chapter 9
Nuclear Changes

Math Skills
Practice, page 289

2. $A = 4$
   $Z = 2$
   $X = \text{He}$
   Alpha decay occurs, and $^{4}_{2}\text{He}$ is produced.
4. $212 = A + 4; A = 208$
   $83 = Z + 2; Z = 81$
   $X = \text{Tl}$
   Alpha decay occurs, and $^{208}_{81}\text{Tl}$ is produced.

Section 1 Review
Math Skills, page 292

4. The product is $^{208}_{84}\text{Po}$.
6. 64.4 minutes.
8. 22 860 years old.

Chapter Review
Building Math Skills, page 309

22. $\frac{1}{8} = \frac{1}{2} \times \frac{1}{2} \times \frac{1}{2}$; three half-lives
    3×5715 years =
    1.71×10^4 years

Chapter 10
Motion

Math Skills
Practice, page 323

2. 22 m/s toward first base

Section 1 Review
Math Skills, page 324

None

Math Skills
Practice, page 328

2. 0.075 m/s^2 toward the shore
4. 0.85 s

Section 2 Review
Math Skills, page 330

4. 2.5 m/s^2 is the acceleration. The graph should be a straight line from 7.0 m/s at the zero line of time to 12 m/s at the 2.0 s line of time (with time on the x-axis and velocity on the y-axis).

Graphing Skills
Practice, page 337

4. 8.0 m/s; from $t = 15.0$ s to $t = 17.5$ s; 0 m/s

Chapter Review
Building Math Skills, page 339

16. 0.3m/s^2
18. $v = \frac{d}{t} = \frac{72\text{ m}}{45\text{ s}} = 1.6\text{ m/s}$ eastward
20. $a = \frac{5.5\text{ m/s} - 14.0\text{ m/s}}{6.0\text{s}} =$ $\frac{-8.5\text{ m/s}}{6.0\text{ s}} = -1.4\text{ m/s}^2$ eastward $= 1.4\text{ m/s}^2$ westward

Chapter 11 Forces

Math Skills
Practice, page 351

2. 0.14 kg

Section 1 Review
Math Skills, page 351

4. 0.26 m/s^2 forward
6. 8.5 kg

Section 2 Review
Math Skills, page 359

6. The force of gravity is inversely proportional to the square of distance. Since the distance is made twice as close, the force of gravity will be four times as great (the square of 2), or 4 million N.

Math Skills
Practice, page 363

2. 6.3 m/s forward

Section 3 Review
Math Skills, page 366

6. 12 kg • m/s eastward

Math Skills
Practice, page 367

2. 3.5 m/s^2 in a backward direction (deceleration)

Chapter Review
Building Math Skills, page 369

18. 2.1 kg
20. 3.7 N

Chapter 12 Work and Energy

Math Skills
Practice, page 379

2. 1 J
4. 3960 J

Math Skills
Practice, page 381

2. 900 MW
4. **a.** 7.20×10^2 J

Math Skills
Practice, page 383

2. MA = 66
4. output force = 78 N

Section 1 Review
Math Skills, page 384

6. MA = 2.40
8. $P = 2.0 \times 10^4$ W (27 hp)

Math Skills
Practice, page 393

2. $PE = 1.4 \times 10^{15}$ J
4. $m = 58$ kg

Math Skills
Practice, page 395

2. $v = 3.3$ m/s

APPENDIX D

Section 3 Review
Math Skills, page 399

8. KE = 900 J

Math Skills
Practice, page 407

2. work input = 4800 J

Section 4 Review
Math Skills, page 408

8. a. useful work output = 780 J
   b. P = 780 W

Chapter 13
Heat and Temperature

Math Skills
Practice, page 424

2. Row 1: 294 K
   Row 2: 115°C, 239°F
   Row 3: –328°F, 73 K
   Row 4: 43°C, 316 K
4. c

Section 1 Review
Math Skills, page 426

6. 184K

Math Skills
Practice, page 434

2. 28 000 J
4. T_f = 145°C
6. 480 J/kg • K

Section 2 Review
Math Skills, page 434

6. 228 J/kg • K

Chapter Review
Understanding Concepts, page 446

2. b

Building Math Skills, page 447

18. 4400 J

Chapter 14
Waves

Math Skills
Practice, page 468

2. 3.00×10^{14} m/s
4. 1.5 m

Section 2 Review
Math Skills, page 471

8. 0.77 m

Chapter Review
Building Math Skills, page 481

20. 3.0 m/s
22. 440 Hz

Building Graphing Skills, page 482

24. a. 9 cm = 0.09 m
    b. 20.0 cm = 0.200 m
    c. 5.00 m/s
    d. T = 0.0400 s

Chapter 15
Sound and Light

Math Skills
Practice, page 519

2. 1.38×10^3 W/m^2

Chapter Review
Building Math Skills, page 521

20. 1.0×10^{-4}m (0.10mm)
22. 250m

Chapter 16
Electricity

Math Skills
Practice, page 543

2. 240 Ω
4. 0.43 A

Section 2 Review
Math Skills, page 545

8. 0.5 A

Math Skills
Practice, page 551

2. 1.6×10^{-2} W
4. 0.62 A

Section 3 Review
Math Skills, page 553

8. The 75 W bulb has more current in it.

Chapter Review
Building Math Skills, page 555

18. $R = \frac{V}{I} = \frac{12\ \text{V}}{0.30\ \text{A}} = 4.0 \times 10^1\ \Omega$

20. $I = \frac{V}{R} = \frac{3.0\ \text{V}}{25\ \Omega} = 0.12\ \text{A}$

Chapter 17
Magnetism
none

Chapter 18
Communication Technology
none

Chapter 19
The Solar System
Chapter Review
Building Math Skills, page 657
24.

Planet	Wt in N
Mercury	270
Venus	620
Earth	690
Mars	260

Chapter 20
The Universe
none

Chapter 21
Planet Earth
none

Chapter 22
The Atmosphere
none

Chapter 23
Using Natural Resources
Chapter Review
Building Math Skills, page 803
18. 3600 days; You would produce 1600 lbs per year—but only 800 lbs per year if you recycled one-half of the trash.

Glossary

A

absolute zero the temperature at which molecular energy is at a minimum (0 K on the Kelvin scale or –273.16°C on the Celsius scale) (423)

acceleration the rate at which velocity changes over time; an object accelerates if its speed, direction, or both change (325)

accretion the accumulation of matter (649)

accuracy a description of how close a measurement is to the true value of the quantity measured (25)

acid any compound that increases the number of hydronium ions when dissolved in water; acids turn blue litmus paper red and react with bases and some metals to form salts (256)

acid precipitation precipitation, such as rain, sleet, or snow, that contains a high concentration of acids, often because of the pollution of the atmosphere (727)

aerobic describes a process that requires oxygen (747)

air mass a large body of air where temperature and moisture content are similar throughout (757)

air pressure the force with which air molecules push on a surface (83)

alkali metal one of the elements of Group 1 of the periodic table (lithium, sodium, potassium, rubidium, cesium, and francium) (121)

alkaline-earth metal one of the elements of Group 2 of the periodic table (beryllium, magnesium, calcium, strontium, barium, and radium) (122)

alloy a solid or liquid mixture of two or more metals (231)

alpha particle a positively charged atom that is released in the disintegration of radioactive elements and that consists of two protons and two neutrons (285)

alternating current an electric current that changes direction at regular intervals (abbreviation, AC) (578)

amino acid any one of 20 different organic molecules that contain a carboxyl and an amino group and that combine to form proteins (170)

amorphous solid a solid in which the particles are not arranged with periodicity or order (71)

amplitude the maximum distance that the particles of a wave's medium vibrate from their rest position (464)

analog signal a signal whose properties, such as amplitude and frequency, can change continuously in a given range (595)

angle of incidence the angle between a ray that strikes a surface and the perpendicular to that surface at the point of contact (507)

angle of reflection the angle formed by the line perpendicular to a surface and the direction in which a reflected ray moves (507)

anion an ion that has a negative charge (115)

antacid a weak base that neutralizes stomach acid (272)

antinode a point in a standing wave, halfway between two nodes; it indicates a position of maximum intensity (477)

Archimedes' principle the principle that states that the buoyant force on an object in a fluid is an upward force equal to the weight of the volume of fluid that the object displaces (81)

asteroid a small, rocky object that orbits the sun, usually in a band between the orbits of Mars and Jupiter (641)

asthenosphere the zone or layer of the mantle beneath the lithosphere where magma may be generated (704)

atmospheric pressure the pressure due to the weight of the atmosphere; also called air pressure or barometric pressure (753)

atmospheric transmission the passage of an electromagnetic wave signal through the atmosphere between a transmitter and a receiver (602)

atom the smallest unit of an element that maintains the properties of that element (39)

atomic mass unit a unit of mass that describes the mass of an atom or molecule; it is exactly one-twelfth of the mass of a carbon atom with mass number 12 (abbreviation, amu) (118)

atomic number the number of protons in the nucleus of an atom; the atomic number is the same for all atoms of an element (116)

autumnal equinox the moment when the sun passes directly above the equator from north to south; day and night are of equal length on the day that the autumnal equinox occurs (761)

average atomic mass the weighted average of the masses of all naturally occurring isotopes of an element (118)

Avogadro's constant equals 6.02×10^{23}; the number of particles in 1 mol (130)

B

background radiation the nuclear radiation that arises naturally from cosmic rays and from radioactive isotopes in the soil and air (299)

barometric pressure the pressure due to the weight of the atmosphere; also called air pressure or atmospheric pressure (753)

base any compound that increases the number of hydroxide ions when dissolved in water; bases turn red litmus paper blue and react with acids to form salts (258)

beat the interference of waves of slightly different frequencies traveling in the same direction (476)

Bernoulli's principle the principle that states that the pressure in a fluid decreases as the fluid's velocity increases (86)

beta particle a charged electron emitted during certain types of radioactive decay, such as beta decay (285)

big bang theory the theory that all matter and energy in the universe was compressed into an extremely small volume that 10 to 20 billion years ago exploded and began expanding in all directions (684)

biology the scientific study of living organisms and their interactions with the environment (6)

black hole an object so massive and dense that not even light can escape its gravity (672)

bleach a chemical compound used to whiten or make lighter, such as hydrogen peroxide or sodium hypochlorite (271)

blue shift an apparent shift toward shorter wavelengths of light caused when a luminous object moves toward the observer (682)

boiling point the temperature at which a liquid becomes a gas (46)

bond angle the angle formed by two bonds to the same atom (146)

bond length the distance between two bonded atoms at their minimum potential energy; the average distance between the nuclei of two bonded atoms (146)

botany the branch of biology that is the study of plants (6)

Boyle's law the law that states that for a fixed amount of gas at a constant temperature, the volume of the gas increases as the pressure of the gas decreases and the volume of the gas decreases as the pressure of the gas increases (89)

buoyant force the upward force exerted on an object immersed in or floating on a liquid (80)

C

carbohydrate any organic compound that is made of carbon, hydrogen, and oxygen and that provides nutrients to the cells of living things (170)

carrier in physics, a wave that can be modulated to send a signal (604)

catalyst a substance that changes the rate of a chemical reaction without being consumed or changed significantly (207)

cathode-ray tube a tube that uses an electron beam to create a display on a phosphorescent screen (606)

cation an ion that has a positive charge (115)

centripetal acceleration the acceleration directed toward the center of a circular path (326)

Charles's law the law that states that for a fixed amount of gas at a constant pressure, the volume of the gas increases as the temperature of the gas increases and the volume of the gas decreases as the temperature of the gas decreases (90)

chemical bond the attractive force that holds atoms or ions together (145)

chemical change a change that occurs when a substance changes composition by forming one or more new substances (55)

chemical energy the energy released when a chemical compound reacts to produce new compounds (397)

chemical equation a representation of a chemical reaction that uses symbols to show the relationship between the reactants and the products (198)

chemical equilibrium a state of balance in which the rate of a forward reaction equals the rate of the reverse reaction and the concentrations of products and reactants remain unchanged (210)

chemical formula a combination of chemical symbols and numbers to represent a substance (41)

chemical property a property of matter that describes a substance's ability to participate in chemical reactions (50)

chemical structure the arrangement of the atoms in a substance (146)

chemical weathering the process in which rocks break down as a result of chemical reactions (726)

chemistry the scientific study of the composition, structure, and properties of matter and the changes that matter undergoes (7)

cinder cone a steep-sloped deposit of solid fragments ejected from a volcano (715)

circuit breaker a switch that opens a circuit automatically when the current exceeds a certain value (552)

cirrus cloud a feathery cloud that is composed of ice crystals and that has the highest altitude of any cloud in the sky (752)

climate the average weather conditions in an area over a long period of time (760)

cluster a group of stars or galaxies bound by gravity (675)

code a set of rules used to interpret data that convey information (593)

cold front the front edge of a moving mass of cold air, usually accompanied by heavy rain (757)

colloid a mixture consisting of tiny particles that are intermediate in size between those in solutions and those in suspensions and that are suspended in a liquid, solid, or gas (226)

combustion reaction the oxidation reaction of an organic compound, in which heat is released (191)

comet a small body of ice, rock, and cosmic dust loosely packed together that follows an elliptical orbit around the sun and that gives off gas and dust in the form of a tail as it passes close to the sun (650)

community a group of species that live in the same habitat and interact with each other (775)

composite volcano a volcano made of alternating layers of lava and pyroclastic material; also called stratovolcano (714)

compound a substance made up of atoms of two or more different elements joined by chemical bonds (39)

compound machine a machine made of more than one simple machine (390)

compression a point of highest density in a longitudinal wave; corresponds to maximum amplitude (464)

computer an electronic device that can accept data and instructions, follow the instructions, and output the results (610)

concave mirror a mirror that is curved inward like the inside of a spoon (509)

concentration the amount of a particular substance in a given quantity of a mixture, solution, or ore (240)

condensation the change of a substance from a gas to a liquid (76)

constructive interference a superposition of two or more waves that produces a greater intensity than the sum of the intensities of the individual waves (475)

continental drift the hypothesis that states that the continents once formed a single landmass, broke up, and drifted to their present locations (702)

convection the movement of matter due to differences in density that are caused by temperature variations; can result in the transfer of energy as heat (428)

convection current the vertical movement of air currents due to temperature variations (429)

convergent boundary the border formed by the collision of two lithospheric plates (706)

conversion factor a ratio that is derived from the equality of two different units and that can be used to convert from one unit to the other (131)

core the central part of Earth below the mantle; also the center of the sun (701)

Coriolis effect the curving of the path of a moving object from an otherwise straight path due to Earth's rotation (755)

covalent bond a bond formed when atoms share one or more pairs of electrons (155)

crest the highest point of a wave (464)

critical mass the minimum mass of a fissionable isotope that provides the number of neutrons needed to sustain a chain reaction (297)

critical thinking the ability and willingness to assess claims critically and to make judgments on the basis of objective and supported reasons (12)

crude oil unrefined petroleum (230)

crust the thin and solid outermost layer of Earth above the mantle (700)

crystalline solid a solid that consists of crystals (71)

cumulus cloud the low-level, billowy cloud that often has a dark bottom and a top that resembles cotton balls (752)

cyclone an area in the atmosphere that has lower pressure than the surrounding areas and has winds that spiral toward the center (760)

D

decibel the most common unit used to measure loudness (abbreviation, dB) (492)

decomposition reaction a reaction in which a single compound breaks down to form two or more simpler substances (191)

density the ratio of the mass of a substance to the volume of the substance; often expressed as grams per cubic centimeter for solids and liquids and as grams per liter for gases (47)

dependent variable in an experiment, the variable that is changed or determined by manipulation of one or more factors (the independent variables) (21)

deposition the process in which material is laid down (728)

destructive interference a superposition of two or more waves whose intensity is less than the sum of the intensities of the individual waves (475)

detergent a water-soluble cleaner that can emulsify dirt and oil (270)

dew point the temperature at which air or a gas begins to condense to a liquid (752)

diffraction a change in the direction of a wave when the wave finds an obstacle or an edge, such as an opening (473)

diffusion the movement of particles from regions of higher density to regions of lower density (237)

digital signal a signal that can be represented as a sequence of discrete values (595)

diode an electronic device that allows electric charge to move more easily in one direction than in the other (602)

disinfectant a chemical substance that kills harmful bacteria or viruses (271)

dispersion in optics, the process of separating a wave (such as white light) of different frequencies into its individual component waves (the different colors) (517)

displacement the change in position of an object (319)

dissociation the separating of a molecule into simpler molecules, atoms, radicals, or ions (259)

distillation a process of separation in which a liquid is evaporated and then the vapor is condensed into a liquid (229)

divergent boundary the boundary between two tectonic plates that are moving away from each other (705)

Doppler effect an observed change in the frequency of a wave when the source or observer is moving (471)

double-displacement reaction a reaction in which a gas, a solid precipitate, or a molecular compound forms from the apparent exchange of atoms or ions between two compounds (195)

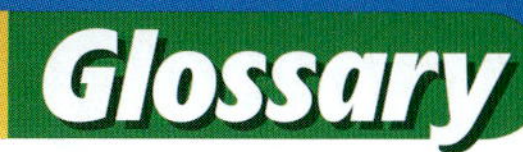

E

eclipse an event in which the shadow of one celestial body falls on another (635)

ecosystem a community of organisms and their abiotic environment (774)

efficiency a quantity, usually expressed as a percentage, that measures the ratio of useful work output to work input (406)

elastic potential energy the energy available for use when an elastic body returns to its original configuration (392)

electrical conductor a material in which charges can move freely and that can carry an electric current (532)

electrical energy the energy that is associated with charged particles because of their positions (550)

electrical insulator a material that does not transfer current easily (532)

electrical potential energy the ability to move an electric charge from one point to another (537)

electric charge an electrical property of matter that creates electric and magnetic forces and interactions (530)

electric field a region in space around a charged object that causes a stationary charged object to experience an electric force (535)

electric motor a device that converts electrical energy into mechanical energy (574)

electrolysis the process in which an electric current is used to produce a chemical reaction, such as the decomposition of water (191)

electrolyte a substance that dissolves in water to give a solution that conducts an electric current (257)

electromagnet a coil that has a soft iron core and that acts as a magnet when an electric current is in the coil (572)

electromagnetic induction the process of creating a current in a circuit by changing a magnetic field (576)

electromagnetic spectrum all of the frequencies or wavelengths of electromagnetic radiation (466)

electromagnetic wave a wave that consists of oscillating electric and magnetic fields, which radiate outward at the speed of light (455)

electron a subatomic particle that has a negative electric charge (106)

element a substance that cannot be separated or broken down into simpler substances by chemical means; all atoms of an element have the same atomic number (39)

empirical formula the composition of a compound in terms of the relative numbers and kinds of atoms in the simplest ratio (162)

emulsion any mixture of two or more immiscible liquids in which one liquid is dispersed in the other (227)

endothermic reaction a chemical reaction that requires heat (187)

energy the capacity to do work (73)

energy level the energy state of an atom (107)

enzyme a type of protein that speeds up metabolic reactions in plants and animals without being permanently changed or destroyed (207)

epicenter the point on Earth's surface directly above an earthquake's focus (710)

equivalence point the point at which the two solutions used in a titration are present in chemically equivalent amounts (267)

erosion a process in which the materials of Earth's surface are loosened, dissolved, or worn away and transported from one place to another by a natural agent, such as wind, water, ice, or gravity (728)

eutrophication an increase in the amount of nutrients, such as nitrates, in a marine or aquatic ecosystem (796)

evaporation the change of a substance from a liquid to a gas (75)

exosphere the outermost region of a planet's atmosphere in which the density is low enough that the lighter atmospheric atoms can escape into space (745)

exothermic reaction a chemical reaction in which heat is released to the surroundings (187)

F

fault a crack in Earth created when rocks on either side of a break move (707)

fission the process by which a nucleus splits into two or more fragments and releases neutrons and energy (295)

flammability the ability of a substance to react in the presence of oxygen and burn when exposed to a flame (50)

fluid a nonsolid state of matter in which the atoms or molecules are free to move past each other, as in a gas or liquid (80)

focal point the point on the axis of a mirror or lens at which all incident parallel light rays converge or diverge (516)

focus the area along a fault at which the first motion of an earthquake occurs (710)

force an action exerted on a body in order to change the body's state of rest or motion; force has magnitude and direction (331)

fossil fuel a nonrenewable energy resource formed from the remains of organisms that lived long ago; examples include oil, coal, and natural gas (783)

free fall the motion of a body when only the force of gravity is acting on the body (354)

freezing point the temperature at which a solid and liquid are in equilibrium at 1 atm pressure (76)

frequency the number of cycles or vibrations per unit of time; also the number of waves produced in a given amount of time (465)

friction a force that opposes motion between two surfaces that are in contact (332)

Glossary

front the boundary between air masses of different densities and usually different temperatures (757)

fuse an electrical device that contains a metal strip that melts when current in the circuit becomes too great (552)

fusion the process in which light nuclei combine at extremely high temperatures, forming heavier nuclei and releasing energy (298)

G

galaxy a collection of stars, dust, and gas bound together by gravity (674)

galvanometer an instrument that detects, measures, and determines the direction of a small electric current (573)

gamma ray the high-energy photon emitted by a nucleus during fission and radioactive decay (286)

gas giant a planet that has a deep, massive atmosphere, such as Jupiter, Saturn, Uranus, or Neptune (641)

Gay-Lussac's law the law that states that the pressure of a gas at a constant volume is directly proportional to the absolute temperature (92)

generator a machine that converts mechanical energy into electrical energy (578)

geocentric describes something that uses Earth as the reference point (647)

geology the study of the origin, history, and structure of Earth and the processes that shape Earth (7)

geostationary orbit a geosynchronous orbit in which a satellite moves in Earth's equatorial plane in the same direction as Earth's rotation such that the satellite remains at an altitude of 35,880 km above a fixed spot on the equator (600)

geothermal energy the energy produced by heat within Earth (786)

global warming a gradual increase in the average global temperatures that is due to a higher concentration of gases such as carbon dioxide in the atmosphere (749)

gravitational potential energy the potential energy stored in the gravitational fields of interacting bodies (392)

greenhouse effect the warming of the surface of Earth and the lower atmosphere as a result of carbon dioxide and water vapor, which absorb and reradiate infrared radiation (748)

group a vertical column of elements in the periodic table (also called family); elements in a group share chemical properties (114)

H

half-life the time required for half of a sample of a radioactive substance to disintegrate by radioactive decay or by natural processes (289)

halogen one of the elements of Group 17 of the periodic table (fluorine, chlorine, bromine, iodine, and astatine); halogens combine with most metals to form salts (126)

hardware the parts or pieces of equipment that make up a computer (614)

harmonic series a series of frequencies that includes the fundamental frequency and integral multiples of the fundamental frequency (494)

heat the energy transferred between objects that are at different temperatures; energy is always transferred from higher-temperature objects to lower-temperature objects (426)

heat engine a machine that transforms heat into mechanical energy, or work (442)

heliocentric sun-centered (647)

heterogeneous composed of dissimilar components (42)

homogeneous describes something that has a uniform structure or composition throughout (42)

humidity the amount of water vapor in the air (751)

hurricane a severe storm that develops over tropical oceans and whose strong winds of more than 120 km/h spiral in toward the intensely low-pressure storm center (760)

hydroelectric energy electrical energy produced by falling water (778)

hydrogen bond the intermolecular force occurring when a hydrogen atom that is bonded to a highly electronegative atom of one molecule is attracted to two unshared electrons of another molecule (234)

hydrosphere the portion of Earth that is water (639)

I

igneous rock rock that forms when magma cools and solidifies (719)

immiscible describes two or more liquids that do not mix with each other (226)

independent variable the factor that is deliberately manipulated in an experiment (21)

indicator a compound that can reversibly change color depending on the pH of the solution or other chemical change (256)

inertia the tendency of an object to resist being moved or, if the object is moving, to resist a change in speed or direction until an outside force acts on the object (346)

infrasound slow vibrations of frequencies lower than 20 Hz (493)

inhibitor a substance that slows down or stops a chemical reaction (207)

inner core the solid, dense center of Earth (701)

intensity the rate at which energy flows through a given area of space (502)

interference the combination of two or more waves of the same frequency that results in a single wave (474)

Internet a large computer network that connects many local and smaller networks all over the world (617)

interstellar matter the gas and dust located between the stars in a galaxy (676)

ion an atom, radical, or molecule that has gained or lost one or more electrons and has a negative or positive charge (115)

ionic bond a bond formed by the attraction between oppositely charged ions (152)

ionization the process of adding or removing electrons from an atom or molecule, which gives the atom or molecule a net charge (302)

ionosphere a region of the atmosphere that is above about 80 km and in which the air is ionized by solar radiation (745)

isotope an atom that has the same number of protons as other atoms of the same element do but that has a different number of neutrons (117)

K

kinetic energy the energy of a moving object due to its motion (73)

kinetic friction the force that opposes the movement of two surfaces that are in contact and are sliding over each other (333)

L

law of reflection the law that states that the angle of incidence is equal to the angle of reflection (507)

length a measure of the straight-line distance between two points (18)

lens a transparent object that refracts light waves such that they converge or diverge to create an image (515)

Le Système International d'Unités the International System of Units, which is the measurement system that is accepted worldwide (15)

light ray a line in space that matches the direction of the flow of radiant energy (506)

light-year the distance that light travels in one year; about 9.5 trillion kilometers (9.5×10^{12} km) (666)

lithosphere the solid, outer layer of Earth that consists of the crust and the rigid upper part of the mantle (703)

longitudinal wave a wave in which the particles of the medium vibrate parallel to the direction of wave motion (461)

loudness the extent to which a sound can be heard (491)

M

magma liquid rock produced under Earth's surface; igneous rocks are made of magma (705)

magnetic field a region where a magnetic force can be detected (567)

magnetic pole one of two points, such as the ends of a magnet, that have opposing magnetic qualities (566)

magnification a change in the size of an image compared with the size of an object (515)

mantle the layer of rock between Earth's crust and core (700)

maria large, dark areas of basalt on the moon (singular, mare) (634)

mass a measure of the amount of matter in an object (18)

mass defect the difference between the mass of an atom and the sum of the masses of the atom's protons, neutrons, and electrons (296)

mass number the sum of the numbers of protons and neutrons in the nucleus of an atom (116)

matter anything that has mass and takes up space (38)

mechanical advantage a quantity that measures how much a machine multiplies force or distance (383)

mechanical energy the sum of the kinetic and potential energy of large-scale objects in a system (396)

mechanical wave a wave that requires a medium through which to travel (455)

medium a physical environment in which phenomena occur (455)

melting point the temperature and pressure at which a solid becomes a liquid (46)

mesosphere the strong, lower part of the mantle between the asthenosphere and the outer core; also the coldest layer of the atmosphere between the stratosphere and the mesopause (745)

metallic bond a bond formed by the attraction between positively charged metal ions and the electrons around them (154)

metal an element that is shiny and that conducts heat and electricity well (121)

metamorphic rock a rock that forms from other rocks as a result of intense heat, pressure, or chemical processes (721)

meteorology the scientific study of Earth's atmosphere, especially in relation to weather and climate (757)

mineral a natural, usually inorganic solid that has a characteristic chemical composition, an orderly internal structure, and a characteristic set of physical properties (718)

miscible describes two or more liquids that can dissolve into each other in various proportions (42)

mixture a combination of two or more substances that are not chemically combined (41)

model a pattern, plan, representation, or description designed to show the structure or workings of an object, system, or concept (9)

modulate to change a wave's amplitude or frequency in order to send a signal (604)

molarity the concentration of a solution in moles of dissolved solute per liter of solution (243)

molar mass the mass in grams of 1 mol of a substance (130)

mole the SI base unit used to measure the amount of a substance whose number of particles is the same as the number of atoms of carbon in 12 g of carbon-12 (130)

molecular formula a chemical formula that shows the number and kinds of atoms in a molecule, but not the arrangement of the atoms (164)

molecule the smallest unit of a substance that keeps all of the physical and chemical properties of that substance; it can consist of one atom or two or more atoms bonded together (40)

mole ratio the relative number of moles of the substances required to produce a given amount of product in a chemical reaction (203)

momentum a quantity defined as the product of the mass and velocity of an object (362)

monomer a simple molecule that can combine with other like or unlike molecules to make a polymer (169)

motion an object's change in position relative to a reference point (318)

N

nebula a large cloud of dust and gas in interstellar space (648)

nebular model a model for the formation of the solar system in which the sun and planets condense from a cloud (or nebula) of gas and dust (648)

net force a single force whose external effects on a rigid body are the same as the effects of several actual forces acting on the body (334)

neutralization reaction the reaction of the ions that characterize acids (hydronium ions) and the ions that characterize bases (hydroxide ions) to form water molecules and a salt (264)

neutron a subatomic particle that has no charge and that is found in the nucleus of an atom (106)

neutron star a star that has collapsed under gravity to the point that the electrons and protons have smashed together to form neutrons (672)

noble gas an unreactive element of Group 18 of the periodic table (helium, neon, argon, krypton, xenon, or radon) that has eight electrons in its outer level (except for helium, which has two electrons) (127)

node in physics, a point in a standing wave that maintains zero amplitude (477)

nonmetal an element that conducts heat and electricity poorly and that does not form positive ions in an electrolytic solution (121)

nonpolar compound a compound whose electrons are equally distributed among its atoms (235)

nonrenewable resource a substance that is consumed faster than it forms and therefore cannot be replaced within a human life span (784)

nuclear chain reaction a continuous series of nuclear fission reactions (296)

nuclear radiation the particles that are released from the nucleus during radioactive decay, such as neutrons, electrons, and photons (284)

nucleus an atom's central region, which is made up of protons and neutrons (106)

O

operating system the software that controls a computer's activities (614)

optical fiber a transparent thread of plastic or glass that transmits light (597)

orbital a region in an atom where there is a high probability of finding electrons (109)

organic compound a covalently bonded compound that contains carbon, excluding carbonates and oxides (165)

oxidation reaction a chemical reaction in which a reactant loses one or more electrons such that the reactant becomes more positive in charge (195)

oxidation-reduction reaction any chemical change in which one species is oxidized (loses electrons) and another species is reduced (gains electrons); also called redox reaction (196)

ozone a gas molecule that is made up of three oxygen atoms (744)

ozone layer the thin layer of the atmosphere at an altitude of 15 to 40 km in which ozone absorbs ultraviolet solar radiation (744)

P

Pangea a single landmass that existed for about 40 million years before it began to break apart and form the continents that we know today (702)

parallel a circuit in which all of the components are connected to each other side by side (549)

pascal the SI unit of pressure; equal to the force of 1 N exerted over an area of 1 m^2 (abbreviation, Pa) (83)

Pascal's principle the principle that states that a fluid in equilibrium contained in a vessel exerts a pressure of equal intensity in all directions (84)

period in chemistry, a horizontal row of elements in the periodic table (114)

period the time that it takes a complete cycle or wave oscillation to occur (465)

periodic law the law that states that the repeating chemical and physical properties of elements change periodically with the atomic numbers of the elements (111)

pH a value used to express the acidity or alkalinity of a solution; it is defined as the logarithm of the reciprocal of the concentration of hydronium ions (261)

phase in astronomy, the change in the illuminated area of one celestial body as seen from another celestial body; phases of the moon are caused by the changing positions of Earth, the sun, and the moon (634)

photon a unit or quantum of light; a particle of electromagnetic radiation that has zero rest mass and carries a quantum of energy (500)

photosynthesis the process by which plants, algae, and some bacteria use sunlight, carbon dioxide, and water to produce carbohydrates and oxygen (746)

physical change a change of matter from one form to another without a change in chemical properties (53)

physical property a characteristic of a substance that does not involve a chemical change, such as density, color, or hardness (45)

physical science the scientific study of nonliving matter (7)

pitch a measure of how high or low a sound is perceived to be depending on the frequency of the sound wave (470)

pixel a picture element, the smallest element of a display image (607)

planet any of the nine primary bodies that orbit the sun; a similar body that orbits another star (630)

plasma a state of matter that starts as a gas and then becomes ionized; it consists of free-moving ions and electrons, it takes on an electric charge, and its properties differ from those of a solid, liquid, or gas (72)

plate tectonics the theory that explains how the outer parts of Earth change over time; explains the relationships between continental drift, sea-floor spreading, seismic activity, and volcanic activity (703)

polar molecule a molecule that has a negative charge on one side and a positive charge on the other (232)

pollution an undesirable change in the natural environment that is caused by the introduction of substances that are harmful to living organisms, or by excessive wastes, heat, noise, or radiation (791)

polyatomic ion an ion made of two or more atoms (156)

polymer a large molecule that is formed by more than five monomers, or small units (169)

potential difference between any two points, the work which must be done against electric forces to move a unit charge from one point to the other (538)

potential energy the stored energy resulting from the relative positions of objects in a system (392)

power a quantity that measures the rate at which work is done (380)

precipitation any form of water that falls to Earth's surface from the clouds; includes rain, snow, sleet, and hail (751)

precision the exactness of a measurement (24)

pressure the amount of force exerted per unit area of a surface (81)

prism a system that consists of two or more plane surfaces of a transparent solid at an angle with each other (517)

product a substance that forms in a chemical reaction (185)

projectile motion the curved path that an object follows when thrown, launched, or otherwise projected near the surface of Earth; the motion of objects that are moving in two dimensions under the influence of gravity (358)

protein an organic compound that is made of one or more chains of amino acids and that is a principal component of all cells (170)

proton a subatomic particle that has a positive charge and that is found in the nucleus of an atom (106)

pure substance a sample of matter, either a single element or a single compound, that has definite chemical and physical properties (41)

R

radar **ra**dio **d**etection **a**nd **r**anging, a system that uses reflected radio waves to determine the velocity and location of objects (504)

radiation the energy that is transferred as electromagnetic waves, such as visible light and infrared waves (429)

radical an organic group that has one or more electrons available for bonding (196)

radioactive decay the disintegration of an unstable atomic nucleus into one or more different nuclides accompanied by either the emission of radiation, nuclear capture or ejection of electrons, or fission (124)

radioactive tracer a radioactive material that is added to a substance so that its distribution can be detected later (301)

radioactivity the process by which an unstable nucleus emits one or more particles or energy in the form of electromagnetic radiation (284)

random-access memory a storage device that allows a computer user to write and read data (abbreviation, RAM) (613)

rarefaction the portion of a longitudinal wave in which the density and pressure of the medium are at a minimum (464)

reactant a substance or molecule that participates in a chemical reaction (185)

reactivity the capacity of a substance to combine chemically with another substance (50)

read-only memory a memory device that contains data that can be read but cannot be changed (abbreviation, ROM) (614)

real image an image of an object formed by light rays that actually come together at a specific location (509)

recycling the process of recovering valuable or useful materials from waste or scrap, or reusing some items (800)

red giant a large, reddish star late in its life cycle (671)

red shift an apparent shift toward longer wavelengths of light caused when a luminous object moves away from the observer (682)

reduction a chemical change in which electrons are gained, either by the removal of oxygen, the addition of hydrogen, or the addition of electrons (196)

reflection the bouncing back of a ray of light, sound, or heat when the ray hits a surface that it does not go through (472)

refraction the bending of a light ray as it passes from one substance to another one with a different density (474)

refrigerant a material used to cool an area or an object to a temperature that is lower than the temperature of the environment (440)

rem the quantity of ionizing radiation that does as much damage to human tissue as 1 roentgen of high-voltage X rays does (300)

renewable resource a natural resource that can be replaced at the same rate as it is consumed, such as food production by photosynthesis (785)

resistance the opposition posed by a material or a device to the flow of current (541)

resonance a phenomenon that occurs when two objects naturally vibrate at the same frequency (495)

respiration the interchange of oxygen and carbon dioxide between living cells and their environment; includes breathing and cellular respiration (747)

Richter scale a scale that expresses the magnitude of an earthquake (713)

rock cycle the series of processes in which a rock forms, changes from one type to another, is destroyed, and forms again by geological processes (722)

S

salt an ionic compound that forms when a metal atom or a positive radical replaces the hydrogen of an acid (265)

satellite a natural or artificial body that revolves around a planet (633)

saturated solution a solution that cannot dissolve any more solute under the given conditions (241)

schematic diagram a graphical representation of a circuit that uses lines to represent wires and different symbols to represent components (547)

science the knowledge gained by observing natural events and conditions in order to discover facts and formulate laws or principles that can be verified or tested (6)

scientific law a summary of many experimental results and observations; a law tells how things work (8)

scientific method a series of steps followed to solve problems including collecting data, formulating a hypothesis, testing the hypothesis, and stating conclusions (13)

scientific notation a method of expressing a quantity as a number multiplied by 10 to the appropriate power (22)

scientific theory an explanation for some phenomenon that is based on observation, experimentation, and reasoning (8)

sedimentary rock a rock formed from compressed or cemented layers of sediment (720)

seismic wave a vibration in rock that travels out from the focus of an earthquake in all directions; seismic waves can also be caused by explosions (710)

seismology the study of earthquakes, including their origin, propagation, energy, and prediction (711)

semiconductor an element or compound that conducts electric current better than an insulator but not as well as a conductor (121)

series the components of a circuit that form a single path for current (549)

shield volcano a large, gently sloped volcano that forms by eruptions of balsatic lava flows (714)

SI Le Système International d'Unités, or the International System of Units, which is the measurement system that is accepted worldwide (15)

signal anything that serves to direct, guide, or warn (592)

significant figure a prescribed decimal place that determines the amount of rounding off to be done based on the precision of the measurement (24)

simple harmonic motion a periodic motion whose path is formed by one or more vibrations that are symmetric about an equilibrium position (459)

simple machine one of the six basic types of machines of which all other machines are composed (385)

single-displacement reaction a reaction in which one element or radical takes the place of another element or radical in a compound (194)

soap a substance that is used as a cleaner and that dissolves in water (269)

software a set of instructions or commands that tells a computer what to do; a computer program (614)

solar system the sun and all of the planets and other bodies that travel around it (632)

solenoid a coil of wire with an electric current in it (571)

solubility the ability of one substance to dissolve in another at a given temperature and pressure; expressed in terms of the maximum amount of solute that will dissolve in a given amount of solvent (239)

soluble capable of dissolving in a particular solvent (239)

solute the substance that dissolves in the solvent (229)

solution a homogeneous mixture of two or more substances uniformly dispersed throughout a single phase (229)

solvent the substance in which the solute dissolves (229)

sonar **so**und **n**avigation **a**nd **r**anging, a system that uses acoustic signals to determine the location of objects or to communicate (497)

sound wave a longitudinal wave that is caused by vibrations and that travels through a material medium (490)

specific heat the quantity of heat required to raise a unit mass of homogeneous material 1 K or 1°C in a specified way given constant pressure and volume (432)

spectator ion an ion that is present in a solution in which a reaction is taking place but that does not participate in the reaction (264)

speed the distance traveled by an object divided by the time interval during which the motion occurred (320)

standing wave a pattern of vibration that simulates a wave that is standing still (477)

star a large celestial body that is composed of gas and that emits light; the sun is a typical star (666)

static friction the force that resists the initiation of sliding motion between two surfaces that are in contact and at rest (333)

stationary front a front of air masses that moves either very slowly or not at all (758)

stratosphere the upper layer of the atmosphere, which lies immediately above the troposphere and extends from 10 km to about 50 km above Earth's surface (744)

stratus cloud a gray cloud that has a flat, uniform base and forms at very low altitudes (752)

strong acid an acid that ionizes completely in a solvent (257)

strong nuclear force the interaction that binds nucleons together in a nucleus (294)

structural formula a formula that indicates the location of the atoms, groups, or ions relative to one another in a molecule and that indicates the number and location of chemical bonds (146)

subduction the process by which one lithospheric plate moves beneath another as a result of tectonic forces (706)

sublimation the process in which a solid changes directly into a gas or a gas changes directly into a solid (75)

substrate the reactant in reactions catalyzed by enzymes (208)

succession the replacement of one type of community by another at a single location over a period of time (778)

summer solstice in the Northern Hemisphere, the moment in the year at which the sun appears to be at the greatest distance north of the equator; the first day of summer (761)

supernova a gigantic explosion in which a massive star collapses and throws its outer layers into space; plural supernovae (671)

surface wave a seismic wave that can move only through solids (711)

suspension a mixture in which particles of a material are more or less evenly dispersed throughout a liquid or gas (225)

synthesis reaction a reaction in which substances combine to form a new compound (190)

T

technology the application of science for practical purposes (7)

tectonic plate a block of lithosphere that consists of the crust and the rigid, outermost part of the mantle; also called lithospheric plate (703)

telecommunication the sending of visual or auditory information by electromagnetic means (594)

telescope an instrument that produces a magnified image of a distant object by using a system of lenses or mirrors (15)

temperature a measure of how hot (or cold) something is; specifically, a measure of the average kinetic energy of the particles in an object (420)

temperature inversion the atmospheric condition in which warm air traps cooler air near Earth's surface (743)

terminal velocity the constant velocity of a falling object when the force of air resistance is equal in magnitude and opposite in direction to the force of gravity (356)

terrestrial planet one of the highly dense planets nearest to the sun; Mercury, Venus, Earth, and Mars (637)

thermal conduction the transfer of energy as heat through a material (428)

thermal energy the kinetic energy of a substance's atoms (73)

thermometer an instrument that measures and indicates temperature (421)

Glossary

thermosphere the uppermost layer of the atmosphere, in which temperature increases as altitude increases; includes the ionosphere (745)

titration a method to determine the concentration of a substance in solution by adding a solution of known volume and concentration until the reaction is completed, which is usually indicated by a change in color (267)

topography the configuration of a land surface, including its relief (762)

total internal reflection the complete reflection that takes place within a substance when the angle of incidence of light striking the surface boundary is less than the critical angle (514)

transformer a device that increases or decreases the voltage of alternating current (581)

transform fault boundary the boundary between tectonic plates that are sliding past each other horizontally (707)

transition metal one of the metals that can use the inner shell before using the outer shell to bond (123)

transpiration the process by which plants release water vapor into the air through stomata; also the release of water vapor into the air by other organisms (751)

transverse wave a wave in which the particles of the medium move perpendicular to the direction the wave is traveling (461)

troposphere the lowest layer of the atmosphere, characterized by a constant drop of temperature with increasing altitude; the part of the atmosphere where weather conditions exist (743)

trough the lowest point of a wave (464)

typhoon a severe tropical cyclone that forms on the western Pacific Ocean and on the China Seas; a hurricane (760)

U

ultrasound any sound wave with frequencies higher than 20 000 Hz (493)

universe the sum of all space, matter, and energy that exists, that has existed in the past, and that will exist in the future (680)

unsaturated solution a solution that is able to dissolve additional solute (240)

V

vaccine a substance prepared from killed or weakened pathogens and introduced into an organism to produce immunity (223)

valence electron an electron that is found in the outermost shell of an atom and that determines the atom's chemical properties (110)

variable a factor that changes in an experiment in order to test a hypothesis (13)

velocity the speed of an object in a particular direction (322)

vent an opening at the surface of Earth through which volcanic material passes (714)

vernal equinox the moment when the sun passes directly above the equator from south to north; day and night are of equal length on the day that the vernal equinox occurs (761)

virtual image an image that forms at a location from which light rays appear to come but do not actually come (508)

viscosity the resistance of a gas or liquid to flow (85)

visible spectrum the portion of the electromagnetic spectrum that includes all of the wavelengths that are visible to the human eye (466)

volume a measure of the size of a body or region in three-dimensional space (18)

W

warm front a front that advances in such a way that warmer air replaces colder air (757)

water cycle the continuous movement of water from the ocean to the atmosphere to the land and back to the ocean (750)

watt the unit used to express power; equivalent to joules per second (abbreviation, W) (380)

wave a periodic disturbance in a solid, liquid, or gas as energy is transmitted through a medium (454)

wavelength the distance from any point on a wave to an identical point on the next wave (464)

weak acid an acid that releases few hydrogen ions in aqueous solution (257)

weathering the natural process by which atmospheric and environmental agents, such as wind, rain, and temperature changes, disintegrate, and decompose rocks (720)

weight a measure of the gravitational force exerted on an object (18)

white dwarf a small, hot, dim star that is the leftover center of an old star (671)

winter solstice in the Northern Hemisphere, the moment in the year at which the sun appears to be at the greatest distance south of the equator; the beginning of winter (761)

work the quantity of energy transferred by a force when it is applied to a body and causes that body to move in the direction of the force (378)

A

absolute zero/cero absoluto la temperatura a la que la energía molecular es mínima (0 K en la escala de Kelvin ó –273.16ºC en la escala de Celsius) (423)

acceleration/aceleración la tasa a la que la velocidad cambia con el tiempo; un objeto acelera si su rapidez cambia, si su dirección cambia, o si tanto su rapidez como su dirección cambian (325)

accuracy/exactitud término que describe qué tanto se aproxima una medida al valor verdadero de la cantidad medida (25)

acid/ácido cualquier compuesto que aumenta el número de iones de hidrógeno cuando se disuelve en agua; los ácidos cambian el color del papel tornasol a rojo y forman sales al reaccionar con bases y con algunos metales (256)

acid precipitation/precipitación ácida precipitación tal como lluvia, aguanieve o nieve, que contiene una alta concentración de ácidos debido a la contaminación de la atmósfera (727)

aerobic/aeróbico término que describe un proceso que requiere oxígeno (747)

air mass/masa de aire un gran volumen de aire que tiene una temperatura y contenido de humedad similar en toda su extensión (757)

air pressure/presión del aire la medida de la fuerza con la que las moléculas del aire empujan contra una superficie (83)

alkali metal/metal alcalino uno de los elementos del Grupo 1 de la tabla periódica (litio, sodio, potasio, rubidio, cesio y francio) (121)

alkaline-earth metal/metal alcalinotérreo uno de los elementos del Grupo 2 de la tabla periódica (berilio, magnesio, calcio, estroncio, bario y radio) (122)

alloy/aleación una mezcla sólida o líquida de dos o más metales (231)

alpha particle/partícula alfa un átomo cargado positivamente, liberado en la desintegración de elementos radiactivos, que está formado por dos protones y dos neutrones (285)

alpha particle/partícula alfa un átomo cargado positivamente, liberado en la desintegración de elementos radiactivos, que está formado por dos protones y dos neutrones (285)

alternating current/corriente alterna una corriente eléctrica que cambia de dirección en intervalos regulares (abreviatura: CA) (578)

amino acid/aminoácido cualquiera de las 20 distintas moléculas orgánicas que contienen un grupo carboxilo y un grupo amino y que se combinan para formar proteínas (170)

amorphous solid/sólido amorfo un sólido en el que las partículas no están ordenadas periódicamente o en orden (71)

amplitude/amplitud la distancia máxima a la que vibran las partículas del medio de una onda a partir de su posición de reposo (464)

analog signal/señal análoga una señal cuyas propiedades, tales como la amplitud y la frecuencia, cambian continuamente en un rango determinado (595)

angle of incidence/ángulo de incidencia el ángulo que se forma entre un rayo que choca contra una superficie y la línea perpendicular a esa superficie en el punto de contacto (507)

angle of reflection/ángulo de reflexión el ángulo formado por la línea perpendicular a la superficie y la dirección en la que se mueve un rayo reflejado (507)

anion/anión un ion que tiene carga negativa (115)

antacid/antiácido una base débil que neutraliza el ácido del estómago (0)

antinode/antinodo un punto en una onda estacionaria, ubicada en el punto medio entre dos nodos; indica una posición de intensidad máxima (477)

Archimedes' principle/principio de Arquímedes el principio que establece que la fuerza flotante de un objeto que está en un fluido es una fuerza ascendente cuya magnitud es igual al peso del volumen del fluido que el objeto desplaza (81)

asteroid/asteroide un objeto pequeño y rocoso que se encuentra en órbita alrededor del Sol, normalmente en una banda entre las órbitas de Marte y Júpiter (641)

asthenosphere/astenosfera la capa sólida y plástica del manto, que se encuentra debajo de la litosfera; está formada por roca del manto que fluye muy lentamente, lo cual permite que las placas tectónicas se muevan en su superficie (704)

atmospheric pressure/presión atmosférica la presión producida por el peso de la atmósfera (753)

atmospheric transmission/transmisión atmosférica el paso de la señal de una onda electromagnética a través de la atmósfera entre el transmisor y el receptor (602)

atom/átomo la unidad más pequeña de un elemento que conserva las propiedades de ese elemento (39)

atom/átomo la unidad más pequeña de un elemento que conserva las propiedades de ese elemento (104)

atomic mass unit/unidad de masa atómica una unidad de masa que describe la masa de un átomo o molécula; es exactamente 1/12 de la masa de un átomo de carbono con un número de masa de 12 (abreviatura: uma) (118)

atomic number/número atómico el número de protones en el núcleo de un átomo; el número atómico es el mismo para todos los átomos de un elemento (116)

autumnal equinox/equinoccio otoñal el momento en el que el Sol pasa directamente encima del ecuador del Norte al Sur; el día y la noche tienen la misma duración en el día en que ocurre el equinoccio otoñal (761)

average atomic mass/masa atómica promedio el promedio ponderado de las masas de todos los isótopos de un elemento que se encuentran en la naturaleza (118)

Avogadro's number/número de Avogadro 6.02×10^{23}, el número de átomos o moléculas que hay en 1 mol (130)

B

background radiation/radiación de fondo la radiación nuclear que surge naturalmente de los rayos cósmicos y de los isótopos radiactivos que están en el suelo y en el aire (299)

barometric pressure/presión barométrica la presión debida al peso de la atmósfera; también se llama presión del aire o presión atmosférica (753)

base/base cualquier compuesto que aumenta el número de iones de hidróxido cuando se disuelve en agua; las bases cambian el color del papel tornasol a azul y forman sales al reaccionar con ácidos (258)

beat/batido la interferencia de ondas que se desplazan en la misma dirección y que tienen frecuencias ligeramente distintas (476)

Bernoulli's principle/principio de Bernoulli el principio que establece que la presión de un fluido disminuye a medida que la velocidad del fluido aumenta (86)

beta particle/partícula beta un electrón con carga, emitido durante ciertos tipos de desintegración radiactiva, como por ejemplo, durante la desintegración beta (285)

big bang theory/teoría del Big Bang la teoría que establece que toda la materia y la energía del universo estaban comprimidas en un volumen extremadamente pequeño que explotó hace aproximadamente 10 a 20 mil millones de años y empezó a expandirse en todas direcciones (684)

biology/biología el estudio científico de los seres vivos y sus interacciones con el medio ambiente (6)

black hole/hoyo negro un objeto tan masivo y denso que ni siquiera la luz puede salir de su campo gravitacional (672)

bleach/blanqueador un compuesto químico que se usa para blanquear o aclarar, tal como el peróxido de hidrógeno o el hipoclorito de sodio (271)

boiling point/punto de ebullición la temperatura y presión a la que un líquido y un gas están en equilibrio (46)

boiling point/punto de ebullición la temperatura y presión a la que un líquido y un gas están en equilibrio (75)

bond angle/ángulo de enlace el ángulo formado por dos enlaces al mismo átomo (146)

bond length/longitud de enlace la distancia entre dos átomos que están enlazados en el punto en que su energía potencial es mínima; la distancia promedio entre los núcleos de dos átomos enlazados (146)

botany/botánica la rama de la biología que se ocupa del estudio de las plantas (6)

Boyle's law/ley de Boyle la ley que establece que para una cantidad fija de gas a una temperatura constante, el volumen del gas aumenta a medida que su presión disminuye y el volumen del gas disminuye a medida que su presión aumenta (89)

buoyant force/fuerza boyante la fuerza ascendente que hace que un objeto se mantenga sumergido en un líquido o flotando en él (80)

C

carbohydrate/carbohidrato cualquier compuesto orgánico que está hecho de carbono, hidrógeno y oxígeno y que proporciona nutrientes a las células de los seres vivos (170)

carrier/portador en física, una onda que puede modularse para enviar una señal (604)

catalyst/catalizador una substancia que cambia la tasa de una reacción química sin ser consumida ni cambiar significativamente (207)

cathode-ray tube/tubo de rayos catódicos un tubo que usa un haz de electrones para crear una representación en una pantalla fosforescente (606)

cation/catión un ion que tiene carga positiva (115)

centripetal acceleration/aceleración centrípeta la aceleración que se dirige hacia el centro de un camino circular (0)

Charles's law/ley de Charles la ley que establece que para una cantidad fija de gas a una presión constante, el volumen del gas aumenta a medida que su temperatura aumenta y el volumen del gas disminuye a medida que su temperatura disminuye (90)

chemical bond/enlace químico la fuerza de atracción que mantiene unidos a los átomos o iones (145)

chemical change/cambio químico un cambio que ocurre cuando una o más substancias se transforman en substancias totalmente nuevas con propiedades diferentes (55)

chemical energy/energía química la energía que se libera cuando un compuesto químico reacciona para producir nuevos compuestos (187)

chemical energy/energía química la energía que se libera cuando un compuesto químico reacciona para producir nuevos compuestos (397)

chemical equation/ecuación química una representación de una reacción química que usa símbolos para mostrar la relación entre los reactivos y los productos (198)

chemical equilibrium/equilibrio químico un estado de equilibrio en el que la tasa de la reacción directa es igual a la tasa de la reacción inversa y las concentraciones de los productos y reactivos no sufren cambios (210)

chemical formula/fórmula química una combinación de símbolos químicos y números que se usan para representar una substancia (41)

chemical property/propiedad química una propiedad de la materia que describe la capacidad de una substancia de participar en reacciones químicas (50)

chemical structure/estructura química la disposición de los átomos en una molécula (146)

chemical weathering/desgaste químico el proceso por medio del cual las rocas se fragmentan como resultado de reacciones químicas (726)

chemistry/química el estudio científico de la composición, estructura y propiedades de la materia y los cambios por los que pasa (7)

chemistry/química el estudio científico de la composición, estructura y propiedades de la materia y los cambios por los que pasa (38)

cinder cone/cono de escorias un depósito con pendiente empinada de fragmentos sólidos expulsados por un volcán (715)

circuit breaker/disyuntor un interruptor que abre un circuito automáticamente cuando la corriente excede un valor determinado (552)

cirrus cloud/nube cirro una nube liviana formada por cristales de hielo, la cual tiene la mayor altitud de todas las nubes en el cielo (752)

climate/clima las condiciones promedio del tiempo en un área durante un largo período de tiempo (760)

cluster/conglomerado un grupo de estrellas o galaxias unidas por la gravedad (675)

code/código un conjunto de reglas que se usan para interpretar datos y transmitir información (593)

cold front/frente frío el borde del frente de una masa de aire frío en movimiento, normalmente acompañado de fuertes lluvias (757)

colloid/coloide una mezcla formada por partículas diminutas que son de tamaño intermedio entre las partículas de las soluciones y las de las suspensiones y que se encuentran suspendidas en un líquido, sólido o gas (226)

combustion reaction/reacción de combustión la reacción de oxidación de un compuesto orgánico, durante la cual se libera calor (191)

comet/cometa un cuerpo pequeño formado por hielo, roca y polvo cósmico que sigue una órbita elíptica alrededor del Sol y que libera gas y polvo, los cuales forman una cola al pasar cerca del Sol (650)

community/comunidad un grupo de varias especies que viven en el mismo hábitat e interactúan unas con otras (775)

composite volcano/volcán compuesto un volcán formado por capas alternas de lava y material piroclástico; también se llama estratovolcán (714)

compound/compuesto una substancia formada por átomos de dos o más elementos diferentes unidos por enlaces químicos (39)

compound machine/máquina compuesta una máquina hecha de más de una máquina simple (390)

compression/compresión un punto de densidad máxima en una onda longitudinal; equivale a la amplitud máxima (464)

computer/computadora un aparato electrónico que acepta información e instrucciones, sigue instrucciones y produce una salida para los resultados (610)

concave mirror/espejo cóncavo un espejo que está curvado hacia adentro como la parte interior de una cuchara (509)

concentration/concentración la cantidad de una cierta substancia en una cantidad determinada de mezcla, solución o mena (240)

condensation/condensación el cambio de estado de gas a líquido (76)

constructive interference/interferencia constructiva una superposición de dos o más ondas que produce una intensidad mayor que la suma de las intensidades de las ondas individuales (475)

continental drift/deriva continental la hipótesis que establece que alguna vez los continentes formaron una sola masa de tierra, se dividieron y se fueron a la deriva hasta terminar en sus ubicaciones actuales (702)

convection/convección el movimiento de la materia debido a diferencias en la densidad que se producen por variaciones en la temperatura; puede resultar en la transferencia de energía en forma de calor (428)

convection current/corriente de convección el movimiento vertical de las corrientes de aire debido a variaciones en la temperatura (429)

convergent boundary/límite convergente el borde que se forma debido al choque de dos placas de la litosfera (706)

conversion factor/factor de conversión una razón que se deriva de la igualdad entre dos unidades diferentes y que se puede usar para convertir una unidad en otra (131)

core/núcleo la parte central de la Tierra, debajo del manto; también, el centro del Sol (701)

Coriolis effect/efecto de Coriolis la desviación de una línea recta que experimentan los objetos en movimiento debido a la rotación de la Tierra (755)

Glosario

covalent bond/enlace covalente un enlace formado cuando los átomos comparten uno más pares de electrones (155)

crest/cresta el punto más alto de una onda (464)

critical mass/masa crítica la cantidad mínima de masa de un isótopo fisionable que proporciona el número de neutrones que se requieren para sostener una reacción en cadena (297)

critical thinking/razonamiento crítico la capacidad y voluntad de evaluar declaraciones críticamente y de hacer juicios basados en razones objetivas y docum entadas (12)

crude oil/petróleo crudo petróleo no refinado (230)

crust/corteza la capa externa, delgada y sólida de la Tierra, que se encuentra sobre el manto (700)

crystalline solid/sólido cristalino un sólido formado por cristales (71)

cumulus cloud/nube cúmulo una nube esponjada ubicada en un nivel bajo, que normalmente es obscura en la parte inferior y cuya parte superior parece una bola de algodón (752)

cyclone/ciclón un área de la atmósfera que tiene una presión menor que la de las áreas circundantes y que tiene vientos que giran en espiral hacia el centro (760)

D

decibel/decibel la unidad más común que se usa para medir el volumen del sonido (abreviatura: dB) (492)

decomposition reaction/reacción de descomposición una reacción en la que un solo compuesto se descompone para formar dos o más substancias más simples (191)

density/densidad la relación entre la masa de una substancia y su volumen; comúnmente se expresa en gramos por centímetro cúbico para los sólidos y líquidos, y como gramos por litro para los gases (47)

dependent variable/variable dependiente en un experimento, la variable que se cambia o que se determina al manipular dos o más factores (las variables independientes) (21)

deposition/deposición el proceso por medio del cual un material se deposita (728)

destructive interference/interferencia destructiva una superposición de dos o más ondas cuya una intensidad menor que la suma de las intensidades de las ondas individuales (475)

detergent/detergente un limpiador no jabonoso, soluble en agua, que emulsiona la suciedad y el aceite (270)

dew point/punto de rocío la temperatura y presión a la que un gas se empieza a condensar para formar un líquido (752)

diffraction/difracción un cambio en la dirección de una onda cuando ésta se encuentra con un obstáculo o un borde, tal como una abertura (473)

diffusion/difusión el movimiento de partículas de regiones de mayor densidad a regiones de menor densidad (237)

digital signal/señal digital una señal que se puede representar como una secuencia de valores discretos (595)

diode/diodo un aparato electrónico que permite que la corriente eléctrica pase más fácilmente en una dirección que en otra (602)

disinfectant/desinfectante una substancia química que elimina bacterias dañinas o virus (271)

dispersion/dispersión en óptica, el proceso de separar una onda que tiene diferentes frecuencias (por ejemplo, la luz blanca) de las ondas individuales que la componen (los distintos colores) (517)

displacement/desplazamiento el cambio en la posición de un objeto (319)

dissociation/disociación la separación de una molécula en moléculas más simples, átomos, radicales o iones (259)

distillation/destilación un proceso de separación por medio del cual un líquido se evapora y, luego, el vapor se condensa en un líquido (229)

divergent boundary/límite divergente el límite entre dos placas tectónicas que se están separando una de la otra (705)

Doppler effect/efecto Doppler un cambio que se observa en la frecuencia de una onda cuando la fuente o el observador está en movimiento (471)

double-displacement reaction/reacción de doble desplazamiento una reacción en la que un gas, un precipitado sólido o un compuesto molecular se forma a partir del intercambio aparente de iones entre dos compuestos (195)

E

eclipse/eclipse un suceso en el que la sombra de un cuerpo celeste cubre otro cuerpo celeste (635)

ecosystem/ecosistema una comunidad de organismos y su ambiente abiótico (774)

efficiency/eficiencia una cantidad, generalmente expresada como un porcentaje, que mide la relación entre la entrada y la salida de trabajo (406)

elastic potential energy/energía potencial elástica la energía disponible para ser usada cuando un cuerpo elástico regresa a su configuración original (0)

electrical conductor/conductor eléctrico un material en el que las cargas se mueven libremente y que conduce una corriente eléctrica (532)

electrical energy/energía eléctrica la energía asociada con partículas que tienen carga debido a sus posiciones (550)

electrical insulator/aislante eléctrico un material que no transfiere corriente con facilidad (532)

electrical potential energy/ energía potencial eléctrica la capacidad de mover una carga eléctrica de un punto a otro (537)

electric charge/carga eléctrica una propiedad eléctrica de la materia que crea fuerzas e interacciones eléctricas y magnéticas (530)

electric field/campo eléctrico una región en el espacio alrededor de un objecto con carga experimente una fuerza eléctrica (535)

electric motor/motor eléctrico un aparato que transforma la energía eléctrica en energía mecánica (574)

electrolysis/electrólisis el proceso por medio del cual se utiliza una corriente eléctrica para producir una reacción química, como por ejemplo, la descomposición del agua (191)

electrolyte/electrolito una substancia que se disuelve en agua y crea una solución que conduce la corriente eléctrica (257)

electromagnet/electroimán una bobina que tiene un centro de hierro suave y que funciona como un imán cuando hay una corriente eléctrica en la bobina (572)

electromagnetic induction/inducción electromagnética el proceso de crear una corriente en un circuito por medio de un cambio en el campo magnético (576)

electromagnetic spectrum/espectro electromagnético todas las frecuencias o longitudes de onda de la radiación electromagnética (466)

electromagnetic wave/onda electromagnética una onda que está formada por campos eléctricos y magnéticos oscilantes, que irradia hacia fuera a la velocidad de la luz (455)

electron/electrón una partícula subatómica que tiene carga negativa (106)

element/elemento una substancia que no se puede separar o descomponer en substancias más simples por medio de métodos químicos; todos los átomos de un elemento tienen el mismo número atómico (39)

empirical formula/fórmula empírica la composición de un compuesto en función del número relativo y el tipo de átomos que hay en la proporción más simple (162)

emulsion/emulsión cualquier mezcla de dos o más líquidos inmiscibles en la que un líquido se encuentra disperso en el otro (227)

endothermic reaction/reacción endotérmica una reacción química que necesita calor (187)

energy/energía la capacidad de realizar un trabajo (73)

energy level/nivel de energía el estado de energía de un átomo (107)

enzyme/enzima un tipo de proteína que acelera las reacciones metabólicas en las plantas y animales, sin ser modificada permanentemente ni ser destruida (207)

epicenter/epicentro el punto de la superficie de la Tierra que queda justo arriba del punto de inicio, o foco, de un terremoto (710)

equivalence point/punto de equivalencia el punto en el que dos soluciones usadas en una titulación están presentes en cantidades químicas equivalentes (267)

erosion/erosión un proceso por medio del cual los materiales de la superficie de la Tierra se aflojan, disuelven o desgastan y son transportados de un lugar a otro por un agente natural, como el viento, el agua, el hielo o la gravedad (728)

eutrophication/eutrofización un aumento en la cantidad de nutrientes, tales como nitratos, en un ecosistema marino o acuático (796)

evaporation/evaporación el cambio de una substancia de líquido a gas (75)

exosphere/exosfera la porción más externa de la atmósfera de un planeta, en la cual la densidad es suficientemente baja como para permitir que los átomos atmosféricos más livianos escapen al espacio (745)

exothermic reaction/reacción exotérmica una reacción química en la que se libera calor a los alrededores (187)

F

fault/falla una grieta en un cuerpo rocoso a lo largo de la cual un bloque se desliza respecto a otro (707)

fission/fisión el proceso por medio del cual un núcleo se divide en dos o más fragmentos y libera neutrones y energía (295)

fluid/fluido un estado no sólido de la materia en el que los átomos o moléculas tienen libertad de movimiento, como en el caso de un gas o un líquido (80)

focal point/punto focal el punto en el eje de un espejo o lente en el que todos los rayos de luz paralelos e incidentes convergen o divergen (516)

Glosario

focus/foco el punto a lo largo de una falla donde ocurre el primer movimiento de un terremoto (710)

force/fuerza una acción que se ejerce en un cuerpo con el fin de cambiar su estado de reposo o movimiento; la fuerza tiene magnitud y dirección (331)

fossil fuel/combustible fósil un recurso energético no renovable formado a partir de los restos de organismos que vivieron hace mucho tiempo; algunos ejemplos incluyen el petróleo, el carbón y el gas natural (783)

free fall/caída libre el movimiento de un cuerpo cuando la única fuerza que actúa sobre él es la fuerza de gravedad (354)

freezing point/punto de congelación la temperatura a la que un sólido y un líquido están en equilibrio a 1 atm de presión (76)

frequency/frecuencia el número de ciclos o vibraciones por unidad de tiempo; también, el número de ondas producidas en una cantidad de tiempo determinada (465)

friction/fricción una fuerza que se opone al movimiento entre dos superficies que están en contacto (0)

front/frente el límite entre masas de aire de diferentes densidades y, normalmente, diferentes temperaturas (757)

fuse/fusible un aparato eléctrico que contiene una tira de metal que se derrite cuando la corriente en el circuito es demasiado elevada (552)

fusion/fusión el proceso por medio del cual núcleos ligeros se combinan a temperaturas extremadamente altas formando núcleos más pesados y liberando energía (298)

G

galaxy/galaxia un conjunto de estrellas, polvo y gas unidos por la gravedad (674)

galvanometer/galvanómetro un instrumento que detecta, mide y determina la dirección de una corriente eléctrica pequeña (573)

gamma ray/rayo gamma el fotón de alta energía emitido por un núcleo durante la fisión y la desintegración radiactiva (286)

gas giant/gigante gaseoso un planeta con una atmósfera masiva y profunda, como por ejemplo, Júpiter, Saturno, Urano o Neptuno (641)

Gay-Lussac's law/ley de Gay-Lussac la ley que establece que la presión de un gas a volumen constante es directamente proporcional a la temperatura absoluta (92)

generator/generador una máquina que transforma la energía mecánica en energía eléctrica (578)

geocentric/geocéntrico término que describe algo que usa a la Tierra como punto de referencia (647)

geology/geología el estudio del origen, historia y estructura del planeta Tierra y los procesos que le dan forma (7)

geostationary orbit/órbita geoestacionaria una órbita geosincrónica en la que el satélite se mueve en el plano ecuatorial de la Tierra en la misma dirección que la rotación de la Tierra, de modo que el satélite permanece a una altitud de 35,880 km sobre un punto fijo en el ecuador (600)

geothermal energy/energía geotérmica la energía producida por el calor del interior de la Tierra (786)

global warming/calentamiento global un aumento gradual en las temperaturas globales promedio debido a una concentración más alta de gases (tales como dióxido de carbono) en la atmósfera (749)

gravitational potential energy/energía potencial gravitatoria la energía potencial almacenada en los campos gravitacionales entre cuerpos que interactúan (0)

greenhouse effect/efecto de invernadero el calentamiento de la superficie terrestre y de la parte más baja de la atmósfera, el cual se produce cuando el dióxido de carbono, el vapor de agua y otros gases del aire absorben radiación infrarroja y la vuelven a irradiar (748)

group/grupo una columna vertical de elementos de la tabla periódica; los elementos de un grupo comparten propiedades químicas (114)

H

half-life/vida media el tiempo que tarda la mitad de una muestra de una substancia radiactiva en desintegrarse por desintegración radiactiva o por procesos naturales (289)

halogen/halógeno uno de los elementos del Grupo 17 (flúor, cloro, bromo, yodo y ástato); se combinan con la mayoría de los metales para formar sales (126)

hardware/hardware las partes o piezas de equipo que forman una computadora (614)

harmonic series/serie armónica una serie de frecuencias que incluye la frecuencia fundamental y los múltiplos integrales de una frecuencia fundamental (494)

heat/calor la transferencia de energía entre objetos que están a temperaturas diferentes; la energía siempre se transfiere de los objetos que están a la temperatura más alta a los objetos que están a una temperatura más baja (426)

heat engine/motor térmico una máquina que transforma el calor en energía mecánica, o trabajo (442)

heliocentric/heliocéntrico centrado en el Sol (647)

heterogeneous/heterogéneo compuesto de componentes que no son iguales (42)

homogeneous/homogéneo término que describe a algo que tiene una estructura o composición global uniforme (42)

humidity/humedad la cantidad de vapor de agua que hay en el aire (751)

hurricane/huracán tormenta severa que se desarrolla sobre océanos tropicales, con vientos fuertes que soplan a más de 120 km/h y que se mueven en espiral hacia el centro de presión extremadamente baja de la tormenta (760)

hydroelectric energy/energía hidroeléctrica energía eléctrica producida por agua en caída (778)

hydrogen bond/enlace de hidrógeno la fuerza intermolecular producida por un átomo de hidrógeno que está unido a un átomo muy electronegativo de una molécula y que experimenta atracción a dos electrones no compartidos de otra molécula (234)

hydrosphere/hidrosfera la porción de la Tierra que es agua (639)

igneous rock/roca ígnea una roca que se forma cuando el magma se enfría y se solidifica (719)

immiscible/inmiscible término que describe dos o más líquidos que no se mezclan uno con otro (226)

independent variable/variable independiente el factor que se manipula deliberadamente en un experimento (21)

indicator/indicador un compuesto que puede cambiar de color de forma reversible dependiendo del pH de la solución o de otro cambio químico (256)

inertia/inercia la tendencia de un objeto a no moverse o, si el objeto se está moviendo, la tendencia a resistir un cambio en su rapidez o dirección hasta que una fuerza externa actúe en el objeto (346)

infrasound/infrasonido vibraciones lentas de frecuencias inferiores a 20 Hz (493)

inhibitor/inhibidor una substancia que desacelera o detiene una reacción química (207)

inner core/núcleo interno el centro sólido y denso de la Tierra (701)

intensity/intensidad la tasa a la que la energía fluye a través de un área determinada de espacio (502)

interference/interferencia la combinación de dos o más ondas de la misma frecuencias que resulta en una sola onda (474)

Internet/Internet una amplia red de computadoras que conecta muchas redes locales y redes más pequeñas por todo el mundo (617)

interstellar matter/materia interestelar el gas y polvo que están entre las estrellas de una galaxia (676)

ion/ion un átomo, radical o molécula que ha ganado o perdido uno o más electrones y que tiene una carga negativa o positiva (115)

ionic bond/enlace iónico una fuerza que atrae a los electrones de un átomo a otro y que transforma un átomo neutro a un ion (152)

ionization/ionización el proceso de añadir o quitar electrones de un átomo o molécula, lo cual da al átomo o molécula una carga neta (302)

ionosphere/ionosfera una región de la atmósfera que está a aproximadamente 80 km sobre la Tierra y en la que el aire está ionizado debido a la radiación solar (745)

isotope/isótopo un átomo que tiene el mismo número de protones (número atómico) que otros átomos del mismo elemento, pero que tiene un número diferente de neutrones (masa atómica) (117)

K

kinetic energy/energía cinética la energía de un objeto debido al movimiento del objeto (394)

kinetic friction/fricción cinética la fuerza que se opone al movimiento de dos superficies que están en contacto y que se deslizan una sobre la otra (333)

law of reflection/ley de la reflexión la ley que establece que el ángulo de incidencia es igual al ángulo de reflexión (507)

length/longitud una medida de la distancia en línea recta entre dos puntos (18)

lens/lente un objeto transparente que refracta las ondas de luz de modo que converjan o diverjan para crear una imagen (515)

light ray/rayo luz una línea en el espacio que corresponde con la dirección del flujo de energía radiante (506)

light-year/año luz la distancia que la luz viaja en un año; aproximadamente 9.5 trillones de kilómetros (9.5×10^{12} km) (666)

lithosphere/litosfera la capa externa y sólida de la Tierra que está formada por la corteza y la parte superior y rígida del manto (703)

longitudinal wave/onda longitudinal una onda en la que las partículas del medio vibran paralelamente a la dirección del movimiento de la onda (461)

longitudinal wave/onda longitudinal una onda en la que las partículas del medio vibran paralelamente a la dirección del movimiento de la onda (710)

loudness/volumen el grado al que se escucha un sonido (491)

Glosario

M

magma/magma roca líquida producida debajo de la superficie terrestre; las rocas ígneas están hechas de magma (705)

magnetic field/campo magnético una región donde puede detectarse una fuerza magnética (567)

magnetic pole/polo magnético uno de dos puntos, tales como los extremos de un imán, que tienen cualidades magnéticas opuestas (566)

magnification/magnificación el aumento del tamaño aparente de un objeto mediante el uso de lentes o espejos (515)

mantle/manto en las ciencias de la Tierra, la capa de roca que se encuentra entre la corteza terrestre y el núcleo (700)

maria/maria las áreas obscuras y grandes de basalto en la Luna (singular: mar) (634)

mass/masa una medida de la cantidad de materia que tiene un objeto; una propiedad fundamental de un objeto que no está afectada por las fuerzas que actúan sobre el objeto, como por ejemplo, la fuerza gravitacional (18)

mass defect/defecto de masa la diferencia entre la masa de un átomo y la suma de la masa de los protones, neutrones y electrones del átomo (296)

mass number/número de masa la suma de los números de protones y neutrones que hay en el núcleo de un átomo (116)

matter/materia cualquier cosa que tiene masa y ocupa un lugar en el espacio (38)

mechanical advantage/ventaja mecánica un número que dice cuántas veces una máquina multiplica una fuerza; se calcula dividiendo la fuerza de salida entre la fuerza de entrada (383)

mechanical energy/energía mecánica la cantidad de trabajo que un objeto realiza debido a las energías cinética y potencial del objeto (396)

mechanical wave/onda mecánica una onda que requiere un medio para desplazarse (455)

medium/medio un ambiente físico en el que ocurren fenómenos (455)

melting point/punto de fusión la temperatura y presión a la cual un sólido se convierte en líquido (46)

melting point/punto de fusión la temperatura y presión a la cual un sólido se convierte en líquido (75)

mesosphere/mesosfera la parte fuerte e inferior del manto que se encuentra entre la astenosfera y el núcleo externo; también, la capa más fría de la atmósfera que se encuentra entre la estratosfera y la termosfera, en la cual la temperatura disminuye al aumentar la altitud (745)

metallic bond/enlace metálico un enlace formado por la atracción entre iones metálicos cargados positivamente y los electrones que los rodean (154)

metalloid/metaloides elementos que tienen propiedades tanto de metales como de no metales; a veces de denominan semiconductores (121)

metamorphic rock/roca metamórfica una roca que se forma a partir de otras rocas como resultado de calor intenso, presión o procesos químicos (721)

meteorology/meteorología el estudio científico de la atmósfera de la Tierra, sobre todo en lo que se relaciona al tiempo y al clima (757)

mineral/mineral un sólido natural, normalmente inorgánico, que tiene una composición química característica, una estructura interna ordenada y propiedades físicas y químicas características (718)

miscible/miscible término que describe a dos o más líquidos que son capaces de disolverse uno en el otro en varias proporciones (42)

mixture/mezcla una combinación de dos o más substancias que no están combinadas químicamente (41)

model/modelo un diseño, plan, representación o descripción cuyo objetivo es mostrar la estructura o funcionamiento de un objeto, sistema o concepto (9)

modulate/modular cambiar la amplitud o la frecuencia de una onda con el fin de enviar una señal (604)

molarity/molaridad una unidad de concentración de una solución, expresada en moles de soluto disuelto por litro de solución (243)

molar mass/masa molar la masa en gramos de 1 mol de una substancia (130)

mole/mol la unidad fundamental del sistema internacional de unidades que se usa para medir la cantidad de una substancia cuyo número de partículas es el mismo que el número de átomos de carbono en exactamente 12 g de carbono-12 (130)

molecular formula/fórmula molecular una fórmula química que muestra el número y los tipos de átomos que hay en una molécula, pero que no muestra cómo están distribuidos (164)

molecule/molécula la unidad más pequeña de una substancia que conserva todas las propiedades físicas y químicas de esa substancia; puede estar formada por un átomo o por dos o más átomos enlazados uno con el otro (40)

mole ratio/razón molar el número relativo de moles de las substancias que se requieren para producir una cantidad determinada de producto en una reacción química (203)

momentum/momento una cantidad que se define como el producto de la masa de un objeto por su velocidad (362)

monomer/monómero una molécula simple que se puede combinar con otras moléculas parecidas o diferentes y formar un polímero (169)

motion/movimiento el cambio en la posición de un objeto respecto a un punto de referencia (318)

N

nebula/nebulosa una nube grande de polvo y gas en el espacio interestelar (648)

nebular model/teoría nebular un modelo de la formación del Sistema Solar en el que el Sol y los planetas se condensan a partir de una nube (o nebulosa) de gas y polvo (648)

net force/fuerza neta una fuerza única cuyos efectos externos en un cuerpo rígido son los mismos que los efectos de varias fuerzas reales ejercidas sobre el objeto (0)

neutralization reaction/reacción de neutralización la reacción de los iones que caracterizan a los ácidos (iones hidronio) y de los iones que caracterizan a las bases (iones hidróxido) para formar moléculas de agua y una sal (264)

neutron/neutrón una partícula subatómica que no tiene carga y que se encuentra en el núcleo de un átomo (106)

neutron star/estrella de neutrones una estrella que se ha colapsado debido a la gravedad hasta el punto en que los electrones y protones han chocado unos contra otros para formar neutrones (672)

noble gas/gas noble un elemento no reactivo del Grupo 18 de la tabla periódica; los gases nobles son: helio, neón, argón, criptón, xenón o radón (127)

node/nodo en física, un punto en una onda estacionaria que mantiene una amplitud de cero (477)

nonmetal/no metal un elemento que es mal conductor del calor y la electricidad y que no forma iones positivos en una solución de electrolitos (121)

nonpolar compound/compuesto no polar un compuesto cuyos electrones se encuentran distribuidos equitativamente entre los átomos (235)

nonrenewable resource/recurso no renovable un recurso que se forma a una tasa que es mucho más lenta que la tasa a la que se consume (784)

nuclear chain reaction/reacción nuclear en cadena una serie continua de reacciones nucleares de fisión (296)

nuclear radiation/radiación nuclear las partículas que el núcleo libera durante la desintegración radiactiva, tales como neutrones, electrones y fotones (284)

nucleus/núcleo la región central de un átomo, la cual está constituida por protones y neutrones (106)

O

operating system/sistema operativo el software (programas de computadora) que controla las actividades de una computadora (614)

optical fiber/fibra óptica una hebra transparente de plástico o vidrio que transmite luz (597)

orbital/orbital una región en un átomo donde hay una alta probabilidad de encontrar electrones (109)

organic compound/compuesto orgánico un compuesto enlazado de manera covalente que contiene carbono, excluyendo a los carbonatos y óxidos (165)

oxidation reaction/reacción de oxidación una reacción química en la que el reactivo pierde uno o más electrones, volviéndose más positivo en cuanto a su carga (195)

oxidation-reduction reaction/reacción de óxido-reducción cualquier cambio químico en el que una especie se oxida (pierde electrones) y otra especie se reduce (gana electrones); también se denomina reacción redox (196)

ozone/ozono una molécula de gas que está formada por tres átomos de oxígeno (744)

ozone layer/capa de ozono la capa de la atmósfera ubicada a una altitud de 15 a 40 km, en la cual el ozono absorbe la radiación solar (744)

P

Pangaea/Pangea una sola masa de tierra que existió durante aproximadamente 40 millones de años y luego comenzó a separarse para formar los continentes, tal como los conocemos en la actualidad (702)

parallel/paralelo cualquier círculo que va hacia el Este o hacia el Oeste alrededor de la Tierra y que es paralelo al ecuador; una línea de latitud (549)

pascal/pascal la unidad de presión del sistema internacional de unidades; es igual a la fuerza de 1 N ejercida sobre un área de 1 m2 (abreviatura: Pa) (83)

Pascal's principle/principio de Pascal el principio que establece que un fluido en equilibro que esté contenido en un recipiente ejerce una presión de igual intensidad en todas las direcciones (84)

period/período en química, una hilera horizontal de elementos en la tabla periódica (114)

period/período en física, el tiempo que se requiere para completar un ciclo o la oscilación de una onda (465)

periodic law/ley periódica la ley que establece que las propiedades químicas y físicas repetitivas de un elemento cambian periódicamente en función del número atómico de los elementos (111)

pH/pH un valor que expresa la acidez o la alcalinidad (basicidad) de un sistema; cada número entero de la escala indica un cambio de 10 veces en la acidez (261)

phase/fase en astronomía, el cambio en el área iluminada de la Luna según se ve desde la Tierra; las fases se producen como resultado de los cambios en la posición de la Tierra, el Sol y la Luna (634)

photon/fotón una unidad o quantum de luz; una partícula de radiación electromagnética que tiene una masa de reposo de cero y que lleva un quantum de energía (500)

photosynthesis/fotosíntesis el proceso por medio del cual las plantas, algas y algunas bacterias utilizan la luz solar, dióxido de carbono y agua para producir carbohidratos y oxígeno (746)

physical change/cambio físico un cambio de materia de una forma a otra sin que ocurra un cambio en sus propiedades químicas (53)

physical property/propiedad física una característica de una substancia que no implica un cambio químico, tal como la densidad, el color o la dureza (45)

physical science/ciencias físicas el estudio científico de la materia sin vida (7)

pitch/altura tona una medida de qué tan agudo o grave se percibe un sonido, dependiendo de la frecuencia de la onda sonora (470)

pitch/altura tona una medida de qué tan agudo o grave se percibe un sonido, dependiendo de la frecuencia de la onda sonora (492)

pixel/pixel el elemento más pequeño de una imagen de visualización (607)

planet/planeta cualquiera de los nueve cuerpos principales que giran en órbita alrededor del Sol; un cuerpo similar que gira en órbita alrededor de otra estrella (630)

plasma/plasma un estado de la materia que comienza como un gas y luego se vuelve ionizado; está formado por iones y electrones que se mueven libremente, tiene carga eléctrica y sus propiedades difieren de las de un sólido, líquido o gas (72)

plate tectonics/tectónica de placas la teoría que explica cómo cambian las partes externas de la Tierra con el tiempo; explica las relaciones entre la deriva continental, la expansión del suelo marino, la actividad sísmica y la actividad volcánica (703)

polar compound/compuesto polar un compuesto cuyas moléculas tienen una carga negativa en un lado y una carga positiva en el otro (232)

pollution/contaminación un cambio indeseable en el ambiente natural, producido por la introducción de substancias que son dañinas para los organismos vivos o por desechos, calor, ruido o radiación excesivos (791)

polyatomic ion/ion poliatómico un ion formado por dos o más átomos (156)

polymer/polímero una molécula grande que está formada por más de cinco monómeros, o unidades pequeñas (169)

potential difference/diferencia de potencial la diferencia de voltaje en el potencial entre dos puntos de un circuito (538)

potential energy/energía potencial la energía que tiene un objeto debido a su posición, forma o condición (392)

power/potencia una cantidad que mide la tasa a la que se realiza un trabajo o a la que se transforma la energía (380)

precipitation/precipitación cualquier forma de agua que cae de las nubes a la superficie de la Tierra; incluye a la lluvia, nieve, aguanieve y granizo (751)

precision/precisión la exactitud de una medición (24)

pressure/presión la cantidad de fuerza ejercida en una superficie por unidad de área (81)

prism/prisma un sistema formado por dos o más superficies planas de un sólido transparente ubicadas en un ángulo unas respecto a otras (517)

product/producto una substancia que se forma en una reacción química (185)

projectile motion/movimiento proyectil la trayectoria curva que sigue un objeto cuando es aventado, lanzado o proyectado de cualquier otra manera cerca de la superficie de la Tierra; el movimiento de objetos que se mueven en dos dimensiones bajo la influencia de la gravedad (358)

protein/proteína un compuesto orgánico que está hecho de una o más cadenas de aminoácidos y que es el principal componente de todas las células (170)

proton/protón una partícula subatómica que tiene una carga positiva y que se encuentra en el núcleo de un átomo (106)

pure substance/substancia pura una muestra de materia, ya sea un solo elemento o un solo compuesto, que tiene propiedades químicas y físicas definidas (41)

R

radar/radar detección y exploración a gran distancia por medio de ondas de radio; un sistema que usa ondas de radio reflejadas para determinar la velocidad y ubicación de los objetos (504)

radiation/radiación la energía que se transfiere en forma de ondas electromagnéticas, tales como las ondas de luz y las infrarrojas (429)

radicals/radicales un grupo orgánico que tiene uno o más electrones disponibles para formar enlaces (196)

radioactive decay/desintegración radiactiva la desintegración de un núcleo atómico inestable para formar uno o más nucleidos diferentes, lo cual va acompañado de la emisión de radiación, la captura o expulsión nuclear de electrones, o fisión (124)

radioactive tracer/trazador radiactivo un material radiactivo que se añade a una substancia de modo que su distribución pueda ser detectada posteriormente (301)

radioactivity/radiactividad el proceso por medio del cual un núcleo inestable emite una o más partículas o energía en forma de radiación electromagnética (284)

random-access memory/memoria de acceso aleatorio un instrumento de almacenaje que permite que los usuarios de las computadoras escriban y lean datos (abreviatura: RAM, por sus siglas en inglés) (613)

rarefaction/rarefacción la porción de una onda sonora en la que la compresión del medio es mínima (464)

reactant/reactivo una substancia o molécula que participa en una reacción química (185)

reactivity/reactividad la capacidad de una substancia de combinarse químicamente con otra substancia (50)

read-only memory/memoria de sólo lectura un instrumento de memoria que contiene información que puede leerse pero que no puede cambiarse (abreviatura: ROM, por sus siglas en inglés) (614)

real image/imagen real la imagen de un objeto que se forma cuando pasan rayos de luz a través de un lente y se cruzan en un punto único (509)

recycling/reciclar el proceso de recuperar materiales valiosos o útiles de los desechos o de la basura; el proceso de reutilizar algunas cosas (800)

red giant/gigante roja una estrella grande de color rojizo que se encuentra en una etapa avanzada de su vida (671)

red shift/desplazamiento al rojo un aparente desplazamiento hacia una longitud de onda de luz mayor, que se origina cuando un objeto luminoso se aleja del observador (682)

reduction/reducción un cambio químico en el que se ganan electrones, ya sea por la remoción de oxígeno, la adición de hidrógeno o la adición de electrones (196)

reflection/reflexión el rebote de un rayo de luz, sonido o calor cuando el rayo golpea una superficie pero no la atraviesa (472)

refraction/refracción el curvamiento de un frente de ondas a medida que el frente pasa entre dos substancias en las que la velocidad de las ondas difiere (474)

refrigerant/refrigerante un material que se usa para enfriar un área o un objeto a una temperatura que es menor que la temperatura del ambiente (440)

rem/rem la cantidad de radiación ionizante que produce el mismo daño a los tejidos humanos que 1 roentgen de rayos X de alto voltaje (300)

renewable resource/recurso renovable un recurso natural que puede reemplazarse a la misma tasa a la que el se consume, como por ejemplo, el alimento que se produce por medio de la fotosíntesis (785)

resistance/resistencia en ciencias físicas, la oposición que un material o aparato presenta a la corriente (541)

resonance/resonancia un fenómeno que ocurre cuando dos objetos vibran naturalmente a la misma frecuencia (495)

respiration/respiración en química, el proceso por medio del cual las células producen energía a partir de los carbohidratos; el oxígeno atmosférico se combina con la glucosa para formar agua y dióxido de carbono (747)

Richter scale/escala de Richter una escala que expresa la magnitud de un terremoto (713)

rock cycle/ciclo de las rocas la serie de procesos por medio de los cuales una roca se forma, cambia de un tipo a otro, se destruye, y se forma nuevamente por procesos geológicos (722)

S

salt/sal un compuesto iónico que se forma cuando el átomo de un metal o un radical positivo reemplaza el hidrógeno de un ácido (265)

satellite/satélite un cuerpo natural o artificial que gira alrededor de un planeta (633)

saturated solution/solución saturada una solución que no puede disolver más soluto bajo las condiciones dadas (241)

schematic diagram/diagrama esquemático una representación gráfica de un circuito, la cual usa líneas para representar cables y diferentes símbolos para representar los componentes (547)

science/ciencia el conocimiento que se obtiene por medio de la observación natural de acontecimientos y condiciones con el fin de descubrir hechos y formular leyes o principios que puedan ser verificados o probados (6)

scientific method/método científico una serie de pasos que se siguen para solucionar problemas, los cuales incluyen recopilar información, formular una hipótesis, comprobar la hipótesis y sacar conclusiones (13)

scientific notation/notación científica un método para expresar una cantidad en forma de un número multiplicado por 10 a la potencia adecuada (22)

sedimentary rock/roca sedimentaria una roca que se forma a partir de capas comprimidas o cementadas de sedimento (720)

seismic wave/onda sísmica una vibración en las rocas que se aleja del epicentro de un terremoto en todas direcciones; las ondas sísmicas también pueden ser originadas por explosiones (710)

seismology/sismología el estudio de los terremotos, incluyendo su origen, propagación, energía y predicción (711)

Glosario

semiconductor/semiconductor un elemento o compuesto que conduce la corriente eléctrica mejor que un aislante, pero no tan bien como un conductor (121)

series/serie los componentes de un circuito que forman un solo camino para la corriente (549)

shield volcano/volcán de escudo un volcán grande que tiene una pendiente suave y se forma por erupciones de flujos de lava basáltica (714)

SI/SI Le Système International d'Unités, o el Sistema Internacional de Unidades, que es el sistema de medición que se acepta en todo el mundo (15)

signal/señal cualquier cosa que sirve para dirigir, guiar o advertir (592)

significant figure/cifra significativa un lugar decimal prescrito que determina la cantidad de redondeo que se hará con base en la precisión de la medición (24)

simple harmonic motion/movimiento armónico simple un movimiento periódico cuya trayectoria se forma por una o más vibraciones que son simétricas respecto a una posición de equilibrio (459)

simple machine/máquina simple uno de los seis tipos fundamentales de máquinas, las cuales son la base de todas las demás formas de máquinas (385)

single-displacement reaction/reacción de sustitución simple una reacción en la que un elemento o radical toma el lugar de otro elemento o radical en el compuesto (194)

soap/jabón una sustancia que se usa como limpiador y que se disuelve en el agua (269)

software/software un conjunto de instrucciones o comandos que le dicen qué hacer a una computadora; un programa de computadora (614)

solar system/Sistema Solar el Sol y todos los planetas y otros cuerpos que se desplazan alrededor de él (632)

solenoid/solenoide una bobina de alambre que tiene una corriente eléctrica (571)

solubility/solubilidad la capacidad de una sustancia de disolverse en otra a una temperatura y presión dadas; se expresa en términos de la cantidad de soluto que se disolverá en una cantidad determinada de solvente (239)

soluble/soluble capaz de disolverse en un solvente determinado (239)

solute/soluto la sustancia que se disuelve en el solvente (229)

solution/solución una mezcla homogénea de dos o más sustancias dispersas de manera uniforme en una sola fase (229)

solvent/solvente la sustancia en la que se disuelve el soluto (229)

sonar/sonar navegación y exploración por medio del sonido; un sistema que usa señales acústicas y ondas de eco que regresan para determinar la ubicación de los objetos o para comunicarse (497)

sound wave/onda de sonido una onda longitudinal que se origina debido a vibraciones y que se desplaza a través de un medio material (490)

specific heat/calor específico la cantidad de calor que se requiere para aumentar una unidad de masa de un material homogéneo 1 K ó 1°C de una manera especificada, dados un volumen y una presión constantes (432)

spectator ions/iones espectadores iones que están presenten en una solución en la que está ocurriendo una reacción, pero que no participan en la reacción (264)

speed/rapidez la distancia que un objeto se desplaza dividida entre el intervalo de tiempo durante el cual ocurrió el movimiento (320)

standing wave/onda estacionaria un patrón de vibración que simula una onda que está parada (477)

star/estrella un cuerpo celeste grande que está compuesto de gas y emite luz; el Sol es una estrella típica (666)

static friction/fricción estática la fuerza que se opone a que se inicie el movimiento de deslizamiento entre dos superficies que están en contacto y en reposo (333)

stationary front/frente estacionario un frente de masas de aire que se mueve muy lentamente o que no se mueve (758)

stratosphere/estratosfera la capa de la atmósfera que se encuentra justo encima de la troposfera y se extiende de aproximadamente 10 km hasta 50 km sobre la superficie de la Tierra; ahí, la temperatura aumenta al aumentar la altitud; contiene la capa de ozono (744)

stratus cloud/nube stratus una nube gris que tiene una base plana y uniforme y que se forma a altitudes muy bajas (752)

strong acid/ácido fuerte un ácido que se ioniza completamente en un solvente (257)

strong nuclear force/fuerza fuerte la interacción que mantiene unidos a los nucleones en un núcleo (294)

structural formula/fórmula estructural una fórmula que indica la ubicación de los átomos, grupos o iones, unos respecto a otros en una molécula, y que indica el número y ubicación de los enlaces químicos (146)

subduction/subducción el proceso por medio del cual una placa de la litosfera se mueve debajo de otra como resultado de las fuerzas tectónicas (706)

sublimation/sublimación el proceso por medio del cual un sólido se transforma directamente en un gas o un gas se transforma directamente en un sólido (75)

substrate/sustrato el reactivo en reacciones que son catalizadas por enzimas (208)

succession/sucesión el reemplazo de un tipo de comunidad por otro en un mismo lugar a lo largo de un período de tiempo (778)

summer solstice/solsticio de verano el primer día del verano (761)

supernova/supernova una explosión gigantesca en la que una estrella masiva se colapsa y lanza sus capas externas hacia el espacio (671)

surface wave/onda superficial una onda sísmica que únicamente se puede mover a través de los sólidos (711)

suspension/suspensión una mezcla en la que las partículas de un material se encuentran dispersas de manera más o menos uniforme a través de un líquido o de un gas (225)

synthesis reaction/reacción de síntesis una reacción en la que dos o más sustancias se combinan para formar un compuesto nuevo (190)

T

technology/tecnología la aplicación de la ciencia con fines prácticos; el uso de herramientas, máquinas, materiales y procesos para satisfacer las necesidades de los seres humanos (7)

tectonic plate/placa tectónica un bloque de litosfera formado por la corteza y la parte rígida y más externa del manto; también se llama placa litosférica (703)

telecommunication/telecomunicación el envío de información visible o audible por medios electromagnéticos (594)

telescope/telescopio un instrumento que produce una imagen aumentada de un objeto distante por medio del uso de un sistema de lentes y espejos (15)

temperature/temperatura una medida de qué tan caliente (o frío) está algo; específicamente, una medida de la energía cinética promedio de las partículas de un objeto (420)

temperature inversion/inversión de la temperatura la condición atmosférica en la que el aire caliente retiene al aire frío cerca de la superficie terrestre (743)

terminal velocity/velocidad terminal la velocidad constante de un objeto en caída cuando la fuerza de resistencia del aire es igual en magnitud y opuesta en dirección a la fuerza de gravedad (356)

terrestrial planet/planeta terrestre uno de los planetas muy densos que se encuentran más cerca del Sol; Mercurio, Venus, Marte y la Tierra (637)

thermal conduction/conducción térmica la transferencia de energía en forma de calor a través de un material (428)

thermal energy/energía térmica la energía cinética de los átomos de una sustancia (73)

thermometer/termómetro un instrumento que mide e indica la temperatura (421)

thermosphere/termosfera la capa más alta de la atmósfera, en la cual la temperatura aumenta a medida que la altitud aumenta; incluye la ionosfera (745)

titration/titulación un método para determinar la concentración de una sustancia en una solución al añadir una solución de volumen y concentración conocidos hasta que se completa la reacción, lo cual normalmente es indicado por un cambio de color (267)

topography/topografía la configuración de una superficie de terreno, incluyendo su relieve (762)

total internal reflection/reflexión total interna

transformer/transformador un aparato que aumenta o disminuye el voltaje de la corriente alterna (581)

transform fault boundary/límite de transformación el límite entre placas tectónicas que se están deslizando horizontalmente una sobre otra (707)

transition metal/metal de transición uno de los metales que tienen la capacidad de usar su orbital interno antes de usar su orbital externo para formar un enlace (123)

transpiration/transpiración el proceso por medio del cual las plantas liberan vapor de agua al aire por medio de los estomas; también, la liberación de vapor de agua al aire por otros organismos (751)

transverse wave/onda transversal una onda en la que las partículas del medio se mueven perpendicularmente respecto a la dirección en la que se desplaza la onda (461)

troposphere/troposfera la capa inferior de la atmósfera, en la que la temperatura disminuye a una tasa constante a medida que la altitud aumenta; la parte de la atmósfera donde se dan las condiciones del tiempo (743)

trough/seno el punto más bajo de una onda (464)

typhoon/tifón un ciclón tropical severo que se forma en el océano Pacífico occidental y en los mares de China; un huracán (760)

U

ultrasound/ultrasonido cualquier onda de sonido que tenga frecuencias superiores a los 20,000 Hz (493)

universe/universo la suma de todo el espacio, materia y energía que existen, que han existido en el pasado y que existirán en el futuro (680)

unsaturated solution/solución no saturada una solución que contiene menos soluto que una solución saturada, y que tiene la capacidad de disolver más soluto (240)

vaccine/vacuna una sustancia que se prepara a partir de organismos patógenos muertos o debilitados y se introduce al cuerpo para producir inmunidad (223)

valence electron/electrón de valencia un electrón que se encuentra en el orbital más externo de un átomo y que determina las propiedades químicas del átomo (110)

Glosario

variable/variable un factor que se modifica en un experimento con el fin de probar una hipótesis (13)

velocity/velocidad la rapidez de un objeto en una dirección dada (322)

vent/chimenea una abertura en la superficie de la Tierra a través de la cual pasa material volcánico (714)

vernal equinox/equinoccio vernal el momento en el que el Sol pasa directamente encima del ecuador del Sur al Norte; el día en que ocurre un equinoccio vernal, el día y la noche tienen la misma duración (761)

virtual image/imagen virtual una imagen que se forma en un punto desde el cual parece que provienen los rayos de luz, pero en realidad no vienen de ahí (508)

viscosity/viscosidad la resistencia de un gas o un líquido a fluir (85)

visible spectrum/espectro visible la porción del espectro electromagnético que contiene todas las longitudes de onda que son visibles para el ojo humano (466)

volume/volumen una medida del tamaño de un cuerpo o región en un espacio de tres dimensiones (18)

W

warm front/frente cálido un frente que avanza de tal manera que el aire más cálido reemplaza al aire más frío (757)

water cycle/ciclo del agua el movimiento continuo del agua: del océano a la atmósfera, de la atmósfera a la tierra y de la tierra al océano (750)

watt/watt (o vatio) la unidad que se usa para expresar potencia; es equivalente a un joule por segundo (abreviatura: W) (380)

wave/onda una perturbación periódica en un sólido, líquido o gas que se transmite a través de un medio en forma de energía (454)

wavelength/longitud de onda la distancia entre cualquier punto de una onda y un punto idéntico en la onda siguiente (464)

weak acid/ácido débil un ácido que libera pocos iones de hidrógeno en una solución acuosa (257)

weathering/meteorización el proceso natural por el que los agentes atmosféricos y ambientales, tales como el viento, la lluvia y los cambios de temperatura, desintegran y descomponen las rocas (720)

weight/peso una medida de la fuerza gravitacional ejercida sobre un objeto; su valor puede cambiar en función de la ubicación del objeto en el universo (18)

white dwarf/enana blanca una estrella pequeña, caliente y tenue que es el centro sobrante de una estrella vieja (671)

winter solstice/solsticio de invierno el comienzo del invierno (761)

work/trabajo la transferencia de energía a un cuerpo por medio de la aplicación de una fuerza que hace que el cuerpo se mueva en la dirección de la fuerza; es igual al producto de la magnitud del componente de una fuerza aplicada en la dirección del desplazamiento por la magnitud del desplazamiento (378)

Index

Note: Page numbers followed by *f* refer to figures, and page numbers followed by *t* refer to tables. A page range followed by *f* or *t* indicates that one or more figures or tables appear within that page range. Boldface page numbers indicate the primary discussion of a topic.

A

B

C

D

E

F

G

H

I

Index

T

U

V

W

Acknowledgments continued from page iv.

Aaron Timperman, Ph.D.
Professor of Chemistry
Department of Chemistry
West Virginia University
Morgantown, West Virginia

Richard S. Treptow, Ph.D.
Professor of Chemistry
Department of Chemistry and Physics
Chicago State University
Chicago, Illinois

Martin VanDyke, Ph.D.
Professor of Chemistry, Emeritus
Front Range Community College
Westminister, Colorado

Text Reviewers

Dan Aude
Magnet Programs Coordinator
Montgomery Public Schools
Montgomery, Alabama

Robert Baronak
Science Teacher
Donegal High School
Mount Joy, Pennsylvania

David Blinn
Secondary Sciences Teacher
Wrenshall High School
Wrenshall, Minnesota

Robert Chandler
Science Teacher
Soddy-Daisey High School
Soddy-Daisey, Tennessee

Cindy Copolo, Ph.D.
Science Specialist
Summit Solutions
Bahama, North Carolina

Linda Culp
Science Teacher
Thorndale High School
Thorndale, Texas

Katherine Cummings
Science Teacher
Currituck County
Currituck, North Carolina

Donna Defrieze
Technical Communications Teacher
Soddy-Daisy High School
Soddy-Daisy, Tennessee

Chris Diehl
Science Teacher
Belleville High School
Belleville, Michigan

Benjamen Ebersole
Science Teacher
Donnegal High School
Mount Joy, Pennsylvania

Jeffrey L. Engel
Science Teacher
Madison County High School
Danielsville, Georgia

Randa Flinn
Science Teacher
Northeast High School
Fort Lauderdale, Florida

Sharon Harris
Science Teacher
Mother of Mercy High School
Cincinnati, Ohio

Gail Hermann
Science Teacher
Quincy High School
Quincy, Illinois

Donald R. Kanner
Physics Instructor
Lane Technical High School
Chicago, Illinois

Edward Keller
Science Teacher
Morgantown High School
Morgantown, West Virginia

Howard Knodle
Science Teacher
Maine South High School
Park Ridge, Illinois

Stewart Lipsky
Science Teacher
Seward Park High School
New York, New York

Mike Lubich
Science Teacher
Maple Town High School
Greensboro, Pennsylvania

Thomas Manerchia
Environmental Science Teacher, Retired
Archmere Academy
Claymont, Delaware

Tammie Niffenegger
Science Chair and Science Teacher
Port Washington High School
Waldo, Wisconsin

Donna Norwood
Science Teacher
Monroe High School
Charlotte, North Carolina

Jennifer Seelig-Fritz
Science Teacher
North Springs High School
Atlanta, Georgia

Aida Semerjibashian
Science Teacher
Pflugerville High School
Pflugerville, Texas

Bert Sherwood
Science/Health Specialist
Socorro ISD
El Paso, Texas

Linnaea Smith
Science Teacher
Bastrop High School
Bastrop, Texas

Dan Trockman
Science Teacher
Hopkins High School
Minnetonka, Massachusetts

Gabriela Waschesky, Ph.D.
Science and Math Teacher
Emery High School
Emeryville, California

Jim Watson
Science Teacher
Dalton High School
Dalton, Georgia

Staff Credits

Executive Editor, High School Sciences and Health
Mark Grayson

Managing Editor
Debbie Starr

Editorial Development Team
Jackie Garrett
Darien Large
Michael Mazza
Marjorie Roueché
Michelle Trautwein

Copyeditors
Dawn Marie Spinozza, *Copyediting Manager*
Anne-Marie De Witt
Simon Key
Jane A. Kirschman
Kira J. Watkins

Editorial Support Staff
Mary Anderson
Soojinn Choi
Jeanne Graham
Shannon Oehler
Stephanie Sanchez
Tanu'e White

Editorial Interns
Kristina Bigelow
Erica Garza
Sarah Ray
Kenneth G. Raymond
Kyle Stock
Audra Teinert

Online Products
Bob Tucek, *Executive Editor*
Wesley M. Bain
Catherine Gallagher
Douglas P. Rutley

Book Design
Kay Selke, *Director of Book Design*

Media Design
Richard Metzger, *Design Director*
Chris Smith, *Developmental Designer*

Cover Design
Kay Selke, *Director of Book Design*

Publishing Services
Carol Martin, *Director*
Jeff Robinson *Manager, Ancillary Design*

Production
Eddie Dawson, *Senior Production Manager*
Beth Sample, *Project Manager*
Teresa McQueen, *Senior Production Coordinator*

Technology Services
Laura Likon, *Director*
Juan Baquera, *Manager*
JoAnn Stringer, *Manager*

Senior Technology Services Analysts
Katrina Gnader
Lana Kaupp

Production Artists
Sara Buller
Margaret Sanchez
Patty Zepeda

eMedia
Melanie Baccus, *eMedia Coordinator*
Ed Blake, *Design Director*
Kimberly Cammerata, *Design Manager*
Lydia Doty, *Senior Project Manager*
Marsh Flournoy, *Technology Project Manager*
Dakota Smith, *Quality Assurance Analyst*
Cathy Kuhles, *Technical Assistant*
Tara F. Ross, *Senior Project Manager*
Ken Whiteside, *Manager, Application Development*

Photo Credits

Chapter 1: Chapter opener image of laser-induced fusion by Roger Ressmeyer/CORBIS; George Washington Carver in lab; Bettmann/CORBIS; Fig. 1A, Hulton Archive/Getty Images; Fig. 1B, Phil Degginger/Color-Pic, Inc.; Fig. 2, AIP Emilio Segrè Visual Archives; Fig. 4, Leonard Lessin/Peter Arnold, Inc.; Fig. 5A, Sheila Terry/Science Photo Library/Photo Researchers, Inc.; Fig. 5B, SuperStock; Fig. 5B(portrait), Bettmann/CORBIS; Fig. 6A, Peter Van Steen/HRW; Fig. 6B, Sam Dudgeon/HRW; Fig. 7, Peter Van Steen/HRW; Fig. 8, Kristian Hilsen/Getty Images/Stone; Fig. 9, BMW of North America, Inc.; Fig. 10, Chris Johns/Getty Images/Stone; Fig. 11, Peter Van Steen/HRW; "Quick Activity," Peter Van Steen/HRW; Fig. 13, Science Photo Library/Photo Researchers, Inc.; Fig. 14A, Roger Ressmeyer/CORBIS; Fig. 14B, Celestial Image Co./Science Photo Library/Photo Researchers, Inc.; Figure 15, all images HRW except, nickles, EyeWire, Inc.; calipers, tape measure, cd, Image Copyright ©2004 Photodisc, Inc.; Fig. 16, Peter Van Steen/HRW; Fig. 20, Sam Dudgeon/HRW; "Skills Practice Lab," (boy, box), Peter Van Steen/HRW; (girl), Sam Dudgeon/HRW.

Chapter 2: Chapter Opener image of glass sculpture by Claire Garoutte/Dale Chihuly Studio; inset image of artist Dale Chihuly on beach with sculpture by Russel Johnson/Dale Chihuly Studio; Fig. 1, Dale Chihuly Studio; Fig. 2, D. Boone/CORBIS; Fig. 3(Earth), Tom Van Sant/The Geosphere Project/Corbis Stock Market; (student), Image Copyright ©2004 Photodisc, Inc.; Fig. 4(c), Sam Dudgeon/HRW; (r), Ken Eward/Science Source/Photo Researchers, Inc.; Fig. 7-8, Sam Dudgeon/HRW; "Science and the Consumer," Peter Van Steen/HRW; Fig. 9, FoodPix/Getty Images; Fig. 10, Index Stock Imagery, Inc.; Fig. 11, Sergio Purtell/HRW; Fig. 11, Comstock; Fig. 12, John Morrison/Morrison Photography; Fig. 13, Digital Image©2004, PhotoDisc; Fig. 14, Rob Boudreau/Getty Images/Stone; "Real World Application," Pascal Goetgheluck/Science Photo Library/Photo Researchers, Inc.; Fig. 18, Brett H. Froomer/Getty Images/The Image Bank; Fig. 16, Benelux Press/Index Stock Imagery, Inc.; Fig. 17, Sam Dudgeon/HRW; Fig. 18A, Klaus Guldbrandsen/Science Photo Library/Photo Researchers, Inc.; Fig. 18B, Charlie Winters; Fig. 18C, Klaus Guldbrandsen/Science Photo Library/Photo Researchers, Inc.; Fig. 19A, John Morrison/Morrison Photography; Fig. 19B, BSIP/Phototake; Fig. 19C, SuperStock; Fig. 20, Charlie Winters/HRW; "Chapter Review," (magnesium), Charles D. Winters; (can), Lance Schriner/HRW; "Skills Practice Lab," Peter Van Steen/HRW; "Viewpoints," HRW Photos.

Chapter 3: Chapter Opener photo of ice sculpture by Keren Su/CORBIS; dry ice photo by Matt Meadows/SPL/Photo Researchers, Inc.; Fig. 1, Getty Images/The Image Bank; Fig. 2(l,c), Sergio Purtell/Foca/HRW; (r), Rich Treptow/Photo Researchers, Inc.; Fig. 3, Digital Image copyright 2004, PhotoDisc; Fig. 4, Andy Sacks/Getty Images/Stone; Fig. 5, Scott Van Osdol/HRW; Fig. 6, Pekka Parvianen/SPL/Photo Researchers, Inc.; Fig. 7(l-r), John Langford/HRW; Paul A. Souders/CORBIS; Tony Freeman/PhotoEdit; Fig. 9, Lori Adamski Peek/Getty Images/Stone; Fig. 10, Charlie Winters/HRW; Fig. 11, Myrleen Ferguson/PhotoEdit; Fig. 12, Scott Van Osdol/HRW; Fig. 13(l-r), Steve Joester/Getty Images/Taxi; Michael Keller/Corbis Stock Market; E. R. Degginger/Color-Pic, Inc.; "Science and the Consumer," Sherman Clark/Getty Images; Fig. 14, Benelux Press/Getty Images/Taxi; Fig. 15, Roine Magnusson/Getty Images/Stone; Fig. 17, Joseph Sohm; ChromoSohm, Inc./CORBIS; "Real World Application," Chris Oxley/CORBIS; Fig. 21, Brian Hagiwara/FoodPix; Fig. 23, Charles D. Winters/Photo Researchers, Inc.; Fig. 27, Charlie Winters; "Chapter Review," Charles D. Winters/Photo Researchers, Inc.; "Skill Builder Lab," Victoria Smith/HRW; "Science in Action," (plasma sphere), Simon Terry/Photo Researchers, Inc.; (lightning), Rohan Sullivan/AP/Wide World Photos, (aurora borealis), Chris Madeley/Photo Researchers, Inc.

Chapter 4: Chapter Opener image of Guggenheim museum in Bilbao, Spain by Rafa Rivas AFP/CORBIS; liquid gold by Torpham/The Image Works; Fig. 1(microscopic), Courtesy JEOL; Fig. 1(cans), Victoria Smith/HRW; Fig 2.(man), Ron Chapple/Getty Images/FPG International; Fig. 2(waterfall), Bill Bachman/Masterfile; Fig. 3(stadium), Douglas Peebles/CORBIS; Fig. 3(marble), CORBIS Images/HRW; Fig. 6, Steven Begleiter/Index Stock; "Quick Activity," Sam Dudgeon/HRW; Fig. 10, SuperStock; Fig. 11, Peter Van Steen/HRW; Fig. 15, Rhonda Sidney/The Image Works; Fig. 19A, Tom Van Sant/Geosphere Project, Santa Monica/Science Photo Library/Photo Researchers, Inc.; Fig. 19B, NASA/Corbis Stock Market; Fig. 22, Mimi Cotter/International Stock Photography; Fig. 23(l), E. R. Degginger/Color-Pic, Inc.; Fig. 23(r), Jerry Mason/SPL/Photo Researchers, Inc.; Fig. 24, Jeff Hunter/Getty Images/The Image Bank; Fig. 25, Peter Van Steen/HRW; Fig. 26, Russ Lappa/Science Source/Photo Researchers, Inc.; Fig. 27, Oullette/Theroux/Publiphoto/Photo Researchers, Inc.; 'Connection to Architecture," Dilip Methta/Contact Press Images/Picture Quest; Fig. 29, Scott Barrow/International Stock Photography; Fig. 30, Rob Boudreau/Getty Images/Stone; Fig. 32, Digital Image copyright 2004, Eyewire; Fig. 33, Sam Dudgeon/HRW; "Did You Know," BETTMANN/CORBIS; Figs. 34, 35, 36, Sam Dudgeon/HRW; "Design Your Own Lab," Peter Van Steen/HRW.

Chapter 5: Chapter Opener photo of breaking bottle by John Bagley, stained glass by Robert Frerck/Getty Images/Stone; FIg. 1A, E. R. Degginger/Color-Pic, Inc.; Fig. 1B, Yoav Levy/Phototake; Fig. 1C, Charles D. Winters; Fig.1D, Sam Dudgeon/HRW; Fig. 2, Sergio Purtell/Foca/HRW; Fig. 5, E. R. Degginger/Color-Pic, Inc.; Fig. 6, Dr. Dennis Kunkel/Phototake; Fig. 7, Sergio Purtell/Foca/HRW; "Quick Lab," Sam Dudgeon/HRW; Fig. 8, Sergio Purtell/Foca/HRW; Fig. 12, Sam Dudgeon/HRW; Fig. 13, Erin Garvey/Index Stock Imagery, Inc.; "Quick Activity," Sam Dudgeon/HRW; Fig. 16, Randall Alhadef/HRW; Fig. 18, Peter Van Steen/HRW; Fig. 20, Getty Images/The Image Bank; Fig. 22, Peter Van Steen/HRW; Fig. 25, Marc Grimberg/Getty Images/The Image Bank; Figs. 27-29, Sam Dudgeon/HRW; Fig. 30, David J. Phillip/AP/Wide World Photos; "Skills Practice Lab," Sergio Purtell/Foca; "Career Feature," (portraits), Steve Fischbach/HRW; (barrels), W. & D. McIntyre/Photo Researchers, Inc.

Chapter 6: Chapter opener image of grilled vegetables by Rita Moss/Getty Images/The Image Bank; burning charcoals by Charles O' Rear/CORBIS; Fig. 1A, 1B Charlie Winters/HRW; Fig. 1C, Charlie Winters; Fig. 2, Peter Van Steen/HRW; Fig. 3, E. R. Degginger/Color-Pic, Inc.; Fig. 6, Peter Van Steen/HRW; Fig. 7A, E. R. Degginger/Color-Pic, Inc.; Fig. 7B, Runk/Schoenberger/Grant Heilman Photography; Fig. 8, Sergio Purtell/Foca/HRW; "Science and the Consumer," Peter Van Steen/HRW; FIg. 10, 11, Sergio Purtell/Foca/HRW; "Connection to Fine Arts," Andy Levin/Photo Researchers, Inc.; Fig. 12, Charlie Winters; Fig. 13, Hank Morgan/Photo Researchers, Inc.; Fig. 14, Sam Dudgeon/HRW; Fig. 15, Visuals Unlimited/John Sohldon; Fig. 17, Charlie Winters; Fig. 18, NASA; FIg. 19, Sergio Purtell/Foca/HRW; Fig. 20, Peter Van Steen/HRW; Fig. 21, Dr. Thomas A. Steitz/Yale University, Fig. 22, Sam Dudgeon/HRW; Fig. 23, SuperStock; Fig. 24, Visuals Unlimited/Steve McCutcheon; Fig. 25, Visuals Unlimited/Tom J. Ulrich; "Skills Practice Lab," Sam Dudgeon/HRW.

Chapter 7: Chapter Opener image of rescue medics by Will & Deni McIntyre/Photo Researchers, Inc.; doctor preparing a shot by Jose Luis Palaez, Inc./CORBIS; Fig. 1, Peter Van Steen/HRW; Fig. 2, Victoria Smith/HRW; Fig. 3-4, Sam Dudgeon/HRW; Fig. 5, Richard Haynes/HRW; Fig. 6, Peter Van Steen/HRW; Fig. 6 (inset), Bruce Iverson; Fig. 7, Sergio Purtell/Foca/HRW; Colin Cuthbert/SPL/Photo Researchers, Inc.; "Real World Application," Sergio Purtell/Foca/HRW; Fig. 9, Image Copyright ©2004 PhotoDisc, Inc./HRW; Fig. 10, Mark Douet/Getty Images/Stone; Fig. 12, Richard Megna/Fundamental Photographs, New York; Fig. 14, Sam Dudgeon/HRW; Fig. 15, Eugene Hecht; Fig. 16, Peter Van Steen/HRW; Fig. 17, Sam Dudgeon/HRW; Fig. 18, Charlie D. Winters/Photo Researchers, Inc.; Fig. 19, Peter Van Steen/HRW; Fig. 20, Charlie Winters/Photo Researchers, Inc.; Fig. 21, Charlie Winters/HRW; Fig. 22, Sam Dudgeon/HRW; "Skills Practice Lab," Peter Van Steen/HRW; "Science in Action," (blood cells), Microworks/Phototake; (blood bank), Jerry Mason/SPL/Photo Researchers, Inc.; (mouse), Black Star.

Chapter 8: Chapter Opener image of Weaver Ants by Philip Chapman/Taxi/Getty Images; helicopter dropping lime by Peter Arnold, Inc.; Fig. 1, Sam Dudgeon/HRW; Fig. 2B, 3B, Sergio Purtell/Foca/HRW; Fig. 4, Sam Dudgeon/HRW; Fig. 6, Charles D. Winters; Fig. 7, Charles D. Winters/Photo Researchers, Inc.; Fig. 8, Yoav Levy/Phototake; Fig. 9, Charlie Winters; Fig. 10, CNRI/Photo Researchers, Inc.; Fig. 11, Charlie Winters; Fig. 13, Frans Lanting/Minden Pictures; Fig. 14, Bob Thomason/Getty Images/Stone; Fig. 15, Sam Dudgeon/HRW; Figs. 16-19, Peter Van Steen/HRW; "Skill Builder Lab," Charlie Winters/HRW.

Chapter 9: Chapter Opener image of the painting "Woman Reading Music", courtesy Rijksmuseum, Amsterdam; man next to X-ray of forgery, Volker Steger/Science Photo Library/Photo Researchers, Inc.; Fig. 2, Bettmann/CORBIS; "Quick Activity" (pennies), Peter Van Steen/HRW; Fig. 5, American Institute of Physics/AIP Emilio Segrè Visual Archives; "Quick Activity" (dominos) Peter Van Steen/HRW; Fig. 9, SuperStock; Fig. 10, Peter Van Steen/HRW; Fig. 11, Howard J. Radzyner/Phototake; Fig. 12, Larry Lefever/Grant Heilman Photography; Fig. 13, Cuthbert/SPL/Photo Researchers, Inc.; "Career Feature" (portraits), Peter Cutts; (article), Reprinted with permission from Science News, ©1998 by Science Service.

Chapter 10: Chapter Opener image of ski jumper by Mike Powell/Getty Images; scoreboard by Rudi Blaha/AP/Wide World Photos; Fig. 1, SuperStock; Fig. 3(l-r), David Madison/Getty Images/Stone; Alan Levenson/Getty Images/Stone; Index Stock Photography, Inc.; Anne Powell/Index Stock Imagery, Inc.; Michael H. Dunn/Corbis Stock Market; Brian Stablyk/Getty Images/Stone; Fig. 5, Steve Coleman/AP/Wide World Photos; Fig. 7, Sergio Purtell/Foca; Fig. 8, Clive Brunskill/Getty Images; Fig. 9, Wernher Krutein/CORBIS Images/HRW; Fig. 10, Roberto SCHMIDT/AFP PHOTO/CORBIS; Fig. 11, Dennis Curran/Index Stock Imagery, Inc.; Fig. 12, Phil Cole/Getty Images; Fig. 13, Sam Dudgeon/HRW; Fig. 16(l-r), SuperStock; SuperStock; ©2004 Ron Kimball Studios; Fig. 17, Sam Dudgeon/HRW; Fig. 18, Michelle Bridwell/HRW; Fig. 19, Digital Image ©2004, PhotoDisc; "Design Your Own Lab," Sam Dudgeon/HRW

Chapter 11: Chapter Opener image of soccer ball by Japack Company/CORBIS; players colliding by Andy Lyons/Allsport/Getty Images; Fig. 1, SuperStock; Fig. 2, Sam Dudgeon/HRW; "Quick Activity," Sam Dudgeon/HRW; "Science and the Consumer," Nicholas Pinturas/Stone; Fig. 3, Peter Van Steen/HRW ; Fig. 4, Sam Dudgeon/HRW; Fig. 5, NASA; Fig. 6, James Sugar/Black Star; Fig. 7, NASA; Fig. 8, Toby Rankin/Masterfile; Fig. 11, Michelle Bridwell/Frontera Fotos; Fig. 12, Richard Megna/Fundamental Photographs; Fig. 16-17, David Madison; Fig. 19, Rene Sheret/Stone; Fig. 20, Yellow Dog Productions/Getty Images/Stone; Fig. 21, Michelle Bridwell/Frontera Fotos; Fig. 23A, Gerard Lacz/Animals Animals/Earth Sciences; Fig. 23B, Image Copyright ©(2004 PhotoDisc, Inc./HRW and Sam Dudgeon/HRW; Fig. 23C, Lance Schriner/HRW; "Design Your Own Lab," and "Viewpoints," HRW Photos.

Chapter 12: Chapter Opener photo of George Rhodes' autokinetic sculpture by Wayne Source; portrait of Alexander Calder by Tony Vaccaro/AKG Photo, London; Fig. 1, Amwell/Getty Images/Stone; Inquiry Lab, Sam Dudgeon/HRW; Figs. 2-3, Peter Van Steen/HRW; Fig. 4 (hammer), Michelle Bridwell/HRW; (pulley), Visuals Unlimited/A. J. Copley; (wheel), Peter Van Steen/HRW; (ramp), Sam Dudgeon/HRW; (wedge), Superstock; (drill bit), Dr. E. R. Degginger/Color-Pic, Inc.; Fig. 5 (hammer) Michelle Bridwell/HRW; (wheelbarrow), John P. Kelly/Getty Images/The Image Bank; (arm), Sam Dudgeon/HRW; Fig. 7, Peter Van Steen/HRW, Fig. 8 (ramp), Sam Dudgeon/HRW; (wedge), Superstock; (drill bit), Dr. E. R. Degginger/Color-Pic, Inc.; "Connection to Social Studies," M. O'Neill/Getty Images/The Image Bank; Figs. 9-10, Peter Van Steen/HRW; Fig. 11, Picture Perfect; Fig. 12, Kindra Clineff/The Picture Cube/Index Stock; Fig. 13, Randy Ury/Corbis Stock Market; Fig. 14, Al Francekevich/Corbis Stock Market; "Real World Applications," Peter Van Steen/HRW; Fig. 15, NASA/Phototake; Fig. 16, Steve Bloom/Picture Perfect; Fig. 17, E. R. Degginger/Color-Pic, Inc.; Fig. 18, AFP/CORBIS; Fig. 20, Getty Images/FPG International; Fig. 21, Henry Groskinsky/Peter Arnold, Inc.; "Inquiry Lab," Sam Dudgeon/HRW; Fig. 23, Visuals Unlimited/Albert J. Copley; Fig. 37, Hank Morgan/Rainbow Inc.; "Chapter Review," (can opener), Peter Van Steen/HRW; "Skill Builder Lab," Peter Van Steen/HRW, "Career Link," Ken Kinzie/Latent Image Photography/HRW.

Chapter 13: Chapter Opener image of forest fire by John M. Roberts/Corbis Stock Market; infrared aerial photo courtesy NOAA; Fig. 1(l), Peter Van Steen/HRW; (c), Sam Dudgeon/HRW; (r), Blair Seitz/Photo Researchers, Inc.; "Quick Activity," Sam Dudgeon/HRW; Fig. 2–3, Sam Dudgeon/HRW; Fig. 6, Peter Van Steen/HRW; Fig. 9, CECOM Night Vision/U. S. Army; "Quick Lab," Sam Dudgeon/HRW; Fig. 10, Sam Dudgeon/HRW; "Quick Activity," Sam Dudgeon/HRW; Fig. 11, Charles D. Winters; Fig. 14, Rod Planck/Photo Researchers, Inc.; Fig. 17, John Maher/Corbis Stock Market; Fig. 19, Courtesy Rheem; "Real World Application," Peter Van Steen/HRW; "Chapter Review," Sam Dudgeon/HRW.

Chapter 14: Chapter Opener image of surfer, International Stock Photography; sunset over beach, Bill Brooks/Masterfile; Fig. 1, SuperStock; Fig. 2, Art Resource, NY; Fig. 3, "Quick Lab," Fig. 6-7, Peter Van Steen/HRW; Fig. 13, Joe Devenney/Getty Images/The Image Bank; Fig. 14, Jeff Hunter/Getty Images/The Image Bank; Fig. 15, Peter Van Steen/HRW; Fig. 17, E. R. Degginger/Color-Pic, Inc.; Fig. 18, Peter Van Steen/HRW; Fig. 19, E. R. Degginger/Color-Pic, Inc.; Fig. 21, Michael Freeman/Bruce Coleman, Inc.; Fig. 22, Neil Nissing/Getty Images/FPG International; Fig. 23, Richard Megna/Fundamental Photographs; "Skills Practice Lab," Sam

Dudgeon/HRW; "Career Link," Peter Van Steen/HRW.
Chapter 15: Chapter Opener photo of Times Square by Paul Hardy/CORBIS; camper by Ron Watts/CORBIS; Fig. 1A, A. Ramey/PhotoEdit; Fig. 2(students speaking, lawnmower, vacuum, dog), Peter Van Steen/HRW; (jet), Peter Gridley/Getty Images/FPG International; (elephant, human), Image Copyright (c)2004 PhotoDisc, Inc.; (dolphin), Doug Perrine/Masterfile; Fig. 4, Tom Pantages Photography; Fig. 5, Thomas D. Rossing; Fig. 6(clarinet), SuperStock; (tuning fork), Sam Dudgeon/HRW; "Quick Lab," Peter Van Steen/HRW; Fig. 8, Benny Odeur/Wildlife Pictures/Peter Arnold, Inc.; Fig. 9(t), Telegraph Colour Library/Getty Images/FPG International; (b), Saturn Stills/Science Photo Library/Photo Researchers; Fig. 10B, E. R. Degginger/Bruce Coleman, Inc.; Fig. 15, Ron Chapple/Getty Images/FPG International; Fig. 16, E. R. Degginger/Animals Animals/Earth Scenes; Fig. 17, Telegraph Colour Library/Getty Images/FPG International; Fig. 18, Claude Gazuit/Photo Researchers, Inc.; Fig. 21, 22, Peter Van Steen/HRW; Fig. 23, Telegraph Colour Library/Getty Images/FPG International; Fig. 24, Peter Van Steen/HRW; Fig. 25A, Leonard Lessin/Peter Arnold, Inc.; Fig. 25B, Sam Dudgeon/HRW; Fig. 26, Richard Megna/Fundamental Photographs; Fig. 30, Ken Kay/Fundamental Photographs; FIg. 30, Guntram Gerst/Peter Arnold, Inc.; Fig. 32, Richard Menga/Fundamental Photographs; Fig. 33, Peter Van Steen/HRW; Fig. 36, Science Photo Library/Photo Researchers, Inc.; Fig. 37, Graham French/Masterfile; "Science In Action" (lasers), Zefa Visual Media/Index Stock Imagery, Inc.; (bog man), Sam Dudgeon/HRW; (butterflies), Yves Gentet.
Chapter 16: Chapter Opener photo of fusion chamber at Sandia National Laboratory by Walter Dickenman, Sandia Lab/David R. Frazier Photolibrary; inset photo of video arcade by DiMaggio/Kalish/Corbis Stock Market; Fig. 1, Michelle Bridwell/HRW; Fig. 2, Peter Van Steen/HRW; Fig. 5, Fundamental Photographs, New York; "Quick Activity," Charles D. Winters/Photo Researchers, Inc.; Fig. 10, Sam Dudgeon/HRW; "Science and the Consumer," Peter Van Steen/HRW; Fig. 13, SuperStock; Figs. 14-16, Sam Dudgeon/HRW; "Schematic Diagram Symbols" Table, HRW Photos; Fig. 17, Sam Dudgeon/HRW; Fig. 18, Peter Van Steen/HRW; Fig. 19, Michelle Bridwell/HRW; "Skills Practice Lab," Peter Van Steen/HRW; "Career Link," Sam Dudgeon/HRW.
Chapter 17: Chapter Opener image of maglev train by Alex Bartel/Science Photo Library/Photo Researchers, Inc.; iron fillings reacting to magnet by Yoav Levy/Phototake; Fig. 2, Breck P. Kent/Animals Animals/Earth Scenes; Fig. 3, "Quick Activities," Peter Van Steen/HRW; Fig. 6, Richard Megna/Fundamental Photographs; "Quick Lab," Mike Fager/HRW; Fig. 19, Peter Van Steen/HRW; "Skills Practice Lab," Sam Dudgeon/HRW.
Chapter 18: GE Americom communication satellite artwork courtesy Lockheed Martin; telecommunications network room by Sam Dudgeon/HRW, courtesy Broadwing, Inc.; Fig. 1A, Michael Newman/PhotoEdit; Figs. 1B-C, Image Copyright ©2004 PhotoDisc, Inc.; Fig. 2-3 Peter Van Steen/HRW; FIg. 4, Andy Christiansen/HRW; Fig. 6, Peter Van Steen/HRW; Fig. 7, Reuters NewMedia Inc./CORBIS; Fig. 8A, Peter Van Steen/HRW; Fig. 8B, Don Mason/Corbis Stock Market; Fig. 10, Lester Lefkowitz/CORBIS; Fig. 14, Bettmann/CORBIS; Fig. 16, Mary Kate Denny/PhotoEdit; "Science and the Consumer," Alexander Tsiaras/Science Source/Photo Researchers, Inc.; "Quick Lab," Peter Van Steen/HRW; Fig. 19(t), Tom Pantages Photography; Fig. 19(b), Los Alamos National Laboratory/Science Photo Library/Photo Researchers, Inc.; "Quick Activity," Peter Van Steen/HRW; Fig. 21, Robert Mathena/Fundamental Photographs; Fig. 22, Telegraph Colour Library/Getty Images/FPG International; Fig. 23, Image Copyright ©2004 Photodisc, Inc.; "Connection to Architecture," Dennis Hallinan/Getty Images/FPG International; Fig. 25, William Taufic/CORBIS; "Real World Applications," HRW; Fig. 26, Michael Newman/PhotoEdit; "Science in Action"(alien parking), Brad Stockton/CORBIS; (telescopes), Dr. Seth Shostak/SPL/Photo Researchers, Inc.
Chapter 19: Chapter opener planet montage courtesy Jim Klemaszewski, Arizona State University/NASA; comet photo; Bob Yen/Getty Images/Liaison; Fig. 1, Lee Cohen/CORBIS; Fig. 2, Anthony Bannister/Gallo Images/CORBIS; Fig. 3(lion), John Foster/Photo Researchers, Inc.; Fig. 3(stars), Roger Ressmeyer/CORBIS; Fig. 7, USGS/NASA; Fig. 8(moons), John Bova/Photo Researchers, Inc.; Fig. 10, Guy Motil/CORBIS; Fig. 12, Mark Robinson, Northwestern University/USGS; "Connection to Social Studies"(Aztec calander), George Holton/Photo Researchers, Inc.; Fig. 13, NASA; Fig. 14, Fred Bavendam/Minden Pictures, Figs. 15-16, NASA; Fig. 17, USGS/SPL/Photo Researchers, Inc.; Fig. 18, NASA/SPL/Photo Researchers, Inc.; Fig. 20(spot), NASA/SPL/Photo Researchers, Inc.; Fig. 20(full disc), NASA; Fig. 21(full disc), NASA/Getty Images/FPG International; Fig. 21(rings), NASA/CORBIS; Fig. 22A-B, NASA; "Real World Application"(probe), JPL/NASA; Fig. 23, NASA; Fig. 24, Telegraph Colour Library/Getty Images/FPG International; Fig. 25, J-L Charmet/Science Photo Library/Photo Researchers, Inc.; Fig. 27, NASA; Fig. 28, John Gleason/Celestial Images; Fig. 30(stony), E.R. Degginger/Bruce Coleman, Inc.; Fig. 30(metallic), Breck P. Kent/Animals Animals/Earth Scenes; Fig. 30(stony-iron), Ken Nichols/Institute of Meteorites; Fig. 31, Jonathan Blair/CORBIS; "Real World Applications"(satellite), NASA/SPL/Photo Researchers, Inc.; Fig. 33, David Nunuk/SPL/Photo Researchers, Inc.; Chapter Review (alien world illustration), John T. Whatmough/JTW Incorporated; "Science in Action" (both), NASA; "Skill Builder Lab"(jar), Peter Van Steen/HRW.
Chapter 20: Chapter Opener photo of Very Large Array radio telescopes by Roger Ressmeyer/CORBIS; radio image of Crab Nebula by R.A. Perely/NRAO; Fig. 1A, Roger Ressmeyer/CORBIS; Fig. 3, Stapelton Collection/CORBIS; Fig. 4, Victoria Smith/HRW; Fig. 7, Jeff Hester and Paul Scowen (Arizona St. University)/NASA; Fig. 9, Anglo-Australian Observatory; "Connection to Social Studies," Tha British Library Picture Library; Fig. 10, Malin/Pasachoff/Caltech/Anglo-Australian Observatory; FIg. 12, John Gleason/Celestial Images; Fig. 13, Dr. Victor Anderson (University of Alabama, KPNO), courtesy W. Keel; Fig. 14A, The Observatories of the Carnegie Institution of Washington; Fig. 14B, NASA; Fig. 15, Jerry Schad/Photo Researchers, Inc.; Fig. 17A, Gemini Observatory, GMOS team; Fig. 17B, Anglo-Australian Observatory; FIg. 17C, Dennis Di Cicco/Peter Arnold, Inc.; Fig. 18, NASA/CXC/SAO/H. Marshall et. al.; "Real World Applications," Arecibo Observatory, Courtesy Dr. Jose Alonso; Fig. 19, R. Williams and the HDF Team (ST Sci)/NASA; Fig. 20(soccer player), Doug Pensinger/Allsport/Getty Images; (field), Bob Long/AP/Wide World Photos; (earth), ESA/PLI/Corbis Stock Market; (galaxies), Dr. Victor Anderson (University of Alabama, KPNO), courtesy W. Keel; Fig. 21, Digital image (c) 1996 CORBIS; Original image courtesy of NASA/CORBIS; NASA/SPL/Photo Researchers, Inc.; Fig. 25, Sam Dudgeon/HRW/Courtesy Dr. Ann Molineux, Texas Memorial Museum, University of Texas at Austin; Fig. 26, Roger Ressmeyer/CORBIS; Fig. 28A, TRW; Fig. 28B, NASA/CXC/SAO; Fig. 29, NASA; "Skills Practice Lab," Dr. Victor Anderson (University of Alabama, KPNO), courtesy W. Keel; "Career Link," (Dr. Cohn portraits), Peg Skorpinski/HRW; (galaxy "chalkboard"), Digital Image copyright (c)2004 PhotoDisc; (nebula), D. Walter(South Carolina State University) and P. Scowen (Arizona State University)/NASA.
Chapter 21: Chapter Opener photo of Wizard Island at Crater Lake, A & L Sinibaldi/Getty Images/Stone; wide shot of Crater Lake, Georg Gerster/Photo Researchers, Inc.; Fig. 4, Charles Palek/Animals Animals/Earth Scenes; Fig. 5, OAR/National Undersea Research Program (NURP)/NOAA; "Quick Activity," Sam Dudgeon/HRW; Fig. 7, Marie Tharp; Fig. 8, Wang Yuan-mao/AP/Wide World Photos; Fig. 9, Bernhard Edmaier/SPL/Photo Researchers, Inc.; Fig. 10, Galen Rowell/CORBIS; Fig. 11, Robin Prange/Corbis Stock Market; Fig. 12, David Parker/Science Photo Library/Photo Researchers, Inc.; "Quick Lab," Sam Dudgeon/HRW; Fig. 14, Mark Downey/Lucid Images; Fig. 16, Simon Kwong/Reuters/TimePix; Fig. 20, Greg Vaughn/Getty Images/Stone; Fig. 21(top), Michael T. Sedam/CORBIS; Fig. 21(center), Orion Press/Getty Images/Stone; Fig. 21(bottom), SuperStock; Fig. 23, Gary Braasch/CORBIS; Fig. 24, John M. Roberts/Corbis Stock Market; Fig. 25A, Breck P. Kent/Animals Animals/Earth Scenes, Fig. 25B, G.R. Roberts Photo Library; "Connection to Social Studies," National Geographic Image Collection/Kenneth Garrett; Fig. 26, Tom Bean/CORBIS; Fig. 27A, Grant Heilman Photography; Fig. 27B, Breck P. Kent/Animals Animals/Earth Scenes; Fig. 28, Harvey Lloyd/Corbis Stock Market; Fig. 29A-B, Fig. 30A, Sam Dudgeon/HRW; Fig. 30B-C, Image Copyright ©2004 PhotoDisc, Inc.; Fig. 30D, Grant Heilman Photography; Fig. 30E, Breck P. Kent/Animals Animals/Earth Scenes, Fig. 30F, SuperStock; Fig. 31, Laurence Parent; Fig. 32, James Kay; Fig. 33, Larry Ulrich/Getty Images/Stone; Fig. 34, Mark Gibson Photography; Fig. 35, Ray Pfortner/Peter Arnold, Inc.; Fig. 36, G.R. Roberts Photo Library; Fig. 37, SuperStock; Fig. 38A, Grant Heilman Photography; Fig. 38B, Visuals Unlimited/Bill Kamin, Fig. 39, Mark Tomalty/Masterfile; "Career Link" (all), Max Aguilera-Hellweg/GEO.
Chapter 22: Chapter Opener image of irrigation truck, Cameron Davidson/Getty Images/Stone; double rainbow, Craig Tuttle/Corbis Stock Market; Fig. 2, Ned Haines/Photo Researchers, Inc.; Fig. 3, NASA; Fig. 6, George Lepp/Getty Images/Stone; Fig. 8, Larry Lefever/Grant Heilman Photography; Fig. 11, Bernard Photo Productions/Animals Animals/Earth Scenes; Fig. 13A, Tom Pantages Photography; Fig. 13B, Runk/Schoenberger/Grant Heilman Photography; Fig. 18A, Photo Courtesy of The Weather Channel; Fig. 18B, Ali Jarekji/REUTERS/TimePix; "Real World Application" (lightning), Telegraph Colour Library/Getty Images/FPG International; Fig. 20, Alan R. Moller/Getty Images/Stone; Chapter Review (weather map), DataStreme Project, American Meteorological Society; "Viewpoints," HRW.
Chapter 23: Chapter Opener photo of blue solar car by William McCoy/Rainbow/Picture Quest; yellow car courtesy California State University, Los Angeles, College of Engineering and Technology; Fig. 3, M. Osf Gibbs/Animals Animals/Earth Scenes; Fig. 4, Tom J. Ulrich/Visuals Unlimited; Fig. 5A, Craig Fugii/©1988 The Seattle Times; Fig. 5B, Raymond Gehman/National Geographic Society Image Collection; Fig. 6(l), Ken M. Johns, The National Audubon Society Collection/Photo Researchers; Fig. 6(c), Glen M. Oliver/Visuals Unlimited; Fig. 6(r), Dr. E. R. Degginger/Color-Pic, Inc.; Fig.7, E. R. Degginger/Animals Animals/Earth Scenes; Fig. 9(trees), Richard Thom/Visuals Unlimited; Fig. 9 (cars), Mark Richards/Photo Edit; Fig. 9(house), Myrleen Ferguson/Photo Edit; Fig. 9 (farm), Peter Dean/Grant Heilman Photography; Fig. 10, Dr. E. R. Degginger/Color-Pic, Inc.; Fig. 14, Bruce Stoddard/Getty Images/FPG International; Fig. 16, Fred Bruemmer/Peter Arnold, Inc.; Fig. 18, Stefan Schott/Panoramic Images, Ltd.; Fig. 19, Telegraph Colour Library/Getty Images/FPG International; Fig. 20, G. R. Roberts Photo Library; Fig. 21, Grant Heilman Photography; "Science and the Consumer," Ulrike Welsch/Photo Edit; Fig. 22A, Warren Bolster/Getty Images/Stone; Fig. 22B, Travelpix/Getty Images/FPG International; Fig. 25, Corbis Images; Fig. 26, Patti Murray/Animals Animals/Earth Scenes; Fig. 27, John Sohlden/Visuals Unlimited; "Quick Lab," Victoria Smith/HRW; Fig. 28-29, Telegraph Colour Library/Getty Images/FPG International; "Science in Action"(fuel cell car), Laurent Gillieron/Keystone/AP/Wide World Photos; (traffic), Andrew Brown; Ecoscene/CORBIS; (plant), Todd Gipstein/CORBIS.

The Periodic Table of the Elements

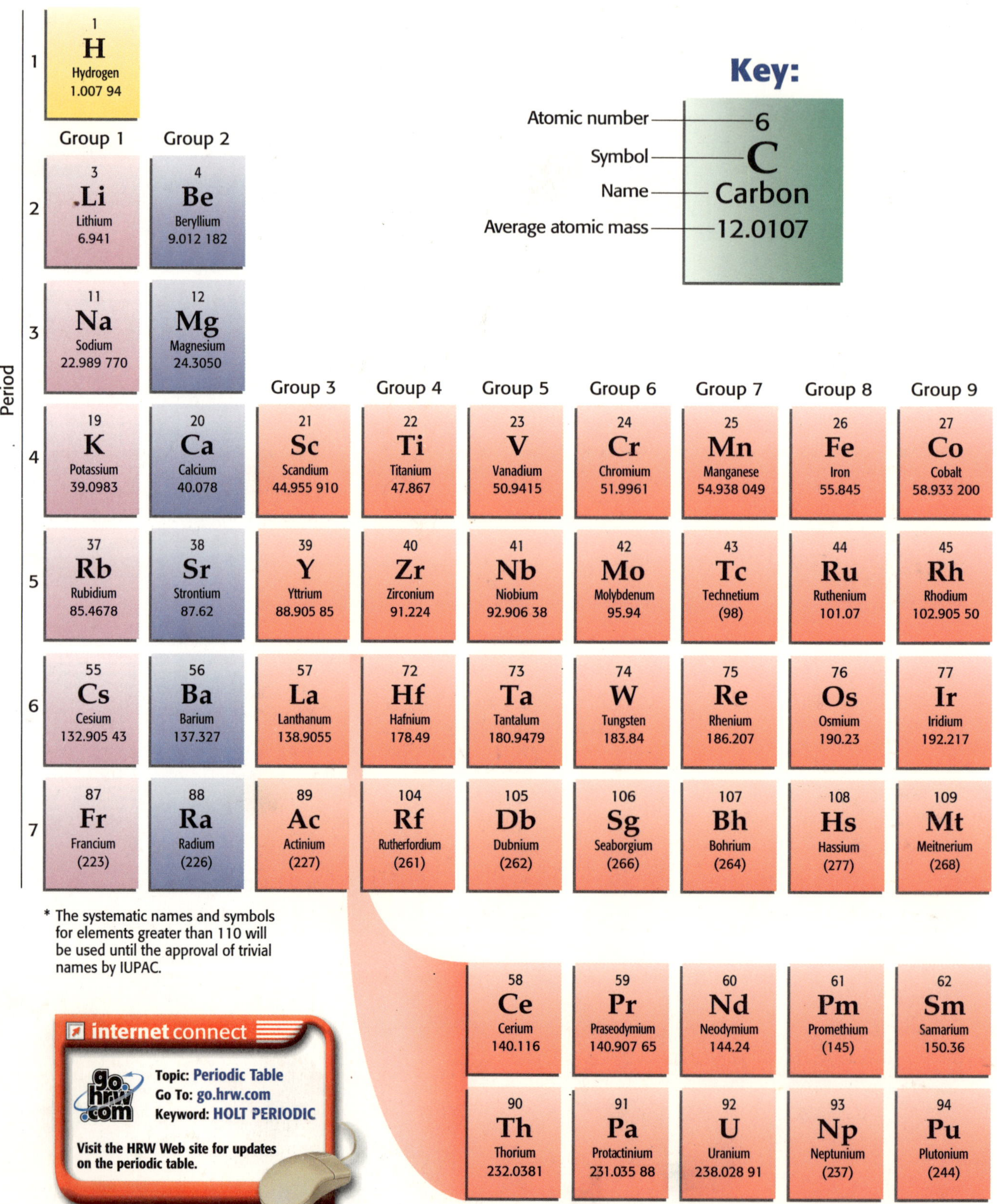

Key:

Atomic number	Symbol	Name	Average atomic mass
6	C	Carbon	12.0107

Period	Group 1	Group 2	Group 3	Group 4	Group 5	Group 6	Group 7	Group 8	Group 9
1	1 H Hydrogen 1.007 94								
2	3 Li Lithium 6.941	4 Be Beryllium 9.012 182							
3	11 Na Sodium 22.989 770	12 Mg Magnesium 24.3050							
4	19 K Potassium 39.0983	20 Ca Calcium 40.078	21 Sc Scandium 44.955 910	22 Ti Titanium 47.867	23 V Vanadium 50.9415	24 Cr Chromium 51.9961	25 Mn Manganese 54.938 049	26 Fe Iron 55.845	27 Co Cobalt 58.933 200
5	37 Rb Rubidium 85.4678	38 Sr Strontium 87.62	39 Y Yttrium 88.905 85	40 Zr Zirconium 91.224	41 Nb Niobium 92.906 38	42 Mo Molybdenum 95.94	43 Tc Technetium (98)	44 Ru Ruthenium 101.07	45 Rh Rhodium 102.905 50
6	55 Cs Cesium 132.905 43	56 Ba Barium 137.327	57 La Lanthanum 138.9055	72 Hf Hafnium 178.49	73 Ta Tantalum 180.9479	74 W Tungsten 183.84	75 Re Rhenium 186.207	76 Os Osmium 190.23	77 Ir Iridium 192.217
7	87 Fr Francium (223)	88 Ra Radium (226)	89 Ac Actinium (227)	104 Rf Rutherfordium (261)	105 Db Dubnium (262)	106 Sg Seaborgium (266)	107 Bh Bohrium (264)	108 Hs Hassium (277)	109 Mt Meitnerium (268)

58 Ce Cerium 140.116	59 Pr Praseodymium 140.907 65	60 Nd Neodymium 144.24	61 Pm Promethium (145)	62 Sm Samarium 150.36
90 Th Thorium 232.0381	91 Pa Protactinium 231.035 88	92 U Uranium 238.028 91	93 Np Neptunium (237)	94 Pu Plutonium (244)

* The systematic names and symbols for elements greater than 110 will be used until the approval of trivial names by IUPAC.

internet connect

Topic: Periodic Table
Go To: go.hrw.com
Keyword: HOLT PERIODIC

Visit the HRW Web site for updates on the periodic table.